Studies in the Scriptures
1922-23

Volume 1
of
17 Volume Set

Studies in the Scriptures 1922-23

Volume 1
of
17 Volume Set

Arthur W. Pink

Sovereign Grace Publishers, Inc.
P.O. Box 4998
Lafayette, IN 47903
2001

A. W. Pink's Studies in the Scriptures,
Volume 1 - 1922-23 - Paperback Edition
Copyright © 2001
By Jay P. Green, Sr.
All Rights Reserved

Volume 1 = ISBN 978-1-58960-230-4

Studies In The Scriptures - 1922
Index

Creation and Restoration	Genesis 1	2
The Saint's Inheritance	1 Peter 1:3-5	7
John's Gospel		9
Counsel to a Preacher		13
The Holy Trinity		14
The Nazarite	Numbers 6:1-4	14
The Sword of Justice Awakened Against God's Fellow		22
John's Gospel		26
The Priest's Place and Portion	Leviticus 6:14-18	33
The Nazarite:	Numbers 6:5	34
The Believer's Hope		42
John's Gospel	John 1:14-16	46
The Nazarite	Numbers 6:6-8	54
The Precious Blood		62
John's Gospel	John 1:19-34	66
The Provisions of Grace for Nazarite Failure	Numbers 6:9-12	73
Grace as it Reigns in the Perseverance of the Saints to Eternal Glory		77
The Antichrist		86
John's Gospel	John 1:35-51	90
The Wisdom of God Displayed in the Way of Salvation		99
The Believer's Response to the Words of the Saviour		106
The Papacy Not the Antichrist		110
John's Gospel	John 2:1-11	116
The Wisdom of God Displayed in the Way of Salvation		123
Confidence in the Lord		131
Human Depravity		131
The Person of the Antichrist		134
John's Gospel	John 2:13-25	141
The Wisdom of God Displayed in the Way of Salvation		148
The Perfections of God		155
Names and Titles of the Antichrist		158
John's Gospel	John 3:1-8	165
The Wisdom of God Displayed in the Way of Salvation		174
The Person of the Antichrist		182
John's Gospel	John 3:9-21	186
Prayer		196
"Assurance of Salvation" and "Full Assurance of Faith"	Heb. 10:22	200
"That Worthy Name"		202
Evil, and How to Meet It		203
Spiritual Preparedness		204

The Career of the Antichrist	206
Christ Mainfested to the Soul	212
John's Gospel .... John 3:21-36	217
"The Way, The Truth, and The Life"	224
The Doom of the Antichrist	230
John's Gospel .... John 4:1-6	236
The Believer and Law or The Bearings of the New Creation	244
Ripe for Heaven	247
Mary, the Mother of Jesus	254
John's Gospel .... John 4:6-10	259
A Christmas Message	267
The Saint and Law	268
The State of the Natural Man	275
The First Christmas Carol	276

Studies In The Scriptures -- 1923
Index

John's Gospel .... John 4:11-19	2
Are Believers Under the Law?	9
Antichrist in the Pslams	13
Exposition on First Peter	20
Anxious Care	26
The Sufferings of This Present Time	32
John's Cospel .... John 4:20-30	34
The Moral Law the Rule of Conduct to Believers	42
Eternal Punishment	45
Exposition of First Peter .... 1 Peter 1:3-5	54
What is it to Believe?	60
The Sinner's Impotency	63
John's Gospel .... John 4:31-42	66
The Antichrist in the Prophets	73
Eternal Punishment	83
Exposition of First Peter	92
John's Gospel .... John 4:43-54	98
Eternal Punishment	107
Antichrist in the Gospels and Epistles	115
Exposition of Peter	124
John's Gospel .... John 5:1-15	130
Antichrist in the Apocalypse	139
The Law and the Saint	148
Exposition of First Peter	155
John's Gospel .... John 5:16-30	162

The Antichrist in Revelation 13		172
The Law and the Saint		177
A Message of Cheer		186
Exposition of First Peter	1 Peter 1:6-9	189
John's Gospel	John 5:31-47	194
Types of the Antichrist		202
The Law and the Saint		210
Exposition of First Peter	1 Peter 1:6-9	219
John's Gospel	John 6:1-13	226
Babylon and the Antichrist		237
The Christian Sabbath		246
John's Gospel	John 6:14-27	258
Antichrist and Babylon		268
The Sabbath		279
Exposition of First Peter		284
John's Gospel	John 6:28-40	290
Antichrist and Bablyon	Rev. 18	298
The Sabbath		303
Exposition of First Peter		308
John's Gospel	John 6:41-59	314
Israel and the Antichrist		323
Exposition of First Peter		328
John's Gospel	John 6:60-71	338
The Antichrist		345
Christian Liberty		347
Exposition of First Peter		353

VOL. I   JANUARY, 1922   No. 1.

STUDIES in the SCRIPTURES

"Search the Scriptures" John 5:39.

A PERIODICAL (MONTHLY "IF THE LORD WILL")
DEVOTED TO BIBLE STUDIES and EXPOSITIONS

ASSOCIATE EDITORS: I. C. HERENDEEN   –   –   ARTHUR W. PINK.
PUBLISHED BY I. C. HERENDEEN,   % Bible Truth Depot, Swengel, Pa.

Price: 10 cents per copy; $1.00 per year. Foreign $1.00 per year.

TO OUR READERS—

We take pleasure in submitting to your prayerful attention this, the first issue of *Studies in the Scriptures,* which we purpose, God willing, to publish monthly. As its name implies, it will be a periodical devoted to opening up the Word of God, and thus we shall endeavor with the Lord's help to minister to the deepest need of the individual believer. We shall "ride no hobbies" but seek to put before the Bible student faithful expositions of and studies in the Holy Scriptures from the pens of the Lord's servants of the past and present. Quality rather than quantity will be our aim. We earnestly covet the prayers of the Lord's people that His blessing may attend our humble efforts to "feed" His "sheep." We are undertaking this work as a ministry to the Lord in obedience, we believe, to His clear leading, and we shall hope, therefore, to have the hearty sympathy and co-operation of all lovers of "the deep things of God." Any criticisms or suggestions tending to the improvement of this periodical will be welcomed and carefully considered. On the other hand, if any receive spiritual profit and blessing from their perusal of this magazine, as we sincerely trust they will, we would be very glad to hear from all such to that effect.

This is entirely a venture of faith and we look to our readers to aid us by sending their own and, if possible, the subscriptions of others at once. We shall further look to them to help us in making the magazine known among their friends, and to this end we shall be glad to furnish free sample copies for gratuitous distribution upon request. Let as many as can do so send postage at least, and as much more as the Lord leads and enables.

"Brethren, pray for us" *(I Thess. 5:25).*
         Faithfully yours,
                 I. C. Herendeen.

CREATION AND RESTORATION
Genesis 1

The manner in which the Holy Scriptures open is worthy of their Divine Author. "In the beginning God created the heaven and the earth," and that is *all* that is here recorded concerning the original creation. Nothing is said which enables us to fix the date of their creation; nothing is revealed concerning their appearance or inhabitants; nothing is told us about the "modus operandi" of their Divine Architect. We do not know whether the primitive heaven and earth were created a few thousands, or many millions of years ago. We are not informed as to *whether they were called into existence* in a moment of time, or whether the process of their formation covered an interval of long ages. The bare fact is stated: "In the beginning God created," and nothing is added to gratify the curious. The opening sentence of Holy Writ is not to be philosophized about, but is presented as a statement of truth to be received with unquestioning faith.

"In the beginning God created." No argument is entered into to *prove* the existence of God: instead, His existence is affirmed as a fact to be believed. And yet, sufficient is expressed in this one brief sentence to expose every fallacy which man has invented concerning the Deity. This opening sentence of the Bible repudiates *atheism,* for it postulates the *existence* of God. It refutes *materialism,* for it *distinguishes between* God and His material creation. It abolishes *pantheism,* for it predicates that which necessitates a *personal* God. *"In the beginning* God created," tells us that He was Himself *before* the beginning, and hence, Eternal. "In the beginning God *created,"* and that informs us He is a *personal being,* for an abstraction, an impersonal "first cause" could not create. "In the beginning God created *the heaven and the earth,"* and that argues He is *infinite* and *omnipotent,* for no finite being possesses the power to "create," and none but an Omnipotent Being could create "the heaven and the earth."

"In the beginning God." *This is the foundation truth of all real theology.* God is the great Originator and Initiator. It is the ignoring of this which is the basic error in all human schemes. False systems of theology and philosophy begin with man, and seek to work up to God. But this is a turning of things upside down. We must, in all our thinking, begin with God, and work down to man. Again, this is true of *the Divine inspiration of the Scriptures.* The Bible is couched in human language, it is addressed to human ears, it was written by human hands, but, in the beginning *God*—"holy men of God spake, moved by the Holy Spirit" *(II Peter 1:21).* This is also true of *salvation.* In Eden, Adam sinned, and brought in death; but his Maker was not taken by surprise: in the beginning God had provided for just such an emergency, for, "the Lamb" was "foreordained before the foundation of the world" *(I Peter 1:20).* This is also true of *the new creation.* The soul that is saved, repents, believes, and serves the Lord; but, in the beginning, God chose us in Christ *(see Eph. 1:4),* and now, "we love Him, because He *first* loved us."

"In the beginning God created the heaven and the earth," and we cannot but believe that these creations were worthy of Himself, that they reflected the perfections of their Maker, that they were exceedingly fair in their pristine beauty. Certainly, the earth, on the morning of its creation, must have been vastly different from its chaotic state as described in Genesis 1:2. "And the earth was *without form and void"* must refer to a condition of the earth much later than what is before us in the preceding verse. It is now over a hundred years ago since Dr. Chalmers called attention to the fact that the word "was" in Genesis 1:2 should be translated "became," and that between the first two verses of Genesis 1 some terrible catastrophe must have intervened. That this catastrophe may have been connected with the apostasy of Satan, seems more than likely; that some catastrophe *did* occur is certain from Isaiah 45:18, which expressly declares that the earth was not *created* in the condition in which Genesis 1:2 views it.

What is found in the remainder of Genesis 1 refers not to the primitive creation but to the *restoration* of that which had fallen into ruins. Genesis 1:1 speaks of the original creation; Genesis 1:2 describes the then condition of the earth six days before Adam was called into existence.

To what remote point in time Genesis 1:1 conducts us, or as to how long an interval passed before the earth *"became"* a ruin, we have no means of knowing; but if the surmises of geologists could be conclusively established, there would be no conflict at all between the findings of science and the teaching of Scripture. The unknown interval between the first two verses of Genesis 1, is wide enough to embrace all the pre-historic ages which may have elapsed; but all that took place from Genesis 1:3 onwards transpired less than six thousand years ago.

"In six days the Lord *made* heaven and earth, the sea, and all that in them is" *(Exod. 20:11)*. There is a wide difference between *"creating"* and *"making:"* to "create" is to call into existence something out of nothing; to "make" is to form or fashion something out of materials *already* existing. A carpenter can "make" a chair out of wood, but he is quite unable to "create" the wood itself. "In the beginning (whenever that was) God *created* the heaven and the earth;" subsequently (after the primitive creation had become a ruin) "the Lord *made* heaven and earth, the sea, and all that in them is." This Exodus scripture settles the controversy which has been raised as to what kind of "days" are meant in Genesis 1, whether days of twenty-four hours, or protracted periods of time. In "six days," that is, literal days of twenty-four hours' duration, the Lord completed the work of restoring and re-fashioning that which some terrible catastrophe had blasted and plunged into chaos.

What follows in the remainder of Genesis 1 is to be regarded not as a poem, still less as an allegory, but as a *literal*, historical statement of Divine revelation. We have little patience with those who labor to show that the teaching of this chapter is in harmony with modern science —as well ask whether the celestial chronometer is in keeping with the timepiece at Greenwich. Rather must it be the part of scientists to bring their declarations into accord with the teaching of Genesis 1, if they are to receive the respect of the children of God. The faith of the Christian rests not in the wisdom of man, nor does it stand in any need of buttressing from scientific *savants*. The faith of the Christian rests upon the impregnable rock of Holy Scripture, and we need nothing more.

Too often have Christian apologists deserted their proper ground. For instance: one of the ancient tablets of Assyria is deciphered, and then it is triumphantly announced that some statements found in the historical portions of the Old Testament have been *confirmed*. But that is only a turning of things upside down again. The Word of God needs no "confirming." If the writing upon an Assyrian tablet agrees with what is recorded in Scripture, that confirms the historical accuracy of the Assyrian tablet; if it disagrees, that is proof positive that the Assyrian writer was at fault. In like manner, if the teachings of science square with Scripture, that goes to show the former are correct; if they conflict, that proves the postulates of science are false. The man of the world, and the pseudo scientist may sneer at our logic, but that only demonstrates the truth of God's Word, which declares, "but the natural man receiveth not the things of the Spirit of God: for they are *foolishness unto him:* neither can he know them, because they are spiritually discerned" *(I Cor. 2:14)*.

Marvelously concise is what is found in Genesis 1. A single verse suffices to speak of the original creation of the heaven and the earth. Another verse is all that is needed to describe the awful chaos into which the ruined earth was plunged. And less than thirty verses more tell of the six days' work, during which the Lord "made heaven and earth, the sea, and all that in them is." Not all the combined skill of the greatest literary genuii, historians, poets, or philosophers this world has ever produced, could design a composition which began to equal Genesis 1. For reconditeness of theme, and yet simplicity of language; for comprehensiveness of scope, and yet terseness of expression; for scientific exactitude, and yet the avoidance of all techinal terms; it is unrivalled, and nothing can be found in the whole realm of literature which can be compared with it for a moment. It stands in a class all by itself. If "brevity is the soul of wit" (i. e., wisdom) then the brevity of what is recorded in this opening chapter of the Bible evidences the *Divine* wisdom of Him Who inspired it. Contrast the labored formulæ of the scientists, contrast the verbose writings of the poets, contrast the meaningless cosmogonies of the ancients and the foolish mythologies of the heathen, and the uniqueness of this Divine account of Creation and Restoration will at once appear. Every line of this opening chapter of Holy Writ has stamped across it the autograph of Deity.

Concerning the details of the six days work we cannot now say very much. The orderly manner in which God proceeded, the ease with which He accomplished His work, the excellency of that which was produced, and the simplicity of the narrative, at once impress the reader. Out of the chaos was brought the "cosmos," which signifies order, arrangement, beauty; out of the waters emerged the earth; a scene of desolation, darkness and death, was transformed into one of light, life, and fertility, so that at the end all was pronounced "very good." Observe that here is to be found the first Divine Decalogue: ten times we read, "And God said, *Let there be*," etc. (*vss. 3, 6, 9, 11, 14, 14, 20, 24, 26, 30*), which may be termed the Ten Commandments of Creation.

In the Hebrew there are just *seven* words in the opening verse of Genesis 1, and these are composed of twenty-eight letters, which is seven multiplied by four. Seven is the number of perfection, and four of creation, hence, we learn that the primary creation was *perfect* as it left its Maker's hands. It is equally significant that there were *seven* distinct stages in God's work of restoring the earth: first, there was the activity of the Holy Spirit (*see 1:2*); second, the calling of light into existence (*see 1:3*); third, the making of the firmament (*see 1:6-9*); fourth, the clothing of the earth with vegetation (*see 1:11*); fifth, the making and arranging of the heavenly bodies (*see 1:14-18*); sixth, the storing of the waters (*see 1:20, 21*); seventh, the stocking of the earth (*see 1:24*). The perfection of God's handiwork is further made to appear in the *seven* times the word "good" occurs here (*see vss. 4, 10, 12, 18, 21, 25, 31*); also the word "made" is found *seven* times in this section (*see 1: 7, 16, 25, 31; 2:2, 3*). Seven times "heaven" is mentioned in this chapter (*see vss. 1, 8, 9, 14, 15, 17, 20*). And, it may be added, that "God" Himself is referred to in this opening section (*see 1:1—2:4*) thirty-five times, which is 7 multiplied by 5. Thus the seal of *perfection* is stamped upon everything God here did and made.

Turning from the literal meaning of what is before us in this opening chapter of Holy Writ, we would dwell now upon that which has often been pointed out by others, namely, the *typical significance* of these verses. The order followed by God in reconstructing the old creation is the same which obtains in connection with the new creation, and in a remarkable manner the one is here made to foreshadow the other. The early history of this earth corresponds with the spiritual history of the believer in Christ. What occurred in connection with the world of old, finds its counterpart in the regenerated man. It is this line of truth which will now engage our attention.

1. "IN THE BEGINNING GOD CREATED THE HEAVEN AND THE EARTH." As we have already observed, the original condition of this primary creation was vastly different from the state in which we view it in the next verse. Coming fresh from the hands of their Creator, the heaven and the earth must have presented a scene of unequaled freshness and beauty. No groans of suffering were heard to mar the harmony of the song of "the morning stars" as they sang together (*see Job 38:7*). No worm of corruption was there to defile the perfections of the Creator's handiwork. No iniquitous rebel was there to challenge the supremacy of God. And no death shades were there to spread the spirit of gloom. God reigned supreme, without a rival, and everything was very good.

So, too, in the beginning of this world's history, God also created man, and vastly different was his original state from that into which he subsequently fell. Made in the image and likeness of God, provided with a helpmate, placed in a garden of delights, given dominion over all the lower orders of creation, "blessed" by his Maker, bidden to be fruitful and multiply and replenish the earth, and included in that which God pronounced "very good," Adam had all that heart could desire. Behind him was no sinful heredity, within him was no deceitful and wicked heart, upon him were no marks of corruption, and around him were no signs of death. Together with his helpmate, in fellowship with his Maker, there was everything to make him happy and contented.

2. "AND THE EARTH BECAME WITHOUT FORM AND VOID, AND DARKNESS WAS UPON THE FACE OF THE DEEP." Some fearful catastrophe must have occurred. Sin had dared to raise its horrid head against God, and with sin came death and all its at-

tendant evils. The fair handiwork of the Creator was blasted. That which at first was so fair was now marred, and what was very good became very evil. The light was quenched, and the earth was submerged beneath the waters of judgment. That which was perfect in the beginning became a ruin, and darkness abode upon the face of the deep. Profoundly mysterious is this, and unspeakably tragic. A greater contrast than what is presented in the first two verses of Genesis 1 can hardly be conceived. Yet there it is: the primitive earth, created by God "in the beginning," had become a ruin.

No less tragic was that which befell the first man. Like the original earth before him, Adam remained not in his primitive state. A dreadful catastrophe occurred. Description of this is given in Genesis 3. By one man *sin entered the world*, and death by sin. The spirit of insubordination possessed him; he rebelled against his Maker; he ate of the forbidden fruit; and terrible were the consequences which followed. The fair handiwork of the Creator is blasted. Where before there was blessing, there now descended the curse. Into a scene of life and joy, entered death and sorrow. That which at the first was "very good," became very evil. Just as the primitive earth before him, so man became a wreck and a ruin. He was submerged in evil and enveloped in darkness. Unspeakably tragic was this, but the truth of it is verified in the heart of every descendant of Adam.

"There was, then, a primary creation, afterward a fall; first, 'heaven and earth,' in due order, then earth without a heaven—in darkness, and buried under a 'deep' of salt and barren and restless waters. What a picture of man's condition, as fallen away from God! How complete the confusion! How profound the darkness! How deep the restless waves of passion roll over the wreck of what was once so fair! 'The wicked are like the troubled sea, when it cannot rest, whose waters cast up mire and dirt.'"—F. W. Grant.

Here, then, is the key to human destiny. Here is the cause of all the suffering and sorrow which is in the world. Here is the explanation of human depravity. Man is not now as God created him. God made man "upright" *(Eccl. 7:29)*, but he continued not thus. God faithfully warned man that if he ate of the forbidden fruit he should surely die. And die he did, spiritually. Man is, henceforth, a fallen creature. He is born into this world "alienated from the life of God" *(Eph. 4:18)*. He is born into this world with a heart that is "deceitful above all things, and desperately wicked" *(Jer. 17:9)*. This is the heritage of The Fall. This is the entail of Adam's transgression. Man is a ruined creature, and "darkness," moral and spiritual, rests upon the face of his understanding *(see Eph. 4:18)*.

3. "AND THE SPIRIT OF GOD MOVED UPON THE FACE OF THE WATERS." Here is where hope begins to dawn. God did not abandon the primitive earth, which had become a ruin. It would not have been surprising, though, if He had. Why should God trouble any further about that which lay under His righteous judgment? Why should He condescend to notice that which was now a desolate waste? Why, indeed? But here was where sovereign mercy intervened. He had gracious designs toward that formless void. He purposed to resurrect it, restore it, refructify it. And the first thing we read of in bringing about this desired end was, "the Spirit of God moved upon the face of the waters." There was *Divine activity*. There was a movement on the part of the Holy Spirit. *And this was a prime necessity.* How could the earth resurrect itself? How could that which lay under the righteous judgment of God bring itself into the place of blessing? How could darkness transform itself into light? In the very nature of the case it could not. The ruined creature was helpless. If there was to be restoration, and a new creation, Divine power must intervene, the Spirit of God must "move."

The analogy holds good in the spiritual realm. Fallen man had no more claim upon God's notice than had the desolated primitive earth. When Adam rebelled against his Maker, he merited naught but unsparing judgment at His hands, and if God was inclined to have any further regard for him, it was due alone to sovereign mercy. What wonder if God had left man to the doom he so richly deserved! But no. God had designs of grace toward him. From the wreck and ruin of fallen humanity, God purposed to bring forth a "new creation." Out of the death of sin, God is now bringing on to resurrection ground all who are united to Christ His Son. And the first thing in bringing this about is *the activity of the Holy Spirit.* And this, again, is *a prime necessity.* Fallen man, in himself, is as helpless as was the fallen earth. The sinner can no more regenerate himself than could the ruined earth lift itself out of the deep which rested upon it. The new creation, like the restoration of the material creation, must be accomplished by God Himself.

4. "And God said, Let there be light: and there was light." First the activity of the Holy Spirit and now the spoken Word. No less than ten times in this chapter do we read "and God said." God might have refashioned and refurnished the earth without speaking at all, but He did not. Instead, He plainly intimated from the beginning that His purpose was to be worked out and His counsels accomplished by the Word. The first thing God said was, "Let there be light," and we read, "There was light." Light, then, came in, was produced by, the Word. And then we are told, "God saw the light, that it was good."

It is so in the work of the new creation. These two are inseparably joined together—the activity of the Spirit and the ministry of the Word of God. It is by these the man in Christ became a new creation. And the initial step toward this was the entrance of light into the darkness. The entrance of sin has blinded the eyes of man's heart and has darkened his understanding. So much so that, left to himself, man is unable to perceive the awfulness of his condition, the condemnation which rests upon him, or the peril in which he stands. Unable to see his urgent need of a Saviour, he is, spiritually, in total darkness. And neither the affections of his heart, the reasonings of his mind, nor the power of his will, can dissipate this awful darkness. Light comes to the sinner *through the Word applied by the Spirit.* As it is written, "The entrance of Thy Words giveth light" *(Ps. 119:130).* This marks the initial step of God's work in the soul. Just as the shining of the light in Genesis 1 made manifest the desolation upon which it shone, so the entrance of God's Word into the human heart reveals the awful ruin which sin has wrought.

5. "And God divided the light from the darkness." Hebrews 4:12 tells us, "The Word of God is quick, and powerful, and sharper than any two-edged sword, piercing even to the *dividing asunder of soul and spirit,* and of the joints and marrow, and is a discerner of the thoughts and intents of the heart." This is not a figurative expression but, we believe, a statement of literal fact. Man is a tripartite being, made up of "spirit and soul and body" *(I Thess. 5:23).* The late Dr. Pierson distinguished between them thus: "The spirit is capable of God-consciousness; the soul is the seat of self-consciousness; the body of sense-consciousness." In the day that Adam sinned, he died spiritually. Physical death is the separation of the spirit from the body; spiritual death is the separation of the spirit from God. When Adam died, his spirit was not annihilated, but it was "alienated" from God. There was a *fall.* The spirit, the highest part of Adam's complex being, no longer dominated; instead, it was degraded, it fell to the level of the soul, and ceased to function separately. Hence, to-day, the unregenerate man is dominated by his soul, which is the seat of lust, passion, emotion. But in the work of regeneration, the Word of God "pierces even to the *dividing asunder* of soul and spirit," and the spirit is rescued from the lower level to which it had fallen, being brought back again into communion with God. The "spirit" being that part of man which is capable of communion with God is *light;* the "soul" when it is not dominated and regulated by the spirit is in *darkness,* hence, in that part of the six days work of restoration which adumbrated the dividing asunder of soul and spirit, we read, "And God divided the light from the darkness."

6. "And God said, Let there be a firmament in the midst of the waters, and let it divide the waters from the waters * * and God called the firmament heaven" *(Gen. 1:6,8).* This brings us to the second day's work, and here, for the first time, we read that "God made" something *(see 1:7).* This was the formation of the atmospheric heaven, the "firmament," named by God "heaven." That which corresponds to this in the new creation, is the impartation of a new nature. The one who is "born of the Spirit" becomes a "partaker of the Divine nature" *(II Peter 1:4).* Regeneration is not the improvement of the flesh, or the cultivation of the old nature; it is the reception of an altogether new

and heavenly nature. It is important to note that the "firmament" was produced by the Word, for, again we read, "And God said." So it is by the written Word of God that the new birth is produced, "Of His own will begat He us *with the Word of Truth*" *(James 1:18).* And again, "Being born again, not of corruptible seed, but of incorruptible, *by the Word of God*" *(I Peter 1:23).*

7. "AND GOD SAID, LET THE WATERS UNDER THE HEAVEN BE GATHERED TOGETHER UNTO ONE PLACE, AND LET THE DRY LAND APPEAR: AND IT WAS SO. AND GOD SAID, LET THE EARTH BRING FORTH GRASS, THE HERB YIELDING SEED, AND THE FRUIT TREE YEILDING FRUIT AFTER HIS KIND, WHOSE SEED IS IN ITSELF" *(Gen. 1:9-11).* These verses bring before us, God's work on the third day, and in harmony with the meaning of this numeral we find that which clearly speaks of *resurrection.* The earth was raised out of the waters which had submerged it, and then it was clothed with vegetation. Where before there was only desolation and death, life and fertility now appeared. So it is in regeneration. The one who was dead in trespasses and sins, has been raised to walk in newness of life. The one who was by the old creation "in Adam," is now by new creation "in Christ." The one who before produced nothing but dead works, is now fitted to bring forth fruit to the glory of God.

And here we must conclude. Much has been left untouched, but sufficient has been said, we trust, to show that the order followed by God in the six days' work of restoration, foreshadowed His work of grace in the new creation: that which He did of old in the material world, typified His present work in the spiritual realm. Every stage was accomplished by the putting forth of Divine power, and everything was produced by the operation of His Word. May writer and reader be more and more subject to that Word, and then shall we be pleasing to Him and fruitful in His service.—*Arthur W. Pink.*

THE SAINTS' INHERITANCE

I PETER 1:3-5

When God made ancient Israel His children (better, "His people"—*Ed.*)—brought them into a covenant relation with Him—He assigned them to an inheritance. That inheritance was, like the enonomy to which it belonged, material and temporal. It was the large and fertile land of Canaan, which they were to possess in security and peace, but into which they were to enter not immediately—not till after a long course of wandering in the wilderness.

When God brings men into the relation of children under the new and spiritual and eternal economy, He assigns to them an inheritance which corresponds with the character of that new dispensation—an inheritance of which they are not to obtain the full possession, till "the end come—the consummation of all things."

The celestial blessedness receives here, and in many other passages of Scripture, the appellation of "the inheritance," for two reasons—to mark its gratuitous nature, and to mark its secure tenure.

An inheritance is something that is not obtained by the individual's own exertions, but by the free gift or bequest of another. The earthly inheritance of the external people of God, was not given them because they were greater or better than the other nations of the earth. It was "because the Lord had a delight in them to love them" *(Deut. 10:15, and see Psa. 44:3).* And the heavenly inheritance of the spiritual people of God is entirely the gift of sovereign kindness: "by grace are ye saved;" "eternal life is the gift of God through Jesus Christ our Lord."

A second idea suggested by the figurative expression, "the inheritance," when used in reference to the celestial blessedness, is *the security* of the tenure by which it is held. No right is more indefeasible than the right of inheritance. If the right of the giver or bequeather be good, all is secure. The heavenly happiness, whether viewed as the gift of the Divine Father, or the bequest of the Divine Son, is "sure to all the seed." If the title of the claimant be but as valid as the right of the original proprietor, *their tenure must be as secure as the throne of God and His Son.*

The idea of the security of this happiness is brought forward, however, more distinctly in the description of the inheritance which immediately follows. It is described as "incorruptible, undefiled, and unfading—reserved in heaven" for Christians, while they "are kept by the power of God through faith." In this description of this inheritance, there are two things which require consideration—the *excellence* of the inheritance itself; and the *security* that the Christian shall in due time enjoy it.

The excellence of the inheritance itself consists, in being "incorruptible, undefiled, and unfading." These epithets may seem in a great degree synonomous, and there is no doubt that permanent, unchanging excellence is the leading idea in them all; yet, on looking a little more closely at them, we shall find that each of them presents that general idea in an instructive and pleasing peculiarity of aspect.

The celestial happiness viewed as an inheritance, is "incorruptible." There is nothing in its own nature which can lead to its dissolution. It is not material, but spiritual. It is not composed of "such corruptible things as silver and gold," but of knowledge and of holiness. It is not "meat and drink,"—it is not costly and splendid apparel—it is not stately buildings, nor extensive estates. It is "joy and peace" and happiness arising from sources which, from their very nature, are inexhaustible—possession of the Divine favor—conformity to the Divine image—intercourse and fellowship with God.

It is not only incorruptible, and therefore everlasting, but it is "undefiled." It is debased by no extrinsic, heterogeneous ingredient. In all our enjoyments on earth, however pure and exalted in themselves, there is a mixture. There is always something wanting—something wrong; and sin, that vilest of all things, taints and pollutes them all. But into heaven there enters "nothing that defileth." There is knowledge, without any mixture of error; holiness, without any mixture of sin; love, without any mixture of malignity; the highest dignities excite there no pride—the richest possessions, no covetousness. The inheritance is undefiled.

Still farther, the heavenly inheritance is "unfading." It "fadeth not away." The garland worn by the blessed is of amaranth —it never withers. The idea here seems to be, *it* not only is everlasting in its own nature, but it will never cease to give happiness to the possessor. How often do worldly possessions wither—cease to give the happiness they once gave to those who continue to hold rather than to enjoy them! It has been beautifully remarked, that "the sweetest earthly music, if heard but for one day, would weary those who are most delighted with it. But the song of heaven, though forever the same, will be forever new."—*Leighton*. Here we are often sated, but never satisfied—there, there is constant satisfaction, but there never will be satiety. Such is the excellence of the celestial inheritance.

"But," may the Christian say, "the inheritance is indeed inestimably precious; but will it ever be mine?" It is as secure as it is precious, says the Apostle. It is "reserved in heaven for you," and you are "kept for it by the power of God through faith." This inheritance is "reserved in heaven" for Christians—that is, it is secured beyond the reach of violence or fraud. Many a person, born to a rich inheritance, has never obtained possession of it, but has lived and died in poverty; but this inheritance is liable to none of the accidents of earth and time. It is "in heaven," under the immediate guardianship of *Divine* power, wisdom, and love.

"But the inheritance may itself be secure, but not secure for me. There may be perfect happiness in heaven, but I may never reach it there." To meet this suggestion the apostle adds, "Ye are kept by the mighty power of God through faith." The apostle's doctrine is, and it is quite accordant with the doctrine of his Master and the other apostles, that all who are begotten again by God shall be preserved to the enjoyment of the inheritance. None of them shall fall in the wilderness. "I give unto My sheep eternal life," says Jesus Christ; "and they shall never perish, neither shall any one pluck them out of My hand. My Father, Who gave them Me, is greater than all; and none can pluck them out of My Father's hand" *(John 10: 28, 29; see also Rom. 8:35-39).*

They are "kept"—preserved safe—amid the many dangers to which they are exposed, "by the power of God." The expression, "power of God," may here refer to the Divine power both as exercised in reference to the enemies of the Christian, controlling their maglignant purposes, and as exercised in the form of spiritual influence on the mind of the Christian himself, keeping him in the faith of the truth, "in the love of God, and in the patient waiting for our Lord Jesus Christ." It is probably to the last that the Apostle principally alludes, for he adds "by faith." It is through the persevering faith of the truth that the Christian is by Divine influence preserved from falling, and kept in possession both of that state and character which are absolutely necessary to the enjoyment of the Heavenly inheritance. The perseverance thus secured to the true Christian is perseverance in faith and holiness, and nothing can be more grossly absurd than for a person living in unbelief and sin, to suppose that he can be in the way of obtaining celestial blessedness.—*John Brown, 1848.*

(The above is taken from Dr. Brown's most helpful exposition of I Peter which is, alas, now out of print. We hope to give other selections from the pen of this Spirit-taught exegete in later issues.—*I. C. H.*)

JOHN'S GOSPEL

Introduction

It is our purpose to give *(D. V.)* a verse by verse exposition of the fourth Gospel in the course of this series of studies, but before turning to the opening verses of chapter 1 it will be necessary to consider John's Gospel as a whole, with the endeavor of discovering its scope, its central theme, and its relation to the other three Gospels. We shall not waste the reader's time by entering into a discussion as to who wrote this fourth Gospel, as to where John was when he wrote it, nor as to the probable date when it was written. These may be points of academical interest, but they provide no food for the soul, nor do they afford any help to an understanding of this section of the Bible, and *these* are the two chief things we desire to accomplish. Our aim is to open up the Scriptures in such a way that the reader will be able to enter into the meaning of what God has recorded for our learning in this part of His Holy Word, and to edify those who are members of the Household of Faith.

The four Gospels deal with the earthly life of the Saviour, but each one presents Him in an entirely different character. Matthew portrays the Lord Jesus as the Son of David, the Heir to Israel's throne, the King of the Jews, and everything in his Gospel contributes to this central theme. In Mark Christ is seen as the Servant of Jehovah, the perfect Workman of God, and everything in this second Gospel brings out the characteristics of His service and the manner in which He served. Luke treats of the humanity of the Saviour and presents Him as the perfect Man contrasting Him with the sinful sons of men. The fourth Gospel views Him as the Heavenly One come down to earth, the eternal Son of the Father made flesh and tabernacling among men, and from start to finish this is the one dominant truth which is steadily held in view.*

As we turn to the fourth Gospel we come to entirely different ground from that which is traversed in the other three. It is true, the period of time which is covered by it is the same as in Matthew, Mark, and Luke, some of the incidents treated of by the "Synoptics" come before us here, and He Who has occupied the central position in the narratives of the first three Evangelists is the same One that is made pre-eminent by John; but otherwise, everything is entirely new. The viewpoint of this fourth Gospel is more elevated than that of the others; its contents bring into view spiritual relationships rather than human ties; and, higher glories are revealed as touching the peerless Person of the Saviour. In each of the first three Gospels Christ is viewed in *human* relationships, but not so in John. The purpose of this fourth Gospel is to show that the One Who was born in a manger and afterward died on the Cross had higher glories than those of King, that He Who humbled Himself to take the Servant place was, previously, "equal with God," that the One Who became the Son of Man was none other than, and ever remains, the Only Begotten of the Father.

Each book of the Bible has a prominent and dominant theme which is peculiar to itself. Just as each member in the human

---

*For a detailed examination of the varied glories of the Saviour as set forth, separately, in each Gospel, see the author's new work "Why Four Gospels?" from the publishers, cloth, $1.00.

body has its own particular function, so every book in the Bible has its own special purpose and mission. The theme of John's Gospel is *the Deity of the Saviour*. Here, as nowhere else in Scripture so fully, the Godhood of Christ is presented to our view. That which is outstanding in this fourth Gospel is the Divine Sonship of the Lord Jesus. In this Book we are shown that the One Who was heralded by the angels to the Bethlehem shepherds, Who walked this earth for thirty-three years, Who was crucified at Calvary, Who rose in triumph from the grave, and Who forty days later departed from these scenes, was none other than the Lord of Glory. The evidence for this is overwhelming, the proofs almost without number, and the effect of contemplating them must be to bow our hearts in worship before "the great God and our Saviour Jesus Christ" *(Titus 2:13)*.

Here is a theme worthy of our most prayerful attention. If the Holy Spirit took such marked care to guard the perfections of our Lord's humanity—seen, for example, in the words of the angel to Mary "that *Holy Thing* which shall be born of thee," "made in *the likeness* of sin's flesh," etc., etc.—equally so has the Inspirer of the Scriptures seen to it that there is no uncertainty touching the Divine Sonship of our Saviour. Just as the Old Testament prophets made known that the Coming One should be a Man, a perfect Man, so did Messianic prediction give plain intimation that He should be *more* than a man. Through Isaiah God foretold "For unto us a Child is born, unto us a Son is given: and the government shall be upon His shoulder: and His name shall be called Wonderful Counsellor, *The Mighty God*, The Everlasting Father, The Prince of Peace." Through Micah He declared, "But thou, Bethlehem Ephratah, though thou be little among the thousands of Judah yet out of thee shall He come forth unto Me that is to be Ruler in Israel; Whose goings forth have been *from the days of eternity*." Through Zechariah He said, "Awake, O sword, against My Shepherd, and against *the Man that is My Fellow*, saith the Lord of Hosts: smite the Shepherd, and the sheep shall be scattered." Through the Psalmist He announced, "The Lord said *unto my Lord*, Sit Thou at My right hand, until I make Thine enemies Thy footstool." And again, when looking forward to the second advent, "Thou art *My Son*; this day have I begotten Thee (or, 'brought Thee forth')." In these days of widespread departure from the faith, it cannot be insisted upon too strongly or too frequently that the Lord Jesus is none other than the Second Person of the Blessed Trinity, co-eternal and co-equal with the Father and the Holy Spirit.

In keeping with the special theme of this fourth Gospel, it is here we have the full unveiling of Christ's Divine glories. It is here that we behold Him dwelling with God before time began and before ever the creature was formed *(see 1:1,2)*. It is here that He is seen as the Creator of all things *(see 1:3)*. It is here that He is denominated the "The Only Begotten of the Father, full of grace and truth" *(1:14)*. It is here we read John the Baptist bore record "that this is the Son of God" *(1: 34)*. It is here that we read "this beginning of miracles did Jesus in Cana of Galilee, and *manifested forth His glory*" *(2: 11)*. It is here we are told that the Saviour said "Destroy this temple, and in three days I will raise it up" *(2:19)*. It is here we learn that "the Father loveth the Son, and hath given all things into His hand" *(3:35)*. It is in this Gospel we hear Christ saying "for as the Father raiseth up the dead, and quickeneth them; even so the Son quickeneth whom He will. For the Father judgeth no man, but hath committed all judgment unto the Son: that all should honor the Son, even as they honor the Father" *(5:21-23)*. It is here we find Him declaring "before Abraham was, I am" *(8:58)*. It is here He affirmed "I and My Father are One" *(10:30)*. It is here He testifies "He that hath seen Me hath seen the Father" *(14:9)*.

Before we take up John's Gospel in detail a few words should also be said concerning the *dispensational* scope of the fourth Gospel. It should be evident at once that this is quite different from the other three. There Christ is seen in human relationships, and as connected with an earthly people, but here He is viewed in a Divine relationship, and as connected with a heavenly people. It is true the mystery of the "Body" is not unfolded here— that is found only in what the Apostle Paul wrote as he was moved by the Holy Spirit —rather is it the Family relationship which is here in view: the Son of God together with the sons of God. It is also true that the "heavenly calling," as such, is not fully unfolded here, yet are there plain intimations of it, as a careful study of it makes apparent. In the first three Gospels Christ is seen connected with the Jews, proclaiming the Messianic Kingdom, a proclamation which ceased, however, as soon as it became evident that the nation had rejected Him. But here in John's Gospel His rejection is anticipated from the beginning, for in the very first chapter we are told "He came unto His own, *and His own received Him not."* The dispensational limitations which obtain in connection with much which is found in the first three Gospels does not, therefore, obtain in John's. Again, in John's Gospel the Saviour is displayed as the Son of God, and as such He can be known only by believers. On this plane, then, the Jew has no priority. The Jew's claim upon Christ was purely a *fleshly* one (arising from the fact that He was "the Son of David"), whereas believers are related to the Son of God by *spiritual* union. The Son of David and Son of Man titles of the Redeemer link Him to the *earth,* but the Son of God connects Him with the Father *in Heaven;* hence, in this fourth Gospel the earthly Kingdom is almost entirely ignored.

As there may be some of our readers who have been influenced by *ultra-*dispensational teaching we deem it well to here call attention to other points which help to fix the true dispensational bearings and scope of this fourth Gospel. There are those who make no distinction between John's Gospel and the "Synoptics," and who insist that this fourth Gospel is entirely Jewish, and has nothing but a remote application to believers of the present dispensation. But this, we are assured, is a serious mistake. John's Gospel, like his Epistles, concerns *the family of God.* In proof of this we request the reader to weigh carefully the following points:

First, in 1:11-13 we read, "He came unto His own, and His own received Him not. But as many as received Him, to them gave He power to become the sons of God, even to them that believe on His name; which were born, not of blood, nor of the will of the flesh, nor of the will of man, but of God." From these verses we may notice three things: first, the Jews as a nation rejected the Sent One of the Father, they "received Him not;" second, a company did "receive Him,'" even those that "believed on His name;" third, this company are here designated "the sons of God," who were "born * * of God." There is nothing which in any wise resembles this in the other Gospels. Here only, in the four Gospels, is the truth of the new birth brought before us. And it is by new birth we enter the family of God. As, then, the family of God reaches out beyond Jewish believers, and takes in all Gentile believers, too, we submit that John's Gospel cannot be restricted to the twelve-tribed people.

Second, after stating that the Word became flesh and tabernacled among us, "and *we* beheld His glory, the glory as of the Only Begotten of the Father (which is a glory that none but *believers* behold!), full of grace and truth," and after summarizing John the Baptist's witness to the Person of Christ, the Holy Spirit through the Evangelist goes on to say, "and of His fulness have all *we* received, and grace for grace." Surely this verse alone establishes the point of *who* it is that is here being addressed. The Jewish nation never received "of His fulness"—*that* can be predicated of *believers* only. The "all we" of verse 16 is the *"as many as"* received Him, to whom gave He power to become *"the sons of God"* of verse 12.

Third, in the 10th chapter of John, we read that the Saviour said "I am the Good Shepherd, and know My sheep, and am known of Mine. As the Father knoweth Me, even so know I the Father: and I lay down My life for the sheep" *(vss. 14, 15).* Immediately following this He went on to say "and *other sheep* I have, which are not of this fold; them also I must bring, and they shall hear My voice, and there shall be one fold, and one Shepherd" *(vs. 16).* Who were these "other sheep"? Before we can answer this, we must ascertain who were the "sheep" referred to by Christ in the first fifteen verses of this chapter. As to who *they* were there can be only one answer: they were not the nation of Israel as such, for they had "received Him not;" no, they were the little company who *had* "received Him," who *had* "believed on His name." But Christ goes on to speak of a further company of believers, "*other* sheep *I have* (speaking as God Who "calleth those things which be not as though they were" [*Rom. 4:17*]), them also I must bring." Clearly, the *"other"* sheep which had not been brought into the fold at the time the Saviour then spake were believers from among the Gentiles, and these, together with the Jewish believers, should be "one fold" (or, better "one flock"), which is the equivalent of one family, the family of God.

Fourth, in John 11:49-52 we read "and one of them, named Caiaphas, being the high priest that same year, said unto them, Ye know nothing at all, nor consider that it is expedient for us, that one Man should die for the people, and that the whole nation perish not. And this spake he not of himself: but being high priest that year, he prophesied that Jesus should die for that nation, and not for that nation only, but that also He should *gather together in one* the children of God that were scattered abroad." This was a remarkable prophecy, and contained far more in it than Caiaphas was aware. It made known the Divine purpose in the death of the Saviour and revealed what was to be the outcome of the great Sacrifice. It looked out far beyond the bounds of Judaism, including within its range believing sinners from the Gentiles. The "children of God that were scattered abroad" were the elect found among all nations. That they were here termed "children of God" while viewed as still "scattered abroad" gives us the *Divine* viewpoint, being parallel with "other sheep I *have*." But what we desire to call special attention to is the declaration that these believers from among the Gentiles were to be "gathered together in one," not into one "Body" (for, as previously said, the Body does not fall within the scope of John's writings), but one family, the family of God.

Fifth, in John 14:1 and 2 we read that Christ said to His disciples "In My Father's House are many mansions: if it were not so, I would have told you. I go to prepare a place for you. And if I go and prepare a place for you, I will come again and receive you unto Myself that where I am, there ye may be also." How entirely different this is from anything that is to be found in the first three Gospels scarcely needs to be pointed out. In them reference is invariably made to the coming of "the Son of Man to the earth (something which is *never* found in John's Gospel), but here it is the first stage in the Second Coming of Christ which is brought into view: it is the rapture of the saints to heaven, and the taking of them to be where Christ now is that is here expressly mentioned. And manifestly this can in no wise be limited to Jewish believers.

Sixth, without attempting to develop this point at any length it should be noticed that the relation which the Holy Spirit sustains to believers in this Gospel is entirely different from what is before us in the first three. Here only do we read of being "born of the Spirit" *(3:5)*. Here only is He denominated their "Comforter" or Advocate *(see 14:16)*, and here only do we read of Him "abiding for ever" with believers *(see 14:16)*.

Seventh, the High Priestly prayer of the Saviour which is recorded in John 17, and found nowhere else in the Gospels, shows plainly that more than Jewish believers are here contemplated, and evidences the wider scope of this fourth Gospel. Here we find the Saviour saying "Father, the hour is come; glorify Thy Son, that Thy Son may also glorify Thee: as Thou hast given Him power over *all flesh*, that He should give eternal life to as many as Thou hast given Him." The "as many as Thou hast given Him" takes in the whole family of God. Again, in verse 20 the Lord Jesus says, "Neither pray I for these alone, but for *them also which shall believe* on Me through their word:" the "these" evidently refer to Jewish believers, while the "them also" looked forward to Gentile believers. Finally, His Words in verse 22 "and the glory which Thou gavest Me I have given them; *that they may be one*, even as We are One" shows, once more, that the whole family of God was here before Him.

In bringing this article to a close we want to prepare the reader for the second of the series. In our next issue we shall (*D.V.*) take up the first section of the opening chapter, and it is our earnest desire that many of our readers will make these verses the subject of prayerful study and meditation. The Bible teacher who becomes a substitute for diligent study on the part of those who hear him is a hindrance and not a help. The business of the teacher is to turn people to the searching of the Scriptures for themselves, stimulating their interest in the Sacred Word, and instructing them *how* to go about it. With this end in view, it will be our aim to prepare a series of questions at the close of each article bearing on the passage to be expounded in the succeeding one, so that the reader may study it for himself during the month which precedes its appearance in this magazine. Below are seven questions on the passage for the portion we shall take up next month, and we earnestly urge our readers to *study* the first thirteen verses of John 1, and to concentrate upon the points raised by our questions.

1. What "beginning" is referred to in John 1:1?

2. How may I obtain a better, deeper, fuller knowledge of God Himself? By studying nature? By prayer? By studying Scripture? Or—how?

3. *Why* is the Lord Jesus here termed "The Word"? What is the exact force and significance of this title?

4. What is the meaning of John 1:4—"The *Life* was the *Light* of men"?

5. The fact that the Saviour is termed "the Light" in 1:7, teaches us *what?*

6. What does John 1:12 teach concerning what a sinner must do to be saved?

7. What is the exact meaning of each clause in 1:13?

Pray over and *meditate* much upon each of these questions, and above all "Search the Scriptures" to find God's answers. Next month, *(D. V.)*, answers to these questions will be found in our exposition of the whole passage.—*Arthur W. Pink.*

COUNSEL TO A PREACHER

As you have expressed a wish for a few of my thoughts on your principal work as a Christian minister, I will endeavor to comply with your request. The work in which you are engaged is of great importance. To declare the whole counsel of God in such a way as to save yourself and them that hear you; or, if they are not saved, to be pure from their blood, is no small matter. The character of the preaching in an age, contributes, more than most other things, to give character to the Christians of that age. A great and solemn trust, therefore, is reposed in us, of which we must shortly give an account.

The work of a Christian minister, as it respects the pulpit, may be distinguished into two general branches; namely, *expounding the Scriptures, and discoursing on Divine subjects.* In this letter I shall offer a few remarks on the former.

I have found it not a little useful, both to myself and to the people, to appropriate one part of every Lord's Day to the *exposition* of a chapter, or part of a chapter, in the Sacred Writings. In this way, during the last eighteen years, I have gone over the greater part of the Old Testament, and some books in the New. It is advantageous to a minister to feel himself necessitated, as it were, to understand every part of Scripture in order to explain it to the people. It is also advantageous to a people, that what they shall hear should come *directly* from the Word of God, and that they should be led to see the scope and connection of the Sacred Writers. For want of this, a great number of Scripture passages are misunderstood and misapplied. In going over the book I have frequently been struck with surprise in meeting with texts, which, as they had always occurred to me, I had understood in a sense utterly foreign from what manifestly appeared to be their meaning *when viewed in connection with the context.*

1. The great thing necessary for expounding the Scripture, is, *to enter into their true meaning.* We may read them, *and talk about them,* again and again, without imparting any light concerning them. If the hearer, when you have done, understands no more of that part of Scripture than he did before, *your labor is lost.*

2. A humble sense of our own ignorance, and of our entire dependance upon God, has also a great influence on our coming at the true meaning of the Word. There are few things which tend more to blind the mind than a conceit of our own powers. Hence we perceive the justness of such language as the following: "Proud, knowing nothing—He that thinketh he knoweth anything, knoweth nothing yet as he ought to know—If any man will be wise, let him first become a fool, that he may be wise."

3. To understand the Scriptures in such a manner as to profitably expound them, it is necessary to be conversant with them *in private;* and to mix, not only faith, but

the prayer of faith with what we read. There is a great difference between reading the Scriptures *as a student,* in order to find something to say to the people, and reading them *as a Christian,* with a view to get good from them to one's own soul. That which is gained in the last of these ways is, beyond all comparison, of the greatest use, both to ourselves and others. That which we communicate will freeze upon our lips, unless we have first applied it to ourselves; or, to use the language of Scripture, "tasted, felt, and handled the Word of Life."—*Extracts from letter by Andrew Fuller, 1824.*

THE HOLY TRINITY

A subject so great and so much above our comprehension as this is, requires to be treated with trembling. Everything we can think or say, concerning the ever blessed God, requires the greatest modesty, fear, and reverence. Were I to hear two persons engaged in a warm contest upon the subject, I should fear for them both. One might in the main be in the right, and the other in the wrong: but if many words were used, they might both be expected to incur the reproof of the Almighty: "Who is this that darkeneth counsel by words without knowledge?"

The people of Israel were forbidden to break through the bounds which were set for them, and to gaze on the visible glory of Jehovah. The Bethshemites, for looking into the Ark, were smitten with death. Such judgments may not befall us in these days; but we may expect others, more to be dreaded. As the Gospel is a spiritual dispensation, its judgments, as well as its blessings, are chiefly spiritual. Where men have employed themselves in curiously prying into things too high for them, they have ordinarily been smitten with a blast upon their minds, and upon their ministry.

There is a greater importance in the doctrine of the Trinity than commonly appears on a superficial inspection of it, chiefly perhaps on account of its affecting our views of the person and work of Christ, which, being the foundation on which the Church is built, cannot be removed without the utmost danger to the building.

It is a subject of pure revelation. If the doctrine be not taught in the oracles of God, we have nothing to do with it; but if it be, whether we can comprehend it or not, we are required humbly to believe it, and to endeavor to understand so much as God has revealed concerning it. We are not required to understand *how* three are one, for this is not revealed. If we do not consider the Father, Son, and Spirit, as being both three and one *in the same sense,* which certainly we do not, we do not believe a contradiction. We may leave speculating minds to lose themselves and others in a labyrinth of conceits, while we learn what is revealed, and rest contented with it. In believing three Divine Persons in one essence, I do not mean that the distinction between the Father, the Son and the Holy Spirit, is the same as that between three human persons; but neither is there any other term that answers to the Scriptural idea; and since Christ is said to be "the express image" of His Father's "*person*," I see nothing objectionable in using this.—*Andrew Fuller, 1824.*

THE NAZARITE

NUMBERS 6:1-4

The appellation Nazarite, signifies a "separated one." Thus, when Jacob invoked blessing on Joseph, he designated him "the Nazarite"—translated in our English Bible, "*Him that was separated* from his brethren" *(Gen. 49:26).* And, indeed, the name is derived from a verb which occurs five times in "the law of the Nazarite," with which this chapter is occupied, and is rendered "to separate" *(vss. 2, 3, 5, 6),* and "to consecrate" *(vs. 12).* In short, "the law of the Nazarite" depicts, in type, true "separation unto the Lord"—first, the perfect separation of Christ, and secondly, that of those who are sanctified in Him.

The ancient Scriptures rehearse separation unto God in numerous types, each enforcing some peculiar aspect of it. The most prominent of these are the separation of Israel as a nation, the separation of the Levitical families, the separation of the cleansed leper, and that of the Nazarite, upon which we are now to meditate. These have all much in common; and yet each distinctly affords its own valuable instruction and admonition for us upon whom the ends of the age are come *(see I Cor. 10:11)*. What the first three have in common with Nazariteship will appear incidentally in any just examination of that type; but it seems necessary particularly to indicate the more prominent points in which this character of consecration differs from those.

The first, the main distinction, is very remarkable. In all the other types we have named, the separation exhibited is *visibly* accomplished through death. In each case the subject of separation dies in his substitute. The nation dies in the Paschal lamb *(Exod. 12)*, the priest in the "ram of consecration" *(Lev. 8)*, and the leper in the slain bird *(see Lev. 14)*.

So the Holy Spirit continually repeats the great truth of the separation of the redeemed unto God by the death of Christ *(see Gal. 1:4)*. God's sentence against sin was executed upon Christ, in His death; and the instant the Holy Spirit brings any man into connection with the death of Christ, he is separated from the world: he has become one of "a holy nation," one of the "royal priesthood;" he was a leper, but infallible truth pronounces him "clean every whit." He enters the path of life, which is truly the path of consecration, because he has been crucified with Christ. This we know upon the testimony of the Holy Spirit: "Our old man was crucified with Christ, that the body of sin might be destroyed, that henceforth we should not serve sin" *(Rom. 6:6)*.

Such an one "died once" in Christ, and yet he "lives unto God." The true Israelite died in the lamb's death, that he might no longer walk in Egypt's way, or eat of Egypt's meat *(see Exod. 12:11; I Cor. 5: 7)*. The true priest died in the ram of consecration, and henceforth presents himself "a living sacrifice, holy and acceptable unto God, which is his reasonable service" *(Num. 18:7; Rom. 12:1)*. The cleansed leper is to "purge himself from all filthiness of the flesh and spirit, perfect holiness in the fear of God" *(Lev. 14:8,9; II Cor. 7:1)*. In a word, truly believing that he was put to death in Christ's crucifixion, the Christian is to "reckon himself to be dead indeed unto sin, but alive unto God in *(Greek, en)* Jesus Christ our Lord" *(Rom. 6:11)*. And because this is true—it is God's reckoning—the Christian is by no means to suffer sin to "reign in his mortal body that he should obey it in the lusts thereof:" and, going beyond the negative, it is demanded of him that he should present himself and his members "*unto God*" in holy and righteous service *(see Rom. 6:12-23)*.

Now, the Nazarite service is in many respects similar to those at which we have glanced, but it is introduced very differently. Let us carefully meditate upon its introduction.

"*And the Lord spake unto Moses saying, speak unto the children of Israel, and say unto them, When a man or woman shall separate themselves to vow a vow of a Nazarite to separate themselves unto the Lord,*" etc. *(vss. 1,2)*.

Thus, death is not, as in the other types, set before us as the introduction to *this* character of separation. To see the reasons for this, it is necessary to observe that our chapter portrays two cases of Nazarite separation: the one imperfect, a "defiled consecration" *(see vss. 9-12)*, the other perfect, a separation of which "the days are fulfilled" *(vss. 13-21)*.

The first represents a believer's separation of himself, which is ever liable to interruption, and ever imperfect. Hence sacrificial death meets us in the type of this as the gracious provision and remedy for defiled consecration *(see vss. 10-12)*.

The second is that of the Lord Jesus, the only perfect Nazarite, and hence sacrificial death meets us as the consummation of unbroken and undefiled consecration *(see vss. 13-17)*. It is obvious that the death of the perfect One lay at the end of His Nazarite course, and was, indeed, its completion, and this could not be represented in the beginning of the typical action. "He was made perfect through suffering" *(Heb. 2:10)*. And, besides this, it will be found that the type, insofar as it refers to believers, is chiefly designed to bring out the truth that their consecration is, in the end, to proclaim the full value and power of His atoning death. This, however, belongs rather to the closing verses of this chapter.

But why, since all true separation of a believer can only begin through death, why is this not visibly introduced in the beginning of the Nazarite ordinance, as well as in the case of failure? The answer will appear in the elucidation of the peculiar nature of consecration displayed in the type.

And first of all it must be observed that Nazar-separation, as seen in the passage before us, was the *voluntary act of an Israelite*. This law is addressed "*To the children of Israel*" *(vs. 2)*. We lay emphasis on the fact that only an Israelite could be a Nazarite: for this shows that while substitutionary death is not rehearsed in the introduction, yet only one who was dead in the Paschal lamb, and who had been baptized into death in the Red Sea, could assume the Nazar's vow in the wilderness; and only as having "passed clean over Jordan"—another symbol of conquered death —could one make himself a Nazarite in the land of Canaan—"the land of the living."

This exhibits, then, a most interesting view of the saint's separation. It tells us that none but crucified, dead, and risen men can take a single step in consecration unto God. Only one on whom God's sentence has been executed can live unto God; and only such an one can have any volition Godward. "He that hath *suffered in the flesh* hath ceased from sin: that he should live to the will of God" *(I Peter 4:1,2)*. Vain are all the religious devotions of unregenerate men. Life's actions cannot be educed from a man "dead *in* sins;" but they can and will be characteristic of the man "dead *to* sin" in Christ; for all such live.

The expression, *"the children of Israel,"* which in our chapter limits Nazariteship, further reminds us of what we are taught very fully by many special examples, namely, that the Christian is a Nazarite *by birth*. This is a prominent point in the case of Samson—"A Nazarite unto God from the womb" *(Judg. 13:5)*, and such, in principle, were Jeremiah *(see Jer. 1:5)*, and the sons of Rechab *(see Jer. 25)*, and John the Baptist *(see Luke 1:15)*. The type had marked fulfillment in Paul, "the pattern of believers"—a Nazarite by birth of God. But, indeed, it is true of all the children of God, that they are born not only to an inheritance, but each to some special service which calls for Nazarite devotion. This is too little felt, and too little manifest in our time: we live in a time of "ease in Zion." May these hints be used to quicken us all to personal devotedness in our special calling.

It must be next observed that the Nazarites *"separate themselves by vow,"* or as it is in the margin, *"make themselves Nazarites."* This is, first, manifestly typical of Christ's voluntary sanctification of Himself. "For their sakes," saith He, "I sanctify Myself" *(John 17:19)*. In the strict sense He only could do this; and in the strict sense He alone "vows and pays His vows," and we look on while He does so in our "presence." It is His to perform, and ours to "praise" *(Psa. 116)*.

Nevertheless, the voluntary action of the Nazarite is in no light sense typical of Christian volition—that is, of Christ's action in the believer. We are, by this picture, introduced to a Christian "walking in newness of life," and "serving in newness of spirit." And in this we see how appropriate it is that His death could only be implied. It is the design of the Holy Spirit here to make the saint's *life*, in its outgoings unto God, the conspicuous thing.

Let us dwell a little on this living of Christ in the believer. We must not suppose that our passage affords any warrant for vow-making. That were to return to legalism. The ritual type pointed to a spiritual reality, not to its own continuance. The type, we repeat, is the portraiture of Christ, and of what a saint ought to be, and will be, insofar as he walks in Him. It exhibits the proper outgoing toward God, of one who can say, "I live, yet I no more, but Christ liveth in me: and the life which I now live in the flesh I live in faith, that of the Son of God Who loved me and gave Himself for me" *(Gal. 2:20)*. Christ is not only the motive of the believer, He is the actor in him. It were well that this great and glorious truth were more fully recognized. It is only in the recognition of this that we can really walk and serve before God. Paul opens out before us the sources and springs or Nazar-life when he says on His own and on our behalf, "We are the circumcision, who worship God in the spirit and rejoice in Christ Jesus, and have no confidence in the flesh."

Once more, in meditating on the introduction to Nazarite devotion, let us lay great stress on the words, "unto the Lord." If the Lord is not set before the soul as its object, it matters nothing how marked our external separation may be. The true intent of consecration is not the display of peculiarities: but these should result from separation "unto the Lord." The external must proceed from internal appreciation of the truth that "He gave Himself for us, that He might redeem us from all iniquity, and purify *unto Himself* a peculiar people zealous of good works" *(Titus 2:14)*. The perfect Nazarite said, "I have set the Lord always before me:" and not a step can be taken in the Nazar-path but as we have the same object—God Himself. It is terrible to find out how far we can go in the externals of the peculiar people from the impulses of nature and the flesh. Even an Elijah, who was certainly a true Nazarite upon the whole, is revealed before us as zealous for himself, while talking of his "jealousy for the Lord God of Hosts" *(I Kings 19:14)*. That jealousy had been real, but it was interrupted when he got occupied with his own dangers and wrongs. True devotedness begins with God; it continues only so long as He is set before the soul; and restoration from failure can only be found in fresh separation "unto the Lord." *"Unto the Lord"* takes precedence of the peculiarities of consecration.

We have already said that Nazarite separation is typical of the devotion of our Lord in His special service, and of ours in Him. It is this which we find specified in such texts as these. "Paul a servant of Jesus Christ *separated unto* the Gospel of God" *(Rom. 1:1)*. "Meditate on these things: *give thyself wholly to them*" *(I Tim. 4:15)*. "Ye know the house of Stephanas that they *have addicted themselves unto the ministry* of the saints" *(I Cor. 16:15)*. Indeed the cases of Samson, and of Jeremiah, and of John the Baptist show that this is the character of service contained in the type.

In this connection it ought to be observed that devotion to one's own service is very pleasing in the sight of the Lord, and that He demands its full acknowledgment among His people. Korah, Dathan and Abiram sought to abolish this distinction of service, and perished before the Lord for their temerity *(see Num. 16)*. And the Holy Spirit demands in the church, the reverent recognition of distinctive devotion in ministry. Speaking of the house of Stephanas, and of others exercising faithfulness as Christian Nazarites, Paul beseeches the Corinthians to "submit themselves to such," and to "acknowledge them that are such" *(I Cor. 16:16,18)*. And to the same effect he exhorts the Thessalonian saints *(see I Thess. 5:12)*. We desire by all means to discourage priestly claims and lordship of God's heritage, but may we be kept also from every approach to "the gainsaying of Korah" *(Jude 10,11; cf. Num. 16)*.

We come now to the particulars of the Nazar-law. These are three in number; they represent separation from nature's enjoyments, from nature's rights, and from nature's sorrows. We shall endeavor to explain the spiritual meaning of each particular, and offer some examples illustrative of each, drawn from the life of the Lord Himself, and from the history of His servants. For while Jesus alone could carry the "Nazarite vow" to its completion, His perfect devotion was in part anticipated by the action of His Spirit in the ancient saints who "waited for His salvation;" and those who have received that salvation in the power of the Holy Spirit have followed Him, in some little measure, in His path of separation.

1. The Nazarite vow demanded separation from wine, and strong drink in every form.

"He shall separate himself from wine and strong drink, and shall drink no vinegar of wine, or vinegar of strong drink, neither shall he drink any liquor of grapes, nor eat moist grapes, or dried. All the days of his separation shall he eat nothing that is made of the vine tree, from the kernels even to the husk" *(Num. 6:3,4)*.

That wine, as a stimulant of nature is viewed as the emblem of nature's gladness scarcely needs proof—"Wine that maketh glad the heart of man" *(Psa. 104:15)*. It is therefore forbidden in the ritual before us, and becomes the representative of all that ministers to the joy of nature, or that stimulates the energies of the flesh.

To see the force of this in its bearing on the Christian's devotion unto the Lord, it must be remembered that the use of wine, of course with self-control, was and is lawful in itself. It is plain that in the case of the Nazarite abstinence from the fruit of the vine, "from the kernel to the husk," belonged to the days of his special separation. And as for the Christian, he is taught that "every creature of God is good," and "nothing unclean of itself." And the apprehension of this is important, because that which is sinful in itself, is disallowed to the Christian, not only insofar as it effects his special service, but always and in any case. But in Christian devotion, represented by our type, we see that which is lawful in itself disallowed and abandoned; and this is *the point* in all the particulars of Nazarite separation.

Here, then, is the great lesson of this portion of Scripture, namely, that Christian devotion demands the rejection of the energies of the flesh, which "profiteth nothing." Some one has well observed that the fleshly nature is sufficiently active to intrude itself, without the aid of stimulants. The Holy Spirit is Himself the power of service in the believer: but, supply nature's excitements, and there is no room for His action. Hence the word "be not drunk with wine wherein is excess; but be filled with the Spirit" *(Eph. 5:18)*. It is certain that the slightest approach to literal drunkenness must be a hindrance to spiritual vigor. But it must not be forgotten that the figure goes much further than the "temperance pledge" of our times. "Strong drink" is the representative of anything which arouses the energy of the flesh, and the flesh is not only unprofitable in service, it is "enmity against God," and therefore cannot *"mind* the things of the Spirit of God" *(Rom. 8:5-8)*. "Total abstinence" from every form of strong drink is well if, like that of the true Nazarite, it is *"unto the Lord;"* but it is possible to abstain from the literal wine, and yet to drink largely, and to inebriety, of all else that excites the flesh. It may be profitable to remember that Nazarite devotion is especially to mark the period of the Bridegroom's absence: for it was of this period in which we are called to serve that He spoke when He said: "The days will come when the Bridegroom shall be taken away from them, and then shall they fast in those days" *(Mark 2:20)*. The time of His absence is the time of the world's rejoicing, but of the weeping and lamentation of a waiting bride *(see John 16:20)*. An apostate Church "lives deliciously," and drinks, and gives to drink of "the cup which she hath filled," but the true spouse refuses the wine of the earth for the "love" that is "better than wine" *(see Rev. 18; Cant. 1:2)*.

But now let us seek some illustrations of this separation unto the Lord, from nature's wine, in the life of the Perfect Nazarite. His was not a few weeks of devotion, but Nazarite life from beginning to end. It was just because of this that, with all the sorrow of His course here below, He could always say, "Thou hast put gladness in My heart, more than in the time that their corn and their wine increased" *(Psa. 4:7)*.

It were easy to multiply instances of His rejection of nature's joy for His Father's work. For our first example of this Nazarite devotion, we turn to His first Passover, as "the child Jesus," when He "tarried behind in Jerusalem." Joseph and Mary, when they missed Him, judging according to *nature,* supposed that He would be found enjoying Himself with "their kinsfolk and acquaintance." But he "was about His Father's business" *(Luke 2)*. In like manner, at the marriage at Cana, Mary counted on nature in her Son—but He refused to drink the joy of maternal approval in His Father's service *(see John 2)*. And so, again, when His brethren expected that He would appreciate the opportunity of the great feast to display Himself, He could say, "My time is not yet" *(John 7)*. We have the perfect vow of the perfect Nazarite in the words in which He refused to eat, at Samaria's well: "My meat is to do the will of Him that sent Me, and to finish His work" *(John 4: 34)*. And every intelligent and thoughtful reader of His life will find the external expression of His internal Nazariteship, in the remarkable saying, "I will drink no more of this fruit of the vine, until that day when I drink it new with you in the Kingdom of God" *(Matt. 26:29)*. He separated Himself from "wine and strong drink," and from all that was "made of the vine tree, from the kernels even to the husk," because "Jehovah was the portion of His cup" *(Psa. 16:5)*. From nature's provisions He drew no comfort in His sorrow, no strength for the oblation of Himself unto God. He went to the Cross, and to death, and passed through Hades, in the power of the Eternal Spirit.

Such was The Nazarite's refusal of all that earth could yield. But let us now glance at a few examples of the same separation from nature's gladdening vine, accomplished by His Spirit in His servants.

One of the most striking displays of this separation from the joys of nature is found in the history of Job. We read that "his sons went and feasted in their houses, every one his day; and sent and called for their three sisters to eat and drink with them" *(Job 1:4)*. Now, few things could be more naturally attractive to a parent than a feast with his children; but Job went not to their feasts. While eating and drinking wine, he was engaged in Nazar-service and worship. "And it was so, when the days of their feasting were gone about, that Job sent and sanctified them, and rose up early in the morning, and offered burnt offerings according to the number of them all: for Job said, It may be that my sons have cursed (or forsaken) God in their hearts. Thus did Job continually" *(Job 1:5)*. This contains a sweet and solemn lesson for true servants. God was Job's object—His glory and His name were precious to his heart; and so, for the Lord's honor among his children, he serves and worships.

What an example for us in these days of religious and worldly gaiety. Too many of the "little children" are following after nature's joys, and, alas, their feasts are not confined to the family. And what are the "fathers" doing? Are they at the feasts, too? Or are they, in the power of unbroken communion with Christ, bringing their Nazarite service to bear on the "little children," that they also may be "sanctified"? And, withal, are the fathers, in the power of the true "burnt offering," dealing with God about all the worldly wines mixed and drunk with such fearful avidity by the children?

We know, of course, the arguments by which it is sought to justify the presence of the believer in the gaieties which they profess to deplore. Their presence, it is said, exerts an influence for good; it is a restraint upon the more thoughtless, and prevents extremes of folly into which young and careless Christians would otherwise fall. But this is the old argument, "Let us do evil that good may come." And, besides, according to Divine argument, testimony against evil is vain while you partake of it, or countenance it. Lot could do nothing for Sodom while *in it*. Abraham, *apart from it*, could plead for it, and for the sake of Abraham, Lot escaped its doom. Job knew this better way. His power was exerted in the presence of the Lord, in separation from his children's gaieties. He knew that he could not both enjoy the wine feast, and act for God's glory in the power of the burnt offering.

Another striking example of separation of this character is that presented in the course of Daniel in the palace of Babylon's king. "Daniel purposed in his heart that he would not defile himself with the king's meat nor with the wine which he drank" *(Dan. 1:8)*, and others with him preferred the "pulse and water." And with what result the whole story tells. Truly the rejection of the fatness and wine of earth was followed by heavenly communion and power. It will not be thought that we advocate either legal or monkish asceticism. The great point is fellowship with Christ, maintained and marked by holy separation from all that drags down and pins the heart to nature and its joy. The New Testament teaches that what we eat or drink, is of no consequence whatever *(see Mark 7:15; I Cor. 8:8)*, save insofar as our eating or drinking may hinder the profit of our own or of another's soul *(see I Cor. 8:10; Rom. 14)*. If we use our liberty "as a cloke of maliciousness" *(I Peter 2:16)*, ruthless of our brother's "stumbling" *(Gal. 5:13; I Cor. 8:9)*, or for the mere gratification of appetite; clearly our consecration is marred *(see Eph. 5:18)*. The Nazarite teaching, however, as we have seen, goes far farther than the regulation of the Christian's food. It demands that separation from natural enjoyments which results from the heart being "established with grace, not with meats" *(Heb. 13)*.

It still remains, to complete our view of this department of Nazarite life, to select some exemplification from the life of the saints of the New Testament. Our limited space compels us to confine ourselves to two expressions contained in Paul's Epistles.

We find a very remarkable expression of his Nazarite renunciation of nature's gladness, in his renunciation of all earthly expectations, which, as a Jew, he had cherished in connection with the advent of Israel's Messiah. "Yea, though we have known Christ after the flesh, yet now henceforth know we Him no more" *(II Cor. 5: 16, cf. Phil. 3)*. All the joy of the earthly was freely abandoned for the better joy of the heavenly hope, and the present blessedness of intimacy with Christ as the head of the new creation—the joy of oneness with Him *(see II Cor. 5:17)*.

To select one more example of this Nazarite spirit. You have it in the pathetic words, "So then death worketh in us, and life in you" *(II Cor. 4:12)*. In the light of the context it seems plain that these words amount to saying, "We, in bearing to you the joys of salvation and life, must lay aside for the present our own enjoyment. Our ministry, by means of which you enjoy the blessings of the life is rendered at the expense of our experience of 'the death.' You are drinking of the gladness of Christ's life, we are tasting the humiliation and sorrow of His death." And this will be the experience of all who serve the saints, with any measure of the devotion represented in the Nazarite.

We must postpone the consideration of the other peculiarities of this type. Meanwhile may the Lord draw us away from creature joys, that we may serve in the power of the Holy Spirit, with the devotion which, so far as His service requires it, refuses even that which is good in itself, because we have learned that His lovingkindness is better than life.

(To be continued, D. V.)
—*From "Grace and Truth" by Chas. Campbell, 1871.*

VOL. 1.   FEBRUARY, 1922   NO. 2.

STUDIES in the SCRIPTURES

"Search the Scriptures" John 5:39.

A PERIODICAL (MONTHLY "IF THE LORD WILL")
DEVOTED TO BIBLE STUDIES and EXPOSITIONS

Associate Editors and Publishers, I. C. HERENDEEN and ARTHUR W. PINK,
Swengel, Pa.
Application for entry as second-class matter at the post office at Swengel, Pa. pending.

Price: 10 cents per copy; $1.00 per year. Foreign $1.00 per year.

TO OUR READERS—

In undertaking the happy task of publishing STUDIES IN THE SCRIPTURES, it is our determination and purpose, with the "help of God," to make it as spiritually helpful and profitable as possible. With this end constantly in view we shall, therefore, be exceedingly conservative in the selection of all articles appearing therein, including in its pages chiefly those of an expository nature, and only such as exalt the adorable Person and finished Work of our Lord and Saviour, Jesus Christ. As stated in the first (January) issue, we mean to "ride no hobbies" of any kind, but, instead, sincerely aim to preserve "the balance of truth." We shall not insert any news items or include anecdotes, but earnestly endeavor to minister to the people of God that which will at once strengthen their faith, deepen their gratitude and feed their souls.

We are counting upon our readers to do all in their power to help us send forth "the light and the truth," by not only sending **at once** their own, but, if such is possible, the subscriptions of others as well. No doubt all will wish to have Brother Pink's most excellent notes on John's Gospel complete, so we advise such to act promptly while the first issues of STUDIES IN THE SCRIPTURES are obtainable. Furthermore, your **prompt** and favorable response when we are just taking up this service to the Lord will be doubly appreciated. Free sample copies will be gladly furnished to all requesting same. Be sure to state the number you can judiciously use.

Yours "holding forth the Word of Life" *(Phil. 2:16),*

I. C. Herendeen.

THE SWORD OF JUSTICE AWAKENED AGAINST GOD'S FELLOW

"Awake, O sword against My Shepherd, and against the Man that is My Fellow, saith the Lord of Hosts" (Zech. 13:7).

I. WHAT KIND OF A SWORD IS THIS?

1. It is a *broad* sword; so broad that it covers all mankind, and hangs over all Christless sinners, who would all have fallen a sacrifice to it, unless Christ had come between them and it. When this sword did awake against Christ, He found it as broad as the curse pronounced against mankind, upon the back of our fall in Adam; which you may read, that you may the better understand what the Man that is God's Fellow underwent, when He substituted Himself in our room, and undertook the punishment for our sins, the curse pronounced against Adam, and in him against all his posterity, and which, in all the parts of it, lighted upon Christ.

2. It is a *long* sword: if we may so call it. Infinite in length from the point to the hilt of the sword: it is as long as eternity. And this makes the punishment of the damned eternal, because the sword of Divine wrath which pierces them, is so long that it never can reach to the hilt, in such finite worms as they are. The duration of the wrath and the curse is eternal; because the sinner, being a mere creature, cannot at one shock meet with the infinite wrath of God, and satisfy justice at once; therefore God supports the poor, damned creature forever under wrath; because it cannot, being finite, satisfy infinite justice. But our Shepherd, being God-Man, the Man God's Fellow; and therefore being of infinite worth and value, of infinite strength and power, *was able* to satisfy justice, and bear all *at once,* that which the elect could never have borne.

3. It is a *bloody and insatiable* sword: this sword of justice was not satisfied with the blood of Sodom and Gomorrah; it was not satisfied with the blood of the old world; it was not satisfied with the blood of bulls, goats, and all the legal sacrifices of old; yea, the blood of the whole creation cannot give it satisfaction, though it were bathed therein; without the shedding of more blood, better blood, there is no remission, no satisfaction to justice, no real satisfaction with God; no salvation of the sinner; therefore, Awake, O sword, against the Man that is My Fellow: till it be drunk with *the blood of this Man,* it never gets a satisfying draught of blood. Well then, says this Man, Lo, I come; let justice take a full draught of My blood: well, "Awake, O sword"; let the blood of this Man, My Fellow, be shed. What say you now, O sword of justice! Are you pleased? Are you satisfied with blood? Yes, I have got my fill of blood; "this is My beloved Son, in Whom I am well pleased"; I am pleased and satisfied to the full with His obedience to the death; I have got all the satisfaction I wanted from My Shepherd, and I have no more to demand of Him or His sheep either.

4. It is a *dreadful, terrible, flaming, and devouring sword:* so it is represented in Genesis 3:24 where it is said, Cherubims were placed, "and a flaming sword, which turned every way to keep the way of the tree of life." The last flame of this sword of justice will be enough to burn up the whole creation; and, O! how terrible will this sword be forever to them that live and die in a Christless state. The dreadfulness of this sword is nowhere to be seen so lively as in its awakening against the Man that was God's Fellow: if human nature trembled at the sight of it—"Now is My soul troubled, and what shall I say?" *(John 12:27).* He saw the dreadful storm coming, the black cloud arising, and so much wrath in it, that He knew not how to express Himself. But the main fight was to be on Mount Calvary, after they nailed Him to the Cross; then, on a sudden, the curtain of heaven is drawn, the sun loses his light; He was now combatting with all the powers of hell and darkness, and therefore the field He was to fight in was dark. The punishment of loss and sense *both was due to us* for sin, therefore He suffered both: the punishment of 'loss', for all comfort now fails Christ; angels appeared before "strengthening" Him; but not an angel dares peep out of heaven for His comfort now; yea, His God fails Him, in respect of His comforting presence: formerly His heart failed Him, in some respects, but now His God: which makes Him cry out "My God, My God, Why hast Thou forsaken Me?" Never was there such a cry in heaven or earth, before or since: yea, now He suffered the punishment of 'sense' also due to us; for now all the wrath of God was poured down immediately upon His soul: all the sluices of Divine fury were opened, and all the waves

and billows of His vengeance passed over Him. Darkness was over all the earth: all things hushed into silence, that Christ might, without interruption grapple with God's wrath, until He cried, "It is finished," and "gave up the ghost"—What think you of this dreadful sword that awaked against our Surety, the Man God's Fellow, when He was to expiate our sins?

5. It is a *living* sword: do you think that God is speaking to a piece of cold iron, when He says, "Awake, O sword"? Nay, this sword is God Himself, the living God: God's justice is God Himself, a just God. Of this living sword you read, "It is a fearful thing to fall into the hands of the living God" *(Heb. 10:31).* They that fall into hell, fall into the hands of the living God; and there they are an everlasting sacrifice to this ever-living sword. Christ, when He came to satisfy justice, fell into the hands of this living God, and if He had not been God's equal, God's Fellow, He could never have got out of His hands again. "Awake, O sword": God is here speaking to Himself. It is as if He had said, Let Me arise in My armour of vengeance and fury, and fall upon My Shepherd, the Man that is My Fellow. It is a living sword that can awake itself. Thus you see, *what* a sword it is that awoke against Christ. O to see and believe this truth, this day!

II. IN WHAT MANNER DID THIS SWORD AWAKE AGAINST CHRIST?

1. The text imports that the sword had been sleeping and must now awake against Him. Christ having no sin of His own to answer for, the sword of justice had nothing to lay to *His* charge; and so was *sleeping,* as it were, with respect to Him, having nothing to do against Him. It was not until He became our Surety and was "made sin for us" that justice had a right to pursue Him. The sword designed against the Son of God had long slumbered: the sword had slumbered above four thousand years after Adam's fall. But now the Lamb must be slain, therefore, "Awake, O sword."

2. "Awake, O sword" imports that the sword of justice *did not rashly* smite the Man that is God's Fellow. A man in his sleep, or half sleeping, may give a rash, unadvised stroke to his fellow; but before God gave the stroke to the Man that is His Fellow, He did *awake* His justice, as it were, out of sleep, and proceeded upon *the maturest deliberation*—"Awake, O sword." It was no unadvised stroke that Christ got by the sword of justice; it was the fruit of a glorious transaction: neither did the sword strike Him without a warrant, by particular orders from the Judge of all; it was warranted to brandish itself against Him.

3. "Awake, O sword" imports that justice was *lively and vigorous* in executing the vengeance due upon our Surety for our sins. Justice did not give Him a sleepy, lazy, drowsy blow; but a strong, lively, awakened blow. As it is said in another case, "Awake, awake, put on strength, O arm of the Lord" *(Isa. 51:9),* so, "awake, O sword," put on strength. Justice arises, as it were, like one out of sleep, puts on its clothes of vengeance and armour of power, rallies its forces, goes forth with war-like robes, and attacks the Man that is God's Fellow with all its force; and acts, like itself, with impartial equity, without sparing our Surety, because of His quality—"God spared not His Own Son."

4. "Awake, O sword," this imports the great *concern and earnestness* that was in God's heart to have His justice satisfied: O sword; "Awake, O sword." God speaks here with affectionate concern: O sword! O justice! Thou must be honored, glorified, and satisfied, one way or another: and seeing I have proposed that My eternal Son should bear the stroke of vengeance in the room of elect sinners; and seeing He has undertaken it, My very heart is set upon the accomplishment of this glorious work; My justice is one of the pearls of My crown; I will not show mercy to the detriment of My justice. A sacrifice I must have, a sacrifice I will have; therefore, "awake, O sword."

III. MANY THINGS MAY BE DEDUCED FROM THIS DOCTRINE BY WAY OF APPLICATION.

1. *The infinite malignity of sin and the dreadful demerit thereof.* Did it overflow the old world with a deluge of water? Did it consume Sodom and Gomorrah with a storm of fire and brimstone? Did it cast angels and men that are under it into Tophet, the place whereof is fire and much wood, which the breath of the Lord doth kindle; so as the smoke of their torments ascend for ever and ever? In all this may the demerit of sin be seen; but much more here in Christ, a sacrifice to the awakened sword of Divine vengeance. Go to Golgotha, and see the Man that is God's Fellow, drinking up the cup of His Father's

indignation! Suffering unto blood! Suffering unto death! For, God spared Him not, being now in the room of sinners: behold the earth trembling under the mighty load of this terrible wrath; for there was a great earthquake while the sword of God's wrath was running through the Man that was His Fellow; the heavens grew dark when this awful spectacle was exposed; the sun was eclipsed, contrary to the common rules of nature, which made an heathen philosopher cry out, "That either the frame of nature was dissolving, or the God of nature suffering." And what shall we that profess to be Christians say to these things? What shall we that are sinners say concerning the abominable evil, sin, which wrought this bloody tragedy? It was sin, and our sin, too; for He was wounded for *our* iniquities; "the Lord hath laid on Him the iniquity of *us* all" *(Isa. 53:6)*. O! how heavy did the Man that is God's Fellow find the weight of sin to be, when it pressed Him to the ground, and made Him sweat great drops of blood! When the sword of wrath, which He endured in our room, was sheathed in Him.

2. *Behold both the goodness and severity of God:* His goodness, in finding out this way of satisfaction to His own justice, and wounding His own Son, that sinners, for whom He was Surety, might not be wounded eternally: and the severity and justice of God, in exacting such a full satisfaction, that though all the elect had been satisfying eternally in hell, justice had not been made to shine so splendidly and gloriously. O if we could think and speak aright of this wonderful mystery! O wonder that we are not more affected with it! That we, miserable wretched sinners, should have been pursued eternally by justice, and could do nothing to avert the stroke of it; and that such a great and glorious person as the Man, God's Fellow, should interpose Himself; and hereupon the Father should spare the poor sinful enemies, and make way for them to escape, by diverting of His justice from pursuing them, and by making it take hold of the Son of His bosom; exacting the debt severely from Him! O wonder that the Lord should pass by the enemies, and satisfy Himself upon His own Son!

3. *Behold herein the holy sovereignty of God, that over-rules all the actions of men, even these wherein they have a most sensible hand, and are inexcusable.* Though Judas that betrayed, and Pilate that condemned, the innocent Son of God, acted most sinfully, yet the Lord Himself had an active over-ruling hand in carrying out their designs. What Judas and Pilate did, was not by guess, but just the execution of God's ancient decree. Here is a principal diamond in Jehovah's crown, that He is able, not only to govern all the natural secondary causes that are in the world in their actions, and order them to His own glory, but even demons, wicked men, and hypocrites, their most corrupt and abominable actions, and make them invariably subservient to the promoting of His own holy ends and purposes, and yet be free of their sin, for which they shall account to Him: and as it was no excuse to the crucifiers of the Son of God, that they did what before was decreed of God; so it shall be no excuse to any man in a sinful course, that God has a hand in everything that really comes to pass, who yet is just and holy in all. This may also stay our hearts, when the Devil and his instruments are, as it were, running mad, that they can do no more than what God permits; nay, some way commissionates them to do: no sword of men or Devils can do any execution, unless God says, "Awake, O sword.".

4. *In this text we may behold what a gloriously well-qualified Redeemer we have;* He is God's Shepherd, the Man His Fellow: behold what interest He has in God! And that both by nature, being God's Fellow; and by covenant, being God's Shepherd. Behold what interest He has in us: and that also both by nature, being Man; and by covenant, by virtue of the covenant of grace, being our Shepherd by God's appointment. O how fit is He, Who is the essential Wisdom of the Father, to reveal the counsel of God's love from eternity! How fit is He, Who is the middle Person of the Godhead, to be the Mediator and Mid-Man. How fit is He Who is the eternal Son of God, to bring many sons to glory! How fit, as God-Man; being Man, to pay man's debt; being God, to give it a value: man, to deal with man; and God to deal with God! What an *able* Saviour must He be, Who is God's Fellow! Able to save to the uttermost. Help is laid upon One that is mighty indeed! What a *willing* Saviour must He be, Who is God's Fellow! He could not have been forced to suffer, nor dragged to the work, if He had not been willing: nay, with cheerful willingness He flew, as it were, upon the point of the sword—"Lo, I come." What a *suf-*

ficient ransom has He given, since He is God's Fellow! O this price of redemption cannot be over-valued! O how *sure* and *permanent* must this redemption be that is managed by the Lord of Hosts and His Fellow!

5. *We may here see the dreadful state of unbelievers, and the damning nature of unbelief.* The sword of Divine justice, the sword of God's wrath, is hanging over the head of all those who come not under the cover of the blood of Christ, that was shed by this awful sword. What a lofty and terrible word is that in Deuteronomy 32: 40, 41—"I lift up my hand to heaven, and say, I live forever; if I whet my glittering sword, and mine hand take hold on judgment; I will render vengeance to mine enemies, and will reward them that hate me. I will make mine arrows drunk with blood." *The sword of God's vengeance must drink either the blood of the sinner, or the blood of the Surety, in the sinner's room.* Now, they who through unbelief, despise and reject Christ, the sacrifice to justice which God has provided, *they must themselves be a sacrifice thereto:* see how fearfully this is set forth in Hebrews 10: 26-31—"If we sin wilfully after that we have received the knowledge of the truth," that is to say, if we wilfully and finally reject Christ, if we live and die in unbelief, refusing the remedy which God has provided, notwithstanding it is made known to us in the glorious Gospel *that there is no other remedy for us but perishing,* "there remaineth no more sacrifice for sins, but a certain fearful looking for of judgment and fiery indignation, which shall devour the adversaries." O sinner, there is not a day that you hear a sermon and have Christ offered, but that if you slight Him you go away with a new load of guilt; hence the Hell of professors shall be the greatest and hottest place in hell. O unbelief, unbelief! For a man to have continued all his days, from his infancy, under the sound of the Word and calls of the Spirit, saying, Come, come to Christ, and yet the man lives and dies never hearkening. This sin of unbelief is worse than the murdering of Christ, for they knew not that He was the Lord of Glory: but this sin wilfully rejects Him, while you know He is the Lord of Glory. The sin of unbelief, what a dreadful thing it is!

6. *See here the comfortable state of believers in Christ.* The believer cannot but be safe and happy, for the stroke of the sword of justice has passed by him, and has fallen upon his Surety, his Shepherd; and the death of the Shepherd is the life of the sheep. Though the sheep may be scattered, and scarred with fatherly chastisements, yet because the Shepherd was smitten with the sword of Divine justice, no stroke of judicial wrath shall ever fall upon them: for Christ has borne their griefs, and carried their sorrows, by His stripes they are healed. Here is a noble foundation for faith: we may even dare to approach a provoked God, an angry Deity, the God Who is a consuming fire, and a flaming sword; because, here is blood, worthy blood, to quench the fire, even the Man that is God's Fellow bleeding and dying in our stead. Here is the atonement and propitiation, and therefore faith may come boldly to the throne of grace.

7. *Hence we may learn what is the great duty of all who hear the Gospel,* namely, to embrace the Man that is God's Fellow; to come to Him as a sacrifice, in whom the sword of Divine justice has been satisfied. Let me then exhort you in the name of the Lord, to this duty. I charge you, to hear the word of salvation, and apply it particularly to your own souls, whoever you are. Is it so, that the sword of the Lord of Hosts is bathed in the blood of the Shepherd, the Man that is God's Fellow, then, if you would not fall a sacrifice to this sword of God's wrath forever, O close with the Man that is God's Fellow, as He that fell a sacrifice to this sword in your room. Have you no apprehension of the wrath of God, and of your dreadful condition by nature, wherein you are lying bound to be a sacrifice to the wrath of God, the Lord's hand being stretched out to lay on the stroke, and the wrath of God abiding on you, liable to the law's sentence, which is the curse of God, and the vengeance of His awakened sword, until once you get the Man that is God's Fellow put in your room? All that the Gospel aims at is this that you should seek to change places with Christ: guilty sinners, here is the way to get your debt paid, your Judge pleased, justice satisfied, God atoned, sin expiated, and everlasting peace and reconciliation between God and you accomplished.

Come then, by the love and good will of God in Christ I adjure and entreat you not to exclude yourselves by unbelief, from all the benefits of this sacrifice, that Christ offered of Himself to the sword of Divine wrath, but accept of His propitiation and lay your poor guilty souls under the protection of the blood of this Man that is God's Fellow. In the name of God, I proclaim the access that you have all to come to Christ, and to look unto, and depend upon Him for salvation; Look unto Him, all ye ends of the earth, and be ye saved. Whosoever will, let him come.—*Extracts from a sermon by Dr. Ralph Erskine, 1725.*

JOHN'S GOSPEL

2. THE DEITY OF CHRIST. 1:1-13.

In our previous article we stated, "Each book of the Bible has a prominent and dominant theme which is peculiar to itself. Just as each member in the human body has its own particular function, so, every book in the Bible has its own special purpose and mission. The theme of John's Gospel is *the Deity of the Saviour.* Here, as nowhere else in Scripture so fully, the Godhood of Christ is presented to our view. That which is outstanding in this fourth Gospel is the Divine Sonship of the Lord Jesus. In this book we are shown that the One Who was heralded by the angels to the Bethlehem shepherds, Who walked this earth for thirty-three years, Who was crucified at Calvary, Who rose in triumph from the grave, and Who forty days later departed from these scenes, was none other than the Lord of Glory. The evidence for this is overwhelming, the proofs almost without number, and the effect of contemplating them must be to bow our hearts in worship before 'the great God and our Saviour Jesus Christ' *(Titus 2:13).*"

That John's Gospel *does* present the Deity of the Saviour is at once apparent from the opening words of the 1st chapter. The Holy Spirit has, as it were, placed the key right over the entrance, for the introductory verses of this fourth Gospel present the Lord Jesus Christ in Divine relationships and unveil His essential glories. Before we attempt an exposition of this profound passage we shall first submit an analysis of its contents. In these first thirteen verses of John 1 we have set forth:—

1. The Relation of Christ to Time—"In the beginning," therefore, Eternal: 1:1.

2. The Relation of Christ to the Godhead—"With God," therefore, One of the Holy Trinity: 1:1.

3. The Relation of Christ to the Holy Trinity—"God was the Word"—the Revealer: 1:1.

4. The Relation of Christ to the Universe—"All things were made by Him"—the Creator: 1:3.

5. The Relation of Christ to Men—Their "Light": 1:4, 5.

6. The Relation of John the Baptist to Christ—"Witness" of His Deity: 1:6-9.

7. The Reception which Christ met with here: 1:10-13.
   (a) "The world knew Him not": 1:10.
   (b) "His own (Israel) received Him not": 1:11.
   (c) A company born of God "received Him": 1:12, 13.

"In the beginning was the Word, and the Word was with God, and the Word was God. The same was in the beginning with God. All things were made by Him; and without Him was not anything made that was made" *(John 1:1-3).* How entirely different is this from the opening verses of the other Gospels! John opens by immediately presenting Christ not as the Son of David, nor as the Son of Man, but as the Son of God. John takes us back to the beginning, and shows that the Lord Jesus had no beginning. John goes behind creation and shows that the Saviour was Himself the Creator. Every clause in these verses calls for our most careful and prayerful attention.

"In the beginning was the Word, and the Word was with God, and the Word was God." Here we enter a realm which transcends the finite mind, and where speculation is profane. "In *the beginning*" is something we are unable to comprehend: it is one of those matchless sweeps of inspiration which rises above the level of human thought. "In the beginning *was the Word*" and we are equally unable to grasp the final meaning of this. A "word" is an expression: by words we articulate our speech. The *Word* of God, then, is Deity expressing itself in audible terms. And yet, when we have said this, how much there is that we leave unsaid! "And the Word was *with God,*" and this intimates His separate personality, and shows His relation to the other Persons of the blessed Trinity. But how sadly incapacitated are we for meditating upon the relations which exist between the different Persons of the Godhead! *"And God was the Word."* Not only was Christ the Revealer of God, but He always was, and ever remains, none other than God Himself. Not only was our Saviour the One through whom, and by whom, the Deity expressed itself in audible terms, but He was Himself co-equal with the Father and the Spirit. Let us now approach the Throne of Grace and there seek the mercy and grace we so sorely need to help us as we turn now to take a closer look at these verses.

"Our God and Father, in the name of Thy dear Son, we pray Thee that Thy Holy Spirit may now take of the things of Christ and show them unto us: to the praise of the glory of Thy grace. Amen."

"In THE BEGINNING," or, more literally, "in beginning," for there is no article in the Greek. In *what* "beginning"? There are various "beginnings" referred to in the New Testament. There is the "beginning" of "the world" *(Matt. 24:21)*; of "the Gospel of Jesus Christ" *(Mark 1:1)*; of "sorrows" *(Mark 13:8)*, which refers to Israel's birth pangs in the coming Tribulation; of "miracles" (or "signs," *John 2:11*), etc., etc. But the "beginning" mentioned in John 1:1 clearly antedates all these "beginnings." The "beginning" of John 1:1 *precedes* the making of the "all things" of 1:3. It is then, *the beginning of creation, the beginning of time.* This earth of ours is old, how old we do not know, possibly millions of years. But "the Word" was before all things. He was not only *from* the beginning, but He was *"in* the beginning." "In beginning:" the absence of the definite article is designed to carry us back to the most remote point that can be imagined. If then, He was before all creation, and He *was,* for *"all things were made by Him;"* if He was "in the beginning," then He was Himself *without beginning,* which is only the negative way of saying He was *eternal.* In perfect accord with this we find, that in His prayer recorded in John 17, He said, "And now, O Father, glorify Thou Me with Thine own self with the glory which I had with Thee *before the world was."* As, then, the Word was "in the beginning," and if in the beginning, *eternal,* and as none but God Himself is eternal, the absolute *Deity* of the Lord Jesus is conclusively established.

"WAS the Word." There are two separate words in the Greek which, in this passage, are both rendered "was:" the one means *to exist,* the other *to come into being.* The latter word (egeneto) is used in 1:3 which, literally rendered, reads, "all things through Him *came into being,* and without Him *came into being* not even one (thing) which has *come into being;"* and again we have this word "egeneto" in 1:6 where we read "there *was* (became to be) a man sent from God, whose name was John;" and again in 1:14, "And the Word *was made* (became) flesh." But here in 1:1 and 1:2 it is "the word *was* (en) with God." As the Word He did not come into being, or begin *to be,* but He *was* "with God" from all eternity. It is noteworthy that the Holy Spirit uses this word *"en,"* which signifies that the Son *personally subsisted,* no less than four times in the first two verses of John 1. Unlike John the Baptist who *"became* (egeneto) a man," the "Word" *was* (en), that is, *existed* with God before time began.

"Was THE WORD." The reference here is to the Second Person in the Holy Trinity, the Son of God. But *why* is the Lord Jesus Christ designated "the Word"? What is the exact force and significance of this title? The first passage which occurs to our minds as throwing light on this question is the opening statement in the Epistle to the Hebrews: "God, Who at sundry times and in divers manners spake in time past unto the fathers by the prophets, hath in these last days spoken unto us by His Son." Here we learn that Christ is the final *spokesman* of God. Closely connected with this is the Saviour's title found in Revelation 1:8—"I am Alpha and Omega," which intimates that He is *God's alphabet,* the One Who spells out Deity, the One Who utters all God has to say. Even clearer, perhaps, is the testimony of John 1:18: "No man hath seen God at any time; the only begotten Son, which is in the bosom of the Father, He hath *declared Him."* The word "declared" means *tell out,* cf. Acts 15:14, and 21:19; it is translated "told" in Luke 24:35. Putting together these three passages we learn that Christ is the One Who is the Spokesman of God, the One Who spelled out the Deity, the One Who has declared or told forth the Father.

Christ, then, is the One Who has made the incomprehensible God intelligible. The force of this title of His found in John 1:1, may be discovered by comparing it with that name which is given to the Holy Scriptures—"the Word of God." What are the Scriptures? They are the *Word* of God. And what does that mean? This: the Scriptures reveal God's mind, express His will, make known His perfections, and lay bare His heart. This is precisely what the Lord Jesus has done for the Father. But let us enter a little more into detail:—

(a) A "word" is a *medium of manifestation*. I have in my mind a thought, but others know not its nature. But the moment I clothe that thought in words it becomes cognizable. Words, then, make objective unseen thoughts. This is precisely what the Lord Jesus has done. As the Word, Christ has made manifest the invisible God.

(b) A "word" is a *means of communication*. By means of words I transmit information to others. By words I express myself, make known my will, and impart knowledge. So Christ, as the Word, is the Divine Transmitter, communicating to us the life and love of God.

(c) A "word" is a *method of revelation*. By his words a speaker exhibits both his intellectual caliber and his moral character. By our words we shall be justified, and by our words we shall be condemned. And Christ, as the Word, reveals the attributes and perfections of God. How *fully* has Christ revealed God! He displayed His power, He manifested His wisdom, He exhibited His holiness, He made known His grace, He unveiled His heart. In Christ, and nowhere else, is God fully and finally told out.

"*And the Word was WITH GOD.*" This preposition "with" seems to suggest two thoughts. First, the Word was in *the presence* of God, He was "with" Him. Second, the Word was *in communion with* God. As we read, "Enoch walked *with* God," that is, he lived in fellowship with Him; so the Word was in fellowship with God. There is a beautiful verse in Proverbs 8 which throws its light on the meaning of "with" in John 1:1, and reveals the blessed relation which obtained from all eternity between the Word and God. The passage begins at 8:22 where "wisdom" is personified. It tells us of the happy fellowship which existed between the Word and God before ever the world was. In 8:30 we read "Then I was *by Him*, as one brought up with Him: and I was daily His delight, rejoicing always before Him." In addition to the two thoughts just suggested, we may add that the Greek preposition "pros" here translated "with" is sometimes rendered "toward," but most frequently, "unto." The Word was toward or unto God. One has significantly said "The word rendered *with* denotes a perpetual tendency, as it were, of the Son to the Father, in unity of essence."

That it is here said "the Word was with God" tells of His *separate personality*: He was not "in" God, but "with" God. Now, mark here the marvelous accuracy of Scripture. It is not said, "the Word was with the Father" as we might have expected, but "the Word was with *God*." The name "God" is common to the three Persons of the Holy Trinity, whereas "the Father" is the special title of the first person only. Had it said "the Word was with the Father" the Holy Spirit had been excluded; but "with God" takes in the Word dwelling in eternal fellowship with both the Father and the Spirit. Observe, too, it does not say, "And God was with God," for while there is a plurality of Persons in the Godhead, there is but "one God," therefore the minute accuracy of "the WORD was with God."

"*And the Word WAS GOD,*" or, more literally, "and God was the Word." Lest the figurative expression "the Word" should convey to us an inadequate conception of the Divine glories of Christ, the Holy Spirit goes on to say "and the Word was *with God*," which denoted His separate personality, and intimated His essential relation to the Godhead. And, as though that were not strong enough, the Holy Spirit expressly adds "and *God was* the Word." Who could express God save He who is God! The Word was not an emanation from God, but He was God. Not merely a manifestation of God, but God Himself made manifest. Not only the revealer of God, but God Himself revealed. A more emphatic and unequivocal affirmation of the absolute Deity of the Lord Jesus Christ it is impossible to conceive.

"*The same was in the beginning with God.*" The "same," that is, the Word; "was," that is, subsisted, not began to be; "in the beginning," that is, before time commenced; "with God," that is, as a distinct Personality. That it is here repeated Christ was "*with* God" seems to be intended as a repudiation of the early

Gnostic heresy that Christ was only an *idea* or *ideal IN* the mind of God from eternity, duly made manifest in time—a horrible heresy which is being re-echoed in our own day. It is not said that the Word was *in* God; He was, eternally *"with* God."

Before we pass on to the next verse, let us seek to make practical application of what has been before us, and at the same time answer the third of the seven questions asked at the close of the previous article; "How may I obtain a better, deeper, fuller knowledge of God Himself? By studying Nature? By prayer? By studying Scripture? Or—how?" A more important question we cannot consider. What conception have you formed, dear reader, of the Being, Personality, and Character, of God? Before the Lord Jesus came to this earth, the world was without the knowledge of the true and living God. To say that God is revealed in Nature is true, yet is it a statement that needs qualifying. Nature reveals the existence of God, but how little it tells of His character. Nature manifests His *natural* attributes—His power, His wisdom, His immutability, etc.; but what does Nature say to us of His *moral* attributes—His justice, His holiness, His grace, His love? Nature, as such, knows no mercy and shows no pity. If a blind saint unwittingly steps over the edge of a precipice he meets with the same fate as if a vile murderer had been hurled over it. If I break Nature's laws, no matter how sincere may be my subsequent repentance, there is no escaping the penalty. Nature conceals as well as reveals God. The ancients had "Nature" before them, and what did they learn of God? Let that altar, which the Apostle Paul beheld in one of the chief centers of ancient learning and culture make answer—"to the UNKNOWN GOD" is what he found inscribed thereon!

It is only in Christ that God is fully told out. Nature is no longer as it left the Creator's hands: it is under the Curse, and how could that which is imperfect be a perfect medium for revealing God? But the Lord Jesus Christ is the Holy One. He was God, the Son, manifest in flesh. And so fully and so perfectly did He reveal God, He could say, "He that hath seen Me hath seen the Father" *(John 14:9)*. Here, then, is the answer to our question, and here is the practical value of what is before us in these opening verses of John's Gospel. If the believer would enter into a better, deeper, fuller knowledge of God, he must prayerfully study *the person and work of the Lord Jesus Christ as revealed in the Scriptures!* Let this be made our chief business, our great delight, to reverently scrutinize and meditate upon the excellencies of our Divine Saviour as they are displayed upon the pages of Holy Writ, then, and only then, shall we "increase in the knowledge of God" *(Col. 1:10)*. The "light of the knowledge of the glory of God" is seen *only* "in the face of Jesus Christ" *(II Cor. 4:6)*.

"All things were made by Him; and without Him was not anything made that was made" *(1:3)*. How this brings out, again, the absolute deity of Christ! Here creation is ascribed to Him, and none but *God* can create. Man, with all his boasting, is unable to bring into existence a single blade of grass. Observe, that the *whole* of creation is here ascribed to the Word—"*all* things were made by Him." This would not be true if He were Himself a creature, even though the first and the highest creature. But nothing is excepted—"*all* things were made *by Him.*" Just as He was before all things, and therefore, *eternal;* so was He the Originator of all things, and therefore, *omnipotent.*

"In Him was life; and the life was the light of men" *(1:4)*. This follows logically from what has been said in the previous verse. If Christ created all things He must be the Fountain of *life*. He is the Life-Giver. We understand "life" to be used here in its widest sense. Creature life is found in God, for "in Him we live and move and have our being;" spiritual or eternal Life, and resurrection life too, are also found "in Him." If it be objected that the Greek word for "life" here is "zoe," and that zoe has exclusive reference to *spiritual* life, we answer, Not always: see Luke 12:15; 16:25 (translated "life-time"), Acts 17:25, etc. where, in each case, "zoe" has reference to human (natural) life, as such. Thus, "zoe" includes within its scope *all* "life."

"*And the Life was THE LIGHT of men.*" What are we to understand by this? Notice two things: this statement in verse 4 follows immediately after the declaration that "all things were made" by Christ, so that it is *creatures,* as such, which are here in view; second, it is "men," as men, not only believers, which are here referred to. The "Life" here is one of the Divine titles of the Lord Jesus, hence, it is equivalent to saying *"God was the Light of men."* It speaks of the relation which Christ sustains to men, all men—He is their "Light." This is confirmed by what we read of in verse 9, "That was the true Light, which *lighteth every man* that cometh into the world." In what sense, then, is Christ as "the Life" the *"Light* of men"? We answer, in that which renders men accountable creatures. Every rational man is morally enlightened. All rational men "show the *work of* the law written in their hearts, their conscience also bearing witness" *(Rom. 2:15).* It is this "light," which lightens every man that cometh into the world, that constitutes them responsible beings. The Greek word for "light" in John 1:4 is "phos," and that it is not restricted to spiritual illumination is plainly evident from its usage in Matthew 6:23, "If therefore the light that is in thee be darkness, how great is that darkness," and also see Luke 13:35; Acts 16:29, etc.

Let no reader infer from what has been said that we are among the number who believe the unscriptural theory that there is in every man a spark of Divine life, which needs only to be fanned, to become a flame. No, we expressly repudiate any such satanic lie. By nature, every man is "alienated from the life of God" because, spiritually, he is "dead in trespasses and sins." Yet, notwithstanding, the natural man is a responsible being before God, to Whom he shall yet give an account of himself; responsible, because the work of God's law is written in his heart, his conscience *also* bearing witness, and this, we take it, is the "light" which is referred to in John 1:4 and the "lighteneth" in John 1:9.

"And the Light shineth in darkness; and the darkness comprehended it not" *(1:5).* This gives us still another of the Divine titles of Christ. In verse 1 He is spoken of as "the Word." In verse 3 as the Maker of all things. In verse 4 as "the Life." Now, in verse 5 as "the Light." With this should be compared I John 1:5 where we read *"God is Light."* The conclusion, then, is irresistible, the proof complete and final, that the Lord Jesus is none other than God, the second Person in the Holy Trinity.

The "Englishman's Greek New Testament" renders the last clause of 1:5 as follows—"and the light in the darkness appears, and the darkness it apprehended not." This tells us of the effects of the Fall. Every man that comes into this world is lightened by his Creator, but the natural man disregards this light, he repels it, and in consequence, is plunged into darkness. Instead of the natural man "living up to the light he has" (which none ever did) he "loves darkness rather than light" *(John 3:19).* The unregenerate man, then, is like one that is blind—he is in the dark. Proof of this appears in the fact that "the Light in the darkness appears, and the darkness it apprehended not." All other darkness yields to and fades away before light, but here *"the darkness"* is so impenetrable and hopeless, it neither apprehends or comprehends. What a fearful and solemn indictment of fallen human nature! And how evident it is that nothing short of a miracle of saving grace can ever bring one "out of darkness into God's marvelous light."

"There was a man sent from God, whose name was John" *(1:6).* The change of subject here is most abrupt. From "the Word" Who was God, the Holy Spirit now turns to speak of the forerunner of Christ. He is referred to as *"a man,"* to show us, by way of contrast, that the One to Whom he bore witness was *more* than Man. This man was "sent from God," so is every man who bears faithful witness to the Person of Christ. The name of this man was "John" which, as etymologists tell us, signifies, "the gift of God."

"The same came for a witness, to bear witness of the Light, that all through Him might believe" *(1:7).* John came to bear witness of "the Light." Weigh well these words: they are solemn, pathetic, tragic. Perhaps their force will be the more evident if we ask a question: When the sun is shining in all its beauty, who are the ones that are unconscious of the fact? Who need to be *told* it is shining? The blind! How tragic, then, when we read that God sent John to "bear witness of the Light"! How pathetic that there should be any need for this! How solemn the statement that men have to be *told* "the Light" is now in their midst! What a revelation of man's fallen condition. The Light shone in the darkness, but the darkness comprehended it not. Therefore, did God send John to bear witness to the Light. God would not allow His beloved Son to come here unrecognized and unheralded. As soon as He was born into this world, He sent the angels to the Bethlehem shepherds to proclaim Him, and just before His public ministry began, John appeared bidding Israel prepare to receive Him.

"The same came *for a witness*." This defines the character of the preacher's office. He is a "witness," and a witness is one who knows what he says and says what he knows. He deals not with speculations, he speaks not of his own opinions, but he testifies to what he knows to be the truth.

"To bear witness *of the Light*." This should ever be the aim of the preacher: to get his hearers to look away from himself to Another. He is not to testify of himself, nor about himself, but he is to "preach Christ" *(I Cor. 1:23)*. This is the message the Spirit of God will own, for Christ has said of Him "He shall glorify *Me*" *(John 16:14)*.

"That all through Him might believe." "That" means "in order that." To "bear witness" defines the character of the preacher's *office:* to "bear witness of the Light" makes known the preacher's *theme;* that "all through Him might believe" speaks of the *design* of his ministry. Men become believers through receiving the testimony of God's witness.

"He was not that Light, but was sent to bear witness of that Light" *(1:8)*. No, John himself was not "that Light," for "light" like "life" is to be found only in God. Apart from God all is darkness, profound and unrelieved. Even the believer has no light *in himself*. What saith the Scriptures? "For ye were sometimes darkness, but now are ye light *in the Lord*" *(Eph. 5:8)*. There is a statement found in John 5:35 which, as it stands in the A. V., conflicts with what is said here in 1:8. In 5:35 when speaking of John, Christ said, "He was a burning and shining *Light*," but the Greek word used here is entirely different from that translated "light" in 1:8, and in the R. V. it is correctly translated "He was *the lamp* that burneth and shineth." This word used of John, correctly translated "lamp," points a striking contrast between the forerunner and Christ as "the Light." A lamp has no inherent light of its own—it has to be supplied! A "lamp" has to be carried by another! A "lamp" soon burns out: in a few hours it ceases to shine.

"That was the true Light, which lighteth every man which cometh into the world" *(1:9)*. Bishop Ryle in his most excellent notes on John's Gospel, has suggested that the adjective "true" has here at least a fourfold reference. First, Christ is the *"true* Light" as the Undeceiving Light. Satan himself, we read, "is transformed into an Angel of light" *(II Cor. 11:14)*, but he appears as such only to *deceive*. But Christ is the *true* Light in contrast from all the false lights which are in the world. Second, as the *"true* Light" Christ is the Real Light. The real light in contrast from the dim and shaded light which was conveyed through the types and shadows of the Old Testament ritual. Third, as the *"true* Light" Christ is the Underived Light: there are lesser lights which are borrowed and reflected, as the moon from the sun, but Christ's "light" is His own essential and underived glory. Fourth, as the *"true* Light," Christ is the Super-eminent Light, in contrast from all that is ordinary and common. There is one glory of the sun, and another glory of the moon, and another of the stars; but all other lights pale before Him Who is *"the* Light." The latter part of this 9th verse need not detain us now, having already received our consideration under the exposition of verse 4. The light which "every man" has by nature is the light of reason and conscience.

"He was in the world, and the world was made by Him, and the world knew Him not" *(1:10)*. "He was in the world" refers, we believe, to His incarnation and the thirty-three years during which He tabernacled among men. Then it is said "and the world was made by Him." This is to magnify the Divine glory of the One Who had become incarnate, and to emphasize the tragedy of what follows, "and the world knew Him not."

"He was in the world." *Who* was? None other than the One Who had made it. And how was He received? The great Creator was about to appear: will not a thrill of glad expectancy run around the world? He is coming not to judge, but to save. He is to appear not as a haughty Despot, but as a Man "holy, harmless, undefiled;" not to be ministered unto, but to minister. Will not such an One receive a hearty welcome? Alas, "the world knew Him not." Full of their own schemes and pursuits, they thought nothing of Him. Unspeakably tragic is this; yet something even more pathetic follows.

"He came unto His own, and His own received Him not" *(1:11)*. How appropriate are the terms here used: note the nice distinction: "He *was* in the world" and, therefore, within the reach of inquiry. But to the seed of Abraham He *"came,"* knocking as it were, at their door for admission; but "they *received Him not."* The world is charged with ignorance, but Israel with unbelief, yea, with a positive refusal of Him. Instead of welcoming the Heavenly Visitant, they drove Him from their door, and even banished Him from the earth. Who would have supposed that a people whose believing ancestors had been eagerly awaiting the appearance of the Messiah for long ages past, would have rejected Him when He came among them! Yet so it was: and should any ask, How could these things be? we answer, This very thing was expressly foretold by their own prophet, that He *should* possess neither form nor comeliness in their eyes, and when they should see Him there would be no beauty that they should desire Him. Ah, would it have been any wonder if He had turned away from such ingrates in disgust! What blessed subjection to the Father's will, and what wondrous love for sinners, that He remained on earth in order that He might later die the death of the Cross!

But if the world "knew Him not," and Israel "received Him not," was the purpose of God defeated? No; indeed, for that *could not be.* The counsel of the Lord *"shall* stand" *(Prov. 19:21).* The marvelous condescension of the Son could not be in vain. So, we read, "but as many as received Him, to them gave He power to become the sons of God, even to them that believe on His name" *(vs. 12).* This tells us of the human side of salvation, what is required of sinners. Salvation comes to the sinner through "receiving" Christ, that is, by "believing on His name." There is a slight distinction between these two things, though in substance they are one. Believing, respects Christ as He is exhibited by the Gospel testimony: it is the personal acceptance as truth of what God has said concerning His Son. Receiving, views Christ as presented to us as God's Gift, presented to us for our acceptance. And "as many as," no matter whether they be Jews or Gentiles, rich or poor, illiterate or learned, receive Christ as their own personal Saviour, to them is given the power or right to become the sons (better "children") of God.

But *who* receive Him thus? Not all by any means. Only a few. And is this left to chance? Far from it. As the following verse goes on to state, "which were born, not of blood, nor of the will of the flesh, nor of the will of man, but of God" *(1:13).* This explains to us *why* the few "receive" Christ. It is because they are born of God. Just as verse 12 gives us the human side, so verse 13 gives us the Divine. The Divine side is the new birth: and the taking place of the new birth is "not of blood," that is to say, it is not a matter of heredity, for regeneration does not run in the veins; "nor of the will of the flesh," the will of the natural man is opposed to God, and he has *no will* Godward until he has been born again; "nor of the will of man," that is to say, the new birth is not brought about by the well-meant efforts of friends, nor by the persuasive powers of the preacher; "but of God." The new birth is a Divine work. It is accomplished by the Holy Spirit applying the Word in living power to the heart. The reception Christ met with during the days of His earthly ministry is the same still: the world "knows Him not;" Israel "receives Him not;" but a little company *do* "receive Him," and who these are Acts 13: 48 tells us—"as many as were ordained to eternal life believed." And here we must stop.

Preparatory to our next article, we are anxious that the reader should study the following questions:

1. In John 1:14 the word "dwelt" signifies "tabernacled." The Word tabernacled among men. It points us back to the Tabernacle of Israel in the wilderness. In *what* respects did the Tabernacle of old typify and foreshadow Christ?

2. "We beheld His glory" *(1:14):* what is meant by this? *what* "glory"? At least a threefold "glory."

3. In what sense was Christ "before" John the Baptist *(see 1:15)?*

4. What is the meaning of 1:16?

5. Why are we told that the Law was *given* by Moses, but that grace and truth *came* by Jesus Christ *(see 1: 17)?*

6. Was there any "grace and truth" *before* Jesus Christ came? If so, what is meant by them *coming by* Jesus Christ?

7. How many contrasts can you draw between Law and Grace?—*Arthur W. Pink.*

THE PRIEST'S PLACE AND PORTION

READ LEVITICUS 6:14-18

These verses present three things to our notice in connection with "the law of the meat-offering," namely, the priest, his place, and his portion.

1. *The Priest.* All the sons of Aaron were priests. They became such by birth. They were born into this highly privileged position. They did not reach it by effort, but simply by birth. Being sons of Aaron, they were, of necessity, priests. They might be disqualified for the discharge of the functions of their position, through bodily blemish or ceremonial defilement *(see Lev. 21:21, 22);* but as to the position itself, it was a necessary result of their being sons of Aaron. Position is one thing; ability to discharge the functions, or capacity to enjoy the privileges thereof, is quite another. A dwarf among the sons of Aaron was deprived of many of the higher priestly dignities; but even a dwarf was "to eat the bread of his God, of the most holy and of the holy." God would not leave the feeblest or most diminutive member of the household without a holy portion. "Only he shall not go in unto the veil, nor come nigh unto the altar, because he hath a blemish, that he profane not My sanctuaries; for I the Lord do sanctify them." A dwarf could not attend upon the altar of God; *but the God of the altar took care of the dwarf.* The two things are Divinely perfect. God's claims have been perfectly answered, and the need of His priestly family perfectly met.

2. *The Place.* The place where the priest was to partake of his portion teaches us a most valuable lesson of practical holiness. *"With unleavened bread* shall it be eaten *in the holy place;* in the court of the Tabernacle of the congregation they shall eat it." That is to say, it is only in the power of personal holiness, and in the immediate presence of God, that we can really partake of our priestly portion. The way in which we get the place exhibits absolute grace. The place which we get demands personal holiness. To speak of effort in reaching the place, is the fallacy of legalism. To think of unholiness in the place is the blasphemy of Antinomianism. I reach the position *only* through grace. I occupy the position *only* in holiness. The pathway to the sanctuary has been thrown open by free grace; but it is to the sanctuary *of God* that grace has opened the pathway. These things must never be forgotten. We want to have them graven on the tablets of the conscience, and hidden in the chambers of the heart.

3. *The Portion.* And now as to the portion. "This is the law of the meat-offering: the sons of Aaron shall offer it before the Lord, before the altar. And he shall take of it his handful, of the flour of the meat-offering, and of the oil thereof, and all the frankincense thereof, and shall burn it upon the altar for a sweet savor, even the memorial of it unto the Lord. And the remainder thereof shall Aaron and his sons eat." The fine flour and oil typify *Christ's perfect manhood,* conceived and anointed by the Holy Spirit. This is the portion of God's priests, to be enjoyed in the sanctuary of the Divine presence, in separation of heart unto God. *It is utterly impossible that we can enjoy Christ anywhere else but in the presence of God, or in any other way than personal holiness.* To speak of enjoying Christ while living in worldliness, indulging in pride, gratifying our lusts, giving a loose rein to our temper and passions, is a fatal delusion. "If we say that we have fellowship with Him, and walk in darkness, we lie and do not the truth" *(I John 1:6).* The two things are wholly incompatible. "Fellowship with God" and "walking in darkness" are as diametrically opposed as heaven and hell. Thus, then, the place of all true priests—all believers—all members of the priestly household is to be within the sacred precincts of the sanctuary, in the immediate presence of God, feeding upon Christ in the power of personal holiness. All this we are taught in "the law of the meat-offering."

But let the reader note particularly that *"all* the frankincense" was consumed on the altar. *Why was this?* Because that frankincense typified the fragrance of Christ's manhood as enjoyed *exclusively by God Himself.* There was that in Christ, as a Man, down here, which *only God* could duly appreciate. Every thought, every look, every word, every movement, every act of "the Man Christ Jesus," emitted a fragrance which weht up directly to the throne of God, and refreshed the heart of Him Who sat thereon. *Not a single atom of Christ's perfectness or preciousness was ever lost.* It might be lost on a cold, heartless world, and even upon carnal and earthly-minded disciples, *but it was not lost upon God.* It *all* went up to Him, according to its true value.

This is a spring of joy and comfort to the spiritual mind. When we think of how the blessed Lord Jesus was depreciated in this world, how little even His own disciples understood or valued Him, how the rarest and most exquisite touches and traits of His perfect humanity were lost upon a rude and unbelieving world, and even upon His own people, what a comfort to remember that He *was* perfectly understood and appreciated *by the One Who sat on the throne!* There was an unbroken line of communication kept up between the heart of Jesus and the heart of God—the cloud of incense was continually ascending to the throne from the only perfect Man that ever trod this cursed and groaning earth. Not a grain of the incense was lost, because *not a grain was entrusted into the hands of the priests.* All went up to God. Nothing was lost. The world might despise and hate; the disciples might fail to understand or appreciate; what then? Was a single ray of Christ's moral glory to go for naught? Surely not; all was duly estimated by Him for Whom it was designed and Who alone could value it aright. This was true in every stage of Christ's precious life down here, and when we reach the end, and see the climax, when one disciple sold Him for thirty pieces of silver, another cursed and swore he knew Him not, all forsook Him and fled, the world nailed Him to an ignominious Cross between two thieves, God showed to the universe how much *He* differed from all the thoughts of men by placing the crucified One on the throne of the Majesty in the heavens.

This much as to the primary application of the incense, which, unquestionably is to Christ. We may also observe that it has *a secondary application to the believer,* which he should seek to understand. True Christianity is the outflow *of the life of Christ* in the believer's practical ways, and this is most precious to God, though it may be lost upon an unbelieving world, and even upon a professing church. There is not a movement of the life of Christ in the believer, not an expression of what He is, not the smallest manifestation of His grace, that does not ascend, directly, as sweet incense, to the throne of God. It may not attract the notice or elicit the applause of this world; it may not get a place in the records of men; *but it goes up to God,* and this is enough for the faithful heart. *God values all that is of Christ,* nothing more, nothing else. There may be much that looks like service—much show—much noise —much that men make a great ado about! But nothing goes up to the throne—nothing is entered in the imperishable records of eternity but that which is the fruit of *the life of Christ* in the soul.

May God the Holy Spirit lead us into the experimental understanding of these things, and bring forth in us, day by day, a brighter and fuller manifestation of *Christ* to the glory of God the Father!— *Charles Campbell, 1872.*

2. THE NAZARITE:

NUMBERS 6:5

HIS ABANDONMENT OF HIS RIGHTS

In a former paper it was our privilege to meditate on the first particular of Nazarite life, namely, "Separation unto the Lord" from the joy which the vines of the earth afford. We come now to the consideration of the second particular of this type of Christ's consecration, and of ours in Him.

The Nazarite vow demanded that during the period of separation he should allow the hair of his head to grow.

"All the days of the vow of his separation there shall no razor come upon his head: until the days be fulfilled, in the which he separateth himself unto the Lord, he shall be holy, and shall let the locks of his hair grow" (Num. 6:5).

In this part of the law of the Nazarite we find a type of the devoted Christian's renunciation of privilege, and his acceptance of shame for the Lord's sake; and in the long unshorn hair we see the symbol of absolute subjection to Christ. That this view of the matter is sustained by Scripture may be made clear by comparison of the text in Numbers with I Corinthians, chapter 11th. The Apostle, in that place, distinctly teaches that it is the privilege of a man to appear in God's presence with his head shorn, and that long hair upon a man is the symbol of shame. "Every man praying or prophesying, having his head covered, dishonoreth his head. For a man ought not to cover his head, forasmuch as he is the image and glory of God. Doth not even nature itself teach you, that, if a man have long hair, it is a shame unto him?" *(vss. 4, 7, 14).* Thus the privilege of the man is to appear shorn, while to wear long hair is to choose shame for one's self, inasmuch as it is the token of voluntary surrender of the place of superior glory.

On the other hand, the same passage shows us that long hair is ordained for the woman, in token of her subjection, and that it is a shame for her to affect or assert the superior place, which she does by appearing in the Lord's presence uncovered, or shorn of her hair. God's ordinance is that "the head of the woman is the man," and upon this ground the inspired Apostle asserts that "every woman that prayeth and prophesieth with her head uncovered dishonoreth her head: for that is even all one as if she were shaven" *(vs. 5).* Her hair, we are taught, "is given her for a covering," which is to be the token of her subjection to her "head," and that subjection is her proper "glory" *(vss. 10, 15).*

It would lead us away from the purpose of our reference to I Corinthians 11, to dwell upon its direct teaching upon the social, or church position to be assumed by the sexes. But we cannot pass on without the remark that it were well for Christian men and women to weigh the instruction given by Infinite Wisdom on this point. That ungodly women, encouraged by ungodly men, should unsex themselves will not surprise anyone versed in prophecy. But a fearful responsibility is incurred by Christian women who, by their public abandonment of their own province, countenance this growing crime, which, going hand in hand with satanic spiritualism, is to end in the widespread rejection of the marriage relation *(see I Tim. 4:3).*

Thus Scripture establishes the meaning of this part of the Nazarite law. The true Nazarite *relinquishes* his rights, at the expense of the shame which ever less or more accompanies such a course; and in this he necessarily clothes himself with the tokens of subjection unto the Lord.

And where shall we find one who properly answers to the type? In Jesus. Yes, only in Him Who, possessing all rights and all glory and all power, yet vowed His vow to empty Himself of all, laid aside His rights, was "covered with shame," and in holy subjection, as the Servant of God, "performed what His lips had spoken," *"Until the days of his separation were ful-* filled" *(see Phil. 2:6-8; cf. Psa. 56:12; 66:13; 116:14, 18).* So completely does this part of the Nazarite ritual find its end in Him—it really represents one whole aspect of His history—that we shrink from illustrative detail, lest we should thereby understate His marvelous self-abandonment to His Father's will. "All the kingdoms of the world, and the glory of them," were His by right, but were freely abandoned, nay, refused, that He might worship and serve only the Lord His God *(see Matt. 4:8-10).* When the Tempter sought to mar His consecration, He was saying in His heart, "Thy vows are upon Me, O God, I will render praises unto *THEE.* For Thou, O God, hast heard My vows: Thou hast given Me the heritage of those that fear Thy name. Thou wilt prolong the King's life: and His years as many generations. He shall abide before God forever. O prepare mercy and truth which may preserve Him. So will I sing praise unto Thy name forever, that I may daily perform My vows" *(Psa. 56:12; 61:5-8).*

All judgment was "committed unto the Son," but He, in the performance of His vow, "judged no man" for He came, a Nazarite, "not to judge but to save" *(John 5:22; 8:15; 12:47).* The homage of the service of all was His due, but He "sought not honor of men," and came "not to be ministered unto but to minister" *(John 5:23, 41; 12:26; 13:4, 14; Matt. 20:28).* All the land was His—"Immanuel's land"—but when refused a place in its villages, He would not put forth His power to assert His right, by bringing down fire upon His rejecters; the despised Nazarite "went to another village" *(Luke 9:53-56).* "He came to His own possessions, and His own people received Him not."

And what shall I say more of the all-renouncing Son of Man? Life was His right, but He became obedient unto death, was led as a lamb to the slaughter, yet opened not His mouth. The sinless One, made sin, "endured the Cross and despised the shame."

The long hair of the Nazarite was the result of his renouncing his privilege. It was, therefore, the type of shame voluntarily incurred in the path of devotion. The shame of Jesus was the token and accompaniment of His self-abnegation, and for the love of the Father, for the perfecting of the work to which He had separated Himself, He "despised the shame."

But though He "despised" it and "hid

not His face from shame and spitting," yet He felt it. How He felt it may be learned from Psalms which were framed by the Spirit for His lips. Thus we find Him rebuking those who put Him to shame, "O ye sons of men, how long will ye turn My glory into shame?" *(Psa. 4:2).* But it is still more affecting to hear Him speak of His shame to Him from Whom and for Whom He had accepted it. Unto God He says, "Thou hast made His glory to cease, Thou hast covered Him with shame" *(Psa. 89:44,45).* And again, "Because for Thy sake I have borne reproach; shame hath covered My face. Thou hast known My shame, My reproach, and My dishonour" *(Psa. 69:7, 19).*

These hints may suffice to direct our eyes to the Perfect Nazarite, on whose head *"no razor came,* until the days were fulfilled, in the which He separated Himself unto the Lord," and who let "the locks of the hair of His head grow." If any one wishes to follow out this aspect of Jesus' life, he will find it profitable especially to follow His history as it is found in John's Gospel, which, more vividly than the others, sets in contrast the rights and renunciations, the glory and the shame of Him "Whom the Father sanctified and sent into the world." We must now notice this peculiar feature of separation to the Lord in His saints.

The flesh protests against everything that pertains to Nazarite separation, and not least decidedly against the relinquishment of rights, with the consequent shame, which is involved in obedience to the Word, *"He shall be holy, and shall let the locks of the hair of his head grow."* That the giving up of obvious privilege should be a constituent of the holiness to which we are called, is, indeed, something that takes nature by surprise, and excites its deepest displeasure. For example, just assume that the Master means what He says on this subject in His sermon on the mount, and you arouse at once the indignation of the majority of His disciples. They can far more easily "cut off the right hand," "pluck out the right eye," "give alms," "fast," "pray" and "strive" than consent to be "poor in spirit," when "smitten on one cheek to turn the other also," to let his "coat" and then "cloak be taken away," to be "compelled to go one mile," far less "two." In fact, there are no texts which disciples are so unwilling to count "literal" as those which demand the relinquishment of our rights for Jesus' sake.

Yet the spirit of Jesus has in all ages produced in His saints this characteristic of Nazar-life. We find it in Abraham's attitude toward Lot, when he said, "Let there be no strife, I pray thee, between thee and me: if thou wilt take the left hand I will go to the right; or if thou depart to the right hand then I will go to the left" *(Gen. 13: 8, 9).* We see the principle illustrated in the lives of Joseph *(see Deut. 33:16; Psa. 105: 17-19),* Mephibosheth *(see II Sam. 19:28-30),* Hezekiah *(see II Kings 18:14-16),* and many others. But, of the ancient saints, David most singularly exemplified this trait of the Nazarite.

Like his Son and Lord, of Whom he was in so many respects typical, David for long years not only suffered deprivation and shame, but refused to stand forth as a man asserting his rights till "the days of his separation were fulfilled" *(Num. 6:13).* Till the Lord's time came he was content to be as "a dead dog" and "as a flea;" and to be pursued by Saul's malignant jealousy, "as when one doth hunt a partridge in the mountains" *(I Sam. 24:14; 26:20).* And when at length he occupies the throne, he is still found refraining from the exercise of his royal prerogative *(see II Sam. 3:39; 16:10).* This, we have no doubt, was because his reign was ordained to be the type not of the millennial power of Christ, but of that period now going on, in which Jesus though crowned, is still as a Nazarite enduring humiliation and wrong in His saints, and delaying the manifest and puissant assertion of His authority. As the exercise of the royal prerogative was delayed till the embellishment of his kingdom under Solomon *(see I Kings 2:5-9),* so the open and triumphant assertion of the rights of Jesus is to await the hour of His coming in power and great glory *(cf. II Sam. 23:3-7; Matt. 16:27; 25:31-46; Rev. 19:14,15, etc.).*

Before taking leave of David, we may profitably refer to one remarkable instance of his devotion, in which we may learn the exercise of his soul towards the Lord, and see his acceptance of shame for His sake. We have in view his action in bringing up the ark from the house of Obed-edom *(see II Sam. 6).* Laying aside all the insignia of his royalty, as a true Nazarite, stripped of all pretensions to glory and privilege in God's presence, "David danced before the Lord with all his might: and David was girded with a linen ephod" *(vs. 14).* Most men would deem the occasion one in which a king should appear in all the splendor of his royalty, and would judge David's appearance and action exceedingly undignified. But David was not present to grace the procession of the ark of God, nor as a patron of religion. What he was manward, and what he was Godward were with him very different things. He took his place before the ark as a worshiper, renouncing all glory for the Lord's sake, rejoicing in Him, and not even in the dignity He had conferred. His was Nazariteship from the heart. The state of his heart and of Michal's are revealed in singular contrast. "Michal, Saul's daughter, looked through a window, and saw David leaping and dancing before the Lord, and she despised him in her heart" *(vs. 16)*. Michal was a true daughter of Saul, who ever cared more for his own dignity than for the Lord's honor *(see I Sam. 15:30)*, and she could not have sympathy with a king who preferred Him Who gave him his crown to the crown itself. So Saul's daughter poured shame upon David for making himself as nothing before the Lord. His reply to her taunt was the language of a Nazarite indeed. "It was before the Lord Who chose me before thy father, and before all his house, to appoint me ruler over the people of the Lord, over Israel: therefore will I play before the Lord. *And I will yet be more vile than thus, and will be base in mine own sight*" *(vss. 21, 22)*. It is ever thus. If we step down from our supposed sphere, or anyway lower ourselves for Jesus' sake, we will have to meet abundant scorn from the world and worldly Christians. But if we are really acting "*before the Lord*," we shall pursue our lowly path, and even go down lower still, not only accepting the shame, but "rejoicing to suffer shame for His name" *(Acts 5:41)*.

It may be well, just here, to offer a word of warning for earnest Christians, which is suggested by Michal's false thoughts of David's behavior. Earnest Christians will not "despise" one another, but they may very much misjudge each other in the matter of separation unto the Lord. And perhaps such misjudgment is especially likely to be formed in regard to the extent and form in which we relinquish our privileges. You may think that I do not go far enough, and I may think that you go too far in this direction. Of course, there are certain things which the Word definitely demands should be given up. But Nazarite law seems to have been instituted for the express purpose of eliciting and directing voluntary devotion; and its Christian use is particularly to stimulate and guide in matters which do not come under the head of positive injunction. The particulars of renunciation will therefore be very different in different cases, and it is exceedingly important that we should abstain from judging one another in regard to things indifferent in themselves. To do so is really to hinder or attempt to hinder another's devotion. One may be led of the Spirit to pursue a course which you are not called to, and another may be led in a way which to you may appear unholy or eccentric; and yet another may be giving up much for the Lord's sake, while there is to your eye little self-renunciation. But you must not make your *ideal* of separation, or the peculiarities of your own devotion, the rule for others. Let us see to it that we neither judge nor despise one another. The great thing is for each of us to act "before the Lord," and in such things to leave His other servants to Him. The Holy Spirit has spoken very decidedly on this subject, by an apostle who himself, as we shall presently see, distanced all other servants in the true Nazar-renunciation of his rights. "Who," says Paul, "who art thou that judgest another's servant? To his own master he standeth or falleth. Yea, he shall be holden up: for God is able to make him stand. One man esteemeth one day above another: another esteemeth every day alike. Let every man be fully persuaded in his own mind. He that regardeth the day regardeth it *unto the Lord;* and he that regardeth not the day, *to the Lord* he doth not regard it" *(Rom. 14)*. So in the matter and form of our renunciations let us act unto the Lord, and we will then be independent of human judgment: and let us leave our fellow-servants to their and our Master, and we shall judge nothing before the time.

From the nature of the economy under which the saints lived before the coming of the Messiah, Nazariteship, in principle, could not be *characteristic* of their whole course, though, as we have sufficiently showed, the Spirit of Christ so wrought in them that the principle found frequent illustrations in their actions, which serve for our types. But when, by the death of Christ, the whole economy was changed, the symbolic Nazariteship ceased, and the reality which it shadowed became a characteristic of devotion to God. The saints in Christ Jesus have looked upon *the Nazarite,* and being "in Him," and partakers of

His Spirit, they confess God's claims by walking as He walked.

Accordingly, it is in the New Testament especially, that we find the saints called to a discipleship which finds its proper expression in the relinquishment of nature's privileges and rights for the Lord's sake, which was once typified by the Israelites who, by vow, was restrained from the "razor," and "let the locks of the hair of his head grow," and which was wont to be illustrated occasionally by ancient saints, through the energy of the Spirit of Christ, Who in these gave adumbration anticipative of the fulfillment in Him.

The best illustration of the principle of Christian abandonment of rights and privileges, in devotion to the Lord, will be found in the writings of the apostle who, as we have frequently had occasion to remark, was ordained to be the pattern of believers. We see Paul, in his position of "Nazarite unto the Lord," in the aspect under consideration, very distinctly in I Corinthians 9, and find that he, not occasionally, but habitually renounced all his own rights and immunities "for the Gospel's sake" *(vs. 23)*. He had "power to eat and to drink," to "take about with him a believing wife," and to "forbear working" *(vss. 4-6)*. He was entitled to support for himself and his family while he journeyed and labored as an apostle of Christ, for "even so hath the Lord ordained that they which preach the Gospel should live of the Gospel" *(vs. 14)*. But to obtain his rights was not Paul's object. He was holy unto the Lord, and for His sake could give up his dues from men. "But I have used none of these things, neither have I written these things that it should be so done unto me: for it were better for me to die, than that any man should make my glorying void" *(vs. 15)*.

Nor was it merely that Paul abandoned his claims to temporal sustenance. His aim was to keep intact *"the head of his consecration,"* in all things. His liberty, and all else that was his own to part with, he would relinquish for Jesus' sake. He was "free from all, yet made Himself the servant of all, that he might gain the more" *(vs. 19)*. He would be "as a Jew," "under law," or "without law," "weak," yes, and "all things to all men," that "by any means he might save some" *(vss. 20-22)*.

It is scarcely necessary to guard against the perversion of such a position which would make this self-devotion in any degree akin to the satanic doctrine that "the end sanctifies the means." Only a mind alienated from the truth of God can gather such a doctrine from the self-abnegation here exhibited. Devotion to Christ never abandons sound principles, never relinquishes truth. It can give up its own comfort, rights and liberty, but, in proportion as it is ready to part with these, it is tenacious of the *truth* of Christ *(Gal. 2:5)*.

But will the devotion which abandons privilege bring honor to those who are thus *"holy unto the Lord"?* No, as in nature "it is a shame for a man to have long hair," so, with fallen nature, it is counted a shame to give up one's rights, and to forbear self-assertion. "Men will praise thee, when thou doest well for thyself," but scorn is reserved for him who will not stand up for his own. Paul found that he was despised for his renunciations. He "ought to have been commended" for these *(II Cor. 12:11)*, but he had to write, "Have I committed an offence in abasing myself that ye might be exalted, because that I have preached to you the Gospel of God freely?" *(II Cor. 11:7)*. Yes, abasement before the Lord, whether in David or in Paul, brings out the scorn of fleshly men. It may be worth while to remark in passing that, in II Corinthians 10 to 12, the reader will find the fullest display and defence of Paul's Nazariteship, and that the singular glorying of the apostle just corresponds to the godly vaunt of the King of Israel, "And I will yet be more vile and base in mine own sight."

One thing will be clear to any who study the point before us, as expounded in Paul's letters; namely, that there is a vast difference between the service of Christ and mere ecclesiastical service. Not to affirm too much or too strongly, we may say that generally pure Christian devotion leads to shame and obloquy, while ecclesiastical devotion—devotion to a Church—usually secures preferment and honor. This is, indeed, too well known. Hence the soul-saddening fact that thousands of men have "chosen the ministry" as "a profession," in which they might attain to eminence, emolument, power and fame, and some "professing Godliness" are not ashamed to speak and write with apparent approbation of men "entering the church," as the only course by which they could hope to emerge from their original obscurity. And the church *does* reward "her sons" *now* with wealth, or honor, according to their zeal in her service, and for her system. But alas she too often pours shame and contempt upon those who are more Christians than "churchmen," those who prefer renunciation for Christ, to the praise that cometh from men. Paul lived to find out that "all they of Asia," where he labored and lost so much for Jesus' sake, were "turned away from him." But the day of glory succeeds the Nazar-shame. Meanwhile, it is not permitted to saints to assume or affect the privileges or immunities of the day of glory. The Church at Corinth once sought to do so, and to their error in this respect, we owe at once the most vivid exhibition of Nazariteship and the most pungent rebuke of its evasion *(see I Cor. 4:8-14)*. Let us be warned, lest, in evading the reproach of Christ, we incur the deeper shame. "If we be reproached for the name of Christ, happy are we; for the Spirit of glory and of God resteth upon us."

The particulars of Nazarite devotion under consideration might, of course, be much more largely illustrated from the New Testament, but the examples adduced may suffice to show what we ought to be, as avowedly consecrated unto the Lord. Our calling demands the cheerful resignation of everything in itself indifferent, and the endurance of shame for Jesus' sake.

Nor is this merely an adjunct of ministerial calling. It is to be characteristic of saints. It is true, as we said before, that nature revolts from such a life; and few, indeed, accept it. The majority of saints habitually "stand up for their rights" in society and in the church; and as in Paul's, so in our day, "brother goeth to law against brother, and that before unbelievers" *(I Cor. 6:6)*. And for all this they have much plausible justification. But the Scripture still protests, "Now, therefore, there is utterly a fault among you, because ye go to law one with another;" and still asks, "Why do ye not rather take wrong? Why do ye not rather suffer yourselves to be defrauded?" *(I Cor. 6:7)*. Our calling and that of the Chief Nazarite is one calling. And so, also, the Holy Spirit testifies. See I Peter 2:19, 21, 23.

If we have at all thoughtfully regarded the Nazariteship of our Lord, or of those to whom attention has been directed as walking in His steps, we must have been struck with the difference between yieldingness and cowardice, between poverty of spirit and meanness of spirit, between renunciation for the truth's sake and the relinquishment of the truth itself. The fact is that the surrender of privilege for Jesus' sake is the exercise of the highest courage; he who is poorest of spirit is ever the boldest, and he who renounces most cheerfully is he who is most unflinching in testimony to truth. Abraham could yield to Lot "right" or "left" for peace sake; but when the five kings fled from the four, and Lot was taken captive, Abraham could, with Godly bravery pursue, and fight, and conquer, and rescue; and then return *to renounce the spoil*. David could be a fugitive, and abase himself more and more before the Lord, but David was a "mighty valiant man," beyond all Israel's men of might. Paul could suffer the loss of all things for Christ, and endure all things for the elect's sake, but among mere men, before him there was none, and after him there has arisen none, to take rank with him as champion of the truth of God. Above all, Jesus could abandon more than all, and go down in His self-renouncing devotion to a deeper shame than any, but truth and righteousness were never obscured, far less abandoned, nay, they were every way established, and illuminated by His Nazarite humiliation. He could suffer every wrong, and be silently led to the slaughter; but though it was the means to the dreadful doom, He would not withhold the confession of the truth, which was, indeed, the confession of His own person and the power and glory which must surely succeed His Nazar-weakness and shame *(see Matt. 26: 63-68)*. All this has a voice for us. If we would be true Nazarites, we must not make its yieldedness as excuse for the evasion of testimony; we must not cloak our cowardice by its honorable name. "For God hath not given us the spirit of cowardice but of power, and of love, and of a sound mind. Be not therefore ashamed of the testimony of our Lord, nor of me, His prisoner; but be thou partaker of the afflictions of the Gospel according to the power of God" *(II Tim. 1:7,8)*. He who can calmly endure the deepest shame, can with intrepidity conquer the mightiest foe; he who can renounce for Christ, can fight and conquer in His name. He who fears the Lord has nothing else to fear.—*Chas. Campbell in "Grace and Truth," 1872.*

(To be continued, D.V.).

STUDIES in the SCRIPTURES

"Search the Scriptures" John 5:39.

A PERIODICAL (MONTHLY "IF THE LORD WILL") DEVOTED TO BIBLE STUDIES and EXPOSITIONS

Associate Editors and Publishers, I. C. HERENDEEN and ARTHUR W. PINK,
Swengel, Pa.

Price: 10 cents per copy; $1.00 per year. Foreign $1.00 per year.

TO OUR SCRIPTURE STUDY FAMILY

"According unto your faith be it unto you" *(Matt. 9:29)*. Faith is the channel through which Omnipotence works. It is that which connects us with Heaven. God alone doeth great marvels, but, frequently, it is in answer to the faith of His people. Israel's victories were wrought through faith. It was Divine grace and power which redeemed them from Egypt, yet are we told, "**Through faith** Moses kept the Passover, and the sprinkling of blood" *(Heb. 11:28)*. Many of the miracles which our Saviour performed were done in response to faith:—"O woman great is **thy faith,** be it unto thee as **thou** wilt"; "And seeing **their faith,** Jesus said unto the sick of the palsy; Son, be of good cheer, thy sins be forgiven thee"; "Thy **faith** hath saved thee".

"According unto your faith be it unto you". God delights in our confidence in Him. We were about to say, God delights to be tested, but that savors strongly of unbelief. Real faith never experiments, and where there **is** faith, there is never any doubt concerning the outcome. God never disappoints those who put their trust in Him. The **quality** of our faith may be gauged by our patience, or lack of it, as we await God's answer. And the **measure** of our faith may be determined by the extent to which we are influenced by the things of sight during the interval of testing.

"According to your faith be it unto you". What a searching word is this! It tests our ways and reveals the state of our hearts. There are difficulties confronting us, circumstances are against us, earthly friends fail us. What then? Shall we allow such things to dishearten and discourage us? If we are walking by faith the things of sight will not disturb us. If our eye is upon God we shall be impervious to all obstacles. If our trust is in the One who possesses **all** power, we shall refuse to be dismayed. If God be for us, who can be against us! According unto your faith, then, be it unto you.

It is in view of this scripture that the editors have decided to increase the number of the pages in this magazine. Were we to be governed by the subscriptions we now have, we should wait until we had twice as many. We believe, though, that it will be more pleasing to the Lord if the next issue is increased to twenty-four pages, feeling assured that God will honor the confidence (fruit of **His own** grace) which we have in Him. "O taste and see that the Lord is good: blessed is the man that trusteth in Thee" *(Psa. 34:8)*. "They trusted in Thee, and were not confounded" *(Psa. 22:5)*.

ARTHUR W. PINK.

STUDIES IN THE SCRIPTURES

A Monthly Periodical Devoted to Bible Studies and Expositions.

Subscription Price: $1.00 per year to any address in the world. Single copies 10 cents.

Change of Address: Please notify us promptly of any change of address, and be certain to give both old and new addresses.

Non-Subscribers receiving this Magazine regularly will understand their subscription has been entered by a friend.

Entered as second-class matter December 15th, 1921 at the post office at Swengel, Pa., under Act of March 3rd, 1879.

CONTENTS

The Believer's Hope 42
Exposition of John's Gospel, continued 46
The Nazarite, continued 54

THE BELIEVER'S HOPE

There are three chief things which the Lord Jesus is said to be unto believers: first, He is our LIFE—"When Christ our life shall appear" (Col. 3:4). We have no "life" apart from Christ; those outside of Him merely exist. Notice that in Revelation 20, after the wicked have been raised, they are yet termed "dead," as they stand before the great white throne. Second, Christ is our PEACE—"For He is our peace" (Eph. 2:14). Outside of Christ men are at enmity against God. "There is no peace saith my God to the wicked." Third, Christ is our HOPE—"Jesus Christ our hope" (I Tim. 1:1). Of unbelievers it is written that they are living in this world "without God and *without hope*" (Eph. 2:12).

If we look at these three statements a little closer it will be found that the first looks backward to the time of our regeneration, the second treats of a present unvarying fact, while the third looks forward to the future, now soon to be realized. The first takes me back to the time when I was "dead in trespasses and sins," but when through the grace of God and the power of the Spirit, I was "born again" and became a new creation in Christ Jesus. The second tells me of what Christ is before God for every believer—"Our peace." He is the One who has made an end forever of the warfare of sin between a holy God and every one that believeth. Because Christ Himself is my peace nothing can change or affect my standing before God. God is forever satisfied with the Crosswork of His blessed Son on my behalf. The third looks forward to the time of our Lord's return, for in Scripture "hope" always respects the future. Just as Christ became my life the moment I believe on Him, just as Christ is my peace before God through all the changing experiences I pass through here below, so, as I look forward to the eternal future, Christ is my hope—all my joyous anticipations and expectations *center in Him.*

According to I Corinthians 13:13. "hope" is one of the three cardinal Christian graces—"Faith, hope and love." It is striking to see how much the New Testament Scriptures have to say about "hope." We "rejoice in *hope* of the glory of God" *(Rom. 5:2)*. We "wait for *the hope* of righteousness by faith" *(Gal. 5:5)*. We "sorrow not, even as others which have no *hope*" *(I Thess. 4:13)*. We are "looking for that blessed *hope*" *(Titus 2:13)*. We have "a strong consolation who have fled for refuge to lay hold upon *the hope* set before us, which hope we have as an anchor of the soul, both sure and steadfast" *(Heb. 6:18, 19)*. Christians are exhorted to "be ready always to give an answer to every man that asketh you a reason for *the hope* that is in you, with meekness and fear" *(I Peter 3:15)*. While the apostle John tells us that "He that hath this *hope* in Him purifieth himself even as He is pure" *(I John 3:3)*. And thus we might continue quoting similar passages, showing what prominence the Holy Spirit has given to the believer's "hope."

The subject of our hope is such a comprehensive one that a small volume might easily be written on this single aspect of our Lord's return. We therefore propose to limit ourselves now to just one line of thought, and that is the various characteristics of the believer's Hope. We shall look at seven of them.

1. It is the Hope of the Gospel.

"Be not moved away from *the hope* of the Gospel" *(Col. 1:23)*. The Gospel embraces far more within its scope than is commonly supposed. The Gospel not only tells us of what Christ has done and what

God has made Him to be to us, besides what He is now doing for us at the right hand of the Majesty on high, but it also makes known what He is going to do for us when He comes again. The hope which the Gospel reveals is that Christ is coming back to receive us unto Himself, that where He is, there we may be also. The hope which the Gospel sets before us is that when He shall appear we shall be like Him, for we shall see Him as He is. Nothing less than this can satisfy God, for He has predestinated us to be conformed to the image of His Son. The hope which the Gospel makes known is, that we shall be forever with the Lord, there where Christ Himself is, throughout the endless ages of eternity. Ah, is not that good news! Is not that glad tidings! Does not such a glorious prospect make you cry "Even so, come, Lord Jesus!"

Yes, this is the hope of the Gospel, and until this is fairly and Scripturally presented we have not fully preached the Gospel. It is greatly to be feared that many of us are preaching but half a Gospel. Is this one reason why God's blessing is absent from much of our evangelistic effort? If we were to faithfully present Christ as the coming One, might not we witness more of the Spirit's power and see sinners aroused from their deadly indifference!

This glorious hope of the Lord Jesus coming to receive us unto Himself, to make us like Himself, and to have us forever with Himself, is something that is peculiar to the Gospel; it is something which the Gospel has brought to light. The Law revealed no such glorious prospect before the people of God. Even the prophets were silent concerning it. Old Testament saints knew nothing of Christ coming *for* His people—that is peculiarly and distinctively the "hope" of the Gospel.

2. It is the Hope of Salvation.

Thus it is denominated in I Thessalonians 5:8. Let us begin reading from verse 5 of this chapter: "Ye are all the children of light, and the children of the day: we are not of the night, nor of darkness." How searching this is! "We are *not of the night*"—reposing, and oblivious to all that is going on around us. No; believers are "the children of the day," and to be slumbering during the day denotes one of two things—sloth or sickness. It is only those who are ill or idle that sleep during the day. O, children of God, if we are of the day *let us be about our Father's business*. As the apostle continues here, "Therefore let us not sleep, as do others; but let us watch and be sober. For they that sleep sleep in the night: and they that be drunken are drunken in the night. But let us, who are of the day, be sober, putting on the breastplate of faith and love, and for an helmet *the hope of salvation*."

It is of first importance that we should remember "salvation" is treated of in a threefold way in the New Testament. There is a past, a present, and a future aspect to salvation. The believer has been saved from the penalty of sin, because on the Cross Christ was punished in his stead. The believer is now being saved from the power of sin, because Christ now lives within him. The believer will soon be saved from the very presence of sin, because Christ is coming to make us like Himself.

Wherever "salvation" is placed in the future for the believer, it never has reference to deliverance from the wrath to come, (for that was effected, immutably, the moment we believed in Christ), but always has reference to the "conforming" us, perfectly and finally, to "the image of God's Son." For example when we read, "Now is our salvation nearer than when we believed" *(Rom. 13:11);* "To them that look for Him (which *all* believers do, though some with a greater degree of intelligence than others) shall He appear the second time without sin unto salvation" *(Heb. 9:28);* or, "Who are kept by the power of God through faith unto salvation ready to be revealed in the last time" *(I Peter 1:5),* the reference is in each case to this third aspect of our salvation, namely, our complete and final deliverance from the presence of sin.

The hope of salvation is described in Philippians 3:20, 21: "For our citizenship, is in heaven, from whence also we look for the Saviour, the Lord Jesus Christ: Who shall change our vile body, that it may be fashioned like unto His glorious body, according to the working whereby He is able even to subdue all things unto Himself." This will be the glorious climax and consummation, when we shall be conformed to the image of God's Son both inwardly and outwardly.

3. It is the Hope of Righteousness.

"For we through the Spirit wait for *the hope* of righteousness by faith" *(Gal. 5:5).*

Notice carefully this verse does not say we hope *for* righteousness, but that we are waiting for the hope *of* righteousness. There is a wide difference between these two things so far as the Christian is concerned personally. Every believer is, even now, righteous before God—not in himself but in Christ. The filthy rags of our righteousness have been covered by the "best robe" of Divine righteousness. Life has been imparted to us, but righteousness has been imputed to us, that is, legally placed to our account. As we read in II Corinthians 5:21, "For He (that is, God) hath made Him (Christ) to be sin for us, who knew no sin, that we might be made the righteousness of God in Him." No, we are not hoping *for* righteousness, for even now the Lord is our righteousness.

But we are waiting for the hope *of* righteousness. Christ was cast out by this world as the *un*-righteousness One, by being condemned to die the shameful death of a malefactor, numbering Him with transgressors. Nevertheless, the Father vindicated Him, by exalting Him to His own right hand in the heavenlies, far above all principality and power and might and dominion and every name that is named. Hence, the Holy Spirit is here to "convict the world" (establish its guilt) not only of sin, but also, said Christ, *"of righteousness* because I go unto My Father" *(John 16:9, 10).*

And Christ is still the rejected One, and because of this "the whole world lieth in the wicked one" *(I John 5:19, R.V.).* And what is the inevitable consequence? Why this, the world is filled with *unrighteousness.* O, how much unrighteousness there is! Diplomatic unrighteousness, when international treaties are treated as scraps of paper. Political unrighteousness, when vital issues are subordinated to party interests. Industrial unrighteousness, when the hire of laborers who have reaped down the fields is, by the rich, "kept back by fraud" *(James 5:4).* Social unrighteousness, when a man's dress and bank balance, rather than character, is made the standard of measurement. Ecclesiastical unrighteousness, when sectarian considerations rather than personal piety are more and more the controlling factor.

Yes, on every side, we witness corruption, chicanery, and unrighteousness. But read Isaiah 3:1: "Behold a king shall *reign in righteousness."* That king is none other than our Lord Jesus Christ. When His kingdom is established on this earth, He will speedily subdue the workers of iniquity, overthrow every opposing force, make an end of every form of injustice, and inaugurate a dispensation characterized by righteousness and peace. As saith the prophet Jeremiah, "Behold, the days come, saith the Lord, that I will raise unto David a *righteous* branch, and a king shall reign and prosper, and shall execute judgment *and justice* in the earth. In his days shall Judah be saved, and Israel shall dwell safely, and this is his name whereby he shall be called, *the Lord our Righteousness" (23:5,6).* For this we wait.

4. IT IS THE HOPE OF OUR CALLING.

"There is one body and one Spirit, even as ye are called in one *hope* of your calling" *(Eph. 4:4).* The subject of the believer's calling, like that of his salvation, may be considered from a threefold viewpoint. As we contemplate the past, we remember how God called us "out of darkness into His marvelous light" *(I Peter 2:9).* II Timothy 1:9 takes us back further still: "Who hath saved us, and *called* us with an holy *calling,* not according to our works, but according to His own purpose and grace, which was given us in Christ Jesus before the world began." Concerning the present we are told, "God hath not *called* us unto uncleanness, but unto holiness" *(I Thess. 4:7).* As to the future, we learn that we shall walk worthy of God "Who hath *called* us unto His kingdom and glory" *(I Thess. 2:12);* and again, we are *"called* that we might receive the promise of eternal inheritance" *(Heb. 2:15).* But what is the hope of our calling? Is it not to hear Him say "Come up hither. Arise, my love, my fair one and come away?"

Inseparably connected with the hope of *our* calling, in Ephesians 1:18, the apostle prays that we may know "what is the hope of *His* calling." As another has pointed out, this is one of the golden links of Ephesians 1 in connection with the word "His." We read of *His* will *(vs. 5), His* grace *(vs. 6), His* blood *(vs. 7), His* good pleasure *(vs. 9), His* glory *(vs. 12), His* inheritance *(vs. 18), His* power *(vs. 19), His* feet *(vs. 22), His* body *(vs. 23),* and *His* calling *(vs. 18).* And what is the hope of His calling? Is it not to come back again and receive us unto Himself?

5. It is the Hope of Glory.

"Christ in you the hope of glory" (Col. 1:27). The glorification of the believer is yet future; hence we read of *the hope of* "glory." Whether asleep in the grave or alive on the earth when our Lord returns, our glorification is equally sure. Concerning the former it is written, "There is one *glory* of the sun, and another *glory* of the moon, and another *glory* of the stars; for one star differeth from another star in glory. So also is the resurrection of the dead ..... it is sown in dishonor, it is *raised in glory*" (I Cor. 15:41,42). Of the latter it is written, he shall "change our vile body, that it may be fashioned like unto *His glorious* body" (Phil. 3:21). Then, and not till then, will the Divine purpose be fully realized—"Whom He did predestinate, them He also called: and whom He called, them He also justified: and whom He justified, them He also *glorified*" (Rom. 8:30). Then will the Divine promise be fulfilled, "When Christ our life shall appear, then shall ye also appear with Him *in glory*" (Col. 3:4); for then "He shall come to be *glorified* in His saints, and to be admired in all them that believe" (II Thess. 1:10). In the meantime, "We rejoice in hope of the glory of God" (Rom. 5:2).

6. It is a Living Hope.

"Blessed be the God and Father of our Lord Jesus Christ, which according to His abundant mercy hath begotten us again unto a living hope, by the resurrection of Jesus Christ from the dead" (I Peter 1:3). It is a living hope in a dying world. How strange that in the face of this, so many believers are looking for death. The King of Glory, not the king of terrors, is our hope.

Christ is the *living* stone upon which we are built. He is the new and *living* way by which we have access into the Holiest of all. He is the *living* water, indwelling us by His Spirit. He is the *living* bread who feeds us by His Word. He is our great High Priest who *ever liveth* to make intercession for us. Because He lives we shall live also. Thus we have a living hope in a dying world.

7. It is a Blessed Hope.

Says the apostle Paul, "Looking for that blessed hope, and the glorious appearing of the great God and our Saviour Jesus Christ" (Titus 2:13). It is a blessed hope, because as we have seen, at His return our Lord receives us unto Himself, that where He is there we may be also. It is a blessed hope, because then our salvation will be consummated, and our vile body shall be fashioned like unto the body of His glory. It is a blessed hope, because then all our miserable failures and divisions will be at an end forever. It is a blessed hope, because then shall Christ present the Church to Himself a glorious Church, not having spot or wrinkle or any such thing. It is a blessed hope to Christ Himself, for then shall He see of the travail of His soul and be satisfied.

Here, then, is the *character* of our Hope. Here are its constituent elements. Here is its sevenfold preciousness told out. It is the Hope of the Gospel—looking forward to the time when the believer shall be delivered from all sin. It is the Hope of Salvation—looking forward to the climax of our redemption. It is the Hope of Righteousness—looking forward to the reign of Christ when all injustice and oppression shall cease. It is the Hope of our Calling—looking forward to the realization of God's eternal purpose concerning us. It is the Hope of Glory—looking forward to the glad Day when the Lord Jesus shall "come to be glorified in His saints, and to be admired in all them that believe." It is a Living Hope—looking forward to that morning without clouds, when by the vivification of the sleeping saints, and the translation of those then alive on the earth, it shall be witnessed that our Saviour *is* "the Resurrection and the Life." It is that Blessed Hope—looking forward to the eternal happiness of the Redeemer and His redeemed.

A closing word now to the unsaved. We have been pondering together the believer's hope, and it is *only the believer*, the one who has been "born again," who has any hope. Every man out of Christ is living in this world "without God *and without hope*" (Eph. 2:12). Therefore, if the Saviour were to come to-day, *you* would face *a closed door!* Then it would be too late to cry for mercy, for the Lord would say, "I know you not." But thank God the door stands wide open to-day. Christ Himself is the Door. Heed what He says, "I am the door: by Me if any man enter in, he shall be saved" (John 10:9).—*Arthur W. Pink.*

JOHN'S GOSPEL

3. THE INCARNATE WORD: JOHN 1:14-18

We first submit a brief Analysis of the passage which is to be before us—John 1: 14-18. We have here:—

1. Christ's Incarnation—"The Word became flesh": 1:14.
2. Christ's Earthly sojourn—"And tabernacled among us": 1:14.
3. Christ's Essential glory—"As of the Only Begotten": 1:14.
4. Christ's Supreme excellency—"Preferred before": 1:15.
5. Christ's Divine sufficiency—"His fulness": 1:16.
6. Christ's Moral perfections—"Grace and truth": 1:17.
7. Christ's Wondrous revelation—Made known "the Father": 1:18.

"And the Word was made (became) flesh, and dwelt among us" (1:14). The Infinite became finite. The Invisible became tangible. The Transcendent became imminent. That which was far off drew nigh. That which was beyond the reach of the human mind became that which could be beholden within the realm of human life. Here we are permitted to see through a veil that, which unveiled, would have blinded us. "The Word became flesh:" He became what He was not previously. He did not cease to be God, but He became Man.

"And the Word became flesh." The plain meaning of these words is, that our Divine Saviour took upon Him human nature. He became a real Man, yet a sinless, perfect Man. As Man He was "holy, harmless, undefiled, separate from sinners" *(Heb. 7:26)*. This union of the two natures in the Person of Christ is one of the mysteries of our faith—"Without controversy *great is the mystery* of Godliness: God was manifest in the flesh" *(I Tim. 3:16)*. It needs to be carefully stated. "The Word" was His Divine title; "became flesh" speaks of His holy humanity. He was, and is, the God-Man, yet the Divine and human in Him were never confounded. His deity, though veiled, was never laid aside; His humanity, though sinless, was a real humanity; for as incarnate, He *"increased* in wisdom and stature, and in favor with God and man" *(Luke 2:52)*. As "the Word" then, He is the Son of God; as "flesh," the Son of Man.

This union of the two natures in the Person of Christ was necessary in order to fit Him for the office of Mediator. Three great ends were accomplished by God becoming incarnate, by the Word being made flesh. First, it was now possible for Him *to die*. Second, He can now be *touched* with the feeling of *our* infirmities. Third, He has left us an *example*, that we should follow *His* steps.

This duality of nature was plainly intimated in Old Testament prediction. Prophecy sometimes represented the coming Messiah as human, sometimes as Divine. He was to be the woman's "seed" *(Gen. 3:15)*; a "prophet" like unto Moses *(see Deut. 18: 18)*; a lineal descendant of David *(see II Sam. 7:12)*; Jehovah's "Servant" *(Isa. 42: 1)*; a "Man of sorrows" *(Isa. 53:3)*. Yet, on the other hand, He was to be "the Branch *of the Lord,* beautiful and glorious" *(Isa. 4: 2)*; He was "the wonderful Counsellor, the Mighty God, the Father of the ages, the Prince of peace" *(Isa. 9:6)*. As *Jehovah* He was to come suddenly to His temple *(see Mal. 3:1)*. The One who was to be born in Bethlehem and be Ruler in Israel, was the One "whose goings forth had been from the days of eternity" *(Mic. 5:2)*. How were these two different sets of prophecy to be harmonized? John 1:14 is the answer. The One born at Bethlehem was the Divine and eternal Word. The Incarnation does not mean that God dwelt in a man, but that God became Man. He became what He was not previously, though He never ceased to be all that He was before. The Babe of Bethlehem was Immanuel—God with us.

"And *the Word* became flesh." It is the design of John's Gospel to bring this out in a special way. The *miracles* recorded therein illustrate and demonstrate this in a peculiar manner. For example: He turns the water into wine—but how? He, Himself, did nothing but *speak the word*. He gave His command to the servants and the transformation was wrought. Again; the Nobleman's son was sick. The father came to the Lord Jesus and besought Him to journey to His home and heal his boy. What was our Lord's response? "Jesus *said unto him,* Go thy way, thy son liveth" *(John 4:50)*, and the miracle was performed. Again; an impotent man was lying by the porch of Bethesda. He desired some one to put him into the pool, but while he was waiting another stepped in before him, and was healed. Then the Lord Jesus passed that way and saw him. What happened? "Jesus *saith unto him*, Rise," etc. The word of power went forth, and the sufferer was made whole. Once more: consider the case of Lazarus, recorded only by John. In the raising of the daughter of Jairus Christ took the damsel by the hand; when He restored to life the widow's son of Nain, He touched the bier. But in bringing Lazarus from the dead He did nothing except speak the word, "Lazarus, come forth." In all of these miracles we see *the Word at work*. The One who had become flesh and tabernacled among men was the eternal and omnipotent—"the great God (the Word) and our Saviour (became flesh) Jesus Christ" *(Titus 2:13)*.

"And dwelt *(tabernacled)* among us." He pitched His tent on earth for thirty-three years. There is here a latent reference to the Tabernacle of Israel in the wilderness. That tabernacle had a typical significance: it foreshadowed God the Son incarnate. Almost everything about the tabernacle adumbrated the Word made flesh. Many and varied are the correspondences between the type and the Anti-type. We notice a few of the more conspicuous.

1. The "tabernacle" was *a temporary appointment*. In this it differed from the temple of Solomon, which was a permanent structure. The tabernacle was merely a tent, a temporary convenience, something that was suited to being moved about from place to place during the journeys of the children of Israel. So it was when our blessed Lord tabernacled here among men. His stay was but a brief one—less than forty years; and, like the type, He abode not long in any one place, but was constantly on the move—unwearied in the activity of His love.

2. The "tabernacle" was *for use in the wilderness*. After Israel settled in Canaan, the tabernacle was superseded by the Temple. But during the time of their pilgrimage from Egypt to the promised land, the tabernacle was God's appointed provision for them. The *wilderness* strikingly foreshadowed the conditions amid which the eternal Word tabernacled among men at His first advent. The wilderness home of the tabernacle unmistakably foreshadowed the manger-cradle, the Nazarite-carpenter's bench, the "nowhere" for the Son of Man to lay His head, the borrowed tomb for His sepulchre. A careful study of the chronology of the Pentateuch seems to indicate that Israel used the tabernacle in the wilderness rather less than thirty-five years!

3. *Outwardly the "tabernacle" was mean, humble, and unattractive in appearance.* Altogether unlike the costly and magnificent temple of Solomon, there was nothing in the externals of the tabernacle to please the carnal eye. Nothing but plain boards and skins. So it was at the Incarnation. The Divine majesty of our Lord was hidden beneath a veil of flesh. He came, unattended by any imposing retinue of angels. To the unbelieving gaze of Israel He had no form nor comeliness; and when they saw Him, their unanointed eyes saw in Him no beauty that they should desire Him.

4. The "tabernacle" was *God's dwelling place*. It was there, in the midst of Israel's camp, He took up His abode. There, between the cherubim upon the mercy-seat He made His throne. In the holy of holies He manifested His presence by means of the Shekinah glory. And during the thirty-three years that the Word tabernacled among men, God had His dwelling place in Palestine. The holy of holies received its anti-typical fulfillment in the Person of the Holy One of God. Just as the Shekinah dwelt between the two cherubim, so on the mount of transfiguration the glory of the God-Man flashed forth from between two men—Moses and Elijah. "We beheld His *glory*" is the language of the tabernacle type.

5. The "tabernacle" was, therefore, *the place where God met with men*. It was termed "the Tent of Meeting." If an Israelite desired to draw near unto Jehovah He had to come to the door of the tabernacle. When giving instructions to Moses concerning the making of the tabernacle and its furniture, God said, "And thou shalt put the mercy seat above upon the ark; and in the ark thou shalt put the testimony that I shall give thee. And *there* I will meet with thee, and I will commune with thee" *(Exod. 25:21, 22)*. How perfect is this lovely type! Christ is the *meeting-place* between God and men. No man cometh unto the Father but by Him (see *John 14:6*). There is but one Mediator between God and men—the Man Christ Jesus (see *I Tim. 2:5*). He is the One who spans the gulf between deity and humanity, because Himself both God and Man.

6. The "tabernacle" was *the center of Israel's camp*. In the immediate vicinity of the tabernacle dwelt the Levites, the priestly tribe: "But thou shalt appoint the Levites over the tabernacle of testimony, and over all the vessels thereof, and over all things that belong to it: they shall bear the tabernacle, and all the vessels thereof; and they shall minister unto it, and shall *encamp round about* the tabernacle" (*Num. 1:50*), and around the Levites were grouped the twelve tribes, three on either side—see Numbers 2. Again; we read, that when Israel's camp was to be moved from one place to another, "Then the tabernacle of the congregation shall set forward with the camp of the Levites *in the midst of the camp*" (*Num. 2:17*). And, once more, "And Moses went out, and told the people the words of the Lord, and gathered the seventy men of the elders of the people, and set them *round about the tabernacle*. And the Lord came down in a cloud and spake unto him" (*Num. 11:24, 25*). How striking is this! The tabernacle was the great *gathering center*. As such it was a beautiful foreshadowing of the Lord Jesus. He is our great *gathering-center*. And His precious promise is, that, "where two or three are gathered together in My name, there am I *in the midst* of them" (*Matt. 18:20*).

7. The "tabernacle" was *the place where the Law was preserved*. The first two tables of stone, on which Jehovah had inscribed the ten commandments were broken (*see Exod. 32:19*); but the second set were deposited in the ark in the tabernacle for safe keeping (*see Deut. 10:2-5*). It was only there, within the holy of holies, the tablets of the Law were preserved intact. How this, again, speaks to us of Christ! It was He who said, "Lo, I come: in the volume of the book it is written of Me; I delight to do Thy will, O My God: yea, *Thy Law is within* My heart" (*Psa. 40:7, 8*). Throughout His perfect life He preserved in thought, word, and deed, the Divine Decalogue, honoring and magnifying God's Law.

8. The "tabernacle" was the *place where sacrifice was made*. In its outer court stood the brazen altar, to which the animals were brought, and on which they were slain. There it was that blood was shed and atonement was made for sin. So it was with the Lord Jesus. He fulfilled in His own Person the typical significance of the brazen altar, as of every piece of the tabernacle furniture. The body in which He tabernacled on earth was nailed to the cruel Tree. The Cross was the altar upon which God's Lamb was slain, where His precious blood was shed, and where complete atonement was made for sin.

9. The "tabernacle" was *the place where the priestly family was fed*. "And the remainder thereof shall Aaron and his sons eat: with unleavened bread shall it be eaten *in the holy place;* in the court of the tabernacle of the congregation they shall eat it. .... The priest that offereth it for sin shall eat it: *in the holy place* shall it be eaten" (*Lev. 6:16, 26*). How deeply significant are these scriptures in their typical import! And how they speak to us of Christ as the Food of God's priestly family to-day, that is, all believers *(see I Peter 2:5)*. He is the Bread of Life. He is the One upon whom our souls delight to feed.

10. The "tabernacle" was *the place of worship*. To it the pious Israelite brought his offerings. To it he turned when he desired to worship Jehovah. From its door the Voice of the Lord was heard. Within its courts the priests ministered in their sacred service. And so it was with the Anti-type. It is *"by Him"* we are to offer unto God a sacrifice of praise (*see Heb. 13:15*). It is in Him, and by Him, *alone*, that we can worship the Father. It is through Him we have access to the throne of grace.

Thus we see how fully and how perfectly the tabernacle of old foreshadowed the Person of our blessed Lord, and why the Holy Spirit, when announcing the Incarnation, said, "And the Word became flesh, and *tabernacled* among us." Before passing on to the next clause of John 1:14, it should be pointed out that there is a series of striking contrasts between the wilderness tabernacle and Solomon's temple in their respective foreshadowings of Christ.

(1) The tabernacle foreshadowed Christ in His first advent; the temple looks forward to Christ at His second advent.

(2) The tabernacle was first, historically; the temple was not built until long afterwards.

(3) The tabernacle was but a temporary erection; the temple was a permanent structure.

(4) The tabernacle was erected by Moses the *prophet* (which was the office Christ filled during His first advent); the temple was built by Solomon the *king* (which is

the office Christ will fill at His second advent).

(5) The tabernacle was used in the *wilderness*—speaking of Christ's humiliation; the temple was built *in Jerusalem*, the "city of the great King" (*Matt. 5:35*)—speaking of Christ's future glorification.

(6) The numeral which figured most prominently in the tabernacle was five, which speaks of *grace,* and grace was what characterized the earthly ministry of Christ at His first advent; but the leading numeral in the temple was twelve which speaks of *government,* for at His second advent Christ shall rule and reign as King of kings and Lord of lords.

(7) The tabernacle was unattractive in its externals—so when Christ was here before He was as "a root out of a dry ground;" but the temple was renowned for its outward magnificence—so Christ when He returns shall come in power and great glory.

"*And we beheld His glory.*" "*We* beheld" refers, directly, to the first disciples, yet it is the blessed experience of all believers to-day. "But we all *beholding,* as in a glass (mirror) *the glory of the Lord*" (*II Cor. 3:18*). The term used in both of these verses seems to point a contrast. In John 12:41 we read, "These things said Isaiah, when he *saw* His glory, and spake of Him," the reference being to Isaiah 6. The Old Testament celebrities only had occasional and passing glimpses of God's glory. But, in contrast from these who only "saw," we—believers of this dispensation—"*Behold* His glory." But more particularly, there is a contrast here between the beholding and the non-beholding of God's glory: the Shekinah glory abode in the holy of holies, and therefore, was *hidden.* But we, now, "*behold*" the Divine glory.

"We beheld *His glory.*" What is meant by this? Ah! who is competent to answer. Eternity itself will be too short to exhaustively explore this theme. The glories of our Lord are infinite, for in Him dwelleth all the fulness of the Godhead bodily. No subject ought to be dearer to the heart of a believer. Briefly defined, "We beheld His glory," signifies, His supreme excellency, His personal perfections. For the purpose of general classification we may say the "glories" of our Saviour are fourfold, each of which is capable of being subdivided indefinitely. First, there are His *essential* "glories," as the Son of God; these are His Divine perfections, as for example, His Omnipotence. Second, there are His *moral* "glories," and these are His human perfections, as for example, His meekness. Third, there are His *official* "glories," and these are His mediatorial perfections, as for example, His priesthood. Fourth, there are His *acquired* "glories," and these are the reward for what He has done. Probably the first three of these are spoken of in our text.

First, "We beheld His glory" refers to His *essential* "glory," or Divine perfections. This is clear from the words which follow: "The glory as of the Only Begotten of the Father." From the beginning to the end of His earthly life and ministry the Deity of the Lord Jesus was plainly evidenced. His supernatural birth, His personal excellencies, His matchless teaching, His wondrous miracles, His death and resurrection, all proclaimed Him as the Son of God. But it is to be noted that these words, "we beheld His *glory,*" follow immediately after the words "tabernacled" among men. We cannot but believe there is here a further reference to the tabernacle. In the tabernacle, in the holy of holies, Jehovah made His throne upon the mercy seat, and the evidence of His presence there was the *Shekinah glory,* frequently termed "The Cloud." When the tabernacle had been completed, and Jehovah took possession of it, we read, "then a *cloud* covered the Tent of the congregation, and *the glory of the* Lord filled the tabernacle" (*Exod. 40:34*). It was the same at the completion of Solomon's temple: "The *Cloud* filled the House of the Lord, so that the priests could not stand to minister because of the Cloud, *for the glory* of the Lord had filled the House of the Lord" (*II Kings 8:10, 11*). Here "the Cloud" and "the Glory" are clearly identified. The Shekinah glory, then, was the standing sign of God's presence in the midst of Israel. Hence, after Israel's apostasy, and when the Lord was turning away from them, we are told, "And *the glory* of the Lord went up from the midst of the city" (*Ezek. 11:23*). Therefore, when we read, "The Word . . . . tabernacled among men, and we beheld His *glory*" it was the proof that none other than Jehovah was again in Israel's midst. And it is a remarkable fact, to which we have never seen attention called, that at either extremity of the Word's tabernacling among men the *Shekinah glory was evidenced*. Immediately following His birth we are told, "And there were in the same country shepherds abiding in the field, keeping watch over their flocks by night. And, lo, the angel of the Lord came upon them, and *the Glory of the Lord shone round about them:* and they were sore afraid" *(Luke 2: 8,9)*. And, at His departure from this world, we read "And when He had spoken these things, while they beheld, He was taken up; and *a Cloud* received Him out of their sight" *(Acts 1:9)*—not "clouds," but "a Cloud!" "We beheld His glory," then, refers, first, to His Divine glory.

Second, there also seems to be a reference here to His *official* "glory," which was exhibited upon the Holy Mount. In II Peter 1:16 we read, "For we have not followed cunningly devised fables, when we made known unto you the power and coming of our Lord Jesus Christ, but were eye witnesses of His *majesty*." The reference is to the Transfiguration, for the next verse goes on to say, "For He received from God the Father honor and *glory,* when there came such a voice to Him from the excellent glory, This is My beloved Son, in Whom I am well pleased." It is the use of the word "glory" here which seems to link the transfiguration-scene with John 1: 14. This is confirmed by the fact that on the Mount, "while He yet spake, a *bright cloud* overshadowed them" *(Matt. 17:5)*.

Third, there is also a clear reference in John 1:14 to the *moral* "glory" or perfections of the God-Man, for after saying "we beheld His glory," John immediately adds (omitting the parenthesis) *"Full of grace and truth."* What marvelous grace we behold in that wondrous descent from heaven's throne to Bethlehem's manger! It had been an act of infinite condescension if the One who was the Object of angelic worship had deigned to come down to this earth and reign over it as King; but that He should appear in weakness, that He should voluntarily choose poverty, that He should become a helpless Babe—such grace is altogether beyond our ken; such matchless love passeth knowledge. O that we may never lose our sense of wonderment at the infinite condescension of God's Son.

In His marvelous stoop we behold His *glory.* Greatness is never so glorious as when it takes the place of lowliness. Power is never so attractive as when it is placed at the disposal of others. Might is never so triumphant as when it sets aside its own prerogatives. Sovereignty is never so winsome as when it is seen in the place of service. And, may we not say it reverently, Deity had never appeared so glorious as when It hung upon a maiden's breast! Yes, we behold His glory—the glory of an infinite condescension, the glory of a matchless grace, the glory of a fathomless love.

Concerning the *acquired* "glories" of our Lord we cannot now treat at length. These include the various rewards bestowed upon Him by the Father after the successful completion of the work which had been committed into His hands. It is of these acquired glories Isaiah speaks, when, after treating of the voluntary humiliation and death of the Saviour, he gives us to hear the Father saying of Christ, "Therefore will I divide Him a portion with the great, and He shall divide the spoil with the strong; *because* He hath poured out His soul unto death" *(Isa. 53:12)*. It is of these acquired glories the Holy Spirit speaks in Philippians 2, where after telling of our Lord's obedience even unto the death of the Cross, He declares, *"Wherefore* God also hath highly exalted Him, and given Him a name which is above every name" *(Phil. 2:9)*. And so we might continue. But how unspeakably blessed to know, that at the close of our great High Priest's prayer, recorded in John 17, we find Him saying, "Father, I will that they also, whom Thou hast given Me, be with Me where I am; that they may behold *My glory*, which Thou hast given Me" *(vs. 24)*!

Before we pass on to the next verse we would point out that there is an intimate connection between the one which has just been before us *(see vs. 14)* and the opening verse of the chapter. Verse 14 is really an explanation and amplification of verse 1. There are three statements in each which exactly correspond, and the latter throw light on the former. First, "in the beginning was the Word," and that is something that transcends our comprehension; but "and the Word became flesh" brings Him within reach of our senses. Second, "and the Word was with God," and again we are unable to understand; but the Word "tabernacled among us," and we may draw near and behold. Third, "and the Word was God," and again we are in the realm of the Infinite; but "full of grace and truth," and here are two essential facts concerning God which come within the range of our vision. Thus by coupling together verses 1 and 14 (reading the verses in between as a parenthesis) we have a statement which is, probably, the most comprehensive in its sweep, the profoundest in its depths, and yet the simplest in its terms, to be found between the covers of the Bible. Put these verses side by side:—

(1) *"In the beginning was the Word:"*
  (a) *"And the Word became flesh"* tells of *the beginning* of His human life.

(2) *"And the Word was with God"*
  (b) *"And tabernacled among us"* shows Him *with men.*

(3) *"And the Word was God"*
  (c) *"Full, of grace and truth,"* and this tells what *God is.*

"John bare witness of Him, and cried, saying, This was He of whom I spake, He that cometh after Me is preferred before Me: for He was before Me" *(1:15).* Concerning the ministry and testimony of John the Baptist we shall have more to say in our next article, D. V., so upon this verse we offer only two very brief remarks. First, we find that here the Lord's forerunner bears witness to Christ's supreme excellency: "He that cometh after me is *preferred* before me," he declares, which, in the Greek, signifies Christ had His *being* "before" John. Second, "For He *was* before me." But, historically, John the Baptist was born into this world three months before the Saviour was. When, then, the Baptist says Christ "was *before*" him, he is referring to His eternal existence, and, therefore, bears witness to His deity.

"And of His fulness have all we recieved, and grace for grace" *(1:16).* The word "fulness" is still another term in this important passage which brings out the absolute Deity of the Saviour. It is the same word which is found in Col. 1:19 and 2:9— "For it pleased the Father that in Him should all fulness dwell;" "For in Him dwelleth all the fulness of the Godhead bodily." The Greek preposition "ek" signifies "out of." Out of the Divine fulness have all we (believers) "received." *What* is it we have "received" from Christ? Ah, what is it *we have not* "received!" It is out of His inexhaustible *"fulness"* we have "received." From Him we have "received" life *(see John 10:28);* peace *(see 14:27);* joy *(see 15:11);* God's own Word *(see 17:14);* the Holy Spirit *(see 20:22).* There is laid up in Christ, as in a great storehouse, *all* that the believer needs both for time and for eternity.

"And grace for grace." Bishop Ryle tells us the Greek preposition here may be translated two different ways, and suggests the following thoughts. First, we have received "grace *upon* grace," that is, God's favors heaped up, one upon another. Second, "grace *for* grace," that is, new grace to supply old grace; grace sufficient to meet every recurring need.

"For the law was given by Moses, but grace and truth came by Jesus Christ" *(1:17).* A contrast is drawn between what was "given" by Moses, and what "came" by Jesus Christ; for "grace and truth" were not merely "given," they *"came by* Jesus Christ," came in all their fulness, came in their glorious perfections. The Law was "given" to Moses, for it was not his own; but "grace and truth" were not "given" to Christ, for *these* were His own *essential* perfections. On looking into this contrast we must bear in mind that the great point here is *the manifestation of God:* God as He was manifested through the Law, and God as He was made known by the Only Begotten Son.

Was not the Law "truth?" Yes, so far as it went. It announced what God righteously demanded of men, and therefore, what men ought to be according to God's mind. It has often been said, the Law is a transcript of God's mind. But how inadequate such a statement is! Did the Law reveal what God *is?* Did it display all His attributes? If it did, there would be nothing more to learn of God than what the Law made known.

Did the Law tell out the *grace* of God? No; indeed. The Law was holy, and the commandment holy, just, and good, but it was utterly opposed to grace. It demanded obedience; it required the strictest doing and continuance of *all* things written in it. And the only alternative was death. Inflexible in its claims, it remitted no part of its penalty. He that despised it "died *without mercy,"* and, *"every* transgression and disobedience received a just recompense of reward" *(Heb. 10:28; see Heb. 2:3).* Such a Law could never justify a *sinner.*

The inevitable effect of the Law on those who receive it is just that which was produced at Sinai, to whom it first came: "And they said unto Moses, Speak *thou* with us, and we will hear: but let not *God* speak with us, lest we die" *(Exod. 20:19).* "Now therefore why should we die? For this great fire will consume us, if we hear the voice of the Lord our God any more, then shall we die" *(Deut. 15:25).* Why such terror? Because "they could not endure that which was commanded" *(Heb. 12:20).* This terror was the testimony which the Law extorts from every sinner, to whom it is brought home *as God's* Law; it is "the ministration of condemnation, and of death" *(II Cor. 3:7, 9).* It has a "glory," indeed, but it is the glory of thunder and lightning, of fire, of blackness, and of darkness, and the sound of the trumpet, and of the voice of words, which only bring terror to the guilty conscience. But, blessed be God, there is "a glory that excelleth" *(II Cor. 3:10).*

In perfect contrast from the Law, *"grace and truth* came by Jesus Christ." The "glory that excelleth" is the glory of "the Word that became flesh, the glory as of the Only Begotten of the Father full of grace and truth." The Law revealed God's justice, but it did not make known His mercy; it testified to His righteousness, but it did not exhibit His grace. It was God's "truth" for the time present, but not the full truth about God Himself. "By the Law is the knowledge of sin;" we never read "by the Law is the knowledge of God." No; the "Law entered that the offense might abound," "sin by the commandment became exceeding sinful." It made known the heinousness of sin: it condemned the sinner, but it did not fully reveal God. It exhibited His righteous hatred of sin and His holy determination to punish it: it exposed the guilt and corruption of the sinner, but for ought *it* could tell him, it left him to his doom. This was "truth," but was it the *whole* "truth?" Was there nothing to hope for in God? Was there no salvation for the sinner, no justification for the condemned, no reconciliation for the enemy? Yes, blessed be God, there was: but the *"truth"* as to all this "came by Jesus Christ," and therefore could He say "I am the Way," and not only so, but **"I am the Truth."**

"Grace *and* truth." These are fitly and inseparably joined together. We cannot have the one without having the other. There are many who do not like salvation by *grace,* and there are those who would tolerate grace if they could have it without the *truth.* The Nazarenes could "wonder" at the *gracious* words which proceeded out of His mouth, but as soon as Christ pressed the *truth* upon them, they "were filled with wrath," and sought to "cast Him down headlong from the brow of the hill whereon their city was built" *(see Luke 4).* Such, too, was the condition of those who sought Him for "the meat that perisheth." They were willing to profit from His *grace,* but when He told them the *truth* some "murmured" at Him, others were "offended," and "many of His disciples went back and walked no more with Him" *(see John 6).* And in our own day, there are many who admire the grace which came by Jesus Christ, and would consent to be saved by it, provided this could be without the intrusion of the truth. But this cannot be. Those who reject the truth, reject grace.

There is, in Romans 5:21, another sentence which is closely parallel, and really, an amplification of these words "grace and truth"—"Grace reigns *through righteousness,* unto eternal life by Jesus Christ our Lord." The grace which saves sinners is no mere moral weakness such as is often to be found in human government. Nor is "the righteousness of God," through which grace reigns, some mere *semblance* of justice. No; on the Cross, Christ was "set forth a *propitiation* (a perfect satisfaction to the broken Law) through faith in His blood, to declare His (God's) *righteousness* for the remission of sins" *(Rom. 3:25).* Grace does not ignore the Law, or set aside its requirements; nay verily, "it *establishes* the Law" *(Rom. 3:31):* establishes it because inseparably linked with "truth"; establishes it because it reigns "through righteousness," not at the expense of it; establishes it because grace tells of a Substitute who kept the Law for and endured the death penalty on behalf of all who receive Him as their personal Saviour.

But was there *no* "grace and truth" *before* Jesus Christ came? Assuredly there was. God dealt according to "grace and truth" with our first parents immediately after their transgression—it was grace that sought them, and provided them with a covering; as it was truth that pronounced sentence upon them, and expelled them from the garden. God dealt according to "grace and truth" with Israel on the Passover night in Egypt: it was grace that provided shelter for them beneath the blood; it was truth that righteously demanded the death of an innocent substitute in their stead. But "grace and truth" were never *fully* revealed till the Saviour Himself appeared. By Him they "came:" in Him they were personified, magnified, glorified.

And now let us notice a few contrasts between Law and Grace:

1. Law addresses men as members of the old creation; Grace makes men members of a new creation.
2. Law manifested what was in Man—sin; Grace manifests what is in God—Love.
3. Law demanded righteousness from men; Grace brings righteousness to men.
4. Law sentences a living man to death; Grace brings a dead man to life.
5. Law speaks of what men must do for God; Grace tells of what Christ has done for men.
6. Law gave a knowledge of sin; Grace puts away sin.
7. Law brought God out to men; Grace brings men in to God.

"No man hath seen God at any time; the Only Begotten Son, which is in the bosom of the Father, He hath declared Him" *(John 1:18).* This verse terminates the Introduction to John's Gospel, and *summarizes* the whole of the first eighteen verses of John 1. Christ has "declared"—told out, revealed, unveiled, displayed the Father; and the One who has done this is "the Only Begotten Son, which *is* in the bosom of the Father." The "bosom of the Father" speaks of proximity, personal intimacy with, and the enjoyment of the Father's love. And, in becoming flesh, the Son did not leave this place of inseparable union. It is not the "Son which *was*," but "which *is* in the bosom of the Father." He retained the same intimacy with the Father, entirely unimpaired by the Incarnation. Nothing in the slightest degree detracted from His own personal glory, or from the nearness and oneness to the Father which He had enjoyed with Him from all eternity. How we ought, then, to honor, reverence, and worship the Lord Jesus!

But a further word on this verse is called for. A remarkable contrast is pointed. In the past, God, in the fulness of His glory, was unmanifested—"No man" had seen Him; but now, God is fully revealed—the Son has "declared" Him. Perhaps this contrast may be made clearer to our readers if we refer to two passages in the Old Testament and compare them with two passages in the New Testament.

In I Kings 8:12 we read, "Then spake Solomon, The Lord said that He would dwell *in the thick darkness."* Again, *"Clouds and darkness* are round about Him" *(Psa. 97:2).* These verses tell not what God is in Himself, but declare that under the Dispensation of Law He was not revealed. What could be known of a person who dwelt in "thick darkness!" But now turn to I Peter 2:9, "But ye are a chosen generation, a royal priesthood, an holy nation, a peculiar people; that ye should show forth the praises of Him who hath called you *out of darkness* into His marvelous *light."* Ah, how blessed this is. Again, we read in I John 1:5, 7, "God is Light, and in Him is no darkness at all .... but if we walk *in the light,* as He is in the light, we have fellowship one with another." And this, because the Father has been fully "declared" by our adorable Saviour.

Once more: turn to Exodus 33:18—"And he said, I beseech thee, show me Thy glory." This was the earnest request of Moses. But was it granted? Read on, "And the Lord said, behold, there is a place by Me, and thou shalt stand upon a rock: and it shall come to pass, while My glory passeth by, that I will put thee in a cleft of a rock, and will cover thee with My hand while I pass by: And I will take away Mine hand, and thou shalt see My back parts: *but My face shall not be seen."* Character is not declared in a person's *"back* parts" but in his face! That Moses saw not the face, but only the back parts of Jehovah, was in perfect accord with the Dispensation of Law in which he lived. How profoundly thankful should we be that the Dispensation of Law has passed, and that we live in the full light of the Dispensation of Grace! How deeply grateful should we be, that we look not on the back parts of Jehovah "for God, who commanded the light to shine out of darkness, hath shined in *our* hearts, to give the light of the knowledge of the glory of God in the *face* of Jesus Christ" *(II Cor.*

4:6). May grace be given us to magnify and adorn that superlative grace which has brought us out of darkness into marvelous light, because the God whom no man hath seen at any time has been fully "declared" by the Son.

We conclude, once more, by drawing up a number of questions on the passage which will be before us, D. V., next month *(John 1:19-34)*, so that the interested reader, who desires to "Search the Scriptures" may give them careful study in the interval.

1. Why did the Jews ask John if he were Elijah, 1:21?
2. What "prophet" did they refer to in 1:21?
3. What are the thoughts suggested by "voice" in 1:23?
4. Why did John cry "in the wilderness" rather than the Temple, 1:23?
5. "Whom ye know not," 1:26—What did this prove?
6. What are the thoughts suggested by the Saviour's title "The Lamb of God," 1:29?
7. Why did the Holy Spirit descend on Christ in the form of a "dove," 1:32?—Arthur W. Pink.

3. THE NAZARITE

Numbers 6:6-8

His Separation from the Defilement of Nature's Sorrow

Under the form of Nazarite abstinence from "wine and strong drink," and from everything "that is made of the vine tree, from the kernels even to the husk," the Holy Spirit has exhibited and enforced the separation of Christ and His saints from creature joy, during the present period of the world's creature worship. By means of the law that the Nazarite must wear his hair unshorn during all the time of his vow of separation, we are impressively taught how Jesus, in lowly obedience to the will of the Father, refused to assert His original and unsurrendered rights, and how we are called to walk in His steps, yielding, for the present, our natural privileges, and refraining from the vindication of our rights, knowing that "this is thankworthy, if a man for conscience toward God endure grief, suffering wrongfully." These particulars of Nazar-life have already been dwelt upon at some length in previous papers.

We would now ponder the third and last trait of Nazarite separation—the most touching of them all—that which reveals the Man of Sorrows, and His suffering saints, rejecting both the luxury and the defilement of natural grief, in willing devotion to God, His Father and their Father, because of the joy and rest even now found in Him, and because of the foretaste He has vouchsafed in the gladness of the day when Christ and His companions in this night of weeping shall be "comforted from grief on every side." The picture of this particular of holy devotion on which we are to look is thus described:

"All the days that he separateth himself unto the Lord he shall come at no dead body. He shall not make himself unclean for his father, or for his mother, for his brother, or for his sister, when they die: because the consecration of his God is upon his head. All the days of his separation he is holy unto the Lord" (Num. 6:6-8).

To the profitable use of this particular of Nazarite consecration it is necessary to observe that legal defilement by the dead divides itself into two parts: these are defilement by contact, and defilement by funeral rites or by the use of any external symbol of mourning. The Nazarite's consecration demanded the most rigid care lest he should contract defilement in either of these ways.

1. He must not approach a dead body. *"All the days that he separateth himself unto the Lord he shall come at no dead body"* (vs. 6). Under the law the slightest contact with death in any form brought defilement of the most serious nature. A striking proof of this is given in the ordinance which provided that if at "the appointed season" for keeping the passover it should be found that any one was "unclean by reason of a dead body," his privilege to observe that institution must be postponed for a whole month *(see Num. 9: 10, 11)*. This is very impressive. The defiled by the dead is a true Israelite, and therefore his privilege is preserved for him by grace, which will not cast him off; and yet because of his defilement he is, by holiness, which must be maintained, for a

month debarred from fellowship with Israel; and when restored to fellowship he can only enjoy it in a narrowed circle.

The nature of defilement by contact with death, and its spiritual significance, may, however, best be gained by an examination of the institution of the sacrifice of the "red heifer," "the ashes" of which were "kept for the congregation of the children of Israel, for a water of separation—a purification for sin.

First, we may learn from this chapter (*Num. 19*) how appropriate it was that the Israelite who essayed to occupy the place of strictest consecration unto the Lord, should be laid under obligation to keep himself far off from death's taint. The law respecting defilement by contact ran thus: "He that toucheth the dead body of any man that is dead, and purifieth not himself, defileth the tabernacle of the Lord; and that soul shall be cut off from Israel: because the water of separation was not sprinkled upon him, he shall be unclean; his uncleanness is yet upon him. This is the law, when a man dieth in a tent: all that come into the tent, and all that is in the tent, shall be unclean seven days. And every open vessel, which hath no covering bound upon it, is unclean. And whosoever toucheth one that is slain with a sword in the open field, or a dead body, or a bone of a man, or a grave, shall be unclean seven days" (*Num. 19:11, 13-16*).

Passing by many of the solemn and interesting topics which these verses suggest, let us confine our inquiries to those points which have more immediate relation to defilement by contact with death. What then is the character of sin against which we are warned by all the texts of the law cited above? A general answer may be found in the apostolic exposition of Numbers 19. "For if the blood of bulls and of goats, *and the ashes of an heifer sprinkling the unclean,* sanctifieth to the purifying of the flesh: how much more shall the blood of Christ, who through the eternal Spirit offered Himself without spot to God, purge your conscience from *dead works* to serve the living God" (*Heb. 9:13, 14*). It is manifest that the moral defilements represented by the uncleanness which the Israelite contracted by touching a dead body, and the like, are included in the *"dead works"* from which the conscience of believers is purged by the blood of Christ. But that "dead works" is a phrase of wider, instead of the widest scope, will be clear when it is considered that the apostle, in the verses just cited, brings together the offerings of the yearly atonement, "the blood of bulls and of goats"—and the sacrifice of the red heifer—"the ashes of an heifer sprinkling the unclean"—as both finding their end in the one offering of Christ. It thus becomes plain that by the phrase "dead works" he designates, at once, all our sins which were represented by all the sins of Israel's year, and which were confessed by Israel's high priest "over the head" of the "scape goat" —"all the iniquities of the children of Israel, and all their transgressions in all their sins" (*Lev. 16:21*)—and all our contracted defilements, which were represented by all the uncleannesses which Israelites contracted by contact with death and the grave; and he shows that the blood of Christ purges our conscience from them all; as another apostle expresses it, "the blood of Jesus Christ, God's Son, cleanseth us from all sin." The expression "dead works," includes all that can by any possibility defile or burden the conscience of the believer.

But the uncleannesses which were, under the law, contracted by death's touch and taint must be regarded as representing the sinful defilements to which the believer is exposed by contagion. It must be remembered that the legal defilement under consideration does not typify the sins of unregenerate men. On the contrary they evidently represent the moral defilement to which the believer is liable through necessary contact with a world full of death— a world full of death in its wider sense—a world spiritually dead and yet dying. Unregenerate men are doubtless represented by the *"dead body,"* and the *"bone of a man"*—they are "dead in sins" (*John 5:25; Eph. 2:5*). And we have the Lord's own warrant for regarding *"a grave"* as the figure of a man who has, in His sight, taken on the most revolting form of death in sin. "Woe unto you, Scribes and Pharisees, hypocrites! for ye are like unto whited sepulchres, which indeed appear beautiful outward, but are within full of dead men's bones and all uncleanness" (*Matt. 23:27*). And the same apostle, who tells us that men in their natural condition are "dead in sins," when testifying and exposing the ruin of all men by sin, declares that "their throat is an open sepulchre" (*Eph. 2; Rom. 3*).

Such *were* believers, "even as others," but such they are no longer. They have been "quickened and raised up together with Christ; by grace they have been saved." Nevertheless, though no longer dead, they dwell in "the region and shadow of death:" and while they dwell here they are necessarily exposed to "uncleanness by reason of the dead;" they are liable to the pestilential breath of the "open sepulchre;" they too often "walk over graves which appear not," and "are not aware of them" *(Luke 11:44)*, until the sickness of conscious sin laid them low.

Such is somewhat of the character of defilement against which the Christian Nazarite is warned in the injunction laid upon his typical representative. *"All the days that he separateth himself unto the Lord he shall come at no dead body."* And our comparison of this text with the others which applied to all Israelites, has shown us that all believers are called to Nazariteship, and all are alike warned against the pollutions of the world. To all believers is the New Testament form of the Nazarite admonition addressed, "Pure religion and undefiled before God and the Father is this ..... *To keep himself unspotted from the world" (James 1:27).*

It may also have struck the reader that both the figures employed in the law, and their New Testament expositions, are well suited to impress upon us the necessity of unwearied vigilance against the pollutions of a defiling world.

Having gathered somewhat of God's view of our surroundings, and learned their defiling character, having heard the admonitions to be on our guard lest we find ourselves unclean by contact with the world, and recognizing the perils of our proximity to corruption, it should seem quite pertinent to ask ourselves what effect these have upon us. To say that the truth we have presented in this paper is not recognized by the mass of Christians is unnecessary. And to urge on Christians in general the acceptance of this truth, and to exhort them to take care lest they should defile themselves in the course of their necessary association with men dead in sins, would be to call upon them to take pains to avoid the spot and the stain while they are deep in the mire. Is this too much to say? Do the Christians of Christendom practically recognize the great foundation truths of our separation from the world, namely this truth, that "Christ gave Himself for our sins, *that He might deliver us from this present evil world?" (Gal. 1:4).* Do Christians generally tremble at the Word of God which saith "Ye adulterers and adulteresses, know ye not that the friendship of the world is enmity with God? Whosoever, therefore, will be the friend of the world is the enemy of God" *(James 4:4).* That Christians generally abstain from the commission of open crime there can be no doubt—and in that matter they are in no way in advance of what we call respectable people, though they be infidels—but that allowed, wherein are they a "peculiar people?" Are they not unequally yoked with unbelievers? While refusing *some* of the world's delights, are they not greedy of *many* pleasures which can only be enjoyed in the congregation of the dead? What worldly society is not largely composed of professing Christians? Are they not members of bodies whose objects are extremely evil; brothers in fraternities whose rites are unspeakably impious, and whose deeds are often such as dare not be revealed even in the world's own feeble light? We say then, that to the mass of Christians it is useless to deal respecting that severity of holiness which condemns "the garments spotted by the flesh," and the touch of "a dead bone." To these, testimony to saintly separation must be addressed on its broader ground. Complete separation from the world's *doom* and the world's *course,* as the very first results of Jesus' death and resurrection—this is the testimony to be delivered to worldly Christians, and not the minute details of holiness which are offered to the eye and claim the holy obedience of the Christian who can intelligently say, "I have been crucified with Christ, and by His Cross the world has been crucified unto me, and I unto the world" *(Gal. 2:20; 6:14).*

But this inference may be drawn from the law of defilement from death, and from the warnings addressed to Christians respecting the spot and stain of sin: If, in God's view, the touch taints, if the spot and stain cannot be tolerated in God's presence, what must be His abhorrence of the Christianity which takes delight in the world's embrace?

Let us turn away from the fearful misrepresentation of Christianity, and from the imperfect representations of Christian devotion—imperfect at the best—to the one true Nazarite who was never "unclean by reason of the dead," who passed through the world without spot or stain, who never contracted pollution in this world of death and corruption. Our space will not permit us to enter on this moral glory of the Lord Jesus in all its parts: enough to say, that our malignant disease could not reach Him. He was not susceptible of death's corrupting taints. The malarious poison of our world could find no pore of entrance into Him. His holiness was in itself absolutely repellent of sin's deadly exhalations. He only could pass through the world without at any time drawing evil to Himself.

If we have rightly interpreted the particular of Nazariteship now before us, it must be obvious that the special danger pointed out is that of defilement from legitimate association with men. And it is just in this point of view that we see the perfect purity of the Son of God, while dwelling in this world of sin and death. Wherever you follow Him you see that He is "undefiled in the way." It is needless to say that death's corruption is everywhere, in the temple and the synagogue, in the house and in the field, on the mountain and on the plain, and on the sea. But at last there is One who goes everywhere on His Father's business, and yet He takes no taint; He contracts no defilement, while everywhere surrounded by corrupting influences. He can eat and drink with the publicans and sinners, and with Simon the Pharisee, and yet He keeps Himself free alike from the pollution of the immorality of the one, and from the pollution of the hypocrisy and hardness of the other. He meets the guile of men, but He touches it not, and there is no guile found in His mouth; He was reviled, but He reviles not again; He has, in a word, no *contact* with the moral evil that assails Him.

We have just said that so far from contracting defilement, His holiness repelled all sin's pollution. And it is impossible in this connection not to recall the remarkable proofs of this which He gave in those instances in which He, in the fulfillment of His saving grace, as the Physician of the sick, and the Life of the dead, came in contact with the ceremonially unclean He touched the leper, saying, "I will, be thou clean," and instead of receiving defilement *from* the leper He sends forth cleansing *to* him. He touches the bier of Nain's dead, and raises the sleeping damsel by the right hand, but instead of contracting uncleanness *from* the dead, He sends forth *to* them life from Himself. He could pass by the *ceremonial* of Nazarite life because the *power* and *reality* were there, and because there was more than Nazarite consecration in Him.

Thus, on the one hand He touches not the morally unclean thing in the world of death, because sin has no power to attract Him; on the other hand, He touches the ceremonially unclean thing, to cleanse and quicken, because there is no affinity between Him and sin; its noxious vapors and all its pollutions flee before His presence. There is something of this Divine rejection of evil taint in all believers *(see I John 5:18)*, but the word they need, as Nazarites following Him in this evil day, and through this evil world, is rather, "Be ye separate, and touch not the unclean thing." But we must now turn to a still more remarkable part of the law of the Nazarite respecting the dead.

2. The Nazarite must not defile himself by any symbol of mourning for his nearest and dearest departed, *"He shall not make himself unclean for his father, or for his mother, for his brother, or for his sister, when they die, because the consecration of his God is upon his head"* (vs. 7).

It might be supposed that these words were merely designed to warn the Nazarite that the injunction of verse 6 extended even to the dead body of his nearest relative. But that verse 7 goes far beyond this will be apparent, if we compare the law respecting "defilement for the dead" which was imposed on Israel's priests. "And the Lord said unto Moses, speak unto the sons of Aaron, and say unto them, There shall none be defiled for the dead among his people: but for his kin, that is near unto him, that is, for his mother, or for his father, and for his son, and for his daughter, and for his brother, and for his sister, a virgin, that is nigh unto him, which hath no husband, for her he may be defiled. But he shall not defile himself, being a chief man among his people, to profane himself. They shall not make baldness upon their head, neither shall they shave off the corner of their beard, nor make any cuttings in their flesh. They shall be holy unto their God" *(Lev. 21:1-6)*. We have quoted this law at length because it shows plainly that *"defilement for the dead"* embraced far more than touch. It shows that to adopt any symbol of mourning, that to exhibit the conventional signs of natural grief, were ceremonial defilement. That this is the design of the law may be confirmed by comparing the marginal rendering of verse four with the example cited, *(Ezek. 24:16,17)*. But we need not leave Leviticus 21 to seek for further proof that mourning for the dead was legal defilement. This is the law for the high priest: "And he that is the high priest among his brethren, upon whose head the anointing oil was poured, and that is consecrated to put on the garments, *shall not uncover his head, nor rend his clothes;* neither shall he go in to any dead body, nor defile himself for his father, or for his mother" *(Lev. 21:10,11; comp. Lev. 10:6,7).*

In the light of these passages we learn the meaning of the Nazar-law, *"He shall not make himself unclean for his father,"* etc. And we further see that the consecration of the Nazarite is of the highest rank; not that of an ordinary priest, but that of the high priest. It is the characteristic of Christ Jesus, the Head of the royal priesthood, which is before us in the law of separation from the defilement of natural sorrow; and that we are called to share with Him this character of separation will be seen presently.

Taking with us these general views of the type, let us now see how this law of the Nazarite appears in the consecration of Christians, in the New Testament.

Believers in Christ Jesus are not called to stoicism; they are permitted to sorrow: and yet they are called away from the sorrow of nature. These statements are by no means contradictory; they are not even so paradoxical as the apostle's descriptions of the characteristics of an approved ministry, one of which is the truly Nazarite trait, "sorrowful, yet always rejoicing" *(II Cor. 6:10).*

We are, we have just said, permitted to sorrow. "Jesus wept." And the Holy Spirit dealing with believer's bereavements forbids not their sorrow *(I Thess. 4:13).* But then He will have our sorrows so ordered that it shall not break in upon the fellowship to which we are called. Let not any bereaved and mourning saint esteem it harsh that we should speak plainly on this subject. We know that it is easy to say how trial should be borne, easy to talk of submission to the stroke which "takes away from thee the desire of thine eyes;" and all this only in such a way as to show that the would-be comforters know not what they say, and in such a way as to induce anything but submission. But shall we not, the rather, seek to learn what He has to say about the sorrow which His love hath brought into our hearts, and learn of Him how to weep? Shall we not receive Himself into the place He has emptied in our hearts and homes? For, really, beloved saint, this is that Nazarite separation from earth's sorrows to which thou art called. He means not to repress thy tears, but that thou shouldst weep thy losses on His bosom, and confess that He is better than father or mother, son or daughter, brother or sister. He brought thy adversity, that thou mightest know Him as *thy* "brother born for adversity."

Let it then be observed that the sorrow of the saint must not be "the sorrow of the world which worketh death." It is not suitable that believers should be like the heathen mourners who "made cuttings in their flesh" *(Lev. 21:5).* The saint in Christ is not to "sorrow, even as others who have no hope." If bereaved saints will enter into the true Nazarite consecration, they will occupy themselves not with their bereavement by itself, but with their bereavement as the occasion of rejoicing in the sure hope that their "asleep in Jesus" "God will bring with Him" *(I Thess. 4:14).* And thus shall they escape the defilement of nature's sorrow; they shall "weep as though they wept not."

Again, it must be observed that our consecration demands that the sorrow of nature shall in no case interrupt our fellowship or interfere with our service. There is a remarkable enforcement of this in a passage to which we before incidentally alluded. Nadab and Abihu, sons of Aaron, had "offered strange fire before the Lord, which He commanded them not," and they "died before the Lord." That Aaron and his surviving sons should be filled with grief, and give every expressive token of it, was most natural. But they were priests, they were engaged in priestly service, and their communion with God must not be interrupted by natural grief: consequently their sorrow is at once put under the restraints of their separation unto the Lord. "And Moses said unto Aaron, and unto Eleasar, and to Ithamar, his sons, Uncover not your heads, neither rend your clothes: lest ye die, and lest wrath come upon all the people: but let your brethren, the whole house of Israel, bewail the burning which the Lord hath kindled" *(Lev. 10:6)*. This is full of instruction. We have each side of the paradox already referred to—"sorrowful yet always rejoicing"—the whole house of Israel bewailing, this is the "sorrowful" side; the priestly joy in the Lord uninterrupted, the covered head, the unrent garments, is the "always rejoicing."

We have found few things more humbling than the discovery that such is the inherent corruption of our nature that its most legitimate sorrow may defile. This is to discover that the rent heart and the whole heart are alike deceitful and desperately wicked. At the same time we must perceive that the "defiling of the head of our consecration" *(Num. 6:9)* is not necessarily brought about by sorrow in itself; but by sorrow *indulged at the expense of communion with God, and at the expense of the service to which we are called.*

That this is the true distinction may be gathered from an incident in the life of our Lord, which is indeed fraught with instruction for the disciple who would fully own His claims. Jesus said to one of His disciples, "Follow Me." But he said, "Lord, suffer me first to go and bury my father." "Jesus said unto him, Follow Me, and let the dead bury their dead; go thou and preach the kingdom of God" *(Matt. 8:21; Luke 9:59)*. The dead in sins may set their bereavements and their funeral ceremonies against Christ's claims. But the man living in Christ's life, is called to a discipleship which follows and serves Him first, and at every cost. This is the truth contained in the Nazarite law, *"He shall not make himself unclean for his father, or for his mother; for his brother, or for his sister, when they die: because the consecration of his God is upon his head."*

Such admonitions are always needed; but they are, perhaps, peculiarly suited to the present time. It may seem ungracious work, but we are convinced that faithfulness demands a testimony against the unholy indulgence of morbid grief which refuses to be comforted, as much as against any other form of defilement. Surely the grandeur of Christian cemeteries, their monuments in the highest style of art, their floral decorations which so speedily proclaim the decay of nature, and much more which the mention of these will recall to every reader, sufficiently tell that Christians have not yet left it to "the dead to bury their dead."

But we need not go to the cemeteries. How many disciples of Jesus are refusing present communion with Him, and neglecting the service to which He is calling them, while they continually rehearse the scenes of the death-bed and of the funeral. They *cherish* their sorrows instead of cherishing *the hope.* They look at the grave and cannot lift up their eyes to Him Who is coming to empty it. Weeping saints, turn from your grief to Him, turn away from death and the grave to resurrection, the glory, honor, immortality and incorruption which He will bring to your sleeping ones when He shall descend from heaven with a shout, when the dead in Christ shall rise first, and when we together with them shall be caught up to the meeting of the Lord in the air, and shall be forever with the Lord. In this hope you will find at once the "steadfastness" of your faith, and the "abounding in the work of the Lord" to which you are called as those *"separated"* and *holy unto the Lord."*

We close by reminding you of the three characteristics of the Christian's consecration of himself as a "living sacrifice, holy and acceptable unto God," which we have found outlined in the Nazarite law: The refusal of nature's joys, the abandonment of nature's rights, and separation from the defilement of nature's sorrow, that they may be *"holy unto the Lord."* And all these are commended to the believer in the words of inspiration, thus: "This I say, brethren, the time is short: it remaineth, that both they that have wives be as though they had none; and they that weep, as though they wept not; and they that rejoice, as though they rejoiced not; and they that buy, as though they possessed not; and they that use this world, as not abusing it: for the fashion of this world passeth away" *(I Cor. 7:29-31)*. —From *"Grace and Truth,"* edited by *Chas Campbell, 1871.*

(To be concluded, D.V.).

All that will live godly in Christ Jesus must suffer persecution. In Ishmael's case it was seen that he that is born after the flesh persecuteth him that is born after the Spirit, and so it is now. You cannot expect to pass through this *vanity fair* without exciting the jeers and sneers of the ungodly. Every David has his Saul, every Nehemiah his Sanballat, and every Mordecai his Haman.—*C. H. Spurgeon.*

VOL. I   APRIL, 1922   NO. 4.

STUDIES in the SCRIPTURES

"Search the Scriptures" John 5:39.

A PERIODICAL (MONTHLY "IF THE LORD WILL")
DEVOTED TO BIBLE STUDIES and EXPOSITIONS

Associate Editors and Publishers, I. C. HERENDEEN and ARTHUR W. PINK,
Swengel, Pa.

Price: **10** cents per copy; **$1.00** per year. Foreign **$1.00** per year.

TO OUR SCRIPTURE STUDY FAMILY

It is our desire to offer a few comments on the motto text of this magazine from John 5:39. The R. V. renders it "Ye search the Scriptures", while giving in the margin "Search the Scriptures" which is the wording of the A. V. The difference between the two is this: "Ye search the Scriptures" is merely a statement of fact; "Search the Scriptures" is an appeal or a command. The grammatical variation is the difference between the indicative and imperative moods of the verb. Devout Christian scholars are about equally divided: many honored names could be cited on either side.

We shall now put the simple facts before the interested reader. As a mere matter of correct translation either the indicative or the imperative form of the verb would be *equally accurate*. How then are we to ascertain which is the right one? To answer this question the chief requirement is not a profound knowledge of Greek or even English grammar, but it is to compare scripture with scripture. The Bible is its own interpreter. Two things must be borne in mind: the *usage* of the indicative and imperative forms of the verbs in the New Testament, and particularly in this Gospel of John; and the *setting* of John 5:39.

John 7:52 is the only other verse in this Gospel where the word "ereunao" (to search, trace or track) occurs—"They answered and said unto him (Nicodemus), Art thou also of Galilee? *Search* (i. e. the Scriptures), and look: for out of Galilee ariseth no prophet". Now we ask, Could the verb here be given in the *indicative*—"Ye search"? Certainly not; and we are fully satisfied that it is equally inadmissible to so render it in 5:39. For similar examples where the verb has exactly the same form in the Greek as in John 5:39, see 14:11 for "believe" and 15:20 for "remember", where in each case the verb is rendered in the *imperative* mood, and where to change it to the indicative would destroy its force: "Ye believe" and "Ye remember" would falsify the Saviour's meaning. To us this is conclusive: the imperative mood is required in each of these three examples.

A word now on the setting of our text. John 5:18 shows the Jews assaulting the Saviour because He made Himself equal with God. From vv. 19-31 the Lord makes a sevenfold affirmation of His absolute Deity. Then, in vv. 32-39 He appeals to four witnesses who avouch His Divine Sonship: first, John the Baptist *(v. 32)*; second, His own works *(v. 36)*; third, the Father Himself *(v. 37)*; and fourth, the Scriptures *(v. 39)*. Christ here appeals to the Scriptures as the final court of authority—*they* "testified" of Him, and that ended the controversy; beyond *them* there was no appeal. This the Jews themselves admitted, and it was on their own belief in their Divine authority He bids them act.

What marvelous dignity does the Saviour here give to the Scriptures! Beyond them there was no appeal; above them there was no higher authority; after them there was no further witness. "For in them YE think"—the pronoun is emphatic. The word "think" does not imply it was a doubtful point, or merely a matter of human opinion. It is rather that Christ said to them, "This is one of the articles of *your* faith: 'ye think' (and rightly so), then act on it. Search those Scriptures (in which ye are assured there is eternal life) and you will find *they* testify of *Me*". The word "think" here means to account. It does not imply a doubt, but signifies an assurance; it practically means *believe*—see Matt. 12:17. 42 for its force.

It is indeed blessed to notice the order in which Christ placed the four witnesses to whose testimony He appealed in proof of His Divine Sonship. First, there was the witness of His own forerunner. Second, there was the witness of His own Divine works. Third, there was the witness of the Father, which had been borne from an opened heaven at the time of His baptism. And fourth, there was the witness of the Scriptures, which had been written by men moved by the Holy Spirit. So that in these last three witnesses there is a remarkable reference made to *the three Persons in the Holy Trinity.*

In making appeal to the Scriptures last, the Saviour indicated that they were of *final* authority. This in itself is more than enough to settle the debated point as to how the verb should be rendered. To give it in the indicative mood, and say "Ye search the Scriptures", would simply be to make a commonplace statement having little or no relevancy to what had been said before, and would be to destroy the climax to which the Saviour was manifestly working. Whereas "Search the Scriptures" *clinches* the argument and beautifully rounds out the whole period.

Assured then of the correctness of the A. V. rendering, we give a very brief word in closing on its application to ourselves. "Search the Scriptures". This is a command from our Lord. The authority of His Godhood is behind it. "Search" He says, not merely "read". The Greek word is one that was used in connection with hunting. It referred to the hunter stalking game. When he discovered the tracks of an animal he concentrated all his attention on the ground before him, diligently searching for other marks which would lead him to his quarry. In a similar way *we* are to study God's Word—minutely examining each word, tracing each occurrence of it, and learning its meaning from its usage. The grand motive for such earnest study is, that the Scriptures *testify of Christ*. May both writer and reader give daily heed to this Divine admonition to "*Search* the Scriptures."

Yours in affectionate bonds,   Arthur W. Pink.

STUDIES IN THE SCRIPTURES

An Unsectarian Monthly Periodical
Devoted to Bible Studies
and Expositions.

Subscription Price: **$1.00** per year to any address in the world. Single copies **10 cents**.

Change of Address: Please notify us promptly of any change of address, and be certain to give both old and new addresses.

Non-Subscribers receiving this Magazine regularly will understand their subscription has been entered by a friend.

Entered as second-class matter December 15th, 1921 at the post office at Swengel, Pa., under Act of March 3rd, 1879.

CONTENTS

The Precious Blood	62
John's Gospel	67
The Provisions of Grace for Nazarite Failure	73
Grace As It Reigns in the Perseverance of the Saints to Eternal Glory	77

THE PRECIOUS BLOOD

Evangelistic Address: by Request

"Without shedding of blood is no remission" *(Heb. 9:22).*

If there is one doctrine of the Bible which Satan hates more than another, it is that of the Atonement. The truth of the atoning death of the Saviour is peculiarly offensive to him. He is quite willing for preachers to exhort their hearers to be good and do good, so long as they maintain a criminal silence about the Cross. The Devil knows full well that it was at Calvary his own death warrant was signed.

If there is one word in the Bible which Satan fears more than another it is, in all probability, the word Blood. If Satan can cause this word to drop out of the preacher's vocabulary he is supremely happy, for he knows full well that once the sinner has fled for refuge to the precious blood of Christ, once he has exercised faith in that blood, he has no more claim upon him. I rarely meditate upon this theme but what I am reminded of the parable of the Sower. How Satan has succeeded in catching away the "seed"!

One fundamental difference between true Gospel preaching and all spurious imitations, is the place that is given to and the emphasis that is laid upon the blood. Man-made systems inculcate morality and good citizenship; they emphasize the importance of honesty, truthfulness, and righteousness; but they one and all ignore the blood.

"Blood" is mentioned in the Bible over four hundred times. It runs through both Testaments like a scarlet thread. The Mosaic ritual was blood, blood, blood on every occasion. The daily Tabernacle worship began with the shedding of blood and it terminated with the same, in the slaying of the morning and evening lamb. The Tabernacle itself, the Book of the Covenant, the priests at their consecration, were all sprinkled with blood. It was the same at the cleansing of the leper.

The blood occupies a prominent place in New Testament teaching. The Lord Jesus spoke of the blood: "This is My blood of the New Covenant, which was shed for many for the remission of sins" *(Matt. 26:28).* Paul spoke of the blood: "But now in Christ Jesus ye who sometimes were far off are made nigh by the blood of Christ" *(Eph. 2:13).* Peter spoke of the blood. "Forasmuch as ye know that ye were not redeemed with corruptible things, as silver and gold, from your vain conversation received by tradition from your fathers; But with the precious blood of Christ, as of a lamb without blemish and without spot' *(I Peter 1:18, 19).* John spoke of the blood "But if we walk in the light, as He is in the light, we have fellowship one with another, and the blood of Jesus Christ His Son cleanseth us from all sin" *(I John 1:7)*

"Without shedding of blood is no remission." This enunciates a cardinal doctrine of the Christian Faith. It is, in fact, the foundation truth of the Gospel. A man may be unsound on many doctrines and his eternal welfare is not jeopardized, but error here is fatal Unless we are clear on *this* truth our souls are in deadly danger.

In developing our theme we shall first, define the terms of our text; second, give illustrations of its central truth in the Old Testament; third, explain its doctrine; and fourth, set forth some of its corollaries.

I. Definition of Terms.

What is meant by "shedding of blood"? An answer to this question is found in Leviticus 17:11, where we are told. "For *the life* of the flesh *is in the blood:* and I have given it to you upon the altar to make an atonement for your souls: for it is the blood that maketh an atonement for the soul." The shedding of blood, then, means a life poured forth, a life laid down on behalf of others, a life given in sacrifice.

What is meant by the word "remission"? And, remission *of what?* The word "remission" means to send away, and the remission here refers to the sending away of the sins of the one who believes in Christ. No doubt the reference is to the scape goat of Israel's annual Day of Atonement. As we read in Leviticus 16:21, 22. "And Aaron shall lay both his hands upon the head of the live goat, and confess over him all the iniquities of the children of Israel, and all their transgressions and all their sins, putting them upon the head of the goat, and shall *send him away* by the hand of a fit man into the wilderness: And the goat shall *bear upon him* all their iniquities unto a land not inhabited." Or, as we read in Psalm 103:12, "As far as the east is from the west, so far hath He *removed* our transgressions from us."

What is the force of the word "without"? It means *apart from*. It signifies that, unless blood is shed, anything and everything else is quite unable to secure or procure the "remission" of sins.

II. ILLUSTRATIONS OF THIS TRUTH.

1. *Blood-shedding in the Garden of Eden.*

"Unto Adam also and to his wife did the Lord God make coats of skins, and clothed them" *(Gen. 3:21)*. Though the word "blood" is not mentioned here, yet, we have a clear and striking illustration of the truth of our text. In order to obtain these skins life must have been taken, and blood must have been shed. Man did not eat the flesh of animals before the Flood, consequently these animals must have been slain in sacrifice. This is the first instance in human history of vicarious suffering, that is, of the innocent dying in the place of the guilty. The first lesson God taught fallen man was, that the way back to Himself was through blood-shedding. It is exceedingly remarkable to find that the first blood ever spilled on this earth was *shed by God Himself!*

Let us go back for a moment to Gen. 3:7: "And the eyes of them both were opened, and they knew that they were naked; and they sewed fig leaves together, and made themselves aprons." Conscious of their shame, Adam and Eve at once sought to hide it by making unto themselves aprons of fig leaves. Instead of at once seeking God, and confessing their guilt and shame, they attempted to *conceal* it both from Him and from themselves. This is the way of the natural man: this is exactly what men have been doing ever since. The last thing the sinner wants to do is to *own* before God his lost and ruined condition. Conscious that something is wrong, he seeks to shelter behind his own works and hide behind the filthy rags of his own righteousnesses.

But *why* are we told that the leaves of these aprons were *fig* leaves? Of what particular interest or importance is it for us today to know that these were *fig* leaves? That there is some important meaning to this is clear, or otherwise the Holy Spirit would not have recorded it. And the way to find out the answer (God's answer) to this question is to compare scripture with scripture. The answer is found in the Gospels, where we read of Christ cursing the *fig* tree, on which He found *nothing but leaves.* What a message has this for all who have ears to hear! That which is manufactured by human efforts as a device to hide our shame *is under the direct Curse of Christ!*

What a striking contrast there was between the aprons of fig leaves made by Adam and Eve and the "coats of skins" supplied by the Lord. Here was the first Gospel sermon, given in figurative form. "Remission" cannot be obtained by human effort. That which clothed Adam and Eve was not manufactured by fallen man, but was *provided by God.* There could be no clothing until life had been taken. And how this incident revealed the Heart of God! All that Adam and Eve deserved was judgment, but in sovereign grace God provided a covering through sacrifice. Sin was covered before our first parents were banished from Eden. God always deals in mercy before He acts in judgment.

2. *Blood-shedding in connection with Abel.*

"And in process of time it came to pass, that Cain brought of the fruit of the ground an offering unto the Lord. And Abel, he also brought of the firstlings of his flock, and of the fat thereof. And the Lord had respect unto Abel and to his offering: But unto Cain and to his offering He had not respect" *(Gen. 4:3-5).* "By *faith* Abel offered unto God a more excellent sacrifice than Cain, by which he obtained witness that he was righteous, God testifying of his gifts; and by it he being dead yet speaketh" *(Heb. 11:4)*. Both Cain and Abel were shapen in iniquity and conceived in sin: both of them were born of fallen parents, and both of them were born *outside* of Eden. There was only one ground of approach to God, and *that* He had made known. "Without shedding of blood is no remission" of sin had been strikingly, if silently, proclaimed by the Lord Himself to our fallen first parents. In clothing them with the coats of skins God taught Adam and Eve four things; namely: that the sinner needed a covering, that a covering manufactured by human toil was worthless, that God Himself must provide the covering, and that this could be obtained only through blood-shedding—either the sinner must die or another must die in his stead. The sinner must put the death of an innocent substitute between himself and God.

Cain and Abel both knew what God's requirements were, for it was "by faith" that Abel offered his sacrifice unto God, and as we are told in Rom. 10:17. "Faith cometh by hearing, and hearing by the word of God". Cain and Abel, then, had *heard*, and it was now solely a question of submitting themselves to God's demands.

It is strange that so many have erred in their conclusions as to why Cain's offering was rejected and Abel's offering accepted. There is nothing whatever in the inspired record to indicate that up to this time Abel was a better man than Cain. Both of them were fallen sinners, and as such neither of them could stand before God. The scripture quoted above from Heb. 11 expressly tells us that the difference lay not in the respective characters of Cain and Abel, but in the offerings they brought to the Lord Abel "offered unto God a more excellent *sacrifice* than Cain".

Cain and Abel stand as the concrete illustrations of two great classes of people. They represent the same two classes as do the Pharisee and the Publican, spoken of by our Lord, going up to the Temple to pray. They are examples of the proud self-righteous on the one hand, and of the broken-spirited penitents on the other.

Cain did not like God's way of salvation. He would not bow to the truth that "without shedding of blood is no remission". He would not acknowledge that death was his due. Instead, he insulted God by bringing to Him the fruits of the ground, the products of his own labors, the works of his own hands—the fruits of that ground that had been *cursed* by God *(Gen. 3:17)*.

Abel presented unto the Lord a bleeding lamb—the "firstlings of his flock and *of the fat thereof"*—which could only be obtained by blood-shedding. What a contrast was presented by these respective offerings! Cain's must have been most attractive to the human eye. No doubt he procured the most luscious fruits and beautiful flowers that were obtainable; while Abel stood there with nothing but a bleeding lamb. And yet God rejected the former and accepted the latter.

By bringing the offering which he did Abel confessed that he could not go to God as he was. He knew that he was outside of Paradise, that sin had come in between himself and a holy God, and that *death*—"the wages of sin"—was his righteous due. Only by owning this and by putting his trust in a substitute could he be accepted by God, for "without shedding of blood is no remission".

3. Blood-shedding in connection with Noah.

"And Noah builded an altar unto the Lord; and took of every clean beast, and of every clean fowl and offered burnt offerings on the altar" *(Gen. 8:20)*. We pass down the stream of human history sixteen hundred years and reach a new dispensation, and it is striking to notice that like the one that preceded it this also opens with blood-shedding. The very first thing that Noah did on coming out of the ark onto the earth which had been swept with the besom of Divine judgment, was to place *blood* between himself and God.

It is blessed to read the sequel: "And the Lord smelled *a sweet savor;* and the Lord said in His heart, I will not again curse the ground any more for man's sake (for the imagination of man's heart is evil from his youth), neither will I again smite any more every thing living, as I have done." On the sixth day of creation God beheld all His works which He had made, and "Behold they were very good". Perfect they were, for nothing short of perfection could come from His hand. Beautiful must those works have been, when Adam and Eve first surveyed them, but we do not read of them sending up a "sweet savor" to God. Why then should we do so here when Noah offered his burnt offerings to Him on the altar? *Wherein* consisted the fragrance of Noah's offering? *He* did nothing to sweeten it. No flowers, with their fine aroma, were added: no fragrant herbs or incense imparted a sweetness to it in God's nostrils. No, it was the *sacrifice itself* that was a "sweet savor", and to *that* man could add nothing. It was, of course, that which spoke to God of *Christ*, for it was Christ's obedience unto death which glorified God as nothing else could do.

And what do we read of next? "And God *blessed* Noah and his sons" *(9:1)*. A welcome sound must this have been, for since the days of paradise God had blessed no man. God *blessed* Adam and Eve on the sixth day; He "blessed" the seventh day, and there His blessing *ended*. An why? Because sin had come in, and never again is it recorded that God bestowed "blessing" on any man until Noah and his sons received it as they came forth out of the ark, and then, only after Noah had built an altar unto the Lord and had offered thereon burnt offerings.

4. *Blood-shedding in connection with Israel in Egypt.*

"For I will pass through the land of Egypt this night, and will smite all the firstborn in the land of Egypt, both man and beast; and against all the gods of Egypt I will execute judgment: I am the Lord. And *the blood* shall be to you for a token upon the houses where ye are: and when *I see the blood,* I will pass over you, and the plague shall not be upon you to destroy you, when I smite the land of Egypt" *(Ex. 12:12 13)*. This is one of the most important chapters in the Old Testament. It brings us to the opening of another dispensation, and it, too, begins with blood-shedding. The angel of death was to visit the land of Egypt that night, for God was to act in judgment and punish sin. The children of Israel were under sentence of death, for God had said, I will "smite *all* the firstborn *in* the land of Egypt". The "firstborn" stands for the natural man: against the natural man God has pronounced sentence of death. Death had to do its work in every household, for death is the wages of sin, and from it there is no escape. Faithfully was the sentence carried out. The "firstborn" in *every* household died that night. This is no slip of the pen. The "firstborn" in the homes of the Israelites died as truly as did those in the homes of the Egyptians, but in the case of the former they *died in the person of a substitute.*

Here was the Gospel in Egypt. Here the truth of our text "without shedding of blood is no remission" was both illustrated and demonstrated. The way of deliverance for Israel was through the death of an innocent lamb, and by the shedding and applying of its blood. When the Israelite had applied the blood to the lintel and posts of his door, God said, "When I see the blood I will pass over *you.*" It was not when I see your genealogical descent from Abraham, nor your circumcision, nor the excellence of your characters, nor, in fact, anything from them, or anything in them. It was something *outside* of them, and that something was BLOOD. The "lamb" was neither of Israel's choosing nor of Moses' recommendation; it was of God's appointment. The remarkable thing is that here in Ex. 12 we behold a whole nation under the blood, and that, too, before they ever came under the Law.

How striking it is to consider the gradation in these four types in which the blood plays so prominent a part. First, the coats of skins teaches us that the shedding of blood is necessary in order to provide a *standing* before God. Second, Abel's offering teaches that the shedding of blood is that which enables God to *accept* the sinner. Third, Noah's sacrifice teaches that the shedding of blood brings *blessing* on those who have faith in it. Fourth, the passover night teaches us that the shedding of blood provides *security* in the midst of judgment.

We cannot now follow this interesting line of truth any further through the typical teaching of the Old Testament Scriptures, nor consider in detail the prominent place it occupies in the New Testament; but in concluding this section we would turn to one passage in the last book of the Bible. In Rev. 7 the apostle John is given to behold a striking scene in heaven. He sees a great multitude which no man could number, who cry with a loud voice, "Salvation to our God which sitteth upon the throne, and unto the Lamb", and in response all the inhabitants of heaven fall before the throne on their faces and worship God. Then we are told that one of the elders inquired, "What are these which are arrayed in white robes? and whence came they?" And he is told, "These are they which came out of great tribulation, and have washed their robes, and made them white *in the blood* of the Lamb. *Therefore* are they before the throne of God" *(vv. 14, 15)*. What marvelous force has the word "therefore" in this connection!

III. AN EXPLANATION OF THIS TRUTH.

I can well imagine that some are saying, I do not understand *why* God should require blood. If He is loving and merciful why should blood-shedding be necessary at all? Let us attempt a detailed, though brief, answer to these questions.

The shedding of blood was imperatively necessary because *death* was the sentence of God's law upon those who broke it. To Adam God said at the beginning, "In the day thou eatest thereof thou shalt surely *die*". Through the prophet he declared, "The soul that sinneth it shall *die*". The wages of sin is *death*. Again and again was this illustrated at varying intervals throughout the Old Testament dispensation. One single sin and Lot's wife is cut off out of the land of the living. One single sin and Moses is debarred from entering the promised land. One single sin and Achan is stoned to death. The Scripture cannot be broken. God cannot lie. Death *must* come upon every transgressor.

As the moral Governor of the universe God must see to it that justice is administered. Sin *ought* to be punished. Not to punish sin would be to overthrow all government, and destroy all moral distinctions. If sin were left unpunished, the universe would be filled with spiritual anarchy. Suppose the Governor of your State became so sentimental that he could not bear the thought of criminals being punished, and tomorrow morning gave orders that all lying in the penitentiaries should be released. How long would he remain Governor? Is it wrong, then, for God THE SUPREME GOVERNOR, to punish sin!

Why is it that "without shedding of blood there is no remission"? Because this was the penalty of God's broken law, because this is what sin deserved, because this is what Divine justice demanded. Nothing short of the death of Christ could secure the remission of our sins. The requirements of the law were "a life *for* a life". By sin we had forfeited our lives, and hence nothing but the laying down of Christ's life could redeem us. The Son of Man *must* be lifted up.

IV. COROLLARIES OF THIS TRUTH.

1. *What is the relation of Repentance to Remission?*

Repentance is not the price which the sinner has to pay, for 'Jesus paid it *all*'. "It is finished" is final. Repentance is the realization of my deep and desperate *need:* it is the acknowledgment of my lost condition. A good example of what evangelical repentance is, is found in the case of the Publican in the Temple.

2. *What is the relation of Faith to Remission?*

In Rom. 3:25 we are told that God hath set forth Christ to be "a propitiation through faith in His blood". To have faith in His blood means to confide in it, to rely upon it; it signifies the turning away from every other ground of confidence for our acceptance before God. Faith in His blood is trusting in its merits, the personal appropriation of its virtues, the applying to myself of its value.

3. *What is the relation of Baptism to Remission?*

And again we say it is not something that is *added* to Christ's blood. There is nothing, absolutely nothing, that we can add to its efficacy. The blood of Christ is all-sufficient. It has *satisfied God,* why does it not satisfy you? Baptism is simply the outward confession and symbolical showing forth of the fact that my sins were dealt with by the death of Christ and were done away with when He arose again from the dead.

4. *What is the relation of Good Works to Remission?*

After what has been said above it will suffice to say that they are not *in order to* our salvation, but rendered *because of* it. The one who has been saved will perform good works out of love and gratitude to the One who has saved him.

And now, dear reader, where do you stand? "Without shedding of blood is no remission". Unless you have, for yourself, exercised faith in the blood of Christ, unless you are relying upon it as the sol ground of your acceptance before God, you are yet in your sins. Morality and religiousness can avail you nothing. There may have been remorse for the past, there may be a historical faith in the facts of Christianity, there may have been going through the form of baptism, and there may be an abundance of legal works, but God says, "Without shedding of blood *is no remission*".

Go back again for a moment to Ex. 12. Consider with me the striking and blessed order of mention that we have there in connection with the *lamb* in vv. 3, 4, and 5. In v. 3 we find God gave instructions that in the tenth day of the month every man of the congregation of Israel was to take "*a* lamb". In v. 4 we are told that "every man according to his eating shall make your count for *the* lamb", but in v. 5 we read, "*Your* lamb shall be without blemish". Has this any voice for you, dear reader? This is precisely the order in which every believer has apprehended Christ. He heard of Him first as *a Saviour;* then, as he continued under the sound of the Gospel, he became convinced that Christ is *the Saviour;* but it was not until he exercised faith in the Lord Jesus for himself that He became a *personal Saviour.* Reader, which is Christ to you—a lamb, the lamb, or your lamb?

—Arthur W. Pink.

JOHN'S GOSPEL

4. THE BAPTIST'S TESTIMONY CONCERNING CHRIST: John 1:19-34.

Following our usual custom, we begin by submitting an Analysis of the passage which is to be before us. In it we have:—

1. The Jew's inquiry of John, and his answers, 1:19-26.
   (1) "Who art thou?" Not the Christ: 19, 20.
   (2) "Art thou Elijah?" No: 21.
   (3) "Art thou that prophet?" No: 21.
   (4) "What sayest thou of thyself?" A "voice", 22, 23.
   (5) "Why baptisteth thou?" To prepare the way for Christ, 24-26.
2. John's Witness concerning Christ, 1:27.
3. Location of the Conference, 1:28.
4. John proclaims Christ as God's "Lamb", 1:29.
5. The purpose of John's baptism, 1:30-31.
6. John tells of the Spirit descending on Christ at His baptism, and foretells that Christ shall baptize with the Spirit, 1:32, 33.
7. John owns Christ's Deity, 1:34.

Even a hurried reading of these verses will make it evident that the personage which stands out most conspicuously in them is John the Baptist. Moreover, we do not have to study this passage very closely to discover, that the person and the witness of the Lord's forerunner is brought before us here in a manner entirely different from what we find in the first three Gospels. No hint is given that His raiment was "of camel's hair", that he had "a leathern girdle about his loins", or that "his meat was locusts and wild honey". Nothing is recorded of his stern Call to Repentance, nor is anything said of his announcement that "the Kingdom of Heaven is at hand". These things were foreign to the design of the Holy Spirit in this fourth Gospel. Again; instead of referring to the Lord Jesus as the One "whose fan is in His hand", and of the One who "will thoroughly purge His floor, and gather His wheat into His garner, but He will burn up the chaff with unquenchable fire" *(Matt. 3:12),* he points to Him as "the Lamb of God which taketh away the sin of the world". All this is most significant and blessed to those who have been divinely taught to rightly divide the Word of Truth.

Without doubt John the Baptist is, in several respects, one of the most remarkable characters that is brought before us in the Bible. He was the subject of Old Testament prophecy *(Isa. 40),* his birth was due to the direct and miraculous intervention of God *(Luke 1:7, 13),* he was "filled with the Holy Spirit even from his mother's womb" *(Luke 1:15),* he was a man "sent from God" *(John 1:6),* he was sent to prepare the way of the Lord *(Matt. 3:3).* Of him the Lord said, "Among them that are born of women there hath not risen a greater than John the Baptist" *(Matt. 11:11):* the reference being to his *positional* "greatness", as the forerunner of the Messiah: to him was accorded the high honor of baptizing the Lord Jesus. That Christ *was* referring to the *positional* "greatness" of John is clear from His next words, "notwithstanding he that is least *in* the Kingdom of Heaven is greater than he". To have a place in the Kingdom of Heaven (i. e., the Messianic Kingdom, yet future) will be a more exalted position than to be heralding the King outside of it, as John was. This, we take it is the key to that word in John 14:28, where we find the Lord Jesus saying, "My Father is *greater* than I"—greater not in His person, but in His position; for, at the time the Saviour uttered those words He was in the place of subjection, as God's "Servant."

Our passage opens by telling of a deputation of priests and Levites sent from Jerusalem to enquire of John as to who he was: "And this is the record of John, when the Jews sent priests and Levites from Jerusalem to ask him, Who art thou?" *(1:19)*. Nothing like this is found in the other Gospels, but it is in striking accord with the character and scope of the fourth Gospel, which deals with spiritual rather than dispensational relationships. The incident before us brings out *the spiritual ignorance* of the religious leaders among the Jews. In fulfillment of Isaiah's prophecy, the Lord's forerunner had appeared in the wilderness, but, lacking in spiritual discernment, the leaders in Jerusalem knew not who he was. Accordingly, their messengers came and enquired of John, "Who art thou?" Multitudes of people were flocking to this strange preacher in the wilderness, and many had been baptized by him. A great stir had been made, so much so that "men mused in their hearts of John, whether he were Christ, or not" *(Luke 3:15)*, and the religious leaders in Jerusalem were compelled to take note of it; therefore, did they send a deputation to wait upon John, to find out who he really was, and to enquire into his credentials.

"And he confessed, and denied not; but confessed, I am not the Christ" *(1:20)*. These words give plain intimation of the spirit in which the priests and Levites must have approached John, as also of the design of "the Jews" who had sent them. To them the Baptist was an interloper. He was outside the religious systems of that day. He had not been trained in the schools of the Rabbins, he had held no position of honor in the temple ministrations, and he was not identified with either the Pharisees, the Sadducees, or the Herodians. From whence then had he received his authority? Who had commissioned him to go forth bidding men to "Repent". By what right did *he* baptize people? One can imagine the tone in which they said to John, "Who art *thou!*" No doubt they expected to intimidate him. This seems clear from the fact that we are here told, "and he confessed, and *denied not*". He boldly stood his ground. Neither the dignity of those who had sent this embassy to John, nor their threatening frowns, moved him at all. "He confessed, and denied not". May like courage be found in us when we are challenged with an "who art thou?"

"But confessed, I am not the Christ". Having taken the firm stand he had, did Satan now tempt him to go to the other extreme? Failing to intimidate him, did the Enemy now seek to make him boastfully exaggerate? Christ had not then been openly manifested: John was the one before the public eye, as we read in Mark 1: 5, "And there went out unto him all the land of Judea, and they of Jerusalem, and were all baptized of him in the river Jordan" (Mark 1:5). Now that the multitudes were flocking to him, and many had become his "disciples" *(cf. John 1:35)*, why not announce that he was the Messiah himself! But he instantly banished such wicked and presumptuous thoughts, if such were presented by Satan to his mind, as most likely they were, or, why tell us that he "confessed I am not the Christ"? May God deliver us from the evil spirit of boasting, and keep us from ever claiming to be anything more than what we really are—sinners saved by grace.

"And they asked him, What then? Art thou Elijah? And he saith, I am not" *(1: 21)*. Why should they have asked John if he were Elijah? The answer is, Because there was a general expectation among the Jews at that time that Elijah would again appear on earth. That this was so, is clear from a number of passages in the Gospels. For instance; when the Lord asked His disciples, "Whom do men say that I the Son of Man am?", they answered, "Some say that Thou art John the Baptist (who had been slain in the interval), some *Elijah,* and others Jeremiah, or one of the prophets" *(Matt. 16:13,14)*. Again; as the Lord Jesus and His disciples came down from the Mount of Transfiguration, He said unto them, "Tell the vision to no man until the Son of Man be raised from the dead". Then, we read, "His disciples asked Him, Why then say the scribes that

Elijah must first come?" (Matt. 17:9,10). This expectation of the Jews had a scriptural foundation, for the last verses of the Old Testament say, "Behold, I will send you *Elijah the prophet* before the coming of the great and dreadful day of the Lord: And he shall turn the heart of the fathers to the children, and the heart of the children to their fathers, lest I come and smite the earth with a curse" *(Malachi 4: 5,6).* This prophecy (which will yet be literally fulfilled) has reference to the return to earth of Elijah, to perform a ministry just before the second advent of Christ, similar in character to that of John the Baptist before the first public appearing of Christ.

When asked, "Art thou Elijah?", John replied, emphatically, "I am not". John had much in common with the Tishbite, and his work was very similar in character to the yet future work of Elijah; nevertheless, he was not Elijah himself. He went before Christ "in the spirit and power of Elijah" *(Luke 1:17),* because he came "to make ready a people prepared for the Lord", as will Elijah just before the Millennium.

Next, John's interrogators asked him, "Art thou that prophet?" *(1:21).* What "prophet"? we may well enquire. And the answer is, The "Prophet" predicted through Moses. This prediction is recorded in Deut. 18:15, 18: "The Lord thy God will raise up unto thee a Prophet from the midst of thee, of thy brethren, like unto Me; unto Him ye shall hearken.....I will raise them up a Prophet from among their brethren, like unto thee, and will put My words in His mouth; and He shall speak unto them all that I shall command thee". This was one of the many Messianic prophecies given in Old Testament times, which received its fulfillment in the person of the Lord Jesus Christ. "Art thou that prophet?", John was asked; and, again, he answered, "No".

"Then said they unto him, Who art thou? that we may give an answer to them that sent us. What sayest thou of thyself?" *(1:22).* Searching questions were these— "*Who* art thou?"; "what sayest thou *of thyself?*" John might have answered, and answered truthfully, "I am the son of Zacharias the priest. I am one who has been filled with the Holy Spirit from my birth". Or, he might have replied, "I am the most remarkable character ever raised up by God and sent unto Israel". "What sayest thou of thyself?" Ah, that was indeed a searching question, and both writer and reader may well learn a lesson from John's reply, and seek grace to emulate his lovely modesty—a lesson much needed in these days of Laodicean boasting.

"He said, I am the voice of one crying in the wilderness, Make straight the way of the Lord, as said the prophet Isaiah" *(1: 23).* Here was John's answer. "What sayest thou of thyself?" "I am the *voice* of one crying in the wilderness", he said. Becoming humility was this. Humility is of great price in the sight of God, and has had a prominent place in the men whom He has used. Paul, the greatest of the apostles, confessed himself "less than the least of all saints" *(Eph. 3:8).* And John here confesses much the same thing, when he referred to himself as "the voice of one crying in the wilderness". Reader, what reply would *you* make to such a query— "What sayest thou *of thyself?*" Surely you would not answer, "I am an eminent saint of God: I am living on a very exalted plane of spirituality: I am one who has been much used of God". Such self-exaltation would show you had learnt little from Him who was "meek and lowly in heart", and would evidence a spirit far from that which should cause us to own that, after all, we are only "unprofitable servants" *(Luke 17:10).*

When John referred to himself as "the voice", he employed the very term which the Holy Spirit had used of him seven hundred years previously, when speaking through Isaiah the prophet—"The voice of him that crieth in the wilderness, Prepare ye the way of the Lord, make straight in the desert a highway for our God" *(Isa. 40:3).* And we cannot but believe this appelation was selected with Divine discrimination. In a former article, when commenting upon one of the titles of the Lord Jesus, found in John 1:7—"The Light"—we called attention to the fact that Christ referred to His forerunner in evident contrast from Himself as "the Light") as "the *lamp* that burneth and shineth" *(John 5:35, R.V.).* And so here, we are satisfied that another contrast is pointed. Christ is "the Word"; John, was but "the voice". What, then, are the thoughts suggested by this figurative title?

In the first place, the word exists (in the mind) *before* the voice articulates it. Such was the relation between Christ and His forerunner. It is true that John was the first to appear before the public eye; yet, as the "Word", Christ had existed from all eternity. Second, the voice is simply the vehicle or medium *by which* the word is expressed or *made known*. Such was John. The object of his mission and the purpose of his ministry, was to bear witness to "the Word". Again; the voice is simply heard but not seen. John was not seeking to display himself. His work was to get men to listen to his God-given message in order that they might *behold* "the Lamb". May the Lord today make more of His servants John-like; just "voices", *heard but not seen!* Finally, we may add, that the word endures *after* the voice is silent. The voice of John has long since been stilled by death, but "the Word" abideth forever. Appropriately, then, was the one who introduced the Messiah to Israel, termed the "voice". What wonderful depths there are in the Scriptures! How much is contained in a single word! And how this calls for prolonged *meditation* and humble prayer!

"The voice of one crying *in the wilderness*". What a position for the Messiah's forerunner to occupy! Surely his place was in Jerusalem. Why then did not John cry in the Temple? Why, because Jehovah was no more there in the Temple. Judaism was but a hollow shell: outward form there was, but no life within. It was to a nation of legalists, Pharisee ridden, and who boasted they were "the children of Abraham", but who neither manifested Abraham's faith nor produced his works, that John came. God would not own the self-righteous formalism of the Jews. Therefore, the one "sent of God" appeared *outside* the religious systems and circles of that day. But why did John preach *"in the wilderness"?* Because the "wilderness" symbolized the spiritual *barrenness* of the Jewish nation. John could only mourn over that which was not of God, and everything about him was in keeping with this: his food was that which he found in the wilderness, and his *prophetic* garment testified to the failure that was evident on every hand.

"And they which were sent were of the Pharisees. And they asked him, and said unto him, Why baptizeth thou then, if thou be not that Christ, nor Elijah, neither that prophet?" (1:24, 25). This final question put to John by the embassy from Jerusalem confirms what we have said upon v. 20. The religious leaders among the Jews were disputing John's right to preach, and challenging his authority to baptize. He had received no commission from the Sanhedrin, hence "why baptizest *thou?*" John does not appear to have answered the last question directly, instead, he turns to them and speaks of Christ.

"John answered them, saying, I baptize with water: but there standeth One among you, whom ye know not" (1:27). John continued to stand his ground: he would not deny that he baptized with water, or more correctly, *in* water, but he sought to get them occupied with something of greater importance than a symbolical rite. There is much to be learned from John's answer here. These men were raising questions about baptism, while as yet they were utter strangers to Christ Himself—how like many today! Of what use was it to discuss with these Pharisee-commissioned "priests and Levites" the *"why"* of baptism, when they were yet in their sins? Well would it be for the Lord's servants and those engaged in personal work for Christ, to carefully heed what is before us here. People are willing to argue about side issues, while the vital and central Issue remains undecided! And only too often the Christian worker follows them into "By-path meadow". What is needed is for us to ignore all irrelevant quibbles, and press upon the lost the claims of *Christ* and their *need* of accepting Him as their Saviour.

"There standeth One among you, whom ye *know not*". How this exposed Israel's condition! How this revealed their spiritual ignorance! And how tragically true, in principle, is this today. Even in this so-called Christian land, while many have heard about Christ, yet in how many circles, yes, and in religious circles too, we may say, "there standeth One among you, whom ye know not"! O the spiritual blindness of the natural man. Christ, by His Spirit, stands in the midst of many a congregation, unseen and unknown.

"He it is, who coming after me is preferred before me, whose shoe's latchet I am not worthy to unloose" (1:27). What a noble testimony was this! How these words of John bring out the Divine glory of the One he heralded! Remember *who* he was. No ordinary man was John the Baptist. The subject of Old Testament prophecy, the son of a priest, born as the result of the direct intervention of God's power, filled with the Holy Spirit from his mother's womb, engaged in a ministry which drew great multitudes unto him, and yet he looked up to Christ as standing on a plane infinitely higher than the one he occupied, as a Being from another world, as One before whom he was not worthy to stoop down and unloose His shoes. He could find no expression strong enough to define the difference which separated him from the One who was "preferred before" him. Again we say, How these words of John bring out the Divine glory of the One he heralded!

"These things were done in Bethabara beyond Jordan, where John was baptizing" *(1:28)*. There is, of course, some good reason *why* the Holy Spirit has been pleased to tell us *where* this conference between John and the Jerusalem delegation took place, whether we are able to discover it or not. Doubtless, the key to its significance is found in the meaning of the proper nouns here recorded. Unfortunately, there is some variation in the spelling of "Bethabara" in the Greek manuscripts; but with Gesenius, the renowned Hebrew scholar, we are firmly inclined to believe this place is identical with "Bethbarah" mentioned in Judges 7:24, and which signifies "House of Passage" which, was so named, to memorialize the crossing of the Jordan in the days of Joshua. It was here, then, (apparently) at a place whose name signified "house *of passage*", beyond Jordan, the symbol of *death*, that John was baptizing as the forerunner of Christ. The meaning of this should not be hard to find. The significance of these names corresponded closely with the religious position that John himself occupied, and with the character of his mission. *Separated* as he was from Judaism, those who responded to his call to repent, and were baptized of him "confessing their sins", *passed out* of the apostate Jewish system, and took their place with the little remnant who were "prepared for the Lord" *(Luke 1:17)*. Well, then, was the place where John was baptizing named "Beth-barah"—House of Passage.

"The next day John seeth Jesus coming unto him, and saith, Behold, the Lamb of God, which taketh away the sin of the world". "Behold the Lamb of God": the *connection* in which these words are found should be carefully noted. It was the day following the meeting between John and the Jerusalem delegation, a meeting which evidently occurred in the presence of others also, for John continues "this is He of whom *I said,* after me cometh a Man which is preferred before me", which is a word for word reference to what he had said to those who had interrogated him on the previous day—see v. 27; when he had also declared to those priests and Levites "which were sent of the Pharisees" *(v. 24)* "there standeth One among you, whom ye know not".

"Behold the Lamb of God". The force of this Call was deeply significant when viewed in the light of its setting. The Pharisees were looking for a "prophet", and they desired a "king" who should deliver them from the Roman yoke, but they had no yearnings for a *Saviour-priest*. The questions asked of John betrayed the hearts of those who put them. They appeared to be in doubt as to whether or not the Baptist was the long promised Messiah, so they asked him, "Art thou *Elijah?* Art thou *that prophet?"* But, be it noted, no enquiry was made as to whether he was the one who should deliver them "from the wrath to come"! One would have naturally expected these *priests* and *Levites* to have asked about the *sacrifice,* but no; apparently they had *no sense of sin!* It was under *these* circumstances that the forerunner of Christ announced Him as "the *Lamb* of God", not as "the *Word* of God", not as "the *Christ* of God", but as THE LAMB. It was the Spirit of God presenting the Lord Jesus to Israel in the very office and character in which they stood in deepest need of Him. They would have welcomed Him on the *throne,* but they must first accept Him on the *altar.* And is it any different today? Christ as an Elijah—a Social-Reformer—will be tolerated; and Christ as a Prophet, as a Teacher of ethics, will receive respect. But what the world needs first and foremost is the Christ of the Cross, where as the Lamb of God He offered Himself as a sacrifice for sin.

"Behold *the Lamb* of God". There before John stood the One whom all the sacrifices of Old Testament times had foreshadowed. It is exceedingly striking to observe the progressive order followed by God in the teaching of Scripture concerning "the Lamb". First, in Gen. 4, we have the Lamb *typified* in the firstlings of the flock slain by Abel in sacrifice. Second, we have the Lamb *prophesied* in Gen. 22:8

where Abraham said to Isaac, "God will provide Himself a lamb". Third, in Ex. 12, we have the lamb slain and its blood *applied*. Fourth, in Isa. 53:7, we have the lamb *personified*: here for the first time we learn that the Lamb would be a Man. Fifth, in John 1:29, we have the Lamb *identified*, learning *who* He was. Sixth, in Rev. 5, we have the Lamb *magnified* by the hosts of heaven. Seventh, in the last chapter of the Bible we have the Lamb *glorified*, seated upon the eternal throne of God, Rev. 22:1. Once more; mark the orderly development in the *scope* of the sacrifices. In Gen. 4 sacrifice is offered for the *individual* —Abel. In Ex. 12 the sacrifice avails for the whole *household*. In Lev. 16, on the annual Day of Atonement, the sacrifice was efficacious for the entire *nation*. But here in John 1:29 it is "Behold the Lamb of God which taketh away the sin *of the world*"—Gentiles are embraced as well as Jews!

"Behold *the Lamb* of God". What are the thoughts suggested by this title? It points to His moral perfections, His *sinlessness*, for He was the "Lamb without blemish and without spot" *(1 Pet. 1:19)*. It tells of His *gentleness*, His voluntary offering Himself to God on our behalf— He was "led" (not driven) as "a lamb to the slaughter" *(Acts 8:28, R.V.)*. But, more especially and particularly, this title of our Lord speaks of *sacrifice*—He was "the Lamb of God which *taketh away the sin* of the world", and this could only be through death, for "without shedding of blood is no remission". There was only one way by which sin could be taken away, and that was *by death*. "Sin" here signifies *guilt* (condemnation) as in Heb. 9:26; and "the world" refers to the world of *believers*, for it is only those who are in Christ for whom there is now "no condemnation" *(Rom. 8:1)*; it is the world of believers, as contrasted from "the world of the ungodly" *(2 Pet. 2:5)*.

"This is He of whom I said, After me cometh a Man which is preferred before me, for He was before me. And I knew Him not: but that He should be made manifest to Israel, therefore am I come baptizing with water" *(1:30, 31)*. Here for the third time John declares that Christ was "preferred before" him—*(see vv. 15, 27, 30)*. It affirmed His pre-existence: it was a witness to His eternality. Then John tells of the purpose of his baptism. It was to make Christ "manifest" to Israel. It was to prepare a people for Him. This people were prepared by taking the place of sinners before God *(Mark 1:5)*, and that is why he baptized in Jordan, the river of death; for, baptized in Jordan they acknowledged that *death was their due*. In this, John's baptism differs from Christian baptism. In Christian baptism the believer does not confess that death is his due, but he shows forth the fact that he *has already* died, died to sin, died *with Christ (Rom. 6:3, 4)*.

"And John bare record, saying, I saw the Spirit descending from heaven like a dove, and it abode upon Him" *(1:32)*. This has reference, of course, to the occasion when Christ Himself was baptized of John in the Jordan, when the Father testified to His pleasure in the Son, and when the Spirit descended upon Him in the form of a dove. *Why* did the Holy Spirit assume *this* form, when descending on Christ? It manifested the *character* of the One on whom He came. The "dove" is the bird of love and sorrow: apt symbol, then, of Christ. The love expressed the sorrow, and the sorrow told out the depths of His love. Thus did the heavenly Dove bear witness to Christ. When the Holy Spirit came upon the disciples on the Day of Pentecost, we read "there appeared unto them cloven tongues like as *of fire*, and it sat upon each of them" *(Acts 2:3)*. "Fire", uniformly signifies Divine *judgment*. There was that in the disciples which needed to be judged—the evil nature still remained within them. But, there was nothing in the Holy One of God that needed judging; hence, did the Holy Spirit descend upon *Him* in the form of a Dove!

"And I knew Him not: but he that sent me to baptize with water, the same said unto me, Upon whom thou shalt see the Spirit descending and remaining on Him, the same is He which baptizeth with the Holy Spirit" *(1:33)*. The word "remaining" is rendered "abiding" in the R. V., and this is one of the characteristic words of this fourth Gospel. The other three Gospels all make mention of the Lord Jesus being anointed by the Holy Spirit, but John is the only one that says the Spirit *"abode"* upon Him. The Holy Spirit did not come upon Him, and then leave again, as with the prophets of old—He "abode" on Christ. This term has to do with the *Divine* side of things, and speaks of *fellowship*. We have the same word again in John 14:10, "Believest thou not that I am in the Father, and the Father in Me? The words that I say unto you, I speak not from Myself, but the Father *abiding* in Me doeth His works" *(R.V.).* So, in John 15, where the Lord Jesus speaks of the fundamental requirement in spiritual fruit-bearing—*fellowship* with Himself—He says, "He that *abideth* in Me, and I in him, the same beareth much fruit" *(John 15:13, R.V.).* That Christ shall "baptize with (or 'in') the Holy Spirit", was another proof of His Godhood.

"And I saw, and bare record that this is the Son of God" *(1:34).* Here the witness of John the Baptist to the person of Christ terminates. It is to be noted that the forerunner bore a seven-fold witness to the excellency of the One he heralded. First, he testified to His *pre-existence*—"He *was* before me", v. 15. Second, He testified to His *Lordship*, v. 23. Third, he testified to His *immeasureable superiority*—"I am not worthy to unloose" His "shoe's latchet", v. 27. Fourth, he testified to His *sacrificial work*—"Behold the Lamb", v. 29. Fifth, he testified to His *moral perfections*—"I saw the Spirit descending from heaven like a *dove*, and it *abode* upon Him", v. 32.

Sixth, he testified to His *Divine right* to "baptize with the Holy Spirit", v. 33. Seventh, he testified to His *Divine Sonship*, v. 34.

The questions below concern the passage which we shall expound in our next article, D. V., namely, John 1:35-51, and to prepare our readers for it we ask them to give these questions their prayerful and careful study:—

1. Why did Christ ask the two disciples of John "What seek ye?" 1:38.
2. What is signified by their reply "Where dwellest Thou"? 1:38.
3. What important practical truth is incorporated in 1:40, 41?
4. What blessed truth is illustrated by "findeth" in 1:43?
5. What is meant by "in whom is no guile"? 1:47.
6. What attribute of Christ does 1:48 demonstrate?
7. To what does Christ refer in 1:51?

—Arthur W. Pink.

4. THE PROVISIONS OF GRACE FOR NAZARITE FAILURE.

Numbers 6:9-12.

It is very remarkable that when the Lord exhibits in type the highest form of separation and devotion to Himself, He anticipates failure, and provides for it all. He knows what we are, and He knows the day will never come, till we see Jesus, when we will not need to be restored in soul; He knows that there will always be sin to be confessed, judged, forgiven, and put away. And so, while He never lowers the claim of His holiness, His grace is ever found amply sufficient for His people's need, even though that need may be the result of His people's sin. And indeed it is just in this abounding grace that His holiness is ever maintained. For grace reigns through Christ, and is thus itself the most glorious display of His holiness; and this is not least seen when its provisions are applied to the purifying of the saint from his defilement. These remarks are delightfully illustrated in the provisions made for the restoration of the Nazarite who had broken his vow of separation.

Our subject divides itself naturally into two parts, I. The Defilement and its Acknowledgment; II. The Gracious Provision for Cleansing.

I. THE DEFILEMENT AND ITS ACKNOWLEDGMENT.

"And if any man die very suddenly by him, and he hath defiled the head of his consecration; then he shall shave his head in the day of his cleansing, on the seventh day shall he shave it" (Num. 6:9).

There are here two things which demand our thoughtful consideration. First, we have to consider the character of defilement; and, secondly, the acknowledgment of the defilement.

1. The defilement is not that gross form of evil which we call deliberate sin. It is contracted by the most natural impulse. "A man dies very suddenly" by the side of a Nazarite, and humanity, we might say, demands that he should put forth his hand. He does so, and he is defiled.

It must be remembered that the law respecting the touch of a dead body was not given as having any value in itself; but was ordained to impress our proneness to moral defilement from our present surroundings, our natural impulses being toward these. And just because the action of the failing Nazarite is so natural, the case serves admirably to represent the ease with which the most devoted Christian may contract defilement, and incur serious spiritual loss through contact with a polluting world —and all this because he has a nature prone to evil. If the Christian had *only* a "Divine nature", no "sudden" event could occasion his defilement. But here we are reminded that though we are "partakers of the Divine nature" we carry with us still the tendency to sin: for the flesh still exists, and its natures and desires are very different from those of the "Divine nature".

Now the Lord would have His saints to know that *natural* impulse may lead to defilement, and mar our consecration to Him. That the sorrow of nature is not forbidden or condemned as evil; and that the evil lies in the *indulgence of nature at the expense of the Lord's claims and service*, is clear enough in the type; but on these points we need not dwell, since they were the subject of extended remark in a former paper. But let it be observed that our sin is not the less sin because it is that of natural impulse. The Christian Nazarite has no right to guide himself by nature and impulse. The Lord, he has said, is his object. He ought then to do everything as to the Lord; and therefore he should "wait on the Lord", that He may direct his every action.

2. The acknowledgment of defilement—as God would have it—is next ordained. "*Then he shall shave his head in the day of his cleansing*". We need not hesitate to say that this "shaving of his head" was the confession that his strength was gone. The secret of Nazarite strength was in the unshorn head. "There hath not", said Samson, madly revealing his secret to the base accomplice of his enemies, "there hath not come a razor on my head; for I have been a Nazarite unto God from my mother's womb: *if I be shaven then my strength will go from me, and I shall become weak, and be like any other man*". We all know what followed. Sleeping upon the lap of Delilah, he was shaven, "and his strength went from him" *(Judges 16:17,19)*. Solemn lesson for us all! Ours is not nature's strength, but the strength of the Lord put forth in our weakness.

While we thus learn the significance of the type from Samson, the case in our text is very different from his. There is a vast difference between being deprived of our strength by the hand of the enemy, and the confession of our failure to maintain our holy separation unto the Lord. It is this confession which is typified in the Nazarite shaving his own head. The Christian, alas, often delays his cleansing and restoration, by postponing his acknowledgment that, by reason of sin's defilement, his strength is gone. How many of us have been in this respect like the Nazarite judge of Israel. "And she said, The Philistines be upon thee, Samson. And he awoke out of his sleep, and said, I will go out as at other times, and shake myself. And he wist not that the Lord was departed from him" *(Judges 16:20)*. But though it may have been so, yet, let us but "confess unto the Lord", and we shall find forgiveness; and when we are weak again, we shall be strong again. There will, indeed, be irreparable loss, for as it is written in the type, so is it fulfilled in Christian experience— "the days that were before shall be lost, because his separation was defiled" *(Num. 6:12)*. But as it was, after all, written of Samson, "Howbeit the hair of his head began to grow again after he was shaven", so it will be in the case of all who confess their defilement and weakness, "in the day of their cleansing".

And these words—"in the day of his cleansing"—what revelations and experiences of grace they recall. "If we confess our sins, He is faithful and just to forgive us our sins, and to cleanse us from all unrighteousness" *(1 John 1:9)*. The day of confession and the day of cleansing are ever but one day. You have but to cry, "Unclean, unclean" and the word shall scarcely fall from your lips, when they shall be closed with the "live coal from off the altar", and your ear shall be saluted with God's testimony, "Lo, this hath touched thy lips: and thine iniquity is taken away, and thy sin purged" *(Isa. 6)*. He delights to have you say, "I have sinned against Thee", but it is that He may drown your confession in mirth and gladness over your return to Him. But on this we need not dwell; for surely all saints know better than we can write it that the day of acknowledgement is "the day of cleansing". And yet it is possible that this paper may be read by some dear child of God who is "keeping silence" concerning sin; to his own great hurt refusing to own his defilement and powerlessness unto the Lord. If so, let him know that his silence imposes silence upon Him, so far as the utterance of comfortable words is concerned, and restrains the stream of His grace; while all the while He is yearning to speak peace and to put forth His power in cleansing. And this brings us to the consideration of the rich provision prepared for us "in the day of our cleansing," which is displayed in the second part of the passage.

II. THE DIVINE PROVISION FOR THE CLEANSED NAZARITE.

It must be considered that the provision here displayed does not typify the first dealing of the Spirit with a sinner in conversion. It rather tells forth what is the privilege of the saint to apprehend, as to the truth of his standing and acceptance in Christ, in the hour of his restoration. It reveals what God thinks of him, and what place He has given him in Christ; and plainly says that thus the pardoned saint *ought* to think, and that thus he *ought* to take his place before God, even the Father of our Lord Jesus. How very far from what they *ought* to be our thoughts are, may thus become apparent. But then, to discover our failure in apprehension in such a light, is to have our apprehension corrected. *Naturally* we would have a period of probationary reformation; and then, when that is successful, we would believe that we are forgiven. But God's way is contrary to our *natural* thoughts. When He says, "Forgiven", He would have us to take it to heart with all joy; when He meets our confession with His cleansing, it is only the due homage to His "faithfulness" and "justice" that we confess our cleansing as readily as we confessed our sin. Nay, more, we shall find that He would have us take high ground at once, not only as forgiven, but as accepted in the Beloved. Accordingly, our thoughts of our place in Christ are instructed in the order of His satisfaction in Christ, and not in the order in which we usually apprehend His suitableness to our need. God provides not for cleansing only, but for the restoration of "the *joy* of His salvation, and "the *joy* of the Lord is our strength".

1. The restoration of Nazarite joy and strength is accomplished in the power of Christ's resurrection. We find this in the ordinance that the cleansed Nazarite should bring his offerings *"on the eighth day" (v. 10).* For the eighth day was not only equal to our "first day of the week", but the ritual transactions for it are ever found to bring into view those aspects of the truth in Christ which can only be discerned in the light of His resurrection. The importance of discerning the cleansing efficacy of our Lord's sacrifice in the light of His resurrection cannot be overrated. His resurrection is God's attestation of the value of completed atonement for us, as certainly as it is the demonstration of His Sonship *(Rom. 1:4).* Accordingly, he who "believes in his heart that God hath raised Him from the dead, shall be saved" *(Rom. 10:9).* In like manner, wherever and however sin has interposed to interrupt our fellowship, our joy, or our service, the restoration to these must be in the apprehension of the atonement in the light of Christ's resurrection; since the intercession or advocacy of Christ with the Father, by which our restoration is effected, is that of One raised again from the dead, and appearing in heaven with His own blood for us. Yes, and when we are restored, our fellowship with Christ, in our renewed course, will depend upon our setting everything in the light of His resurrection. Why is it that the apostle, in declaring his holy ambition of intimacy with Christ, sets His resurrection before His sufferings and death? "I count all things but loss..... that I may know Him, and *the power of His resurrection,* and the fellowship of His sufferings, being made conformable unto His death" *(Phil. 3:8-10).* It is just because the latter can only be known as we take our stand before God *"on the eighth day",* only as we know that we are risen with Christ, being "begotten again by His resurrection from the dead".

Thus, when we worship as restored saints, it is God's desire that we should do so in the full assurance that our condition, so far from being estimated according to our falls, our sins and failures, is just that of Christ in heaven; it is His purpose that we should think of ourselves according to the value and efficacy of the sacrifice of Christ, that is evermore witnessed by His session at the right hand of the Majesty on high; for He reached that seat through the *purgation of our sins (Heb. 1:3).*

2. Let us consider the offerings of the restored one. They are sacrifices of humiliation and joy.

(1) *"He shall bring two turtles, or two young pigeons, to the door of the tabernacle of the congregation" (v. 10).* It is generally recognized that the different grades of the same kind of offering represent the degree of apprehension. And this grade, though not the lowest, is yet far from the

highest *(see Lev. 1)*. We see in this that, when He calls us to receive the truth concerning our place in Christ in all its fulness, God well knows that our apprehension of it will be lower, when we are just returning from our aberrations, than in periods of sustained communion. The "bullock" upon the altar represents the fullest apprehension. But at the same time it is blessed to observe that it is the same truth of our acceptance, and the same atonement on which that rests, which are typified, whatever the grade of offering. The Father proclaims us to be *"AS CHRIST IS"*, irrespective of the feebleness of our thoughts about Him. He who brings Christ with him is welcomed at *"the door of the tabernacle of the congregation"*, nay, "in the holiest of all", not according to the measure of his thoughts, but according to what Christ is.

(2) *"And the priest shall offer the one for a sin offering" (v. 11)*. This is quite distinct from the thought of the special sin, or touch of defilement, which occasioned the interruption of the Nazarite's consecration. How that is dealt with appears in the appointment of the trespass offering, in the next verse. The truth of this part of the ritual is that the restored Christian finds both his joy and his strength in God's presence, because the sin in the flesh, which alone renders trespass possible, was wholly and fully judged in Christ, when God "made his soul an offering for *sin*". And thus it is that God blends our deepest humiliation with our most perfect restoration from every fall. His arrangement in our passage speaks to us thus: "You, when you have erred, would rather regard the special act of sin as that which most called for My judgment, and the forgiveness of that act as the special desideratum of your happiness in My presence, but I would have you give glory to My holiness, and to its satisfaction by My sinless Son 'made sin for you'; I would have you to see in the light of His sin-bearing death the vileness of the evil thing from which trespasses spring forth". Thus His glory demands that in every instance in which we meet Him, in His restoring love, we should first adore the grace which dealt with *"SIN IN THE FLESH"*, and learn that our forgiven trespass may well serve to warn us of the fountain of evil from which it sprang; while we are constrained to confess that as surely as He is our sin offering, we are "The righteousness of God in Him" *(2 Cor. 5: 21)*.

(3) *"And the priest shall offer the other for a burnt offering"*. The sin offering brings before the soul God's judgment of what He abhors; and shows that judgment fully accomplished in Jesus' death. The burnt offering proclaims the ineffable excellence of the same sacrifice, as not only exhausting God's judgment, but as yielding Him infinite delight. The one takes us back to God's love to us, in righteousness "bruising and putting to grief" His Son; but the other continually repeats the voice from heaven, "This is My beloved Son in whom I am well pleased". The Father, by the figurative "burnt offering", when He brings us back to His presence, restores joy and "strengthens us with strength in our souls", telling us that what the true "offering of sweet smelling savor" is to Him, *that we are to Him;* He would assure us that we are the children of His good pleasure, even as Jesus is the Son of His good pleasure. And it is in this apprehension of His good pleasure in Christ that God's joy becomes our joy. We are apt to imagine that when we return to Him He will postpone our joy of acceptance, till we approve ourselves by future well doing. He seeks to fill us with the assurance that we are on the same terms with Him—that is Christ's terms with Him—as before we were defiled by touching the unclean thing.

(4) *"And he (the priest) shall make atonement for him in that he sinned by the dead" (v. 11)*. We here learn that whether Christ's sacrifice is viewed in relation to sin, or in relation to the Father's pleasure, it is an "atonement" for us. And we may well deeply value this truth, for much has been, and is being said and written which is calculated to unsettle the souls of Christians respecting the fulness of Christ our righteousness. While we see Him as our atonement for sin, we behold Him as our atonement for acceptance. Ours is no mere negative standing—as though our sins were cancelled by His death, and that were all; but ours is a positive standing in Him, according to *all* the infinite merits of His whole work, which was finished when He offered Himself a sweet smelling savor unto God *FOR US*.

(5) *"And shall hallow his head the same day. And he shall consecrate unto the Lord the days of his separation" (vv. 11.*

12). The restored soul, having been replenished with Divine joy and strength, is at once to re-enter the path of devotion and separation. It is most interesting to observe that this is, in the type, seen first as the result of the priest's action, and then is demanded of the restored Nazarite. The latter is appropriately viewed as flowing out of the former. The priest "shall hallow his head the same day", and the Nazarite himself "shall consecrate unto the Lord the days of his separation". So Jesus purges the conscience, or washes the feet, and then we can go forth in holy separation unto the Lord, with renewed vigor. And this, be it observed, as if there had been no failure. There is to be no despair, and no looking back. "Forgetting those things which are behind, and reaching forth unto those things which are before, I press toward the mark for the prize of the high calling of God in Christ Jesus" *(Phil. 3: 13, 14).*

But this is by no means to ignore our confessed failure, for

(6) *"And he shall bring a lamb of the first year for a trespass offering" (v. 12).* It need scarcely be said that the prominence given to "sin" over "trespass" does not at all lead to any light views of the latter. On the contrary, by the prominence to the source of the action, the heinousness of the action itself is brought into full view. It is clear, from the clause concerning the trespass offering, that the special act of sin cannot be lightly regarded by the restored soul. The truth is, that at no moment is any sin so perfectly abhorred by us as just when we are rejoicing in the recovery of what we lost by it. This is strikingly brought out by the place of "the trespass offering" here; for it is just when the Nazarite resumes his "separation unto the Lord" that he is seen judging his "trespass", and confessing its forgiveness by bringing the appropriate "offering".

Nor is it only that we get the most vivid view of our sins when our souls are fully restored. We may easily perceive, through the place assigned to the trespass offering, that the saint enters anew upon the path of devoted separation, with the profitable use of his forgiven failure—deeper abhorrence of evil, a deeper distrust of self, and a deeper dependence upon Him who, having restored his soul, *makes* him to walk in the paths of righteousness for His name's sake.

We must surely adore Him who alone could bring together such various things as we have harmoniously joined in this most valuable portion of His Word. Sin and judgment meet upon Him who knew no sin—judgment is exhausted and sin is put away: confession, forgiveness, and cleansing come together, because God is faithful and just. Self-judgment, and renewed consecration are joined in the power of known acceptance in the Beloved. Forgiven trespass, and tenderness of conscience, unite to induce a more careful walk with God. And God is glorified in all that He so sweetly blends and harmonizes, through Jesus Christ our Lord. And yet, while adoring all this grace, we must not forget the solemn warning to which we before adverted, namely, that irreparable loss is sustained by every touch of the unclean thing. Grace does not repair the loss incurred by our failure in separation. God's ways in the government of His redeemed are not stultified by the freeness and fulness of His grace. *"But the days that were before shall be lost, because his separation was defiled" (v. 12).*

The end.

—From *"Grace and Truth"* edited by *Chas. Campbell, 1871.*

GRACE AS IT REIGNS IN THE PERSEVERANCE OF THE SAINTS TO ETERNAL GLORY.

It appears, from the preceding chapters, that the state of believers, whether considered as relative, or as real, in their Justification, Adoption, and Sanctification, is highly exalted; and that the privileges attending it are of incomparable excellence, and of infinite worth. In each of these particulars it has also been proved that grace reigns; and that the exceeding riches of grace are manifested.

The believer, notwithstanding, who knows himself, will be ready to inquire with great solicitude, "How shall I persevere in this happy state? By what means shall I attain the desired end? What provision has the Lord made, that, after all, I shall not come short of the expected bliss? Grace, I thankfully acknowledge, has done great things for me: to reigning grace I owe myself unspeakably obliged. But if grace, as a sovereign, do not still exert her power, I not only possibly may, but certainly shall, finally miscarry." Thus will every Christian conclude, when he considers the number and power, the malice and subtilty, of his inveterate spiritual enemies, compared with his own inherent strength to resist them. For the World, the Flesh, and the Devil are combined against him. These, in their several ways, assault his peace and seek his ruin. These attempt, in various forms, to cause him to wallow in the mire of sensuality, as the filthiest brute; or to puff him up with pride, as Lucifer. By insinuating wiles and open attacks, with the craft of the serpent, or the rage of a lion, they endeavor to compass his ruin: and, alas, how small his ability, considered in himself, to resist and overcome! The corruption of nature, even in the regenerate, renders the believer's desires after that which is good, too often exceedingly languid, and enervates all his moral powers. His pious frames are fickle and uncertain to the last degree; nor can he with safety, place the least confidence in them.

This humbling truth was exemplified in the case of Peter. *"Though all men shall be offended because of Thee, yet will I never be offended........Though I should die with Thee, yet will I not deny Thee"* *(Matt. 26:33-35)* was his confident language. But, alas! in a very little while his frame of mind is altered. His courage fails. His pious resolutions hang their enfeebled heads: and, notwithstanding his boasted fidelity, he cannot watch with Christ so much as one hour, though there be the greatest necessity for it. He is brought to the trial, and, like Samson, his locks are shorn; his presumed strength is gone. He trembles at the voice of a silly maid; and, shocking to think! denies his Lord with dreadful oaths and horrid imprecations. Such are the inherent abilities of those who are to fight against the World, the Flesh, and the Devil. Such, considered in themselves, are the best of saints.

Now, can these unstable and impotent creatures hope to persevere, and to attain eternal life? Can those who know not how to trust their own hearts for a moment; *(see Prov. 28:26)*, whose moral strength, in a comparative view, is mere weakness; who are continually surrounded with crafty, powerful, and unwearied adversaries, rationally expect a complete victory and everlasting crown? Yes; these very persons "can do all things through Christ" *(Phil. 4:13)* strengthening them. God can enable even a worm to thrash the mountains. They shall not only come off victorious, but be "more than conquerors" over all their enemies. Nor can this appear strange, or in the least incredible, when it is considered that Omnipotent "Grace reigns" —that the love, the power, the wisdom, the promises, the covenant, and faithfulness of God—that all the Divine Persons in the eternal Trinity, and every Perfection in the Godhead, are concerned in their preservation, and engaged to maintain it.

The *love* of God is engaged for their everlasting security. Having chosen them to life and happiness, as a primary fruit of His own eternal favor, His love must abate, or His purpose be rendered void, before they can finally fall. But if "the Lord of Hosts hath purposed" who shall "disannul it?" If "His hand be stretched out" for the execution of His gracious designs, "who shall turn it back" before the end be accomplished? *(Isa. 14:27)*. As He "thought, so shall it come to pass;" and as He "purposed, so shall it stand" *(Isa. 14:24)*. Nor shall His love to their persons ever abate. For "He rests", He takes the highest complacency in the exercise of "His love", and in all its favored objects. Such is Jehovah's delight in His people, that "He rejoices over them with singing" *(Zeph. 3: 17)*, and takes a Divine pleasure in doing them good. His love is as unchangeable as Himself, and unalterably fixed upon them. Consequently, though the manifestations of it may vary, yet, while infinite Wisdom is capable of directing, and almighty power of executing His gracious purposes toward them, they shall never perish. Agreeable to which, we hear the apostle exulting in God's immutable love; affirming, that nothing in the heights above, nor anything in the depths beneath; nothing present, nor anything future, should be able to separate him from it *(Rom. 8:38, 39)*.

The *power* of God is also engaged on the behalf of all those who are "begotten" "again unto a lively hope" *(1 Pet. 1:3)*. They are "kept" by it as in a garrison, "through faith unto salvation" *(1 Pet. 1:5)*. His power surrounds them as a fiery wall, to be their protection and the destruction of their adversaries *(see Zech. 2:5)*. Omnipotence itself is their shield, and keeps them night and day *(see Isa. 27:3)*. As Omnipotence is their guard, so Omniscience is their guide; the honor of Divine wisdom being concerned in their preservation. For if a regenerate soul, one that has been rescued out of Satan's hand, were finally to fall and perish forever; it would argue, if not a want of power in God to maintain the conquest, yet a change of resolution; and so would bring no honor to the wisdom of His first design. It is no reputation to the wisdom of an artificer to suffer a work, by which he determined to manifest, in the ages to come, his exquisite skill, and upon which his affections were placed, to be dashed in pieces before his eyes, by an inveterate enemy, when he had power to have prevented it. Now the Scriptures inform us that, in the method of redemption, the wisdom of God is peculiarly concerned, is greatly diversified, and in the most wonderful manner displayed. Jehovah "abounded in all wisdom and prudence", in forming the stupendous plan, and in choosing suitable means to attain the wonderful end. But if any of the chosen, redeemed, and called, were to be finally miserable, how could this appear?

The *promises* of God, those "exceeding great and precious promises" *(2 Pet. 1:4)* which are made to His people, afford them strong consolation respecting this matter. For the Father of Mercies has declared that He will "confirm them to the end" *(1 Cor. 1:8)*, and "preserve them unto His heavenly kingdom" *(2 Tim. 4:18)*. That the "righteous shall hold on his way" and grow "stronger and stronger" *(Job 17:9)*; that they shall "not depart from Me" but "fear Me for ever" *(Jer. 32:39, 40)*; that as they are in His hand and in the hand of Christ, they shall never be plucked thence; and, consequently, they shall "never perish" *(John 10:27-29)*. Yes, the blessed God has repeatedly and solemnly declared that He will never, no never, leave them nor forsake them *(Heb. 13:5)*. And the reason is, not because they are worthy, or any way better than others, but for the glory of His own eternal name, and because He hath chosen them to be His peculiar people. "For the Lord will not forsake His people for His great name's sake: because it hath pleased the Lord to make" them "His people" *(1 Sam. 12:22)*. These promises, with many others of a similar kind, are yea and amen; are made, and unalterably confirmed, "in Christ Jesus". Divine faithfulness is pledged in them, and infinite power is engaged to perform them. These promises, let Christians exult in the cheerful thought! these promises were made by Him that cannot lie; to which He has annexed—amazing to think!—His most solemn oath; with this professed design, that every sinner who flees "for refuge to lay hold upon the hope set before" him might have a "strong consolation" *(Heb. 6:18)*. Now the promise and oath of God, being two immutable things, must ascertain the believer's final happiness.

Jehovah's *covenant* with His people in Christ affords another glorious attestation to the comfortable truth. That covenant which is ordered in all things, which is stored with heavenly promises, replete with spiritual blessings, and absolutely sure; that covenant of peace which shall never be removed, runs thus: "And they shall be My people, and I shall be their God: And I will give them one heart, and one way, that they may fear Me forever, for the good of them, and of their children after them: And I will make an everlasting covenant with them, that I will not turn away from them, to do them good; but I will put My fear in their hearts, that they shall not depart from Me" *(Jer. 32: 38-40)*. The stability of the new covenant is here asserted in the strongest terms. This gracious covenant is entirely different from that which was made with our great progenitor Adam; the condition of which was perfect obedience, and the promise of life was suspended on that condition. It is also very different from that which was made with the people of Israel at Sinai; which, being broken by them, was abrogated by the Lord Himself. The language of this is *testamentary*. It consists of absolute promises, requires no condition to be performed by man, and is perpetual. Here that sovereign Being, who cannot lie, declares in the strongest manner, that those who are included in this covenant *shall not depart from Him,* and that He will *never cease to do them good.* Security greater than this is not to be conceived, nor can be had. It would indeed be absurd to suppose, that God should make a new and better covenant than that which He made with Adam, or with Israel at Sinai—a covenant without conditions to be performed by man; a covenant which displays rich goodness and boundless grace—and that, after all, the covenantees should be as liable to the dreadful forfeiture of life and happiness, as our first father, when under the covenant of works. Nay, if the new covenant had been conditional; if perseverance and immortal happiness had depended on our performance of any condition, whether greater or less; our state, as believers, would have been much more hazardous than Adam's was, while under the covenant of works; because of the very great disparity between that state of uprightness in which he was created, and ours of corruption, into which we are fallen. Perfect obedience was easier to him than the least condition would be to us.

The *faithfulness* and inviolable *veracity* of God give further assurance of the saint's perseverance. The rocks, though of adamant, shall melt away; the everlasting mountains shall be removed; yea, the whole terraqueous globe itself shall disappear; but the faithfulness of God in executing His covenant, and the veracity of God in performing His promises, are unchangeable and eternal. "The Lord is faithful, who shall establish you, and keep you from" the destructive power of every "evil" *(2 Thess. 3:3)*; and He has declared that He will not suffer His faithfulness to fail *(Psa. 89:33)*. Yea, He hath sworn by His holiness, by the glory of all His perfections, that He will be faithful to His covenant of promises, respecting Christ and His chosen seed. So that if there be immutability in the purpose of God, if any stability in His covenant, if any fidelity in His promises, the true believer shall certainly persevere. Rejoice then, ye feeble followers of the Lamb. The basis of your confidence and consolation is strong and firm. Stronger than all the troubles of life; stronger than all the fears of death; and stronger than the terrors of approaching judgment. Why should you not dismiss every slavish apprehension when the power of God, of truth, and of grace, has made such ample provision for your deliverance from every evil that you had any reason to fear; and for the enjoyment of every blessing you ought to desire, whether in this or a future world?

The *merit* of the Redeemer's blood, His *intercession* for His people, and His *union* with them, strongly argue their final preservation, and heighten their assurances of it. *The merit of His blood*. For, is it probable that He who so loved them as to give His life a ransom for them; that He who so suffered such tortures of body and horrors of soul in their stead; that He who drank the very dregs of the cup of wrath, on purpose that joy and bliss might be their portion forever—is it probable, I say, that He should ever suffer those who are in the most emphatic sense His *peculiar, His purchased people,* and His own property, to be taken from Him by craft or power, and that by the most abhorred of beings and His greatest enemy? Such a supposition is very absurd. Such an event would be highly injurious to the Saviour's character. What, will not He who underwent so much for them in the Garden and on the Cross; who bore the Curse and suffered the pains of Hell in their stead, even while they were enemies, protect them, now they are become, by converting grace, His friends? Why was He willing to be at such an amazing expense in their purchase, if, after all, He permit their avowed enemy to make them his easy prey? That be far from Him! The thought be far from us! No; while there is compassion in His heart, or power in His hand; while His name is *Jesus,* and His work *salvation;* He must "see of the travail of His soul and be" completely "satisfied" *(Isa. 53:11)*. It cannot be, that one soul for whom He gave His life and spilled His blood; whose sins He bore and whose curse He sustained, should ever finally perish. For if that were the case, Divine justice, after having exacted and received satisfaction at the hand of the Surety, would make a demand on the principal; in other words, would require double payment. Besides, the faithfulness of Christ to His engagements is greatly interested in the everlasting happiness of all His redeemed. For we cannot forget who it is that says, "For I came down from heaven, not to do Mine own will, but the will of Him that sent Me. And this is the Father's will which hath sent Me, that of all which He hath given Me *I should lose nothing,* but should raise it up again at the last day" *(John 6:38, 39)*. Now if Jesus, to whom the elect were given, and by whom they were redeemed, became responsible for them to the Father at the last day, as His own declarations import; were He not to fully execute the Divine will, in raising up all that were committed to His care, He would (I speak it with reverence) fail in the performance of His own engagements. Consequently, either His power, or His faithfulness, would be impeached: a supposition of which is absurd, and the assertion blasphemy.

The *intercession* of Christ for His people, in the heavenly sanctuary, affords another evidence of the glorious truth. This intercession is founded on His perfect atonement for all their sins; and it is a firm foundation for that purpose. So that, notwithstanding all the accusations of Satan lodged against them, notwithstanding all their weakness and all their unworthiness, the intercession of Jesus the Son of God, of Jesus Christ the righteous, must afford them the highest security. "Their Redeemer is strong; the Lord of Hosts is His name: He shall thoroughly plead their cause" *(Jer. 50:34).* And as every believer is interested in this intercession, so Jesus, the Advocate, is never denied in His suit *(see John 17:20, etc.).* His plea is always valid, and always effectual to the end intended; which is, as He expressly informs us, that their faith fail not; and that they may be preserved from destructive evil. Our ascended Redeemer is not, in this part of His mediatorial undertaking, like a mere petitioner, who may or may not succeed; for, to all the blessings He solicits on their behalf He has a previous right. He can claim them, in virtue of the promise made to Him and His spiritual seed, having, as their Substitute, fully performed the conditions of the everlasting covenant. Yes, believer, the compassion of Him who bled on the Cross, and the power of Him who pleads on the Throne, ascertain your final felicity.

That ineffable *union* which subsists between Christ and His people involves the truth for which I am pleading, and clearly evinces the important point. For as every believer is a member of that mystical body of which He is the Head; so, while there is life in the Head, the members shall never die, neither by the wiles of craft, nor by the assaults of power. For He who rules over all, with an unremitting regard to the church, declares concerning His people, "Because I live, ye shall live also" *(John 14:19).* His life, as Mediator, is the cause and support of theirs; and they are the fulness and glory of Him who filleth all in all *(see Eph. 1:22, 23).* As it is written, Christ is our life, and "Your life is hid with Christ in God" *(Col. 3:3, 4).* Your life is "hid" like the most valuable treasure in a secret place. "With Christ"; committed to His guardianship, and lodged under His care, who is able to keep that which is intrusted to His hands. "In God"; the bosom of the Almighty is the sacred repository in which the jewel is safely kept. Cheering thought! For Jesus, the Guardian, will never be bribed to deliver up His charge to the power of an enemy; nor shall any sacrilegious hand ever be able, by secret fraud, or open violence, to rifle the casket where Jehovah lays up His jewels. The life of believers is "bound in the bundle of life with the Lord" their God *(I Sam. 25: 29),* and the bond of that union shall never be broken, the mysterious connection shall never be dissolved. For "He that is joined unto the Lord is one spirit" *(I Cor. 6:17)* with Him, and, therefore, absolutely inseparable.

The *indwelling* of the Holy Spirit in believers furnishes them with another cogent argument in proof of the joyful truth. He is in them "a well of water springing up into everlasting life" *(John 4:14).* As a Guide and Comforter, He is given to abide with them forever *(See John 14:16).* His design, in regeneration, is their complete holiness and everlasting happiness. His gracious purpose, in taking up His residence in them, is to fit them for sublimer enjoyments, to secure their perseverance, to guard them through life, and conduct them to glory. By Him they are "sealed unto the day of redemption" *(Eph. 4:30),* and He is "the earnest of our inheritance" *(Eph. 1:14).* Now as an earnest is part of the whole, and is given in assurance of enjoying the whole; and as the Holy Spirit is called "the Earnest" of our everlasting "inheritance"; the words must import the utmost certainty of our future bliss, if possessed of this earnest. Otherwise, which would be shocking to affirm, it must be esteemed precarious, as not answering the end for which it was given.

The *word and ordinances* of God, on which it is both the duty and privilege of believers to attend, happily subserve the great design. By these, as through the whole, the great Agent of the covenant works in a way suited to the nature of a rational being. For though the saints are kept by the invincible power of God, yet not by means merely physical but "through faith" *(I Peter 1:5).* Whatever, therefore, is adapted to increase and confirm our faith in the great Redeemer, at the same time tends to our preservation. This the Word and ordinances do. In the Divine Word, believers have many great and precious promises to encourage them; many exhortations to direct and animate them in the performances of duty; many warnings given, and dangers pointed out, to deter them from evil; many examples of suffering patience and victorious faith for their imitation, comfort, and support whenever they come into similar circumstances; and many glorious things affirmed concerning that inheritance which God has provided for them, in order to raise their affections to heavenly things, and to invigorate their hope of eternal blessedness; all which are adapted to promote their edification, and to preserve them in the way of peace. The *ordinances* of God in general, which are compared to green pastures, in which the sheep of Christ delight both to feed and to rest *(Psa. 23:2)*, being adapted to nourish their souls, and to increase the vigor of their spiritual life, must be happily conducive to their preservation. By a suitable attendance on Divine institutions, believers have their faith confirmed, their holiness advanced, and their hope brightened. In them they have the bread of God dispensed, by which they are nourished up to life eternal. On those appointments of Heaven, therefore, is their duty and their blessing to attend: nor can they, without the slightest presumption, expect preservation in the faith, while they neglect the salutary means. Nor are the Divine *chastisements* without their use in this respect. For the children of God are chastened of their Father, that they "should not be condemned with the world" *(I Cor. 11:32).*

On the whole, then, we have the utmost reason to conclude with Paul, that wherever God begins a "good work" He will certainly "perform it until the day of Jesus Christ" *(Phil. 1:6).* For He that formed the Universe is not such an inconsistent Builder, as to lay the foundation of a sinner's complete happiness in His own eternal purpose, and in the blood of His only Son, and then leave His work unfinished. No; it shall never be said by His infernal enemies, Here God began to build, but was not able to finish. He once loved, redeemed, regenerated, and designed to have saved those wretched souls. But His love abated; His purpose altered, or, which is more to our honour and His disappointment, we have rendered His plan of operation abortive; and now we torment with a vengeance, myriads that were once high in Jehovah's favor, and numbered among His children. But though this be the consequence of the opposite doctrine, Lucifer himself, with all his pride and enmity, will never entertain such a thought, nor thus blaspheme His Maker.

The following quotation may serve to exhibit, in a compendious view, the substance of the foregoing paragraphs: "Since we stand not, like Adam, upon our own bottom, but are branches of such a vine as never withers; members of such a head as never dies; sharers in such a Spirit as cleanseth, healeth, and purifieth the heart; partakers of such promises as are sealed with the oath of God—since we live, not by our own life, but by the life of Christ; are not led or sealed by our own spirit, but by the Spirit of Christ; do not obtain mercy by our own prayers, but by the intercession of Christ; stand not reconciled to God by our own endeavors, but by the propitiation wrought by Christ; who loved us when we were enemies, and in our blood; who is both willing and able to save to the uttermost, and to preserve His own mercies in us; to whose office it belongs to take order that none who are given unto Him be lost—undoubtedly, that life of Christ in us, which is thus underpropped, though it be not privileged from temptations, no, not from backslidings, yet it is an abiding life. He who raised our soul from death, will either preserve our feet from falling, or if we do fall, will heal our backslidings, and will save us freely."

Some, perhaps, may be ready to object: "If the preservation of believers depend upon God, in the manner asserted, they have no occasion to be at all careful how they live. No great harm can befall them, for they are certain of being finally safe." In answer to which I shall only observe; that the strength of this objection was long since tried, by Satan, upon our Lord Himself. But as it appeared of no force to Him, though the tempter proposed it as the necessary consequence of those promises made by the Father to Christ, as Man and Mediator, respecting His preservation; so it appears to have as little in the present case. The major proposition in the Devil's argument was; if Thou art the Son of God, His angels will certainly preserve Thee: Thou canst not be injured. And his conclusion was, therefore, without any danger, Thou mayest cast Thyself down from this eminence. So, in the present case, the argument contained in the objection, is, If you be a child of God and in union with Christ, your perseverance must be certain. For, being the charge of Omnipotence, it is impossible you should finally fall. Therefore, you may safely bid adieu to all circumspection. You need not fear sin, or its consequences; nor is there any occasion to be solicitous about walking with God in the ways of holiness. But as our Lord, who had not the least doubt of the special care of His Father over Him, rejected Satan's proposal with the utmost abhorrence; knowing it was a temptation to evil, and that the argument used to enforce it was an abuse of the Scripture: so the believer, though fully persuaded that grace reigns in every part of his salvation: and though it strongly appears in that special care of God, which is incessantly exercised over him in his preservation to eternal life; yet he is well convinced, that he must not continue in sin that grace may abound. On every such suggestion, therefore, he will from his heart say, "God forbid!" Besides, there are many important purposes answered, by walking in the ways of obedience, respecting the Christian himself, his neighbour, and his God; which, having been considered already, I shall not here particularly mention.

Nor, can it, with any propriety, be objected against the doctrine for which I am pleading; "That the saints are exhorted to pray for the continual aids of grace; for Divine support in times of trial; and for protection against their enemies", as if it argued their state uncertain, with reference to the final event. For Christ, who was absolutely sure of happiness, nor could possibly fail of enjoying the reward that was promised to Him, as Mediator; or come short of possessing that glory which He had with the Father before the world was; yet prayed for it with as much fervor as any saint can possibly do for the most desirable blessing *(John 17:1, 5)*. A noble example this, of the assurance of faith, respecting our eternal state; and of the unreserved reliance on the Divine promises, being perfectly consistent with earnest and constant prayer for the fulfillment of them! Besides, whoever dares to act on the principal of this objection has no reason to consider himself as a Christian; but rather as dead in sin, and in the broad way to final ruin.

But notwithstanding the Lord has promised that His people shall never perish; yet He has nowhere engaged that they shall not fall into sin, and as moral evil is provoking to the eyes of His holiness, they are bound to use the utmost caution, lest by disobedience they move Him to use the scourge. For the frowns of a father will be hard to bear; as their spiritual peace and joyful communion with him will be much interrupted, by such disobedience and chastisement for it. The children of God, when careless in their walk and guilty of backsliding, have severely smarted under His correcting hand. The sorrowful confessions and bitter complaints of David, after his scandalous intrigue with Uriah's wife, are a standing incontestable proof of this observation. Their persuasion of interest in the everlasting covenant has been terribly shaken, if not lost for a season, so as to wound their hearts with keenest anguish; till, after many prayers and great watchfulness, they have been again indulged with the smiles of Jehovah's countenance, and with the joys of His salvation. The remembrance of this, and a consideration how God the Father and His incarnate Son are dishonored, the Holy Spirit grieved, the glorious Gospel reproached, weak believers offended, and the hands of the wicked strengthened, by the careless conduct of Christian professors, afford a sufficient reason for those multiplied cautions, which are given to the disciples of Christ in the Book of God, that they indulge not any criminal passion in the least degree; without supposing that their final happiness depends on the steadiness of their walk, or on the goodness of their conversation. For our perseverance in faith and holiness depends on the excellency of our state; as being in covenant with God, His adopted children and the members of Christ; not upon any obedience and endeavors.

Hence you may learn, believer, that as the enemies of your soul are inveterate, subtle and powerful, and your spiritual frames inconstant, it is highly necessary that you should live under the continual remembrance of those awakening considerations. What more advisable, what more necessary for you, than to walk circumspectly; to watch and pray, lest you enter into temptation! A sense of your own weakness and insufficiency should ever abide on your mind and appear in your conduct. As the corruption of nature is an enemy that is always near you, and always in you while on earth; and as it is very strongly disposed to second every temptation from without; you should keep your heart with all diligence *(see Prov. 28:26; 4:23; Jer. 17:9)*. Watch, diligently watch, over all its imaginations, motions and tendencies. Consider whence they arise, and to what they incline, before you execute any of the purposes formed in it. For such is the superlative deceitfulness of the human heart that he who trusteth in it is a fool; ignorant of his danger, and unmindful of his best interests. This consideration should cause every child of God to bend the suppliant knee, with the utmost frequency, humility, and fervor; to live, as it were, at the "throne of grace" *(Heb. 4:16)*; nor depart thence till far from the reach of danger. Certain it is, that the more we see of the strength of our adversaries, and of the danger we are in from them, the more shall we exercise ourselves in fervent prayer. Can you, O Christian, be cool and indifferent, be dull and careless, when the World, the Flesh, and the Devil, are your implacable and unwearied opposers? Dare you indulge yourself in carnal delights, or in a slothful profession, while the enemies of your peace and salvation are ever active and busy in seeking to compass your fall, your disgrace, and, if possible, your eternal ruin? "Awake, thou that sleepest" *(Eph. 5:14)*! Mistake not the field of battle for a bed of rest. "Be sober; be vigilant" *(1 Pet. 5:8)*.

Are there, notwithstanding the believer's weakness and the power of his enemies, such strong assurances given of his perseverance, complete victory, and final happiness? then, though with fear and trembling he should often reflect on his own insufficiency, he may rely on a faithful God, as his unerring Guide and invincible Guard, with confident joy. The remembrance of that will be a constant motive to humility and watchfulness. The exercise of this will maintain peace and consolation of soul; will be an inexhaustible source of praise, in spite of all the attempts of inveterate malice in his enraged foes. For the Almighty says, "Fear not: I am thy shield" forever to defend thee; and "Thy exceeding great reward" to render thee completely happy. While "the eternal God is thy refuge," and the "everlasting arms" thy support, there is no occasion to fear. "If God be for us, who can be against us?" *(Rom. 8:31)*. When the gates of hell and the powers of earth united, assail the believer, menacing destruction to both body and soul, then the "name", the promises, the oath, and the attributes of Jehovah are "a strong tower", an impregnable fortress: and, conscious of his own inability to resist the enemy, he "runneth into it, and is safe" from every attack, however crafty or violent. The righteous man, the real Christian, "dwelleth on high", out of the reach of every evil. "His place of defence is the munitions of rocks"; immovable as their solid foundations; inaccessible as their lofty ridges. Nor shall the favored inhabitants of this everlasting fortress ever be obliged to surrender for want of provisions. A fulness of living bread, and streams of living water, are united with invincible strength. For, it is added, "Bread shall be given him; his waters shall be sure" *(Isa. 33:16)*. He shall want neither nourishment nor protection; outward defence, nor inward comfort. Happy, then, thrice happy they that are under the Reign of Grace! Every attribute of Deity is engaged to promote their felicity. All the eternal counsels terminate in their favor; and Providence in the whole course of events respecting them, has a special regard to their advantage. Thus Divine grace appears and reigns in the perseverance of true believers. For grace promotes the means necessary to it; grace applies them; and omnipotent grace crowns them with success, to its own eternal honor and praise.—*From "The Reign of Grace" by Abraham Booth, 1768.*

(The Bible Truth Depot, Swengel, Pa. have re-published this most valuable and helpful work, which was out of print; and same is obtainable from them at **$1.00**, postpaid. We trust our readers will be sure to procure a copy for the spiritual profit and blessing they will derive therefrom.)

VOL. I   MAY   1922   NO. 5.

STUDIES in the SCRIPTURES

"Search the Scriptures" John 5:39.

A PERIODICAL (MONTHLY "IF THE LORD WILL")
DEVOTED TO BIBLE STUDIES and EXPOSITIONS

Associate Editors and Publishers, I. C. HERENDEEN and ARTHUR W. PINK,
Swengel, Pa.

Price: 10 cents per copy; $1.00 per year. Foreign $1.00 per year.

TO OUR SCRIPTURE STUDY FAMILY

The instant and hearty response which has been accorded *Studies in the Scriptures*, and the numerous letters already to hand telling of the spiritual profit and blessing derived from the ministry of its pages, furnish abundant cause for praise and thanksgiving to "the God of all grace". The leading of the Lord in undertaking the publication of this periodical was so clear and definite that we were not left in any uncertainty as to His will in the matter, and the many evidences since of His approval and blessing have greatly cheered and encouraged our hearts. It was to be expected, of course, that if He wished us to take up such a ministry He would prepare hearts to receive it, and so He has: to Him alone be all the praise.

The precious things the Lord has so graciously given us to put before His people in the first four issues are but samples of what are in store for future issues, if the Lord will. In addition to Brother Pink's exceptionally helpful and illuminating exposition of John's Gospel, appearing, D. V., in each issue, there is also to be found in this number the first installment of a very timely and important series of articles from his pen on "The Antichrist." Doubtless many believers are desirous of having a better knowledge of what the Scriptures teach concerning this "Man of Sin", this "Son of Perdition", and we believe all such will receive just the help they have been looking for from our brother's exhaustive and detailed, but withal clear and lucid, examination of the Word of God on this subject.

In this issue we also begin a shorter series of articles by Jonathan Edwards on "The Wisdom of God Displayed in the Way of Salvation". These are of more than ordinary value and merit from the pen of this servant of God so widely used of Him in the past. We trust our readers will give both series a *patient* and *careful* reading for only thus can the most help be gotten from them. They are the results of much study and searching of Scripture, and each one would do well to re-read them slowly and thoughtfully.

We sincerely trust our friends will at once consider it to be both their privilege and their duty to do what they can in bringing this magazine to the notice of such as would appreciate its ministry and be profited thereby. If you derive help and blessing from this publication, will you not speak of and recommend it to others that they, too, might have an opportunity of sharing these "good things" with us? We would rejoice to be able to minister to a large number of the Lord's people every month, and especially to pastors, missionaries, Sunday School teachers and other Christian workers.

Studies in the Scriptures will be true to its title. It will contain no news items, no anecdotes, no denunciations of higher criticism and the other heresies, but, instead, helpful and constructive expositions of God's Word such as will, we feel confident, provide real food for the souls of believers. Sample copies for judicious distribution will be sent, gladly, to those requesting same. Be sure to specify the number you wish. Above all, pray for us.

Yours "in the Beloved",
I. C. Herendeen.

STUDIES IN THE SCRIPTURES

Subscription Price: $1.00 per year to any address in the world. Single copies 10 cents.

Change of Address: Please notify us promptly of any change of address, and be certain to give both old and new addresses.

Non-Subscribers receiving this Magazine regularly will understand their subscription has been entered by a friend.

Copies lost in the mail duplicated on request.

All new subscriptions will be dated back to January, 1922.

Entered as second-class matter December 15th, 1921 at the post office at Swengel, Pa., under Act of March 3rd, 1879.

CONTENTS

The Antichrist	86
John's Gospel	91
The Wisdom of God Displayed in the Way of Salvation	99
The Believer's Response to the Words of the Saviour	106

THE ANTICHRIST

1. INTRODUCTION.

Across the varied scenes depicted by prophecy there falls the shadow of a figure at once commanding and ominous. Under many different names, like the aliases of a criminal, his character and movements are set before us. It is our intention to write a series of papers concerning this one who will be the full embodiment of human wickedness and the final manifestation of satanic blasphemy. Many others have made reference to this mysterious personage in their general expositions of prophecy, but so far as our examination of the literature on this subject has carried us (and we have endeavored to make it as thorough as possible) there seem to have been very few attempts made to furnish a *complete* delineation of this Prince of Darkness. We do not know of any exhaustive treatment of the subject, and for this reason, and also because there is no little confusion in the minds of many concerning the character and career of the coming Man of Sin, these papers are now submitted to the attention of Bible students.

For upwards of twelve years we have studied diligently and prayerfully what the Scriptures teach about the Pseudo-Christ. The deeper we have carried these studies, the more surprised we are at the prominent place which is given in the Bible to this Son of Perdition. There is an amazing wealth of detail which, when carefully collected and arranged, supplies a vivid biography of the one who is shortly to appear and take the government of the world upon his shoulders. The very fact that the Holy Spirit has caused so much to be written upon the subject at once denotes its great importance. The *prominence* of the Antichrist in the prophetic Scriptures will at once appear by a glance at the references that follow.

The very first prophecy of the Bible takes note of him, for in Gen. 3:15 direct reference is made to the Serpent's "Seed". In Exodus a striking type of him is furnished in Pharaoh; the defier of God; the one who cruelly treated His people; the one who by ordering the destruction of all the male children, sought to cut off Israel from being a nation; the one who made fair promises only to break them; the one who met with such a drastic end at the hands of the Lord. In the prophecy of Balaam, the Antichrist is referred to under the name of "Asshur" *(Num. 24:22)*,—in future articles evidence will be given to prove that "Asshur" and the Antichrist are one and the same person. There are many other remarkable types of the Man of Sin to be found in the historical books of the Old Testament, but these we pass by now, as we hope to devote a separate paper to their consideration.

In the book of Job he is referred to as "the Crooked Serpent" *(Job. 26:13)*: with this should be compared Isa. 27:1 where, as "the Crooked Serpent" he is connected with the Dragon, though distinguished from him. In the Psalms we find quite a number of references to him; as "the Bloody and Deceitful Man" *(5:6)*; "the Wicked (One)" *(9:17)*; "the Man of the Earth" *(10:18)*; the "Mighty Man" *(52:1)*; "the Adversary" *(74:10)*; "the Head over many countries" *(110:6)*; "the Evil Man" and "the Violent Man" *(140:1)*, etc., etc. Let the student give special attention to Psalms 10, 52 and 55.

When we turn to the Prophets there the references to this Monster of Iniquity are so numerous that were we to cite all of them, even without comment, it would take us quite beyond the proper bounds of this introductory article. Only a few of the more prominent ones can, therefore, be noticed.

Isaiah mentions him: first as the "Assyrian", "the Rod" of God's anger *(10:5)*; then as "the Wicked" *(11:4)*; then as "the King of Babylon" *(14:11-20 and cf 30:31-33)*; and also as the "Spoiler"—Destroyer *(16:4)*. Jeremiah calls him "the Destroyer of the Gentiles" *(4:7)*; the "Enemy", the "Cruel One" and "the Wicked" *(30:14 and 23)*. Ezekiel refers to him as the "Profane Wicked Prince of Israel" *(21:25)*, and again under the figure of the "Prince of Tyre" *(28:2-10)*, and also as "the chief Prince of Meshech and Tubal" *(38:2)*. Daniel gives a full delineation of his character and furnishes a complete outline of his career. Hosea speaks of him as "the King of Princes" *(8:10)*, and as the "Merchant" in whose hand are "the balances of deceit" and who "loveth to oppress" *(12:7)*. Joel describes him as the Head of the Northern Army, who shall be overthrown because he "magnified himself to do great things" *(2:20)*. Amos terms him the "Adversary" who shall break Israel's strength and spoil her palaces *(3:11)*. Micah makes mention of him in the fifth chapter of his prophecy *(see v. 6)*. Nahum refers to him under the name of "Belial" *(Heb.)* and tells of his destruction *(1:15)*. Habakkuk speaks of him as "the Proud Man" who "enlargeth his desires as hell, and is as death, and cannot be satisfied, but gathereth unto him all nations, and heapeth unto him all peoples" *(2:5)*. Zechariah describes him as "the Idol Shepherd" upon whom is pronounced God's "woe", and upon whom descends His judgment *(11:17)*.

Nor is it only in the Old Testament that we meet with this fearful character. Our Lord Himself spoke of him as the one who should "come in his own name", and who would be "received" by Israel *(John 5:43)*. The apostle Paul gives us a full length picture of him in 2 Thess. 2, where he is denominated "the Man of Sin, the Son of Perdition," whose coming shall be "after the working of Satan with all power and signs and lying wonders". The apostle John mentions him by name, and declares that he will deny both the Father and the Son *(1 John 2:22)*. While in the Apocalypse, the last book in the Bible, all these lines of prophecy are found to converge in "the Beast" who shall ultimately be cast, together with the False Prophet, into the lake of fire, there to be joined a thousand years later by the Devil himself, to suffer for ever and ever in that fire specially "prepared" by God.

The appearing of the Antichrist is a most appalling and momentous subject, and in the past, many well meaning writers have deprived this impending event of much of its terror and meaning, by confusing some of the antichrists that have already appeared at various intervals on the stage of human history, with that mysterious being who will tower high above all the sons of Belial, being no less than Satan's counterfeit and opposer of the Christ of God, who is infinitely exalted above all the sons of God. It promotes the interests of Satan to keep the world in ignorance of the coming Super-man, and there can be no doubt that he is the one who is responsible for the general neglect in the study of this subject, and the author, too, of the conflicting testimony which is being given out by those who speak and write concerning it.

There have been three principal schools among the interpreters of the prophecies pertaining to the Antichrist. The first have applied these prophecies to persons of *the past*, to men who have been in their graves for many centuries. The second have given these prophecies a *present* application, finding their fulfillment in the Papacy which still exists. While the third give them a *future* application, and look for their fulfillment in a terrible being who is yet to be manifested. Now, widely divergent as are these several views, the writer is assured there is an element of truth in each of them. Many, if not the great majority of the prophecies—not only those pertaining to the Antichrist, but to other prominent objects of prediction—have at least a twofold, and frequently a threefold fulfillment. They have a local and immediate fulfillment: they have a continual and gradual fulfillment: and they have a final and exhaustive fulfillment.

In the second chapter of his first epistle the apostle John declares, "Little children, it is the last time: and as ye have heard that Antichrist shall come, *even now* are there many antichrists; whereby we know that it is the last time" *(v. 18)*. In strict harmony with this, the apostle Paul affirmed that the "mystery of iniquity" was *"already"* at work in his day *(2 Thess. 2:7)*. This need not surprise us, for many centuries before the apostles, the wise man declared, "The thing that *hath been,* is that *which shall be;* and that which *is* done is that which *shall be* done: and there is no new thing under the sun" *(Ecc. 1:9).* History works in cycles, but as each cycle is completed we are carried nearer the goal and consummation of history. There have been, then, and there exist today, many antichrists, but these are only so many forecasts and foreshadowings of the one who is yet to appear. But it is of first importance that we should distinguish clearly between *an* antichrist and *the* Antichrist. As we have said, there have already been many antichrists, but the appearing of the Antichrist is yet future.

The first school of interpreters referred to above, have lighted upon Antiochus Epiphanes as the one who fulfills the prophecies respecting the Antichrist. As far back as the days of Josephus *(see his "Antiquities")* this view found ardent advocates. Appeal was made to the title he assumed *(Epiphanes signifying "Illustrious");* to his opposition to the worship of Jehovah; to his remarkable military achievements; to his diplomatic intrigues; to his defiling of the Temple; to his sacrificing of a pig in the holy of holies; to his setting up of an image; and to his cruel treatment of the Jews. But there are many conclusive reasons to prove that Antiochus Epiphanes could not possibly be the Antichrist, though undoubtedly he was, in several respects, a striking type of him, inasmuch as he foreshadowed many of the very things which this coming Monster will do. It is sufficient to point out that Antiochus Epiphanes had been in his grave for more than a hundred years when the apostle wrote 2 Thess. 2.

Another striking character who has been singled out by those who believe that the Antichrist has already appeared and finished his course, is Nero. And here again there are, admittedly, many striking resemblances between the type and the antitype. In his office of emperor of the Romans; in his awful impiety; in his consuming egotism; in his bloodthirsty nature; and in his ferocious and fiendish persecution of the people of God, we discover some of the very lineaments which will be characteristic of the Wicked One. But again it will be found that this man of infamous memory, Nero, did nothing more than foreshadow that one who shall far exceed him in satanic malignity. Positive proof that Nero was not the Antichrist is to be found in the fact that he was in his grave before John wrote the thirteenth chapter of the Revelation.

The second school of interpreters, to whom reference has been made above, apply the prophecies concerning the Antichrist to the papal system, and see in the succession of the popes the fac-simile of the Man of Sin. Attention is called to Rome's hatred of the Gospel of God's grace; to her mongrel combination of political and ecclesiastical rule; to her arrogant claims and tyrannical anathemas upon all who dare to oppose them; to her subtlety, her intrigues, her broken pledges; and last, but not least, to her unspeakable martyrdoms of those who have withstood her. The pope, we are reminded, has usurped the place and prerogatives of the Son of God, and his arrogance, his impiety, his claims to infallibility, his demand for personal worship, all tally exactly with what is postulated of the Son of Perdition. Antichristian, Roman Catholicism unquestionably is, yet, even this monstrous system of evil falls short of that which shall yet be headed by the Beast. We expect to devote a separate section to a careful comparison of the papacy with the prophecies which describe the character and career of *the* Antichrist.

The third school of interpreters believe that the prophecies relating to the Lawless One have not yet received their fulfillment, and cannot do so until this present Day of Salvation has run its course. The Holy Spirit of God, whose presence here now prevents the final outworking of the Mystery of Iniquity, must be removed from these scenes before Satan can bring forth his Masterpiece of deception and opposition to God. Many are the scriptures which teach plainly that the manifestation of the Antichrist is yet future, and these will come before us in our future studies. For the moment we must continue urging upon our readers the importance of this subject and the timeliness of our present inquiry.

The study of Antichrist is not merely one of interest to those who love the sensational, but it is of vital importance to a right understanding of dispensational truth. A true conception of the predictions which regard the Man of Sin is imperatively necessary for an adequate examination of that vast territory of unfulfilled prophecy. A single passage of scripture will establish this. If the reader will turn to the beginning of 2 Thess. 2 he will find that the saints in Thessalonica had been waiting for the coming of God's Son from heaven, because they had been taught to expect their gathering together unto Him before God launches His judgments upon the world, which will distinguish the "Day of the Lord". But their faith had been shaken and their hope disturbed. Certain ones had erroneously informed them that "that day" *had* arrived, and therefore, their expectation of being caught up to meet the Lord in the air had been disappointed. It was to relieve the distress of these believers, and to repudiate the errors of those who had disturbed them, that, moved by the Holy Spirit, the apostle wrote his second epistle to the Thessalonian church.

"Now we beseech you, brethren, by the coming of our Lord Jesus Christ, and by our gathering together unto Him, That ye be not soon shaken in mind, or be troubled, neither by spirit, nor by word, nor by letter as from us, as that the day of Christ is at hand. Let no man deceive you by any means: for that day shall not come, except there come a falling away first, and that Man of Sin be revealed, the Son of Perdition; Who opposeth and exalteth himself above all that is called God, or that is worshipped; so that he as God sitteth in the temple of God, showing himself that he is God. Remember ye not, that, when I was yet with you I told you these things? And now ye know what withholdeth that he might be revealed in his time. For the mystery of iniquity doth already work: only He who now letteth (hindereth) will let, until He be taken out of the way. And then shall that Wicked One be revealed, whom the Lord shall consume with the spirit of His mouth, and shall destroy with the brightness of His coming: Even him whose coming is after the working of Satan with all power and signs and lying wonders, And with all deceivableness of unrighteousness in them that perish; because they received not the love of the truth, that they might be saved. And for this cause God shall send them strong delusion, that they might believe a lie: That they all might be damned who believed not the truth, but had pleasure in unrighteousness" *(2 Thess. 2:1-12)*,

We have quoted this passage at length to show that the Day of the Lord cannot come until after the Rapture *(v. 1)*, after the Apostasy *(v. 3)*, and after the appearing of the Man of Sin *(v. 3)*, whose character and career are here briefly but graphically sketched. The Antichrist is to run his career of unparalleled wickedness *after* all Christians have been removed from these scenes, for it is under him, as their leader, that all the hosts of ungodliness shall muster to meet their doom by the summary judgment of God. Has, then, the Wicked One been revealed? or must we still say, as the apostle said in his day, that while the "mystery of iniquity" is even now working, there is something "withholding" (restraining), that he should be revealed "in his time"? The vital importance of the answer which is given to these questions will farther appear when we connect with this description of the Antichrist given in 2 Thess. 2 the other prophecies which reveal the exact length of time within which his course must be accomplished. Our reason for saying this is because the majority of the prophecies yet unfulfilled *are to be fulfilled* during the time that the Antichrist is the central figure upon earth. Moreover, the destruction of the Antichrist and his forces will be the grand finale in the age-long conflict between the Serpent and the woman's Seed, as He returns to set up His kingdom.

The dominant view which has been held by Protestants since the time of the Reformation is that the many predictions relating to the Antichrist describe, instead, the rise, progress, and doom of the papacy. This mistake has led to others, and given rise to the scheme of prophetic interpretation which has prevailed throughout Christendom. When the predictions concerning the Man of Sin were allegorized, consistency required that all associated and collateral predictions should also be allegorized, and especially those which relate to his doom, and the kingdom which is to be established on the overthrow of his power. When the period of his predicted course was made to measure the whole duration of the papal system, it naturally followed that the predictions of the *associated events* should be applied to the history of Europe from the time that the Bishop of Rome became recognized as the head of the Western Churches.

It was, really, this mistake of Luther and his contemporaries in applying to Rome the prophecies concerning the Antichrist which is responsible, we believe, for the whole modern system of post-millennialism. The reformers were satisfied that the Papacy had received its death blow, and though it lingered on, the Protestants of the sixteenth century were confident it could never recover. Believing that the doom of the Roman hierarchy was sealed, that the kingdom of Satan was rocking on its foundations, and that a brief interval would witness a complete overthrow, they at once seized upon the prophecies which announced the setting up of the kingdom of Christ as immediately following the destruction of the Antichrist, and applied them to Protestantism. It is true that some of them did not seem to fit very well, but human ingenuity soon found a way to overcome these difficulties. The obstacle presented by those prophecies that announced the *immediate* setting up of Christ's kingdom, following the overthrow and destruction of Satan's, was surmounted by an appeal to the analogy furnished in the overthrow of Satan's kingdom—if this was a tedious process, a gradual thing which required time to complete, why not so with the other? If the rapidly waning power of the papacy was sufficient to guarantee its ultimate extermination, why should not the progress of the Reformation presage the ultimate conquering of the world for Christ!

If, as it seemed clear to the reformers, the papacy was the Man of Sin, and St. Peter's was the "temple" in which he usurped the place and prerogatives of Christ, then, this premise established, all the other conclusions connected with their scheme of prophetic interpretation must logically follow. To establish the premise was the first thing to be done, and once the theory became a settled conviction it was no difficult thing to find scriptures which appeared to confirm their view. The principal difficulty in the way was to dispose of the predictions which limited the final stage of Antichrist's career to forty-two months, or twelve hundred and sixty days. This was accomplished by what is known as the 'year-day' theory, which regards each of the 1260 days as 'prophetic days', that is, as 1260 years, and thus sufficient room was afforded to allow for the protracted history of Roman Catholicism.

Without entering into further details, it is evident at once that, if this allegorical interpretation of the prophecies regarding Antichrist can be proven erroneous, then the whole post-millennial and 'historical' schemes of interpretation fall to the ground, and thousands of the voluminous expositions of prophecy which have been issued during the past three hundred and fifty years are set aside as ingenious but baseless speculations. This, of itself, is sufficient to demonstrate the importance of our present inquiry.

Not only is the *importance* of our subject denoted by the prominent place given to it in the Word of God, and not only is its *value* established by the fact that a correct understanding of the person of Antichrist is one of the chief keys to the right interpretation of the many prophecies which yet await their fulfillment, but the *timeliness* of this inquiry is discovered by noting that the Holy Spirit has connected the appearing of the Antichrist with the Apostasy: "Let no man deceive you by any means: for that day shall not come, except there come *a falling away* (the 'Apostasy') first, and that Man of Sin be revealed, the Son of Perdition" *(2 Thess. 2:3)*. These two things are here joined together, and if it can be shown that the Apostasy is already far advanced, then we may be certain that the manifestion of the Man of Sin cannot be far distant.

There is little need for us to make a lengthy digression here and give a selection from the abundance of evidence to hand, which shows that the Apostasy *is* already far advanced. The great majority of those whom we are addressing have already had their eyes opened by God to discern the Christ-dishonoring conditions which exist on almost every side. It will be enough to barely mention the gathering of the "tares" into bundles, which is taking place before our eyes; the rapid spread of Spiritism, with its "seducing spirits and doctrines of demons", and the significant and solemn fact that thousands of those who are ensnared by it are they who have *departed* from the formal profession of the faith *(1 Tim. 4:1)*; the "form of godliness" which still exists, but which alas! in the vast majority of instances "denies its power"; the alarming development and growth of Roman Catholicism in this land, and the lethargic indifference to this by most of those who bear the name of Christ; the denial of every cardinal doctrine of the faith once delivered to the saints, which is now heard in countless pulpits of every denomination; the "scoffing" which is invariably met with by those who teach the imminent return of the Lord Jesus; and the Laodicean spirit which is now the very atmosphere of Christendom, and from which few, if any, of the Lord's own people are entirely free—these, and a dozen others which might be mentioned, are the proofs which convince us that the time must be very near at hand when the Divine Hinderer shall be removed, and when Satan shall bring forth his Son to head the final revolt against God, ere the Lord Jesus returns to this earth and sets up His kingdom. This, then, shows the need of a prayerful examination of what God has revealed of those things "which must *shortly* come to pass". The very fact that the time when Satan's Masterpiece shall appear is rapidly drawing nearer, supplies further evidence of the importance and timeliness of our present inquiry.

The *practical value* of these preliminary considerations should at once be apparent. What we have written in connection with this incarnation of Satan who is shortly to appear, is not the product of a disordered imagination but the subject of Divine revelation. The warning given that the appearing of the Antichrist cannot be far distant springs not from the fears of an alarmist, but is required by the Signs of the Times which, in the light of Scripture, are fraught with significant meaning to all whose senses are exercised to discern both good and evil. The many proofs that the manifestation of the Man of Sin is an event of the near future are so many *calls to God's own children* to be ready for the Return of the Saviour, for before the Son of Perdition can be revealed the Lord Himself must first descend into the air and catch away from these scenes, unto Himself, His own blood-bought people. Therefore, it behooves each one of us to make "our calling and election *sure*", and to heed that urgent admonition of the Saviour "Let your loins be girded about, and your lights burning; and ye yourselves like unto men that wait for their Lord" *(Luke 12:35, 36)*.

—*Arthur W. Pink.*

JOHN'S GOSPEL

5. CHRIST AND HIS FIRST DISCIPLES.
John 1:35-51.

We first submit a brief Analysis of the passage which is to be before us. We would divide it as follows:—

1. John points to Christ as God's Lamb, 1:35, 36.
2. The effect of this on two of His disciples, 1:37
3. Christ's searching question, the disciples' reply and communion with Christ, 1:38, 39.
4. The effect of this on Andrew, 1:40-42.
5. Christ finds and calls on Philip to follow Him, 1:43, 44.
6. The effect of this on Philip, 1:45, 46.
7. The meeting between Christ and Nathanael, 1:47-51

The central truth of the passage we are about to study is, How the first of Christ's disciples were brought into saving contact with Him. It may be that some of our readers have experienced a difficulty when studying these closing verses of John 1 and as they have compared their contents with what is found in Mark 1:16-20—"Now as He walked by the sea of Galilee, He saw Simon and Andrew his brother casting a net into the sea: for they were fishers. And Jesus said unto them, Come ye after Me, and I will make you to become fishers of men. And straightway they forsook their nets, and followed Him. And when He had gone a little farther thence, He saw James the son of Zebedee, and John his brother, who also were in the ship mending their nets. And straightway He called them: and they left their father Zebedee in the ship with the hired servants, and went after them" *(cf. Matt. 4:18-22; Luke 5:1-11)*. Many have wondered how to harmonize John 1:35-42 with Mark 1:16-20. But there is nothing *to* harmonize, because there is *no* contradiction between them. The truth is, that Mark and John are not writing on the same subject. Mark treats of something which happened at a later date, than that of which John writes. John tells us of the *conversion* of these disciples whereas Mark (as also Matthew and Luke) deals with their *call to service*—a service which concerned the lost sheep of the house of Israel, and which had, therefore, a *dispensational* significance and value. That John omits the call to service (which each of the other three evangelists record) brings out, again, the special character of his Gospel, for he treats not of dispensational but of *spiritual* relationships, and therefore was it reserved for him to describe *the conversion* of these first disciples of Christ.

It is deeply interesting and instructive to mark attentively the manner in which these first disciples found the Saviour. They did not all come to Him in the same way, for God does not confine Himself to any particular method—He is *sovereign* in this, as in everything. It had been well if this had been kept in mind, for then had many a doubt been dispelled and many an heartache removed. How many there are who have listened to the testimony of some striking conversion, and have reproached themselves and made themselves miserable because *their* experience was a different one. How many churches there are which have their annual two weeks "protracted" Meetings and then conduct themselves as though there were no other souls that needed salvation during the remaining fifty weeks of the year! How many there are who imagine no sinner can be saved except at a "mourner's bench"! But all of these are so many ways of *limiting* God, that is, holding limited conceptions of God.

Of the four cases of Conversion described in our passage (we say *four*, for the two mentioned in verse 35 are linked together) *no two were alike!* The first two heard a preacher proclaiming Christ as "the Lamb of God", and, in consequence, promptly sought out the Saviour for themselves. Simon Peter, the next one, was "brought" to Christ by his brother, who had followed and found the Saviour on the previous day. Philip, the third one, seemed to have no believer to help him, perhaps no fellow creature who cared for his soul; and of him we read, "Jesus went forth into Galilee and *findeth* Philip, and saith unto him, Follow Me" *(1:43)*. While the last, Nathanael, was sought out by his now converted brother Philip, and was warmly invited to come and see Christ for himself; and while making for Him, the Saviour, apparently, advanced toward and met the seeking one. Putting the four together we may observe that the first found Christ as the result of *a preacher's message*. The second and the fourth found Christ as the result of *the personal work* of a believer. In the case of the third there was *no human instrument* employed by God. The fact that the first came to Christ as the result of the ministry of John the Baptist, seems to show that God puts the *preaching* of the Word as of first importance in the saving of sinners. The fact that God honored the personal efforts of two of these early converts, shows He is pleased to give a prominent place to *personal work* in His means of saving souls. The fact that Philip was saved apart from all human instrumentality, should teach us that God has not reached the end of His resources even though preachers should prove unfaithful to their calling, and even though individual believers are too apathetic to go forth bidding sinners come to Christ.

It is also to be noted that not only did these first converts find the Saviour in a variety of ways, but also that Christ Himself *dealt* differently with each one. For the two mentioned in v. 35 there was a searching question to test their motives in following Christ—"What seek ye?" For Simon Peter there was a striking declaration to convince him that Christ knew all about him, followed by a gracious promise to reassure his heart. For Philip there was nothing but a peremptory command—"Follow Me". While for Nathanael there was a gracious word to disarm him of all prejudice and to assure his heart that the Saviour stood ready to receive him. Thus did the Great Physician deal with each man according to his individual peculiarities and needs.

Finally, observe how this passage brings out the *suitability* of Christ for all kinds of men.* It is blessed to behold here, how the Saviour drew to Himself men of such widely different types and temperaments. There are some superficial sceptics who sneeringly declare that Christianity only attracts those of a particular type—the effeminate, the emotional, and the intellectually feeble. But such an objection is easily refuted by the facts of common observation. Christ has been worshipped and served by men and women of every variety of temperament and calling. Those who have delighted to own His name as The Name "which is above every name" have been drawn from every walk of life, as well as from every nation and tribe under the sun. Kings and queens, statesmen and soldiers, scientists and philosophers, poets and musicians, lawyers and physicians, farmers and fishermen have been among the number who have cried,

---

*For the central thought of this paragraph, as also of the preceding, we are indebted to the commentary of Dr. Dod, in which, however, are some things we cannot commend.

"Worthy is the Lamb". And in the cases of these early converts we find this principle strikingly illustrated.

The unnamed disciple of v. 35 is, by common consent, regarded as John, the writer of this fourth Gospel. John was the disciple who leaned on the Master's bosom, devoted and affectionate. He was "the disciple whom Jesus loved": he was, apparently, the only one of the twelve who stood by the Cross as the Saviour was dying. Andrew seems to have been a man with a calculating mind, what would be termed today, of a practical turn: no sooner had he come to Christ, than he goes at once and finds his brother Simon, tells him the good news that they had found the Messiah, and brought him to Jesus; and, *he* was the one to observe the lad with the five barley loaves and two small fishes, when the hungry multitude was to be fed *(John 6:8,9)*. Simon Peter was hot-headed, impulsive, full of zeal. Philip was sceptical and materialistic: he was the one to whom our Lord put the test question, "Whence shall we buy bread, that these may eat?", to which Philip replied, "Two hundred pennyworth of bread is not sufficient for them, that every one of them may take *a little*" *(John 6:5,7)*; and again, Philip was the one who said to Christ, "Lord, *show us* the Father, and it sufficeth us" *(John 14:8)*. Nathanael, of whom least is known, was, evidently of a meditative and retiring disposition, whose life was lived in the background, but of an open and frank nature, one "in whom was no guile". How radically different, then, were these men in type and temperament, yet each of them found in Christ that which met his need and satisfied his heart! We regard these first converts as representative and illustrative cases, so that it behooves us to study each separately and in detail.

"Again the next day after John stood, and two of his disciples" *(1:35)*. This is the place to ask the question, *What* was the fruitage of John's mission? What results accrued from his ministry? They were very similar to what may be expected to attend the labors of a servant of God who is used by his Master, today. John had borne faithful witness to Christ: how had his ministry been received? In the first place, the religious leaders of his day *rejected* the testimony of God *(Luke 7:30)*. In the second place, great crowds were attracted, and men of all sorts attended upon his ministry *(Luke 3:7-15)*. In the third place, only a few were *really* affected by his message, and stood ready to receive the Messiah when He appeared. It has been much the same all through the ages. When God sends forth a man to take an active and prominent part in His service, the religious leaders look upon him with suspicion, and hold aloof in their fancied superiority. On the other hand, the vulgar, curious crowds, ever hungering for the novel and sensational, are attracted; but comparatively few are really touched in their consciences and hearts.

"Again the next day after John stood, and two of his disciples; and looking upon Jesus as He walked, he saith, Behold the Lamb of God" *(1:35, 36)*. Once more the Lord's forerunner heralds Him as "the Lamb of God" *(cf. v. 29)*. This teaches us that there are times when the servant of God needs to *repeat* the same message. It also informs us that the central and vital truth which God's messenger must press, unceasingly, is the *sacrificial* work of Christ. Never forget, brother preacher, that your chief concern is to present your Master as "the *Lamb* of God"! Notice, also, we are told, "John *stood,* and two of his disciples, and *looking* upon Jesus as He walked, he saith, *Behold* the Lamb of God". The words we have placed in italics call attention to a most important moral principle: if we would "look upon Jesus", if we would "Behold the Lamb", we must *stand still,* that is, all fleshly activity must cease; we must come to the end of ourselves. This was the first truth which God taught Israel after they had been delivered from Egypt: as they were being pursued by the Egyptians, and came to the Red Sea, God's servant cried, "Fear ye not, *stand still,* and see the salvation of the Lord" *(Ex. 14:13)*.

"And the two disciples heard Him speak" *(1:37)*. These two men were John and Andrew. By calling they were fishermen. They had already attached themselves to John, and had not only been baptized but were eagerly awaiting the promised Messiah and Saviour. At last the day arrived when their teacher, whom they trusted as God's prophet, suddenly checked them in their walk, and no doubt with almost breathless interest, laid his hand upon them, and pointing to a passing Figure, cried, "Behold the Lamb of God"! There, in actual bodily form, was the One for whom the ages had waited. There, within reach of their own eyes, was the Son of God, who was to offer Himself as a Sacrifice for sin. There, right before them, was He of whom one of these very two men later wrote, "That which was from the beginning, which we have heard, which we have seen with our eyes, which we have looked upon, and our hands have handled, of the Word of Life" *(1 John 1:1)*.

How often this experience has been duplicated—duplicated *in principle,* we mean. How many of us used to hear Christ spoken of while as yet we had no personal knowledge of Him! We sat under a preacher who magnified His excellencies, we heard men and women singing "Thou O Christ art all I want, more than all in Thee I find", and we were impressed by the testimonies of God's saints as they bore witness to that Friend who sticketh closer than a brother. As we listened, our hearts yearned for a similar experience, but as yet we had no personal acquaintance with Him. When one day, perhaps we were waiting on the ministry of one of God's servants, or may be we were alone in our room reading a portion of the Scriptures, or perhaps down on our knees crying to God to reveal His Son to us, or possibly, we were attending to the daily round of duty, when suddenly He who until then had been only a Name, was revealed to us by God as a *living reality.* Then we could say with one of old, "I *have* heard of Thee by the hearing of the ear: but *now* mine eye seeth Thee" *(Job 42:5).*

And what is the consequence of such an experience? Ah, now the soul has been awakened, it feels some action is demanded of it. Such an one can no longer sit and *listen* to descriptions of Christ—he must rise and seek Him on his own account. Individual acquaintance with this unique and Divine Person is now desired above everything. The one thus awakened now seeks the Lord with all his heart. Thus it was with these two disciples of John. As they heard their master say "Behold the Lamb of God", we read, "they *followed* Jesus" *(v. 37).*

"Then Jesus turned and saw them following, and saith unto them, What seek ye?" *(1:38).* No sincere soul seeks or follows after Christ in vain. "Seek and ye shall find" is His own blessed promise. Accordingly, we find the Saviour turning to and addressing these enquiring souls. "What seek ye?", He says to them. At first sight this question strikes us as strange. Some, perhaps, have regarded it as almost a rebuff; yet it cannot be that. Personally, we look upon these words of our Lord as designed to test the *motive* of these two men, and to help them understand their own *purpose.* There are a great variety of motives and influences which make people become the outward and professed followers of Christ. In the days of which our passage treats, many soon "followed" Christ because the crowd streamed after Him and carried them along with it. Many "followed" Him for what they could get—the loaves and fishes, or the curing of their ailments and the healing of their loved ones. For a time many "followed" Him, doubtless, because it was the popular and the respectable thing to do. But a few "followed" because they felt their deep need of Him, and were attracted by the perfections of His Person.

So it was then, and so it is now. Christ desired to be followed intelligently or not at all—that is, He will not accept formal or superstitious worship. What He wants is the heart—the heart that seeks Him for Himself! Hence the heart-searching question was put to these two men, "What seek ye?" What, dear reader, would be *your* answer to such a question? What seekest thou? The true answer to this question reveals your spiritual state. Let no one suppose he is not seeking anything. Such were an impossibility. Every heart has its object. If your heart is not set upon Christ Himself, it is set upon something which is not Christ. *"What* seek ye?" Is it gold, fame, ease and comfort, pleasure, or—what? On what is your *heart* set? Is it an increased knowledge of Christ, a more intimate acquaintance with Him, a closer walk with Him? Can you say, in measure at least, "As the hart panteth after the waterbrooks, so panteth my soul after Thee, O God" *(Psa. 42:1)!*

It is beautiful to notice the reply made to these two earnest souls. "Master", they said, "Where dwellest Thou?" It seems strange that their answer to the Lord's query has puzzled so many who have pondered it. Most of the commentators have quite missed the point of these words and failed to see any direct connection between the question put by the Saviour and the reply He received. "Where dwellest Thou?" Let us emphasize each word separately.

"*Where* dwellest Thou?" How pathetic and tragic! What a question to ask the Son of God! How it brought out His humiliation! There was no need to ask where Caiaphas or Pilate dwelt, for everybody knew. But who among men cared to know, or could have told these two men, if asked, where *Christ* dwelt?

"Where *dwellest* Thou?" This was no question of mere idle curiosity. It showed that they longed to be *with Him*. What they desired was *fellowship,* as would have been made more evident if the translators had rendered it "Where *abidest* Thou?", for "abiding" ever has reference to communion.

"Where dwellest *Thou?*" they asked, in answer to "*What* seek ye?" It was not a "what" but an "whom" that their hearts were set upon. It was not a blessing, but the Blesser Himself that their hearts sought.

Unspeakably blessed is it to listen to the Saviour's response to the request made by these two inquiring souls: "He saith unto them, Come and see" *(1:39)*. Ah, He knew their desires. He had read their hearts. He discerned that they sought His presence, His person, His fellowship. And He never disappoints *such* longings. "Come" is His gracious invitation. "Come" was a word which assured them of His welcome. "Come" is what He still says to all who labor and are heavy laden.

"And see" or "look": this was, we believe, a further word to *test* them. When Christ conducted these two men to His dwelling-place, would a brief visit suffice them? No, indeed. Mark the remainder of the verse, "they came and saw where He dwelt, and abode with Him that day: for it was about the tenth hour". So fully had He won their confidence, so completely had He attracted their hearts to Himself, that though this was the first day of meeting with the Saviour, they *abode* with Him. Yes, they "abode" with *Him*. This is the word which uniformly speaks of *spiritual fellowship*. They abode with Him that day: for it was about the tenth hour; that is 4 P. M. We doubt not they remained with Him that night, but this is not expressly stated, and why? Ah, the Holy Spirit would not say they abode with *Him* "that night", for there *is no night* in His presence! Notice, too, the name of the place where He dwelt is not given. They "abode with Him", where this is we are not told: He was but a *stranger* here, and those who follow *Him* must be strangers too. "They abode *with* Him." How blessed! *His* abiding place was *theirs* too. And so shall it be for all believers throughout eternity. Has He not said, "I will come again, and receive you unto Myself; that where I am, *there* ye may be also" *(John 14:3)*?

"One of the two which heard John speak, and followed him, was Andrew, Simon Peter's brother. He first findeth his own brother Simon, and saith unto him, We have found the Messiah, which is, being interpreted, the Christ" *(1:40, 41)*. How this tells of the *satisfaction* which these two disciples had found in Christ! They wished to share with others their newborn joy! Andrew now sought out his brother Simon, and said to him, "We have found the Christ". That it is here said "*He* first findeth his own brother", implies that John (who ever seeks to hide himself, never once mentioning himself by name) did the same with *his* brother, James, a little later. This is the happy privilege of every young believer—to tell others of the Saviour he has found. For this no college training is required, and no authority from any church need be sought. Not that we despise either of these, but *all* that is needed to tell a perishing sinner of the Saviour is a heart acquaintance with Him yourself. It was not that Andrew went forth as a preacher, for *that* work he needed training, training by Christ Himself. But he set out to bear simple yet earnest witness of the Saviour he had found. The one whom he sought was his own brother, and this illustrates the fact that our personal responsibility *begins* with those nearest to us. Witness should first be borne in our own family circle.

"And he brought him to Jesus. And when Jesus beheld him, He said, Thou art Simon the son of Jona (or, perhaps better, 'the son of John'): thou shalt be called Cephas, which is by interpretation, A stone" *(1:42)*. Here we find the Lord giving Simon a blessed promise, the force of which must be sought in what he was by nature. By natural temperament Simon was fiery and impetuous, rash and unstable. What would *such* a man's thoughts be, when he first heard Andrew? When he learned that Christ was here, and received invitation to go to Him, when he knew that the Master was seeking loyal and devoted servants, would he not say, That is all right for steady, reliable Andrew, but not for such as me? Would he not say, Why, I would be a stumbling-block to the cause of Christ: my impetuous temper and hasty tongue will only hinder not help? If such thoughts passed through his mind, as we think most likely, then how these words of Christ which now fell on his ears must have re-assured his heart: "When Jesus *beheld* him, He said, Thou art Simon the son of John". Thus the Lord showed that He was already thoroughly acquainted with Simon. But, He adds, "Thou shalt be called A stone." "Cephas", was Aramaic and signifies "a rock". "Petros" is the Greek and signifies "a stone". Peter is the English form of both Cephas and Petros. How blessed, then, was this promise of our Lord! "Thou art Simon" (his natural name), vacillating and unstable. Yes, I *know* all about you, "But thou shalt be called Cephas" (his new name), "a rock", fixed and stable. Christ, thus, promised to undertake for him. What a blessed fulfillment did this promise receive after the Saviour's resurrection!

We believe, though, there is a deeper meaning in this verse, and one which has a wider application, an application to all believers. In these verses which treat of the third "day", we have that which belongs, strictly, to the Christian dispensation. Peter must be viewed as a *representative* character. Thus viewed, everything turns upon *the meaning* of the proper nouns here. Simon means "hearing". Son of Jona is, correctly rendered we believe, in the R. V. "son of John", and John signifies "God's gift". We become Christians by *hearing* God's Word *(Rom. 10:17)*, and this spiritual hearing is *God's gift*, and every believer becomes a *stone*, comp. "Ye also, as living stones, are built up a spiritual house" *(1 Pet. 2:5)*.

"The day following Jesus would go forth into Galilee, and findeth Philip, and saith unto him, Follow Me" *(1:43)*. How precious is this! What a lovely illustration of His own declaration "The Son of Man is come *to seek* and to save that which was lost" *(Luke 19:10)*. How it shows us the Good Shepherd going after this lone sheep of His! What we read of here is equally true of every case of genuine conversion. Whether the Lord uses a human instrument or not, it is Christ Himself who seeks out and finds each one who, subsequently, becomes His follower. Our seeking of Him is only the reflex action of His first seeking of us, just as we love Him because He *first* loved us.

"Now Philip was of Bethsaida, the city of Andrew and Peter. Philip findeth Nathanael, and saith unto him, We have found Him, of whom Moses in the law, and the prophets, did write, Jesus of Nazareth, the Son of Joseph" *(1:44, 45)*. Here, again, we see the effect that Christ's revelation of Himself has upon the newly born soul. The young believer partakes of the spirit of the One in whom he has believed. The compassion of the Saviour for the lost, now fills his heart. There is a going out of his affections toward the perishing. He cannot remain silent or indifferent. He must tell others of the Saviour he has found, or rather, of the Saviour who has found him. Alas, that so many believers have become discouraged in the blessed work of telling others of the Saviour. So often their efforts seem to meet with no response. Those whom they approach are so indifferent, if not resentful. And the witnessing convert becomes disheartened. Perhaps these lines may catch the eye of some who have grown weary in this work. Then permit us to ask this question: Did you *promptly* welcome the advances some earnest Christians made to *you?* Did you accept the Saviour *without* delay? Ah, was not God "longsuffering" to youward? Did He not send one after another to speak to you about your soul? Then why be so impatient and petulant toward those who are now as *you* once were! "But", you may say, "I have spoken to some of my loved ones about Christ so often, and it all seems of no avail". Then, stay your soul on these promises: "Cast thy bread upon the waters: for *thou shalt* find it after many days" *(Ecc. 11:1)*. "And let us not be weary in well doing; for in due season we shall reap, *if we faint not*" *(Gal. 6:9)*. "Therefore, my beloved brethren, be ye steadfast, unmoveable, *always* abounding in the work of the Lord, forasmuch as *ye know* that your labor is not in vain in the Lord" *(1 Cor. 15:58)*.

"And Nathanael said unto him, Can there any good thing come out of Nazareth?" *(1:46)*. The one who seeks to win souls must expect to be met with objections. Many a sinner is hiding behind queries and quibbles. How then shall we meet them? Learn from Philip. All that he said to Nathanael in reply to his question, was, "Come and see". He invited his brother to come and *put Christ to the test* for himself. This is the wise way: do not be turned aside by the objections of the one to whom you are speaking, but continue to press upon him *the claims of Christ*, and then trust God to bless His own Word, in His own good time.

"Jesus saw Nathanael coming to Him, and saith of him, Behold an Israelite indeed in whom is no guile" *(1:47)*. Nathanael was honest and open. His question to Philip was no mere evasion, or hypocritical quibble; rather was it the voicing of a genuine difficulty. This must not be forgotten in our dealings with different souls. We must not conclude that *all* questions put to us are asked in a carping spirit. There are some people, many perhaps, who have *real* difficulties. What they need is light, and in order to obtain this they need to come to Christ. So in every case we cannot err if we present Christ and His claims upon every soul we meet. Nathanael was an "Israelite, indeed, in whom was no guile". We take it, he illustrates in his person one of the qualifications for becoming a good ground hearer of the Word, namely, to receive that Word into "an honest and good heart".

"Nathanael saith unto Him, Whence knowest Thou me? Jesus answered and said unto him, Before that Philip called thee, when thou wast under the fig tree, I saw thee" *(1:48)*. How this incident evidences the Deity of Christ! It displayed His *omniscience*. Christ saw Nathanael, and read his heart, *before* he came to Him. And, dear reader, He sees and reads each of us, too. Nothing can be hid from His all-seeing eye. No guise of hypocrisy can deceive Him.

"Nathanael answered and saith unto Him, Rabbi, Thou art the Son of God; Thou art the King of Israel" *(1:49)*. This was sure evidence that a Divine work had been wrought in Nathanael's soul. The eyes of his understanding were opened to behold the Divine glory of the Saviour. And promptly does he confess Him as "the Son of God". It is significant that in this fourth Gospel we find there are just *seven* who bear witness to Christ's Deity. First, John the Baptist *(1:34)*; second, Nathanael *(1:49)*; third, Peter *(6:69)*; fourth, the Lord Himself *(10:36)*; fifth, Martha *(11:27)*; sixth, Thomas *(20:28)*; seventh, the writer of this Gospel *(20:31)*.

"Jesus answered and said unto him, Because I said unto thee I saw thee under the fig tree, believest thou? Thou shalt see greater things than these. And He saith unto him, Verily, verily, I say unto you, Hereafter ye shall see the heaven open, and the angels of God ascending and descending upon the Son of Man" *(1:50, 51)*. Nathanael had been deeply impressed by what he had just witnessed, namely, this manifestation of Christ's Omniscience. But, says the Lord, he should yet see greater things. Yea, the time should come when he should behold an open heaven, and the earth directly connected with it. He should see that to which in the far past, the dream and vision of Jacob had pointed: that which should be the antitype of the latter which linked earth to heaven, should be Christ Himself, and Nathanael with all believers, will see "the angels of God ascending and descending upon the Son of Man", which, of course, will be in the Millennium.

It only remains for us to point out that here in the last half of John 1 we have four very remarkable *typical pictures*, treating of four distinct Dispensations. The first is found in 1:19-28. The second begins at 1:29—"The next day"—and ends at 1:34. The third begins at 1:35—"Again the next day"—and ends at 1:42. The fourth begins at 1:43—"The day following"—and runs to the end of the chapter.

I. In John 1:19-28 we have a typical picture of the O. T. Dispensation.

1. Note the mention of the "priests and Levites" *(v. 19)*, as representing the whole Levitical economy.
2. Note that "Jerusalem" is referred to here in this section *(v. 19)*, but in none of the others.
3. Note how Israel's spiritual state during O. T. times is here pictured by the ignorance and lack of discernment of the Jews *(v. 19)*.
4. Note the reference here to "Elijah", and "that Prophet" who was to be like unto *Moses (v. 21)*.
5. Note that John is here seen in the *wilderness (v. 23)*, symbolical of Israel's spiritual barrenness up to the time of Christ's appearing.
6. Note how accurately John's words "There standeth One among you, whom ye know not" *(v. 26)*, depicted Israel's blindness to the presence of

Jehovah in their midst all through the O. T. era.

7. Note that John bears witness to One who was to come *"after"* him (*v. 27*): such was the witness borne to Christ during O. T. times.

II. In John 1:29-34 we have a typical picture of *the Messianic Dispensation* (embracing the period of Christ's public ministry on earth) intimated here by the words "The *next* day" (*v. 29*).

1. Note "John seeth Jesus coming unto him" (*v. 29*): this gives the historic beginning of *that* dispensation, for "the law and the prophets were until John" (*Luke 16:16*).
2. John proclaims Christ as "the Lamb of God" (*v. 29*): it was to offer Himself in sacrifice that He had come here.
3. "After me" (*v. 30*): that is, after John the Baptist, who represented in his own person the terminal of the O. T. dispensation.
4. "And I knew Him not" (*v. 31*): this represents the ignorance of the Jews when Christ appeared.
5. "He shall be made manifest *to Israel*" (*v. 31*): cf. Matt. 15:24, "I am not sent but unto the lost sheep of the house of Israel".
6. "The Spirit.....abode upon *Him*" (*v. 32*), and upon no others during that dispensation.
7. "This is the Son of God" (*v. 34*): it was as such Israel rejected Him.

III. In John 1:35-43 we have a typical picture of the *Christian Dispensation*, intimated by "Again the *next* day" (*v. 35*).

1. "The next day after, John *stood*" (*v. 35*): the *end* of John's *activities* were now reached: cf. v. 39 "the tenth hour"—the full measure of Israel's responsibility (cf. the *ten* commandments) was now reached.
2. There is here a turning away from Judaism, represented by John, and a following of the Lord Jesus (*vv. 35-37*): note Jesus "walked"—this was in contrast from John who "stood".
3. It is as "the Lamb of God" Christians first know Christ (*v. 36*).
4. "They followed Jesus" (*v. 37*): this is

what the Christian walk is,—"He has left us an example that we should follow His steps" (*1 Peter 2:21*).

5. Believers now *"abide"* with Christ (*v. 39*): that is, they enjoy *communion* with Him, meanwhile hidden from the world.
6. Christianity is to be propagated by personal efforts of individual believers (*vv. 40, 41*).
7. Unto Simon Christ said "Thou shalt be called a *stone*" (*v. 42*): it is as "living stones" that believers of *this* dispensation are "built up a spiritual house" (*1 Pet. 2:5*), which is "a habitation of God through the Spirit" (*Eph. 2:22*).

IV. In John 1:43-51 we have a typical picture of the *Millennium*, intimated by "The day following" (*v. 43*).

1. Note "Jesus would *go forth* into Galilee" (*v. 43*): this going forth, speaks of His *open manifestation* in contrast from the secret "dwelling" (apart from the world) of the previous day. And "into *Galilee*", cf. Isa. 9:1.
2. *"Findeth* Philip" (*v. 43*): at the beginning of the Millennium Christ will "find" the *lost* Ten Tribes. Note also that "Philip was of Bethsaida" (*v. 44*), and Bethsaida means "house of *nets*", which speaks of *the sea*—the standing symbol of the Gentiles.
3. O. T. prophecy will then be completely fulfilled and vindicated, (*see v. 45*), and notice "the son of *Joseph*"—it was through Joseph that the Lord Jesus acquired the legal right to David's throne.
4. "Israelite *indeed*" (*v. 47*): in the Millennium the favored Nation shall no longer be *Jacob-like*, but like unto that which his new name signified.
5. Note the reference here to the "fig tree" (*v. 48*)—the standing symbol of Israel.
6. Christ is *now* owned as Son of God and King of *Israel*" (*v. 49*).
7. Heaven and earth shall then be in direct contact with each other (*v. 51*).

The following questions are given to be studied during this month, so as to prepare the reader for our next article on John 2: 1-11:—

1. "And the third day" *(2:1)*—after what? And *why* mention *which* "day"?
2. Why is a marriage scene introduced at this point?
3. Why is the "mother" of Jesus so prominent?
4. What is signified by the two statements made by the Lord to His mother in 2:4?
5. What is the typical significance of the "*six* waterpots of *stone*" *(2:6)?*
6. Of what is "wine" *(2:10)*, the emblem?
7. What are the central lessons to be learned from this first miracle of Christ?

—*Arthur W. Pink.*

THE WISDOM OF GOD DISPLAYED IN THE WAY OF SALVATION

Eph. 3:10—"To the intent that now unto the principalities and powers in heavenly places, might be known by the church the manifold wisdom of God".

(The following is a blessed and most illuminating exposition, given 200 years ago by the renowned Jonathan Edwards—a man widely used of God. It will require close reading, and will well repay a re-reading. We are dividing it into several installments, each of which will increase in interest, till at the close the heart of the believer will be filled with wonderment and praise.—*Editors*).

Introduction.

The apostle is speaking in the context of the glorious doctrine of the redemption of sinners by Jesus Christ; and how it was in a great measure kept hid in the past ages of the world. It was a mystery that before they did not understand, but now it was in a glorious manner brought to light: "By revelation He made known unto me the mystery (as I wrote afore in few words; whereby when ye read ye may understand my knowledge in the mystery of Christ), which in other ages was not made known unto the sons of men, as it is now revealed unto His holy apostles and prophets, by the Spirit" *(vv. 3-5)*. And again; "Unto me who am less than the least of all saints is this grace given, that I should preach among the Gentiles the unsearchable riches of Christ; and to make all men see what is the fellowship of the mystery, which from the beginning of the world hath been hid in God, who created all things by Jesus Christ" *(vv. 8,9)*.

In the text the apostle informs us, that what Christ had accomplished towards His church, in the work of redemption, had not only in a great measure unveiled the mystery to the church in this world; but God had more clearly and fully opened it to the understanding even of the angels themselves; and that this was one end of God in it, to discover the glory of His wisdom to the angels: "*To the intent* that now unto the principalities and powers in heavenly places, might be known by the church the manifold wisdom of God".

One end of revealing God's counsels concerning the work of redemption, is making known God's *wisdom*. It is called *manifold* wisdom; because of the manifold glorious ends that are attained by it. The excellent designs, hereby accomplished, are very manifold. The wisdom of God in this is of vast extent. The contrivance is so manifold, that one may spend an eternity in discovering more of the excellent ends and designs accomplished by it; and the multitude and vast variety of things that are, by Divine contrivance, brought to conspire to the bringing about those ends.

We may observe, *to whom* it is that God would manifest His wisdom, by revealing the mystery of our redemption;—and they are not only men, but the *angels*. "To the intent that now unto the *principalities and powers in heavenly places,* might be known —the manifold wisdom of God". The angels are often called principalities and powers, because of the exalted dignity of their nature. The angels excel in strength and wisdom. Those who are the *wise men* of the earth are called *princes* in the style of the apostle: "Howbeit we speak wisdom among them that are perfect, yet not the wisdom of this world nor of *the princes* of this world". "Which none of the *princes* of this world knew; for had they known it, they would not have crucified the Lord of Glory" *(1 Cor. 2:6,8)*. So the angels are called principalities for their great wisdom. They may also be so-called for the honor God has put upon them, in employing them as His ministers and instruments, wherewith He governs the world: and therefore are they called thrones, dominions, principalities and powers—Col. 1: 16.

They are called principalities and powers in *heavenly* places, as distinguishing them from those that are in places of *earthly* power and dignity. The offices or places of dignity and power that the angels sustain, are not earthly but *heavenly*. They are in places of honor and power *in the heavenly city* and the *heavenly kingdom*.

One end of God in revealing His design or contrivance for redemption, as He hath so fully and gloriously done by Jesus Christ, is that the angels in heaven may behold the glory of His wisdom by it. Though they are such bright intelligences, and do always behold the face of God the Father, and know so much; yet here is matter of instruction for them. Here they may see more of the Divine wisdom than ever they had seen before. It was a new discovery of the wisdom of God to them.

The *time* when this display of the wisdom of God was especially made to the angels is, when Christ introduced the Gospel Dispensation, implied in those words, "To the intent that *now* unto the principalities", etc., When Christ came into the world and died, and actually performed the work of redemption—when He had fully and plainly revealed the counsels of God concerning it; and accordingly introduced the evangelical dispensation, and erected the Gospel church—then the angels understood more of the mystery of man's redemption, and the manifold designs and counsels of Divine wisdom, than ever they had done before.

In the foregoing verse the apostle, after speaking of revealing this wisdom of God to man, "And to make all *men* see, what is the fellowship of this mystery", etc., speaks of this mystery as a thing from the beginning kept hid till now, "The mystery, which from the beginning of the world had been hid in God—that now", etc. In this verse he mentions another end, namely, that He may, at the same time, make the *angels* also see God's wisdom in His glorious scheme of redemption—"now", at this time, implies that it was previously a mystery kept hid from them in comparison of what it is now. And here is room enough for the angels to discover more and more to all eternity of the wisdom of God in this work.

Observe the *medium* by which the angels come by this knowledge, namely, the church—"That now unto the principalities —might be known *by the church*",—i. e., by the things they see done *in* the church, or *towards* the church: and by what they see *concerning* the church. So hath it pleased the sovereign God, that the angels should have the most glorious discoveries of Divine wisdom by His doings toward His church, a sort of beings much inferior to themselves. It hath pleased God to put this honor upon us.

The wisdom of God appearing in the way of Salvation by Jesus Christ, is far above the wisdom of the angels. For here it is mentioned as one end of God in revealing the contrivance of our salvation, that the angels thereby might see and know how great and manifold the wisdom of God is; to hold forth the Divine wisdom to the angels' view and admiration. But why is it so, if this wisdom be not higher than their own wisdom? It never would have been mentioned as one end of revealing the contrivance of redemption, that the angels might see how manifold God's wisdom is; if all the wisdom to be seen in it was no greater than their own. It is mentioned as a wisdom such as they had never seen before, not in God, much less in themselves. That *now* might be known how manifold the wisdom of God is; now, four thousand years since the creation.—In all that time the angels had always beheld the face of God; and had been studying God's works of creation; yet they never, till that day, had seen anything like that; never knew how *manifold* God's wisdom is, as now they know it by the church.

SECTION I.

WONDERFUL THINGS DONE, BY WHICH SALVATION IS PROCURED.

Such is the choice of the person chosen to be our Redeemer,—the substituting of Him in our room; His incarnation—His life—His death—and exaltation. And,

1. We will consider the *choice of the person* to be our Redeemer. When God designed the redemption of mankind, His great wisdom appears in that He pitched upon His own, His only-begotten Son, to be the person to perform the work. He was a Redeemer of God's own choosing, and therefore He is called in Scripture, God's *Elect*, Isa. 42:1. The wisdom of choosing this person to be the Redeemer, appears in His being every way a *fit* person for this undertaking. It was necessary, that the person who is to be the Redeemer, should

be a *Divine* person.—None but a *Divine* person was sufficient for this great work. The work is infinitely unequal to any creature. It was requisite, that the Redeemer of sinners, should be Himself infinitely *holy*. None could take away the infinite evil of sin, but One that was infinitely far from and contrary to sin Himself. Christ is a fit person upon this account.

It was requisite, that the person, in order to be sufficient for this undertaking, should be one of infinite *dignity* and *worthiness*, that He might be capable of meriting infinite blessings. The Son of God is a fit person on this account. It was necessary, that He should be a person of infinite *power* and *wisdom*; for this work is so difficult, that it requires such an One. Christ is a fit person also upon this account. It was requisite, that He should be a person infinitely *dear* to God the Father, in order to give an infinite value to His transactions in the Father's esteem, and that the Father's love to Him might balance the offence and provocation by our sins. Christ is a fit person upon this account. Therefore is He called *the Beloved*, Eph. 1:6: "We are accepted in the *Beloved*".

It was requisite that the person should be one that could act in this as of *his own absolute right;* one that in Himself, was not a servant or subject; because, if he is one that cannot act of his own right, he cannot merit anything. He that is a servant, and that can do no more than he is bound to do, cannot merit. And then he that has nothing that is absolutely his own, cannot pay any price to redeem another. Upon this account Christ is a fit person; and none but a Divine person can be fit.— And He must be a person also of infinite *mercy* and *love;* for no other person but such a one would undertake a work so difficult for a creature so unworthy as man. Upon this account also Christ is a fit person. It was requisite that He should be a person of unchangeable, perfect, *truth* and *faithfulness;* otherwise He would not be fit to be depended upon by us in so great an affair. Christ is also a fit person upon this account.

The wisdom of God in choosing His eternal Son, appears, not only in that He is a fit person; but in that He was the *only* fit person of all persons, whether created or uncreated. No *created* person, neither man, nor angel, was fit for this undertaking; for we have just now shown, that he must be a person of infinite holiness, dignity, power, wisdom; infinitely dear to God; of infinite love and mercy; and one that may act of his own absolute right. But no creature, how excellent soever, has any one of these qualifications. There are three *uncreated* persons, the Father, Son, and Holy Spirit; and Christ alone of these is a suitable person for a Redeemer. It was not meet, that the Redeemer should be God the *Father;* because He, in the Divine economy of the persons of the Trinity, was the person that holds the rights of the Godhead, and so was the person offended, whose justice required salvation; and was to be appeased by a Mediator. It was not meet it should be the *Holy Spirit*, for in being Mediator between the Father and the saints, He is in some sense so between the Father and the Spirit. The saints, in all their spiritual transactions with God, act by the Spirit; or rather, it is the Spirit of God that acts in them; they are the temples of the Holy Spirit. The Holy Spirit dwelling in them is their principle of action, in all their transactings with God. But in these their spiritual transactings with God, they act by a *Mediator*. These spiritual and holy exercises cannot be acceptable, or avail anything with God, as from a fallen creature, but by a Mediator. Therefore Christ, in being Mediator between the Father and the saints, may be said to be Mediator between the Father and the Holy Spirit, that acts in the saints. And therefore it was meet, that the Mediator should not be either the Father or the Spirit, but a middle person between them both. It is the Spirit in the saints, that seeks the blessing of God, by faith and prayer; and, as the apostle says, with groanings that cannot be uttered: "Likewise the Spirit also helpeth our infirmities: for we know not what we should pray for as we ought: but the Spirit Himself maketh intercession for us, with groanings that cannot be uttered" *(Rom. 8:36).* The Spirit in the saints seeks Divine blessings of God, by and through a Mediator; and therefore that Mediator must not be the Spirit, but another person.

It shows a Divine wisdom to *know* that Christ was a fit person. No other but one of *Divine* wisdom could have known it. None but one of infinite wisdom could have thought of Him to be a Redeemer of sinners. For He, as He is God, is one of the first persons offended by sin; against whom man, by his sin, had rebelled. Who but God infinitely wise could ever have thought of *Him* to be a Redeemer of sinners; against whom they had sinned, to whom they were enemies, and of whom they deserved infinitely ill? Who would ever have thought of Him as One that should set His heart upon men, and exercise infinite love and pity toward them, and exhibit infinite wisdom, power, and merit in redeeming them? We proceed,

2. To consider the *substituting* of this person in our room. After choosing the person to be our Redeemer, the next step of Divine wisdom is, to contrive the way how He should perform this work. If God had declared who the person was, that should do this work, and had gone no further; no creature could have thought which way this person could have performed the work. If God had told them, that His own Son must be the Redeemer; and that He alone was a fit person for the work; and that He was a person every way fit and sufficient for it,—but had proposed to *them* to contrive a way how this fit and sufficient person should succeed—we may well suppose that all created understandings would have been utterly at a loss.

The first thing necessary to be done, is, that this Son of God should become our Representative and Surety; and so be substituted in the sinner's room. But who of created intelligences would have thought of any such thing as the eternal and infinitely beloved Son of God being substituted in the room of sinners? His standing instead of the sinner, a rebel, an object of the wrath of God? Who would have thought of a person of infinite glory representing sinful worms that had made themselves by sin infinitely provoking and abominable?

For, if the Son of God be substituted in the sinner's room, then his sin must be charged upon Him: He will thereby take the guilt of the sinner upon Himself; He must be subject to the same law that man was, both as to the commands, and threatenings: but who would have thought of any such thing concerning the Son of God? But we proceed,

3. To consider the *incarnation* of Jesus Christ. The next step of Divine wisdom in contriving how Christ should perform the work of redeeming sinners, was in determining His incarnation. Suppose God had revealed His counsels thus far to created understandings, that His own Son was the person chosen for this work, that He had substituted Him in the sinner's room, and appointed Him to take the sinner's obligations, and guilt on Himself— and had revealed no more, but had left the rest of them to find out; it is no way probable, that even then they could ever have thought of the way, whereby this person might actually have performed the work of redemption. For if the Son of God be substituted in the sinner's stead, then He takes the sinner's obligations on Himself. For instance, He must take the obligations the sinner is under to perform *perfect obedience* to the Divine law. But it is not probable, that any creature could have conceived how that could be possible.—How should a person who is the eternal Jehovah, become a servant, made under law, and perform obedience even to the law of man?

And again, if the Son of Man be substituted in the sinner's stead, then He comes under the sinner's obligation to suffer the punishment which man's sin deserved. And who could have thought that to be possible? For how should a Divine person, who is essentially, unchangeably, and infinitely happy, suffer pain and torment? And how should He who is the object of God's infinitely dear love, suffer the wrath of His Father? It is not to be supposed, that created wisdom ever would have found a way how to have got over these difficulties. But Divine wisdom hath found a way, namely, by the incarnation of the Son of God. That the Word should be made flesh, that He might be both God and Man, in one person: what created understanding could have conceived that such a thing was possible? Yet these things could never be *proved* to be *impossible*. This distinction, duly considered will show the futility of many Socinian objections.

And if God had revealed to them, that it was possible, and even that it should be, but left them to find out *how* it should be; we may well suppose that they would all have been puzzled and confounded, to conceive of a way for so uniting a man to the eternal Son of God, that they should be but one person; that one who is truly a man in all respects, should indeed be the very same Son of God, that was with God from all eternity. This is a great mystery to us. Hereby, a person that is infinite, omnipotent, and unchangeable, is become, in a sense, a finite, a feeble man; a man subject to our sinless infirmities, passions, and calamities! The great God, the sovereign of heaven and earth, is thus become a worm of the dust: "I am a worm, and no man" *(Psa. 22:6).* He that is eternal and self-existent, is by this union born of a woman! He who is the great original Spirit, is clothed with flesh and blood like one of us! He who is independent, self-sufficient, and all-sufficient, now is come to stand in need of food and clothing: He becomes poor, "hath not where to lay His head"; stands in need of the charity of men, and is maintained by it. It is far above us, to conceive *how* it is done. It is a great wonder and mystery to us; but it was no mystery to Divine wisdom.

4. The next thing to be considered is, the *life* of Christ in this world. The wisdom of God appears in the circumstances of His life, and in the work and business of His life.

(1) The *circumstances* of His life. If God had revealed that His own Son should be incarnate, and should live in this world in the human nature; and it had been left to men to determine what circumstances of life would have been most suitable for Him, human wisdom would have determined that He should appear in the world in a most magnificent manner; with very extraordinary outward ensigns of honor, authority, and power, far above any of the kings of the earth: that here He should reign in great visible pomp and splendor over all nations. And thus it was that men's wisdom *did* determine before Christ came. The wise, the great men among the Jews, Scribes and Pharisees, who are called "princes of this world", *did* expect the Messiah should thus appear. But the wisdom of God shows quite otherwise: it shows that when the Son of God became man; He should begin His life in a stable; for many years dwell obscurely in a family of low degree in the world; and be in low outward circumstances; that He should be poor, and not have where to lay His head: that He should be maintained by the charity of some of His disciples; that He should "grow up as a tender plant, and as a root out of a dry ground" *(Isa. 52:2):* that He should "not cry, nor lift up, nor cause His voice to be heard in the streets" *(Isa. 42:2):* that He should come to Zion in a lowly manner, "riding on an ass, and the colt the foal of an ass": that He should be "despised and rejected of men, a Man of sorrows, and acquainted with grief".

And now the Divine determination in this matter is made known, we may safely conclude that it is far the most suitable; and that it would not have been at all suitable for God, when He was manifest in the flesh, to appear with earthly pomp, wealth, and grandeur. No! these things are infinitely too mean and despicable, for the Son of God to show as if He affected or esteemed them. Men, if they had had this way proposed to them, would have been ready to condemn it as foolish, and very unsuitable to the Son of God. But "the foolishness of God is wiser than men" *(1 Cor. 1: 25),* "and God hath brought to nought the wisdom of this world, and the princes of this world" *(1 Cor. 2:6).* Christ by thus appearing in mean and low outward circumstances in this world, has poured contempt upon all worldly wealth and glory; and has taught us to despise it. And if it becomes mean men to despise them, how much more does it become the Son of God! And then Christ hereby hath taught us to be lowly in heart. If He who is infinitely high and great, was thus lowly; how lowly should we be, who are indeed so vile!

(2) The wisdom of God appears in the *work* and business of the life of Christ. Particularly, that He should obey the law of God, under such great temptations: that He should have conflicts with, and overcome for us, in a way of obedience, the powers of earth and hell; that He should be subject to, not only the *moral* law, but the *ceremonial* also, that heavy yoke of bondage. Christ went through the time of His public ministry, in delivering to us Divine instructions and doctrines. The wisdom of God appears in giving us such a One to be our prophet and teacher, who is a Divine person: who is Himself the very wisdom and word of God; and was from all eternity in the bosom of the Father. His Word is of greater authority and weight than if delivered by the mouth of an ordinary prophet. And how wisely ordered that the same should be our teacher and Redeemer; in order that His relations and offices, as Redeemer, might the more sweeten and endear His instructions to us. We are ready to give heed to what is said by those who are dear to us. Our love to their persons makes us to delight in their discourse. It is therefore wisely ordered, that He who has done so much to endear Him-

self to us, should be appointed our great Prophet, to deliver to us Divine doctrines.

5. The next thing to be considered is the *death* of Christ. This is a means of salvation to poor sinners, that no other but Divine wisdom would have pitched upon; and when revealed, it was doubtless greatly to the surprise of all the hosts of heaven, and they never will cease to wonder at it. How astonishing is it, that a person who is blessed forever, and is infinitely and essentially happy, should endure the greatest sufferings that ever were endured on earth! That a person who is the supreme Lord and Judge of the world, should be arraigned, and should stand at the judgment-seat of mortal worms, and then be condemned. That a person who is the living God, and the Fountain of life, should be put to death. That a person who created the world, and gives life to all His creatures, should be put to death by His own creatures. That a person of infinite majesty and glory, and so the object of the love, praises, and adorations of angels, should be mocked and spit upon by the vilest of men. That a person infinitely good, and who is love itself, should suffer the greatest cruelty. That a person who is infinitely beloved of the Father, should be put to inexpressible anguish under His own Father's wrath. That He who is King of heaven, who hath heaven for His throne, and the earth for His footstool, should be buried in the prison of the grave. How wonderful is this! And yet this is the way that God's wisdom hath fixed upon, as the way of sinners' salvation; as neither unsuitable nor dishonorable to Christ.

6. The last thing done to procure salvation to sinners, is Christ's *exaltation*. Divine wisdom saw it needful, or most expedient, that the same person who died upon the Cross, should sit at His right hand, on His own throne, as Supreme Governor of the world; and should have particularly the absolute disposal of all things relating to man's salvation, and should be the Judge of the world. This was needful, because it was requisite that the same person who purchased salvation, should have the bestowing of it; for it is not fit, that God should at all transact with the fallen creature in a way of mercy, but by a Mediator. And this is exceedingly for the strengthening of the faith and comfort of the saints, that He who hath endured so much to purchase salvation for them, has all things in heaven and in earth delivered unto Him; that He might bestow eternal life on them for whom He purchased it. And that the same person that loved them so greatly as to shed His precious blood for them, was to be their final Judge.

This then was another thing full of wonders, that He who was man as well as God; He who was a servant, and died like a malefactor; should be made the sovereign Lord of heaven and earth, angels and men; the absolute disposer of eternal life and death; the supreme Judge of all created intelligent beings, for eternity: and should have committed to Him all the governing power of God the Father; and that, not only as God, but as the God-Man, not exclusive of the human nature.

As it is wonderful, that a person who is truly *Divine* should be humbled so as to become a servant, and to suffer as a malefactor; so it is in like manner wonderful, that He who is the God-Man, not exclusive of His manhood, should be exalted to the power and honor of the great God of heaven and earth. But such wonders as these has infinite wisdom contrived, and accomplished in order to our salvation.

SECTION II.

In This Way of Salvation God is Greatly Glorified.

God has greatly glorified Himself in the work of creation and providence. All His works praise Him, and His glory shines brightly from them all: but as some stars differ from others in glory, so the glory of God shines brighter in some of His works than others. And amongst all these, the work of redemption is like the sun in his strength. The glory of the Author is abundantly the most resplendent in this work.

I. Each *attribute* of God is glorified in the work of redemption. How God has exceedingly glorified His *wisdom*, may more fully appear before we have done with this subject. But more particularly,

1. God hath exceedingly glorified His *power* in this work. It shows the great and inconceivable power of God to unite natures so infinitely different, as the Divine and human nature, in one person. If God can make one who is truly God, and one that is truly man, the self-same person, what is it that He cannot do? This is a greater and more marvelous work than creation.

The power of God most gloriously appears in man's being actually saved and redeemed in this way. In his being brought out of a state of sin and misery, into a conformity to God; and at last to the full and perfect enjoyment of God. This is a more glorious demonstration of Divine power, than creating things out of nothing, upon two accounts. One is, the *effect is greater and more excellent*. To produce the new creature is a more glorious effect, than merely to produce a creature.—Making a holy creature, a creature in the spiritual image of God, in the image of the Divine excellencies, and a partaker of the Divine nature—is a greater effect than merely to give being. And therefore as the effect is greater, it is a more glorious manifestation of power.

And then, in this effect of the actual redemption of sinners, *the term from which, is more distant from the term to which,* than in the work of creation. The term from which, in the work of creation, is *nothing*, and the term to which, is *being*. But the term from which, in the work of redemption, is a state *infinitely worse than nothing*, and the term to which, *a holy and a happy being*, a state infinitely better than mere being. The terms in the production of the last, are much more remote from one another than in the first.

And then the production of this last effect, is a more glorious manifestation of power than the work of creation; because, though in creation, the terms are very distant—as *nothing* is very remote from *being*—yet there is no opposition. "Nothing" makes no opposition to the creating power of God. But in redemption, the Divine power *does* meet with and overcome great opposition. There is a great opposition in a state of sin to a state of grace. Men's lusts and corruptions are exceedingly opposite to grace and holiness; and greatly resist the production of the effect. But this opposition is completely overcome in actual redemption.

Besides, there is great opposition from Satan. The power of God is very glorious in this work, because it therein conquers the strongest and most powerful enemies. Power never appears more illustrious than in conquering. Jesus Christ, in this work, conquers and triumphs over thousands of demons, strong and mighty spirits, uniting all their strength against Him: "When a strong man armed keepeth his palace, his goods are in peace: but when a stronger than he shall overcome him, he taketh from him all his armour wherein he trusted and divideth his spoil" *(Luke 11:21)*. "And having spoiled principalities and powers, He made a show of them openly, *triumphing over them* in the Cross" *(Col. 2:15)*.

2. The *justice* of God is exceedingly glorified in this work. God is so strictly and immutably just, that He would not spare His beloved Son when He took upon Him the guilt of men's sins, and was substituted in the room of sinners. He would not abate Him the least mite of that debt which justice demanded. Justice should take place, though it cost His infinitely dear Son His precious blood; and His enduring such extraordinary reproach, and pain, and death in its most dreadful form.

3. The *holiness* of God is also exceedingly glorious in this work. Never did God so manifest His hatred of sin as in the death and sufferings of His only begotten Son. Hereby He showed Himself unappeasable to sin, and that it was impossible for Him to be at peace with it.

4. God hath also exceedingly glorified His *truth* in this way, both in His threatenings and promises. Herein is fulfilled the threatenings of the law, wherein God said, "In the day thou eatest thereof thou shalt surely die". And "cursed is every one that continueth not in all things written in the book of the law to do them". God showed hereby, that not only heaven and earth should pass away, but, which is more, that the blood of Him who is the eternal Jehovah should be spilt, rather than that one jot or tittle of His word should fail, till all be fulfilled.

5. And lastly, God has exceedingly glorified His *mercy* and *love* in this work. The mercy of God was an attribute never seen before in its exercise, till it was seen in this work of redemption, or the fruits of it. The goodness of God appeared toward the angels in giving them being and blessedness. It appeared glorious toward man in his primitive state, a state of holiness and happiness. But now God hath shown that He can find in His heart to love sinners who deserve His infinite hatred. And not only hath He shown that He can love them, but loved them so as to give them more and do greater things for them than ever He did for the holy angels, that never

sinned nor offended their Creator. He loved sinful men so as to give them a greater gift than ever He gave the angels; so as to give His own Son, and not only to give Him to be their possession and enjoyment, but to give Him to be their sacrifice. And herein He has done more for them, than if He had given them all the visible worlds; yea, more than if He had given them all the angels, and all heaven besides. God hath loved them so, that hereby He purchased for them deliverance from eternal misery, and the possession of immortal glory.

II. Each *person* of the Trinity is exceedingly glorified in this work. Herein the work of redemption is distinguished from all the other works of God. The attributes of God are glorious in His other works; but the three persons of the Trinity are distinctly glorified in no work as in this of redemption. In this work every distinct person has His distinct parts and offices assigned Him. Each one has His particular and distinct concern in it, agreeable to their distinct, personal properties, relations, and economical offices. The redeemed have an equal concern with and dependence upon each person in this affair, and owe equal honor and praise to each of them.

The Father appoints and provides the Redeemer, and accepts the price of redemption. The Son is the Redeemer and the price. He redeems by offering up Himself. The Holy Spirit immediately communicates to us the thing purchased; yea, and He is the good purchased. The sum of what Christ purchased for us is holiness and happiness. The Holy Spirit is the sum of all that Christ purchased for man: "He was made a curse for us, that we might receive the promise of the Spirit, through faith" *(Gal. 3:13, 14).*

The blessedness of the redeemed consists in partaking of Christ's fulness which consists in partaking of that Spirit, which is given not by measure unto Him. This is the oil that was poured upon the Head of the church, which ran down to the members of His body, to the skirts of His garment. Thus we have an equal concern with and dependence upon each of the persons of the Trinity, distinctly; upon the Father, as He provides the Redeemer, and the person of whom the purchase is made; the Son as the purchaser, and the price; the Holy Spirit as the good promised.—*Jonathan Edwards.*

(*To be continued, D. V.*).

THE BELIEVER'S RESPONSE TO THE WORDS OF THE SAVIOUR.

I have been much impressed lately with the rich and varied fullness of the written Word of God, and its nice adaptation to our every want. I have specially observed that the Holy Spirit not only *bears to* us the words of Jesus, and *applies* them to our heart according to our need, but that He also *gives us discernment* of their suitableness, and then *supplies* the very words in which we may respond; and then, further, as we respond, *brings, by the response itself,* deeper comfort to our aching hearts, and fills the void in us from the Saviour's fulness.

Let me endeavor to illustrate this by some examples from the Christian's favorite Psalm *(23);* viewing some of its sentences as responses to certain words of Christ.

The Lord says, "I am the Good Shepherd". The saint in Christ answers, "The Lord is my Shepherd, I shall not want".

The Lord says, "The Good Shepherd giveth His life for the sheep"; and hearken: He says again, "By Me if any one enter in, he shall be saved, and shall go in and out, and find pasture". What shall I say to this? Here is the answer of my soul: "I shall not want: He maketh me to lie down in green pastures: He leadeth me beside the still waters".

The Lord saith, "He that is *bathed* needeth not save to wash his feet . . . Know ye what I have done unto you?" (*cf. John 13 with 1 John 1:9-2:1*). Now what shall I say to this? I will say, "He restoreth my soul, and maketh me to walk in the paths of righteousness for His name's sake". What a pledge I here confess, *"His name!".* It is a large, long name—for what we call His *names,* are, I may say, and with reverence, but syllables of His Name. Well, then, "Good Shepherd", "Great Shepherd of the sheep" are precious syllables of that *Name,* for the sake of which He will "*make* me walk in the paths of righteousness".

But let me not pass away from this word too rapidly. By what means will He make me, and thee, my fellow-saint, to walk in the paths of righteousness? It is thus: "And when He putteth forth His own sheep, *He goeth before them,* and the sheep hear His *voice*". "My sheep", says the Lord Jesus, "hear My *voice,* and I know them, and they follow Me." I know My sheep and am known of Mine". He knows them, they know Him; He goes before them, they follow Him; He speaks, they know His voice and *hear* it. *So* He "maketh them to walk". May we keep the eye fixed on Him, the ear opened to His voice.

But now He speaks again, "He that followeth Me shall not walk in darkness, but shall have the light of life". Nay, more than this, He is saying: "I am the Resurrection and the Life: he that believeth in Me though he were dead yet shall he live, and whosoever liveth and believeth in Me shall never die". And still He speaks: Ah, He is asking, "Believest thou this?" What response shall I give? I have already ofttimes, when He so spake, and I would, and do here and now, confess to Him: "Yea, Lord: I believe that Thou art the Christ, the Son of God which should come into the world". But I know that He wants a further answer now, for He is repeating these words to my soul, evidently in exact adaptation to the dark path by which He is leading me, down in the deep vale of humiliation, where but for His sweet voice uttering words of life, I hear only the echoes of death. And here the Spirit supplies the very words which *match* those of my Lord to me: "Yea, though I walk through the valley of the shadow of death, I will fear no evil: for Thou art with me; Thy rod and Thy staff they comfort me".

Furthermore, He said to me, when I came to Him perishing with hunger, "He that cometh to Me shall never hunger, and he that believeth on Me shall never thirst". Thou hast exceeded Thy word, O Christ, and I may well say to Thee, blessed Lord, "Thou preparest a table before me in the presence of mine enemies: Thou anointest my head with oil: my cup runneth over".

Nay, more, Thou hast anticipated all my need: "What shall I eat and what shall I drink, and wherewithal shall I be clothed?" Thou sayest, "Your Father knoweth that ye have need of all these things. Seek ye first the kingdom of God and His righteousness *and all these things shall be added unto you".* Good is Thy word, and therefore I will say, "Surely goodness and mercy shall follow me all the days of my life".

Crowning all Thy words of love which Thou hast spoken to my troubled heart, is this one superior word, "In my Father's house are many mansions: if it were not so I would have told you: I go to prepare a place for you. And if I go and prepare a place for you, I will come again, and receive you unto Myself; that where I am there ye may be also". So Thou hast spoken; and I will crown all my confession of Thine unfathomable love with this one word, *"And I will dwell in the house of the Lord forever".*

Dear fellow-partners in the affliction and kingdom and patience of Jesus, may He fill you with His comfortable words, and cause your lips to overflow with responsive songs —songs supplied by Himself. For after this fashion He "giveth songs in the night".
—*Charles Campbell, 1871.*

Although the main matter of regeneration lies within, yet it manifests itself without. Say, then, has there been a change in you in the exterior? Do you think that others who look at you would be compelled to say, This man is not what he used to be? Do not your companions observe a change? Have they not laughed at you for what they think to be your hypocrisy, your puritanism, your sternness? Do you think now that if an angel should follow you into your secret life, should track you to your closet and see you on your knees, that he would detect something in you that he could never have seen before? For, mark, there must be a change in the outward life, or else there has been no change within. In vain you bring me to the tree, and say that the tree's nature is changed. If I still see it bringing forth wild grapes, it is a wild vine still. And if I mark upon you the apples of Sodom and the grapes of Gomorrah, you are still a tree accursed and doomed, notwithstanding all your fancied experience. The proof of the Christian is in the living. To other men, the proof of our conversation is not what we feel but what we do.—*C. H. Spurgeon.*

VOL. I JUNE, 1922 NO. 6.

STUDIES in the SCRIPTURES

"Search the Scriptures" John 5:39.

A PERIODICAL (MONTHLY "IF THE LORD WILL")
DEVOTED TO BIBLE STUDIES and EXPOSITIONS

Associate Editors and Publishers, I. C. HERENDEEN and ARTHUR W. PINK,
Swengel, Pa.

Price: 10 cents per copy; $1.00 per year. Foreign $1.00 per year.

TO OUR SCRIPTURE STUDY FAMILY

It is our desire to offer a few remarks in this editorial upon how to read this magazine to the best advantage. Perhaps they are not needed by many of our readers, but possibly there are others who will find them timely.

Those who have given a careful reading to the first five issues will have discovered that *Studies in the Scriptures* differs, in several respects, from many other religious periodicals. There is little in this publication that will appeal to the popular reader. Our purpose is not to entertain but to instruct. We are not writing for the great mass of superficial people, who have no capacity for anything save that which is shallow; but are seeking to minister to those who have a hunger for the deeper things of God, and who are prepared to make a sacrifice to obtain these.

If this magazine be read as a newspaper is read, little profit to the soul will be obtained. What we solicit from our subscribers is this: First, that before taking up any article herein the reader will lift up his or her heart to God, and earnestly ask Him for a spirit of discernment to recognize His truth and an open heart to receive it. Second, that to this end the reader will study each article with an open Bible before him, turning to each passage quoted to see whether or not the writer *proves* what he says by a "thus saith the Lord". And third, that he read slowly, critically and thoughtfully what is presented in these pages.

God has said in His Word, "He that believeth shall not make haste" *(Isa. 28:16)*, and if ever there was a time when His children needed to give special heed to this admonition it is now. The children of God are infected with the spirit of the world. The mad rush which characterizes everything around us: the awful hustle and bustle of the ungodly as they rush headlong to eternal death, has affected the members of the Household of Faith; and few, if any of us, are free from it. One of our most urgent needs is to be *delivered from* this *feverish* spirit, for it is rapidly sapping the spiritual vitality of many of God's people. The irreverent speed at which the Holy Scriptures are read in the average pulpit; the rate at which sacred songs are commonly sung; the unholy manner in which many rush into the presence of the Most High God, and gabble off the first words that come to their lips, are so many examples of this infection. And, alas, the same spirit possesses most of us when we read the Word of God, and expositions of that Word. We earnestly ask our readers to make a prayerful study of the words "stand", "sit", "wait", "tarry" as they are found in Holy Writ.

The title of this magazine implies that it is designed not for lazy people, or for those who are so busily occupied with the things of this world, that they have no time (in reality, *no heart*) for the things of God. No, it is published for the benefit of those who are, or who wish to become, *students* of Scripture. The articles herein call for study, thoughtful perusal, prolonged meditation.

Finally, let not this magazine become a substitute for your own daily study of God's Word: rather let it be an incentive for further search on *your* part to discover the priceless treasures hidden therein.

"And now, brethren, I commend you to God, and to the Word of His grace, which is able *to build you up*, and to give you an inheritance among them which are sanctified" *(Acts 20:31).*

Yours in the Fellowship of the Word,
Arthur W. Pink.

STUDIES IN THE SCRIPTURES

Subscription Price: **$1.00** per year to any address in the world. Single copies 10 cents.

Change of Address: Please notify us promptly of any change of address, and be certain to give both old and new addresses.

Non-Subscribers receiving this Magazine regularly will understand their subscription has been entered by a friend.

Copies lost in the mail duplicated on request.

All new subscriptions will be dated back to January, 1922.

Entered as second-class matter December 15th, 1921 at the post office at Swengel, Pa., under Act of March 3rd, 1879.

CONTENTS

The Papacy not the Antichrist	110
John's Gospel (2:1-11)	116
The Wisdom of God Displayed in the Way of Salvation	123
Confidence in the Lord	131
Human Depravity	131

THE PAPACY NOT THE ANTICHRIST

"I am come in My Father's name, and ye receive Me not: if another shall come in his own name, him ye will receive" *(John 5:43)*. These words were spoken by the Lord Jesus Christ, and the occasion on which they were uttered and the connection in which they are found, invest them with peculiar solemnity. The chapter opens by depicting the Saviour healing the impotent man who lay by the pool of Bethesda. This occurred on the Sabbath day, and the enemies of Christ made it the occasion for a vicious attack upon Him: "Therefore did the Jews persecute Jesus, and sought to slay Him, because He had done these things on the Sabbath day" *(v. 16)*. In vindicating His performance of this miracle on the Sabbath, the Lord Jesus began by saying, "My Father worketh hitherto, and I work" *(v. 17)*. But this only served to intensify their enmity against Him, for we read, "Therefore the Jews sought the more to kill Him, because He not only had broken the Sabbath, but said also that God was His Father, making Himself equal with God" *(v. 18)*. In response, Christ then made a detailed declaration of His Divine glories. In conclusion He appealed to the varied witnesses which bore testimony to His Deity:—the Father Himself *(v. 32)*; John the Baptist *(v. 33)*; His own works *(v. 36)*; and the Scriptures *(v. 39)*. Then He turned to those who were opposing Him and said, "And ye will not come to Me, that ye might have life. But I know you, that ye have not the love of God in you. I am come in My Father's name, and ye receive Me not: if another shall come in his own name, him ye will receive" *(vv. 40, 42, 43)*. And this was immediately followed by this searching question—"How can ye believe which receive honor (glory) one of another, and seek not the honor (glory) that cometh from God only?" *(v. 44)*.

Here is the key to the solemn statement which begins this article. These Jews received glory from one another; they did not seek it from God, for they had not the love of God in them. Therefore it was that the One who had come to them in the Father's name, and who "received *not* glory from men" *(v. 41)* was rejected by them. And just as Eve's rejection of the word of God's truth laid her open to accept the serpent's lie, so Israel's *rejection* of the true Messiah has prepared them, morally, to *receive* the false Messiah, for he will come in his own name, doing his own pleasure, and *will* "receive glory from men". Thus will he thoroughly appeal to the corrupt heart of the natural man.

The future appearing of this one who shall "come in his own name" was announced, then, by the Lord Himself. The Antichrist will be "received", not only by the Jews, but also by the whole world; received as their acknowledged Head and Ruler; and all the modern pleas for and movements to bring about a federation of the churches and a union of Christendom, together with the present-day efforts to establish a League of Nations—a great United States of the World—are but preparing the way for just such a character as is portrayed both in the Old and New Testaments.

There will be many remarkable correspondences between the true and the false Christ, but more numerous and more striking will be the *contrasts* between the Son of God and the Son of Perdition. The Lord Jesus came down from Heaven, whereas the Antichrist shall ascend from the bottomless Pit *(Rev. 11:7)*. The Lord Jesus came in His Father's name, emptied Himself of His glory, lived in absolute dependence upon God, and refused to receive honor from men; but the Man of Sin will come in his own name, embodying all the pride of the Devil, opposing and exalting himself not only against the true God, but against everything that bears His name, and his deepest craving will be to receive honor and homage from men.

Now since this parallel, with its pointed contrasts, was drawn by our Lord Himself in John 5:43, how conclusive is the proof which it affords that the Antichrist will be a single individual being as surely as Christ was! In further proof of this I John 2:18 may be cited: "Little children, it is the last hour: and as ye heard that Antichrist cometh, even now hath there arisen many antichrists; whereby we know that it is the last hour" *(R. V.)*. Here *the* Antichrist is plainly distinguished from the many who prepare his way. The verb "cometh" here is a remarkable one, for it is the very same that is used of the Lord Jesus Christ in reference to *His* first and second Advents. The Antichrist, therefore, is also "the coming one", or "he that cometh". This defines his relation *to the world*—which has long been expecting some Conquering Hero—as "the Coming One" defines the relation of the Christ of God *to His Churches*, whose Divinely inspired hope is the return of the Lord from Heaven.

Nor does this by any means exhaust the proof that the coming Antichrist will be a single individual being. The expressions used by the apostle Paul in 2 Thess. 2—"the Man of Sin", "The Son of Perdition", "he that opposeth and exalteth himself", "the Wicked One whom the Lord shall consume with the spirit of His mouth", "he whose coming is after the working of Satan"—all these point as distinctly to a single individual as did the Messianic predictions of the Old Testament point to the person of our Lord Jesus Christ.

Now, in accordance with these texts, and many others which might be quoted, we find that all the Christian writers of the first six centuries (that is all who make reference to the subject) regarded the Antichrist as a real person, a specific individual. We might fill many pages by giving extracts from their works, but three must suffice. The first is taken from a very ancient document, entitled "The Teaching of the Apostles", which probably dates back to the beginning of the second century:—

"For in the last days the false prophets and the destroyers shall be multiplied, and the sheep shall be turned into wolves, and love shall be turned into hate. For when lawlessness increases, they shall hate and persecute and deliver up one another; and then shall appear the world-deceiver as Son of God, who shall do signs and wonders, and the earth shall be delivered into his hands, and he shall do lawless deeds such as have never yet been done since the beginning of the world. Then shall the race of men come into the fire of trial, and many shall be offended and shall perish, but they who have endured in their faith shall be saved under the very curse itself".

Our second quotation is taken from the writings of Cyril, who was Bishop of Jerusalem in the fourth century:

"This aforementioned Antichrist comes when the times of the sovereignty of the Romans shall be fulfilled, and the concluding events of the world draw nigh. Ten kings of the Romans arise at the same time in different places, perhaps; but reigning at the same period. But after these, the Antichrist is the eleventh, having, by his magic and evil skill, violently possessed himself of the Roman power. Three of those who have reigned before him, he will subdue; the other seven he will hold in subjection to himself. At first he assumes a character of gentleness (as if a wise and understanding person), pretending both to moderation and philanthropy; deceiving, both by lying miracles and prodigies which come from his magical deceptions, the Jews, as if he were the expected Messiah. Afterwards he will addict himself to every kind of evil, cruelty, and excess, so as to surpass all who have been unjust and impious before him; having a bloody and relentless and pitiless mind, and full of wily devices against all, and especially against believers. But having dared such things three years and six months, he will be destroyed by the second glorious coming from heaven of the truly begotten Son of God, who is our Lord and Saviour, Jesus the true Messiah; who, having, destroyed Antichrist by the Spirit of His mouth, will deliver him to the fire Gehenna".

Our last quotation is made from the

writings of Gregory of Tours, who wrote at the end of the sixth century A. D.:—

"Concerning the end of the world, I believe what I have learnt from those who have gone before me. Antichrist will assume circumcision, asserting himself to be the Christ. He will then place a statue to be worshipped in the Temple at Jerusalem, as we read that the Lord has said, 'Ye shall see the abomination of desolation standing in the holy place'".

Our purpose in making these quotations is not because we regard the voice of antiquity as being in any degree authoritative: far from it; the *only* authority for us is "What saith the Scriptures?". Nor have we presented these views as curious relics of antiquity—though it is interesting to discover the thoughts which occupied some of the leading minds of past ages. No; our purpose has been simply to show that the early Christian writers uniformly held that the Antichrist would be a real person, a Jew, one who should both simulate and oppose the true Christ. Such continued to be the generally received doctrine until what is known as the Dark Ages were far advanced.

It is not until we reach the fourteenth century (so far as the writer is aware) that we find the first marked deviation from the uniform belief of the early Christians. It was the Waldenses,—so remarkably sound in the faith on almost all points of doctrine—who, thoroughly worn out by centuries of the most relentless and merciless persecutions, published about the year 1350 a treatise designed to prove that the system of Popery was the Antichrist. It should however be said in honor of this people, whose memory is blessed, that in one of their earliest books entitled "The Noble Lesson", published about 1100 A. D., they taught that the Antichrist was an individual rather than a system.

Following the new view espoused by the Waldenses it was not long before the Hussites, the Wycliffites and the Lollards —other companies of Christians who were fiercely persecuted by Rome—eagerly caught up the idea, and proclaimed that the Pope was the Man of Sin and the papacy the Beast. From them it was handed on to the leaders of the Reformation who soon made an earnest attempt to systematize this new scheme of eschatology. But rarely has there been a more forcible example of the tendency of men's beliefs to be moulded by the events and signs of their own lifetime. In order to adapt the prophecies of the Antichrist to the Papal hierarchy, or the line of the Popes, they had to be so wrested that scarcely anything was left of their original meaning.

"The coming Man of Sin had to be changed into a long succession of men. The time of his continuance, which God had started with precision and clearness as forty-two months *(Rev. 13:5)*, or three years and a half, being far too short for the line of Popes, had to be lengthened by an ingenious, but most unwarrantable process of first resolving it into days, and then turning these days into years.

"The fact that, in the 13th chapter of the Apocalypse, the first Beast or secular power, is supreme while the second Beast or ecclesiastical power is subordinate, had to be ignored; since such an arrangement is opposed to all the traditions of the Roman system. Also the circumstances that the second Beast is a prophet and not a priest, had to be kept in the background; for the Roman church exalts the priest, and has little care for the prophet. Then, again, the awful words pronouncing sentence of death upon every one who worshipped the Beast and his image, and receives his mark in his forehead or in his hand *(Rev. 13)*, seemed—and no wonder—too terrible to be applied to every Roman Catholic, and, therefore, had to be explained away or suppressed" *(G. H. Pember).*

Nevertheless, by common consent the Reformers applied the prophecies which treat of the character, career, and doom of the Antichrist, to Popery, and regarded those of his titles which referred to him as "the Man of Sin, the Son of Perdition", the "King of Babylon" and "the Beast", as only so many names for the head of the Roman hierarchy. But this view, which was upheld by most of the Puritans too, must be brought to the test of the one infallible standard of Truth which our gracious God has placed in our hands. We must search the Scriptures to see whether these things be so or not.

Now we shall hold no brief for the pope, nor have we anything good to say of that pernicious system of which he is the head. On the contrary, we have no hesitation in denouncing as rank blasphemy the blatent assumption of the pope as being the infallible vicar of Christ. Nor do we hesitate to declare that the Papacy has been marked, all through its long history, by impious arrogance, awful idolatry, and unspeakable cruelty. But, nevertheless, there are many scriptures which prevent us from believing that the Papacy and the Antichrist are indentical. The Son of Perdition will eclipse any monstrosities that have sprung from the waves of the Tiber. The Bible plainly teaches us to look for a more terrible personage than any Hildebrand or Leo.

Undoubtedly there are many points of analogy between Antichrist and the popes, and without doubt the Papal system has foreshadowed to a remarkable degree the character and career of the coming Man of Sin. Some of the parallelisms between them were pointed out by us in the previous paper, and to these many more might be added. Not only is it evident that Roman Catholicism is a most striking type and harbinger of that one yet to come, but the cause of truth requires us to affirm that the Papacy is an *antichrist,* doubtless, the most devilish of them all. Yet, we say again, that Romanism is not *the* Antichrist. As it is likely that many of our readers have been educated in the belief that the pope and the Antichrist are identical, we shall proceed to produce some of the numerous proofs which go to show that such is not the case. That the Papacy cannot possibly be the Antichrist appears from the following considerations:—

1. The term "Antichrist" whether employed in the singular or the plural, denotes a person or persons, and *never a system.* We could speak correctly of an anti-Christ*ian* system, just as we may refer to a Christian organization; but it is just as inadmissible and erroneous to refer to any system or organization as "the Antichrist" or "an antichrist", as it would be to denominate any Christian system or organization "the Christ", or "a Christ". Just as truly as *the Christ* is the title of a single person, the Son of God, so *the Antichrist* will be a single person, the son of Satan.

2. The Antichrist will be a lineal descendant of Abraham, *a Jew.* We shall not stop to submit the proof for this, as that will be given in our next article, D. V.; suffice it now to say that none but a full-blooded Jew could ever expect to palm himself off on the Jewish people as their long-expected Messiah. Here is an argument that has never been met by those who believe that the pope is the Man of Sin. So far as we are aware no Israelite has ever occupied the Papal See —certainly none has done so since the seventh century.

3. In line with the last argument, we read in Zech. 11:16, 17, "For, lo, I will raise up a Shepherd *in the land,* which shall not visit those that be cut off, neither shall seek the young ones, nor heal that that is broken, nor feed that that standeth still: but he shall eat the flesh of the fat, and tear their claws in pieces. Woe to the Idol Shepherd that leaveth the flock! The sword (of Divine judgment) shall be upon his arm (his power), and upon his right eye (intelligence): his arm shall be clean dried up, and his right eye shall be utterly darkened". *"The* land" here is, of course, Palestine, as is ever the case in Scripture with this expression. This could not possibly apply to the line of the Popes.

4. In 2 Thess. 2:4 we learn that the Man of Sin shall sit "in the Temple of God", and St. Peter's at Rome cannot possibly be called *that*. The "Temple" in which the Antichrist shall sit will be the rebuilt temple of the Jews, and that will be located not in Italy but in Jerusalem. In later articles it will be shown that the Mosque of Omar shall yet be replaced by a Jewish Temple before our Lord returns to the earth.

5. The Antichrist will be *received by the Jews*. This is clear from the passage which heads the first paragraph of this article: "I am come in My Father's name, and ye receive Me not: if another shall come in his own name, him *ye* will receive"; but the *Jews* have never yet owned allegiance to any pope.

6. The Antichrist will make a Covenant with the Jews. In Dan. 9:27 we read, "And he shall confirm the covenant with many for one week". The one referred to here as making this seven-year Covenant is "the Prince that shall come" of the previous verse, namely, the Antichrist, who will be the Head of the ten-kingdomed Empire. The nation with whom the Prince will make this covenant is the people of Daniel, as is clear from the context—see v. 24. But we know of no

record upon the scroll of history of any pope having ever made a seven-year Covenant with the Jews!

7. In Dan. 11:45 we read, "And he shall plant the tabernacles of his palace between the seas, in the glorious holy mountain; yet he shall come to his end, and none shall help him". The person referred to here is, again, the Antichrist, as will be seen by going back to v. 36 where this section of the chapter begins. There we are told, "The king shall do according to his will; and he shall exalt himself, and magnify himself above every god, and shall speak marvelous things against the God of gods, and shall prosper till the indignation be accomplished; for that that is determined shall be done". This is more than sufficient to identify with certainty the one spoken of in the last verse of Dan. 11. The Antichrist, then, will plant the tabernacles of his palace "between the seas", that is, between the Mediterranean and the Red Sea. By no species of ingenuity can this be made to apply to the pope, for his palace, the Vatican, is located in the capital city of Italy.

8. The Antichrist cannot be revealed until the mystic Body of Christ and the Holy Spirit have been removed from the earth. This is made clear by what we read in 2 Thess. 2. In verse three of that chapter the apostle refers to the revelation of the Man of Sin. In verse four he describes his awful impiety. In verse five he reminds the Thessalonians how that he had taught them these things by word of mouth when he was with them. And then, in verse six he declares "And now ye know what withholdeth that he might be revealed in his time". And again he said, "For the mystery of iniquity doth already work: only He who now letteth (hindereth) will let until He be taken out of the way". There are two agencies, then, which are hindering, or preventing the manifestation of the Antichrist, until "his time" shall have come. The former agency is covered by the pronoun "what", the latter by the word "He". The former, we are satisfied, is the mystical Body of Christ; the latter being the Holy Spirit of God. At the Rapture both shall be "taken out of the way", and then shall the Man of Sin be revealed. If, then, the Antichrist cannot appear before the Rapture of the saints and the taking away of the Holy Spirit, then, here is proof positive that the Antichrist *has not yet appeared*.

9. Closely akin to the last argument is the fact that quite a number of definite scriptures place the appearing of the Antichrist at that season known as the End-Time. Dan. 7 and 8 make it plain that the Antichrist will run his career at the very end of this age (we do not say this 'dispensation' for *that* will end at the Rapture), that is, during the great Tribulation, the time of "Jacob's trouble". Dan. 7:21-23 declares, "I beheld, and the same horn made war with the saints, and prevailed against them; Until the Ancient of days came, and judgment was given to the saints of the Most High; and the time came that the saints possessed the kingdom". Dan. 8:19 places his course *(see 8:23-25)* at "the last end of the indignation", i. e. of God's wrath against Israel and the Gentiles. Dan. 9 shows that he will make his seven-years' Covenant with the Jews at the beginning of the last of the seventy "Weeks" which is to bring in "the end" of Israel's sins and "finish the transgression" *(9:24)*. If the time of the Antichrist's manifestation is yet future then it necessarily follows that Rome cannot be the Antichrist.

10. The Antichrist will deny both the Father and the Son: "He is Antichrist, that denieth the Father and the Son" *(I John 2:22)*. This scripture does not speak of virtual, but of actual and formal denial. But Rome has always maintained in her councils and creeds, her systems of faith and worship, that there are three persons in the Godhead. Numerous and grievous have been her departures from the teaching of Holy Scripture, yet since the time of the Council of Trent *(1563 A. D.)* every Roman Catholic has had to confess "I believe in God the Father . . . . and in the Lord Jesus Christ . . . . and in the Holy Ghost, the Lord and Giver of life, which proceedeth from the **Father** and the Son".

As a system Romanism is a go-between. The 'priest' stands between the sinner and God; the 'confession' between him and the throne of grace; 'penance' between him and godly sorrow; the 'mass' between him and Christ; and 'purgatory' between him and Heaven. The pope acknowledges both the Father and the Son: he confesses himself to be both the servant of God and His worshipper; he blesses the people not in his own name, but in that of the Holy Trinity.

11. The Antichrist is described as the one "who opposeth and exalteth himself above all that is called God, or that is worshipped; so that he as God sitteth in the Temple of God, showing himself that he is God" *(2 Thess. 2:4)*. This is what the popes have never done. Not even Leo ventured to deify himself or supersede God. The popes have made many false and impious claims for themselves; nevertheless, their decrees have been sent forth as from the 'vice-gerent' of God, the 'vicar' of Christ—thus acknowledging a Divine power *above* himself.

12. In Rev. 13:2, 4 we read, "And the beast which I saw was like unto a leopard, and his feet were as the feet of a bear, and his mouth as the mouth of a lion: and *the dragon gave him* his power, and his seat, and great authority .... and they *worshipped the dragon* which gave power unto the beast". By comparing these verses with Rev. 12:9 we learn that the Dragon is none other than Satan himself. Now by almost common consent this first beast of Rev. 13 is the Antichrist. If, then, Romanism be the Antichrist, where, we may ask, shall we turn to find anything answering to what we read of here in Rev. 13:4—"And they *worshipped the dragon* which gave power unto the beast"!

13. This same 13th chapter of Revelation informs us that the Antichrist (the first Beast) shall be *aided* by a second Beast who is denominated "the False Prophet" *(Rev. 19:20)*. The False Prophet, we are told "exerciseth all the power of the First Beast before him, and causeth the earth and them which dwell therein to worship the *First* Beast" *(Rev. 13:12)*. If the First Beast be the Papacy, then who is the False Prophet who "causeth the earth and them which dwell therein to worship" her?

14. Again; we are told that this False Prophet shall say to them that dwell on the earth "that they should make an image to the Beast, which had the wound by a sword and did live" *(Rev. 13:14)*. Further, we are told, "And he had power to give life unto the image of the Beast, that the image of the Beast should both speak, and cause that as many as would not worship the image of the Beast should be killed" *(Rev. 13:15)*. Where do we find anything in Popery which in anywise resembles this?

15. In Dan. 9:27 we are told that the Antichrist "shall cause the *sacrifice* and the *oblation* to *cease*". And again in 8:11 we read, "Yea, he magnified himself even against the Prince of the host, and by him the daily sacrifice was *taken away*". If Romanism is the Antichrist how can these scriptures be made to square with the oft repeated *"Sacrifice* of the Mass"?

16. The *dominion* of the Antichrist shall be *world-wide*. The coming Man of Sin will assert a supremacy which shall be unchallenged and universal. "And all the world wondered after the Beast" *(Rev. 13:3)*. "And power was given him over *all* kindreds, and tongues, and nations" *(13:7)*. It hardly needs to be pointed out that half of Christendom, to say nothing of Heathendom, is *outside* the pale of Rome, and is antagonistic to the claims of the Papacy. Again; in 13:17 we read "No man might buy or sell, save he that had the mark, or the name of the Beast, or the number of his name": and when, we ask, has any pope exercised such commercial supremacy that *none* could buy or sell without his permission?

17. The *duration* of Antichrist's career, after he comes out in his true character, will be *limited* to forty-two months. There are no less than six scriptures which, with a variety of expression, affirm this time restriction. In Dan. 7:25 we learn that this one who shall "speak great words against the Most High", and who shall "think to change times and laws," will have these "given into his hand until a time, and times, and the dividing of time:" that is, for three years and a half—cf. Rev. 12:14 with 12:6. And again in Rev. 13:5 we are told, "And there was given unto him a mouth speaking great things and blasphemies; and power was given unto him to continue *forty and two months*" *(Rev. 13:5)*. Now it is utterly impossible to make this harmonize with the protracted history of Romanism by any honest method of computation,

18. In Rev. 13:7, 8 we read, "And it was given unto him to make war with the saints, and to overcome them: and power was given him over all kindreds, and tongues, and nations. And *all* that dwell upon the face of the earth shall worship him, *whose names are not written* in the

book of life of the Lamb slain from the foundation of the world." Here we are expressly told that the only ones who will not "worship the Beast", i. e. the Antichrist, are they whose names are written in the Lamb's book of life. If then the pope is the Antichrist, all who do not worship him must have their names written in the Lamb's book of life—an absurdity on the face of it, for this would be tantamount to saying that all the infidels, atheists, and unbelievers of the last thousand years who were outside of the pale of Roman Catholicism are saved.

19. In 2 Thess. 2:11, 12 we are told, "For this cause God shall send them strong delusion, that they should believe a lie: that *they all* might be damned who believed not the truth, but had pleasure in unrighteousness". The context here shows that "believing a lie" means accepting the claims of the Antichrist. Those who believe his claims will "receive" him *(John 5:43)*, and not only so, they will "worship" him *(Rev. 13:8)*; and 2 Thess. 2: 12 declares that *"all"* who do this will be "damned". If, then, the pope is the Antichrist, then it necessarily follows that *all* who have "believed" his lying claims, that *all* who have "received" him as the vicar of Christ, that, *all* who have "worshipped" him, will be eternally lost. But the writer would not for a moment make any such sweeping assertion. He, together with thousands of others, believes firmly that during the centuries there have been many Roman Catholics who, despite much ignorance and superstition, have been among that number that have exercised faith in the blood of Christ, and that lived and died resting on the finished work of Christ as the alone ground of their acceptance before God, and who because of this shall be forever with the Lord.

20. That the Antichrist and the Papacy are totally distinct is unequivocally established by the teaching of Rev. 17. Here we learn that there shall be ten kings who will reign "with the Beast" *(v. 12)*, and act in concert with him *(vv. 13, 16)*. Then we are told "these shall hate the Whore (the papacy), and shall make her desolate and naked, and shall eat her flesh, and burn her with fire" *(v. 16)*. Instead of the Antichrist and the Papacy being identical, the former shall destroy the latter; whereas, the Antichrist shall be destroyed by Christ Himself, see 2 Thess. 2:8.

Perhaps a word of explanation is called for as to why we have entered into such lengthy details in presenting some of the many proofs that the Papacy is not the Antichrist. Our chief reason for doing so was because we expect that many who will read this paper are among the number who have been brought up in the belief which was commonly taught by the Reformers and which has prevailed generally since their day. For those readers who had already been established on this point, we would ask them to please bear with us for having sought to help those less fortunate. Our next paper, D. V., will be one of more general interest, for in it we shall discuss the *person* of the Antichrist—*who* he will be, from *whence* he will spring, and what marks will serve to *identify* him.—*Authur W. Pink.*

JOHN'S GOSPEL

6. CHRIST'S FIRST MIRACLE—John 2:1-11.

First of all we will give a brief and simple Analysis of the passage before us:—

1. The Occasion of the Miracle: a marriage in Cana v. 1.
2. The Presence there of the Mother of Jesus v. 2.
3. The Saviour and His Disciples Invited v. 2.
4. Mary's Interference and Christ's Rebuke vv. 3, 4.
5. Mary's Submission v. 5.
6. The Miracle Itself vv. 6-8.
7. The Effects of the Miracle vv. 9-11.

We propose to expound the passage before us from a threefold viewpoint: first, its *typical* significance, second its *prophetic* application, third, its *practical* teaching. It is as though the Holy Spirit had here combined three pictures into one. We might illustrate it by the method used in printing a picture in colors. There is first the picture itself in its black-edged outline; then, on top of this, is filled in the first coloring—red, or yellow, as the case may be; finally, the last color—blue or brown—may be added to the others, and the composite and variegated picture is complete. To use the terms of the illustration, it is our purpose to examine, separately, the different tints and shadings in the Divine picture which is presented to our view in the first half of John 2.

I. THE TYPICAL SIGNIFICANCE.

It is to be carefully noted that this second chapter of John opens with the word "and", which indicates that its contents are closely connected with what has gone before. One of the things that is made prominent in John 1 (following the Introduction, which runs to the end of v. 18) is the *failure of Judaism*, and the turning away from it to Christ. The failure of Judaism (seen in the ignorance of the Sanhedrin) is made plain by the sending of priests and Levites from Jerusalem to enquire of John who he was *(1:19)*. This is made still more evident by the pathetic statement of the Baptist, "there standeth One among you, whom ye know not" *(1:26)*. All this is but an amplification of that tragic word found in 1:11—"He came unto His own, and His own received Him not". So blind were the religious leaders of Israel, that they neither knew the Christ of God who stood in their midst, nor recognized His forerunner to whom the Old Testament Scriptures bore explicit witness.

Judaism was but a dead husk, the heart and life of it were gone. Only one thing remained, and that was the setting of it aside, and the bringing in "of a better hope". Accordingly, we read in Gal. 4:4, "But when the fulness of time was come, God sent forth His Son". Yes, the fulness of God's time *had* come. The hour was ripe for Christ to be manifested. The need for Him had been fully demonstrated. Judaism must be set aside. A typical picture of this was before us in John 1. The Baptist wound up the Old Testament system ("The law and the prophets were *until John*"—Luke 16:16), and in John 1:35-37 we are shown two (the number of competent testimony) of His disciples leaving John, and following the Lord Jesus.

The same principle is illustrated again in the chapter now before us. A marriage-feast is presented to our view, and the central thing about it is that *the wine had given out*. The figure is not difficult to interpret: "Wine" in Scripture is the emblem of *joy* as the following passages will show: "And wine that *maketh glad* the heart of man" *(Psa. 104:15);* "And the vine said unto them, Should I leave my wine, *which cheereth God and man?" (Judges 9:13).* How striking, then, is what we have here in John 2! How accurate the picture. Judaism still existed as a religious system, but it ministered no comfort to the heart. It had degenerated into a cold, mechanical routine, utterly destitute of joy in God. Israel had lost the joy of their espousals.

"And there were set there six waterpots of stone, after the manner of the purifying of the Jews" *(v. 6).* What a portrayal of Judaism was this! Six is the number of *man,* for it was on the sixth day man was made, and of the coming Superman it is written "Let him that hath understanding count the number of the beast: for it is the number of a man; and his number is six hundred sixty and six" *(Rev. 13:18).* Yes, there were *six* waterpots standing there, not seven, the perfect number. All that was left of Judaism was of the flesh; God was not in it. As we read later on in this Gospel, the "feasts of the Lord" *(Lev. 23:2)* were now only "the feast of *the Jews*" *(2:13, etc.).*

Observe, too, that these six waterpots were of "stone", not silver which speaks of redemption, nor of gold that tells of Divine glory. As we read in Isa. 1:22, "Thy silver is become dross", and again in Lam. 4:1, "How is the gold become dim?" Profoundly significant, then, were these waterpots of *"stone".* And what is the more noticeable, *they were empty.* Again, we say, what a vivid portrayal have we here of Israel's condition at that time! No wonder the wine had given out! To supply *that* Christ was needed. Therefore, our chapter at once directs attention to Him as the One who alone can provide that which speaks of joy in God. Thus does John 2 give us another representation of the failure of Judaism, and the turning away from it to the Saviour. Hence, it opens with the word "and", as denoting the continuation of the same subject which had been brought out in the previous chapter.

In striking accord with what we have just suggested above, is the further fact, that in this scene of the Cana-marriage feast, the mother of Jesus occupies such a prominent position. It is to be noted that she is not here called by her personal name —as she is in Acts 1:14—but is referred to as "the mother of Jesus". She is, therefore, to be viewed as a *representative* character. In this chapter Mary occupies the same position as the Baptist did in John 1. She stands for *the Nation of Israel*. Inasmuch as through her the long promised "Seed" had come, Mary is to be regarded here as gathering up into her person the entire Abrahamic stock. If confirmation of this be needed, the reader may be directed to Rev. 12, where the "woman" who gives birth to the Man-Child, and afterwards flees into the "wilderness", where she is preserved for 1260 days, is plainly the Jewish Remnant. As, then, the Jewish Remnant is termed the "woman"—the woman who gave birth to the Saviour—we are fully warranted in contemplating the "mother of Jesus" in this representative capacity, and as illustrating the attitude of Israel toward Christ.

What, then, does the Holy Spirit record here of Mary? Were her actions on this occasion in keeping with the representative character she filled? They certainly were. The record is exceedingly brief, but what is said is enough to confirm our line of interpretation. The mother of Jesus exhibited a woful lack of spiritual discernment. It seems as if she presumed so far as to *dictate* to the Lord. Apparently she ventured to order the Saviour, and tell Him what to do. No otherwise can we account for the reply that He made to her on this occasion— "Woman, what have I to do with thee?" It was a pointed rebuke, and as such His words admonished her for her failure to render to Him the respect and reverence which, as the Lord of glory, were His due.

We believe that this unwonted interference of Mary was prompted by the same carnal motive as actuated His unbelieving "brethren" (i. e. other sons of Mary and Joseph) on a later occasion. In John 7:2-5 we read, "Now the Jews' feast of tabernacles was at hand. His brethren therefore said unto Him, Depart hence, and go into Judea, that Thy disciples also may see the works that Thou doest. For there is no man that doeth anything in secret, and he himself seeketh to be known openly. If Thou do these things, show Thyself to the world. For neither did His brethren believe in Him".

Mary wanted the Saviour to openly display His power and glory, and, accordingly, she was a true representative of the Jewish Nation. Israel had no thought and had no heart for a suffering Messiah; what they desired was One who would immediately set up His kingdom here on earth. Thus, in Mary's ignorance (at that time) of the real character of Christ's mission, in her untimely longing for Him to openly display His power and glory, and in Christ's word of rebuke to her "What have I to do with thee?", we have added evidences of the typical significance of this scene at the Cana marriage-feast— *the setting aside of Israel after the flesh.*

II. THE PROPHETIC APPLICATION.

What is recorded here in the first part of John 2 looks beyond the conditions that obtained in Israel at that time. The miracle which Christ performed at Cana possessed a *prophetic* significance. Like so much that is found in Scripture, the passage before us needs to be studied from a twofold viewpoint: it's *immediate* and its *remote* applications. Above, we have sought to bring out what we believe to be the direct significance of this incident, in its typical and representative suggestiveness. Now we would turn for a moment to contemplate its more distant and prophetic application.

"And the third day": so our chapter opens. The Holy Spirit presents to our view a *third day scene*. The third day is the day of *resurrection*. It was on the third day that the earth emerged from its watery grave, as it was on the third day the barren earth was clothed with vegetable life *(Gen. 1:9, 11)*. There is an important scripture in Hosea 6:2 which should be placed side by side with John 2:1: *"After two days* will He revive us: *in the third day* He will raise us up, and we shall live in His sight". For almost two thousand years (two Days with God—*see 2 Pet. 3: 8)* Israel has been without a king, without a priest, without a home. But the second "Day" is almost ended, and when the third dawns, their renaissance shall come. Israel, as a nation, is to be raised from the dead *(Ezek. 37)*, and under the millennial rule of Christ will again occupy the land which once flowed with milk and honey.

This second chapter of John presents us with a prophetic foreshadowing of the future. It gives us a typical picture of Christ *in the Millennium*—the Third Day, following the two days (the two thousand years) of Israel's dispersion. Then will Israel *invite* Jesus to come to them: for, not until they say "Blessed is He that cometh in the name of the Lord" will He return to the earth. Then will the Lord be *married* to the new Israel, Millennial Israel—see Isa. 54; Hosea 2, etc. Then will Christ turn the water into wine—fill Israels' hearts with joy. Then will Israel say to the Gentiles (their servants), "Whatsoever *He* saith unto you, do". Then will Israel render unqualified obedience to Jehovah, for He will write His law in their hearts *(Jer. 31:33)*. Then will Christ "manifest His glory" *(John 2: 11)*—cf. Matt. 25:31; and thus will the best wine be reserved for Israel until the last.

If further proof be needed to establish the fact that these opening verses of John 2 furnish us with a prophetic picture of the Millennium, it is to be found in v. 1, "And the third day". The "third day" after what? The answer to this question is found, of course, in the previous chapter. In our last article we called attention to the *four "days"* which are referred to in John 1. The fourth beginning at v. 43 "the next day" and running to the end of the chapter; the third beginning at v. 35 "again, the next day" and running to the end of v. 42; the second, beginning at v. 29 "the next day" and running to the end of v. 34; and the first, beginning at v. 19 and running to v. 28 as v. 29 implies. Thus, by adding together these four "days" in John 1 to the "third day" of John 2:1, we learn that John 2 presents us with a *seventh day* scene, and this is, of course, the Millennium. The six days work of God in Gen. 1. foreshadowed the six thousand years of human toil, and the seventh day when God rested, pointed to the Millennium, the Seventh Day, when a groaning creation shall be delivered from its bondage, and when the earth shall rest from war for a thousand years. The same thing is brought out in Matt. 17:1, 2, "And *after six days* Jesus . . . . was transfigured"; the Transfiguration, as is well known, gives a miniature representation of Christ in His millennial glory. So, here, in John 2, the seventh day (the four days of John 1 plus the three of John 2:1) portrays Christ in millennial connections, manifesting His glory and gladdening the hearts of men.

Having touched, somewhat briefly, upon the typical and prophetic significance of this miracle, we turn now to consider,

III. THE PRACTICAL TEACHING.

"And the third day there was a marriage in Cana of Galilee; and the mother of Jesus was there: And both Jesus was called, and His disciples, to the marriage" *(vv. 1, 2)*. Christ here sanctifies the marriage relationship. Marriage was ordained by God in Eden and in our lesson, the Saviour, for all time, set His stamp of approval upon it. To be present at this marriage was almost Christ's first public appearance after His ministry commenced. By gracing this festive gathering, our Lord distinguished and glorified this sacred institution. Observe that Christ was *invited* to be there. Christ's presence is essential to a happy marriage. The marriage where there is no place for our Saviour and Lord cannot be blest of God: *"Whatsoever* ye do . . . . do *all* to the glory of God" *(I Cor. 10:31)*.

"And when they wanted wine, the mother of Jesus saith unto Him, They have no wine" *(v. 3)*. Mary's words seem to indicate two things: first, she ignored His Deity. Was she not aware that He was more than Man? Did she not know that He was God manifest in the flesh? and, therefore, omniscient. *He* knew that they had no wine. Second, it appears as though Mary was seeking to exert her parental authority, by suggesting to Him what He ought to do under the circumstances.

"Jesus saith unto her, Woman, what have I to do with thee?" *(v. 4)*. This is an elliptical expression, and in the Greek literally reads, "What to Me and thee?" We take it that the force of this question of our Lord's was, What is there common to Me and thee—cf. Matt. 8:29 for a similar grammatical construction. It was not that the Saviour resented Mary's inviting His aid, but a plain intimation that she must allow Him to act in His own way. Christ here intimated that His season of subjection to Mary and Joseph *(Luke 2: 51)*, was over, His public ministry had now commenced and she must not presume to dictate to Him.

Many of our readers, no doubt, have wondered why Christ here addressed His mother as "Woman". Scholars tell us that at the time our Lord used this word it would not sound harsh or rough. It was a designation commonly used for addressing females of all classes and relationships, and was sometimes employed with great reverence and affection. Proof of this is seen in the fact that while on the Cross itself Christ addressed Mary as "Woman", saying, "Behold thy Son" *(John 19:26 and see also 20:13, 15).*

But we believe our Lord chose this word with Divine discrimination, and for at least two reasons. First, because He was here calling attention to the fact that He was more than Man, that He was none less than the Son of God. To have addressed her as "mother" would have called attention to *human* relationships; but calling her "woman" showed that *God* was speaking to her. We may add that it is a significant fact that the two times Christ addressed His mother as "woman" are both recorded in the Gospel of *John* which sets forth His Deity.

Again, the employment of this term "woman" denotes Christ's omniscience. With prophetic foresight He anticipated the horrible idolatry which was to ascribe Divine honors to her. He knew that in the centuries which were to follow, men would entitle her the Queen of angels and the Mother of God. Hence, He refused to use a term which would in any wise countenance the monstrous system of Mariolatry. Christ would here teach us that Mary was only a *woman*—"Blessed *among* women" *(Luke 1:38),* but not "blessed *above* women".

"Mine hour is not yet come" *(v. 4)* became the most solemn watchword of His life, marking the stages by which He drew nigh to His death. *Seven* references are made in this Gospel to that awful "hour". The first is in our present passage in John 2:4. The second is found in 7:30—"Then they sought to take Him: but no man laid hands on Him, because *His hour* was not yet come". The third is found in 8:20—"And no man laid hands on Him, for *His hour* was not yet come". The fourth is in 12:23—"And Jesus answered them, saying, *The hour* is come, that the Son of Man should be glorified." The fifth is in 12:27—"Now is My soul troubled; and what shall I say? Father, save Me from *this hour:* but for this cause came I unto *this hour."* The sixth is in 16:32—"Behold, *the hour* cometh, yea, is now come, that ye shall be scattered, every man to his own, and shall leave Me alone: and yet I am not alone, because the Father is with Me". The seventh is in 17:1—"These. words spake Jesus, and lifted up His eyes to heaven, and said, Father, *the hour* is come; glorify Thy Son, that Thy Son also may glorify Thee". This "hour" was the hour of His *humiliation.* It was the "hour" of His suffering. But *why* should Christ refer to this "hour" when Mary was seeking to dictate to Him? Ah, surely the answer is not far to seek. That awful "hour" to which He looked forward, was the time when He *would be subject* to *man's* will, for then He would be delivered up into the hands of sinners. But until this, He was not to be ordered by man; instead, He was about His *Father's* business, seeking only to do *His* will.

"His mother saith unto the servants, Whatsoever He saith unto you, do". This is very beautiful. Mary meekly accepted the Lord's rebuke, recognized His rights to act as He pleased, and left the matter entirely in His hands. There is an important and much neglected lesson here for each of us. How prone *we* are to dictate to God! How often we are disposed to tell Him *what* to do! This is only another evidence of that detestable self-will which still operates in the believer unless Divine grace subdues it. Our plain duty is to commit our way unto the Lord and then leave Him to supply our need in His own good time and way.

We turn now to consider the Miracle which Christ performed here at Cana. And first, a few words upon the *occasion* of it. The Lord Jesus recognized in this request of Mary's a call from His Father. He discerned in this simple act of furnishing the wedding-guests with wine a very different thing from what His mother saw. The performing of this miracle marked an important crisis in the Saviour's career. His act of turning the water into wine would alter the whole course of His life. Hitherto He had lived in quiet seclusion in Nazareth, but from this time on He would become a public and marked character. From henceforth He would scarcely have leisure to eat, and His opportunities for retired communion with the Father would be only when others slept. If He performed this miracle, and manifested forth His glory, He would become the gazing stock of every eye, and the common talk of every tongue. He would be followed about from place to place, thronged and jostled by vulgar crowds. This would provoke the jealousy of religious leaders, and He would be spied upon and regarded as a public menace. Later, this would eventuate in His being seized as a notorious criminal, falsely accused, and sentenced to be crucified. All of this stood out before Him as He was requested to supply the needed wine. But He did not shrink. He had come to do the will of God, no matter what the cost. May we not say it reverently, that as He stood there by Mary's side and listened to her words, that *the Cross* challenged Him. Certainly it was here anticipated, and hence His solemn reference to His "hour" yet to come.

In the second place, the *manner* in which the Miracle was performed is deserving of our closest attention. "And there were set there six waterpots of stone, after the manner of the purifying of the Jews, containing two or three firkins apiece. Jesus saith unto them, Fill the waterpots with water. And they filled them up to the brim. And He saith unto them, Draw out now, and bear unto the governor of the feast. And they bare" *(vv. 6-8).* Christ was the One to work the miracle, yet the "servants" were the ones who seemed to do everything. *They* filled the waterpots, *they* drew off the wine, *they* bore it to the governor of the feast. There was no visible exhibition of the putting forth of Divine power. Christ pronounced no magical formula: He did not even command the water to become wine. What was witnessed by the spectators was men at work, not God creating out of nothing. And all this speaks loudly to us. It was a parable in action. The means used were human, the result was seen to be Divine.

This was Christ's first miracle, and in it He shows us that God is pleased to use human instrumentality in performing the wonders of His grace. The miracle consisted in the supplying of wine and, as previously pointed out, wine symbolizes joy in God. Learn then, that the Lord is pleased to employ human agents in bringing joy to the hearts of men. And *what* was the element Christ used on this occasion in producing the wine? It was *water.* Now "water" is one of the symbols of the written Word *(see Eph. 5:26).* And how may we His servants, today, bring the wine of joy unto human hearts? By ministering the Word, preaching the Gospel to a perishing world. To these "servants" Christ's command to fill those six empty waterpots of stone with water, might have seemed meaningless, if not foolish; but their obedience made them fellow-workers in the miracle! And to the wise of this world, who put their trust in legislation, and social amelioration, it seems useless to go forth unto the wicked with nothing more in our hands than a Book written almost two thousand years ago. Nevertheless, it has pleased God "by the foolishness of preaching to save them that believe"—foolish, that is, in the estimate of the worldly wise. Here then is blessed instruction for the servants of God today. Let us go forth with the Water of Life, implicitly obeying the commands of our Lord, and He will use us to bring the wine of Divine joy to many a sad heart.

In the third place, consider the *teaching* of this Miracle. In it we have a striking picture of *the regeneration of a sinner.* First, we see the condition of the natural man before he is born again: he is like an empty waterpot of stone—cold, lifeless useless. Second, we see the worthlessness of man's religion to help the sinner. Those waterpots were set apart "after the manner of the purifying of the Jews"— they were designed for ceremonial purgation; but their valuelessness was shown by their emptiness. Third, at the command of Christ they were filled with water, and water is one of the emblems of the written Word: it is the Word which God uses in quickening dead souls into newness of life. Observe, too, these waterpots were filled "up to the brim"— God always gives good measure; with no niggardly hand does He minister. Fourth, the water produced wine, "good wine" *(v. 10):* symbol of the Divine joy which fills the soul of the one who has been "born of water". Fifth, we read *"This* beginning of miracles did Jesus". That is precisely what the new birth is—a "miracle". And not only so, it is always the *"beginning* of miracles" for the one newly born: regeneration is ever the *initial* work of grace. Sixth, observe "this beginning of miracles did Jesus in Cana of Galilee, and *manifested forth His glory".* It is thus, in the regeneration of dead sinners, that the "glory" of our Saviour and Lord is "manifested". Seventh, observe, "And His disciples *believed* on Him". A dead man cannot believe. But the first movement of the newly born soul is to turn to Christ. Not that we argue an interval of time between the two, but as cause stands to effect so the work of regeneration precedes the act of believing in Christ—cf. 2 Thess. 2:13: first, "Sanctification of the Spirit", which is the new birth, *then* "belief of the truth."

But is there not even a deeper meaning to this beginning of Christ's miracles? Is it not profoundly significant that in this first miracle which our Saviour performed, the "wine", which is the symbol of *His shed blood*, should be so prominent! The marriage-feast was the occasion of joy and merriment; and does not God give us here something more than a hint that in order for His people to be joyous, the precious blood of His Son must be first poured forth! Ah, that is the foundation of every blessing we enjoy, the ground of all our happiness. Hence did Christ *begin* His supernatural works of mercy by producing that which spoke of His sacrificial death.

"When the ruler of the feast had tasted the water that was made wine, and *knew not* whence it was: (but the *servants* which drew the water *knew;*) the governor of the feast called the bridegroom" (*v. 9*). This parenthetical statement is most blessed. It illustrates an important principle. It was the *servants*—not the "disciples", nor yet Mary—who were *nearest* to the Lord on this occasion, and who possessed the knowledge of His mind. What puzzled the "ruler of the feast", was no secret to these "servants". How different are God's ways from ours! The Lord of Glory was here as "Servant". In marvelous grace He came "not to be ministered unto, but to minister": therefore, are those who are humble in service, and those engaged *in* the humblest service, *nearest to Him*. This is their reward for turning their backs upon the honors and emoluments of the world. As we read in Amos 3:7— "Surely the Lord God will do nothing, but He revealeth His secret unto (Ah, unto whom?) *His servants* the prophets". It is like what we read of in Psa. 103:7—"He *made known* His ways unto Moses"; and who was Moses? Let Scripture answer: "Now the man Moses was *very* meek *above all* the men who were upon the face of the earth" (*Num. 12:3*)! Yes, "the *meek* will He guide in judgment, and the *meek* will He teach His way" (*Psa. 25:9*).

Those who determine to occupy the position of authority (as *Mary* did here) are not taken into the Lord's secrets. Those who wish to be in a place like the *"ruler* of the feast", know not His thoughts. But those who humble themselves to take the *servant* position, who place themselves at Christ's disposal, are the ones who share His counsels. And in the day to come, when He will provide the true wine of the Kingdom, those who have served Him during the time of His absence, shall then be under Him the dispensers of joy. Has He not promised, "If any man *serve Me,* him will My Father *honor"?*

"And saith unto Him, Every man at the beginning doth set forth good wine; and when men have well drunk, then that which is worse: but thou hast kept the good wine until now" (*v. 10*). This illustrates the ways of men and the ways of God. The world (and Satan also) gives its best first, and keeps the worst for the last. First the *pleasures* of sin—for a season—and then the *wages* of sin. But with God it is the very opposite. He brings His people into the wilderness before He brings them into the promised inheritance. First the Cross and then the crown. Fellow believer, for us, the best wine is yet to be: "The path of the just is as the shining light, that shineth *more and more* unto the perfect day" (*Prov. 4:18*).

One more observation on this passage and we must close. What a message is there here for the unsaved! The natural man has a "wine" of his own. There is a carnal happiness enjoyed which is produced by "the pleasures of sin"—the merriment which this world affords. But how fleeting this is! How unsatisfying! Sooner or later this "wine", which is prest from "the vine *of the earth"* (*Rev. 14:18*), gives out. The poor sinner may be surrounded by gay companions, he may be comfortably circumstanced financially and socially, yet the time comes when he discovers he has "no wine". Happy the one who is conscious of this. The discovery of our own wretchedness is often the turning point. It prepares us to look to that One who is ready "to give unto them beauty for ashes, the oil of *joy* for mourning, the garment of praise for the spirit of heaviness" (*Isa. 61:3*). Unbelieving friend, there is only One who can furnish the true "wine", the "good wine", and that is the Lord Jesus Christ. *He* can satisfy the longing soul. *He* can quench the thirst of the heart. *He* can put a song into thy mouth which not even the angels can sing, even the song of Redemption. What then must *you* do? What price must you pay? Ah, dear friend, listen to the glad tidings of grace: *"Believe* on the Lord Jesus Christ, and thou shalt be *saved"!* That is all—"Only believe" (Mark 5:36).

And now, once more, we give a number of questions to prepare the interested student for the lesson to follow. Next month we shall give an exposition (D. V.) of the remaining portion of John 2. Study, then, and prayerfully meditate on the following questions:—

1. *Why* is the Cleansing of the temple referred to just here?—Note its place in the other Gospels.
2. Why did not Christ *drive out* "the doves"? v. 16.
3. What was indicated by the Jews' demand for a "sign"? v. 18.
4. Why did Christ point them forward to His *resurrection?* vv. 18-21.
5. Did the Lord's own disciples believe in the promise of His resurrection? If not, why? v. 22.
6. What solemn warning does v. 23 point?
7. What does v. 25 prove concerning Christ?

—Arthur W. Pink.

THE WISDOM OF GOD DISPLAYED IN THE WAY OF SALVATION

SECTION III.

THE GOOD ATTAINED BY SALVATION IS WONDERFULLY VARIOUS AND EXCEEDING GREAT

Here we may distinctly consider the *variety* and the *greatness* of the good procured for men.

1. The good procured by salvation is wonderfully *various.* Here are all sorts of good procured for fallen men, that he *does* or *can* really need, or is *capable* of. The wisdom of God appears in the way of salvation, in that it is most worthy of an infinitely wise God, because every way perfect and sufficient. We, in our fallen state, are most necessitous creatures, full of wants: but they are here all answered. Every sort of good is here procured; whatever would really contribute to our happiness, and even many things we could not have thought of, had not Christ purchased them for us, and revealed them to us. Every demand of our circumstances, and craving of our natures, is here exactly answered.—For instance,

1. We stand in need of *peace* with God. We had provoked God to anger, His wrath abode upon us, and we needed to have it appeased. This is done for us in this way of salvation; for Christ, by shedding His blood, has fully satisfied justice, and appeased God's wrath, for all that shall believe in Him. By the sentence of the law we were condemned to hell; and we needed to have our sins pardoned that we might be delivered from hell. But in this work, pardon of sin and deliverance from hell, is fully purchased for us.

2. We needed not only to have God's wrath appeased, and our sins pardoned; but we needed to have the *favor* of God. To have God, not only not our enemy, but our Friend. Now God's favor is purchased for us by the righteousness of Jesus Christ.

3. We needed not only to be delivered from hell, but to have some *satisfying happiness* bestowed. Man has a natural craving and thirst after happiness; and will thirst and crave until his capacity is filled. And his capacity is of vast extent; and nothing but an infinite good can fill and satisfy his desires. But, notwithstanding, provision is made in this way of salvation to answer those needs, there is a satisfying happiness purchased for us; that which is fully answerable to the capacity and cravings of our souls.

Here is food procured to answer all the appetites and faculties of our souls. God has made the soul of man of a spiritual nature; and therefore he needs a corresponding happiness; some spiritual object, in the enjoyment of which he may be happy. Christ has purchased the enjoyment of God, who is the great and original Spirit, as the portion of our souls. And He hath purchased the Spirit of God to come and dwell in us as an eternal principle of happiness.

God hath made man a rational intelligent creature; and man needs some good that shall be a suitable object to his understanding, for him to contemplate; wherein he may have full and sufficient exercise for his capacious faculties, in their utmost extent. Here is an object that is great and noble, and worthy of the exercise of the noblest faculties of the rational soul.—God Himself should be theirs, for them forever to behold and contemplate; His glorious perfections and works are most worthy objects; and there is room enough for improving them, and still to exercise their faculties to all eternity. What object can be more worthy to exercise the understanding of a rational soul, than the glories of the Divine Being, with which the heavenly intelligences, and even the infinite understanding of God Himself is entertained?

Our souls need some good that shall be a suitable object of the will and affections; a suitable object for the choice, the acquiesence, the love, and the joy of the rational soul. Provision is made for this also in this way of salvation. There is an infinitely excellent Being offered to be chosen, to be rested in, to be loved, to be rejoiced in, by us: even God Himself, who is infinitely lovely, the fountain of all good; a fountain that can never be exhausted, where we can be in no danger of going to excess in our love and joy: and here we may be assured ever to find our joy and delight in enjoyments answerable to our loves and desires.

4. There is all possible enjoyment of this object, procured in this way of salvation. When persons entirely set their love upon another, they naturally desire to *see* that person: merely to hear of the person, does not satisfy love. So here is provision made that we should see God, the object of our supreme love. Not only that we should hear and read of Him in His Word, but that we should see Him with a spiritual eye here: and not only so, but that we should have the satisfaction of seeing God face to face hereafter. This is promised in Matt. 5:8—"Blessed are the pure in heart, for they shall see God." It is promised that we shall not see God, as through a glass darkly, as we do now, but face to face—I Cor. 13:12. That we shall see Christ as He is —I John 3:2.

We naturally desire not only to see those whom we love, but to *converse with* them. Provision is made for this also, that we should have spiritual conversation with God while in this world; and that we should be hereafter admitted to converse with Christ in the most intimate manner possible. Provision is made in this way of salvation, that we should converse with God much more intimately, than otherwise would have been possible for us, for now Christ is incarnate, is in our nature: He is become one of us, whereby we are under advantages for an immensely more free and intimate converse with Him, than could have been, if He had remained only in the Divine nature; and so in a nature infinitely distant from us.—We naturally desire not only to converse with those whom we greatly love, but to *dwell* with them. Provision, through Christ, is made for this. It is purchased and provided that we should dwell with God in His own house in heaven, which is called our Father's house—to dwell forever in God's presence, and at His right hand.

We naturally desire to have a *right* in that person whom we greatly love. Provision is made, in this way of salvation that we should have a right *in* God; a right *to* Him. This is the promise of the covenant of grace, "that He will be our God." God, with all His glorious perfections and attributes, with all His power and wisdom, and with all His majesty and glory, will be ours; so that we may call Him our inheritance, and the portion of our souls: what we can humbly claim by faith, having this portion made over to us by a firm instrument; by a covenant ordered in all things and sure. And we may also hereby claim a right to Jesus Christ. Love desires that the right should be *mutual*. The lover desires, not only to have a right to the beloved, but *that the beloved should have a right to him:* he desires to be his beloved's, as well as his beloved should be his. Provision is also made for this, in this wise method of salvation, that God should have a special propriety in the redeemed, that they should be in a distinguishing manner *His*, that they should be His *peculiar* people. We are told that God sets apart the godly for Himself, Psa. 4:3. They are called God's jewels. The spouse speaks it with great satisfaction and rejoicing, "My beloved is mine, and I am his" *(S. of S. 2:16)*.

Love desires to stand in some *near relation* to the beloved. Provision is made by Christ, that we should stand in the nearest possible relation to God; that He should be our Father, and that we should be His children. We are often instructed in the Holy Scriptures, that God is the Father of believers, and that they are His family; and not only so, but they stand in the nearest relation to Christ Jesus. There is the closest union possible. The souls of believers are married to Christ. The church is the bride, the Lamb's wife. Yea, there is yet a nearer relation than can be represented by such a similitude. Believers are the very members of Christ, members of His flesh and of His bones, Eph. 5:30. Yea, this is not near enough yet, but *they are one spirit*, 1 Cor. 6:17.

Love naturally inclines to a *conformity* to the beloved. To have those excellencies, upon the account of which He is beloved, copied in ourselves. Provision is made in this way of salvation, that we may be conformed to God; that we shall be transformed into the same image. "We all, with open face beholding as in a glass the glory of the Lord, are changed into the same image from glory to glory" (*2 Cor. 3:18*). And hereafter we shall see Him as He is and be like Him.

It is the natural desire of love to *do something* for the beloved, either for his pleasure or honor. Provision is made for this also in this way of salvation; that we should be made instruments of glorifying God, and promoting His kingdom here, and of glorifying Him to all eternity.

5. In this way of salvation, provision is made for our having *every sort of good* that man naturally craves; as honor, wealth, and pleasure. Here is provision made that we should be brought to the highest honor. This is what God has promised, *that those that honor Him, He will honor*. And that true Christians shall be kings and priests unto God. Christ has promised, that as His Father has appointed unto Him a kingdom, so He will appoint unto them, that they may eat and drink at His table in His kingdom. He has promised to crown them with a crown of glory, and that they shall sit with Him in His throne: that He will confess their names before His Father, and before His angels: that He will give them a new name, and that they shall walk with Him in white. Christ has also purchased for them the *greatest wealth*. All those that are in Christ are rich. They are *now* rich. They have the *best* riches; being rich in faith, and the graces of the Spirit of God. They have gold tried in the fire. They have durable riches and righteousness. They have treasure in heaven, where neither thief approacheth, nor moth corrupteth, an inheritance incorruptible, undefiled, and that fadeth not away. They are possessors of all things.

Christ has also purchased *pleasure* for them; pleasures that are immensely preferable to all the pleasures of sense, most exquisitely sweet and satisfying. He has purchased for them fulness of joy, and pleasures for evermore at God's right hand; and they shall drink of the river of God's pleasure.

6. Christ has purchased all needed good *both for soul and body*. While we are here, we stand in need of these earthly things; and of these Christ has purchased all that is best for us. He has purchased for the body, that God should feed and clothe us. "How much more shall He *feed* you, O ye of little faith!" (*Matt. 6:26*). How much more shall He *clothe* you! Christ has purchased, that God should take care of us, and provide what is needed of these things, as a father provides for his children: "Casting all your care upon Him, for He careth for you" (*1 Pet. 5:7*).

7. Christ has purchased good that is suitable for His people *in all conditions*. There is, in this way of salvation, respect had to, and provision made for, all circumstances that they can be in. Here is provision made, for a time of affliction, for a time of poverty and pinching want, for a time of bereavement and mourning, for spiritual darkness, for a day of temptation, for a time of persecution, and for a time of death. Here is such a provision made that is sufficient to carry a person above death, and all its terrors; and to give him a complete triumph over that king of terrors. Here is enough to sweeten the grave and make it cease to seem terrible. Yea, enough to make death in prospect to seem desirable; and in its near approach to be not terrible but joyful.

8. There is provision made in this way of salvation for the life and blessedness of soul and body *to all eternity*. Christ has purchased, that we should be delivered

from a state of temporal death, as well as *spiritual* and *eternal*. The body of the saints shall be raised to life. He has purchased all manner of perfection for the body of which it is capable. It shall be raised a spiritual body in incorruption and glory, and be made like Christ's glorious body, to shine as the sun in the kingdom of His Father, and to exist in a glorified state in union with the soul to all eternity.

9. But man in his fallen state still needs something else in order to his happiness, than that these aforementioned blessings should be purchased for him; namely, he needs to be *qualified* for the possession and enjoyment of them. In order to our having a title to *these* blessings of the covenant of grace (so that we can scripturally *claim* an interest in them), there is a certain condition must be performed by us. We must *believe* in the Lord Jesus Christ, and *accept* of Him as offered in the Gospel for a Saviour. But, as we cannot do this of ourselves, Christ has purchased this also for all the elect. He has purchased, that they shall have faith given them; whereby they shall be (actively) united to Christ, and so have a (pleadable) title to His benefits.

But still something further is necessary for man in order to his coming to the actual possession of the inheritance. A man, as soon as he has believed, has a title to the inheritance: but in order to come to the actual possession of it, he must *persevere* in a way of holiness. There is not only a gate which must be entered; but there is a narrow way which must be travelled, before we can arrive at heavenly blessedness; and that is the way of universal and persevering holiness. But men, after they have believed, cannot persevere in a way of holiness, of themselves. But there is sufficient provision made for this also, in the way of salvation by Jesus Christ. The matter of a saint's perseverence is sufficiently secured by the purchase that Christ has made.

But still there is something else needful in order to qualify a person for the actual entering upon the enjoyments and employments of a glorified estate, namely, that he should be made *perfectly holy;* that all remainders of sin should be taken away; for there cannot any sin enter into heaven. No soul must go into the glorious presence of God, with the least degree of the filth of sin. But there is provision made: for Christ has purchased that all sin shall be taken away out of the hearts of believers at death; and that they should be made perfectly holy: whereby they shall be fully and perfectly qualified to enter upon the pleasures and enjoyments of the new Jerusalem.

Christ has purchased all, both objective and inherent good: not only a portion to be enjoyed by us; but all those inherent qualifications necessary to our enjoyment of it. He has purchased not only justification, but sanctification and glorification; both holiness and happiness.—Having considered the good attained in the way of salvation as *manifold* and various, I now proceed as proposed,

II. To consider the good attained for us by this way of salvation, as *exceeding great*. There is not only every sort of good we need, but of every sort in *that degree*, so as to answer the extent of our capacity, and the greatest stretch of our desires, and indeed of our conceptions. They are not only greater than our conceptions are here, but also greater than ever they could be, were it not that God's relation, and our own experience, will teach us. They are greater than the tongue of angels can declare, the *deliverance* that we have in it is exceeding great; it is deliverance from guilt, from sin itself, from the anger of God, and from the miseries of hell.

How great is the *good conferred!* The objective good is the infinite God, and the glorious Redeemer, Jesus Christ. How great is the love of the Father, and the Son! And how near the relation between them and the true believer! How close the union, how intimate the communion, and ultimately how clear will be the vision in glory!

There are great *communications* made to the believing soul on earth, but how much greater in heaven! Then their conformity to God will be perfect, their enjoyment of Him will be full, their honor great and unsullied, and the glory of body and soul ineffable. The riches of the Christian are immense; all things are included in his treasure. Pleasures unspeakably and inconceivably great await him; rivers of delight, fulness of joy; and all of infinite duration!

The benefit procured for us, is *doubly* infinite. Our deliverance is an infinite benefit, because the evil we are delivered from is infinite; and the positive good bestowed is eternal; namely, the full enjoyment of all those blessings merited.

SECTION IV.

How Angels Are Benefitted by the Salvation of Men.

So hath the wisdom of God contrived this affair, that the benefit of what He has done therein should be so extensive, as to reach the elect angels. It is for men that the work of redemption is wrought out; and yet the benefit of the things done in this work is not confined to them, though all that is properly called *redemption,* or included in it, is confined to men. The angels cannot partake in this, having never fallen; yet they have great indirect benefit by it.—God has so wisely ordered, that what has been done in this directly and especially for men, should redound to the exceeding benefit of all intelligent creatures who are in favor with God. The benefit of it is so diffusive as to reach heaven itself. So great and manifold is the good attained in this work, that those glorious spirits who are so much above us, and were so highly exalted in happiness before, yet should receive great addition hereby. I will show *how* in some particulars.

1. The angels hereby see a great and wonderful manifestation of the glory of God. The happiness of angels as well as of men consists very much in beholding the glory of God. The excellency of the Divine Being is a most delightful subject of contemplation to the saints on earth; but much more to the angels in heaven. The more holy any being is, the more sweet and delightful will it be to him to behold the glory and beauty of the Supreme Being. Therefore the beholding of the glory of God must be ravishing to the holy angels, who are perfect in holiness, and never had their minds leavened with sin. The manifestations of the glory of God, are as it were the food that satisfies the angels; they live thereon. It is their greatest happiness.

It is without doubt much of their employment to behold the glory of God appearing in His works. Therefore this work of redemption greatly contributes to their happiness and delight, as the glory of God is so exceedingly manifested by it. For what is done, is done in the sight of the angels, as is evident by many passages of Holy Scripture. And they behold the glory of God appearing herein with entertainment and delight, as it is manifest by 1 Pet. 1:12. "Which things the angels desire to look into".

The angels have this advantage, that now they may behold the glory of God in the face of Jesus Christ, where it shines with a peculiar lustre and brightness. "Great is the mystery of godliness: God was manifest in the flesh, justified in the Spirit, seen of angels" *(1 Tim. 3:16).* Perhaps all God's attributes are more gloriously manifested in this work, than in any other that ever the angels saw. There is certainly a fuller manifestation of some of His attributes, than ever they saw before; as is evident by the text. And especially, it is so with respect to the mercy of God, that sweet and endearing attribute of the Divine nature. The angels of heaven never saw so much grace manifested before, as in the work of redemption; nor in any measure equal to it. How full of joy doth it fill the hearts of the angels to see such a boundless and bottomless ocean of love and grace in their God! And therefore with what rejoicing do all the angels praise Christ for His being slain! "And I beheld, and I heard the voice of many angels round about the throne, and the beasts and the elders: and the number of them was ten thousand times ten thousand, and thousands of thousands; saying with a loud voice, Worthy is the Lamb that was slain to receive power, and riches and wisdom, and strength, and honor, and glory, and blessing" *(Rev. 5:11, 12).*

2. They have this benefit by it, that hereby Jesus Christ, God-Man, is become their head. God, subsisting in three persons, Father, Son and Holy Spirit, was the King of angels, and would have been, if it had not been for our redemption. But it was owing to what was done in this work, that Jesus Christ, as God-Man, becomes the head of the angels. Christ is now not only the head of angels simply as God, but as God-Man: "And ye are complete in Him, who is the head of all principality and power" *(Col. 2:10).* "Which He wrought in Christ, when He raised Him from the dead, and set Him at His own right hand in heavenly places, far above all principality and power, and might and dominion, and every name that is named, not only in this world, but also in that which is to come. And hath put all

things under His feet, and gave Him to be the head over all things to the church" (*Eph. 1:20-22*).

This is a part of the exaltation and glory of Christ which God confers on Him as His reward. And not only so, but it is greatly to the angels' benefit. It is God's manner in His dealings with His elect creatures, in the same works wherein He glories Himself, or His Son, greatly to benefit them. The same dealings of His that are most for His glory, shall be most for their good. That Christ, God-Man, should be made the head of the angels, is greatly to their benefit several ways,

(1) Because they become hereby more nearly *related* to so glorious a person, the Son of God, than otherwise they would have. The angels esteem it a great honor done them to be related to such a person as Jesus Christ, God-Man, who is an infinitely honorable person.

The angels, by Christ becoming their head, are with the saints gathered together in one in Christ, Eph. 1:10. They, by virtue hereof, though Christ be not their Redeemer as He is ours, have a right and propriety in this glorious person, as well as we. He is theirs; though not their Saviour, yet He is their head of government, and head of influence.

(2) Again, this is greatly to their *benefit;* as they are under advantages for a far more intimate converse with God. The Divine nature is at an infinite distance from the nature of angels, as well as from the nature of man. This distance forbids a familiarity and intimacy of intercourse. It is therefore a great advantage to the angels, that God is come down to them in a created nature; and in that nature is become their Head; so that their intercourse and enjoyment may be more intimate. They are invited by the similar qualifications of the created nature, with which the Son of God is invested.

(3) It is for the benefit of the angels, as hereby the elect of mankind are gathered into their society. Christ, by the work of redemption, gathers in the elect of mankind to join the angels of heaven. Eph. 1:10, "That in the dispensation of the fulness of times, He might gather together in one all things in Christ, both which are in heaven, and which are on earth, even in Him". Men are brought in to join with the angels in their work of praising God; to partake with them of their enjoyments. The angels greatly rejoice at this. They rejoice when but one person is gathered in, as Christ teaches us, Luke 15:10: "Likewise I say unto you, There is joy in the presence of the angels of God over one sinner that repenteth". The heavenly society is made more complete by this accession of the saints to it; they contribute to the happiness of each other. The angels rejoice that others are added to join them and assist them in praising God; and thus the vacancy by the fall of angels is filled up.

(4) It tends to make the angels to prize their happiness the more, when they see how much it cost to purchase the same happiness for man. Though they knew so much, yet they are not incapable of being taught more and more the worth of their own happiness. For when they saw how much it cost to purchase the same happiness for man; even the precious blood of the Son of God; this tended to give them a great sense of the infinite value of their happiness. They never saw such a testimony of the value of the eternal enjoyment of God before.

Thus we have shown, how the wisdom of God appears in the work of redemption in the good ends attained thereby, with respect to God, men, and good angels.

But are there any good ends obtained with respect to *bad* angels, God's grand enemies? Undoubtedly there are, as may appear from the few following considerations. Satan and his angels rebelled against God in heaven, and proudly presumed to try their strength with His. And when God by His almighty power overcame the strength of Satan, Satan still hoped to get the victory by subtlety. Though he could not overcome by power, yet he hoped to succeed by craft; and so by his subtlety to disappoint God of His end in creating this lower world. God therefore has shown His great wisdom in overthrowing Satan's design. He has disappointed the devices of the crafty, so that they cannot perform their enterprise; He has carried their counsel headlong.

1. Satan thought to have disappointed God of His glory, which He designed in creating this lower world; and to make mankind be for his own glory, in setting up himself god over them. Now Christ, by what He has done in the work of redemp-

tion, has overthrown Satan; and utterly frustrated him as to this end. God is exceedingly glorified in the elect, to the surprise of angels and demons. God by redemption has all the glory that He intended, and more than either men, angels, or demons imagined that God intended. God might have glorified His justice in the destruction of all mankind. But it was God's design in creating the world, to glorify His goodness and love; and not only to be glorified eventually but to be served and glorified actually by men. Satan intended to frustrate God of this end; but, by the redemption of Jesus Christ, his design is confounded.

2. Another design of the Devil, was to gratify his envy in the utter destruction of mankind. But, by the redemption of Jesus Christ, this malicious design of Satan is crossed: because all the elect are brought to their designed happiness; which is much greater than ever Satan thought it was in God's heart to bestow on man. And though some of mankind are left to be miserable, yet that does not answer Satan's end; for this also is ordered for God's glory. No more are left miserable than God saw meet to glorify His justice upon.

One end why God suffered Satan to do what he did in procuring the fall of man, was that His Son might be glorified in conquering that strong, subtle, and proud spirit, and triumphing over him. How glorious doth Christ Jesus appear in baffling and triumphing over this proud king of darkness, and all the haughty confederate rulers of hell! How glorious a sight is it to see the meek and patient Lamb of God leading that proud, malicious, and mighty enemy in triumph! What songs doth this cause in heaven! It was a glorious sight in Israel to see David carrying the head of Goliath in triumph to Jerusalem. It appeared glorious to the daughters of Israel, who came out with timbrels and with dances, and sang, "Saul hath slain his thousands, and David his ten thousands". But how much more glorious to see the Son of David, the Son of God, carrying the head of the spiritual Goliath, the champion of the armies of hell, in triumph to the heavenly Jerusalem! It is with a principal view to this, that Christ is called, "The Lord of Hosts, or armies, and a Man of War" *(Ex. 15:13)*. And Psa. 24:8, "Who is this King of Glory? The Lord strong and mighty, the Lord mighty in battle".

SECTION V.

IN THIS WAY OF SALVATION WONDERFUL GLORY REDOUNDS TO GOD, AS THE EFFECT OF DIVINE WISDOM.

1. By this contrivance for our redemption, God's greatest dishonor is made an *occasion* of His greatest glory. Sin is a thing by which God is greatly dishonored; the nature of its principle is enmity against God, and contempt of Him. And man, by his rebellion, has greatly dishonored God. But this dishonor, by the contrivance of our redemption, is made an occasion of the greatest manifestation of God's glory that ever was. Sin, the greatest evil, is made an occasion of the greatest good. It is the nature of a principle of sin that it seeks to dethrone God: but this is hereby made an occasion of the greatest manifestation of God's royal majesty and glory that ever was. By sin, man has slighted and despised God: but this is made an occasion of His appearing the more greatly honorable. Sin casts contempt upon the authority and law of God: but this, by the contrivance of our redemption, is made the occasion of the greatest honor done to that same authority, and to that very law. It was a greater honor to the law of God that Christ was subject to it, and obeyed it, than if all mankind had obeyed it. It was a greater honor to God's authority that Christ showed such great respect, and such entire submission to it, than the perfect obedience of all the angels in heaven. Man by his sin showed his enmity against the holiness of God; but this is made an occasion of the greatest manifestation of God's holiness. The holiness of God never appeared to so great a degree, as when God executed vengeance upon His own dear Son.

2. So has the wisdom of God contrived that those attributes are glorified in man's salvation, whose glory seemed to require his *destruction*. When man had fallen, several attributes of God seemed to require his destruction. The justice of God requires, that sin be punished as it deserves: but it deserves no less than eternal destruction. God proclaims it as a part of the glory of His nature, that He will no wise clear the guilty, Ex. 34:7. The holiness of God seemed to require man's destruction; for God by His holiness infinitely hates sin. This seemed to require, therefore, that God should mani-

fest a proportionable hatred of the sinner; and that He should be forever an enemy unto him. The truth of God seemed also to require man's destruction; for eternal death was what God had threatened for sin, one jot or tittle of which threatening cannot by any means pass away. But yet so has God contrived, that those very attributes not only allow of man's redemption, and are not inconsistent with it, but they are glorified in it. Even vindictive justice is glorified in the death and sufferings of Christ. The holiness of God, or His holy hatred of sin, that seemed to require man's damnation, is seen in Christ's dying for sinners. So herein also is manifested and glorified the truth of God, in the theatenings of the law.

3. Yea, it is so ordered now that the glory of these attributes *requires* the salvation of those that believe. The justice of God that required man's damnation, and seemed inconsistent with his salvation, now as much requires the salvation of those that believe in Christ, as ever before it required their damnation. Salvation is an absolute debt to the believer from God, so that he may in justice demand it, on account of what his Surety has done. For Christ has satisfied justice fully for his sin; so that it is but a thing that may be challenged, that God should now release the believer from the punishment; it is but a piece of justice, that the creditor should release the debtor, when he has fully paid the debt. And again, the believer may demand eternal life, because it has been merited by Christ, by a merit of condignity. So is it contrived, that that justice that seemed to require man's destruction, now requires his salvation.

So also the truth of God that seemed to require man's damnation, now requires his salvation. At the same time that the threatening of the law stands good, there is a promise of eternal life to many who have broken the law. They both stand good at the same time; and the truth of God requires that both should be fulfilled. How muchsoever they seem to clash, yet so is the matter contrived in this way of salvation, that both are fulfilled, and do not interfere one with another.

At the very time that God uttered the threatening, "In the day thou eatest thereof thou shalt surely die"; and at the time that Adam had first eaten the forbidden fruit, there was then an existing promise, that many thousands of Adam's race should obtain eternal life. This promise was made to Jesus Christ, before the world was. What a difficulty and inconsistence did there seem to be here! But it was no difficulty to the wisdom of God, that the promise and the threatening should be both fully accomplished to the glory of God's truth in each of them. Psa. 85: 10, "Mercy and truth are met together, righteousness and peace have kissed each other".

4. Those very attributes which seemed to require man's destruction, are *more glorious* in his salvation, than they would have been in his destruction. The revenging justice of God is a great deal more *manifested* in the death of Christ, than it would have been if all mankind had been sufferers to all eternity. If man had remained under the guilt and imputation of sin, the justice of God would not have had such a *trial*, as it had, when His own Son was under the imputation of sin. If all mankind had stood guilty, and justice had called for vengeance upon them, that would not have been such a trial of the inflexibleness and unchangeableness of the justice of God, as when His own Son, who was the object of His infinite love, and in whom He infinitely delighted, stood with the imputation of guilt upon Him.

This was the greatest trial that could be to manifest whether God's justice was perfect and unchangeable, or not; whether God was so just that He would not upon any account abate of what justice required; and whether God would have any respect unto persons in judgment.

So the *majesty* of God appears much more in the sufferings of Christ than it would have done in the eternal sufferings of all mankind. The majesty of a prince appears greater in the just punishment of great personages under the guilt of treason, than of inferior persons. The sufferings of Christ have this advantage over the eternal sufferings of the wicked, for impressing upon the minds of the spectators a sense of the dread majesty of God, and His infinite hatred of sin; namely, that the eternal sufferings of the wicked never will be seen actually accomplished, and finished; whereas they have seen that which is equivalent to those eternal sufferings actually fulfilled and finished in the sufferings of Christ.

5. Such is the wisdom of this way of salvation, that the more any of the elect have dishonored God, the more is God glorified in this redemption. Such wonders as these are accomplished by the wisdom of this way of salvation. Such things as these, if they had been proposed to any created intelligence, would have seemed strange and unaccountable paradoxes, till the counsels of Divine wisdom concerning the matter were unfolded.

So sufficient is this way of salvation, that it is not inconsistent with any of God's attributes to save the chief of sinners. However great a sinner any one has been, yet God can, if He pleases, save without any injury to the glory of any one attribute. And not only so, but the more sinful any one has been, the more doth God glorify Himself in his salvation. The more doth He glorify His power, that He can redeem one in whom sin so abounds, and of whom Satan hath such strong possession. The greater triumph has Christ over His grand Adversary, in redeeming and setting at liberty from his bondage those that were his greatest vassals. The more doth the sufficiency of Christ appear, in that it is sufficient for such vile wretches.

The more is the sovereignty and boundless extent of the mercy of God manifested, in that it is sufficient to redeem those that are most undeserving. Rom. 5:20, "Where sin abounded, grace did much more abound".—*Jonathan Edwards.*
(To be continued, D. V.).

CONFIDENCE IN THE LORD

How many arguments God has used to work in us this trust. Sometimes the Scriptures teach us to argue from the less to the greater: "If God so clothe the grass of the field, which to day is, and to morrow is cast into the oven, shall He not *much more* clothe *you*, O ye of little faith?" *(Matt. 6:30).* Sometimes the Scripture teaches us to argue on the contrary, from the greater to the less: "He that spared not His own Son, but delivered Him up for us all, how shall He not also *with Him* freely give us all things?" *(Rom. 8:32)*—if God has given us His Christ, will He not with Him freely give us all things? Sometimes the Scripture teaches us to argue from things past. God hath been your Shield and Helper, He hath delivered from the mouth of the lion and bear, and this uncircumcised Philistine shall be as one of them *(see I Sam. 17:37).* Sometimes Scripture teaches us to argue from things past and present to things to come: "Who *hath* delivered from so great a death, and *doth* deliver; in Whom we trust that He will *yet* deliver" *(II Cor. 1:10).* Sometimes the Scripture teaches us to argue from things to come to things present: *"Fear not,* little flock; *for* it is your Father's good pleasure to give you the Kingdom" *(Luke 12:32).*—If He give a Kingdom, will He not give daily bread? Will He not preserve you while He hath a mind to use you? Thus our unbelief is overpowered by Divine argument to press us to trust God. —*Thos. Manton, 1660.*

HUMAN DEPRAVITY

In looking into the composition of the human mind, we observe various passions and propensities, and if we inspect their operations, we shall see in each a marked aversion from the true God. For example: Man loves to *think,* and cannot live without thinking; but he does not love to think of God—"God is not in all his thoughts." Man delights in *activity,* is perpetually in motion; but has no heart to act for God. Men take pleasure in con*versation,* and are never more cheerful than when engaged in it; but if God and religion be introduced, they are usually struck dumb, and discover an inclination to drop the subject. Men greatly delight in hearing and telling *news;* but if the glorious news of the Gospel be sounded in their ears, it frequently proves as unwelcome as Paul's preaching at Athens. In short, man feels the necessity of *a god;* but has no relish for the true God.—*Andrew Fuller, 1824.*

VOL. I   JULY, 1922   NO. 7

STUDIES in the SCRIPTURES

"Search the Scriptures" John 5:39.

A PERIODICAL (MONTHLY "IF THE LORD WILL") DEVOTED TO BIBLE STUDIES and EXPOSITIONS

Associate Editors and Publishers, I. C. HERENDEEN and ARTHUR W. PINK,
Swengel, Pa.

Price: **10 cents per copy; $1.00** per year. Foreign **$1.00** per year.

TO OUR SCRIPTURE STUDY FAMILY—

The special aims of this magazine are to quicken interest in the Word of God, to produce a conviction of the deep importance of studying it, and to provide help to that end. To neglect the daily reading of the Scriptures is to sin against their Author and is to impoverish our own souls. One of the most urgent needs of the Christian is to give a regular, diligent, prayerful, meditative attention to the Holy Oracles. If the Lord wills, it is our purpose to publish (a few months hence) a series of articles on How to Read and Study the Scriptures, and we shall greatly value the prayers of our friends that the writer may have wisdom from God to make them simple and helpful. In the meantime, we would earnestly press upon all who are anxious to gain a deeper insight into the things of God the need of living much in the 119th Psalm.

In several striking ways the Holy Spirit has given peculiar prominence to this Psalm. It is by far the longest chapter in the whole Bible. Its literary structure is unique. It has 176 verses, which are divided into twenty-two sections, each of eight verses. Twenty-two is the number of the letters in the Hebrew alphabet, and each section of this Psalm begins with one of those letters. The first eight verses each begin with the first letter of the Hebrew alphabet; each of the second eight verses begin with the second letter; each of the third eight verses with the third letter, and so on to the end of the Psalm. These are surface features which at once arrest the attention, and denote there is something here of unusual importance. What this is, is not hard to discern. The whole Psalm rehearses the excellencies of *the Word of God*, and the saints' delight and profit therein.

In the Massorah (critical notes inserted in the margins of the Old Testament by ancient Hebrew scribes) the rubric on Psalm 119:112 is as follows, "Throughout the whole of the Great Alphabet (i. e. the Alphabetic Psalm, 119) there is in every verse one of the following ten expressions: 'Way, Testimony, Precepts, Commandments, Saying, Law, Judgment, Righteousness, Statutes, Word', which correspond to the Ten Commandments; except one verse, in which there is none of these; namely, verse 122" (from the Companion Bible). Thus reference is made to God's Word—under various names—in all save one of its 176 verses!

The Psalm opens with a double "Blessed"—see the first word of verses 1 and 2. There is only one other Psalm that does, namely, the 32nd. The Psalm begins with a description of the way to true blessedness—just as the whole Book of Psalms begins. Blessedness is what we all aim at, but most of us are either ignorant or careless in heeding the way that leadeth to this; therefore does the Holy Spirit first set us right as to what a "blessed" man really is.

We had intended making a few comments on one or two outstanding features in this most important Psalm, but we will defer these till another time, if the Lord will. Let each subscriber read slowly and thoughtfully through the whole Psalm and make its petitions the substance of his own supplications to God.

                   Cordially,

                             A fellow-student of the Word,
                                  Arthur W. Pink.

STUDIES IN THE SCRIPTURES

Subscription Price: **$1.00** per year to any address in the world. Single copies **10** cents.

Change of Address: Please notify us promptly of any change of address, and be certain to give both old and new addresses.

Non-Subscribers receiving this Magazine regularly will understand their subscription has been entered by a friend.

Copies lost in the mail duplicated on request.

All new subscriptions will be dated back to January, 1922.

Entered as second-class matter December 15th, 1921 at the post office at Swengel, Pa., under Act of March 3rd, 1879.

CONTENTS

The Person of the Antichrist (continued) 134
John's Gospel (John 2:13-25) 141
The Wisdom of God Displayed in the Way of Salvation (continued) 148
The Perfections of God 155

THE PERSON OF THE ANTICHRIST

In our last paper we pointed out how that the Antichrist is not a system of evil, nor an anti-Christian organization, but instead, a single individual being, a person yet to appear. In support of this we appealed to the declaration of our Lord recorded in John 5:43; "I am come in My Father's name, and ye receive Me not: if another shall come in his own name, him ye will receive". Here the Saviour both compares and contrasts the Man of Sin with Himself. The point of comparison is that, like the Saviour, he shall offer himself to Israel; the contrast is, that unlike Christ who was rejected by the Jews, the false messiah shall be "received" by them. If, then, the Antichrist may be compared and contrasted with the Christ of God, he, too, must be a person, an individual being.

Again; we called attention to the expression used by the apostle Paul in 2 Thess. 2:—"The Man of Sin", "the Son of Perdition", "he that opposeth and exalteth himself", "the Wicked One whom the Lord shall consume with the spirit of His mouth", "he whose coming is after the working of Satan"—all these point as distinctly to a single individual as did the Messianic predictions of the Old Testament point to the person of our Lord Jesus Christ. Assured, then, that "the Antichrist" signifies a specific individual, our next concern is to turn to the Scriptures and learn what God has been pleased to reveal concerning this Personification of Evil.

I. THE ANTICHRIST WILL BE A JEW.

The Antichrist will be a *Jew*, though his connections, his governmental position, his sphere of dominion, will by no means confine him to the Israelitish people. It should, however, be pointed out that there is no express declaration of Scripture which says *in so many words* that this daring Rebel *will be* "a Jew"; nevertheless, the hints given are so plain, the conclusions which must be drawn from certain statements of Holy Writ are so obvious, and the requirements of the case are so inevitable, that we are forced to believe he *must* be a Jew. To these 'hints,' 'conclusions' and 'requirements' we now turn.

1. In Ezek. 21:25-27 we read: "And thou, profane wicked prince of Israel, whose day is come, when iniquity shall have an end, Thus saith the Lord God; Remove the diadem, and take off the crown: this shall not be the same: exalt him that is low, and abase him that is high. I will overturn, overturn, overturn it: and it shall be no more until he come whose right it is, and I will give it him". The dispensational place and scope of this passage is not hard to determine. The time-mark is given in v. 25: it is "when iniquity shall have an end". It is the End-Time which is in view, then, the End of the Age, when "the transgressors are come to the full" *(Dan. 8:23 and cf. 11:36*—"Till the indignation be accomplished"). At that time Israel shall have a "Prince", a Prince who is "crowned" *(v. 26)*, and a Prince whose "day" is said to be "come" when "iniquity shall have an end". Now, as to *who* this "Prince" is, there is surely no room for doubt. The only "Prince" whom Israel will have in that day, is the Son of Perdition, here termed their "Prince" because he will be masquerading as "Messiah *the Prince*" *(see Dan. 9:25)!* Another unmistakeable mark of identification is here given, in that he is expressly denominated "thou, *profane wicked* Prince"—assuredly, it is the Man of Sin

who is here in view, that impious one who shall "oppose and exalt himself above all that is called God". But what should be noted, particularly, is that this profane and wicked character is here named "Prince *of Israel*". He must, therefore, be of the Abrahamic stock, a *Jew!*

2. In Ezek. 28:2-10 a remarkable description is given us of the Antichrist under the figure of "the Prince of Tyrus", just as in vv. 12-19 we have another most striking delineation of Satan under the figure of "the king of Tyrus". In a later paper we hope to show that, beyond a doubt, it is the Antichrist who is in view in the first section of this chapter. There is only one thing that we would now point out from this passage: in v. 10 it is said of him "Thou shalt die the deaths of the *uncircumcised*", which is a very strong hint that he *ought not* to die the deaths of the "uncircumcised" because *he* belonged to the Circumcision! Should it be said that this verse cannot apply to the Antichrist because he will be destroyed by Christ Himself at His coming, the objection is very easily disposed of by a reference to Rev. 13:14, which tells of the Antichrist being wounded to death by a sword and rising from the dead—which is prior to his ultimate destruction at the hands of the Saviour.

3. In Dan. 11:36, 37 we are told, "And the king shall do according to his will; and he shall exalt himself, and magnify himself above every god, and shall speak marvelous things against the God of gods, and shall prosper till the indignation be accomplished: for that that is determined shall be done. Neither shall he regard "the God of his fathers". This passage, it is evident, refers to and describes none other than the coming Antichrist. But what we wish to call special attention to is the last sentence quoted—"The God of his fathers". What are we to understand by this expression? Why, surely, that he is *a Jew,* an Israelite, and that his fathers after the flesh were Abraham, Isaac and Jacob—for such is the invariable meaning of "the fathers" throughout the Old Testament Scriptures.

4. In Matt. 12:43-45 we have another remarkable scripture which will be considered briefly, in a later section of this article, when we shall endeavor to show that "The Unclean Spirit" here is none other than the Son of Perdition, and that the "house" from which he goes out and into which he returns, is the Nation of Israel. If this can be established, then we have another proof that he will be *a Jew,* for this "house", which is Israel, is here termed by Antichrist *"my* house". Just as Solomon was of "the House of David", so Antichrist shall be of the House of Israel.

5. In John 5:43 we have a further word which helps us to fix the nationality of this coming One. In speaking of the false messiah, the Lord Jesus referred to him as follows, *"Another"* shall come in his own name". In the Greek there are four different words all translated "Another" in our English versions. One of them is employed but once, and a second but five times, so these need not detain us now. The remaining two are used frequently, and with a clear distinction between them. The first "allos" signifies "another" *of the same kind or genus*—see Matt. 10:23; 13:24; 26:71, etc. The second, "heteros", means "another" *of a totally different kind.* —see Mark 16:12; Luke 14:31; Acts 7:18; Rom. 7:23. Now the striking thing is that the word used by our Lord in John 5:43 is "allos", another of the *same* genus, not "heteros", another of a different order. Christ, the Son of Abraham, the Son of David, had presented Himself to Israel, and they rejected Him; but "another" of the *same* Abrahamic stock should come to them, and him they would "receive". If the coming Antichrist were to be a Gentile, the Lord would have employed the word "heteros"; the fact that He used "allos" shows that he will be a *Jew.*

6. The very name "Antichrist" argues strongly his *Jewish* nationality. This title "Antichrist" has a double significance. It means that he will be one who shall be *"opposed"* to Christ, one who will be His enemy. But it also purports that he will be a *mock* Christ, an *imitation* Christ, a *pro-*Christ, a *pseudo* Christ. It intimates that he will ape Christ. He will pose as the real Messiah of Israel. In such case he *must* be a *Jew.*

7. This mock Christ will be "received" by Israel. The Jews will be deceived by Him. They will believe that he is indeed their long expected Messiah. They will accept him as such. Proofs of this will be furnished in a later article, D. V. But if this pseudo Christ succeeds in palming

himself off on the Jews as their true Messiah he *must* be a *Jew*, for it is unthinkable that they would be deceived by any Gentile.

Ere passing to the next point, we may add, that it was the common belief among Christians during the first four centuries A. D., that the Antichrist would come from the tribe of Dan. Whether this will be the case or no, we do not know. Gen. 49:17, 18 may have ultimate reference to this Son of Perdition. Certainly Dan is the most mysterious of all the twelve tribes.

II. THE ANTICHRIST WILL BE THE SON OF SATAN.

That Satan will have a son ought not to surprise us. The Devil is a consummate *imitator* and much of his success in deceiving men is due to his marvelous skill in counterfeiting the things of God. Below we give a list of his imitations:—

Do we read of Christ going forth to sow the "good seed"? *(Matt. 13:24)*, then we also read of the enemy going forth to sow his "tares"—an imitation wheat *(Matt. 13:25)*. Do we read of "the children of God", then we also read of "the children of the wicked one" *(Matt. 13:38)*. Do we read of God *working in* His children "both to will and to do of His good pleasure" *(Phil. 2:13)*, then we are also told that the Prince of the power of the air is "the spirit that now *worketh in* the children of disobedience" *(Eph. 2:2)*. Do we read of the Gospel of God, then we also read that Satan has a gospel—"Another gospel, which is not another" *(Gal. 1:6,7)*. Did Christ appoint "apostles", then Satan has his "apostles" too *(2 Cor. 11:13)*. Are we told that "the Spirit searcheth all things, yea, the *deep things* of God" *(1 Cor. 2:10)*, then Satan also provides *his* "deep things" *(see Greek of Rev. 2:24)*. Are we told that God, by His angel, will "seal" His servants in their foreheads *(Rev. 7:3)*, so also we read that Satan, by his angels, will set a "mark" in the "foreheads" of his devotees *(Rev. 13:16)*. Does the Father seek "worshippers" *(John 4:23)*, so also does Satan *(Rev. 13:4)*. Did Christ quote scripture, so also did Satan *(Matt. 4:6)*. Is Christ the Light of the world, then Satan also is transformed as an "angel of light" *(2 Cor. 11:14)*. Is Christ denominated *"the Lion of the tribe of Judah" (Rev. 5:5)*, then the Devil is also referred to as "a roaring *lion*" *(I Peter 5:8)*. Do we read of Christ and "His angels" *(Matt. 24:31)*, then we also read of the Devil and "*his*" angels *(Matt. 25:41)*. Did Christ work miracles, so also will Satan *(2 Thess. 2:9)*. Is Christ seated upon a "Throne", so also will Satan be *(Rev. 2:13, Gk.)*. Has Christ a Church, then Satan has his "synagogue" *(Rev. 2:9)*. Has Christ a "bride", then Satan has his "whore" *(Rev. 17:16)*. Has God His "Vine", so has Satan *(Rev. 14:19)*. Does God have a city, the new Jerusalem, then Satan has a city, Babylon *(Rev. 17:5; 18:2)*. Is there a "mystery of godliness" *(1 Tim. 3:16)*, so also there is a "mystery of iniquity" *(2 Thess. 2:7)*. Does God have an only-begotten Son, so we read of "the Son of Perdition" *(2 Thess. 2:3)*. Is Christ called "the Seed of the woman", then the Antichrist will be "the seed of the serpent" *(Gen. 3:15)*. Is the Son of God also the Son of Man, then the son of Satan will also be "the Man of Sin" *(2 Thess. 2:3)*.

Is there a Holy Trinity, then there is also an Evil Trinity *(Rev. 20:10)*. In this Trinity of Evil Satan himself is supreme, just as in the Blessed Trinity the Father is (governmentally) supreme: note that Satan is several times referred to as a *father (John 8:44, etc.)*. Unto his son, the Antichrist, Satan gives his authority and power to represent and act for him *(Rev. 13:4)* just as God the Son received "all power in heaven and earth" from *His* Father, and uses it for His glory. The Dragon (Satan) and the Beast (Antichrist) are accompanied by a third, the False Prophet, and just as the third person in the Holy Trinity, the Spirit, bears witness to the person and work of Christ and glorifies Him, so shall the third person in the Evil Trinity bear witness to the person and work of the Antichrist and glorify him *(see Rev. 13:11-14)*.

Now the Antichrist will be a man, and yet more than man, just as Christ was Man and yet more than man. The Antichrist will be the 'Superman' of whom the world, even now, is talking, and for whom it is looking. The Wicked One who is to be revealed shortly, will be a supernatural character, he will be the son of Satan. His twofold nature is plainly declared in 2 Thess. 2:3—"The Man of Sin, the Son of Perdition". In proof of these assertions we ask for a careful attention to what follows.

1. "And I will put enmity between thee

and the woman, and between *thy Seed* and her seed; it shall bruise thy head, and thou shalt bruise his heel" *(Gen. 3: 15)*. It is to be noted that there is here a *double* "enmity" spoken of: God says, "I will put enmity between thee and the woman", that is, between Satan and Israel, for Israel was the woman that bore Christ *(Rev. 12)*; *"And* between thy seed and her seed". Observe particularly that *two* "seeds" are here spoken of; "Thy seed" (the antecedent is plainly the "Serpent") and "her seed", the woman's Seed. The woman's "Seed" was Christ, the Serpent's "Seed" will be the Antichrist. The Antichrist, then, will be more than a man, he will be the actual and literal Seed of that old Serpent, the Devil; as Christ was, according to the flesh, the actual and literal Seed of the woman. "Thy seed", Satan's seed, refers to a specific individual, just as "her seed" refers to a specific Individual.

2. "In that day the Lord with His sore and great and strong sword shall punish Leviathan the piercing Serpent, even Leviathan that crooked Serpent; and he shall slay the Dragon that is in the sea" *(Isa. 27:1)*. To appreciate the force of this we need to attend to the context, which is unfortunately broken by the chapter division. In the closing verses of Isa. 26 we hear God saying, "Come, My people, enter thou into thy chambers, and shut thy doors about thee: hide thyself as it were for a little moment, until the indignation be overpast" *(26:20)*. These words are addressed to the elect remnant in Israel. Their ultimate application will be to those on earth at the end of this Age, for it is the time of God's "indignation" *(cf. Dan. 8:19 and 11:36)*. It is the time when "the Lord cometh out of His place to punish the inhabitants of the earth for their iniquity: the earth also shall disclose her blood, and shall no more cover her slain" *(26:21)*— notice "iniquity", singular number, not "iniquities". It is their worshipping of Satan's Man which is specifically referred to. Then, immediately following we read, *"In that day* the Lord . . . shall punish Leviathan the piercing Serpent". The connection, then, makes it plain that it is just before the Millennium when God shall punish the Crooked Serpent, the Antichrist. Now the very fact that the Wicked One is here denominated "the piercing and crooked Serpent" hints strongly that he will be *the son* of "that old Serpent, the Devil".

3. In the first two sections of Ezek. 28 two remarkable characters are brought before us. The second who is described in vv. 12-19 has received considerable attention from Bible students of the last two generations, and since the late Mr. G. H. Pember pointed out that what is there said of "the king of Tyrus" could be true of no earthly king or mere human being, and must outline a character that none but Satan himself (before his fall) could fill*, this view has been adopted by most of the leading Bible teachers. But little attention has been paid to the character described in the first ten verses of this chapter.

Now just as what is said in Ezek. 28 or "the king of Tyrus" can only apply fully to Satan himself, so, what is said of "the prince of Tyrus" manifestly has reference to the Antichrist. The parallelisms between what is said here and what we find in other scriptures which describe the Son of Perdition are so numerous and so evident, that we are obliged to conclude that it is the same person which is here contemplated. We cannot now attempt anything like a complete exposition of the whole passage (though we hope to give one later) but will just call attention to some of the outstanding marks of identification:

First, the Lord God says to this personage, "Because thine heart is lifted up, and thou hast said I am a god, I *sit* in the *seat* of God"—cf. 2 Thess. 2:4. Second, "Behold thou art *wiser* than Daniel"—cf. Dan. 8:23, and 7:8, "Behold, in this horn were *eyes* like the eyes of men, and a mouth speaking great things", which intimates that the Antichrist will be possessed of extraordinary intelligence. Third, it is said of this character, "With thy wisdom and with thine understanding thou hast gotten thee *riches,* and hast gotten gold and silver into *thy treasures*" *(v. 4—cf. Psa. 52:7; Dan. 11:38)*.

Sufficient has been said, we trust, to show that under the figure of this "prince of Tyrus" we may discern clearly the unmistakeable features of the coming Antichrist. But the particular point we would make here, is this, that as Satan is termed "the *king* of Tyre", in the second section of this chapter the Antichrist is re-

---

*See also the chapter on Satan's Origin in the writer's "Satan and His Gospel" obtainable from the Bible Truth Depot, Swengel Pa. at **20 cents.**

ferred to as "the *prince* of Tyre". Antichrist, then, is related to Satan as "prince" is to "king", that is, as *son* is to his *father*.

4. In Matt. 12:43 the Antichrist is called "The Unclean Spirit", not merely *an* unclean spirit, but *"the* Unclean Spirit". We cannot now stop and submit the evidence that it *is* the Antichrist who is here in view, for this is another passage which we hope to consider carefully in a later article. But in the writer's mind there is no doubt whatever that none other than the Beast is here in view. If this be the case, then we have further evidence that the coming One will be no mere man indwelt by Satan, but a fallen angel, an evil spirit, the incarnation of the Devil.

5. "Ye are of your father the Devil, and the lusts of your father ye will do. He was a murderer from the beginning, and abode not in the truth, because there is no truth in him. When he speaketh a lie, he speaketh of his own; for he is a liar, and the *father* of it" *(John 8:44)*. Here is still another proof that the Antichrist will be superhuman, the offspring of Satan. In the Greek there is the definite article before the word "lie"—the lie, "the Lie". There is but one other passage in the New Testament where "the Lie" is mentioned, and that is *in* 2 Thess. 2:11, where again the definite article is found in the Greek, and there the reference is unmistakeable.

A threefold reason may be suggested as to *why* the Antichrist should be termed "the Lie". First, because his fraudulent claim to be the real Christ will be the greatest falsehood palmed off upon humanity. Second, because he is the direct antithesis of the real Christ, who is "the Truth" *(John 14:6)*. Third, because he is the son of Satan who is the *arch* liar. But to return to John 8:44: "When he (the Devil) speaketh (concerning) the Lie, he speaketh of his own". His "own" what? His "own" *son*—the remainder of the verse makes this very plain—"for he (the Devil) is a liar *and the father of it*", i. e., of "the Lie". The Lie, then, is *Satan's* "*son*"!

"That day shall not come, except there come a falling away (the Apostasy) first, and that Man of Sin be revealed, *the Son of Perdition*" *(2 Thess. 2:3)*. Nothing could be plainer than this. Here the Antichrist is expressly declared to be superhuman—"the Son of Perdition". Just as the Christ is the Son of God, so Antichrist will be the son of Satan. Just as in Christ dwelt all the fulness of the Godhead bodily, and just as Christ could say "He that hath seen Me, hath seen the Father", so the Antichrist will be the full and final embodiment of the Devil. He will not only be the incarnation of the Devil, but the consummation of his wickedness and power.

7. In Rev. 13:1 (R. V.) we read, "And he (the Dragon—see context) stood upon the sand of the sea"—symbolic of taking possession of the Nations: "And I saw a Beast coming up out of the sea, having ten horns and seven heads, and on his horns ten diadems, and upon his heads names of blasphemy." It is deeply significant to mark how these two things are here linked together *as cause and effect*. The coming forth of the Beast (the Antichrist) is immediately connected with the Dragon! But this is not all. Notice the description that is here given of him: he has "ten horns (fulness of power) and seven heads (complete wisdom)" and this is exactly how Satan himself is described in Rev. 12:3—"And behold, a great red Dragon, having *seven heads* and *ten horns,* and *upon his heads names of blasphemy"!* Does not a linking of these scriptures prove beyond all doubt that the Antichrist will be an *exact replica* of Satan himself!

But one other thing, even more startling, remains to be considered, and that is,

III. THE ANTICHRIST WILL BE JUDAS REINCARNATED.

1. In Psalm 55 much is said of the Antichrist in his relation to Israel. Among other things we read there "The words of his mouth were smoother than butter, but war was in his heart: his words were softer than oil, yet were they drawn swords" *(v. 21)*. The occasion for this sad plaint is given in the previous verse—"He hath put forth his hands against such as be at peace with him: he hath *broken his covenant*". The reference is to Antichrist breaking his seven-year Covenant with the Jews *(see Dan. 9:27; 11:21-24)*. Now if the entire Psalm be read through with these things in mind, it will be seen that it sets forth the sorrows of Israel and the sighings of the Godly remnant during the End-Time. But the remarkable thing is that when we come to vv. 11-14 we find

that which has a *double* application and fulfillment—"wickedness is in the midst thereof: deceit and guile depart not from her streets. For it was not an enemy that reproached me; then I could have borne it: neither was it he that hated me that did magnify himself against me; then I would have hid myself from him: But it was thou, a man mine equal, my guide, and mine acquaintance. We took sweet counsel together, and walked unto the house of God in company". These verses describe not only the base treachery of Judas toward Christ, but they also announce how He shall yet, when reincarnated in the Antichrist, *betray and desert Israel*. The relation of Antichrist to Israel will be precisely the same as that of Judas to Christ of old. He will pose as the friend of the Jews, but later he will come out in his true character. In the Tribulation period, the Nation of Israel shall taste the bitterness of betrayal and desertion by one who masqueraded as a "familiar friend". Hence, we have here the first hint that the Antichrist will be Judas reincarnated.

2. "And your covenant with Death shall be disannuled, and your agreement with Hell shall not stand; when the overflowing scourge shall pass through, then ye shall be trodden down by it" *(Isa. 28:18)*. The "Covenant" referred to is that seven-year one which is mentioned in Dan. 9:27. But here the one with whom this Covenant is made is termed "Death" and "Hell". This is a title of the Antichrist, as "the Resurrection and the Life" is of the true Christ. Nor is this verse in Isa. 28 the only one where the Son of Perdition is so denominated. In Rev. 6 a fourfold picture of him is given—the antithesis of the fourfold portrayal of the Lord Jesus in the Gospels. Here he is seen as the rider on differently colored horses, which bring before us four stages in his awful career, and when we come to the last of them the Holy Spirit exposes his true identity by telling us, "and his name that sat on him was Death, and Hell followed with him" *(Rev. 6:8)*. Now "Hell" or "hades" is the place which receives the souls of the dead, and the fact that this awful name is here applied to Antichrist intimates that he has *come from there*.

3. Above we referred to Matt. 12:41-43 to prove that Antichrist will be a super-human being, a fallen and unclean "spirit"; we turn to it again in order to show that this coming Incarnation of Satan has previously been upon earth. The history of this "Unclean Spirit" is divided into three stages. First, as having dwelt in "a man"; second, as having gone out of a man, and walking through dry places, seeking rest and finding none—this has reference to his present condition during the interval between his two appearances on earth. Third, he says, "I will *return* to my house". This Unclean Spirit, then, who has already been here, who is now away in a place where rest is not to be found, is to come back again!

4. In John 17:12 we have a word which, more plainly still, shows that the Antichrist will be Judas reincarnated, for here he is termed by Christ "The Son of Perdition". But first, let us consider the teaching of Scripture concerning Judas Iscariot. Who was he? He was a "man" *(Matt. 26:24)*. But was he *more* than a man? Let Scripture make answer. In John 6:70 we read, "Have not I chosen you twelve, and one of you *is a Devil?*" It is hardly necessary to say that in the Greek there are two different words for "Devil" and "demon". There are *many* demons, but only *one* Devil. Further, in no other passage is the word "devil" applied to any one but to Satan himself. Judas then was the Devil incarnate, just as the Lord Jesus was God incarnate. Christ Himself *said so*, and we dare not doubt His word.

As we have seen in John 17:12 Christ termed Judas "the Son of Perdition", and 2 Thess. 2:3 we find that the Antichrist is *similarily designated*—"That Man of Sin be revealed, *the Son of Perdition*". These are the only two places in all the Bible where his name occurs, and the fact that Judas was termed by Christ not *a* "son of perdition", but *"the* Son of Perdition", and the fact that the Man of Sin is so named prove that they are *one and the same person*. What other conclusion can a simple and unprejudiced reader of the Bible come to?

5. In Rev. 11:7 we have the first reference to "the Beast" in the Apocalypse: "The Beast that ascendeth out of the bottomless pit". Here the Antichrist is seen issuing forth from the Abyss. What is the Abyss? It is the abode of lost spirits, the place of their incarceration and torment—see Rev. 20:1-3, and Luke 8:31, "deep" is "abyss" and cf. Matt. 9:28. The question naturally arises, How did he get

there? and *when* was he sent there? We answer, When Judas Iscariot died! *The Antichrist will be Judas Iscariot reincarnated*. In proof of this we appeal to Acts 1:25 where we are told, "that he may take part of this ministry and apostleship from which Judas by transgression fell, that he might go *to his own place*". Of no one else in all the Bible is it said that at death he went "to his own place". Put these two scriptures together: Judas went "to his own place", the Beast *ascends* out of the Abyss.

6. In Rev. 17:8 we read, "The Beast that thou sawest was, and is not; and shall ascend out of the Bottomless Pit, and go into perdition." This verse is generally understood to refer to the revived Roman Empire, and while allowing that such an application is warrantable, yet we are persuaded it is a mistake to *limit* it to this. In the Apocalypse, the Roman Empire and its final and satanic Head are very closely connected, so much so, that at times it is difficult to distinguish between them. But in Rev. 17 they are distinguishable. In v. 8 we are told that the Beast "shall ascend out of the Bottomless Pit", and that he shall go into perdition". In v. 11 we are told, "And the Beast that was, and is not, even he is the eighth, and is of the seventh, and goeth into perdition". Now nearly all expositors are agreed that the Beast of v. 11—the "eighth" (head, and form of government of the Roman Empire)—is the Antichrist himself; then why not admit the same of v. 8? In both, the designation is the same—"the Beast"; and in both, we are told he "goeth into perdition".

We take it, then, that what is predicated of "the Beast" in 17:8 is true of *both* the Roman Empire and its last head, the Antichrist: of the former, in the sense that it is infernal in its character. Viewing it now as a declaration of the Antichrist, what does it tell us about him? Four things. First, he "was". Second, he "is not". Third, he shall "ascend out of the Bottomless Pit". Fourth, he shall "go into perdition". The various time marks here concern the Beast in his relation to *the earth*. First, he "was", i.e., on the earth.

Second, he "is not", i. e. now on the earth *(cf. Gen. 5:24*, "Enoch *was not* for God took him"; that is, "Was not" any longer *on the earth)*. Third, he shall "ascend out of the Bottomless Pit," where he now is, which agrees with 11:7. Fourth, he shall "go into perdition". We learn then from this scripture that at the time the Apocalypse was written the Beast "was not" then on the earth, but that *he had been on it formerly*. Further, we learn that in John's day the Beast was then in the Bottomless Pit but should yet ascend out of it. Here then is further evidence that the Antichrist who is yet to appear *has been on earth before*.

7. "And the Beast was taken, and with him the False Prophet that wrought miracles before him, with which he deceived them that had received the mark of the Beast, and them that worshipped his image. These both were cast alive into the lake of fire burning with brimstone" *(Rev. 19:20)*. This gives the last word concerning the Antichrist. It makes known the terrible fate which awaits him. He, together with his ally, will be cast alive into the lake of fire. This is very striking, and confirms what has been said above, namely, that the Antichrist will be one who has already appeared on earth, and *has been* in "the Abyss" during the interval which precedes his return to the earth. And how remarkably Rev. 19:20 corroborates this. The Antichrist will not be cast, eventually into the Abyss, as Satan will be at the end of the Millennium *(Rev. 20:1-3)*, but into the lake of fire which is the *final* abode of the damned. Why is it that he shall not be cast into the Abyss at the return of Christ? It must be because he has *already* been there. Hence, the judgment meted out to him is final and irrevocable, as will be that of the Devil a thousand years later, see Rev. 20:10.

Our next article, D. V., will be devoted to an examination and consideration of the many Names and Titles which are given to the Antichrist in the Word of God, and we would urge the student to diligently search the Scriptures for himself to see how many of these he can find—there are over twenty.—*Arthur W. Pink*.

JOHN'S GOSPEL

7. THE CLEANSING OF THE TEMPLE—
John 2:13-25.

"After this He went down to Capernaum, He, and His mother, and His brethren, and His disciples: and they continued there not many days" *(John 2:12)*. This verse comes in as a parenthesis between the two incidents of the Cana marriage-feast and the Cleansing of the Temple. Like everything else in this chapter, it may be studied from a two-fold viewpoint, namely, its immediate application and its remote. In both of these applications the reference to *Capernaum* is the key, and Capernaum stands for two things—Divine favor and Divine judgment, see Matt. 11:23.

Taking the immediate application first, this verse tells us that for a short season Israel occupied the position of being in God's peculiar favor. The mother of Jesus (as we saw in our last article) stands for the Nation of Israel, and particularly for Israel's *privileges*—for she was the one most honored among women. "His brethren" represents the Nation of Israel in *unbelief*; proof of this is found in John 7:5. "His disciples" were the little remnant in Israel who *did* believe in Him, see 2:11. With these, the Lord Jesus went down to Capernaum; but they "continued there not many days". Not for long was Israel to enjoy these special favors of God. Soon Christ would leave them.

But this twelfth verse also has a prophetic significance. Its double application being suggested by the twofold meaning of Capernaum. Capernaum, which was exalted to heaven, was to be brought down to hell. Hence the force of "He went *down* to Capernaum". So it was with the Nation of Israel. They had been marvelously favored of God, and they should be as severely punished. They should go *down* into the place of punishment—for this is what Capernaum speaks of. And this is exactly where the Jews have been all through this Christian dispensation, which, as all careful students of Scripture know is a *parenthetical* one, not being noticed in Old Testament prophecies, but *coming in between* the predictions which speak of Israel's dispersion and Israel's restoration; coming in between the sixty-ninth and the seventieth weeks of Daniel *(Dan. 9:24-27)*, for the sixty-ninth has already been fulfilled, whereas the seventieth is yet future. How perfectly in accord with this, then, that John 2:12 should come in as a parenthesis *between* the marriage-feast and the Temple Cleansing. And how blessed to note that as the mother, brethren, and disciples of Christ (who represented, respectively, the Nation of Israel privileged, but unbelieving, and the little remnant who did believe) went *down* to Capernaum—the place of Divine judgment—that the Lord Jesus *went with them*. So it has been throughout this parenthetical Christian dispensation. The Jews have suffered severely, under the chastisements of God, but the Lord has been *with them* in their dispersion—otherwise they had been utterly consumed long, long ago. The statement "they continued there *not many days*" is also in perfect keeping with its prophetic significance and application. Only *two* "Days" shall Israel abide in that place of which Capernaum speaks; on the third "Day" they shall be delivered—see Hosea 6:2.

Let us now give a brief and simple Analysis of the passage which is to be before us: the Cleansing of the Temple:—

1. The Time of the Cleansing, v. 13.
2. The Need of the Cleansing, v. 14.
3. The Method of the Cleansing, vv. 15, 16.
4. The Cause of the Cleansing, v. 17.
5. The Jews' demand for a Sign and Christ's reply, vv. 18-22.
6. Christ's miracles in Jerusalem and the unsatisfactory result, vv. 23, 24.
7. Christ's knowledge of the human heart, v. 25.

We shall study this passage in a manner similar to that followed in our exposition of the first half of John 2, considering first, the *typical* meaning of the Cleansing of the Temple; second, its *prophetic* significance; the third, its *practical* suggestions.

I. THE TYPICAL MEANING.

The first of the questions which we placed at the end of our last article, and which we asked our readers to meditate on in preparation for this article, was, "*Why* is the Cleansing of the Temple referred to just here?" The careful student will have noticed that in each of the other

Gospels, the Cleansing of the Temple is placed right at the close of our Lord's public ministry, as one of the last things He did before His apprehension. But here, the Holy Spirit has placed Christ's Cleansing of the Temple almost at the beginning of His public ministry. This has led the majority of the commentators to conclude that these were two totally different occasions and incidents, separated by a space of three years. In support of this conclusion some plausible arguments are advanced, but we are not at all sure of their validity. Personally, we are strongly inclined to believe that what is recorded in Matt. 21:12, 13 is the same incident as is before us here in John 2, and that the Holy Spirit has ignored the chronological order (as is so often the case in the Gospels) for His own good reasons. What these reasons may be we shall suggest below. Before advancing them, let us first state why we regard the Cleansing of the Temple here in John 2 as being identical with that which is described in Matt. 21:12, 13, and the parallel passages in Mark and Luke.

The points of likeness between the two are so striking that unless there is irrefutable evidence that they are separate incidents, it seems to us the most natural and the most obvious thing to regard them as one and the same. We call attention to seven points of resemblance.

First, Matthew places the Cleansing of the Temple at the beginning of the *Passover* week, and John tells us that "the Jews' *Passover* was at hand" *(2:12).*

Second, Matthew mentions those that "*sold* and bought" being in the Temple *(21:12);* John says the Lord found in the Temple "those that *sold* oxen", etc. *(2:14).*

Third, Matthew refers to the presence of those that "sold *doves*" *(21:12);* John also speaks of the "*doves*" *(2:16).*

Fourth, Matthew tells us that Christ "*overthrew* the tables of the money-changers" *(21:12);* John also tells us that Christ "*overthrew* the tables" *(2:15).*

Fifth, Matthew mentions that Christ "*cast out all* that sold and bought in the Temple" *(21:12);* John declares He "*drove them all out* of the Temple" *(2:15).* Note, in the Greek it is the *same* word here translated "drove" as is rendered "cast out" in Matthew!

Sixth, Matthew declares Christ said "My house shall be called a house of prayer; but ye have made it a den of thieves" *(21:15);* John records that the Lord said, "Make not My Father's house a house of merchandise" *(2:16).* We have no doubt that the Lord made *both* of these statements in this same connection, but John records the one which expressly affirmed His Divine Sonship. In each case Christ declared the Temple was God's.

Seventh, Matthew records how Christ spent that night in Bethany, and next morning He returned to Jerusalem, and was in the Temple teaching, when the chief priests and elders of the people came to Him and said, "By what authority *doest Thou these things?*" *(21:23).* John also records it that after Christ had cleansed the Temple, the Jews said to Him, "What sign showest Thou unto us, seeing that *Thou doest these things?*" *(2:18).*

If, then, our conclusion is correct, that this Cleansing of the Temple occurred at the close of our Lord's ministry, the question returns upon us, *Why* has the Holy Spirit taken this incident out of its chronological setting and placed it by the side of our Lord's miracle where He changed the water into wine? We believe the answer to this question is not far to seek. We suggest that there was a double reason for placing this incident in juxtaposition with the Cana marriage-feast scene. First, it furnished added proof of the abject failure of Judaism; second, it completed the prophetic picture of Christ in the Millennium which John 2 supplies. We shall enlarge upon each of these points below.

In the previous articles of this series we have pointed out how that in the opening portion of John's Gospel two things are noticed repeatedly—the setting aside of Judaism, and the turning away from it to Christ. This was emphasized at some length in our last paper, where we showed that the giving out of the wine at the Cana marriage-feast, and the presence of the six waterpots of stone standing there empty, symbolized the spiritual condition of Israel at that time—they had lost the joy of their espousals and were devoid of spiritual life.

In the passage which is now before us, an even darker picture still is presented to view. Here all figures and symbols are dropped, and the miserable state of Judaism is made known in pointed and plain terms. Up to this stage, Israel's miserable condition spiritually, had been expressed by *negatives;* the Messiah was there in their midst, but, said His forerunner to the Jerusalem embassy, Him "ye know *not*" *(1:26);* so, again, in the first part of chap. 2, "They have *no* wine" *(2:3).* But here, in the second half of John 2, the *positive* evil which existed is fully exposed —the Temple was profaned.

"And the Jews' passover was at hand, and Jesus went up to Jerusalem" *(2:13).* Here is the first key to that which follows. The *"Lord's* passover" *(Ex. 12:11)* had degenerated into "the passover of *the Jews".* But this is not the particular point upon which we would now dwell. What we would call attention to, particularly, is the time-mark given here. Two things are linked together: the Passover and the Cleansing of the Temple. Now the reader will recall at once, that one of the express requirements of God in connection with the observance of the Passover was, that all leaven must be rigidly excluded from the houses of His people. The Passover was a busy time for every Jewish family: each home was subjected to a rigorous examination, lest ceremonial defilement, in the form of leaven should be found therein. "No leaven in your houses" was the requirement of the Law.

Now the center of Israel's ceremonial purity was the Temple, the Father's House. Israel gloried in the Temple, for it was one of the chief things which marked them off from all other nations, as the favored people of God. What other race of people could speak of Jehovah dwelling in their midst? And now Jehovah Himself was there, incarnate. And what a sight met His eye! The House of Prayer had become a house of merchandise; the holy place of worship was now "a den of thieves". Behold here the light shining in the darkness and exposing the real nature of things. No doubt the custodians of the Temple would have stood ready to excuse this reproach upon God's honor. They would have argued that these money-changers and cattle dealers, in the Temple courts, were there as a convenience to those who came to the Temple to worship. But Christ lays bare their real motive: "Den of thieves" tells us that the love of money, *covetousness,* lay at the bottom of it all.

And what is "covetousness"? What is the Divine symbol for it? Let us turn the light of Scripture on these questions. Notice carefully what is said in 1 Cor. 5.

Writing to the Corinthian believers, the Holy Spirit through the apostle Paul says, "Your glorying is not good. Know ye not that a little leaven leaveneth the whole lump? Purge out therefore the old leaven, that ye may be a new lump, as ye are unleavened. For even Christ our Passover is sacrificed for us: Therefore let us keep the feast, not with old leaven, neither with the leaven of malice and wickedness; but with the unleavened bread of sincerity and truth". To what was he referring here under the figure of "leaven"? Mark what follows: "I wrote unto you in an epistle not to company with fornicators: yet not altogether with the fornicators of this world, or with the covetous, or extortioners, or with idolaters" *(vv. 9, 10). Leaven,* then, here refers (among other things) to *covetousness, extortion and idolatry.* Now go back again to John 2. The feast of the passover was at hand, when all leaven must be removed from Israel's dwellings. And there in the Temple, were the cattle dealers and the money-changers, actuated by *covetousness* and practicing *extortion.* What horrible desecration was this! Leaven in the Temple of God!

But let us turn on the light of one more passage. In Col. 3:5 we read, "Covetousness, which is *idolatry".* Ah, does not this reveal the emptiness of Israel's boast! The Nation prided itself upon its Monotheism, —they worshipped not the many gods of the heathen. The Jews boasted that they were free from idolatry. Yet *idolatry*— "covetousness"—*was* the very thing the Son of God found in His Father's House. Note again, the force of 1 Cor. 5:10, covetousness, extortion, and idolatry are the three things there mentioned under the symbol of "leaven". Here, then, is the first reason why the Holy Spirit has placed this incident just where He has in this Gospel. It furnishes a striking climax to what has gone before. Put together these three things, and see what a glaring picture they give us of Judaism: first, a *blinded priesthood (John 1:19-26);* second, a *joyless Nation* (no "wine", *John 2:3);* third, a *desecrated Temple.*

There is a deeper meaning yet to this picture of the defiled Temple which Christ cleansed, that furnishes, we believe, an additional reason why the Holy Spirit has placed it side by side with the Cana marriage-scene. And this leads us to consider

II. Its Prophetic Significance.

In our last article we pointed out, how that what is recorded in John 2:1-11 furnishes us with a sevenfold view of Christ in the Millennium. The Cana marriage to which the Lord Jesus was invited, foreshadowed His coming marriage to restored Israel *(Isa. 54)*, after they shall have asked Him to return to them. The "third day" *(John 2:1)*, the unquestioning obedience of the servants *(2:7)*, the supplying of the good wine (symbol of joy), the "manifesting forth His glory" *(2:11)*, all typify that which shall find its ultimate fulfillment in the Millennium. But *before* Christ will come back to earth and gladden Israel's hearts with the wine of the Kingdom, the way for this must be prepared by a preliminary work of Divine judgment—"All things that offend" must first be "gathered out of His Kingdom" *(Matt. 13:41)*. And it is this which is prefigured in the second half of John 2.

After this Christian dispensation has closed, and before the Millennium begins, there intervenes the Tribulation period, when the Antichrist will be the central actor in the coming drama of Divine judgment, and when Israel as a nation will be at their greatest distance from God. Even now the stage is being rapidly set, and preparations for the fulfilling of the prophetic Word are going on apace. Jews are returning to Palestine in increasing numbers, the Hebrew language will soon become the dominant tongue in that land, and a separate Jewish State will, most probably, soon be an accomplished thing. A great revival of Judaism has long been looked for by students of prophecy, and it may be that even in our own lifetime a re-built Jewish temple shall replace the Moslem Mosque. Certain it is that when the coming Super-man makes his Covenant with the Jews *(Dan. 9:27)*, their new temple will then be standing in Jerusalem.

There is little room to doubt that, when the Jews erect their temple in Jerusalem, that their ancient system of worship will be revived, and that the blood of beasts will once more flow from their altars. But this will be regulated and dominated by the Antichrist. The prophetic scriptures make it clear that he will be in the position to do this. Unlimited power will be his; homage will be demanded from all his subjects, and none will be able to "buy or sell, save he that had the mark, or the name of the Beast, or the number of his name" *(Rev. 13:17)*.

Not for long, though, will the Jews be suffered to continue thus. In the midst of Daniel's seventieth week, the Antichrist will throw off this religious mask, break his covenant with Israel, and endeavor to stamp out everything that witnesses to the true and living God. As we are told in 2 Thess. 4, he is the one "who opposeth and exalteth himself above all that is called God, or that is worshipped; so that he as God sitteth in the temple of God, showing himself that he is God". An image will be made to the Antichrist, and his vicegerent will have power to "give life unto the image of the beast, that the image of the beast should both speak, and cause that as many as would not worship the image of the beast should be killed. And he causeth all, both small and great, rich and poor, free and bond, to receive a mark in their right hand, or in their foreheads" *(Rev. 13:15, 16)*. This image will be placed, we doubt not, in Israel's re-built temple, and it was to this that our Lord referred, when He said, "When ye therefore shall see *the abomination of desolation* spoken of by Daniel the prophet, stand in the holy place, (whoso readeth, let him understand:) Then let them which be in Judea flee into the mountains" *(Matt. 24:15, 16)*.

From these scriptures, then, we learn that there is to be another Temple in Jerusalem; that in all probability, oxen shall be sold and bought in it *(cf. "buy and sell"* in Rev. 13:17); that it shall be made an house of merchandise, and that, worst of all, it shall be defiled and profaned by the idolatrous image and worship there of the Antichrist. History will repeat itself. There is to be another "Temple" which will need cleansing!

There is one other line in this prophetic picture which should not be overlooked in this connection. In verses 23 and 24 we read, "Now when He was in Jerusalem at the passover, in the feast, many believed in His name, when they saw the miracles which He did. But Jesus *did not commit Himself unto them*". How strikingly this foreshadowed the day to come! When the Jews rebuild their Temple, and restore the ancient order of sacrifices, they will do so in the name of Jehovah. But He will not accept their worship, nor will He "commit Himself *unto them*".

Finally, the prophetic significance of Christ's Cleansing the Temple no doubt carries us forward into the Millennium itself, when as Zechariah's prophecy announces "Yea, every pot in Jerusalem and in Judah shall be holiness unto the Lord of Hosts: and all they that sacrifice shall come and take of them, and seethe therein: and in that day there shall be no more the Canaanite (which means 'trafficker') in the house of the Lord of Hosts" *(14:21)*. Taking John 2 as a whole we may observe that Christ gave a typical foreshadowing of the *power* of the Kingdom by working a miracle; second, He provided the *joy* of the Kingdom by supplying the wine; third, He made manifest His *title* to the Kingdom by exhibiting His Divine authority.

We turn now to consider

III. THE PRACTICAL LESSONS.

1. We see here the holy zeal of Christ for the Father's House. "Worshippers coming from remote parts of the Holy Land, found it a convenience to be able to purchase on the spot the animals used in sacrifice. Traders were not slow to supply this demand, and vying with one another they crept nearer and nearer to the sacred precincts, until some, under pretense of driving in an animal for sacrifice, made a sale within the outer court. This court had an area of about 14 acres, and was separated from the inner court by a wall breast high, and bearing intimations which forbade the encroachment of Gentiles on pain of death. Round this outer court ran marble colonnades, richly ornamented and supported by four rows of pillars, and roofed with cedar, affording ample shade to the traders.

There were not only cattle-dealers and sellers of doves, but also money-changers; for every Jew had to pay to the Temple treasury an annual tax of half a shekel, and this tax could be paid only in the sacred currency. No foreign coin, with its emblem of submission to an alien king, was allowed to pollute the Temple. Thus there came to be need of money-changers, not only for the Jew who had come up to the feast from a remote part of the empire, but even for the inhabitant of Palestine, as the Roman coinage had displaced the shekel in ordinary use.

Cattle-dealers and money-changers have always been notorious for making more than their own out of their bargains, and facts enough are on record to justify our Lord calling this particular market 'a den of thieves'. The poor were shamefully cheated, and the worship of God was hindered and impoverished instead of being facilitated and enriched. The worshipper who came to the Temple seeking quiet and fellowship with God had to push his way through the touts of the dealers, and have his devotional temper dissipated by the wrangling and shouting of a cattle-market. Yet although many must have lamented this, no one had been bold enough to rebuke and abolish the glaring profanation" *(Dr. Dods)*. But the Lord Jesus Christ could not suffer His Father's House to be reproached thus. Zeal for God consumes Him and without hesitation He cleanses the Temple of those who defiled it.

2. "And when He had made a scourge of small cords, He drove them all out of the Temple, and the sheep, and the oxen; and poured out the changers' money, and overthrew the tables" *(v. 15)*. How this brings out the *Deity* of Christ! First, He identifies Himself with the Temple, terming it "My Father's House", and thus affirming His Divine Sonship. This was something which none other had dreamed of doing. Neither Moses, Solomon nor Ezra, ever termed the Tabernacle or the Temple *his* "Father's house". Christ alone could do this. Again; mark the result of His interference. One man, single handed, takes a whip and the whole crowd flee in fear before Him. Ah, this was no mere man. It was the terror of *God* that had fallen upon them.

3. This incident brings before us a side of Christ's character which is almost universally ignored to-day. We think of the Lord Jesus as the gentle and compassionate One. And such He was, and still is. But this is not all He is. God is *Light*, as well as Love. God is *inflexibly righteous*, as well as infinitely gracious. God is *holy*, as well as merciful. And we do well to remind ourselves of this. Scripture declares "it is a fearful thing to fall into the hands of the living God", as all who defy Him will yet discover. Scripture speaks of "the *wrath* of the Lamb", and our lesson furnishes us with a solemn illustration of this. The unresisting money-changers and cattle-dealers, fleeing in terror before His flashing eye and upraised hand, give warning of what shall happen when the

wicked stand before the Throne of His Judgment.

4. This incident rebukes the present-day desecration of the House of Prayer. If the holy anger of the Lord Jesus was stirred when He beheld the profanation of that House which was to be a "House of Prayer", if the idolatrous commercialization of it caused Him to cleanse it in such a drastic manner, how must He now regard many of the edifices which have been consecrated to His name! How tragically does history repeat itself. The things which are now done in so many church-houses—the ice cream suppers, the bazaars, the moving picture turns and other forms of entertainment—what are these but idolatrous commercialization of these "houses of prayer"! No wonder that such places are devoid of spirituality and strangers to the power of God. The Lord will not tolerate an unholy mixture of worldly things with spiritual.

5. One of the questions we drew up at the close of our last article, was, "Why did not Christ *drive out* the 'doves'?" The answer to this is found in Isa. 52:13, where God through His prophet, declared of the Messiah then to come, "Behold, My servant shall deal prudently". The "prudence" of Christ was strikingly evidenced by His mode of proceedure on this occasion of the Cleansing of the Temple. The attentive reader will observe that He distinguished, carefully, between the different objects of His displeasure. The oxen and sheep He *drove out,* and these were in no danger of being lost by this treatment. The money of the changers He *threw on the ground,* and this could be easily picked up again and carried away. The doves He simply ordered to be *taken away:* had He done more with *them,* they might have flown away, and been lost to their owners. Thus, the perfect One combined wisdom with zeal. How differently would Moses or Elijah have acted under similar circumstances! But even in His anger, Christ dealt in *prudence.* Christ *rebuked* all, yet none were really injured, and nothing was lost. O that we may learn of Him Who has left us such a perfect example.

6. "Then answered the Jews and said unto Him, What sign showest Thou unto us seeing that Thou doest these things?" *(v. 18).* This demand for a "sign" evidenced their blindness, and gave proof of what the Baptist had said—"There standeth One among you whom ye know not" *(1:26).* To have given *them* a sign, would only have been to confirm them in their unbelief. Men who could desecrate God's House as they had, men who were so utterly devoid of any sense of what was due Jehovah, were judicially blinded, and Christ treats them accordingly: "Jesus answered and said unto them, Destroy this temple, and in three days I will raise it up" *(v. 19).* He spoke in language which was quite unintelligible to them. "Then said the Jews, Forty and six years was this temple in building, and wilt Thou rear it up in three days? But He spake of the temple of His body" *(vv. 20, 21).* But why should the Lord express Himself in such ambiguous terms? Because, as He Himself said on another occasion, "Therefore speak I to them in parables: because they seeing see not; and hearing they hear not, neither do they understand" *(Matt. 13:13).* Yet, in reality, our Lord's reply to these Jews was much to the point. In raising Himself from the dead He would furnish the final proof that He was God manifest in the flesh, and if God, then the One Who possessed the unequivocal right to cleanse the defiled Temple which bore His name. It is very significant to compare these words of Christ here with what we find in Matt. 21: 24-27, spoken, we doubt not, on the same occasion. When challenged as to His authority, Matthew tells us He appealed to the witness of His *forerunner,* which was primarily designed for the Jews after the flesh. But John mentions our Lord's appeal to His own *resurrection,* because this demonstrated His Deity, and has an evidential value for the whole household of faith.

7. Another of the questions asked at the close of our previous article was, "Did the Lord's own disciples believe in the promise of His resurrection?" The answer is, No, they did not. The evidence for this is conclusive. The death of the Saviour shattered their hopes. Instead of remaining in Jerusalem till the third day, eagerly awaiting His resurrection they retired to their homes. When Mary Magdalene went to tell His disciples that she had seen the risen Christ, they "believed not" *(Mark 16:11).* When the two disciples returned from Emmaus and reported unto the others how the Saviour had appeared unto them and had walked with them, we are told, "neither believed they them" *(Mark*

16:13). The testimony of these eye-witnesses "seemed to them as idle tales" *(Luke 24:11)*. But how is this to be explained? How can we account for the persistent unbelief of these disciples? Ah, is not the answer to be found in the Lord's teaching in the Parable of the Sower? Does He not there warn us, that the great Enemy of souls comes and *catches away* the "seed" sown! And this is what had taken place with these disciples. They had heard the Saviour say He *would* raise up the temple of His body in three days, but instead of treasuring up this precious promise in their hearts, and being comforted by it, they had, through their unbelief, allowed the Devil to snatch it away. Their unbelief, we say, for in verse 22 we are told, "When therefore He was risen from the dead, His disciples remembered He had said this unto them; and they believed the Scriptures, and the word which Jesus had said." It was not until *after* He had risen that they "remembered" and "believed" the word which Jesus had said. And what was it that enabled them to "remember" it then? Ah, do we not recall what Christ had said to them on the eve of His crucifixion, "But the comforter, the Holy Spirit, whom the Father will send in My name, He shall teach you all things, *and bring all things to your remembrance,* whatsoever I have *said* unto you" *(John 14:26)*. What a striking and beautiful illustration of this is given us here in John 2:22!

8. "Now when He was in Jerusalem at the passover, in the feast, many believed in His name, when they saw the miracles which He did. *But Jesus did not commit Himself unto them,* because He knew all" *(vv. 23, 24)*. What a word is this! How it evidences human depravity! Fallen man is a creature that God will not trust. In Eden Adam showed, that man after the flesh, is not to be trusted. The Law had proved him still unworthy of the confidence of God. And now this same character is stamped upon him by the Lord Jesus Himself. As another has said, "Man's affections may be stirred, man's intelligence informed, man's conscience convicted; but still God cannot trust him." *(J. E. B.)* Man in the flesh is condemned. Only a new creation avails before God. Man must be "born again".

9. "Jesus did not *commit Himself* unto them" *(v. 24)*. The Lord's example here is a warning for us. We do well to remember that all is not gold that glitters. It is not wise to trust in appearances of friendliness on short acquaintance. The discrete man will be kind to all, but intimate with few. The late Bishop Ryle has some practical counsels to offer on this point. Among other things he said, "Learn not to place yourself rashly in the power of others. Study to develop a wise and happy moderation between universal suspiciousness and that of making yourself the sport and prey of every pretender and hypocrite".

10. "Jesus did not commit Himself unto them, because He knew all and needed not that any should testify of man: *for He knew what was in man*" *(vv. 24, 25)*. Here we are shown the Saviour's perfect knowledge of the human heart. These men could not impose upon the Son of God. He knew that they were only "stony ground" hearers, and therefore, not to be depended upon. They were only intellectually convinced. Our Lord clearly discerned this. He knew that their profession was not from the heart. And reading thus their hearts He manifested His *omniscience*. The force of what is said in these closing words of John 2 will be made more evident if we compare them with 1 Kings 8:39: "Hear Thou in heaven Thy dwelling-place, and forgive, and do, and give to every man according to his ways, whose heart Thou knowest; for Thou, *even Thou only*, knowest the hearts of all the children of men".

It only remains for us to point out how that there is a series *of most striking contrasts* between the two incidents recorded in the first and second parts of this chapter—the making of water into wine at the Cana marriage-feast, and the Cleansing of the Temple. 1. In the one we have a *festive* gathering; in the other a scene of Divine *judgment*. 2. To the former the Lord Jesus was *invited;* in the latter He took the initiative *Himself*. 3. In the former case He employed *human instruments;* in the latter He acted all *alone*. 4. In the former He *supplied* wine; in the latter He *emptied* the Temple. 5. In the former, His act of making the wine was *commended;* in the Cleansing of the Temple, He was *challenged*. 6. In the former Christ pointed forward to His *death (see 2:4);* in the latter He pointed forward to His *resurrection (see 2:19, 21)*. 7. In the former He "manifested forth His *glory*" (*2:11*); in the latter He manifested His "*zeal*" for His Father's House (*2:17*).

In conclusion, we have again drawn up a number of questions to be prayerfully studied and meditated upon in preparation for the next lesson, when we shall, D. V., give an exposition of the first portion of John 3.

1. Why is Nicodemus referred to in this connection? v. 1.
2. Why are we told he came to Jesus "by night"? v. 2.
3. Was Nicodemus' conclusion justifiable? v. 2.
4. *Why* cannot a man "see" the Kingdom of God except he be "born again"? v. 3.
5. What did Nicodemus' ignorance demonstrate? v. 4.
    What does "born of water" mean? v. 5.
7. In what other ways is the blowing of the Wind analogous with the activities of the Holy Spirit in regeneration? v. 8. —*Arthur W. Pink.*

THE WISDOM OF GOD DISPLAYED IN THE WAY OF SALVATION

Continued.

SECTION VI.

How the Wisdom of God Appears in the Manner and Circumstances of Obtaining the Good Intended

We now come to take notice of some wonderful circumstances of the attainment of our good, hereby; which shows the great wisdom of this contrivance.

1. So hath God contrived in this way, that a sinful creature should become not guilty; and that he who has no righteousness of his own, should become righteous. These things, if they had been proposed, would have appeared contradictions to any but the Divine understanding.

If it had been proposed to any created intelligence, to find out a way in which a *sinful* creature should not be a *guilty* creature, how impossible would it have been judged, that there should be any way at all. It would doubtless have been judged impossible but that he who has committed sin, must stand guilty of the sin he has committed; and if sin necessarily obliges to punishment, it must oblige him who has committed it. If punishment and sin be inseparable, then that punishment and the sinner are inseparable. If the Law denounces death to the person who is guilty of sin, and if it be impossible that the law should not take place, then he who has committed sin must die. Thus any created understanding would have thought.

And if it had been proposed, that there should be some way found out, wherein man must be righteous without fulfilling righteousness himself; so that he might reasonably and properly be looked upon and accepted as a righteous person, and adjudged to the reward of righteousness, and yet have no righteousness of his own, but the contrary—that he should be righteous by the righteousness of the law, by a perfect righteousness, and yet have broken the law, and done nothing else but break it—this doubtless would have been looked upon as impossible and contradictious.

But yet the wisdom of God has truly accomplished each of these things. He hath accomplished that men, though sinners, should be without guilt, in that He hath found a way that the threatenings of the law should truly and properly be fulfilled, and punishment be executed on sin, and yet not on the sinner. The sufferings of Christ answer the demands of the law, with respect to the sins of those who believe in Him; and justice is truly satisfied thereby. And the law is fulfilled and answered by the obedience of Christ, so that His righteousness should properly be our righteousness. Though not performed by us, yet it is properly and reasonably accepted for us, as much as if we had performed it ourselves. Divine wisdom has so contrived, that such an interchanging of sin and righteousness should be consistent, and most agreeable with reason, with the law, and God's holy attributes. For Jesus Christ has so united Himself to us, and us to Him, as to make Himself ours, our Head. The love of Christ to the elect is so great, that God the Father looks upon it proper and suitable to account Christ and the elect as one; and according to account what Christ does and suffers, as if they *did* and *suffered* it. That love of Christ which is so great as to render Him willing to put Himself in the stead of the elect, and to bear the misery that they deserved, does, in the Father's account, so unite Christ and the elect, that they may be looked upon as legally one.

2. It shows wonderful wisdom that our good should be procured by such seemingly unlikely and opposite means, as the humiliation of the Son of God. When Christ was about to undertake that great work of redemption, He did not take that method that any creature-wisdom would have thought the most proper. Creature-wisdom would have determined that in order to His effectually and more gloriously accomplishing such a great work, He should rather have been exalted higher, if it had been possible, instead than humbled so low. Earthly kings and princes, when they are about to engage in any great and difficult work, will put on their strength, and will appear in all their majesty and power, that they may be successful. But when Christ was about to perform the great work of redeeming a lost world, the wisdom of God took an opposite method, and determined that He should be humbled and abased to a mean state, and appear in low circumstances. He did not deck Himself with glory, but laid it aside. He emptied Himself. "Being in the form of God—He made Himself of no reputation, and took on Him the form of a servant, and was made in the likeness of men: and being found in fashion as a man, He humbled Himself, and became obedient unto death, even the death of the cross" *(Phil. 2:6-8).* Creature-wisdom would have thought that Christ, in order to perform this great work, should deck Himself with all His strength; but Divine wisdom determined, that He should be made weak, or put on the infirmities of human nature.

And why did Divine wisdom determine that He should become thus weak? It was that He might be subject to want, and to suffering, and to the power and malice of His enemies. But then what advantage could it be to Him in this work, to be subject to the power and malice of His enemies? It was the very design on which He came into this world, to overthrow His enemies. Who would have thought that this was the way to overthrow them, that He should become weak and feeble, and for that very end that He might be subject to their power and malice? But this is the very means by which God determined, that Christ should prevail against His enemies, even that He should be subject to their power, that they might prevail against Him, so as to put Him to disgrace, and pain, and death.

What other but Divine wisdom could ever have determined, that this was the way to be taken in order to being successful in the work of our redemption! This would have appeared to creature-wisdom the most direct course to be frustrated that could be devised. But indeed it was the way to glorious success, and the only way. "The foolishness of God is wiser than men" *(1 Cor. 1:25).* God has brought strength out of weakness, glory out of ignominy and reproach. Christ's shame and reproach are the only means by which a way is made to our eternal honor.

The wisdom of God hath made Christ's humiliation the means of our exaltation; His coming down from heaven is that which brings us to heaven. The wisdom of God hath made life the fruit of death. The death of Christ was the only means by which we could have eternal life. The death of a person who was God, was the only way by which we could come to have life in God. Here favor is made to arise out of wrath; our acceptance into God's favor out of God's wrath upon His own Son. A blessing rises out of a curse; our everlasting blessedness, from Christ being made a curse for us. Our righteousness is made to rise out of Christ's imputed guilt. He was made sin for us, that we might be made the righteousness of God *(2 Cor. 5:21).* By such wonderful means hath the wisdom of God procured our salvation.

3. Our sin and misery, by this contrivance, are made an occasion of our greater blessedness. This is a very wonderful thing. It would have been a very wonderful thing if we had been merely restored from sin and misery, to be as we were before; but it was a much more wonderful thing that we should be brought to a higher blessedness than ever; and that our sin and misery should be the occasion of it, and should make way for it.

(1) It was wonderful that *sin* should be made the occasion of our greater blessedness for sin deserves misery. By our sin we had deserved to be everlastingly miser-

able; but this is so termed by Divine wisdom, that it is made an occasion of our being more happy. It was a strange thing that sin should be the occasion of anything else but misery: but Divine wisdom has found out a way whereby the sinner might not only escape being miserable, but that he should be happier than before he sinned; yea, than he would have been if he had never sinned at all. And this sin and unworthiness of his, are the occasion of this greater blessedness.

(2) It was a wonderful thing that man's own *misery* should be an occasion of his greater happiness. For happiness and misery are contraries; and man's misery was very great. He was under the wrath and curse of God, and condemned to everlasting burnings. But the sin and misery of man, by this contrivance, are made an occasion of his being more happy, not only than he was before the fall, but than he would have been if he never had fallen.

Our first parents, if they had stood and persevered in perfect obedience, till God had given them the fruit of the tree of life as a seal of their reward, would probably have been advanced to higher happiness: for they before were but in a state of probation for their reward. And it is not to be supposed but that their happiness was to have been greater after they had persisted in obedience, and had actually received the reward, than it was while they were in a state of trial for it. But by the redemption of Christ, the sin and misery of the elect are made an occasion of their being brought to a higher happiness than mankind would have had if they had persisted in obedience till they had received the reward. For,

1st. Man is hereby brought to a greater and nearer *union* with God. If man had never fallen, God would have remained man's Friend; he would have enjoyed God's favor, and so would have been the object of Christ's favor, as he would have had the favor of all the persons of the Trinity. But now Christ becoming our Surety and Saviour, and having taken on Him our nature, occasions between Christ and us a union of a quite different kind, and a nearer relation than otherwise would have been. The fall is the occasion of Christ becoming our Head, and the Church His body. And believers are become His brethren, and spouse, in a manner that otherwise would not have been. And by our union with Christ we have a greater union with God the Father. We are sons by virtue of our union with the natural Son of God. "When the fulness of time was come, God sent forth His son, made of a woman, made under the law, to redeem them that were under the law, that we might receive the adoption of sons. And because ye are sons, God hath sent forth the spirit of His Son into your hearts, crying, Abba, Father" *(Gal. 4:4-6)*. And therefore Christ has taught us, in all our addresses to God, to call Him our Father, in like manner as He calls Him Father: "Go tell My brethren, Behold I ascend to My Father, and your Father" *(John 20:17)*.

This is one of the wonderful things brought about by the work of redemption, that thereby our separation from God is made an occasion of a greater union than was before, or otherwise would have been. When we fell, there was a dreadful separation made betwixt God and us, but this is made an occasion of a greater union: "Neither pray I for these alone, but for them also which shall believe on Me through their word; that they all may be one, as Thou Father art in Me, and I in Thee; that they also may be one in Us: that the world may believe that Thou hast sent Me. And the glory which Thou gavest Me I have given them; that they may be one, even as We are one: I in them and Thou in Me, that they may be made perfect in one" *(John 17:20-23)*.

2ndly. Man now has greater *manifestations* of the *glory* and *love* of God, than otherwise he would have had. In the manifestations of these two things, man's happiness principally consists. Now, man by the work of redemption, has greater manifestation of both, than otherwise he would have had. We have already spoken particularly of the glory of God, and what advantages even the angels have by the discoveries of it in this work; but if *they* have such advantages much more will *man*, who is far more directly concerned in this affair than they. Here are immediately greater displays of the love of God, than man had before he fell; or, as we may well suppose, than he would have had, if he had never fallen. God now manifests His love to His people, by sending His Son into the world, to die for them. There never would have been any such testimony of the love of God, if man had not fallen.

Christ manifests His love, by coming into the world, and laying down His life. This is the greatest testimony of Divine love that can be conceived. Now, surely, the greater discoveries God's people have of His love to them, the more occasion will they have to rejoice in that love. Here will be a delightful theme for the saints to contemplate to all eternity which they never could have had, if man never had fallen, namely, the dying love of Christ. They will have occasion now to sing that song forever, "Unto Him that loved us, and washed us from our sins in His own blood, and hath made us kings and priests unto God and His Father; to whom be glory and dominion forever. Amen" *(Rev. 1:5,6)*.

3rdly. Man now has greater *motives* offered him to love God than otherwise he would have had. Man's happiness consists in mutual love between God and man; in seeing God's love to him, and in reciprocally loving God. And the more he sees of God's love to him, and the more he loves God, the more happy must he be. His love to God is as necessary in order to his happiness, as the seeing of God's love to him; for he can have no joy in beholding God's love to him, any otherwise than as he loves God. This makes the saints prize God's love to them; for *they love Him*. If they did not love God, to see His love to them would not make them happy. But the more any person loves another, the more will he be delighted in the manifestations of that other's love. There is provision therefore made for both in the work of redemption. There are greater *manifestations* of the love of God to us, than there would have been if man had not fallen; and also there are greater *motives* to love Him than otherwise there would have been. There are greater *obligations* to love Him, for God has done more for us to win our love. Christ has died for us.

Again, man is now brought to a more universal and immediate and *sensible dependence* on God, than otherwise he would have been. All his happiness is now *of* Him, *through* Him, *in* Him. If man had not fallen, he would have had all his happiness of God by his own righteousness; but now it is by the righteousness of Christ. He would have had all his holiness of God, but not so sensibly; because then he would have been holy from the beginning, as soon as he received his being; but now, he is first sinful and universally corrupt, and afterwards is made holy. If man had held his integrity, misery would have been a stranger to him; and therefore happiness would not have been so sensible a derivation from God, as it now is, when man looks to God from the deeps of distress, cries repeatedly to Him, and waits upon Him. He is convinced by abundant experience, that he has no place of resort but God, who is graciously pleased, in consequence of man's earnest and persevering suit, to appear to his relief, to take him out of the miry clay and horrible pit, set him upon a rock, establish his goings, and put a new song into his mouth. By man's having thus a more immediate, universal, and sensible dependence, God doth more entirely secure man's undivided respect. There is a greater motive for man to make God his all in all,—to love Him, and to rejoice in Him, as his only portion.

4thly. By the contrivance for our salvation, man's sin and misery are but an occasion of his being brought to a more full and free *converse* with and *enjoyment* of God than otherwise would have been. For as we have observed already, the union is greater; and the greater the union, the more full the communion, and intimate the intercourse. Christ is come down to man in his own nature; and hereby he may converse with Christ more intimately, than the infinite distance of the Divine nature would allow. This advantage is more than what the angels have. For Christ is not only in a *created* nature, but He *is in man's own nature*. We have also advantages for a more full *enjoyment* of God. By Christ's incarnation, the saints may see God with their bodily eyes, as well as by an intellectual view. The saints, after the day of judgment, will consist of both body and soul: they will have outward as well as spiritual sight. It is now ordered by Divine wisdom that God Himself, or a Divine person, should be the principal entertainment of both these kinds of sight, spiritual and corporeal: and the saints in heaven shall not only have an intellectual sight of God, but they shall see a Divine person as they see one another; not only spiritually, but outwardly. The body of Jesus Christ will appear with that transcendent majesty and beauty, which is exceedingly expressive of the Divine majesty, beauty, and glory. The body of Christ shall appear with the glory of God upon it, as Christ tells us: "The Son of Man shall come in the glory of His Father" *(Matt. 16:27)*. Thus to see God will be a great happiness to the saints. Job comforted himself that he should see God with his bodily eyes: "And though after my skin worms destroy this body, yet in my flesh shall I see God".

5thly. Man's sin and misery is made an occasion of his greater happiness, as he has now a greater relish of happiness, by reason of his knowledge of both. In order to happiness, there must be two things, namely, union to a proper object, and a relish of the object. Man's misery is made an occasion of increasing both these by the work of redemption. We have shown already, that the union is increased; and so is the relish too, by the knowledge man now has of evil. These contraries, good and evil, heighten the sense of one another. The forbidden tree was called the tree of knowledge of good and evil; of *evil*, because by it we came to the experience of evil; of *good*, because we should never have known so well what good was, if it had not been, for that tree. This teaches us to prize good, and makes us the more to relish and rejoice in it. The saints know something what a state of sin and alienation from God is. They know something what the anger of God is, and what it is to be in danger of hell. And this makes them the more exceedingly to rejoice in the favor and in the enjoyment of God.

Take two persons; one who never knew what evil was, but was happy from the first moment of his being, having the favor of God, and numerous tokens of it; another who is in a very doleful and undone condition. So the saints in heaven will forever the more rejoice in God, and in the enjoyment of His love, for their being brought to it out of a most lamentable state and condition.

SECTION VII.

Some Wonderful Circumstances of the Overthrow of Satan

The wisdom of God greatly and remarkably appears in so exceedingly baffling and confounding all the subtlety of the old Serpent. Power never appears so conspicuous as when opposed, and conquering opposition. The same may be said of wisdom; it never appears so brightly, and with such advantage as when opposed by the subtlety of some very crafty enemy; and in baffling and confounding that subtlety. The Devil is exceeding subtle. The subtlety of the serpent is emblematical of his *(Gen. 3:1)*. He was once one of the bright intelligences of heaven, and one of the brightest, if not the very brightest of all. And all the demons were once morning stars, of a glorious brightness of understanding. They still have the same faculties, though they ceased to be influenced and guided by the Holy Spirit of God; and so their heavenly wisdom is turned into hellish craft and subtlety. God in the work of redemption hath wondrously baffled the utmost craft of the demons, though they are all combined to frustrate God's designs of glory to Himself, and goodness to men. The wisdom of God appears very glorious herein. For,

1. Consider the weak and seemingly despicable means and weapons that God employs to overthrow Satan. Christ poured the greatest contempt upon Satan in the victory that He obtained over him, by reason of the means of His preparing Himself for it, and the weapons He hath used. Christ chooses to encounter Satan in the human nature, in a poor, frail, afflicted state. He did as David did. David when going against the Philistines refused Saul's armour, a helmet of brass, a coat of mail, and his sword. No, he puts them all off. Goliath comes mightily armed against David, with a helmet of brass upon his head, a coat of mail weighing five thousand shekels of brass, greaves of brass upon his legs, and a target of brass between his shoulders; a spear, whose staff was like a weaver's beam; and the spear's head weighing six hundred shekels of iron. And besides all this, he had one bearing a shield before him. But David takes nothing but a staff in his hand, and a shepherd's bag and a sling; and he goes against the Philistine. So the weapons that Christ made use of were his poverty, afflictions and reproaches, sufferings and death. His principal weapon was His cross: the instrument of His own reproachful death. These were seemingly weak and despicable instruments, to wield against such a giant as Satan. And doubtless the Devil disdained them as much as Goliath did David's stave and sling. But

with such weapons as these has Christ, in a human, weak, mortal nature, overthrown and baffled all the crafts of hell.

Such disgrace and contempt has Christ poured upon Satan. David had a more glorious victory over Goliath for his conquering him with such mean instruments; and Samson over the Philistines, for killing so many of them with such a despicable weapon as the jaw-bone of an ass. It is spoken of in Scripture as a glorious triumph of Christ over the Devil, that He should overcome him by such a despicable weapon as His cross: "Blotting out the handwriting of ordinances that was against us, which was contrary to us, and took it out of the way, nailing it to His cross: and having spoiled principalities and powers, He made a shew of them openly, triumphing over them in it" *(Col. 2:14, 15)*. God shows His great and intimate wisdom in taking this method, to confound the wisdom and subtlety of His enemies. He hereby shows how easily He can do it, and that He is infinitely wiser than they. "God hath chosen the foolish things of the world, to confound the wise; and God hath chosen the weak things of the world, to confound the things that are mighty: and the base things of the world, and things that are despised, hath God chosen; yea, and things that are not, to bring to naught things that are" *(I Cor. 1:27, 28)*.

2. God has hereby confounded Satan with his own weapons. It is so contrived in the work of redemption, that our grand enemy should be made a means of his own confusion; and that, by those very things whereby he endeavors to rob God of His glory, and to destroy mankind, he is made an instrument of frustrating his own designs. His most subtle and powerful endeavors for accomplishing his designs are made a means of confounding them, and of promoting the contrary. Of this, I will mention but two instances. First; his procuring man's fall is made an occasion of the contrary to what he designed. Indeed he has hereby procured the ruin of multitudes of mankind, which he aimed at. But in this he does not frustrate God's design from all eternity to glorify Himself; and the misery of multitudes of mankind will prove no content to him, but will enhance his own misery.

What Satan did in tempting man to fall, is made an occasion of the contrary of what he intended, in that it gave occasion for God to glorify Himself the more; and gave occasion for the elect being brought to higher happiness.

The happy state of man was envied by Satan. That man who was of earthly origin should be advanced to such honors, when he who was originally of a so much more noble nature should be cast down to such disgrace, his pride could not bear. How then would Satan triumph, when he had brought him down!

The Devil tempted our first parents with this, that if they would eat of the forbidden fruit, they should be as gods. It was a lie in Satan's mouth; for he aimed at nothing else but to fool man out of his happiness, and make him his own slave and vassal, with a blinded expectation of being a god. But little did Satan think that God would turn it so, as to make man's fall an occasion of God's becoming man; and so an occasion of our nature being advanced to a state of closer union to God.

By this means it comes to pass, that one in man's nature now sits at the right hand of God, invested with Divine power and glory, and reigns over heaven and earth with a Godlike power and dominion. Thus is Satan disappointed in his subtlety. As he intended that saying, *"Ye shall be as gods"*, it was a lie, to decoy and befool man. Little did he think, that it would be in such manner verified by the incarnation of the Son of God. And this is the occasion also of all the elect being united to this Divine person, so that they become one with Christ. Believers are as members and parts of Christ, yea, the church is called Christ. Little did Satan think, that his telling that lie to our first parents, "Ye shall be as gods", would be the occasion of their being members of Christ the Son of God.

Again, Satan is made a means of his own confusion in this:—It was Satan's design, in tempting man to sin, to make man his captive and slave forever; to have plagued, and triumphed over him. And this very thing is a means to bring it about, that man instead of being his vassal shall be his judge. The elect, instead of being his captives, to be forever tormented and triumphed over by him, shall sit as judges to sentence him to everlasting torment. It has been the means, that one in man's nature should be his supreme Judge. It was man's nature that Satan so envied, and sought to make a prey of. But Jesus Christ at the last day shall come in man's nature; and the demons shall be all brought to stand trembling at His bar: and He shall judge, and condemn them, and execute the wrath of God upon them. And not only shall Christ in the human nature judge the demons, but all the saints shall judge them with Christ as assessors with Him in judgment: "Know ye not that we shall judge angels?" *(1 Cor. 6:3)*.

In another instance Satan is made a means of his own confusion; that is, in his procuring the death of Christ. Satan set himself to oppose Christ as soon as He appeared. He sought, by all means, to procure His ruin. He set the Jews against Him. He filled the minds of the scribes and Pharisees with the most bitter persecuting malice against Christ. He sought by all means to procure His death; and that He might be put to the most ignominious death. We read that "Satan entered into Judas", and tempted him to betray Him *(Luke 22:3)*. And Christ speaks of His sufferings as being the effects of the power of darkness: "When I was daily with you in the temple, ye stretched forth no hands against Me, but this is your hour and the power of darkness" *(Luke 22:53)*. But Satan hereby overthrows his own kingdom. Christ came into the world to destroy the works of the Devil. And this was the very thing that did it, namely, the blood and death of Christ. The Cross was the Devil's own weapon; and with this weapon he was overthrown: as David cut off Goliath's head with his own sword.

Christ thus making Satan a means of his own confusion was typified of old by Samson's getting honey out of the carcase of the lion. There is more implied in Samson's riddle, "Out of the eater came forth meat, and out of the strong came forth sweetness", than ever the Pharisees explained. It was verified by Christ in a far more glorious manner. God's enemies and ours are taken in the pit which they themselves have digged: and their own soul is taken in the net which they have laid. Thus we have shown, in some measure, the wisdom of this way of salvation by Jesus Christ.

SECTION VIII.

The Superiority of This Wisdom to That of the Angels

The wisdom of this contrivance appears to have been above the wisdom of the angels by the following things.

1. It appears that the angels did not fully comprehend the contrivance, till they saw it accomplished. They knew that man was to be redeemed, long before Christ came into the world: but yet they did not fully comprehend it until they saw it. This is evident by the expression in the text, *"That now might be known unto the principalities"—the manifold wisdom of God:* i. e., Now the work is actually accomplished by Jesus Christ. Which implies that it was now new to them. If they understood no more of it now, than they had all along, the apostle would have expressed himself so; for he is speaking of it as a mystery, in a measure kept hid until now.

Now it is to be considered, that the angels had four thousand years to contemplate this affair; and they did not want inclination and desire to understand and look into it, as the Scripture teaches us. They had also a great deal to put them upon an attentive contemplation of it. For when it was made known that God had such a design, it must appear a new and wonderful thing to them. They had seen their fellow-angels destroyed without mercy; and this redeeming of the fallen sinful creature, was quite a new thing. It must needs be astonishing to them, when God had revealed this design of mercy to them presently after the fall; and had given an intimation of it, in saying, "The seed of the woman shall bruise the serpent's head". They knew that God had such a design; for they were, from the beginning, ministering spirits, sent forth to minister to those that were the heirs of salvation. They were present at the institution of the typical dispensation, that was so full of shadows of Gospel truth: Psa. 69:17.

The angels contemplating the contrivance of our redemption was typified by the posture of the cherubims over the mercy-seat, which was the lid of the ark. These emblems were made bending down towards the ark and mercy-seat. This is what the apostle Peter is thought to have some reference to, in 1 Pet. 1:12. Yet the angels, though for four thousand years they had been studying this contrivance, did not fully comprehend it till they saw it accomplished. This shows that the wisdom of it is far above theirs; for if they could not fully comprehend it after it had been revealed that there was such a design

—and after much of it had already been made known in the Old Testament—how much less could they have found it out of themselves?

Consider for what end this wisdom of God was made known unto the angels, namely, that they might admire and prize it. It was made known to them, that they might see how manifold, how great and glorious, it is; that they might see the unspeakable "depths of the riches of the wisdom and knowledge of God", as the apostle expresses it, Rom. 11:33. It was manifested to them that they might see the glory of God in it, and how great and wonderful the mystery was. "Great is the mystery of godliness: God was manifest in the flesh, justified in the Spirit, seen of angels" *(1 Tim. 3:16).* Now if the wisdom of it were not far above their own understanding, this would not be shown them for the express purpose that they might admire and praise God for it.

2. It appears to be above the wisdom of the angels, because they are still contemplating it; and endeavoring to see more and more of it. Indeed there is room for their faculties to employ themselves to all eternity. It is evident from 1 Pet. 1:11, 12 that they are still employing themselves in endeavoring to see more and more of God's wisdom appearing in the work of redemption, "Searching what or what manner of time the Spirit of Christ which was in them did signify, when it testified beforehand of the sufferings of Christ, and the glory that should follow. Unto whom it was revealed, that not unto themselves, but unto us they did minister the things which are now reported unto you by them that have preached the Gospel unto you, with the Holy Spirit sent down from heaven; which things the angels desire to look into". They still desire to look into it, after they have seen it accomplished. They do not so perfectly comprehend all the wisdom that is to be seen in it; but they are contemplating, looking into it, that they may see more and more; but there will still be room enough in this work to employ the angelical understandings.—*Jonathan Edwards.*

(To be concluded, D. V.).

THE PERFECTIONS OF GOD

Just views of the Divine character lie at the foundation of all true religion. Without them it is impossible, in the nature of things, to love God, or to perceive the fitness of our being required to love Him, or the evil of not loving Him, or the necessity of such a Saviour and such a salvation as the Gospel reveals. We may be terrified by the fear of the wrath to come, and delighted with the hope of escaping it through Christ; but if this terror and this hope have no respect to the character of God as holy, just, and good, there can be no hatred of sin *as sin,* nor love to God *as God,* and consequently no true religion. "This is life eternal, to know Thee the only true God, and Jesus Christ Whom Thou hast sent." God is a Spirit, and cannot be known by sense, nor by any means but those in which He has been pleased to manifest Himself.—*Andrew Fuller, 1824.*

Now, dear children of God, if any of you are in bondage under the Law, why do you remain so? Let the redeemed go free. Are you fond of wearing chains? Are you like Chinese women that delight to wear little shoes which crush their feet? Do you enjoy slavery? Do you wish to be captives? You are not under the Law, but under grace; will you allow your unbelief to put you under the Law? You are not a slave. Why tremble like a slave? You are a child; you are a son; you are an heir; live up to your privileges. You are members of the household of God; then be not as a stranger. I hear Ishmael laughing at you; let him laugh. Tell your Father of him, and He will soon say, "Cast out this bondwoman and her son." Free grace is not to be mocked by human merit; neither are we to be made sad by the forebodings of the legal spirit. Our soul rejoices, and, like Isaac, is filled with holy laughter; for the Lord has done great things for us whereof we are glad. To Him be glory for ever and ever. Amen.—*C. H. Spurgeon.*

STUDIES in the SCRIPTURES

"Search the Scriptures" John 5:39.

A PERIODICAL (MONTHLY "IF THE LORD WILL") DEVOTED TO BIBLE STUDIES and EXPOSITIONS

Associate Editors and Publishers, I. C. HERENDEEN and ARTHUR W. PINK,
Swengel, Pa.

Price: 10 cents per copy; $1.00 per year. Foreign $1.00 per year.

TO OUR SCRIPTURE STUDY FAMILY—

We called attention last month to the importance of the 119th Psalm, and the need for the believer to live daily in its atmosphere. If we would grow in grace and in the knowledge of the Lord, and if we are seeking a better understanding of God's Word, we must read and re-read this Psalm until we make its language our own.

Two things stand out prominently here: the petitions of the Psalmist for God to illumine him and enable him to subject himself to the teaching of Scripture, and the happy consequences and blessed results which comes to one who does this. We single out a few verses which illustrate each of these points:—

"*O that my ways were directed* to keep Thy statutes" *(v. 5)*. "With my whole heart have I sought Thee: *O let me not wander* from Thy commandments" *(v. 10)*. "*Open Thou mine eyes,* that I may behold wondrous things out of Thy law" *(v. 18)*. "*Teach me, O Lord,* the way of Thy statutes; and I shall keep it unto the end" *(v. 33)*. "*Make me to go* in the path of Thy commandments" *(v. 35)*. "*Incline my heart* unto Thy testimonies" *(v. 36)*. "*Give me understanding,* that I may learn Thy commandments" *(v. 73)*. "*Order my steps* in Thy Word: and let not any iniquity have any dominion over me" *(v. 133)*.

A careful reading of these verses will show how deeply the Psalmist realized his own waywardness and sinfulness, and because of this how conscious he was that he needed Divine grace to abound toward him. He realized his own inability to behold the wonders and glories of the written Word. He knew that God must open his eyes, quicken his soul, incline his heart and give him understanding, if he was to make progress in spiritual things. And this is *our* deepest need. To acknowledge before God our ignorance and helplessness: to cry to Him for light and strength.

Then, too, the verses quoted above teach us that our desire and design in studying the Scriptures is not to obtain more light and knowledge for the mere sake of it, but that it may be turned to practical account in our daily lives. The Psalmist prayed to be taught God's statutes that he might "keep" them *(v. 33)*. His earnest desire was that his steps might be ordered in the Word, so that "iniquity" should not have dominion over him *(v. 133)*. This, too, should be our motive and aim— first to *know* and then to *do* the Will of God.

Turning now to the second line of truth running through this Psalm, it is blessed to note the experiences of the one who maintains such an attitude before God:—

"*I have rejoiced* in the way of Thy testimonies, as much as in all riches" *(v. 14)*. "Thy testimonies also *are my delight and my counsellors*" *(v. 24)*. "*This is my comfort in my affliction:* for Thy Word hath quickened me" *(v. 50)*. "*I have more understanding than all my teachers;* for Thy testimonies are my meditation. Thy Word *is a lamp unto my feet, and a light unto my path*" *(v. 105)*. "*Great peace* have they which love Thy law" *(v. 165)*.

What encouragement do these afford! What a blessed reward for supplicating God and being subject to His Word! A heart filled with joy *(v. 14)*, boldness given to testify *(v. 46)*, comfort afforded in affliction *(v. 50)*, deep and more lasting satisfaction than thousands of gold and silver could give *(v. 72)*, light on the path *(v. 105)*, great peace for the soul *(v. 165)*. Again we exclaim, What glorious compensation! What an incentive *for us* to emulate the Psalmist and take a lowly place before God and subject our lives to His Word. May this be, increasingly, our experience, to the praise of the glory of His grace.

Yours in His happy service,
Arthur W. Pink.

STUDIES IN THE SCRIPTURES

Subscription Price: $1.00 per year to any address in the world. Single copies 10 cents.

Change of Address: Please notify us promptly of any change of address, and be certain to give both old and new addresses.

Non-Subscribers receiving this Magazine regularly will understand their subscription has been entered by a friend.

Copies lost in the mail duplicated on request.

All new subscriptions will be dated back to January, 1922.

Entered as second-class matter December 15th, 1921 at the post office at Swengel, Pa., under Act of March 3rd, 1879.

CONTENTS

Names and Titles of Antichrist 158
John's Gospel (John 3:1-8) 165
The Wisdom of God Displayed in the Way of Salvation (concluded) 174

4. NAMES AND TITLES OF THE ANTICHRIST

There is a distinct science of nomenclature, a system of names, in the Word of God. Probably every name found in Scripture has either a historic, a symbolic, or a spiritual significance. The names are inseparably bound up with the narrative, and it frequently happens that the meaning of a proper noun is a key to an important passage. Names are not employed by the Holy Spirit in a loose and careless manner —of course not!—but with definite design. A variety of names for the same individual are not given in order to prevent monotonous repetition, but because the significance of each separate appellation is best fitted to express what is recorded in any given instance. "Devil" and "Satan" are not synonyms, nor are they used at haphazard, but with Divine discrimination. Upon the meaning of names found in Holy Writ rests a whole scheme of interpretation; even the order in which names occur is not fortuitous but designed, and constitutes a part of each lesson taught, or each truth presented.

There is here a wide field opened for study, a field which few have made serious effort to explore. It is strange that it has been so neglected, for again and again the Holy Spirit calls attention to the importance and meaning of names. In the first book of the Bible we find that children and places were given meaningful names, which called to remembrance incidents, experiences, characteristics of interest and importance. Examples are given where names were changed to harmonize with a change in the person, place, experience, or situation where it occurred. Abram and Sarai will at once occur to mind. For a place, take Luz, which was changed to Bethel—"House of God"—because by reason of a vision he received there it became *that* to Jacob. Jacob's name is changed to Israel; and in the New Testament an example is furnished in Simeon being re-named Peter. In Heb. 7:1,2 the Holy Spirit calls attention to the significance of the names Melchizedek and Salem (Jerusalem). These are sufficient to show the importance of this line of study.

Names are used in Scripture with marvelous discrimination, and it was this fact which first demonstrated to the writer the *verbal* inspiration of Scripture. The precision with which names are used in the Bible is especially noticeable in connection with the Divine titles. The names Elohim and Jehovah are found on the pages of the Old Testament several thousand times, but they are never used loosely or interchangeably. Over three hundred names and titles are given to the Lord Jesus Christ, and each has its own distinctive significance, and to substitute any other for the one used would destroy the beauty and perfections of every passage where they are found.

Names are employed to express character; titles are used to denote relationships. It is only as we make a careful study of the various and numerous names and titles of the Lord Jesus Christ, that we are in a position to appreciate His infinite excellencies and the manifold relationships which He sustains. From an opposite standpoint the same is equally true of the Antichrist. As we pay careful attention to the different names and titles which are given to him, we then discover what a marvelously complete delineation the Holy Spirit has furnished us with of the person, the character, and career of this monster of wickedness. It is unfortunate that the great variety of names bestowed upon him has led some brethren to the conclusion that they must belong to separate persons, and has led them to apportion these out to different individuals; only confusion can result from this. There is almost as much ground to make the Devil and Satan different persons, as there is to regard (as some do) the Beast and the Antichrist as separate entities. That the Devil and Satan are names belonging to *the same* person, and that the Beast and the Antichrist is *the selfsame* individual, is proven by the fact that identically the same characteristics under each is found belonging to the one as to the other. Instead of apportioning these names to different persons, we must see that they denominate the same individual, only in different relationships, or as giving us various phases of his character.

An old writer has said the name Devil is most suggestive of his character. If "d" is taken away *evil* is left. If "e" is taken away *vile* is left. If "v" is taken away *ill* is left. And if "i" is taken away and the next letter be aspirated, it tells of *hell*. It is equally true of the Antichrist: his names reveal his character, expose his vileness, and forcast his career and doom.

The names and titles given to the Antichrist are far more numerous than is commonly supposed. We propose to give as complete a list as possible, and offer a few comments on their significations. We shall not expatiate on them at equal length, for that is not necessary; instead, we shall say the most on those cognomens which are of the greater importance, or, which because of their ambiguity call for a more detailed elucidation.

1. THE ANTICHRIST.

"Who is a liar but he that denieth that Jesus is the Christ? He is *Antichrist*, that denieth the Father and the Son" (*1 John 2:22*). This name introduces to us one of the most solemn and foreboding subjects in the Word of God. It brings before us one of the persons in the Trinity of Evil. At every point he is the antithesis of Christ. The word "Antichrist" has a double significance. Its primary meaning is one who is *opposed* to Christ; but its secondary meaning is one who is *instead of* Christ. Let not this be thought strange, for it accords with the two stages in his career. At first he will pose as the true Christ, masquerading in the livery of religion. But, later, he will throw off his disguise, stand forth in his true character, and set himself up as one who is against God and His Christ.

Not only does *anti*-christ denote the antagonist of Christ, but it tells of one who is instead of Christ. The word signifies another Christ, a pro-Christ, an *alter christus,* a pretender to the name of Christ. He will seem to be and will set himself up as the true Christ. He will be the Devil's counterfeit. Just as the Devil is an *Antitheos*—not only the adversary of God, but the *usurper* of the place and prerogatives of God, demanding worship; so the Son of Perdition will be *anti-christ*—not only the antagonist and opponent of Christ, but His rival: assuming the very position and prerogatives of Christ; passing himself off as the rightful claimant to all the rights and honors of the Son of God.

2. THE MAN OF SIN, THE SON OF PERDITION.

"Let no man deceive you by any means: for that day shall not come, except there come a falling away first, and that *Man of Sin* be revealed, *the Son of Perdition*" *(2 Thess. 2:3)*. This double appellation is probably the most awful, the most important, and the most revealing title given to the Antichrist in all the Bible. It diagnoses his personality and exposes his awful character. It tells us he will be possessed of a twofold nature: he will be a man, and yet more than a man. He will be Satan's parody of the God-Man. He will be an incarnation of the Devil. The world today is talking of and looking for the Superman. This is exactly what the Antichrist will be. He will be the Serpent's masterpiece.

"That Man of Sin". What a frightful name! The sin of man will culminate in the Man of Sin. The Christ of God was sinless; the Christ of Satan will not only be sinful, but the Man *of* Sin. "Man of Sin" intimates that he will be the living and active embodiment of every form and character of evil. "Man of Sin" signifies that he will be sin itself personified. "Man of Sin" denotes there will be no lengths of wickedness to which he will not go, no forms of evil to which he will be a stranger, no depths of corruption that he will not bottom.

"The Son of Perdition". And again we are forced to exclaim, what a frightful name! Not only a human degenerate, but the offspring of the Dragon. Not only the worst of human kind, but the incarnation of the Devil. Not only the most depraved of all sinners, but an emanation from the Pit itself. "Son of Perdition" denotes that he will be the culmination and consummation of satanic craft and power. All the evil, malignity, and cunning and power of the Serpent will be embodied in this terrible monster.

3. THE LAWLESS ONE.

"And then shall be revealed *the Lawless One,* whom the Lord Jesus shall slay with the breath of His mouth, and bring to nought by the manifestation of His coming" *(II Thess. 2:8 R. V.).* This is another name of the Antichrist which makes manifest his awful character. Each of his names exhibits him as the antithesis of the true Christ. The Lord Jesus was the Righteous One; the Man of Sin will be the Lawless One. The Lord Jesus was "made under the law" *(Gal. 4:4);* the Antichrist will oppose all law, being a law unto himself. When the Saviour entered this world, He came saying, "Lo I come to do Thy will, O God" *(Heb. 10:9);* but of the Antichrist it is written "And the king shall do according to *his* will" *(Dan. 11:36).* The Antichrist will set himself up in direct opposition to all authority, both Divine and human.

4. THE BEAST.

"And when they shall have finished their testimony *the Beast* that ascendeth out of the bottomless pit shall make war against them, and shall overcome them, and kill them" *(Rev. 11:7).* This is another name which reveals the terrible nature and character of the Antichrist and which places him in sharp antithesis from the true Christ. "The Beast" is the title by which he is most frequently designated in the Revelation: there are at least thirty references to him under this name in the last book of the Bible. The Greek word signifies a wild beast. This name "the Beast" contrasts the Antichrist from the true Christ as "the Lamb"; and it is a significant fact that by far the great majority of passages where the Lord Jesus is so designated are also found here in the Apocalypse. The "Lamb" is the Saviour of sinners; the "Beast" is the persecutor and slayer of the saints. The "Lamb" calls attention to the gentleness of Christ; the "Beast" tells of the ferocity of the Antichrist. The "Lamb" reveals Christ as the "harmless" One *(Heb. 7:26);* the "Beast" manifests the Antichrist as the cruel and heartless one. Under the Law lambs were ceremonially clean and used in sacrifice, but beasts were unclean and unfit for sacrifices.

It is a point of interest to note that there is one other very striking contrast between the persons in the Holy Trinity, and the persons in the trinity of evil. At our Lord's baptism the Holy Spirit descended upon Him in the form of a *dove,* and the first mention of the Holy Spirit in Scripture represents Him as "brooding" like a dove over the waters which covered the pre-Adamic earth *(Gen. 1:2).* How remarkable are these symbols—a "Lamb" and a "Dove"! A Dove, not a hawk or an eagle. The gentle, harmless, cooing "dove". Over against this the Devil is termed "the *Dragon*". What a contrast—the Dove and the Lamb, the Dragon and the Beast!

5. THE BLOODY AND DECEITFUL MAN.

"Thou shalt destroy them that speak leasing: the Lord will abhor the *Bloody and Deceitful Man*" *(Psa. 5:6).* The Psalm from which this verse is quoted contains a prayer of the godly Jewish remnant, offered during the Tribulation period. In proof of this assertion observe that in v. 2 God is owned and addressed as "King". In v. 7 intimation is given that the Temple has been rebuilt in Jerusalem, for turning away from it when it has been defiled by "the Abomination of Desolation", the remnant say, "But as for me I will come into *Thy* House in the multitude of Thy mercy: and in Thy fear will I worship toward *Thy* Holy Temple". While in v. 10 we find them praying for the destruction of their enemies, which is parallel with Rev. 6:10. It is during that time the faithful remnant will exclaim, "Thou shalt destroy them that speak leasing: the Lord will abhor the Bloody and Deceitful Man".

The Bloody and Deceitful Man views the Antichrist in relation to the Jews. In the earlier stages of his public career he poses as their friend and benefactor. He recognizes their rights as a separate State and appears anxious to protect their autonomy. He makes a formal covenant with them *(Dan. 9:27)* and their peace and security seem assured. But a few years later he comes out in his true character. His fair speeches and professions of friendship are seen to be false. He breaks his covenant *(Psa. 55:20)* and turns upon the Jews in fury. Their benefactor is now their worst enemy. The protector of their interests now aims to cut them off from being a nation in the earth *(Psa. 83:4)*. And thus is he rightfully denominated by them "the Bloody and Deceitful Man".

6. THE WICKED ONE.

"*The Wicked* (One) in his pride doth persecute the poor: the *Wicked* (One), through the pride of his countenance, will not seek after God" *(Psa. 10:2, 4)*. This entire Psalm is about the Wicked One. The opening verse gives the key to its dispensational scope. It contains the cry of the Jewish remnant during the Tribulation period, here denominated "Times of Trouble" *(cf. Jer. 30:7)*. So desperate is the situation of the true Israel, it seems as though Jehovah must have deserted them —"Why standest Thou afar off, O Lord? Why hidest Thou Thyself in times of trouble?" *(v. 1)*. Then follows a remarkably full description of their arch-enemy, the Wicked One. His pride *(v. 2)*, his depravity: "He abhorreth the Lord" *(v. 3 margin)*; his blasphemy: "All his thoughts are, There is no God" *(v. 4 margin)*; his grievous ways, *(v. 5)*; his consuming egotism, *(v. 6)*; his deceitfulness, *(v. 7)*; his treachery, *(v. 8)*; his cruelty, *(vv. 9, 10)*; his complacent pride, *(v. 11)*, are each described. Then the Remnant cry, "Arise, O Lord; O God, lift up Thine hand: forget not the humble. Break Thou the arm of the Wicked and Evil One" *(vv. 12 and 15)*. The whole Psalm should be carefully studied.

7. THE MAN OF THE EARTH.

"To judge the fatherless and the oppressed, that *the Man of the Earth* may no more oppress" *(Psa. 10:18)*. The "Wicked One" describes his character; the "Man of the Earth" defines his position. The one speaks of his awful depths of depravity; the other of his vast dominions. The sphere of his operations will be no mere local one. He will become World-Emperor. He will be a king of kings and lord of lords *(Rev. 13:7)*. When the true Christ appeared on earth, Satan offered Him "all the kingdoms of the world and the glory of them" if He would fall down and worship him. When the false Christ appears, this offer will be repeated, the conditions will be met, and the tempting gift will be bestowed *(Rev. 13:2)*. In consequence of this he shall be "the Man of the Earth"; just as later, Christ shall be "King over all the earth" *(Zech. 14:7)*.

8. THE MIGHTY MAN.

"Why boasteth thou thyself in mischief, O *Mighty Man*" *(Psa. 52:1)*. This is another Psalm which is devoted to a description of this fearful character. Here again we have mention of his boastfulness *(v. 1)*, his deceitfulness *(v. 2)*, his depravity *(v. 3)*, his egotism *(v. 4)*, his riches *(v. 7)*. His doom is also announced *(v. 5)*. This title, the Mighty Man, refers to his immense wealth and possessions, and the power which they confer upon their possessor. It also points a striking contrast: Christ was the Lowly Man, not having where to lay His head; the Antichrist will be the Mighty Man, of whom it is said, "Lo, this is the man that made not God his strength; but trusted in the abundance of his riches, and strengthened himself in his substance" *(Psa. 52:7)*.

9. THE ENEMY.

"Because of the voice of *the Enemy*, because of the oppression of the Wicked: for they cast iniquity upon me, and in wrath they hate me" *(Psa. 55:3)*. This is another title used of the Antichrist in connection with Israel, a title which recurs several times both in the Psalms and the prophets. It points a designed contrast from that *Friend* that "sticketh closer than a brother". This Enemy of Israel oppresses them sorely. His duplicity and treachery are here referred to. Concerning him Israel shall exclaim, "The words of his mouth were smoother than butter, but war was in his heart: his words were softer than oil, yet were they drawn swords" *(Psa. 52:21)*. Let the student be on the lookout for passages in the Old Testament which make mention of the Enemy.

10. THE ADVERSARY.

"They said in their hearts, Let us destroy them together: they have burned up all the synagogues of God in the land. We see not our signs: there is no more any profit: neither is there any among us that knoweth how long. O God, how long shall *the Adversary* reproach? Shall the Enemy blaspheme Thy name forever?" *(Psa. 74:8-10).* This title occurs in several important passages. In Isa. 59:19 we read, "So shall they fear the name of the Lord from the west, and His glory from the rising of the sun. When the Adversary shall come in like a flood, the Spirit of the Lord shall lift up a standard against him". Lam. 4:11,12 is another scripture which obviously speaks of the End-Time. "The Lord hath accomplished His fury; He hath poured out His fierce anger, and hath kindled a fire in Zion, and it hath devoured the foundations thereof. The kings of the earth, and all the inhabitants of the world, would not have believed that the Adversary and the Enemy should have entered into the gates of Jerusalem". In Amos 3:11 we read, "Therefore thus saith the Lord God; an Adversary there shall be even round about the land; and he shall bring down thy strength from thee, and thy palaces shall be spoiled". This is a title which intimates his satanic origin, for the Greek word for Devil means adversary.

11. THE HEAD OVER MANY COUNTRIES.

"He shall judge among the heathen, he shall fill the places with the dead bodies; he shall wound *the Head over many countries"* *(Psa. 110:6).* The context here shows that it must be the Antichrist which is in view. The Psalm opens by the Father inviting the Son to sit at His right hand until His enemies shall be made His footstool. Then follows the affirmation that Jehovah will display His strength out of Jerusalem, and make His people Israel willing in the day of His power. Then, following Jehovah's oath that Christ is a Priest forever after the order of Melchizedek (which contemplates the exercise of His millennial and royal priesthood), we read, "The Lord at thy right hand shall strike through kings in the day of His wrath. He shall judge among the heathen, He shall fill the places with the dead bodies; He shall wound the Head over many countries". The "Day of His wrath" is the closing portion of the Tribulation period, and in the Day of His wrath He wounds this Head over many countries. The Head over many countries refers to the Man of Sin as the Cæsar of the last world-empire, prior to the establishment of the Messianic Kingdom.

12. THE VIOLENT MAN.

"Deliver me, O Lord, from the Evil Man: preserve me from *the Violent Man*" *(Ps. 140:1).* This is another Psalm which expresses the plaintive supplications of the godly remnant in the "time of Jacob's trouble". Three times over the Antichrist is denominated the Violent Man. In v. 1 the remnant pray to be delivered from him. In v. 4 the petition is repeated. In v. 11 his doom is foretold. Cry is made for God to take vengeance upon this bloody persecutor: "Let burning coals fall upon them: let them be cast into the fire; into deep pits, that they rise not up again. Let not an evil speaker be established in the earth: evil shall hunt the Violent Man to overthrow him" *(Psa. 140:10,11).* The Violent Man is a name which fully accords with his Beast-like character. It tells of his ferocity and rapacity.

13. THE ASSYRIAN.

"*O Assyrian,* the rod of Mine anger, and the staff in their hand is Mine indignation ...Wherefore it shall come to pass, that when the Lord hath performed His whole work upon mount Zion and on Jerusalem, I will punish the fruit of the stout heart of *the King of Assyria,* and the glory of his high looks" *(Isa. 10:5, 12).* We cannot here attempt an exposition of the important passage in which these verses occur— that we hope to give in later articles, when we purpose to treat in detail of the Antichrist in the Psalms, and the Antichrist in the Prophets—suffice it now to point out that it treats of the End-Time *(see vv. 12, 20),* and that the leading characteristics of the Man of Sin can be clearly discerned in what is here said of the Assyrian. Almost all pre-millennial students of prophecy are agreed that "the King" of Isa. 30:33 is the Antichrist, and yet in the two verses which precede, this "King" is identified with "the Assyrian".

14. THE KING OF BABYLON.

"Thou shalt take up this proverb against *the King of Babylon,* and say, How hath the oppressor ceased! the golden city ceased!" *(Isa. 14:4).* We do not wish to anticipate what we hope to discuss at length in our future studies, enough now to state it is our firm conviction that Scripture plainly teaches that there will be another Babylon which will eclipse the importance and glories of the one of the past, and that Babylon will be one of the headquarters of the Antichrist. He will have three: Jerusalem will be his *religious* headquarters, Rome his *political,* and Babylon his *commercial.* For those who desire to anticipate our future expositions, we recommend them to make a minute study of Isa. 10, 11, 13, 14; Jer. 49-51; Zech. 5, and Rev. 18.

15. SON OF THE MORNING.

"How art thou fallen from heaven O Lucifer, *Son of the Morning!* How art thou cut down to the ground, which didst weaken the nations" *(Isa. 14:12).* "Lucifer" is a Latin word which signifies the "morning star". "All the ancient versions and all the Rabbins make the word a noun denoting the *bright one,* or, more specifically, *bright star,* or according to the ancients more specifically still, the *Morning Star* or harbinger of daylight" (Dr. J. A. Alexander). This term "Lucifer" has been commonly regarded as one of the names of Satan, and what is here said of the Morning Star is viewed as describing his apostasy. Against this interpretation we have nothing to say, except to remark that we are satisfied it does not exhaust this remarkable scripture. A detailed exposition must be reserved for a later paper. Sufficient now to point out that however Isa. 14 looks back to the distant past when, through pride, Satan fell from his original estate, it most evidently looks forward to a coming day and gives another picture of the Antichrist. In this same passage "Lucifer" is termed "the *Man* that did make the earth to tremble" *(v. 16),* and in his blasphemous boast "I will be like the Most High" *(v. 14),* we have no difficulty in identifying him with the Man of Sin of 2 Thess. 2:3, 4. The force of this particular title "Morning Star" is seen by comparing it with Rev. 22:16, where we learn that this is one of the titles of the God-Man. The "Morning Star" speaks of Christ coming to usher in the great Day of rest for the earth. In blasphemous travesty of this Satan will send forth the mock messiah to usher in a false millennium.

16. THE SPOILER.

"Let mine outcasts dwell with thee, Moab; be thou a covert to them from the face of *the Spoiler:* for the Extortioner is at an end, *the Spoiler* ceaseth, the oppressors are consumed out of the land. And in mercy shall the throne be established: and He shall sit upon it in truth in the tabernacle of David, judging, and seeking judgment, and hasting righteousness" *(Isa. 16:4, 5).* It will be observed that the verse in which the Antichrist is spoken of as the Spoiler comes immediately before the one where we read of the throne being established, a reference, of course, to the setting up of the Messianic Kingdom. These two things synchronize: the destruction of Antichrist, and the beginning of the real Messiah's reign; hence we read here "the Spoiler ceaseth". A further reference to the Man of Sin under this title of the Spoiler is found in Jer. 6:26: "O daughter of My people, gird thee with sackcloth, and wallow thyself in ashes: make thee mournings, as for an only son, most bitter lamentation: for *the Spoiler* shall suddenly come upon thee". This is another title which views the Anti-Christ in connection with Israel. After the return of many of the Jews to Palestine, and after their rights have been owned by the Powers, and their security and success seem assured; their enemy, filled with satanic malice, will seek their extermination. "The Spoiler" contrasts him with the Lord Jesus who is the great Restorer *(see Psa. 69:4).*

17. THE NAIL.

"In that day, saith the Lord of hosts, shall *the Nail* that is fastened in the sure place be removed, and be cut down, and fall; and the burden that was upon it shall be cut off: for the Lord hath spoken it" *(Isa. 22:25).* The last ten verses of this chapter should be read carefully. They furnish a striking foreshadowment of the End-Time. Shebna was holding some office *over* (note "government" in v. 21) Israel. Apparently he was a usurper. God announced that he should be set aside in shame, and the man of His choice—Eliakim—should take his place. These historical figures merge into prophetic characters. In v. 22 we read that God says, "And the key of the house of David will I lay upon His shoulder, so He shall open, and none shall shut; and He shall shut, and none shall open". As we know from Rev. 3:7 this refers to none other than the Lord Jesus, and of Him it is here said, "And I will fasten Him as a Nail in a sure place; and He shall be for a glorious throne to His father's house" (*v. 23*). Then, in the closing verse of the chapter we read, "In that day, saith the Lord of hosts, shall the Nail that is fastened in a sure place be removed, and be cut down, and fall". Just as Eliakim foreshadowed Christ, so Shebna pointed forward to the Antichrist; and just as in v. 23 we have a prophecy announcing the establishment of Messiah's Kingdom, so in v. 25 we have foretold the overthrow of the false messiah's kingdom.

18. THE BRANCH OF THE TERRIBLE ONES.

"Thou shalt bring down the noise of strangers, as the heat in a dry place; even the heat with the shadow of a cloud; *the Branch of the terrible ones* shall be brought low" (*Isa. 25:5*). The first five verses of this chapter contemplate the Enemy's stronghold—Babylon—and the remainder of the chapter pictures the blessedness of the millennial era. In the fifth verse the Antichrist's overthrow is announced: "The Branch of the terrible ones shall be brought low". With this should be compared Isa. 14:19, where of Lucifer it is said, "Thou art cast out of thy grave like an abominable Branch". This points another contrast. The "Branch" is one of the Messianic names: "Behold, I will bring forth My Servant, the Branch" (*Zech. 3:8*); "Behold the man whose name is the Branch" (*Zech. 6:12*). By placing together Isa. 4:2 and Isa. 14:19 the anthithesis will be more evident. Of Christ it is said, "The Branch of the Lord shall be *beautiful and glorious*"; Antichrist is called "an *abominable* Branch": Christ is "the Branch *of the Lord*"; Antichrist is "the Branch *of the terrible ones*".

19. THE PROFANE AND WICKED PRINCE OF ISRAEL.

"And thou, *profane wicked Prince of Israel*, whose day is come, when iniquity shall have an end, thus saith the Lord God; remove the diadem, and take off the crown; this shall not be the same: exalt him that is low, and abase him that is high. I will overturn, overturn, overturn it: and it shall be no more, until He come whose right it is; and I will give it Him" (*Ezek. 21:25-27*). The Profane and Wicked Prince of Israel here can be none other than the Antichrist, we are expressly told that his day shall be "when iniquity shall have an end". The reference is, of course, to Israel's "iniquity", and their iniquity shall *end* at the appearing of the Messiah (*see Dan. 9:24*) when "He shall be a priest upon His throne" (*Zech. 6:13*). Here in Ezekiel we see how the Son of perdition shall ape the Christ of God, for he, too, will be a priest-king: "Remove the *diadem*" refers to the insignia of his priesthood (in every other place in the O. T. where occurs the Hebrew word here translated "diadem" it is rendered "mitre"— worn only by the high priest of Israel); "take off the crown" is the symbol of his kingship.

20. THE LITTLE HORN.

"I considered the horns, and, behold, there came up among them another *Little Horn*, before whom there were three of the first horns plucked up by the roots: and, behold, in this Horn were eyes like the eyes of man, and a mouth speaking great things" (*Dan. 7:8*). For a full description of the Antichrist under this title see Dan. 7:8-11, 21-26; 8:9-12, 23-25. We must reserve our comments on these verses till a later article. "*Little* Horn" refers to the lowly political origin of the Antichrist, and describes him as he is before he attains governmental supremacy.

21. THE PRINCE THAT SHALL COME.

"And after threescore and two weeks shall Messiah be cut off, but not for Himself: and the people of *the Prince that shall come* shall destroy the city and the sanctuary" (*Dan. 9:26*). This title connects the Antichrist with the Roman Empire in its final form, and presents him as the last of the Cæsars.

22. THE VILE PERSON.

"And in his estate shall stand up *a Vile Person*, to whom they shall not give the honor of the kingdom: but he shall come in peaceably, and obtain the kingdom by flatteries" (*Dan. 11:21*). This contrasts the Antichrist from "the *Holy* One of Israel". His identity is established by noting what is predicated of him.

23. THE WILFUL KING.

"And *the King* shall do according *to his will*; and he shall exalt himself, and magnify himself above every god, and shall speak marvelous things against the God of gods, and shall prosper till the indignation be accomplished: for that that is determined shall be done" *(Dan. 11:36)*. The Antichrist will not only be the High Priest of the world's religion, but he will be King supreme at the head of its government.

24. THE IDOL SHEPHERD.

"For, lo, I will raise up a *Shepherd* in the land, which shall not visit those that be cut off, neither shall seek the young ones, nor heal that that is broken, nor feed that that standeth still: but he shall eat the flesh of the fat, and tear their claws in pieces. Woe to *the Idol Shepherd* that leaveth the flock! The sword shall be upon his arm, and upon his right eye: his arm shall be clean dried up, and his right eye shall be utterly darkened" *(Zech. 11:16,17)*. This is in evident contrast from the Good Shepherd who gave His life for His sheep. The Idol Shepherd of deluded Israel will prove himself the monster Desolator, who shall bring upon that people the severest tribulations ever experienced by that race.

25. THE ANGEL OF THE BOTTOMLESS PIT.

"And they had a king over them, which is *the Angel of the bottomless pit,* whose name in the Hebrew tongue is Abaddon, but in the Greek tongue hath his name Apollyon" *(Rev. 9:11)*. "Abaddon" and "Apollyon" mean *Destroyer.* It is the "Spoiler" of Isa. 16:4 rendered "Destroyer" in Jer. 4:7. That his name is here given in the Hebrew and the Greek shows that he will be connected with both the Jews and the Gentiles.

Other names of the Antichrist which the student may look up are, "The Rod of God's anger" *(Isa. 10:12)*; "The Unclean Spirit" *(Matt. 12:43)*; "The Lie" *(2 Thess. 2:11)*; "A Star" *(Rev. 8:10 and 9:1)*; and "The Vine of the Earth" *(Rev. 14:18)*.

In our next article we shall deal with the *genius* of the Antichrist, and point out the many striking *comparisons and contrasts* between him and the Christ of God. Let the student see how many points of resemblance and opposition he can find.—*Arthur W. Pink.*

JOHN'S GOSPEL

3. CHRIST AND NICODEMUS. JOHN 3:1-8.

We begin with the usual Analysis of the passage that is to be before us:—

1. The Person of Nicodemus, v. 1.
2. The official Position of Nicodemus, v. 1.
3. The Timidity of Nicodemus, v. 2.
4. The Reasoning of Nicodemus, v. 2.
5. The Need of Nicodemus, v. 3.
6. The Stupidity of Nicodemus, v. 4.
7. The Instructing of Nicodemus, vv. 5-8.

"There was a man of the Pharisees, named Nicodemus, a ruler of the Jews: The same came to Jesus by night, and said unto Him, Rabbi, we know that Thou art a teacher come from God: for no man can do these miracles that Thou doest, except God be with him" *(vv. 1,2.).* Nicodemus was a "ruler of the Jews", which means, most probably, that he was a member of the Sanhedrim. As such, he is to be viewed here as a representative character. He gives us another phase of the spiritual condition of Judaism. First, he came to Jesus "by night" *(v. 2)*; second, he was altogether lacking in spiritual discernment *(vv. 4, 10)*; third, he was dead in trespasses and sins, and therefore, needing to be "born again" *(v. 7)*. As such, he was a true representative of the Sanhedrim—Israel's highest ecclesiastical court. What a picture, then, does this give us again of Judaism! For the Sanhedrim it was *nighttime,* they were in the dark. And like Nicodemus, their representative, the Sanhedrim were devoid of all spiritual discernment, and had no understanding in the things of God. So, too, like Nicodemus, the other members of the Sanhedrim were destitute of spiritual light. Again we say, What light does this cast upon Judaism at that time! So far, we have seen a *blinded* Priesthood *(1:21,26)*; second, a *joyless* Nation *(2:3)*; third, a *desecrated* Temple *(2:16)*; and now we have a spiritually *dead* Sanhedrim.

A brief word now upon the prophetic application. The second chapter closed, it will be remembered, with a scene which foreshadowed the re-built Temple of the Jews, defiled by Antichrist; and the ultimate banishment of the "Trafficker" from the Millennial Temple. So, I take it, we have a *double* foreshadowing here. The Tribulation period is prefigured by the "night-time". Again; at the close of John 2 we saw many professing the name of the Lord, but Christ refusing to commit Himself unto them. This suggests the Lord disowning the worship offered to Him in the Tribulation by the majority section of the Jews. But from other scriptures we learn there will be a *Godly Remnant* who will separate themselves from the Nation as a whole; a remnant though marked by much spiritual ignorance shall, nevertheless, honestly seek Christ, and who at the beginning of the Millennium will be born again. These are the ones here represented by Nicodemus, and it is most significant that we are told he was "a Pharisee", which means a *Separatist:* as such he accurately typified the godly remnant, separated unto God. The meaning of his name is also very suggestive. "Nicodemus" at once calls to mind the "Nicolaitanes": the former signifies "Victor of the people", the latter, "Victor of the laity". We believe that in its final application the "Nicolaitanes" refer to the officers of the Antichrist. In contrast from them, Nicodemus, victor of the people, tells us that the despised and persecuted godly remnant of the last days shall be the *true* "victors". Finally; we know from later scriptures that Nicodemus was eventually born again. Thus will it be with the godly remnant who emerge from the Tribulation, and who will form the nucleus from which will spring the regenerated Millennial Israel.

"The same came to Jesus by night". And *why* did Nicodemus come to the Lord Jesus by night? Was it because he was ashamed to be seen coming to Him? Did he approach Christ secretly, under cover of the darkness? This is the view generally held, and we believe it to be the correct one. Why else should we be told that he came "by night"? What seems to confirm the popular idea is that each time Nicodemus is referred to in the Gospel afterwards, it is *repeated* that he came to Jesus "by night". In John 7:50, 51 we read, "Nicodemus saith unto them, (He that came to Jesus by night, being one of them,) Doth our Lord judge any man, before it hear him, and know what he doeth?" And again in John 19:39 we are told, "And there came also Nicodemus, which at the first came to Jesus by night, and brought a mixture of myrrh, and aloes, about a hundred pound weight". What is the more noticeable is that something *courageous* is recorded of Nicodemus: his boldness in reprimanding the Sanhedrim, and his intrepidity in accompanying Joseph of Arimathea at a time when all the apostles had fled. It seems as though the Holy Spirit has emphasized these bold acts of Nicodemus by reminding us that at first he acted timidly. One other thing which appears to confirm our conclusion is his use of the personal pronoun when Nicodemus first addressed the Saviour: "Rabbi", he said, *"we* know that Thou art a teacher come from God". Why speak in the plural number unless he hesitated to commit himself by expressing *his own* opinion? and so preferred to shelter behind the conclusion drawn by others, hence the "we".

"The same came to Jesus by night, and said unto Him, Rabbi, we know that Thou art a teacher come from God: for no man can do these miracles that Thou doest except God be with him" *(v. 2)* This was true, for the miracles of Christ differed radically from those performed by others before or since. But this very fact warns us that we need to examine carefully the credentials of other miracle-workers. Is the fact that a man works miracles a sure proof that he comes from God, and that God is with him? To some the question may appear well-nigh superfluous. There are many who would promptly answer in the affirmative. How could any man perform miracles "except God be with him"? It is because this superficial reasoning obtains so widely that we feel it incumbent upon us to dwell upon the point. And it is because there *are* men and women today that work miracles, who (we are fully persuaded) *are not* "sent of God", that a further word on the subject is much needed.

In these times men and women can stand up and teach the most erroneous doctrines, and yet if they proffer as their credentials the power to perform miracles of healing, they are widely received and hailed as the servants of God. But it is generally overlooked that Satan has the power to work miracles, too, and frequently the great Deceiver of souls bestows this power on his emissaries in order to beguile the unstable and confirm them in error. Let us not forget that the magicians of Egypt were able, up to a certain point, to duplicate the miracles of Moses, and whence obtained they this power unless from that old Serpent, the Devil! Let us not forget the warning of the Holy Spirit in 2 Cor. 11:13, 14, "For such are false apostles, deceitful workers, transforming themselves into the apostles of Christ. And no marvel: for Satan himself is transformed into an angel of light." And, finally, let us not forget it is recorded in Scripture that of the Antichrist it is written, "Even him, whose coming is after the working of Satan with all power and signs and lying wonders" *(2 Thess. 2:9).* Yes, Satan *is* able to work miracles, and also to deliver this power to others. So, then, the mere fact that a certain teacher works miracles is no proof that he is "come from God".

It is because we are in danger of being beguiled by these "deceitful workers" of Satan, who "transform themselves into the apostles of Christ", that we are exhorted to "believe not every spirit, but try the spirits whether they are of God: because many false prophets are gone out into the world" *(1 John 4:1).* And it should not be forgotten that the church at Ephesus was commended by Christ because they had heeded this exhortation, and in consequence had "tried them which say they are apostles, and are not, and hast found them liars" *(Rev. 2:3).* "But", it will be asked, "*how* are we to *test* those who come unto us in the name of Christ?" A most important and timely question. We answer, *not* by the personal *character* of those who claim to come from God, for as *2 Cor. 11: 14, 15* tells us, "Satan himself is transformed into an angel of light, therefore it is no great thing if his ministers also be transformed as *the ministers of righteousness*". And *not* by their power to work miracles. How then? Here is the Divinely inspired answer, "To the law and to the testimony: if they speak not according to *this word,* it is because there is no light in them" *(Isa. 8:20).* They must be tested by the written Word of God. Does the profest servant of God teach that which is in accord with the Holy Scriptures? Does he furnish a "Thus saith the Lord" for every assertion he makes? If he does not, no matter how winsome may be his personality, nor how pleasing his ways, no matter how marvelous may be the "results" that he "gets", God's command is, "If there come any unto you, and bring not *this doctrine* (this teaching), receive him not into your house, neither bid him Godspeed" *(2 John 10).* Let us emulate the Bereans, of whom it is recorded in Acts 17:11 "They received the Word with all readiness of mind, and searched the Scriptures daily, whether those things were so".

And how did the Lord receive Nicodemus? Notice, He did not refuse him an audience. It was night-time, and no doubt the Saviour had put in a full day, yet He did not seek to be excused. Blessed be His name, there is no unacceptable time for a sinner to seek the Saviour. Nighttime it was, but Christ readily received Nicodemus. One of the things which impresses the writer as he reads the Gospels, is the blessed *accessibility* of the Lord Jesus. He did not surround Himself with a bodyguard of attendants, whose duty it was to insure his privacy and protect Him from those who would be a nuisance. No; He was easily reached, and blessedly approachable—quite unlike some "g r e a t" preachers we know of.

And what was Christ's response to Nicodemus's address? This "ruler of the Jews" hailed Him as "a Teacher come from God", and such is the only conception which many a sinner has of Him today. A Teacher of ethics is the popular conception of the Christ of God. But it is not as a Teacher the sinner must first approach Christ. What the sinner needs is to be "born again", and in order to this he must have a *Saviour.* And it is of these very things our Lord speaks to Nicodemus—see verses 3 and 14. Of what value is *teaching* to one who is "*dead* in trespasses and sins", and who is even now, under the condemnation of a holy God! A saved person is a fit subject for teaching, but what the unsaved needs is preaching, preaching which will expose their depravity, exhibit their deep need of a Saviour, and then (and not till then) reveal the One who is mighty to save.

Christ ignored Nicodemus's address, and with startling abruptness said, "Verily, verily, I say unto thee, Except a man be born again, he cannot see the kingdom of God". This brings us to the central truth of the passage before us—the teaching of our Lord upon the New Birth. Here we find that He speaks of first, the supreme Importance of the new birth *(v. 3);* second, the Instrument of the new birth— "water" *(v. 5);* third, the Producer of the new birth—"the Spirit" *(v. 5);* fourth, the imperative Necessity of the new birth—"except .... cannot enter" *(v. 5)*; fifth, the Character of the new birth—a new nature, "spirit" *(v. 6)*; sixth, the obvious Imperativeness of the new birth *(v. 7)*; seventh, the Process of the new birth *(v. 8)*. Let us consider each of these points separately.

1. The supreme *importance* of the New Birth. This is exhibited here in a number of ways. To begin with, it is profoundly significant that the new birth formed the first subject of the Saviour's teaching in this Gospel. In the first two chapters we learn of a number of things He *did*, but here in John 3 is the first discourse of Christ recorded by this apostle. It is not *how* man should live that we are first instructed by Christ in this Gospel, but how men are *made alive* spiritually. A man cannot live before he is born; nor can a dead man regulate his life. No man can live Godwards until he has been born again. The importance of the new birth, then, is shown here, in that the Saviour's instruction upon it is placed at the *beginning* of His teaching in this Gospel. Thus we are taught it is of basic, fundamental importance.

In the second place, the *importance* of the new birth is declared by the solemn terms in which Christ spoke of it, and particularly in the manner in which He prefaced His teaching upon it. The Lord began by saying, "Verily, verily", which means "Of a truth, of a truth". This expression is only employed by Christ when He was about to mention something of a momentous nature. The double "verily" denoted that what He was about to say was of solemn and weighty significance. Let the reader learn to pay special attention to what follows these "verily, verily's" of the Saviour, found only in John.

In the third place, Christ here plainly intimated the supreme *importance* of the new birth by affirming that "Except a man be born again, he *cannot* see the kingdom of God" *(v. 3)*. If then the Kingdom of God cannot be seen until a man is born again, the new birth is shown to be a matter of vital moment for every descendant of Adam.

"Except a man be born again, he cannot see the kingdom of God" *(v. 3)*. There is some doubt in our mind as to exactly what is referred to here by "the kingdom of God". In the first place, this expression occurs no where else in this Gospel but here in John 3:3, 5. In the second place, this fourth Gospel, unlike the other three, generally speaking, ignores dispensational relationships, and treats of spiritual things. For this reason we think "the kingdom of God" in this passage has a moral force rather than a dispensational one. It seems to us that Romans 14:17 helps us to understand the significance of the term we are here studying, "For the kingdom of God is not meat and drink; but righteousness, and peace, and joy in the Holy Spirit". In the third place, the kingdom of God could not be "seen" by Nicodemus except by new birth, hence it could not be the Messianic kingdom for that was not then (or now) set up. We take it, then, that the "kingdom of God" in John 3 refers to the *things* of God, spiritual things, which are discerned and enjoyed by the regenerate here upon earth (*cf. I Cor. 2:10, 14*). The word for "see" in the Greek is "eidon", which means "to know or become acquainted with". The full force, then, of this first word of Christ to Nicodemus appears to be this: "Except a man be born again he cannot come to know the things of God". Such being the case, the new birth is seen to be a thing of profound importance.

"Nicodemus saith unto Him, How can a man be born when he is old? can he enter the second time into his mother's womb, and be born?" *(v. 4)*. What a verification was this of what the Lord had just told Nicodemus. Here was proof positive that this ruler of the Jews was altogether lacking in spiritual discernment, and quite unable to know the things of God. The Saviour had expressed Himself in simple terms, and yet this master of Israel altogether missed His meaning. How true it is that "The natural man receiveth not the things of the Spirit of God; for they are foolishness unto him: neither can he know them, because they are spiritually discerned" *(I Cor. 2:14)*, and in order to have spiritual discernment a man must be born again. Till then he is blind, and unable to *see* the things of God.

2. The *instrument* of the New Birth. "Jesus answered, Verily, verily, I say unto thee, Except a man be born of water and of the Spirit, he cannot enter into the kingdom of God" *(v. 5)*. Regeneration is a being born "of water". This expression has been the occasion of wide difference

of opinion among theologians. Ritualists have seized upon it as affording proof of their doctrine of baptismal regeneration, but this only evidences the weakness of their case when they are obliged to appeal to such a proof text. However, it may be just as well if we pause here and give the scriptural refutation of this widely held heresy.

That baptism is in no wise essential to salvation, that it does not form one of the conditions which God requires the sinner to meet, is clear from many considerations, First, if baptism be necessary to salvation then no one was saved before the days of John the Baptist, for the Old Testament will be searched from beginning to end without finding a single mention of "baptism". God, who changes not, has had but one way of salvation since Adam and Eve became sinners in Eden, and if baptism is an indispensable prerequisite to the forgiveness of sins, then all who died from Abel to the time of Christ are eternally lost. But this is absurd. The Old Testament Scriptures plainly teach otherwise.

In the second place, if baptism be necessary to salvation, then every professing believer who has died during this present dispensation is eternally lost, if he died without being baptized. And this would shut heaven's door upon the repentant Thief, as well as all the Quakers and members of the Salvation Army, the vast majority of whom have never been baptized. But this is equally unthinkable.

In the third place, if baptism be necessary to salvation, then we must utterly ignore every passage in God's Word which teaches that salvation is by grace and not of works, that it is a free gift and not bought by anything the sinner does. If baptism be essential to salvation, it is passing strange that Christ Himself never baptized any one *(see John 4:2)*, for He came to "save His people from their sins". If baptism be essential to salvation, it is passing strange that the apostle Paul when asked point blank by the Philippian jailor, "What must I do to be saved?" answered by saying, "Believe on the Lord Jesus Christ, and thou shalt be saved". Finally, if baptism be essential to salvation, it is passing strange the apostle Paul should have written to the Corinthians, "I thank God I baptized none of you, but Crispus and Gaius" *(1 Cor. 1:14)*.

If then the words of Christ "born of water" have no reference to the waters of baptism, *what* do they signify? Before replying directly to this question, we must observe how the word "water" is used in other passages in this Gospel. To the woman at the well Christ said, "Whosoever drinketh of the *water* that I shall give him shall never thirst; but the *water* that I shall give him shall be in him a well of *water* springing up into everlasting life" *(John 4:14)*. Was this literal "water"? One has but to ask the question to answer it. Clearly, "water" is here used *emblematically*. Again; in John 7:37, 38 we are told "In the last day, that great day of the feast, Jesus stood and cried, saying, If any man thirst, let him come unto Me, and drink. He that believeth on Me, as the Scripture hath said, out of his belly shall flow rivers of living *water*." Here, too, the word "water" is *not* to be understood literally, but emblematically. These passages in John's Gospel are sufficient to warrant us in giving the word "water" in John 3:5 a figurative meaning.

If then the Lord Jesus used the word "water" emblematically in John 3:5, to *what* was He referring? We answer, The *Word* of God. *This* is ever the instrument used by God in regeneration. In every other passage where the *instrument* of the new birth is described, it is *always* the Word of God that is mentioned. In Psa. 119:50 we read, "For Thy *word* hath *quickened* me". Again, in 1 Cor 4:15 we find the apostle saying, "I have *begotten* you *through the Gospel*". Again, we are told "Of His own will *begat* He us with (what?—baptism? no but with) the *Word* of truth" *(James 1:18)*. Peter declares, "Being *born again*, not of corruptible seed, but of incorruptible by *the Word of God*, which liveth and abideth for ever" *(1 Peter 1:23)*.

The new birth, then, is by the Word of God, and one of the *emblems* of the Word, is *"water"*. God employs quite a number of emblems to describe the various characteristics and qualities of His Word. It is likened to a "lamp" *(Psa. 119:105)* because it illumines. It is likened unto a "hammer" *(Jer. 23:29)* because it breaks up the hard heart. It is likened unto "water" because it *cleanses*: see Psa. 119:9; John 15:3; Eph. 5:26. "Born of water" means born of the cleansing and purifying Word of God.

3. The *Producer* of the New Birth". "Born of water, and *of the Spirit" (John 3:5)*. The Holy Spirit of God is the begetter, the Word is the "seed" *(1 John 3: 9)* He uses. "That which is born of the flesh is flesh*:* and that which is *born of the Spirit* is spirit" *(John 3:6)*. And again, "It is *the Spirit that quickeneth;* the flesh profiteth nothing" *(John 6:33)*. Nothing could be plainer. No sinner is quickened except by the Spirit; and no sinner is quickened apart from the Word.

The order which is followed by God in the new creation is the same He observed in the restoring of the old creation. A beautiful illustration of this is found in Gen. 1. The opening verse refers to the original creation of God. The second verse describes its subsequent condition, after it had been ruined. Between the first two verses of Gen. 1 some terrible calamity intervened—most probably the fall of Satan—and the fair handiwork of God was blasted. The Hebrew of Gen. 1:2 literally reads, "And the earth *became* a desolate waste". But six days before the creation of Adam, God began the work of restoration, and it is indeed striking to observe the order He followed. First, "darkness abode upon the face of the deep" *(Gen. 1:2)*; second, "And the Spirit of God moved upon (Hebrew 'brooded over') the waters"; third, "And God *said*, Let there be light" *(Gen. 1:3)*; fourth, "And there was light". The order is exactly the same in the new creation. First, the unregenerate sinner is in darkness, the darkness of spiritual death. Second, the Holy Spirit moves upon, broods over, the conscience and heart of the one He is about to quicken. Third, *the Word* of God goes forth in power. Fourth, the result is "light"—the sinner is brought out of darkness into God's marvelous light. The Holy Spirit, then, is the One who produces the new birth.

4. The imperative *necessity* of the New Birth. "*Except* a man be born of water and of the Spirit, *he cannot enter into the kingdom of God*" *(3:5)*. By his first birth man enters this world a sinful creature, and because of this he is estranged from the thrice Holy One. Of the unregenerate it is said, "Having the understanding darkened, being *alienated from the life of God* through the ignorance that is in them, because of the blindness of their heart".

Unspeakably solemn is this. When Adam and Eve fell they were banished from Paradise, and each of their children were born outside of Eden. That sin shuts man out from the holy presence of God, was impressively taught to Israel. When Jehovah came down on Sinai to give the Law unto Moses (the mediator), the people were fenced off at the base of the Mount, and were not suffered to pass on pain of death. When Jehovah took up His abode in the midst of the chosen people, He made His dwelling place inside the holy of holies, which was curtained off, and none was allowed to pass through the veil save the high priest, and he but once a year as he entered with the blood of atonement. Man then is *away from God*. He is, in his natural condition, where the prodigal son was —in the far country, away from the father's house—and except he be born again he cannot enter into the kingdom of God.

"Except a man be born of water and of the Spirit, he *cannot* enter into the kingdom of God". This is not an arbitrary decree, but the enunciation of an abiding principle. Heaven is a prepared place for a prepared people. And this in the very nature of the case. An unregenerate man who has no relish at all for spiritual things, who is bored by the conversation of believers, who finds the Bible dull and dry, who is a stranger to the Throne of Grace, would be *wretched* in heaven. Such a man could not spend eternity in the presence of God. Suppose a fish were taken out of the water, and laid upon a salver of gold; suppose further that the sweetest of flowers surrounded it, and that the air was filled with their fragrance; suppose, too, that the strains of most melodious music fell upon its ears, would that fish be happy and contented? Of course not. And why? Because it would be out of harmony with its environment; because it would be lacking in capacity to appreciate its surroundings. *Thus* would it be with an unregenerate soul in heaven.

Once more. The new birth is an imperative necessity because the natural man is altogether devoid of spiritual life. It is not that he is ignorant and needs instruction: it is not that he is feeble and needs invigorating: it is not that he is sickly and needs doctoring. His case is far, far worse. He is *dead* in trespasses and sins. This is no poetical figure of speech; it is a solemn reality, little as it is perceived by the majority of people. The sinner is spiritually lifeless and needs quickening. He is a spiritual corpse, and needs bringing from death unto life. He is a member of the old creation, which is under the Curse of God, and unless he is made a new creation in Christ, he will lie under that Curse to all eternity. What the natural man needs above everything else is life, Divine life; and as birth is the gateway to life, he *must* be born again, and except he be born again, he *cannot* enter the kingdom of God. That is final.

5. The *character* of the New Birth. But what is the new birth? Precisely what is it that differentiates a man who is dead in sins from one who has passed from death unto life? Upon this point there is much confusion and ignorance. Tell the average person that he must be born again and he thinks you mean that he must reform, mend his manner of life, turn over a new leaf. But reformation concerns only the outer life. And the trouble with man is within. Suppose the mainspring of my watch were broken, what good would it do if I put in a new crystal and polished the case until I could see my face in it? None at all, for the seat of the trouble is inside the watch. So it is with the sinner. Suppose that his deportment was irreproachable, that his moral character was stainless, that he had such control of his tongue that he never sinned with his lips, what would all this avail while he still had (as God says he has) a *Heart* that is "deceitful above all things, and desperately wicked"? The new birth, then, is something more than reformation.

Others suppose, and there are thousands who do so, that being born again means *becoming religious*. Tell the average church-goer that "Except a man be born again, he cannot see the kingdom of God", and these solemn words afford him no qualms. *He* is quite at ease, for he fondly imagines that he *has been* born again. He will tell you that he has *always* been a Christian: that from early childhood he has believed in Christianity, has attended church regularly, nay, that he is a church-member, and contributes regularly toward the support of the Gospel. He is very religious. Periodically he has happy feelings; he says his prayers regularly, and on Sunday's he reads his Bible. What more can be required of him! And thus many are lulled to sleep by Satan. If such an one should read these lines, let him pause and seriously weigh the fact that it was to a man eminently *religious* that the Saviour was addressing when He declared, "Except a man be born of water and of the Spirit, he cannot enter into the kingdom of God". Nicodemus was not only a religious man, he was a *preacher*, and yet it was to him Christ said, "Marvel not that I said unto thee, *Ye* must be born again".

There are still others who believe that the new birth is *a change of heart,* and it is exceedingly difficult to convince them to the contrary. They have heard so many preachers, orthodox preachers, speak of a change of heart, that they have never thought of challenging the scripturalness of this expression, yet it *is* unscriptural. The Bible may be searched from Genesis to Revelation, and nowhere does this expression "change of heart" occur upon its pages. The sad thing is that "change of heart" is not only *un*scriptural, but it is *anti*scriptural, untrue, and therefore, utterly misleading. In the one who has been born again there is no change of heart though *there is* a change of life, both inward and outward. The one who is born again now loves the things he once hated, and he hates now the things he once loved; and, in consequence, his whole line of conduct is radically affected. But, nevertheless, it remains true that his old heart (which is deceitful above all things, and desperately wicked) remains in him, *unchanged,* to the end.

What, then, is the new birth? We answer, It is not the removal of anything from the sinner, nor the changing of anything within the sinner; instead, it is the communication of something to the sinner. The new birth is the impartation of the new nature. When I was born the first time I received from my parents *their* nature: so, when I was born again, I received from God *His* nature. The Spirit of God begets within us a spiritual nature: as we read in 2 Pet. 1:4, "Whereby are given unto us exceeding great and precious promises: that by these ye might be *partakers of the Divine nature*".

It is a fundamental law which inheres in the very nature of things that like can only produce like. This unchanging principle is enunciated again and again in the first chapter of Genesis. There we read,

"And the earth brought forth grass, and herb yielding seed *after his kind,* and the tree yielding fruit, whose seed was in itself, *after his kind*" (1:12). And again, "And God created great whales, and every living creature that moveth, which the waters brought forth abundantly, *after their kind,* and every winged fowl *after his kind*" (1:21). It is only the blindness and animus of infidelistic evolutionists who affirm that one order of creatures can beget another order radically different from themselves. No; that which is born of the vegetable is vegetable; that which is born of the animal is animal. And that which is born of sinful man is a sinful child. A corrupt tree cannot bring forth good fruit. Hence, "That which is born of the flesh *is flesh.*" It cannot be anything else. Educate and cultivate it all you please, it remains flesh. Water cannot rise above its own level, neither can a bitter fountain send forth sweet waters. That which is born of the flesh is flesh; it may be refined flesh, it may be beautiful flesh, it may be religious flesh. But it is still flesh. On the other hand, "That which is born of the Spirit *is spirit*". The child always partakes of the nature of his parents. That which is born of man is human; that which is born of God is divine. That which is born of man is sinful, that which is born of God is spiritual.

Here, then, is the character or nature of the new birth. It is not the reformation of the outward man, it is not the education of the natural man, it is not the purification of the old man, but it is the creation of a new man. It is a Divine begetting *(James 1:18)*. It is a birth of the Spirit *(John 3: 6)*. It is a being made a new creation *(2 Cor. 5:17)*. It is becoming a partaker of the Divine nature *(2 Pet. 1:4)*. It is a being born into God's family. Every born again person has, therefore, *two* natures within him: one which is carnal, the other which is spiritual. These two natures are contrary the one to the other *(Gal. 5:17)*, and in consequence, there is an unceasing warfare going on within the Christian. It is only the grace of God which can subdue the old nature; and it is only the Word of God which can feed the new nature.

6. The *obvious imperativeness* of the New Birth. "Marvel not that I said unto thee, Ye must be born again". Without doubt, Nicodemus was startled. The emphatic statements of Christ staggered him. The vital importance and imperative necessity of the new birth were points which had never exercised his conscience or engaged his serious attention. He was amazed at the Saviour's searching declarations. Yet he ought not to have been. Really, there was no cause for him to stand there in open-mouthed wonderment. *"Marvel not"*, said Christ. It was as though the Lord had said, "Nicodemus, what I have said to you should be obvious. If a man is a sinner, if because of sin he is blind to the things of God, if no amount of religious cultivation can change the essential nature of man, then it is *patent* that his deepest need is to be born again. Marvel not: it is a self-evident truth."

That entrance into the kingdom of God is only made possible by the new birth, that is, by the reception of the Divine nature, follows a basic law that obtains in every other kingdom. The realm of music is entered by birth. Suppose I have a daughter, and I am anxious she should become an accomplished musician. I place her under the tuition of the ablest instructor obtainable. She studies diligently the science of harmony, and she practices assiduously hours every day. In the end, will my desires be realized? will she become an accomplished musician? That depends upon one thing—was she *born* with a musical nature? Musicians are born, not manufactured. Again; suppose I have a son whom I desire should be an artist. I place him under the instruction of an efficient teacher. He is given lessons in drawing; he studies the laws of color-blending; he is taken to the art galleries and observes the productions of the great masters. And what is the result? Does he blossom out into a talented artist? And again it depends solely on one thing—was he *born* with the nature and temperament of an artist? Artists are born and not manufactured. Let these examples suffice for illustrating this fundamental principle. A man *must* have a musical nature if he is to enter the kingdom of music. A man *must* have an artistic nature if he is really to enter the realm of art. A man *must* have a mathematical mind if he is to be a mathematician. There is nothing to "marvel" at in this: it is self-evident; it is axiomatic. So, in like manner, a man *must* have a spiritual nature before he can enter the spiritual world: a man *must* have God's own nature before he can enter God's kingdom. Therefore "Marvel not ....ye *must* be born again".

7. The *process* of the New Birth. "The wind bloweth where it listeth, and thou hearest the sound thereof, but canst not tell whence it cometh, and whither it goeth: so is every one that is born of the Spirit" *(3:8)*. A comparison is here drawn between the wind and the Spirit. The comparison is a *double* one. First, both are *sovereign in their activities;* and second, both are *mysterious in their operations*. The comparison is pointed out in the word "so". The first point of analogy is found in the words "where listeth" or "pleaseth"; the second is found in the words "canst not tell".

The wind *bloweth* where it pleaseth.... *so is every one that is born of the Spirit"*. The wind is *irresponsible:* that is to say, it is sovereign in its action. The wind is an element altogether beyond man's control. The wind neither consults man's pleasure, nor can it be regulated by his devices. So it is with the Spirit. The wind blows where it pleases, when it pleases, as it pleases. So it is with the Spirit.

Again; the wind is *irresistible.* When the wind blows in the fulness of its power it sweeps everything before it. Those who have looked upon the effects of a tornado just after it has passed, know something of the mighty force of the wind. It is so with the Spirit. When He comes in the fulness of His power, He breaks down man's prejudices, subdues his rebellious will, overcomes all opposition.

Again; the wind is *irregular.* Sometimes the wind blows so softly it scarcely rustles a leaf, at other times it blows so loudly that its roar can be heard miles away. So it is in the matter of the new birth. With some the Holy Spirit works so gently His work is imperceptible to onlookers; with others His action is so powerful, radical, revolutionary, His operations are patent to many. Sometimes the wind is only local in its reach, at other times it is widespread in its scope. So it is with the Spirit. Today He acts on one or two souls, tomorrow, He may—as at Pentecost —"prick in the heart" a whole multitude. But whether He works on few or many He consults not man; He acts as *He* pleases.

Again; the wind is *invisible*. It is one of the very few things in Nature that is invisible. We can *see* the rain, the snow, the lightning's flash; but not so the wind. The analogy holds good with the Spirit. His Person is unseen.

Again; the wind is *inscrutable*. There is something about the wind which defies all effort of human explanation. Its origin, its nature, its activities, are beyond man's ken. Man cannot tell whence it cometh or whither it goeth. It is so with the activities of the Holy Spirit. His operations are conducted secretly; His workings are profoundly mysterious.

Again; the wind is *indispensable*. If a dead calm were to continue indefinitely all vegetation would die. How quickly *we* wilt when there is no wind at all! Even more so is it with the Spirit. Without Him there could be no spiritual life at all.

Finally, the wind is *invigorating*. The life-giving properties of the wind are illustrated every time a physician orders his sick patient to retire to the mountains or to the seaside. It is so, again, with the Spirit. He is the One who strengthens with might in the inner man. He is the One who energizes, revives, empowers.

How marvelously full was the figure employed by Christ on this occasion. How much is suggested by this single word "wind". Let the above serve as an example of the great importance and value of prolonged meditation upon every word of Holy Writ.

God has thrown an impenetrable veil over the beginnings and processes of life. That we live we know, but *how* we live we cannot tell. Life is evident to the consciousness and manifest to the senses, but it is profoundly mysterious in its operations. It is so with the new life born of the Spirit. To sum up the teaching of this verse: "The wind bloweth"—there is the fact. "And thou hearest the sound thereof"—there is the evidence of the fact. "But knowest not whence"—there is the mystery behind the fact. The one born again knows that he has a new life, and enjoys the evidences of it, but *how* the Holy Spirit operates upon the soul, subdues the will, creates the new life within us, belongs to the deep things of God.

Below will be found a number of questions bearing on the passage which is to be before us next month, D. V. In the meantime let each reader who desires to become a "Workman that needeth not to be ashamed" diligently study the whole passage *(John 3:9-21)* for himself, paying particular attention to the points raised by our questions:—

1. What does v. 9 go to prove?
2. What solemn warning does v. 10 point?
3. What is the force of the contrast between earthly things and heavenly things in v. 12?
4. How are we to understand v. 13 in view of Enoch's and Elijah's experiences?
5. What Divine attribute of Christ is affirmed in v. 13?
6. What is the connection between v. 14 and the context?
7. Why was a "serpent" selected by God to typify Christ on the Cross? v. 14.

Study carefully the first nine verses of Numbers 21.—*Arthur W. Pink.*

(No doubt our readers will be glad to know that the author has published a booklet containing the substance of the above entitled *The New Birth,* which the Lord has been pleased to own in blessing to many. Price is **7 cents** per copy, or **75 cents** per dozen, postpaid. Order from the Bible Truth Depot, Swengel, Pa.—I. C. H.)

THE WISDOM OF GOD DISPLAYED IN THE WAY OF SALVATION

(Concluded.)

Section IX.

The Subject Improved.

I. Hence we may learn the blindness of the world, that the wisdom appearing in the work of redemption is no more admired in it. God has revealed this His glorious design and contrivance to the world; sends forth His Gospel, and causes it to be preached abroad, in order to declare to the world that His infinite wisdom has been engaged for man's salvation. But how little is it regarded! There are some who have their eyes opened to behold the wondrous things of the Gospel, who see the glory of God in, and admire the wisdom of it. But the greater part are wholly blind to it. They see nothing in all this that is any way glorious and wonderful. Though the angels account it worthy of their most engaged and deep contemplation; yet the greater part of men take little notice of it. It is all a dull story and dead letter to many of them. They cannot see anything in it above the wisdom of men. Yea, the Gospel to many seems foolishness.

Though the light that shines in the world be so exceeding glorious, yet how few are there who do see it. The glory of God's wisdom in this work is surpassing the brightness of the sun: but so blind is the world that it sees nothing. It does not know that the Sun of righteousness shines.

Thus it has been in all ages, and wherever the Gospel has been preached, ministers of the Word of God in all ages have had occasion to say, Who hath believed our report, and to whom is the arm of the Lord revealed? Thus the prophets were sent to many with that errand: "Go and tell this people, Hear ye indeed, but understand not; and see ye indeed, but perceive not. Make the heart of this people fat, and their ears heavy, and shut their eyes; lest they should see with their eyes, and hear with their ears, and understand with their heart, and convert, and be healed" *(Isa. 6: 9, 10).*

When Christ that glorious prophet came, and more fully revealed the counsels of God concerning our redemption, how many were then blind! how much did Christ complain of them! How blind were the scribes and Pharisees, the most noted sect of men among the Jews for wisdom: they beheld no glory in that Gospel which Christ preached unto them; which gave Him occasion to call them fools and blind *(Matt. 23:17).* So it was again in the apostles' time. In all places where they preached, some believed, and some believed not *(Acts 28:24).* "As many as were ordained to eternal life believed" *(Acts 13:48).* "The elect obtained it, but the rest were blinded" *(Rom. 11:7).* So it is still in those places where the Gospel is preached. There are few who see the glory of the Gospel. God has a small number whose eyes He opens, who are called out of darkness into marvelous light, and who have an understanding to see the wisdom and fitness of the way of life. But how many are there who sit under the preaching of the Gospel all their days, yet never see any Divine wisdom or glory in it! To their dying day they are unaffected with it. When they hear it, they see nothing to attract their attention, much less excite any admiration. To preach the Gospel to them will serve very well to lull them to sleep; but produces very little other effect upon them. This shows the exceeding wickedness of the heart of man. How affecting the thought, that infinite wisdom should be set on work, so as to surprise the angels, and to entertain them from age to age; and that to men, though so plainly set before them, it should appear foolishness! "The preaching of the cross is to them that perish foolishness" *(2 Cor. 1:18)*.

II. This is a great confirmation of the truth of the Gospel. The Gospel stands in no need of external evidences of its truth and divinity. It carries its own light and evidence with it. There is that in its nature that sufficiently distinguishes it, to those who are spiritually enlightened from all the effects of human invention. There are evident appearances of the Divine perfections; the stamp of Divine glory, of which this of the Divine wisdom is not the least part.

There is as much in the Gospel to show that it is no work of men, as there is in the sun in the firmament. As persons of mature reason who look upon the sun, and consider the nature of it, its wonderful height, its course, its brightness and heat, may know that it is no work of man; so, if the Gospel be duly considered, if the true nature of it be seen, it may be known that it is no work of man, and that it must be from God. And if the *wisdom* appearing in the Gospel be duly considered, it will be seen as much to excel all human wisdom, as the sun's light excels the lights of fires of our own kindling. The contrivance of our salvation is of such a nature that no one can rationally conclude that man had any hand in it. The nature of the contrivance is such, so out of the way of all human thoughts, so different from all human inventions; so much more sublime, excellent, and worthy, that it does not savor at all of the craft or subtlety of man: it savors of God only.

If any are ready to think man might have found out such a way of salvation for sinners—so honorable to God, to His holiness and authority—they do not well consider the scantiness of human understanding. Mankind were of a poor capacity for any such undertaking; for till the Gospel enlightened the world, they had but miserable notions of what was honorable to God. They could have but poor notions of what way would be suitable to the Divine perfections; for they were wofully in the dark about these Divine perfections themselves, till the Gospel came abroad in the world. They had strange notions about a Deity. Most of them thought there were many gods. "They changed the glory of the incorruptible God into an image made like to corruptible man, and to birds, and fourfooted beasts, and creeping things" *(Rom. 1:23)*. They attributed vices to God. Even the philosophers, their wisest men, entertained but imperfect notions of the Supreme Being. How then should men find out a way so glorious and honorable to God, and agreeable to His perfections, who had not wisdom enough to get any tolerable notions of God, till the Gospel was revealed to them. They groped in the dark. Their notions showed the infinite insufficiency of man's blind understanding for any such undertaking, as the contriving of a way of salvation every way honorable to God, and suitable to the needs of the fallen creature.

But since the Gospel has told what God's counsels are, and how He has contrived a way for our salvation, men are ready to despise it, and foolishly to exalt their own understanding; and to imagine they could have found out as good a way themselves. When, alas! men, of themselves, had no notion of what was honorable to God, and suitable for a Divine Being. They did not so much as think of the necessity of God's law being answered, and justice satisfied. And if they had, how dreadfully would they have been puzzled to have found out the way how! Who would have thought of a trinity of persons in the Godhead; and that one should sustain the rights of the Godhead; and another should be the Mediator; and another should make application of redemption? Who would have thought of such a thing as three distinct persons, and yet but one God? All the same Being, and yet three persons! Who would have thought of this, in order to have found out a way for satisfying justice? Who would have thought of a way for answering the law, the law that threatened eternal death, without the sinner's suffering eternal death? And who would have thought of any such thing as a Divine person *suffering the wrath of God?* And if they had, who would have contrived a way *how* he should suffer, since the Divine nature cannot suffer?

Who would have thought of any such thing as God becoming man; two natures and but one person? These things are exceedingly out of the way of human thought and contrivance. It is most unreasonable to think that the world, who, till the Gospel enlightened them, were so blind about the nature of God and Divine things, should contrive such a way that should prove thus to answer all ends; every way to suit what the case required; most glorious to God, and answerable to all man's necessities. Everything is so fully provided for, and no absurdity to be found in the whole affair, but all speaking forth the most perfect wisdom. That there should be no infringement upon holiness or justice; nothing dishonorable to the majesty of God; no encouragement to sin, all possible motives to holiness; all manner of happiness provided; and Satan so confounded and entirely overthrown; how truly wonderful!

And if we suppose that all this notwithstanding was the invention of men, whose invention should it be? Who should be pitched upon as the most likely to invent it? It was not the invention of the Jews; for they were the most bitter enemies to it. The wise men among them, when they first heard of it, conceived malice against it, and persecuted all that held this doctrine. It was not the invention of the heathen; for they knew nothing about it, till the apostles preached it to them; and it appeared a very foolish doctrine to the wise men among them. The doctrine of Christ crucified was not only to the Jews a stumbling-block but also to the Greeks foolishness *(1 Cor. 1:23)*. Besides, it was contrary to all their notions about a Deity, and they knew nothing about the fall of men, and the like, till the Gospel revealed it to them.

It was not the invention of the apostles; for the apostles, of themselves, were no way capable of any such learned contrivance. They were poor fishermen and publicans, and obscure and illiterate sort of men, till they were extraordinarily taught. They were all surprised when they first heard of it. When they heard that Christ must die for sinners, they were offended at it; and it was a long while before they were brought fully to receive it.

There is but one way left; and that is, to suppose that Christ was a mere man, a very subtle crafty man, and that He invented it all: but this is as unreasonable as the rest; for it would have been all against Himself, to invent a way of salvation by His own crucifixion, a most tormenting and ignominious death.

III. How great a sin they are guilty of who despise and reject this way of salvation! When Christ has manifested such unsearchable riches of wisdom; when all the persons of the Trinity have as it were held a consultation from all eternity in providing a way of salvation for us sinful, miserable worms;—a way that should be sufficient and every way suitable for us; —a way that should be in all things complete, whereby we might have not only full pardon of all our sins, and deliverance from hell; but also full blessedness in heaven forever:—how must God needs be provoked, when, after all, men reject this way of salvation!

When salvation comes to be preached, and is offered to them in this way; when they are invited to accept of its benefits, and yet they despise and refuse it; they thus practically deny it to be a wise way, and call this wisdom of God foolishness. How provoking it must be, when such a poor creature as man shall rise up, and find fault with that wisdom which is so far above the wisdom of angels! This is one thing wherein consists the heinousness of the sin of unbelief, and it implies a rejecting and despising of Divine wisdom in the way of salvation by Jesus Christ. Unbelief finds fault with the wisdom of God in the choice of the person, for performing this work. It dislikes the person of Christ. It sees no form nor comliness in Him, nor beauty wherefor it should desire Him.

That person whom the wisdom of God looked upon as the fittest person of any, the *only* fit person, is despised and rejected by unbelief. Men, through unbelief, find fault with the salvation itself that Christ has purchased; they do not like to be saved as Christ would save. They do not like to be made holy, and to have such a happiness as is to be had in God for a portion.

It may not be amiss here to mention two or three ways whereby persons are guilty of a provoking contempt of the wisdom of God in the way of salvation.

1. They are guilty of a provoking contempt, who live in a *careless neglect* of their salvation; they who are secure in their sins, and are not much concerned about either salvation or damnation. This is practically charging God with folly. Its language is, that all is in vain, and to no purpose; that God has contrived and consulted for our salvation, when there was no need of it. They are well enough as they are. They do not see any great necessity of a Saviour. They like that state they are in, and do not much desire to be delivered out of it. They do not thank Him for all His consultation and contrivance, and think He might have spared His cost. God has greatly minded that, which they do not think worth minding; and has contrived abundantly for that which they do not trouble their heads about.

2. They are guilty of a provoking contempt of the wisdom of this way of salvation, who go about to *contrive ways of their own*. They who are not content with salvation by the righteousness of Christ, which God has provided, are for contriving some way of being saved by their own righteousness. These find fault with the wisdom of God's way, and set up their own wisdom in opposition to it. How greatly must God be provoked by such conduct!

3. Those that entertain discouraged and *despairing apprehensions* about their salvation, cast contempt on the wisdom of God. They think that because they have been such great sinners, God will not be willing to pardon them; Christ will not be willing to accept of them. They fear that Christ, in the invitations of the Gospel, does not mean such wicked creatures as they are; that because they have committed so much sin, they have sinned beyond the reach of mercy. They think it is in vain for them to seek for salvation. These cast contempt on the wisdom of God in the way of salvation, as though it were not all-sufficient;— as though the wisdom of God had not found out a way that was sufficient for the salvation of great sinners.

SECTION X.

THE MISERY OF UNBELIEVERS

Unbelievers have no portion in this matter. There is a most glorious way of salvation, but you, who are unbelievers, have no interest in it. The wisdom of God hath been gloriously employed for the deliverance of men from a miserable, doleful state; but you are never the better for it, because you reject it. If you continue in that state, this wisdom will do you no good.

Christ is a glorious person; every way fit to be a Saviour of sinners; a person who has power sufficient, wisdom sufficient, merit sufficient, and love sufficient for perfecting this work. And He is the *only* fit person; but you have no right in Him; you can lay claim to no benefit by His power, wisdom, love, or merits. This wisdom of God hath found out a way whereby this Saviour might satisfy justice, and fulfill the law for us: a way whereby He might be capable of suffering for us: but you have no lot in the incarnation, death, and sufferings of Jesus Christ.

The wisdom of God hath contrived a way of salvation that there should be procured for us perfect and everlasting happiness. Here is that happiness procured which is most suitable to our nature, and answerable to the salvation of our souls. Here is a most glorious portion, namely, the Divine Being Himself, with His glorious perfections. Here it is purchased, that we should see God face to face; that we should converse and dwell with God in His own glorious habitation; that we should be the children of God, and be conformed to Him. Here are the highest honors, the most abundant riches, the most substantial satisfying pleasures for ever more. Here we have prepared all needed good, both for the souls and bodies of sinners: all needed earthly good things, while here; and glory, for both body and soul hereafter, forever.

But you are never the better for all this. You have no lot nor portion in any of it. Notwithstanding all this rich provision, you may remain in the same miserable state and condition, in which you came into the world. Though the provision of the Gospel be so full, yet your poor soul remains in a famishing, perishing state. You remain dead in trespasses and sins; under the dominion of Satan; in a condemned state, having the wrath of God abiding on you, and being daily exposed to the dreadful effects of it in hell. Notwithstanding all this provision, you remain wretched and miserable, poor and blind and naked. O that you might turn to God through Jesus Christ, be numbered among His disciples and faithful followers and so be entitled to their privileges! They have an interest in this glorious Saviour, and are entitled to all the ineffable blessedness of His kingdom, so far as their capacities will admit: but you remain without Christ, being aliens from the commonwealth of Israel, strangers to the covenant of promise, having no well-grounded hope, and without God in the world. Further consider a few things:—

First. It argues the *great misery* of sinners, that the wisdom of God should be exercised to such a degree and order to find out a way to deliver them from it. Their case surely was most deplorable, since it required infinite wisdom to find out a way for their deliverance. The wisdom of angels is not sufficient—nothing but Divine wisdom could reach and remedy their case. And all the persons of the Trinity did enter into a consultation about it. If man's misery were not very great, Divine wisdom would not have been exercised for his deliverance from it. God would not contrive and do things so wonderful in a trivial affair. If the salvation of a sinner were not a great salvation, from an exceeding great misery, it is not to be supposed, that God's wisdom should be more signalized in this affair than in any other whatever.

But so it is; this contrivance seems to be spoken of in Scripture as the masterpiece of Divine wisdom. This wisdom of redemption is represented as most wonderful, and spoken of in Scripture in the most exalted manner of any work of God. Doubtless therefore salvation is a great thing; and consequently the misery which sinners are saved from, is a great and unspeakable misery. Now this is the misery that you are all in, to remain in a natural condition. This is the condemnation you lie under. This is the wrath of God that abides upon you. The wisdom of God knew it to be a very doleful thing for a person to be in a natural state, and therefore did so exercise itself to deliver miserable sinners out of it. But this is the state that many among us do yet remain in.

Secondly. Consider that if you continue in the state you are in, you will be so far from being the better for this contrivance, that you will be much *more miserable* for it. The justice and wisdom of the way of salvation will be your condemnation. "This is the condemnation, that light is come into the world, and men loved darkness rather than light" *(John 3:19)*. If you continue in the state that you are now in, it would have been better for you, if Christ had never died for sinners; if God had left all mankind to perish, as He did the fallen angels. Your punishment then would have been light in comparison with what it will be now. You will have greater sins by far to answer for; and all your sins will be abundantly the more aggravated.

Since I have been upon this subject, I have observed, that the work of redemption is an occasion of the elect being brought to greater happiness than man could have had, if he had not fallen. And it is also true as to reprobates, that it will be the occasion of their having greater misery than they would have had, if there had been no redemption. "For we are unto God a sweet savor of Christ, in them that are saved, and in them that perish. To the one we are a savor of death unto death; and to the other we are a savor of life unto life" *(2 Cor. 2:15)*. If you perish at last, you will be the more miserable for the benefits of the Gospel being so glorious, and that because your crime in rejecting and despising them will be the more heinous. "How shall we escape, if we neglect so great salvation?" *(Heb. 2:3)*.

Thirdly. Whilst you continue an unbeliever, *the more you hear* of this way of salvation, your condition will become the more miserable. The longer you sit under the preaching of the Gospel, the more doleful does your case grow. Your guilt continually increases, for your refusals of the Gospel, and your rejections of this way of salvation are so much the oftener repeated. Every time you hear the Gospel preached, you are guilty of a renewed rejection of it, the guilt of which therefore you will have lying upon you. And the more you hear of the suitableness and glory of this way, the greater is your guilt who still continue to reject it. Every new illustration of the wisdom and grace of God in redemption, adds to your guilt: "O Jerusalem, Jerusalem, how often would I have gathered thy children together, even as a hen gathereth her chickens under her wings, but ye would not" *(Matt. 23:37)*. What adds to your misery is, that as long as it continues it is a growing evil.

Fourthly. Consider the danger there is, that you will never have any lot or portion in this matter; seeing there are but few that have. Christ has told us that strait is the gate and narrow is the way that leadeth unto life, and few there be that find it. There have been but few in all ages of the world. Many seek; and many hope that they shall obtain. There are few that intend to be damned; while many hope that they shall some way or other find means to escape eternal misery. But after all, there are but few saved; or obtain the benefits of redemption.

SECTION XI.

EXHORTATION TO COME TO CHRIST.

I conclude with a use of exhortation to come to Christ, and accept of salvation in this way. You are invited to come to Christ, heartily to close with Him, and trust in Him for salvation: and if you do so; you shall have the benefit of this glorious contrivance. You shall have the benefit of it all; as much as if the whole had been contrived for you alone. God has already contrived everything that is needful for your salvation; and there is nothing wanting but your consent. Since God has taken this matter of the redemption of sinners into His own hands, He has made thorough work of it; He has not left it for you to finish. Satisfaction is already made, righteousness is already wrought out; death and hell are already conquered. The Redeemer has already taken possession of glory, and keeps it in His hands to bestow on them who come to Him. There were many difficulties in the way, but they are all removed. The Saviour has already triumphed over all, and is at the right hand of God, to give eternal life to His people.

Salvation is ready brought to your door; and the Saviour stands, knocks, and calls that you will open to Him, that He might bring it in to you. There remains nothing but your consent. All the difficulty now remaining is with your own heart. If you perish now, it must be wholly at your door. It must be because you would not come to Christ that you might have life; and because you virtually choose death rather than life: "He that sinneth against Me, wrongeth his own soul: all they that hate Me love death" *(Prov. 8:36)*. All that is now required of you, is, that your heart should close with Christ as a Saviour. Here consider,

1. That the wisdom of God has so contrived, that He hath forestalled all your *objections*. If you make objections against Christ and the way of salvation, they must be all unreasonable. You cannot reasonably object that your sins are of such a nature, that God's honor will not allow your pardon. It is true God insists upon His own honor. He is a God that will be honored, and His majesty shall be vindicated: and when sinners cast contempt upon Him, His honor requires vengeance. But God has so contrived this way, that His honor may be repaired by the punishment of sin without the sinner's suffering, how great so ever the sin be. Herein lies the wisdom of this way, that there is a sufficiency for the greatest and most heinous transgressors.

You cannot object that God will not be willing to accept you, for the Mediator's sake; for He hath chosen His own Son to be a Mediator, to cut off any such objections. So you may be sure that God will receive you if you go to Him through Christ. You cannot object that God the Father had not given sufficient assurance of salvation to believers; for the principal things, those which would have been most difficult to believe, are already fulfilled: God hath already given His Son to die for us. This, before it was accomplished, was much more strange, and difficult to believe, than that He should give eternal life to sinners after Christ died for them: "He that spared not His own Son, but delivered Him up for us all, how shall He not with Him freely give us all things?" *(Rom. 8:32)*.

There is no room to doubt but that if we accept of Christ, God will give eternal life; for He hath given it already into the hands of our Saviour for us. He hath intrusted Him with the whole affair. He hath given all things into His hand, that He might give eternal life to as many as should come to Him. The Father has appointed Him who died for believers, to be the Judge, to have the whole determination of the matter, and the disposal of the reward, in His own hand. And you cannot doubt but that Christ will be willing to bestow eternal life on them for whom He purchased it. For if He is not willing to bestow it, surely He never would have died to purchase it. Who can think that Christ would be so desirous of sinners being saved, as to undergo so much for them; and not be willing to let them have it, when He had obtained it for them? Consider,

2. The wisdom of God hath contrived that there should be in the *person* of the Saviour all manner of attractives to draw us to Him. He has in Him all possible excellency. He is possessed of all the beauty and glory of the Godhead. So that there can be no manner of excellency, nor degree of excellency that we can devise, but what is in the person of the Saviour. But yet so redundant has the wisdom of God been in providing attractives in order that we should come to Christ, it hath so ordered that there should also be all human excellencies in Him. If there be anything attractive in this consideration, that Christ is one in our own nature, one of us; this is true of Christ. He is not only in the Divine, but in the human nature. He is truly a Man, and has all possible human excellencies. He was of a most excellent spirit; wise and holy, condescending and meek, and of a lowly, benign, and benevolent disposition.

Again: The wisdom of God hath chosen a person of great love to sinners, and who should show that love in the most endearing manner possible. What more *condescending* love can there be, than the love of a Divine person to such worms of the dust? What *freer* love can there be than love to enemies? What *greater* love can there be, than dying love? And what more endearing *expression* of love, than dying for the beloved? And the wisdom of God hath so contrived, that Christ shall sustain that office which should most tend to endear Him to us, and draw us to Him: the office of a Redeemer from eternal misery, and the Purchaser of all happiness.

And if all this be not enough to draw us, the wisdom of God hath ordered more; it hath provided us with a Saviour that should offer Himself to us in the most endearing relation. He offers to receive us as friends. To receive us to a union to Himself, to become our spiritual Husband and portion for ever. And the wisdom of God has provided us a Saviour that woos in a manner that has the greatest tendency to win our hearts. His word is most attractive. He stands at our door and knocks. He does not merely command us to receive Him: but He condescends to apply Himself to us in a more endearing manner. He entreats and beseeches us in His Word and by His messengers.

3. The wisdom of God hath contrived that there should be all manner of attractives in the *benefits* that Christ offers you. There are not only the excellencies of the person of Christ to draw you to Him, but the desirable benefits He offers. Here is what is most suitable to the cravings of the human nature. Men when distressed and burdened, long for ease and *rest:* here it is offered to us in Christ. "Come unto Me", says He, "All ye that labor and are heavy laden, and I will give you rest". Men when in fear of danger, long for *safety:* here it is provided for us in Christ. God promises that He will become a shield and buckler, a strong rock and high tower to those that trust in Him. Those that mourn need *comfort:* Christ tells us that "He came to comfort those that mourn" *(Isa. 61:2).* The blind need to have their eyes opened. The light is sweet to men: Christ offers to anoint our eyes with eyesalve that we may see glorious light. He will be our sun, and the light of God's countenance. What is more dear to men than *life?* Christ hath purchased for men, that they should live forever: "He asked life of Thee, and Thou gavest it Him, even length of days for ever and ever". How greatly is a crown prized and admired by the children of men! And Christ offers this:—not a corruptible crown, but an incorruptible and far more glorious crown than any worn by earthly kings: a crown of glory, the lustre of which shall never fade nor decay; with an everlasting kingdom. Do men love *pleasures?* Here are pleasures for evermore. What could there be more to draw our hearts to Jesus Christ, and to make us willing to accept of Him for our Saviour, with all His unspeakable benefits?—*Jonathan Edwards.*

The end.

VOL. I   SEPTEMBER. 1922   NO. 9

STUDIES in the SCRIPTURES

"Search the Scriptures" John 5:39.

A PERIODICAL (MONTHLY "IF THE LORD WILL")
DEVOTED TO BIBLE STUDIES and EXPOSITIONS

Associate Editors and Publishers, I. C. HERENDEEN and ARTHUR W. PINK,
Swengel, Pa.

Price: **10** cents per copy; **$1.00** per year. Foreign **$1.00** per year.

TO OUR SCRIPTURE STUDY FAMILY—

"These were more noble than those in Thessalonica, in that they received the word with all readiness of mind, and searched the Scriptures daily, whether those things were so" *(Acts 17:11)*. This verse points a contrast between the Jews in Berea and the conduct of the Jews in Thessalonica. If the first nine verses of Acts 17 be read, it will be seen that in Thessalonica the apostle Paul entered the Jewish synagogue and for three Sabbath days reasoned with them out of the Scriptures. The result was that "some of them believed", while "others believed not". But when Paul preached in the synagogue at Berea he met with a people who were more cautious and critical. They were not captious or prejudiced but on the other hand, they were not going to be deceived by any false teachers who came along, no matter how great his reputation or how convincing his reasoning. They received the word with "all readiness of mind", that is, they were eager for the Truth, and listened attentively to the preacher; yet, they "searched the Scriptures daily", and that, for the express purpose of ascertaining *"whether* (if) those things *were so"*. And the Holy Spirit commends them for this diligence and pronounces them "noble".

There is here an important lesson for us today. Acts 17:11 is recorded for our instruction and imitation. We do well to follow the noble example of those Bereans. When we are about to hear a servant of God, we should go, not full of doubt and suspicion that we shall hear error propounded; instead, we ought to receive the message "with all readiness of mind". But then comes in our responsibility to *test what we have heard*. God requires us to "search the Scriptures daily" with the object of confirming or refuting what the preacher told us. This is our only safeguard. No preacher is infallible. It is human to err, and it is the bounden duty of every person to bring to the test of God's Word every sermon they hear and every book they read.

Observe that the Bereans went at their task in no half-hearted way. They were dead in earnest. They not only read the Scriptures, but they *"searched"* them; and they "searched" them not merely once or twice, but *"daily"*. This is what is most needed now. Let us be *Berean*-Christians—daily searchers of the Scriptures—then shall we be forewarned of error and able to detect false teaching. Let us be *Berean*-Christians, then shall we be grounded in the Truth and able to recognize "sound doctrine" when we hear it. Let us be *Berean*-Christians, then shall we be numbered among the nobility of God.

                                           Yours by wondrous grace,
                                                   Arthur W. Pink.

STUDIES IN THE SCRIPTURES

Subscription Price: **$1.00** per year to any address in the world. Single copies **10 cents.**

Change of Address: Please notify us promptly of any change of address, and be certain to give both old and new addresses.

Non-Subscribers receiving this Magazine regularly will understand their subscription has been entered by a friend.

Copies lost in the mail duplicated on request.

All new subscriptions will be dated back to January, 1922.

Entered as second-class matter December 15th, 1921 at the post office at Swengel, Pa., under Act of March 3rd, 1879.

CONTENTS

The Person of the Antichrist	182
John's Gospel (John 3:9-21)	186
Prayer	196
"Assurance of Salvation," and "Full Assurance of Faith"	200
"That Worthy Name"	202
Evil, and How to Meet It	203
Spiritual Preparedness	204

THE PERSON OF THE ANTICHRIST

5. THE GENIUS AND CHARACTER OF THE ANTICHRIST.

For six thousand years Satan has had full opportunity afforded him to study fallen human nature, to discover its weakest points, and to learn how best to make men do his bidding. The Devil knows full well how to dazzle men by the attraction of power, and how to make them quail before its terrors. He knows how to gratify the craving for knowledge and how to satisfy the taste for refinement and culture: he can delight the ear with melodious music and the eye with entrancing beauty. If he could transport the Saviour from the wilderness to a mountain, in a moment of time, and show Him all the kingdoms of the world and their glory, he is no novice in the art of presenting alluring objects before his victims today. He knows how to stimulate energy and direct inquiry, and how to appease the craving for the occult. He knows how to exalt men to dizzy heights of worldly greatness and fame, and how to control that greatness when attained, so that it may be employed against God and His people.

It is true that up to now Satan's power has been restrained, and his activities have been checked and often counteracted by the Spirit of God. The brightest fires of the Devil's kindling can burn but dimly whilever God sheds around them the power of heavenly light. They require *the full darkness of night* in order to shine in the full strength of their deceiving brightness; and that time is coming. The Word of God reveals the fact that a day is not far distant when Divine restraint will be removed; the light of God will be withdrawn; and then shall "darkness cover the earth and gross darkness the people" *(Isa. 60:2).* Not only will that which has hindered the full development of the Mystery of Iniquity be removed, but God will "send them strong delusion, that they should believe the Lie" *(2 Thess. 2:13),* and Satan will take advantage of this; he will then make full use of all the knowledge which he has acquired during the last six thousand years.

Satan will become incarnate and appear on earth in human form. As we have shown in previous chapters, the Antichrist will not only be the Man of Sin, but also "the Son of Perdition", the Seed of the Serpent. The Antichrist will be the Devil's masterpiece. In him shall dwell all the fulness of the Devil bodily. He will be the culmination and consummation of Satan's workings. The world is now talking of and looking for the Superman; and the Devil is soon to supply him. The Antichrist will be no ordinary person, but one possessed of extraordinary talents. He will be endowed with superhuman powers. With the one exception of the God-Man he will be the most remarkable personage who has ever appeared upon the stage of human history. But to particularize:

1. HE WILL BE AN INTELLECTUAL GENIUS.

He will be possessed of extraordinary intelligence. He will be the Devil's imitation of that blessed One "in whom are hid all the treasures of wisdom and knowledge" *(Col. 2:3).* This Son of Perdition will surpass Solomon in wisdom. In Dan. 7:20 he is represented as "A horn that had eyes". It is a double symbol. The "horn" prefigures strength; "eyes" speak of intelligence. Again, in Dan. 8:23 he is referred to as "A King of fierce countenance", who shall "understand dark sentences". That which baffles others shall be simple to him. The Hebrew word here translated "dark sentences" is the same as the one rendered "hard questions" in I Kings 10:1, where we read of the Queen of Sheba coming to Solomon with her "hard questions" in order to test his wisdom. It is also the word that is used of Samson's riddle in Judges 14. It indicates that the Antichrist will be master of all the secrets of occult science. Ezek. 28:3 declares of him, "Behold, thou art wiser than Daniel; there is *no secret* that they can hide from thee". This will be one of his most alluring attractions. His master mind will captivate the educated world. His marvelous store of knowledge, his acquaintance with the secrets of nature, his superhuman powers of perception, will stamp him as an intellectual genius of the first magnitude.

2. HE WILL BE AN ORATORICAL GENIUS.

In Dan. 7:20 we are told that he has "a mouth that spake very great things". As a wizard of words he will surpass Demosthenes. Here also will the Devil imitate that One "who spake as never man spake". The people were "astonished" at Christ's doctrine *(Matt. 7:28)*, and said "Whence hath this man this wisdom?" *(Matt. 13:54)*. So will it be with this daring counterfeiter: he will have a mouth speaking very great things. He will have a perfect command and flow of language. His oratory will not only gain attention but command respect. Rev. 13:2 declares that his mouth is "as the mouth of a lion" which is a symbolic expression telling of the majesty and awe-producing effects of his voice. The voice of the lion excels that of any other beast. So the Antichrist will outrival orators ancient and modern.

3. HE WILL BE A POLITICAL GENIUS.

He will emerge from obscurity, but by dint of his diplomatic skill he will win the admiration and compel the co-operation of the political world. In the early stages of his career he appears as "a *little* horn" (or power), but it is not long before he climbs the ladder of fame, and by means of brilliant statesmanship ascends its topmost rung. Like the majority of politicians, he **will not scruple to employ questionable methods**; in fact it will be by diplomatic chicanery and intrigue that he will win his early successes. Dan. 11:21 tells us that at first they will not give to him the honor of the kingdom, but "he shall come in peaceably, and obtain the kingdom by flatteries". Once he gains the ascendancy none will dare to challenge his authority. Kings will be his pawns and princes his playthings.

4. HE WILL BE A COMMERCIAL GENIUS.

"And through his policy also he shall cause craft to prosper in his hand" *(Dan. 8:25)*. Under his regime everything will be nationalized, and none will be able to buy or sell without his permission *(Rev. 13:17)*. All commerce will be under his personal control, and this will be used for his own aggrandizement. The wealth of the world will be at his disposal. There are several scriptures which call attention to this. For example in Psa. 52:7 we read, "Lo, this is the man that made not God his strength; but trusted *in the abundance of his riches;* and strengthened himself in his substance". Again in Dan. 11:38 we are told, "But in his estate shall he honor the god of forces (Satan) : and a god whom his fathers knew not shall he honor with gold, and silver, and with precious stones, and pleasant things." Even plainer is Dan. 11:43, "But he shall have power over *the treasures of gold and of silver,* and over *all* the precious things of Egypt". In the last verse of Dan. 11 mention is made of his place". He will be wealthier than Croesus. Ezek. 28:4, 5 speaks of him thus, "With thy wisdom and with thine understanding thou hast gotten thee riches, and hast gotten gold and silver into thy treasures: By thy great wisdom and by thy traffic hast thou increased thy riches, and thine heart is lifted up because of thy riches". Thus will he be able to wield the sceptre of financial power and outdo Solomon in all his glory.

5. HE WILL BE A MILITARY GENIUS.

He will be endowed with the most extraordinary powers, so that "he shall destroy wonderfully, and shall prosper, and practice, and shall destroy the mighty and the holy people" *(Dan. 8:24)*. Before his exploits the fame of Alexander and Napoleon will be forgotten. None will be able to stand before him. He will go "forth conquering and to conquer" *(Rev. 6:2)*. He will sweep everything before him so that the world will exclaim, "Who is like unto the beast? who is able to make war with him?" *(Rev. 13:4)*. His military exploits will not be confined to a corner, but carried out on a vast scale. He is spoken of as the man who will "shake kingdoms" and "make the earth to tremble" *(Isa. 14: 16)*.

6. HE WILL BE A GOVERNMENTAL GENIUS.

He will weld together opposing forces. He will unify conflicting agencies. Under the compelling power of his skill the world Powers will be united. The dream of a League of Nations will then be realized. The Orient and the Occident shall no longer be divided. A marvelous symbolic picture of this is given us in Rev. 13:1, 2: "And I stood upon the sand of the sea, and saw a Beast rise up out of the sea, having seven heads and ten horns, and upon his horns ten crowns, and upon his heads the name of blasphemy. And the Beast which I saw was like unto a leopard, and his feet were as the feet of a bear, and his mouth as the mouth of a lion: and the Dragon gave him his power, and his seat, and great authority". Here we find the forces of the Roman, the Grecian, the Medo-Persian, and the Babylonian empires coalesced. He will be the personal embodiment of the world's political authority in its final form. So completely will the world be swayed by the hypnotic spell cast over it by the Beast that the ten kings of the Roman empire in its ultimate form shall "give their kingdoms unto him" *(Rev. 17:17)*. He will be the last great Caesar.

7. HE WILL BE A RELIGIOUS GENIUS.

He will proclaim himself God, demanding that Divine honors should be rendered to him and sitting in the Temple shall show himself forth that he is God *(2 Thess. 2: 4)*. Such wonders will he perform, such prodigious marvels will he work, the very elect would be deceived by him did not God directly protect them. The Man of Sin will combine in himself all the varied genius of the human race, and what is more, he will be invested with all the wisdom and power of Satan. He will be a master of science, acquainted with all of nature's forces, compelling her to give up for him her long held secrets. "In this master-piece of Satan", says one, "will be concentrated intellectual greatness, sovereign power and human glory, combined with every species of iniquity, pride, tyranny, wilfulness, deceit, and blasphemy, such as Antiochus Epiphanes, Mohammed, the whole line of popes, atheists, and deists of every age of the world have failed to unite in any individual person".

"All the world wondered after the Beast" *(Rev. 13:3)*. His final triumph shall be that, wounded by a sword, he shall live again *(Rev. 13:3)*. He shall raise himself from the dead, and so wonder-struck will men be at this stupendous marvel they will readily pay him Divine homage, yea, so great will be his dazzling over men, they will worship his very image *(Rev. 13:14, 15)*.

Having contemplated something of the *genius* of Satan's prodigy, let us now consider his *character*. In doing so we shall view him in the light of the Character of the Lord Jesus. Christ is the Divine plumb-line and standard of measurement by which all character must be tested.

In our last article we pointed out how that the distinguishing title of the coming Super-Man—*the Antichrist*—has a double significance, inasmuch as it points to him as the imitator of Christ and the opponent of Christ. Hence, in studying his character, we find a series of comparisons and a series of contrasts drawn between the false christ and the true Christ; and these we now propose to set before the reader.

Comparisons between Christ and the Antichrist.

Satan is the master-counterfeiter, and in nothing will this appear more conspicuously than in his next great move. He is now preparing the stage for his climactic production, which will issue in a blasphemous imitation of the Divine incarnation. When the Son of Perdition appears he will pose as the Christ of God, and so perfect will be his disguise, the very elect would be deceived, were it not that God will grant them special illumination. It is this disguise, this simulation of the true Christ which we shall now examine, pointing out the various parallelisms which Scripture furnishes:

1. Christ was the subject of Old Testament prophecy: so also is the Antichrist; many are the predictions which describe this coming one, see especially Dan. 11: 21-45.

2. The Lord Jesus was typified by many Old Testament characters such as Abel, Joseph, Moses, David, etc. So also will the Antichrist be: such characters as Cain,

Pharaoh, Absalom, Saul, etc., foreshadow the Man of Sin. We hope to devote a separate paper to this most fascinating and totally neglected branch of our subject.

3. Christ was revealed only at God's appointed time: such will also be the case with the Antichrist. Of the one we read, "But when *the fulness of time was come,* God sent forth His Son" *(Gal. 4:4)*; of the other it is said, "And now we know what withholdeth that he might be *revealed in his time*" *(2 Thess. 2:6)*.

4. Christ was a Man, a real Man, "the Man Christ Jesus" *(1 Tim. 2:5)*; so also will the Antichrist be—"the Man of Sin" *(2 Thess. 2:3)*.

5. But Christ was more than a man: He was the God-Man; so also will the Antichrist be more than a man: the Super-man.

6. Christ was, according to the flesh, a Jew *(Rom. 1:3)*; so also will the Antichrist be—for proofs see article three, section one.

7. Christ will make a covenant with Israel *(Heb. 8:8)*; so also will the Antichrist *(Dan. 9:27)*.

8. Christ is our "Great High Priest"; so Antichrist will yet be Israel's great high priest *(Ezek. 21:26)*.

9. Christ was and will be the King of the Jews *(Matt. 2:1)*; so also will the Antichrist be *(Dan. 11:36)*.

10. Christ will be the King of kings *(Rev. 17:14)*; so also will the Antichrist be *(Rev. 17:12, 13)*.

11. Christ wrought miracles: of Him it is said "approved of God among you by miracles and wonders and signs" *(Acts 2: 22)*; so also will the Antichrist, concerning whom it is written, "whose coming is after the working of Satan with all power and signs and lying wonders" *(2 Thess. 2:9)*.

12. Christ's public ministry was limited to three years and a half; so also will the Antichrist's final ministry be *(Rev. 13:5)*.

13. Christ is shown to us riding a "white horse" *(Rev. 19:11)*; so also is the Anti-Christ *(Rev. 6:2)*.

14. Christ will return to the earth as Prince of Peace *(Isa. 9:6,7)*; so also will the Antichrist introduce an Era of peace *(Dan. 11:21)*; it is to this that 1 Thess. 5:3 directly refers.

15. Christ is entitled "the Morning Star" *(Rev. 22:16)*; so also is the Antichrist *(Isa. 14:12)*.

16. Christ is referred to as Him "which was, and is, and is to come" *(Rev. 4:8)*; the Antichrist is referred to as him that "was, and is not; and shall ascend out of the bottomless pit" *(Rev. 17:8)*.

17. Christ died and rose again; so also will the Antichrist *(Rev. 13:3)*.

18. Christ will be the object of universal worship *(Phil. 2:10)*; so also will the Antichrist *(Rev. 13:4)*.

19. The followers of the Lamb will be sealed in their foreheads *(Rev. 7:3; 14: 1)*; so also will the followers of the Beast *(Rev. 13:16, 17)*.

20. Christ has been followed by the Holy Spirit who causes men to worship Him; so the Antichrist will be followed by the anti-spirit—the false prophet—who will cause men to worship the Beast *(Rev. 13: 12)*.

There is no need for us to make any comments on these striking correspondences: they speak for themselves. They show the incredible lengths to which God will permit Satan to go in mimicking the Lord Jesus. We turn now to consider:

Contrasts between Christ and the Antichrist.

I. In their respective Designations.

1. One is called the Christ *(Matt. 16: 16)*; the other the Antichrist *(1 John 4:3)*.

2. One is called the Man of Sorrows *(Isa. 53:3)*; the other the Man of Sin *(2 Thess. 2:3)*.

3. One is called the Son of God *(John 1:34)*; the other the Son of Perdition *(2 Thess. 2:3)*.

4. One is called the Seed of the woman *(Gen. 3:15)*; the other the seed of the Serpent *(Gen. 3:15)*.

5. One is called the Lamb *(Isa. 53:7)*; the other the Beast *(Rev. 11:7)*.

6. One is called the Holy One *(Mark 1:24)*; the other the Wicked One *(2 Thess. 2:8)*.

7. One is called the Truth *(John 14:6)*; the other the Lie *(John 8:44)*.

8. One is called the Prince of Peace *(Isa. 9:6)*; the other the wicked, profane Prince *(Ezek. 21:25)*.

9. One is called the glorious Branch *(Isa. 4:2)*; the other the abominable Branch *(Isa. 14:19)*.

10. One is called the Mighty Angel *(Rev. 10:1)*; the other is called the Angel of the Bottomless Pit *(Rev. 9:11)*.

11. One is called the Good Shepherd *(John 10:11)*; the other is called the Idol Shepherd *(Zech. 11:17)*.

12. One has for the number of His name (the gematria of "Jesus") 888; the other has for the number of his name 666 *(Rev. 13:18)*.

II. In their respective Careers.

1. Christ came down from heaven *(John 3:13)*; Antichrist comes up out of the bottomless pit *(Rev. 11:7)*.

2. Christ came in Another's Name *(John 5:43)*; Antichrist will come in his own name *(John 5:43)*.

3. Christ came to do the Father's will *(John 6:38)*; Antichrist will do his own will *(Dan. 11:36)*.

4. Christ was energized by the Holy Spirit *(Luke 4:14)*; Antichrist will be energized by Satan *(Rev. 13:4)*.

5. Christ submitted Himself to God *(John 5:30)*; Antichrist defies God *(2 Thess. 2:4)*.

6. Christ humbled Himself *(Phil. 2:8)*; Antichrist exalts himself *(Dan. 11:36)*.

7. Christ honored the God of His fathers *(Luke 4:16)*; Antichrist refuses to *(Dan. 11:37)*.

8. Christ cleansed the temple *(John 2:14:16)*; Antichrist defiles the temple *(Matt. 24:15)*.

9. Christ ministered to the needy *(Luke 4:18)*; the Antichrist robs the poor *(Psa. 10:8,9)*.

10. Christ was rejected of men *(Isa. 53:7)*; Antichrist will be accepted by men *(Rev. 13:4)*.

11. Christ leadeth the flock *(John 10:3)*; Antichrist leaveth the flock *(Zech. 11:17)*.

12. Christ was slain for the people *(John 11:51)*; Antichrist slays the people *(Isa. 14:20)*.

13. Christ glorified God on earth *(John 17:4)*; Antichrist blasphemes the name of God in heaven *(Rev. 13:6)*.

14. Christ was received up into heaven *(Luke 24:51)*; Antichrist goes down into the lake of fire *(Rev. 19:20)*.—Arthur W. Pink.

JOHN'S GOSPEL

9. CHRIST and NICODEMUS (Continued)

John 3:9-21.

We begin with an Analysis of the passage which is to be before us:—

1. The Dullness of Nicodemus, vv. 9, 10.
2. The Unbelief of Nicodemus, vv. 11, 12.
3. The Omnipresence of Christ, v. 13.
4. The Necessity for Christ's Death, vv. 14, 15.
5. The Unspeakable Gift of God, v. 16.
6. The Purpose of God in sending Christ, v. 17.
7. Grounds of Condemnation, vv. 18-21.

In our last article we dealt at length with Nicodemus's interview with Christ, and sought to bring out the meaning of our Lord's words on that occasion. We saw how the Saviour insisted that the new birth was an imperative *necessity;* that, even though Nicodemus were a Pharisee, a member of the Sanhedrim, nevertheless, unless he was born again he could not see the kingdom of God, i. e. come to know the things of God. We also saw how the Lord explained the *character* of the new birth as a being "born of water (the Word) and of the Spirit"; that regeneration was not a process of reformation or the improving of the old man, but the creating of an altogether new man. That which is born of the flesh is flesh, and no artifices of men can ever make it anything else. If a sinner is to enter the kingdom of God he *must* be born again. Finally, we saw how the Saviour likened the *operations* of the Spirit in bringing about the new birth to the sovereign but mysterious action of the wind. The Saviour had used great plainness of speech, and one had thought it impossible for an intelligent man to miss His meaning. But observe the next verse.

"Nicodemus answered and said unto Him, How can these things be?" *(v. 9).* How this reveals the natural man! It is true that Nicodemus was an educated man and, doubtless, one of examplary moral character; but something more than education and morality are needed to understand the things of God. God has spoken plainly, and in simple terms, yet notwithstanding, the natural man, unaided, has no capacity to receive what God has recorded in His Holy Word. Even though God became incarnate and spoke in human language, men understood Him not. This is demonstrated again and again in this Gospel. Christ spoke of raising the temple of His body, and they thought He referred to the Temple standing in Jerusalem. He spoke to the Samaritan woman of the "living water", and she supposed Him to be referring to the water of Jacob's well. He told the disciples He had meat to eat they knew not of, and they thought only of material food *(4:32)*. He spoke of Himself as the Living Bread come down from heaven which, said He, "is My flesh, which I will give for the life of the world", and the Jews answered, "How can this man give us His flesh to eat?" *(6:51,52)*. He declared, "Yet a little while am I with you, and then I go unto Him that sent Me. Ye shall seek Me, and shall not find Me; and where I am, thither ye cannot come", and His auditors said, "Whither will He go, that we shall not find Him? Will He go unto the dispersed among the Gentiles?" *(7:33-35)*. Again, He said, "I go My way, and ye shall seek Me, and shall die in your sins: whither I go, ye cannot come"; and the Jews replied, "Will He kill Himself? because He saith, Whither I go, ye cannot come?" *(8:21,22)*. He declared, "If ye continue in My Word, then are ye My disciples indeed; and ye shall know the truth, and the truth shall make you free", and they answered, "We be Abraham's seed, and were never in bondage to any man: how sayest thou, Ye shall be made free?" *(8:31-33)*. And so we might continue through this Gospel. What a commentary upon human intelligence; what a proof of man's stupidity and blindness!

And Nicodemus was no exception. Master in Israel he might be, yet was he ignorant of the A. B. C. of spiritual things. And why? What is the cause of the natural man's stupidity? It is because he is in the dark: "The way of the wicked is as darkness: they know not at what they stumble" *(Prov. 4:19)*. The testimony of the New Testament is equally explicit: "Having the understanding darkened, being alienated from the life of God through the ignorance that is in them, because of the blindness of their heart" *(Eph. 4:18)*. How humbling all this is. How it exposes the folly of the proud boasting of men upon their fancied wisdom and learning! The natural man is in the dark because he is blind. Yet how rarely is this stressed by the modern pulpit. How very rarely do most of the Bible teachers of the day emphasize and press the blindness of the natural man, and his deep need of Divine illumination! These things are not palatable we know, and a faithful exposition of them will not make for the popularity of those who preach them; yet are they sorely needed in these days of Laodicean complacency. Let any one who desires to follow the example which our Saviour has left us, read through the four Gospels at a sitting, with the one purpose of discovering how large a place *He* gave in His preaching to the depravity of man, and most probably the reader will be greatly surprised.

"How can these things be?" Nicodemus was at least honest. He was not ashamed to own his ignorance, and ask questions. Well for many another if they would do likewise. Too many are kept in ignorance by a foolish pride which scorns to take the place of one seeking light. Yet this is one of the prime requirements in any who desire to learn. It applies as much to the believer as to the unbeliever. If the Christian refuses to humble himself, if he disdains the attitude of "What I see not, teach Thou me" *(Job 34:32)*; if he is unwilling to receive instruction from those taught of God, and above all, if he fails to cry daily to God "Open Thou mine eyes, that I may behold wondrous things out of Thy law", he will not, and cannot, grow in the knowledge of the truth.

"Jesus answered and said unto him, Art thou a Master of Israel, and knowest not these things?" *(v. 10)*. It is to be noted that our Lord here employed the same term in interrogating Nicodemus as this Ruler of the Jews used at the beginning when addressing Christ, for in the Greek the word for "teacher" in v. 2 is the same as the one rendered "master" in v. 10. It is exceedingly striking to observe that in the brief record of this interview we find the Lord employing just seven times the very expressions used by Nicodemus himself. We tabulate them thus:

1. Nicodemus declared, *"We know"*, v. 2.
   Christ said, "That which *we know we speak"* (Gk.), v. 11.
2. Nicodemus said, *"Thou art a Teacher"*, v. 2.
   Christ said, *"Thou art a teacher"*, v. 10.
3. Nicodemus said, *"Except* God *be* with him", v. 2.
   Christ said, *"Except* a man *be"*, v. 3.
4. Nicodemus asked, "How can *a man be born?"* v. 4.
   Christ answered, "Except *a man be born"*, v. 5.
5. Nicodemus asked, *"Can he enter?"* v. 4.
   Christ answered, *"He cannot enter"*, v. 5.
6. Nicodemus asked *"How* can?" v. 9.
   Christ asked, *"How* shall?" v. 12.
7. Nicodemus asked, "How can *these things* be?" v. 9.
   Christ asked, "Knowest not *these things?"* v. 10.

It is really startling to behold this remarkable correspondency between the language of Nicodemus and the words of the Saviour, and surely there is some important lesson to be learned from it. What are we to gather from this employment by Christ of the terms first used by Nicodemus? Does it not illustrate a principle and teach a lesson for all Christian workers? Let us state it this way: Christ met this man on his own ground, and made his own language the channel of approach to his heart. How simple, yet how important. Have we not often been puzzled to know how to approach some person in whose soul we were interested? We wondered just where was the place to begin. Well, here is light on the problem. Make *his own utterances* the starting point of your address. Turn his own words around against him, and whenever possible invest them with a deeper meaning and a higher application.

"Jesus answered and said unto him, Art thou a master of Israel, and knowest not these things?" What a rebuke this was! It was as though the Lord had said, "You a teacher, and yet untaught yourself? You a lightholder, and yet in the dark! You a master of Israel, and yet ignorant of the most elementary spiritual truths!" How searching, and how solemn! To what extent is this true of the writer and the reader? Ah, must we not all of us hang our heads in shame? How little we know of what we ought to know. How blind we are! So blind that we need to be *guided* into the truth *(John 16:13)!!* Is not our sorest need that of going to the great Physician and seeking from Him that spiritual "eyesalve", so that He may anoint our eyes that we can see *(Rev. 3:18)?* God forbid that the haughtiness of Laodiceanism should prevent us.

Ere passing on to the next verse let us point out one more lesson from that now before us:—v. 10. Even a religious teacher may be ignorant of Divine truth. What a solemn warning is this for us to put no confidence in any man. Here was a member of the Sanhedrim, trained in the highest theological schools of his day, and yet having no discernment for spiritual things. Unfortunately he has had many successors. The fact that a preacher has graduated with honors from some theological center is no proof that he is a man taught of the Holy Spirit. No dependence can be placed on human learning. The only safe course is to emulate the Bereans, and bring everything we hear from the platform and pulpit, yes, and everything we read in religious magazines, to the test of the Word of God, rejecting everything which is not clearly taught in the Holy Oracles.

"Verily, verily, I say unto thee, We speak that we do know, and testify that we have seen; and ye receive not our witness" *(v. 11).* As pointed out above, this was Christ's reply to what Nicodemus had said in his opening statement. "We know that Thou art a Teacher come from God" declared this representative of the Sanhedrim. In response, our Lord now says, "We speak that *we do know,* and testify that we have seen". At a later stage in the conversation, Nicodemus had asked, "How can these things be?" *(v. 9).* What Christ had said concerning the new birth had struck this ruler of the Jews as being incredible. Hence this solemn and emphatic declaration—"We speak that we do know, and testify that we have seen". Christ was not dealing with metaphysical speculations or theological hypotheses, such as the Jewish doctors delighted in. Instead, He was affirming that which He knew to be a

Divine reality, and testifying to that which had an actual existence and could be seen and observed. What an example does our Lord set before all His servants! The teacher of God's Word must not attempt to expound what is not already clear to himself, still less must he speculate about Divine things, or speak of that of which he has no experimental acquaintance. Rather must he speak that which he knows and testify that which he has seen.

"And ye receive not our witness". There is an obvious connection between this statement and what is recorded in the previous verse. There we find Christ chiding Nicodemus for his ignorance of Divine truth; here He reveals the *cause* of such ignorance. The reason a man does not *know* the things of God, is because he *receives not* God's witness concerning them. It is vitally important to observe this order. First receiving, then knowledge: first believing what God has said, and then an understanding of it. This principle is illustrated in Heb. 11:3—"Through faith we understand". This is the *first* thing predicated of faith in this wonderful faith chapter. Faith is the root of perception. As we believe God's Word, He honors our faith by giving us a *knowledge* of what we have believed. And, if we believe not His Word we shall have no understanding whatever of Divine things.

"If I have told you earthly things, and ye believe not, how shall ye believe, if I tell you heavenly things?" (*v. 12*). This is closely connected with the previous verse. There, the Lord Jesus lays bare the cause of man's ignorance in the things of God; here He reveals the condition of *growth* in knowledge. God's law in the spiritual realm corresponds with that which operates in the natural world: there is first the blade, then the ear, and last the full corn in the ear. God will not reveal to us a higher truth until we have thoroughly apprehended the simpler one first. This, we take it, is the moral principle that Christ here enunciated. "Earthly things" are evident and in measure comprehensible, but "heavenly things" are invisible and altogether beyond our grasp until divinely revealed to us. As to the local or immediate reference, we understand by the "earthly things" the new birth which takes place here upon earth, and the Lord's reference to the "wind" as an illustration of the Spirit's operations in bringing about the new birth. These were things that Nicodemus ought to have known about, for Ezek. 36: 25-27 speaks plainly of the yet future regeneration of God's earthly people Israel. If, then, Nicodemus believed not God's Word concerning these earthly things of what avail would it be for Christ to speak to him of "heavenly things"? We pause to apply this searching principle to ourselves.

Why is it that our progress is so slow in the things of God? What is it that retards our growth in the knowledge of the truth? Is not the answer to these and all similar questions stated above: "if I have told you earthly things, and ye believe not, how shall ye believe, if I tell you heavenly things?" The earthly things are things pertaining to the earthly realm. They are the things which have to do with our present life here upon earth. They are the commands of God which are for the regulation of our daily walk down here. If we believe not *these*, that is, if we do not appropriate them and submit ourselves to them, if we do not receive and heed them, then will God reveal to us the higher mysteries—the "heavenly things"? No, indeed, for that would be setting a premium on our unbelief and casting pearls before swine.

Why is it that we have so little light on many of the prophetical portions of Scripture? Why is it that we know so little of the conditions of those who are now "present with the Lord"? Why is it that we are so ignorant of what will form our occupation in the Eternal State? Is it because the prophecies are obscure? Is it because God has revealed so little about the Intermediate and Eternal States? Surely not. It is because we are in no condition to receive illumination upon these things. Because we have paid so little earnest heed to the "earthly things" (the things pertaining to our earthly life, the precepts of God for the regulation of our earthly walk) God withholds from us a better knowledge of "heavenly things," things pertaining to the heavenly realm. Let writer and reader bow before God in humble and contrite confession for our miserable failures, and seek from Him that needed grace that our ways may be more pleasing in His sight. Let our first desire be, not a clearer apprehension of the Divine mysteries, but a more implicit obedience to the Divine requirements. As we turn to God's Word, let our dominant motive be that we may learn God's mind *for us* in order that we may do it, and not that we may become wise in recondite problems. Let us remember that "Strong meat belongeth to them that are of full age, even those *who by reason of use* have their senses (spiritual senses) *exercised* to discern both good and evil" *(Heb. 5:14)*.

"And no man hath ascended up to heaven, but He that came down from heaven, even the Son of Man which is in heaven" *(v. 13)*. The connection between this verse and the preceding one seems to be as follows. The "heavenly things" to which the Lord had referred had not till then been clearly revealed to men. To ascend to heaven, and penetrate the hidden counsels of God, was an utter impossibility to fallen man. Only the Son, whose native residence was heaven, was *qualified* to reveal heavenly things.

But what did the Lord mean when He said, *"No man* hath ascended up to heaven"? This verse is a favorite one with many of those who believe in "Soul Sleep" and "Annihilation". There are those who contend that between death and resurrection man ceases to be. They appeal to this verse and declare it teaches *no* man, not even Abel or David, has yet gone to heaven. But it is to be noted that Christ did not say, "No man hath *entered* heaven", but, "No man hath *ascended* up to heaven". This is an entirely different thing. "Ascended" no man had, or ever will. What is before us now is only one of ten thousand examples of the minute and marvelous accuracy of Scripture, lost, alas! on the great majority who read it so carelessly and hurriedly. Of Enoch it is recorded that he "was *translated* that he should not see death" *(Heb. 11:5)*. Of Elijah it is said that he *"went up* by a whirlwind into heaven" *(2 Kings 2:11)*. Of the saints who shall be raptured to heaven at the return of Christ, it is said that they shall be *"caught up"* (*1 Thess. 4: 17*). Of Christ alone is it said that He *"ascended"*. This at once marks His uniqueness, and demonstrates that in *all* things He *has* "the pre-eminence"!

But observe further that the Lord said, "Even the Son of Man *which is* in heaven". In heaven, even while speaking to Nicodemus on earth. This is another evidence of His Deity. It affirmed His Omnipresence. It is remarkable to see that every essential attribute of Deity is predicated of Christ in this Gospel, the special object of which is to unveil His Divine perfections. His *eternality* is argued in 1:1. His Divine *glory* is mentioned in 1:14. His *omniscience* is seen in 1:48 and again in 2:24, 25. His *omnipotence* was demonstrated by the miracles He performed. His matchless *wisdom* is borne witness to in 7:46. His unchanging *love* is affirmed in 13:1. And so we might go on indefinitely.

"And as Moses lifted up the serpent in the wilderness, even so must the Son of Man be lifted up" *(v. 14)*. Christ had been speaking to Nicodemus about the imperative necessity of the new birth. By nature man is dead in trespasses and sins, and in order to obtain life he must be born again. The new birth is the impartation of Divine life, *eternal life,* but for this to be bestowed on men, the Son of Man *must* be lifted up. Life could come only out of death. The sacrificial work of Christ is the basis of the Spirit's operations and the ground of God's gift of eternal life. Observe that Christ here speaks of the lifting up of the Son of *Man,* for atonement could be made only by One in the nature of him who sinned, and only as Man was God's Son capable of taking upon Him the penalty resting on the sinner. No doubt there was a specific reason why Christ should here refer to His sacrificial death as a "lifting up". The Jews were looking for a Messiah who should be lifted up, but elevated in a manner altogether different from what the Lord here mentions. They expected Him to be elevated to the Throne of David—as He *will* yet be—but before this, He must be lifted up upon the Cross of Shame, enduring the judgment of God upon His people's sin.

To illustrate the character, the meaning, and the purpose of His death, the Lord here refers to the well-known incident in Israel's wilderness wanderings which is recorded in Num. 21. Israel was murmuring against the Lord, and He sent fiery serpents among the people, which bit them so that some of the people died and many others were sorely wounded from their poisonous bites. In consequence, they confessed they had sinned, and cried unto Moses for relief. He, in turn, cried unto God, and the Lord bade him make a serpent of brass, fix it on a pole, and tell the bitten Israelites to look to it in faith and they should be healed. All of this was a striking forshadowing of Christ being lifted up on the Cross in order that He might save, through the look of faith, those who were dying from sin. The type is a remarkable one and worthy of our closest study.

A "serpent" was a most appropriate figure of that deadly and destructive power, the origin of which the Scriptures teach us to trace to *the* Serpent, whose "seed" sinners are declared to be. The *poison* of the serpent's bite, which vitiates the entire system of its victim, and from the fatal effects of which there was no deliverance, save that which God provided, strikingly exhibited the awful nature and consequences of *sin*. The *remedy* which God provided was the exhibition of *the destroyer destroyed*. Why was not one of the actual serpents spiked by Moses to the pole? Ah, *that* would have marred the type: that would have pictured judgment executed on the sinner himself; and, worse still, would have misrepresented our sinless Substitute. In the type chosen there was the likeness of a serpent, not an actual serpent, but a piece of brass *made* like one. So, the One who is the sinner's Saviour was sent "in the likeness of sin's flesh" *(Rom. 8:3, Gk.)*, and God "made Him to be sin for us, who knew no sin; that we might be made the righteousness of God in Him" *(2 Cor. 5:21)*.

But how could a *serpent* fitly typify the Holy One of God? This is the very last thing of all we had supposed could, with any propriety, be a figure of Him. True, the "serpent" did not, could not, typify Him in His essential character, and perfect life. The brazen serpent only foreshadowed Christ as He was "lifted up". The lifting up manifestly pointed to the Cross. What was the "serpent"? It was the reminder and emblem of *the Curse*. It was through the agency of that old Serpent, the Devil, that our first parents were seduced, and brought under the Curse of a Holy God. And on the Cross, dear reader, the holy Son of God, incarnate, was made a curse for us. We would not dare make such an assertion, did not Scripture itself expressly affirm it. In Gal. 3:13 we are told, "Christ hath redeemed us from the curse of the law, being made a Curse for us". There was no flaw, then, in the type. The foreshadowing was perfect. A "serpent" was the only thing in all Nature which could accurately prefigure the crucified Saviour made a Curse for us.

But *why* a "serpent" of *brass?* That only brings out once more the perfect accuracy of the type. "Brass" speaks of two things. In the symbolism of Scripture brass is the emblem of *Divine judgment*. The *brazen* altar illustrates this truth, for on it the sacrificial animals were slain, and upon it descended the consuming fire from heaven. Again; in Deut. 28, the Lord declared unto Israel, that if they would not hearken unto His voice and do His commandments *(v. 15)*, that His curse should come upon them *(v. 16)*, and as a part of the Divine judgment with which they should be visited, He warned them, "And thy heaven that is above thy head shall be *brass*" *(v. 23)*. Once more, in Rev. 1, where Christ is seen as *Judge*, inspecting the seven churches, we are told, "His feet were like unto fine *brass*" *(v. 15)*. The "serpent", then, spoke of the *Curse* which sin entailed; the "brass" told of God's *judgment* falling on the One made sin for us. But there is another thought suggested by the brass. Brass is harder than iron, or silver or gold. It told, then, of Christ's mighty strength, which was able to *endure* the awful judgment which fell upon Him— a mere creature, though sinless, would have been utterly consumed.

From what has been said, it will be evident that when God told Moses to make a serpent of brass, fix it upon a pole, and bid the bitten Israelites look on it and they should live, that He was preaching to them the Gospel of His grace. We would now point out seven things which these Israelites were *not* bidden to do.

1. They were not told to *manufacture some ointment as* the means of healing their wounds. Doubtless, that would have seemed much more reasonable to them. But it would have destroyed the type. The religious doctors of the day are busy inventing spiritual lotions, but they effect no cures. Those who seek spiritual relief by such means are like the poor woman mentioned in the Gospel: she "suffered many things of many physicians, and had spent all that she had, and was nothing bettered but rather grew worse" *(Mark 5:26)*.

2. They were not told to *minister to others* who were wounded, in order to get relief for themselves. This, too, would have appealed to their sentiments as being more practical and more desirable than gazing at a pole, yet in fact it had been

most impracticable. Of what use would it be for one to jump into deep water to rescue a drowning man if he could not swim a stroke himself! How then can one who is dying and unable to deliver himself, help others in a similar state? And yet there are many today engaged in works of charity with the vain expectation that giving relief to others will counteract the deadly virus of sin which is at work in their own souls.

3. They were not told to *fight the serpents*. If some of our moderns had been present that day they would have urged Moses to organize a Society for the Extermination of Serpents! But of what use had that been to those who were *already* bitten and dying? Had each stricken one killed a thousand serpents they would still have died. And what does all this fighting of sin amount to! True, it affords an outlet for the energy of the flesh; but all these crusades against intemperance, profanity and vice, have not improved society any, nor have they brought a single sinner one step nearer to Christ.

4. They were not told to make *an offering to the serpent* on the pole. God did not ask any payment from them in return for their healing. No, indeed. Grace ceases to be grace, if any price is made for that which it brings. But how frequently is the Gospel perverted at this very point! Not long ago the writer preached on human depravity, addressing himself exclusively to the unsaved. He sought by God's help to show the unbeliever the terribleness of his state and how desperate was his need of a Saviour to deliver him from the wrath to come. As we took our seat, the pastor of the church rose and announced an irrelevant hymn and then urged everybody present to "re-consecrate themselves to God". Poor man! That was the best he knew. But what pitiful blindness! Other preachers are asking their hearers to "Give their hearts to Jesus"—another miserable perversion. God does not ask the sinner to *give* anything, but to *receive* HIS CHRIST.

5. They were not told to *pray* to the serpent. Many evangelists urge their hearers to go to the "mourner's bench" or "penitent form" and there plead with God for pardoning mercy, and if they are dead in earnest they are led to believe that God has heard them for their much speaking. If these "seekers after a better life" believe what the preacher has told them, namely, that they have "prayed through" and have now "got forgiveness", they feel happy, and for a while continue treading the clean side of the Broad Road with a light heart; but the almost invariable consequence is that their last state is worse than the first. O dear reader, do not make the fatal mistake of substituting prayer for faith in Christ.

6. They were not told to *look at Moses*. They *had* been looking to Moses, and urging him to cry to God on their behalf; and when God responded, He took their eyes from off Moses, and commanded them to look at the brazen serpent. Moses was the Law-Giver, and how many today are looking to him for salvation. They are trusting in their own imperfect obedience to God's commandments to take them to heaven. In other words, they are depending on their own works. But Scripture says emphatically, "Not by works of righteousness which we have done, but according to His mercy He saved us" *(Titus 3:5)*. The Law was given by Moses, but *grace and truth* came by Jesus Christ, and Christ alone can save.

7. They were not told to look at *their wounds*. Some think they need to be more occupied with the work of examining their own wicked hearts in order to promote that degree of repentance which they deem a necessary qualification for salvation. But as well attempt to produce heat by looking at the snow, or light by peering into the darkness, as seek salvation by looking to self for it. To be occupied with myself is only to be taken up with that which God has condemned, and which already has the sentence of death written upon it. But, it may be asked, "Ought I not to have that godly sorrow which worketh repentance *before* I trust in Christ?" Certainly not. You cannot have a godly sorrow till you are a godly person, and you cannot be a godly person until you have submitted yourself to God and obeyed Him by believing in Christ. *Faith* is the beginning of all godliness.

We have developed the seven points above with the purpose of exposing some of the wiles by which the Enemy is deceiving a multitude of souls. It is greatly to be feared that there are many in our churches today who sincerely think they are Christians, but who are sincerely mistaken. Believing that I am a millionaire will not make me one; and believing that I am saved, when I am not, will not save me. The Devil is well pleased if he can get the awakened sinner to look at anything rather than Christ—good works, repentance, feelings, resolutions, baptism, anything so long as it is not Christ Himself.

Turning now from the negative to the positive side, let us consider, though it must be briefly, one or two points in the type itself. First, Moses was commanded by God to make a serpent of brass—it was of *The Lord's providing*—and the spiritual significance of this we have already looked at. Second, Moses was commanded to fix this brazen serpent upon a pole. Thus was the Divine remedy *publically exhibited* so that all Israel might look on it and be healed. Third, the Lord's promise was that "it shall come to pass, that every one that is bitten, when he looketh upon it, shall live" *(Num. 21:8)*. Thus, not only did God here give a foreshadowing of the *means* by which salvation was to be wrought out for sinners, but also the *manner* in which the sinner obtains an interest in that salvation, namely, *by looking away from himself to the Divinely appointed object of faith*, even to the Lord Jesus Christ. How blessed this was: the brazen serpent was "lifted up" so that those who were too weak to crawl up to the pole itself, and perhaps too far gone to even raise their voices in supplication could, nevertheless, lift up their eyes in simple faith in God's promise and be healed.

Just as the bitten Israelites were healed by a look of faith, so the sinner may be saved by looking to Christ by faith. Saving faith is not some difficult and meritorious work which man must perform so as to give him a claim upon God for the blessing of salvation. It is not on account of our faith that God saves us, but it is through means of our faith. It is in believing we *are* saved. It is like saying to a starving man, He that eats of this food shall be relieved from the pangs of hunger, and be refreshed and strengthened. Eating is no meritorious performance, but, from the nature of things, eating is the indispensable *means* of relieving hunger. To say that when a man believes he shall be saved, is just to say that the guiltiest of the guilty, and the vilest of the vile, is *welcome* to salvation, and shall assuredly obtain salvation, if he will but receive it in the only way in which, from the nature of the case, it can be received, namely, by personal faith in the Lord Jesus Christ, which means believing what God has recorded concerning His Son in the Holy Scriptures. The moment a sinner does that *he is saved,* just as God said to Moses, "It *shall* come to pass, that every one that is bitten, *when* he looketh upon it *shall live*".

"*Every one* that is bitten". No matter how many times he may have been bitten; no matter how far the poison had advanced in its progress toward a fatal issue, if he but *looked* he should "live". Such is the Gospel declaration: *"Whosoever believeth* shall not perish, but have everlasting life". There is no exception. The vilest wretch on the face of the earth, the most degraded and despised, the most miserable and wretched of all human kind, who believes in Christ shall be saved by Him with an everlasting salvation. No sin but unbelief can bar the sinner's way to the Saviour. It is possible that some of the Israelites who heard of the Divinely appointed remedy made light of it; it may be that some of them cherished wicked doubts as to the possibility of them obtaining any relief by looking at a brazen serpent; some may have hoped for recovery by the use of ordinary means; no matter, if these things were true of some of them, and later they found the disease gaining on them, and then they lifted up a believing eye to the Divinely erected standard, *they too* were healed. And should these lines be read by one who has long procrastinated, who has continued for many long years in a course of stouthearted unbelief and impenitence, nevertheless, the marvelous grace of our God declares to you, that *"whosoever believeth* shall not perish, but have everlasting life". It is still the "accepted time"; it is still "the day of salvation". Believe now, and *thou* shalt be saved.

Man became a lost sinner by a *look,* for the first thing recorded of Eve in connection with the fall of our first parents it that "When the woman *saw* that the tree was good for food" *(Gen. 3:6)*. In like manner, the lost sinner is saved by a look. The Christian life *begins* by looking: "*Look* unto Me, and be ye saved, all the ends of the earth: for I am God, and there is none else" *(Isa. 45:22)*. The Christian life *continues* by looking: "Let us run with patience the race which is set before us, *looking* unto Jesus the Author and Finisher of faith" *(Heb. 12:2)*. And at the *end* of the Christian life we are still to be looking for Christ: "For our citizenship is in heaven; from whence also we *look* for the Saviour, the Lord Jesus Christ" *(Phil. 3:20)*. From first to last, the one thing required is *looking* at God's Son.

But perhaps right here the troubled and trembling sinner will voice his last difficulty—"Sir, I do not know that I am looking in the correct way". Dear friend, God does not ask you to look *at your look,* but at CHRIST. In that great crowd of bitten Israelites of old there were some with young eyes and some with old eyes that looked at the Serpent; there were some with clear vision and some with dim vision; there were some who had a full view of the Serpent by reason of their nearness to the uplifted type of Christ; and there were, most probably, others who could scarcely see it because of their great distance from the pole, but the Divine record is "It shall come to pass, that *every one* that is bitten, when he *looketh* upon it, shall live". And so it is today. The Lord Jesus says, "Come unto Me, all ye that labor and are heavy laden, and I will give you rest". He does not define the *method* or the *manner* of coming, and even if the poor sinner comes groping, stumbling, falling, yet, if only he *will* "come" there is a warm welcome for him. So it is in our text: it is "Whosoever believeth" —nothing is said about the *strength* or the *intelligence* of the belief, for it is not the character or degree of faith that saves, but Christ Himself. Faith is simply the eye of the soul that looks off unto the Lord Jesus. Do not rest, then, on your faith, but on the Saviour Himself.

"For God so loved the world, that He gave His only begotten Son, that whosoever believeth in Him, should not perish but have everlasting life" *(3:16)*. Christ had just made mention of His death, and had affirmed that the Cross was an imperative necessity; it was not "the Son of Man *shall* be lifted up", but "the Son of Man *must* be lifted up". There was no other alternative. If the claims of God's throne were to be met, if the demands of justice were to be satisfied, if sin was to be put away, it could only be by some sinless One being punished in the stead of those who should be saved. The righteousness of God required this: the Son of Man *must* be lifted up.

But there is more in the Cross of Christ than an exhibition of the righteousness of God; there is also a display of His wondrous *love*. V. 16 explains v. 14, as its opening word indicates. V. 16 takes us back to the very foundation of everything. The great Sacrifice was provided by Love. Christ was God's love-gift. This at once refutes an error that once obtained in certain quarters, namely, that Christ died in order that God might be induced to pity and save men. The very opposite is the truth. Christ died because God *did* love men, and *was* determined to save them that believe. The death of Christ was the supreme demonstration of God's love. It was impossible that there should be any discord among the Persons of the Godhead in reference to the salvation of men. The will of the Godhead is, and necessarily must be, one. The Atonement was not the cause, but the effect, of God's love: "In this was manifested the love of God toward us, because that God sent His only begotten Son into the world, that we might live through Him. Herein is love, not that we loved God, but that He loved us, and sent His Son to be the propitiation for our sins" *(1 John 4:9, 10)*. From what other source *could* have proceeded the giving of Christ to save men but from LOVE—pure sovereign benignity!

The Love of God! How blessed is this to the hearts of believers, for only believers can appreciate it, and they but very imperfectly. It is to be noted that here in John 3:16 there are seven things told us about God's love: first, the *tense* of His love—"God so *loved*". It is not God *loves,* but He "loved". That He loves us now that we are His children, we can, in measure, understand; but that He should have loved us *before* we became His children passes knowledge. But He did. "God commendeth His love toward us, in that, *while we were yet sinners* Christ died for us" *(Rom. 5:8)*. And again: "Yea, I have loved thee with *an everlasting love:* therefore with loving kindness have I drawn thee" *(Jer. 31:3)*. Second, the *magnitude* of His love—"God *so* loved". None can define or measure that little word "so". There are dimensions to the breadth and length, and depth, and height of His wondrous love, that none can measure. Third, the *scope* of God's love—"God so loved *the world*". It was not limited to the narrow bounds of Palestine, but it flowed out to sinners of the Gentiles, too. Fourth, the *nature* of God's love—"God so loved the world that *He gave*". Love, real love, ever seeks the highest interest of others. Love is unselfish: it gives. Fifth, the *sacrificial character* of God's love—"He gave *His only begotten Son*." God spared not His BEST. He freely delivered up Christ, even to the death of the Cross. Sixth, the *design* of His love—"That whosoever believeth on Him *should not perish*". Many died in the wilderness from the bites of the serpents: and many of Adam's race will suffer eternal death in the lake of fire. But God purposed to have a people who "should not perish". Who this people are is made manifest by their "believing" on God's Son. Seventh, the *beneficence* of God's love—"But have *everlasting life*". This is what God imparts to every one of His own. Ah, must we not exclaim with the apostle, "Behold, *what manner of love* the Father hath bestowed upon us"! *(1 John 3:1)*. O dear Christian reader, if ever you are tempted to *doubt* God's love go back to the Cross, and see there how He gave up to that cruel death His "only begotten Son".

"For God sent not His Son into the world to condemn the world; but that the world through Him might be saved" *(3: 17)*. This verse enlarges upon the beneficent nature and purpose of God's love. Unselfish in its character—for *love* "seeketh not her own"—it ever desires the good of those unto whom it flows forth. When God sent His Son here it was not to "condemn the world", as we might have expected. There was every reason why the world should have been condemned. The heathen were in an even worse condition than the Jews. Outside the little land of Palestine, the knowledge of the true and living God had wellnigh completely vanished from the earth. And where God is not known and loved, there is no love among men for their neighbors. In every Gentile nation idolatry and immorality were rampant. One has only to read the second half of Rom. 1 to be made to marvel that God did not then sweep the earth with the besom of destruction. But no; He had other designs, gracious designs. God sent His Son into the world that the world through Him "might be saved". It is to be remarked that the word "might" here does not express any uncertainty. Instead, it declares the *purpose* of God in the sending of His Son. In common speech the word "might" signifies a contingency. It is only another case of the vital importance of ignoring man's dictionaries and the way he employs words, and turning to a concordance to see how the Holy Spirit uses each word in the Scriptures themselves. This word "might"—as a part of the verb —expresses *design*. When we are told that God sent His Son into the world that through Him "the world might be saved", it signifies that "through Him the world *should be* saved", and this is how it is rendered in the R. V. For other instances we refer the reader to 1 Pet. 3:18—"Might bring us to God" implies no uncertainty whatever, but tells of the object to be accomplished. For further examples see Gal. 4:5; Tit. 2:14; 2 Pet. 1:4, etc., etc.

"He that believeth on Him is not condemned: but he that believeth not is condemned already, because he has not believed in the name of the only begotten Son of God". For the believer there is "no condemnation" *(Rom. 8:1)*, because Christ was condemned in His stead—the "chastisement of our peace" was upon Him. But the unbeliever is "condemned already". By nature he is a "child of *wrath*" *(Eph. 2:3)*, not corruption merely. He enters this world with the Curse of a sin-hating God upon him. If he hears the Gospel and receives not Christ he incurs a new and increased condemnation through his unbelief. How emphatically this proves that the sinner is *responsible* for his unbelief!

"And this is the condemnation, that light is come into the world, and men loved darkness rather than light, because their deeds were evil" *(3:19)*. Here is the *cause* of man's unbelief: he loves the darkness, and therefore hates the light. What a proof of his depravity! It is not only that men are *in* the dark, but they *love* the darkness—they prefer ignorance, error, superstition, to the light of truth. And the reason why they love the darkness and hate the light is because their deeds are evil.

"For every one that doeth evil hateth the light, neither cometh to the light, lest his deeds should be reproved. But he that doeth truth cometh to the light, that his deeds may be made manifest, that they are wrought in God" *(3:20, 21)*. Here is the final test. *"Every one* that doeth (practices) evil, hateth the light, neither cometh to the light", and why?—"lest his deeds should be reproved". *That* is why men refuse to read the Scriptures. God's Word would condemn them. On the other hand, "he that doeth truth," which describes what is characteristic of every believer, "cometh to the light"—note the perfect tense—he comes *again and again* to the light of God's Word. And for what purpose? To learn God's mind, that he may cease doing the things which are displeasing to Him, and be occupied with that which is acceptable in His sight. Was not this the final word of Christ to Nicodemus, addressed to his *conscience?* This ruler of the Jews had come to Jesus "by night", as though his deeds would not bear the light!

For the benefit of those who would prepare for the next lesson we subjoin the following questions:

1. What does the "much water" teach? v. 23.
2. What was the real purpose of the Jews in coming to John and saying what is recorded in v. 26?
3. What is the meaning of v. 27?
4. What vitally important lesson for the Christian is taught in v. 29?
5. What is the meaning of v. 33?
6. What is meant by the last half of v. 34?
7. How does v. 35 bring out the Deity of Christ?—Arthur W. Pink.

PRAYER

In an idle tale, which amused the childhood of many of our readers, there is a worse than foolish fancy of a wishing-cap, which, when the possessor wore it, invested him with the power of obtaining, instantaneously, whatever he desired. Men sometimes appear to regard the promises of God to answer prayer, as serving a similar purpose. As though they meant that a man, whatever his character, had only to work himself up to a blind and presumptuous confidence, and Omnipotence stood pledged to the accomplishment of his wishes, and unless his selfish desires were gratified, he would almost be entitled to impugn the Divine varacity. If this is not the spirit in which men frequently address a throne of grace, or in which they are admonished to make experiments in prayer, it is, at all events, on some such misconception that infidelity bases its objection to the Christian doctrine, and the ridicule of the Christian practice of making our requests known unto God. "Is it for a moment to be supposed", they ask, "that the will of the Eternal is to be changed by the will of His creature, or that the order of nature and the course of Providence are to be interrupted or reversed, in obedience to the capricious demand of a vain mortal?" No, caviller, it is not for a moment to be supposed. No supposition could be more impious—none more inconsistent with the doctrine of Scripture—none more utterly repugnant to the convictions of a child of God. In this, as in almost every case, the objections of infidelity are based upon the grossest ignorance or misconception of what is taught in the Word of God.

We have no desire to evade, but rather court the fullest investigation of every article of our faith, claiming, however, that every article be taken in the scriptural statement of it. We avow the fullest confidence in God as a God who heareth prayer, in His repeated promises to answer our supplication, and in the recorded testimony of His people that God hath heard them. "This is the confidence that we have in Him, that if we ask anything according to His will He heareth us". Nor do we use language in any hidden and indirect sense, in avowing His confidence. Nor do we in any way modify the promises on which that confidence rests. We receive these promises as meaning *all*, and precisely *what* they affirm. But we claim, as a matter of simple justice, that they be considered in their scriptural light and connections, and then it will be clearly seen that they are very far from teaching that the will of God is to be subject to the caprice of His creatures, or that He binds Himself to comply with their selfish desires.

In order to a just view of these promises we must remember to whom they are addressed; for the same scriptures which contain the promise, also contain assurances, equally emphatic, that there are certain descriptions of persons whose prayers are an abomination to God. Thus He says of one class, "Then shall they call upon Me but I will not answer, then shall they seek Me early but shall not find Me". It is asked regarding the hypocrite, "Will God hear his cry when trouble cometh upon him?" Again, we are taught, "The Lord is far from the wicked, but He heareth the cry of the righteous". Without multiplying examples, we direct attention to the fact, that all the promises of God to hear and answer prayer are addressed to *believers*, whose highest ambition is that their wills should be in strict harmony with God's will. The promise, for example, "Ask and ye shall receive, seek and ye shall find, knock and it shall be opened unto you", is addressed, not to men indiscriminately, but to the disciples of Christ. Such promises can be urged by the people of God only when they are in their proper position of submission to the will of God. So one of them says, "If I regard iniquity in my heart the Lord will not hear me." So the confidence expressed in a passage quoted above, is the confidence of those who can say in the context, "Now are we the sons of God"; and their confidence was this express limitation, "If we ask anything *according to His will* He heareth us". The promise of a loving Father to His child must not be appropriated by His enemies.

In order to a just view of these promises we must take into account the scriptural conditions of all true prayer; for, surely, it would be most unreasonable to consider God as bound to any other conditions. We are taught in Scripture that "we know not what we should pray for as we ought"; and, on this account, we are assured that "the Spirit helpeth our infirmities"; nay, that "the Spirit itself maketh intercession for us", and this is true prayer—prayer in the Spirit. This harmonizes with the view given above of the character of those to whom the promises are made. The Spirit who helps our infirmities, and makes intercession for us, is the Spirit of adoption whereby we cry Abba, and He maketh intercession for us *according to the will of God*. We do not ask at present *how* the Spirit helpeth our infirmities, or guides our desires into the channel of prayer; but this is the prayer to which the promise is given, and, therefore, "This is the confidence that we have in Him, that if we ask anything according to His will, He heareth us".

Another scriptural condition of true prayer is, that it be offered in the name of Christ. He is the only medium through which prayer can be either offered or answered. "No man", He says, "cometh unto the Father but by Me". He is the advocate and high priest who ever liveth to make intercession for us; and it is on this same consideration that the promise turns, "Verily I say unto you, Whatsoever ye shall ask the Father *in My name* He will give it you". He is the only way whereby we have access to the Father, the only sacrifice through whose blood we have boldness to enter into the holiest, the only high priest through whose intercessions our plea can be accepted. All this is acknowledged in all true prayer. We disclaim all pretension to be heard on our own account, and claim to be accepted and answered only for His sake. We profess our faith in the testimony of God concerning Him, that in Him we have pardon, peace, and eternal life. This implies our renunciation of all that opposes the will of *His* Father, and *our* Father. And who that knows the meaning of all this, could for a moment think of profaning the holy name of Jesus, by using it as a plea for anything that is not in harmony with the will of the Father? When we rest our cause upon His intercession, who would presume to expect His advocacy of a right that contravenes the Divine will? Thus, whether we consider the parties to whom the promises are made, or the scriptural conditions of true prayer, which originates in the intercession of the Spirit, is offered in the name of Jesus, and depends on His advocacy, the Scriptures are very far from teaching that the will of God can be controlled by the caprice or selfishness of His creatures.

They teach, on the contrary, that all the interests of His creatures are involved in the prevalence of His will. The happiness and perfection of His people consist in conforming their wills to His, and all true prayer may be summed up in this, "Thy will be done". No child of God can deliberately ask anything contrary to the will of God, or inconsistent with **His glory.** So far as true prayer is the intercession of the Spirit, it must be according to the will of God. And if, in the obscurity of this present state, a believer asks anything in the name of Jesus, regarding which the will of God is not known, the very fact of asking in that name implies that it is asked in submission to the will of the Father. The end in view is still that God's will may be done, however we may be mistaken regarding the time, means, or manner of its accomplishment; and thus, "if we know that He heareth us whatsoever we ask, we know that we have the petitions that we desired of Him". When Paul was subject to a bodily affliction which, in his own view, disqualified him for the service to which he was called, he besought the Lord thrice that it might be removed, and received the assurance, "My grace is sufficient for thee, for My strength is perfected in weakness". His prayer was answered, though in a way very different from what he expected. He had the petition which he desired of Him, not in the removal of the affliction, but in the assurance that the affliction would be made subservient to the very end which Paul feared it would hinder; and fully satisfied with the answer, he said, "Most gladly therefore will I rather glory in my infirmity, that the power of Christ my rest upon me".

The child of God can never cease ardently to desire whatever he knows to be according to the will of God, and subservient to His glory. If his power were equal to his desire the object of it would at once be accomplished. But, while he is conscious that he is utterly destitute of such power, all that remains is that his inefficient will should go out and indentify itself with the will of Him who speaks, and it is done; and, since he has a Divine warrant for it, his ardent desire assumes the form and finds the utterance of confident supplication in a name that always prevails.

Here it may be demanded: "If, then, it is the will of God that is done, what does prayer avail, or how does it affect the issue?" If it availed nothing, the child of God could not do less than utter his ardent desire, "Thy will be done". But we are told that "the effectual, fervent prayer of a righteous man, availeth much". Nor will the infidel be warranted in disputing the truth of this, because a poor, short-sighted mortal, like himself, cannot explain *how* it avails, or *why* the Spirit of God should make the prayer of the believer the vehicle of His intercession. The will of God must be accomplished in all things; all creatures combined could not thwart it. Yet God has been pleased to assign an important place to the agency of His servants in carrying out His purposes. They are "laborers together with Him" in carrying out His designs, though He no more needs their cooperation that He who fed thousands with five small loaves, needs the cooperation of the husbandman or the influence of sunshine and showers in giving bread to all that live. But if God has left room for the agency of our labors in the accomplishment of His designs, why not also for the agency of our prayers? If, for example, He employs Paul's preaching to the Gentiles as a means of their salvation, why not also employ Paul's prayers for them? If an objector demands, "Would they not have been saved if Paul had not prayed?" it is a sufficient reply to ask, "Would they not have been saved if Paul had not preached?" All difficulties that can be suggested lie no more against prayer than they do against any other form of creature agency. There is only this distinction, that a sanctified spirit, going out in unison with the Divine will, and, in loving dependence, laying hold on the outstretched arm of Omnipotence, is the most sublime act of creature agency, and one to which it becomes God to give the first place among all the secondary causes which He is pleased to employ. And it surely does not diminish our sense of His wisdom, while it sheds new glory on His condescending love, that in His providential arrangements for the execution of His sovereign will, He should have made provision for fulfilling the promise of His Son, "Whatsoever ye shall ask the Father in My name He will give it you". That He has made such provision, we have the amplest proof. Neither in the inspired nor in the uninspired records of the people's experience, their written nor their unwritten testimony, can an instance be found in which their confidence has been disappointed. A host of worthies of all ages and countries, whose testimonies are not to be impeached, and, least of all, by those who, from the nature of the case, can have no counter experience, unite in the grateful expression of the common experience, "But, verily, God hath heard me; He hath attended to the voice of my prayer. Blessed be God, who hath not turned away my prayer, nor His mercy from me."

Much, it is true that has the sound of prayer in human ears, falls dead and ineffectual; for God is not deceived by words upon the lips when there is not behind them a soul intent on the accomplishment of His will and the manifestation of His glory. To many professed suppliants it may be said, "Ye ask and receive not, because ye ask amiss, that ye may consume it upon your lusts." Their prayers, if not an empty sound, are the breathings of selfishness; or, when not the utterance of selfishness, the doubt in their heart belies the supplication of their lips. There is a plain direction regarding prayer which is, often misunderstood or misapplied. The direction is, "Let him ask in faith, nothing wavering;" and the misapprehension is, that a man whose habitual state is one of distrust or unbelief, has only to "work himself up" to a firm belief on any given occasion in order to claim the promise which belongs to the prayer of faith. But the word "wavering" in that direction relates not to a man's state of mind with reference to a particular object, but to his character or habitual state of mind; for it is added, "He that wavereth is like a wave of the sea, driven of the wind and tossed." Not more positive is God's promise to hear the prayer of the believer than is His assurance of the vanity of the prayer of the waverer. "Let not that man think that he shall receive anything of the Lord." Men cannot come and insult God by making experiments in prayer, pretending to plead with Him in order that they may see what the result will be. The prayer of faith can be offered only by a believer; the Spirit makes intercession only in the heart where He dwells; and prayer, in accordance with the will of God, can only come from a soul whose ruling desire and aim is that the will of God may be done. As Leighton has it, "He that hath nothing of the Spirit of God cannot pray at all; he may howl as a beast in his necessity or distress, or may speak words of prayer, as some birds learn the language of men, but pray he cannot." And again, "Only the children call God their *Father*, and cry unto Him as their Father; and therefore many a poor, unlettered Christian, far outstrips your school rabbies in this faculty; because it is not effectually taught in those lower academies. They must be taught in the school of God as children of His house, who speak His language. Men may give spiritual rules and directions in this, and such as may be useful, drawn from the Word, which furnishes us with all needed precepts; but you have still to bring these into the seat of this faculty of prayer, the heart, and stamp them upon it, and so to teach it to pray, without which there is no prayer. This is the prerogative royal of Him who framed the heart of man within him."

In His last discourse with His disciples before He suffered, the Lord makes this the condition on which He promises the answer, "If ye abide in Me, and My words abide in you." Then only is the heart the receptacle, and then only are our words the utterance of the very mind of Jesus. Then, as has been remarked, "prayer in the name of Christ is such as is offered in the nature, mind, and spirit of Christ." Then the unlimited promise of the fulfillment of prayer will be understood, not as referring to spiritual blessings only, but to all that can possibly concern the children of God or affect His glory, were it an interest insignificant as the hairs of their head, which are all numbered. If prayer proceeds from our own will, the promise cannot be claimed, even though it relate to spiritual blessings which may be sought after, no less than earthly blessings, in a selfish spirit; but, when the incitement to prayer is derived from an inward Divine operation, *that* prayer is truly offered in the name of the Lord, and has the fulfillment in itself; for, where God incites to prayer, there of course, in His veracity and faithfulness, He gives to him who prays.— *From "Waymarks in the Wilderness".*

When Jesus stands up to fight He wars by non-resistance. He says, "My Kingdom is not of this world, else would My servants fight." He conquers by flight rather than by fight. He taught His people when persecuted in one city to flee to another; and never did He bid them form bands, and battle with their persecutors. That is not according to Christ's law or example. A fighting church is the Devil's church, but a bearing and enduring church—*that* is Christ's church. His parents fled with Him by night, and took Him down into Egypt that He might be sheltered there.—*C. H. Spurgeon.*

"ASSURANCE OF SALVATION,"
and
"FULL ASSURANCE OF FAITH"

Heb. 10:22.

Assurance of salvation makes its possessor unspeakably happy. We do not mean the doctrine, but the possession of assurance. It is good to know that the privilege of assurance is the doctrine of Scripture. But you may be able to prove beyond a doubt that the Word of God warrants the believer's assurance, and yet you may not yourself be assured of salvation, or your assurance may be but fitful, and unfruitful of joy, peace, happy worship, and holy obedience.

Now, we believe that this often arises from the absence of "the full assurance of faith" in those who have "assurance of salvation". For these two things, though connected, are not the same. "Assurance of salvation" is simply faith that we are saved. It is the settled conviction of the truth of the testimony of God that He "has given unto us", who believe, "eternal life". A ruined soul betakes himself to Christ, and believes that he "shall never perish"; that he is forever safe in Him. Thus, "assurance of salvation" is just another name for "faith in Jesus".

Now, while "full assurance of faith" cannot exist without "assurance of salvation", it may be found that the latter exists without the former. At any rate the former is far more than the latter. We wish to avoid nice distinctions, but we may observe that "assurance of salvation", is faith, and that "full assurance" is faith's complement. The man who has "assurance of salvation" accepts a testimony to blessings in Christ, and rests on Him for these, it may be, without knowing much more about what these are, beyond the mere fact that he is safe; but the man who has "full assurance of faith", takes up the blessings in Christ and lays them on his heart, and knows their power. The one believes in the unsearchable riches of grace, the other enters the Treasure-House and appropriates all he finds suited to his need. The one is content to know that salvation is secured in Christ; the other revels in Christ's fullness, his soul is ravished by His person, and satiated by His sacrifice. The one has eternal life; the other has, at least in larger measure, the end of eternal life; namely, fellowship with the Father, and with His Son Jesus Christ.

Now, our object in this paper is to suggest the way by which the believer in Christ may *enjoy* "full assurance of faith", and have it *maintained* in his soul, an actual living happiness; a stream of joy, causing fruit to spring forth in which "the Father is glorified". And before we go on we would distinctly state what we have already implied, that we write for those who know the doctrine, and have approved it because it is according to the Word, but who do not possess it in heart, or who do not habitually live in it; and O how vain is the knowledge of it in the head without its peace in the heart!

In the first place, then, let our thoughts rest on the word *"faith"*—"full assurance of *faith."* We fear that, in adjusting the doctrine, this, its essence, is practically lost sight of, for it is, in the argument, regarded as mere *assent* to the truth propounded. Now, faith is not a mere assent to the truth, nor is it the mere persuasion of truth. Faith not only believes what is spoken, but it takes Christ to be what He is said to be; it takes God at His Word—it confides—it trusts; and so we may safely say it is found only in those who are convinced of the adaptation of the word and the suitableness of Christ to their condition; for only to convicted souls is it at first "given to believe on His name", and only as there is fresh conviction of need does any soul receive *confidingly* fresh revelations of grace. Indeed, while in one aspect of it faith is *"confidence"*, in another aspect faith is *"conviction."* This we judge is the true sense of the only formal definition of faith given by the Holy Spirit. "Now, faith is the *confidence* of things hoped for, the *conviction* of things not seen" *(Heb. 11:1)*. Faith is the confidence which rests in the truth revealed, it is the conviction of truth testified, whether the testimony be to the soul's emptiness, nakedness, or to the grace which saves, clothes and fills. This latter is the conviction of truth, which exactly fits the conviction of need: cf. John 16:8-11.

Now, "assurance" is not what the memory or the head carries, it is what our *faith* carries; it is according to the measure of our confidence in "the unseen things", which are "freely given to us of God", and our conviction of their reality. And *"full* assurance of faith", is full freighted faith", or rather "faith's full freight".

No better proof or illustration of this can be found than that which is contained in the connection in which the expression "full assurance of faith" occurs. When Paul said, "Let us draw near with a true heart in full assurance of faith", he had been lading the faith of the saints whom he addressed with a perfect sacrifice, precious blood, an all-sufficient High Priest, and the testimony of the Holy Spirit, that these availed to the remission of their sins, their entrance into the holiest of all, and their worship there: Hebrews 10:10-20. These things realized in confidence, these things grasped by faith, constitute the "full assurance of faith". Saints with faith thus laden are like their ancient types, the sons of Aaron, who having been washed and clothed, and sprinkled with the blood of the ram of consecration, and with the anointing oil,—sweet symbol of the testimony of the Holy Spirit—held forth their hands, upon which were laid the excellent sacrifices, and with hands thus freighted found themselves emboldened to enter into the holy place, and to take their stand in the presence of the Holy One who dwelt therein *(Lev. 8)*. It is because their faith carries a sacrifice which leaves "no more conscience of sin", it is because their faith carries "the witness of the Holy Spirit", that there is in heaven itself "no more remembrance of sins and iniquities", it is because faith carries the priestly power of Christ into God's presence, that the apostle demands that saints should "enter with boldness into the Holiest of all", and "draw near with a true heart".

"Full assurance of faith," we repeat then, is faith's full load. Now faith can always carry—not all we read—but all that God the Holy Spirit reveals to us; for the Holy Spirit ever enlarges faith as He gives it more to carry. But, as to the fact of Christian experience, too often slowness of heart to receive *all* that God has spoken, and self-closed eyes and ears prevent His larger revealing. We stop short with a very little of the things addressed to faith; or, instead of receiving them in "confidence", we adjust them in argument, and admire the beauty and harmony of the doctrine, as men may admire a perfect cluster of fine grapes of which, for lack of appetite, they do not eat. In all this there is, of course, no assurance of faith.

It follows from all that has been said that assurance will ever be proportioned to our *abiding in Christ,* and to the measure in which *His Word abides in us.* We put these two things together by His own express warrant: "If ye abide in Me, and My words abide in you, ye shall ask what ye will and it shall be done unto you" *(John 15:7).* So again, the apostle John couples these two things: "Let that therefore abide in you which ye have heard from the beginning. If that which ye have heard from the beginning shall abide in you, ye also shall abide in the Son, and in the Father. And this is the promise which He hath promised us—even eternal life" *(I John 2:24, 25).* From the last quoted passage we may see that the retention of the words of Jesus involves the assurance of "the promise", the assurance of eternal life; while by means of the word abiding in us, we abide in the Father and the Son"; and this abiding in Christ is of the very nature of full assurance of faith. Thus, assurance can only be possessed and maintained by the word of God laid on the heart, that is, the word received with *"confidence",* and the word of God is only received thus according to the *conviction* of need.

Dear reader, do not, we pray you, dismiss this paper as merely expository of certain terms. Do you hold the assurance of salvation merely as the just conclusion of a cogent argument? Or is it in you "the conviction of things not seen"? the conviction of absolute perfection in Christ, meeting the conviction of your needy condition? If any man holds assurance *merely* as a satisfactorily proved doctrine it will do him no good; and it will be well if he does not fall into the mischievous absurdity which we have heard thus uttered: "Believe that you are saved, and you are saved." This is "faith *in* assurance", not "assurance *of* faith". The word which we are to hold fast is—"Believe in the Lord Jesus Christ and thou shalt be saved". Assurance rests on its object. We are not called to faith in faith; but to faith in Christ.

We do not ask then of any, What is your opinion as to assurance? But we ask, "What think ye of Christ?" What do you believe, on God's Word? To what extent are you convinced of the adaptation of its revelations *to your need,* and to what extent do you *confide* in these? And then another question arises: To what extent are you acquainted with the things offered to faith in the Word? Mere knowledge will not bring assurance to the soul; but then you must know what God has revealed, in order that you may confide. Assurance must ever be simply as much and no more than that which is known and believed; and "full assurance of faith", is faith full-charged with the things unseen.—*Charles Campbell, 1871.*

"THAT WORTHY NAME"

"Yours in the name of *Jesus.*" How many who owe **their all, both for time** and eternity, to the peerless One, refer thus to Him who was *"God* manifest in the flesh" *(1 Tim. 3:6)!* It is "Jesus" this, and "Jesus" that. But is it becoming for worms of the dust, for sinners, even for sinners saved by grace, to *thus* speak of *Him?* Jesus is the Lord of Glory, and surely it is due the dignity and majesty of His person that this be recognized and owned, even in our references to Him in common speech. Those who despise and reject the Saviour, speak of Him as "The Carpenter," "The Nazarene," as "Jesus." But should those who have been given an "understanding, that we may know Him that is true" *(1 John 5:20),* ignore His Lordship? In a word, can we who have been redeemed by His precious blood do less than confess Him as the *"Lord Jesus Christ"?*

In John 13:13 we find Him saying, "Ye call Me *Master and Lord:* and ye say well; for so I am." Surely this is enough for the *believer.* If our blessed Redeemer declares we *"say well"* when we call Him "Master and Lord" can we afford to speak of Him in terms on which His approval is *not* stamped? Never once do we find any of the apostles addressing Him as "Jesus" while He was with them on earth. When He exhorted them to make request for an increase of laborers, He bade them "Pray ye therefore *the Lord* of the harvest, that He will send forth laborers into His harvest" *(Matt. 9:38).* When He sent forth the disciples to secure the ass on which He was to ride into Jerusalem, He ordered them to say, *"The Lord* hath need of him" *(Luke 19:31).* And again, when He required the use of the upper room, it was, *"The Master* saith, My time is at hand; I will keep the passover at thy house with My disciples" *(Matt. 26:18).*

It may be objected to what we have contended for above that the Gospel narratives commonly refer to our Lord simply as "Jesus." It was "Jesus" who was led of the Spirit into the wilderness to be tempted of the Devil. It was "Jesus" who was moved with compassion as He beheld the sufferings and sorrows of humanity. It was "Jesus" who cleansed the leper, healed the sick, and raised the dead. This is true, and the explanation is not far to seek. It was *the Holy Spirit of God* who, thro' the pens of the evangelists, *thus* refers to Him, *and this makes all the difference.* Let us illustrate. What would be thought of one of the subjects of King George the fifth, referring to the reigning monarch of Great Britain and saying, "I saw *George* pass thro' the city this morning"? If then it would be entirely incongruous for one of his subjects to speak thus of the King of England, how much more is it to refer to *the King of kings* simply as "Jesus"? But now, King George's *wife* could refer to and speak of *her husband* as "George" with perfect propriety. Thus it is that *the Holy Spirit* in the Gospel narratives refers to our Lord by His personal name.

Once more "Jesus" was the Name of our Lord *in humiliation.* Said the angel to Joseph, "Thou shalt call His name Jesus: for He shall save His people from their sins" *(Matt. 1:21),* and in order to save His people from their sins He had to die the death of the Cross. But it is to be noted that when Peter addressed the Jews on the day of Pentecost, he said, "Therefore let all the house of Israel know assuredly, that God hath made that same Jesus, whom ye have crucified, *both Lord and Christ" (Acts 2:36).* Hence it is that the Saviour is referred to as Christ, Christ Jesus, Jesus Christ, or Lord Jesus Christ, and never simply as "Jesus" except when reference is made (either direct, by way of implication, or in contrast) to His humiliation and suffering.

Our modern hymns are largely responsible for the dishonor that is now so generally cast upon "That Worthy Name." And we cannot but raise our voice in loud protest against much of the trash (for that is the correct term) that today masquerades under the name of hymns and religious songs. It is sad and shocking to find professing Christians singing, "A little talk with Jesus makes it right." Fancy saying, "A little talk with *God* makes it right"! and yet Jesus was and is *"God blessed for ever" (Rom. 9:5)*. Such unseemly *familiarity* as "a little talk" with "The mighty God" is horrible.

"There's not a friend like *the lowly Jesus*" is utterly erroneous, and nigh akin to blasphemy. There is no "lowly" Jesus to-day, except the one created by the imagination and sentimentality of the moderns. Instead of being "lowly," the Lord Jesus Christ is seated "on the right hand of the Majesty on high" *(Heb. 1:3)*, from whence He will shortly descend in flaming fire to take vengeance on them that know not God and obey not His gospel *(II Thess. 1:7, 8)*.

Above we have said that the apostles never once addressed our Lord simply as "Jesus." Mark, now, *how they did* refer to the Blessed One. "And Peter answered Him, and said, *Lord*, if it be Thou, bid me come unto Thee on the water" *(Matt. 14:28)*. "Then came Peter to Him, and said, *Lord*, how oft shall my brother sin against me, and I forgive him?" *(Matt. 18:21)*. "And they were exceeding sorrowful, and began every one of them to say unto Him, *Lord*, is it I?" *(Matt. 26:22)*. "And when His disciples James and John saw this, they said, *Lord*, wilt Thou that we command fire to come down from heaven, and consume them?" *(Luke 9:54)*. "And they rose up the same hour, and returned to Jerusalem, and found the eleven gathered together, and them that were with them, saying, *the Lord* is risen indeed" *(Luke 24:33, 34)*. "Thomas saith unto Him, *Lord*, we know not whither Thou goest" *(John 14:5)*. "Therefore that disciple whom Jesus loved saith unto Peter, It is *the Lord*" *(John 21:7)*.

In marked contrast with the manner in which the apostles referred to and spoke of their Lord, note how others particularly His *enemies*, referred to Him. "And *the multitude* said, This is *Jesus* the prophet of Nazareth of Galilee" *(Matt. 21:11)*. "And hearing *the multitude* pass by, he asked what it meant. And *they* told him, that *Jesus* of Nazareth passeth by" *(Luke 18:36, 37)*. "And there was in their synagogue a man with *an unclean spirit;* and he cried out, saying, Let us alone; what have we to do with Thee, Thou *Jesus of Nazareth?*" *(Mark 1:23, 24)*. "And when he was gone out into the porch, another *maid* saw him and said unto them that were there, This fellow was also with *Jesus of Nazareth*" *(Matt. 26:71)*.

Christian reader, Will you refer to and speak of the Son of God as did His *enemies* and the *demons*, namely, as "Jesus," or will you call Him "Master and Lord" as did His apostles, concerning whom He said "ye say well?" Let us ask God to deliver us from this flippant, careless, irreverent manner of confessing His Son. Let us own our Saviour as "Lord" during the time of His rejection by the world. Let us remember His own words, "For the Father judgeth no man, but hath committed all judgment unto the Son: That all should honor the Son, *even as they honor the Father*" *(John 5:22, 23)*. Let us remember it is written, "For by *thy words* thou shalt be justified, and by *thy words* thou shalt be condemned" *(Matt. 12:37)*.— Arthur W. Pink.

EVIL, AND HOW TO MEET IT

There is, probably, no more necessary and salutary lesson for the saints of God today than how to meet evil. It is assuredly a time of evil, and we pass through a scene of evil. "Evil men and seducers", said the apostle, "shall wax worse and worse, deceiving, and being deceived". This state of things has ripened into full development. But it has a blessing in its train for those who are in the secret of the Lord. In Matt. 5 the Lord's words are full of abounding consolation: "Blessed are ye, when men shall revile you, and persecute you, and shall say all manner of evil against you falsely, for My sake. Rejoice, and be exceeding glad: for great is your reward in heaven: for so persecuted they the prophets which were before you". Now, the question arises, what are properly our relation and attitude towards evil?

The first answer is *endurance*. As the aged apostle instructed Timothy, his son in the faith, "Thou therefore endure hardness, as a good soldier of Jesus Christ" *(2 Tim. 2:3);* and again, "But watch thou in all things, endure affliction" *(2 Tim. 4:5)*. What a needed word does the Spirit of God give us, beloved, in **Heb. 12:3**: "Consider Him that *endured* such contradiction of sinners against Himself, lest ye be wearied and faint in your minds". His words and His example are in perfect harmony, and pregnant with richest blessing to those who have an ear for His voice, and eyes to behold the Divine beauty and moral glory of His ways.

The second answer is found in the Lord's words in Matt. 5:39: "But I say unto you, That ye *resist not* evil: but whosoever shall smite thee on the right cheek, turn to him the other also". Herein, beloved, is another wholesome and needful lesson. We are to make no resistance. "If, when ye do well, and suffer for it, ye take it patiently, this is acceptable with God" *(1 Pet. 2:20)*. Three things here coalesce: good done, suffering borne, patience manifested; *"This is acceptable with God".*

The third answer is seen in Paul's word to the Romans, 12:9: *"Abhor* that which is evil; cleave to that which is good". With this we may connect the Lord's commendation to the church at Ephesus: "Thou canst not bear them which are evil" *(Rev. 2:2)*. We ought to have a perfectly clear discernment and abhorrence of evil. Every form of evil is repugnant to the nature of God, and should be intolerable to us. "Beloved, follow not that which is evil, but that which is good. He that doeth good is of God: but he that doeth evil hath not seen God" *(3 John 11).*

The fourth is recorded in I Thess. 5:22: *"Abstain from all appearance* of evil". A lesson most important for us to learn: the outward aspect of evil, its mere semblance, is morally defiling. We must "eschew evil"—that is, shun it, flee from it, and everything that carries the character of it in any degree in its aspect. It is not enough to do no evil, and to mean no evil; we must give no countenance to it, or that which suggests it even in appearance only. It is, it must be, obnoxious to Him who is the Holy and the True.

Lastly, in Rom. 12:21: "Be not overcome by evil, but *overcome* evil with good". The evil and the good are side by side in this world. The evil has to be endured; it is not to be resisted, but to be hated, abhorred, eschewed, every appearance of it abstained from. We are to make no compromises with it, give no countenance to it, yield to it in no respect and in no degree. What then? Scripture supplies the Divine answer. *Overcome it.* Overtop the evil with good. Rise above it, and keep above it in the power and practice of that which is good. Beloved, "Follow not that which is evil, but that which is good" *(3 John 11).*

The Lord give His saints to be both endurers and overcomers in relation to the prevailing evil of this evil day.—*Extracts from Words in Season, June 1889.*

SPIRITUAL PREPAREDNESS

"O, that they were wise, that they would consider their latter end" *(Deut. 32:29).*

It is not so much to be stood upon who is happy now, but who shall be happy at last. If men would frequently consider this, it would much rectify all the mistakes in the world. If we would inure our minds not to look to things as they seem at present, or relish to the flesh, or appear now to such short-sighted creatures as we are, but as they will be judged of at Christ's appearing: how soon would this vain show be over, and the face of things changed, and what is rich, and pleasant, and honorable now, appear base and contemptible at the latter end! Then shall we see that there is an excellency in oppressed Godliness, that exalted wickedness and folly is but shame and ruin. Do but translate the scene from the world's judgment to Christ's tribunal, and you will soon alter your opinions concerning wisdom and folly, misery and happiness, liberty and bondage, shame and glory; the mistaking of which notions pervert all mankind, and there is no rectifying the mistake but by a carrying of our mind seriously to the last review of all things: for then we shall judge things not by what they seem now, but by what they will be hereafter. Solomon tells us, "Hear counsel and receive instruction that thou mayest be wise in thy latter end" *(Prov. 19:20).* That is true wisdom, to be found wise at last. The time will come when we shall wish and say in vain, Oh, that we had laid up treasure in heaven, that we had labored for the meat that perisheth not, that we had esteemed despised holiness, that we had set less by all the vanities of the world, that we had imitated the strictest and most mortified believer, for only those are esteemed and have honor in that day.
—*Thos. Manton, 1660.*

VOL. I OCTOBER, 1922 NO. 10

STUDIES in the SCRIPTURES

"Search the Scriptures" John 5:39.

A PERIODICAL (MONTHLY "IF THE LORD WILL")
DEVOTED TO BIBLE STUDIES and EXPOSITIONS

Associate Editors and Publishers, I. C. Herendeen and Arthur W. Pink,
Swengel, Pa.

Price: 10 cents per copy; $1.00 per year. Foreign $1.00 per year.

TO OUR SCRIPTURE STUDY FAMILY—

It is our desire to send out this magazine free of charge to at least one hundred missionaries. Our hearts go out to these servants of God, who are laboring for Him "in the regions beyond"; many of whom rarely have an opportunity to listen to any oral ministry of the Word. We would like to share with them some of the good things which our Father is so graciously giving to us. We already have a number on our free list, but feel impressed that the Lord would have us add to them. We are praying for guidance that we may be brought into touch with those who really appreciate expositions of Scripture.

The purpose of this editorial is to take our readers into our confidence that they may have fellowship in this work. Let it be clearly understood that this is in nowise an appeal for money—such appeals we shall make only at the Throne of Grace—and we hope none will send any unless they are definitely prompted of God to do so. But first, we shall be thankful if any members of our Scripture-study-family are led to join us in prayer that the Lord will bring us into touch with those of His servants who would be helped by this magazine. Second, we shall appreciate it if our readers will send us the names and addresses of missionaries *known to them personally* whom they have good reason to believe would read and enjoy *Studies in the Scriptures*. There are many preachers in this country who are too busy or too something else to take the time to give a careful reading to such a publication as this, and we fear there may be such abroad. On the other hand, we are satisfied there must be many who would be glad to receive our little paper did they but know of its existence, and especially if it was sent to them free of charge. *These* are the ones we are praying to locate, and we shall value any help from our readers to this end. Finally, let us pray daily for those who are toiling in the dark and difficult places of the earth that God will strengthen their hands, cheer their hearts, and fire their souls with a holy zeal to proclaim the unsearchable riches of Christ.

Yours with love to all the saints,
Arthur W. Pink
I. C. Herendeen

STUDIES IN THE SCRIPTURES

Subscription Price: $1.00 per year to any address in the world. Single copies 10 cents.

Change of Address: Please notify us promptly of any change of address, and be certain to give both old and new addresses.

Non-Subscribers receiving this Magazine regularly will understand their subscription has been entered by a friend.

Copies lost in the mail duplicated on request.

All new subscriptions will be dated back to January, 1922.

Entered as second-class matter December 15th, 1921 at the post office at Swengel, Pa., under Act of March 3rd, 1879.

CONTENTS

The Career of the Antichrist 206
Christ Manifested to the Soul 212
John's Gospel (John 3:21-36). 217
The Way, the Truth, and the Life 224

6. THE CAREER OF THE ANTICHRIST.

We now come to the most interesting and yet the most difficult part of our subject. When will the Antichrist be manifested? where will he appear? what will he do? are questions which readily occur to all who have given any thought to the matter. It is not our purpose to seek to satisfy the idly curious, still less is it to gratify those who love the sensational. We are well aware that our present theme is one that appeals strongly to the curiously inclined, and were it not for the importance of our inquiry we would leave it alone. But without due regard to the person and place of the coming Superman, it is impossible to understand the eschatology of either the Old or New Testaments.

The chief difficulty is to arrange in chronological sequence the many passages which treat of the Antichrist. It is by no means easy to discover the precise order in which the prophecies which deal with the Man of Sin will receive their fulfillment. There is great need for much prayerful study along this line. We can only write according to the light we now have, and our readers must examine for themselves what we say in the light of the Scriptures. It ill becomes any one to be dogmatic where the Word itself does not plainly state the exact time when certain prophecies are to be fulfilled.

In this article we are placed somewhat at a disadvantage, because we shall be obliged to give brief expositions of many scriptures where it will be impossible for us to pause and furnish proofs or reasons for each interpretation. For example, it is our firm conviction that the Assyrian of Isa. 10, the King of Babylon of Isa. 14, the Little Horn of Dan. 7, the Little Horn of Dan. 8, and the first Beast of Rev. 13, each and all view the Antichrist himself in different relationships. There are some Bible students who may take issue with us on these points, and complain because that in this article we make assertions without endeavoring to prove them. We regret this, but would ask all to bear with us patiently. In the later articles of this series we purpose devoting separate studies to the Antichrist in the Psalms, in the Prophets, in the Gospels and Epistles, and in the Apocalypse; when we shall endeavor to examine each passage separately and attempt to give scriptural proofs for every interpretation adopted.

While it is admittedly difficult, and perhaps impossible, to fit each prophecy concerning the Antichrist into its proper chronological place, *we are* able to determine the relative position of most of them. The career of the Antichrist is divided into two distinct parts, and there is a clearly defined dividing line between them. In previous articles we have pointed out how that the name "Antichrist" has a double meaning, signifying one who imitates Christ, and one who is opposed to Christ. This double meaning to His name corresponds exactly with the two chief parts in his career. In the first, he poses as the true Christ, claiming to be indeed the Messiah of Israel. This claim will be backed up with the most imposing credentials, and all excepting God's elect will be deceived. He will sit in the Temple (a rebuilt temple in Jerusalem) showing himself forth to be God, and Divine honors will be paid him. But at a later stage he will throw off his mask, and appear in his true character as the opponent of Christ and the defier of God,

Then, instead of befriending the Jews, he will turn against them and seek to exterminate them from the earth. Thus, with many of the scriptures which describe the person and career of the Antichrist it is a comparatively easy matter to decide whether they belong to the first or to the second stage of his history. But beyond this it is difficult, with some scriptures at least, to go.

We shall now consider, first the *time* of Antichrist's appearing. It is hardly necessary for us to enter into a lengthy argument to show that the Antichrist (as such) has not already appeared. Many antichrists have already come and gone, and some are in the world even now; the same is equally true of the many false prophets foretold in Scripture; but all of these are but the forecasts and foreshadowings of *the* Antichrist and *the* False Prophet, who are yet to be revealed, and who will receive their final overthrow by the Lord Jesus at His return to the earth. Before *the* Antichrist can appear the Holy Spirit must be "taken out of the way" *(2 Thess. 2:7)*; the old Roman Empire must be revived and assume its final form—divided under "ten kings"—*before* the "Little horn" comes into prominence *(Dan. 7:24*—he rises *"after* them")*: Israel must be restored to their land and the Temple be rebuilt, etc., etc.

At the present time the ultimate development of "the Mystery of Iniquity" is being hindered. God's people are the salt of the earth, and their presence here stays the corruption of the "carcase" *(Matt. 24: 28*—The "Carcase" is the antithesis of the "Body" of Christ). The saints are the light of the world, and while they remain in it it is impossible for darkness to *cover* the earth and gross darkness the people *(Isa. 60:2)*. The Spirit of God is here indwelling believers, and His holy presence checks the final outworking of Satan's plans. But when all believers of this dispensation have been "caught up to meet the Lord in the air" *(1 Thess. 4:16)*, and the Holy Spirit has departed from the earth, all restraint will be removed, and Satan will be allowed to bring forth his false christ, who will be "revealed in his time" *(2 Thess. 2:6)*, and it would seem that even now signs are not wanting to show that God has already given permission to Satan to prepare the stage of action for the ghastly consummation of his evil efforts. There can be no doubt but that the Devil has desired to reveal the Son of Perdition long before this, so that by means of him he may reduce the whole world to submission. But the restraining hand of God, now so soon to be removed, has held him back.

The time, then, when the Antichrist will be revealed is after this present Dispensation of Grace has run its course; after the Mystical Body of Christ has been completed; after the whole company of God's people have been caught up to meet the Lord in the air; after the Holy Spirit has departed from the world. How soon after we cannot say for certain. The majority of prophetic students seem to think that the last great Caesar will come into prominence almost immediately after the rapture of the saints. Personally, we believe there will be an interval, long or short, between the two. As there was a period of thirty years after the birth of the Lord Jesus—a period of silence—before His public ministry commenced, so there may be a similar interval between the Rapture and the Revelation of Antichrist.

The Antichrist will enter the arena of public affairs sometime *before* the beginning of Daniel's seventieth week, for at the beginning of it he makes a seven-years' covenant with the Jews, then in their land. But at that point he will be the Dictator of the world's policies, and as he begins in comparative obscurity (at least from a governmental standpoint), some time—probably years—must be allowed for his gradual rise to political supremacy. His meteoric course will not be terminated until the Lord Himself descends to earth to usher in the Millennium. Just as the reign of Saul preceded that of David, so shall that of Antichrist antedate that of the true Christ.

We turn now to consider the *place* of Antichrist's appearing. So far as the writer is aware there are only two scriptures which give direct information upon this point, and they are each found in the prophecy of Daniel. We refer to the passages which speak of "the Little Horn". In Dan. 7:7, 8 we read, "After this I saw in the night visions, and, behold, a fourth beast, dreadful and terrible, and strong exceedingly; and it had great iron teeth: it devoured and break in pieces, and stamped the residue with the feet of it: and it was diverse from all the beasts that were before it; and it had ten horns. I considered the horns, and, behold, there came up among them another little horn". This "fourth Beast" is the last world-empire, prior to the setting up of the Messianic kingdom. This empire will, at first, be ruled over by ten kings—the "ten horns" of v. 7 are defined as "ten kings" in v. 24. After them arises another, the "Little Horn," which signifies another "king", see v. 24. He is termed "little" because at that stage his kingdom is but small with that of the others, and the power he then wields is insignificant when contrasted from the ten kings. But not for long will he remain weak and insignificant. Soon the ten kings will themselves own allegiance to this eleventh—see Rev. 17:12, 13. We reserve for a later article the proofs that this "Little Horn" *is* the Antichrist, asking our readers to study carefully the description furnished of him in Dan. 7:8, 20-27; 8:9-12, 23-25.

Taking it for granted (at the moment) that the Little Horn of Dan. 7 is the Antichrist let us see how what is there said of him helps us to determine the quarter from which he will arise. In Dan. 7:7 the "fourth Beast" is described, and in 7:23 we are told, "the fourth beast shall be the fourth *kingdom* upon earth, which shall be diverse from all kingdoms, and shall devour the whole earth, and shall tread it down, and break it in pieces". This Kingdom will be divided into ten parts, over which will be the ten kings *(7:24)*. This kingdom will be, we believe, the old Roman Empire revived in its final form, and divided into two great halves—the Eastern and the Western. This fourth kingdom will include within itself all the territory and will perpetuate all the dominant characteristics of the other three which have preceded it, i. e., the Babylonian, the Medo-Persian, and Grecian. Turning now to Dan. 7:8 we are told, "I considered the horns, and, behold, there came up *among them* another little horn". The Antichrist, then, will have his rise within the limits of the old Roman Empire. This narrows considerably our circle of inquiry. The next question is, Can we determine from which part of the empire he will arise—the Eastern or the Western? Dan. 8 furnishes light upon this point.

In Dan. 8:8, 9 we read, "Therefore the he-goat waxed very great: and when he was strong, the great horn was broken; and for it came up four notable ones toward the four winds of heaven. And out of one of them came forth a little horn, which waxed exceeding great, toward the south, and toward the east, and toward the pleasant land." Now v. 21 of this same chapter tells us, "The rough goat is the king (kingdom) of Grecia", and v. 22 informs us "and the great horn that is between his eyes is the first king. Now that being broken, whereas four stood up for it, four kingdoms (or kings) shall stand up out of the nation." This, of course, refers to the act of Alexander the Great who divided his kingdom into four parts—Greece, Egypt, Syria, and the rest of the domains of Turkey; under his four great generals: Ptolemy, Cassander, Lysimachus, and Seleucus. This, again, very appreciably narrows our circle of inquiry. Dan. 7 tells us the Little Horn is to arise in a part of the territory covered by the old Roman Empire, which Empire gradually included within its domains that of the preceding empires. Now here in Dan. 8 we learn that the Little Horn will spring from that part of the revived Roman Empire which was included in the Grecian Empire. But this is not all that Dan. 8 tells us. The Grecian Empire is here viewed as disintegrated into four parts or kingdoms, from which of *these* parts, then, may we expect him to issue—Macedonia, Egypt, Syria, or Thrace? This question, we believe, receives answer in Dan. 8:9 where we are told, that the Little Horn "waxed exceeding great toward the south, and toward the east, and toward the pleasant land". Practically all students are agreed that "the south" here refers to Egypt, the "east" to Persia and Greece, and "the pleasant land" to Palestine, hence it would seem that the country from which Antichrist will first be manifested is *Syria*. It will be noted that nothing is said in Dan. 8:9 about the Little Horn "waxing great" toward *the north*, and we believe the reason for this is because *that* is the quarter from whence he shall arise. This is confirmed by the fact that "the king of Assyria" in Isa. 10:12 is clearly none other than the Antichrist. We may say this was the current view of Christian writers on prophecy through the first ten centuries A. D. The late Mr. W. B. Newton in his splendid "Aids to the Study of Prophetic Inquiry" has succinctly summarized the various arguments of the ancients in the following language:—

"In the first place, as Nimrod—the founder of Babel, that is, the Tower of Babylon—a savage tyrant and cruel oppressor of men, was the first person who declared open war against God; so it is meet that there should arise from the self-same Babylon, the last and most atrocious persecutor of the saints—the Antichrist. Moreover, seeing that Nebuchadnezzar and Antiochus Epiphanes—two monsters who bore down upon the people of God with an overwhelming power of destruction, and who were the antichrists of the Old Testament and remarkable types of the Antichrist which is to come; seeing, I say, that these monarchs reigned in Babylon, it is fitting that the true Antichrist of the New Testament should arise from the same Babylon.

"Besides, no place can be pointed out more meet for the nativity of Antichrist than Babylon, for it is the City of the Devil—always diametrically opposed to Jerusalem, which is deemed the City of God; the former city, that is, Babylon, being the mother and disseminator of every kind of confusion, idolatry, impiety—a vast sink of every foul pollution, crime, and iniquity—the first city in the world which cut itself off from the worship of the true God—which reared the city of universal vice,—which perpetually (according to the record of Holy Writ) carries on the mystery of iniquity, and bears imprinted on her brow the inscription of blasphemy against the name of God. The consummation, therefore, of impiety, which is to have its recapitulation in Antichrist, could not break forth from a more fitting place than Babylon".

Having dwelt at some length on the *time* and the *place* of the Antichrist's appearing, we shall attempt to give now a brief outline of the leading events in his *career*. We have seen that the scriptures which help us to determine the direction from which he will arise, speak of him under the title of the "Little Horn". Now the first thing this title denotes is that he is a *king*, king of Assyria. Some, no doubt, will wonder how a Jew will succeed in obtaining the throne of Syria. Several answers might be suggested, such, for example, as heading a successful rebellion—the spectacle of an obscure plebian speedily rising to the rank of national Dictator, has been forcibly exhibited before our own eyes in Russia. But on this point we are not left to speculation. Dan. 11:21 tells us that the "Vile Person" will "come in peaceably, and obtain the kingdom by flatteries". With this agrees Rev. 6:2, where the Antichrist is seen riding a white war-horse, and with bow in hand, but with no arrow fitted to it. The symbol suggests bloodless victories.

As soon as this Jew acquires the crown of Syria he will speedily enlarge his dominions. As Rev. 6:2 tells us, he will go forth "conquering, and to conquer", and as we are told further in Hab. 2:5, "He is a proud man, neither keepeth at home, who enlargeth his desire as hell, and is as death, and cannot be satisfied, but gathereth unto him all nations, and heapeth unto him all people". The first thing which is predicated of him (as "the Little Horn") is that "he shall subdue three kings" *(Dan. 7:24)*. As to what "kings" these may be, appears to be intimated in Dan. 8:9 where we are told, "And out of one of them came forth a little horn, which waxed exceeding great toward the south, and toward the east, and toward the pleasant land". He "waxes great" first toward the south, that is, most probably, by a victorious expedition into Egypt. Next, he is seen moving "toward the east", reducing, to what extent we are not told, the dominions of Persia and Greece; finally he turns his face "toward the pleasant land", which is Palestine. Without being dogmatic, we would suggest that the three kings he subdues are those of Egypt, Persia, and Greece.

Having subdued the three kings by his military prowess a "league" is made with him *(see Dan. 11:23)*. Probably it is the remaining seven kings of the revived Roman Empire, plus the three vassals of the Antichrist who take the place of the kings he had deposed, that enter into this League with the Little Horn, or king of Assyria; but he "shall work deceitfully, and shall become strong with a small people" *(Dan. 11:23)*. So strong does he become that in a short time he rises to political supremacy, and the whole of the ten kings shall "give their kingdom unto the Beast" *(Rev. 17:17)*, and he will then be recognized as the imperial Emperor. Thus as King of kings he will dictate the policies of Europe and Asia.

"The Little Horn will revive in himself all the personified glory of Babylon, Medo-Persia, Greece and Rome. And let not this be regarded as an event incredible. We are to remember that Antichrist will be Satan's masterpiece; furnished with every auxiliary of influence and wealth, for wresting the sceptre from the hands of Him who won it by His humiliation on the Cross. Thus it is said he will 'resist the

God of gods'. The accumulated and restored honors of each royal successor are thus to crown the brow of this last and greatest of Gentile monarchs. And so shall he stand in his unrivalled magnificence till the Stone shall smite him and his power, and grind all to powder" *(Mrs. G. Needham).*

After the Antichrist has acquired the political sovereignty of the prophetic earth he will then enter upon his religious role, claiming to be the Christ of God and demanding Divine honors. At first sight it appears strange, if not incongruous, that a military despot should be found filling the character of a religious impostor. But history shows that there is a point at which one character readily merges into the other. Political ambition, intoxicated by success, finds it an easy step from self-glorification to self-deification, and the popular infatuation as easily passes from the abject adulation of the tyrant to the adoration of the god. Or again; a religious impostor, encouraged by the ascendancy he has acquired over the minds of men, grasps the sceptre of secular power and becomes the most arbitrary of despots. Rev. 13:4 makes it plain that the military prowess of the Antichrist first induces them to render him Divine homage: "And they worshipped the Dragon which gave power unto the Beast: and they worshipped the Beast, saying, Who is like unto the Beast? who is able to make war with him?" But no ordinary honors will suffice him. His religious ambitions are as insatiable as his political, for he will "oppose and exalt himself above all that is called God, or that is worshipped; so that he as God sitteth in the temple of God, showing himself that he is God" *(2 Thess. 2:4).* This claim to be God Himself, incarnate, will be backed up by imposing credentials, for his coming will be, "after the working of Satan, with all power and signs and lying wonders" *(2 Thess. 2:9).* These miracles will be no mere pretenses, but prodigies of power.

The Jews, previously returned to Palestine, and with temple in Jerusalem rebuilt, will receive this Son of Perdition as their long-promised Messiah" *(John 5:43).* In imitation of the true Christ who will, at His return to the earth, "make a new covenant with the House of Israel and with the House of Judah" *(Heb. 8:8, compare Jer. 31 and Ezek. 36),* the Antichrist will make a covenant with the Jews *(see Dan. 9:27 and 11:22).* Under a seven years' treaty, and in the guise of friendship, he will gain ascendancy in Jerusalem, only later to throw off the mask and break the covenant.

About seven months after the Antichrist, the "Prince" (i. e. of the Roman Empire) of Dan. 9:27 has made the Covenant with the Jews he will begin to "practice" in Jerusalem *(Dan. 8:24).* This we believe is the explanation of the two thousand three hundred days of Dan. 8:14 which has puzzled so many of the commentators. This two thousand three hundred days is the whole period during which the false messiah will practice in Jerusalem and have power over the "sanctuary": two thousand three hundred days is seven years less seven months and ten days.

There, in Jerusalem, he will pose as the Christ of God, the Prince of Peace. The world will suppose that the long looked-for Millennium has arrived. There will be every indication that the eagerly desired Golden Age has, at last, dawned. The great Powers of Europe and Asia will have been united under the ten-kingdomed Empire. It will be expected that the League of Nations will guarantee the peace of the earth. For a season quietness and amity will prevail. None will dare to oppose the mighty Emperor. But not for long will the hideous war-spectre hide himself. Soon will the "white horse" of Rev. 6 be found to change his hue. A "red horse" will go forth, and then "peace shall be taken from the earth" *(Rev. 6).* At the very time the world is congratulating itself that all is well, and the slogan of the hour is "Peace and Safety", *then* "sudden destruction cometh upon them" *(I Thess. 5:3).*

In the midst of the seven years the Antichrist will throw off his mask, break his covenant with Israel, and stand forth as the most daring idolater who has ever trodden this earth. After he has "practiced" in Jerusalem for two years and five months, he will "take away the daily sacrifice" *(Dan. 8:11; 9:27)* from the Temple, and in its place rear an image to himself in the holy place, which is the "abomination of desolation" referred to by Christ *(see Matt. 24:15).*

This brings us to the great dividing line in his career, to which reference was made near the beginning of this article. It is a point not only of interest but of considerable importance to ascertain what it is that causes this startling change of front, from posing as the true Christ to that of the open defier of God. There are several scriptures which throw light on this point. Satan will cause the Man of Sin to crown his daring imitation of the Christ of God by being slain and rising again from the dead.

Both the Old and the New Testaments refer to the death of the Antichrist, and attribute it to the *sword*. In Rev. 13:14 we read that the false Prophet shall say to them that dwell on the earth "that they should make an image to the Beast, which had the wound by the *sword* and did live". In harmony with this we read in Zech. 11: 17, "Woe to the Idol Shepherd that leaveth the flock! The *sword* shall be upon his arm, and upon his right eye". It is to be noted that before we are told here that "the sword shall be" upon him, that he "leaveth the flock" and the previous verse tells us that he was raised up "in *the* Land", which can only mean that he was ruling in Palestine. Hence it is clear that he leaves the Land before he receives his death wound by the sword. In perfect accord with this is what we read in Isa. 37:6, 7 (in a later article we hope to treat at length of the future Babylon, restored; the connection of Antichrist with it, and the typical and prophetical significance of Isa. 37 and 38): "Behold, I will send a blast upon him, and he shall hear a rumour, and return to his own land; and I will cause him to fall *by the sword* in his own land".

Leaving Palestine, the Antichrist will "return to his own land", that is, the land of his nativity—Assyria—which confirms what we have said previously about Assyria being the country where Antichrist will first be manifested. There, in his own land, he will fall by the sword. Most probably he will be slain there by his political enemies, envious of his power and chafing under his haughty autocracy. In death he will be hated and dishonored, and burial will be refused him. It is to this that Isa. 14 (speaking of the King of Babylon, see v. 4) refers: "But thou art cast out of thy grave like an abominable branch, and as the raiment of those that are slain, thrust through *with a sword*, that go down to the stones of the pit. As a carcase trodden under feet, thou shalt not be joined with them in burial, because thou hast destroyed thy land, and slain thy people" *(vv. 19, 20)*. But his enemies will suddenly be filled with consternation and then admiration, for to their amazement this one slain by the sword shall rise from the dead, and his deadly wound will be healed —note how this is implied in Isa. 14, for v. 25 shows him once more in the land of the living, only to meet his final doom at the hands of the Lord Himself. It is to this amazing resurrection of the Antichrist that Rev. 13:3, 4 refer "And I saw one of his heads as it were wounded to death; and his deadly wound was healed: and all the world wondered after the Beast. And they worshipped the Dragon which gave power unto the Beast: and they worshipped the Beast, saying, Who is like unto the Beast? who is able to make war with him?" Details of his resurrection are supplied in Rev. 9, from which we gather that just as Christ was raised from the dead by God the Father, so the Antichrist will be raised from the dead by his father the Devil, see v. 1 where the fallen "Star", which refers to Satan, is given the "key of the bottomless pit", and when this is opened there comes out of it the mysterious "locusts" whose king is the Destroyer *(v. 11)*, the Antichrist.

A further reference to the resurrection of the Antichrist, his coming forth from the Bottomless Pit is found in Rev. 17:8: "The Beast that thou sawest was, and is not; and shall ascend out of the Bottomless Pit, and go into Perdition: and they that dwell on the earth shall wonder, whose names were not written in the book of life from the foundation of the world, when they behold the Beast that was, and is not, and yet is". It is to be noted that the earth-dwellers wonder *when they behold* the Beast that was (alive), and is not (now alive), and yet is (raised again). The world will then be presented with the spectacle of a man raised from the dead. All know him, for this career and amazing progress were eagerly watched; his wonderful achievements and military campaigns were the subjects of daily interest; his transcendent genius elicited their admiration. They had witnessed his death. They stood awe-struck, no doubt, at the downfall of this King of kings. And now he is made alive; his wound of death is healed; and the whole world wonders and worships him.

It is about this time, apparently, that the "False Prophet" *(Rev. 13:11-16)*, the third person in the Trinity of Evil will appear on the scene. From a number of scriptures it is evident that the Antichrist will not spend all his time in Palestine during the last three and a half years of his career. It seems that shortly after the middle of the "Week" the Beast will turn his face again toward Babylon, leaving the False Prophet to act as his vicegerent, compelling all in Jerusalem to worship the image of the Beast under pain of death *(Rev. 13:15)*. It is to be noted that Hab. 2:5 tells us that the Antichrist is "a proud man, *neither keepeth at home,* who enlargeth his desire as hell, and is as death, and cannot be satisfied, but gathereth unto him all nations, and heapeth unto him all people".

The reason for the Antichrist's return to Babylon is not far to seek. Having thrown off his mask of religious pretension, he now stands forth as the Defier of God. His first move now will be to blot out from the earth everything that bears His name. To accomplish this the Jewish race must be utterly exterminated, and to this end he will put forth all his power to banish Israel from the earth. He will make war with the saints (the Jewish saints) and prevail against them *(Dan. 7:21; 8:24)*: this is the going forth of the "red horse" of Rev. 6:4.

Those of the godly remnant who are left will "flee to the mountains" *(Matt. 24:16)*, and there they will be hunted like partridges. It is then they will cry, "Keep not Thou silence, O God: hold not Thy peace, and be not still, O God. For, lo, Thine enemies make a tumult: and they that hate Thee have lifted up the head. They have taken crafty counsel against Thy people, and consulted against Thy hidden ones. They have said, Come, and let us *cut them off from being a nation;* that the name of Israel may be no more in remembrance" *(Psa. 83:1-4).* Then, because many of the Jews will be found in that day dwelling in Babylon *(see Jer. 50:8; 51: 6, 45; Rev. 18:4)* the Antichrist will go thither to wreak his vengeance upon them. But not for long will he be suffered to continue his blasphemous and bloody course. Soon will heaven respond to the cries of the faithful remnant of Israel, and terrible shall be the punishment meted out on their last enemy. This, however, must be left for consideration in our next article, when we shall treat, D. V., of the last days and doom of the Antichrist.—*Arthur W. Pink.*

CHRIST MANIFESTED TO THE SOUL.

"He that hath My commandments, and keepeth them, he it is that loveth Me; and he that loveth Me shall be loved of My Father, and I will love him, and manifest Myself to him. Judas saith unto Him, not Iscariot, Lord, how is it that Thou wilt manifest Thyself unto us, and not unto the world? Jesus answered and said unto him, If a man love Me he will keep My words; and My Father will love him, and We will come unto him, and make our abode with him" *(John 14:21-23).*

There are many Christians at the present day who are longing for that manifestation of Christ which is promised here. They believe in Christ, and look forward to the time when they shall stand in His presence and see Him as He is. Christ is dear to them now; they love His name; they prize His Word; they delight at times in praise and prayer; they build their hopes on Christ and on Christ alone; and yet there are special blessings promised by Christ, to which they have not attained. There is a near communion, an uninterrupted fellowship, and unbroken assurance of Christ's favor, of which they read in the Word of God, and of which they hear some Christians speak, to which they themselves are strangers. They have almost reached the cloudless land; they have thought, at times, that one more upward step would bring them there, and yet another and another frowning cliff still keeps them from the Beulah of their hopes. During a few brief moments of their pilgrimage, Christ has drawn near, but now again the heavens are closed, and no answer comes back to their fervent prayers.

What then, let us ask, is the nature of this Divine manifestation; what are some of its concomitants or consequences; and what is the condition on which it is to be secured? And may the result of our inquiries be a richer, fuller, more glorious manifestation of the Saviour than we have ever yet enjoyed, even the presence of the Saviour in every reader's heart!

It is obvious, at the outset, that it is not a personal manifestation which is promised. In olden times, the Son of God did actually draw near to men. In the Garden of Eden, He walked and talked with Adam. On the plains of Mamre, He appeared to Abraham. At Horeb, He spoke face to face with Moses. Many of the patriarchs could say: "We have both seen the Lord and heard His voice."

So, too, after Christ's ascension into heaven, he appeared to Paul and to John—to Paul as he journeyed to Damascus—to John on the isle of Patmos.

But these were extraordinary manifestations of Jesus, and are not to be expected by all His followers, that is, not to be expected in the present life. The time is coming when we shall see Him—see Him in all His glory, and by the sight be transformed into His likeness. The time is coming when we shall stand in His very presence, and talk with Him, as friend talketh with friend. But as yet the heavens are closed. As yet, we are obliged to say: "Whom having not seen, we love; in whom, though now we see Him not, yet believing, we rejoice with joy unspeakable and full of glory" *(1 Peter 1:8)*.

The manifestation now promised is very different from this. The open vision we could not bear. Moses, we read, "hid his face, for he was afraid to look upon God." Paul, we are told, "could not see for the glory of the light;" and John when the Saviour approached him, "fell at His feet as dead." No, not to the outward eye, but to the inner sense is the revelation made. It is a manifestation to the spirit—an epiphany to the soul, less glorious than that for which we wait, and yet most real and precious.

Nor does the manifestation here promised partake of the nature of a vision. This is another and a very common way in which God of old drew near to men. Every one recalls at once the vision which Jacob saw at Bethel—the delight and wonder of our childhood days.

"As he went toward Haran," we read, "he lighted on a certain place, and tarried there all night; and he took the stones of that place, and put them for his pillows, and lay down to sleep. And he dreamed, and behold a ladder set up on earth, and the top of it reached to heaven: and the angels of God ascended and descended upon it. And, behold, the Lord stood above it, and talked with him" *(Gen. 28: 10-12)*. What a glorious manifestation was this! A shining way begirt on either side by angels, and leading up to the very throne of God.

But still more glorious was the vision of Isaiah, who saw the Lord sitting upon a throne high and lifted up, while His train filled the temple; above, the seraphim crying to one another, and saying, "Holy, holy, holy, is the Lord of hosts; the whole earth is full of His glory." The books of the New Testament, as well as those of the Old, are rich in visions in which Christ appeared, and spoke with men.

And yet it is not in dreams that Christ vouchsafes to come to us. Enthusiasts there are who claim this. Some persons may have visions as real and as authoritative as those seen by Peter and Ananias of old. But the vision is not promised. It is not in the night season only that Christ draws near. It is a continuous presence which He pledges, even an abiding in the believer's heart.

And now we are prepared to state, so far as it can be stated in words, what the promised revelation is. Some of our readers already know. Some of you have thus met Christ in the closet. Some of you are walking with Him, day by day, and hour by hour; and those of you who have not been thus favored, see what the manifestation is in your very consciousness of need. You see that it consists in a vivid realization of the Saviour's being and nearness, in a deep and abiding sense of His favor and His love. This is what is meant by the manifestation of Jesus. By the power of the Spirit, He makes His Word so true and luminous, that as we read it, He Himself seems to draw near. The whole biography of Jesus becomes in this way a present reality. We see His form. We hear His words. We follow Him to the Garden and to the Cross. We stand with Him on Olivet. With the disciples we gaze upon Him as He ascends to heaven. By faith we follow Him within the veil, and see Him still as our ever-living Intercessor, pleading in our behalf the merits of His atoning sacrifice. The world cannot understand this, and yet the Holy Spirit does so illumine the Word as to make its truth living and real. Hence Christ is manifested chiefly through the Word; chiefly when, in obedience to the Word, we walk in the way of His commands.

We say chiefly, and yet perhaps we ought to say only. Sometimes nature seems to be a clearer medium of revelation. Sometimes, when walking amidst the beautiful creations of His hand, we seem most impressed with a sense of Christ's presence and glory. Those wonderful manifestations of which Edwards and Brainerd speak in their diaries, were not made in their closets, nor in the house of God. They were given to them in the great temple of nature—beneath the over-arching woods. And yet even here the Word was the medium of revelation; for it was while meditating not on nature, but on Christ, that Christ drew near.

Yes, it is through the Word that His glory shines. This is the oracle through which He speaks. Nature's voices are conflicting, contradictory, obscure. The inner light we cannot trust. How many thousands has it led astray! To the written Word we must resort, if we would really see our Saviour.

Take, for example, one of the beautiful narratives of Mark's Gospel, one through which perhaps some readers of this volume first became acquainted with the Redeemer's saving power. Jesus was going toward a certain house, and much people followed and thronged Him. And a certain woman, which had been sick twelve years, and had suffered many things of many physicians, and had spent all that she had, and was nothing bettered, but rather grew worse, when she heard of Jesus, came in the press behind and touched His garment; for she said, If I may but touch His clothes I shall be whole. And immediately she felt in her body that she was healed of her plague.

"A long time sick." In this respect first, her case struck you like your own. "And had suffered many things of many physicians, and had spent all that she had." How this part of the narrative came home to you! Your resort to the thousand vanities of the world for peace—your numberless endeavors to obtain rest for your weary soul—your spending all that you had —your utter despair of salvation, till you took up this precious narrative and read these now marvellous and saving words: *"If I may but touch the hem of His garment."* You knelt in your closet. You felt that you could kneel, as did the woman, before thronging multitudes, if they had been around you. You touched in faith the Saviour's clothes. Your burden of guilt and shame was gone. Christ seemed to stand before you, and as you rose from your knees, His words of calm and merciful assurance, "Thy faith hath saved thee, go in peace" thrilled your soul with transporting joy. It was not a history. It was a reality. It is a reality still. Christ now stands in that narrative before us. That touch of faith today is accompanied today with a Divine and saving power.

Thus through all the narratives of the New Testament may we commune with Jesus. Thus in the epistles may we behold His glory. Thus in the Apocalypse may we rise to His very throne, stand with the great multitude upon the crystal sea, and enjoy even on earth the worship and the rapture of heaven.

2. But it is time to turn to the concomitants or consequences of such a manifestation, and among them we mention, in the first place, a new and glorious apprehension of the person of the Redeemer.

The Christian life often begins with a belief in doctrines. The believer's peace often flows at first from an apprehension of truth rather than from an apprehension of the Lord. "Being justified by faith, we have peace with God." How many seem, for years, to go no farther than this; busying themselves about the philosophy of salvation, about the manner in which the righteousness of Christ meets the demands of a broken law—almost forgetting the gracious person through whom this righteousness has been provided!

But it is one thing to believe in a truth about Jesus, while it is quite another thing to believe in Him. It is one thing to find peace in believing an abstraction, but quite another thing by believing in a personal Redeemer and resting the weary heart on His compassionate breast. The one faith leaves the Christian comparatively cold, and loveless, and comfortless. There is a hardness and rigidity to his character, a disagreeable regularity to his life. The other brings warmth and freshness, and beauty and power. By communing with a living Saviour the soul grows into the Saviour's likeness, and reflects the Saviour's sympathy, and grace, and love.

The coldness of philosophy is proverbial, and much that is called theology deserves no better name. There may be truth there, and truth fashioned into a system symetrical and beautiful; but it lacks the warmth and the power of life. In the New Testament, truth is never separated from Jesus. It is not the atonement there, so much as the atoning Saviour; not justification or sanctification, so much as Jesus the Justifier, Jesus imparting the spirit of holiness to those who cleave in faith and love to Him. The great design of the Gospel history is to make known a living Redeemer, and to bring us into His communion and fellowship.

Now, when Christ is manifested in the way here promised, the manifestation is often marked by a conception of the Saviour's person at once new and glorious. From the cold region of dogmas, and from the chilling atmosphere of heartless observances, the soul is lifted to a rapt communion with its Lord and life. Once distant, He now seems near. Once seldom thought of as a direct object of love or worship, the soul now sings of Him alone. And what a new power it gives to doctrines once believed in, though coldly; what new meaning to ordinances once observed, though as ends rather than as means! Now, through both doctrines and ordinances the Saviour reveals Himself, making His presence both a reality and a joy. The promised manifestation brings out in bold relief the personality of Jesus, and makes a living Christ the object of the believer's reverence and trust.

Another consequence of this manifestation is an assurance of Christ's favor. How much would I give for it, perhaps some reader is saying! How earnestly have I sought it in days and months that are past! You hope that Christ loves you, but you do not believe it. Or, you do believe it, but do not know it—know it in the New Testament sense of the term. St. John often uses that word know. "We know that we have passed from death unto life". "Hereby know we that we are in Him". It is a most precious knowledge, a gift which should be coveted by every child of God. And it always comes with the manifestation of which we speak. Not only through the Word does Christ appear, but He speaks—speaks as really to our inward ear as He spoke to John or Mary when on earth. "As the Father hath loved Me, so have I loved you". "Satan hath desired to have you, that he may sift you as wheat: but I have prayed for thee, that thy faith fail not". "Let not your heart be troubled: ye believe in God, believe also in Me. I go to prepare a place for you. And if I go and prepare a place for you, I will come again, and receive you unto Myself; that where I am there ye may be also". "I am the good Shepherd, and know My sheep, and am known of Mine. And I gave unto them eternal life, and they shall never perish, neither shall any pluck them out of My Father's hand". Would you ask anything more than to have these precious words spoken to you by Jesus? And yet you do hear them when Christ draws near; hear them whenever you open your Bible; hear them whenever you kneel in your closet to pray. Yes, they remain with you engraven on your memory and on your heart, and ever-present assurance of your Saviour's faithfulness and love.

Intimately connected with this assurance, and following it as another consequence of the Saviour's manifestation, we mention comfort and support in trials, especially in those trials which, on account of their peculiar nature, are beyond the reach of human sympathy and love—the trials of desertion and loneliness from which Jesus Himself suffered so keenly; heart trials, domestic trials, secret griefs, too sacred to be breathed in the ear of man—all these trials in which nothing can sustain us but that sympathy which Christ's own presence gives.

The work of the Saviour in this respect was beautifully foreshadowed in the history of the Hebrew youths, who, for their faithfulness to God, were cast into the fiery furnace. "Did we not cast three men bound into the midst of the fire?" asked the astonished king. His counsellors answered and said: "True, O king". "But lo", he replied, "I see four men loose, walking in the midst of the fire, and they have no hurt: and the form of the fourth is like the Son of God".

In the lives of God's children how repeatedly has this history been realized! How often to the afflicted has Christ appeared, bringing a consolation and support which earth has no power to give! The experience of St. Paul at Rome stands on the sacred page an ever-enduring illustration. "At my first answer no man stood with me, but all men forsook me; notwithstanding the Lord stood with me, and strengthened me". This is not an imaginary, but a real presence, bringing with it a sustaining power well-nigh Divine.

And in the last great trial, how precious

is the Saviour's presence then! For then, unless Christ be manifested, to what or to whom can we turn? On earthly friends we can no longer lean. From human experience we can no longer gather consolation. Unless we have Christ, we must step down alone into the dark river, and alone enter the region and shadow of death. And yet, it is here that the Saviour manifests most triumphantly His power, staying the sinking soul, and enabling it in all its feebleness to rejoice over the last great enemy. What death could be more painful than Stephen's? Stones were his pillows; enemies and murderers were the watchers around his bed; and yet what death more peaceful! What departure more serene! "And they stoned Stephen, calling upon God and saying, Lord lay not this sin to their charge. And when he had said this he fell asleep". What made the martyr so calm in death? "Being full of the Holy Ghost, he looked up stedfastly into heaven, and saw the glory of God, and Jesus standing at God's right hand". How often has the victory been thus achieved! How often have the words "Jesus", "Saviour", "Redeemer", "Lord", uttered as though the Saviour were full in view, fallen from the lips of the departing! How often has the lifted eye, and the rapt expression, the countenance illumined with the glory already revealed—how often has all this taught us that heaven really opens on the dying, that the precious promise of the Master, "Lo! I am with you alway", is gloriously fulfilled!

But enough has been said, we trust, to induce the reader to demand the condition of the Saviour's manifestation—to ask for the key to an experience so elevated and full of strength. "Tell me", we can hear some reader saying, "Tell me on what terms my Lord will thus draw nigh?"

But are you ready for the announcement? Are you ready for the sacrifice?—ready to empty that proud and self-complacent heart of thine, that the Redeemer may have room wherein to dwell? You have sought His presence by prayer; you have sought it by the study of the Word; you have sought it perhaps by sacramental observances and ritual conformity; and yet you have sought it in vain. The reason is, your obedience has not been entire. Prayer is good. The study of the Word is good. The Lord's Supper, when rightly observed, is a most precious means of grace. But before any of these can become in the highest degree efficacious, they must be used by a thoroughly devoted heart. Listen to the Saviour's terms: "He that hath My commandments, and keepeth them, he it is that loveth Me: and he that loveth Me shall be loved of My Father, and I will love him, and will manifest Myself to him". And again, "If a man love Me, he will keep My words", that is, the least of Thy commandments, "And My Father will love him, and we will come unto him, and make our abode with him".

Nor are these terms found only here. The Saviour seeks and saves us in our lost estate, putting no bar between us and His full forgiveness; but when He has forgiven He expects us to love and to obey. The faith through which He so freely justifies does not destroy the necessity of obedience. It is only its herald and forerunner. Faith is the root of which obedience is the beautiful flower and fruit. And it is only when faith has issued in obedience; in an obedience beautified and perfected by love; in an obedience which stumbles not at sacrifices, and halts not when the way is rough and dark; in an obedience that cheerfully bears the cross and shame—it is only then that this highest promise of the Gospel is fulfilled; it is only then that Jesus comes and dwells in the believer's heart.

Does not some reader see that he has failed at just this point—where faith passes into obedience? Do you not see that this is just the spot where decay has assailed your comfort—that this is just the region where darkness has settled over your hopes? Are there no wrongs in the past left unrepaired, no duties in the present left unperformed? Does not conscience speak of some one sin unjudged and unmortified? God imputes sin to none who are standing under the value of Christ's blood; and yet sin is in us, and that sin must be resisted and condemned. "Let not sin therefore reign in your mortal body, that ye should obey it in the lusts thereof". We must resist it if we would know and feel that Christ is near.

"*He that hath My commandments, and keepeth them, he it is that loveth Me: and he that loveth Me shall be loved of My Father, and I will love him, and will manifest Myself to him*".

When love for the Saviour shall lead us to keep His holy Word—lead us to an immediate, unreserved, unhesitating obedience —lead us to say, in the spirit of entire self-surrender and sacrifice, "Thy will, not mine, be done", then farewell forever to doubt and darkness, to loneliness and sorrow! Then shall we mourn no more an absent Lord. Then shall we walk as seeing Him who is invisible, triumphant over every fear, victorious over every foe. Then, according to the promise, shall our path shine brighter and brighter unto the perfect day, leading from height to height of holiness and happiness until we appear in the unveiled presence of the King.

"I need Thy presence every passing hour;
What but Thy grace can foil the tempter's power?
Who like Thyself my Guide and stay can be?
Through cloud and sunshine, O! abide with me!

"I fear no foe with Thee at hand to bless;
Ills have no weight, and fears no bitterness:
Where is death's sting? Where, grave, thy victory?
I triumph still, if Thou abide with me."
—From *"Waymarks in the Wilderness"*.

JOHN'S GOSPEL

10. CHRIST MAGNIFIED BY HIS FORERUNNER. John 3:21-36.

We give first a brief Analysis of the passage which is to occupy our attention. Here we see:

1. The Lord Jesus and His Disciples in Judea, v. 22.
2. John baptizing in Arnon, vv. 23, 24.
3. The attempt to provoke John's jealousy, vv. 25, 26.
4. The humility of John, vv. 27, 28.
5. The joy of John, v. 29.
6. The preeminence of Christ, vv. 30-35.
7. The inevitable alternative, v. 36.

Another typical picture is presented in the passage before us, though its lines are not so easily discernible as in some of the others which we have already looked at. But there is this in common between them, that like the previous ones, the scene here has a *double* significance, portraying as it does the then condition of Judaism, and foreshadowing the glories and blessedness of the Millennium.

The spiritual state of Judaism as it existed at the time of our Lord's sojourn on earth is revealed in three pathetic statements; first, the Jews were occupied with the externals of religion *(v. 25)*; second, they were envious of the results attending the ministry of Christ *(v. 26)*; third, they rejected the testimony of the Saviour *(v. 32)*. How pointedly did these things expose the condition of Israel as a nation! With no heart for the Christ of God, and ignorant, too, of the position occupied by His forerunner *(v. 28)*, they were concerned only with matters of ceremonialism. Religious they were, but for a Saviour they felt no need. They preferred to wrangle over questions of "purification", rather than go to the Lord Jesus for the Water of Life. But this was not all. They were *jealous* of the outward success that attended the ministry of the Lord Jesus in its early stages. How this revealed their hearts! Plainer still is what we read of them in v. 32—the testimony of Christ they "received not". The Saviour was not only "despised" by them, He was "rejected", too. Once more, then, is the awful condition of Judaism made manifest before our eyes. But following this, another picture, a bright one, is spread before us, and to it we would now direct attention.

The first part of John 3 is devoted to a record of the conversation which passed between Christ and Nicodemus, in which the Saviour expounded the need and nature of the new birth. This, in its prophetic foreshadowing, looks forward to the regeneration of Israel, which shall take place at the beginning of the Millennium. What follows here gives us a striking and blessed picture of the conditions that shall obtain when Christ has returned and set up His kingdom. Nicodemus points forward to the godly remnant of the Jews, which in the Tribulation period shall be separated from the mass of their fellows (who shall be in unholy alliance with the Antichrist), and who are eventually born again, and from these spring the regenerated Israel of the Kingdom. Another millennial foreshadowing is, therefore, given in the closing verses of John 3. Note these seven details:—

First, the Lord and His disciples are seen once more in "the land of Judea" and there *"He tarried with them"* (v. 22). Thus will it be in the Millennium. Christ will then dwell with a regenerated Israel in the land of Judea. Second, there the Lord (through His disciples, cf. 4:2) and John the Baptist were baptizing *(v. 23)*. This was not Christian baptism, but that which was indispensable for entrance into the MESSIANIC KINGDOM—see Matt. 3: 1, 2, 5, 6. Third, it was said *"all come to Him"* (v. 26). Thus will it be in that glad Day: in Zech. 14:16 we read, "And it shall come to pass that *every one* that is left of *all* the nations which came against Jerusalem shall even go up from year to year to worship the King, the Lord of Hosts, and to keep the feast of tabernacles". Fourth, here for the only time in this Gospel is the Lord Jesus referred to as "the Bridegroom"—a title never found in connection with the Church; and it is here said that He *"hath* the Bride". How marvelously accurate! The new, regenerated Israel is to be His "Bride", and not until the Millennium will He possess her. Fifth, it is in *this* connection we read of the Bridegroom's "friend" saying, "This my joy therefore is fulfilled" *(v. 29)*. The Millennium will be, supremely, a time of rejoicing. Sixth, it is highly significant that only here do we read, "God giveth not the Spirit by measure" *(John 3:34)*. Thus will it be in the Millennium: then it shall come to pass that the Lord will "pour out His spirit upon *all flesh*" *(Joel 2:28)*. Seventh, then, and not till then, will it be fully manifested that the Father not only loveth the Son, but "hath given all things *into His hand"* (v. 35). How wonderfully complete, then, is this prophetic foreshadowment.

"After these things came Jesus and His disciples into the land of Judea; and there He tarried with them, and baptized" *(3:22)*. This must be read in the light of John 4:2. By linking these two verses together an important principle is established: what is done by the servants of Christ *by His authority* is as though it had been done by Christ immediately. It is the same as what we read of in 2 Cor. 5:20: "Now then we are ambassadors for Christ, as though God did beseech you by us: *we* pray you *in Christ's stead,* be ye reconciled to God". It is the same in prayer. When we really pray to the Father in the name of Jesus Christ, it is as though Christ Himself were the suppliant.

"And John also was baptizing in Aenon near to Salim, because there was much water there: and they came, and were baptized" *(3:23)*. The meaning of the names of these places—like all others in Scripture—is deeply significant. Aenon signifies "place of springs", Salim means "peace". What a blessed place for John to be in! These names point a striking contrast from "the wilderness of Judea" and "the region round about Jordan" *(cf. Matt. 3:1, 5)*, which speak of drought and death. Surely there is a most important lesson taught us here, and a most precious one too. The place of drought and death was where God had called the forerunner of Christ to labor, and as he there bore faithful witness to the Lord Jesus it became *to him* a place of "springs" (refreshment) and "peace"! Such is ever the experience of the obedient servant of God.

"John *also* was baptizing". There is a word of great practical importance here for many a servant of God. The Lord Jesus was there in Judea in person, and His disciples were with Him, baptizing. The crowds which at first attended the preaching of John had now deserted him, and were thronging Christ *(v. 26)*. What then does the Lord's forerunner do? Does he decide that his work is now finished, and that God no longer has need of him? Does he become discouraged because his congregations were so small? Does he quit his work and go on a long vacation? Far, far from it. He faithfully persevered: "John *also* was baptizing". Has this no message for us? Perhaps these lines may be read by some who used to minister to big crowds. But these are no more. Another preacher has appeared, and the crowds flock after him. What then? Must you then conclude that God has set you aside? Are you suffering this experience to discourage you? Or, worse still, are you *envious* of the greater success attending the labors of another? Ah, fellow-servants of Christ, take to heart this word —"John *also* was baptizing". His season of popularity might be over: *his* light might be eclipsed with that of a greater: the crowds might have become thin; but, nevertheless, he plodded on and faithfully persevered in the work God had given him to do! "And *let us* not be weary in well doing: for in due season we shall reap, *if we faint not" (Gal. 6:8).* John performed his duty and fulfilled his course.

"John also was baptizing in Aenon near to Salim, *because* there was *much water* there". This is one of the many verses in the New Testament which plainly intimates the *mode* of baptism. If baptism were by sprinkling or by pouring, *"much* water" would not be required. The fact that John baptized in Aenon *"because* there was much water there" strongly implies that the scriptural form of baptism is immersion. Bnt the one who desires to know and carry out God's mind is not left to mere inferences, forceful though they may be. The very word "baptized" (both in the Greek and in English) signifies "to dip or immerse". The Greek words for "sprinkling and pouring" are entirely different from the one for baptize. Again; the example of our blessed Lord Himself ought to settle all controversy. No unprejudiced mind can read Matt. 3:16 without seeing that the Lord Jesus was immersed. Finally, the Testimony of Rom. 6 is unequivocal and conclusive. There we read, "We are *buried* with Him *by baptism* into death" *(v. 3).*

"Then there arose a question between some of John's disciples and the Jews about purifying" *(3:25).* The "Jews" mentioned here are the same as those we read of in 1:19, who sent a delegation unto the Baptist to inquire who he was. There is a slight difference between the ancient Greek MSS, and following a variation of reading the R. V. says, "There arose therefore a questioning on the part of John's disciples with *a Jew* about purifying". But we are thoroughly satisfied that here, as in the great majority of instances, the A. V. is preferable to the R. V. Clearly it is "the Jews" of 1:19 who are before us again in 3:25. This is seen from what we read in v. 28: "Ye yourselves bear me witness, *that I said,* I am not the Christ, but that I am sent before Him". The Baptist reminds them of the testimony he bore before their representatives on the previous occasion, for John 3:28 corresponds exactly with John 1:20 and 23.

"And they came unto John, and said unto him, Rabbi, He that was with thee beyond Jordan, to whom thou bearest witness, behold, the same baptizeth, and all men come to Him" *(3:26).* What was the object of these Jews? Was not their motive a malicious one? Were they not seeking to make John envious? It would certainly appear so. Why tell him of the outward success of Christ's ministry if it were not to provoke the jealousy of his harbinger? And cannot we detect the Enemy of souls behind this! This is ever a favorite device with him, to make one servant of the Lord envious at the greater success enjoyed by another. And alas! how frequently does he gain his wicked ends thus. It is only those who seek not honor of men, but desire only the glory of their Lord, that are proof against such attacks.

A striking example of the above principle is found in connection with Moses, who "was very meek, above all the men which were upon the face of the earth" *(Num. 12:3).* In Num. 11:26, 27 we read, "But there remained two of the men in the camp, the name of the one was Eldad, and the name of the other Medad: and the Spirit rested upon them: and they were of them that were written, but went not out unto the tabernacle: and they prophesied in the camp. And there ran a young man, and told Moses, and said, Eldad and Medad do prophesy in the camp": now notice what follows—"And Joshua the son of Nun the servant of Moses, one of his young men, answered and said, My lord Moses, forbid them". Even Joshua was jealous for his master's sake. But how blessedly did Moses rebuke him: "And Moses said unto him, Enviest thou for my sake? Would God that *all* the Lord's people were prophets, that the Lord would put His Spirit upon them"!

The same unselfish spirit is seen in that one who referred to himself as "less than the least of all saints" *(Eph. 3:8).* While the beloved apostle was a prisoner in Rome, many of the brethren waxed confident, and were bold to speak the word without fear. True, some preached Christ of envy and strife, and some also of good will. How then did the apostle feel? Did he think these others were seeking to take advantage of his absence? Was he jealous of *their* labors? Not so: he said: "Notwithstanding * * I therein *do rejoice,* yea, and will rejoice" *(Phil. 1:14-18).* So, again, he learns of the ministry of Philemon in refreshing the saints, and to him he writes, *"We* have *great joy* and consolation *in thy* love, because the bowels of the saints are refreshed *by thee,* brother" *(Philemon 7).* May more of this spirit be found in us and in other of the Lord's servants, as we learn of how God is using them.

"John answered and said, A man can

receive nothing, except it be given him from heaven" *(3:27)*. It is beautiful to see how John conducted himself on this occasion. His reply was most becoming. First, he bows to God's sovereign will *(v. 27)*. Second, he reminds his tempters of his previous disclaimer of any other place being his save that of one "sent before" the Lord *(1:28)*. Third, he declared that Israel (the "Bride") belonged to Christ, not to himself *(v. 29)*. Fourth, he affirms that his own joy was fulfilled in seeing men turning to the Lord Jesus *(v. 29)*. Finally, he insists that while Christ must "increase", *he* must "decrease" *(v. 30)*. Blessed self-abnegation was this.

"John answered and said, A man can receive nothing, except it be given him from heaven" *(3:27)*. John was not at all surprised at the lack of spiritual perception in these Jews. The things of God cannot be discerned by the natural man. Before a man can even "receive" spiritual things they must first be "given him from heaven". And in the bestowment of His gifts God is sovereign. We are fully satisfied that the contents of this twenty-seventh verse contains the key to much that is puzzling. There are some brethren, beloved of the Lord, who do not see the truth of believer's baptism; there are others who stumble over the subject of predestination; there are yet others who have no light on prophetic and dispensational truth. What may be as clear as sunlight to us, is dark to them. But let us not be puffed up by our superior knowledge. Let us remember the admonition of the apostle Paul, "For who maketh thee to differ from another? and what hast thou that thou didst not *receive?* now if thou didst *receive* it why dost thou glory (boast), as if thou hadst not received it? *(1 Cor. 4:7)*.

But on the other hand, there is no excuse for ignorance in the things of God. Far from it. God has plainly made known His mind. His blessed Word is here in our hands. The Holy Spirit has been given to us to guide us into *all* truth. And it is our responsibility to believe and understand all that is recorded for our learning: "And if any man think that he knoweth anything, he knoweth nothing yet as he *ought* to know" *(1 Cor. 8:2)*. Nevertheless, there is the Divine side, too; and *this* is what is before us here in John 3:27. What did the Lord Jesus say in response to the unbelief of the cities wherein His mightiest works were done?

"Jesus answered and said, I thank Thee, O Father, Lord of heaven and earth, because Thou has hid these things from the wise and prudent, and *hast revealed* them unto babes. Even so, Father: for so it seemed good in Thy sight" *(Matt. 11:25, 26)*. What did He say to Peter, when that apostle bore such blessed testimony to His Messiahship and Deity? "Jesus answered and said unto him, Blessed art thou, Simon Bar-Jona: for flesh and blood hath not *revealed it* unto thee, but *My Father* which is in heaven" *(Matt. 16:17)*. And what is recorded of Lydia? "And a certain woman named Lydia, a seller of purple, of the city of Thyatira, which worshipped God, heard us: *whose heart the Lord opened,* THAT (in order that) she attended unto the things which were spoken of Paul" *(Acts 16:14)*.

And yet God is not capricious. If it is not "given" to us the fault is all our own. We "have not" because we "ask not" *(James 4:2)*. Or, we "find" not because we are too lazy to "search" diligently for the precious things of God. Here is His sure promise, provided we meet the conditions annexed to it: "My son, if thou wilt *receive* My words, and hide My commandments with thee; So that thou incline thine ear unto wisdom, and apply thine heart to understanding; yea, if thou criest after knowledge, and liftest up thy voice for understanding; If thou *seekest* her as silver, and *searchest* for her as for hid treasures; *then* shalt thou understand the fear of the Lord, and *find the knowledge of God*" *(Prov. 2:1-5)*.

"Ye yourselves bear me witness, that I said, I am not Christ, but that I am sent before Him" *(3:28)*. John now announces what he was not, and what he was. He was but the messenger before the face of Christ, His forerunner. A subordinate place, therefore, was *his*. How blessed was this. These Jews were seeking to stir up the pride of John. But the Lord's servant takes his proper place before them. He reminds them that he was only one "sent before" Christ.

"He that hath the bride is the Bridegroom: but the friend of the Bridegroom, which standeth and heareth Him, rejoiceth greatly because of the Bridegroom's voice: this my joy therefore is fulfilled" *(3:29)*. The first thing which claims our attention here is the opening sentence of this verse. Who is meant by the "bride" which the Lord Jesus even then was said to *"have"?*

In seeking the answer to this question, particular attention should be paid to the *connection* in which this statement is found, the *circumstances* under which it was made, and also to the *person* who uttered it. The *connection* in which this occurs is discovered by going back to John 3:22, 23. The disciples of Jesus, as well as John himself, were "baptizing". This was not Christian baptism, for that was not instituted until after the death and resurrection of the Saviour. This baptism, therefore, was *kingdom* baptism, and was one of the conditions of entrance into it *(cf. Matt. 3)*. The circumstances under which this statement was made is seen in that John 3:29 formed part of the Baptist's reply to those who were seeking to arouse his envy over the fact that the crowds were now flocking to Christ. The *person* who uttered it was not Paul the apostle to the Gentiles, but John the Baptist, whose ministry was *confined* to Israel, and who here styles himself "the friend of the Bridegroom". Mr. C. E. Stuart in his commentary, says upon this verse, "The 'bride' here is only a figure—certainly not the church", and with the latter part of this statement we are in hearty accord.

A "bride" is a young wife, and we believe that the "Bride" is *Millennial Israel*. A common objection against this is, How can this be, seeing that Israel is a divorced wife? The answer is, that the divorced wife and the bride are quite distinct. *Apostate* Israel is the "divorced wife"; the *new* Israel will be the "Bride". The new Israel, Millennial Israel, will grow out of the godly remnant of Jews that pass through the Tribulation undefiled. They will constitute the nucleus of those who shall be in the Messianic kingdom. This was the kingdom announced by the Baptist—'announced' we say, not 'offered'—announced because the King Himself was about to appear before Israel. The great demand was that Israel should repent, and manifest their repentance by taking their place, symbolically, in death—this is what baptism in the Jordan signified. Had the entire Nation obeyed John's call, then, within a few years, the Kingdom would have been established. But the Nation as a whole repented not. Nevertheless, there was a remnant who *did so* even then, and these—regenerated Jews—represented that regenerated Israel who shall yet be the Bride of Christ.

When the Baptist said "He that hath the bride, is the Bridegroom", he was not referring to the Church, the Body of Christ, for of that he knew nothing whatever, nor did any one else save the Triune God. At that time Christ was not forming a church, but as "the Minister of the Circumcision" He was presenting Himself to Israel. A repenting and believing few gathered around Him, and in the day to come the godly remnant of the Tribulation period shall augment that number, and *together* form that company from which shall come the Millennial Israel, "the Bride". That the twelve apostles *are* connected with Christ in an *earthly* relationship (though also, of course, members of the Household of Faith, and of the Family of God) is clear from the words of the Saviour: "Jesus said unto them, Verily I say unto you, That ye which have followed Me, in the regeneration, (a title of the Millennium) when the Son of Man shall sit in the throne of His glory, *ye also* shall sit upon twelve thrones, judging the twelve tribes *of Israel*" *(Matt. 19:28)*. This is something which the apostle Paul—the apostle of the Gentiles, the one through whom God made known the truth of the one Body—will never do.

"He that *hath* the Bride" was the language of faith. The company who will form the "Bride" was then far from being complete; only a nucleus was there, but *faith* viewed the purpose of God concerning Israel as *already accomplished*. But "he that *hath* the Bride" rules out the one Body, for *that* did not begin to be formed until several years later. If further proof of the correctness of what we have written be asked for, it is at once forth-coming in the very next sentence: "But *the friend of the Bridegroom*, which standeth and heareth Him, rejoiceth greatly because of the Bridegroom's voice: this *my* joy therefore is fulfilled". Without a doubt this refers to John the Baptist himself. But in no possible sense was *he* associated with heralding the truth of the church which is the Body of Christ. His own language, as recorded in John 1:31 is final: "But that he should be made manifest *to Israel*, therefore, *am I come* baptizing with water".

Let it be clearly understood that in this article we are neither denying nor affirming that the Body of Christ will be His *heavenly* bride. *That* does not fall within the compass of the present passage. What we have attempted to do is to give a faithful exposition of John 3:29, and the "Bride" there plainly refers to a company of regenerated Israelites, a company not yet completed. The work of gathering out *that* company has been *interrupted* by the rejection of Christ by the Jewish nation as a whole, and this has been followed by the present *parenthetical period*—parenthetical, because *outside* the scope of Old Testament prophecy. But after the Body of Christ has come "in the unity of the faith, and the knowledge of the Son of God, unto a perfect *man*, unto the measure of the stature of the fulness of Christ" *(Eph. 3:13)* God will *resume* His work with Israel and *complete* that company which is to be gathered out from them.

"But the friend of the Bridegroom, which standeth and heareth him, rejoiceth greatly because of the Bridegroom's voice" *(v. 29).* This is very blessed. Notice first, how we have repeated here what we called attention to when considering John 1:35-37: the two disciples of John "stood" before they heard their master "speak" and say "Behold the Lamb of God". The order is the same in the verse now before us—"Which standeth *and* heareth Him". Standing signifies the cessation of activity: it denotes an act of concentrated attention. The principle illustrated is a deeply important one. It is one which needs to be pressed in this day of hustling and bustling about, which is only the product of the *energy of the flesh.* We must "stand" before we can "hear *Him*".

"This my joy therefore is fulfilled". How precious is this! Joy of heart is the fruit of being *occupied with Christ"!* It is standing and hearing *His voice* which delights the soul. But again we say that the all-important prerequisite for this is a cessation of the activities of the flesh. *His* voice cannot be heard if we are rushing hither and thither in fellowship with the fearful bedlam all around us. The "better part" is not to be like Martha—"cumbered about *much serving"*—but is to "sit" at the feet of the Lord Jesus like Mary did, *hearing* His word *(see Luke 10:38-42).* Notice, too, the tense of the verbs in John 3:29: "Stand*eth* and hear*eth*". The perfect tense expresseth *continuous* action: again and again, daily, this must be done, if our joy is to be filled full. Is not our failure at this very point the explanation of our joyless lives?

"He must increase, but I must decrease" *(3:30).* Blessed climax was this to the lovely modesty of John, and well calculated to crush all party feeling and nip in the bud any jealousy there might be in the hearts of his own disciples. In principle this is inseparably connected with what he had just said before in the previous verse. The more I "decrease" the more shall I delight in standing and hearing the voice of that blessed One who is Altogether Lovely. And so, conversely. The more I stand and hear *His* voice, the more will He "increase" before me, and the more shall I "decrease". I cannot be occupied with two objects at one and the same time. To "decrease" is, we take it, to be less and less occupied with ourselves. The more I am occupied with Christ, the less shall I be occupied with myself. Humility is not the product of direct cultivation, rather is it a *bi-product*. The more I *try* to be humble, the less shall I attain unto humility. But if I am truly occupied with that One who was "meek and lowly in heart", if I am constantly beholding *His* glory in the mirror of God's Word, then shall I be "changed into *the same image* from glory to glory, even as by the Spirit of the Lord" *(2 Cor. 3:18).*

The passage now before us contains the final testimony of the Baptist to the Lord Jesus Christ. In it the Saviour and His servant are sharply contrasted. In witnessing to the manifold glories of his Master, John the Baptist draws a seven-fold contrast. First, John was one who could receive *nothing*, except it were given him from heaven, v. 27; whereas Christ was the One to whom the Father "hath given *all things*", v. 35. Second, Jesus was the Christ, whereas John was only one "sent before Him", v. 28. Third, Christ was the "Bridegroom", whereas John was but the "friend" of the Bridegroom, v. 29. Fourth, Christ must "increase", whereas John himself must "decrease", v. 30. Fifth, John was "of the earth", whereas the Lord Jesus had come "from above", and "is above all", v. 31. Sixth, John had only a measure of the Spirit, but of Christ it is witnessed. "God giveth not the Spirit by measure unto Him", v. 34. Seventh, John was but a servant, whereas the Saviour was none less than the Son of the Father, v. 35. What a blessed and complete testimony was this to the immeasurable superiority of the Lord of Glory!

"He that cometh from above is above all: he that is of the earth is earthly, and speaketh of the earth: He that cometh from heaven is above all" *(3:31)*. John now witnesses to the person, the glory, and the testimony of Christ. It seems to us that John is here giving point to one of the seven contrasts contained in this testimony which he here drew between Christ and himself. "Earth and earthly" must not be understood to signify "world and worldly". John was of the earth, and spoke of things which pertain to the earth. But the Lord was from heaven, and is above all. All other messengers that God has sent had much earthiness about them, as those of us who are His servants now have much of it. We are limited by our finite grasp. The bodies of death in which we dwell are a severe handicap. Our vision is largely confined to the things of earth. But there were no limitations to the Lord Jesus: He was the Son of God from heaven, pure, perfect, omniscient.

"And what he hath seen and heard, that he testifieth" *(3:32)*. The testimony which Christ bore was a perfect one. The prophets received their messages from the Holy Spirit, and they spoke of things they *had not* "seen"—see Matt. 13:17. There are things which the angels desire to look into, but they were too mysterious for them to fathom—see 1 Pet. 1:12. But our Lord Jesus Christ knows "heavenly things" by His own perfect knowledge, for He hath ever dwelt in the bosom of the Father. *He* knew the mind of God for He is God.

"And no man receiveth His testimony" *(3:32)*. How radically different was this word of John from that of the Jews who declared "all men come to Him", v. 26! One lesson we may draw from this is the unreliability of statistics which seek to tabulate spiritual results. Those Jews were looking at the outward appearance only, and from that point of view the cause of Christ seemed to be prospering in an extraordinary way. But the Lord's forerunner looked beneath the surface, at the true spiritual results, and his verdict was "no man receiveth His testimony". Beware then of statistics, they depend largely on the one who compiles them. Some, who are sanguine, will say everything that is pleasing and encouraging; others, who are more serious and severe in their judgment, will say much that is depressing.

"No man receiveth His testimony". This is not to be understood without qualification, for the very next words declare "he that *hath* received His testimony hath set to His seal that God is true". It is evident that what John meant was that *comparatively* none received the testimony of Christ. Compared with the crowds which came to Him, compared with the nation of Israel as a whole, those who "received" Christ's testimony were so few, that they were as though none at all received it. And is it not the same today? In this favored land Christ is preached to multitudes, and many there are who hear about Him; but, alas! how few give evidence of having really received His testimony into their hearts!

And *why* is it that men receive not the testimony of this One who "cometh from heaven" *(v. 31)*, who testifies of what He has seen and heard *(v. 32)*, and who has the Spirit without measure *(v. 34)*, yea, who is none other than the Son beloved of the Father *(v. 35)*? It is because they are *earthly*. The message is too heavenly for them. They have no relish for it. They have hearts only for things below. Others are too learned to believe anything so simple: it is still to the Jews a stumblingblock, and to the Greeks foolishness. They will not believe God; and how can *they* while "they receive honor from men"! With others it is *pride* that hinders. They think themselves good enough already. They are pharisaical. They are too highborn to see their need of being born again. They are too haughty to take the place of empty-handed beggars and receive God's gift. But the root reason for rejecting the testimony of Christ is that "men loved darkness rather than light, because their deeds were evil" *(8:19)*. Men are so depraved their hearts are hardened and their understandings are darkened, and therefore, do they prefer the darkness to the light.

"He that hath received His testimony hath set to his seal that God is true" *(3:33)*. To "set to his seal" means to certify and ratify. By faith in the Lord Jesus the believer has come to know God as a *reality*. Hitherto he heard of and talked about an unknown God, but now he knows God for himself, and declares his faith in His fidelity. God says, "He that believeth on the Son hath everlasting life", and the believer finds that God is true, for he lives now in newness of life. The Lord says, "He that believeth on Him is not condemned", and the believer *knows* it is so, for the burden of guilt is gone from his conscience. Those who receive Christ's testimony as true, take it unto themselves. They rest their souls upon it. They make it their own. They allow nothing to make them doubt what He has said. No matter whether they can thoroughly understand it or no; no matter whether it seems reasonable or unreasonable, they implicitly believe it. Whether their *feelings* respond or not, makes no difference—the Son of God has spoken, and that is enough.

"For he whom God hath sent speaketh the words of God: for God giveth not the Spirit by measure unto Him" *(3:34)*. The Lord Jesus Christ was sent here by God, and He spoke only the words of God. Testimony to this fact was borne to Him by the Father on the Mount of Transfiguration: "This is My beloved Son, in whom I am well-pleased: hear ye Him". And Christ differed from every other messenger sent from God—in *all* things *He* has "the preeminence". Others *had* the Spirit "by measure". They knew but fragments of the truth of God. To them the Spirit came and then went again. Moreover their gifts varied: one had a certain gift from the Spirit, another an entirely different gift. But God gave not the Spirit "by measure" unto Christ. The Lord Jesus knew the full truth of God, for He Himself is the Truth. On Him the Spirit did not come and go; instead, we read, He *"abode* upon Him" *(John 1:32)*. And further: Christ was endowed with *every* Divine gift. In contrast from the fragmentary communications of God through the prophets, *(see Heb. 1:1)*, Christ fully and finally received the mind of God. We believe that the full meaning of these words that Christ had the Spirit "without measure" is a statement that is strictly parallel with what we read in Col. 2:9: "For in Him dwelleth *all the fulness* of the Godhead bodily".

"The Father loveth the Son, and hath given all things into His hands" *(3:35)*. What a glorious testimony was this! Christ was more than a messenger or witness for God, He was the "Son" beloved of the Father. Not only so, He was the One into whose hand the Father had "given all things." How this brings out, again, the absolute Deity of Christ! To none but to One absolutely equal with Himself could the Father give *"all things"*.

"He that believeth on the Son hath everlasting life: and he that believeth not the Son shall not see life: but the wrath of God abideth on him" *(3:36)*. Here is the Inevitable Alternative. Salvation comes through believing, believing on the Son. How Divinely simple! Those who believe on the Son have "everlasting life" as a present possession, though the full enjoyment as well as the full manifestation of it are yet future. But those who believe not the Son "shall not see life", neither enter into it nor enjoy it; instead, the wrath of a sin-hating God "abideth" on them. It is upon them even now, and if they believe not, it shall abide on them for ever and ever. How unspeakably solemn! How it behooves every reader to seriously and honestly face the question—To which class do I belong?—to those who believe on the Son, or to those who believe not on the Son?

The following questions are concerning next month's lesson:

1. What are we to learn from the statement that "Jesus Himself baptized not"? 4:2.
2. Why did the Lord "leave Judea" when He knew the Pharisees were jealous? 4:3.
3. What prophetic foreshadowing do we have in John 4:3, 4?
4. Why was it that Christ "must needs" go through Samaria? 4:4.
5. What are we to learn from the fact that the meeting between Christ and the Samaritan woman occurred at a *"well"?* 4:6.
6. Why are we told that it was *"Jacob's* well? 4:6.
7. What is suggested by the "sixth hour"? 4:6.—*Arthur W. Pink.*

"THE WAY, THE TRUTH, AND THE LIFE"

Many are attracted by the beauty of the last discourse of Jesus with His disciples before He went to suffer, who cannot appropriate its wealth of heavenly consolation. To them it is like a fountain pouring in living joy from the lofty and inaccessible rock. The traveller stops to gaze with delight on its sparkling beauty, though he cannot reach its waters to quench his thirst. But to the Church of God, what

To that Adamic creation we all belong naturally and physically. Were I an angel, I should belong to the angelic creation, another and earlier order of intelligent existences, though equally with us creatures, and equally under creature obligations. But I am a man, and thus belong to the human family, the material creation; and that which, as we have seen, pertains to the creature as such pertains to me, because I am a creature. Unless God could cease to be Creator, He could not cease to have creatorial rights or claims; and unless I could cease to be His creature, I could not cease to owe Him creatorial obligations; He is our "faithful Creator" *(1 Pet. 4:19)*.

But it may be asked, (1) Is there not for us a change of relationship? (2) Are not our old creation debts all gone in the Cross? (3) Are not the things of the old creation passed away and replaced by a new creation? (4) Have we not died out of all that we have referred to, our old man being crucified with Christ? (5) Are we not redeemed from the curse of the law, being dead to it by the body of Christ?

Such questions, deeply interesting as they are, indicate no small degree of confusion in the inquirer's mind. A sound nomenclature is in these things of the first importance. Unless penalty be distinguished from debt, person from nature, that which is physical from that which is spiritual, the old man from the so-called old creation, and creature-obligations from the demands of the Mosaic law, no clear and correct conclusions are possible.

Now let us see, (1) What "change of relationship" is possible between a creature and his Creator as such. My son may become my servant or master; but he can never cease to be my son. New and added relations there may be, and there are, between God and us; but those which He has formed are as eternal as Himself. Sin never changed the fact of man's creatureship, though it constituted him a sinner; grace has not changed it, though it has made him a son of God; and neither will glory for ever and for ever. Adam innocent, Adam a sinner, Adam a believer, Adam in glory by-and-by, in no one of these conditions more than in another was, and is, and will be a human being, intelligent, and therefore responsible, under, and never from under creature-obligations, whether in a state of probation in Eden, a state of failure in the world, or in the perfected state in the Father's house, when "spirit and soul and body" *(1 Thess. 5:23)* will be glorified with Christ. Equally so is a sinner alive in this scene under these obligations; and should he go down to perdition will never drown them in the lake of fire, though he will then be where their breach is as irremediable as their validity is irrevocable.

(2) The obligations referred to, constituting our original indebtedness to God, belong to our creatureship, not to our sinnership, if we may use the word. Thus while the penalty of every default, in other words, the sins we have committed, has been borne by Christ, the Divinely-provided Substitute, the ever-existing responsibility we are under as creatures remains untouched, being uninvalidated by the work of the Cross.

(3) Scripture never speaks of the "old creation", or of old debts, or old indebtedness, as some do, for the palpable reason that the creation referred to, and the obligations attaching to us therein, are never obsolete, nor ever will be.

The new creation is entirely a spiritual creation, and is only *in Christ*, who is "the Beginning of the creation of God" *(Rev. 3:14)*. Hence it is an entire mistake to regard it as having come in successionally to take the place of the physical or natural creation. That which is moral does not supplant or replace that which is material. It is an essentially new character and Divine order of blessing superadded to what went before, which latter God will yet clear of its ruin, and of which we shall be witnesses for eternity. So far from the natural creation being set aside, I could not possibly be a new creation unless I were generically of the Adamic, for it is us from such, and not from angels, is formed a new creation, essentially heavenly and constituted for heaven, having Christ, its glorified Head already there, is over all, God blessed forever! The eternal state will consist of a new heaven and a new earth, when the tabernacle of God will be with men, and He will dwell with them and be their God!

(4) That we have died in the death of Christ is unquestionable truth to faith; but let us not be misled. This is never predicated of us as creatures, but as men in the flesh; that is, as sinners under broken responsibilities. In His death we have died, and in His resurrection are risen. Our old man is crucified with Christ; its history is thus

thought of meeting with Him; or you may have envied them their unreflecting enjoyment of existence, undisturbed by thoughts of a terrible hereafter. But the truth still remains, that it sums all the pitiful and appalling desolation of your condition, that you are "without God". In contrast with this stands the immortal blessedness of the children of God, who are partakers of His nature, sharers of His counsel, the agents of His will, and the heirs of all that infinite love can bestow upon finite beings, of His own bliss and glory. The only alternative that is open to you is to be without God or in God, and that is just the alternative of heaven or hell. You are now without God, and the question is, How can one so estranged from God be reconciled to Him? How can a child of wrath become a child of God? Your sin raises a barrier between you and God which you cannot surmount. If God were to receive you as you are, by a mere act of clemency, He would (do you not shudder at the impious thought?) declare Himself to be as indifferent to the evil of sin as you are, make Himself a partaker of your guilt, and join with you in the overthrow of all righteousness. Can anything be more impossible than this?

In this awful strait, Christ meets your case. You are like a poor outcast, perishing on some solitary and barren rock of the ocean. It would only mock your misery to lead you to that rock's giddy brink, and across an awful chasm, impassable as the great gulf fixed between Abraham and Dives, show you the smiling home of a Father in the midst of a land of teeming abundance. Some men speak of Christ as though He were only a guide come to show us the way; but what could a guide do for that poor outcast but tantalize him with the view of inaccessible happiness? The Gospel proclaims to you that the awful chasm is bridged over—Christ has borne our sins in His own body on the tree, and has satisfied every claim of Divine justice against the sinner; and now He proclaims, "I am the way". The way is open to your reconciliation with God; and by that open way a Father stands, with outstretched arms, crying to the poor perishing outcast, "Return unto Me".

You are a lost wanderer in a pathless desert, perishing in a waste, howling wilderness; and what would it avail you if a guide should take you by the hand and conduct you to the fartherest border of the desert, only to leave you at the foot of a frowning rampart of inaccessible rocks, towering up mountain high, around whose summit lightnings forever flashed and thunders rolled, while beyond this insurmountable barrier of your guilt Paradise lay in the eternal sunshine of God's love? Who can silence these awful thunders, and cleave a way for you through that mountain barrier? The Gospel proclaims that Christ has put away sin by the sacrifice of Himself so that justice, fully satisfied, no longer forbids our approach. Christ Himself proclaims, "I am the way". But you must remember He is the *only way*. To attempt to win God's favor by anything of your own, is as if the outcast on the rock, turning from the way of sure escape, should, in his pride of heart, attempt to leap across the awful chasm, only to plunge into its horrible darkness, and be engulfed in its wrathful billows. "I am the way", He says; "No man cometh unto the Father but by Me".

CHRIST IS THE TRUTH.—The discovery of a way to any place would be no value to one who had no desire to go there, who would not or could not go. This is your case, sinner, when Christ reveals Himself to you as the way to the Father. Desolate and wretched as you must forever be without God, you would take any way rather than the way that leads to Him. You would, perhaps, prefer annihilation to meeting with God, because your heart is estranged from its proper centre, and you are full of errors and misconceptions regarding Him. The belief of Satan's lie regarding the character of God was the source of all the pollution and wretchedness of fallen man. You hate His holiness, you dread His justice, you deny His love. You regard Him as your enemy—an austere tyrant, who thwarts and opposes you, and at whose hands you expect nothing but destruction. Consequently, though every barrier is removed, you will not come unto Him until your views of God's character are wholly changed.

Now Christ meets you with the intimation, "I am the truth". He is not merely a teacher come to reveal a doctrine regarding God. He is Himself *the* truth—the truth is in Jesus. "He that hath seen Me", He says, "hath seen the Father". He is the revelation of God, and the sum of the revelation is, "God is love". God speaks in the gracious words of Him who spake as never man spake. God acts in those mighty deeds of grace, and help, and healing; "The Father that dwelleth in Me, He doeth the works". You see the pity of God in the tenderness of the compassion of the Man of sorrow. You see the grace and mercy of God when you see the Holy One stretching out a helping hand to the fallen, till He become known as the friend of sinners. You see the long-suffering love of God when you see Jesus led like a lamb to the slaughter; and if, on the cross, Jesus declares God's righteous hatred of sin, He also manifests the unfathomable wonder of God's love to the sinner. Look upon the crucified One and hear Him say, "He that hath seen Me hath seen the Father"; and is this He whom you account your enemy, against whose oppressions you revolt, from whose severity you shrink in guilty fear? What cruel wrong you have been doing to the God and Father of our Lord Jesus Christ. One look at *the truth*, one glance at God in Christ, must surely awaken in your contrite hearts the resolution, "I will arise and go to my Father". Well, then, there is none to forbid. The way is open, and Christ Himself is the assurance of the welcome that awaits you; He is the truth.

CHRIST IS THE LIFE.—Though the way to a place were known, though all its attractions and advantages were revealed, and a thousand motives for going there were urged, all would be unavailing to him who could not go there, who had no eye for its attractions, and no capacity to use or enjoy its advantages. This is your case, sinner. You are not only guilty and estranged from God, you are dead in trespasses and sins. The only life you know has its objects in this world, and its enjoyment in the lusts of the flesh, the lusts of the eye, and the pride of life. What could such a life be in the presence of God? His very perfections would be its dread and its destruction. "Except a man be born again he cannot see the kingdom of God". Here, also, Christ meets you, not with proposals to invigorate the old nature, to refine its grossness, or repair its defects, but to be a new and Divine life to you. He says, "I am the life"—the overflowing fountain from which every stream is filled, the vine which sends its power to the remotest branch, that it may bring forth fruit.

When you consider that it is His own life that He communicates to the believer—it is "*Christ in you*, the hope of glory"—you will perceive that this is precisely what you need to fit you for the presence and enjoyment of God. You are, by the very fact of receiving it, a child of God, not only in name, but in nature; for out of His fulness have all we received, and grace for grace. Grievously, alas! this life is hindered in its manifestation through this body of sin and death. But it is there—he that believeth on the Son *hath* life. And in what heavenly perfection shall that life be manifested when all that now obscures it is removed and it finds a fitting organization in a body fashioned like unto Christ's glorious body; for when He shall appear we shall be like Him. But remember that as Christ is *the way*, and there is no other, so Christ is *the life*, and there is no other; for "he that believeth not the Son shall not see life, but the wrath of God abideth on him".

Christ is the way, the truth, and the life. What more do you need? You are guilty and condemned. Well, there, here is Christ, who hath put away sin by the sacrifice of Himself. The way is open for your reconciliation to God. In your estrangement you shrink from God in guilty fear. Well, then, in Christ you behold God pleading with you to return, conquering enmity by tenderness, meeting all your sin with the riches of His grace, hastening to greet the returning prodigal, stretching out the arms of paternal welcome, and rejoicing over the lost found. You are dead in trespasses and sins. Well, then, here is life, Divine life, in all its holy affections and spiritual power. He offers Himself now in all His fulness to your confidence. Believing in Him, you are in the presence of God as Christ is; complete in Him, made meet for the inheritance of the saints in light—a child of God, and, if a child, then an heir—an heir of God, and a joint-heir with Christ. What could be added to all this? and yourself being judge, how can you escape if you neglect so great salvation?—*From "Waymarks in the Wilderness" edited by James Inglis.*

VOL. I NOVEMBER, 1922 No. 11

STUDIES in the SCRIPTURES

"Search the Scriptures" John 5:39.

A PERIODICAL (MONTHLY "IF THE LORD WILL")
DEVOTED TO BIBLE STUDIES and EXPOSITIONS

Associate Editors and Publishers, I. C. HERENDEEN and ARTHUR W. PINK,
Swengel, Pa.

Price: **10** cents per copy; **$1.00** per year. Foreign **$1.00** per year.

TO OUR SCRIPTURE STUDY FAMILY—

In this editorial we desire to draw from God's Word a few thoughts upon prayer. We shall aim to be as simple as possible. Psalm 86 will form the basis of our meditation. This Psalm is a Psalm of supplication, and like all other scripture it is written for our learning. A thoughtful perusal of it will show *the various grounds* on which the Psalmist supplicated God.

The Psalm opens as follows: "Bow down thine ear, O Lord, hear me". Here is a cry made that God will hearken to the believer. The suppliant is conscious of God's greatness. He recognizes that for God to regard *him*, for Jehovah to pay any attention to *him* would be an act of gracious condescension on the part of the high and lofty One that inhabitest the praises of eternity. It is equally meet that we too should recognize and own God's sovereign majesty. We shall now dwell briefly on the seven *different pleas* here made by the Psalmist:—

1. HE PLEADS HIS OWN POVERTY.

"O Lord, hear me FOR *I am poor and needy* (v. 1). This is the first reason advanced by the Psalmist *why* the great God should hear him, and it is one which is employed a number of times in different Psalms, see 70:5; 109:21,22. How different is this from the haughty Laodicean pride which prevails so widely today. How many are now saying, "I am rich, and increased with goods, and have need of nothing" (Rev. 3:17). May Divine grace deliver writer and reader from the spirit of self-sufficiency. May the Holy Spirit work in us an ever-deepening realization of our utter nothingness and unworthiness. Re-read the first verse of this Psalm and learn that our poverty and need is an argument of appeal to *plead before God*. Remember that the *first* beatitude of the Saviour was, "Blessed are the *poor* in spirit".

2. HE PLEADS HIS OWN HOLINESS.

"Preserve my soul FOR *I am holy*" (v. 2). To the carnal mind this seems in direct conflict with what has been before us in the previous verse—how this proves that the carnal mind is utterly incompetent to understand the things of God! "I am holy" seems to breathe the spirit of boasting. And yet there is no incongruity here. With perfect propriety and fidelity can a child of God say "I am poor and needy," and then in the next breath exclaim "I am holy". He is holy *by imputation;* holy not in himself, but *in Christ*. Thus does the apostle address the Hebrews: "*Holy* brethren, partakers of the heavenly calling" (3:1). Miserable failures in ourselves are we all; but faultless and spotless in Christ. This, too, we may *plead* before God.

3. HE PLEADS HIS IMPORTUNITY.

"Be merciful unto me, O Lord, FOR I cry unto Thee *daily*" (v. 3). What a blessed example the Psalmist has set us. Well for us to take this word to heart. This saint of Old Testament times was *continually* supplicating God. Thus should it be with us. Not only on Sundays, nor simply at the mid-week prayer-meeting, but "*daily*"—as often as a sense of need presses upon our spirits. And *who* is it that creates within us this sense of need? Surely it is none other than the indwelling Holy Spirit. If then we have the least desire to approach God, we have an additional pledge that we shall be heard of Him.   *(Concluded on page 252.)*

STUDIES IN THE SCRIPTURES

Subscription Price: $1.00 per year to any address in the world. Single copies 10 cents.

Change of Address: Please notify us promptly of any change of address, and be certain to give both old and new addresses.

Non-Subscribers receiving this Magazine regularly will understand their subscription has been entered by a friend.

Copies lost in the mail duplicated on request.

All new subscriptions will be dated back to January, 1922.

Entered as second-class matter December 15th, 1921 at the post office at Swengel, Pa., under Act of March 3rd, 1879.

CONTENTS

The Doom of the Antichrist	230
John's Gospel (John 4:1-6)	236
The Believer and Law	244
Ripe for Heaven	247

---

7. THE DOOM OF THE ANTICHRIST.

If there is a measure of difficulty attending the placing and elucidation of some of the prophecies which depict the various phases and stages of the Antichrist's career, the cloud lifts as the end is neared. And this is in full accord with many other things which pertain to the closing days of the Age. The nearer we come to the blessed event of our Lord's return to this earth, the more light has God seemed to cast on those things which immediately precede the Second Advent. It is as though, at first, God furnishes only a bare outline, but ultimately He fills in the details for us. It is thus with the end of the Antichrist. The Holy Spirit has been pleased to supply us with a most comprehensive and vivid description of the closing scenes in the career of the Son of Perdition. It is with mingled feelings that we turn and ponder what has thus been recorded for our learning.

The awful course which is followed by the Man of Sin cannot but shock us. The frightful hypocrisy, the shocking duplicity and treachery, the terrible cruelty, and the amazing impiety of this Monster of wickedness, make us marvel at the forbearance of God, who endures "with much long-suffering the vessels of wrath fitted to destruction". But when we come to the final scenes, and behold the Antichrist openly challenging heaven, publicly defying God, and making a deliberate and determined effort to prevent the Lord Jesus returning to this earth, we are well nigh rendered speechless by the unthinkable lengths to which sin will go. On the other hand, as we learn that all of this is the ending of that long dismal night which precedes the Day of Christ, the Millennium, we see that it is but the dark background to bring into more vivid relief the glories of the God-Man. The destruction of the Antichrist will be followed at once by the setting up of the Messianic Kingdom which shall bring peace and blessing to all the earth. And the contemplation of this cannot but fill us with joy and thanksgiving.

"The end of the Man of Sin marks an era of sublimest interest to the believing children of God. It shall be the day of our triumphant manifestation, and the Jubilee of all creation. The day, Oh, Hallelujah! when Satan's crown of pride shall be smitten, and his glory trailed in the dust; when his long-continued and persistent temptations shall have an end; and his power receive the wounding from which it shall never recover itself. That blessed, blessed day, when He whose right it is, shall reign, and the kingdom of Israel be no more overturned and dishonored. The sweet, sweet day, when the mockings, the scourgings, the bonds, the imprisonments, the afflictions, and the torments of the great multitude 'of whom the world was not worthy,' shall cease to annoy forever, and the whole earth be at rest, and break forth into gladness" *(Mrs. G. Needham)*.

But before that blessed Day arrives, the last hour of the night of Christ's absence has to run its course, and as the darkest hour precedes the dawn, so the last hour of this "night" shall be the most foreboding of all. The period which immediately precedes the return of Christ to the earth will witness the most awful events ever chronicled. It was of this period that Daniel spoke when he said, "There shall be a time of trouble, such as never was since there was a nation even to that same time" *(12:1)*. It was to this same time that Christ referred when He declared, "For in those days shall be affliction, such as was not from the beginning of the creation which God created unto this time, neither shall be. And except that the Lord had shortened those days, no flesh should be saved: but for the elect's sake, whom He hath chosen, He hath shortened the days" *(Mark 13:19, 20)*. This is "the hour of temptation which shall come upon all the world" *(Rev. 3:10)*. It will be a time of unparalleled wickedness, and a time of unprecedented suffering. It is the time when God shall avenge the murder of His Son, when He shall take to task a world that has so long despised His Word, and trampled His commandments under foot. The very Antichrist will be one of the instruments of His vengeance—"the rod of His anger" *(Isa. 10:5)*.

It is because men received not the love of God's truth He shall send them strong delusion that they should believe the Devil's lie. It is because men had "pleasure in unrighteousness" they shall be deceived by the Lawless One. It is because Israel refused that blessed One who came in His Father's name that they shall receive the one who comes in his own name. This is why the Antichrist will, for a season, be suffered to prosper, and apparently to defy God with impugnity. But when God has used him to perform His own pleasure, then shall He empty upon his kingdom and upon his subjects the vials of His wrath. Just as God has set the bounds of the sea, saying thus far shalt thou go and no further, so has He fixed the limits to which He will allow the Antichrist to go. And when that limit is reached the Son of Perdition will find himself as helpless to pass beyond what God has decreed as a worm would be beneath the foot of an elephant. This will be made evident as we proceed.

At the close of our last article we followed the career of the Antichrist to the point where he turns upon the Jewish people and seeks to cut them off from being a nation. Fearful will be his assaults upon them, and bitter will be their wailings. It is at that time the Remnant will cry, "O God; why hast Thou cast us off forever? why doth Thine anger smoke against the sheep of Thy pasture? Remember Thy congregation, which Thou hast purchased of old; the rod of Thine inheritance, which Thou hast redeemed; this mount Zion, wherein Thou hast dwelt. Lift up Thy feet unto the perpetual desolations; even all that the Enemy hath done wickedly in the sanctuary. Thine enemies roar in the midst of Thy congregations; they set up their ensigns for signs. A man was famous according as he had lifted up axes upon the thick trees. But now they break down the carved work thereof at once with axes and hammers. They have cast fire into Thy sanctuary, they have defiled by casting down the dwelling place of Thy name to the ground. They said in their hearts, Let us destroy them together; they have *burned up all the synagogues of God in the land*. We see not our signs: there is no more any profit neither is there any among us which knoweth how long. O God, how long shall the Adversary reproach? Shall the Enemy blaspheme Thy name forever? Why withdrawest Thou Thy hand, even Thy right hand? Pluck it out of Thy bosom" *(Psa. 74:1-11)*.

It is at this same time that the prophecy of Amos 8 will receive its final fulfillment: "The Lord hath sworn by the excellency of Jacob, Surely I will never forget any of their works. Shall not the land tremble for this, and every one mourn that dwelleth therein? and it shall rise wholly as a flood; and it shall be cast out and drowned, as by the flood of Egypt. And it shall come to pass in that day, saith the Lord God, that I will cause the sun to go down at noon, and I will darken the earth in the clear day: And I will turn your feasts into mourning, and all your songs into lamentation; and I will bring up sackcloth upon all loins, and baldness upon every head; and I will make it as the mourning of an only son, and the end thereof as a bitter day. Behold, the days come, saith the Lord God, that I will send a famine in the land, not a famine of bread, nor a thirst for water, but of hearing the words of the Lord: And they shall wander from sea to sea, and from the north even to the east, they shall run to and fro *to seek the word of the Lord, and shall not find it*. In that day shall the fair virgins and the young men faint for thirst" *(Amos. 8:7-13)*. How remarkably does Psa. 74 interpret this prophecy of Amos! The reason why the godly Remnant shall run to and fro to "seek the word of the Lord" and shall not find it, and the meaning of the "famine of *hearing* the words of the Lord" is that "all the synagogues in the land" shall have been burned up.

But not for long will this frightful persecution continue: "Therefore thus saith the Lord God of hosts, O My people that dwellest in Zion, be not afraid of the Assyrian: he shall smite thee with a rod, and shall lift up his staff against thee, after the manner of Egypt. For yet *a very little while*, and the indignation shall cease, and Mine anger in their destruction" *(Isa. 10: 24, 25)*. Once the Antichrist turns upon Israel his days are numbered, for to touch that nation is to touch the apple of God's eye *(Zech. 2:8)*. God shall respond to the cries of the faithful Remnant and shall "stir up a scourge for him" *(Isa. 10:26)*. What this "scourge" is we learn from Dan. 11:40: "And at the time of the end shall the king of the south push at him; and the king of the north (the Antichrist) shall come against him (i. e. the king of the south) like a whirlwind, with chariots, and with horsemen, and with many ships; and he shall enter into the countries, and shall overflow, and pass over" *(Dan. 11:40)*.

The king of the south who pushes at—assails—the Antichrist is the king of Egypt. The Antichrist, here termed "the king of the north", i. e. Assyria, shall leave Babylon, and marshalling his imperial forces, which he has ready for immediate action, shall lead them against him (the king of Egypt) like a whirlwind. The rapidity of his movements and the immensity of his armies, is intimated by the words, "He shall enter into the countries, and shall overflow and pass over". His progress will be as the rushing of an overwhelming torrent from the mountains, that spreads over the land, and carries everything before it. "He shall enter also into the glorious land, and many countries shall be overthrown" *(Dan. 11:41)*. His route from Babylon to Egypt will take him through Palestine, the land which is soon to be the glory of all lands; and, although we are not told here what he will do there at that time, his hand will, no doubt, be heavy upon it, as also upon the many other countries which he will overthrow. "But these shall escape out of his hand, even Edom, and Moab, and the chief of the children of Ammon" *(Dan. 11:41)*. These three peoples will escape his fury. The reason for *their* escape seems to be a double one. In Ps. 83, which describes an event at a little earlier period, we are told, "they have taken crafty counsel against Thy people, and consulted against Thy hidden ones. They have said, Come, and let us cut them off from being a nation; that the name of Israel may be no more in remembrance. For they have consulted together with one consent, they are confederate against Thee: the tabernacles of *Edom*, and the Ishmaelites; of *Moab*, and the Hagarenes; Gebal, and *Ammon*, and Amalek; the Philistines with the inhabitants of Tyre; Assur (the Assyrian) also is joined with them" *(Psa. 83:3-8)*. Thus we see that these three peoples acted in concert with the Antichrist, when a determined effort was made to utterly exterminate the Jewish people. The Antichrist, therefore, spares these submissive allies of his when he goes forth to overthrow the other countries.

So much for the human side as to why "these shall escape out of his hand, even Edom, and Moab, and the chief of the children of Ammon". But there is a Divine side, too. These peoples are spared at that time in order that they may be dealt with later by God Himself. Thus did Jehovah declare of old through Balaam the heathen prophet: "There shall come a Star out of Jacob, and a Sceptre shall rise out of Israel, and shall smite the corners of Moab, and destroy all the children of Sheth. And Edom shall be a possession, Seir also shall be a possession for his enemies" *(Num. 24:17, 18)*. This will be right at the beginning of the Millennium. Israel, too, shall be used by God in this work of judgment upon their ancient enemies: "But they shall fly upon the shoulders of the Philistines toward the west; they shall spoil them of the east together: they shall lay their hand upon Edom and Moab; and the children of Ammon shall obey them" *(Isa. 11:14)*.

"He shall stretch forth his hand also upon the countries: and the land of Egypt shall not escape. But he shall have power over the treasures of gold and of silver, and over all the precious things of Egypt: and the Libyans and the Ethiopians shall be at his steps" *(Dan. 11:42, 43)*. The victorious King will then take possession of those countries which were overthrown by him during his march from Babylon to Egypt. Having now reached this land which dared to "push at him"—the land never completely subjugated by the previous kings of the north referred to in the earlier part of Dan. 11—its king and subjects must now bow before his iron sceptre. He becomes master of its treasures of gold, silver, and precious things. The Libyans and Ethiopians, who were the allies of Egypt, will be compelled to follow in his train. Thus will he crush this Egyptian rebellion, and demonstrate once more his military prowess. Yet not for long will he be permitted to defy Heaven with impugnity.

"But tidings out of the east and out of the north shall trouble him: therefore he shall go forth with great fury to destroy, and utterly to make away many" *(Dan. 11:44)*. What these troublous tidings are we learn from Jer. 51. A serious attack will be made upon his Babylonian headquarters, and during his absence from there, the kings of Ararat, Minni, and Ashchenaz— no doubt emboldened by the insubordination of Egypt—will besiege and capture one end of the Capital. The time is nigh at hand when God shall utterly destroy that City of the Devil, and a preliminary warning of this is now given: "And I will render unto Babylon and to all the inhabitants of Chaldea all their evil that they have done in Zion in your sight, saith the Lord. Behold, I am against thee, O destroying mountain, saith the Lord, which destroyeth all the earth: and I will stretch out Mine hand upon thee, and roll thee down from the rocks, and will make thee a burnt mountain. And they shall not take of thee a stone for a corner, nor a stone for foundations; but thou shalt be desolate forever, saith the Lord" *(Jer. 51:24-26)*.

As a beginning to this end, the Lord says, "Set ye up a standard in the land, blow the trumpet among the nations, prepare the nations against her, call together against her the kingdoms of Ararat, Minni, and Ashchenaz (all situated in the vicinity of Armenia); appoint a captain against her; cause the horses to come up as the rough caterpillers. Prepare against her the nations with the kings of the Medes, the captains thereof, and all the rulers thereof, and all the land of his dominion. And the land shall tremble and sorrow: for every purpose of the Lord shall be performed against Babylon, to make the land of Babylon a desolation without an inhabitant. The mighty man of Babylon hath forborn to fight, they have remained in their holds: their might hath failed: they became as women: they have burned their dwelling places; her bars are broken" *(Jer. 51:27-30)*.

It is this ominous news—the "tidings" which "trouble him" of Dan. 11:44—which reaches the ears of Babylon's King, then absent in Egypt. The alarming tidings that part of the city has already been destroyed arouses him to fierce anger, for we are told, "therefore he shall go forth with great fury to destroy, and utterly to make away many" *(Dan. 11:44)*. As he nears the capital, "one post shall run to meet another, and one messenger to meet another, to show the King of Babylon that his city is taken at one end, and that the passages are stopped, and the reeds they have burned with fire, and the men of war are affrighted" *(Jer. 51:31,32)*. The end is not far distant: "For thus saith the Lord of hosts, the God of Israel; the daughter of Babylon is like a threshing floor, it is time to thresh her: yet a little while, and the time of her harvest shall come" *(Jer. 51:33)*. God now calls on the Jews who are found dwelling within that city to leave at once, lest they be caught in the storm of His fierce anger: "My people, go ye out of the midst of her, and deliver you every man his soul from the fierce anger of the Lord" *(Jer. 51:45)*. A graphic description of Babylon's destruction is found at the end of Jer. 51 and also in Rev. 18.

The fury of the Antichrist at the destruction of Babylon will know no bounds. Enraged at his loss, and incensed against God, he will now turn his face toward Palestine, and at the head of his vast forces will bear down upon the glorious land. Even so, it is *God* who is directing him and his blinded dupes—directing him to finish the work of judgment upon Israel, and directing him to his awful doom. Habakkuk gives a fearful description of the spirit in which the King of Babylon and his hosts shall fall upon the dwellers of Palestine:—"For, lo, I raise up the Chaldeans, that bitter and hasty nation, which shall march through the breadth of the land, to possess the dwelling places that are not theirs. They are terrible and dreadful: their judgment and their dignity shall proceed of themselves. Their horses also are swifter than the leopards, and are more fierce than the evening wolves: and their horsemen shall spread themselves, and their horsemen shall come from far; they shall *fly* as the eagle that hasteth to eat.

(How this verse anticipates the cruel aerial war-weapons!). They shall come all for violence: their faces shall sup up as the east wind, and they shall gather the captivity as the sand. And they shall scoff at the kings, and the princes shall be a scorn unto them: they shall deride every stronghold; for they shall heap dust, and take it. Then shall his mind change, and he shall pass over, and offend, imputing this his power unto his god" (Note how this last verse serves to identify the "Chaldean" with the "King" of Dan. 11:38, 39). So terrible will be this onslaught that we are told, "And it shall come to pass, that in all the land, saith the Lord, two parts therein shall be cut off and die; but the third shall be left therein" *(Zech. 13:8)*.

His course is vividly sketched by Isaiah in the tenth chapter of his prophecy: "He is come to Aiath, he is passed to Migron; at Mickmash he hath laid up his carriages: They are gone over the passage: they have taken up their lodging at Geba; Ramah is afraid; Gibeah of Saul is fled. Lift up thy voice, O daughter of Galim: cause it to be heard unto Laish, O poor Anathoth. Madmena is removed; the inhabitants of Gebim gather themselves to flee. As yet shall he remain at Nob that day" *(Isa. 10:28-32)*. Nob is his camping-ground for that day, and it is there he will "plant the tabernacles of his palace between the seas in the goodly holy mountain" *(Dan. 11:45)*. Nob must be some elevation commanding a distant view of Jerusalem from the west. As he stands on the hill that night and looks at the Holy City, he "shall shake his hand against the mount of the daughter of Zion, the hill of Jerusalem" *(Isa. 10:32)*.

We now come to the closing scene. The following morning the Man of Sin leads his forces to the famous Armageddon, there awaiting his final re-inforcements before attacking Jerusalem. It is of this that Joel speaks: "Proclaim ye this among the Gentiles; Prepare war, wake up the mighty men, let all the men of war draw near; let them come up: Beat your plowshares into swords, and your pruning hooks into spears: let the weak say, I am strong. Assemble yourselves, and come all ye heathen, and gather yourselves together round about: thither cause Thy mighty ones to come down, O Lord. Let the heathen be wakened, and come up to the valley of Jehoshaphat; for there will I sit to judge all the heathen round about. Put ye in the sickle, for the harvest is ripe: come, get you down; for the press is full, the fats overflow; for their wickedness is great. Multitudes, multitudes in the valley of decision: for the day of the Lord is near in the valley of decision" *(Joel 3:9-14)*.

It is to this that Micah refers: "Now also many nations are gathered against thee, that say, Let her be defiled, and let our eye look upon Zion. But they know not the thoughts of the Lord, neither understand they His counsel: for *He* shall gather them as the sheaves into the floor" *(4:10, 11)*. But it is not in the valley that the battle is fought, but around Jerusalem, where the Beast and his armies deliver the final blow of God's judgment on that city ere the Deliverer appears. It is then that God will say, "O Assyrian, the rod of Mine anger, and the staff in their hands is Mine indignation. I will send him against an hypocritical nation, and against the people of My wrath will I give him a charge, to take the spoil, and to take the prey, and to tread them down like the mire of the streets. Howbeit he meaneth not so, neither doth his heart think so; but it is in his heart to destroy and cut off nations not a few. For he saith, Are not my princes altogether kings? Is not Calno as Carchemish? It not Hamath as Arpad? Is not Samaria as Damascus? As my hand hath found the kingdoms of the idols, and whose graven images did excel them of Jerusalem and of Samaria; Shall I not, as I have done unto Samaria and her idols, so do to Jerusalem and her idols? Wherefore it shall come to pass, that when the Lord hath performed His whole work upon mount Zion and on Jerusalem, I will punish the fruit of the stout heart of the King of Assyria, and the glory of his high looks" *(Isa. 10:5-12)*. The Antichrist is but the Lord's instrument after all. Just as Moses picked up and held in his hand the rod which became a serpent, so shall this offspring of the Serpent be wielded by the hand of God to accomplish His predetermined counsels.

Once again, though, the Beast appears to be successful. Jerusalem falls before his onslaught as Jehovah had foretold that it should—"For I will gather all nations against Jerusalem to battle; and the city shall be taken, and the houses rifled, and the women ravished; and half of the city shall go forth into captivity, and the residue of the people shall not be cut off from the city" *(Zech. 14:2)*. Intoxicated by their success, it is then that the heathen shall rage and the people imagine a vain thing: "The kings of the earth set themselves, and the rulers take counsel together, against the Lord, and against His anointed, saying, Let us brake their bands asunder, and cast away their cords from us" *(Psa. 2:2, 3)*.

And then comes the grand finale. The heaven will open and from it will descend the King of kings and Lord of lords, seated on a white horse, with His eyes "as a flame of fire" *(Rev. 19:11, 12)*. Attending Him will be the armies of heaven, also seated on white horses *(Rev. 19:14)*. Far from being appalled at this awe-inspiring spectacle, the Beast and the kings of the earth and their armies shall gather together to "make war against Him that sat on the horse, and against His armies" *(Rev. 19: 19)*. "Then shall the Lord go forth, and fight against those nations, as when He fought in the day of battle" *(Zech. 14:3)*. At last the Christ of God and the christ of Satan will confront each other. But the instant the conflict begins, it is ended. The Foe will be paralyzed, and all resistance cease.

Scripture has solemnly recorded the end of various august evil personages. Some were overwhelmed by waters; some devoured by flames; some engulfed in the jaws of the earth; some stricken by a loathsome disease; some ignominiously slaughtered; some hanged; some eaten up of dogs; some consumed by worms. But to no sinful dweller on earth, save the Man of Sin, "the Wicked One", has been appointed the terrible distinction of being consumed by the brightness of the personal appearing of the Lord Jesus Himself. Such shall be his unprecedented doom, an end that shall fittingly climax his ignoble origin, his amazing career, and his unparalleled wickedness.

"Hitherto proud boastings have issued from the lips of Satan's king; but now he falls helplessly to the ground, blasted by the lightening which streams from the King of kings; and together with the False Prophet and in the full sight of his countless armies, he is seized by the angels of the Lord, to be hurled alive into the lake which burneth with fire and brimstone" *(G. H. Pember)*.

The overthrow of the Antichrist is described as follows:—"But with righteousness shall He judge the poor, and reprove with equity for the meek of the earth: and He shall smite the earth with the rod of His mouth and *with the breath of His lips shall He slay the Wicked*" *(Isa. 11:14)*.

"And through his policy also he shall cause craft to prosper in his hand; and he shall magnify himself in his heart, and by peace shall destroy many: he shall also stand up against the Prince of princes; but *he shall be broken without hand*"—an expression which always refers to that which is supernatural *(Dan. 8:25)*.

"And he shall plant the tabernacles of his palace between the seas in the glorious holy mountain; yet shall he *come to his end, and none shall help him*" *(Dan. 11:45)*.

"And then shall that Wicked (One) be revealed, whom the Lord *shall consume with the spirit of His mouth, and shall destroy with the brightness of His coming*" *(2 Thess. 2:8)*.

"And the Beast was taken, and with him the False Prophet that wrought miracles before him, with which he deceived them that had received the mark of the Beast, and them that worshipped his image. These both were *cast alive into a lake of fire burning with brimstone*" *(Rev. 19:20)*.

"For Tophet is ordained of old; yea, *for the King it is prepared;* he hath made it deep and large: the pile thereof is fire and much wood; *the breath of the Lord, like a stream of brimstone, doth kindle it*" *(Isa. 30:33)*.

"And the Devil that deceived them was cast into the lake of fire and brimstone, where the Beast and the False Prophet are, and (they) *shall be tormented day and night for ever and ever*" *(Rev. 20: 10)*.

Frightful, too, shall be the doom meted out to the followers of the Antichrist. Zech. 14 tells us, "And this shall be the plague wherewith the Lord will smite all the people that have fought against Jerusalem; Their flesh shall consume away while they stand upon their feet, and their eyes shall consume away in their holes, and their tongues shall consume away in their mouth. And it shall come to pass in that day, that a great tumult from the Lord shall be among them; and they shall lay hold every one on the hand of his neighbour, and his hand shall rise up against the hand of his neighbour" *(vv. 12, 13)*. So, also Rev. 19: 21 declares, "And the remnant were slain with the sword of Him that sat upon the horse, which sword proceeded out of His mouth: and all the fowls were filled with their flesh".—*Arthur W. Pink.*

JOHN'S GOSPEL

II. CHRIST AT SYCHAR'S WELL: John 4:1-6.

We begin with the usual Analysis of the passage that is to be before us. In it we see:—

1. The Lord's knowledge of the Pharisees' jealousy, v. 1.
2. The disciples of the Lord baptizing, v. 2.
3. The Lord leaving Judea and departing into Galilee, v. 3.
4. The Constraint of Divine grace, v. 4.
5. The journey to Sychar, v. 5.
6. The Saviour's weariness, v. 6.
7. The Saviour resting, v. 6.

Like the first three chapters of John, this fourth also furnishes us with another aspect of the deplorable spiritual state that Israel was in at the time the Lord was here upon earth. It is remarkable how complete is the picture supplied us. Each separate scene gives some distinctive feature. Thus far we have seen, first, a blinded Priesthood *(1:19, 26)*; second, a joyless Nation *(2:3)*; third, a desecrated Temple *(2: 14)*; fourth, a spiritually-dead Sanhedrim *(3:7)*; fifth, the person of Christ despised *(3:26)* and His testimony rejected *(3:32)*. Now we are shown the heartless indifference of Israel toward their semi-heathen neighbors.

Israel had been highly privileged of God, and not the least of their blessings was a written revelation from Him. But though favored with much light themselves, they were selfishly indifferent toward those who were in darkness. Right within the bounds of their own land (for Samaria was a part of it), dwelt those who were semi-heathen, yet had the Jews no love for their souls and no concern for their spiritual welfare. Listen to the tragic plaint of one of their number: "The Jews have no dealings with the Samaritans" *(John 4:9)*. The heartless indifference of the favored people of God toward the Samaritans is intimated further in the surprise shown by the disciples when they returned and found the Saviour talking with this Samaritan woman *(see 4:27)*. It was, no doubt, in order to rebuke them that the Saviour said, "Say not ye, There are yet four months, and then cometh harvest? Behold, I say unto you, Lift up *your* eyes, and look on the fields; for they are white already to harvest" *(4: 35)*. Thus, this heartless neglect of the Samaritans gives us another glimpse of Israel's state at that time.

But not only does John 4 give us another picture of the miserable condition the Jews were in, but, once more, it contains a prophetic foreshadowing of the future. In the closing verses of the previous chapter we are shown the person of Christ despised *(3:26)* and His testimony rejected *(3:32)*. This but anticipated the final rejection of Christ by the Nation as a whole. Now in marvelous consonance with this, the very next thing we see is *Christ turning to the Gentiles!* The order here, as everywhere, is perfect. As we all know, this is exactly what happened in God's dispensational dealings with the earth. No sooner did the old dispensation end, end with Israel's rejection of Christ, than God turned in mercy to the Gentiles *(Rom. 11, etc.)*. This is intimated in our lesson, first, by the statement made in v. 3: the Lord Jesus *"left Judea,* and departed again into *Galilee"*—cf. Matt. 4:15—"Galilee of the *Gentiles"!* Second, in the fact that here the Lord Jesus is seen occupied not with the Jews but with the Samaritans. And third, by what we read of in v. 40—"And He abode *there* two days." How exceedingly striking is this! "He abode there *two days".* Remember that word in 2 Pet. 3:8, which declares "One day is with the Lord as a thousand years, and a thousand years as one day". Two "Days", then, or 2,000 years is the length of time that Christ was to be away from the Jews in Judea. How perfect and accurate is this dispensational picture!

But this is not all that we have here. In our last article we also pointed out how that the closing verses of John 3 supply us with a striking sevenfold picture of Christ in the Millennium. The same line of truth is continued here, and another line is added to the picture. The Millennium will be a time of great blessing, not only for the Jews, but for the Gentiles too. As we read in Acts 15:14-17, "Simeon hath declared how God at the first did visit the Gentiles, to take out of them a people for His name (this, during the present dispensation). And to this agree the words of the prophets; As it is written, After this (this dispensation) I will return, and will build again the tabernacle of David which is fallen down; and I will build again the ruins thereof, and I will set it up: That the residue of them might seek after the Lord, and *all the Gentiles,* upon whom My name is called, saith the Lord, who doeth all these things". A striking foreshadowment of this is found here. Not only does the poor woman who spoke to the Lord at the well find in Him the One who alone can satisfy the heart, but others were brought to Him too. Yea, we read "And *many* of the Samaritans of that city believed on Him for the saying of the woman" *(4:39),* and again "And many more believed because of His own word" *(4:41).* How marvelously in accord with this prophetic application is the testimony of these Samaritans recorded in 4:42, "And (they) said unto the woman, Now we believe, not because of thy saying: for we have heard Him ourselves, and know that this is indeed the Christ, *the Saviour of the world".* What evidences are these—to those with anointed eyes—of the Divine inspiration of the Scriptures?

At the close of the seventh article of this series we called attention to the importance of noticing the relation of one passage to another. This is a principle which has been sadly neglected by Bible students. Not only should we be diligent to examine each verse in the light of its context, but also each passage as a whole should be studied *in its relation to* the complete passage which precedes and follows it. By attending to this it will often be found that the Holy Spirit has placed in juxtaposition two incidents—miracles, parables, conversations, as the case may be—in order to point a contrast, or a series of contrasts between them. Such we saw was plainly the case with what we have in the first and second halves of John 2, where a sevenfold contrast is to be noted. Another striking example is before us here. There is a manifest antithesis between what we have in the first half of John 3 and the first half of John 4.

As we study John 3 and 4 together, we discover *a series of striking contrasts.* Let us look at them. First, in John 3 we have "a man of the Pharisees *named* Nicodemus": in John 4 it is an *unnamed woman* that is before us. Second, the former was a man of rank, a "Master of Israel": the latter was a woman of the lower ranks, for she came "to draw water". Third, the one was a favored Jew: the other was a despised Samaritan. Fourth, Nicodemus was a man of high reputation, a member of the Sanhedrim: the one with whom Christ dealt was a woman of dissolute habits. Fifth, Nicodemus sought out Christ: here Christ seeks out the woman. Sixth, Nicodemus came to Christ "by night": Christ speaks to the woman at midday. Seventh, to the self-righteous Pharisee Christ said, "Ye must be born again": to this sinner of the Gentiles He tells of "the gift of God". How much we miss by failing to compare and contrast what the Holy Spirit has placed side by side in this wondrous revelation from God! May the Lord stir up all of us to more diligent *study* of His Word.

"When therefore the Lord knew how the Pharisees had heard that Jesus made and baptized more disciples than John, (though Jesus Himself baptized not, but, His disciples,) He left Judea, and departed again into Galilee" *(4:1-3).* Even at that early date in Christ's public ministry the Pharisees had begun to manifest their opposition against Him. But this is not difficult to understand, for the teaching of the Lord Jesus openly condemned their hypocritical practices. Moreover, their jealousy was aroused at this new movement, of which He was regarded as the head. The Baptist was the son of a priest that ministered in the Temple, and this would entitle him to some consideration. But here was a man that was regarded as being no more than the son of a carpenter, and who was *He* to form a following! And, too, He was of Nazareth, now working in Judea! And "out of Nazareth," they taught, "could arise no prophet" *(John 7: 52).* A spirit of rivalry was at work, and the report was being circulated that "Jesus was making and baptizing more disciples than John". Every one knew what crowds had flocked to the preaching and baptizing of that Elijah-like prophet, crying in the wilderness. Was it to be suffered then, that this One of poor parentage should eclipse the Baptist in fame? Surely not: that could not be allowed at any cost.

"When therefore the Lord knew

He left Judea". What a word is this! There is no hint of any one having informed Him. That was not necessary. This One who had humbled Himself to the infinite stoop of taking upon Him the form of a servant, was none other than *"The Lord"*. This One whom the Pharisees contemptuously regarded as the Nazarene-carpenter, was none other than the Christ of God, in whom "dwelt all the fulness of the Godhead bodily". 'The Lord *knew"*, at once displays His omniscience. Nothing could be, and nothing can be, hidden from Him.

"The Pharisees had heard that Jesus made and baptized more disciples than John". It is important to observe the order of the two verbs here for they tell us who, alone, are eligible for baptism. When two verbs are linked together thus the first denotes the action, and the second *how* the action was performed. For example: suppose I said, "He poured oil on him and anointed him". You could not say, "He anointed him and poured oil on him", unless the anointing and the pouring were two different acts. Therefore, the fact that "baptizing" here comes after, and not before, the verb "made", proves that they were *"disciples"* first, and were "baptized" subsequently. It is one of many passages in the New Testament which, uniformly, teaches that only one who is already a believer in Christ is qualified for baptism.

"Though Jesus Himself baptized not, but His disciples". This is but a parenthetical statement, nevertheless, it is of considerable importance. It has been well said by the late Bishop Ryle, "This verse intimates that baptism is neither the first nor the chief thing about Christianity. We frequently read of Christ preaching and praying, once of His administering the Lord's Supper, but 'baptize' He did not—as though to show us that baptism has nothing to do with salvation".

"He left Judea, and departed again into Galilee". This is exceedingly solemn. To cherish the spirit of jealousy and rivalry is to drive away the Lord. When the Saviour sent forth the twelve on their mission to the cities of Israel, He bade them "and whosoever will not receive you, when ye go out of that city, shake off the very dust from your feet for a testimony against them" *(Luke 9:5).* And again; when sending forth the seventy, He said to them, "But into whatsoever city ye enter, and they receive you not, *go your ways* out into the streets of the same, and say, Even the very dust of your city, which cleaveth on us, we do wipe off against you" *(Luke 10:10, 11).* But before He did this, He first set them an example. If "no man" would receive His testimony in Judea *(3:32),* then He would *leave* for other parts. He would not stay to cast pearls before swine.

No doubt the preaching of the Lord Jesus in Judea, and especially the circumstance of baptizing many of the people (through the instrumentality of His disciples) had greatly angered the Jewish rulers, and probably they had already taken steps to prevent the progress of this One whose teaching so evidently conflicted with theirs, and whose growing influence over the minds of the people threatened to weaken their authority. Our Lord knew this, and because His hour was not yet come, and much was to be done by Him before He finished the work the Father had given Him to do, instead of waiting until He should be driven out of Judea, He left that district of His own accord, and retired into Galilee, which, being remote from Jerusalem, and under the governorship of Herod, was more or less outside of their jurisdiction and less subject to the power of the Sanhedrim.

"In going from Judea into Galilee, our Lord's most direct route lay through Samaria, which was a district of Palestine, bounded on the south by Judea, and on the north by Galilee, on the west by the Mediterranean Sea, and on the east by the river Jordan. It was possible to go from Judea into Galilee by crossing the Jordan, and passing through Perea; but this was a very circuitous route, though some of the stricter Jews seemed to have been in the habit of taking it, to avoid intercourse with the Samaritans. The direct route lay through Samaria" *(Dr. J. Brown).*

Samaria was a province allotted to Ephraim and the half tribe of Manassah in the days of Joshua *(see Josh. 16 and 17, and particularly 17:7).* After the revolt of the ten tribes, the inhabitants of this district had generally ceased to worship at the Temple in Jerusalem, and following first the wicked idolatry introduced by Jeroboam the son of Nebat *(see 1 Kings 12:25-33, and note "Shechem" in v. 25),* they fell an easy prey to the Gentile corruptions introduced by his successors. After the great body of the ten tribes had been carried away captives, and their district left almost without inhabitant, the king of Assyria planted in their province a colony of various nations *(2 Kings 17:24)* who, mingling with the few original inhabitants of the land, formed unto themselves a strange medley of a religion, by combining the principles and rights of Judaism with those of oriental idolaters. As the inspired historian tells us, they "feared the Lord, and made unto themselves of the lowest of them priests of the high places, which sacrificed for them in the houses of the high places. They feared the Lord, and served their own gods, after the manner of the nations who carried them away from thence. So these nations feared the Lord, and served their graven images, both their children, and their children's children: as did their fathers, so do they unto this day" *(2 Kings 17:32, 33, 41)*. Thus, the original dwellers in Samaria were, to a great extent, heathenized.

At the time of the return of the remnant of Israel from the Babylonian captivity, the Samaritans offered to enter into an alliance with the Jews *(Ezra 4:1, 2)*, and on being refused *(Ezra 4:3)* they became the bitter enemies of the Jews and their most active opposers in the rebuilding of their Temple and capital *(see Neh. 4 and 6)*. According to Josephus *(see his "Antiquities" XI:7,2; XIII:9)*, at a later date Manasseh the son of Jaddua the high priest, contrary to the law, married the daughter of Sanballat, the chief of the Samaritans, and when the Jews insisted that he should either repudiate his wife, or renounce his sacred office, he fled to his father-in-law, who gave him an honorable reception, and by the permission of Alexander the Great built a temple to Jehovah on mount Gerizim, in which Manasseh and his posterity officiated as high priests, in rivalry to the Divinely instituted ritual at Jerusalem—see also 1 Macc. 3:10.

The Samaritans received as Divine the five books of Moses, and probably, also, some at least of the prophetic oracles; but they did not acknowledge the authenticity of the historical books written by the Jews, whom they regarded as their worst enemies. The natural consequence of all these circumstances was, that the Jews and Samaritans regarded each other with much more rancorous dislike than either of them did the idolatrous nations by which they were surrounded. Hence, when his enemies said unto Christ, "Say we not well that Thou art *a Samaritan*" *(John 8:48)*, we can understand better the venom behind the insult. Hence, too, it makes us bow our hearts in wonderment to find the Lord Jesus representing Himself as "a certain Samaritan" *(Luke 10:33)* as we learn of the depths of ignominy into which He had descended and of how He became the despised and hated One in order to secure our salvation.

"And He must needs go through Samaria" *(4:4)*. The needs be was a moral and not a geographical one. There were two routes from Judea to Galilee. The more direct was through Samaria. The other, though more circuitous, led through Perea and Decapolis to the southern shores of Gennesaret. The former was the regular route. But the reason why the Lord "must" go through Samaria, was because of a Divine *needs be*. From all eternity it had been ordained that *He should* go through Samaria. Some of God's elect were there, and these *must* be sought and found—cf. the Lord's own words in John 10:16, "And other sheep I have, which are not of this fold, them also I *must* bring". We shall never appreciate the Gospel until we go back to the basic truth of *predestination*, which puts God first, which makes the choice His before it is ours, and which, in due time, brings His grace to bear upon us with irresistible power.

"Election is of *persons*—predestination is of *things*. All the great movements of the universe are regulated by God's will,—But if the great movements, then the small movements, for the great depend upon the small. It was predestinated that our Saviour should go through Samaria, because there was a chosen sinner there. And she *was* a chosen sinner, for if not she never would have chosen God, or known Jesus Christ. The whole machinery of grace was therefore set in motion in the direction of one poor lost sinner, that she might be restored to her Saviour and to her God. That is what we wish to see in our own experience—to look back of ante-mundane ages, and date our eternal life from the covenant. To say:

"Father 'twas Thy love that knew us
Earth's foundation long before
That same love to Jesus drew us

By its sweet constraining power,
And will keep us
Safely now and ever more."
(Dr. G. S. Bishop).

It is not difficult to understand *why* the Lord must *needs* go through Samaria. There were those in Samaria whom the Father had given Him from all eternity, and these He "must" save. And, dear reader, if you are one of God's elect there is a *needs be* put on the Lord Jesus Christ to save *you*. If you are yet in your sins, you will not always be. For years you may have been fleeing from Christ; but when His time comes He will overtake you. However you may kick against the pricks and contend against Him; however deeply you may sin, as the woman in our passage, He will most surely overtake and conquer you. Yea, even now He is on the way!

"Then cometh He to a city of Samaria, which is called Sychar, near to the parcel of ground that Jacob gave to his son Joseph. Now Jacob's well was there. Jesus therefore, being wearied with His journey, sat thus on the well: and it was about the sixth hour" (*vv. 5, 6*). How truly human was the Lord Jesus! He would in all points be like unto His brethren, so He did not exempt Himself from fatigue. How fully then, can He sympathize with the laborer today who is worn out with toil! To the Saviour, a long walk brought weariness, and weariness needed rest, and to rest He "sat thus" on the well. He was, apparently, more worn than the disciples, for *they* continued on into the village to buy food. But He was under a greater mental strain than they. He had a weariness they knew nothing about.

"Of the Son of Man being in heaven, whilst upon earth, we have learnt in the previous chapter (*3:13*). Now, though Divine, and therefore in heaven, He was truly a man upon earth. This mystery of His person none of us can fathom (*Matt. 11:27*). Nor are we asked to. We have to believe it. . 'Perfect God, and perfect Man: of a reasonable soul and human flesh subsisting'—such has been the language of confession of the western part of Christendom for many an age. Now there are some conditions incident to humanity. There are others, in addition, connected with *fallen* humanity, such as liability to sickness, to disease, and even to death. To these last, of course, the holy Son of God, *was not*, though a man, subject; yet, as being a man He was able to die, and willingly gave up His life for His people. But to sickness and bodily decay, as the Holy One, in whom was no sin, He was not, and *could not have been*, subject. On the other hand, from conditions incident to humanity, as hunger, thirst and weariness, He was not exempt. In the wilderness He was hungry. On the Cross He was thirsty. Here at the well He was weary. Into what circumstances, then, did He voluntarily come, and that in obedience and love to His Father, and in love to His own sheep! He, by whom the worlds were made, was sitting a weary man by Jacob's well, and there at first alone. One word from the throne, and the whole angelic host would have flown to minister to Him. But that word was not spoken. For God's purpose of grace to souls in Samaria was to be worked out at Sychar" (C. E. Stuart).

"Jesus therefore being *wearied*." This brings out the *reality* of Christ's humanity. He was just as really and truly Man as He was God. In stressing His absolute Deity, we are in danger of overlooking the reality of His humanity. The Lord Jesus was perfect Man: He ate and drank, labored and slept, prayed and wept. And what a precious thought is there here for Christian workers: the Saviour knew what it was to be "weary"—not weary *of* well doing, but weary *in* well doing. But it is blessed to see how the Holy Spirit has guarded the glory of Christ's person here. Side by side with this word upon His humanity, we are shown His Divine omniscience—revealed in His perfect knowledge of the history of the woman with whom He dealt at the well. This principle meets us at every turn in the Gospels. At His birth we behold His humiliation—lying in a *manger*—but we discover His Divine glory, too, for the angels were sent to announce the One born as "Christ the Lord". See Him *asleep* in the boat, exhausted from the toil of a heavy day's work: but mark the sequel, as He rises and stills the storm. Behold Him by the grave side of Lazarus, groaning in spirit and weeping: and then bow before Him in worship as He, by a word from His mouth, brings the dead to life. So it is here: "wearied with His journey", and yet displaying His Deity by reading the secrets of this woman's heart.

"Jesus therefore being wearied with His journey, sat thus *on the well*". This illustrates another important principle, the application of which is often a great aid to the understanding of a passage, namely, noticing *the place* where a particular incident occurred. There is a profound significance to *everything* in Scripture, even the seemingly insignificant details. The character of the place frequently supplies the key to the *meaning* of what is recorded as occurring there. For instance: the children of Israel were *in Egypt* when the Lord delivered them. Egypt, then, symbolizes the place where we were when God apprehended *us*, namely, *the world* in which we groaned under the merciless task-masters that dominated us. John the Baptist preached *in the wilderness*, for it symbolized the spiritual barrenness and desolation of Israel at that time. When the Lord Jesus enunciated the laws of His kingdom, He went up into *a mountain*—a place of elevation, symbolic of His *throne* of authority from which He delivered His manifesto. When He gave the parables which set forth the Kingdom in its 'mystery form' as it relates to the *Gentiles*, He "sat by the *sea side*" (*cf. Isa.* 17:12, 13; *Ezek.* 26:3; *Dan.* 7:2, 3; *Rev.* 17:5, for the "sea" in its symbolic significance). The first four parables of Matt. 13 pertain to the *public* profession of Christianity, hence these were given in the hearing of the "great multitudes"; but the next two concerned only the Lord's own people, so we read "Then Jesus sent the multitude away, and *went into the house*: and His disciples came unto Him" (*Matt. 13:36*). When the Lord portrayed the poor sinner as the one to whom He came to minister (under the figure of the good "Samaritan") He represented him as a certain man who "went *down* from Jerusalem (foundation of peace) to Jericho (the city of the curse)". So, again, in Luke 15 the prodigal son is seen in "the *far country*" (away from the father), and there feeding on the husks which the swine did eat—another picture giving us *the place* where the sinner is morally.

The above examples, selected almost at random, illustrate the importance of observing *the place* where each event happened, and *the position* occupied by the chief actors. This same principle receives striking exemplification in the passage before us. The meeting between the Saviour and this Samaritan adulteress occurred at Sychar which means "purchased"—so was the "gift of God" that He proffered to her. And, as He revealed to her her soul's deep need He sat "on the well". The "well" was *a figure of Himself*, and its water was the emblem of *the salvation* that is to be found in Him. Our authority for these statements is Isa. 12:3, "Therefore with joy shall ye draw water out of *the wells* (Heb. 'the well') *of salvation*". What a remarkable statement is this! It is the key to the typical significance of many an Old Testament passage. The "well" of the Old Testament Scriptures foreshadowed Christ and what is to be found in Him. We shall now turn to some of the Old Testament passages where the "well" is mentioned, and discover how remarkably and blessedly they foreshadowed this One who gave the water of life to the woman of Samaria.

1. The first time the "well" is mentioned in Scripture, is in Gen. 16:7, 13, 14. "But Abram said unto Sarai, Behold, thy maid is in thy hand; do to her as it pleaseth thee. And when Sarai dealt hardly with her, she fled from her face. And the angel of the Lord found her by a fountain of water in the wilderness . . . . And she called the name of the Lord which spake unto her, Thou God seest me: for she said, Have I also here looked after Him that seeth me? Wherefore the well was called The well of Him that liveth and seeth me." Note the following points: First, the "well" (the "fountain of water" of v. 7 is termed the "well" in v. 14) was the place where the angel of the Lord *found* this poor outcast. So *Christ* is where God meets the sinner, for "no man cometh unto the Father" but by Him. Second, this well was located in the wilderness—fit symbol of *this world*. The "wilderness" well depicts the state of heart we were in when first met with by Christ! Third, the "well" was the place where *God* was *revealed*. Hagar, therefore, termed it, "the well of Him that liveth and seeth me". So, again, Christ is *the Revealer of God*—"He that hath seen Me, hath seen the Father".

2. In Gen. 21:14-19 we read, "And Abraham rose up early in the morning, and took bread and a bottle of water, and gave it unto Hagar, putting it on her shoulder, and the child, and sent her away: and she departed, and wandered in the wilderness of Beersheba. And the water was *spent* in the bottle, and she cast the child under one of the shrubs. And she went, and sat her down over against him a good way off,

as it were a bow shot: for she said, Let me not see the death of the child. And she sat over against him: and lift up her voice, and wept. And God heard the voice of the lad; and the angel of God called to Hagar out of heaven, and said unto her, What aileth thee, Hagar? Fear not; for God hath heard the voice of the lad where he is . . . . and God *opened her eyes,* and she saw *a well of water*". How inexpressibly blessed is this in its typical suggestiveness! Notice again the following points: First, we have before us again an outcast, and one whose water was spent, for she had but "a bottle": like the prodigal son, she "began to be in want". Second, she had cast away her child to die, and there she sat *weeping*. What a picture of the poor, desolate, despairing sinner! Third, *God* "opened her eyes", and what for? In order that she might *see* the "well", that had been there all the time! Ah, was it not so with thee, dear Christian reader? It was not thine own mental acumen which discovered that One of whom the "well" here speaks. It was God who *opened* thine eyes' to *see* Him as the One who alone could meet thy desperate and deep need. What do we read in Prov. 20:12—"The hearing ear, and *the seeing eye,* the Lord hath made even both of them". And again in 1 John 5:20, we are told, "And we know that the Son of God is come, and hath *given us an understanding,* that (in order that) we may know Him that is true".

3. In this same chapter the "well" is mentioned again in another connection: "And Abraham took sheep and oxen, and gave them unto Abimelech; and both of them made *a covenant.* And Abraham set seven ewe lambs of the flock by themselves. And Abimelech said unto Abraham, What mean these seven ewe lambs which thou hast set by themselves? And he said, For these seven ewe lambs shalt thou take of my hand, that they may be a witness unto me, that I have digged this well. Therefore he called that place *the well of the oath;* because there they sware both of them" *(Gen. 21:27-31).* Here we find the "well" was the place of the "Covenant" *(v. 27),* which was ratified by an "Oath" *(v. 31).* And what do we read in Heb. 7:20-22?—"And inasmuch as not without *an oath* He was made priest: (for those priests were made without an oath; but this with an oath by Him that said unto Him, The Lord sware and will not repent, Thou art a priest forever after the order of Melchisedec:) By so much was Jesus made a Surety of a better *Covenant".*

4. In Gen. 24:10-12 we read, "And the servant took ten camels of the camels of his master and departed; for all the goods of his master were in his hand: and he arose, and went to Mesopotamia, unto the city of Nahor. And he made his camels to kneel down without the city by *a well* of water at the time of the evening, even the time that women go out to draw water. And he said, O Lord God of my master Abraham, I pray Thee, send me good speed this day". Not only is each typical picture perfect, but the order in which they are found evidences Divine design. In the first scriptures we have glanced at, that which is connected with the "well" suggested the meeting between the Saviour and the *sinner.* And in the last passage, the covenant and the oath speak of that which tells of the sure ground upon which our eternal preservation rests. And from that point, every reference to the "well" has that connected with it which is appropriate of *believers* only. In the last quoted passage, the "well" is the place of *prayer:* so, the believer asks the Father in *the name of Christ,* of whom the "well" speaks.

5. In Gen. 29:1-3 we read, "Then Jacob went on his journey, and came into the land of the people of the East. And he looked, and behold a well in the field, and, lo, there were three flocks of sheep lying by it; for out of that well they watered the flocks". This is very beautiful. How striking is the contrast between this typical scene and the first that we looked at in Gen. 16. There, where it is a *sinner* and Christ which is in view, the "well" is located in the *wilderness*—figure of the barrenness and desolation of the sinner. But here, where the *sheep* are in view, the "well" is found in the *field*—suggesting the "green pastures" into which the Good Shepherd leads His own. Notice there were "three flocks of sheep" that were lying by this "well", their position denoting *rest,* that rest which Christ gives His own. The *three* flocks may prefigure the Old Testament saints, New Testament saints, and the Millennial company of believers. Here in the *field* were the three flocks lying *"by it"*—the well. It is only *in Christ* that we find rest.

6. In Ex. 2:15-17 we are told, "Now when Pharaoh heard this thing, he sought

to slay Moses. But Moses fled from the face of Pharaoh, and dwelt in the land of Midian: and he sat down by a well. Now the priest of Midian had seven daughters: and they came and drew water, and filled the troughs to water their father's flock. And the shepherds came and drove them away: but Moses stood up and helped them, and watered their flock." How marvelous is this type. First, Pharaoh the king of Egypt prefigures Satan as the god of this world, attacking and seeking to destroy the believer. From him Moses "fled". How often the great Enemy frightens us and gets us on the run. But how blessed to note the next statement here: fleeing from Pharaoh to Midian, where he now dwells, the first thing that we read of Moses is "he sat down by a well". Thank God there is One to whom we can flee for refuge—the Lord Jesus Christ to whom the "well" pointed. To this well the daughters of Jethro also came, for water. But the shepherds came and *drove them away*. How many of the "undershepherds" to-day are, by their infidelistic teaching, driving many away from Christ. Nevertheless, God still has a Moses here and there, who will *"stand up and help"* those who really desire the Water of Life. But be it noted, before we can "help" others we must first be resting on the well for ourselves, as Moses was.

7. "And from thence they went to Beer: that is the well whereof the Lord spake unto Moses, Gather the people together and I will give them water. Then Israel sang this song, Spring up, O well; *sing ye unto it*" *(Numbers 21:16, 17)*. What a word is this! The well is personified. It is made the object of song. It evokes praise. No interpreter is needed here. Beloved reader, are you "singing" unto *the* "Well"?

8. "Now Jonathan and Ahimaaz stayed by En-rogel; for they might not be seen to come into the city: and a wench went and told them; and they went and told king David. Nevertheless a lad saw them, and told Absalom: but they went both of them away quickly, and came to a man's house in Bahurim, which had a well in his court: *whither they went down*. And the woman took and spread a covering over the well's mouth, and spread ground corn thereon; and *the thing was not known*" *(2 Sam. 17: 17-19)*. Here we find the "well" providing *shelter* and *protection* for God's people.

Notice there was a "covering" over its mouth, so that Jonathan and Ahimaaz were *hidden* in the well. So it is with the believer—"Your life is *hid with Christ* in God" *(Col. 3:3)*. How striking is the last sentence quoted above, "And the thing was not known!" The world is in complete ignorance of the believer's place and portion in Christ!

9. "And David longed, and said, O that one would give me drink of the water of the well of Bethlehem, which is by the gate!" *(2 Sam. 23:15)*. Nothing but water from the well of *Bethlehem* would satisfy David.

10. "Drink waters out of thine own cistern, and running waters out of *thine own well*" *(Prov. 5:15)*. What a blessed climax is this. The "Well" is our own, and from its "running waters" we are invited to drink."

We sincerely pity any who may regard all of this as fanciful. Surely such need to betake themselves to Christ for "eyesalve" that their eyes may be enabled to behold "wondrous things" out of God's Law. To us this study has been unspeakably blessed. And what meaning it all gives to John 4:6—"Jesus, therefore, being wearied with His journey sat thus on *the well*".

But there is one other word here that we must not overlook, a word that gives added force to the typical character of the picture before us, for it speaks of the *character* of that Salvation which is found *in* Christ. "Now *Jacob's* well was there" *(John 4:6)*. There are three things in connection with this particular "well" that we need to consider. First, this well was *purchased* by Jacob, or more accurately speaking, the "field" in which the well was located was purchased by him. "And Jacob came to Shalem a city of *Shechem,* which is in the land of Canaan, when he came from Padan-Aram and pitched his tent before the city, and he *bought* a parcel of a field, where he had spread his tent, at the hand of the children of Hamor, Shechem's father, for an hundred pieces of money" *(Gen. 33:18, 19)*. The word "Sychar" in John 4:6 signifies *purchased*. What a well-chosen and suited place for Christ to speak to that woman of the *"gift* of God"! But let it never be forgotten that this "gift" costs *us* nothing, because it cost *Him* everything.

Second, the "parcel of ground" in which was this well, was afterwards taken by

Joseph with *"sword* and *bow"*: "And Israel said unto Joseph, Behold, I die: but God shall be with you, and bring you again unto the land of your fathers. Moreover I have *given* to thee one portion above thy brethren, which I took out of the hand of the Amorite with *my sword* and with my bow" *(Gen. 48:21,22)*.—that this is the same "parcel of ground" referred to in Gen. 33 is clear from John 4:5. The reference in Gen. 48 must be to a later date than what is in view in Gen. 33. The Amorites were seeking to rob Jacob of his well, and therefore an appeal to arms was necessary. This, we believe, foreshadowed the present interval, during which the Holy Spirit (while Satan is yet the "Prince of this world" and ever seeks to oppose and keep God's Jacobs away from the "well") is bringing salvation to souls by means of the "sword" *(Heb. 4:12)*.

Third, this portion purchased by Jacob, and later secured by means of the "sword and bow" was *given to Joseph (see Gen. 48: 21,22)*. This became a part of Joseph's "birthright", for said Jacob "I have given to thee the one portion *above* thy brethren". But this ought to have been to Reuben, Jacob's "firstborn", yet through his fall into grievous sin it was transferred to Joseph *(see 1 Chron. 5:1)*. How marvelously accurate the type! Christ the Second Man takes the inheritance which the first man forfeited and lost through sin! Putting these three together, we have: the "well" purchased, the "well" possessed, the "well" enjoyed.

And here we must stop. In our next article we shall, D. V., consider carefully each sentence in vv. 7-11. Let the student ponder prayerfully:—

1. What are we to learn from the fact that the Saviour was the first to speak? v. 7.
2. Why did He begin by asking her for a drink? v. 7.
3. Was it merely a drink of water He had in mind? If not, what was it?
4. What is the force and significance of the parenthetical statement of v. 8?
5. What does the woman's answer *(v. 9)* go to prove?
6. What was the "gift of God"? v. 10.
7. Why does Christ liken salvation to "living *water*"? Enumerate the different thoughts suggested by this figure.—*Arthur W. Pink.*

THE BELIEVER AND LAW

or

The Bearings of the New Creation

Few subjects are to the saints of God more interesting or more weighty than the new creation; but we may also add that few are less generally understood. We all know that "God said, Let us make man in Our image, after Our likeness;" and we read, "So God created man in His own image, in the image of God created He him" *(Gen. 1:26,27)*. We all accept that in the exercise of creatorial rights God was entitled to put the man He had created (an intelligent being, able to know and do His will) under any conditions He saw fit to impose. Indeed, we may go further, and say that in the very nature of things the relations of an intelligent creature to His Creator require that he should receive and observe a revelation of His will. Thus we find that the Lord God had no sooner placed His creature in the Garden He had planted for him than He *"commanded* the man". He was entitled to man's obedience, for he was His handiwork; to his confidence, for He had done him nothing but good; and to his dependence, for He was not only the source of his being, but his Sustainer and his Supplier through evening shade and morning sheen. Alas, how soon he fell! And how deep his fall! We do not dwell on the dismal story. "Where art thou?" and "What is this that thou hast done?" tell their own tale more impressively than any human language, and indicate conclusively that obedience, confidence and dependence, the vested rights of God in His creature, had been flagitiously denied Him. That which man owed to God, the true debt of his nature, he failed to pay, and in consequence brought its righteously ordained but terrible penalty upon himself and his prospective race. The righteousness of God demanded the imposition of a penalty, and no less did the holiness of God require that its rigorousness should mark His eternal abhorrence of sin. The Divine commentary upon this is, "By one man sin entered into the world, and death by sin; and so death passed upon all men, for that all have sinned" *(Rom. 5:12)*.

To that Adamic creation we all belong naturally and physically. Were I an angel, I should belong to the angelic creation, another and earlier order of intelligent existences, though equally with us creatures, and equally under creature obligations. But I am a man, and thus belong to the human family, the material creation; and that which, as we have seen, pertains to the creature as such pertains to me, because I am a creature. Unless God could cease to be Creator, He could not cease to have creatorial rights or claims; and unless I could cease to be His creature, I could not cease to owe Him creatorial obligations; He is our "faithful Creator" *(1 Pet. 4:19)*.

But it may be asked, (1) Is there not for us a change of relationship? (2) Are not our old creation debts all gone in the Cross? (3) Are not the things of the old creation passed away and replaced by a new creation? (4) Have we not died out of all that we have referred to, our old man being crucified with Christ? (5) Are we not redeemed from the curse of the law, being dead to it by the body of Christ?

Such questions, deeply interesting as they are, indicate no small degree of confusion in the inquirer's mind. A sound nomenclature is in these things of the first importance. Unless penalty be distinguished from debt, person from nature, that which is physical from that which is spiritual, the old man from the so-called old creation, and creature-obligations from the demands of the Mosaic law, no clear and correct conclusions are possible.

Now let us see, (1) What "change of relationship" is possible between a creature and his Creator as such. My son may become my servant or master; but he can never cease to be my son. New and added relations there may be, and there are, between God and us; but those which He has formed are as eternal as Himself. Sin never changed the fact of man's creatureship, though it constituted him a sinner; grace has not changed it, though it has made him a son of God; and neither will glory for ever and for ever. Adam innocent, Adam a sinner, Adam a believer, Adam in glory by-and-by, in no one of these conditions more than in another was, and is, and will be a human being, intelligent, and therefore responsible, under, and never from under creature-obligations, whether in a state of probation in Eden, a state of failure in the world, or in the perfected state in the Father's house, when "spirit and soul and body" *(1 Thess. 5:23)* will be glorified with Christ. Equally so is a sinner alive in this scene under these obligations; and should he go down to perdition will never drown them in the lake of fire, though he will then be where their breach is as irremediable as their validity is irrevocable.

(2) The obligations referred to, constituting our original indebtedness to God, belong to our creatureship, not to our sinnership, if we may use the word. Thus while the penalty of every default, in other words, the sins we have committed, has been borne by Christ, the Divinely-provided Substitute, the ever-existing responsibility we are under as creatures remains untouched, being uninvalidated by the work of the Cross.

(3) Scripture never speaks of the "old creation", or of old debts, or old indebtedness, as some do, for the palpable reason that the creation referred to, and the obligations attaching to us therein, are never obsolete, nor ever will be.

The new creation is entirely a spiritual creation, and is only *in Christ,* who is "the Beginning of the creation of God" *(Rev. 3:14).* Hence it is an entire mistake to regard it as having come in successively to take the place of the physical or natural creation. That which is moral does not supplant or replace that which is material. It is an essentially new character and Divine order of blessing superadded to what went before, which latter God will yet clear of its ruin, and of which we shall be witnesses for eternity. So far from the natural creation being set aside, I could not possibly be a new creation unless I were generically of the Adamic; for it is us from such, and not from angels, is formed a new creation, essentially heavenly and constituted for heaven, having Christ, its glorified Head already there, is over all, God blessed forever! The eternal state will consist of a new heaven and a new earth, when the tabernacle of God will be with men, and He will dwell with them and be their God!

(4) That we have died in the death of Christ is unquestionable truth to faith; but let us not be misled. This is never predicated of us as creatures, but as men in the flesh; that is, as sinners under broken responsibilities. In His death we have died, and in His resurrection are risen. Our old man is crucified with Christ; its history is thus

forever closed in the Cross; but the person, the living sentient being, the accountable creature, continues, being born again, and a new creation in Christ, having then a new order of responsibilities super-imposed and connected with the former, which have now new motives, and give a higher character.

(5) The curse of the law is not at all a question of creature-obligations as such. Five and twenty centuries rolled by (during which those obligations were in full force, however unfulfilled) ere the law and its condemnation came in; then only to one people of all the nations of the earth, and to them only because they in their self-sufficiency entered into a covenant of works. Says the apostle, "It was *added* because of transgressions" (Gal. 3:19).

Let us recapitulate, then, the conclusions we submit to the reader for his prayerful consideration:

I. Man as a creature owes to God obedience, confidence and dependence. So long as I am a creature, I am under this inherent obligation; it is my debt to God. I have not ceased, and shall never cease to be, a creature; therefore I shall never cease to owe this debt.

II. Man as born into the world is also a sinner as to his nature, and every default of his debt to God is a committed sin, accordingly, by nature and by practice we are sinners and sinful.

III. But Christ became the Divine Substitute of them that believe, as such bore the penalty of our sins, which penalty we had incurred by default of our obligations to God. In His death He also ended for faith our history (not as creatures, but) as men in the flesh—sinners under judgment. Through grace we as believers have in consequence received eternal forgiveness of our sins. We also reckon that in His death we died, and thus our old man was crucified; moreover, we are *in* Christ a new creation, essentially heavenly.

We have here three distinct things—man as a creature, man as a sinner, and man as a believer. To the first belong characteristically the creature responsibilities; to the second belongs the penalty for his sins; to the third belong remission of sins and new creation.

The first did not (looked at alone) call for Christ's death, and Christ's death has nothing necessarily to say to it. The second brought in the work of Christ in atonement, in whose death we are accounted to have died, and have thus put off the old man, which is crucified with Him, that the body of sin might be destroyed. The third is that into which I am brought as the result of the resurrection of Christ, and which is so wonderful in its character that the apostle predicates of *our bodies* that even now they are members of Christ and temples of the Holy Ghost.

Thus two of these things, the first and third, remain to me. (1) That I am as I have been from birth, and ever shall be, a creature owing to God obedience, confidence and dependence; my original obligation maintained in its immutable validity, and which indissolubly attaches to me in common with every intelligent creature, be he man or angel, and in whatever condition of existence. (2) That new and distinct order of purely spiritual blessedness which is only in Christ (involving relationship to the Father as a son, union with Christ by the Holy Ghost given, and eternal glory), which I came into for eternity by the death and resurrection of Christ, in whom I have died and am risen. But the same being in its very essence a heavenly thing, it awaits its blissful consummation when this corruptible shall put on incorruption, and this mortal shall put on immortality; when the natural body shall be changed into a spiritual body, being fashioned like unto the glorified body of the Lord Jesus Christ, who is Himself the beginning of the creation of God!

In no respect whatever are these two things incompatible with each other, nor do the obligations and responsibilities pertaining to the second (incomparably higher though they be in character) set aside or weaken those which are inherent in the first; but entwined together they subsist in perfect harmony, in Divinely established order, and in eternal duration. Even amid the wondrous blessedness of the Father's house, where the unsullied joy is as perpetual as profound, in the dignity and the grace of a seat in the throne of Christ as being of His body, though enraptured in the ineffable delight and ecstatic bliss of His own presence (heaven's crowning joy to my soul), throughout all eternity shall I love to *obey* Him who formed me by the skill of His hand, shall love to *confide* in Him who won me with the love of His heart, and shall love to *depend* upon Him who Divinely upholds me for His own glory for ever and ever!—*William Reid.*

Adopted from the Bible Scholar, March 1901.

RIPE FOR HEAVEN

Many of the children of God, who ought to be rejoicing in the liberty of the Gospel, are enthralled in some form of legal bondage. Comparatively few of these are exulting in a finished salvation, with the self-abasing, but soul-satisfying consciousness that "we are complete in Him in whom dwelleth all the fulness of the Godhead bodily." If the only consequences of this were the over-clouding of their joy and the disturbance of their peace, the evil would be worthy of every effort to correct it. How much more when, in addition to this, it dishonors their Lord, while it cramps all their energies, obscures their graces, and leaves their position in the world uncertain both to themselves and others.

One of the most subtle forms of the evil may be thus stated, even when there is a distinct knowledge of the grounds on which God justifies the ungodly, after the soul has tasted the blessedness of "the man whose transgression is forgiven, whose sin is covered," and has rejoiced in hope of the glory of God, there is an impression that much remains to be done before the soul is, to use a common expression, "ripe for heaven". The impression seems to be that after his justification, the believer must undergo a process of sanctification, and that for this reason he is left for a time amid the trials and conflicts of a hostile world. The wide prevalence of this notion appears in public teaching and in the mutual exhortations of Christians, and, if possible, more distinctly in their prayers; for they may very often be heard pleading that they may be made meet, but are rarely heard giving thanks to the Father, who *hath* made us meet to be partakers of the inheritance of the saints in light.

One might suppose that those who are toiling on under this impression, would be staggered by their experience and observation. Their progress must at the best be unsatisfactory. They cannot know when the process is completed. They see others, in whose Christian character they have the fullest confidence, cut off apparently in very various stages of the process; and if the completion of it be what men style "perfect sanctification", in how few cases, so far as we can judge, is any such state of preparation for glory attained? On their death-beds, the most eminent saints appear most humbled in view of their own attainments, most dissatisfied with all that they are in themselves. *There,* self is most completely renounced, and their parting triumph is not in what they are, but in what Christ is. Besides, how can we with confidence say to a man—to a dying man—"Believe on the Lord Jesus Christ and thou shalt be saved," when we do not know if his life may be prolonged beyond the instant of believing? "Justification", they say, "is an act completed at once, but sanctification is a progressive work;" and there can be no objection to the expression in speaking of our growth in holiness, and the manifestation of it in this life. But if this be said with reference to our preparation for glory, and if such a preparation be the grand object of the believer's life in the flesh, then it is difficult to know how Paul could say, "To me to live is Christ, and to die is gain. But, if I live in the flesh, this is the fruit of my labor; yet what I shall choose I wot not; for I am in a straight betwixt two; having a desire to depart and be with Christ, which is far better; nevertheless to abide in the flesh is more needful for you. And, having this confidence, I know that I shall abide and continue with you all, for your furtherance and joy of faith." Especially difficult is it to know how Paul could use such language when in a subsequent portion of the same epistle he says, "Not as though I had already attained, either were already perfect." How, in short, could believers either have a desire to depart, or long for the coming of the Lord, while the very fact that they are in the body was the proof that the process was not completed which should fit them for His coming? A person who had spent a lifetime in reaching a boasted consciousness of perfect sanctification, upon a death-bed, was betrayed into a fit of ungoverned anger. She found the labor of so many years frustrated in a moment, and would have died in despair had not the Spirit of God in her extremity, brought home this truth to her heart, "Jesus Christ is of God made unto us wisdom and righteousness, and sanctification and redemption."

The confusion and vagueness of prevailing views on this subject, which is of unspeakable moment to us, warrant us in inviting a patient consideration of a passage in the epistle to the Colossians, which seems to give an unambiguous answer to all inquiries regarding the believer's preparation for glory. "Giving thanks unto the Father who hath made us meet to be partakers of the inheritance of the saints in light" *(Col. 1:12)*. The apostle tells these "saints and faithful brethren at Colosse," of his unceasing prayers for them; and the matter of his prayers shows that he was very far from regarding them as perfect either in knowledge or in grace, yet he does not pray that they may be made meet for the inheritance, but speaks of himself and them as already "made meet for the inheritance of the saints in light." From the manner in which this occasion of thanksgiving is introduced, it appears that Paul considered, or rather the Holy Spirit teaches, that their gratitude for such meetness was intimately connected with their advancement in grace, knowledge and spiritual fertility. For he does not inform them that *he* gave thanks for them on this behalf, but that he does not cease to pray that *they* might walk worthy of the Lord unto all pleasing—giving thanks to the Father for what He had actually accomplished in them. At any rate, whether it be regarded as a statement of Paul's thanksgiving, or of Paul's prayer that their gratitude might be awakened, this much is clear, that the occasion of thanksgiving is that the Father had actually made Paul and the saints at Colosse meet to be partakers of the inheritance of the saints in light. We may, therefore, at once proceed to inquire: In what does our meetness to be partakers of that inheritance consist? and then we shall see how it is an occasion of gratitude to believers that such meetness is actually bestowed upon them, and not an occasion of prayerful solicitude that they may yet attain it.

But it will clear our way to the consideration of these questions, if we inquire first of all, what is the inheritance spoken of? An inheritance is a possession or dignity which we do not acquire by our labor or merits, nor purchase with money, but to which we lawfully succeed in virtue of our relationship to another. Primarily, it is that to which a child succeeds in virtue of his relationship to his father, as a son inherits the estate of his father, or as the son of a king inherits the crown. In this case the inheritance becomes ours in virtue of our being sons of God. So Peter speaks of the God and Father of our Lord Jesus Christ having begotten us again unto a lively hope, to an inheritance that is incorruptible, undefiled, and that fadeth not away. So Paul speaks of the Spirit witnessing with our spirits that we are the sons of God— and then he argues, "if sons, then heirs, heirs of God and joint-heirs with Christ."

When we inquire more distinctly, what is this inheritance of the sons of God? the next verse explains it as the kingdom of God's dear Son; or, more accurately, "of the Son of His love." Those who are joint-heirs with Christ, must share His kingdom. "He hath made us kings and priests unto God," and the inheritance of kings is a crown, a throne, a kingdom. The blessedness which lies before us is not merely to be subjects of the King of kings but to sit with Him on His throne, to reign with Him for ever and ever. Such is the dignity of our inheritance, and we cannot doubt its glory and blessedness. As to its extent, we are joint heirs with Him whom God hath appointed heir of *all things*. Our destiny is bound up with His. The inheritance of the saints in light must be holy. The term "in light" describes, not the saints, though they are children of light, but the inheritance, which thus stands in contrast with the empire of darkness from which they are delivered; and it describes, not only the glory with which it is radiant, but the effulgence of knowledge, truth, purity, and joy, in which it lies, bathed in a perpetual sunshine of the Divine presence.

We shall now find a shorter and clearer answer to the question, What constitutes meetness for the inheritance of the saints in light?

Nothing can be more plain than that fallen man, in his natural state, cannot enjoy it. A child of wrath cannot, as such, be a partaker of the inheritance of the children of God. The rejecter of Christ cannot be a joint heir with Christ. A mind at enmity with God can have no relish for the joys of the inheritance, and no sympathy with the saints. The presence of impurity would taint its holiness; the presence of darkness would throw a shadow athwart the kingdom of light, vitiating its whole character. Only think of a man with the wrath of God abiding on him, sitting with Christ on His throne! think of the horror of a guilty soul in the unclouded sunshine of the Divine presence, where its hideousness would stand revealed in the contrast of spotless holiness! so that, as one expresses it, "he would plunge for relief into the gloom of hell." But when we know what the inheritance is, no argument is needed to enforce the Lord's declaration, "Except a man be born again he cannot see the kingdom of God." Now the question is, What is necessary to make a fallen, guilty man meet to be a partaker of the inheritance of the saints in light?

If we were to answer, first of all, the forgiveness of sins, it might be said that the forgiveness of sins is not so much meetness for the inheritance, as the removal of a disqualification. Yet there can be no question that guilt is a disqualification that must be removed, and it will be seen that, when it is removed in the manner provided in the gracious purpose of God, meetness for the inheritance necessarily follows. Nothing could be more monstrous than to suppose a guilty and condemned being enjoying eternal life in spite of God; or standing in the highest place of favor, and at the same time, the wrath of God abiding on him. So the Gospel meets the sinner, first of all, with a proclamation of forgiveness. But then, it is forgiveness of such a character, and provided in such a way, that it is the first link of a chain of blessings which cannot possibly be dissevered, the whole of which is *salvation*. The forgiveness of the Gospel is not a mere act of clemency which remits the penalty of sin, as might be supposed if we were to take our idea of God's forgiveness of the sinner, from man's forgiveness of his offending fellow, when he either forgoes his revenge or sets aside the sentence of justice. There is, indeed, love passing knowledge, there are Divine riches of mercy in the forgiveness of sins by God, but there is justice also gloriously manifested and truth completely vindicated in the act. God displays the riches of His mercy, not in forgoing vengeance or setting aside the claims of justice, but in setting forth His Son to be a propitiation through faith in His blood, in laying our sins upon Him, and meeting every claim against the sinner. But when we consider how and by whom all this is accomplished, it must be evident that the love displayed in it, and the glory that redounds to God, are infinitely greater in this than in any other sphere of the Divine operation. The obedience of Christ for guilty man, is of an infinitely more exalted character than any obedience of unfallen man could have been. There is not only a removal of every obstruction, but there is a ground laid for the communication of blessing which may manifest the grace and attest the faithfulness and righteousness of God.

The results of this interposition of Divine mercy must evidently prove as beneficial to those who are the objects of it as it is honoring to Him by whom it has been made. So that it by no means tells the whole truth about this redemption, even the forgiveness of sins, to say that we are reinstated in the place from which man fell. The innocence of man would have been something infinitely inferior to the righteousness of God. Now "He hath made Him to be sin for us who knew no sin, that we might be made the *righteousness* of God in Him" *(2 Cor. 5:21)*. The rank, favor, or position before God, which would have been the just acknowledgment or reward of the most perfect creature righteousness, must be infinitely beneath that of the believer in Christ. No one can suppose that Adam, if he had never fallen, could have been exalted to the throne on which Christ shall sit, or attain the glory with which He is now crowned. But it is evident that redemption, accomplished through the blood of Christ, the forgiveness of sin, procured as we have seen it is, means, not merely deliverance from the curse and remission of the guilt of sin, placing us in the position we would have occupied if we had never sinned at all; but implies our exaltation to the place of favor and love which He who is our righteousness occupies. It is not merely that the thunder is silenced, but the light of God's countenance shines forth. It is not merely that hell has lost its prey, but that we have, in Christ, a perfect and indefeasible title to the inheritance of the saints in light.

But an inheritance implies sonship. And this leads us to another view of our standing in Christ. It is not necessary to speak at length, here, of the condition of fallen man, or of the family to which he belongs; but, in speaking of God's gracious design concerning those who were lost and undone by sin, an apostle exclaims, "Behold what manner of love the Father hath bestowed upon us, that we should be called the sons of God" (1 John 3:1). The obstruction to our being called "sons of God" was removed, as we have seen, by the only-begotten and well-beloved Son of God. "God gave His Son to be the propitiation for our sins." But you will observe, that after He had died for our sins, had been forsaken by the Father, and was made a curse for us, there is a peculiar sense in which He was acknowledged to be the Son of God; for it is to His resurrection from the dead that the acknowledgment in the second Psalm is applied, "Thou art My Son, *this day* have I begotten Thee." So Paul says, He was "declared to be the Son of God with power, according to the spirit of holiness, by the resurrection from the dead." Not that He then became the Son of God; but, in a peculiar relation to us, after all that had taken place, He was then declared or proved to be the Son of God. And then, as in Him we have redemption, even the forgiveness of sins, so in Him we are sons of God. After His resurrection, and not before it, He recognizes the relationship as common to Him and His people:—"Go, tell My brethren," He says, "that I ascend to My Father, and to your Father; and to My God and your God" (John 20:17). Up to this point, He is spoken of as the "Only begotten Son," for it may be seen in the Scriptures that wherever this designation is employed, it is with reference to what precedes His resurrection from the dead. But from this point, He is the first-born among many brethren, the elder brother of the many sons whom He is bringing to glory. All that He had endured for us was in order that we might receive the adoption of sons. "Wherefore", says the apostle, "thou art no more a servant but a son; and if a son, then an heir of God through Christ." The believer's title to the inheritance is complete in Christ, —"For ye are all the children of God by faith in Christ Jesus." This is not a prospective but a present distinction of every believer; "Now are we the sons of God." His title can never be defeated or even disputed; and yet it seems, according to the prevailing doctrine, that all this may be true of a man, and yet he is not made meet for the inheritance; he must pass through a certain course of training and discipline; there is a process of sanctification before he is qualified to be a partaker of the inheritance. We could easily suppose such a thing in human relations as a man, having a claim to a position, nay, actually occupying a position for which he is not qualified; but how can we suppose such an anomaly in the express arrangement of God, and especially in His gracious undertaking of human salvation. This much, however, is settled, and in this believers may confidently exult, that the inheritance is theirs; *that* cannot be questioned, unless the righteousness of God, which is the basis of their claim, be disputed; unless the title of Christ, in whom they are made the sons of God, is disputed. And this much being settled, they need not fear to have their qualification for the inheritance investigated.

In what, beyond their title to the inheritance, does meetness for it consist? Evidently they must be saints if they obtain the inheritance of saints; but *that* they are as believers, and as soon as they believe, they are sanctified by that very blood in which they have the forgiveness of sins. Evidently, also, they must be children of *light* who obtain the inheritance in light; but *that* also they are, by the very fact that they are believers: "Ye are all the children of light, and of the day: we are not of the night nor of darkness." But these may appear very vague and general statements of their qualifications, and we may willingly meet the most minute investigation. It is further evident, that in order to the enjoyment of an inheritance which is incorruptible, undefiled, and that fadeth not away,—an everlasting kingdom, a crown of unfading glory,—we must have eternal life; but *that* also the believer has in the very act of believing; for we are assured that "he that believeth on the Son of God hath everlasting life." This, in fact, is the very record which God gave of His Son, "that God hath given unto us eternal life, and this life is in His Son;" so that "he that hath the Son, hath life." But that new life which the believer has in Christ is not a restoration of the life we had lost; it is nothing less than the life of Christ. "He is our life," as truly as our righteousness,—the infinite fountain of life from which every stream is filled. But is its perpetuity its only characteristic in which we can now rejoice? Is it, as yet, a feeble spark which must be fanned into a flame;

an infantile life, which must be cherished and nursed to maturity? There is, indeed, a body of sin and death through which its presence is now manifested, and the manifestation of it may be feeble, infantile, and obscure, like the sunbeam making its way through an opaque medium; the sunbeam itself is not dim, though it may be dimmed in its shining; and the removal of the opaque body would at once make it manifest in its perfection. So, also, of this everlasting life which the believer has. If *He* is our life, there can be no defect in the life itself, though its manifestation may be obstructed by a mortal body. It is, in itself, as perfect as it can ever be, and he who hath life in the Son of God, is made meet to be a partaker of an inheritance which is its proper sphere.

We have already seen that only the sons of God can obtain the inheritance, and we have seen that believers are all the sons of God through faith in Christ Jesus. Can it be supposed that they are sons in name, but not in nature? Then it might be supposed that a man had a claim to the inheritance without meetness for it; but, then, that would be to suppose that sonship was a mockery, and not a reality. This is very far from being the teaching of the Word of God; for *there* we are taught that we become sons of God by being born again. This does not mean a gradual improvement or purification of the old nature, but the communication of a new nature. It is styled a "new creation." The Almighty agent of it is the Spirit of God, the means employed in it is the Word of God, which is His testimony of Christ, and we thus come to the same point as before—faith in Christ; for we are taught "to as many as received Him, to them gave He power to become sons of God, even to them that believe on His name; which were born, not of blood, nor of the will of the flesh, nor of the will of man, but of God." They are born of God—born of the Spirit. Now, does any man suppose that that which is born of God requires to be gradually purified or perfected? Will any man speak of sanctification as a progressive work in this new man, this son of God? It is indeed true, that the old nature remains what it ever was, and opposes all the desires, tendencies, and affections of the new nature; for "that which is born of the flesh is flesh," neither more nor less; and so the believer, as long as he is in the flesh, is called upon, "through the Spirit, to mortify the deeds of the body." But it is none the less true, that "that which is born of the Spirit is spirit." The new life is of the same nature as its source. The child partakes of the nature of his Father. Many a weary conflict, indeed, must the Spirit maintain against the flesh; and many an humbling occasion of confession may the Christian have, who finds in his experience that nature is nature still. But that which is born of the Spirit is spirit also, unaffected and uncontaminated by the vileness in the midst of which it exists, and which it seeks continually to renounce and subdue. "Whosoever is born of God doth not commit sin. He cannot sin, because he is born of God." The new nature is not only in itself perfect, so that no motion of sin can proceed from it; but it cannot be defiled from without. It is true, that we still bear outwardly the image of the earthy. The body is dead, because of sin; but the Spirit is life because of righteousness. We are now the sons of God, though it doth not appear what we shall be. The *real*, with the believer, is not the *apparent;* but it is not the less real. So, by the very fact that, as soon as we have, in Christ, a title to the inheritance, we are also, as sons, made meet for the inheritance. The real will, at last, be the apparent: there will be a manifestation of the sons of God; we shall bear the image of the heavenly; when He "shall appear, we shall be like Him, for we shall see Him as He is."

Yes, we are now sons of God by faith in Christ Jesus, and the spirit of adoption is the earnest of the inheritance. We are one with Christ, and joint-heirs with Him. The inheritance is His kingdom; and though it is now true that He has gone to receive a kingdom and to return, it is true *now* that He is a King; all the usurpations of Satan can not invalidate His title. But if we are one with Him, then it is true of believers that they are made kings and priests unto God, though they do not now reign, nor enjoy the inheritance. When the glorious destiny of the saints is considered, it cannot, for a moment be supposed that any conceivable improvement of nature could qualify them for occupying the exalted place in which they shall be Christ's partners. Adam, in the perfection of his nature, would no more have been qualified for that exalted destiny, than he could, by any perfection of his own obedience, have deserved it. And, in looking forward to that destiny of glory, we can only expect to fill it as we receive from Christ's fulness. The soul would shrink from that exceeding and eternal weight of glory which angels could not sustain, were it not that our completeness is in Christ, "who, of God, is made unto us wisdom, and righteousness, and sanctification, and redemption." But surely He who has made Him all this to us, hath, by the very fact, made us meet to be partakers of the inheritance of the saints in light. We do not undervalue the importance of our present growth in knowledge and in grace, when we say that no attainment of ours can qualify us, any more than it can entitle us to reign with Him. No, as it is *His* joy and glory we shall share, *His* throne on which we shall sit, and with *Him* we shall reign, so it is in *His* holiness we shall be arrayed, and in *His* wisdom and *His* strength we shall fill our places in the administration of *His* kingdom. But for the present, knowing all this, and rejoicing in all this, we should seek to "walk worthy of the Lord unto all pleasing, being fruitful in every good work, and increasing in the knowledge of God; strengthened with all might, according to His glorious power, and unto all patience and longsuffering with joyfulness."—*From "Waymarks in the Wilderness" edited by James Inglis.*

(Continued from front page.)

4. HE PLEADS THE SOURCE OF HIS CONFIDENCE.

"Rejoice the soul of Thy servant, FOR *unto Thee,* O Lord, do I lift up my soul" *(v. 4).* We might paraphrase it thus: "Unto Thee, O Lord, do I lift up my soul, *therefore* rejoice the soul of Thy servant". The force of this can best be gathered by pointing a contrast. The worldling rejoices when his material possessions increase; and when they diminish and decay he is saddened and depressed, for *they* are the only source of *his* happiness. But the believer has a different Source of joy. He turns away from everything down here and looks off unto the Lord. Therefore, he pleads, 'disappoint me not'—"rejoice the soul of Thy servant."

5. HE PLEADS THE LORD'S GOODNESS.

"FOR Thou, Lord, *art good,* and ready to forgive; and plenteous in mercy unto all them that call upon Thee. Give ear, O Lord, unto my prayer; and attend to the voice of my supplications" *(vv. 5,6).* Here the reason precedes the petition. Assured of God's goodness and mercy he is emboldened to ask Him to attend to the voice of his supplications. This is something of which we ever need to remind ourselves. What a God is ours! Full of goodness, the sum of all excellency, abounding in mercy to His unworthy creatures. Meditate much on God's perfections and it will encourage thee to seek His face and ask blessings at His bounteous hand.

6. HE PLEADS GOD'S GREATNESS.

"In the day of my trouble I will call upon Thee: for Thou wilt answer me . . . FOR *Thou art great,* and doest wondrous things; Thou art God alone" *(vv. 7, 10).* Nothing is too hard for the Lord. Infinite power and infinite wisdom are His; and matchless grace and fathomless love direct them. Because God is "great" He doeth "wondrous things". The remembrance of this is a source of unfailing confidence to the child of God. Take a concordance, dear reader, and look up the passages in the New Testament where we are told "He is able", and your faith will be strengthened.

7. HE PLEADS GOD'S PREVIOUS KINDNESS TO HIM.

"Show me a token for good, that they which hate me may see it, and be ashamed: BECAUSE Thou, Lord, *hast* holpen me, and comforted me." This is the Psalmist's final plea. He encourages himself by recalling how God had helped and comforted him in the past. Let us remember that the Lord is *the same* yesterday and today and forever. The apprehension of this will soothe the troubled breast. The One who heard thy cry as a perishing sinner will surely heed the call of His believing child. The One who has faithfully supplied thine every need all these years will not forsake thee now. This was how the apostle Paul encouraged himself: "Who delivered us from so great a death, and doth deliver: in whom we trust *that He will yet* deliver us" *(2 Cor. 1:10).*

Arthur W. Pink.

GLEANINGS IN GENESIS
By Arthur W. Pink

We take pleasure in announcing that the second and last volume of this important work is now off the press. It contains twenty-two expositions, seven of which are devoted to Joseph as a type of Christ, in which the author shows there are no less than one hundred points of comparison between them. The price of this book is **$1.00 postpaid.**

VOL. I   DECEMBER, 1922   NO. 12

STUDIES in the SCRIPTURES

"Search the Scriptures" John 5:39.

A PERIODICAL (MONTHLY "IF THE LORD WILL")
DEVOTED TO BIBLE STUDIES and EXPOSITIONS

Associate Editors and Publishers, I. C. HERENDEEN and ARTHUR W. PINK,
Swengel, Pa.

Price: 10 cents per copy; $1.00 per year. Foreign $1.00 per year.

TO OUR SCRIPTURE STUDY FAMILY—

The present issue completes the first year of this publication. We have every cause to be unfeignedly thankful to our ever-faithful God for His abundant mercies. He has brought us into touch with many of His people whom we have never seen in the flesh. He has given us numerous evidences that this magazine has brought blessing to its readers. He has fully supplied our every need. For all of which we are filled with gratitude and praise.

As we look forward to the next year we contemplate no radical changes. Our chief aim will be to stir up the people of God to "search the Scriptures" prayerfully, diligently, and systematically. We shall endeavor to give encouragement and help to this end. As far as possible we shall avoid that which is sectarian and controversial, seeking to be constructive rather than destructive. The Lord willing, our studies in John's Gospel and our articles on the Antichrist will be continued, except that we may substitute a Gospel address now and again in place of an Antichrist article in every issue.

In the January number we shall commence a series of verse by verse expositions of First Peter by Dr. John Brown: these will be found, we believe, most illuminating and edifying. In addition, there will be occasional topical studies on important subjects. We ask the reader's most careful attention to the one in the present issue —"The Saint and the Law" by Andrew Bonar, of blessed memory.

ALL SUBSCRIPTIONS are dated from January. Therefore it is NOW TIME to renew if you wish the 1923 issues sent to you. The postal laws do not permit us to continue subscriptions after same have expired. Will you then please attend to YOUR RENEWAL PROMPTLY. If you do not want to miss any numbers send in your renewal AT ONCE. And if *you* have found *Studies in the Scriptures* a blessing to your soul will you not send in *an extra subscription* with your own?

We are anxious to increase our circulation. As soon as the number of subscriptions justifies the additional expense (a matter of three hundred dollars) we shall *increase the size* of the type, using 28 instead of 24 pages for the same amount of material, and thus making it easier for elderly people to read. This will require three hundred additional subscriptions! Join us in prayer about this.

Wishing all our friends and readers the compliments of the season, we remain,

Yours by grace,
Arthur W. Pink
I. C. Herendeen

STUDIES IN THE SCRIPTURES

Subscription Price: $1.00 per year to any address in the world. Single copies 10 cents.

Change of Address: Please notify us promptly of any change of address, and be certain to give both old and new addresses.

Non-Subscribers receiving this Magazine regularly will understand their subscription has been entered by a friend.

Copies lost in the mail duplicated on request.

All new subscriptions will be dated back to January, 1922.

Entered as second-class matter December 15th, 1921 at the post office at Swengel, Pa., under Act of March 3rd, 1879.

CONTENTS

Mary, the Mother of Jesus	254
John's Gospel (John 4:6-10)	259
A Christmas Message	267
The Saint and the Law	268
The State of the Natural Man	275
The First Christmas Carol	276

MARY, THE MOTHER OF JESUS

"Fear not Mary: for thou hast found favor with God" *(Luke 1:30).*

What is our conception of the person and character of the mother of our Lord Jesus Christ? Surely this question is something more than the inquiry of idle curiosity. Is it not a question of practical importance? The mother of Jesus could not have been commonplace. The most highly favored of all Adam's race could have been no ordinary woman. She must have been a noble character, and a reverent study of her cannot fail to be both instructive and profitable.

While it is sadly true that the Roman Catholics have unduly and unwarrantably exalted her; while it is true that they have ascribed to her a glory which belongs alone to her blessed Son, and have rendered to her a worship which Holy Scripture nowhere authorizes; yet it is also true that Protestants have gone to the opposite extreme. We have failed to give her memory that veneration and esteem which it merits; we have grossly neglected the study of the character of what was probably the holiest woman who ever trode this earth. We are, I believe, paying the price of the Romish perversion. While it is true that they have made too much of her, we Protestants have made too little of her. Nothing is said of her in our theological text-books, ministers in the pulpit are nearly all of them silent upon the subject, while Christians in general scarcely ever mention her name. We ought not to ignore the mother of our Saviour—the one whom Scripture declares "found favor with God"—one who is twice hailed as "blessed among women."

On the other hand we must carefully guard against the danger of unduly exalting her to a position for which she has no title. Mary is not the Madonna. She is no Queen of Heaven. She was only a woman. It is a striking fact of the Gospel narratives that, while we find our Saviour making frequent mention of His "Father," yet He is silent about His mother. So far as the sacred record goes, never once do we find Him uttering that name which is the sweetest of all to a mother's ear. Twice He addressed her as "Woman"— once at the marriage feast, and again while He hung upon the Cross. And though at first it seems strange that He should employ such a term, yet as we now look back over the centuries and trace the dark development of Mariolatry, we see an evidence of His omniscient foresight in refusing to use a word which would have in any wise lent countenance to such idolatry. We shall now note some of the outstanding characteristics in Mary's character.

1. OBSERVE HER BEAUTIFUL SUBMISSIVENESS. This is strikingly brought out in Luke 1:38, "And Mary said, Behold the handmaid of the Lord, *be it unto me according to Thy word.*" There is far more that is worthy of deep admiration in these words than at first sight appears. An angel from the Lord had just announced to her the fact of the miraculous conception, and a moment's reflection will show us that it was no light matter for Mary to become the mother of our Lord in this mysterious and unheard of way. As the late Bishop Ryle said in commenting upon these words, "It brought with it, no doubt, at a distant date, great honor; but it brought with it for the present no small danger to Mary's reputation, and no

small trial to Mary's faith." And yet in full view of this difficulty and danger, she willingly submitted to God's good pleasure. She freely acquiesced and received the honor thus laid upon her with all its attendant perils and inconveniences. "Be it unto me according to Thy word." What beautiful submissiveness! What holy resignation! Not my will, but Thine be done, is virtually what she said. O that Mary's spirit might be ours. Let us earnestly pray to God for His grace, so that in times of difficulty and adversity we, too, may say, "Be it unto me according to Thy word."

2. CONSIDER HER INTELLECTUAL POWER.

This may be gathered from the beautiful poem she has bequeathed us. "And Mary said, My soul doth magnify the Lord, and my spirit hath rejoiced in God my Saviour. For He hath regarded the low estate of His handmaiden: for, behold, from henceforth all generations shall call me blessed. For He that is mighty hath done to me great things, and holy is His name. And His mercy is on them that fear Him from generation to generation. He hath showed strength with His arm; He hath scattered the proud in the imagination of their hearts. He hath put down the mighty from their seats, and exalted them of low degree. He hath filled the hungry with good things, and the rich He hath sent empty away. He hath holpen His servant Israel, in remembrance of His mercy; as He spake to our fathers, to Abraham, and to his seed for ever" (Luke 1:46-55).

With what a mighty intellect must this woman have been endowed! What a sublime songstress and wondrous poetess she was! Have you ever considered this fact? What a sanctified mind she possessed! Think about the one who could produce such a beautiful lyric. Study the Magnificat this Christmas, and the more you study it, the more will you be ready to place Mary among the sweetest songstresses of history. Remember that she belonged to the poorer classes, and that books were very much dearer and rarer then than they are now. Probably the Old Testament was her only literary guide. O what a lesson for us! It was the Word of God which built up her intellect. It was from the pure rivers of Scripture that she filled her soul. What an example for you and me. She ennobled her mind, clarified her spiritual perceptions by pondering the Oracles of God. We, too, may have our understandings enlightened, our minds developed, our intellectual faculties cultivated by drawing from the same Source from which she derived her inspiration. The mightiest intellects of the ages have been those that were schooled in the Scriptures of Truth.

3. PONDER HER MARVELLOUS KNOWLEDGE OF THE SCRIPTURES.

One of the outstanding features of the earthly life of our Lord was His deep love for and reverence of the Scriptures. From whence did He derive His inspiration? The human answer is, from mother's example! A study of the Magnificat reveals the wonderful knowledge which Mary possessed of God's Word. In it she quotes from Genesis, Exodus, 1st Samuel, Job, Psalms, Isaiah, Jeremiah, Habakkuk and Malachi. What an acquaintance with God's Oracles she must have had! It is evident that the mind of the mother of Israel's Messiah was stored with Scripture, and so, when out of the abundance of the heart her mouth spoke, she gave vent to her feelings *in the language of Holy Writ*. Let us, too, so search and study, ruminate and meditate upon the contents of the Bible that the word of Christ may dwell in us richly.

Not only is Mary's knowledge of the Word evidenced by her ready quotation of it, but it is also apparent that she was acquainted with its historical portions, especially of God's dealings with His ancient people Israel. She speaks of Jehovah as One whose "mercy is on them that fear Him from generation to generation" —as One who "scattereth the proud in the imagination of their heart"—as One who "hath put down the mighty from their seats, and exalted them of low degree." She remembered how Israel's God had put down Pharaoh and the Canaanites, Sennacherib and Haman, Nebuchadnezzar and Belshazzar. She remembered how He had exalted Joseph and Moses, Samuel and David, Esther and Daniel. We, too, do well to examine the "footsteps of the flock." Such study throws light on God's methods of dealings with His people. For He is without variableness or shadow of turning. Israel's God is our God, and He is the same yesterday and today and forever. Such study will teach us what to expect, will check unwarrantable assumptions, and encourage us when cast down. Happy the man or woman whose mind is stored with such knowledge.

Note, also, what a firm grasp she had of *the promises* of God. She ends her song by declaring that Jehovah "hath holpen His servant Israel, *in remembrance* of His mercy, *as He spake to our fathers*, to Abraham and to his seed for ever." Those words show plainly that she remembered the promise of old which God gave to the father of all who believe—"In thee shall all the families of the earth be blessed," and she regarded the approaching birth of her Son as the fulfilment of His promise. It is of the deepest importance to our peace of mind that we emulate Mary in this respect. God's promises are the daily manna that we should feed upon as we journey through the wilderness. We are to walk by faith, and faith leans hard upon the promises.

Probably Mary was unequalled for her insight into God's Word. What an example she has left for every mother! The greatest and grandest thing which you mothers can do is to train and teach your children to reverence and love the Holy Bible, and you can best accomplish this by setting before them a pious and practical example.

4. Behold her beautiful Modesty.

"And Mary said, Behold the handmaid of the Lord" *(Luke 1:38)*. And again, "For He hath regarded the low estate of His handmaiden" *(Luke 1:48)*. What humility these words breathe! She does not call herself the Madonna, but is content to be the "handmaid of the Lord." She does not speak of her dignified position, and enthrone herself as an object for worship, but speaks of her "low estate." This is not ostentation, but meekness incarnate. Rightly has she been termed the "Moss-rose of Palestine." How her retiring quiet-heartedness rebukes many of her sisters to-day! Can we imagine anything more repulsive to her than the worship which the Roman Catholics offer her? One so humble, so meek and lowly is the Mother of Modesty rather than the Queen of Heaven. Her very lowliness is an unanswerable argument against the system of Mariolatry.

Once again, here is an example we do well to heed. Humbleness of mind is of great price in the sight of God, and a fundamental condition of growing in the knowledge of Divine Truth. Humility is the highest of all the Christian graces, and has ever characterized the most eminent saints. Let us seek to be lowly in our own eyes, and esteem others more highly than ourselves.

5. Mark her lively Thankfulness.

The Magnificat is really a hymn of praise, a song of thanksgiving. No words can express more aptly the believer's gratitude for the redeeming mercy of God. What lively thankfulness Mary here displays! "My soul doth magnify the Lord, and my spirit hath rejoiced in God my Saviour." She was not occupied with herself and the great honor conferred upon her, but instead, her heart was lifted up in gratitude to God. "For He that is mighty hath done to me great things" is no contradiction of this fact, but points back to the past. She reviews her blessings and recognises that every good and perfect gift cometh down from the Father of lights. We, too, do well to walk in Mary's steps in this matter, and seek to cultivate a thankful spirit. Gratitude and praise are the only rent which God asks for our enjoyment of His mercy. Thankfulness has been a prominent characteristic in God's most distinguished saints in every age. Let us rise from our beds every morning with the deep conviction that we are debtors, and that every day we enjoy infinitely more mercies than ever we deserve. To rejoice in God, to find all our springs in Him, to rise above our circumstances, to refuse to be cast down in soul, to magnify the Saviour, is what brings the greatest honor and glory to His name, and is what convinces the world that we drink from a spring of which they know not.

6. Study her admirable Reflectiveness.

"And when she heard him, she was troubled at his saying, and *cast in her mind* what manner of salutation this should be" *(Luke 1:29)*. Perhaps nothing is so characteristic of Mary as this quality of reflectiveness. How she ruminated, pondered, meditated. "But Mary kept all these things *and pondered them in her heart*" *(Luke 2:19)*. She weighed these sayings in her heart, and sought to fathom their meaning. That is the place to keep the words of God. Things kept in the head are quickly lost, but pondered in the heart they remain and abide. Thy Word have I hid in mine heart that I might not sin against Thee. "And He went down with them, and came to Nazareth, and was subject unto them: but His mother *kept all these things in her heart*" *(Luke 2:51)*.

How we all need to take this lesson to heart. In these days of stress and turmoil, hurry and bustle, meditation has become almost a lost art. We have no time for serious reflection and spiritual rumination. But we must make time: the well-being of our souls demands it. Meditation stands to reading as mastication does to eating. One of the characteristics of the "blessed man" *(Ps. 1)* is, that in God's Law "doth he meditate day and night." It is of little use to hear great preachers and read great books unless we diligently store up their sayings and ponder them over in our hearts.

7. Emulate her sublime Trustfulness.

"And blessed is she that believeth: for there shall be a performance of those things which were told her of the Lord." Luke 1:45. This statement proves that Mary was a woman of simple, childlike faith. She was a true believer, and accepted at its face value the Word of God. When Sarah was informed that the Lord would give her a son she doubted and mocked. When an angel of the Lord appeared to Zechariah in the temple and gave him a similar communication, his faith also broke down, and as the result he was struck dumb. But how different with Mary! She readily believed the word of Jehovah. She is one of the company of believing women. Are you? Will you be found a member of the household of faith this Christmas-tide? If so, it will be a truly happy one.

Note, also, the attitude which Mary displayed toward Christ at the marriage-feast in Cana of Galilee. "His mother said unto the servants, Whatsoever He saith unto you, do it" *(John 2:5)*. What simple trustfulness! What calm and absolute confidence! What perfect submission to His will and word! A word from her Son would be quite sufficient. She had complete faith in Him. She never questioned the wisdom of His commands. Can this be said of us? Are we, like the mother of our Lord, ever ready to respond promptly to His every word?

8. Yet, note her Fallibility.

"And when they had fulfilled the days, as they returned, the Child Jesus tarried behind them in Jerusalem, and Joseph *and His mother knew not of it*" *(Luke 2:43)*. In other words, Mary was ignorant of the whereabouts of her Son. How different is this to the Roman Catholic conception of the "Mother of God"! She was fallible like ourselves, but how can this fact be harmonized with the Popish interpretation of her person? And, moreover, let me call your attention again to her words in Luke 1:47 "And my spirit hath rejoiced in God *my Saviour.*" Yes, she was not only fallible, but she was also, a sinner. She, too, was a member of our fallen race, and like us all, she needed a Saviour. What a smashing blow this is to Mariolatry!

9. Think of the Sorrow and Anguish she endured.

Like her Son, Mary was not unacquainted with grief. "And when she saw him (the angel of the Lord) she was *troubled* at His saying" *(Luke 1:29)*. This was but the forerunner of many troubles. What sorrow it must have caused her when, because there was no room in the inn, she had to lay her newly-born Child in a manger! What anguish must have been hers when she learned of Herod's attempt to destroy her Infant's life! What trouble was given her when she was forced on His account to flee into a foreign country and sojourn for several years in the land of Egypt! What a remarkable prophecy that was of old Simeon's, "Yea, a sword shall pierce through thy own soul also" *(Luke 2: 35)*. What piercings of soul must have been hers when she saw her Son despised and rejected of men! What grief must have wrung her heart when she witnessed Him persecuted by His own nation! If Christ was the Man of Sorrows, it is certainly true that His mother was the Woman of Sorrows.

10. View her Devotion and Love.

"Now there stood by the Cross of Jesus His mother" *(John 19:25)*. After the days of His infancy and childhood, and during all the public ministry of Jesus, we see and hear so little of Mary. Her life was lived in the background, among the shadows. But now, when the supreme hour strikes of her Son's agony, when the world has cast out the Child of her womb, she stands there by the Cross! Who can fitly portray such a picture? Mary was nearest to the cruel tree. Bereft of faith and hope, baffled and paralyzed by this strange scene, yet bound with the golden chain of love to the Dying One, there she stands. Try and read the thoughts and emotions of that mother's heart. O what a sword it was that pierced her soul then! Never such bliss at a human birth, never such sorrow at an inhuman death.

Here we see displayed the Mother-heart. She is the dying Man's mother. The One who agonizes there on the Cross is *her* child. She it was who first implanted kisses on that brow now crowned with thorns. She it was who guided those hands and feet in their first infantile movements. No mother ever suffered as she did. His disciples may desert Him, His friends may forsake Him, His nation may despise Him, but His mother stands by His side. She was the one that was nearest to the Cross. Who can analyze or fathom the love of the Mother-heart!

11. GAZE UPON HER MARVELLOUS FORTITUDE.

"There *stood* by the Cross of Jesus His mother." The crowds are mocking, the thieves are taunting, the priests are jeering, the soldiers are callous and indifferent, the Saviour is bleeding, dying, and there is His mother beholding this horrible mockery. What wonder if she had swooned at such a sight. What wonder if she had turned away from such a spectacle. What wonder if she fled from such a scene. But no! There she is: she does not crouch away, she does not faint, she does not even sink to the ground in her grief—she *stands*. Her action and attitude are unique. In all the annals of the history of our race there is no parallel. What transcendent courage. She stood by the Cross of Jesus—what marvellous fortitude.

12. BE REMINDED AGAIN OF HER HUMANITY.

Mary is no proud Madonna, crowned with diadem. The Word of God presents no such Mary. She is the Mother of Sorrows. If you would see the real Mary, go yonder to Calvary, and view her standing by the Cross of Jesus. She is human, she is a woman, she is a real member of our fallen race; and that scene on Golgotha's rugged heights portrays her not as the Queen of Angels, but as the Woman of the stricken heart.

And learn too another lesson. *She* stood by the Cross. *She* needed a Saviour. What an example! If we would be saved from our sins we, too, must take our stand by the Cross. If we would be cleansed from our iniquities we, too, must draw near to that Dying One. If we would be delivered from the wrath to come we, too, must accept the Lord Jesus as our Saviour.

13. THINK OF HER BLESSEDNESS.

"Blessed art thou among women" *(Luke 1:42)*. "For henceforth, all generations shall call me blessed" *(Luke 1:48)*. Note, she is not blessed *above* all women (which would make her more than human), but blessed "*among* all women," which singles her out as the most highly honored of our race. And *is* she not blessed among women? Assuredly. While it is true that by a woman sin entered this world, that by woman came the greatest of all curses to this earth, that by woman the first Adam lost Paradise; yet, let us not forget that it was also by a woman came the Saviour, that by woman came the greatest of all blessings to this earth, that by woman came the last Adam who regained Paradise. Yes, Mary, thou art indeed "blessed among women."

14. FINALLY, APPRECIATE HER DEVOUTNESS.

"Those all continued with one accord in prayer and supplication with the women and *Mary the mother of Jesus*" *(Acts 1:14)*. Here we see Mary engaged in prayer. What a different Mary to the one the Roman Catholics present! In Matt. 2:11 we read, "And when they (the wise men) were come into the house, they saw the young child with Mary His mother, and fell down and worshipped *Him*"—not "them"! They worshipped the Lord Jesus, not His mother. Mary is not to be worshipped as if she is God, for in the Scripture quoted above from the "Acts," we find her worshipping God herself. This is the last glimpse which the Bible affords us of Mary. The final picture is Mary at a prayer-meeting. How significant! How instructive! What an example!

Mary then, is one of the most remarkable characters presented in the Bible and one of the holiest women who ever trod our earth, though at the same time fallible and needing a Saviour herself. Let us pray that the spiritual graces so richly displayed by her may also adorn our characters, and that through the merits of our Redeemer's sacrifice it may be said of each of us, "Thou hast found favor with God."

This unique character-study of the mother of the Saviour may be had in booklet form (attractively gotten up and in a size which will just go in an ordinary envelope) for **5 cents** a copy, **60 cents** a dozen, from

BIBLE TRUTH DEPOT, SWENGEL, PA.

JOHN'S GOSPEL

12. CHRIST AT SYCHAR'S WELL.
(Continued). John 4:6-10.

First, a brief Analysis of the passage which is to be before us:—

1. The Woman of Samaria, v. 7.
2. The Saviour's request, v. 7.
3. The Saviour's solitariness, v. 8.
4. The Woman's surprise, v. 9.
5. The Woman's prejudice, v. 9.
6. The Saviour's rebuke, v. 10.
7. The Saviour's appeal, v. 10.

In the last article we pointed out the deep significance underlying the words of John 4:4—"He *must needs* go through Samaria". It was the constraint of sovereign grace. From all eternity it had been foreordained that the Saviour should go through Samaria. The performing of God's eternal decree required it. The Son, incarnate, had come here to do the Father's will—"Lo, I come to do *Thy* will, O God." And God's will was that these hated Samaritans should hear the Gospel of His grace from the lips of His own dear Son. Hence, "He must *needs* go through Samaria". There were elect souls there, which had been given to Him by the Father, and these also He *"must* bring" *(see John 10:16).*

"Now Jacob's well was there. Jesus therefore, being wearied with His journey, sat thus on the well" *(v. 6).* Observe, particularly, that the Lord Jesus was beforehand with this woman. *He* was at the well first! "I am found of them that sought Me not" *(Isa. 65:1)* is the language of the Messiah in the prophetic word centuries before He made His appearance among men, and this oracle has been frequently verified. His salvation is not only altogether *unmerited* by those to whom it comes, but at first, it is always *unsought (see Rom. 3:11),* and of every one who is numbered among His peculiar people it may be as truly said, as of the apostles, "Ye have not chosen Me, but I have chosen you" *(John 15:16).* When we were pursuing our mad course of sin, when we were utterly indifferent to the claims and superlative excellency of the Saviour, when we had no serious thought at all about our souls, He —to use the apostle's peculiarly appropriate word—"apprehended" us *(Phil. 3:12). He* "laid hold of" us, aroused our attention, illumined our darkened understanding, that we might receive the truth and be saved by it. A beautiful illustration of this is before us here in John 4.

Yes, the Lord was beforehand with this woman. He was found of one that sought Him not. It was so with the idolatrous Abraham *(Josh. 24)* in the land of Chaldea: the Lord of glory appeared to him while he was yet in Mesopotamia *(Acts 7:2).* It was so with the worm Jacob, as he fled to escape from his brother's anger *(Gen. 28: 10, 13).* It was so with Moses, as he went about his shepherd duties *(Ex. 3:1,2).* In each instance the Lord was found by those who sought Him not. It was so with Zacchaeus, hidden away amid the boughs of the trees—"Zacchaeus, make haste, and come down", was the peremptory command, for, said the Lord, "Today I *must* abide at thy house" *(Luke 19:5).* It was so with Saul of Tarsus, as he went on his way to persecute the followers of the Lamb. It was so with Lydia, "whose heart *the Lord opened,* that she might attend unto the things which were spoken of Paul" *(Acts 16:14).* And, let us add, to the praise of the glory of God's grace, but to our own unutterable shame, it was so with the writer, when Christ "apprehended" him; apprehended him when he was altogether unconscious of his deep need, and had no desire whatever for a Saviour. Ah, blessed be His name, *"We* love Him, *because* He *first* loved us"!

But let not the false conclusion be drawn that the sinner is, therefore, irresponsible. No so. God has placed within man a moral faculty, which discerns between right and wrong. Men *know* that they are sinners, and if so they need a Saviour. God now commands *all* men, everywhere, to "repent", and woe be to the one who disobeys. And again we read, "And this is *His commandment,* That we should believe on the name of His Son Jesus Christ" *(1 John 3:23),* and if men refuse to "believe" their blood is on their own heads. Christ receives *all* who come to Him. The Gospel announces eternal life to "whosoever believeth". The door of mercy stands wide open. But, notwithstanding, it remains that men love darkness rather than light, and so strong is their love for the darkness and so deep-rooted is their antipathy against the light, that, as the Lord declared, "No man can come to Me, except the Father which sent Me draw him" *(John 6:44).* Here, again, is the Divine side, and it is this we are now pressing.

"And it was about the *sixth* hour. There cometh a woman of Samaria to draw water" *(vv. 6, 7)*. This means it was the sixth hour after sunrise, and would be, therefore, midday. It was at the time the sun was at its greatest height and heat. Under the glare of the oriental sun, at the time when those exposed to its strong rays were most weary and thirsty, came this woman to draw water. The hour corresponded with her spiritual condition—weary and parched in her soul. "The *sixth* hour". What a significant line is this in the picture! Six invariably speaks of man in the flesh.

"*There cometh* a woman of Samaria to draw water" *(v. 7)*. This was no accident. She chose this hour because she expected the well would be deserted. But, in fact, she went to the well that day, at that time, because *God's* hour had struck when she was to meet the Saviour. Ah, our least movements are directed and over-ruled by Divine providence. It was no accident that the Midianites were passing by when Joseph's brethren had made up their minds to slay him *(Gen. 37:28)*, nor was it merely a coincidence that these Midianites were journeying to Egypt. It was no accident that Pharaoh's daughter went down to the river to bathe, nor that she "saw" the ark, which contained the infant Moses, "among the flags" *(Ex. 2:5)*. It was no accident that at the very time Mordecai and the Jews were in imminent danger of being killed, that Ahasuerus could not sleep, and that he occupied himself with reading the court records, which told of how, aforetime, Mordecai had befriended the king; and which led to the deliverance of God's people. No; there are no accidents in a world that is presided over by a living, reigning God!

"There cometh a woman of Samaria *to draw water*". To "draw water" was her object. She had no thought of anything else, save that she should not be seen. She stole forth at this hour of the mid-day sun because a woman of her character—shunned by other women—did not care to meet any one. The woman was unacquainted with the Saviour. She had no expectation of meeting *Him*. She had no idea she would be converted that day—that was the last thing *she* would expect. Probably she said to herself, as she set forth, "No one will be at the well at this hour". Poor desolate soul. But there *was* One there! One who was *waiting* for her—"sitting *thus* on the well". He knew all about her. He knew her deep need, and He was there to minister to it. He was there to overcome her prejudices, there to subdue her rebellious will, there to *invite Himself* into her heart.

"Jesus saith unto her, Give me to drink" *(v. 7)*. Link together these two statements: "Jesus, therefore, being *wearied* with His journey . . . . . Jesus *saith* unto her, Give Me to drink". There was everything to make Him "weary". Here was the One who had been the Center of Heaven's glory, now dwelling in a world of sin and suffering. Here was the One in whom the Father delighted, now enduring the contradiction of sinners against Himself. He had, in matchless grace, come "unto His own", but with base indifference they "received Him not." He was not wanted here. The ingratitude and rebellion He met with, the jealousy and opposition of the Pharisees, the spiritual dulness of His own disciples—yes, there was everything to make Him "weary". But, all praise to His peerless name, He never wearied in His ministry of grace. There was never any love of ease with Him: never the slightest selfishness: instead, nothing but one unbroken ministry of love. Fatigued in body He might be, sick at heart He must have been, but not too weary to seek out and save this sin-sick soul.

"Jesus saith unto *her*". How striking is the contrast between what we have here and what is found in the previous chapter! There we are shown Nicodemus coming to Christ "by night", under cover of the darkness, so that he might guard *his reputation*. Here we behold the Lord Jesus speaking to this harlot in the full light of day—it was midday. Verily, *He* "made Himself of *no reputation*"!

"Jesus saith unto her, Give Me to drink" *(v. 7)*. The picture presented is unspeakably lovely. Christ seated on the well, and what do we find Him doing? Sitting alone with this poor outcast, to settle with her the great question of eternity. He shows her *herself*, and reveals *Himself!* This is exactly what He does with every soul that He calls to Himself. He takes us apart from the maddening world, exposes to us our desperate condition, and then makes known to us in whose Presence we are, leading us to ask from Him that precious "gift" which He alone can impart. Thus did He deal here with this Samaritan adulteress. And how this incident makes manifest the wondrous grace and infinite patience of the Saviour in His dealings with sinners! Tenderly and patiently He led on this woman, step by step, touching her heart, searching her conscience, awakening her soul to a consciousness of her deep need. And how this incident also brings out the depravity of the sinner—his spiritual blindness and obstinacy; his lack of capacity to understand and respond to the Saviour's advance; yea, his slowness of heart to believe!

"Jesus saith unto her, Give Me to drink". The first thing the Saviour did (note that He took the initiative) was to ask this woman for a drink of cold water—considered the very cheapest gift which this world contains. How the Son of God had humbled Himself! Among the Jews it was considered the depth of degradation even to hold converse with the Samaritans; to be beholden to them for a favor would not be tolerated at all. But here we find the Lord of glory asking for a drink of water from one of the worst in this city of the Samaritans! Such was His condescension that the woman herself was made to marvel.

"Give Me to drink". Here was the starting point for the Divine work of grace which was to be wrought in her. Every word in this brief sentence is profoundly significant. Here was no "ye must be." The very *first* word the Saviour uttered to this poor soul, was *"give"*. It was to *grace* He would direct her thoughts. "Give Me", He said. He immediately calls the attention of the sinner to Himself—"Give *Me.*" But what was meant by "Give Me *to drink*"? To what did the Saviour refer? Surely there can be no doubt that His mind was on something other than literal water, though, doubtless, the first and local significance of His words had reference to literal water. Just as the "weariness" of the previous verse has a deeper meaning than physical fatigue, so this "Give Me to drink" signifies more than slaking His thirst. This world was a dry and thirsty land to the Saviour, and the only refreshment He found here was in ministering of His grace to poor needy sinners, and receiving from them their faith and gratitude in return. This is fully borne out in the sequel, for when the disciples returned and begged Him to eat, He said unto them, "I have meat to eat that ye know not of" (*v. 32*). When then, the Saviour said to this woman, "Give Me to drink", it was refreshment of spirit He sought.

"Give Me to drink". But how could she, a poor, despised and blinded sinner, "give" to *Him?* Ah, she could not. She must first ask of Him. She had to receive herself, before she could give. In her natural state, she had nothing. Spiritually, she was poverty-stricken; a bankrupt. And this it was that the Saviour would press upon her, in order that she might be led to *ask* of Him. When, then, the Saviour said, "Give Me to drink" He was making a demand of her with which, at that time, she was *unable* to comply. In other words, He was bringing her face to face with her *helplessness*. We are often told that God never commands us to do what we have no ability to perform, but He does, and that for two very good reasons: first, to awaken us to a sense of our impotency; second, that we might seek from Him the grace and strength we need to do that which is pleasing in His sight. What was the Law—that Law that was "holy, just and good"—given for? Its summarized requirements were, "Thou shalt love the Lord with all thy heart . . . . and thy neighbour as thyself". But what man ever did this? What man *could* do it? Only one—the God-man. Why, then, was the Law given? On purpose to reveal man's *impotency*. And why was that? To bring man to cast himself at the foot of God's omnipotency: "The things which are *impossible* with men, *are* possible with God" (*Luke 18:27*). This is the first lesson in the school of God. This is what Christ would first teach this needy woman, v. 10 establishes that beyond a doubt—"Jesus answered and said unto her, If thou knewest the gift of God, and who it is that saith to thee, Give Me to drink; thou wouldest have *asked of Him*". But it was the moral impossibility which Christ put before this woman that aroused her curiosity and interest.

"For His disciples were gone away unto the city to buy meat" (*v. 8*). This was no mere coincidence, but graciously ordered by the providence of God. Christ desired this poor soul to be *alone* with Himself! This Gospel of John presents Christ in the very highest aspect in which we can contemplate Him, namely, as God manifest in the flesh, as the eternal Word, as Creator of all things, as the Revealer of the Father. And yet there is none of the four Gospels in which this glorious Person is so frequently seen alone with the sinners as here in John. Surely there is Divine design in this. We see Him alone with Nicodemus; alone with this Samaritan woman; alone with the convicted adulteress in John 8; alone with the man whose eyes He had opened, and who was afterwards put out of the synagogue *(John 9:35)*. Alone with God is where the sinner needs to get—with none between and none around him. This is one reason why the writer, during the course of four pastorates, never made use of an "inquiry room", or "penitent form". Another reason was, because he could find nothing resembling them in the Word of God. They are human inventions. No priest, no intermediary is necessary. Bid the sinner retire by himself, and get alone with God and His Word.

"For His disciples were gone away unto the city to *buy* meat". The word "buy" here, points a contrast. Occurring just where it does it brings into relief the "gift" of God to which the Saviour referred, see vv. 10 and 14. Another has suggested to the writer, that the action of the disciples here furnishes a striking illustration of 3 John 7: "taking nothing of the Gentiles". These disciples of Christ did not beg, but bought.

"Then saith the woman of Samaria unto Him, How is it that Thou, being a Jew, askest drink of me, which am a woman of Samaria? For the Jews have no dealings with the Samaritans" *(v. 9)*. The Saviour's request struck this woman with surprise. She knew the extreme dislike which Jews cherished towards Samaritans. It was accounted a sin for them to have any friendly intercourse with that people. The general tendency of this antipathy may be judged from the following extracts made from the Jewish rabbins by Bishop Lightfoot:—"It is prohibited to eat the bread, and to drink the wine of the Samaritan". "If any one receives a Samaritan into his house, and ministers to him, he will cause his children to be carried into captivity." "He who eats the bread of a Samaritan, is as if he ate swine's flesh".

Aware of this extreme antipathy, the Samaritan woman expresses her amazement that a person, whom, from His dress and dialect, she perceived to be a Jew, should deign to ask, much less receive a favor from a Samaritan—"How is it that Thou, being a Jew, askest drink of me, which am a woman of Samaria?" Ah, "little did she think", to borrow the words of one of the Puritans, "of the glories of Him who sat there before her. He who sat on the well owned a Throne that was placed high above the head of the cherubim; in His arms, who then rested Himself, was the sanctuary of peace, where weary souls could lay their heads and dispose their cares, and then turn them to joys, and to guild their thorns with glory; and from that holy tongue, which was parched with heat, should stream forth rivulets of heavenly doctrine, which were to water all the world, and turn deserts into a paradise" *(Jeremy Taylor)*.

"Then saith the woman of Samaria unto Him, How is it that Thou being a Jew, askest drink of me?" In a previous article we have pointed out the sevenfold contrast which exists between the cases of Nicodemus and this Samaritan woman. Here we call attention to a striking analogy. The very first word uttered by Nicodemus in response to the Saviour's initial statements was "How?" *(3:4);* and the very first word of this woman in reply to Christ's request was "How?". Both of them met the advances of the Saviour with a sceptical "How": there were many points of dissimilarity between them, but in this particular they concurred. In His dealings with Nicodemus, Christ manifests Himself as the "truth"; here in John 4, we behold the "grace" that came by Jesus Christ. "Truth" to break down the religious prejudices of a proud Pharisee; "grace" to meet the deep need of this Samaritan adulteress.

"We are full of 'how's'. The truth of God, in all its majesty and authority, is put before us; we meet it with a *how!* The grace of God, in all its sweetness and tenderness, is unfolded to our view; we reply with a *how?* It may be a theological 'how', or a rationalistic 'how', it matters not, the poor heart will reason instead of believing the truth, and receiving the grace of God. The *will* is active, and hence, although the conscience may be ill at ease, and the heart be dissatisfied with itself, and all around, still the unbelieving 'how' breaks forth in one form or another. Nicodemus says, 'How can a man be born when he is old?' The Samaritan says, 'How canst Thou ask drink of me?' " *(C. H. M.)*.

Thus it is ever. When the Word of God

declares to us the utter worthlessness of nature, the heart, instead of bowing to the holy record, sends up its unholy reasonings. When the same truth sets forth the boundless grace of God, and the free salvation which is in Christ Jesus, the heart, instead of receiving the grace, and rejoicing in the salvation, begins to reason as to *how* it can be. The fact is, the human heart is *closed* against God,—against the truth of His Word, and against the grace of His heart. The Devil may speak, and the heart will give its ready credence. Man may speak, and the heart will greedily swallow what he says. Lies from Satan and nonsense from men all meet with a ready reception by the foolish sinner; but the moment *God* speaks, whether it be in the authoritative language of *truth*, or in the winsome accents of *grace*, all the return the heart will make is an unbelieving, rationalistic, infidelistic *"How?"* Anything and everything for the natural heart save the truth and grace of God. How deeply humbling all this is! How it ought to make us hide our faces with shame! How it should make us heed that solemn word in Ezek. 16:63, "And thou shalt know that I am the Lord: that thou mayest remember, and be confounded, and never open thy mouth (in self-extenuation) any more because of thy shame, when I am pacified toward thee for all that thou hast done, saith the Lord God".

"Then saith the woman of Samaria unto Him, How is it that Thou, being a Jew, askest drink of me, which am a woman of Samaria?". How completely this manifested the *blindness* of the natural heart—*"Thou* being a *Jew"*. She failed to discern the excellency of the One talking to her. She knew not that it was the Lord of glory. She saw in Him nothing but a "Jew". She was altogether ignorant of the fact that He who had humbled Himself to take upon Him the form of a servant, was none other than the Christ of God. And Christian readers, it was thus with each of us before the Holy Spirit quickened us. Until we were brought out of darkness into God's marvelous light, we "saw in Him no beauty that we should desire Him". All that this poor woman could think of was the *old prejudice*—"Thou a Jew . . . . . me a woman of Samaria". So it was with you and me. When the sinner first comes into the presence of God the latent enmity of the carnal mind is stirred up, and, until Divine grace has subdued us, all we could do was to prevaricate and raise objections.

"Jesus answered and said unto her, If thou knewest the gift of God, and who it is that saith to thee, Give Me to drink?: thou wouldest have asked of Him, and He would have given thee living water" *(v. 10)*. Our Lord was not to be put off with her "how?". He had answered the "how" of Nicodemus, and He would now answer the "how" of this woman of Sychar. He replies to Nicodemus, eventually, by pointing to Himself as the great Antitype of the brazen serpent, and by telling him of the Love of God in sending His Son into the world. He replies to the woman, likewise, by telling her of "the *gift* of God". It is beautiful to observe the spirit in which the Saviour answered this poor outcast. He did not enter into an argument with her about the prejudices of the Samaritans, nor did He seek to defend the Jews for their heartless treatment of them. Nor did He deal roughly with her and reproach her for her woeful ignorance and stupidity. No; He was seeking her salvation, and with infinite patience He bore with her slowness of heart to believe.

"Jesus answered and said unto her, If thou knewest the *gift* of God and *who* it is that saith to thee, Give Me to drink". There is where the root of the trouble lay. Man neither knows his need, nor the One who can minister to it. This woman was ignorant of "the *gift* of God". The language of *grace* was an unknown tongue. Like every other sinner in his natural state, this Samaritan thought *she* was the one who must do the giving. But salvation does not come to us in return for *our* giving. God is the Giver; all we have to do is receive. "If thou knewest the gift of God". What is this? It is salvation: it is eternal life: it is the "living water" spoken of by Christ at the end of the verse.

"If thou knewest the gift of God, and *who it is* that saith to thee, Give Me to drink?" But this woman did not know Who it was that spoke to her, nor of the marvelous condescension of this One who had asked her for a "drink". Had she done so, she, in turn, would have "asked of Him". He was ready to give, if she would but take the place of a receiver, and thus make *Him* the Giver; instead of her wanting to take the place of a giver and make Him the Receiver.

"Thou wouldest have asked of Him". It is blessedly true that the only thing between the sinner and eternal life is an "ask". But asking proceeds from knowing. "If thou *knewest* . . . thou wouldest have *asked.*" But O how reluctant the sinner is to take this place. God has to do much for him and in him before he is ready to really "ask". The sinner has to be brought to a realization of his awful condition and terrible danger: he must see himself as lost, undone, bound for the lake of fire. He has to be made to see his desperate need of a Saviour. Again, God has to show him the utter vanity and worthlessness of everything in this world, so that he experiences an acute "thirst" for the Water of Life. He has to be driven to despair, until he is made to wonder whether God can possibly save such a wretch as he. He has to be stript of the filthy rags of his own self-righteousness, and be made willing to come to God just as he is, as an empty-handed beggar ready to receive Divine charity. He has to really come into the presence of Christ and have personal dealings with Him. He has to make definite request for himself. This, in part, is what is involved, before the sinner will "ask." Before we *ask,* God has to deal with the conscience, enlighten the understanding, subdue the rebellious will, and open the heart, the door of which is fast closed against Himself. All of this is what Christ did with this woman of our lesson. We are not saved because of our seeking; we have to be sought. "And who it is that saith to thee": notice, particularily, this *"who* it is," not *"what* it is"—it is not doctrine any more than doing. It is personal dealings with Christ that is needed; with Him who is the Source and Giver of "life".

Attention has often been called to the striking contrast in the manner of our Lord's speech with Nicodemus and His method of dealing with this poor Samaritan adulteress. The Lord did not deal with souls in any mechanical, stereotyped way, as it is to be feared many Christian-workers do today. No; He dealt with each according to the condition of heart they were in. Christ did not begin with the Gospel when dealing with Nicodemus. Instead, He said, "Marvel not that I said unto thee, Ye must be born again". There is no good news in a "ye must be". If a man must be born again, what is *he* going to do in order that he *may be?* What does all his past life amount to?—no matter how full of deeds of benevolence, acts of kindness, and religious performances. Just nothing: a *new beginning* has to be made. But not only is an entirely different order of life imperative, but man has to be "born from above". What, then, can the poor sinner do in the matter? Nothing, absolutely nothing. To tell a man he "must be born again" is simply a shut door in the face of all fleshly pretentions; and that is precisely what Christ intended with Nicodemus.

But *why* shut the door before Nicodemus? It was because he belonged to the Pharisees. He was a member of that class, one of whom Christ portrayed as standing in the Temple and saying to God "I thank Thee, that I am not as other men are, extortioners, unjust, adulterers," etc. *(Luke 18:11).* Nicodemus was not only a highly respectable and moral man, but he was deeply religious. And what he most needed was just what he heard, for the Lord Jesus never made any mistakes. Nicodemus prided himself upon his respectability and religious standing: evidence of this is seen in his coming to Jesus "by night"—he was conscious of how much he risked by this coming; he feared he was endangering his reputation among the people by visiting this Nazarene. Therefore his self-righteousness must be smashed up; his religious pride must be broken down. The force, then, of what our Lord said to this ruler of the Jews was, "Nicodemus, with all your education and reformation, morality and religion, you have not begun to live that life which is pleasing to God *for that* you must be born again". And this was simply to prepare the way *for* the Gospel; to prepare a self-righteous man to receive it.

How entirely different was our Lord's speech with this woman at the well! To her He never so much as mentions the need for the new birth; instead, He tells her at once of the "gift of God". In the case of this woman there was no legalistic and religious platform to be swept away. Her moral character and religious standing were already gone. But it was far otherwise with Nicodemus. It is very evident that he felt he *had* something to stand upon and glory in. What he needed to know was, that, all of this in which he prided himself was worthless before God. Even though a master of Israel, he was utterly *unfit* to enter *God's* kingdom, and nothing could show him this quicker than for the Lord to say unto him "Ye must be born again".

Do what you will with nature, educate,

cultivate, sublimate it as much as you please; raise it to the loftiest pinnacle of the temple of science and philosophy; summon to your aid all the ornaments and ordinances of the legal system, and all the appliances of man's religion; make vows and resolutions of moral reform; weary yourself out with the monotonous round of religious duties; betake yourself to vigils, fastings, prayers, and alms, and the entire range of *"dead* works", and after all, yonder Samaritan adulteress is as near to the kingdom of God as you, seeing that you as well as she *"must* be born again". Neither you nor she has one jot or tittle to present to God, either in the way of title to the kingdom, or of capacity to enjoy it. It is, and must be, *all of grace*, from beginning to end.

What, then, is the Remedy? That to which Christ, at the close, pointed out to Nicodemus: "As Moses lifted up the serpent in the wilderness, even so must the Son of Man be lifted up: that whosoever believeth in Him should not perish, but have eternal life". But for whom was this brazen serpent intended? Why for *any* bitten creature, just because he was bitten. The wound was the title. The title to what? To look at the serpent. And what then? He that looked, *lived*. Blessed Gospel, "look and live". True for Nicodemus: true for the woman of Sychar: true for every bitten son and daughter of Adam. There is no limit, no restriction. The Son of Man has been lifted up, that *whosoever looks to Him,* in simple faith, might have what Adam in innocency never possessed, and what the law of Moses never proposed, even "everlasting life".

The Gospel meets men on a common platform. Nicodemus had moral character, social standing, religious reputation; the woman at the well had nothing. Nicodemus was at the top of the social ladder; she was at the bottom. You could hardly get anything higher than a "Master in Israel", and you could scarcely get anything lower than a Samaritan adulteress; yet so far as standing before God, fitness for His holy presence, title to heaven was concerned, they were both on one common level. But how few understand this! So far as standing before God was concerned there was "no difference" between this learned and religious Nicodemus and the wretched woman of Sychar. To Nicodemus Christ said, "Ye must be born again"; this brief statement completely swept away the foundation from under his feet. Nothing less than a new nature was required from him; and nothing more was needed for her. Uncleanness could not enter heaven, nor could Phariseeism. Each must be born again. True, there was a great difference morally and socially between Nicodemus and this woman—that goes without saying. No sensible person needs to be told that morality is better than vice, that sobriety is preferable to drunkenness, that it is better to be an honorable man than a thief. But none of these will save, or contribute anything toward the salvation of a sinner. None of these will secure admittance into the kingdom of God. Both Nicodemus and the Samaritan adulteress were dead; there was no more spiritual life in the one than in the other.

"Jesus answered and said unto her, If thou knewest the gift of God, and who it is that saith to thee, Give Me to drink; thou wouldest have asked of Him, and He would have given thee living water". There are some who regard the "living water" here as the Holy Spirit, and there is something to be said in favor of this view; but personally, while not dissenting from it, we think that more is included within the scope of our Lord's words. We believe the "living water" has reference to *salvation,* salvation in its widest sense, with all that it embraces. The figure of "water" is most suggestive, and like all others which are found in Scripture calls for prayerful and prolonged meditation in order to discover its fulness and beauty. At least seven lines of thought appear to be suggested by "water"—living water—as a figure of the salvation which Christ gives:—

1. Water is *a gift from God*. It is something which man despite all his boasted wisdom, is quite unable to create. For water we are absolutely dependent upon God. It is equally so with His salvation, of which water is here a figure. 2. Water is something which is *indispensable to man*. It is not a luxury, but a vital necessity. It is that without which man cannot live. It is equally so with God's salvation—apart from it men are eternally lost. 3. Water is that which meets a *universal need;* it is not merely a local requirement, but a general one. *All* are in need of water. It is so with God's salvation. It is not merely some particular class of people, who are more wicked than their fellows, but all who

are outside of Christ are lost. 4. Water is that which first *descends from the heavens*. It is not a product of the earth, but comes down from above. So is it with salvation: it is "of the Lord". 5. Water is a *blessed boon*: it cools the fevered brow, slakes the thirst, refreshes and satisfies. And so does the salvation which is to be found in Christ. 6. Water is something of which *we never tire*. Other things satiate us, but not so with water. It is equally true of God's salvation to the heart of every one who has really received it. 7. Water is *strangely and unevenly distributed by God*. In some places there is an abundance; in others very little; in others none at all. It is so with God's salvation. In some nations there are many who have been visited by the Dayspring from on high; in others there are few who have passed from death unto life; while in others there seem to be none at all.

"He would have given thee living water". How blessed this is! The living water is without money and without price: it is a "gift". This gift can be obtained from Christ alone. This gift can be procured from Christ only by asking, asking Him for it. How blessed the gift! How wondrous the Giver! How simple the terms! Here, then, was the Christ of God preaching to this poor fallen woman the Gospel of His grace. Here was the Messiah in Israel winning to Himself a despised Samaritan. This is hardly what *we* would have looked for. And how the *unexpected* meets us again and again in these Gospels! How vastly different were things from what we had imagined them! Here was the Son of God, incarnate, born into this world; and where would we expect to find His cradle? Why, surely in Jerusalem, the "city of the great king". Instead, He was born in Bethlehem, which was "little among the thousands in Judah". Yes, born in Bethlehem, and cradled in a *manger*—the very last place we had looked for Him! And for what purpose has He visited this earth? To offer Himself as a sacrifice for sins. To whom shall we go to learn more about this? Surely, to the priests and Levites. Ah, and what do we learn about them in this very Gospel? Why, *they* were the very ones who knew not the One who stood in their midst *(John 1:26).* No, if we would learn about Him who had come to be the great Sacrifice, we must turn away from the priests and Levites, and go yonder into the "wilderness"—the last place, again, we would think of—and listen to that strange character clad in raiment of camel's hair, with a leathern girdle about his loins; and *he* would tell us about the Lamb of God which taketh away the sin of the world. Once more: suppose it had been *worship* we had desired to learn about, whither had we betaken ourselves? Why, surely, to the Temple—*that*, of all places, must be where the Lord God is worshipped in the truest form. But again would our quest have been in vain, for the Father's house was now but "a house of merchandise". Whom had we sought out if instruction in the things of God had been our desire? Why, surely, one of those best qualified to teach us would be Nicodemus, "a Master in Israel". But again would we have met with disappointment.

Now if *we* would have gone to Nicodemus to learn of the things of God, who among us would have imagined these very truths being revealed by a weary Traveller by one of Samaria's wells, to an audience of one! Who were the Samaritans to be privileged thus? Should we not expect to find this much-favored woman, and a people so highly honored, as being the descendants of some race of age-long seekers after God? Would we not conclude they must be the offspring of men who for long centuries had lived in one continued and supreme endeavor to purge their thoughts and ceremonies from every false and impure admixture? But read again 2 Kings 17 for the inspired account of the unlovely origin of the Samaritans. *They* were two thirds heathen! Ah, after reading this chapter would *we* not have expected to find *worship* in Jerusalem and *idolatry* in Samaria! Instead of which, we find idolatry in Jerusalem, and (before we are through with John 4) the true worship in Samaria. And what does all this go to prove? It shows that the wisdom of this world is foolishness with God. It demonstrates how utterly incompetent we are for drawing conclusions and reasoning about *spiritual* things. It exemplifies what was said long ago through Isaiah: "For My thoughts, are not your thoughts, neither are My ways your ways, saith the Lord" *(55: 8).* How foolish are man's reasonings; how wise God's "foolishness"!

And here we must stop. Next month, D. V., we shall continue our study of this wondrous and blessed chapter. In the meantime, let the student prayerfully ponder the following questions:—

1. What particular trait of the sinner's heart is manifested by the woman in her next statement? v. 11—we do not mean her blindness or stupidity.
2. What spiritual truth did she unconsciously voice when she said, "The well is deep"? v. 11.
3. What God-dishonoring principle was enunciated by her in v. 12?
4. To what was Christ referring when He said, "This water"? v. 13.
5. How does v. 14 bring out the eternal security of the believer?
6. What did the woman mean by her words in v. 15?
7. Why did Christ say to her, "Go, call thy husband"? v. 16.

—Arthur W. Pink.

A CHRISTMAS MESSAGE

"There was no room for them in the inn" (Luke 2:7).

This was said of the Infant Christ and His mother.

It is not only an historical fact, but a prophecy of that reception which the blessed Saviour has had in all ages past, and which He has to-day.

There is "no room" for Him in the *hearts* of men. It may be, that even the heart of the one who is now reading this message has been so filled with the things of this world—business, society, pleasure, and material success that there has been no time for thinking seriously of the adorable Saviour, Jesus of Nazareth, and His righteous claims.

This is the season of exchanging gifts, and it is a time of good cheer, and joy, and festivity, and merry making, all in connection with the presumed anniversary of the birth of the *Saviour of men;* and yet the sad, sad thing is, that many, very many of those who will enter so enthusiastically into these festivities have no room at all in their hearts for the *Saviour Himself.*

They may say prayers to Him.

They may sing His praises.

They may read and hear His Word with respect.

But *He* is not real to their *hearts.*

All is mere *formality* with them.

They do not *know* Him as *their* Saviour. Their *hearts* have never really come in contact with Him in an *experimental* way.

He is not *"precious"* to them *(1 Peter 2:7).*

They have not been *"born again"* (John 3:3-7).

And how many, alas, will join in all this Christmas gayety, amid scenes and sounds of shameless revelry and drunkenness, and profanity!

O, the desperate wickedness of the heart! (Jer. 17:9).

And yet, there is the solemn Word of God, that if men do not give that blessed One, born in Bethlehem, the place in their hearts, which His person, His love, and His atoning work on the cross, justly demand, there will be no place of forgiveness for them, of escape from that awful and unending judgment which He went to the cross to save them from.

If we have *"no room"* for Him, how can we expect Him to have any room for us?

Surely there is no room in heaven for the Christ rejector!

His room will be in the place of infinite distance from the Saviour, in "the lake that burneth with fire and brimstone," no matter what Satan and his learned servants may do to expunge the appalling fact from God's Word.

Do we not need that *Saviour* whose nativity the world is celebrating?

Can you think that He would have come into the world, and have gone to that shameful cross, if God could have saved men in any other way?

Think of *"trying to get to heaven"* by your own endeavors in view of that cross!

Every one who is trusting in his *"trying,"* is denying the testimony of the cross, and does not yet see his deep need!

He is denying the word of the Saviour, who said: "I am the *Way,* the *Truth,* and the *Life;* no man cometh unto the Father, but by *Me*" (John 14:6).

He is denying the word of the Apostle, who said: "Neither is there salvation in any other, for there is *none other name* under heaven, given among men, whereby we must be saved" (Acts 4:12).

Oh, it is a truth that we *must receive*—that the Christ of the New Testament, has opened heaven for us, *only by the blood of His cross;* and we must open our *hearts* to

Him, that He may come in, and *reign* there as our *Saviour* and *Lord,* or remain unsaved forever.

They only, who are truly trusting in His *death* for their salvation, can truly appreciate and celebrate *His birth.*

Giving and receiving gifts and making merry in connection with His birthday, while *rejecting Himself—the "unspeakable gift" of God,* is not only most inconsistent, but *most sinful.* (This article can be had in tract form—40¢ per 100). —M. S.

THE SAINT AND THE LAW

"God imputeth righteousness without works", says the Holy Spirit, speaking through Paul *(Rom. 4:6);* and he who is in possession of this righteousness is "a blessed man". This righteousness is at once Divine and human; "the righteousness of God" *(Rom. 1:17);* "the righteousness of Him who is our God and Saviour" *(2 Pet. 1:1, see Greek);* the righteousness of Him whose name is "Jehovah our righteousness" *(Jer. 23:6).* It is "righteousness without the law" *(Rom. 3:21);* yet righteousness which has all along been testified to by "the law and the prophets". It is the "righteousness which is of faith" (i. e. which was got by believing) *(Rom. 10:6);* "without the deeds of the law" *(Rom. 3: 28),* yet arising out of a fulfilled law. It is the righteousness, not of the Father, or of Godhead, but of the Son, the Christ of God, the God-man; who, by His obedient life and death, magnified the law and made it honorable.

Thus, then, on believing the Divine testimony concerning this righteousness, we are no longer "under the law", but "under grace" *(Rom. 6:14);* we are "dead to the law by the body (the crucifixion, or crucified body) of Christ"; we are "delivered from the law, that being dead wherein we were held" *(Rom. 7:6).*

It appears, then, that the Gospel does not change the law itself, for it is holy, and just, and good; that grace does not abate the claims, nor relax the penalties of law. The law remains the same perfect code, with all its old breadth about it, and all its eternal claims. For what is the purport of the Gospel, what is the significance of grace? Is it perfect obedience on our part to the perfect law? That would be neither Gospel nor grace. Is it a perfect obedience to a relaxed, a less strict law? That would be the ruin of law on the one hand, and the exaction of an obedience on the other, which no sinner could render. Is it imperfect obedience to an unrelaxed, unmodified law? That would be salvation by *sin,* not by *righteousness.* Or lastly, is it imperfect obedience to a relaxed and imperfect law? That would be the destruction of all government, the dishonor of all law; it would be the setting up "the throne of iniquity", and "framing mischief by law" *(Psa. 94:20).* The demand of the law is *perfection.* Between *everything* and *nothing* the Bible gives us our choice. If we are to be saved by law, it *must be wholly by the law;* if not wholly by the law, it must be wholly without the law.

But while it is clear the law is not changed, and cannot be changed, either in itself or in its claims, it is as clear that our relations to the law, and the law's relations to us, *are* altered, upon our believing on Him who is "the end (or fulfilling) of the law for righteousness to every one that believeth". If, indeed, the effect of Christ's death had been to make, what is called "evangelical obedience to a milder law", our justifying righteousness, then there would be a change in the law itself, though not in our relation to it, which would in that case remain the same, only operating on a lower scale of duty. But if the end of Christ's life and death be to substitute His obedience for ours entirely, in the matter of justification, so that His doings meet everything in law that our doings should have met, then the relationships between us and the law is altered; we are placed upon a new footing in regard to it, while it remains unchanged and unrelaxed.

What, then, is this new relationship between us and law, which faith establishes?

There are some who speak as if in this matter there is the mere breaking up of the old relationship, the cancelling of the old covenant, without the substitution of anything new. They dwell on such texts as these: "Not under the law", "delivered from the law", "without the law", affirming that a believing man has nothing more to do with law at all. They call that "improper teaching" which urges obedience to law in the carrying out of a holy life; they brand as "bondage" the regard to law which those pay who, studying Moses and the prophets, and specially the Psalms of Him who tasted the blessedness of the man to whom the Lord imputeth righteousness without works *(Psa. 32:1)*, are drinking into the spirit of David, or more truly, into the spirit of the greater than David, the Only-Begotten of the Father, who speaks, in no spirit of bondage, of the laws and statutes and judgments of the Father.

Our old relationship to law (so long as it continued) made justification by law a necessity. The *doing* was indispensable to the *living*, so long as the law's claims over us personally were in force. We strove to obey, in order that we might live; for this is *law's* arrangement, the *legal* order of things; so long as this order remained there was no hope. It was impossible for us to "obey and live"; and as the law could not say to us, "live and obey", it could do nothing for us. Only that which could reverse this order in our case, which could give *life in order to obedience*, would be of any service to us. This the Gospel steps in to do. Not first obedience and then life, but first life and then obedience.

This argues no weakness or imperfection in the law. For if any law could have given life, this law would have done it *(Gal. 3:21)*. But law and life, in the case of the sinner, are incompatible. It is the very perfection of the law that makes life impossible under it, unless in the case of entire and ceaseless obedience, without a flaw. "By the law is the knowledge of sin"; and where sin is, law proclaims death, not life.

So long, then, as the old relationship continued between us and law; or, in the apostle's words, so long as we were "under law", there was nothing but condemnation and an evil conscience, and the fearful looking for of judgment. But with the change or relationship there came pardon and liberty and gladness. "Christ hath redeemed us from the curse, being made a curse for us" *(Gal. 3:13)*; and so we are no longer under the law, but under grace. The law is the same law, but it has lost its hold on us, its power over us. It can not cease to challenge perfect obedience from every being under heaven, but to us its threat and terror are gone. It can still say "Obey", but it cannot now say "Disobey and perish".

Our new relationship to the law is that of Christ Himself to it. It is that of men who have met all its claims, exhausted its penalties, satisfied its demands, magnified it, and made it honorable. For our faith in God's testimony to Christ's surety-obedience has made us one with Him. The relation of the law to Him is its relation to us who believe in His name. His feelings toward the law ought to be our feelings. The law looks on us as it looks on Him; we look on the law, as He looked on it. And does He not say, "I delight to do Thy will, O My God; yea, THY LAW is within My heart" *(Psa. 40:8)*!

Some speak as if the servant were greater than the Master, and the disciple above his Lord; as if the Lord Jesus honored the law, and His people were to set it aside; as if He fulfilled it for us, that we might not need to fulfill it; as if He kept it, not that we might keep it, but that we might not keep it, but something else in its stead, they know not what.

The plain truth is, we might either keep it or break it. Which of these men ought to do let those answer who speak of the believer having nothing more to do with law. There is no midway. If it be not a saint's duty to keep the law, he may break it at pleasure, and go on sinning because grace abounds.

The word *duty* is objected to as inconsistent with the liberty of forgiveness and sonship. Foolish and idle cavil! What is duty? It is a thing *due by me to God;* that line of conduct which *I owe to God*. And do these objectors mean to say that, because God has redeemed us from the curse of the law, therefore we *owe* Him nothing, we have no *duty* now to Him? Has not redemption rather made us *doubly debtors?* We *owe* Him more than ever, and we owe His holy law more than ever; more honor, more obedience. Duty has been *doubled*, not *cancelled*, by our being delivered from the law; he who says that duty has ceased, because deliverance has come, knows nothing of duty, or law, or deliverance. The greatest of all debtors in the universe is the redeemed man, the man who can say, "the life that I now live in the flesh, I live by the faith of the Son of God, who loved me, and gave Himself for me". What a strange sense of gratitude these men must have who suppose that, because love has cancelled the penalties of law, and turned away its wrath, therefore reverence and obedience to that law are no longer *due*. Is *terror* in their estimation the only foundation of duty; and when love comes in and terror ceases, does duty become a bondage?

No, they may say, but there is something higher than duty, there is privilege; it is that we contend for. I answer, the privilege of what? Of obeying the law? *That* they cannot do away with; for they are no longer under the law, but under grace. What privilege, then? Of imitating Christ? Be it so. But how can we imitate Him whose life was one great law-fulfilling without keeping the law? What privilege, again we ask? Of doing the will of God? Be it so. And what is law but the revealed will of God? And has our free forgiveness released us from the privilege of conformity to the revealed will of God?

But what do they mean by thus rejecting the word duty, and contending for that of privilege? Privilege is not something distinct from duty, nor at variance with duty; but it is duty *and something more;* it is duty influenced by higher motives; duty uncompelled by terror or suspense. In privilege the *duty* is all there; but there is something superadded, in the shape of motive and relationship, which exalts and enobles duty. It is my duty to obey government; it it my privilege to obey my parents. But in the latter case is duty gone because privilege has come in? Or has not the loving relationship between parent and child only intensified the duty by superadding the privilege, and sweetening the obedience by the mutual love? "The love of Christ *constraineth*". There is something more than both duty and privilege added.

Let men who look but at one side of a subject say what they will, this is the truth of God, that we are liberated from the law just in order that we may keep the law; we get the "no condemnation", in order that *"the righteousness of the law* may be fulfilled in us" *(Rom. 8:4);* we are delivered from "the mind of the flesh", which is enmity to God, and not subject to His law, on purpose that we may be *subject to His law (Rom. 8:7);* nay, that we may "with the mind *serve the law* of God" *(Rom. 7:25);* that we may be "doers of the law" *(James 4:11).* These objectors may speak of obedience to the law as bondage, or of the law itself being abolished to believers; here are the words of the Holy Ghost; the law of God is just the law of God, that very law which David loved, and in which David's Son delighted; and what delighting in it, serving it, doing it, are, it would be well for such men meekly and lovingly to learn.

"Do we make void the law by faith? God forbid: yea, we *establish* the law" *(Rom. 3:31);* that is, we set it on a firmer basis than ever. That law, "holy, and just, and good", thus doubly established, is now for us, not *against* us. Its aspect toward us is that of friendship and love, and so we have become "the *servants* of righteousness" *(Rom. 6:18);* "yielding our members *servants* to righteousness" *(Rom. 6:19);* we are not men delivered from service but delivered from one kind of service, and by that deliverance introduced into another, "that we should *serve* in newness of spirit, and not in the oldness of the letter" *(Rom. 7:6);* as "the Lord's *freemen*" *(1 Cor. 7:22),* yet Christ's *servants* *(1 Cor. 7:22).* Thus, obligation, duty, service, obedience, still remain to the believing man, though no longer associated with bondage and terror, but with freedom, and gladness, and love. The law's former bearing on us is altered, and, with that, the *nature* and spirit of the service are altered, but the service itself remains, and the law which regulates that service is confirmed, not annulled.

Some will tell us here that it is not *service* they object to, but service regulated by *law*. But will they tell us what is to regulate service, if not law? *Love,* they say. This is a pure fallacy. Love is not a *rule* but a *motive*. Love does not tell me *what* to do; it tells me *how* to do it. Love constrains me to do the will of the Beloved One; but to know what that will is I must go elsewhere. The law of our God is *the will* of the Beloved One, and were that expression of His will withdrawn, love would be utterly in the dark; it would not know what to do. I might say I love my Master, and I love His service, and I want to do His bidding, but I must know *the rules of His house,* that I may know *how* to serve Him. Love without law to guide its impulses would be the part of will-worship and confusion, unless upon the supposition of an inward miraculous illumination as an equivalent for law. Love goes to the law to learn the Divine *will,* and love delights in the law, as the exponent of that will; and he who says that a believing man has nothing more to do with law, save to shun it as an old enemy, might as well say that he has nothing to do with the will of God.

For the Divine law and the Divine will are substantially one: the former being the outward manifestation of the latter. And it is *"the will* of our Father which is in heaven" that we are to do *(Matt. 7:21)*, or proving by loving obedience what is that "good, and acceptable, and perfect *will of God*" *(Rom. 12:2)*. Yes, it is "he that doeth *the will* of God that abideth forever" *(1 John 2:17)*; it is to *"the will of God"* that we are to live *(1 Pet. 4:2)*; "make you perfect in every good work *to do His will*" *(Heb. 13:21)*; and fruitfulness in every good work springs from being "filled with the knowledge of His *will*" *(Col. 1:9, 10)*.

As to the oneness of the Divine *will* and Divine *law*, I need only quote the words of Him who came to fulfill the law, "Lo, I come: in the volume of the Book it is written of Me, I delight to do *Thy will*, O My God: yea, *Thy law* is within My heart" *(Psa. 40:7, 8; Heb. 10:7)*.

If *law* be not *will*, what is it? And if will has not uttered itself in law, in what has it spoken? *Truth* is the utterance of the Divine *mind*, but law is the utterance of the Divine *will*. When a father teaches his child, we see simply *mind meeting mind;* but when he commands, or gives rules, we see *will* meeting *will*. When parliament publishes reports of proceedings, or the like, there is simply the expression of its *mind;* when it passes an act, there is the declaration of its *will*.

I ask attention to this the real meaning of law, because it is the key to the solution of the question before us. That question is really not so much concerning the *law* of God as concerning His *will;* and the theology which would deny the former would set aside the latter. Conformity to the will of God can only be carried out by observance of His law, for we know His will only through His law.

I do not see how a crooked will is to be straightened unless by being brought into contact with the perfect *will* of God; nor do I see how that will is to be brought to bear upon us, for the rectification of our will, unless by the medium of the revealed law. *Will* must be brought to bear upon *will*, the Divine upon the human will, and this must be through that part of revelation which embodies *will*, unless some miraculous power be put forth in us apart altogether from the truth of God; and he who affirms this may also affirm that peace is to be dropped into us apart from the Gospel of peace. The Divine volition, embodied in a force or power which we call gravitation, rules each motion of unconscious planets, and this same Divine volition or will, embodied in intelligent law, is that which regulates the movements of our conscious wills, straightening them and keeping them straight, though without wrong done to their nature, or violation of their true freedom.

Should it be said that will and law are now *embodied in Christ,* and that it is to this model we are to look; I ask, What do we see in Christ? The fulfiller of the law. He is the embodiment and perfection of law-fulfilling. We cannot look at Him without seeing the perfect law. God has given us these two things in these last days, the law and the living model; but was the living model meant to *supersede* the law? Was it not to illustrate and enforce it? We see the law now, not merely in the statute-book, but in the person of the King Himself. But is the statute-book thereby annihilated, and its statutes made void? Were Christ's expositions of the law in the fifth, sixth, and seventh chapters of Matthew, intended to over-rule or abrogate the law itself? No; but to show its breadth and purity. And when He thus expounded the law, did He say to His disciples, "But *you* have nothing to do with the law; it is set aside for all that shall believe in My name"? Did He not liken to a wise man every one who should hear these sayings and do them *(Matt. 7:24);* nay, did He not say, "Think not that I am come to destroy the law or the prophets, I am not come to destroy but to fulfill .... Whosoever, therefore, shall break *one of these least commandments,* and shall teach men so, he shall be called least in the kingdom of heaven; but whosoever *shall do and teach them,* the same shall be called great in the kingdom of heaven" *(Matt. 5:17-19)*. Now one would think this should settle the question. For the Lord is speaking of the law and its commandments, lesser and greater, and He is speaking of it as binding on those who are heirs of the kingdom of heaven.

Should it be said that it is only exemption from obligation to the moral law or ten commandments that is pleaded for, and not the law or will of God in general, I answer, The ten commandments are the summary or synopsis of God's will as to the regulation of man's life; and every other part of the Bible is in harmony with this moral law.*

If the objection is to the use of the word "law", or "commandment" as implying bondage, I answer, Obedience to law is true liberty; perfect obedience to perfect commandments is perfect liberty. And there must be some dislike of the law's strictness where this dislike of obligation is felt; nay, there must be ignorance of the Gospel as well as law, in such a case; ignorance of that very redemption from the curse of the law for which the objectors profess such zeal, ignorance of the complete "righteousness without the law" which we have in Christ. I am persuaded of this, that where there is this shrinking from the application of law as our rule of life, there is a shrinking from *perfect conformity to the will of God;* nay, more, there is *unbelief in the Gospel,* the want of a *full consciousness* of the perfect forgiveness which the believer of that Gospel brings; for were there this full consciousness of pardon, there would be no dread of law, there would be no shrinking from Sinai's thunders, no wish to be exempted from the broadest application of Sinai's statutes. In all Antinomianism, whether practical or theological, there is some mistake both as to law and Gospel.

But why object to such words as law, and commandments, and obedience? Does not the apostle speak of "the *law* of the spirit of life"? *(Rom. 8:2).* Does he not say, "This is His *commandment,* that we should believe on the name of His Son Jesus Christ" *(1 John 3:23);* and is not "the *new commandment"* said to be only a repetition of "the *old commandment,* which we have heard from the beginning"? *(1 John 2:7);* and does he not speak of *"obedience* unto righteousness" *(Rom. 6:16),* and of *"obedience* to the faith"? *(Rom. 1:5).*

When the apostle is exhorting Christians in the twelfth and thirteenth of the Romans, is he not giving precepts and laws? Nay, and does he not found his exhortations on the ten commandments? "For this, Thou shalt not kill, Thou shalt not steal, Thou shalt not covet; and if there be *any other commandment,* it is briefly comprehended in the same, Thou shalt love thy neighbour as thyself. Love worketh no ill to his neighbour, therefore, love is the *fulfilling of the law" (Rom. 13:9, 10).* The ten commandments are here presented as our guide and rule, which guide and rule *love* enables us to follow: for the apostle does not say "love is exemption from the law, or love is the abrogation of the law", "but "love is the fulfilling of the law". Love does not supersede law, nor release us from obedience to it; it enables us to obey. Love does not make stealing or coveting, or any such breach of law, *no sin in a Christian,* which would seem to be the meaning which some attach to this passage; but it so penetrates and so constrains us, that not reluctantly or through fear, but right joyfully, we act towards our neighbor in all things, great and small, as the Lord bids us to do. Yes, Christ "hath redeemed us from the curse of the law", but certainly not from the law itself; for that would be to redeem us from a Divine rule and guide; it would be to redeem us from that which is "holy and just and good".

In other epistles the same reference occurs to the ten commandments, as the basis of a true and righteous life. Thus in speaking of the family relationship, the apostle introduces the moral law as the foundation of obedience *(see Eph. 6:1-3),* where writing to those who are *in the Lord,* and not Jews, but Gentiles, he demands obedience and honor in the name of *the fifth commandment.* Yet surely, if any duty might have been left to the impulses of Christian love, without reference to law, it would be that of a believing child to its parent. Was the apostle, then, a legalist when he referred the Ephesians to the moral law as a rule of life? Did he not know that they were "not under the law, but under grace"? In the epistle of James we find similar appeals to the moral law as the rule of Christian life. That he is speak-

---

*Besides, the ten commandments were for *redeemed* Israel. The Sinaitic code began with redemption, "The Lord thy God redeemed thee, *therefore I command* thee this day" *(Deut. 15:15).* Redemption forms a new obligation to law-keeping, as well as puts us in a position for it. And was it not to Sinai and its burnings that the apostle referred when he said "Wherefore we receiving a kingdom which cannot be moved, let us have grace, whereby we may serve God acceptably with reverence and godly fear: For our God is a consuming fire" *(Heb. 12: 28, 29).* Some would, perhaps, call this legality and bondage, a motive unfit to be addressed to a saint, so that exemption from compliance with *any Bible statute,* or from the obligation of submitting ourselves to *any Bible truth,* might be pleaded for as properly as exemption from the law. For the law cannot be cut out of the Bible and set aside by itself, while all else remains in force. Either all must go or none.

ing of the ten commandments is evident, for he quotes *two of them (2:11)* as specimens of what he calls the law. This law he bids his Christian brethren "look into" *(1: 25)*, "continue in it" *(1:25)*, "fulfill" it *(2: 8)*, "keep" it *(2:10)*, be "doers" of it *(4:11)*. And this law he calls "the law of liberty" *(2:12)*: nay, "the perfect law of liberty" *(1:25)*, carrying us back to the Psalmist's experience, "I will walk *at liberty,* for I seek Thy precepts" *(119:45)*; for law is bondage only to the unforgiven; all true obedience is liberty, and all true liberty consists in obedience to law. This law, moreover, the apostle so delights in that he calls it "the royal law" *(2:8)*, the "perfect law" *(1:25)*, pronouncing those blessed who are "not forgetful hearers, but *doers* of the work" *(1:25)*. Had this apostle forgotten that we were "not under the law, but under grace"? But he was writing to Jews, some say. Yes, but to *believing Jews,* just as Paul was when writing to "the Hebrews", and when writing to "the Romans also *(see 2:17-29)*. And do men mean to say there is one Gospel for the Jew and another for the Gentile; that the Jew is still "under the law" and *not under grace;* and that in Christ Jesus all nations of men are not entirely ONE *(Eph. 2:14- 22, Gal. 3:28)*?

If the objection to the believer's use of the law be of any weight it must apply to *everything in the form of precept,* for the reasons given against our having anything to do with the moral law are founded upon its *preceptive* or *commanding* character. The law, in itself, is admitted to be good, and breaches of it are sin, as when a man steals or lies; but then, the form in which it comes of *do* or *do not,* makes it quite unsuited for a redeemed man! Had it merely said "stealing is wrong", it might have been suitable enough; but when it issues its precepts, *"Thou shalt not* steal", it becomes unmeet; and one who is *"not* under the law, but under grace" must close his ears against it, as an intruder and a tyrant.

Of angels this is said to be the highest felicity, that they do *His commandments,* hearkening unto the voice of His word" *(Psa. 103:20)*; just as of those from whom the Lord has "removed transgression as far as the east is from the west", it is said that "they remember *His commandment* to do them" *(Psa. 103:12, 18)*. But if this theory of the total disjunction of the law from believers be true, then angels must be in bondage, as they also be so to whom Paul refers as specimens of the blessed men whose transgressions are forgiven by the imputation of "righteousness without works." *(Rom. 4:6)*. To unforgiven men law is bondage, but is it so to the forgiven? Do pardoned men hate or love it? Do they dread it or delight in it? Do they disobey or obey it? Do they dismiss it from their thoughts and consciences, or do they make it their "meditation all the day"? Yet there are men who speak of law as abrogated to a believer, who look with no favor on those who listen to it, but pity them as ill-taught, ill-informed men, who if in Christ at all, are only Christians of the lowest grade, the least in the kingdom of heaven.

And this is said to be the proper effect of a believed Gospel! This is called an essential part of higher Christianity; and is reckoned indispensable to the right appreciation of a saint's standing before God. The realization of it is a proof of true spirituality, and the denial of it an evidence of imperfect knowledge and a cramped theology!

We can find no such spirituality, no such Christianity in the Bible. This is license, not liberty; it is freedom *to* sin, not freedom *from* sin. It may be spiritual sentimentalism, but it is not spirituality. It is sickly religionism, which, while professing a higher standing than mere law, is departing from that healthy and authentic conformity to the will of God which results from the love and study of His statutes. It is framing a new and human standard, in supplement, if not in contradiction, of the old and the Divine.

This dislike of the law as a rule of life, and a guide to our knowledge, both of what is right and what is wrong, bodes nothing good. It bears no resemblance to the apostle's delight in the law of God after the inward man, but looks like a dread of its penalty and searchlight. Nay, it looks more like the spirit of Antichrist than of Christ; the spirit of him whose character is lawlessness (anomia, "without law"), than of Him who, as the obedient Son, ever did the Father's will, in accord with the holy law: "I delight to do Thy will, O My God: yea, Thy *law* is within my heart" *(Psa. 40:8)*. It is granted that "the law worketh wrath" *(Rom. 4:15)*, and yet that to a believing man legal threats of condemnation have no terror. It is granted that, in the matter of forgiveness and acceptance, law is to him nothing, save as seen fulfilled in his Surety; that law has no claim upon him which should break his peace, or trouble his conscience, or bring him into bondage; that law can only touch him and deal with him in the person of his Substitute; that the righteousness in which he stands before God is a "righteousness without the law", and "without the deeds of the law;" that the sin which still remains in him does not give the law hold over him, or any right to enforce its old claims or threats. It is granted that it is in grace alone he stands, and rejoices in hope of the glory of God, in a condition at all times to take up the challenge, "Who shall lay anything to the charge of God's elect?" "Who is he that condemneth?" But admitting fully all this, we ask, "What is there in this to disjoin him from the law, or exempt him from obedience to it? And should he not feel and cry, as did the redeemed men of other days, "O that my ways were directed to keep Thy *statutes*" *(Psa. 119:5)*; "O let me not wander from Thy *commandments*" *(Psa. 119:10)*; "I have rejoiced in the way of Thy *testimonies*" *(119:14)*; "My soul breaketh for the longing it hath unto Thy *judgments*" *(119:20)*; "Make me to understand the way of Thy *precepts*" *(119:27)*; "I will run in the way of Thy *commandments* when Thou shalt enlarge my heart" *(119:13)*.

Should any one say that it is not to *service*, but to *bondage* they object, I answer, No one contends for bondage. It is in the spirit of adoption and filial love that we obey the law, even as the Son of God obeyed it. But it is somewhat remarkable that the word which the apostle uses, in reference to *his* connection with the law, is not that for *priestly* service, or ministration, but for *menial offices*, "that we should *serve* in newness of spirit" *(Rom. 7:6)*; "with the mind I myself *serve* the law of God" *(Rom. 7:25)*; "yielding your members *servants* to righteousness" *(6:19)*; so that, as the strictest conformity to the law was that in which he delighted so it is that in which he calls upon us to delight.

When he speaks of not being "under the law", but "delivered from the law", his meaning is so obvious that it is somewhat difficult to misunderstand him. His whole argument is to show how the law affected a sinner's standing before God, either in condemning or justifying. He shows that it cannot be the latter but only the former; and that, for justification, we must go to something else than law, for "by the deeds of the law shall no flesh be justified". In everything relating to our justification, everything connected with pardon or the giving of a "good conscience", we are not under law. But does this release us from conformity to the law? Does this make it less a duty to walk according to its precepts, or make our breaches of law no longer sin? Does our being, in this sense, "delivered from the law" cancel the necessity of loving God and man? The summing up of the law is, "Thou shalt love the Lord thy God with all thy heart, and thy neighbor as thyself". Is a saint not under obligation so to love? Would the fulfillment of this be bondage, and inconsistent with the spirit of adoption? Is liberty claimed for a Christian either to love or not to love, as he pleases? If he does not love, is he not sinning? Or does his not being under law, but under grace, make the want of love no crime? Is obedience a matter of option, not of obligation? If it is answered, No; we will love God with all our heart, but not because the law enjoins; I answer, This looks very like the spirit of a froward child, who says to a parent, I will do such and such a thing because I please, but not because you bid me.

At the common objections to the observance of the Sabbath take for granted that that day is a curse and not a blessing—bondage, not liberty—so the usual objections to the keeping of the law are seen that it is in itself an evil, not a good—an enemy and not a friend.

Say what men will, obedience to law is liberty, compliance with law is harmony, not discord. The *force* of law does not need always to be *felt*, but its object, whether felt or unfelt, is to keep everything in its proper place, and move in its proper course, so that one man's liberty, may not interfere with another man's liberty, but each have the greatest amount of actual freedom which creaturehood is capable of, without harm to itself or others. Law does not interfere with true liberty, but only with that which is untrue, promoting and directing the former, discouraging only the latter.

As with the orbs of heaven, so with us. Obedience to their ordered courses is not simply a necessity of their *being*, but of their *liberty*. Let them snap their cords, and choose for themselves the unfettered range of space; then not only is order gone, and harmony gone, and beauty gone, but *liberty* is gone; for that which keeps men in freedom is obedience to the forces of their constitution, and non-departure from their appointed orbits. Disobedience to them, departure from these, would bring about immediate collision of star with star, the stoppage of their happy motions, the extinction of their joyful light, havoc and death, star heaped on star in universal wreck.—*Andrew Bonar, 1860.*

THE STATE OF THE NATURAL MAN

"I will take away the heart of stone" *(Ezek. 36:26).*

Every man that comes to be converted hath a heart of stone; and what is that? insensible, inflexible. Insensible, he hath *no feeling* of his condition; inflexible, *he will not be moved* and wrought upon by the Word, and the Spirit, and Providence. How many means are wasted upon him, and to no purpose! "The heart is deceitful above all things, and desperately wicked; who can know it?" *(Jer. 17:9).* It invents all kinds of shifts and excuses to elude God, or rather to cheat itself. When God comes to work upon man, it slides away from under His hand as if salvation itself should not save them.

But is not the New Testament more favorable to man than the Old? Or, is not man grown better now that there is so much of God's grace discovered? I answer, There is a perfect harmony between the Testaments: here he is styled "a child of wrath by nature" *(Eph. 2:3),* the elect as well as others were so. Here you will find him to be "a servant of sin" *(Rom. 6:17).* Never such an imperious master as sin is, never such a willing servant as man is. Sin never leaves commanding, and we love to work, and therefore are at its beck. Here you will find him to be represented as a man that hath a "blind understanding," and a "hard heart," and one that is "alienated from the life of God" *(Eph. 4:18).* Here you will find him to be one that is an "enemy to the Law of God," "enmity" itself *(see Rom. 8:7),* one that neither will nor can "please God." One that is blind, and knows not what to do: II Peter 1:9: "He that lacketh these things is blind," and with such a blindness as is far worse than bodily. A man that is blind in his bodily eyes, would think it to be a great happiness to have a fit guide: as in Acts 13:11, when Elymas was smitten blind, "he sought about for somebody to lead him by the hand" but he that is spiritually blind, cannot endure to have a guide; or if one would lead him, and direct him in the right way, he is angry. And as the Scripture represents him as blind, so "without strength" *(Rom. 5:6),* "dead in trespasses and sins" *(Eph. 2:1),* yea, worse than dead; a dead man doth no more hurt, his evil dieth with him; but there is a life of resistance and rebellion against God that goeth along. I have spoken but little, yet put all together, and then it shows *what a miserably wretched creature man is.*

The Scripture doth not speak this by hyperbole, nor once or twice, but everywhere, where it speaks of this matter, it sets out man to be blind, hard, dead, obstinate, and averse from God. Certainly man contributes little to his own conversion, if the Word of God sets him out everywhere to be such an one; he cannot hunger and thirst after Christ, that drinks in iniquity like water. Nothing in his nature to carry him to grace, who is *altogether* sinful.

If the Scripture had only said that man had accustomed himself to sin, and was not *born* in sin: if it had said that man is very prone, and not *greedy* and *thirsty* in iniquity: if it had only said that man did often think evil, but not *continually*: if the Scripture had said that man was somewhat obstinate, but not *a stone, an adamant,* and like the nether millstone: that he had been indifferent to God and the world, God and the flesh, and not a professed *enemy*: that he had been a captive of sin, and not a *servant* of sin: that man had been weak and not *dead*: only a neuter and not a *rebel*: then there might have been something in man; and the work of conversion and reducing to God had not been so great. But the Scripture saith quite the contrary, that man is all this and much more, therefore this clears it up, that his conversion *is not in himself,* but it is God Who *must* work this good in him, or else he can never be renewed.—*Thomas Manton, 1660.*

(Dr. Manton who is, perhaps, one of the best known of the Puritans, was Sir Oliver Cromwell's personal chaplain.)

THE FIRST CHRISTMAS CAROL

"Glory to God in the highest, and on earth peace, good will toward men" *(Luke 2:14).*

It is superstitious to worship angels; it is but proper to love them. Although it would be a high sin, and an act of misdemeanor against the Sovereign Court of Heaven to pay the slightest adoration to the mightiest angel, yet it would be unkind and unseemly, if we did not give to holy angels a place in our heart's warmest love. In fact, he that contemplates the character of angels, and marks their many deeds of sympathy with men, and kindness towards them, cannot resist the impulse of his nature—the impulse of love towards them. The one incident in angelic history, to which our text refers, is enough to weld our hearts to them forever.

How *free from envy* the angels were! Christ did not come from heaven to save their compeers when they fell. When Satan, the mighty angel, dragged with him a third part of the stars of heaven, Christ did not stoop from His throne to die for them; but He left them to be reserved in chains and darkness until the last great day. Yet angels did not envy men. Though they remembered that He took not up angels, yet they did not murmur when He took up the seed of Abraham; and though the blessed Master had never condescended to take the angel's form, they did not think it beneath them to express their joy when they found Him arrayed in the body of an infant.

How *free, too, they were from pride!* They were not ashamed to come and tell the news to humble shepherds. Methinks, they had as much joy in pouring out their songs that night before the shepherds, who were watching with their flocks, as they would have had if they had been commanded by their Master to sing their hymn in the halls of Caesar. Mere men, men possessed with pride, think it a fine thing to preach before kings and princes; and think it great condescension now and then to have to minister to the humble crowds. Not so the angels. They stretched their willing wings, and gladly sped from their bright seats above, to tell the shepherds on the plain by night, the marvelous story of an Incarnate God.

And mark *how well they told the story,* and surely you will love them! Not with the stammering tongue of him that tells a tale in which he hath no interest; nor with the feigned interest of a man that would move the passions of others, when he feeleth no emotion himself; but with joy and gladness, such as angels only can know. They sang, "Glory to God in the highest, and on earth peace, good will toward men". Methinks, they sang it with gladness in their eyes; with their hearts burning with love, and with breasts as full of joy as if the good news to man had been good news to themselves. And, verily, it was good news to them, for the heart of sympathy makes good news to others, good news to itself.

Do you not love the angels? Ye will not bow before them, and there ye are right; but will ye not love them? Doth it not make one part of your anticipation of heaven, that in heaven you shall dwell with the holy angels, as well as with the spirits of just men made perfect? Oh, how sweet to think that these holy and lovely beings are our guardians every hour! They keep watch and ward about us, both in the burning noon-tide, and in the darkness of the night. They keep us in all our ways; they bear us up in their hands, lest at any time we dash our feet against stones. They unceasingly minister unto us who are the heirs of salvation; for know ye not, that "the angel of the Lord encampeth round about them that fear Him"?

—*C. H. Spurgeon, December 1857.*

"Glory to God in the highest" *(Luke 2: 14).* The angels were no Arminians, they sang, "glory *to God* in the highest." They believe in no doctrine which uncrowns Christ, and puts the crown upon the heads of mortals. They believe in no system of faith which makes salvation dependent upon the creature, and, which really gives the creature the praise, for what is it less than for a man to save himself, if the whole dependence of salvation rests upon his own free will? No, my brethren; there may be some preachers, that delight to preach a doctrine that magnifies man; but in their gospel angels have no delight. The only glad tidings that made the angels sing, are those that put God first, God last and God midst, and God without end, in he salvation of His creatures, and put the crown wholly and alone upon the hea of Him Who saves without a helper. "Glory *to God* in the highest," is the angels' song.— *C. H. Spurgeon.*

VOL. II   JANUARY. 1923   NO. 1

STUDIES in the SCRIPTURES

"Search the Scriptures" John 5:39.

A PERIODICAL (MONTHLY "IF THE LORD WILL")
DEVOTED TO BIBLE STUDIES and EXPOSITIONS

Associate Editors and Publishers, I. C. Herendeen and Arthur W. Pink,
Swengel, Pa.

Price: 10 cents per copy; $1.00 per year. Foreign $1.00 per year.

TO OUR SCRIPTURE STUDY FAMILY—

By the time this is read another year will have sped its course: to some wearisomely, to others all too swiftly. Another milestone has been passed, and we are that much nearer the end of our journey. No matter what our lot has been during the past twelve months, no matter how mysterious the trials and testings we have been called on to endure, each child of God can say, Surely "goodness and mercy" have followed me throughout the entire course of the three hundred and sixty-five days now past. And how blessed to know as we face the year before us, with all its unknown joys and sorrows, that *"goodness and mercy"* will continue to follow us all the days of our lives! What, then, should be our response? Verily, unquestioning confidence in that One who maketh *all things* "work together for good" to His own.

As intimated in our last editorial we contemplate no radical changes. Our dominating desire is to feed the sheep and lambs. We do not believe there is any *food* for the soul in exposing and criticising systems of error—necessary as that may sometimes be—so we shall continue to keep our pages clear of declamations and denunciations. It will be our aim, with God's gracious help, to bring forth things "new and old". In these days there are some who are glorying in the new light they have received. While not disparaging their productions, it seems to us there is a real need at present to recover some of the truths known and practiced by our fathers, and which are, largely lost to the rising generation. Among these are the teachings of God's Word concerning the believer's relation to the Law and the place the Sabbath should have in this dispensation. We beg our readers to examine in the light of Holy Writ the article in this issue on "Are believers under the Law?" This will be followed by other articles, D. V., from well-known servants of God, now no more with us.

For some time past we have pondered the advisibility of enlarging our magazine. The small type used during 1922 has been a trial to many of our readers, but to use a larger and to increase the spacing between the lines meant that we must cut down the material, unless more pages were added; and this latter meant quite an increase in the cost of production. But after prayerful deliberation the editors are in entire accord to extend the size of *Studies in the Scriptures* without further delay. At the moment of writing (October 31st) we have less than a dozen subscriptions entered for 1923, so this is a step entirely by faith. Nor are we expecting to increase the price. We have every confidence in our ever-faithful God to supply our every need. What is done we do solely for His glory and the blessing of His dear people, so we may safely leave the issue with Him who doeth all things well.

We are obliged to state, however, that the postal regulations do not permit us to continue sending this magazine to those whose subscriptions have expired. The present issue is sent out to many as a sample copy and will not be repeated. If, then, you desire *Studies in the Scriptures* for 1923 please send in your subscription at once.

Trusting that the increase in size will bring increased blessing to our friends, and with the old time wish of a "Happy New Year", I remain,

Yours by grace,
Arthur W. Pink.

IMPORTANT NOTICES

Subscription Price: $1.00 per year to any address in the world. Single copies **10 cents.**

Change of Address: Please notify us promptly of any change of address, and be certain to give both old and new addresses.

Non-Subscribers receiving this Magazine regularly will understand their subscription has been entered by a friend.

Copies lost in the mail duplicated on request.

All new subscriptions will be dated back to January, 1923.

Entered as second-class matter December 15th, 1921 at the post office at Swengel, Pa., under Act of March 3rd, 1879.

CONTENTS

John's Gospel (John 4:11-19) 2
Are Believers Under the Law? 9
Antichrist in the Psalms 13
Exposition of First Peter 20
Anxious Care 26
Spiritual Preparedness 32

JOHN'S GOSPEL

13. CHRIST AT SYCHAR'S WELL.
(Continued). John 4:11-19.

In viewing the Saviour's conversation with this Samaritan woman as a sample case of God's gracious dealings with a sinner, we have seen, thus far: First, that the Lord took the initiative, being the first to speak. Second, that His first word to her was "Give"—directing her thoughts at once to *grace;* and that His next was "Me"—leading her to be occupied with *Himself.* Third, that He brings her face to face with her helplessness, by asking her for a "drink," which in its deepest meaning, signified that He was seeking her faith and confidence to refresh His spirit. Fourth, this was met by an exhibition of the woman's prejudice, which, in principle, illustrated the enmity of the carnal mind against God.

Fifth, Christ then affirmed that she was ignorant of the way of salvation and of His own Divine glory. Sixth, He referred to eternal life under the expressive figure of "living water." Seventh, He assured her that this living water was offered to her as a "gift," on the condition that she would "ask" for it, and thus take the place of a receiver. This brief summary brings us to the end of verse 10, and from that point we will now proceed, first, presenting an Analysis of the verses which immediately follow:—

1. The Woman's Ignorance, v. 11.
2. The Woman's Insolence, v. 12.
3. The Saviour's gracious Promise, vv. 13, 14.
4. The Woman's Prejudice Overcome, v. 15.
5. The Saviour's Arrow for the Conscience, v. 16.
6. The Saviour's Omniscience Displayed, vv. 17, 18.
7. The Woman's Dawning Perception, v. 19.

As we read the first section of this blessed narrative we were struck with the amazing condescension of the Lord of Glory, who so humbled Himself as to converse with this fallen woman of Samaria. Now, as we turn to consider the section which follows, we cannot fail to be impressed with the wondrous patience of the Saviour. He had invited this wretched creature to ask from Him, and He promised to give her living water; but instead of promptly closing with His gracious offer, the woman continued to raise objections. But Christ did not turn away in disgust, and leave her to suffer the merited results of her waywardness and stubbornness; He bore with her stupidity, and with Divine long-sufferance wore down her opposition, and won her to Himself.

"The woman saith unto Him, Sir, Thou hast nothing to draw with, and the well is deep: from whence then hast Thou that living water?" *(v. 11)*. Four things are brought out by this statement. First, her continued blindness to the glory of Him who addressed her. Second, her occupation with material things. Third, her concentration on the means rather than the end. Fourth, her ignorance of the Source of the "living water." Let us briefly consider each of these separately.

In v. 9 we find that this woman referred to Christ as "a Jew." In replying, the Saviour reproached her for her ignorance by saying, "If thou knewest the gift of God, and *who* it is that saith to thee, Give me to drink; thou wouldest have asked of Him" *(v. 10)*. It is true she had never before met the Lord Jesus, but this did not excuse her. It was because she was blind that she saw in Him no beauty that she should *desire* Him. And it is only unbelief which prevents the sinner today from recognizing in that One who died upon the Cross the Son of God, and the only One who could save him from his sins. And unbelief is not a thing to be pitied, but blamed. But now that Christ had revealed Himself as the One who dispensed the "gift" of God, the Samaritan woman only answered "Sir, *Thou hast nothing* to drawn with"! Poor woman, how little she knew as yet the Divine dignity of that One who had come to seek and to save that which was lost. How complete was her blindness. And how accurately does she picture *our* state by nature. Exactly the same was our condition when God, in infinite mercy, began His dealings with us—our eyes were closed to the perfections of His beloved Son, and "We hid as it were our faces from Him."

"Sir, Thou hast nothing *to draw with.*" How this shows the trend of her thoughts. Her mind was centered upon wells and buckets! And this, again, illustrates a principle of general application. This woman is still to be viewed as a representative character.

Behold in her an accurate portrayal of the sinner, as we see her mind concentrated upon *material things*. Her mind was occupied with the world—its duties and employments—and hence she could not rise to any higher thoughts: she could not discern *who* it was that addressed her, nor *what* He was offering. And thus it is with all who are of the world: they are kept away from the things of Christ, by the things of time and sense. The Devil uses just such things to keep the soul from the Saviour. "Let it be what it may, let it be only a waterpot, he cares not, so long as it occupies the mind to the exclusion of the knowledge of Christ. He cares not for the instrument, so that he gains his own ends, to draw the mind away from the apprehension of spiritual things. It may be pleasure, it may be amusement, gain, reputation, family duties, lawful employments, so that it keeps the soul from fixing on Christ. This is all he wants. A waterpot will serve his purpose, just as well as a palace, so that he can blind them, 'lest the light of the glorious Gospel of Christ, who is the image of God, should shine unto them'" (J. N. Darby).

Ah, dear friend, Is there anything which has thus been keeping you away from Christ—from seeking His great salvation, and obtaining from Him the "living water"? That thing may be quite innocent and harmless, yea, it may be something praiseworthy in itself. Even lawful employments, family duties, may keep a soul from the Saviour, and hinder you from receiving His priceless gift. Satan is very subtle in the means he employs to blind the mind. Did you ever notice that, in the Parable of the Sower, the Lord tells us that the things which "choke the Word" are "the *cares* of this world, and the deceitfulness of riches" *(Matt. 13:22)*?

Should an unsaved soul read these lines we ask you to *see yourself* in the case of this woman, as far as we have yet considered it. Her thoughts were on the purpose which had brought her to the well—a lawful and necessary purpose, no doubt, but one which occupied her mind to the exclusion of the things of Christ! She could think of nothing but wells and buckets—she was, therefore, unable to discern the love, the grace, the winsomeness of that blessed One who sought her salvation. And how many a man there is today so busily occupied with making a living for his family, and how many a woman so concerned with the duties of the home—lawful and necessary things—that Christ and His salvation are *crowded out!* So it was with this Samaritan woman. She thought only of her *bodily* need: her mind was centered on the common round of daily tasks. And thus it is with many another now. They are too busy to take time to study the things of God. They are too much occupied with *their* "waterpots" to listen to the still small voice of God.

"Sir, Thou hast nothing to draw with." These words illustrate another principle which, in its outworkings, stand between many a sinner and salvation. The woman's mind was centered on *means*, rather than the end. She was occupied with something to "draw with," rather than with Christ. And how many today are concerned far more with their own efforts and doings than with the Saviour Himself. And even where their eyes are not upon their own works, they are frequently turned to the evangelist, or to the 'inquiry room' or 'the mourner's bench.' And where this is not the case, the Devil will get them occupied with their own repentance and faith. Anything, so long as he can keep the poor sinner from looking to *Christ alone.*

And, too, we may observe how this woman was *limiting* Christ to the use of means. She supposed He could not provide the "living water" unless He had something to "draw with." And how many imagine they cannot be saved except in some 'Revival Meetings,' or at least in a church-house. But when it pleases God to do so, He acts independently of all means (the Word excepted). When He desires to create a world, He speaks and it is done! He rains manna from heaven; furnishes water out of the rock, and supplies honey from the carcase of the lion!

"The woman saith unto Him, Sir, Thou hast nothing to draw with and the well is deep: from whence then hast Thou that living water?" *(v. 11).* She continues to raise objections, and press her questions. No sooner had the Lord answered one than she brings forward another. The Lord had replied to her "How?" by telling of the "gift" of God, the "living water." Now she asks "Whence?" this was to be obtained. She knew not the *Source* from whence this "living water" proceeded. All she knew was that the well was deep.

"The well is deep." And there is a deep meaning in these words. The well *is* deep—far deeper than our hands can reach down to. From whence then shall man obtain the "living water"? *How* shall he procure "eternal life"? By keeping the Law? Nay, verily, for "by the deeds of the law there shall no flesh be justified" *(Rom. 3:20).* Is it by cultivating the best that is within us by nature? No, for "in my flesh dwelleth no good thing" *(Rom. 7:18).* Is it by living up to the light we have, and doing the best we know how? No, for we are "without strength" *(Rom. 5:6).* What then? Ah, dear reader, listen: This "living water" is not a wage to be earned, a prize to be sought, a crown to be won. No; it is a gift, God's free gift in Christ: "The gift of God is eternal life through Jesus Christ our Lord" *(Rom. 6:23);* yes; the well *is* deep. Into awful depths of suffering had the Saviour to descend before the life-giving Water could be furnished to sinners.

"Art Thou greater than our father

Jacob, which gave us the well, and drank thereof himself, and his children, and his cattle?" *(v. 12)*. As another has said, "How little she knew, as yet, of the One she was addressing. The well might be deep, but there is something deeper still, even her soul's deep need; and something deeper than that again, even the grace that had brought Him down from heaven to meet her need. But so little did she know of Him, that she could ask, 'Art Thou greater than our father Jacob, which gave us the well?' She knew not that she was speaking to Jacob's God—to the One who had formed Jacob and given him all that he ever possessed. She knew nothing of this. Her eyes were yet closed, and this was the true secret of her *'How?'* and her *'Whence?'*"

How much this explains! When we find people asking questions, unbelieving questions, concerning the things of God, it is a sure sign that they need to have their eyes opened. The rationalist, the critic, and the infidel are blind. It is their very blindness that causes them to ask questions, raise difficulties, and create doubts. They deem themselves very clever, but they do only exhibit their folly. However, in the case of this Samaritan woman her questions proceeded not from a bold infidelity, but from nature's blindness and ignorance, and therefore the Lord dealt patiently with her. He knew how to silence a rationalist, and ofttimes He dismissed a carping critic in a summary manner. But there were also occasions when, in marvelous condescension and gracious patience, He waited on an ignorant inquirer, for the purpose of resolving his difficulties and removing his fears. And thus it was at the well at Sychar. He was not to be put off with her quibbling, nor could He be wearied by her dullness. He bore with her (as He did with each of us) in marvelous longsufferance, and left her not until He had fully met the deep need of her soul by the revelation of Himself.

"Art Thou greater than our father Jacob, which gave us the well, and drank thereof himself?" *(v. 12)*. Once again we may discover here a deeper significance than what appears on the surface. Attention is called to the *antiquity* of the well from which Jacob and his children drank. Beautiful is the underlying spiritual lesson. The "Well" is as old as man the sinner. The salvation of which the "water" of this "Well" speaks, had refreshed the hearts of Abel and Enoch, Noah and Abraham, and all the Old Testament saints. God has had but one way of salvation since sin entered the world. Salvation has always been by grace, through faith, altogether apart from human works. The Gospel is no novelty: it was "preached before unto Abraham" *(Gal. 3:8)*. Yea, it was preached to Adam and Eve in the Garden of Eden, when, clothing our fallen first parents with coats of skins *(Gen. 3:21)*, God made known the fact that "without shedding of blood is no remission," and that through the death of an innocent substitute a covering was provided which fitted the guilty and the defiled to stand unabashed in the presence of the thrice holy One, because "accepted in the Beloved."

"Jesus answered and said unto her, Whosoever drinketh of this water shall thirst again" *(v. 14)*. The Lord Jesus was not to be put off. He was determined to reveal Himself to this sin-sick soul. "Whosoever drinketh of this water shall thirst again." The seat of the "thirst" within man lies too deep for the waters of this earth to quench. The "thirst" of man's soul is a spiritual one, and that is why material things are unable to slake it. Earth's deepest well may be fathomed and drained, and the needy soul remain thirsty after all. Men and women may take their fill of pleasure, yet will it fail to satisfy. They may surround themselves with every comfort and luxury that wealth can provide, and the heart still be empty. They may court the honors of the world, and climb to the highest pinnacle of human fame, but the plaudits of men will leave an aching void behind them. They may explore the whole realm of philosophy and science, until they become as wise as Solomon, but like Israel's king of old, they will discover that all under the sun in only "vanity and vexation of spirit." Over all the wells of this world's providing must be written, "Whosoever drinketh of this water shall thirst again."

This is true not only of the material, the mental, and the social realms, but of the religious, too. Man may awaken within us certain desires, but he cannot satisfy them. Man may exhort and persuade, and we may make resolutions, amend our lives, become very religious, and yet "thirst again." The religious systems of human manufacture hold not the Water of Life. They do but disappoint. Nothing but the "living water" can quench our thirst and satisfy our hearts, and only *Christ* can give this.

"Whosoever drinketh of this water shall *thirst again.*" What an awful illustration of this is furnished in Luke 16. There the Saviour sets before us a man clothed in purple and fine linen, who fared sumptuously every day. He drank deeply of the wells of this passing world; but he thirsted again. O see him, as the Son of God lifts the veil which hides the unseen; see him lifting up his eyes in hell torments, craving, but craving in vain, a single drop of water to cool his parched tongue. There is not so much as a drop of water in hell! There he thirsts, and the unspeakably dreadful thing is that he will thirst *forever and ever.* Fearfully solemn is this for all; but perfectly appalling for the children of ease and luxury, and they who spend their time going from well to well of this world, and giving no serious thought to an eternity of burning in the lake of fire. O that it may please God to cause some such to give these lines a thoughtful consideration, and arrest their attention, and lead them to the Lord Jesus Christ, the Giver of that living water of which whosoever drinketh shall never thirst.

"But whosoever drinketh of the water that I shall give him shall never thirst" *(v. 14).* Here is satisfaction to the soul. The one who has *asked* and *received* is now satisfied. The Lord goes on to say, "But the water that I shall give him shall be in him a well of water springing up into everlasting life." The believer now has a well of living water within, ever fresh, ever flowing, ever springing up toward its native source, for water always seeks its own level. But let us weigh each expression. "Whosoever *drinketh.*" What is drinking? It is ministering to a felt need. It is a personal act of appropriation. It is a taking into myself that which was, previously, without me. "Of the water that I shall *give* him." This "water" is "eternal life," and this is not bought or won, but is received as a "gift," for the "gift of God is eternal life through Jesus Christ our Lord." "Shall never thirst:" here the Lord speaks according to the *fulness* of the gift bestowed: as to our *enjoyment* of it, that is conditioned upon the way in which faith maintains us in fellowship with the Giver. "Never thirst" denotes a satisfying portion. "Never thirst" argues the eternal security of the recipient. Were it possible for a believer to forfeit salvation through unworthiness, this verse would not be true, for every lost soul *will* "thirst," thirst for ever in hell. "Shall be in him a well of water springing up into everlasting life": this "gift," this "living water," is a present possession, imparted by grace, and is something within the believer.

"But whosoever drinketh of the water that I shall give him shall never thirst." To borrow again the language of the eloquent Puritan: "Here we labour, but receive no benefit; we sow many times, and reap not; we reap, and we do not gather in; or gather in, and do not possess; or possess and do not enjoy; or if we enjoy, we are still unsatisfied: it is with anguish of spirit and circumstances of vexation. A great heap of riches makes neither our clothes more warm, our meat more nutritive, nor our beverage more palatable. It feeds the eye but never fills it. Like drink to a person suffering from dropsy, it increases the thirst and promotes the torment. But the grace of God fills the furrows of the heart; and, as the capacity increases, it grows itself in equal degrees, and never suffers any emptiness or dissatisfaction, but carries contentment and fulness all the way; and the degrees of augmentation are not steps and near approaches to satisfaction, but increasings of the capacity. The soul is satisfied all the way, and receives more, not because it wanted any, but that it can now hold the more, being become more receptive of felicity; and in every minute of sanctification, there is so excellent a condition of joy that the very calamities, afflictions, and persecutions of the world, are turned into felicities by the activity of the prevailing ingredient: like a drop of water falling into a tun of wine, it is ascribed into a new form, losing its own nature by a conversion in one more noble. These were the waters which were given us to drink, when, with the rod of God, the Rock, Christ Jesus, was smitten. The Spirit of God moves forever upon these waters; and, when the angel of the covenant had stirred the pool, whosoever descends hither shall find health and peace, joys spiritual, and the satisfaction of eternity" (Jeremy Taylor).

"The woman saith unto Him, Sir, give me this water, that I thirst not, neither come hither to draw" *(v. 15)*. She is still more or less in the dark. The natural mind is occupied with natural things, and it contemplates everything through that medium; it is confined to its own little circle of feelings and ideas; and can neither see nor feel anything beyond it; it lives in its own cramped realm, finds there its own enjoyment and employment, and if left to itself, will live and die there. Poor woman! The Saviour of sinners was before her, but she knew Him not. He was speaking words of grace to her, but as yet, she did not fully comprehend. He had asked for a drink, and she had replied with a *"How?"*. He had told her of God's gift, and she had replied with a *"Whence?"*. He had spoken of an everlasting well, and she seeks only to be spared the trouble of coming hither to draw.

And yet while all that we have just said above is no doubt true, nevertheless, as we take a closer look at this last statement of the woman, we may detect signs more hopeful. Her words afford evidence that the patient dealing of Christ with her was not in vain, yea, that light was beginning to illumine her darkened understanding. Note, she now appropriates His word, and says, "Sir, *give* me to drink." Relief from daily toil was, no doubt, the thought uppermost in her mind; yet, and mark it well, she was now *willing* to be indebted to a "Jew" for that! There was still much ignorance; but her prejudice was being overcome; her heart was being won. What, then, is the next step? Why, her *conscience* must be reached. A sense of need must be created. And how is this accomplished? By a conviction of sin. The first thought in connection with salvation, the prime meaning of the word itself, is that of *deliverance* from something. Salvation implies danger, and the sinner will not flee to Christ as a Refuge from the wrath to come until a due sense (not merely of wretchedness, but) of guilt is upon him. There can be no blessing till there is conviction and confession of sin. It is not until we discover our case to be truly *desperate* that we betake ourselves to Christ—until then, we attempt to prescribe for ourselves. Herein lies the force of the Saviour's next word. "Jesus saith unto her, Go, call thy husband, and come hither" *(v. 16)*. It is strange that so many have missed the point of this. A little meditation will surely discern not only the solemnity, but the blessedness, of this word from the Saviour, to the woman whose heart was slowly opening to receive Him. It is mainly a matter of finding the proper emphasis. Two things the Lord bade her do: the first was solemn and searching; the second gracious and precious. *"Go,"* He said, "Call thy husband"—that was a word addressed to her conscience. "And *come hither"*—that was a word for her heart. The force of what He said was this: If you really want this living water of which I have been telling you, you can obtain it only as a poor, convicted, contrite sinner. But not only did He say "Go," but He added "Come." She was not only to go and call her husband, but she was to come back to Christ *in her true character*. It was a marvelous mingling of "grace" and "truth." Truth for her conscience; grace for her heart. Truth which required her to come out into the light in her proper character, as a self-confessed sinner; grace which invited her to return to the Saviour's side. Well may we admire the wonderful ways of Him "in whom are hid all the treasures of wisdom and knowledge" *(Col. 2:3)*.

"The woman answered and said, I have no husband. Jesus saith unto her, Thou hast well said I have no husband: For thou hast had five husbands; and he whom thou now hast is not thy husband: in that saidst thou truly" *(vv. 17, 18)*. How this exhibits the Deity of Christ! He revealed His omniscience. He knew all about this woman—her heart, her life, her very thoughts; nothing could be hid from Him. She might be a complete stranger to Him in the flesh, yet was He thoroughly acquainted with her. It was the same with Peter: the Saviour knew him thoroughly the first time they met, see 1:42 and our comments thereon. So, too, He saw Nathanael under the fig tree before he came to Him. And so, dear reader, He knows all about you. Nothing can be concealed from His all-seeing eye. But this will not trouble you if everything has been brought out into the light, and confessed before Him.

"The woman saith unto Him, Sir, I perceive that Thou art a prophet" *(v. 19)*. Though the goal was not yet reached, here was the turning point. The secrets of her heart and life had been laid open to her by One she had never seen before. The Lord struck the cord to the conscience of the sinner, and it vibrated. In her previous utterance, "Sir, give me to drink," we have proof that her prejudice was being overcome and her heart was beginning to open. Here we see how, through the exercise of conscience, her understanding was being enlightened.

"The woman saith unto Him, Sir, I perceive that Thou art a prophet." A "prophet" is God's spokesman. This poor soul now recognized the Voice of God. He had spoken more deeply than any man to her soul. The Divine arrow of conviction had pierced her conscience, and the effect is striking: "I *perceive*." Her eyes were beginning to open: she sees something. She discovers herself to be in the presence of some mysterious personage whom she owns as God's spokesman. It was through her conscience the light began to enter! And it is ever thus. O dear reader, have you experienced this for yourself? Has *your* conscience been in the presence of that Light which makes all things manifest? Have you seen yourself as guilty, undone, lost, Christless, hell-deserving? Has the arrow ever entered your conscience? Christ has various arrows in His quiver. He had an arrow for Nicodemus, and He had an arrow for this adulteress. They were different arrows, but they did their work. "He that doeth truth cometh to the light, that his deeds may be made manifest" *(3:21)* was the arrow for the master in Israel. "Go, call thy husband" was His arrow for this Samaritan woman. The question of sin and righteousness must be settled in the presence of God. Has, then, this vital and all-important matter been settled between *your* soul and God? If so, you will be able to appreciate the sequel—the remainder of this wonderful and blessed narrative.

There is a principle here of great importance to the believer. An exercised conscience precedes intelligence in the things of God. Spiritual illumination comes through the heart, more than through the mind. They who are most anxious to have a better understanding of the Holy Oracles need to pray earnestly for God to put His fear upon them, that they may be more careful in avoiding the things which displease Him. One of our deepest needs is a more sensitive conscience. In Heb. 5:11-13 we read of those who were "dull of hearing" and incapacitated to receive the deeper things of God. "Dulness of hearing" does not mean they were suffering from a stupified mind, but rather from a calloused conscience. The last verse of Heb. 5 speaks of those who *were* qualified to receive the deeper truths: "but strong meat belongeth to them that are of full age, even those who by reason of use *have their senses exercised* to discern both good and evil". Thus it was for our learning that we are shown that perception of spiritual things came to the Samaritan woman through, and as the result of, a conscience active in the presence of God.

As preparation for the next article we ask the interested reader to ponder the following questions:—

1. What is signified by "salvation is of the Jews"? v. 22
2. What is signified by worshipping "in spirit and in truth"? v. 24
3. Make a careful study of passages both in the Old and New Testaments which speak of "worship".
4. What is implied by the woman's words in v. 25?
5. What constrained the disciples to remain silent? v. 27
6. What is the force of the "then" in v. 28?
7. What principle is illustrated by the woman leaving her water-pot?—*Arthur W. Pink.*

ARE BELIEVERS UNDER THE LAW?

With respect to the liberty and privileges of the Gospel, it is a truth full of the richest consolation that those who believe in Jesus are freed, not only from the ceremonial yoke of the Mosaic dispensation, but from the condemning power of the law considered as moral. It is by faith in Christ that believers live. All their hope is derived from His righteousness which being imputed to them they are accepted of God on account of it. Being "not under the law" as a covenant, "but under grace", sin hath no more dominion over them. But surely it does not follow that they are no longer under obligation to love God with all their heart, soul, mind, and strength, or their neighbor as themselves. The prodigal son, when forgiven and accepted, was not less obliged to conform to the orders of his father's house than before he left it, but rather the more so. Though the law is dead to a believer, and a believer to it, as *a term of life,* yet he is under perpetual and indissoluble obligations to conform to it as *a rule of conduct.*

To satisfy a serious and sincere mind on this subject one would think it were sufficient to read the ten commandments in the twentieth chapter of

Exodus. Is a believer any more than an unbeliever, allowed to have more Gods than one? May he make to himself a graven image and fall down and worship it? Will the Lord hold him guiltless if he take His name in vain? Is he not obliged to keep holy the Sabbath day? Is he at liberty to dishonor his parents, or kill his neighbors, or commit adultery, or steal, or bear false witness, or covet anything belonging to another? Surely the things which are required by all these precepts must approve themselves to every man's conscience, unless it be perverted and seared as with a hot iron.

But in order to set aside the authority of the ten commandments as a rule of duty to the believer, it has been objected that they do not contain the whole of it. If this were granted, yet it would not follow but they are binding as far as they go; but if so, why pretend to be delivered from the law? The new commandment of Christ to love one another, does not include the whole of duty, and yet we are not free from obligation to comply with it. If the ten commandments were admitted to be binding as far as they go, their comprehending the whole of duty would be a question of comparatively small importance; but the manifest design of the objector is, by undermining their perfection to overturn their authority, that having freed himself from this disagreeable yoke he may establish what he calls Christian liberty.

To show the perfection, then, as well as the authority of the ten commandments, let it suffice to have recourse to our Saviour's exposition of them. If that exposition be faithful, they are reducible to two, answering to the tables of stone on which they were written, and consisting in "love to God with all the heart, soul, mind, and strength, and to our neighbor as ourselves". But love to God and our neighbor comprehends every act of duty that can possibly be performed. Love is the fulfilling of the law, and of all that God requires of man. It is the principle of all positive obedience: for he that loveth God supremely, willingly obeys Him in whatever forms He shall prescribe. The new commandment of love to the brethren is comprehended in the old commandment; For he that loveth God cannot but love His image wherever it is seen. Hence the former is enforced by the latter *(see Gal. 5:13-15; Rom. 13:8-12)*. All the graces of the Spirit, as repentance, faith, hope, charity, patience, temperance, goodness, etc. are but so many modifications of love. He that loveth God cannot but be grieved for having dishonored Him; cannot but believe His Word, and embrace His way of saving sinners through the death of His Son; cannot but build his expectations upon His promises; cannot but love those that love Him; cannot but take everything well at His hand; in short, cannot but deny himself for His sake, and aspire to be of His mind who causeth His sun to shine upon the evil and the good, and sendeth His rain upon the just and upon the unjust. Upon this great principle, therefore, as our Lord observed, *hangs all the law and the prophets,* and, indeed, the whole of true religion.

'Yes,' say some, 'We must be ruled by a *principle* of love; but not by the law as requiring it. The love of Christ constrains the believer to be zealous in the performance of good works'. It is true, we shall never love without a principle, nor run in the way of God's commandments unless constrained to do so by a gracious enlargement of heart. Nor does anything afford so powerful a motive to it as the dying love of Christ. But to make that the rule which is the moving spring of obedience, is to confound things essentially different. "The way of God's commandments" is the same whether our hearts be "enlarged to run therein" or not. To confound the rule with the moving cause, or to make a rule of the latter to the exclusion of that which is afforded by the commandment is to reduce our obligations to the standard of our inclinations, or to consider ourselves as bound to yield just so much obedience to God as we do yield, and no more; and this is the same thing as professing to live free from sin. Moreover, to make that the rule of obedience which is the moving cause of it, is the same thing as for a son to say to his father, 'Sir, I will do what you desire me when I feel inclined to do so, but I will not be *commanded*'. Whatever may be argued against the authority of God, I believe there are few if any parents who could put up with such language from their own children.

In addition to the above, let the following particulars be duly considered:—

1. If we be not under the moral law as a rule of life, we are not *obliged* to love either God or man, and it is no sin to be destitute of love to both. But such a state of things can never exist. The obligation to love God supremely, and our neighbor as ourselves, is founded in our relation to Him and one another, and cannot possibly be dissolved while God is God and man is man. To suppose the contrary, is to suppose that the King of the universe can abdicate His throne, and leave His subjects at liberty to hate and rebel against Him with impugnity. If all the fathers of families in the world could dispense with filial affection in their children, and all the princes in the world with loyal attachment in their subjects, it were less unnatural, and infinitely less mischievous, than for God to dispense with the requirement of our loving Him supremely, and each other as ourselves.

2. Believers are represented as subject to commit sin, and as actually committing it every day of their lives. The petition for daily forgiveness, in the Lord's prayer, supposes this; and John teaches, that "if we say we have no sin, we deceive ourselves, and the truth is not in us". But all sin implies a law of which it is the breach: *"Where no law is, there is no transgression"*. Believers, therefore, must be under some law. And that this is no other than the moral law, is evident from the definition which is given of sin by the apostle John, that it is "the transgression of the law". This is the same as saying, that every sin which is committed, whether by believers or unbelievers, is a deviation from that Divine rule. The sum is, if believers daily break the law they must of necessity be under it as a rule of duty. If the law were abrogated, or its authority superseded so as to be no longer a rule of duty to believers, it could be no medium to *them* by which to come at the knowledge of sin. That by which sin is known must be a living rule. To say otherwise, is as absurd as to judge of the criminality of a prisoner by a statute which had long since been repealed.

3. One great and leading design of our Lord in His sermon on the Mount was to vindicate the precepts of the moral law from the false glosses of the Jewish Rabbis, and to show that in their most spiritual meaning they were binding upon His followers. Coming into the world as He did, to introduce a new dispensation, He was aware that men might suppose His mission was at variance with Moses and the Prophets. To prevent such conceits, He speaks in the most decided language—"Think not that I am come to destroy the law or the prophets: I am not come to destroy, but to fulfill. For verily I say unto you, Till heaven and earth pass, one jot or one tittle shall in no wise pass from the law, till all be fulfilled!" He also goes on to warn His followers against those who should *"break the least of the commandments, and teach men so;"* and to

declare that "except their righteousness exceeded that of the scribes and Pharisees, they should in no case enter into the kingdom of heaven!" To say that we need the righteousness of Christ to be imputed to us, is to speak truth, but not the truth of this saying, the manifest design of which is to inculcate a purer morality than that which was taught and practised by the Jewish leaders. Had this Sermon been heard by many a modern audience, it would have been condemned as legal, and the preacher pronounced a poor graceless wretch, who knew nothing of the Gospel.

4. Believers are exhorted, in the New Testament, to love one another on the express ground of its being a requirement of the moral law. "Brethren, we have been called unto liberty; only use not liberty for an occasion to the flesh, but by love serve one another. *For all the law* is fufilled in one word, *even in this,* Thou shalt love thy neighbour as thyself. But if ye bite and devour one another, take heed that ye be not consumed one of another" *(Gal. 5:13-15).* If the "liberty" possessed by the Galatians consisted in a freedom from obligation to obey the precepts of the moral law, it is passing strange that these very precepts should be *urged as an authority* against their using liberty as an occasion to the flesh. Paul, whatever some of his professed admirers have been, was assuredly a better reasoner than this would make him. The liberty of the Gospel, includes an exemption from the precepts of the ceremonial law, and from the curse or condemning power of the moral law; and these were privileges of inestimable value. They were, however, capable of abuse; and to guard against this, the holy *precept* of the law, notwithstanding the removal of its penalty, is held up by the apostle in all its native and inalienable authority. To the same purpose the apostle, writing to the believing Romans, inculcates brotherly love and purity, *from the authority of the moral law.* "Owe no man anything, but love one another; for he that loveth another hath fulfilled the law. For this, Thou shalt not commit adultery, Thou shalt not kill, Thou shalt not steal, Thou shalt not bear false witness, Thou shalt not covet; and if there be any other commandment, it is briefly comprehended in this saying, Thou shalt love thy neighbor as thyself. Love worketh no ill to his neighbor, therefore, *love is the fulfilling of the law*" *(Rom. 13:8-10).* If any man can read this passage without perceiving that the precepts of the moral law are still binding on believers, he must be proof against evidence; and with such a person it is in vain to reason. If God give him not repentance to the acknowledging of the truth, he must e'en go on, and abide the consequences.

5. Believers are either under the law, (in the sense in which we plead for it) or *without law.* By the language of the apostle there can be no medium. There is no other way of exonerating ourselves from the charge of being *without law to God* but by acknowledging that we are *under the law to Christ (I Cor. 9:21).* Such was the acknowledgment of Paul in behalf of the primitive Christians: "To them that are without law, as without law, (being not without law to God, but under the law to Christ,) that I might gain them that are without law." His words plainly intimate a change, indeed, in its administration; but not of the thing itself. Formerly it was administered by Moses, and attended with that terrific aspect which properly pertains to it when addressed to transgressors: now it is administered by Christ, who has placed it at the foundation of His legislative code, and by divesting it of its curse, has rendered it to the believer a friendly guide. But the thing itself is the same, and will remain so

when heaven and earth shall have passed away.

6. Those who have the greatest aversion to the law being a rule of life, are yet very willing that others should make it a rule of their conduct towards them! Whether they are bound to love their neigbours as themselves, or not, if they are treated unkindly or unjustly, even by their brethren, they are as much alive to resentment as any other people. But if they be not obliged to love others, why should others be obliged to love them; and why should they be offended with them for the contrary? And if the second table of the law be mutually binding, on what ground can we plead exemption from the first?—*Extract from Antinomianism by Andrew Fuller, 1814.*

"When they affirm that the law is still the rule of life, if they mean that it still declares the mind of God as to what man ought to be and do, there can be no objection to the expression; but if they mean that the believer is required to walk according to this rule in order to salvation, and that he will be judged and condemned if he fails in conformity to its demands, nothing can be more false."—*Dr. James H. Brookes in "The Way Made Plain."*

8. ANTICHRIST IN THE PSALMS

The references to the Man of Sin in the book of Psalms are, for the most part, more or less incidental ones. With rare exceptions he comes into view only as he is related to Israel, or as he affects their fortunes. One cannot appreciate the force of what is there said of him except as that is examined in the light of its prophetic setting. The time when the Antichrist will be in full power is during the Tribulation period, and it is not until we discover, by careful searching, which of the Psalms describe the Time of Jacob's trouble, that we know where to look for their last great Troubler.

Politically and ecclesiastically the Antichrist may be viewed in a three-fold connection: first, as he is related to the Gentiles; second, as he is related to the apostate Jewish nation; third, as he is related to the godly Jewish Remnant, who separate themselves from their unbelieving brethren. More details are furnished us in the Psalms upon this third relationship than upon the other two, though we have occasional allusions to Antichrist's connections with the Gentiles and the Jewish nation as a whole.

The second Psalm gives us a brief but vivid picture of that which will wind up the Tribulation period, and while the Antichrist is not directly named, yet the light which other scriptures throw upon it reveals the dreadful personality who heads the rebellion there described. This second Psalm is prophetic in its character and has, like most (if not all) prophecy, a *double* fulfillment.

"Why do the heathen rage, and the people imagine a vain thing? The kings of the earth set themselves, and the rulers take counsel together, against the Lord, and against His anointed, saying, Let us break their bands asunder, and cast away their cords from us" *(Psa. 2:1-3)*. A part of this passage is found quoted in Acts 4, but it is striking to note where the quotation ceases. Peter and John had been arraigned before the religious authorities of Israel, because that in the name of Jesus Christ they had healed an impotent man. The apostles boldly and faithfully vindicated themselves, and after being admonished and threatened were allowed to depart to their own company. Then it was that they "lifted up their voice to God with one accord, and said, Lord, Thou art God, which hast made heaven, and earth, and the sea, and all that in them is: Who by the mouth of Thy servant David hath said, Why did the heathen rage, and the people imagine vain things? The kings of the earth stood up, and the rulers were gathered together against the Lord, and against His Christ" *(Acts 4:24-26)*. Notice they quoted only the first two verses of Psalm 2, and *this* they did not say was now "fulfilled." What they did say was, "For of a truth against Thy holy child Jesus, whom Thou hast anointed, both Herod, and Pontius Pilate, with the Gentiles, and the people of Israel, were gathered together, for to do whatsoever Thy hand and Thy counsel determined before to be done" *(v. 28)*. In the apprehension of Christ and in His trials before the Jewish and Gentilish authorities, this prophecy through David had received a partial fulfillment, but its final one is yet future. The time when Psalm 2 is to receive its complete accomplishment is intimated in the middle section —it is just prior to the time when Christ returns to the earth as "King," and receives the heathen for His inheritance and the uttermost parts of the earth for His possession; in other words, it is just before the dawn of the Millennium, namely, the end of the Tribulation period.

As we re-read this second Psalm in the light of Rev. 16:14 and 19:19 we find that it depicts the final act in the blatant and defiant career of the last great Caesar. It is an act of insane desperation. The Son of Perdition will gather his forces and make a concerted effort to prevent the Christ of God entering into His earthly inheritance. This we believe is evident from the terms of the Psalm itself.

The Psalm opens with an interrogation: "*Why* do the heathen (the Gentiles) rage (better, "tumultuously assemble"), and the people (Israel) imagine (meditate) a vain thing?" The fact that this is put in the form of a question is to arrest more quickly the reader's attention, and to emphasize the unthinkable impiety of what follows. "The kings of the earth set themselves, and the rulers take counsel together, against the Lord, and against His anointed." Notice that this rebellion is staged not only against the Lord but also against His "Anointed," that is, His Christ. The madness of this effort (headed by Antichrist) is intimated in v. 4: "He that sitteth in the heavens shall laugh: the Lord shall have them in derision." The futility of this movement is seen in v. 6: "Yet have I set My King upon My holy hill of Zion." The "yet" here has the force of "notwithstanding:" it shows the aim and the object which the insurrectionists had in view, namely, an attempt to *prevent* Christ returning to earth to set up His millennial kingdom. The response of heaven is noted in v. 5: "Then shall He speak unto them in His wrath, and vex them in His sore displeasure." This is enlarged upon in Rev. 19:20, 21. Psalm 2, then, brings us to the *end* of the Antichrist's history and treats only of the closing events in his awful career. In the other Psalms where he is in view earlier incidents are noted and his dealings with the Jews are described.

The next Psalm in which the Antichrist appears is the fifth. This Psalm sets forth the petitions which the godly Remnant of Israel will make to God during the Tribulation period. It would carry us beyond our present bounds to attempt anything like a complete exposition of this Psalm in the light of its prophetic application. We shall do little more than generalize.

The Tribulation period is the time when Satan is given the freest rein, when lawlessness abounds, and when to the unbelieving heart it would seem that God had vacated His throne. But the eye of faith recognizes the fact that Jehovah is still ruling amid the armies of the heavens and among the inhabitants of the earth. Hence the force of the Divine title in v. 2—the remnant address Jehovah as "My *King* and my God." The most awful wickedness and rebellion is going on around them, but they are fully assured that God is quite able to cope with the situation. "The Wicked shall not stand in Thy sight: Thou hatest all workers of iniquity. Thou shalt destroy them that speak leasing: the Lord will abhor the bloody and deceitful man" *(vv. 5, 6)*.

The "Bloody and Deceitful Man" is plainly the Man of Sin. He is denominated "bloody" by virtue of his military ferocity; he is called "deceitful" because of his political duplicity. One after another of his opponents will fall before him: through a sea of blood will he advance to his imperial throne. Utterly unreliable will be his word, worthless his promises. A manifest incarnation of that one who is the father of lies will he be. Most completely will he deceive the Jews. At first posing as their friend; later, standing forth as their arch-enemy. All doubt as to the identity of this "Bloody and Deceitful Man" is removed by what is said of him in v. 9, "for there is no faithfulness in his mouth."

From Psalm 5 we turn to Psalm 7 where we find the godly Jewish Remnant crying unto the Lord against their persecutors, chief of which is the Antichrist. This is clear from the first two verses, where the change from the plural to the singular number is very significant—"O Lord my God, in Thee do I put my trust: save me from all *them* that persecute me, and deliver me: Lest *he* tear my soul like a lion, rending it in pieces, while there is none to deliver." The Remnant plead their innocency before God and call down upon themselves the Enemy's curse if they have acted unjustly—"O Lord my God, If I have done this; if there be iniquity in my hands; if I have requited him that did evil unto me, or spoiled mine adversary unto emptiness; Let the Enemy pursue my soul, and overtake it" *(vv. 4-6*, Jewish translation). This at once serves to identify the individual of v. 2 who would tear their souls like a lion" (not "like a *bear*")—showing his kinship with that awful one who "goeth about as a roaring lion, seeking whom he may devour." Observe, too, the word he *"was* at peace," but now "without cause *is* mine enemy." Clearly it is the Antichrist that is here in view, and, as manifested in the second half of Daniel's seventieth week, when he shall have thrown off his mask and stood forth revealed in all his dreadfulness. The twelfth verse goes on to say, "If he turn not, he will whet his sword; he hath bent his bow and made it ready." It is this which causes the Remnant to cry, "O Lord my God, in Thee do I put my trust: save me from all them that persecute me, and deliver me" *(v. 1)*. The fourteenth verse unmistakeably identifies this end-time Enemy of Israel, and again stamps him as a worthy son of "the father of lies" —"Behold, he travaileth with iniquity, and hath conceived mischief, and brought forth falsehood." In the sixteenth verse the Remnant express their assurance of the certain fate of their Foe: "His mischief shall return upon his own head, and his violent dealing shall come down upon his own pate."

The eighth Psalm is closely connected with the seventh. In the last verse of the seventh we hear the Remnant saying, "I will praise the Lord according to His righteousness: and will sing praise to the name of the Lord most high." This anticipates the time when they shall be delivered from their awful Enemy, and when the glorious Millennium shall have dawned—"The Lord *most high*" is His distinctive millennial title. Psalm 8 follows this with a lovely millennial picture, when Jehovah will be worshipped because His name is then "excellent in *all* the earth." Then shall the Remnant say, "Out of the mouth of babes and sucklings hast Thou ordained strength because of Thine enemies, that Thou mightest still *the Enemy and the Aveng-*

er" (v. 2). The "Enemy and the Avenger," more literally "the Foe and the Revenger," is one of the many names of the Antichrist.

Much in the ninth Psalm also anticipates millennial conditions and celebrates the overthrow of the Man of Sin. Sings the Remnant, "For Thou hast maintained my right and my cause; Thou satest in the throne judging right. Thou hast rebuked the heathen, Thou hast destroyed the Wicked" (vv. 4, 5). That the Wicked, or Lawless One, is the Antichrist, is clear from the next verse: "The destructions of the Enemy are come to a perpetual end: and their cities hast Thou destroyed." We hope to show in a later article that "their cities" which God will destroy are the cities of Antichrist and the False Prophet, namely, Babylon and Rome. Again; in vv. 15, 16 of this Psalm we read, "The heathen are sunk down in the pit that they made: in the net which they hid is their own foot taken. The Lord is known by the judgment which He executeth: the Wicked is snared in the work of his own hands!" This refers to the destruction of the Antichrist and his forces at Armegeddon.

In the tenth Psalm we have the fullest description of the Antichrist found in any of the Psalms. This Psalm is divided into four sections: first, the Cry of the Remnant (v. 1); second, the Character of the Antichrist (vv. 2-11); third, the Cry of the Remnant renewed (vv. 12-15); fourth, the Confidence of the Remnant (vv. 16-18). In its opening verse we discover its dispensational key—the "Times of Trouble" (cf. Jer. 30:7) being the great Tribulation. Observe now what is here said of the Wicked One. In v. 2 we read, "The Wicked in his pride doth persecute (R. V. "hotly pursue") the poor." The "poor" (referred to in this Psalm seven times—vv. 2, 8, 9, 9, 10, 14, and "humble" in v. 17 should be "poor"—emphasizing the *completeness* of their poverty) are the faithful Remnant who have refused to receive the mark of the Beast, and as the result are suffered to neither "buy nor sell" (*see* Rev. 13:17). In vv. 3, 4 we are told, "For the Wicked (One) boasteth of his heart's desire, and curseth, yea, abhorreth the Lord (see Hebrew). The Wicked, through the pride of his countenance, will not seek after God: all his thoughts are—no God." This tells of his frightful impiety and reveals his satanic origin. In v. 6 his consuming egotism is depicted: "He hath said in his heart, I shall not be moved: for I shall never be in adversity." Then follows a description of his awful wickedness: "His mouth is full of cursing and deceit and fraud: under his tongue is mischief and vanity. He sitteth in the lurking places of the villages: in the secret places doth he murder the innocent: his eyes are privily set against the poor." Notice in this last verse the mention of "the secret places." It was to them our Lord referred in His Olivet Discourse, when He said, "Wherefore if they shall say unto you, Behold, he is in the desert; go not forth: Behold, he is in the *secret chambers;* believe it not." This whole Psalm will well repay the most minute study.

In the opening verse of the fourteenth Psalm we have what we doubt not is another reference to the Antichrist, here called *"The* Fool." He is the archfool, who, in his blatant defiance, says in his heart—"no God." The mark of identification is found in the marginal reading of Psalm 10:4: "All his thoughts are—no God." Does not this title point out another contrast between Christ and the Antichrist: One is "the wonderful Counsellor," the other is "the Fool"!

In the seventeenth Psalm, which contains the confession of the Remnant (pleading their innocency before God), reference is again made to the Antichrist. "By the word of God's lips" will the believing Jews be "kept from the paths of the Destroyer." This is another of his titles which points a contrast: Christ is the Saviour; Antichrist the Destroyer. That it is the Antichrist who is here in view is clear from what follows in vv. 12 and 13, where we read, "Like as a lion that is greedy of his prey, and as it were a young lion lurking in secret places. Arise, O Lord, disappoint him, cast him down: deliver my soul from the Wicked, by Thy sword." The "Wicked" is here in the singular number. Note again the reference to the "secret places," about which we shall have something to say, D. V., in our exposition of Matt. 24, vv. 25 and 26 when we treat of the Antichrist in the Gospels.

We pass over several Psalms which contain incidental allusions to the Wicked One and turn now to the thirty-sixth. The wording of the first verse is somewhat ambiguous, and we believe its force comes out better by rendering it, with the Sept., Syriac and Vulgate, "the transgression of the Wicked saith within his heart, that there is no fear of God before his eyes." He defies Jehovah and fears not Elohim. "For he flattereth himself in his own eyes, until his iniquity be found to be hateful" *(v. 2)*. Haughty conceit fills him, but in the end he shall reap as he has sown. "The words of his mouth are iniquity and deceit; he hath left off to be wise, and to do good" *(v. 3)*. This refers to his treacherous dealings with the Jews, and takes note of the two great stages in his career; first, when he poses as Israel's friend, later when he comes out in his true character as their enemy. V. 4 describes his moral character: "he deviseth mischief upon his bed; he setteth himself in a way that is not good; he abhorreth not evil."

The thirty-seventh Psalm, which in its ultimate application has to do with the godly Remnant in the Tribulation period, contains a number of references to the Antichrist. In the seventh verse the Remnant are exhorted to "rest in the Lord and wait patiently for Him" (i. e. for His personal appearing) and to "fret not because of him who prospereth in his way, because of the Man who bringeth wicked devices to pass"—a manifest allusion to the Man of Sin. In the tenth verse they are assured, "for yet a little while, and the Wicked shall not be: yea, thou shalt diligently consider his place, and it shall not be." In vv. 12 and 13 we read, "the Wicked plotteth against the just, and gnasheth upon him with his teeth. The Lord shall laugh at Him: for He seeth that his day is coming." This brings out the satanic malice of Antichrist against the people of God, and also marks the Lord's contempt for him as He beholds the swiftly-approaching doom of this one who has so daringly defied Him. The end of the Wicked is noticed in v. 35. "I have seen the Wicked in great power, and spreading himself like a green bay tree. Yet he passed away, and, lo, he was not: yea, I sought him, but he could not be found." The whole of this wondrous Psalm calls for close study. It throws a flood of light on the experiences of the Remnant amid the awful trials of the end of the age.

"I said, I will take heed to my ways, that I sin not with my tongue: I will keep my mouth with a bridle, while the Wicked is before me" *(Psa. 39:1)*. This sets forth the resolutions of the Remnant in view of the troublesome presence of the Wicked One; while in v. 8 they are seen praying that they may not be made the reproach of the Foolish One—"Deliver me from all my transgressions: make me not the reproach of the Foolish."

The forty-third Psalm opens with the plaintive supplications of the Remnant in view of the contempt and opposition of the Jewish nation as a whole, at the head of which will be the false Messiah: "Judge me, O God, and plead my cause against an ungodly nation: O deliver me from the deceitful and unjust Man. For Thou art the

God of my strength: why dost Thou cast me off? Why go I mourning because of the oppression of the Enemy?" The allusion to the deceit and injustice of the Man of Sin views, of course, his breaking of the covenant.

In the forty-fourth Psalm we are given to hear more of the bitter lamentations of the Remnant, betrayed as they have been by the one who posed as their benefactor, and scorned as they are by their fellow-Jews: "Thou makest us a byword among the heathen, a shaking of the head among the people (Israel). My confusion is continually before me, and the shame of my face covered me, For the voice of him that reproacheth and blasphemeth; by reason of the Enemy and Avenger."

The fiftieth Psalm is one of deep interest in this connection. It announces the response of Jehovah to the cries of His faithful people. It declares that "God shall come, and shall not keep silence: a fire shall devour before Him, and it shall be tempestuous round about Him" *(v. 3)*. It promises that He will gather His saints together unto Him *(v. 5)*. It contains an expostulation with Israel as a whole *(see vv. 7-14)*. And then, after bidding His people call upon Him "in the Day of Trouble" and assuring them He will deliver them, God addresses their Enemy as follows:—"But unto the Wicked God saith, What hast thou to do to declare My statutes, or that thou shouldest take My covenant in thy mouth? Seeing thou hatest instruction, and casteth My words behind thee. When thou sawest a thief, then thou consentedst with him, and hast been partaker with adulterers. Thou givest thy mouth to evil, and thy tongue frameth deceit. Thou sittest and speakest against thy brother; thou slanderest thine own mother's son" *(vv. 16-22)*. First, God rebukes the Antichrist for his hypocrisy, referring to the time when, at the beginning of his career, he had (like Satan in tempting the Saviour) come declaring God's statutes and taking the Divine Covenant in his mouth *(v. 16)*. Second, He charges him with his treachery when, at the midst of the seventieth week, he had cast God's words behind him *(v. 17)*. Third, He exposes his depravity and shows that he is altogether destitute of any moral sensibility *(vv. 18-20)*. Fourth, He reminds him of how he had congratulated himself that he should continue on his vile course with impugnity and escape the due reward of his wickedness *(v. 21)*. Finally, He announces the certainty of retribution and the fearful doom which awaits him *(v. 22)*.

The fifty-second continues and amplifies what has just been before us from the closing verses of the fiftieth Psalm. Here again the Antichrist is indicted by God—no doubt through the Remnant. "Why boastest thou thyself in mischief, O mighty man? The goodness of God endureth continually. Thy tongue deviseth mischiefs; like a sharp razor, working deceitfully. Thou lovest evil more than good; and lying rather than to speak righteousness. Selah. Thou lovest all devouring words, O thou deceitful tongue. God shall likewise destroy thee forever, and pluck thee out of thy dwelling place, and root thee out of the land of the living. Selah. The righteous also shall see, and fear, and shall laugh at him: Lo, this is the Man that made not God his strength; but trusted in the abundance of his riches, and strengthened himself in his wickedness" *(vv. 1-7)*. The pride, the enmity, the treachery, the moral corruption, and the vaunting of the incarnate Son of Perdition are all noticed and charged against him. The certainty of his doom, and his degradation before those he had persecuted, is graphically depicted.

The prophetic application of the fifty-fifth Psalm first found its tragic realization in the treachery of Judas against the Lord Jesus, but its final accomplishment yet awaits a coming day. In it we may see a pathetic description of the heart-pangs of the Remnant, mourning over the duplicity of the mock Messiah. Driven out of Jerusalem, they bewail the awful wickedness now holding high carnival in the holy city: "Wickedness is in the midst thereof: deceit and guile depart not from her streets. For it was not an enemy that reproached me; then I could have borne it: neither was it he that hated me that did magnify himself against me; then I would have hid myself from him: But it was thou, a man mine equal (i. e. a Jew), my guide, and mine acquaintance" *(vv. 11-13)*. Thus will the Jews in a coming day be called upon to endure the bitter experience of betrayal and desertion by one whom they regarded as their friend. Concerning their Enemy the Remnant exclaim, "He hath put forth his hand against such as be at peace with him: he hath broken his covenant. The words of his mouth were smoother than butter, but war was in his heart: his words were softer than oil, yet were they drawn swords" *(vv. 20, 21)*. The reference is to the seven-year Treaty which the final Cæsar makes with Palestine, and which after three and one half years is treated as 'a scrap of paper'. But such treachery will not go unpunished. In the end Antichrist and his abettors will be summarily dealt with by the Judge of all the earth: "But Thou, O God, shalt bring them down into the pit of destruction: bloody and deceitful men shall not live out half their days" *(v. 23)*.

Psalm seventy-one contains another of the Remnant's prayers during the end-time. "Deliver me, O my God, out of the hand of the Wicked, out of the hand of the unrighteous and cruel Man" *(v. 4)*. The reference is, again, to the Man of Sin who has acted unjustly, and whose fiendish delight it will be to persecute the people of God.

In Psalm seventy-two we find expressed the confidence of the Remnant. They are there seen anticipating that joyful time when God's King shall reign in righteousness. With glad assurance they exclaim: "He shall judge Thy people with righteousness, and Thy poor with judgments. The mountains shall bring peace to the people, and the little hills Thy righteousness. He shall judge the poor of the people, He shall save the children of the needy, and shall break in pieces the Oppressor" *(vv. 2-4)*. Mighty as their Enemy appeared in the eyes of men, and invincible as he was in his own estimation, when God's appointed time comes he shall be broken in pieces as easily as the chaff is removed by the on-blowing wind.

The seventy-fourth Psalm makes reference to the violence of the Antichrist against the believing Remnant: "They said in their hearts, Let us destroy them together: they have burned up all the synagogues of God in the land. We see not our signs: there is no more any profit: neither is there any among us that knoweth how long. O God, how long shall the Adversary reproach? Shall the Enemy blaspheme Thy name forever?" *(vv. 8-10)*. This contemplates the time when the Man of Sin and his lieutenants will make a desperate effort to cut off Israel from the earth and abolish everything which bears the name of God. Note it does not say "all the synagogues" will be burned up, but the "synagogues *of God*," that is, where the true and living God is owned and worshipped.

The eighty-third Psalm carries us to a point a little nearer the end. Not only will the synagogues of God be all destroyed, but an attempt will be made to exterminate those who still worship God in secret. Listen to the tragic pleadings of this Satan-hunted company, "Keep not Thou silence, O God: hold not Thy peace, and be not still, O God. For, lo, Thine enemies make a tumult: and they that hate Thee have lifted up the head. They have taken crafty counsel against Thy people, and consulted against Thy *hidden ones*. They have said, Come, and let us cut them off from being a nation; that the name of Israel may be no more in remembrance" *(vv. 1-4)*. As to who is responsible for this the verses following show. In v. 5 we read, "For they have consulted together with one consent; they are confederate against Thee." The word "confederate" means "leagued together." Then will be realized man's dream of a League of Nations. It is remarkable that just *ten* nations are here named—see vv. 6-8. "Assur" in v. 8 is "the Assyrian" —the Antichrist in his king-of-Babylon character. This verse is one of the few passages in the Psalms which shows the Antichrist in connection with the Gentiles. Psalm 110:6 also contains a reference to him as related to the Gentiles—"He hath stricken the Head over many countries" *(R. V.)*.

The one hundred and fortieth appears to be the last of the Psalms that takes note of the Antichrist. There we hear once more the piteous cries of the Remnant to God: "Deliver me, O Lord, from the Evil Man: preserve me from the Violent Man: Keep me, O Lord, from the hands of the Wicked; preserve me from the Violent Man; who hath purposed to overthrow my goings .... Grant not, O Lord, the desires of the Wicked: further not his wicked device" *(vv. 1, 4, 8)*.

Thus we have glanced at no less than *twenty* Psalms in which allusion is made to the Antichrist. This by no means exhausts the list; but sufficient has been noted to show what a prominent place is there given to this dreadful monster. Let it not be supposed that we are denying the *present* value and application of the Psalms to ourselves. Nothing is more foreign to our desire. We not only firmly believe that *all* Scripture is given by inspiration of God and is "profitable for doctrine," but we readily and gladly unite with the saints of all ages in turning to this precious portion of God's Word to provide us with language suited to express to God the varying emotions of our hearts. But while allowing fully the experimental and doctrinal value of the Psalmter for us today, it needs to be pointed out that many of the Psalms have a prophetic significance, and will be used by another company of believers after the Church which is the body of Christ has been removed from these scenes of sin and suffering. We would urge those of our readers who are interested in dispensational truth to restudy these lyrics of David with a view to discovering how much they reveal of things to come. In our next article (March issue) we shall, D. V., deal with the Antichrist in the Prophets.—*Arthur W. Pink.*

EXPOSITION OF FIRST PETER

Introduction.

Among the apostolical letters, the first Epistle of the apostle Peter has always held a high place in the estimation of the Church. The authenticity and genuineness of the Epistle, and its apostolic origin and consequent Divine inspiration, rest on the most satisfactory evidence. It is alluded to in the second Epistle bearing Peter's name; the great antiquity of which is undoubted.

Like the letters of Paul, this composition holds a middle place between the treatise or discourse and the familiar Epistle. It is not, like the Epistles to the Romans, Galatians, and Hebrews, principally occupied with one great doctrinal theme. It more resembles the minor Pauline epistles, with this difference, that the doctrinal and the practical statements are more commingled. There is comparatively little discussion or argument in it. It is—as the author himself describes it (5:12)—a testimony and an exhortation.

This Epistle is distinguished for great tenderness of manner, and for bringing forward prominently the most consolatory parts of the Gospel. The apostle wrote to those who were in affliction. He was himself an old man. He expected soon to be with the Saviour. He had nearly done with the conflicts and toils of life. It was natural that he should direct his eye onward and upward, and dwell on those things in the Gospel which were adapted to support and comfort the soul. There is, therefore, scarcely any part of the New Testament where the ripe and mellow Christian will find more that is adapted to his matured feelings, or to which he will more naturally turn.

This Epistle holds an intermediate place between those of the great apostle to the Gentiles and that of James the apostle of the Circumcision. It resembles both in a greater degree than they resemble each other.

With respect to the time when this Epistle was written, we have not the means of arriving at absolute certainty. The probability seems to be, that its true date is about A. D. 65, the eleventh year of Nero's reign, two or three years before the apostle's martyrdom, which is generally supposed to have taken place A. D. 67.

It may be proper here to say a word as to the meaning of the epithet General or Catholic, which since the fourth century has been given to this Epistle, as well as to the second Epistle of Peter, and the Epistles of James, John, and Jude. This is not a question of vital importance (for the appellation has no claim to Divine authority), and it is well it is so, for there seems no means of determining it with anything like certainty. The term appears originally to have meant an Epistle, directed not to one church, but to all, or at any rate to many churches,—a description which belongs to five of the seven Epistles so distinguished; the other two being addressed to individuals.

The object of the apostle in this Epistle is plainly to confirm the disciples in the faith, profession, and obedience of the Gospel; by deepening their conviction that the source of happiness, and the foundation of the everlasting kingdom of God, were contained in that faith of the Redeemer which had been announced to them, and received by them into their hearts; that that doctrine was indeed the everlasting unchangeable Word of God, and that, therefore, they ought to aim at appropriating it with childlike simplicity, that so they might continually advance towards "the measure of the stature of the fulness of Christ:" and to exhort them to maintain their stedfastness in the faith under all persecutions, and a corresponding course of conduct, by which they would "shine as lights in the world," and refute the false accusations against Christianity and Christians.

DISCOURSE I

"Peter, an apostle of Jesus Christ, to the strangers scattered throughout Pontus, Galatia, Capadocia, Asia, and Bithynia, Elect according to the foreknowledge of God the Father, through sanctification of the Spirit, unto obedience and sprinkling of the blood of Jesus Christ: Grace unto you, and peace, be multiplied" *(I Peter 1:1, 2).*

Peter describes himself as "An apostle of Jesus Christ." The word apostle signifies a person sent by another, a messenger. The term is, in the New Testament, generally employed as the descriptive appellation of a comparatively small class of men, to whom Jesus Christ entrusted the organization of His Church, and the dissemination of His religion among mankind. At an early period of His ministry, "He ordained twelve" of His disciples "that they should be with Him." These He named apostles. The characteristic features of the apostles as official men were, that they had seen the Lord, and been eye and ear witnesses of what they testified to the world; that they had been called and chosen *immediately* by Christ; that they were infallibly inspired to declare His doctrine and laws; that they possessed the power of working miracles; and that their commission was, strictly speaking, catholic, extending to the whole Church,—to the whole world.

It must be obvious from this scriptural account of the apostolical office, that the apostles had—could have, in the strict sense of the term—no successors. Their qualifications were supernatural, and their work once performed, remained in the infallible record of the New Testament for the advantage of the Church and the world in all future ages. They are the only authoritative teachers of Christian doctrine and law. All official men in Christian churches can legitimately claim no higher place than that of expounders of the doctrines, and administrators of the laws, found in their writings. Few things have been more injurious to the cause of Christianity, than the assumption, on the part of ordinary office-bearers in the Church, of the peculiar prerogatives of "the holy apostles of our Lord Jesus." Much that is said of the latter is not at all applicable to the former, and much that admits of being thus applied, can be so, in accordance with truth, only in a very secondary and extenuated sense.

To this, the highest and holiest office ever held by mere man, the author of this Epistle had been called by his Master; and it appears that, in the exercise of its important functions, his labors were chiefly, though not exclusively, devoted to his "brethren, his kinsmen according to the flesh" *(Gal. 2:8, 9)*. Though there is no ground for the assertion, that Peter was the Prince of the Apostles or had even a permanent presidency among them, yet there can be no doubt he stood very high in the estimation of his brethren, being among those who "seemed to be pillars."

The persons to whom the Epistle is addressed come next to be considered. They are described first, generally, as "elect," or chosen, and then, particularly, both as to their external circumstances and to their spiritual state and character. With regard to the former, they are "the strangers scattered abroad throughout Pontus, etc." With regard to the latter, they are "elect according to the foreknowledge of God the Father, through sanctification of the Spirit, unto obedience and sprinkling of the blood of Jesus Christ."

It has been, and is, a question among expositors who are the persons to whom this Epistle is addressed. It is plainly addressed to Christians, and to Christians resident in the countries specified; but, according to one class of interpreters, it is addressed to Jewish converts resident in these regions; by another class, it is considered as addressed to the Gentile converts resident there; by a third class, it is considered as addressed to those who are called "proselytes of the gate,"—persons by birth Gentiles, but who had embraced Judaism and had afterwards been converted to Christianity.

We apprehend that the true view of the matter is, that the Epistle was addressed to the Christian converts, generally, whether Jews or Gentiles, residing in the countries mentioned. As a majority of these were Jews, and as Peter was not only a Jew, but the apostle of the Circumcision, it is not wonderful that the circumstances and duties of the persons addressed are spoken of, so frequently, I had almost said so uniformly, in language referring to the peculiarities of the Jewish economy.

These persons are described,—first, generally, as "elect," or chosen. It appears to me a doctrine not only very plainly revealed in Scripture, but necessarily resulting from the principles of natural religion, that all who enjoy the blessings of Christianity, the saving benefits of pardon, sanctification, and eternal life, do so in consequence of the sovereign free love of God, which, like Himself, is necessarily eternal; or, in other words, were elected from unbeginning ages to the happiness bestowed on them. This doctrine is taught with peculiar plainness in the first chapter of the Epistle to the Ephesians: "Blessed be the God and Father of our Lord Jesus Christ, who hath blessed us with all spiritual blessings in heavenly places in Christ; according as He hath chosen us in Him before the foundation of the world, that we should be holy and without blame before Him: in love having predestinated us unto the adoption of children by Jesus Christ to Himself, according to the good pleasure of His will" *(vv. 3-5).*

At the same time, I apprehend, the word "elect" here, and in a number of other places in the New Testament, does not refer directly to what has been termed the electing decree *(Rom. 9:11)*, but to the manifestation of it in the actually *selecting* certain individuals from amidst a world lying in wickedness, that they may be set apart to God, and become His peculiar people. This is the election which our Lord speaks of when He says, "Because ye are not of the world, but I have chosen"—selected—"you out of the world, therefore the world hateth you" *(John 15:19)*; and the apostle Paul speaks plainly of the election and vocation of the Corinthians as the same thing *(I Cor. 1:26-29)*. As Israel, as a nation, was selected to be a peculiar people to Jehovah, so true Christians are, as individuals, selected to be a part of God's spiritual "purchased inheritance" or peculiar people.

These selected or chosen persons are described, first, as to their external condition. They are represented as "strangers scattered abroad." The appellation is borrowed from the term generally given to Jews dwelling in Gentile lands *(John 7:35)*. The situation of Christians, while on earth, does not resemble that of Israel dwelling in peace and security in Canaan, but that of Israelites sojourning among strangers and enemies. The selected people of God, while here below, are not gathered into one place, assembled together as citizens of the same city. They will be so by and by, but now they are "strangers," "pilgrims," "sojourners," being a small minority among a people whose habits of thought and feeling, whose pursuits and whose pleasures, are altogether alien from theirs; and "scattered" strangers, as being not merely far from home, but often far from each other, and but imperfectly enjoying the comfort and support arising from intimate communion with persons of kindred sentiments and affections. Such was the external state of the Christians to whom this Epistle was addressed—such is the external state of true Christians still.

The particular description of the spiritual state of these selected and dispersed strangers now requires our attention. They are "elect according to the foreknowledge of God"—they are "elect through sanctification of the Spirit"—they are "elect unto obedience and sprinkling of the blood of Jesus."

They are "elect according to the foreknowledge of God." Here is the doctrine of election very plainly stated. They were selected from the rest of mankind, not because they were better than others. They were selected in accordance with the sovereign will of Him "to whom all His works are known from the beginning of the world." They are the "called" or chosen "according to His purpose;" and the purpose in reference to His choice of them stands, "not of works, but of Him that calleth." No cause can be assigned for them being selected rather than others, but the sovereign free love of God. "He hath mercy on whom He will have mercy;" "He hath compassion on whom He will have compassion." When the Lord set His love on Israel, and chose them to be His peculiar people, the cause was not in them, but in Himself; it was just because He loved them—"because He had a delight in them to love them;" and it is equally true that the selection of certain individuals who enjoy the better blessings of the better economy, can be traced by us to nothing but the sovereign kindness of Him who "worketh all things according to the counsel of His own will."

They are "elect through sanctification of the Spirit." Sanctification means here, as usually in the New Testament, separation—setting apart; and sanctification of the Spirit means spiritual separation (that is, by the regenerating work of the Holy Spirit—Eds.). When Israel was chosen to be God's people, in being separated from all nations, they were marked by a great variety of external distinctions. They lived in a country of their own, were distinguished by peculiar civil laws and customs, and were warned to abstain from all intimate intercourse of any kind with the surrounding nations. The peculiar people of God, under the new dispensation, are also separated from the rest of mankind: but their separation is of a spiritual kind.

They are "elect according to the Divine foreknowledge, and by the separation of the Spirit, unto obedience." The full expression is "the obedience of faith," or the obedience of the truth; and to obey the faith or the truth, is just to believe the Gospel and live under its influence. That the New Testament writers used the word "obedience" simply when they mean "the obedience of faith," is evident from Rom. 6:16, 17. When Israel became the peculiar people of God, by His selecting them according to His sovereign good pleasure, and externally separating them to Himself, it was that they might be subject to His laws. In like manner, when individuals are selected by God to form a part of His peculiar people under the better economy, according to His foreknowledge, and by the Holy Spirit setting them apart, it is that they may obey its law—that they may believe the Gospel, and give up their whole inner and outer man to be regulated by its influence—it is that, taught by "the grace of God, which brings salvation," they may "deny ungodliness and worldly lusts, and live soberly, righteously, and godly, in this present world; looking for that blessed hope, and the glorious appearing of the great God and our Saviour Jesus Christ: who gave Himself for us, that He might redeem us from all iniquity, and purify unto Himself a peculiar people, zealous of good works."

Still farther, they are, "elect—unto the sprinkling of the blood of Jesus Christ." When Israel were chosen to be God's people, and externally set apart for this purpose, it was not only that they might be subject to His law, but that they might share in the effects of that law's expiatory offering —that, being sprinkled with the blood of the sacrifices by which that covenant was ratified, their ceremonial guilt might be pardoned, their ceremonial pollution removed, and that they might be fitted for external fellowship with Jehovah as their God and King. When God, in accordance with His sovereign purpose of mercy, selects individuals, and sets them spiritually apart for His people, it is that, through the faith of the Gospel, they may be personally interested in the blessings procured by the death of Jesus Christ as propitiatory sacrifice for the sins of men—that their sins may be forgiven them, that the jealousies of guilt may be removed, that they may be enabled and disposed with a true heart to approach to God, as rich in mercy, ready to forgive, "God in Christ reconciling the world to Himself;" and in spiritual fellowship with Him, with minds conformed to His mind, and wills conformed to His will, serve Him with their souls and bodies, which are His, not only because they are made by Him, but because they have been "redeemed" to Him, "not by corruptible things as silver and gold, but by the precious blood, the blood of Christ, as of a lamb without blemish and without spot."

Such is the apostle's description of the spiritual state, character, and circumstances of those whom he addresses. They are selected by God according to His own sovereign purpose, and spiritually set apart for Him, that, believing the Gospel, they may enjoy all the blissful results of the death of Jesus Christ the Just One, in the room of the unjust.

The benevolent wish or prayer which the apostle presents for those to whom he writes, now calls for our consideration: "Grace unto you, and peace, be multiplied."

"Grace" is free favor—sovereign kindness—the principle in the Divine mind from which all blessings to sinful men flow. The word is often used as a general name for those blessings which flow from this sovereign kindness. Grace here plainly is the grace of God. The prayer, "grace be multiplied unto you," implied that they were already objects of the grace of God, and is equivalent to—'God loves you, and has given you proofs of His love. Had He not loved you, would He have selected you—would He have spiritually set you apart for Himself—would He have brought you to the obedience of the truth—would He have sprinkled you with the blood of Jesus? May you have continued, increasing, and multiplied proofs that God loves you, in the continuance, and increase, and multiplication of all heavenly and spiritual blessings!'

"Peace" is not so much a different thing from "grace," as a different view of the same thing. We call spiritual blessings "grace," as springing from God's sovereign kindness. We call them "peace," as calculated to tranquillise our minds and make us happy. The prayer, "Peace be multiplied to you," is equivalent to—'You already enjoy peace and happiness.' For "they who believe, do enter into rest." "May your happiness be continued—may it increase." May "the peace of God, which passeth all understanding, keep your hearts and minds in Christ Jesus."

Having thus, very cursorily, considered the interesting topics suggested by this passage of Scripture, let us, my brethren, endeavor to turn them to practical account. A great majority of us are professors of Christianity. Does the description given in the text suit us? Have we any satisfactory evidence that we have been selected by God—called by His grace—spiritually separated to His service—that we have believed the truth, and are enjoying the happy consequence of the belief of the truth, in having the heart sprinkled from an evil conscience by the blood of Christ? Do we feel that *here* we are "strangers of the dispersion," and are waiting for "the gathering together," at the period when all the citizens of heaven shall be assembled in the New Jerusalem, where all the children of God shall be brought home to their Father's house? If this be the case with you, brethren, then let your conduct correspond with your privileges; and "may grace and peace be multiplied to you, and to all the Israel of God."

If it be otherwise, we call on you now to obey the truth, and, through the obedience of the truth, to submit your hearts and consciences to the pacifying and purifying influence of the atoning blood of Jesus. We know nothing about the purpose of God in reference to individuals till that purpose is manifested in its execution; but we do know the purpose of God in reference to lost men generally, and we proclaim it as the appointed means of gathering from men the elect of God. "God so loved the world, that He gave His only begotten Son, that whosoever believeth in Him, should not perish, but have everlasting life. God sent not His Son into the world to condemn the world, but that the world through Him might be saved" *(John 3:16, 17)*. "Be it known unto you, men and brethren, that through this Man is preached unto you the forgiveness of sins: and by Him all who believe are justified from all things, from which they could not be justified by the law of Moses."—Dr. John Brown, 1849.

(To be continued, D. V.)

ANXIOUS CARE

"Ye cannot serve God and mammon. Therefore I say unto you, Take no thought for your life" *(Matt. 6:24, 25)*.

Foresight and foreboding are two very different things. It is not that the one is an exaggeration of the other, but the one is opposed to the other. The more a man looks forward, in the exercise of foresight, the less he does so in the exercise of foreboding. And the more he is tortured by anxious thoughts about a *possible* future, the less clear vision has he of a *likely* future, and the less power to influence it. When Christ here, therefore, enjoins the abstinence from thought for our life and for the future, it is not for the sake of getting away from the pressure of a very unpleasant command that we say, He does not mean to prevent the exercise of wise and provident foresight and preparation for what is to come. When this English version of ours was made, the phrase "taking thought" meant solicitous anxiety, and that is the true rendering and proper meaning of the original. The idea is, therefore, that here there is forbidden for a Christian not the careful preparation for what is likely to come, nor the foresight of the storm, and taking in sail while yet there is time, but the constant occupation and distraction of the heart with gazing forward, and fearing, and being weakened thereby; or, to come back to words already used, foresight is commanded, and, *therefore,* foreboding is forbidden. My only object now, is to endeavor to gather together by their link of connection, the whole of those precepts which follow my text to the close of the chapter; and to try to set before you, in the order in which they stand, and in their organic connection with each other, the reasons which Christ gives for the absence of anxious care from our minds.

I mass them all into three. If you notice, the whole section, to the end of the chapter, is divided into three parts, by the threefold repetition of the injunction, "take no thought." *"Take no thought for your life, what ye shall eat, or what ye shall drink; nor yet for your body, what ye shall put on."* The reason for the command as given in this first section follows:—*Is not the life more than meat, and the body than raiment?* The expansion of that runs on to the close of the thirtieth verse.

Then there follows another division

or section of the whole, marked by the repetition of the command, "take no thought,"—saying, *"What shall we eat? or, What shall we drink? or, Wherewithall shall we be clothed?"* The reason given for the command in this second section is *("For after all these things do the Gentiles seek:) for your heavenly Father knoweth that ye have need of all these things. But seek ye first the kingdom of God."*

And then follows a third section, marked by the third repetition of the command, *"take no thought for the morrow."* The reason given for the command in this third section is—*"For the morrow shall take thought for the things of itself."*

Now if we try to generalize the lessons that lie in these three great divisions of the Sermon on the Mount, we get, I think, these,—anxious thought is contrary to all the lessons of nature; which show it to be unnecessary. That is the first, the longest section. Then, secondly, anxious thought is contrary to all the lessons of revelation or religion; which show it to be heathenish. And lastly, anxious thought is contrary to the whole scheme of Providence; which shows it to be futile. You do not *need* to be anxious. It is *wicked* to be anxious. It is *of no use* to be anxious. Let us try now simply to follow the course of thought in our Lord's illustration of these three principles.

The first is the consideration of THE TEACHING OF NATURE. *"Take no thought for your life, what ye shall eat, or what ye shall drink; nor yet for your body, what ye shall put on. Is not the life more than meat, and the body than raiment?"* And then comes the illustration of the fowls of the air and the lilies of the field.

The whole of these four or five verses fall into these general thoughts: You are obliged to trust God for your body, for its structure, for its form, for its habitudes, and for the length of your being; you are obliged to trust Him for the foundation—trust Him for the superstructure. You are obliged to trust Him, whether you will or not, for the greater—trust Him gladly for the less. You cannot help being dependent. After all your anxiety, it is only directed to the providing of the things that are needful for the life; the life itself, though it be a natural thing, comes direct from God's hands; and laborious days, and sleepless nights, is but to adorn a little more beautifully or a little less beautifully, the allotted span; it is but to feed a little more delicately or a little less delicately, the body which God has given you! What is the use of being careful for food and raiment, when down below these necessities there lies the awful question,—for the answer to which you have to hang helpless, in implicit, powerless dependence upon God,—Shall I live, or shall I die? Shall I have a body instinct with vitality, or a body crumbling amid the clods of the valley? After all your work, your anxiety gets but such a little way down; like some passing shower of rain, that only softens an inch of the hard-baked surface of the soil, and has nothing to do with fructifying the seed that lies far below the reach of its useless moisture. Anxious care is foolish; for far beyond the region within which your anxieties move, there is the greater region in which there must be entire dependence upon God. "Is not the life more than meat? Is not the body more than raiment?" You *must* trust Him for that; you may as well trust Him for all the rest.

Then there is another thought. Look at God's ways of doing with all His creatures. The animate and the inanimate creation are appealed to, the fowls of the air and the lilies of the field, the one in reference to food and the other in reference to clothing, which are the two great wants already spoken of by Christ in the previous verses. I am not going to linger at all on the exquisite beauty of these illustrations. Every sensitive heart and pure eye dwells upon them with delight. The fowls of the air, the lilies of the field, "they toil not, neither do they spin;" and then, with what an eye for the beauty of God's universe,— "Solomon, in all His glory, was not arrayed like one of these"! Now, what is the force of this consideration? It is this,—There is a specimen, in an inferior creation, of the same principles which *you* can trust, you men who are "better than they." And not only that:—There is an instance, not only of God's giving things that are necessary, but of God's giving more, lavishing *beauty* upon the flowers of the field. I do not think that we sufficiently dwell upon the moral and spiritual uses of beauty in God's universe. That everywhere His loving, wooing hand should touch the flower into grace, and deck all barren places with glory and with fairness—what does *that* reveal to us about Him? It says to us, He does not give scantily: it is not the mere measure of what is wanted, absolutely needed, to support a bare existence, that God bestows. He taketh pleasure in the prosperity of His servants. Joy, and love, and beauty, belong to Him; and the smile upon His face that comes from the contemplation of His own fairness flung out into His glorious creation, is a prophecy of the gladness which comes into His heart from His own holiness and more ethereal beauty adorning the spiritual creatures whom He has made flash back His likeness. The flowers of the field are so clothed that we may learn the lesson that it is a fair Spirit, and a loving Spirit, and a bountiful Spirit, and a royal heart, that presides over the bestowments of creation, and allots gifts to men.

But notice further, how much of the force of what Christ says here, depends on the consideration of *the inferiority of these creatures who are thus blessed;* and also notice what are the particulars of that inferiority. We read that, *"they sow not, neither do they reap, nor gather into barns,"* as if it marked out a particular in which their free and untoilsome lives were superior to ours. It is the very opposite. It is part of the thing that marks them as lower than we, that they have not to work for the future. They reap not, they sow not, they gather not;—are you not much better than they? Better in this, amongst other things, that God has given us the privilege of influencing the future by our faithful toil, by the sweat of our brow, and the labor of our hands. These creatures labor not, and yet they are fed. And the lesson for us is—Much more may we, whom God has blessed with the power of work, and gifted with force to mould the future, be sure that He will bless the exercise of the prerogative by which He exalts us above inferior creatures, and makes us capable of toil. *You* can influence tomorrow. What you can influence by work, fret not about, for you *can* work. What you cannot influence by work, fret not about, for it is vain. "They toil not, neither do they spin." You are lifted above them because God has given you hands, that can grasp the tool or the pen. Man's crown of glory, as well as man's curse and punishment, is, "in the sweat of thy brow shalt thou eat bread." So learn what you have to do with that great power of anticipation. It is meant to be the *guide of wise work.* It is meant to be the support for far-reaching, strenuous action. It is meant to elevate us above mere living from hand to mouth; to ennoble the whole being by leading to and directing toil that is blessed because there is no anxiety in it, labor that will be successful since it is according to the will of God who has endowed us with the power of putting it forth.

Then there comes another inferiority: *"Your heavenly Father feedeth them."* They cannot say *"Father!"* and yet they are fed. You are above them by the prerogative of toil. You are above them by the nearer relation which you sustain to your Father in heaven. He is their Maker, and lavishes His goodness upon them: He is your Father, and He will not forget His child. *They* cannot trust: *you* can. *They* might be anxious, if they could look forward, for they know not the hand that feeds them: but *you* can turn round, and recognize the source of all blessings. So doubly ought you to be guarded from care by the lesson of that free joyful Nature that lies round about you, and say, No fear of famine, nor of poverty, nor of want; for He feedeth the ravens when they cry. No reason for distrust! Shame on me if I am anxious! For every lily of the field blows its beauty, and every bird of the air tells its song without sorrowful foreboding, and yet there is no *Father* in heaven to them!

And the last inferiority is this: *"To-day it is, and tomorrow it is cast into the oven."* Their little life is thus blessed and brightened. Oh, how much greater will be the mercies that belong to them who have a longer life upon earth, and who never die! The lesson is not—These are the plebeians in God's universe, and you are the aristocracy, and you may trust Him; but it is,—They, by their inferior place, have lesser and lower wants, wants but for a bounded being, wants that stretch not beyond earthly existence, and that for a brief span. They are blessed in the present, for the oven tomorrow saddens not the blossoming today. You have nobler necessities and higher longings, wants that belong to a soul that never dies, to a nature which may glow with the consciousness that God is your Father, therefore, you are "better than they;" and "shall He not much more clothe you, O ye of little faith?"

And now, in the second place, there is here another general line of considerations tending to dispel all anxious care—the thought that IT IS CONTRARY TO ALL THE LESSONS OF RELIGION OR REVELATION WHICH SHOW IT TO BE HEATHENISH. There are three clauses devoted to the illustration of this thought: *"After all these things do the Gentiles seek";—"Your heavenly Father knoweth that ye have need of all these things;"—"Seek ye first the kingdom of God, and His righteousness, and all these things shall be added unto you."*

The first contains the principle, that solicitude for the future is at bottom heathen worldly-mindedness. The heathen tendency in us all leads to an over-estimate of material good, and it is a question of circumstances whether that shall show itself in heaping up earthly treasures, or in anxious care. They are the same plant, only the one is growing in the tropics of sunny prosperity, and the other in the arctic zones of chill penury. The one is the sin of the worldly-minded rich man, the other is the sin of the worldly-minded poor man. The character is the same turned inside out! And therefore, the words "ye cannot serve God and Mammon," stand in this chapter in the center between our Lord's warning against laying up treasures on earth, and His warnings against being full of cares for earth. He would show us thereby that these two apparently opposite states of mind in reality spring from that one root, and are equally, though differently, serving Mammon. We do not sufficiently reflect upon that. We say, Perhaps, this intense solicitude of ours is a matter of temperament, or of circumstances. So it may be: but the Gospel was sent to help us to cure worldly temperaments, and to master circumstances. But *the* reason why we are troubled about the things of this life, lies here, that our hearts have got an earthly direction, that we are at bottom heathenish in our lives, and in our desires. It is the very characteristic of the Gentile (that is to say, of the heathen) that earth should bound his horizon. It is the very characteristic of the worldly man that all his anxieties on the one hand, and all his joys on the other, should be 'cribbed, cabined, and confined' within the narrow sphere of the visible. When a Christian is living in the foreboding of some earthly sorrow to come down upon him, and is feeling as if there would be nothing left if some earthly treasure were swept away, is it not, in the very root of it, idolatry—wordly-mindedness? Is it not clean contrary to all our profession that for us "there is none upon earth that we desire besides Thee"? Anxious care rests upon a basis of heathen worldly-mindedness.

Anxious care rests upon a basis, too, of heathen misunderstanding of the character of God. *"Your heavenly Father knoweth that you have need of all these things."* The heathen thought of God is that He is far removed from our perplexities, either ignorant of our struggles, or unsympathizing with them. The Christian has the double armour against anxiety—the name of the Father, and the conviction that the Father's knowledge is co-extensive with the Father's love. He who calls us His children thoroughly understands what His children need. And so, anxiety is contrary to the very name by which we have learned to call God, and to the pledge of pitying care and perfect knowledge of our frame which lies in the words "our Father." Our Father is the name of God, and our Father intensely cares for us, and lovingly does all things for us.

And then, still further, Christ points out here, not only what is the real root of this solicitous care—something very like worldly-mindedness, h e a t h e n worldly-mindedness; but He points out what is the one counterpoise of it —*"Seek ye first the kingdom of God."* It is of no use only to tell men that they *ought* to trust, that the birds of the air might teach them to trust, that the flowers of the field might preach resignation and confidence to them. It is of no use to attempt to scold them into trust, by telling them that this trust is heathenish! You must fill the heart with a supreme and transcendent desire after the one supreme object; and then there will be no room and leisure left for the anxious care after the lesser. Have inwrought into your being, Christian man, the opposite of that heathen over-regard for earthly things. "Seek ye first the kingdom of God." Let all your spirit be stretching itself out towards the Divine and blessed reality, longing to be a subject of that kingdom, and a possessor of that righteousness; and 'the cares that infest the day' shall steal away from out of the sacred pavilion of your believing spirit. Fill your heart with desires after what is worthy of desire; and the greater having entered in, all lesser objects will range themselves in the right place, and the "glory that excelleth" will outshine the seducing brightness of the paltry present. Oh! it is want of love, it is want of earnest desire, it is want of firm conviction that God, God only, God by Himself, is enough for me, that makes me careful and troubled. And therefore, if I could only attain unto that sublime and calm height of perfect conviction, that He is sufficient for me, that He is ever with me,—the satisfying object of my desires and the glorious reward of my searchings—let life and death come if they may; let riches, poverty, health, sickness, all the antitheses of human circumstances storm down upon me in quick alternation, yet in them all I shall be content and peaceful. God is beside me! And His presence brings in its train whatsoever things I need.

You cannot cast out the sin of foreboding thoughts by any power short of the entrance of Christ and His love. The blessings of faith and felt communion leave no room nor leisure for anxiety.

Finally, Christ here tells us, that thought for the morrow is CONTRARY TO ALL THE SCHEME OF PROVIDENCE, WHICH SHOWS IT TO BE VAIN. *"The morrow shall take thought for the things of itself. Sufficient unto the day is the evil thereof."*

I interpret these two clauses as meaning this: Tomorrow has anxieties enough of its own, after and in spite of all the anxiety about it today by which you try to free it from care when it comes. *Every* day will have its evil, have it to the end. And every day will have evil enough for all the strength a man has to cope with it. So that it just comes to this: Anxiety,—it is all vain. After all your careful watching for the corner of the heaven where the cloud is to come from, there *will be* a cloud, and it will rise somewhere, but you never know in what quarter. The morrow shall have its own anxieties. After all your fortifying of the castle of your life, there will be some little postern left unguarded, some little weak place in the wall left uncommanded by a battery; and there, where you never look for him, the inevitable intruder will come in! After all the plunging of the hero in the fabled waters that made him invulnerable, there was a little spot on the heel, and the arrow found its way *there!* There is nothing certain to happen, says the proverb, but the unforeseen. Tomorrow *will have* its cares, spite of anything that anxiety and foreboding can do. It is God's law of providence that man should be disciplined by sorrow; and to try to escape from that law by any forecasting prudence, is utterly hopeless, and madness.

And what does your anxiety do? It does not empty tomorrow, brother, of its sorrows; but, Ah! it empties today of its strength. It does not make you escape the evil, it makes you unfit to cope with it when it comes. It does not bless tomorrow, and it robs today. For every day has its own burden. Sufficient for each day is the evil which properly belongs to it. Do not add tomorrow's to today's. Do not drag the future into the present. The present has enough to do with its own proper concerns. We have always strength to bear the evil when it comes. We have not strength to bear the foreboding of it. As thy day, thy strength shall be. In strict proportion to the existing exigencies will be the God-given power; but if you cram and condense today's sorrows by experience, and tomorrow's sorrows by anticipation, into the narrow round of the one four-and-twenty hours, there is no promise that as *that* day thy strength shall be! God gives us (His name be praised!) power to bear all the sorrows of His making; but He does not give us power to bear the sorrows of our own making, which *the anticipation* of sorrow most assuredly is.

Then: contrary to the lessons of Nature, contrary to the teachings of Religion, contrary to the scheme of Providence; weakening your strength, distracting your mind, sucking the sunshine out of every landscape, and casting a shadow over all the beauty— the curse of our lives is that heathenish blind, useless, faithless, needless anxiety in which we *do* indulge. Look forward, my brother, for God has given you that royal and wonderful gift of dwelling in the future, and bringing all its glories around your present. Look forward! Not for life, but for heaven; not for food and raiment, but for the righteousness after which it is blessed to hunger and thirst, and wherewith it is blessed to be clothed. Not for earth, but for heaven, let your forecasting gift of prophecy come into play. Fill the present with quiet faith, with patient waiting, with honest work, with wise reading of God's lessons of nature, of providence, and of grace, all of which say to us, Live in God's future, that the present may be bright: work in the present, that the future may be certain! *They* may well look around in expectation, sunny and unclouded, of the blessed time to come, whose hearts are already "fixed, trusting in the Lord." He to whom there is a present Christ, and a present Spirit, and a present Father, and a present forgiveness, and a present redemption, may well live expiating in all the glorious distance of the unknown to come, sending out (if I may use such a figure)—sending out from His placid heart over the weltering waters of this lower world, the peaceful seeking dove, his meek hope, that shall come back again from its flight with some palm-branch broken from the trees of Paradise between its bill, and he that has *no* such present, *has* a future, dark, chaotic, heaving with its destructive ocean, and over it there goes forever-black-pinioned, winging its solitary and hopeless flight, the raven of his anxious thoughts, and finds no place to rest, and comes back again to the desolate ark with its foreboding croak of evil in the present and evil in the future. Live in Christ, "the same yesterday, and today, and forever," and *His* presence shall make all *your* past, present, and future—memory, enjoyment, and hope—to be bright and beautiful, because all are centered in Him!—*Dr. Alexander Maclaren.*

THE SUFFERINGS OF THIS PRESENT TIME

"For I reckon that the sufferings of this present time are not worthy to be compared with the glory which shall be revealed in us" *(Rom. 8:18).*

By this we are reminded that the present time is a time of suffering, and that this world is to believers as a field of battle. The shortness, too, of the period of suffering, is indicated. It is limited to the *present* life, respecting which man is compared to a flower which cometh forth and is cut down; to a shadow that fleeth and continueth not. It is in the present time exclusively that sufferings are to be endured by the children of God.

Christians often dwell upon their own sufferings, while they overlook the sufferings of their Lord, to whom they must be conformed. They forget their sins, on account of which they receive chastisement that they may not be condemned with the world, and for which they must also partake of their bitter fruits. But as there is no proportion between what is finite, however great it may be, and what is infinite, so their afflictions here, even were their lives prolonged to any period, and although they had no respite, would bear no proportion to their future glory either in intensity or duration. The felicity of that glory is sovereign, but their afflictions here are not insupportable. They are always accompanied with the compassion and the consolations of God. "As the sufferings of Christ abound in us, so our consolation also aboundeth by Christ." The patriarch Jacob, a fugitive from his father's house, constrained to pass the night without a covering, with stones only for his pillow, enjoyed a vision excelling all with which he had been before favored. This is recorded to show that the believer, in his tribulation, often experiences more joy and peace than in his prosperity. God never permits the sufferings of His people to be extreme.—*Robert Haldane.*

VOL. II   FEBRUARY, 1923   NO. 2

STUDIES in the SCRIPTURES

"Search the Scriptures" John 5:39.

A PERIODICAL (MONTHLY "IF THE LORD WILL")
DEVOTED TO BIBLE STUDIES and EXPOSITIONS

Associate Editors and Publishers, I. C. HERENDEEN and ARTHUR W. PINK,
Swengel, Pa.

Price: 10 cents per copy; $1.00 per year. Foreign $1.00 per year.

TO OUR SCRIPTURE STUDY FAMILY—

In the present issue of our magazine appears the first of three articles on the Eternal Punishment of the Wicked. The theme is unspeakably solemn, yet is it one which occupies a prominent place in Holy Writ. God has not left us in ignorance concerning the future destiny of either the saved or the lost. The same Bible which tells of the eternal glory awaiting the redeemed, also announces the eternal torment reserved for the damned. In fact the latter is referred to far more frequently than the former, and fuller details are given of the one than of the other.

The existence of heaven and the existence of hell are established by the same authority. They stand or fall together. We cannot consistently believe in the one and disbelieve in the other. None of us have seen either of them. None of us have ever spoken to any one who has visited either of them. All that we can now know of the abode of believers or unbelievers is what God has been pleased to reveal concerning each of them in His Word. Let us then believe, unquestioningly, *all* that He has made known.

Not only is all Scripture "given by inspiration of God," but all Scripture is *"profitable* for doctrine, for reproof, for correction, for *instruction* in righteousness" *(2 Tim. 3:16).* We cannot ignore any subject dealt with in the Bible without being impoverished. If we decline to study, prayerfully and diligently, what God has revealed concerning that which awaits the lost, we shall be the losers. If we refuse to dwell on those solemn scriptures which describe the future of the wicked because we find their contemplation distasteful and harrowing to our feelings, we shall not be "throughly furnished unto all good works." On the other hand, if we ponder carefully what has been said on this solemn theme we shall gain a clearer apprehension of the awfulness of sin, we shall have a deeper appreciation of that costly Sacrifice which was needed to deliver us from the wrath to come, and we shall be (or ought to be) awakened to our responsibilities toward those who are fast hastening to "the blackness of darkness forever."

We trust that these articles will receive the most careful attention of our readers, and that they may bring forth much fruit to the praise of the glory of Him who loved us and gave Himself for us. Let each Christian reader join with the editors in earnest prayer that God may be pleased to use these articles on Eternal Punishment to the snatching of brands from the burning.

                                              Yours by Grace,
                                                  Arthur W. Pink.

IMPORTANT NOTICES

All new subscriptions will be dated back to January, 1923.

Set of twelve issues for 1922, unbound, $1.00.

Note: We cannot break a set or now supply any *single* 1922 issues.

Subscription Price: **$1.00** per year to any address in the world. Single copies 10 cents.

Change of Address: Please notify us promptly of any change of address, and be certain to give both old and new addresses.

Non-Subscribers receiving this Magazine regularly will understand their subscription has been entered by a friend.

Copies lost in the mail duplicated on request.

Entered as second-class matter December 15th, 1921 at the post office at Swengel, Pa., under Act of March 3rd, 1879.

CONTENTS

John's Gospel (John 4:20-30)	34
The Moral Law the Rule of Conduct to Believers	42
Eternal Punishment	45
Exposition of First Peter (I Peter 1:3-5)	54
What Is It to Believe?	59

JOHN'S GOSPEL

14. CHRIST AT SYCHAR'S WELL.
(Continued). John 4:20-30.

In our last article we continued our exposition of John 4 down to the end of v. 19. It is of surpassing interest to follow the course of the Saviour's dealings with the poor Samaritan adulteress—the Divine patience, the infinite grace and tenderness, the faithful application of the truth to her heart and conscience. We have been struck, too, with the expose of human depravity which this instance furnishes: not simply with the dissolute life of the woman, but with her prejudice, her stupidity, her occupation with material things, her procrastination—all so many exhibitions of what is in us by nature: "As in water face answereth to face, so the heart of man to man" (*Prov. 27:* 19). In the attitude of this sinner toward Christ we see an accurate portrayal of our own past history. Let us now resume at the point where we left off in our last.

We append an Analysis of the passage which is to be before us:—

1. The Place of Worship, vv. 20, 21.
2. Worshippers sought by the Father, vv. 22, 23.
3. The Character of acceptable Worship, v. 24.
4. The woman's desire for Christ, v. 25.
5. Christ fully reveals Himself, v. 26.
6. The disciples' surprise and silence, v. 27.
7. The gratitude and zeal of a saved soul, vv. 28-30.

"Our fathers worshipped in this mountain; and ye say, that in Jerusalem is the place where men ought to worship" (*v. 20*). This woman was not yet regenerated, though she was on the very eve of being so. She was at that point where it is always very difficult (if not impossible) for us to determine on which side of the line a person stands. Regeneration is an instantaneous act and experience, but preceding it there is a process, sometimes brief, usually more or less protracted. During this process or transitional stage there is a continual conflict between the light and the darkness, and nothing is very clearly defined. There is that which is the fruit of the Spirit's operations, and there is that which springs from the activities of the flesh. We may detect both of these at this point in John 4. In the previous verse the woman had said, "Sir, I perceive that Thou art a prophet." This evidenced the fact that light was beginning to illumine her understanding: there was the dawning of spiritual intelligence. But immediately following this we discover the workings of the flesh—"*Our* fathers worshipped in this mountain; and *ye* say, that in Jerusalem is the place where men ought to worship." Here was the enmity of the carnal mind showing itself again. It was a return to the old prejudice, which was voiced at the commencement of the conversation—see v. 9. The subject of *where* to worship was one of the leading points of contention between the Jews and the Samaritans. The Lord had introduced a very disquieting theme. He had spoken directly to her conscience; He had been convicting of sin. And when a sinner's conscience is disturbed, instinctively he seeks to throw it off. He endeavors to turn aside the sharp point of the accusing shaft, by occupying his mind with other things.

There is little doubt that this woman raised the subject of worship at this stage for the purpose of diverting a theme of conversation which was far from agreeable or creditable to her. "Sir, I perceive that Thou art a prophet," she had said, and so, glad of an opportunity to shift the discourse from a subject so painful, she introduces the great point of controversy between the Jews and the Samaritans, that she might hear His opinion respecting it. And, too, the woman was really interested in the friendly advances of this mysterious Stranger who had spoken to her so graciously and yet so searchingly: and doubtless she was anxious to know how *He* would decide the age-long dispute. It is no uncommon thing for persons living in sin, not merely to pretend, but really to *have* an interest in, and a zeal for, what they term 'religion'. Speculation about points in theology is frequently found in unnatural union with habitual neglect of moral duty. Ofttimes a sinner seeks protection from shafts of conviction which follow the plain violation of the law of God, by discussions respecting orthodoxy and heterodoxy. Ah, "who can understand the errors" of that deceitful and desperately wicked thing, the human heart!

In this question of the woman we may discover an underlying principle of general application. Her conscience had been exercised over sin, in the presence of God, and the effect upon her, as upon most quickened souls, was to be concerned with the matter of "worship"—*where* to worship is the question which now engages the attention. Really, it is only *self* again in one of its ten thousand forms. First the sinner is conscious of his prejudice; then he is occupied with his sins; then he turns to his own repentance and faith; and then where to worship—anything but Christ Himself! So it was with this woman here. The Lord had pointed out what it was that kept her from asking for the "gift of God," namely, *ignorance*. True, she was clear on some points. She was versed in the contention between the Jews and the Samaritans; she had been instructed in the difference between Jerusalem and Gerizim; she knew all about "father Jacob." But there were two things she did not know: "The *gift* of God" and *"who* it was that was speaking to her." As yet she knew not Christ as the all-sufficient Saviour for lost sinners. Her mind was engaged with the problem of where to worship.

Was it not thus with most of us? Following our first awakening, were we not considerably exercised over the conflicting claims of the churches and denominations? Where ought I to worship? Which denomination shall I join? In what church shall I seek membership? Which is the most scriptural of the different sects? These are questions which the majority of us faced, and probably many sought the solution to these problems long before they had found rest in the finished work of Christ. After all it was only another 'refuge' in which we sought shelter from the accusing voice which was convicting us of our lost condition.

"Our fathers worshipped in *this* mountain; and ye say, that *in Jeru-*

salem is the place where men ought to worship"—some worship here; some worship there; where *ought* we to worship? Important as this question is, it is not one to be discussed by a convicted sinner. The all-important thing for him is to find himself in the presence of a revealed Saviour. Let this be deeply pondered, clearly understood, and carefully borne in mind. "A convicted sinner can never become a devoted saint, until he finds his happy place at the feet of a revealed Saviour" (C. H. M.) Irreparable damage has been done to souls by occupying them with churches and denominations, instead of with a Saviour-God. If the sinner joins a church before he has accepted Christ he is in greater danger than he was previously. The church can neither save nor help to save. Many regard the Church as a stepping stone *to* Christ, and frequently they find it but a stumbling-stone away *from* Christ. No stepping stones to Christ are needed. He has come all the way from heaven to earth, and is so near to us that no stepping stones are required. Mark how strikingly this is illustrated in one of the Old Testament types:

"An altar of earth thou shalt make unto Me, and shalt sacrifice thereon thy burnt offerings, and thy peace offerings, thy sheep, and thine oxen: in all places where I record My name I will come unto thee, and I will bless thee. And if thou wilt make Me an altar of stone, thou shalt not build it of hewn stone: for if thou lift up thy tool upon it, thou hast polluted it. Neither shalt thou go up by steps unto Mine altar, that thy nakedness be not discovered thereon" *(Ex. 20:24-26)*. It is to be noted that these instructions concerning "the altar" follow immediately on the giving of the Law, for it foreshadowed that which was to succeed the Legal dispensation, namely, the Cross of Christ, on which the great Sacrifice was offered. Note also it was expressly prohibited that the altar of stone should not be built from *hewn* stones. The stones must have no human tools lifted up upon them; no human labor should enter into their preparation. Neither were there to be any steps up to God's altar. Any attempt to climb up to God will only expose our shame. Indeed, steps *up* are not necessary for us, for the Lord Jesus took all the steps *down* to where we lay in our guilt and helplessness.

What stepping-stone did this woman of Samaria require? None at all, for Christ was there by her side, though she knew Him not. He was patiently dislodging her from every refuge in which she sought to take shelter. He was seeking to bring her to the realization that she was a great sinner, and He a great Saviour, come down here in marvelous grace to save her, not only from the guilt and penalty of sin, but also from its dominion and power. What could "this mountain," or that "Jerusalem" do for her? Was it not obvious that a prior question, of paramount importance, claimed her serious attention, namely, What she was to do with her sins?—how she was to be saved? What relief could places of worship afford her burdened heart and guilty conscience? Could she find salvation in Gerizim? Could she procure peace in Jerusalem's temple? Could she worship the Father in spirit and in truth in either the one or the other? Was it not plain that she needed salvation before she could worship anywhere?

"Jesus saith unto her, Woman, believe Me, the hour cometh, when ye shall neither in this mountain, nor yet at Jerusalem, worship the Father" *(v. 21)*. The Lord turned her attention to a subject of infinitely greater importance than the place of worship, even the nature of acceptable worship; assuring her that the time was at hand when controversies respecting the place of worship would be obsolete. "The hour cometh, when ye shall neither in this mountain, nor yet at Jerusalem, worship the Father." The meaning of this evidently is that 'The time is just at hand when the public worship of God the Father should not be confined to any one place, and when the controversy as to whether Jerusalem or Gerizim had the better claim to that honor would be superceded.'

"Ye worship ye know not what: we know what we worship: for salvation is of the Jews" *(v. 22)*. Here we see 'truth' mingling with 'grace.' Christ not only dealt in tenderness but in faithfulness. He was, and is, "the faithful and true Witness." The Lord, in a very brief word, settled the disputed point—the Samaritans were wrong; the Jews right; the former were ignorant, the latter well instructed. Christ then added a reason to what He had just said—*"For* salvation is of the Jews." We take it that "salvation" here is equivalent to "the Saviour," that is, the Messiah. In this way was the word used by Simeon—"Lord, now lettest Thou Thy servant depart in peace, according to Thy word: For mine eyes have seen Thy *Salvation."* *(Luke 2:29, 30)*. So, too, the word was used by John the Baptist—"And all flesh shall see the *Salvation* of God" *(Luke 3:6)*. The force then of Christ's declaration was this: The Saviour, the Messiah, is to arise from among the Jews, and therefore the true worship of Jehovah is to be found among them.

It may be inquired, Why should the Lord Jesus refer to Himself under the impersonal word "salvation"? A moment's reflection will show the propriety of it. Christ was continuing to press upon this woman the fact that she was a sinner, and therefore it was useless to occupy her mind with questions about places of worship. What she needed was salvation, and this salvation could only be had through the knowledge of God revealed as Father, in the face of Jesus Christ. Such is the ground, and the only ground, of true spiritual worship. In order to worship the Father we must know Him; and to know Him is salvation, and salvation is eternal life.

What a lesson is there here for every Christian worker respecting the proper manner to deal with anxious souls. When we are speaking to such, let us not occupy them with questions about sects and parties, churches and denominations, creed and confessions. It is positively cruel to do so. What they need is salvation—to know God, to believe on the Lord Jesus Christ. Let us shut them up to this one thing, and refuse to discuss anything else with them until they have received the Saviour. Questions about church-membership, the ordinances, etc., have their place and interest; but manifestly they are not for convicted sinners. Too many are so foolishly anxious to swell the ranks of *their* party, that they are in grave danger of thinking more about getting people to join *them,* than they are about leading anxious souls simply and fully to Christ. Let us study diligently the example of the perfect Teacher in His dealings with the woman of Sychar.

"But the hour cometh, and now is, when the true worshippers shall worship the Father in spirit and in truth: for the Father seeketh such to worship Him" *(v. 23)*. Here is the point which the Lord now presses upon this anxious soul. A new order of things was about to be established, and under it God would be manifested not as Jehovah (the Covenant-keeping God) but as "the Father," and then the great question would not be *where* to worship, but *how.* Then, the worshipper at Jerusalem will not be accounted the true worshipper because he worships there, nor the worshipper at Gerizim the false worshipper because he worships there; the one who worships in spirit and in truth, no matter where he may worship, he and he alone, is the genuine worshipper.

To "worship in *spirit,"* is to worship spiritually; to "worship in *truth,"* is to worship truly. They are not two different kinds of worship, but two aspects of the same worship. To worship spiritually, is the opposite of mere external rights which pertained to the flesh; instead, it is to give to God the homage of an enlightened mind and an affectionate heart. To worship Him truly, is to worship Him according to the Truth, in a manner suited to the revelation He has made of Himself; and, no doubt, it also carries with it the force of worshipping truly, not in pretense, but sincerely. Such, and such alone, are the acceptable worshippers.

"God is a Spirit: and they that worship Him must worship Him in spirit and in truth" *(v. 24)*. This is a most important verse and treats of a most important but sadly misunderstood subject, namely, that of Worship. Much of that which is termed "worship" to-day is fleshly rather than spiritual, and is external and spectacular, rather than internal and reverential. What are all the ornate decorations in our church-houses for? the stained glass windows, the costly hangings and fittings, the expensive organs! But people at once reply, 'But God's House must be beautiful, and He surely loves to have it so.' But why will not such objectors be honest, and say. 'We love to have it so, and therefore, God should too'? Here, as everywhere else, God's thoughts are entirely different from man's. Look at the tabernacle which was made according to the pattern which Jehovah Himself showed to Moses in the mount! 'Yes,' people reply, 'but look at Solomon's temple!' Ah, *Solomon's*, truly. But look at it, and what do we see? Not one stone left upon another? Ah, dear reader, have you ever stopped to think what the future holds for this world and all its imposing structures? The world, and all that is therein, will be burned up! Not only the saloons and the picture shows, but also its magnificent cathedrals and stately churches, erected at enormous expense, while half of the human race was hastening to the Lake of Fire without any knowledge of Christ! Does this burning up of them look as though God esteemed them very highly? And if His people pondered this, would they be so ready to put so much of their money in them? After all, is it not the lust of the flesh, and the lust of the eye—denominational pride—which lies behind it all?

"God is a Spirit: and they that worship Him must worship Him in spirit and in truth." Note how emphatic this is—MUST. There is no alternative, no choice in the matter. This "must" is final. There are three "musts" in this Gospel, equally important and unequivocal. In John 3: 7 we read, "Ye *must* be born again." In John 3:14, "The Son of Man *must* be lifted up." In John 4:24, "God *must* be worshipped in spirit and in truth." It is indeed striking to observe that the first of these has reference to the work of God the Spirit, for He is the One who effects the new birth. The second "must" has reference to God the Son, for He was the One who had to die in order for atonement to be made. The third "must" respects God the Father, for He is the Object of worship, the One who "seeketh" worshippers. And this order cannot be changed. It is only they who have been regenerated by God the Spirit, and justified by the Atonement of God the Son, who can worship God the Father: "The sacrifice of the wicked is an abomination to the Lord" *(Prov. 15:8)*.

What is worship? We answer: First, it is the *action of the new nature* seeking, as the sparks fly upward, to return to the Divine and heavenly source from which it came. Worship is one of the three great marks which evidences the presence of the new nature—"We are the circumcision, which worship God in the spirit, and rejoice in Christ Jesus, and have no confidence in the flesh" *(Phil. 3:3)*—in the Greek there is no article before "spirit" or "flesh;" the spirit refers to the new nature, which is born of the Spirit.

In the second place, Worship is the *activity of a redeemed people*. Israel did not worship Jehovah in Egypt; there they could only "sigh," and "cry," and "groan" *(see Ex. 2:23, 24)*. It is not until Israel had passed through the Red Sea that we are told "Then sang Moses and the children of Israel this song unto the Lord, and spake, saying, *I will sing unto the Lord*" *(Ex. 15:1)*; and note, this was the Song of Redemption—the words "redeemed" and "redemption" are not found in Scripture until this chapter is reached: see v. 13.

In the third place, Worship *proceeds from the heart*. "This people draweth nigh unto Me with their mouth, and honoreth Me with their lips; but their *heart* is far from Me. But *in vain do they worship Me*" *(Matt. 15:8, 9)*. Worship is a redeemed heart *occupied with God*, expressing itself in adoration and thanksgiving. Read through the Redemption Song, expression of Israel's worship, in Ex. 15, and notice the frequent repetition of "Thou," "Thee," and "He." Worship, then, is the occupation of the heart with a *known God;* and everything which *attracts* the flesh and its senses, *detracts* from real worship.

"God is a spirit: and they that worship Him must worship Him in spirit and in truth" *(v. 24)*. There is no choice in the matter. This emphatic "must" bars out everything which is of the flesh. Worship is not by the eyes or the ears, but "in spirit," that is, from the *new nature*. The more spiritual is our worship the less formal and the less attractive to the flesh will it be. O how far astray we have gone! Modern "worship" (?) is chiefly designed to render it pleasing to the flesh: a 'bright and attractive service,' with beautiful surroundings, sensuous music, and entertaining talks. What a mockery and a blasphemy! O that we all would heed that pointed word in Psa. 89:7; "God is greatly to be feared in the assembly of the saints, and to be had in reverence of all them that are about Him"—how different things would then be.

Is a choir needed to 'lead' worship? What choir was needed to aid the Saviour and His apostles as they sung that hymn in the upper room, ere going forth into the Garden? *(Matt. 26:30)*. What choir was needed to assist the apostles, as with bleeding backs they sang praises to God in the Philippian dungeon? Singing to be acceptable to God *must* come from the heart. And *to whom* do the choirs sing—to God, or to the people? The attractiveness of singing has been substituted for "the foolishness of preaching." The place which music now holds in many of our public services is a solemn "sign of the times" to those who have eyes to see. But is music wrong? Has not God Himself bestowed the gift? Surely, but what we are now complaining about is church singing that is professional and spectacular, that which is of the flesh, and rendered to please the ear of man. The *only* music which ever passes beyond the roof of the church in which it is rendered is that which issues from born again people who "sing with grace in their hearts *unto the Lord*."

"God is a spirit: and they that worship Him must worship Him in spirit and in truth." We must worship "in spirit," and not merely with the physical senses. We cannot worship by admiring grand architecture, by listening to the peals of a costly organ or the anthems of a highly trained choir. We cannot worship by gazing at pictures, smelling of incense, counting of beads. We cannot worship with our eyes or ears, noses or hands, for they are all "flesh," and *not* "spirit." Moreover, spiritual worship must be distinguished sharply from *soulical* worship, though there are few today who discriminate between them. Much, very much, of our modern so-called worship is soulical, that is, emotional. Music which makes one "feel good," touching anecdotes which draw tears, the magic oratory of a speaker which thrills his hearers, the clever showmanship of professional evangelists and singers who aim to 'produce an atmosphere' for worship (?) and which are designed to move the varied emotions of those in attendance, are so many examples of what is soulical and not spiritual at all. True worship, spiritual worship, is decorous, quiet, reverential, occupying the worshipper with God Himself; and the effect is to leave him not with a nervous headache (the inevitable reaction from the high tension produced by soulical activities) but with a peaceful heart and a rejoicing spirit.

"The woman saith unto Him, I know that Messias cometh, which is called Christ: when He is come, He will tell us all things" *(v. 25)*. Here is the Saviour's reward for His gracious patience in dealing with this woman. Slowly but surely the Word had done its work. At last this poor soul has been driven from every false refuge, and now she is ready for a revealed Saviour. She is through with her prevarications and procrastinations. She had asked *"How?"*, and Christ had graciously answered her. She had inquired *"Whence?"*, and has received a kindly reply. She had said, *"Where?"*, and this difficulty had been disposed of too. And now her questions ceased. She speaks with greater confidence and assurance—"I know that Messias cometh." This was tantamount to saying, "I want *Christ.*"

"Jesus saith unto her, I that speak unto thee am He" *(v. 26)*. For the seventh and last time (in this interview) the Lord addressed this soul whose salvation He sought and won. The moment the Samaritan woman expressed her desire for Christ, He answers, "You have Him; He is now speaking to you." Nothing more was needed. The Saviour of sinners stood revealed. That was enough. All was settled now. "It was not a mount nor a temple; Samaria nor Jerusalem. She had found Jesus—a Saviour-God. A detected sinner and a revealed Saviour have met face to face, and all is settled, once and for ever. She discovered the wonderful fact that the One who had asked her for a drink, knew all about her—could tell her all that ever she did, and yet He talked to her of salvation. What more did she want? Nothing" *(C. H. M.)*.

"And upon this came His disciples, and marvelled that He talked with the woman: yet no man said, What seekest Thou? or, Why talkest Thou with her?" *(v. 27)*. Once again we may discern the providential dealings of God, regulating and directing the slightest movements of His creatures. These disciples of Christ left the Saviour seated on the well, while they went into the city to buy meat *(v. 8)*. Had they remained they would only have been in the way. The Lord desired to have this woman alone with Himself. His purpose in this had now been accomplished. Grace had achieved a glorious victory. Another brand had been plucked from the burning. The poor Samaritan adulteress had now been brought out of sin's darkness into God's marvelous light. The woman had plainly expressed her desire for the Christ to appear, and the Lord had revealed Himself to her. "And *upon this* came His disciples." Though they had not been permitted to hear what had been said between Christ and this woman, they returned in time to witness the happy finale. They needed to be taught a lesson. They must learn that the saving grace of God was not limited to Israel, that it was reaching out to sinners of the Gentiles, too. They "marvelled" as they beheld their Master talking to this despised Samaritan, but they held their peace. A Divine constraint arrested them. None of them dared to ask Him a question at that moment.

"The woman then left her waterpot, and went her way into the city" *(v. 28)*. Here is the blessed climax. The patient work of the condescending Saviour was now rewarded. The darkness was dissipated: "The light of the knowledge of the glory of God in the face of Jesus Christ" *(2 Cor. 4:6)* now shone into the heart of this believing sinner. Four times had this woman referred directly to herself, and it is striking to note the contents and order of her respective statements. First, she *acknowledged her thirst*—"Give me this water *that* (in order that) *I thirst not*" *(v. 15)*. Second, she *confessed her sin*—"I have no husband" *(v. 17)*. Third, she evidenced *a dawning intelligence*—"I perceive" *(v. 19)*. Fourth, she *avowed her faith*—"I know that Messias cometh" *(v. 25)*. Finally, she leaves her waterpot and goes forth to testify of Christ.

"The woman then left her waterpot and went her way into the city." Notice carefully the word "then," which is parallel with the "upon this" of the previous verse. Both look back to what is recorded in v. 26—"Jesus saith unto her, I that speak unto thee am." It will be noted that the final word of this verse is in italics, which signifies there is no corresponding word in the Greek. Omitting the word "he" the verse as it reads in the A. V. is unintelligible. We are satisfied that the correct reading would give "Jesus saith unto her, *I am* that speaketh unto thee." It was the enunciation of the sacred "I am" title of Jehovah *(see Ex. 3:14)*; it was the solemn affirmation that *God* was addressing her soul. It is a parallel utterance to John 8:58. The pronunciation of this ineffable Name was attended with awe-inspiring effects *(cf. John 18:6)*. This explains, here, the silence of the disciples who marvelled when they found their Master talking with the woman, but asked Him no question. It accounts for that Divine constraint resting upon them. Moreover, it gives added force and significance to what we read of in v. 28—"The woman *then* left her waterpot." The weary Traveller by the well stood revealed as God manifest in the flesh.

"The woman then left her waterpot." Ah, was not that a lovely sequel! She "left her waterpot" because she had now found a well of "living water." She had come to the well for literal water; *that* was what she had desired, and on what her mind was set. But now that she had obtained salvation, she thought no more of her "waterpot." It is ever thus. Once there is a clear *preception* of Christ to the soul, once He is *known* and received as a personal Saviour, there will be a turning away from that on which before the carnal mind was centered. Her mind was now stayed upon Christ, and she had no thought of well, water, or waterpot. The Messias' glory was now her end and aim. Henceforth, "for to me to live *is Christ*" was her object and goal. She knew the Messiah now, not from hearsay, but from the personal revelation of Himself, and immediately she began to proclaim Him to others.

"And went her way into the city, and saith to the men, Come, see a man, which told me all things that ever I did: is not this the Christ?" *(vv. 28, 29)*. How beautiful! Transformed from a convicted sinner into a devoted saint. The work done had been thorough—nothing could be put to it, nor anything taken from it: because *God* had done it *(Ecc. 3:14)*. There was no placing this woman on probation. There was no telling her she must hold out faithful to the end if she would be saved—wretched perversion of men! No; she *was* saved; saved for all eternity. Saved by grace through faith, apart from any works of her own. And now that she is saved, she wants to tell others of the Saviour she had found. The love of Christ constrained her. She now had **His** nature within her, and therefore has she a heart of compassion for the lost.

"Christian reader, be this our work, henceforth. May our grand object be to invite sinners to come to Jesus. This woman began at once. No sooner had she found Christ for herself, than she forthwith entered upon the blessed work of leading others to His feet. Let us go and do likewise. Let us by word and deed—'by all means,' as the apostle says—seek to gather as many as possible around the Person of the Son of God. Some of us have to judge ourselves for lukewarmness in this blessed work. We see souls rushing along the broad and well-trodden highway that leadeth to eternal perdition, and yet, how little are we moved by the sight! How slow are we to sound in their ears, that true, that proper Gospel note, 'Come!' O, for more zeal, more energy, more fervor! May the Lord grant us such a deep sense of the value of immortal souls, the preciousness of Christ, and the awful solemnity of eternity, as shall constrain us to more urgent and faithful dealing with the souls of men" (C. H. M.)

"And saith to the men, Come, see a man, which told me all things that ever I did: is not this the Christ?" (vv. 29, 30). "*Come*" was the word of invitation that this newly born soul extended to those men. It was a word she had learned from Christ's own lips (v. 16). It is the great word of the Gospel. It is the word which has resulted in peace to countless hearts. The last recorded words of this woman show her now as an active servant for Christ. It is remarkable to find that this final word of the woman was her seventh—the *perfect* number. Seven times, no more and no less, had Christ spoken to her—telling of the perfectness of His work in dealing with her. Six times she spoke to Him (the number of man in the flesh) before she was fully saved; and then to this is added the last recorded word when she went forth to tell others of the One who had saved her; making seven in all—this last one, the *seventh*, evidencing the *perfect work* which Christ had wrought in her!

Our next lesson, D. V., will be devoted to John 4:31-42. Let the interested reader study the following questions:—

1. What is the central theme of verses 31-42?
2. What does verse 31 reveal to us about the disciples?
3. What did Christ mean when He said that doing the will of God provided Him with "meat to eat"? vv. 32, 34.
4. What "work" of the Father did Christ "finish"? v. 34.
5. In applying what is said in v. 38 to ourselves what should be the effect upon us?
6. What dispensational picture can you discover in this passage?—note the "two days" of v. 40.
7. What does "the Saviour of the world" signify? v. 42.

—*Arthur W. Pink.*

THE MORAL LAW THE RULE OF CONDUCT TO BELIEVERS

First: There is no dispute on the ground of our acceptance with God. We are not justified on account of anything inherent, whether before, in, or after believing; but merely for the sake of the righteousness of Christ, believed in and imputed to us. As a medium of life, or, as a covenant, believers are dead to the law, and the law to them, being united to another husband.

Secondly: The question is not, Whether the whole of Christian obedience be *formally* required in the Ten Commandments? Certainly it is not. Neither the ordinance of baptism, nor that of the supper, are expressly required by them; and there may be other duties which they do not, in so many words inculcate;—but the question is, Whether it be not *virtually* required by them? and, Whether they be not *binding* on believers? If we allow our Saviour to be a just expositor, the sum of the Ten Commandments is, *The love of God with all the heart, soul, mind and strength, and of our neighbor as ourselves;* and this includes all the obedience that can possibly be yielded by a creature. If we love God with all our hearts, we shall comply with every positive institute and particular precept which He hath enjoined in His Word; and all such compliance contains just so much obedience as it contains love to Him, and no more. Let an instance of Christian obedience be produced, if it can, which is not comprehended in the general precepts of love.

In objecting to the perfection of the Ten Commandments, our adversaries would seem to hold with an extensive rule; but the design manifestly is to undermine their authority, and that without substituting any other competent rule in the place of them. In what follows, therefore, I shall endeavor to prove both the authority and perfection of the law; or that the commandments of God; whether we consider them as ten or two, are still *binding* on Christians; and virtually contain the whole revealed will of God, as to the matter of obedience.

First: To prove that the Ten Commandments are binding, let any person read them, one by one, and ask his own conscience as he reads, Whether it would be any sin to break them? Is the believer at liberty to have other gods besides the true God? Would there be no harm in his making to himself a graven image, and falling down to worship it? Is it any less sin for a believer to take God's name in vain than for an unbeliever? Are believers at liberty to profane the Sabbath, or to disobey their parents, or to kill their neighbors, or to commit adultery, or to steal, or to bear false witness, or to covet what is not their own? Is this, or any part of it, the liberty of the Gospel? Every conscience which is not seared as with a hot iron, must answer these questions in the negative.

Secondly: It is utterly inconsistent with the nature of moral government, and of the great designs of mercy, as revealed in the Gospel, that believers should be freed from obligation to love God with all their hearts; and their neighbors as themselves. The requirement of love is founded in the nature of the revelation between God and a rational creature; and cannot be made void so long as the latter exists, unless the former were to deny himself. The relation between a father and son is such, that an obligation to love is indispensable; and should the son on having offended his father, be forgiven and restored, like the prodigal to his family, to pretend to be free on this account, were an outrage on decency. Every one must feel that his obligations, in such a case, are increased, rather than diminished.

Thirdly: It was solemnly declared by our Saviour. *That He came, not to destroy the law, but to fulfill it;* yea, *that heaven and earth should pass away, but not a jot or tittle of the law should fail.* A considerable part of His Sermon on the Mount was taken up in pointing out the true meaning of its particular precepts, and in enforcing them upon His disciples. To the same purpose the apostle Paul, after dwelling largely on justification by faith in Christ, in opposition to the works of the law asks, *Do we then make void the law through faith? God forbid; yea, we establish the law.* But if the law ceases to be binding on believers, Christ did come to destroy its authority over them, and faith does make it void in respect of them. The faith of those who set Moses and Christ at variance, has manifestly this effect:—it is therefore, in opposition to the faith taught by our Saviour and the apostle Paul.

Fourthly: In executing the great work of redemption, our Saviour invariably did honor to the law: it was written in His heart. He did not ask for the salvation of His chosen at the expense of the law; but laid down His life to satisfy its righteous demands. Now, the essence of true religion is for the *same mind to be in us which was in Christ Jesus.* Hence He prayed that they all might be *one*, as the Father was in Him, and He in the Father, that they might be *one* in both. The Lawgiver and the Saviour were one; and believers must be of one mind with the former as well as with the latter; but if we depreciate the law, which Christ delighted to honor, and deny our obligations to obey it, how are we of His mind! Rather, are we not of that mind which is "enmity against God, which is not subject to the law of God, neither indeed can be"?

Fifthly: The apostle, in what he writes to the Romans and to the Galatians (two Epistles in which he largely excludes the idea of justification by the works of the law) enforces *brotherly love as the requirement of the law. Love one another,* says he, *for love is the fulfilling of the law—Brethren, we have been called unto liberty; only use not liberty as an occasion to the flesh, but by love, serve one another; for all the law is fulfilled in one word: Thou shalt love thy neighbor as thyself.* If the liberty of the primitive Christians consisted in being delivered from an obligation to obey the precepts of the law, the reasoning of the apostle is self-contradictory:—'Ye are not obliged to love one another, because God in His law requires it; therefore, love one another because God in His law requires it'!!

Sixthly: If the law be not a rule of conduct to believers, and a perfect rule too, they are under no rule; or, which is the same thing, are lawless. But, if so, they commit no sin; for *where no law is, there is no transgression;* and in this case they have no sins to confess either to God or to one another; nor do they stand in need of Christ as an Advocate with the Father; nor of daily forgiveness through His blood. Thus it is, that, by disowning the law, men utterly subvert the Gospel. I am aware, that those who deny the law to be the rule of a believer's conduct, some of them, at least, will not pretend to be lawless. Sometimes they will profess to make the Gospel their rule; but the Gospel, strictly speaking, is not a rule of conduct, but a message of grace, providing for our conformity to the rule previously given. To set aside the moral law as a rule, and to substitute the Gospel in its place, is making the Gospel a new law; and affords a proof how Antinomianism and Neonomianism, after all their difference, can occasionally agree: The Scriptures teach us, that *by the law is the knowledge of sin:* which clearly implies, that there is no sin but what is a breach of that rule. Hence sin is defined as *the transgression of the law.* But if sin be the transgression of the law, the authority of the law must be still binding; for no crime or offense attaches to a breach of the law which is abrogated or repealed; nor can it be known by such a law how much any man hath sinned, or whether he hath sinned at all. Moreover, if there be no sin but what is a transgression of the law, there can be no rule binding on men which is not comprehended in that law.

Seventhly: The apostle writes as if there were no medium between being under the law to Christ, and without law *(1 Cor. 9:21).* If we be not the one, we are the other. Paul declares himself under *the* law to Christ; which implies that Christ has taken the precepts of the moral law as the first principles of His legislative code. Believers, therefore, instead of being freed of obligation to obey it, are under greater obligations to do so than any men in the world. To be exempt from this, is to be without law, and, of course, without sin; in which case we might be without a Saviour, which is utterly subversive of all religion.—I have been told, that believers are not to be ruled by the law, but by love; and that it is by the influence of the Spirit that they are moved to obedience, rather than by the precepts of the law. To this I answer, (1) if a believer be ruled by love in such a way as to exclude obligation, this is the same as if a son should say to his father, 'I have no obligation to oblige you, Sir: I will do your business from love; but I will not be commanded!' That is, what he pleases he will do, and no more. But no parent could bear such an answer from a child: and how can we suppose that God will bear it from us! *If I be a father, where is my honor?* (2) The question is not, What *moves* or *causes* obedience?—but, What is the *rule* of it? It is allowed, that all true obedience is caused by the influence of the Holy Spirit; but that to which He influences the mind was antecedently required of us: *He leadeth us in the way that we should go.* (3) If the influence of the Holy Spirit on the mind be made the rule of obligation, and that influence be effectual, it will follow that believers are without sin; for whatever they are effectually influenced to do, they do; and if this be all they are obliged to do, then do they comply with their whole duty, and so are sinless. Thus, methinks, we have arrived at a state of sinless perfection by a sort of back way! But, *let us not deceive ourselves: God is not mocked; whatsoever a man soweth, that shall he also reap.*

But after all, my dear friends, evidence, even that which is drawn from the Word of God, will have little or no influence on minds which have drunk deeply into the corrupt principles of Antinomianism. Where men have found out the secret of happiness without holiness, there is something so bewitching in it, that you might almost as well encounter insanity, as hope, by reasoning, to convince them. Indeed, I know of no characters to whom the words of the prophet, though spoken immediately of idolators, will more fully apply: "He feedeth on ashes: a deceived heart hath turned him aside, that he cannot deliever his soul, nor say, Is there not a lie in my right hand?" There are, however, degrees in this kind of infatuation; and I doubt not but many sincere minds have been infected with it. If some of this description should be recovered, it is worth our utmost attention; and even those whose prejudices are the most inveterate, are not beyond the reach of omnipotent grace. *Andrew Fuller, 1793.*

ETERNAL PUNISHMENT

This time we take up our pen to write on one of the most solemn truths taught in the Word. And ere we began we turned to the Lord and earnestly sought that wisdom and grace which we are conscious we sorely need; making request that we might be preserved from all error in what we shall say, and that nothing may find a place in these pages which shall be displeasing to that Holy One, "whose we are, and whom we serve." O that we may write in the spirit of One who said, "Who knoweth the power of Thine anger, even according to Thy fear, so is Thy wrath" *(Psa. 90:11).*

The subject before us is one that needs stressing in these days. The great majority of our pulpits are silent upon it, and the fact that it has so little place in modern preaching is one of the signs of the times, one of the many evidences that the Apostasy must be near at hand. It is true that there are not a few who are praying for a world-wide Revival, but it appears to the writer that it would be more timely, and more scriptural, for prayer to be made to the Lord of the harvest, that He would raise up and thrust forth laborers who would fearlessly and faithfully preach those truths which are calculated to bring about a revival.

While it is true that all genuine revivals come from God, yet He is not capricious in the sending of them. We are sure that God never relinquishes His sovereign rights to own and to bless where and as He pleases. But we also believe that here, as everywhere, there is a direct connection between cause and effect. And a revival is the effect of a previous cause. A revival, like a genuine conversion, is wrought of God *by means of the Word*—the Word applied by the Holy Spirit, of course. Therefore, there is something more needed (on our part) than prayer: the Word of God must have a place, a prominent place, *the* prominent place. Without *that* there will be no Revival, whatever excitement and activities of the emotions there may be.

It is the deepening conviction of the writer that what is most needed to-day is a wide proclamation of those truths which are the least acceptable to the flesh. What is needed to-day is a scriptural setting forth of *the character of God*—His absolute sovereignty, His ineffable holiness, His inflexible justice, His unchanging veracity. What is needed to-day is a scriptural setting forth of *the condition of the natural man*—his total depravity, his spiritual insensibility, his inveterate hostility to God, the fact that he is "condemned already" and that the wrath of a sin-hating God is even now abiding upon him. What is needed to-day is a scriptural setting forth of *the alarming danger in which sinners are* —the indescribably awful doom which awaits them, the fact that if they follow only a little further their present course they shall most certainly suffer the due reward of their iniquities. What is needed to-day is a scriptural setting forth of *the nature of that punishment which awaits the lost*—the awfulness of it, the hopelessness of it, the unendurableness of it, the endlessness of it. It is because of these convictions that by pen as well as by voice we are seeking to raise the alarm.

It may be thought that what we have said in the above paragraph stands in need of qualification. We can imagine some of our readers saying, Such truths as these may be needed by the lost, but surely you do not wish to be understood as saying that these subjects ought to be pressed upon the Lord's people! But that is exactly what we do mean and do say. Re-read the Epistles, dear friends, and note what place each of these subjects has in them! It is just because these truths have been withheld so much from public ministrations to the saints that we now find so many backboneless, sentimental, lop-sided Christians in our assemblies. A clearer vision of the awe-inspiring attributes of God would banish much of our levity and irreverence. A better understanding of our depravity by nature would humble us, and make us see our deep need of using the appointed means of grace. A facing of the alarming danger of the sinner would cause us to "consider our ways" and make us more diligent to make *our* "calling and election sure." A realization of the unspeakable misery which awaits the lost (and which each of us fully merited) would immeasureably deepen our gratitude, and bring us to thank God more fervently that *we* have been snatched as brands from the burning and delivered from the wrath to come; and too, it will make us far more earnest in our prayers as we supplicate God on behalf of the unsaved. Moreover, scriptural and searching addresses along these lines would, in some cases at least, lay hold of those who have a form of godliness but who deny the power thereof. They would have some effect on that vast company of professors who are "at ease in Zion." They would, if God were depended upon, arouse the indifferent, and cause some who are now careless and unconcerned to cry, "What must I do to be saved?" Remember that the ground must be *plowed* before it is ready to be sowed: and the truths mentioned above are needed to prepare the way for the Gospel.

Concerning the eternal punishment of the wicked there are few, it seems, who realize the vital importance of a ringing testimony to this truth, and fewer still who apprehend the deep seriousness of what is involved in a denial of it. The importance of a clear witness to this doctrine may be seen by noting what a prominent place it holds in the Word; and contrariwise, the seriousness of denying it is evidenced by the fact that such denial is a rejection of God's truth. The need of giving this solemn subject a prominent place in our witness is apparent, for it is our bounden duty to warn sinners of their fearful peril and bid them flee from the wrath to come. To remain silent is criminal; to substitute anything for it is to set before the wicked a *false* hope. The great importance of expounding this doctrine, freely and frequently, also appears in that, excepting the Cross of Christ, nothing else so manifests the heinousness of sin, whereas every modification of eternal punishment, only serves to minimize the evil of it.

We propose to deal with our present theme under the following divisions. First, we shall examine briefly some of the leading objections brought against the truth of eternal punishment. Second, we shall classify various passages which treat of the destiny of the lost, showing that death seals the sinner's doom, that his condition is then beyond hope, that the punishment awaiting him is interminable. Third, we shall examine those scriptures which throw light upon *the nature* of the punishment which awaits the lost. Finally, we shall seek to make a practical application of the whole subject.

I. OBJECTIONS CONSIDERED

In taking up the objections made against the truth of eternal punishment it would be a hopeless task were we to attempt to notice every argument which the fertile mind of unbelief (under the control of Satan, as it is) has devised. We shall, however, consider those of greatest weight, and those which have received the widest acceptance among unbelievers. These we shall classify as follows: First, deductions drawn from the Divine perfections. Second, passages appealed to by Universalists. Third, passages appealed to by Annihilationists. Fourth, assertions that punishment is not penal and retributive but disciplinary and remedial.

1. DEDUCTIONS DRAWN FROM THE DIVINE PERFECTIONS.

(1) God is *love*. From this scriptural premise the conclusion is drawn that He will never cast any of His creatures into endless woe. But we must remember that the Bible also tells us that "God is light," and between light and darkness there can be no fellowship. Divine love is not a sentimental passion which over-rides moral distinctions. God's love is a *holy* love, and because it is such He hates all evil; yea, it is written, "Thou hatest all workers of iniquity" *(Psa. 5:6)*. Startling as it may sound, it is nevertheless a fact, that the Scriptures speak much more frequently of God's anger and wrath, than they do of His love and compassion. Let any one consult Young's or Strong's Concordance and they may verify this for themselves. To argue, then, that because God is love, He will not inflict eternal

torment on the wicked, is to ignore the fact that God is light, and is to asperse His holiness.

(2) God is *merciful*. Man may be a sinner, and holiness may require that he should be punished, but it is argued that Divine mercy will intervene, and if the punishment be not entirely revoked it is imagined that the sentence will be modified and the term of punishment be shortened. We are told that the *eternal* torment of the lost cannot be harmonized with a God of mercy. But if by the mercy of God be meant that He is too tenderhearted to apportion such miseries to His creatures, then we might as logically reason that seeing God's mercy, like all His attributes, is *infinite*, therefore, none of His creatures will be permitted to suffer at all. Yet this is manifestly erroneous. Facts deny it. His creatures *do* suffer, ofttimes excruciatingly, even in this life. Look out on the world to-day and mark the untold misery which abounds on every hand, and then remember that, however mysterious all this may be to us, nevertheless, it *is* all permitted by a merciful God. So, too, read in the Old Testament the accounts of the deluge, the destruction of Sodom and Gomorrah by fire and brimstone from heaven, the plagues upon Egypt, the judgments which were visited upon Israel, and then bear in mind that these *were not prevented* by the mercy of God! To reason, then, that because God is merciful He will not cast into the lake of fire every one whose name is not found written in the book of life, is to fly in the face of all God's judgments in the past!

(3) God is *just*. It is often said it would be unjust for God to sentence any of His erring creatures to *eternal* perdition. But who are *we* to pass judgment upon the justice of the decisions of the All-Wise? Who are *we* to say what is consistent or inconsistent with *God's* righteousness? Who are *we* to determine what shall best vindicate the Divine benevolence or equity? Sin has so enfeebled our power of righteous judgment, so darkened our understanding, so dulled our conscience, so perverted our wills, so corrupted our hearts, that we are quite *incompetent* to decide. We are ourselves so infected and affected by sin that we are altogether incapable of estimating its due merits. Imagine a company of criminals passing judgment on the equity and goodness of the law which had condemned them! The truth of the matter is—and how often is it lost sight of!—that God is not to be measured by human standards.

But have we realized that to deny the *justice* of eternal punishment is also to repudiate the *grace* of God? If endless misery be unjust, then exemption from it must be the sinner's *right*, and if so, his salvation could never be attributed to grace, which is *un*merited favor! Moreover, to deny the justice of eternal punishment is to fly in the face of Christian consciousness, which universally witnesses to the fact that punishment, and only punishment, is all that *each* of us deserves. Moreover, if the sinner has despised and rejected eternal happiness, is there any reason why he should complain against the justice of eternal misery? Finally, if there is an *infinite* evil in sin—as there is—then infinite punishment is its due reward.

(4) God is *holy*. Because God is infinitely holy, He regards sin with infinite abhorrence. From this scriptural premise it has been erroneously concluded that, therefore, God will ultimately triumph over evil by banishing every last trace of it from the universe; otherwise, it is said, His moral character is gone. But against this sophistry we reply; God's holiness did not prevent sin *entering* His universe, and He has permitted it to *remain* all these thousands of years, therefore a holy God *can* and *does* co-exist with a world of sin! To this it may be an-

swered: There are good and sufficient reasons *why* sin should be allowed now. Quite so, is our rejoinder; and who knows *what* these reasons are? Conjecture we may; but who *knows?* God has not told us in His Word. Who, then, is in the position to say that there may not be *eternal* reasons—*necessities*—for the continued existence of sin? That God will triumph over evil is most certainly true. His triumph will be manifested by incarcerating every one of His foes in a place where they can do no more damage, and where in their torments His holy hatred of sin will shine for ever and ever. The lake of fire so far from witnessing to Satan's victory, will be the crowning proof of his utter defeat.

2. THE PASSAGES APPEALED TO BY UNIVERSALISTS.

Universalists may be divided, broadly, into two classes: those who teach the ultimate salvation of every member of Adam's race, and those who affirm the ultimate salvation of all creatures, including the Devil, the fallen angels, and the demons. The class of passages to which both appeal are verses where the words "all," "all men," "all things," "the world" are to be found. The simplest way to refute their contentions on these passages is to show that such terms are *restricted*, usually modified by what is said in the immediate context.

The issue raised by Universalists narrows itself down to the question of whether "all men" and "all things" are employed, in passages which speak of salvation, in a *limited* or *unlimited* sense. Let us, then, point to a number of passages where these general terms occur, but where it is impossible to give them an absolute force or meaning:

"And there went out unto him *all* the land of Judea, and they of Jerusalem, and were *all* baptized of him in the river of Jordan, confessing their sins" *(Mark 1:5).* "And as the people were in expectation, and *all men* mused in their hearts of John, whether he were the Christ or not" *(Luke 3:15).* "And they came unto John, and said unto him, Rabbi, He that was with thee beyond Jordan, to whom thou barest witness, behold the same baptizeth, and *all* come to Him" *(John 3:26).* "And early in the morning He came again into the temple, and *all the people* came unto Him; and He sat down, and taught them" *(John 8:2).* "For thou shalt be His witness unto *all men* of what thou hast seen and heard" *(Acts 22:15).* "Ye are our epistle written in our hearts, known and read of *all men*" *(2 Cor. 3:2).*

In none of the above passages has "all," "all men," "all the people" an unlimited scope. In each of those passages these general terms have only a relative meaning. In Scripture "all" is used in two ways: meaning "all *without exception*" (occurring infrequently), and "all *without distinction*" (its general significance), that is, all classes and kinds—old and young, men and women, rich and poor, educated and illiterate, and in many instances Jews and Gentiles, men of all nations. Very frequently the "all" has reference to all *believers*, all *in Christ*.

What we have just said concerning the relative use and restricted meaning of the terms "all" and "all men" applies with equal force to "all things." In Scripture this is another expression which often has a very limited meaning. We give a few examples of this: "For one believeth that he may eat *all things*: another, who is weak, eateth herbs" *(Rom. 14:2).* "For meat destroy not the work of God. *All things* indeed are pure" *(Rom. 14:20).* "I am made *all things* to all, that I might by all means save some" *(1 Cor. 9:22).* "*All things* are lawful for me, but all things are not expedient" *(1 Cor. 10:23).* "Tychicus, a beloved brother and faithful minister in the Lord, shall make known to you *all things*" *(Eph. 6:21).*

"I can do *all things* through Christ which strengtheneth me" (*Phil. 4:13*). In each of these passages "all things" has a restricted force.

Another class of passages appealed to by Universalists are verses where "the world" is mentioned. But a careful examination of *every* passage where this term occurs in the New Testament will show that we are *not obliged* to understand it as referring to the entire human race, because in a number of instances it means far less. Take the following examples. "For the bread of God is He which cometh down from heaven and giveth life unto *the world*" (*John 6:33*). Mark that here it is not a matter of *proffering* "life" to the world, but of *giving* "life." Does Christ "give life"—spiritual and eternal life, for that is what is in view —to every member of the human family? "If thou do these things, show Thyself to *the world*" (*John 7:4*). Here it is plain that "the world" is an indefinite expression—show Thyself in public, to men in general, is its obvious meaning here. "The Pharisees therefore said among themselves, Perceive ye how we prevail nothing? Behold, *the world* is gone after Him" (*John 12: 19*). Did the Pharisees mean that the entire human race had "gone after" Christ? Surely not. "First, I thank my God through Jesus Christ for you all, that your faith is spoken of throughout *the whole world*" (*Rom. 1:8*). Must this mean that the faith of the Roman saints was known and spoken of by all the race of mankind? Did all men everywhere "speak" of it? Did one man out of every ten thousand in the Roman Empire know anything about it? "The word of the truth of the Gospel, which is come unto you, as it is in *all the world*" (*Col. 1:5,6*). Does "all the world" here mean, absolutely and unqualifiedly, all mankind? Had all men everywhere heard the Gospel? Surely the meaning of this verse is, that the Gospel, instead of being confined to the land of Judea and the lost sheep of the house of Israel, had gone forth abroad without restraint, into many places. "And *all the world* wondered after the beast" (*Rev. 13:3*). That the reference here cannot be to all men without exception we know from other scriptures, which tell us of a godly remnant of the Jews who will refuse to render allegiance to the Antichrist.

It will be seen, then, from the passages cited above that there is nothing in the words themselves which compel us to give an unlimited meaning to "all men," "all things," "the world." Therefore when we insist that "the world" which is saved, and the "all men" who are redeemed, are the world *of believers* and the all men *who receive Christ* as their personal Saviour, instead of interpreting the Scriptures to suit ourselves we are explaining them in strict harmony with other passages. On the other hand, to give to these terms unlimited scope and to make them mean all without exception is to interpret them in a way which manifestly clashes with the many passages which plainly teach *there are* those who will be finally lost.

One other remark may be made upon Universalism before turning to our next sub-division, and that is, the very fact that Universalism is so popular with the wicked, is proof irresistible, that it is not the system taught in the Bible. 1 Cor. 2:14 tells us "the natural man *receiveth not* the things of the Spirit of God: for they are foolishness unto him: neither can he know them, because they are spiritually discerned." That the natural man *does receive* the teaching that every one will ultimately be saved, is a sure sign it does not belong to "the things of the Spirit of God." The wicked hate the light, but love the darkness; hence, while they deem as "foolishness" the truth of God and reject it, they esteem as reasonable the Devil's lies, and greedily devour them.

3. Passages appealed to by the Annihilationists.

Truth is one: consistent: eternally unchanged. Error is hydra-headed, inconsistent and contradictory, ever varying in its forms. So determined are men to persuade themselves that the eternal punishment of the wicked is a myth, the enmity of the carnal mind has devised a variety of ways of ridding themselves of this truth which is so hateful to them. "God hath made man upright; but they have sought out many inventions" *(Eccl. 7:29)*. One of these inventions is the theory that at death the wicked pass into oblivion, and that after their resurrection and judgment at the Great White Throne, they are annihilated in the lake of fire. Incredible as this view appears, nevertheless it has had and still has many advocates and adherents; and what is even more unthinkable, the Word of God is appealed to in support of it. It is because of this that we make a brief notice of it here.

The first class of passages to which they appeal are verses where "death" is mentioned. Death is regarded in the most absolute sense. Death they take to mean the passing from existence into non-existence; an utter extinction of being. Death is applied to the soul as well as the body. How, then, is this error to be met? We answer, By an appeal to God's Word. The meaning of a word is to be defined not from its derivation, not from its employment by heathen writers, not from the definition supplied by a standard English distionary, nor from the lexicons, but from its *usage in the Holy Scriptures*. What, then, does death mean as used by the Holy Spirit?

Let us turn first to 1 Cor. 15:36: "Thou fool, that which thou sowest is not quickened, except it *die*." Here is the Holy Spirit's illustration and type of the death and resurrection of a believer. Now, does the living germ in the seed sown *become extinct* before it brings forth fruit? Surely not. There is a decaying, of course, of its outer shell—and therein lies the analogy with the death of man—but the living germ within dies not, otherwise there could be no harvest. Death, then, according to this illustration of the Holy Spirit is not annihilation. The same illustration was used by our Lord. Said He, "Except a corn of wheat fall into the ground and *die*, it abideth alone: but if it *die*, it bringeth forth much fruit" *(John 12:24)*. The stalk and ear of corn in harvest time are but the life-germ fully developed. So it is with man. The body dies; the soul lives on. Note how this comes out, unmistakeably, in the Saviour's words as recorded in Matt. 10:28: "And fear not them which kill the body, but are not able to kill the soul: but rather fear Him which is able to destroy both soul and body in hell." The "soul" man is *unable* to kill! But God is able—and mark carefully the distinction—"to *destroy* (not kill) both soul and body in hell." As the word "destroy" is another word mis-used and erroneously defined by the Annihilationists, a few words must be said upon it.

As used in Scripture the words "destroy," "destruction," "perish" etc. never signify cessation of existence. In Matt. 10:7 one of the principle Greek words for "destroyed" is rendered "the *lost* sheep of the house of Israel." Those Israelites had not ceased to be, but were away from God! In Mark 2:22 the same word is translated "marred" in connection with "bottles" of skins which the new wine burst. So, too, the word "perish" never signifies annihilation in Scripture. In 2 Pet. 3:6 we read, "The world that then was, being overflowed with water, *perished*." The "world" that perished, whether the reference be to the pre-Adamic earth or the world destroyed by the Flood, was not reduced to nothing. When, then, Scripture speaks of the wicked as perishing and as being destroyed, it is in order to expose the error of those who assert that they have a gospel for those who die unsaved. That the wicked have "perished" excludes *all* hope of their subsequent salvation. 1 Tim. 5:6 tells us there is a living-death even now—"She that liveth in pleasure is *dead while she liveth*"—so will there be in eternity.

The absurdity and unscripturalness of Annihilationism are easily exposed. If at death the sinner passes out of existence, why resurrect him in order to annihilate him again? Scripture speaks of the "punishment" and "torment" of the wicked; but any one can see that annihilation is not these! If annihilation were all that awaits the wicked, they would never *know* that they *had* received their just deserts and the "due reward" of their iniquities! Scripture speaks of *degrees* of punishment for the lost; but annihilation would make this impossible: annihilation would level all distinctions and ignore all degrees of guilt. In Isa. 33:14 we are told, "Who among us shall dwell with the devouring fire? Who among us shall dwell with everlasting burnings?" So far from sinners being annihilated they shall *dwell* with the devouring fire! Scripture speaks again and again of the "wailing and gnashing of teeth" of those who are cast into hell, and this, at once, gives the lie to those who affirm extinction of being.

4. THE THEORY THAT THE PUNISHMENT OF THE WICKED IS DISCIPLINARY AND REMEDIAL.

There are those who allow that the wicked will be cast into hell, and yet they insist that the punishment is corrective rather than retributive. A sort of Protestant Purgatory is invented, the fires of which are to be purifying rather than penal. Such a conception is grossly dishonoring to God. Some who hold this view make a great pretense of honoring Christ, yet in reality they greatly dishonor Him. If men who died rejecting the Saviour are yet to be saved, if the fires of hell are to do for men what the blood of the Cross failed to effect, then why was the Divine Sacrifice needed at all—*all* might have been saved by the disciplinary sufferings of hell, and so God *could have* spared His Son. Again; if God compassionates His enemies and cherishes nothing but gracious designs of infinite pity toward those who have despised and rejected His Son, we may well ask, Then why does He take such dreadful measures with them? If loving discipline be all that they need, cannot Divine wisdom devise some gentler measure than consigning them to the "torment" of the *lake of fire* for "the ages of the ages"? This is an insuperable difficulty in the way of the theory we are now refuting. But once we see that the lake of fire is the place of *punishment,* not discipline, and that it is Divine *wrath* and not love that casts the reprobate into it, then the difficulty entirely disappears.

Utterly inconsistent though it be, there are those who argue that the fires of hell owe their disciplinary efficacy to the blood of Christ. These enemies of the truth have been well answered by Sir Robert Anderson: "Such punishment, therefore, must be the penalty due to their sins; else it were unrighteous to impose it. If, then, the lost are ultimately to be saved, it must be either because they shall have satisfied the penalty; or else through redemption—that is, because Christ has borne that penalty for them. But if sinners can be saved by satisfying Divine justice in enduring the penalty due to sin, Christ need not have died. If, on the other hand, the redeemed may yet be doomed, though ordained to eternal life in Christ, themselves to endure the penalty for sin, the foundations of our faith are destroyed. It is not, I repeat, the providential or disciplinary, but the *penal* consequences of sin, which follow the judgment. We can therefore understand how the sinner may escape his doom through his debt being paid vicariously, or we can (*in theory*, at all events) admit that he may be discharged on payment personally of 'the uttermost farthing'; but that the sinner should be made to pay a portion of his debt, and then released because some one else had paid the whole before he was remitted to punishment at all,—this is absolutely inconsistent with both righteousness and grace." (Human Destiny).

Again; if it be true that the damned in the lake of fire are still the objects of Divine benevolence; that as the creatures of His hand, the Lord still looks upon them with the most benign regard, and the unquenchable fire is nothing more than a rod in the hand of a wise and loving Father, we ask, How can this be harmonized with the manner in which Scripture uniformly speaks of unbelievers? God has not left us in ignorance of how He regards those who have openly and persistently defied Him. Again and again the Bible makes known to us the solemn fact that God looks upon the wicked as cumberers of the earth, as repugnant to Him. They are represented as "dross" not gold *(Psa. 119: 119)*; as worthless "chaff" *(Matt. 3: 12)*; as "vipers" *(Matt. 12:34)*; as "vessels unto dishonor" and "vessels of wrath" *(Rom. 9:21, 22.)*; as those who are to be made the Lord's *footstool (1 Cor. 15:27)*; as "trees whose fruit withereth, without fruit, twice dead, plucked up by the roots" *(Jude 12)* and therefore fit for nothing but the fire; as those who will be "spued out of the Lord's mouth" *(Rev. 3:16)*, that is, as objects of revulsion. Some of these passages describe Jewish reprobates, others sinners of the Gentiles; some refer to those who lived in a byegone dispensation, others belong to the present; some speak of men this side of the grave, some of those on the other side. Our purpose in calling attention to them is to show *how God regards His enemies*. The estimate expressed in the above passages (and they might easily be multiplied) cannot be harmonized with the view that God still looks upon them in love and entertains only the most tender regards for them.

Another class of passages may be referred to in this connection. "For I lift up My hand to heaven, and say, I live forever. If I whet my glittering sword, and mine hand take hold on judgment; I will render vengeance to mine enemies, and will reward them that hate Me. I will make mine arrows drunk with blood, and My sword shall devour flesh; and that with the blood of the slain and of the captives, from the beginning of revenges upon the enemy" *(Deut. 32:40-42)*. Can this be made to square with the theory that God has nought but compassion towards those who have despised and defied Him?

"Because I have called, and ye have refused; I have stretched out My hand, and no man regarded; But ye have set at nought all My counsel, and would none of My reproof; I also will laugh at your calamity; I will mock when your fear cometh; When your fear cometh as desolation, and your destruction cometh as a whirlwind; when distress and anguish cometh upon you. Then shall they call upon Me, but I will not answer; they shall seek Me early, but they shall not find Me" *(Prov. 1:24-28)*. Is this the language of One who still has designs of mercy toward His enemies?

"I have trodden the winepress alone; and of the people there was none with Me: for I will tread them in Mine anger, and trample them in My fury; and their blood shall be sprinkled upon My garments, and I will stain all My raiment" *(Isa. 63:3)*. Weigh this carefully, and then ask if such treatment is meted out toward those unto whom the Lord cherishes nought but compassion.

Should it be said, Each of these passages is from the Old Testament, it would be sufficient to say, True, but it is the same God as the New Testament reveals that is there speaking. But consider one verse from the New Testament also. The Christ of God is yet going to say to men, "Depart from Me, ye cursed, into everlasting fire" *(Matt. 25:41)*. Is it thinkable that the Son of God would pronounce this awful malediction upon those who are merely appointed to a season of disciplinary chastisement, after which they will be forever with Him in perfect bliss!

Thus we have sought to show that the various objections brought against eternal punishment will not stand the test of Holy Writ; that, though often presented in a plausible form, and with the avowed intention of vindicating the Divine character, yet, in reality, they are nothing more than the reasonings of that carnal mind which is enmity against God.—*Arthur W. Pink.*

(To be continued, D. V.)

EXPOSITION OF FIRST PETER
I Peter 1:3-5
I. OF THE BLESSINGS ACKNOWLEDGED

Let us then, consider, in the first place, the blessings which the apostle here so gratefully acknowledges.

§1.—Divine Sonship

The first of these is the privilege of being children of God, "God, even the God and Father of our Lord Jesus Christ, hath begotten us again." When it is said, God hath "begotten us," the meaning is, "God hath made us His children;" and when it is said that God hath "again," anew, a second time, "begotten us," the meaning is, 'we were His children in one sense before, but in another, a higher, a better sense, a sense in which we were not His children, He has now made us His children.'

As His rational creatures, the objects of His kind providential care, all men are the children of God. "Have we not all one Father? Hath not one God created us?" He is "the Father of the spirits of all flesh." "We are all His offspring."¹ But, as Christians, we have become the children of God in a sense in which all men are not his children. The appellation, children of God, as applied to true Christians in a mystical, spiritual sense, like most of their peculiar appellations, is borrowed from one of the titles bestowed on the peculiar people of God under the former economy: "Israel," said Jehovah, "is my son, my firstborn." "Ye are the children of the Lord your God," says Moses. Jehovah is spoken of as "the Rock that begat them."²

When Christians are represented as the children of God, there are two ideas suggested by the appellation. They are brought by Him into the relation of children—and they are formed by Him to the character of children.

The relation in which every human being stands to God in the present state, previously to his being personally connected with Jesus Christ as the Saviour, is that in which a violator of the law, convicted and condemned, stands to his sovereign. He is the appropriate object of Divine displeasure; in the language of Scripture, "The wrath of God abideth on him."³ His ultimate happiness, if he remains in this state, is incompatible with the honor of God, the good order of his moral administration, and the well-being of his rational and accountable subjects.

But in the case of genuine Christians, a change of state takes place. The obedience to the death of God's

---
¹Mal. 2:10; Acts 17:26-28.
²Exod. 4:22; Deut. 14:1; 32:18.
³John 3:36.

incarnate Son, makes the salvation of sinners consistent with, conducive to, the illustration of the perfections of the Divine character, and subservient to the interests of the Divine government. Faith in Christ is that which, according to the Divine constitution, interests the individual sinner in the "obedience to death" of God's Son. On believing the truth, then, the individual who was condemned is no longer condemned—he is forgiven; he who was a sentenced criminal, is now a beloved child. The relation in which he now stands to God, is that of a son to a father. God no longer frowns on him—He smiles on him. He no longer curses him—He blesses him. He was "angry" with him *(Psa. 7:11)*, but He now comforts him.[1]

When God makes men His children, He not only brings them into the relation of children, but He forms them to the character of children. When He gives men the privilege of being His children He "sends forth into their hearts the Spirit of his Son," who forms in them an habitual temper and disposition, which may be termed "the spirit of adoption."[2] Our sentiments in reference to God, while in our natural condition, are not child-like. Our state is that of condemned criminals, and our character corresponds with our state. The leading feelings of the unrenewed man towards God, are dislike, and jealousy, and fear—"the fear that hath torment." But when God makes us His children, He forms us to the affectionate, confiding character of children. While He leads us to "sanctify Him in our hearts," and to fear Him without being afraid of Him, He disposes us to love Him as infinitely amiable and infinitely kind; and to trust in Him, as perfectly knowing what is good for us—perfectly able to secure our welfare—perfectly disposed to make us happy.

To be thus brought into the state and formed to the character of God's children, form the two great elements of true happiness, as they form the two grand fundamental blessings of the Christian salvation. They are most intimately connected together. The being brought into the state of children is absolutely necessary to the being formed to the character of children. It is impossible to form a slave to the character of a freeman, without making him free. And the formation of us to the character of children, is the great design of God in bringing us into the state of children. He regards and treats us as His children, that we may regard Him and treat Him as our Father.

We become the children of God—both in reference to state and character, to condition and disposition—through the belief of the truth; and this belief of the truth is produced and maintained by the influence of the Holy Spirit. We are "the children of God by faith in Christ Jesus." We are "begotten" or "born" again, "not of corruptible seed, but of incorruptible, by the word of God, which liveth and abideth forever." It is through the faith of the truth that the condemned sinner is forgiven and justified: "He that believeth is not condemned, and can never come into condemnation;" while on him that believeth not, "the wrath of God abideth." And it is through the faith of the truth that the unholy sinner is sanctified. The heart is "purified by the faith." It is through the knowledge and belief of the truth, with regard to God's character as a Father, that we are formed to the disposition and feelings of children. And this faith of the truth is the result of the influence of the Divine Spirit; so that, when born again—born from above—we are "born of the Spirit."[3] So much for the illustration of this first bless-

---

[1] Is. 12:1.
[2] Gal. 4:4-7; Rom. 8:15.

[3] Gal. 3:26; I Peter 1:23; John 3:18. Acts 15:9.

ing, for which the apostle presents his acknowledgments.

§2.—THE INHERITANCE PROVIDED FOR THEM.

The second blessing is the future inheritance which God has provided for us as His children. He has "begotten us again to an inheritance,"—that is, that we may obtain an inheritance, etc. "If children," says the apostle, "then heirs."[1]—that is, "if He bring us into the relation and form us to the character of children, He will give us the treatment of children."

When God made ancient Israel His children—brought them into a covenant relation with Him—He assigned to them an inheritance. That inheritance was, like the economy to which it belonged, material and temporal. It was the large and fertile land of Canaan, which they were to possess in security and peace, but into which they were to enter not immediately—not till after a long course of wandering in the wilderness.

When God brings men into the relation of children under the new and spiritual and eternal economy, He assigns to them an inheritance which corresponds with the character of that new dispensation—an inheritance of which they are not to obtain the full possession, till "the end come—the consummation of all things." The inheritance here is obviously the celestial blessedness, properly so called —the final state of good men—that state which, commencing with the resurrection, is to be continued unchanged, except by indefinite progress, forever and ever. What is figuratively termed "the inheritance" *(v. 4)*, is literally described *(v. 5)*, "as the salvation ready or prepared to be revealed in the last time."

Of that state we can form but very inadequate conceptions, for it has not yet been "revealed." It does not yet appear what we shall be;[2] it will be fully unveiled by-and-by, but not till "the last time"—the period of "the glorious appearing of our Lord Jesus Christ." But we may form correct conceptions, so far as they go; and it is of the greatest importance that we should do so. It is a state of complete freedom from evil, both moral and physical, in all its forms, and in all its degrees; and it is a state of perfect holy happiness, suited to a spiritual nature, endowed with intellect and affection and active power, united to a material frame, every way suited to minister to its progressive improvement and enjoyment; a state in which every capacity of blessedness shall be filled to overflowing, and in which the growing capacity shall never outrun the increasing blessedness.

Knowledge and holiness are the two great elements of the celestial happiness. The holy spirits of the just made perfect, clothed upon with their house from heaven—the immortal, incorruptible, powerful, glorious resurrection body, shall be perfectly conformed to God, so far as their limited capacities admit, in knowledge and purity and happiness. God's mind shall be their mind—God's will, their will—God's happiness, their happiness. They shall "know Him as He is—and they shall be like Him."[3] This is, I am persuaded, the justest view we can take of the celestial happiness. This is "the inheritance."

The celestial blessedness receives here, and in many other passages of Scripture, the appellation of "the inheritance," for two reasons—to mark its gratuitous nature, and to mark its secure tenure.

An inheritance is something that is not obtained by the individual's own exertions, but by the free gift or bequest of another. The earthly inheritance of the external people of God, was not given them because they were greater or better than the other na-

---
[1] Rom. 8:17.
[2] I John 3:3.
[3] Ibid. 3:2.

tions of the earth. It was "because the Lord had a delight in them to love them." "They got not the land in possession by their own sword, neither did their own right hand save them; but Thy right hand, and Thine arm, and the light of Thy countenance, for Thou hadst a favor unto them."[1] And the heavenly inheritance of the spiritual people of God is entirely the gift of sovereign kindness. "By grace are we saved;" "eternal life is the gift of God through Jesus Christ our Lord."[2]

A second idea suggested by the figurative expression, "the inheritance," when used in reference to the celestial blessedness, is the security of the tenure by which it is held. No right is more indefeasible than the right of inheritance. If the right of the giver or bequeather be good, all is secure. The heavenly happiness, whether viewed as the gift of the Divine Father, or the bequest of the Divine Son, is "sure to all the seed." If the title of the claimant be but as valid as the right of the original proprietor, their tenure must be as secure as the throne of God and His Son.

The idea of the security of this happiness is brought forward, however, more distinctly in the description of the inheritance which immediately follows. It is described as "incorruptible, undefiled, and unfading—reserved in heaven" for Christians, while they "are kept by the power of God through faith."

In this description of the inheritance, there are two things which require consideration—the excellence of the inheritance itself; and the security that the Christian shall in due time enjoy it.

The excellence of the inheritance itself, consists in being "incorruptible, undefiled, and unfading." These epithets may seem in a great degree synonymous, and there is no doubt that permanent, unchanging excellence is the leading idea in them all; yet, on looking a little more closely at them, we shall find that each of them presents that general idea in an instructive and pleasing peculiarity of aspect.

The celestial happiness viewed as an inheritance, is "incorruptible." There is nothing in its own nature which can lead to its dissolution. It is not material, but spiritual. It is not composed of "such corruptible things as silver and gold," but of knowledge and of holiness. It is not "meat and drink," —it is not costly and splendid apparel —it is not stately buildings, nor extensive estates. It is "joy and peace" and happiness arising from sources which, from their very nature, are inexhaustible,—possession of the Divine favor—conformity to the Divine image—intercourse and fellowship with God.

It is not only incorruptible, and therefore everlasting, but it is "undefiled." It is debased by no extrinsic, heterogeneous ingredient. In all our enjoyments on earth, however pure and exalted in themselves, there is a mixture. There is always something wanting—something wrong; and sin, that vilest of all things, taints and pollutes them all. But into heaven there enters "nothing that defileth." There is knowledge, without any mixture of error—holiness, without any mixture of sin—love, without any mixture of malignity; the highest dignities excite there no pride—the richest possessions, no covetousness. The inheritance is undefiled.

Still farther the heavenly inheritance is "unfading!" It "fadeth not away." The garland worn by the blessed is of amaranth—it never withers. The idea here seems to be, It not only is everlasting in its own nature, but it will never cease to give happiness to the possessor. How often do worldly possessions wither,—cease to give the happiness they once gave to

---

[1] Ps. 44:3.
[2] Eph. 2:5; Rom. 6:23.

those who continue to hold rather than to enjoy them! It has been beautifully remarked, that "the sweetest earthly music, if heard but for one day, would weary those who are most delighted with it. But the song of Heaven, though forever the same, will be forever new."[1] Here we are often sated but never satisfied—there, there is constant satisfaction, but there never will be satiety. Such is the excellence of the celestial inheritance.

'But,' may the Christian say, 'the inheritance is indeed inestimably precious; but will it ever be mine?' It is as secure as it is precious, says the apostle. It is "reserved in heaven for you," and you are "kept for it by the power of God through faith."

This inheritance is "reserved in heaven" for Christians—that is, it is secured beyond the reach of violence or fraud. Many a person, born to a rich inheritance, has never obtained possession of it, but has lived and died in poverty; but this inheritance is liable to none of the accidents of earth and time. It is "in heaven," under the immediate guardianship of DIVINE power, wisdom, and love.

'But the inheritance may itself be secure, but not secure for me. There may be perfect happiness in heaven, but I may never reach it there.' To meet this suggestion the apostle adds, "Ye are kept by the mighty power of God through faith." The apostle's doctrine is, and it is quite accordant with the doctrine of his Master and the other apostles, that all who are begotten again by God shall be preserved to the enjoyment of the inheritance. None of them shall fall in the wilderness. "I give unto My sheep eternal life," says Jesus Christ; "and they shall never perish, neither shall any one pluck them out of My hand. My Father, who gave them Me, is greater than all; and none can pluck them out of My Father's hand."[3] "Who shall separate us from the love of Christ? shall tribulation, or distress, or persecution, or famine, or nakedness, or peril, or sword? Nay, in all these things we are more than conquerors, through Him that loved us. For I am persuaded, that neither death, nor life, nor angels, nor principalities, nor powers, nor things present, nor things to come, nor height, nor depth, nor any other creature, shall be able to separate us from the love of God, which is in Christ Jesus our Lord."[4]

They are "kept"—preserved safe—amid the many dangers to which they are exposed, "by the power of God." The expression, "power of God," may here refer to the divine power both as exercised in reference to the enemies of the Christian, controlling their malignant purposes, and as exercised in the form of spiritual influence on the mind of the Christian himself, keeping him in the faith of the truth, "in the love of God, and in the patient waiting for our Lord Jesus Christ." It is probably to the last that the apostle principally alludes, for he adds "by faith." It is through the persevering faith of the truth that the Christian is by divine influence preserved from falling and kept in possession both of that state and character which are absolutely necessary to the enjoyment of the heavenly inheritance.

The perseverance thus secured to the true Christian is perseverance in faith and holiness, and nothing can be more grossly absurd than for a person living in unbelief and sin, to suppose that he can be in the way of obtaining celestial blessedness.

So much for the illustration of the second blessing for which the apostle gives thanks—the future inheritance which God has provided for His children.

---

[1] Leighton.　　[3] John 10:28.　[4] Rom. 8:35-39.

§3.—THE LIVING HOPE OF THE INHERITANCE.

Let us now proceed to consider the third of these blessings: The living or lively hope of the inheritance, through the resurrection of Christ Jesus from the dead. God hath "begotten us again to a lively hope"—that is, in making us His children, He has excited in us an influential and enduring hope of final and complete happiness.

Mankind in their natural state are said to "have no hope"[1]—that is, they are without any well-grounded rational hope of final happiness. This is true of all men without exception, of the elect of God as well as of others. They have broken the Divine law; they have incurred the Divine displeasure. They are guilty, and depraved, and miserable. They deserve everlasting destruction; if mercy interpose not, they must meet with their desert.

It is then an inquiry of very deep moment, how is the well-grounded hope of final happiness excited and maintained in the human mind? Now there are two questions which must be resolved, in order to our distinctly apprehending the truth on this subject; the first, what is the ground of the hope referred to in our text? and the second, how is an individual brought to cherish the hope of final happiness on this ground?

With reference to the former of these questions, it is obvious that the ground of hope is not anything in the sinner himself. It is not that he is innocent; it is not that he is less guilty than others. It is not that a great change has been produced, or is to be produced, on him. When he looks at himself in the light of the Divine law, a sinner may well perceive abundant reason for fear, abundant reason for despair; but he can never perceive any sufficient reason for hope.

The ground of hope is not in us, but in God. The ground of the sinner's hope—(and the ground of the saint's hope is just the ground of the sinner's hope; for what is a saint but a saved sinner?)—is sometimes represented as the sovereign benignity of God; sometimes as the obedience to death, the finished work, the perfect atonement, of Christ; and sometimes as the free untrammelled revelation of mercy in the word of the truth of the gospel. These are all but different aspects of the same thing, and the truth on this subject may be thus stated: The ground —the sole ground—of a sinner's hope is the sovereign mercy of God, manifested in consistency with, in glorious illustration of, His righteousness, in the obedience to death of His Son Jesus Christ, the just one in the room of the unjust, of which we have a plain and well-accredited account "in the word of the truth of the gospel." The ground of hope is exhibited in such passages of Scripture as the following:—"God so loved the world, that He gave His only begotten Son, that whosoever believeth in Him might not perish, but have everlasting life." "The righteousness of God without the law is manifested, being witnessed by the law and the prophets; even the righteousness of God, which is by the faith of Christ unto all and upon all them that believe; for there is no difference: for all have sinned, and come short of the glory of God; being justified freely by God's grace, through the redemption that is in Christ Jesus; whom God hath set forth as a propitiation through faith in His blood." "It is a faithful saying, and worthy of all acceptation, that Christ Jesus came into the world to save sinners; of whom I am chief." "God is in Christ, reconciling the world to Himself, not imputing their trespasses to them; for He hath made Him to be sin for us, who knew no sin, that we might be made the righteousness of God in Him." "The blood of Jesus Christ, His Son, cleanseth us from all sin. He is

[1] Eph. 2:12.

able to save to the uttermost them that come unto God by Him, seeing He ever liveth to make intercession for them."[1]—*John Brown.*

(To be continued, D. V.)

WHAT IS IT TO BELIEVE?

Addressed to One who is "No Sceptic"

You tell me, my dear friend, that you are "no sceptic"; but were I to ask you *what* it is you believe, I fear the answer would be very vague. Allow me then, in much love and a yearning tenderness for your soul, which none can understand or appreciate, who have not learned its value at the cross of Christ to tell you what it is to believe in Jesus. It is from God's own Word I would draw instruction, and may the Holy Spirit, whose office it is to apply that Word, open your heart to receive His teachings.

From St. Mark we learn that when the Lord Jesus first came into Galilee, "preaching the Gospel of the Kingdom of God," He proclaimed the time fulfilled, and that kingdom at hand, saying, "Repent ye, and believe the Gospel." John the Baptist had before this exhorted to repentance, but he only added, "For the kingdom of heaven is at hand,"—for although, to the opened understanding, the coming Saviour is found as the theme of all the Jewish scriptures, the "*Gospel,*" glad tidings of a Saviour *come,* had not yet reached the ears of the people. Though the shepherds had repeated it as they heard it from angelic lips at the birth of Jesus, their report had not probably spread far, and very likely where it was heard, made little impression on those who had not heard the heavenly harmony.

But now the long looked-for Messiah had come. On the banks of the Jordan many must have witnessed the wondrous opening of the heavens, with the descent of the Holy Spirit like a dove upon the beloved Son, in whom the Father pronounced Himself well pleased. What a foundation for faith was this! Yet "He came to His own, and His own received Him not." Few, very few, were His disciples, even after mighty works had shown forth His power. Here and there, indeed, was one whose enlightened spirit, "Waiting for the consolation of Israel," could recognize in the houseless stranger their expected King, and who could even take up the enraptured strain of the prophet—prepared for utterance in that day, when the rebuke of His people shall be taken away— "Lo! This is our God; we have *waited for Him,* and He will save us: This is Jehovah—we have waited for Him; we will be glad and rejoice in His salvation." But worldliness had for the most part beclouded the minds of the Jews, and the Lord might still say, as in the days of Isaiah, "Israel doth not know, My people doth not consider."

After this Divine endorsement of His mission, Jesus went about into all their cities and villages, teaching in their synagogues, and preaching the Gospel of the Kingdom. We find Him everywhere—instant in season and out of season, by day and by night, on the mountain top, by the sea shore, in houses and by the wayside, in tenderest compassion ministering to suffering humanity, and by miracles of beneficence manifesting His power as the Son of God.

Having thus prepared the way, He began to look for *faith* in the hearts of those who saw the wonderful works and unprecedented love exhibited in their midst. "Believest thou that I am able to do this?" "Only believe." "Believest thou this?" "Dost thou believe on the Son of God" and the like words were ever falling from His lips as the demand of His heart, for faith. And

[1] John 3:16; Rom. 3:21-25; 1 Tim. 1:15. 2 Cor. 5:19, 21; Heb. 7:25.

here and there a few were found who satisfied His soul, and drew faith's blessing from Him. Such were blind Bartimeus, the centurion, and many others, of whose faith everybody in this land has heard, but whose faith so few follow. "But when He came into His own country," where His earthly origin was known, **few believed on Him.** Though marveling at the power and wisdom of His works and words, the result was only perplexity. "From whence hath this man this knowledge and these mighty works?" "Is not this the carpenter's son? From whence then are all these things?" And we are told, "He could there do no mighty work because of their unbelief."

As the hour approached, when He should be "lifted up," He gradually unfolded His salvation, and claimed His place as Saviour of the world. "As Moses lifted up the serpent in the wilderness, even so must the Son of Man be lifted up, that whosoever believeth in Him should not perish but have everlasting life" *(John 3:14, 15).* "Verily, verily, I say unto you, He that believeth on Me hath everlasting life" *(John 6:47).* "And whosoever liveth and believeth in Me shall never die" *(John 11:26).* At length the time was fully come when, after the deep agony of Gethsemane, the Saviour betrayed by one disciple, and forsaken by all, was led away amidst scorn and derision, to be mocked, and scourged, and spit upon, and crucified. On the cross He completed the work He had left the bosom of the Father to accomplish. After a walk of absolute perfection upon earth, speaking such words as never man spoke, and doing such deeds as God only could perform,—after human cruelty had exhausted its ingenuity in devices to increase the anguish and ignominy of His death, He could say, "It is finished." Then, and not till then, He bowed His head and gave up the ghost. Then, and not till then, He laid down of Himself the life no man could take from Him. The weight of a world's sin and misery was upon Him, and reproach had broken His heart. He looked for some to take pity, but there was none, and for comforters, but not one was there; and beyond all this, even His Father's face was hidden, and in the mysterious depths of that desertion He was left to cry, "My God, My God, Why hast Thou forsaken Me?"

Thus was accomplished the wondrous work of man's redemption. The debt which justice claimed was fully paid. God henceforth was manifestly "just," and yet "the Justifier of him who believeth in Jesus." The penalty of God's broken law was suffered by the Sinless, that the sinner might be saved, and in the Divine munificence of blessing, the disciples who had followed the footsteps of Jesus during His short ministry on earth, were permitted to see their Saviour and ours, after "He was declared to be the Son of God, with power by the resurrection from the dead," be convinced "by many infallible proofs" that He was really alive, and to be assured by His own voice, that because "He lived they should live also." Then, in all the majesty of His Godhead, He announced *"All power"* to be His "in heaven and in earth," and sent them forth to bear witness to what they had seen, and to preach the fully accomplished Gospel, the glad tidings of a free salvation to every creature. "He that believeth shall be saved."

Now what is it to believe? Those who came to be cured of Him whilst on earth would have found no difficulty in answering this question. True, the father of the dumb demoniac when he cried out with tears, "Lord, I believe," added, "Help, Lord, mine unbelief." But was not this a strong testimony of faith in the great Healer? For who but God could be expected to influence the heart? Well is it for every trembling sinner who can repeat the prayer! *True faith is operative:* "I will arise and go to my father," said the famishing prodigal, and he did so, else what would have availed the knowledge that "plenty of bread, and to spare" awaited him? And what would have been the advantage to any of the sufferers alluded to, had they been satisfied with the bare report of Jesus' power, although not doubting it? Had they sat still and said, like some who are "no sceptics," "We believe in Jesus Christ," would such faith have healed them? Ah! my friend, the devils believe more than you do! They desired to escape the holiness which they hated: "We know Thee who Thou art, the Holy One of God," they exclaimed in the same breath with *"Let us alone."* One of these when he saw Jesus afar off, ran and worshipped Him *(Mark 5:6)* but he cried with a loud voice, *"What have I to do with Thee,* Jesus, Son of the Most High God?" And what, dear friend, have you had to do with Him? Have *you* ever worshipped Him, knowing that He is the very Christ, the Holy One of God?

To believe, we see from hence, is more than an assent of the understanding: it is more than faith in the mere existence of Christ: it is more than a knowledge of His deity; for multitudes *saw* Him, but were reproached as "faithless and perverse;" furthermore, the demons *knew* Him to be the Son of God.

To believe in Jesus Christ is not to adopt certain opinions in regard to Him, or His works. It is not to assent to any scheme of doctrine, or to the abstract truth of His existence: but, in the words of a recent writer, *It is 'to hold living relations with a Living Person.'* It is to come to Him, as when He was on earth they did who needed and desired His aid—knowing their necessity, and believing His power. To seek Him as a living Saviour is to believe in Him. Faith is not what we feel or see, it is a simple trust. We are to look confidently to Him for salvation, and then, for all we need; to lean on Him, as a child leans upon a parent. Throughout His Word He reiterates the gracious invitation, "Come unto Me," freely offering rest to the weary, comfort to the mourner, and eternal salvation to the trembling sinner. And with what tender solicitude He laments over those whom He would in nowise cast out, "Ye will not come to Me that ye might have life."

Now since you are no sceptic, my dear friend, you believe generally in the truth of these things, and have never doubted the authenticity of the Bible. Why then, let me ask you in all lovingkindness, why then have you not "Come to the Lord Jesus"? Is it not worth your while? Are you so happy, so satisfied with your portion here and your hope for the hereafter, that you need not this provision of God's mercy? Alas! no; so far from this, the questions seem a cruel irony. Disguise it as you will there is but one answer—*because of unbelief.* A peace that passeth all understanding here and Eternal Bliss hereafter are freely offered. Why are they not yours? Alas, alas, *because you desire them not!* You do not appreciate their value, and have not discovered your need; you are feeding on the husks of this world, complainingly indeed, yet unwilling to "Arise and go" to your Father's house where is "bread enough and to spare." Your eyes have not opened to your lost condition in the sight of God, and you have given small thought to the glorious Being who cries, "Come unto Me," and have never searched His Word to learn either your own state, or the treasures of His grace. Is not this the truth? Are not these things so?

That you are a sinner you will not deny. Even your own imperfect standard of excellence far exceeds your attainments, and there is much in your heart you would shrink from exposing to any human eye. Have you ever considered that "The Lord looketh upon the heart"—that all is naked and open to Him with whom we have to do? If we could ill bear to be weighed in the balance of earthly justice, if the thoughts and intents of our hearts, stripped of all the glories in which we enwrap them, would be condemned even by the world's morality—how shall we stand the searching eye of Him, in whose sight the very heavens are not clean? How much blacker must appear the sinful nature we bear, in the clear light of His Holiness! But blessed be His mercy, as He sees us, He saw a perishing world, and the wonderful history of redemption records His tender pity. There is ample provision made for salvation.

There are but two classes in the world, *believers and unbelievers.* Whosoever is not *for* Jesus Christ is *against* Him: He hath Himself affirmed this. The one class "have eternal life," the other is "condemned already" *(John 3:15, 18).* According to the Word of God, there is no middle ground. How then can any one, having access to the Scriptures, bear to live in doubt for an hour on so momentous a question? Are you a believer—that is, a child of God; or an unbeliever, living under condemnation? Rest not, I beseech you, my beloved friend, until you have settled this most important of all queries, involving life or death eternal! Go to the Word of God as you have never before approached it, with a fixed purpose to test your own thoughts by that Word. You will there find in the grace of God, in the person and cross of Christ, a revelation of your desperate condition, and of that which meets it all. And there you will find that your ruin and God's remedy suit each other so exactly, that you shall no longer need to ask, "What is it to believe?".—*Adapted from Grace and Truth, Vol. I, 1871.*

How little room is there for Christ *in general conversation.* We talk about many things; a man may nowadays talk on any subject he pleases. Speech is free in this land, but, ah! how little room is there for *Christ* in general talk! Even on Sunday afternoons how little room there is for Christ in some professed Christians' houses. They will talk about ministers, tell queer anecdotes about them—perhaps invent a few; they will talk about the Sunday School, or the various agencies in connection with the church, but how little they talk about *Christ!* And if some one should in conversation make this remark, "Could we not speak upon the Godhead and manhood, the finished work and righteousness, the ascension, or the second advent of our Lord Jesus Christ," people would say "Why, that man is quite a fanatic, or else he would not think of introducing such a subject as that into general conversation."—*C. H. Spurgeon.*

THE SINNER'S IMPOTENCY

All power is denied to man to convert himself to God, or to do anything which is spiritually good. He cannot know *(see I Cor. 2:14);* he can not believe *(see John 6:44);* he can not obey *(see Rom. 8:7).* Nay, to instance in single acts: he can not think a good thought of himself *(see II Cor. 3:5);* he can not speak a good word—"How can ye, being evil, speak good things?" *(Matt. 12:34).* He can not do anything *(see John 15:5)*—Christ doth not say "no great thing," but "without Me ye can do *nothing.*" Well, then, when man can neither know, nor believe, nor obey, nor think, nor speak, nor do anything without grace, surely man is "without strength," wholly impotent and unable to turn himself to God. Therefore he is shut up to sovereign grace. —*Thos. Manton, 1660.*

VOL. II   MARCH, 1923   NO. 3

STUDIES in the SCRIPTURES

"Search the Scriptures" John 5:39.

A PERIODICAL (MONTHLY "IF THE LORD WILL")
DEVOTED TO BIBLE STUDIES and EXPOSITIONS

Associate Editors and Publishers, I. C. HERENDEEN and ARTHUR W. PINK,
Swengel, Pa.

Price: 10 cents per copy; $1.00 per year. Foreign $1.00 per year.

TO OUR SCRIPTURE STUDY FAMILY

This issue contains the second article on Eternal Punishment. It aims to present the teaching of God's Word on the Destiny of the wicked, showing the awful punishment which awaits them. The subject is unspeakably solemn yet is it one which urgently needs pressing upon the unconcerned. Moreover, many who have been misled or disturbed by the various and specious denials of the endless suffering of the lost, ought to have this article placed in their hands. In the past, whenever considerable numbers of souls were brought out of darkness into God's marvellous light, the faithful preaching of this truth was one of the principal agencies honored by the Holy Spirit. We believe that the Lord will be pleased to use these articles to convict sinners of their need of a Refuge from the coming wrath. Therefore, we have printed an extra quantity of this March issue. These may be had for ten cents per copy, or six copies for fifty cents. We trust that many of our readers will order some, to hand out to their unsaved friends.

We are glad to announce that our printers are now binding some 1922 sets for us. We are hoping they will be in our hands by February 15th. We shall then have, D. V., a limited number of January to December 1922 bound volumes of *Studies in the Scriptures*. The price will be $1.50, cash with order. These have been bound particularly for the benefit of our new subscribers who may desire the back numbers. We regret that we cannot accept for binding the unbound copies of our old subscribers, as it is now too late, arrangements being already completed and under way.

During the last few weeks many letters have come to hand from different States and lands, telling of the help and blessing received during 1922 from the reading of *Studies in the Scriptures*. Some have had their faith strengthened, others have been encouraged to study God's Word more diligently for themselves, some have been comforted, and many tell of how their souls have been fed. This has drawn out our hearts in fervent praise and thanksgiving to the One from Whom cometh every good and perfect gift. The glory is His alone. We have only given out what we first received, and in giving out we are equally dependent on the Lord's grace to own and to bless. *We* may plant or water, but *God only* giveth "the increase." All praise to Him, then, for whatever spiritual fruit this publication may have brought forth.

But not only have these cheering letters filled us with gratitude, they have also exercised us. There are thousands more of God's dear children in this country (not to speak of those in distant lands) who are receiving no real soul-nourishing food in the churches they attend, and who would welcome such a magazine as this *did*

(Continued on page 96.)

IMPORTANT NOTICES

All new subscriptions will be dated back to January, 1923.

Set of twelve issues for 1922, unbound, $1.00. Bound, $1.50.

Note: We cannot break a set or now supply any **single** 1922 issues.

Subscription Price: $1.00 per year to any address in the world. Single copies 10 cents.

Change of Address: Please notify us promptly of any change of address, and be certain to give both old and new addresses.

Non-Subscribers receiving this Magazine regularly will understand their subscription has been entered by a friend.

Copies lost in the mail duplicated on request.

Entered as second-class matter December 15th, 1921 at the post office at Swengel, Pa., under Act of March 3rd, 1879.

CONTENTS

John's Gospel (John 4:31-42) 66
The Antichrist in the Prophets .. 73
Eternal Punishment 83
Exposition of First Peter 92

JOHN'S GOSPEL

15. CHRIST IN SAMARIA.

John 4:31-42.

We begin with the usual Analysis of the passage which is to be before us. In it we see:—

1. The Disciples' Solicitude, v. 31.
2. The Disciples' Ignorance, v. 32.
3. The Disciples Instructed, vv. 34-38.
4. The Samaritan Converts, v. 39.
5. The Samaritans' Request, v. 40.
6. The Samaritan Converts added unto, v. 41.
7. The Samaritans' Confession, v. 42.

Verses 31-38 form a parenthesis and tell us something of what transpired during the interval that followed the woman's leaving the well and the Samaritans coming to Christ because of her testimony to Him. They record a conversation which took place between the Lord and His disciples. The disciples, it will be remembered, had "gone away unto the city to buy meat," and had returned from their quest, to find their Master engaged in conversation with a woman of Samaria. They had marvelled at this, but none had interrogated Him on the matter. As they had heard the Saviour pronounce the ineffable "I am" title *(v. 26)*, a Divine restraint had fallen upon them. But now the interview between the Lord Jesus and the Samaritan harlot was over. Grace had won a glorious victory. A sinner had been brought out of darkness into God's marvelous light, and in consequence, had gone forth to tell others the good news which meant so much to her own heart.

Once more the Saviour was left alone with His disciples. They had returned in time to hear His closing words with the woman, and had seen the summary effect they had on her. They had witnessed that which should have corrected and enlarged their cramped vision. They had been shown that whatever justification there might have been in the past for the Jews to have "no dealings with the Samaritans," this no longer held good. The Son of God had come to earth, "full of grace and truth," and the glad tidings concerning Him must be proclaimed to all people. This was a hard lesson for these Jewish disciples, but with infinite patience the Lord bore with their spiritual dullness. In what follows we have a passage of great practical importance, which contains some weighty truths upon service.

"In the meanwhile His disciples prayed Him, saying, Master, eat" *(v. 31).* A little earlier in the day, the disciples had left their Master sitting on the well, wearied from the long journey. Accordingly, they had procured some food, and had returned to Him with it. But He evidenced no desire for it. Instead of finding Christ weary and faint, they discovered Him to be full of renewed energy. He had received refreshment which they knew not of. This they could not understand, and so they begged Him to eat of that which they had brought Him. Their request was a kindly one. Their appeal to Him was well meant. But it was merely the amiability of the flesh. The 'milk of human kindness' must not be mistaken for the fruit of the Spirit. Sentimentality is not spirituality.

"But He said unto them, I have meat to eat that ye know not of" *(v. 32)*. This was scarcely a rebuke: it was more a word of instruction for their enlightenment. Their minds were upon material things; the Lord speaks of that which is spiritual. "Meat" was used here as a figurative expression for that which satisfied. Christ's heart had been fed. His spirit had been invigorated. What it was that had refreshed Him we learn from His next utterance. It was something the disciples "knew not of." Not yet had they discovered that the One who gives out the things of God is also a receiver. In dispensing spiritual blessing to others, one is blest himself. Peace and joy are a part of the reward which comes to him who does the will of God. The obedient servant has "meat to eat" that those not engaged in service know nothing bout. These, and other principles of service, were what the Lord would now press upon His disciples.

"Therefore said the disciples one to another, Hath any man brought Him ought to eat?" *(v. 33)*. This confirmed what Christ had just said: disciples of His they might be, but as yet they were very ignorant about spiritual things. Their minds evidently dwelt more upon material things, than the things of God. They knew very little about the relation of Christ to the Father: their thoughts turned at once to the question as to whether or not any *man* had "brought Him ought to eat." Even good men are sometimes very ignorant; yea, the best of men are, until taught of God. "How dull and thick brain'd are the best, till God rend the veil, and enlighten both the organ and the object" (John Trapp, 1650, A. D.). But let us not smile at the dullness of those disciples; instead, see in them an exhibition of our own spiritual stupidity, and need of being taught of God.

"Jesus saith unto them, My meat is to do the will of Him that sent Me, and to finish His work" *(v. 34)*. What did Christ mean? In what sense is doing the will of God "meat" to the one who performs it? What is the *Father's* "work"? And *how* was Christ "finishing" it? The answer to these questions must be sought in the setting of our verse, noting its connection with what has gone before and what follows. We must first ascertain the leading subject of the passage of which this verse forms a part.

As we proceed with our examination of the passage it will become more and more evident that its leading subject is *service*. The Lord was giving needed instruction to His disciples, and preparing them for their future work. He sets before them a concise yet remarkably complete outline of the fundamental principles which underlie all acceptable service for God. The all-important and basic principle is that of absolute obedience to the will of God. The servant must do the will of his master. This the perfect Servant Himself exemplified. Note how He refers to God. He does not say here, "My meat is to do the will of the Father," but "the will of *Him that sent Me*." That shows it is *service* which is in view.

Now what was "the will" of the One who had sent Christ into the world? Was it not to deliver certain captives from the hands of the Devil and bring them from death unto life? If there is any doubt at all on the point John 6:36 and 39 at once removes it—"For

I came down from heaven, not to do Mine own will, but the will of Him that sent Me. And *this is* the Father's will which hath sent Me, that of all which He hath given Me I should lose nothing, but should raise it up again at the last day." This at once helps us to define *the Father's* "work"—"and finish His work," which must not be confounded with the work that was peculiarly the Son's: though closely related, they are quite distinct. The "will" of the Father was that all those He had "given" to the Son should be saved; His "work" had been in *appointing* them unto salvation—"For God hath not appointed us to wrath, but to obtain salvation by our Lord Jesus Christ" *(1 Thess. 5:9).* Appointment unto salvation *(see also 2 Thess. 2:13)* is peculiarly the work of the Father; the actual saving of those appointed is the work of the Son, and in the saving of God's elect the Son *finishes* the "work" of the Father. An individual example of this had just been furnished in the case of the Samaritan woman, and others were about to follow in the "many" who should believe on Him because of her testimony *(v. 39),* and the "many more" who would believe because of His own word *(v. 41).*

How all this casts its own clear light on v. 4 of this chapter, and explains to us the force of the "must" there. The Lord had not journeyed to Samaria to gratify His own desire, for "He pleased not Himself." In infinite grace the Son of God had condescended to lay aside (temporarily) His glory and stooped to the place of a Servant; and in service, as in everything else, He is our great Exemplar. He shows us *how* to serve, and the first great principle which comes out here is that, joy of heart, satisfaction of soul, sustenance of spirit—"meat"—is to be found in doing the will, performing the pleasure, of the One who sends forth. Here, then, the perfect Servant tells us what *true* service is—the simple and faithful performance of that which has been marked out for us by God. Our "meat"—the sustenance of the laborer's heart, the joy of his soul—is not to be sought in results (the "increase") but in doing the will of Him that sent us forth. That was Christ's meat, and it must be ours, too. This was the first lesson the Lord here teaches His disciples about Service. And it is the first thing which each of us who are His servants now, need to take to heart.

"Say not ye, There are yet four months, and then cometh harvest? Behold, I say unto you, Lift up your eyes, and look on the fields; for they are white already to harvest" *(v. 35).* It is very evident that it is the subject of Service which is still before us, and the principle enunciated in this verse is easily perceived. However, let us first endeavor to arrive at the local force of these words, and their particular significance to the disciples, before we reduce them to a principle of application to ourselves.

"Say not ye, There are yet four months, and then cometh harvest? Behold, I say unto you, Lift up your eyes, and look on the fields; for they are white already to harvest" *(v. 35).* There is no need to conclude that the disciples had been discussing among themselves the condition of the fields through which they had walked on their way to the city to buy meat; though they may have done so. Rather does it seem to us that the Lord continued to instruct His disciples in figurative language. There seems no doubt that the Saviour had in mind the spiritual state of the Samaritans and the estimate formed of them by His disciples. Possibly, the Samaritans who had listened to the striking testimony of the woman now saved were on their way toward the well, though yet some considerable distance away, and pointing to them the Saviour said to the disciples, "Lift up your eyes" and behold their state.

"Say not ye, There are yet four months, and then cometh harvest?" Any pious Jew who was familiar with the Old Testament Scriptures knew that in a coming day the Gentiles were to receive blessing from God: numerous were the passages that foretold this. But the turning of God to the Gentiles, and of them to Him, was represented as being consequent upon the restoration of Israel and the establishment of Messiah's kingdom in their midst—see such passages as Zech. 8:23; 14, etc. But the Lord here makes known, what the Old Testament prophecy did not reveal, namely, that there was to be an ingathering from among the Gentiles before the Messianic kingdom was set up.

"Lift up your eyes, and look on the fields; for they are white already to harvest." This was plainly a rebuke. The disciples regarded Samaria as a most unlikely field to work in; at best much sowing would be required, and then a long wait, before any ripened grain could be expected. They deemed the Samaritans fit to trade with, but apparently they never dreamed of telling them that the Messiah was just outside their gates! Must they not have hung their head in shame when they discovered how much more faithful and zealous had been this woman than they? Here, then, is a further reason why Christ "must needs go through Samaria"—to teach His disciples a much needed *missionary* lesson.

What, now, is the application to us of the principle contained in this verse? Surely it is this: we must not judge by appearances. Ofttimes we regard certain ones as hopeless cases, and are tempted to think it would be useless to speak to *them* about Christ. Yet we never know what seeds of Truth may have been lodged in their hearts by the labors of other sowers. We never know what influences may be working: ofttimes those who seem to us the most unlikely cases, when put to the test are the most ready to hear of the Saviour. We cannot tell how many months there are to harvest!

36"And he that reapeth receiveth wages, and gathereth fruit unto life eternal: that both he that soweth and he that reapeth may rejoice together" (v. 36). If the previous verse contained a rebuke, here was a word to encourage. "He that reapeth receiveth wages" seems to mean, This is a work in which it is indeed a privilege to be engaged, for the laborer receives a glorious reward, inasmuch as he "gathereth fruit unto life eternal." The reward is an eternal one, for not only do those saved through the labors of the reaper receive eternal life, but because of this the joy of both will be eternal too. "That both he that soweth and he that reapeth may rejoice together." The sower may have labored hard toward the salvaton of souls, and yet never be permitted to witness in this life the success which God gave to his efforts. The reaper, however, is witness of the ingathering; nevertheless, both sower and reaper shall rejoice together in the everlasting salvaton of those garnered through their joint efforts.

And herein is that saying true, One soweth, and another reapeth" (v. 37). There is a timely warning here. To "reap" is not everything, blessed as the experience is: to "sow" is equally important. The bountiful crop garnered at Sychar was, under God, the result of the labors of earlier sowers. These Samaritans were already informed about the appearing of the Messiah, and for this knowledge they were indebted to the faithful ministry of earlier servants of God. That one sows and another reaps had been exemplified in the case of the converted adulteress. Christ had met the need which the testimony of the prophets had awakened within her.

How gracious of the Lord to recognize and own the labors of those earlier sowers! Apparently their work had counted for little. They had sown the seed, yet seemingly the ground on which it had fallen was very unpromising. But now, under the beneficent influence of the Sun of righteousness, came the harvest, and the Lord is not slack to remind His disciples of their indebtedness to the labors of those who had gone before. Doubtless, Philip would recall these words of Christ in a coming day *(see Acts 8)*. And what comfort is there here for the sower to-day! His labors may seem to go for nothing, but if he is diligent in sowing the proper "seed," let him know that sooner or later all faithful service is rewarded. *He* may not "reap," but "another" *will*—"Therefore, my beloved brethren, be ye stedfast, unmoveable, a l w a y s abounding in the work of the Lord, forasmuch as ye know that your labor *is not in vain* in the Lord" *(1 Cor. 15: 58)*.

"I sent you to reap that whereon ye bestowed no labor: other men labored, and ye are entered into their labors" *(v. 38)*. There is no doubt a historical reference here which points us back to what is recorded in Matt. 10, from which we learn that the Lord had sent forth the twelve apostles to "preach," and to "heal the sick" *(vv. 7, 8)*. This was in Judea, and the success of their labors is indicated in John 4:1, 2—they had made and baptized many disciples. One can imagine the elation of the disciples over their success, and it was to repress their vanity that Christ here says to them, "I sent you to reap that whereon ye bestowed no labor: other men labored, and ye are entered into their labors." He reminds them that they had prospered because others had labored before them. It was a word encouraging to the sower, sobering to the reaper. We may observe, in passing, that when *the Lord sends us* forth to "reap," He directs us to fields which have already been sown. It should also be noted that the toil of the sower is more arduous than that of the reaper: when Christ says, "Other men *labored,* and ye (the reapers) are entered into their (the sowers') labors" He used a word which signified "to toil to the point of exhaustion," indeed it is the same word which is used of the Saviour at the beginning of this chapter, when we read, "Jesus therefore, being *wearied* with His journey." Luther was wont to say, "The ministry is not an idle man's occupation." Alas that so often it degenerates into such.

Sowing and reaping are two distinct departments of Gospel ministry, and spiritual discernment (wisdom from God) is requisite to see which is the more needed in a given place. "To have commenced sowing at Sychar would have indicated a want of discernment as to the condition of souls in that city. To have concluded from their success at Sychar, that all Samaria was ready to receive the Lord, would have been manifestly erroneous, as the treatment He met with in one of the villages of Samaria at a later period of His life clearly demonstrates. This, surely, can speak to us, where sowing and reaping may go on almost side by side. The work in one place is no criterion of what that in another place should be; nor does it follow, that the laborer, highly blessed in one locality, has only to move to another, to find that field also quite ready for his reaping-hook" *(C. E. Stuart)*.

"And many of the Samaritans of that city believed on Him for the saying of the woman, which testified, He told me all that ever I did" *(v. 39)*. At first glance it looks as though this verse introduces a change of subject, yet really it is not so. This verse, as also the two following, enunciates and illustrates other principles of *service*. In the first place, we are shown how that God is pleased to use feeble messengers to accomplish mighty ends. Frequently He employs weak instruments to make manifest His own mighty power. In this, as in everything else, the Lord's thoughts and ways are very different from ours. He employed a shepherd lad to vanquish the mighty Goliath. He endowed a Hebrew slave with more wisdom than all the magicians of Babylon possessed. He made the words of Naaman's servants to have greater effects upon their august master than did those of the renowned Elisha. In making selection for the mother of the Saviour, He chose not a princess, but a peasant woman. In appointing the heralds of the Cross, fisherman were the ones called. And so a mighty work of grace was started there in Sychar by a converted harlot. "How unsearchable are His judgments, and His ways past finding out!"

"And many of the Samaritans of that city believed on Him for the saying of the woman, which testified, He told me all that ever I did." The full force of this can only be appreciated as we go back to what is told us in verses 28 and 29. She did not say, 'Of what use can I be for Christ?—I who have lost character with men, and have sunken into the lowest depths of degradation!' No; she did not stop to reason, but with a conscience that had been searched in the presence of the Light and its burden of guilt removed; with a heart full of wonderment and gratitude to the One who had saved her, she immediately went forth to serve and glorify Him. She told what she knew; she testified of what she had found, but in connection with a *Person*. It was *of Him* she spoke; it was *to Him* she pointed. "*He* told me," she declared, thus directing others to that One who had dealt so blessedly with her. But she did not stop there. She did not rest satisfied with simply telling her fellow-townsmen of what she had heard, nor Whom she had met. She desired others to meet with Him for themselves. "*Come*" she said; Come *to Him* for yourselves. And God honored those simple and earnest words: "Many of the Samaritans of that city believed on Him for (because of) the saying of the woman." Thus are we shown the great *aim* in service, namely, to bring souls into the presence of Christ Himself.

"So when the Samaritans came unto Him, they besought Him to abide with them; and He abode there two days. And many more believed because of His Word; and they said to the woman, Now we believe, not because of thy speaking: for we have heard for ourselves, and know that this is indeed the Saviour of the world" (*vv. 40-42, R.V.*). We have quoted from the R. V. because we believe it is the more correct here. The A. V. makes these Samaritans say, "For we have heard Him ourselves, and know that this is indeed the Christ, the Saviour of the world." The majority of the Greek MSS. do not contain the words "the Christ" in v. 42. These Samaritans had learned from the lips of the woman *who* He was, "the Christ;" now they had discovered for themselves *what* He was—the One who met their deepest need, "the Saviour."

The above scripture places Samaria in striking contrast from the unbelief and rejection of the Judeans and those dwelling in Jerusalem, where so many of His mighty works had been done, and where it might be expected multitudes would have received Him. Here in Samaria was a people who seemed most unpromising; no record is given of Christ performing a single miracle there; and yet many of these despised Samaritans received Him. And is it not much the same to-day? Those whom we would think were most disposed to be interested in the things of God are usually the most indifferent; while those whom we are apt to regard as outside, if not beyond, the reach of God's grace, are the very ones that are brought to recognize their deep need, and become, ultimately, the most devoted among the followers of the Lamb.

Let us now seek to gather up into a

terse summary the leading lessons of the verses which have been before us. The whole passage has to do with *service*, and the fundamental principles of service are here enunciated and illustrated. First, we learn the *essential requirement* of service, as illustrated in the example of the Samaritan woman—a personal acquaintance with the Saviour, and a heart overflowing for Him. Second, we are taught the *spirit* in which all service should be carried on—the faithful performance of the task alotted us; finding our satisfaction not in results, but in the knowledge that the will of God has been done by us. Third, we are shown the *urgency* of service—the fields already white unto harvest. Fourth, we have *encouragement* for service—the fact that we are gathering "fruit unto life eternal." Fifth, we learn about the *interdependence* of the servants—"one soweth and another reapeth:" there is mutual dependence one on the other: a holy partnership between those who work in the different departments of spirtual agriculture. Sixth, we have a *warning* for servants: they who are used to do the reaping must not be puffed up by their success, but must remember that they are entering into the labors of those who have gone before. Finally; we are taught here the *aim* ever to be kept in view, and that is to bring souls into the presence of *Christ*, that they may become independent of us, having learned to draw directly from Him.

It now remains to be pointed out how the passage which has been before us also contains a very striking dispensational picture. It furnishes an accurate typical view of this present Age, which comes in parenthetically between God's dealings with Israel in the past, and His dealings with Israel in the future, when the kingdom of the Messiah will be set up on the earth. A careful study and analysis of our passage will reveal seven lines in the typical picture:—

First, attention is called to the *parenthetical* character of the present dispensation. This is seen in the fact that John 4:4-42 describes what took place outside of Judea and Galilee, in Samaria. Second, the approximate length of this present period is defined in v. 40 where we are told that the Lord Jesus "abode there *two days*," which, dispensationally considered, signifies two thousand years. Third, the *worldwide missionary* need is signified in the Lord's words in v. 35. Fourth, the *distinctive characteristic* of this Age is seen in *the absence* of any public miracles. There is no hint of Christ performing any miracles here in Samaria: nor is He doing so publicly in the world to-day. Fifth, the *means employed* are indicated in vv. 39 and 41, where we are told that it was the woman's testimony, and the Word which caused many of the Samaritans to "believe." Thus it is throughout this dispensation. It is the personal testimony of believers and the preaching of the Word, which are the Divinely appointed means for the propagation of Christianity. Sixth, we may note the *striking prominence of the Gentiles* in this typical picture: "Many of the *Samaritans . . . believed on Him.*" While there is a remnant of Israel "according to the election of grace" (typified in the few disciples who were with Christ), nevertheless, it is the Gentile element which predominates in the saved of this Age. Seventh, mark that Christ is owned here not as "The Son of Man," nor as "The Son of David," but as "The Saviour *of the World.*" This title does not mean that Christ is the Saviour of the human race, but is a general term, used in contradistinction from Israel, including all believing Gentiles scattered throughout the earth.

Thus, once more, we discover that with marvelous skill the Holy Spirit has caused this historical narrative which traces the actions of the Saviour in Samaria, and which records the instructions He there gave to His disciples, to embody a perfect dispensational outline which sets forth the leading features of this present Dispensation of Grace, during which God is taking out of the Gentiles a people for His name. This should cause us to search more diligently for the hidden beauties and harmonies of Scripture.

Below are the questions for the next lesson:—

1. How does v. 43 bring out the perfections of Christ?
2. How does "the Galileans received Him" (v. 45) confirm "no honor in His own country" (Galilee) of v. 44?
3. Why are we told Christ was in Cana when He healed the nobleman's son? v. 46.
4. Why are we told the nobleman belonged to Capernaum? v. 46.
5. In what way does v. 48 apply to us to-day?
6. What does the word "yesterday" in v. 52 tell us about the nobleman?
7. What typical picture can you find in this passage? Note the repeated mention of Galilee.

—*Arthur W. Pink.*

9. THE ANTICHRIST IN THE PROPHETS

The references to the Antichrist in the Prophets are numerous; nor is this to be wondered at. It is there, more than anywhere else in Scripture, that we learn of the future of both Israel and the Gentiles. It is there we have the fullest information concerning End-time conditions, and the completest description of the varied parts which the leading characters shall play in those days. It would carry us beyond the scope designed for these articles were we to examine *every* passage in the Prophets which makes mention of the Man of Sin and the numerous roles he will fill. Yet we do not desire to pass by any of the more important allusions to him. We shall, therefore, make a selection, and yet such a selection that we trust a complete outline at least will be supplied. Certain scriptures, notably those which view the Antichrist in connection with Babylon, will be waived now, because they will receive separate consideration in a later article of this series.

One other introductory remark needs to be made. We are conscious that this article will probably be somewhat unsatisfactory to a few of our readers, inasmuch as we shall be obliged to take a good deal for granted. It is manifest that we cannot here attempt to give a complete analysis of the passages where the different allusions to the Antichrist occur, nor should this be necessary. We are writing to Bible students, therefore we shall ask *them* to turn to the different places from which we quote and examine the contexts so as to satisfy themselves that they treat of End-time conditions. While in most instances the context will show that we are not reading into the Scriptures what is not there, yet in a few cases they may fail us. This is sometimes true with passages which contain prophecies concerning Christ. It is often the case in the prophets that the Holy Spirit is treating of something near at hand and then, without any warning, projects the view into the distant future. But just as the New Testament enables us to determine *which* Old Testament passages speak of Christ, so other scriptures help us to identify the person of the Antichrist in verses where there is but an indefinite and passing allusion to him.

1. ANTICHRIST IN ISAIAH.

A brief notice is taken of the Man

of Sin in chapter 16. The opening verses make it clear that conditions in the Tribulation period are being described. They intimate how that the persecuted Jews flee to the land of Moab for refuge—"Hide the outcasts; bewray not him that wandereth," makes this clear. These "outcasts" are definitely identified in v. 4, where Jehovah terms them *"Mine* outcasts." The same verse goes on to tell *why* they were "outcasts," outcasts from **Palestine:** "Let Mine outcasts dwell with thee, Moab; be thou a covert to them from the face of the Spoiler: for the Extortioner is at an end, the Spoiler ceaseth, the oppressors are consumed out of the land." Here the destruction of the Antichrist is noted. A further proof that these verses describe what immediately precedes the Millennium is found in the next verse, which conducts us to the beginning of the Millennium itself: "And in mercy shall the throne be established: and He shall sit upon it in truth in the tabernacle of David, judging, and seeking judgment, and hasting righteousness." Thus, in the light of other scriptures, there is little room for doubt that *the* Spoiler and *the* Extortioner refer to none other than the Son of Perdition.

In 22:25 we have another incidental reference to the Antichrist. For our comments on this verse we refer the reader to the fourth article of this series, section 17.

"In that day the Lord with His sore and great and strong sword shall punish Leviathan the piercing Serpent, even Leviathan that crooked Serpent; and He shall slay the Dragon that is in the sea" *(Isa. 27:1).* This chapter is by no means easy to analyze: its structure seems complex. That its contents point to a yet future date is intimated by its opening words—compare other verses in Isaiah where "in that day" occur. As one reads the chapter through it will be found that there is a peculiar alternation between references to the Tribulation period and conditions in the Millennium. The closing verse clearly refers to the end of the Tribulation period. So, also, does the first verse with which we are now chiefly concerned.

Leviathan, the piercing Serpent, is, we believe, one of the names of the Antichrist, compare the article in July 1922 issue, II, 2. A comparison with a passage in Job confirms this conclusion. It is generally agreed that "leviathan" in Job 41 refers to the crocodile, yet the commentators do not appear to have seen in it anything more than a description of that creature. But surely a whole chapter of Scripture would scarcely be devoted to describing a reptile! Personally, we are satisfied that under the figure of that treacherous and cruel monster we have a remarkable silhouette of the Prince of darkness. Note the following striking points:

In verses 1 and 2 (of Job 41) the strength of Leviathan is referred to. In v. 3 the question is asked "will he speak *soft words* unto thee?": this is meaningless if only a crocodile is in view; but it is very pertinent if we have here a symbolic description of Antichrist. In v. 4 the question is put, "Will he *make a covenant* with thee?": this, too, is pointless if nothing but a reptile is the subject of the passage; but if it looks to some Monster more dreadful, it serves to identify. "None is so fierce that dare stir him up" *(v. 10):* how closely this corresponds with Rev. 13:4—"Who is able to make war with the Beast?" "His teeth are terrible round about" *(v. 14):* how aptly this pictures the fierceness and cruelty of the Antichrist! "His heart is as firm as a stone; yea, as hard as a piece of the nether millstone" *(v. 24):* how accurately this portrays the moral depravity of the Antichrist! "When he raiseth up himself the mighty are afraid . . . . the sword of him that layeth at him cannot hold . . . . the arrow cannot make him flee" *(vv. 25, 26, 28)*: how these words suggest the invincibility of Antichrist so far as human power is concerned. "Upon earth there is not his like, who is made without fear. He beholdeth all high things: he is a king over all the children of pride" *(vv. 33, 34)*. Surely these last verses remove all doubt as to *who* is really before us here! The whole of Job 41 should be studied carefully, for we are assured that it contains a remarkable but veiled amplification of Isa. 27:1.

In Isa. 33 there is another reference to the Antichrist. This chapter, like so many in Isaiah, passes from a notice of Tribulation conditions to the Millennial state and back again. The opening verse reads, "Woe to thee that spoileth, and thou wast not spoiled; and dealest treacherously, and they dealt not treacherously with thee! When thou shalt cease to spoil, thou shalt be spoiled; and when thou shalt make an end to deal treacherously, they shall deal treacherously with thee." This is evidently a judgment pronounced upon the head of the false messiah. Two things serve to identify him: he is the great Spoiler, and the one who shall deal treacherously with Israel. It is in view of the perfidy and rapacity of their Enemy that the godly remnant cry, "O Lord, be gracious unto us; we have waited for Thee: be Thou their arm every morning, our salvation also in *the time of trouble*" *(v. 2)*. A further word concerning the Antichrist is found in v. 8: "The highways lie waste, the wayfaring man ceaseth: he hath broken the covenant, he hath despised the cities, he regardeth no man." The last three statements in this verse make it certain who is there in view. It is the Antichrist displayed in his true colors; the one who breaks his covenant with Israel, sacks their cities, and defies all human government to resist him.

A brief notice must be taken of 57:9 ere we turn from Isaiah. In this chapter we find God arraigning Israel for their horrid idolatries and wickedness. The opening verse again makes it clear that it is the Tribulation period which is in view: "The righteous perisheth, and no man layeth it to heart," etc. Following this we have the various indictments which God makes against the unfaithful Jews—"But draw near hither, ye sons of the sorceress, the seed of the adulterer and the whore" *(v. 3, etc.)*. The remainder of the chapter continues in the same strain. Among the many charges which God brings against Israel is this: "And thou wentest to the King with ointment, and didst increase thy perfumes, and didst send thy messengers far off, and didst debase thyself even unto hell" *(v. 9)*. It is evident that as this chapter is describing the sins of Israel committed in the End-time that "the King" here must be the false messiah. Incidentally this verse furnishes one of the many proofs that the Antichrist will be king over the Jews.

2. ANTICHRIST IN JEREMIAH.

In the 4th chapter of this prophet there is a vivid description of the fearful afflictions which shall come upon the inhabitants of Palestine. Doubtless, what is there said received a tragic fulfillment in the past. But like most, if not all prophecy, this one will receive a later and final accomplishment. There are several statements found in it which indicate that it treats of the End-time. The plainest of these is found in the closing verse, where we read, "For I have heard a voice as of a woman in travail, and the anguish as of her which bringeth forth her first child, the voice of the daughter of Zion." It is the "birth-pangs" of Matt. 24:8 (see Greek) which is in view. The sore trials which Israel shall then undergo are tragically depicted: "Blow ye the trumpet in the land: cry, gather together, and say, Assemble yourselves, and let us go into the defenced cities. Set up the standard toward Zion: retire, stay not: for I will bring evil from the north, and a great destruction. The Lion is come up from his thicket, and the **Destroyer of the Gentiles** is on his way; he is gone forth from his place to make thy land desolate; and thy cities shall be laid waste, without an inhabitant" *(vv. 5-7).* The Destroyer of the Gentiles now turns to vent his fiendish malignity upon the holy land. Destruction is in his heart. Terrible shall be his onslaught: "Behold, he shall come up as clouds, and his chariots shall be as a whirlwind: his horses are swifter than eagles. Woe unto us! for we are spoiled" *(v. 13).* Fearful will be the devastations his fury shall accomplish: The whole city shall flee for the noise of the horsemen and bowmen: They shall go into thickets, and climb up upon the rocks: every city shall be forsaken, and not a man dwell therein" *(v. 29).*

In 6:26, 27 there is a remarkable statement made concerning the Antichrist: "O daughter of My people, gird thee with sackcloth, and wallow thyself in ashes: make thee mourning, as for an only son, most bitter lamentation: for the Spoiler *(Destroyer, as in 4:7)* shall suddenly come upon us." This Spoiler is "the Destroyer of the Gentiles." But it is what follows in the next verse which is so striking: "I have set thee for a tower and a fortress among My people, that thou mayest know and try their way." Here we learn that, after all, the Antichrist is but a tool in the hands of Jehovah. It is *He* who sets him in the midst of Israel to "try" them. A parallel statement is found in Isa. 10:5, 6, where the Lord says of the Assyrian *"I will send him* against a hypocritical nation." It reminds us very much of what we read concerning Pharaoh in Rom. 9:17. He was "raised up" by God to accomplish *His* purpose. Even so shall it be with this one whom Pharaoh foreshadowed. He shall be an instrument in God's hand to chastise recreant Israel.

Chap. 15 contains brief allusions to the Antichrist. In **v. 8** we have a similar statement to what was before us in the last passage. Speaking to Israel God says, "I have brought upon them against the mother of the young men a Spoiler at noonday: I have caused him to fall upon it suddenly, and terrors upon the city." It is the Lord, then, (behind Satan) who brings this Spoiler against them. After His purpose has been accomplished, after the Antichrist has done what (unknown to himself) God has appointed, we read how that the Lord assures His people, "I will deliver thee out of the hand of the Wicked, and I will redeem thee out of the hand of the Terrible" *(v. 21).* Thus will God demonstrate His supremacy over the Son of Perdition.

25:38 takes us back a little and notices the awful desolation which the Antichrist brings upon the land of Israel: "He hath forsaken his covert, as the lion: for their land is desolate because of the fierceness of the Oppressor, and because of his fierce anger."

3. ANTICHRIST IN EZEKIEL.

We shall notice here but two passages in this prophet. First, in 21:25-27—"And thou, profane wicked Prince of Israel, whose day is come, when iniquity shall have an end, Thus saith the Lord God; Remove the diadem, and take off the crown: this shall not be the same: exalt him that is low, and abase him that is high. I will overturn, overturn, overturn it; and it shall be no more, until He come whose right it is; and I will give it Him."

So far as we are aware, all pre-millennial students regard this passage as a description of the Antichrist. It pictures him as Satan's parody of the Son of Man seated upon "the throne of His glory." It sets Him forth as the priest-king. Just as in the Millennium the Lord Jesus will "be a *Priest upon His throne*" *(Zech. 6:13),* so will the Antichrist *combine* in his person the headships of both the civil and religious realms. He will be what the popes have long aspired to be—head of the World-State, and head of the World-Church.

"And thou, O deadly wounded Wicked One, the Prince of Israel, whose day is come, in the time of the iniquity of the end; thus saith the Lord: remove the mitre, and take off the crown" (*R. V.*). This is clearly Israel's last king, ere the King of kings and Lord of lords returns to the earth. He is here termed "the Prince of Israel" as the true Christ is denominated "Messiah the Prince" in Dan. 9:25. The description "O *deadly wounded* Wicked One" looks forward to Rev. 13:12, where we read, "The first Beast whose *deadly wound* was healed"! "Remove the *mitre* and take off the *crown*" point to his assumption of both priestly and kingly honors. The Heb. word for "mitre" here is in every other passage used of the head-dress of Israel's high priest! Finally, the statement that his "day is come . . . . in the time of the iniquity of the end" establishes, beyond a doubt, the indentity of this person.

In the opening verses of Ezek. 28 we have a striking view of the Man of Sin under the title of "the Prince of Tyre," just as what is said of "the King of Tyre" in the second half of the chapter is an esoteric allusion to Satan. First, we are told his "heart is lifted up" (*v. 2*), which is precisely what is said to his father, the Devil, in v. 17. Second, he makes the boast "I am God" and "I sit in the seat of God" (*v. 2*), which is parallel with 2 Thess. 2:4. Third, it is here said of him, "Behold, thou art wiser than Daniel; there is no secret that they can hide from thee" (*v. 3*), which intimates he will be endowed with superhuman wisdom by that one of whom this same chapter declares, "Thou sealest up the sum, full of wisdom" (*v. 12*). Fourth, it is said of him, "By thy wisdom and by thine understanding thou hast gotten thee riches, and hast gotten gold and silver into thy treasures" (*v. 4*). Thus will he be able to dazzle the worshippers of Mammon by his Croesus-like wealth, and out-do Solomon in the glory of his kingdom. Finally, his death by the sword is here noted, see vv. 7, 8.

4. ANTICHRIST IN DANIEL.

It is here that we find the fullest description of the Man of Sin. First, he is looked at under the figure of "the little horn." As there has been some dispute whether this expression really applies to him, we propose to examine the more carefully what is here said of "the little horn." Personally, we have long been convinced that this expression refers to none other than the Antichrist. There are a number of plain marks which make it comparatively easy to recognize his person, whenever Scripture brings him before us. For example: his insolent and blasphemous pride; his exalting himself against and above God; his impious and cruel warfare against the people of God; his sudden, terrible, and supernatural end. Let us compare these features with what is said of "the little horn" in Dan. 7 and 8.

We turn first to Dan. 7. In vv. 7 and 8 we read, "After this I saw in the night visions, and behold a fourth beast, dreadful and terrible, and strong exceedingly; and it had great iron teeth: it devoured and brake in pieces, and stamped the residue with the feet of it: and it was diverse from all the beasts which were before it; and it had ten horns. I considered the horns, and, behold, there came up among them another *little horn*, before whom there were three of the first horns plucked up by the roots: and, behold, in this horn were eyes like the eyes of man, and a mouth speaking great things." This refers to the *rise* of "the little horn" within the bounds of the Roman Empire, for that is what is represented by the "fourth beast." The first thing said of the little horn is that he has "eyes like the eyes of man," which speak of intelligence, and "a mouth speaking great things"—the Heb. word signifies "very great," and the reference is, no doubt, to his lofty pretensions and his daring blasphemies.

In 7:21 it is further said of him that he "made war with the saints, and prevailed against them." This contemplates his persecution of the godly Jews, and agrees perfectly with Rev. 13:7: "And it was given unto him to make war with the saints, and to overcome them." In v. 25 we are told, "He shall speak great words against the Most High." Surely this serves to *identify* this "little horn" as the first beast of Rev. 13: "And there was given unto him a mouth speaking great things and blasphemies" *(v. 5)*. If further proof be needed, it is supplied by the remainder of verse 25: "And shall wear out the saints of the Most High . . . . and they shall be given into his hand until a time and times and the dividing of time." A "time" equals a year *(see Dan. 4:23 and Rev. 12:14, and cf. 12:6)*, so that a "time and times and the dividing of time" would be three and one-half years during which the saints are given into his hand. This corresponds exactly with Rev. 13:5, where of the first Beast, the Antichrist, it is said, "And power was given unto him to continue forty and two months"—in a later article we shall give a number of proofs to show that the first Beast of Rev. 13 *is* the Antichrist.

In Dan. 8 the Little Horn is before us again, and that it is *the same* dread personage as in chapter 7 appears from what is predicted of him. First, he is referred to as "a king of fierce countenance" *(8:23)*, which agrees with "whose *look* was *more stout* than his fellows" *(7:20)*. Second, it is said of him that he "waxed exceeding great (first) towards the south, and (second) towards the east, and (third) toward the pleasant land" *(8:9)*, which agrees with "there came up among them another little horn, before whom there were *three* of the first horns plucked up" *(7:8)*. Third, it is said that he "shall destroy the mighty and the holy people" *(8:24)*, which agrees with "and the same horn made war with the saints and prevailed against them" *(7:21)*. There should, then, be no doubt whatever that the "little horn" of Dan. 7 and the "little horn" of Dan. 8 refer to one and the same person. Their moral features co-incide: both, from an insignificant beginning, become great in the end: both persecute the people of God: both are stricken down by direct interposition of God. We may add that Messrs. B. W. Newton, James Inglis, G. H. Pember, Sir Robert Anderson, Drs. Tregelles, J. H. Brookes, Haldeman, and a host of other devout scholars and students, take the same view, namely, that the "little horn" of Dan. 7 and 8 and the Man of Sin are one and the same person.

Let us now consider briefly what is revealed concerning the Antichrist under this title of his, the "little horn." We confine ourself to Dan. 8:23-25.

First, he is "a king of fierce countenance." This we believe is a literal description of his facial expression, though we are satisfied that it also has a moral significance. In Deut. 28:50 we read of "a nation of fierce countenance, which shall not regard the person of the old nor show favor to the young." In the light of this scripture it seems clear that when the Antichrist is denominated the "King of fierce countenance" the reference is not only to his actual features, but that it also intimates he will be empowered to face the most perplexing and frightful dangers and the most appalling scenes of horror without flinching or blanching. It is significant that the reference in Deut. 28:50 is to the *Romans*, while what is said of the Antichrist in Dan. 8:23 relates, specially, to his connections with *Greece*. The two dominant characteristics of these Powers will be combined in the Man of Sin. There will be concentrated in him the irresistible will of the Romans and the brilliant intellect of the Greeks.

Second, we are told that he shall be able to "understand dark sentences." The Heb. noun for "dark sentences" is used of Samson's *riddle (Judges 14: 12)*, of the Queen of Sheba's "hard questions" *(1 Kings 10:1)*, and of the *dark sayings* of the wise *(Prov. 1:6)*, which are too profound to be understood by the simple. This characteristic of the King of fierce countenance, that he shall be able to "understand dark sentences," suggests an attempted rivalry of Christ as the Revealer of secret things. This is one of the fascinations by which the Antichrist will dazzle humanity. He will present himself as one in whom are hidden treasures of wisdom and knowledge. He will bewitch the world by his solutions of the enigmas of life, and most probably by his revelation of occult powers implanted in men hitherto unsuspected by most, and of forces and secrets of nature previously undiscovered.

Third, it is said "And his power shall be mighty, but not by his own power" *(8:24)*. This is explained in Rev. 13:2, where we are told, "And the Dragon *gave him his* power, and his throne, and great authority." Just as we read of the Lord Jesus, "The Father that dwelleth in Me, He doeth the works" *(John 14:10)*, so shall the Son of Perdition perform his prodigies by power from his father, the Devil. This is exactly what 2 Thess. 2:9 declares, "Whose coming is after the working of Satan with all power and signs and lying wonders." Thus will men be deceived by the miracles he performs.

Fourth, he will "destroy wonderfully, and shall prosper, and practise, and shall destroy the mighty and the holy people" *(8:24)*. This has received enlargement in the previous article, where we have given several illustrations from the Psalms of the Antichrist persecuting Israel.

Fifth, "And through his policy also he shall cause craft to prosper in his hand" *(8:25)*. The Heb. word for "policy" denotes wisdom and understanding. It was the word used by David to Solomon, when he said, "Only the Lord give thee *wisdom*" *(1 Chron. 22:12)*, as it is also employed by Huram when writing to Solomon: "Blessed be the Lord God of Israel, that made heaven and earth, who hath given to David the king a wise son, endued with *prudence*" *(2 Chron. 2:12)*. The Heb. word for "craft"—"He shall cause craft to prosper"—is the one employed by Isaac when speaking to Esau concerning Jacob: "Thy brother came with *subtilty*" *(Gen. 27:35)*. It has in view the chicanery and treacherous methods the Antichrist will employ. "By peace shall destroy many" *(v. 25)* refers to the fact that he will pose as the Prince of peace, and after gaining men's confidence—particularly that of the Jews—will take advantage of this to spring his bloody schemes upon them.

Sixth, it is said "He shall also stand up against the Prince of princes" *(8: 25)*. This unmistakably identifies him with the Beast of Rev. 19:19, where we are told, "And I saw the Beast, and the kings of the earth, and their armies, gathered together to make war *against Him* that sat on the horse, and against His army."

Seventh, "But he shall be broken without hand" *(8:25)*. This expression means that he shall come to his doom without *human* intervention or instrumentality—see Dan. 2:45; 2 Cor. 5: 1, etc. That the King of fierce countenance shall be *"broken* without hand" refers to his destruction by the Lord Himself—"And He shall smite the earth with the rod of His mouth, and with the breath of His lips shall He slay the Wicked" *(Is. 11:4)*.

We turn now to Dan. 9:26, 27. This forms a part of the celebrated prophecy of the seventy "weeks" or hebdomads. We cannot now attempt an exposition of the whole prophecy: sufficient to point out its principal divisions and examine that part of it which bears on our present theme.

The prophecy begins with v. 24 and concerns the seventy hebdomads, a word signifying "sevens." Each "hebdomad" equals seven years, so that a period of 490 years in all is here comprehended. These seventy "sevens" are divided into three portions: First, seven "sevens" which concerned the re-building of Jerusalem, following the Babylonian captivity. Second, sixty-two "sevens" unto "Messiah the Prince," that is, unto the time when He formally presented Himself to Israel as their King: this receiving its fulfillment in the so-called Triumphal Entrance into Jerusalem." Third, the last "seven" which is severed from the others. It should be carefully noted that we are expressly told that *"after* threescore and two weeks (which added to the preceding seven would make sixty-nine in all up to this point) shall Messiah be *cut off."* The reference is to the Cross, when Christ was "cut off" from Israel and from the land of the living. This occurred *after* the sixty-ninth week and before the seventieth began.

The sixty-ninth terminated with the formal presentation of Christ to Israel as their "Prince." This is described by Matthew (the distinctively *Jewish* Gospel) in chapter 21. The rejection of their Prince caused the break between Christ and Israel. It is very striking to note that (following the Rejection) Matthew records three distinct proofs or evidences of this break. The first is found in Matt. 21:19 in the cursing of the "fig tree," which signified the rejection of *the Nation*. The second was His sorrowful announcement from the brow of Olivet that the time of Israel's visitation was past and her overthrow now certain *(Matt. 23:37 and cf. Luke 19:41-44)*. This was the abandonment of *the City*. The third was His solemn pronouncement concerning the Temple: "Behold your House is left unto you desolate. For I say unto you, Ye shall not see Me henceforth, till ye shall say, Blessed is He that cometh in the name of the Lord" *(Matt. 23:38, 39)*. This was the giving up of *the Sanctuary*.

The entire Christian dispensation (which began with the crucifixion of Christ) is passed by unnoticed in this prophecy of the seventy "weeks." It comes in, parenthetically, between the sixty-ninth and the seventieth. What follows in Dan. 9:26, 27 concerns what will happen *after* the Christian dispensation is ended, when God again takes up Israel and accomplishes His purpose concerning them. This purpose will be accomplished by means of sore judgment, which will be God's answer to Israel's rejection of His Son. But let us examine more closely the form this judgment will take.

The judgment of God upon the people who were primarily responsible for the "cutting off" of their Messiah was to issue in the *destruction* of their "city and sanctuary" *(9:26)*. This destruction was to be brought about by the people of a Prince who should subsequently appear, and be himself destroyed. The "Prince" here is the Antichrist, but the Antichrist connected with and at the head of the Roman Empire in its final form.* Now we know that it was the Romans who destroyed Jerusalem and the temple in A. D. 70, but that "the Prince" here does not refer to the one who then headed the Roman armies is clear from the fact that Dan. 9:27 informs us this Prince is to play his part in the yet future seventieth week—further proof is furnished in that v. 26 carries us to "the end" (i. e. of Israel's "desolations") which is to be marked by a "flood," and Isa. 28:14, 15 in-

---
*It is the Man of Sin who is to be the last great Cæsar: this will be made clear in our study of the Antichrist in the Revelation.

timates that this is to be after Israel's covenant with Antichrist: "Wherefore hear the word of the Lord, ye scornful men, that rule this people which was in Jerusalem. Because ye have said, We have made a covenant with Death, and with Hell are we at agreement; when the overflowing scourge shall pass through it, it shall not come unto us: for we have made lies our refuge, and under falsehood have we hid ourselves." To this God replies, "Your covenant with Death shall be disannulled, and your agreement with Hell shall not stand; when the overflowing scourge shall pass through, then ye shall be trodden down by it" *(v. 18).* The "overflowing scourge" is, literally, "the scourge coming in like *a flood.*"

A few words remain to be said on 9:27: "And he shall confirm the covenant with many for one week: and in the midst of the week he shall cause the sacrifice and the oblation to cease, and for the overspreading of abominations he shall make it desolate, even until the consummation, and that determined shall be poured upon the desolate." The subject of this verse is the Antichrist, "the Prince that shall come" of the previous verse. By the time he appears on the scene large numbers of Jews will have been carried back to their land *(cf. Isa. 18).* With them the Prince makes a covenant, as of old Jehovah made one with Abraham, and as Christ will yet do with Israel, see Jer. 31. This will be regarded by God with indignation, as "a covenant with Death, and an agreement with Sheol." But while this covenant is accepted by the majority of the Jews, God will again reserve to Himself a remnant who will refuse to bow the knee to Baal: hence the qualification, "He shall confirm the covenant with *many*," not all.

"In the midst of the week he shall cause the sacrifice and the oblation to cease." The returned Jews will rebuild their temple and there offer sacrifices. But these, so far from being acceptable to God, will be an offense. There seems a clear reference to this in the opening verses of Isa. 66, which describe conditions just before the Lord's appearing *(see v. 15).* And here the Lord says, "He that killeth an ox is as if he slew a man; he that sacrificeth a lamb, as if he cut off a dog's neck," etc. *(v. 3).* But three and a half years before the end, the Prince will issue a decree demanding that the sacrifices must cease, and the worship of Jehovah be transferred to himself, for it is at this point he shall "exalt himself above all that is called God, or that is worshipped" *(2 Thess. 2:4).* The fact that we are here told that *he* causes the sacrifices and the oblation to cease, at once identifies this Prince of the Romans as the Antichrist—cf. 8:11. The remaining portion of 9:27 will be considered when we come to Matt. 24:15.

We turn now to Dan. 11, which is undoubtedly the most difficult chapter in the book. It contains a prophecy which is remarkable for its fulness of details. Much of it has already received a most striking fulfillment, but like other prophecies, we are fully satisfied that this one yet awaits its final accomplishment. That Dan. 11 treats of the Antichrist all pre-millennial students are agreed, but as to how much of it refers to him there is considerable difference of opinion. A small minority, from whom we must dissent, confine the first thirty-five verses to the past. Others make the division in the middle of the chapter and regard all from v. 21 onwards as a description of the Man of Sin, and with them the writer is in hearty accord. A few consider the entire chapter, after v. 2, as containing a prediction of the Antichrist under the title of "The King of the North," and while we are not prepared to unreservedly endorse this, yet it is fully allowed that there is not a little to be said in its favor.

We shall here confine ourself to the

second half of Dan. 11. Our present limits of space, however, will permit of nothing more that brief notes upon it. Commencing at v. 31 we read, "And in his estate shall stand up a vile person, to whom they shall not give the honor of the kingdom: but he shall come in peaceably, and obtain the kingdom by flatteries." The history of this "vile person" is here divided into three parts: first, the means by which he obtains the kingdom: vv. 21, 22; second, the interval which elapses between the time when he makes a covenant with Israel, the taking away of the daily sacrifice and the setting up of the abomination of desolation: vv. 23—31; third, the brief season when he comes out in his true colors and enters upon his career of open defiance of God, reaching on to his destruction: vv. 32-45. Thus from v. 21 to the end of the chapter we have a continuous history of the Antichrist.

"In his estate shall stand up a vile person . . . . he shall come in peaceably, and obtain the kingdom by flatteries." This epithet "the vile person" is a manifest antithesis from "the *Holy One of God.*" This twenty-first verse takes notice of the Man of Sin posing as the Prince of peace. He shall achieve what his antitype, Absalom, tried but failed to do—"Obtain the kingdom by flatteries."

"And with the arms of a flood shall they be overflown from before him, and shall be broken; yea, also the Prince of the Covenant" *(v. 22).* This "Vile Person" is denominated "the Prince of the Covenant," which, at once, identifies him with the "Prince" of 9:26, 27. Then we are told in v. 23 "And after the league made with him he shall work deceitfully: for he shall come up, and shall become strong with *a small* people." This "league" or "covenant" is doubtless the seven-years-treaty confirmed with Israel, which is made at an early point in the Antichrist's career, and which corresponds with the fact that at the first he appears as a *"little horn,"* the "small people" being the Syrians—cf. our remarks on Dan. 8:8, 9 in article six.

Vv. 25 and 26 describe his victory over the king of Egypt. Then, in v. 28 we read, "Then shall he return into his land with great riches." *His* land is Assyria. The mention of "great riches" corresponds with what we are told of the Antichrist in Psa. 52:7; Ezek. 28:4, etc.

"And arms shall stand on his part, and they shall pollute the sanctuary of strength and shall take away the daily sacrifice, and they shall place the abomination that maketh desolate." This is clear evidence that these verses are treating of that which takes place during the seventieth week. The mention of polluting the Sanctuary is an unmistakable reference to "the abomination of desolation," i. e. the setting up of an idol to the Antichrist in the Temple. Note the repeated use of the plural pronoun in this verse; the "they" refer to the Antichrist *and* the False Prophet, cf. Rev. 13. It is significant that in the next verse *(v. 32)* there is an allusion made to the faithful remnant—"The people that do know their God."

"And the king shall do according to his will; and he shall exalt himself, and magnify himself above every god, and shall speak marvelous things against the God of gods, and shall prosper till the indignation be accomplished: for that that is determined shall be done" *(v. 36).* That "the King" here is the "Vile Person" is not only indicated by the absence of any break in the prophecy, as also by the connecting "and" with which the verse opens, but is definitely established by the fact that in v. 27 (note context) the Vile Person is expressly termed a "king"! The contents of this thirty-sixth verse clearly connects "the king" with the Man of Sin of 2 Thess. 2:3, 4, and also as definitely identifies him with the "little horn"—cf. 7:23 and 8:25. The remaining verses of Dan. 11

have been before us in previous articles and need not detain us now.

5. ANTICHRIST IN THE MINOR PROPHETS.

Here a wide field for study is opened, but we must content ourself with but a few selections and brief comments on them. *Hosea* makes several references to the Man of Sin. In 8:10 he is termed "the King of princes," as such he is Satan's imitation of the King of kings. In 10:15 he is named "the King of Israel," which shows his connection with the Jews. In 12:7 he is called a "Merchant" or Trafficker, and of him it is said, "The balances of deceit are in his hands: he loveth to oppress," with this should be compared Rev. 6:5. These words denote his twofold character in connection with the Jews: first he makes them believe he is the true Christ; second, he ultimately stands forth as their great Enemy.

Joel alludes to him as the head of the "northern army," i. e. the Assyrian. And here God declares that He will "drive him into a land barren and desolate, with his face toward the east sea; and his stink shall come up, and his ill savor shall come up, because he has magnified to do great things" *(2: 20)*.

Amos speaks of him as "an Adversary" which shall be "even round about the land; and he shall bring down thy strength from thee, and thy palaces shall be spoiled" *(3:11)*. That this is referring to the End-time is clear from the verses that follow, where we read, "That in the day that I shall visit the transgressions of Israel upon him," etc. *(v. 14)*.

Micah terms him "the Assyrian," and of him it is said, when he "shall come into our land, and when he shall tread in our palaces, then shall we raise against him seven shepherds, and eight principal men . . . . thus shall he deliver us from the Assyrian" *(5:5,6)*.

Nahum has this to say of him: "There is one come out of thee, that imagineth evil against the Lord, a wicked counseller. Thus saith the Lord; Though they be quiet, and likewise many, yet thus shall they be cut down, when *he* shall pass through. Though I have afflicted thee, I will afflict thee no more . . . . for the Wicked shall no more pass through thee" *(1:11, 12, 15)*. These verses contain another of the many antithesis between Christ and the Antichrist. The One is the "Wonderful Counseller" *(Isa. 9:6)*; the other, the "Wicked Counseller."

Habakkuk describes him as one whose "soul is lifted up" and "is not upright in him," and as one who "transgresseth by wine," as "a proud man, neither keepeth at home, who enlargeth his desire as hell, and is as death, and cannot be satisfied, but gathereth unto him all nations, and heapeth unto him all people" *(2:4, 5)*.

Zechariah denominates him "the Idol Shepherd that leaveth the flock," and then pronounces judgment upon him —"The sword shall be upon his arm, and upon his right eye" *(11:17)*.

In our next article we shall consider the Antichrist in the Gospels and Epistles.—*Arthur W. Pink.*

ETERNAL PUNISHMENT

(Continued)

Having disposed of the principal objections brought against the truth of Eternal Punishment, we now turn to consider

II. THE DESTINY OF THE WICKED

There is deep need for us to approach this solemn subject *impartially*, and *dispassionately*. Let writer and reader cry earnestly to God that all prejudices and preconceptions may be removed from our minds. It ill becomes us to sit at the feet of Infinite Wisdom determined to hold fast to our foregone conclusions. Nothing can be more insulting to God than to presume to examine His Word, *professing* a desire to learn His mind, when we have already settled to our own satisfaction what it will say. Some one has said that we ought to bring our minds to the Scriptures as blank paper is brought to the printing press, that it may receive only the impress of the type. May such grace be vouchsafed to us all that we may ever present our minds to the Holy Spirit's teaching that only the impress may be left which God has designed. May our only desire be to hear "What saith the Lord?"

1. The Certainty of their Judgment.

It is written "It is appointed unto men once to die, but after this the judgment" *(Heb. 9:27)*. This is one of the many verses which refute the errors of the Annihilationists, who make the judgment of the sinner to be, itself, death. But here death and judgment are clearly distinguished. The one follows the other.

The fact of a future judgment for sinners is established by numerous passages. In Eccl. 11:9 we read, "Rejoice, O young man, in thy youth; and let thy heart cheer thee in the days of thy youth, and walk in the ways of thine heart, and in the sight of thine eyes: *but* know thou, that for all these things God *will* bring thee into judgment." Again, in Eccl. 12:14 we are told, "For God *shall* bring every work into judgment, with every secret thing, whether it be good, or whether it be evil." The New Testament witnesses to the same truth: "He hath appointed a day, in the which He will judge the world in righteousness by that man whom He hath ordained" *(Acts 17:31)*. The judgment itself is described in Rev. 20:11-15.

Of the certainty of this coming judgment we are left in no doubt—"The Lord *knoweth how* to deliver the godly out of temptations, and to reserve the unjust unto the day of judgment to be punished" *(2 Pet. 2:9)*. It will be impossible for the sinner to evade it. Escape there will be none—"How can ye escape the damnation of hell?" *(Matt. 23:33)*. Resistance, individually or collectively, will be futile—"Though hand join in hand, the wicked shall not be unpunished" *(Prov. 11:21)*. No confederacy of His foes shall hinder God from taking vengeance upon them.

2. Death Seals the Sinner's Fate.

Scripture teaches plainly that man's opportunity for salvation is limited to the period of his earthly life. If he dies unsaved his fate is sealed inexorably. There are two passages in the New Testament most generally relied upon by those who affirm that *there is* for the lost a hope beyond death. These are both found in the 1st Epistle of Peter. A brief notice then shall be taken of them.

"For Christ also hath once suffered for sins, the just for the unjust, that He might bring us to God, being put to death in the flesh, but quickened by the Spirit: By which also He went and preached unto the spirits in prison; Which sometime were disobedient, when once the longsuffering of God waited in the days of Noah, while the ark was a preparing" *(3:18-20)*. But these verses make no reference whatever to any preaching heard by those who had already passed out of this life. They simply tell us that the Spirit of God preached through Noah, while the ark was being built, to those who were disobedient; and because they refused to respond to that preaching they are now "spirits in prison." It was not Christ who Himself "preached," but the Holy Spirit, as is plain from the opening words of v. 19 —"By which also:" the "by which" points back to "the Spirit" at the end of v. 18. That the Holy Spirit *did* address Himself to the antedeluvians we know from Gen. 6:3—'My *Spirit* shall not always strive with man." The Spirit strove through Noah's preaching. That Noah was a "preacher" we learn from 2 Pet. 2:5.

The second passage is found in 1 Pet. 4:6: "For for this cause was the Gospel preached also to them that are dead." But this need not detain us. The Gospel *was* preached, not is now being preached! That such passages as these are appealed to only serves to show how untenable and impossible is the contention they are supposed to support.

That death seals the doom of the lost, we may prove negatively by the fact—and this is conclusive of itself,—that we have not a single instance described in either the Old Testament or the New of a sinner being saved *after* death. Nor is there a single passage which holds out any promise of this in the future. But there are passages which contain positive teaching to the contrary. Several of these are now submitted.

We turn first to Prov. 29:1: "He, that being often reproved hardeneth his neck, shall suddenly be destroyed, and that *without remedy.*" This is so explicit and unequivocal it needs no words of ours either to expound or enforce it. Once the rebellious sinner is "cut off" he is "without remedy." Nothing could be clearer: at death his doom is sealed.

Again, in Matt. 9:6 we read, "But that ye may know that the Son of Man hath power *on earth* to forgive sins, (then saith He to the sick of the palsy) Arise, take up thy bed, and go unto thine house." Why did not the Lord simply say, "The Son of Man hath power to forgive sins," and then stop? That would have been sufficient reply to His critics. The only reason that we can suggest why the Saviour should have added the qualifying words—"The Son of Man hath power *on earth* to forgive sins"—was because He would give us to understand that after a sinner *leaves* the "earth" the Son of Man (Christ in His mediatorial character) has not the "power" (or "authority" as exousia really means) to forgive sins!

A similar instance to the above is found in John 12:25: "He that loveth his life shall lose it; and he that hateth his life in this world shall keep it unto life eternal." Notice that the antithesis would be complete *without* the restricting words "in this life"—"He that loveth his life shall lose it; and he that hateth his life shall keep it unto life eternal." Again, we say, that the only reason we can see why Christ added the qualifying clause, "He that hateth his life *in this world* shall keep it unto life eternal" was in order to show that destiny is fixed once we leave this world.

In 2 Cor. 5:10, which speaks of believers, we have another example of this careful employment of qualifying language: "We must all appear before the judgment seat of Christ; that every one may receive the things done in his body." The saints are to be dealt with not merely according to what they have done, but that they may receive "the things done *in the body.*" What they have done *after* they left the body and prior to the resurrection is not taken into account.

In John 8:21 it is recorded how that Christ said to His enemies, "I go My way, and ye shall seek Me, and shall die in your sins; whither I go, ye cannot come." Observe carefully the order of the last two clauses. Once they *died* in their sins, it was impossible for them to go to heaven. The solemn force of this verse comes out even more clearly if we contrast with it John 13:36: "Simon Peter said unto Him, Lord, whither goest Thou? Jesus answered him, Whither I go, thou canst not follow Me *now;* but thou shalt follow Me afterwards." Mark the absence of the qualifying "now" in

John 8:21. To Peter it was said, as to a representative saint, "Thou shalt follow Me (to heaven) afterwards;" but to the wicked, Christ declared, "Whither I go, *ye cannot come*"!

3. WHAT AWAITS THE SINNER AT DEATH.

We naturally turn for light on this to the teaching of the Lord, for more was said through Him than through any other concerning the future of the wicked. Nor shall we turn in vain to the record of His words. In Luke 16 we find Him drawing aside the veil which hides from us what lies beyond death. He tells us of a rich man who died "and was buried" *(v. 22)*. But he had not ceased to exist. So far from it, the Lord went on to say, "And in hell he lift up his eyes, being in torments." That Christ was here describing the actual experience of this rich man after death there is no good reason to doubt; to say otherwise, is to be guilty of blasphemously charging the Son of God with using language which He knew would mislead countless numbers of those who later would read the record of His words. No one who comes to this passage with an unprejudiced mind would ever suppose that it gave anything else than a plain and simple picture of what befalls the wicked after death. It is only those who have previously arrived at the foregone conclusion that there is no torment for the unbeliever after death, who approach this passage determined to explain away its obvious meaning, who rule out of it what is there and read into it what is not there.

"In Hades he lift up his eyes, being in torments." The Greek word here translated hell is "Hades," which is a generic term for the unseen world, into which the souls of all pass at death. No doubt it is due to the fact that the souls of saints as well as sinners are represented as entering Sheol at death that caused the translators to render it "grave" in many instances. But the fact that in both the Hebrew and the Greek there is an entirely different word used for "grave" ought to have prevented such a mistake. The Holy Spirit has carefully preserved the distinction between the two terms throughout. A careful examination of every passage in the Old and New Testaments where these words occur will show that many things are said of the "grave" (Heb. "queber;" Gk. "mnemeion") which could never be said of "Sheol" or "Hades;" and many things are said of the latter which are never predicated of the former. For example: both the Hebrew and Greek words for "grave" occur in the *plural* again and again; Sheol and Hades never do so. The Hebrew and Greek words for "grave" are frequently referred to as the *possession* of individuals—"*My* grave" *(Gen. 50:5)*; "grave of Abner" *(2 Sam. 3:32)*; "His own (Joseph's) new tomb" *(Matt. 27:60)*; "The sepulchres of the righteous" *(Matt. 23:39)*, etc. In Gen. 50:5 we read, "In my grave which I have *digged* for me;" of "mnemeion" we read, "And he laid it in his own new tomb, which he had *hewn out* in the rock" *(Matt. 27:60)*. Sheol and Hades are never so referred to. The *body* enters "queber" and "mnemion," but it is *never* said to enter Sheol or Hades. Sufficient has been said to demonstrate that Sheol or Hades *is not* the grave. We may, therefore, confidently affirm that neither Sheol or Hades should ever be rendered "grave" or "the grave."

Hades refers to the same place as Sheol. Their indentification is unequivocally established by a comparison of Psa. 16:10 with Acts 2:27: "Thou wilt not leave My soul in Sheol" *(Psa. 16:10)*, is "Thou shalt not leave My soul in Hades" in Acts 2:27. But it is important to bear in mind that Sheol or Hades had *two* compartments, reserved respectively for the saved and the lost. And "between" these two, our Lord tells us there is, "a great gulf fixed" *(Luke 16:26)*. The compartment we are now considering is that which receives the souls of the wicked. In this, Christ declares, is a "flame" which torments. This is in perfect harmony with the teaching of the Old Testament concerning Sheol. In Deut. 33:22 we read, "For a *fire* is kindled in Mine anger, and shall burn unto the lowest Sheol." Again; in the parable of the tares our Lord said, "I will say to the reapers, Gather ye together first the tares, and bind them in bundles to burn them" *(Matt. 13:30)*. The explanation of this is found in vv. 40-42 of the same chapter: "As therefore the tares are gathered and burned in the fire; so shall it be in the end of this age. The Son of Man shall send forth His angels, and they shall gather out of His kingdom all things that offend, and them which do iniquity; And shall cast them into *a furnace of fire:* there shall be wailing and gnashing of teeth." As this takes place at the end of this age and before the millennial reign begins, the "furnace of fire" must refer to Hades rather than the Lake of Fire.

Returning then to the teaching of Luke 16 concerning the experience of the wicked immediately after death, we read, "And in hell he lift up his eyes, being in torments." Here we have a sentient being, a conscious person, in a definite place; suffering there excruciatingly. He was in "torments." So great was his anguish he begged that one might "dip the tip of his finger in water and cool my tongue" *(v. 24)*. But such alleviation was denied him. He was bidden to "remember" how he had lived—a worshipper of Mammon. Such, we are assured, will be the doom of every one that dies in his sins.

4. THE UTTER HOPELESSNESS OF THE LOST.

Thus far we have seen, first, that the judgment of the wicked is certain; second, that death seals their doom; third, that at death the souls of unbelievers go to Hades, into that compartment of the unseen world reserved for the lost, there to be tormented in the flame. There they remain until the end of the Millennium, when they shall be resurrected and brought before the Great White Throne to receive their final sentence. We, therefore, devote a separate section to show that after the wicked are brought out of Hades there is even then, no hope whatever of their salvation.

The first scripture we appeal to in proof of this is John 5:29: "All that are in the graves shall hear His voice, and shall come forth; they that have done good, unto the resurrection of life; and they that have done evil, unto the resurrection of damnation." This is the solemn announcement of the Son of God. Let His words be well weighed. Here He tells us, briefly, what awaits the sum total of the dead. They are divided into two classes: they that have done good, and they that have done evil. For the one there is the "resurrection of life;" for the other the "resurrection of damnation." For evil-doers there is no resurrection of probation, and no resurrection of salvation; but simply and solely the resurrection *of damnation*. How this removes the very foundation on which any might desire to build a future hope for the wicked!

In 1 Thess. 4:13 we read, "But I would not have you to be ignorant, brethren, concerning them which are asleep, that ye sorrow not, even as others which have *no hope*." Here the apostle draws a contrast between the Christian grieving over the death of *believing* loved ones, and the heathen who mourned the loss of their dear ones. The Christian may sorrow over the departure of a saved relative or friend, but he can also comfort himself with the blessed hope presented to him in the Scriptures, the hope of being re-united at the coming of the

Lord. This hope the heathen, and the unsaved in Christendom who mourn the loss of unsaved friends, have not. Yea, they have *"no* hope." This is not weakened at all by the fact that in Eph. 2:12, 13 we read of those once "without hope" who had, nevertheless, been "made nigh by the blood of Christ." The Ephesian scripture speaks of those alive in the world, and while *here* there is always a hope they may be saved; though while they remain unsaved they are "without hope," that is, without any scripturally-warranted hope. But the Thessalonian passage speaks of those who have passed out of this world unsaved, and for them there is *"no* hope." Whatever vain hopes the wicked may now cherish, in the day to come, the very "expectation of the wicked shall *perish" (Prov.* 10: 28)!

Another scripture which proves the hopeless state of those who have rejected God's truth is to be found in Heb. 10:26-29: "For if we sin wilfully after that we have received the knowledge of the truth, there remaineth no more sacrifice for sins, But a certain fearful looking for of judgment and fiery indignation, which shall devour the adversaries. He that despised Moses' law died without mercy under two or three witnesses: Of how much sorer punishment, suppose ye, shall he be thought worthy, who hath trodden under foot the Son of God, and hath counted the blood of the covenant, wherewith he was sanctified, an unholy thing, and hath done despite unto the spirit of grace?" For our present purpose we need not stop to consider of whom this passage is specifically speaking. Sufficient to know that it treats of those who have wilfully resisted the light. For these we are told "there remaineth *no more* sacrifice for sins." If there remaineth no more sacrifice for sins, then they must themselves suffer the Divine penalty for them. What that penalty is this same passage tells us: it is "fiery indignation" which shall devour them. It is a judgment *"without* mercy." It is a "punishment" *sorer* than that which befell him that despised Moses' law.

"For he shall have judgment *without mercy,* that hath showed no mercy; and mercy rejoiceth against judgment" *(James 2:13).* It is true that the apostle is here writing to saints, but in the verse we have just quoted there is a noticeable change in his language, and here he is obviously speaking of the unsaved. In the previous verse he had said, "Ye," but now he changes to "he." He that hath showed no mercy (to his fellowmen) shall have "judgment without mercy" from God; and this, in spite of the fact that "mercy rejoiceth against judgment." The last clause is plainly for the purpose of adding solemnity to what precedes. Judgment "without mercy" is language which looks back to Isa. 27:11, where we read, "It is a people of no understanding: therefore He that made them will not have mercy on them, and He that formed them will show them *no* favor." If, then, this judgment is "without mercy" how it closes the door against all possibility of a final reprieve, or even a modification of the dread sentence! And how it exposes the baselessness of that hope which is cherished by many, viz., that in the last great Day they think to cast themselves upon the mercy of that One whom they now despise and defy! Vain will it be to cry for mercy then. Of old God said to Israel, "Therefore will I also deal in fury: Mine eye shall not spare, neither will I have pity: and though they cry in Mine ears with a loud voice, yet *will I not hear them."* So it will be at the last Judgment. One other scripture may be considered in this connection: "Raging waves of the sea, foaming out their own shame; wandering stars, to whom is reserved the blackness of darkness forever" *(Jude 13).* Unspeakably solemn is this. This verse is referring to the future portion of those who now turn "the grace of our God into lasciviousness" and deny "the only Lord God and our Lord Jesus Christ" *(Jude 4)*. Unto them is reserved "the *blackness of darkness* forever." The endless night of their doom shall never be relieved by a single star of hope. Thus have we sought to show how the Word of God by a variety of expressions, each of which is unambigious and conclusive, reveals the utter hopelessness of those taking part in "the resurrection of damnation." We shall next consider

5. THE LAST ABODE OF THE LOST.

This is given at least two different names in the New Testament: "Gehenna" and "Lake of Fire." Let us now examine the teaching of Scripture concerning them.

First, "Gehenna" is the Grecianized form of the Hebrew for "valley of Hinnom," which was a deep gorge on the east of Jerusalem. This valley of Hinnom was first used in connection with idolatrous rites *(2 Chron. 28:3)*. Later it became a burial ground *(Jer. 7:31)*, or more probably a crematorium. Still later it became the place where the garbage of Jerusalem was thrown and burned (Josephus). Its fires were kept constantly alight so as to consume the filth and rubbish deposited therein.

Second, this valley of Hinnom foreshadowed the great garbage-receptacle of the universe—Hell, just as other places and persons in the Old Testament Scriptures adumbrated other objects more vile—for example, the "king of Tyre" in Ezek. 28. Just as what is there said of this king has in view one more sinister than he, so what is said of the valley of Hinnom symbolized that which was far more awful. We can no more limit Gehenna to the valley outside of Jerusalem than we can restrict "the king of Tyre" to a mere man of the past.

Third, the valley of Hinnom our Lord used as an emblem of Hell, and stamped with the hall-mark of His authority the wider and more solemn scope of the word. It should be carefully noted that when speaking of Gehenna He never referred to the mere literal valley outside of Jerusalem, but employed it to designate the place of eternal torments.

Fourth, Gehenna, in its New Testament usage, refers to a *place*. "And if thy right eye offend thee, pluck it out, and cast it from thee: for it is profitable for thee that one of thy members should perish, and not that thy whole body should be *cast into* Gehenna" *(Matt. 5:29. See also Matt. 18:9)*.

Fifth, the fire of Gehenna is *eternal*. "And if thy hand offend thee, cut it off: it is better for thee to enter into life maimed, than having two hands to go into Gehenna, into the fire that *never shall be quenched:* where their worm dieth not, and the fire is not quenched" *(Mark 9:43, 44)*.

Sixth, Gehenna is the place in which *both soul and body* are destroyed. "And fear not them which kill the body, but are not able to kill the soul: but rather fear Him which is able to destroy *both* soul and body in Gehenna" *(Matt. 19: 28)*. This passage is most important, for more than any other it enables us to gather the real scope of this term. The fact that the "soul" as well as the body is destroyed there, is proof positive that our Lord was not referring to the valley of Hinnom. So, too, the fact that the "body" is destroyed there, makes it certain that "Gehenna" is not another name for "Hades." In pondering this solemn verse we should remember that "destroy" does not mean to annihilate. Some have raised a quibble over the fact that Christ did not here expressly say that God *would* "destroy both soul and body in hell," but merely said "Fear Him *which is able to.*" This admits of a simple and conclusive reply. Surely it is apparent on the surface that Christ is not here predicating of God a power which none can deny, but which, notwithstanding, He will never exert! He was not simply affirming the omnipotence of God, but uttering a solemn threat which will yet be executed. That such was His meaning is established beyond the shadow of doubt when we compare Matt. 10:28 with the parallel passage in Luke 12:5: "But I will forewarn you whom ye shall fear: fear Him, which after He hath killed hath power to cast into hell; yea, I say unto you, fear Him." This threat we know *will be* fulfilled.

Seventh, Gehenna is *identical with the Lake of Fire*. There are four things which indicate this, and taken together they constitute a cumulative but clear proof. First, the fact that in Gehenna God "destroys" both soul *and body (Matt. 10:28)*. This shows the wicked who are there destroyed have already received their resurrection bodies. Second, the fact that the fire of Gehenna is *eternal:* it will "never be quenched" *(Mark 9:43).* This is nowhere said of the fires of sheol or hades. Third, in Isa. 30:33 we learn that "Tophet" is ordained for "the king"—it is "the king" of Dan. 11:36, that is the Antichrist, "the Assyrian" of Isa. 30:30. Now "Tophet" is another name for the valley of Hinnom, as may be seen by a reference to Jer. 7:31, 32. In Rev. 19:20 we are told that the Beast (the Antichrist) together with the False Prophet will be "cast alive into a lake of fire burning with brimstone." Thus by comparing Isa. 30:33 with Rev. 19:20 we learn that Gehenna and the Lake of Fire are one and the same. Finally, notice *the absence* of "Gehenna" in Rev. 20:14, "And death and hades were cast into the lake of fire." The meaning of this is *the people* whom death and hades had seized—"death" capturing the body; "hades" claiming the soul. That the casting of "death and hades" into the Lake of Fire refers to *their captives* is clear from the concluding words of the verse—"This is the second death." i. e. for *their* victims. Note then that we are not told that "Gehenna" was cast into the Lake of Fire because Gehenna and the Lake of Fire are one and the same place.

We shall now offer a few remarks upon the Lake of Fire and brimstone. The following analysis indicates the teaching of Scripture concerning it.

First, it is the place which finally receives the Beast and the False Prophet: Rev. 19:20.

Second, it is the place which finally receives the Devil: Rev. 20:10.

Third, it is the place which finally received *all* whose names are not found written in the book of life: Rev. 20:15 and cf. 21:8.

Fourth, it is a place of "torment:" Rev. 20:10.

Fifth, it is a place whose torment is ceaseless and interminable, "day and night for ever and ever:" Rev. 20:10, and cf. 14:11.

Sixth, it is also termed "The Second Death:" Rev. 20:14; 21:8, etc.

Seventh, it has "no power" on the people of God: Rev. 20:6 and cf. 2:11.

In the sixth item above we have pointed out that the Lake of Fire is also denominated "The Second Death." At least three reasons may be suggested for this. First, this designation intimates that the endless torments of the Lake of Fire are the penalty and wages of sin." "The wages of sin is death." Second, the use of this appellation calls attention to the fact that all who are cast into the Lake of Fire will be eternally *separated* from God. As the first death is the separation of the soul from the body, so the second death will be the eternal separation of the soul from God—"Punished with everlasting destruction *from the presence of* the Lord" *(2 Thess. 1:9).* Third, such a title emphasizes the *dreadfulness* of the Lake of Fire. To the normal man death is the object he fears above all others. It is that from which he naturally shrinks. It is that which he most dreads. When, then, the Holy Spirit designates the Lake of Fire the "Second Death" He is emphasizing the fact that it is an object of horror from which the sinner should flee.

6. THE ETERNALITY OF THE SUFFERINGS OF THE LOST.

Upon this point the language of Scripture is most explicit. In Matt. 25:41 we read of *"everlasting* fire." In Matt. 25:46 of *"everlasting* punishment." In Mark 6:29 of *"eternal* damnation." And in 2 Thess. 1:9 of *"everlasting* destruction." We are aware that the enemies of God's truth have sought to tamper with this word rendered everlasting and eternal. But their efforts have been entirely futile. The impossibility of rendering the Greek work by any other English equivalent appears from the following evidence:

The Greek word is "aionios" and its meaning and scope has been definitely defined for us by the Holy Spirit in at least two passages. "While we look not at the things which are seen, but at the things which are not seen: for the things which are seen are temporal; but the things which are not seen are *eternal" (2 Cor. 4:18).* Here a contrast is drawn between things "seen" and things "not seen," between things "temporal" and things "eternal." Now it is obvious that if the things "temporal" should last forever, there would be no antithesis between them and the things "eternal." It is equally obvious that if the things "eternal" are merely "age-long," then they cannot be properly contrasted with things that are temporal. The difference between things temporal and things eternal in this verse is as great as the difference between the things "seen" and the things "not seen."

The second example, which is of the same character as the one furnished in 2 Cor. 4:18, is equally conclusive. In Philemon 15 we read, "For perhaps he therefore departed *for a season,* that thou shouldest receive him *forever."*

Here the Greek for "forever" is aionios. The apostle is beseeching Philemon to receive Onesimus, who had left his master, and whom Paul had sent back to him. When the apostle says "receive him forever," his evident meaning is, *never* banish him, *never* sell him, *never* again send him away. "Aionios" is here contrasted with "for a season," showing that it means just the opposite of what that expression signifies.

Eternal or everlasting is the one and unvaried meaning of aionios in the New Testament. The same word translated "everlasting destruction," "everlasting punishment," "everlasting fire," is rendered *"everlasting* life" in John 3:16; "the *everlasting* God" in Rom. 16:26; *"eternal* salvation" in Heb. 5:9; "His *eternal* glory" in 1 Pet. 5:10. No argument needs to be made to prove that in these passages it is impossible to fairly substitute any other alternative for everlasting and eternal. And it is thus with the other class of passages. The "everlasting fire" will synchronize with the existence of "the everlasting God." The "everlasting punishment" of the lost will continue as long as the "everlasting life" of believers. The "eternal damnation" of the wicked will no more have an end than will the "eternal salvation" of the redeemed. The "everlasting destruction" of unbelievers will prove as interminable as the "everlasting glory" of God. To deny the former is to deny the latter. To affirm the everlastingness of God is to prove the endlessness of the misery of His enemies.

7. THE FINALITY OF THEIR STATE.

The doom of those who shall be cast into the Lake of Fire is irrevocable and final. Many independent considerations prove this. Forgiveness of sins is limited to life on this earth. Once the sinner passes out of this world there remaineth "no more sacrifice for sins." The fact that at death the soul of the wicked goes at once into the "furnace of fire" *(Matt. 12:42)* witnesses to the fixity of his future state. The fact that, later, his resurrection is one "of damnation" *(John 5:29)* excludes all possibility of a last-hour reprieve. The fact that he is cast soul and body into a lake of fire argues that then he receives his final portion. The fact that the Lake of Fire is denominated the "Second Death" denotes the hopelessness of his situation. Just as the first death cuts him off forever from this world, so the second death cuts him off forever from God.

In Phil. 3 the apostle Paul speaks of the enemies of the Cross of Christ, and moved by the Holy Spirit he tells us that their *"end is destruction" (v. 19).* Stronger and more unequivocal language could not be used. There is nothing beyond the "end." And the end of the enemies of the Cross of Christ is "destruction" not salvation. The Greek word here translated "end" is "telos." It is found in the following passages: "Of His kingdom there shall be *no end" (Luke 1:33);* "Christ is the *end* of the law for righteousness to every one that believeth" *(Rom. 10:4)*; "Having neither beginning of days nor *end* of life" *(Heb. 7:3)*; "I am .... the Beginning and the *End*, the First and the Last" *(Rev. 22:13).*

As we have already seen, the twentieth chapter of Revelation describes the final judgment of the wicked before the Great White Throne, after which they are cast into the Lake of Fire. The chapters which follow—the last two in the Bible—may be read carefully and searched diligently, but they will not be found to contain so much as a single hint that those cast into the Lake of Fire shall ever be delivered from it. Instead, we find in the very last chapter of God's Word the solemn statement, "He that is unjust *let him be unjust still:* and he which is filthy, *let him be filthy still" (Rev. 22:11).* Thus the finality of their condition is expressly affirmed on the closing page of Holy Writ.—*Arthur W. Pink.*

(To be concluded, D. V.)

EXPOSITION OF FIRST PETER

The second question is, how is the sinner brought to cherish the hope of eternal life on this ground? Now, if the preceding remarks have been understood, there can be no difficulty in answering this question. The free sovereign mercy of God, manifested in a consistency with his righteousness, is revealed in the Gospel; and it can only be by that Gospel being understood and believed, that the individual sinner can obtain the hope of eternal life. If I believe this revelation, I hope for eternal life, and I hope for eternal life on this ground. If I do not believe this revelation, I either have no hope of eternal life, or, if I have, it is a hope built on another and a false foundation. It is in the faith of the truth that the sinner finds hope. Not that the sinner's faith is the ground of his hope, but that it is through believing alone that he can discover the ground on which his hope must rest. When Elisha's servant was overwhelmed with fears lest his master should fall into the hands of the Syrians, these fears were turned into assured hope, when, with enlightened eyes, he beheld the heavenly host with which they were surrounded. His hope rested, not on his seeing that host, but on their being there; but still his seeing them there was in the nature of things necessary to his hope.[1] In like manner the sinner's hope rests entirely on God's free sovereign kindness, manifested in harmony with his righteousness; but it is only in the belief of the truth that this sovereign kindness can be apprehended as a ground of hope.

---

[1] 2 Kings 6:15-17.

The ground of hope never varies. The ground of the hope of eternal life to an aged and accomplished saint, just about to enter Paradise, is the very same as to the most guilty and depraved of men who has just been brought to the knowledge and faith of the truth. "The beginning of our confidence" is the end of our confidence. Our first hope is our last hope.

It follows of course that the great means of maintaining and strengthening hope, is just the continued and the increasing faith of the truth. At the same time it is plain from Scripture, that as the faith of the truth uniformly produces holiness as well as hope, unholy tempers are in their own nature calculated to cloud our hope; and holy tempers and conduct to strengthen it, not by adding to its foundation, but by affording evidence that we have built on that foundation.

There are two other questions respecting this hope, which, though not of such vital importance as those which I have now endeavored briefly and plainly to answer, are yet of very considerable interest at all times, and particularly at present, when much darkening counsel by words without knowledge, on this subject, seems to me to prevail.[1] Is the hope of eternal life connected with the faith of the Gospel? And does every believer enjoy an unclouded hope of eternal life?

With regard to the first question, I unhesitatingly reply in the affirmative. The Gospel cannot be believed without, in the degree in which it is believed, producing the hope of eternal life. It is not only not necessary that a sinner should wait till the faith of the Gospel has proved its efficacy in a moral transformation of his nature, before he begin to cherish the hope of salvation, but he cannot believe the Gospel without cherishing that hope; and it is through means of this hope that the Gospel believed, in a great measure, works that moral change. To believe the Gospel, and to despair of salvation, are two utterly incompatible states of mind. We hold, then, that every believer, according to the measure of his faith, has the hope of eternal life.

And in this principle we also find the true answer to the second question; 'Does every believer enjoy the unclouded hope of eternal life?' He does enjoy that hope according to the measure of his faith. If he is strong in faith, he abounds in hope. But as every believer in the present state has but an imperfect apprehension both of the truth and of its evidence, and is still to a certain extent under the influence of false views, every believer, while in the present state, is imperfect both in holiness and in hope. At the same time, his imperfection in both is not more his misfortune than his fault. A perfect faith of a completely understood Gospel would produce unshaken, unclouded hope, and enable the Christian at all times, in all circumstances, to "rejoice in the hope of the glory of God."

This hope of eternal life, grounded on the sovereign mercy of God manifested, in harmony with his holiness and righteousness, through the mediation of Christ, revealed in the Gospel; and excited, maintained and strengthened by the faith of the Gospel, is described here as "a lively," or rather "a living hope." The hope of the Christian is a "living" hope, in opposition both to a dead and a dying hope —in opposition to the dead hope of the hypocrite, and the dying hope of the self-deceiver.

The apostle James speaks of "a dead faith" which, on examination, turns out to be no faith at all, but merely a man's saying he has faith.[2] There is also a dead hope, which is in reality

---

[1] The reference here is to the speculations about Universal Pardon, which, at the time this discourse was delivered, December 1830, were very prevalent in this country.

[2] James 2:17.

no hope at all, but merely a profession of it. A mere professed hope, founded on a mere professed faith, is a dead thing—it can make a man neither holy nor happy—it cannot animate to duty—it cannot support under suffering. But the hope of the Christian is "a living hope." It fills him with joy and peace in the degree in which it prevails; and it leads him to purify himself, even as He in whom he places his confidence is pure. The hope of eternal life is the well-grounded expectation of perfect holy happiness. Now is it not perfectly plain, so plain as to need no illustration, that this must be a living operative hope, and that, just in the degree in which it exists, it must make him in whom it dwells both holy and happy? It will induce a man to submit to the greatest evils rather than renounce the faith of Christ; and it will keep him cheerful and happy amidst all the sacrifices which he may be called on to make in the cause of his Saviour.

This hope is termed "a *living* hope," not only in opposition to a *dead* hope, but also in opposition to *dying* hopes. There are many hopes which are not merely professed, but really entertained, that will never be realized. This is true both as to worldly hopes and as to religious hopes. With regard to worldly hopes, have we not all from experience discovered the truth of the remark,—"They are not living, but lying, dying hopes. They often die before us, and we live to bury them, and see our own folly and simplicity in trusting to them, and at the utmost they die with us when we die, and can accompany us no farther."¹ With regard to religious hopes, it is a happy thing when all of them, not founded on the faith of the truth, die before we die; for till these dying hopes expire, the living hope cannot exist. All hopes of eternal life, excepting that which we have been endeavoring to describe, will most assuredly expire when we expire, and make those who relied on them ashamed and confounded world without end. But this hope lives in death. This hope remains unshaken by all the calamities which can befall the believer here; for he knows nothing can separate him from the love of God. Death and judgment and eternity do not destroy, they fulfill this hope; and as the object of the hope is ever-enduring holy happiness, it is plain that hope as well as enjoyment must continue forever.

This "hope maketh not ashamed," that is, it never disappoints; and, if you would know the reason, you will find the apostle Paul assigning it, from the 5th to the 10th verse of the 5th chapter of the Epistle to the Romans: "Hope maketh not ashamed, because the love of God is shed abroad in our hearts by the Holy Ghost, which is given unto us. For when we were yet without strength, in due time Christ died for the ungodly. For scarcely for a righteous man will one die; yet peradventure for a good man some would even dare to die. But God commendeth His love toward us, in that, while we were yet sinners, Christ died for us. Much more then, being now justified by His blood, we shall be saved from wrath through Him. For if, when we were enemies, we were reconciled to God by the death of His Son; much more, being reconciled, we shall be saved by His life."

This living hope is produced "by" means of "the resurrection of Christ Jesus from the dead." The resurrection of our Lord Jesus Christ is one of the most striking and satisfactory proofs of the divinity of His mission, and, of course, of the truth of all its doctrines; and, among the rest, of that grand characteristic doctrine of His Gospel on which the hope of eternal life is founded. It is, indeed, not so much one evidence as "a cloud of witnesses." It is the fulfillment of Old Testament predictions respecting the Messiah, and thus proves Him to be

---

¹Leighton.

the Messiah—it is the fulfillment of His own predictions, and therefore proves Him to be a true prophet. It is God determining the controversy between Him and His unbelieving countrymen. He declared Himself to be the Son of God, and they put Him to death because He declared Himself to be the Son of God; and God interposed, and by doing for Him what none but God could have done, proved that He was right, and they were wrong. Most powerfully was Jesus Christ demonstrated to be the Son of God by the resurrection from the dead.[1]

But there is a more intimate connection than this between the resurrection of Christ from the dead, and the hope of eternal life. Christ's resurrection from the dead is a clear proof of the reality and efficacy of His atoning sacrifice. He "who was given for our offences, has been raised again for our justification."[2] When God "brought again from the dead our Lord Jesus, that great Shepherd of the sheep, by the blood of the everlasting covenant," He manifested Himself to be "the God of peace," the pacified Divinity. He "raised Him from the dead, and gave Him glory, that our faith and hope might be in Himself." Had Jesus not risen, "our faith had been vain; we should have been still in our sin,"[3] and without hope. (But now that He has risen)—

> "Our surety freed, declares us free,
> For whose offenses He was seized;
> In His release our own we see,
> And joy to view Jehovah pleased."

But even this is not all. Our Lord's resurrection is to be viewed not only in connection with His death, but with the following glory. Raised from the dead, He has received "all power in heaven and on earth, that He may give eternal life to as many as the Father had given Him." How this is calculated to encourage hope, may be readily apprehended. "Because He lives, we shall live also." Having the keys of death and the unseen world, He can and will raise us from the dead, and give us eternal life. He sits at the right hand of God. Our life is hid with Him in God; and when He who is our life shall appear, we shall appear with Him in glory. We are not yet in possession of the inheritance; but He, our head and representative, is. We see not yet all things put under us; but we see Him, the Captain of our salvation, for the suffering of death, crowned with glory and honor.[4] The resurrection of Christ, when considered in reference to the death which preceded, and the glory which followed it, is the grand means of producing and strengthening the hope of eternal life.

Let us all beware of false hopes. Let him who never hoped, now receive the truth in the love of it, and begin to hope. Let those who have believed abound in hope. There is, there can be, no danger of hoping too confidently, if the hope be but placed on the right foundation. "We desire that every one of you do show the same diligence, to the full assurance of hope unto the end;[5] that ye be not slothful, but followers of them who through faith and patience inherit the promises."—*J. Brown.*

---

[1] Rom. 1:4.
[2] Rom. 4:25.
[3] Heb. 13:20; 1 Pet. 1:21; 1 Cor. 15:17.
[4] John 14:19; Rev. 1:18; Col. 3:3; Heb. 2:9.
[5] Heb. 6:11, 12.

(Continued from page 65.)

they but know of its existence. These have been laid on our hearts. We are not thinking now of the great crowd of self-sufficient, who are satisfied with what they have or what they are getting. Nor do we have in mind those who are so busy with worldly or fleshly church-activities, they have no time for that which calls for diligent study and prayerful meditation. No; we refer to the little companies of really spiritual ones who are to be met with in different places, the ones and the twos scattered here and there, who are willing to *"buy the Truth"*—buy it not with dollars and cents, but with time and study and prayer. We refer to those who would gladly spend an hour or two each week on a magazine that would give them a better knowledge of God's Word, and that would endear to their hearts the Christ of that Word.

How, then, are we to reach those who would value and profit by *Studies in the Scriptures?* Shall we resort to the methods employed by worldly newspapers and magazines? Are we to use the Lord's money for advertising? Shall we offer prizes to those who send us in the largest number of new subscriptions? Rather than do these we would discontinue our publication. We do not feel such ways are pleasing to the Lord, and we are sure they do not honor Him. What, then, is the more excellent way? Surely it is an humble but confident dependence on God. If *we* are not acquainted with many of them, *the Lord* knows each one who really needs and who would prize a magazine devoted exclusively to Bible study. We are asking Him daily to bring us into touch with such, or to bring them into touch with us. In answering our petitions, God may, or He may not (as seemeth Him best), use human media. Though by no means limited to them, the Lord is usually pleased to employ human instruments for the accomplishment of the counsels of His grace. So, we are also asking Him—if such be His sovereign pleasure—to lay it on the hearts of our readers to tell others about *Studies in the Scriptures*. We believe you will be doing *a service* to the Lord and to His people in speaking a word to those who are *hungry* for the Truth, and in describing to them the nature of this little publication. If your own soul is being blessed by reading its pages, why not make an effort to bring others into the circle of blessing? First, by recommending the magazine to Sunday School teachers, Christian workers, or 'shut-in' saints, in your own church, or immediate circle. Second, by making mention of it in your letters to Christian friends at a distance. Third, by joining us in daily prayer that God will bring us into touch with those who would appreciate it.

Let not the reader imagine this to be a veiled appeal for financial help. Nothing is further from our purpose. Were we in pecuniary straits that would be spread only before God. Last year He graciously supplied our every need, and we are confident that He will do so this year. No, our hearts' desire is that our circulation may be extended that God shall be glorified and an increasing number of His saints share with us the precious things He is pleased to give from His Word. We are also hoping to double our *free list* to missionaries. If our readers can help in this by sending in names and addresses of missionaries whom they *know* would value this magazine we shall be glad to send it to them gratis. Should the sender wish to have fellowship in this good work we shall allocate their gifts in this way.

Quite a number of our readers have already acted on the above suggestions. They have loaned out their copies, and spoken to others they thought would be interested. Several subscriptions have come in as the result of letters written to them by our friends. Others, when they sent in their renewal, kindly added two or three besides. To all of them we take this opportunity of expressing our cordial thanks. We pray that enrichment of soul will be theirs for this service to God, as we doubt not it will. As the Lord enables, every effort will be made by us to make *Studies in the Scriptures* increasingly profitable. Ours is a happy ministry, yet it involves solemn responsibilities. We, therefore, covet the daily prayers of our readers that God will prevent anything creeping into this magazine which would in any wise dishonor Him or injure His people. May it be ours to bring glory to the peerless name of Him who loved us and gave Himself for us.

With Christian greetings,

Yours by grace,
Arthur W. Pink,
I. C. Herendeen.

STUDIES in the SCRIPTURES

"Search the Scriptures" John 5:39.

A PERIODICAL (MONTHLY "IF THE LORD WILL")
DEVOTED TO BIBLE STUDIES and EXPOSITIONS

Associate Editors and Publishers, I. C. Herendeen and Arthur W. Pink,
Swengel, Pa.

Price: 10 cents per copy; $1.00 per year. Foreign $1.00 per year.

THE MIRACLE OF CHRIST'S DEATH

A short time ago the editor was making a study of certain passages in Hebrews which bear upon the Death of Christ, and one outcome of his meditations was the opening up of what to him, is a new line of thought. Other passages in the New Testament came to mind, familiar passages, but passages which now carried a new emphasis. We have therefore decided to present this line of thought, in a brief form now, for the consideration of our readers.

Much has been written (not too much, though) on the miraculous birth of Christ, the miraculous works of Christ, and the miraculous resurrection of Christ. But where shall we turn for a treatise on *the miraculous Death* of Christ? We have read not a little upon the infinite value of that Death, on the vicarious nature of it, on the atoning sufficiency of it. But strange to say, little or nothing appears to have been said on the *miracle* of Christ's *death*. No doubt the very word "miracle" applied to the death of our Saviour, has a strange sound as it falls on the ear of the reader. And yet it *was* a miracle. One has but to have it pointed out, and it is at once apparent to every spiritual intelligence. In the humble judgment of the writer, the Death of Immanuel was *the* miracle of all miracles.

Far be it from us to attempt an intellectual analysis of the holy person of the God-man—the Lord preserve us from such irreverence. Yet, we need to remind ourselves that the death of Christ was something more than the physical dissolution of His body. It was a *person* who died—"*Christ died* for the ungodly". It was the God-man who died. Not that we would lead our readers to the heretical (if not the blasphemous) conclusion that His soul and spirit passed into the realm of unconsciousness. Far be the thought. Such is not the case at the death of a man, far less could it be so with the God-man. We shall not attempt an analysis or definition of death, but having sought to guard against a false inference from our words, we wish to press it upon the reader's attention, that the Lord Jesus, the Son of God *Himself*, actually *died*. And *His* death was a stupendous marvel.

The death of Christ was entirely *unique*. His holy *person* is different from every other person in the universe. His *birth* was different from every other birth. His *life* was different, not only in degree but in kind, *radically* different, from every other life before or since; and His *death* was entirely different from every other death. Every other person who has been born into this world, was born that he might live; but the Christ of God was born *in order to die!* That was the central purpose in the Divine counsels. That is why the Beloved of the Father became incarnate. The

(Continued on page 128.)

IMPORTANT NOTICES

All new subscriptions will be dated back to January, 1923.

Set of twelve issues for 1922, unbound, $1.00. Bound, $1.50.

Note: We cannot break a set or now supply any **single** 1922 issues.

Subscription Price: $1.00 per year to any address in the world. Single copies 10 cents.

Change of Address: Please notify us promptly of any change of address, and be certain to give both old and new addresses.

Non-Subscribers receiving this Magazine regularly will understand their subscription has been entered by a friend.

Copies lost in the mail duplicated on request.

Entered as second-class matter December 15th, 1921 at the post office at Swengel, Pa., under Act of March 3rd, 1879.

CONTENTS

John's Gospel (John 4:43-54)	98
Eternal Punishment	107
The Antichrist in the Gospels and Epistles	115
Exposition of First Peter	124

JOHN'S GOSPEL

16. CHRIST IN GALILEE.

John 4:43-54.

What has been before us from v. 4 to the end of v. 42 in this chapter is in the nature of a parenthesis, inasmuch as these verses record what occurred in Samaria, which was outside the sphere of Christ's regular ministry in Judea and Galilee. Here in the last twelve verses of the chapter we are brought onto familiar ground again. It would seem then, that we may expect to find a continuation of what was before us in the first three chapters of John's Gospel, namely, historical events and practical teaching· in both of which the Divine and moral glories of the Lord Jesus are displayed, and beneath the narrative of which we may discern hidden yet definitely defined typical and prophetical pictures.

We saw in our earlier studies two things are made very prominent in the opening chapters of this Gospel. First, the failure of Judaism, the deplorable condition of Israel. Some solemn portrayals of this have already been before us. In the second place, we have seen the Holy Spirit drawing our attention away from Israel to Christ; and then at the beginning of chapter four a third principle has been illustrated, namely, a turning from Judaism to the Gentiles. Furthermore, we have observed that not only do we have depicted in these opening sections of our Gospel the sad spiritual state of Israel at the time our Lord was here upon earth, but the narrative also furnishes us with a series of striking foreshadowings of the future. Such is the case in the concluding section of John 4.

Here, once more, we are reminded of the pitiable condition of Judaism during the days of Christ's public ministry. This is brought out in a number of particulars, which will become more evident as we study them in detail. First, we have the express testimony of the Lord Himself that He had no honour "in His own country." This was in vivid contrast from His experiences in Samaria. Second, while we are told that "the Galilæans received Him," it was not because they recognized the glory of His person, or the authority and life-giving value of His words, but because they had been impressed by what they had seen Him do at Jerusalem. Third, there is the declaration made by Christ to the nobleman—intended, no doubt, for the Galilæans also—"except ye see signs and wonders, ye will not believe." All of this serves to emphasize the condition of the Jews—their inability to recognize in the Lord Jesus the Christ of God, and their failure to set to their seal that what He spake was the truth.

The prophetic foreshadowing of these verses we reserve for the close. It is the practical lessons taught by this passage which will occupy our attention in the body of this article. Before pondering these we submit an Analysis of this closing section of John 4:—

1. Christ goes into Galilee, v. 43.
2. Christ's tragic plaint, v. 44.
3. Christ received by the Galilæans, v. 45.
4. The nobleman's request of Christ, vv. 46, 47.
5. Christ's reply, vv. 48-50.
6. The nobleman's journey home, vv. 50-53.
7. This miracle Christ's second in Galilee, v. 54.

"Now after two days He departed thence, and went into Galilee" *(v. 43)*. Different indeed are God's ways from ours. During those days spent in Samaria many had believed on Christ to the saving of their souls. And now the Saviour leaves that happy scene and departed into a country where He had received no honour. How evident it is that He pleased not Himself! He had come here to do the will of the Father, and now we see Him following the path marked out for Him. Surely there is an important lesson here for every servant of God today: no matter how successful and popular we may be in a place, we must move on when God has work for us elsewhere. The will of the One who has commissioned us must determine all our actions. Failure must not make us lag behind, nor success urge us to run before. Neither must failure make us fretful and feverish to seek another field, nor success cause us to remain stationary when God bids us move on. The one, perhaps, is as great a temptation as the other; but if we are following on to know the Lord, then shall we know when to remain and when to depart.

"Now after two days He departed thence, and went into Galilee" *(v. 43)*. This resumes and completes what is said in vv. 3 and 4. The Lord, accompanied by His disciples, left Judea because of the jealousy and enmity of the Pharisee. He "departed again into Galilee" *(v. 3)*. But before He goes there, "He must needs go through Samaria" *(v. 4)*. We have learned something of the meaning of that "must needs." But the need had now been met, so the Lord Jesus departed from Samaria and arrives at Galilee. The religious leaders in Jerusalem regarded Galilee with contempt *(see 7: 51, 58)*. It was there that "the poor of the flock" were to be found. The first three Gospels record at length the Galilæan-ministry of the Redeemer, but John's gives only a brief notice of it in the passage now before us.

"For Jesus Himself testified, that a prophet hath no honour in his own country" *(v. 44)*. The reference is to what is recorded in Luke 4. At Nazareth, "where He had been brought up," He entered the synagogue and read from Isa. 60, declaring "This day is this scripture fulfilled in your ears." Those who heard Him "wondered," and said, "Is not this Joseph's son?" They were totally blind to His Divine glory. The Lord replied by saying "Ye will surely say unto Me this proverb, Physician, heal thyself: whatsoever we have heard done in Capernaum, do also here in Thy country. And He said, Verily I say unto you, no prophet is accepted in His own country" *(Luke 4:23, 24)*. Proof of this was furnished immediately after, for when Christ referred to God's sovereign dealings of old in connection with Elijah and Elisha, we are told, "And all they in the synagogue, when they heard these things, were filled with wrath, And rose up, and thrust Him out of the city, and led Him unto the brow of the hill whereon their city was built, that they might cast Him down headlong" *(vv. 28, 29)*. Thus was He dishonoured and insulted by those among whom His pre-ministerial life had been lived.

He was without honour in "His own

country," that is, Galilee; and yet we now find Him returning there. Why, then, should He return thither? The answer to this question is found in Matt. 4: "Now when Jesus had heard that John was cast into prison, He departed *into Galilee;* and leaving Nazareth, He came and dwelt in Capernaum, which is upon the sea coast, in the borders of Zebulon and Naphthali: *that it might be fulfilled* which was spoken by Isaiah the prophet, saying, The land of Zabulon, and the land of Naphthali, by the way of the sea, beyond Jordan, *Galilee of the Gentiles;* The people which sat in darkness saw a great light; and to them which sat in the region and shadow of death light is sprung up" *(vv. 12-16)*. This furnishes us with another instance of the obedience of the perfect Servant. In the volume of the Book it was written of Him. Prophecy is not only an intimation of what will be, but a declaration of what shall be. Prophecy makes known the decrees of God. As, then, Christ had come here to do the will of God, and God's will (revealed in the prophetic word) had declared that the people in Galilee who walked in darkness, should see a great light, etc. *(Isa. 9:1,2)* the Lord Jesus Christ goes there.

"For Jesus Himself testified, that a prophet hath no honour in his own country." How this reveals to us the heart of the Saviour! He was no stoic, passing through these scenes unmoved by what He encountered. He was not insensible to the treatment He met with, He *"endured* such contradiction of sinners against Himself" *(Heb. 12:3)*. The indifference, the unbelief, the opposition of Israel, told upon Him, and caused His visage to be "marred more than any man" *(Isa. 52: 14)*. Hear Him, as by the spirit of prophecy, He exclaims, "I have labored in vain, I have spent My strength for nought, and in vain: yet surely My judgment is with the Lord, and My reward with My God" *(Isa. 49:4)*. So here, when we hear Him testifying, "A prophet hath no honour in his own country," we can almost catch the sob in His voice. For two days He had experienced the joys of harvest. His spirit had been refreshed. The "meat" which had been ministered to His soul consisted not only of the consciousness that He had done the will of the One who had sent Him, but also of the faith and gratitude of the woman who had believed on Him. This had been followed by the Samaritans beseeching Him to tarry with them, and the consequent believing of many of them because of His word. But such joyful harvesting was only for a very brief season. Two days only did He abide in Samaria. Now, He turns once more to Galilee, and He goes with sad foreboding.

"For Jesus Himself testified, that a prophet hath no honour in his own country." His use of the word "prophet" here is very suggestive. It was the word that the woman had used when her perceptive faculties began to be illumined *(v. 19)*. There, in Samaria, He *had been* honored. The Samaritans believed His bare word, for no miracles were performed before them. But now in Galilee He meets with a faith of a very inferior order. The Galilæans received Him *because* they *had seen* "all the things that He did at Jerusalem at the feast" *(v. 45)*. So, too, the nobleman's house *(v. 53)* did not believe until a miracle had been performed before their eyes. Thus a solemn contrast is pointed. In Galilee He is not honoured for His person's and word's sake; in Samaria He was. As a Prophet He was not honoured in Galilee; as a Miracle-worker He was "received." This principle is frequently exemplified today. There is many a servant of God who is thought more highly of abroad than he is at home. It is a true saying that 'familiarity breeds contempt.' Ofttimes a preacher is more respected and appreciated when visiting a distant field than he is by his own flock.

"Then when He was come into Galilee, the Galilæans received Him, having seen all the things that He did at Jerusalem at the feast: for they also went unto the feast" (v. 45). How this brings out the fickleness and the shallowness of human nature. For upwards of twenty years the man Christ Jesus had lived in Galilee. Little or nothing is told us about those years which preceded His public work. But we know that He did all things well. His manner of life, His ways, His deportment, His every act, must have stood out in vivid contrast from all around Him. Had His fellow-townsmen possessed any spiritual discernment at all they must have seen at once that Jesus of Nazareth was indeed the Holy One of God. But they were blind to His glory. The perfect life He had lived quietly among them was not appreciated. As the Son of God incarnate He was unknown and unrecognized.

But now things were changed. The humble Carpenter had left them for a season. He had commenced His public ministry. He had been to Jerusalem. There He had sternly corrected the Temple abuses. There He had performed such miracles that "many believed on His name" (2:23). Many of the Galilæans who were in attendance at the Feast had also witnessed His wonderful works, and they were duly impressed. On their return home they would doubtless tell others of what they had witnessed. And now that the Lord Jesus returns to Galilee, He is at once "received." Now that His fame had spread abroad the people flocked around Him. Such is human nature. Let a man who has lived in comparative obscurity leave his native place, become famous in some other state or country, and then return to his home town, and it is astonishing how many will claim friendship, if not kinship, with him. Human nature is very fickle and very superficial, and the moral of all this is to warn us not to place confidence in any man, but to value all the more highly (because of the contrast) the faithfulness of Him who changes not.

"So Jesus came again into Cana of Galilee, where He made the water wine. And there was a certain nobleman, whose son was sick at Capernaum" (v. 46). Why should we be told *where* the Lord was when He performed the miracle of healing the nobleman's son? Why, after mentioning Cana, is it added, "Where He made the water wine"? And why tell us in the last verse of the chapter, "This is again the second miracle that Jesus did when He was come out of Judea into Galilee"? Surely it is apparent at once that we are to place the two miracles that were wrought at Cana side by side. The Holy Spirit indicates there is some connection between them, something which they have in common. Following this hint, a close study of the record of these two miracles reveals the fact that there is a series of striking comparisons between them, apparently seven in number.

In the first place, both were *third day* scenes: in 2:1 we read, "And the third day there was a marriage in Cana of Galilee;" and in 4:43 we are told, "Now after two days He departed thence, and went into Galilee." Second, when Mary came to Christ and told Him they had no wine, He *rebuked* her *(2:4)*, so when the nobleman asked Christ to come down and heal his sick child the Lord *rebuked* him *(4:48)*. Third, in each case we see the *obedient response* made by those whom the Lord commanded (2:7 and 4:50). Fourth, in both miracles we see *the Word at work:* in each miracle the Lord did nothing but speak. Fifth, in both narratives mention is made of the *servant's knowledge* 2:9 and 4:51). Sixth, the sequel in each case was that they who witnessed the miracle *believed:* in the one we read

"And His disciples believed on Him" *(2:11)*; in the other we are told "And himself believed, and his whole house" *(4:53)*. Seventh, there is a designed similarity in the way in which *each narrative concludes:* in 2:11 we are told "This beginning of miracles did Jesus in Cana of Galilee," and in 4:54, "This is again the second miracle which Jesus did, when He was come out of Judea into Galilee." Here is another example of the importance of comparing two incidents which are placed side by side in Scripture (sometimes for the purpose of comparison, at others in order to point a series of contrasts); here we have an example of comparison between two miracles which, though separated in time and in the narrative, both occurred at the same place, and are the only miracles recorded in the New Testament as being wrought in Cana.

"And there was a certain nobleman, whose son was sick at Capernaum" *(v. 46)*. The word "nobleman" signifies a royal officer: probably he belonged to Herod's court; that he was a man of station and means is evident from the fact that he had servants *(v. 51)*. But neither rank nor riches exempt their possessor from the common sorrows of human kind. Naaman was a great man, but he was a leper *(2 Kings 5:1)*. So here was a nobleman, yet his son lay at the point of death. The rich have their troubles as well as the poor. Dwellers in palaces are little better off than they who live in cottages. Let Christians beware of setting their hearts on worldly riches: as Bishop Ryle well says, "They are uncertain comforts, but certain cares." No doubt this nobleman had tried every remedy which money could procure. But money is not almighty. Many invest it with an imaginary value that it is far from possessing. Money cannot purchase happiness, nor can it ensure health. There is just as much sickness among the aristocracy as there is among the common artisans.

"When he heard that Jesus was come out of Judea into Galilee, he went unto Him" *(v. 47)*. This domestic trial was a blessing in disguise, for it caused the anxious father to seek out Christ, and this resulted in him believing, and ultimately his whole house believed. God uses many different agents in predisposing men to receive and believe His Word. No doubt these lines will be read by more than one who dates his first awakening to the time when some loved one lay at death's door—it was then he was made to think seriously and saw the need for preparing to meet God. It is well when trouble leads a man *to* God, instead of away from God. Affliction is one of God's medicines; then let us beware of murmuring in time of trouble.

"And besought Him that He would come down, and heal his son: for he was at the point of death" *(v. 47)*. This nobleman evidently had a measure of faith in the ability of the great Physician, otherwise he had not sought Him at all. But the measure of his faith was small. He had probably learned of the miracles which the Lord had performed at Jerusalem, and hearing that He was now in Galilee—only a few miles distant—he goes to Him. The weakness of his faith is indicated in the request that the Lord should "come down" with him to Capernaum. He believed that Christ could heal close by, but not far away; at short range, but not at a distance. How many there were who thus limited Him. Jairus comes to Christ and says, "My little daughter lieth at the point of death: I pray Thee, *come and lay Thy hands on her*, that she may be healed; and she shall live" *(Mark 5:23)*. The woman with the issue of blood said, "If I may *touch* but His clothes, I shall be whole" *(Mark 5:28)*. So, too, Martha exclaimed, "Lord, if Thou hadst *been here*, my brother had not died" *(John 11:21)*. But let us not censure them, rather let us condemn our own unbelief.

But different far was the faith of the centurion that sought the Lord on behalf of his sick servant, and who said, "Lord, I am not worthy that Thou shouldst come under my roof: but speak the word only, and my servant shall be healed" *(Matt. 8:8)*. It seems to us this is the reason why (or one reason, at least) we are told here in John 4 that the nobleman came from Capernaum, so that we should link the two together and note the comparisons and contrasts between them. Both resided at Capernaum: both were Gentiles: both were men of position: both came to Christ on behalf of a sick member of his household. But in Matt. 8 the centurion simply spread his need before Christ and refrained from dictating to Him;, whereas the nobleman bids the Saviour "come down" to Capernaum. In Matt. 8 we find that the Lord offered to accompany the centurion—"Jesus saith unto him, I will come and heal him" *(v. 7)*. He does the very opposite here in John 4. In Matt. 8 the centurion declines the Lord's offer and says, "Speak the word only;" whereas the nobleman meets Christ's rebuke by repeating his original request—"Sir, come down ere my child die" *(v. 49)*. Thus we see again the value of observing the law of Comparison and Contrast.

"Then said Jesus unto him, Except ye see signs and wonders, ye will not believe" *(v. 48)*. This was a rebuke. Not only was the faith of this nobleman weak, but he so far forgot himself as to dictate to the Lord Jesus, and tell Him what to do. The force of Christ's reply seems to be this: 'You are demanding signs of Me *before* you will *fully* trust your boy's case into My hands.' This is a serious mistake which is made by many seeking souls. We must not be so wickedly presumptuous as to tell God *how* to act and *what* to do. We must state no terms to the Lord Most High. He must be left to work in His own way. "Except ye see signs and wonders ye will not believe." How this brings out the *omniscience* of Christ! He knew this man's heart. A measure of faith he had, but he was afraid to fully commit himself. The Lord knew this, and so addressed Himself to the suppliant accordingly.

"Except ye see signs and wonders ye will not believe." How searching this is! Is it not a word that many of us need? Is it not at this very point we most often fail? We ask God for a certain thing, and we have a measure of faith that it will be given us; but in the interval of waiting the bare word of God is not sufficient for us—we crave a "sign." Or again; we are engaged in some service for the Lord. We are not without faith that our labors will result in some fruitage for Him, but ere the fruit appears we become impatient, and we long for a "sign." Is it not so? Is it true of *you*, dear reader, that "except ye see signs and wonders, ye will not believe"? Ah, have we not all of us cause to cry, "Lord, help Thou mine unbelief." Fellow-worker, God has declared that His Word *shall not* return unto Him void *(Isa. 55:11)*. Is not that sufficient? Why ask for "signs"? Fellow-Christian, God has declared that if we ask anything according to His will, He heareth us *(1 John 5:15)*. Is not His promise enough? Why, then, crave for "signs"?

"The nobleman saith unto Him, Sir, come down ere my child die" *(v. 49)*. While it is evident that the nobleman was still slow of heart to commit himself, unreservedly, into the hands of Christ; nevertheless, it is good to see the spirit in which he received the Lord's rebuke. Though he was a nobleman he did not become angry when corrected; instead, he "suffered the word of exhortation," and with commendable importunity continued to plead his suit.

"The nobleman saith unto Him, Sir,

come down ere my child die." Bishop Ryle has a helpful word on this: "There is here a salutary lesson for the young. Sickness and death come to the young as well as the old. But the young are slow to learn this lesson. Parents and children are apt to shut their eyes to plain facts, and act as if the young never die young. The gravestones in our cemeteries show how many there are who never reached to man's estate at all. The first grave ever dug on earth was for a young man! The first one who ever died was not a father, but a son! He, then, who is wise will never reckon confidently on long life. It is the part of wisdom to be prepared."

We trust these words will come home to the hearts of Christian parents who read this article. In the action of this father who came to Christ on behalf of his child there is an example which you will do well to emulate. If you are not deeply concerned about the soul's welfare of your children, who is likely to be? It is *your* bounden duty to teach them the Word of God; it is your holy privilege to bring them in prayer to God. Do not turn over to a Sunday School teacher what is incumbent upon you. Teach your little ones the Scriptures from their earliest infancy. Train them to memorize such verses as Psa. 9:17, Jer. 17:9, Rom. 6:23, etc., and God has promised to honor them that honor Him. Be not discouraged if you are unable to detect any response, but rest on the promise, "Cast thy bread upon the waters, and thou shalt find it again after many days."

"The nobleman saith unto Him, Sir, come down ere my child die." How the response of Christ to this request brought out the perfections of Jehovah's Servant! This "nobleman," remember, occupied a high social position; most likely he was a member of Herod's court. To any man governed by fleshly considerations and principles, this would have been a tempting opportunity to make a favorable impression in society; it offered a chance to gain a footing in high places, which a man of the world would have quickly seized. But the Lord Jesus never courted popularity, nor did He ever toady to people of influence and affluence. He ever refused to use the ways of the world. He "condescended to men of low estate," and was the Friend not of princes and nobles, but of "publicans and sinners." Well may each servant of God take this to heart.

"Jesus saith unto him, Go thy way; thy son liveth" *(v. 50)*. The Lord never turns away a soul that truly seeks Him. There may be much ignorance (as indeed there is in all of us), there may be much of the flesh mixed in with our appeals, but if the heart is really set on Him, He always responds. And not only so, invariably He does far more for us than we ask or think. It was so here. He not only healed the son of this nobleman, but He did so immediately, by the word of His power.

"Jesus saith unto him, Go thy way; thy son liveth." This nobleman was a Gentile, for there were no "nobles" among the Jews; and in harmony with each similar case, the Lord healed this son from a distance. There are three, possibly four, different cases recorded in the Gospels, where Christ healed a Gentile, and in each instance He healed from a distance. There was a dispensational reason for this. The Jews were in covenant relationship with God, and as such "nigh" to Him. But the Gentiles, being "aliens from the commonwealth of Israel, and strangers from the covenants of promise" were "far off" *(Eph. 2:12, 13)*, and this fact was duly recognized by the Saviour.

"And the man believed the word that Jesus had spoken unto him" *(v. 50)*. Here, once more, we are shown the Word *(John 1:1, 14)* at work. This comes out prominently in the miracles described in this Gospel. The Lord does not go down to Capernaum and take the sick boy by the hand. Instead, He speaks the word of power and he is healed instantly. The "words" He spake were "spirit and life" *(John 6:63)*. And this imparting of life at a distance by means of the word has a message *for us* today. If Christ could heal this dying boy who was at least ten miles away by the word of His mouth, He can give eternal life today by His word even though He is away in heaven. *Distance is no barrier to Him.*

"And the man believed the word that Jesus had spoken unto him, and he went his way." This is very blessed. It shows us the power of the spoken word not only on the boy that was healed, but on his father, too—"Faith cometh by hearing, and hearing by the word of God" *(Rom. 10:17)*. The nobleman had heard the word of God from the lips of the Son of God, and real faith, saving faith, was now begotten within him. He raises no objections, asks no questions, makes no demurs; but with implicit confidence in what he had heard, he believed, and went his way. No "signs" were needed, no feelings required to impart assurance. "He believed, and went his way." This is how salvation comes to the sinner. It is simply a matter of taking God at His word, and setting to our seal that He is true. The very fact that it is *God's* word guarantees its truthfulness. This, we believe, is the only instance recorded in the New Testament where a "nobleman" believed in Christ—"not many noble are called" *(1 Cor. 1:26)*.

"And as he was now going down, his servants met him, and told him, saying, Thy son liveth. Then enquired he of them the hour when he began to amend. And they said unto him, Yesterday at the seventh hour the fever left him" *(vv. 51, 52)*. The word "yesterday" brings out a striking point. Cana and Capernaum were only a comparatively short distance apart: the journey could be made in about four hours. It was only one hour after midday when the Saviour pronounced the sick boy healed. Such implicit confidence had the nobleman in Christ's word, he did not return home *that* day at all!

I can picture the father on his way back home, going along happy and rejoicing. If some one had enquired as to the occasion of his joy, he would have been told it was because his child, at the point of death, had been restored. Had the enquirer asked *how* the father *knew* his child was now well, his answer would have been, 'Because I have the word of Christ for it— what more do I need!' And, dear reader, we too, shall be full of peace and joy if we rest on the sure word of God *(Rom. 15:13)*. The father's enquiry of his servants was not because of unbelief, but because he delighted to hear a recountal of what God had wrought. As John Wesley remarked on this verse, "The more exactly the works of God are considered, the more faith is increased."

"So the father knew that it was at the same hour, in the which Jesus said unto him, Thy son liveth: and himself believed, and his whole house" *(v. 53)*. The nobleman's faith here is not to be regarded as any different from what is attributed to him in v. 50: it is simply a repetition, brought in here in connection with his house believing, too. It is a very rare thing to find a believing wife and believing children where the father, the head of the house, is himself an unbeliever. What an example does this incident furnish us of the mysterious workings of God! —a boy brought to the point of *death* that a whole house might have *eternal life.*

We turn now to consider the prophetic foreshadowment which is found in the passage that has been before us. Once more we discern beneath the historical narrative a clearly defined typical picture. Before we point out its various lines we would offer a word of counsel to those of our readers who are desirous of pursuing this line of study for themselves in connection with other scriptures. With few exceptions, it is *not everything* in a passage which contributes to the typical or prophetic picture which it may contain. The first thing to be sought in every part of God's Word is its practical teaching—its message for *our own* hearts and lives. For God's Word is specifically designed as a lamp unto our feet and a light unto our path as we pass through this "dark place."

When studying a passage to discover its typical significance great care and caution is needed, and spiritual discernment is essential if we are to know what belongs to the typical picture and what does not. The principle which determines this is not an arbitrary one, but is to be drawn from the general analogy of Scripture. In the passage before us we have a prophetic foreshadowment in connection with *Gentiles*, hence that which is decidedly *Jewish* in the passage contributes nothing to the picture.

In our last paper we saw that John 4:30-42 contains a striking picture of this *present Age*, hence in the verses that follow we would naturally expect to find that which prefigures the Age to come, the Millennium. Such is the case. John 4:43-54 gives us a typical foreview of God's dealings with the Gentiles in the Day to come. Should any one ask, But how do you know that it is a typical picture of *Gentiles*, rather than of Israel? We answer, Because of the *repeated mention* of "Galilee." No less than five times do we have "Galilee" spoken of: vv. 43, 45, 46, 47, 54, and in the light of Isa. 9:2, "Galilee *of the Gentiles*," no room is left for doubt.

Once more we find seven lines in the typical picture. First, "Galilee" tells us it is the Gentiles who are here in view. Second, the words *"after two days"* is a time mark which enables us to fix the application. The "two days" point to the present Age; which ends at the return of Christ to the earth. *"After two days,"* then, brings us to the Millennium. Third, the "Galilæans *received Him" (v. 45)*: thus will it be in the Millennium—Acts 15:17. Fourth, the nobleman (a Gentile)—still emphasizing this central characteristic of the picture—journeys to Christ because he had *"heard"* of Him *(v. 47)*; so it will be with the Gentiles during the Millennium—"In those days it shall come to pass, that ten men shall take hold out of all languages of the nations, even shall take hold of the skirt of him that is a Jew, saying, We will go with you: for we have *heard* that God is with you" *(Zech. 8:23)*. Fifth, Christ displays His grace toward the Gentiles by healing the nobleman's son. Sixth, this healing occurred at the seventh hour *(v. 52)*. This is very striking indeed, and is another sure key to the interpretation of this type. The "seventh hour" here is in designed contrast from the "sixth hour" of v. 6; and note the marvelous accuracy there —*"about* the sixth hour," for as a matter of fact *that* to which this "sixth hour" pointed did not actually arrive till after the death of Christ. As we have seen, what occurred there in Samaria foreshadowed God's dealings in the present Age, which, in 1 Cor. 4:3 (margin) is denominated *"man's* Day," hence the *sixth* hour, for six is the number of man. But in the picture now before us, it is the Millennium which is in view, hence the *seventh* hour. Seventh, the unquestioning obedience of this nobleman to the command of Christ "Go thy way" *(v. 50)* furnishes a striking example of the Gentiles subject to the governmental power and authority of Christ during the Millennium.

Let the reader study carefully the following questions in preparation for the next lesson:—

1. What is the meaning of "Bethesda," and what is the signifi-

cance of the "five porches"? v. 2.

2. Why are we told the impotent man had suffered thirty-eight years? v. 5.

3. Why did Christ ask the impotent man such a question as is recorded in v. 6?

4. What does the man's answer denote? v. 7.

5. What important principle is illustrated in v. 11?

6. What moral perfection of Christ is seen in v. 13?

7. What typical picture can you see here? Note the reference to "the sabbath."—*Arthur W. Pink.*

ETERNAL PUNISHMENT
(Concluded)

In the last two articles we have considered some of the principal sophistries which unbelief has brought against the truth of eternal punishment, and have also examined the teaching of Scripture concerning the Destiny of the wicked. We approach now the most solemn aspect of our subject, namely:

III. THE NATURE OF PUNISHMENT AWAITING THE LOST.

1. THE PORTION OF THE WICKED IMMEDIATELY AFTER DEATH.

We turn first to the teaching of our Lord found in Luke 16. Here we learn the following facts: First, that in Hades the lost are in full possession of all their faculties and sensibilities. They *see*, for the rich man saw Abraham afar off, and Lazarus in his bosom *(v. 23)*. They *feel*, for he was in "torments" *(v. 24)*. They *cry for mercy*, for he asked—but in vain—for a drop of water to cool his tongue *(v. 24)*. They are in possession of *memory*, for the rich man was bidden to "remember" what he had received during his lifetime on earth *(v. 25)*. It is impossible for them to join the redeemed: there is "a great gulf fixed between them" *(v. 26)*.

Unspeakably solemn is all this. Not only will the lost be tormented in flames, but their anguish will be immeasureably increased by a sight of the redeemed being "comforted." Then shall they *see* the happy portion of the blest which they despised, preferring as they did the pleasures of sin for a season. And how the retention of "memory" will further augment their sufferings! With what unfathomable sorrows will they recall the opportunities wasted, the expostulations of parents and friends slighted, the warnings of God's servants disregarded, the invitations of God's grace refused. And then to know there is no way of escape, no means of relief, no hope of a reprieve! Their lot will be unbearable; their awful portion, beyond endurance. The Son of God has faithfully forewarned that "there shall be wailing and gnashing of teeth" *(Matt. 13:42)*. It is very significant that Christ referred to this just *seven* times—denoting the *completeness* of their misery and anguish: see Matt. 8:12; 13:42, 50; 22:13; 24:51; 25:30; Luke 13: 28.

2. THE FINAL PORTION OF THE WICKED.

(1) This is spoken of as *being "punished with everlasting destruction from the presence of the Lord"* (2 Thess. 1: 9). None but one who really knows God can begin to estimate what it will mean to be eternally banished from the Lord. Forever separated from the Fount of all goodness! *Never* to enjoy the light of God's countenance! *Never* to bask in the sunshine of His presence. This, this is the most awful of all. 2 Thess. 1:9 furnishes clear intimation that the judgment of Matt. 25, with its eternal sentence, looks beyond the Assize at

the beginning of the Millennium. "Destruction from the presence of the Lord" is parallel with *"depart* from Me ye cursed."

(2) The final portion of the wicked is spoken of as *"everlasting punishment"* (Matt. 25:46). In 1 John 4:18 the same Greek word is rendered "torment." This term announces the satisfying of God's justice. In the punishing of the wicked God vindicates His outraged majesty. Herein punishment differs from correction or discipline. Punishment is not designed for the good of the one who suffers it. It is intended for the enforcing of law and order: it is necessary for the preservation of government.

(3) The final portion of the wicked is spoken of as *a "tormenting."* This is proven by the fact that the everlasting fire into which the wicked depart is "prepared for the Devil and his angels" *(Matt. 25:41)* which emphasizes the awfulness of this punishment, rather than specifies who are going to endure it. This verse sets forth the *severity* of the punishment of the lost. If the everlasting fire be "prepared for *the Devil* and his angels," then how intolerable it will be! If the place of eternal torment into which all unbelievers shall be cast is *the same* as that in which God's *arch-enemy* will suffer, how dreadful that place must be.

That this everlasting fire, prepared for the Devil and his angels, produces the most awful suffering is clear from Rev. 20:10, where we are told that Satan shall be "tormented day and night for ever and ever." No doubt this torment will be both internal and external, mental and physical. The word occurs for the first time in the New Testament in Matt. 8:6: "Lord, my servant lieth at home sick of the palsy, *grievously tormented."* The same word occurs again in Rev. 9:5 where we read of infernal locusts, issuing from the Pit, and which are given power to torment men, the nature of which is explained as "the torment of a scorpion, when he striketh a man." So intense will be the suffering caused therefrom "men shall seek death and shall not find it, and they shall desire to die, and death shall flee from them" *(Rev. 9:6).* This torment, then, cannot mean less than the most excruciating pain which we are now capable of conceiving. How much the pains of Hell will exceed the pains of earth we know not.

(4) The final portion of the wicked is spoken of as *"suffering the vengeance of eternal fire" (Jude 7).* But many say this is merely a figurative expression. We ask, How do they know that? Where has God told them so in His Word? Personally we believe that when God says "fire" He means "fire." We refuse to blunt the sharp edge of His Word. Was the Deluge figurative? Was it figurative "fire and brimstone" which descended from heaven and destroyed Sodom and Gomorrah? Were the plagues upon Egypt figurative ones? Is it figurative fire which shall yet burn this earth, and cause the very elements to "melt with fervent heat"? No; in each of these cases we are obliged to take the words of Scripture in their literal signification. Let those who dare affirm that Hell-fire is non-literal answer to God. We are not their judges; but we refuse to accept their toning down of these solemn words. Literal fire in Hell presents no difficulty at all to the writer. The lost will have literal *bodies* when they are cast into Hell. The "angels" also have bodies; and for all we know to the contrary, the Devil has too.

But the question is often asked, How can the bodies of the lost be tormented eternally by literal fire? Would not the fire utterly consume them? Even though we were unable to furnish an answer to this question, we should still believe that Scripture meant what it said. But we are satisfied that God's Word answers this question. In Ex. 3 we read of the bush in the wilderness burning with fire, and yet was not consumed! In Dan. 3 we read of the three Hebrews being cast into the fiery furnace of Babylon, yet were they not consumed! Why was this? Because, in some way unknown to us, *God preserved* the bush, and the bodies of the three Hebrews. Is God, then, *unable* to preserve the bodies of the damned from being consumed? Surely not. But we are not left even to this unescapable inference. In Mark 9:47-49 we are told, "It is better for thee to enter into the kingdom of God with one eye, than having two eyes to be cast into hell fire, where their worm dieth not, and the fire is not quenched. For every one shall be *salted with fire.*" The expression "salted with fire" confirms what we have said above. Salt is a *preservative;* hence, when we are told that "every one" who is cast into Gehenna shall be "salted with fire" we learn that the very fire itself so far from consuming shall preserve. If it be asked, How can this be? We answer, Because *that* fire is "prepared" by God *(Matt. 25:41).*

(5) The final portion of the wicked is described as *an association with the vilest of the vile.* "But the fearful, and unbelieving, and the abominable, and murderers, and whoremongers, and sorcerers, and idolaters, and all liars, shall have their part in the lake which burneth with fire and brimstone" *(Rev. 21:8).* O dear reader, weigh well this solemn language. You may be a person of culture and refinement: judged by moral standards your life may be exemplary and spotless: you may pride yourself on your honesty and truthfulness: you may be very particular in your choice of friends and very careful to avoid the company of the profane and vicious: you may even be religious, and look down in scorn and pity upon the idolaters of heathendom; but God says that if you die in unbelief your portion shall be with "the fearful, and unbelieving, and the abominable, and murderers, and whoremongers, and sorcerers, and idolaters, and all liars." Think of what it will mean to spend eternity in the Prison-house of the universe with Cain, and Pharaoh, and Judas! Think of what it will mean to be shut up with the vile Sodomites! Think of being incarcerated forever with every blasphemer who has ever lived!

(6) The final portion of the wicked is described as *"the blackness of darkness forever"* (Jude 13). Unrelieved will be their fearful sufferings; interminable their torments. No means of escape. No possibility of a reprieve. No hope of deliverance. Not one will be found who is able to befriend them and intercede with God for them. They had the offer of a Mediator often made them in this world; but no such offer will be made them in the Lake of Fire. "There is *no peace,* saith my God, to the wicked." There will be no resting-place in Hell; no secret corner where they can find a little respite; no cooling fountain at which they may refresh themselves. There will be no change or variation of their lot. Day and night, forever and ever, shall they be punished. With no prospect of any improvement they will sink down into blank despair.

(7) The final portion of the wicked will be *beyond the creature's power of resistance.* "And whosoever shall fall on this stone shall be broken: but on whomsoever it shall fall, *it will grind him to powder"* (Matt. 21:44). There are many who now say, If at the end I find myself in Hell, I will bear it as well as I can, as if by strength of will and firmness of mind they shall, in measure at least, be able to support themselves. But alas! Their resolutions will count for nothing.

It is common with men in this world to shun calamities, but if they find this is impossible, they set themselves to bear it: they fortify their spirits and resolve to support themselves under it as well as they can. They muster up all their courage and resolution in the determination to keep their hearts from sinking. But it will be utterly vain for sinners to do this in the Lake of Fire. What would it help a worm which was about to be crushed by some great rock, to collect its strength and endeavor to set itself to bear up against its weight, and so seek to prevent itself from being crushed? Much less will a poor damned soul be able to support itself under the weight of the wrath of Almighty God. No matter how much the sinner may now harden himself, in order to endure the pains of Hell, the first moment he shall feel the flames, his heart will melt like wax before the furnace—"Can thine heart endure, or can thine hands be strong, in the days that I shall deal with thee? I the Lord have spoken it, and will do it" *(Ezek. 22:14)*.

If such then be the case with impenitent sinners, that they can neither escape their punishment, nor deliver themselves from it, nor bear up under it, what will become of them? I answer in the words of another:—

"They will wholly sink down into eternal death. There will be that sinking of heart, of which we now cannot conceive. We see how it is with the body when in extreme pain. The nature of the body will support itself for a considerable time under very great pain, so as to keep from wholly sinking. There will be great struggles, lamentable groans and panting, and it may be convulsions. These are the strugglings of nature to support itself under the extremity of the pain. There is, as it were, a great lothness in nature to yield to it; it cannot bear wholly to sink. But yet sometimes pain of body is so very extreme and exquisite, that the nature of the body cannot support itself under it; however loth it may be to sink, yet it cannot bear the pain; there are a few struggles, and throes, and pantings, and it may be a shriek or two, and the nature yields to the violence of the torments, sinks down, and the body dies. This is the death of the body. *So it will be with the soul in Hell;* it will have no strength or power to deliver itself; and its torment and horror will be so great, so mighty, so vastly disproportioned to its strength, that having no strength in the least to support itself, although it be infinitely contrary to the nature and inclination of the soul utterly to sink; yet it will sink, it will utterly and totally sink, without the least degree of remaining comfort, or strength, or courage, or hope. And though it will never be annihilated, its being and perception will never be abolished: yet such will be the infinite depth of gloominess that it will sink into, that it will be in a state of death, eternal death.

"The nature of man desires happiness; it is the nature of the soul to crave and thirst after well-being; and if it be under misery, it equally pants after relief; and the greater the misery is, the more easily doth it struggle for help. But if all relief be withholden, all strength overborne, all support utterly gone; then it sinks into the darkness of death. We can conceive but little of the matter; we cannot conceive what that sinking of the soul in such a case is. But to help your conception, imagine yourself to be cast into a fiery oven, all of a glowing heat, or into the midst of a glowing brick-kiln, or of a great furnace, where your pain would be as much greater than that occasioned by accidentally touching a coal of fire, as the heat is greater. Imagine also that your body were to lie there for a quarter of an hour, full of fire, as full within and without as a bright coal of fire, all the while full of quick sense; what horror would you feel at the entrance of such a furnace! And how long would that quarter of an hour seem to you! If it were to be measured by a glass, how long would the glass seem to be running! And after you had endured it for one minute, how overbearing would it be to you to think that you had yet to endure the other fourteen.

"But what would be the effect on your soul, if you knew you must lie there enduring that torment to the full for twenty-four hours! And how much greater would be the effect, if you knew you must endure it for a whole year, and how vastly greater still, if you knew you must endure it for a thousand years! O then, how would your heart sink, if you thought, if you knew, that you must bear it forever and ever! That there would be no end! That after millions of millions of ages, your torment would be no nearer to an end, than ever it was; and that you never, never should be delivered! But your torment in Hell will be immeasureably greater than this illustration represents. How then will the heart of a poor creature sink under it! How utterly inexpressible and inconceivable must the sinking of the soul be in such a case." (Jonathan Edwards).

Such, in brief, is the portion awaiting the lost:—eternal separation from the Fount of all goodness; everlasting punishment; torment of soul and body; endless existence in the Lake of Fire, in association with the vilest of the vile; every ray of hope excluded; utterly crushed and overwhelmed by the wrath of a sin-avenging God. And let us remember in *Whose* Word these solemn statements are found! They are found in the Word of Him who is *faithful*, and therefore has He written in plain and positive language, so that none need be *deceived*. They are found in the Word of Him who *cannot lie*, and therefore He has not employed the language of *exaggeration*. They are found in the Word of Him who says what He means and means what He says, and therefore the writer, for one, dares do nothing else than receive them at their face value. We turn now to:

IV. THE APPLICATION OF THE SUBJECT.

1. In what has been before us *we learn* HOW *the Character and Throne of God will be vindicated.* What can be too severe a judgment upon those who have despised so great a Being as the Almighty? If he that is guilty of treason against an earthly government deserves to lose his life, what punishment can be great enough for one who has preferred his own pleasure before the will and glory of a God who is infinitely good? To despise infinite excellence merits infinite misery. God has commanded the sinner to repent, He has courted him with overtures of grace, He has bountifully supplied his every need, and He has presented before him the Son of His love—His choicest treasure—and yet men persist in their wicked course. No possible ground, then, will the sinner have to appeal against the sentence of the Judge of all the earth, seeing that He not only tendered mercy toward him, but also bore with him in so much patience when He might justly have smitten him down upon the first crime he ever committed and removed him to Hell upon the first refusal of His proffered grace.

That God shall punish every rebel against Himself is required by the very perfections of His high sovereignty. It is but meet that He should display His governmental supremacy. The creature has dared to assert its independency: the subject has risen up in arms against his King; therefore, the rights of God's throne must be vindicated—"I know that the Lord is greater than all gods: for in the thing wherein they dealt proudly He is above them" *(Ex. 18:11).* When Pharaoh dared to pit himself against Jehovah. God manifested His authority by destroying him at the Red Sea. Another king He turned into a beast, to make him know that the Most High ruleth in the kingdom of men. So, when the history of this world is wound up, God will make a full and final manifestation of His sovereign majesty. Though He now *endures* (not "loves") with much longsuffering the vessels of wrath fitted to destruction; it is that, in the coming Day, He may "show His wrath and make His power known" *(Rom. 9:22)*.

2. What has been before us *serves to expose the folly and madness of the greater part of mankind,* in that for the sake of present momentary gratification, they run the serious risk of enduring all these eternal torments. They prefer a small pleasure, or a little wealth, or a little earthly honor and fame (which lasts but "for a season") to an escape from the Lake of Fire. If it be true that the torments of Hell are everlasting, what will it profit a man if he gain the whole world and lose his own soul? How mad men are who hear and read of these things and pretend to believe them, who are alive but a little while, a few short years at most, and yet who are careless about what becomes of themselves in the next world, where there is neither change nor end! How mad are they who hear that if they go on in sin, they shall be eternally miserable, and yet are not moved, but hear it with as much indifference as if they were not concerned in the matter at all! And yet for all they know to the contrary, they may be in fiery torments before another week is at an end!

How sad to note that this unconcern is shared by the great majority of our fellows. Age makes little difference. The young are occupied with pleasures, the middle-aged with worldly advancement, the aged with their attainments or lack of them; with the first it is the lust of the flesh, with the second it is the lust of the eyes, with the third it is the pride of life, which banishes from their minds all serious thoughts of the life to come. "The heart of the sons of men is full of evil, and *madness* is in their heart while they live, and after that they go to the dead" *(Eccl. 9:3).* O the blinding power of sin! O the deceitfulness of riches! O the perversity of the human heart! Nothing so reveals these things as the incredible sight of men and women enjoying themselves and being at rest, while they are suspended over the eternal burning by the frail thread of mortality, which may be snapped at any moment.

3. What has been before us *ought to make every unsaved reader to tremble* as he scans these pages. These things are no mere abstractions, but dread realities, as countless thousands have already discovered to their bitter cost. They may not seem real to you now, but in a short time at most—should you continue to reject the Christ of God—they will be *your* portion. You, too, shall lift up your eyes in Hell, and behold the saints in heaven. You, too, shall crave a drop of water to alleviate your fearful agony; but it will be in vain. You, too, shall cry for mercy; but then it will be too late. O unsaved reader, we pray you not to throw this aside and seek to dismiss the subject from your thoughts. That is how thousands before you have acted, and the very memory of their folly only accentuates their misery. Far better had you be made wretched now for a time, than that you should weep and wail and gnash your teeth forever. Far better that you have your present false peace broken, than that you should be a stranger to real peace for all eternity.

"Except ye repent, ye shall all likewise perish." Whoever you are, whether young or old, whether rich or poor, whether religious or irreligious, if you are in a Christless state, then this is what awaits you at the end of your present course. This, this is the Hell over which *you* now hang, and into which you are ready to drop this very moment. It is vain for you to flatter yourself with hopes that you shall avoid it, or to say in your heart, Perhaps it may not be; perhaps things have been represented worse than they really are. These things are according to the Word of Truth, and if you will not be convinced by that Word when presented to you by men in the name of God, then God Himself will yet undertake to prove to you that these things *are so*.

Think it not strange that God should deal so severely with you, or that the wrath you shall suffer shall be so great. For great as it is, it is no greater than the mercy which you now despise. The love of God, His marvellous grace in sending His own Son to die for sinners, is every whit as great and wonderful as this inexpressible wrath. You have refused to accept Christ as the Saviour from the wrath to come, you have despised God's dying love, why then should you not suffer wrath as great as that grace and love which you have rejected? Does it still seem incredible that God should so harden His heart against a poor sinner as to bear down upon him with infinite power and merciless wrath? Then pause and ask, Is it any greater than it is for me to harden my heart against Him, against infinite mercy, against the Son of His love? O dear friends, face this question of Christ Himself, "How can ye escape the damnation of Hell?" *(Matt. 23:33).* There is only one way of escape, and that is *to flee to the Saviour.* If you would not fall into the hands of the living God, then cast yourself into the arms of the Christ who died—"Kiss the Son, lest He be angry, and ye perish from the way, when His wrath is kindled but a little. Blessed are all they that put their *trust* in Him" *(Psa. 2:12).*

4. What has been before us *ought to make every professing Christian diligently examine himself.* Weigh carefully the tremendously solemn issues which turn on whether or not you have *really* passed from death unto life. You cannot afford to be uncertain. There is far too much at stake. Remember that you are prejudiced in your own favor. Remember that you have a treacherous heart. Remember that the Devil is the great *Deceiver* of souls. Remember that *"there is* a way that seemeth right unto a man, but the end thereof are the ways of death" *(Prov. 14:12).* Remember it is written that "Many shall say unto Me in that day, Lord, Lord, have we not prophesied in Thy name? and in Thy name have cast out devils? and in Thy name done many wonderful works?" And that He will answer them, "I never knew you: depart from Me, ye that work iniquity" *(Matt. 7:22, 23).*

There are many who now wear the guise of saints, who appear like saints, and their state, both in their own eyes and that of their neighbors is satisfactory. And yet they have on only sheep's clothing; at heart, they are wolves. But no disguise can deceive the Judge of all. *His* eyes are as a flame of fire: they search the hearts and try the reins of the children of men. Wherefore, let each take earnest heed that he be not deceived. Compare yourself with the Word of God, for that is the rule by which you will be tried. Test your works, for it is by those you will be made manifest. Inquire whether you are really living a Christian life; whether or not the fear of God is upon you; whether or not you are mortifying your members which are upon the earth; whether or not you are "denying ungodliness and worldly lusts," and whether you are living "soberly, righteously, and godly in this present world," for it is thus that "grace" teaches the saints to live. Cry unto God earnestly and frequently that He will reveal you to yourself, and discover to you whether you are building upon the Rock, or upon the sand. Make the Psalmist's prayer yours— *"Search me,* O God, and know my heart; try me, and know my thoughts. And see if there be any wicked way in me, and lead me in the way everlasting" *(Psa. 139:23, 24)*. God will search you hereafter, and make fully manifest what you are, both to yourself and to others. Let each of us, then, humbly request Him to search us now. We have urgent *need* of Divine help in this matter, for our heart is "deceitful above all things, and desperately wicked."

5. What has been before us should *cause those who really enjoy the full assurance of faith to praise God with a loud voice*. To each of you we say, God has given you wonderful cause for gratitude and thanksgiving. You, too, justly deserved to suffer the full weight of the wrath of a sin-hating and sin-avenging God. It is not long since *you* loved darkness rather than light. It is only a short time ago since *you* turned a deaf ear to both God's commands and entreaties. It is only a few years at most since *you* despised and rejected His beloved Son. What marvelous grace was it then that snatched *you* as a brand from the burning! What wondrous love was it that delivered you from the wrath to come! What matchless mercy it was that changed you from a child of Hell *(Matt. 23:15)* to a child of God! O how you should praise the Father for having ever set His love upon you. How you should praise the Son for having died to save you from the Lake of Fire. How you should praise the blessed Spirit for having quickened you into newness of life. And how your appreciation ought to be expressed now in a life that is glorifying to the triune God. How diligently ought you to seek to learn what is well-pleasing in His sight. How earnestly you should seek His will. How quick should you be to run in the way of His commandments. Let your life correspond with the praises of your lips.

6. What has been before us *ought to stir up all of God's people to a deepened sense of their duty*. Fellow-Christian, have you no obligations toward your godless neighbors? If God has made clear these solemn truths to you, does it not deepen your responsibility toward the unsaved? If you have no love for souls, it is greatly to be feared that your own soul is in imminent danger. If you can witness, unmoved, men and women hurrying down the broad road which leadeth to destruction, then it is seriously to be doubted if you have within you the Spirit of that One who wept over Jerusalem. It is true you have no power of your own to save a soul from death, but are you faithfully giving out that Word which is the instrument which God uses to bring souls from death unto life? Are you supplicating God as you ought and *depending* on Him to bless your efforts to point the lost to the Lamb of God? Are you as fervent as you should be in your cries to God on behalf of the lost? Alas, must you not join the writer as he hangs his head in shame? Is there not reason for each of us to ask God to give us a clearer vision of that indescribably awful portion which awaits every Christ rejector, and to enable us to act in the power of such a vision!

7. What has been before us *will yet be the occasion of profoundest praise to God*. Whatever difficulties the eternal punishment of the wicked may present to us now—and it is freely granted that *it is* difficult for our reason to grasp it, and that of necessity, for we are incapable of discerning the infinite malignity of sin, and therefore unable to see what punishment it really deserves—yet. in the Day to come it will be far otherwise. When we behold God's righteous dealings with His enemies. when we hear the sentences being given according to their works, when we see how justly and thoroughly they deserve merciless wrath, and stand by as they are cast into the Lake of Fire, so far from shrinking back in horror our hearts will give vent to

gladsome praise. Just as of old the overthrow of God's enemies at the Red Sea caused His people to burst forth in worshipful song, so in the coming Day we shall be moved to rejoicing when we witness the final display of God's holiness and justice in the overthrow and punishment of all who have defied Him. Remember that in the destruction of the wicked God will be *glorified,* and *this* it is which will be the occasion of the rejoicing of His people. Not only will God be "clear" when He judges *(Psa. 51:4),* but His perfections will be *magnified* in the sentences pronounced.—*Arthur W. Pink.*

10. ANTICHRIST IN THE GOSPELS AND EPISTLES

The Old and New Testaments have many things in common—far more than some teachers of "dispensational" truth seem to be aware of—but there are also some noticeable contrasts between them. Speaking generally, the one is principally prophetic; the other mainly didactic. There is far more said in the former about the future of Israel than there is in the latter. Much more space in the Old Testament than in the New is devoted to describing the conditions which shall obtain in the Tribulation period. And far more was revealed through the prophets about the Antichrist than was made known through the apostles. It is in full keeping with this that we find there is one book in the New Testament which is a noticeable exception, and that is the one which is peculiarly prophetic in its character and contents, namely, the Revelation. There, perhaps, more is told us concerning the person and career of the Man of Sin than in all the rest of the New Testament put together.

The passages which refer directly to the Antichrist in the four Gospels are few in number; but in addition to these there are several indirect references to him, and these call for a more careful examination because of their apparent obscurity. The writer believes there may be other passages in the Gospels treating of the Man of Sin in his varied relations, and which contain an *esoteric* view of him, but which the Holy Spirit has not yet been pleased to reveal unto students of prophecy. Let not the reader then regard this article as in any-wise a complete or exhaustive treatment of the subject, rather let its brief hints bestir him to make prayerful and patient examination for himself.

The Antichrist receives an even more scant notice in the Epistles than he does in the four Gospels. So far as we have been able to discover he is alluded to only in 2 Thess. 2 and in John's Epistles. The reason for this is not difficult to discover. The Epistles concern those who are members of the Body of Christ, and by the time the Antichrist appears upon the stage of human history, they shall be far above these scenes—with their blessed Lord in the Father's House. Nevertheless "all Scripture" is profitable for our instruction and necessary for our enlightenment. God has been pleased to reveal much concerning those things which must shortly come to pass, and it may be that they who now ignore or neglect the study of the prophetical portions of Scripture will be overtaken by surprise when, in a coming day, they shall behold with wonder the fulfillment of prophecy; and possibly *this* surprise (due to culpable ignorance) is included in what the apostle refers to when he speaks of not being "*ashamed* before Him at His coming" *(1 John 2: 28).* Certainly it is our duty as well as privilege to examine diligently *all* that God has been pleased to make known in His Word.

1. Passing by the typical teaching of Matt. 2, which will come before us in a later article, we turn first to Matt. 12 which is one of the most important chapters in that book, supplying as it does one of the principal keys to its dispensational interpretation. In it is recorded the first great break between the Jews and Christ, which eventually terminated in their crucifying Him. In v. 14 we read, "Then the Pharisees went out, and held a council against Him, how they might destroy Him." This is the first time we read of anything like this in Matthew's Gospel. Following this we read, "Then was brought unto Him one possessed with a demon, blind, and dumb; and He healed him, insomuch that the blind and dumb both spake and saw" *(v. 22)*. Up to that time this was by far the most remarkable miracle our Lord had performed. Its effect upon those who witnessed it was general and deep—"And all the people were amazed, and said, Is not this the Son of David?" *(v. 23)*. It *must be* the long-promised Messiah who now stood in their midst. But the Pharisees were blinded by their hatred of Him, and committed the sin for which there is no forgiveness: "This fellow doth not cast out demons, but by Beelzebub the prince of the demons" *(v. 24)*. Then, following His reply to their awful blasphemy and terming them "a generation of vipers" *(v. 34)*, our Lord uttered a prophetic parable which bears directly on our present theme:

"When the unclean spirit is gone out of a man, he walketh through dry places, seeking rest, and findeth none. Then he saith, I will return into my house from whence I came out; and when he is come, he findeth it empty, swept, and garnished. Then goeth he, and taketh with himself seven other spirits more wicked than himself, and they enter in and dwell there: and the last state of that man is worse than the first. Even so shall it be also unto this wicked generation" *(vv. 43-45)*. The first thing to note concerning this mysterious and remarkable passage is its setting. This, as we have sought to indicate above, has to do with Christ's solemn pronouncement on those who had determined to destroy Him, and who were guilty of the unpardonable sin. In it He declares the judgment which God shall yet send upon apostate Israel.

Our next concern is to ascertain the meaning of this parabolic utterance. The central figure is "The unclean spirit." This "unclean spirit" is viewed here in three connections: first, as indwelling a man; second, as going out of the man; third, as returning to the man and indwelling him again. In v. 44 the "man" is termed by the unclean spirit "my house." This "man" unquestionably represents Israel, for at the close of the parable Christ says, "Even so shall it be also unto this wicked generation." Who, then, is referred to by "the unclean spirit"? We believe that it is the Son of Perdition. The following reasons lead us to this conclusion: First, mark attentively the use of the definite article: it is not simply *an* unclean spirit, but *"the* unclean spirit." Second, note his threefold relation to Israel. At the time the Saviour uttered these words the Son of Perdition was then present in Israel's midst. But a little later he was no longer so. When he hanged himself he passed out of these scenes into the next world: as Acts 1:25 compared with Rev. 11:7 tells us, into the Pit. His present state in the Abyss is graphically and solemnly depicted—"He walketh through dry places, seeking rest, and findeth none" *(v. 43)*. Then, he says, "I will *return* into *my house* from whence I came out." This, we are satisfied, refers to the re-incarnation of the Son of Perdition, when he appears on earth for the last time as the Man of Sin. Then, in a special sense, will Israel be *his* "house." A third reason why we believe "The Unclean Spirit" is the Son of Perdition is furnished by Zech. 13:2—"And it shall come to pass in that day, saith the Lord of hosts, that I will cut off the names of the idols out of the land, and they shall no more be remembered: and also I will cause the prophets and *the unclean spirit* to pass out of the land." Clearly this verse speaks of the End-time. What follows is very striking. Vv. 3 and 4 concern the prophets who shall prophesy falsely. But in v. 5 there is a noticeable change from the plural to the singular number: "But *he* shall say, I am no prophet," etc. The only antecedent to this pronoun is "The Unclean Spirit" of v. 2, which here in v. 5 is shown to be no mere abstraction but a definite person. And then in v. 6 the question is asked, "What are these wounds in thine hands?" We believe this intimates that God will even permit the Man of Sin to imitate the Saviour to the extent that he will appear with *wounds in his hands:* thus will he be the better able to pose as the true Christ.

When the Son of Perdition returns to Israel, he finds his house "empty, swept, and garnished." This depicts the moral and spiritual state of the Jews at the time the Antichrist is manifested. Though clean from the horrible idolatries which defiled them of old, and though adorned with all that temporal prosperity will bring them, Israel, nevertheless, will be devoid of the Shekinah-glory, and have no Holy Spirit indwelling them. Next, we are told, "Then goeth he, and taketh with himself seven other spirits more wicked than himself, and they enter in and dwell there." We believe that this has a double meaning. One plus seven equals eight; and in Scripture eight signifies *a new beginning*. This is in keeping with the *re-*incarnation of the Son of Perdition. But we think there is also a reference here to Satan's blasphemous imitation of what we are told in Rev. 5:6, where we read of the Lamb having seven eyes, which are *the seven spirits of God."* Just as the Christ of God will come back to earth endued with the Spirit of God in the sevenfold plentitude of His power, so will the Antichrist present himself to Israel in the sevenfold fulness of satanic power and uncleanness. Then, indeed, shall Israel's last state be worse than their first—i. e. when they rejected Christ in the days of *Judas.*

2. We turn now to Matt. 24, which contains a lengthy forecast concerning the end of this Age. Here we find our Lord describing the conditions which shall obtain during the Tribulation period. Christ announces with considerable detail those things which are to precede His own return to the earth. The whole chapter sets forth the Master's answers to three questions asked by His disciples, namely, as to when the Temple was to be destroyed, what was to be the sign of His coming, and of the end of the Age *(see v. 3)*. A similar, but by no means identical prophecy, is to be found in Luke 21. The main difference between them being that Luke 21 treats of conditions which obtained *prior* to the destruction of Jerusalem in A. D. 70—it is not until v. 25 that the Tribulation period is reached; whereas *the whole* of Matt. 24 is yet *future.*

It is striking to note that our Lord begins His prophecy by saying, "Take heed that no man deceive you, for many shall come in My name, saying I am Christ; and shall deceive many" *(vv. 4,5)*. The significance of this appears by comparing v. 11, "And many false prophets shall arise, and shall deceive many." These false christs and false prophets are to head up in *the* Antichrist and *the* False Prophet, who will be the arch-deceivers. When we reach v. 15 a clear allusion is made to the Man of Sin: "When ye therefore shall see the abomination of desolation, spoken of by Daniel the prophet, stand in the holy place, whoso readeth, let him understand." This reference of Christ to "the abomination of desolation" which is to "stand in the holy place," looks back to Dan. 12:11: "And from the time that the daily sacrifice shall be taken away, and the abomination that maketh desolate set up, there shall be a thousand two hundred and ninety days." This, in turn, carries us back to Dan. 9:27: "And in the midst of the week he shall cause the sacrifice and the oblation to cease, and for the overspreading of abominations he shall make it desolate." With these verses should be compared Rev. 13:11-15, where we are told that the False Prophet who shall perform great wonders, will command men that "they should make an image to the beast." The False Prophet will have "power to give life unto the image of the beast, that the image of the beast should both speak, and cause that as many as would not worship the beast should be killed." By linking these scriptures together the following facts are brought out:

First, an "image" is going to be made to the Antichrist *(Rev. 13:15)*. Second, this "image" will "stand in the holy place" *(Matt. 24:15)*, that is, in the re-built Temple at Jerusalem. Third, this "image" will possess supernatural power, for it shall be able to "speak" *(Rev. 13:15)*. Fourth, this "image" unto the beast shall be an object of worship, and those who refuse to worship it shall be killed *(Rev. 13:14, 15)*. Fifth, this "image" is termed by Christ "the abomination of desolation." The term "abomination" is an Old Testament expression connected with idolatry, and signifies some special idol or false god *(see Deut. 7:26; 1 Kings 11:5-7)*. Sixth, this "abomination" or idol-god will be set up during the middle of Daniel's seventieth week, or three and one half years from the end of Antichrist's career. This is clear from Dan. 12:11 and 9:27. The taking away of "the daily sacrifice" occurs when the Antichrist throws off his mask and stands forth as the Defier of heaven. In the re-built Temple of the Jews sacrifices shall once more be offered by them to God. These their King suffers, while he is posing as the Christ. But when he drops his religious pretensions and defies heaven as well as earth, the "sacrifices" will be taken away, and in their place worship to an image of himself will be substituted. Seventh, the setting up of this "image" to the Antichrist will, most probably, be attended with supernatural phenomenon. We gather this from Dan. 9:27, where we read, "And he shall cause the sacrifice and the oblation to cease, and for the overspreading of abominations he shall make it desolate." Now the word here translated "overspreading" is never so rendered elsewhere. Seventy times is this word translated "wing" or "wings." It is the word used of the wings of the cherubim in Ex. 25:20 and Ezek. 10:5, etc. And in Psa. 18:10 we read of Jehovah that "He rode upon a cherub, and did fly: yea, He did fly upon the wings of the wind."

One profound Hebrew scholar has rendered the last clause of Dan. 9:27 as follows, "And upon the wing of abominations he shall come desolating." Remembering that "abomination" has reference to an idol or false god, the force would then be "upon the wing of a false god shall he come desolating." Now in view of Psa. 18:10 it is highly probable that Dan. 9:27 refers to *a satanic imitation* of the Chariot of the Cherubim. This is strengthened by 1 Cor. 10:20—"The things which the Gentiles sacrifice, they sacrifice to *demons*, and not to God." Thus showing the demoniacal nature of the "idols" or "abominations" worshipped. If this view be correct, then the Antichrist will be supernaturally borne aloft (by invisible demons), and apparently descending from on high (in blasphemous mimicry of Mal. 3:1) will finally persuade the world to worship him as God. The apostate Jews will, no doubt, believe that their eyes at last behold the long-awaited sign from heaven, and the return of the Glory to the Temple. For it is thither the false christ will be borne, and there his image set up. We believe that the words of 2 Thess. 2:4, "He as God sitteth in the temple of God, *showing himself that HE IS GOD*" may, most likely, have reference to this same event.

Coming back now to the words of Christ, Matt. 24:15 will, we trust, be much more intelligible. What our Lord there said was designed specially for the godly Jewish remnant who will be in Palestine during the Tribulation period. When the "abomination of desolation" is set up in the holy place, whoso *readeth* should "understand." How wondrously this agrees with other scriptures, and what a value it places upon the written Word! No supernatural revelation will be granted —these all *ceased* when the Canon of Scripture closed. Then, as now, "understanding" is made dependent upon the *reading* of what God *has* revealed.

What, then, is it that those godly Jews should "understand"? Why, that a crisis has been reached. That the Antichrist now stands fully revealed for the impious impostor that he is. And now that his character is clearly manifested, let them beware. Let them turn to Rev. 13:14, 15, and they will discover that *death* awaits them should they tarry any longer in Jerusalem. Therefore, says Christ, "Let them which be in Judea flee into the mountains: let him that is on the housetop not come down to take anything out of his house . . . . for then shall be great tribulation, such as was not since the beginning of the world to this time, no, nor ever shall be" *(Matt. 24: 16-21)*. How marvellously one scripture throws light on another! How clearly does Rev. 13:14, 15 explain the need for this hurried flight of the faithful remnant!

There is one other reference to the Antichrist in this 24th chapter of Matthew, namely, in vv. 23-26: "Then if any man shall say unto you, Lo, here is Christ, or there; believe it not. For there shall arise false christs, and false prophets, and shall show great signs and wonders; insomuch that, if it were possible, they shall deceive the very elect. Behold, I have told you before. Wherefore if they shall say unto you, Behold, *he* is in the desert; go not forth: behold, *he* is in the secret chamber; believe it not." The reference to the "great signs and wonders" is explained, at least in part, in Rev. 13. We have already seen that the False Prophet will have power to give "life" or "breath" unto the image of the Beast, so that the image shall speak *(v. 15)*. In addition, it is recorded how that "He doeth great wonders, so that he maketh fire come down from heaven on the earth in the sight of men, and deceiveth them that dwell on the earth by those miracles which he had power to do in the sight of the beast" *(vv. 14, 14)*.

We had hoped to be able to say something further on the "secret chambers" of Matt. 24:26, but in the absence of any clear light from other scriptures, we refrain from speculations of our own. It seems plain, however, that the reference is to the *occult* powers and activities of the Wicked One, who ever loveth darkness rather than light.

3. Our next passage will be the first eight verses of Luke 18, where in a parable the Lord gives us another view of the Antichrist: "And He spake a parable unto them, that men ought always to pray, and not to faint; Saying, There was in a city a judge, which feared not God, neither regarded man: And there was a widow in that city; and she came unto Him, saying, Avenge me of mine adversary. And he would not for awhile: but afterward he said within himself, Though

I fear not God, nor regard man; yet because this woman troubleth me, I will avenge her, lest by her continual coming she weary me. And the Lord said, Hear what the unjust judge saith. And shall not God avenge His own elect, which cry day and night unto Him, though He bear long with them? I tell you that He will avenge them speedily. Nevertheless when the Son of Man cometh, shall He find faith on the earth?"

Like many of Christ's parables, this one is plainly prophetic in its character. It looks forward to a coming day: it treats of conditions which are to obtain during the Tribulation period. This is easily seen from the context. Luke 18 opens with the word "and," and the last eighteen verses of the previous chapter, with which the 18th is thus connected, treat of those things which are to immediately precede the establishing of the Messiah's Kingdom —note particularly v. 26. So, too, the closing words of the parable now before us read, "When the Son of Man *cometh*, shall He find faith on the earth?"

Having thus pointed out the time when this prophetic parable is to receive its fulfillment, our next concern is to ascertain the significance of its terms. The parable revolves around a "widow" and an "unjust judge." Once we discover *who* are represented by these, everything will be simple. Our task ought not to be difficult seeing that we have already learned the time when these characters are to appear.

The "widow" in Scripture is ever the figure of desolation, loneliness, weakness. Dispensationally, *Israel* is the widow, spiritually dead as she now is to her Divine Husband. Here in the parable of Luke 18 it is the new Israel, the "Israel of God," the faithful remnant, which is in view. To quote one scripture is sufficient to establish this: "Fear not; for thou shalt not be ashamed: neither be thou confounded; for thou shalt not be put to shame: for thou shalt forget the shame of thy youth, and shalt not remember the reproach of *thy widowhood* any more. For thy Maker is thine Husband; the Lord of Hosts is His name; and thy Redeemer the Holy One of Israel; the God of the whole earth shall He be called. For the Lord hath called thee as *a widow* forsaken and grieved in spirit, and a wife of youth, when thou wast refused, saith thy God. For a small moment have I forsaken thee; but with great mercy shall I gather thee" *(Isa. 54: 4-7)*. These are the words which Christ will speak to the remnant right at the beginning of the Millennium, after they have made Isa. 53 their own repentant confession.

In our article on the Antichrist in the Psalms attention was repeatedly directed to passages which treat of the condition of the godly Jewish remnant during the Tribulation period. We saw that their lot is to be a bitter one. Severe will be their testings; terrible their sufferings. Not the least painful of their experiences will be the fierce opposition of their unbelieving brethren. Just as the worst enemies of the Saviour were found among His brethren according to the flesh, and just as the most relentless persecutors of the saints during this dispensation have been those who professed to be the followers of Christ, so the most merciless foes of the Jewish remnant will be the unbelieving portion of their own nation. These, too, are noticed in our parable: *they* are the "adversary" against which the "widow" appeals to the "Judge"—"Avenge me of mine adversary" is her plea.

In the light of what has been said above it is easy to discover who is represented by the one to whom the "widow" appeals—appeals no doubt some little time before the end of the Tribulation period is reached. Clearly it is the Antichrist himself, and what is here said of him establishes this beyond a reasonable doubt. First, he is termed "a Judge," so that he is viewed as being in the position of *authority:* we may add, it is the same word as rendered "Judge" in James 5:9 which speaks of the Lord Jesus. Second, he is represented as being located in a certain "city": whether this is Jerusalem or Babylon, we cannot say; but we rather think it is the latter. In the third place, it is said of this Judge that he "feared not God, neither regarded man." We need not tarry to point out how fully this accords with what is elsewhere said of the Man of Sin. Godlessness and lawlessness are the two most prominent elements in his character. In the fourth place, the Lord specifically terms him "the *unjust Judge*" *(v. 6)*. The word signifies "unrighteousness." This word points an antithesis between him and the true Christ who shall reign in righteousness. In the fifth place, his *callousness* is noted in the words "and he would not for awhile" *(v. 4)*. The Greek verb of v. 3 signifies that the widow came to this "Judge" again and again. But in his hard-heartedness he repeatedly turned a deaf ear to her entreaties. Such will be the brutal indifference of the Antichrist to the sufferings of the faithful Jews. In the sixth place, his *untruthfulness* and *treachery* are clearly implied. In v. 5 this unjust Judge is represented as saying, "Because this widow troubleth me, I will avenge her," etc.; but that he fails to keep his word is clear from what we read in the seventh verse—"Shall not *God avenge* His own elect?" etc. The Antichrist does not avenge him, but God will. Finally, his *doom* is hinted at in the words last quoted. When God "avenges" the elect remnant the Antichrist will be destroyed together with those of his followers who had persecuted them.

There is only one difficulty in the way of the above interpretation and that is the appeal of the Jewish remnant *to the Antichrist.* Can it be possible that they should seek help from him! But is there any real difficulty in this? Let us consult our own experience for answer. How often, in the hour of trial, do *we* turn to the arm of flesh for relief! Even the Apostle Paul appealed to Cæsar! But lest this be thought an invention of ours to meet a pertinent objection against the interpretation advanced above, note carefully the wording of the seventh verse: "And shall not God avenge His own elect, which cry day and night unto Him, *though He bear long with them?*" Do not the words "bear long with them" intimate that though they had cried unto God day and night, yet they had *also* sought help from some one else. Even clearer is the testimony of Isa. 10:20—"And it shall come to pass in that day that the remnant of Israel and such as are escaped of the house of Jacob, shall *no more* again *stay upon him that smote them;* but shall stay upon the Lord"!

4. "I am come in My Father's name, and ye receive Me not: if another shall come in his own name, him ye will receive" *(John 5:43).* This scripture has already been before us (see article in July issue I 5) so it need not detain us long. It speaks of the Antichrist in connection with unbelieving Israel. It draws a double contrast between the Son of God and the Son of Perdition. The Christ of God, in lowly condescension, came not in His own name, but in that of His Father—in perfect subjection; but the christ of Satan, in lofty arrogance, shall come in his own name. This will at once appeal to the corrupt hearts of fallen men. The very meekness of the Lord Jesus was an offense to the Jews; but the pride and egotism of the Man of Sin will make him acceptable to them. By the apostate Nation Christ was not received. As we read in this same Gospel, "He came unto His own, and His own received Him not" *(1:11).* But the Antichrist shall be welcomed by them—*"Him* ye *will* receive," says the

Lord. They will receive him as their long-expected Messiah. They will receive him as their King. They will receive him as the promised Deliverer. His yoke will be accepted. Divine honors will be paid him. But bitterly will they rue it; and terrible will be God's judgment upon them.

5. "Ye are of your father the Devil, and the lusts of your father ye will do. He was a murderer from the beginning, and abode not in the truth, because there is no truth in him. When he speaketh the Lie, he speaketh of his own (son): for he is a liar, and the father of it" *(John 8:44)*. The Greek word for "lie" is "pseudos." It occurs in the New Testament just nine times—the number of *judgment*. It always has reference to that which is opposed to the truth. It is a fit appellation for the Antichrist, who is the son of him who is the Arch-liar, the Devil. The Christ of God is "The Truth;" the christ of Satan, "The Lie." That this is one of the many names of the Man of Sin is clear from 2 Thess. 2. There we are told that his coming is "after the working of Satan with all power and signs and lying wonders and with all deceivableness of unrighteousness in them that perish; because they received not the love of the truth, that they might be saved." Then we are told, "And for this cause God shall send them strong delusion that they should believe the Lie (cf. the July 1922 article, II 5).

Upon John 8:44 we cannot do better than quote from Sir Robert Anderson: "'To speak a lie' is not English. In our language the proper expression is 'to tell a lie.' But no one would so render the Greek words here. It is not the false in the abstract which is in view, but a concrete instance of it. And thus the connection is clear between Satan the liar and Satan the murderer. He is not the instigator of all murders, but of *the* murder, there and then in question, the murder of the Christ; he is not the father of *lies*, but the father of *the* Lie. In 2 Thess. 2:11 it is again *the* Lie of John 8:44. God does not incite men to tell lies or to believe lies. But of those who reject '*the* truth,' it is written, 'He shall send them strong delusion that they should believe *the* Lie.' Because they have rejected the Christ of God, a judicial blindness shall fall upon them that they should accept the Christ of humanity, who will be Satan incarnate" (The Silence of God).

6. "While I was with them in the world, I kept them in Thy name: those that Thou gavest Me I have kept, and none of them is lost, but the Son of Perdition; that the Scripture might be fulfilled" *(John 17:5)*. That our Lord was referring to the Antichrist is unequivocally established by 2 Thess. 2:3, where the Man of Sin is denominated "the Son of Perdition." That Judas, here termed the Son of Perdition, was more than a man is clear from John 6:70 where we read, "Have not I chosen you twelve, and one of you is a Devil?" In no other passage is the word "Diabolos" applied to anyone but Satan himself. Just as the Lord Jesus was God incarnate, so will Judas be the Devil incarnate; and, as we have shown in our July article (third main section) Judas will be reincarnated in the Antichrist.

Perhaps one other word should be said on John 17:12 before we pass from it. Some have thought that this verse weakens the doctrine of the absolute security of the saints, but in fact it does nothing of the kind. Notice Christ did not say, "Those that Thou gavest Me I have kept, and none of them is lost *except* the Son of Perdition," instead, He said, "None of them is lost *but* the Son of Perdition." The word "but" is used adversatively, not exceptively; that is to say, Judas is here *opposed to* those that were given to Christ (for other scriptures with a similar construction see Matt. 12:4, Acts 27:22, Rev. 21:27). This interpretation is unequivocally established by John 18:

9—"Of them which Thou gavest Me have I lost *none*."

7. 2 Thess. 2 contains the chief passage in the Epistles concerning the Antichrist. Here he is denominated "that Man of Sin, the Son of Perdition" *(v. 3)*. It is solemnly true that all men are sinners *(Rom. 3:23)*, but the Antichrist will be more than a sinner, he will be the Man *of Sin*. As such he will be the direct opposite of Christ, who was the *Holy One* of God. Sin in all its terrible satanic treachery, daring blasphemy, and tremendous appeal to the corrupt hearts of men, will be consummated in this frightful monster. For fuller notes on the force of these titles we again refer the reader to the fourth article of this series, section II.

Concerning the Man of Sin it is said, "Who opposeth and exalteth himself above all that is called God, or that is worshipped; so that he as God sitteth in the temple of God, showing himself that he is God" *(v. 4)*. Here he reaches the climax of his frightful blasphemy. He will assume Divine honors, and under pain of death *(Rev. 13:15)* will d - mand the worship of all. In vindication of his impious claims he will compel men to regard his mandates as transcending all laws and customs, whether of human or Divine origin *(Dan. 7:25)*. For a season the Almighty will suffer his satanic impiety, the Hinderer having been taken out of the way *(v. 7)*. No lightning flash will strike down his blasted form to the dust. The earth will not open her mouth to swallow him up alive. The Angel of the Lord, who smote Herod with death for a much milder blasphemy, will restrain His hand from the hilt of the sword. For a season Heaven will remain silent while this haughty rebel is doing according to his will. But at the appointed hour "the Lord shall consume (him) with the spirit of His mouth, and shall destroy with the brightness of His coming" *(v. 8)*.

"Even him whose coming is after the working of Satan with all power and signs and lying wonders" *(v. 9)*. The Antichrist will be the culmination and consummation of Satan's craft and genius. He will be endowed with super-human energy so that he shall perform miracles which will be no mere pretenses, but prodigies of power. By means of these miracles and signs he will deceive the entire world. No doubt he will mock the miracles of Christ, as of old Jannes and Jambres duplicated the miracles of Moses. His marvelous deeds will reach their climax in his own resurrection from the dead.

8. "Who is a liar but he that denieth that Jesus is the Christ? He is antichrist, that denieth the Father and the Son" *(1 John 2:22)*. For our comments on the significance of this name "the Antichrist" we refer our readers to the fourth article of this series. There it will be seen that we understand this official title to have a double significance, corresponding to the two main divisions in his career. First, he will pose as the true Christ; later he will stand forth as the avowed opponent of Christ. The above verse presents him as the Arch-apostate. He will, eventually, repudiate the distinguishing truth of *Judaism*, namely, that "Jesus is the Christ;" as he will also set himself against that which is vital in *Christianity*—the revelation of "the Fa- er and the Son."

9. A brief word upon 1 John 4:3 and we must conclude. "And every spirit that confesseth not that Jesus Christ is come in the flesh is not of God: and this is that spirit of Antichrist, whereof ye have heard that it should come; and even now already is it in the world." It is to the last clause we would here direct attention. The spirit of Antichrist, that which is preparing the way for his appearing is even now already "in the world." This statement is parallel with 2 Thess. 2: 7, "For the mystery of iniquity *doth already work:* only He who now letteth

(hindereth) will let, until He be taken out of the way." The Mystery of Iniquity, which concerns the incarnation of Satan, is the direct antithesis of "the Mystery of Godliness" *(1 Tim. 3:16)* which has to do with the Divine incarnation. Just as there was a long preparation by God preceding the advent of His Son, so the Devil is now paving the way for the advent of the Son of Perdition. The Mystery of Iniquity "doth *already* work;" so in 1 John 4:3 of the spirit of Antichrist we read, "Even now *already* is it in the world"! How far advanced the preparations of Satan now are for the bringing forth of his Masterpiece is becoming increasingly evident to those who are granted wisdom to discern the signs of the times. In our next article we shall, D. V., consider the Antichrist in the Apocalypse.—*Arthur W. Pink*.

EXPOSITION OF PETER

II.—OF THE ACKNOWLEDGMENT OF THESE BLESSINGS.

The devout acknowledgment of these blessings comes now to be considered: "Blessed be the God and Father of our Lord and Saviour Jesus Christ, which, according to his abundant mercy, hath begotten us again unto a lively hope, by the resurrection of Jesus Christ from the dead, to an inheritance incorruptible, and undefiled, and that fadeth not away, reserved in heaven for you, who are kept by the power of God through faith unto salvation, ready to be revealed in the last time." This devout acknowledgment naturally leads the mind to reflect on God as the author of these blessings—on the character in which he bestows them, "the God and Father of our Lord and Saviour Jesus Christ,"—on the principle in which the bestowal of these blessings originates, "abundant mercy"—on their vast magnitude and inestimable value—and on the proper manner of Christians expressing their sense of this magnitude and value.

1.—*God is the author of these blessings.*

The first remark suggested by this devout acknowledgment is, that God is the author of the blessings acknowledged. This is not only implied in making the acknowledgment—for when we return thanks for a favor, to whom do we offer our acknowledgment but to him who has bestowed it?—but it is distinctly expressed: God has begotten us again. God has provided us an inheritance. God has given us a living hope.

God is the author of all good. All the holiness and all the happiness in the universe come from him. "Every good gift and every perfect gift is from above, and cometh down from the Father of lights." In the new creation, "All things are of God."[1] The blessings enjoyed by Christians are all the free gifts of his sovereign goodness. He makes us his children. He brings us into the relation of children. He forms us to the character of children. When we are brought into the relation of children, our sins are forgiven, and we are justified freely by God's grace. But "who can forgive sins, but God only?" "It is God that justifieth."[2] The sentence of the law can be remitted only by the great Lawgiver. The privilege of being the sons of God can be conferred by none but God. As it is God who brings us into the relation of children, it is God who forms us to the character of children. "For we are His workmanship, created anew in Christ Jesus." It is God who, by the agency of his own Spirit, through the instrumentality of his own word understood

[1] James i. 17. 2 Cor. v. 18.
[2] Mark ii. 7. Rom. viii. 33.

and believed, transforms the character of a condemned felonious slave into that of a beloved and dutiful child. It is HE who takes "the hard and the stony heart out of our flesh, and gives us a heart of flesh." It is HE who disposes us to venerate, and esteem, and love, and trust him. It is HE who enables us cheerfully to obey his commandments, and submit to his appointments. It is HE who sends forth his Spirit into our hearts, teaching us to cry, "Abba, Father."¹

As it is God who makes us his children, bringing us into the filial relation, forming us to the filial character, so it is God who has provided, and who will bestow on his people, the inheritance corresponding to the relation into which he has brought them, and the character to which He has formed them. "It is the FATHER's good pleasure to give them the kingdom." The final happiness of the saints is entirely the result of DIVINE love, and wisdom, and power. "Eternal life is the gift of God."² God himself is, indeed, if I may use the expression, the very substance of the celestial blessedness. To know him—to see him as he is—to find in him the adequate object of all our unbounded capacities of knowledge, and affection, and enjoyment—to love him, and to be loved by him, and to know that we are loved by him—to be like him, having no mind different from his, no will opposed to his—to enter into his joy, and thus to have our joy made full—this is the inheritance; and who can thus give us God, but God himself?

And all that was necessary, in order to make the communication of such a happiness to such creatures as we are—guilty, righteously condemned—consistent with the honor of the divine character; and all that is necessary to make such depraved creatures as we are, capable of such a happiness, is the work, not of men nor of angels, but of God. His love originated the purpose—his wisdom formed the plan—his power will work out the accomplishment, of his people's salvation.

As the inheritance is his gift, so also is the hope of the inheritance. It is God who gives us the living hope. The ground of that hope is HIS sovereign kindness—that kindness is displayed in harmony with righteousness, in HIS giving HIS Son to be the propitiation for the sins of men. This display of his sovereign kindness is made in HIS revelation of HIS will by "holy men who spoke as they were moved by HIS Spirit;" and this revelation, in the belief of which alone the condemned sinner can find hope, is understood and believed by the individual sinner, in consequence of the effectual working of HIS Spirit. It was HE who "delivered his Son for our offences." It was HE who "raised him again for our justification." It is He who disposes us to believe this revelation of mercy. It is HE who thus gives us "good hope through grace." Every measure of the living hope, from the faint dawn which opens on the mind of the sinner coming to the knowledge of the truth, to the clear unclouded radiance which enlightens the mind of him who has received "the full assurance of understanding," every measure of this living hope is the gift of God; and we end as we began the illustration of this particular with the sublime declaration of the apostle respecting the new creation, "All things are of God." "Of HIM, and through him, and to him, are all things." "God is all in all."³

§ 2.—*It is as the God and Father of our Lord Jesus Christ, that God bestows these blessings.*

The second remark suggested by this devout acknowledgment is, that in bestowing the favors here acknowledged,

---

¹ Eph. ii. 10. Ezek. xi. 19. Gal. iv. 6.
² Luke xii. 32. Rom. vi. 23.

³ Rom. iv. 25. 2 Thess. ii. 16. 2 Cor. v. 18. Rom. xi. 36. 1 Cor. xv. 28.

God acts in the character of "the God and Father of our Lord Jesus Christ." God is infinitely holy, and cannot but disapprove sin—cannot but loathe and abhor it in a degree of which we can form no adequate conception. God is inflexibly just, and can "by no means clear the guilty." He is "not a God that hath pleasure in wickedness, neither shall evil dwell with him. The foolish shall not stand in his sight; and he hates the workers of iniquity." "Snares, fire and brimstone, and a furious tempest will he rain on the wicked; this pertains to them as a portion of their cup."[1] How is it then, that this holy and righteous God blesses sinful men with all heavenly and spiritual blessings? How is it that he makes *them* his children; gives them a heavenly inheritance, and cheers them with a living hope?

It is as "the God and Father of our Lord Jesus Christ," that he does all this. In the riches of his sovereign mercy he determined to save an innumerable multitude of sinful men, and in the depth of his wisdom he formed a plan for realizing the determination of his mercy, not merely in consistency with, but in glorious illustration of, his holiness and justice. The leading feature in that plan is, the appointment of his only begotten Son to be the representative of those who were to be saved, to be dealt with as they deserved to be dealt with, that they might be dealt with as he deserved to be dealt with. The second person of the glorious Trinity is essentially his Father's equal—possessed of the same divine essence and perfections; but in this assumed character he is the Father's inferior; he acts a subordinate part in the economy of salvation. God, essentially considered, in the person of the Father, is the God of "the Mediator between God and men;" and he is his Father, not merely essentially, as he is the second person of the Trinity, but also economically, as he is the head of the chosen family—"the first-born among many brethren."

The great truth intended to be taught us by God being represented as the author of spiritual blessings to men, in the character of the God and Father of our Lord Jesus Christ, is this—that it is only as viewed in connection with him; or, as the inspired writers usually express it, as "in him," that we sinners can obtain any saving blessing from God. The order is, "all things are ours, we are Christ's, Christ is God's." He is our God because he is his God, our Father because he is his Father.[2] Take the blessings mentioned in the text as an illustration. God makes us his children, that is, he pardons our sins, he receives us into his favor, he conforms us to his image. Now, how does he do this? He gives "us redemption in Christ, the forgiveness of sins." He makes us "accepted in the beloved." "We are his workmanship, created anew in Christ Jesus unto good works." He gives us an inheritance. How? in Christ. "In him," says the apostle, "we have obtained an inheritance." He makes us to "sit in heavenly places in him."[3] He gives us a living hope. How? While "without Christ," viewed as unconnected with Christ, there is no hope for man; all his well-grounded expectations of happiness must be founded on what Christ has done, and is doing, as the representative of his people. While in the new creation, all things are "of God," all things are "through Christ Jesus." It is as well pleased with Him, that God is well pleased with us; and it is as his God and Father, that he blesses us "with all heavenly and spiritual blessings in him."

3.—*These blessings originate in the "abundant mercy" of God.*

The third remark suggested by this

---

[1] Exod xxxiv. 7. Psal. v. 4, 5; xi. 6.
[2] 2 Cor. iii. 22, 23. John xx. 17.
[3] Eph. i. 3-13.

devout acknowledgment is, that in the bestowing of these blessings on us by God, there is a remarkable display of the divine benignity. It is "according to his abundant mercy, that he begets us again unto a lively hope, by the resurrection of Jesus Christ from the dead, to an inheritance incorruptible, and undefiled, and that fadeth not away, reserved in heaven for you, who are kept by the power of God through faith unto salvation; ready to be revealed in the last time." This remark invites us into a very wide field of most interesting and improving illustration; but I must satisfy myself with merely opening to you a few tracks of thought, which you will do well to pursue in private meditation.

Think on the character of him who bestows these blessings,—the absolute, independent Jehovah, perfectly, infinitely, unchangeably happy in himself. How could the self-incurred ruin of guilty mankind affect his interest? It might illustrate his holiness, his righteousness, his faithfulness, but how could it disturb his peace, or lessen his blessedness? It is impossible to conceive the communication of saving blessings to man, to originate in any principle in the divine mind but sovereign benignity. If man is saved, it is "only because God had a delight in him to love him."

Think on the nature of the blessings, —the very highest which can be conferred on creatures, the noblest in their own nature, and in their measure limited by nothing but the capacity of the recipient. "Behold, what manner of love" is this,[1] to be God's sons, to see him as he is, to be like him, and all this forever and ever!

Think on the character of those on whom they are bestowed,—sinners, guilty, depraved, righteously condemned; deserving everlasting destruction; in the state in which mercy finds them, forgetters, haters, contemners of God. Surely the mercy which confers such blessings on such sinners is abundant mercy, and the apostle may well say, "Behold what manner of love the Father hath bestowed on us, that we should be called the sons of God."

Think of the number of those on whom these blessings are bestowed,— "the nations of the saved" are a numerous host.[2] The sons who are to be brought to glory are "many sons." They are "a great multitude, an innumerable company, out of every kindred, and people, and tongue, and nation;" and all these are blessed up to their largest capacity of enjoyment, during the whole eternity of their being. Is not this abundant mercy?

Once more, think of the means through which the blessings are communicated,—the incarnation, the sacrifice of God's own Son. He did not spare him, he delivered him up for us all, that he with him might freely give us all things. "Herein surely is love, not that we loved God but that God loved us, and sent his Son to be the propitiation for our sins." "God so loved the world, that he gave his only begotten Son, that whosoever believeth in him might not perish, but have everlasting life."[3]

Surely it is in his "abundant mercy" that "God, even the Father of our Lord Jesus Christ, has blessed us with all heavenly and spiritual blessings."

---

[1] 1 John iii. 1.
[2] Rev. xxi. 24; vii. 9.
[3] 1 John iv. 10. John iii. 16.

(Continued from page 97.)

work which was given Him to do, the counsels of the Godhead, could be accomplished fully by Him *dying*.

It will thus be seen that the death of Christ was far more than a brutal murder. And, too, the death of the Saviour was more than a *passive suffering* at the hands of wicked men. Every member of Adam's fallen race who has passed out of this world into the next was *passive* in death. Even the suicide is no exception. However he may plan his death, and whatever means he may employ to end his life, in death itself he is passive. It could not be otherwise. When the king of terrors lays his clammy hand upon him, no man can successfully resist. Neither will-power, wealth, the skill of science, nor the ministrations of loved ones can cope with death. Man, then, is passive, helpless, impotent, when death gathers him into his cold embrace. But it was far otherwise with the Prince of life. In death He was *active*, not passive; the *Victor*, not the victim.

Herein lies the uniqueness (in part, at least) of the death of the God-man. First, He was born to die. He had received "commandment" from His Father to die *(John 10:18)*, and thus He "became *obedient* unto death, even the death of the Cross" *(Phil. 2:8)*. To Christ death was a *duty*, His official duty, His mediatorial duty, His priestly duty. Second, at Calvary, He not only "suffered" at the hands of men, but He "*offered Himself* without spot to God" *(Heb. 9:14)*. Many are the scriptures which prove this. He "*laid down* His life" *(John 10:18)*. He "*gave Himself*" for the Church *(Eph. 5:25)*. He "*poured out* His soul unto death" *(Isa. 53:12)*. He "*dismissed* (Gk.) His spirit" *(Matt. 27:50)*.

Herein lies both the *uniqueness* of His death and the *glory* of the Cross. The Cross was the place of a *glorious victory*—a victory over the weakness of sinless flesh, over the agonies of suffering, over the worst that men and Satan could do. When we think of the *extent* and *awful intensity* of the sufferings which Christ endured, it will at once be apparent that those sufferings would have overpowered all the *active* powers of any but a Divine person. And yet, *after* all the suffering was over, Christ was in full and unimpaired possession of all His faculties—the "loud voice", the head erect till "bowed", demonstrate that. It is evident, then, that "no man" was able to take His life from Him *(John 10:18)*. Christ was not victimized by death, but was victorious over "him that had the power of death, that is, the Devil" *(Heb. 2:14)*.

Christ died, not from a broken heart, not from the spear-thrust of the Roman soldier, not from the "bruising" of the Serpent, but, because He "laid down His life." And it was a stupendous marvel, a miracle of miracles, for the Prince of life to *die*. Surely, it was far more wonderful that Immanuel should die, than that *He* should rise again. It "was not possible" that death should hold *Him* *(Acts 2:24)*, but how marvellous that HE *should enter* the realm of death! He could only enter it by an act of His own volition. And we repeat, herein lies the *glory* of the Cross *(Gal. 6:14)*. In any other event we should have cause to be ashamed of our Master. If He died merely as a passive and helpless sufferer, then no subsequent glory could redeem His previous defeat. But He did not so die. He was triumphant *in* death, and the resurrection was simply *the coming forth of* the Mighty Victor. The Cross is glorious not because of the subsequent resurrection and enthronement, but in *itself*. Let us remember it is "Christ crucified", not Christ risen, who is said to be "the power of God" *(1 Cor. 1:23, 24)*. And nowhere was the *power* of God more evident; nowhere was the *power* of God more gloriously displayed, than at the Cross, when the Son of God "laid down *His* life". And let us not forget that when, in the Revelation, we first see all heaven moved to profoundest praise, it is not at the appearing of the King of kings crowned with many diadems, but at the sight of the "Lamb" standing "*as it had been slain*" *(Rev. 5:6, 12)*!

May the fruit of this little article be, that all who read it shall exclaim with ever-deepening wonderment and praise, "God forbid that I should glory, save in *the Cross* of our Lord Jesus Christ" *(Gal. 6:14)*.

—Arthur W. Pink.

VOL. II   MAY, 1923   NO. 5

STUDIES in the SCRIPTURES

"Search the Scriptures" John 5:39.

A PERIODICAL (MONTHLY "IF THE LORD WILL")
DEVOTED TO BIBLE STUDIES and EXPOSITIONS

Associate Editors and Publishers, I. C. HERENDEEN and ARTHUR W. PINK,
Swengel, Pa.

Price: 10 cents per copy; $1.00 per year. Foreign $1.00 per year.

TO OUR SCRIPTURE STUDY FAMILY

"O wretched man that I am! who shall deliver me from the body of this death?" (Rom. 7:24).

This is the language of a regenerate soul. The unregenerate man is wretched indeed, but he is a stranger to the wretchedness *here expressed,* for he knows nothing of the experience which evokes this wail. The whole context is devoted to a description of the *conflict* between the two natures in the child of God. "I *delight* in the Law of God after the inward man" (v. 22), is true of none but born again persons. But the one thus "delighting", discovers "another law in his members": this reference must not be limited to his physical members, but is to be understood as including all the various parts of his carnal personality. This "other law" is discoverable in the memory, the imagination, the will, the heart, etc.

This "other law", says the apostle, *warred against* the law of his mind (the new nature), and not only so, it brought him "into captivity to the law of sin" (v. 23). To what *extent* he was brought into "captivity" is not defined. But brought into captivity he was, as is every believer. The wandering of the mind when reading God's Word, the issuing from the heart (Mark 7:21) of evil thoughts when we are engaged in prayer, the horrible images which sometimes come before us in the sleep-state—to name no others—are so many examples of being "brought into captivity to the Law of Sin". "If the evil principle of our nature prevails in exciting one evil thought, it has taken us captive So far it has conquered, and so far are we defeated, and made a prisoner" (Robert Haldane).

It is the consciousness of this *warring* within him and this being brought into captivity to sin, which causes the believer to exclaim, "O wretched man that I am"! This is a cry brought about by a deep realization of indwelling sin. It is the confession of one who *knows* that in his natural man there dwelleth no good thing. It is the mournful plaint of one who has discovered something of the horrible sink of iniquity which is in his own heart. It is the groan of a Divinely-enlightened man who now hates himself—his natural self—and longs for deliverance.

Nor is this only the experience of a back-slidden Christian. The one who is truly *in communion* with Christ will also emit this groan, and emit it daily and hourly. Yea, the closer he draws to Christ, the more will he discover the corruptions of his old nature, and the more earnestly will he long

(Continued on page 160.)

IMPORTANT NOTICES

All new subscriptions will be dated back to January, 1923.

Set of twelve issues for **1922**, unbound, $1.00. Bound, $1.50.

Note: We cannot break a set or now supply any **single** 1922 issues.

Subscription Price: $1.00 per year to any address in the world. Single copies 10 cents.

Change of Address: Please notify us promptly of any change of address, and be certain to give both old and new addresses.

Non-Subscribers receiving this Magazine regularly will understand their subscription has been entered by a friend.

Copies lost in the mail duplicated only if we are notified Promptly.

Entered as second-class matter December 15th, 1921 at the post office at Swengel, Pa., under Act of March 3rd, 1879.

CONTENTS

John's Gospel (John 5:1-15) 130
Antichrist in the Apocalypse 139
The Law and the Saint 148
Exposition of First Peter 155

JOHN'S GOSPEL

17. Christ at the Pool of Bethesda, John 5:1-15

We begin with the usual Analysis:—

1. Jesus in Jerusalem at the feast. v. 1
2. The pool of Bethesda and the sick congregated about it, vv. 2-4
3. The impotent man and Christ's healing of him, vv. 5-9
4. The healed man and his critics, vv. 10-12
5. The man's ignorance, v. 13
6. Christ's final word with him, v. 14
7. The man confesses Jesus, v. 15

In the passage before us we are brought once more onto strictly Jewish ground, and again we are shown the terrible spiritual state of Israel at the time the Lord Jesus was here upon earth. The scene introduced to us is indeed a pathetic one. The background is the pool of Bethesda, around which lay a great multitude of impotent folk. The great Physician approaches this crowd of sufferers, who were not only sick but helpless. But there was no more stir among them than in the quiet waters of the Pool. *He* was neither wanted nor recognized. Addressing one of the most helpless of the sufferers, the Lord asks him if he is desirous of being made whole. Instead of responding to the sympathetic Inquirer with a prompt request that He would have mercy upon him, the poor fellow thought only of the pool and of some man to help him into it. In sovereign grace the Saviour spoke the life-giving word, and the man was immediately and perfectly healed. Yet even then he was still ignorant of the Divine glory of his Benefactor. The healing took place on the Sabbath day, and this evoked the criticism of the Jews; and when they learned that it was Jesus who had performed the miracle "they sought to slay Him". All of this speaks loudly of the condition of Judaism, and tells of the rejection of the Christ of God.

"After this there was a feast of the Jews" (v. 1). "After this" or, as it should be, "After these things", is an expression which is as characteristic of John's Gospel as "Then" is of Matthew, "Immediately" of Mark, and "It came to pass" of Luke. It occurs seven times in this Gospel (3:22; 5:1; 5:14; 6:1; 7:1; 11:11; 21:1) and nine times in the Apocalypse. "It gives one the thought of Jesus acting according to a plan and times marked out 'in the volume of the Book' (Psa. 40:7) and of which He renders an account in John 17" (M. Taylor).

"After this there was a feast of the Jews; and Jesus went up to Jerusalem" (v. 1). There is nothing to indicate which of the Feasts this was. Some think it was the Passover, but this we believe is most unlikely, for when *that* feast is referred to in John it is expressly mentioned by name: see 2:13;

6:4; 11:55. Others think it was the feast of Purim, but as that was a human invention and not of Divine institution we can hardly imagine the Lord Jesus going up to Jerusalem to observe it. Personally we think it much more likely that the view of almost all the older writers is the correct one, and that it was the feast of Pentecost which is here in view. Pentecost occurred fifty days after the Passover, and the feast mentioned in John 5:1 follows the Passover mentioned in 2:13. Pentecost is one of the three great annual Feasts which the law required every male Israelite to observe in Jerusalem (Deut. 16), and here we see the Lord Jesus honoring the Divine Law by going up to Jerusalem at the season of its celebration. Doubtless there was a typical reason why the name of this feast should not be given here, for that to which the feast of Pentecost pointed received no fulfillment in the days of our Lord's earthly ministry—contrast Acts 2:1.

"Now there is at Jerusalem by the sheep market a pool, which is called in the Hebrew tongue Bethesda, having five porches" (v. 2). We believe the reference here is to the sheep "gate" of Neh. 3:1. At first glance Neh. 3 does not seem to be very interesting reading, and yet there is much in it that is precious. It describes the rebuilding of the walls of Jerusalem in the days when a remnant of Israel returned from the Babylonian captivity. Various portions in the work of reconstruction were allotted to different individuals and companies. These portions or sections were from gate to gate. Ten gates are mentioned in the chapter. The first is the sheep gate (v. 1) and the last is "The gate Miphkad" which means "judgment", and speaks, perhaps, of the judgment-seat of Christ; and then the chapter concludes by saying, "And between the going up of the corner *unto the sheep gate* repaired the goldsmiths and the merchants". Thus the circle is completed, and at the close we are brought back to the point from which we started—"The *sheep* gate". This is the gate through which the sacrificial animals were brought to the temple—the "lamb" predominating, hence its name. The sheep gate, then, points us at once to Christ, and tells of His Cross.

Now in the light of what we have just said, how exceedingly significant and blessed to note that we are here told the Pool which was called Bethesda, meaning *mercy*, was by the "sheep" (gate). It is only in Christ that the poor sinner can find mercy, and it is only through His sacrifice on the Cross that this mercy is now obtainable for us in Him. What an instance is this of the great importance of noting carefully every little word in Scripture! There is nothing trivial in the Word of God. The smallest detail has a meaning and value; every name, every geographical and topographical reference, a message. As a further example of this, notice the last words of the verse—"having five porches". The number of the porches here is also significant. In Scripture the numerals are used with Divine design and precision. Five stands for *grace* or *favor*. When Joseph desired to show special favor to his brother Benjamin we read, "And he took and sent messes unto them from before him: but Benjamin's mess was *five* times so much as any of theirs" (Gen. 43:34); and again we are told, "To all of them he gave each man changes of raiment; but to Benjamin he gave three hundred pieces of silver, and *five* changes of raiment" (Gen. 45:22). *Five* and its multiples are stamped on every part of the tabernacle. It was with *five* loaves the Lord Jesus fed the hungry multitude. The *fifth* clause in the Lord's prayer is, "*Give* us this day our daily bread". The *fifth* Commandment was the only one with a promise attached to it; and so we might go on. Thus we see the perfect propriety of *five* porches (colonnades) around the pool of *Mercy*, situated "*by the sheep* (gate)"!

"In these lay a great multitude of impotent folk, of blind, halt, withered, waiting for the moving of the water" (v. 3). What a picture of the Jewish nation at that time! How accurately does the condition of that multitude of sufferers describe the spiritual state of Judaism as it then existed! God had dealt with their fathers in sovereign mercy and marvelous grace, but the Nation as such appropriated it not. A few here and there took the place of lost sinners, and were saved, but the "great multitude" remained in their wretchedness. Israel as a people were *impotent*. They had the Law, made their boast in it, but were unable to keep it. Not only were they impotent, but "blind"—blind to their own impotency, blind to their wretchedness, blind to their desperate need, and so blind to the Divine and moral glories of the One who now stood in their midst "they *saw* in Him *no* beauty that they should desire Him". A third word describing their condition is added, "halt": the term signifies one who is lame, crippled. Israel had the Law but they were unable to walk in the way of God's commandments. A blind man is able to grope his way about: but a cripple cannot walk at all. Again; we are told this "great multitude" were "withered". This, no doubt, refers to those whose hands were paralyzed (cf Matt. 12:10; Luke 6:6), and as a description of Israel it tells us that they were totally incapacitated to work for God. What a pitiable picture! First, a general summing up of their state—"impotent". Second, a detailed diagnosis under three descriptive terms—"blind" (in their understandings and hearts), "halt" (crippled in their feet, so that they were unable to walk), "withered" (in their hands so that they were unable to work). Third, a word that speaks of their response to the prophetic word—"*waiting*"; waiting for the promised Messiah, and all the time ignorant of the fact that He was there in their midst! Who but the Spirit of God could have drawn so marvelously accurate a picture in such few and short lines!

We must not, however, limit this picture to Israel, for it is equally applicable and pertinent to sinners of the Gentiles too. Israel in the flesh was only a sample of fallen man as such. What we have here is a pointed and solemn delineation of human depravity, described in physical terms. True, its dispensational application is first to Israel, but its moral application is to the whole of Adam's fallen race. Let every reader see here a portrait of what he or she is by nature. The picture is not flattering we know. No; it is drawn by One who searcheth the innermost recesses of the human heart, and is presented here to humble us. The natural man is *impotent*—"without strength" (Rom. 5:6). This sums up in a single word his condition before God: altogether helpless, unable to do a single thing for himself. Then follows an amplification of this impotency, given in three (the number of full manifestation) descriptive terms. First, he is *blind*. This explains the lethargic indifference of the great multitude today—sporting on the very brink of the Pit, because *unable to see* the frightful peril that menaces them; making merry as they hasten down the Broad Road, because incompetent to discern the eternal destruction which awaits them at the bottom of it. Yes, blind indeed is the natural man: "The way of the wicked is as darkness: they know not at what they stumble" (Prov. 4:19).

"Halt": lame, crippled, unable to walk. How inevitably this follows the other! How can one who is spiritually blind walk the Narrow Way that leadeth unto life? "The eye affecteth the heart" (Lam. 3:51), and out of the heart are the issues of life (Prov. 4:23); if then the eye be evil, the body also is full of darkness (Luke 11:34).

Halt—lame—a cripple—if, then, such an one is ever to come to Christ he *must* indeed be "drawn" (John 6:44).

"Withered"—blind eyes, crippled feet, paralyzed hands: unable to see, unable to walk, unable to work. How striking is the order here! Consider them inversely: a man cannot perform good works unless he is walking with God; and he will not begin to walk with God until the eyes of his heart have been opened to see his need of Christ. This is the Divine order, and it never varies. First the eyes must be opened, and then an illumined understanding prepares us to walk worthy of the vocation wherewith we are called; and that, in turn, equips us for acceptable service for God. But so long as the eyes are "blind" the feet will be "halt" and the hands "withered".

"Waiting for the moving of the water". Surely this is not hard to interpret. This Pool was the object in which the great multitude placed all their hopes. They were waiting for its waters to be "troubled" so that its curative property might heal them. But they waited in vain. The one invalid who is singled out from the crowd had been there "a long time", and little had it availed him. Is it not thus with the *ordinances* of the religious world? How many there are—a "great multitude" indeed—which place their faith in the waters of baptism, or in the 'mass' and 'extreme unction'! And *a long time* all such will have to wait before the deep need of their *souls* will be met.

"For an angel went down at a certain season into the pool, and troubled the water: whosoever then first after the troubling of the waters stepped in was made whole of whatsoever disease he had" (v. 4). We return now to the Jewish application of our passage. The waters of this pool reflect the Sinaitic law, which was "given by the disposition of angels"; that law which promised "life" to him who did all that it enjoined. But whoever kept the law? Whoever obtained life by meeting its demands? None of Adam's fallen race. The law was "weak through the flesh". A perfect man could keep it, but a sinner could not. Why, then, was the law given? That the offense might abound; that sin might be shown to be exceeding sinful; that the sinner might discover his sinfulness. His very efforts to keep the law, and his repeated failures to do so, would but make manifest his utter helplessness. In like manner, when the angel troubled the water of Bethesda so that the first to step into it might be made whole, this only magnified the sufferings of those who lay around it. How could those who were "impotent" *step in!* Ah, they could not. Was, then, God mocking man in his misery? Nay, verily. He was but preparing the way for that which was "better" (Heb. 11:40). And this it is which is brought before us in what follows.

"And a certain man was there, which had an infirmity thirty and eight years" (v. 5). How this serves to confirm our interpretation of the previous verse, and what an illustration it furnishes us again of the deep significance of every word of Scripture. Why should the Holy Spirit have been careful to tell us the exact length of time this particular sufferer had been afflicted? What is the meaning and message of this "thirty and eight years"? Are we left to guess at the answer? No, indeed. Scripture is its own interpreter if we will but take the trouble to patiently and diligently search its pages and compare spiritual things with spiritual (1 Cor. 2:13). Thirty eight years was exactly the length of time that Israel spent in the wilderness after they came under law at Sinai (see Deut. 2:14). There it was, in the Wilderness of Sin, that of old Israel manifested their "impotency"—blind, halt, withered—under law.

"When Jesus saw him lie, and knew that he had now been a long time in that case, He saith unto him, Wilt thou be made whole?" (v. 6). Here is Light shining in the darkness, but the darkness comprehended it not. The very shining of the Light only served to reveal how great was the darkness. There was a great multitude of sick ones lying around that disappointing Pool, and here was the great Physician Himself abroad in the land. Bethesda thickly surrounded, and Christ Himself passing by unheeded! Truly the "darkness comprehended not". And is it any different today? Here is human Religion with all its cumbersome machinery and disappointing ordinances *waited on*, and the grace of God slighted. Go yonder to India with its myriad temples and sacred Ganges; visit Thibet, the land of praying-wheels; turn and consider the devotees of Mohammed and their holy pilgrimages; come nearer home, and look upon the millions of deluded Papists with their vigils and fasts, their beads and holy water; and then turn in to the religious performances in many of the Protestant churches, and see if there is any difference in the underlying principles which actuate them. They one and all fail, utterly fail, to meet the deep need of the soul. One and all they are unable to put away sin. And, too, sad to say, they one and all supplant the Christ of God—*He* is not wanted; *He* passes by unnoticed.

Such is fallen human nature. The whole world lieth in the wicked one (1 John 5:19), and were it not for sovereign grace every member of Adam's race would perish eternally. Grace is the sinner's only hope. Desert he has none. Spirituality he has none. Strength he has none. If salvation is to come to him, it *must be* by grace, and grace is unmerited favor shown toward the hell-deserving. And just because grace is this, God exercises His sovereign prerogative in bestowing His favors on whom He pleases—"For He saith to Moses, I will have mercy on whom I will have mercy, and I will have compassion on whom I will have compassion" (Rom. 9:16). And let none murmur against this and suppose that any one is wronged thereby. Men prate about God being unjust, but if justice, real justice, bare justice, be insisted on, hope is entirely cut off for all of us. Justice requires that each should receive his exact due; and what, dear reader, is your due, my due, but judgment! Eternal life is a gift, and if a gift it can neither be earned nor claimed. If salvation is God's gift, who shall presume to tell Him the ones on whom He ought to bestow it? Was salvation provided for the angels that fell? If God has left them to reap the due reward of their iniquities, why should He be charged with injustice if He abandons to themselves those of mankind who love darkness rather than light. It is not that God *refuses* salvation to any who truly seek it. Not so; there is a Saviour for every sinner who will repent and believe. But if out of the great multitude of the impenitent and unbelieving God determines to exercise His sovereign grace by singling out a few to be the objects of His irresistible power and distinguishing favors, who is wronged thereby? Has not God the right to dispense His charity as seemeth best to Himself (Matt. 20:15)? Certainly He has.

The sovereignty of God is strikingly illustrated in the passage now before us. There lay a "great multitude" of impotent folk: all were equally needy, all equally powerless to help themselves. And here was the great Physician, God Himself incarnate, infinite in power, inexhaustible resources at His command. It had been just as easy for Him to have healed the entire company as to make a single individual whole. *But He did not.* For some reason not revealed to us, He passed by the "great multitude" of sufferers and singled out one man and healed him. There is nothing whatever in the narrative to indicate that this "certain man" was any different from the others. We are not told that *he* turned to the Saviour and cried "Have mercy on *me*". He was just as blind as were the others to the Divine glory of the One who stood before him. Even when asked "Wilt thou be made whole?" he evidenced no faith whatever; and after he had been healed "He wist not who it was" that had healed him. It is impossible to find *any* ground in the man himself for Christ singling him out for special favor. The *only* explanation is the mere sovereign pleasure of Christ Himself. This is proven beyond the shadow of a doubt by His own declaration immediately afterwards— "For as the Father raiseth up the dead, and quickeneth them; even so the Son quickeneth *whom He will*" (v. 21).

This miracle of healing was a parable in action. It sets before us a vivid illustration of God's work of grace in the spiritual realm. Just as the condition of that impotent multitude depicts the depravity of Adam's fallen race, so Christ singling out this individual and healing him, portrays the sovereign grace of Him who singles out and saves His own elect. Every detail in the incident bears this out.

"When Jesus saw him lie, and knew that he had been now a long time in that case" (v. 6). Note the individuality of this. We are not told that he saw *them*—the "great multitude"—but *him*. The eyes of the Saviour were fixed on that one who, out of all the crowd, had been given to Him by the Father before the foundation of the world. Not only are we told that Christ "saw him", but it is added, "And knew that he had been now a long time in that case". Yes, He knew all about him; had known him from all eternity—"I am the good Shepherd, and *know* My sheep" (John 10:11). And then we read, "And *saith* unto him". It was not the man who spoke first, but Christ. The Lord always takes the initiative, and invites Himself. And it was thus with you, Christian reader, when sovereign grace sought you out. You, too, were lying amid the "great multitude of impotent folk", for by nature you were a child of wrath, "even as others" (Eph. 2:3). Yes, you were *lying* in all the abject misery of a *fallen* creature—blind, halt, withered—unable to do a thing for yourself. Such was your awful state when the Lord, in sovereign grace, drew near to you. O thank Him now that He did not pass you by, and leave you to the doom you so richly deserved. Praise Him with a loud voice for His distinguishing grace that singled *you* out to be an object of His sovereign mercy. But we must now consider the force of the Saviour's question here:

"He saith unto him, Wilt thou be made whole" (v. 6). Does it seem strange that such a question should be put to that sufferer? Would not being made whole be the one thing desired above all others by one who had suffered for thirty-eight years? Was not the very fact that he was lying there by the pool an indication of what he wished? Why, then, ask him "Wilt thou be made whole?" Ah, the question is not so meaningless as some might suppose. Not always are the wretched willing to be relieved. Invalids sometimes trade on the sympathy and indulgence of their friends. Others sink so low that they become despondent and give up all hope, and long for death to come and relieve them. But there is something much deeper here than this.

Did not the Saviour ask the question to impress upon this man the utter helplessness of his condition! Man must be brought to recognize and realize his impotency. While ever we console ourselves we will do better next time, that is a sure sign we have not come to the end of ourselves. The one who promises himself that he will amend his ways and turn over a new leaf, has not learned that he is "without strength". It is not till we discover we are helpless, that we shall abandon our miserable efforts to weave a robe of righteousness for ourselves. It is not till we learn we are impotent that we shall look *outside* of ourselves to Another.

No doubt one reason why Christ selected so many incurable cases on which to show forth His power, was in order to have suitable objects to portray to us the irreparable ruin which sin has wrought and the utter hopelessness of man's natural estate. The Saviour, then, was pressing upon the man the need of being made whole. But more: when the Saviour said, "Wilt thou *be made* whole?" it was tantamount to asking, 'Are you willing to put yourself, just as you are, into My hands? Are you ready for Me to do for you what you are unable to do for yourself? Are you willing to be My debtor?'

"The impotent man answered Him, Sir, I have no man, when the water is troubled, to put me into the pool: but while I am coming, **another steppeth** down before me" (v. 7). How sadly true to life. When the great Physician said "Wilt thou be made whole?" the poor sufferer did not promptly answer, 'Yea Lord; undertake for me'. And not thus does the sinner act when first brought face to face with Christ. The impotent man failed to realize that Christ could cure him by a word. He supposed he must get into the Pool. There are several lines of thought suggested here, but it is needless to follow them out. The poor man had more faith in means than he had in the Lord. And, too, his eye was fixed on "man", not God: he was looking to human kind for help. Again we would exclaim, How true to life! Moreover, he thought that *he* had to do something—"While *I am* coming". How this uncovers the heart of the natural man. How pathetic are the closing words of this verse! What a heartless world we live in. Human nature is full of selfishness. Christ is the only unfailing Friend of the friendless.

"**Jesus saith unto him, Rise, take up thy bed, and walk**" (v. 8). If the Saviour waited until there was in the sinner a due appreciation of His person, none would ever be saved. The sufferer had made no cry for mercy, and when Christ inquired if he were willing to be made whole there was no faith evidenced. But in sovereign grace the Son of God pronounced the life-giving word, yet was it a word that addressed the human responsibility of the subject. A careful analysis of the command of Christ reveals three things. First, there must be *implicit confidence in His word*. "Rise" was the peremptory command. There must be a hearty recognition of His authority, and immediate response to His orders. "Believe on the Lord Jesus Christ, and thou shalt be saved" is something more than a gracious invitation; it is a command (1 John 3:23). Second, "Take up thy bed"—a cotton pallet, easily rolled up. There was to be no thought of failure, and no provision made for a relapse. How many there are who take a few feeble steps, and then return to their beds! The last state of such is worse than the first. If there is faith in the person of Christ, if there is a submission to His Divine authority, then the new life within will find an outlet without: and we shall no longer be a burden to others, but able to shoulder our own burdens. Third, "And walk". I like that word coming here. It is as though the Saviour said, 'You were unable to walk *into* the water: you could not walk *in order to be* cured, but now that you are made whole, "walk"'! There are duties to be faced of which we have had no previous experience, and we must proceed to discharge them in faith; and in that faith in which He bids us do them will be found the strength needed for their performance.

"**And immediately the man was made whole, and took up his bed, and walked: and on the same day was the sabbath**" (v. 9). How blessed! The cure was both instantaneous and complete. Christ does not put the believing sinner into a salvable state. He *saves*.

saves us with a perfect and eternal salvation the moment we believe: "I know that, whatsoever God doeth, it shall be forever: nothing can be put to it, nor anything taken from it" (Ecc. 3:14). We need hardly say that we are here shown, once more, the Word at work. The Saviour did nothing but speak, and the miracle was accomplished. It is thus the Son of God is revealed to us again and again in this fourth Gospel.

"The Jews therefore said unto him that was cured, It is the sabbath day: it is not lawful for thee to carry thy bed" (v. 10). How true to life again! The one who surrenders to his Lord must expect to encounter criticism. The one who regulates his life by the Word of God will be met by the opposition of man. And it is the *religious* world that will oppose most fiercely. Unless we subscribe to *their* creed and observe *their* rules of conduct, persecution and ostracism will be our lot. Unless we are prepared to be brought into bondage by the traditions of the elders we must be ready for their frowns. Christ was not ignorant of the current teaching about the sabbath, and He knew full well what would be the consequences should this healed man carry his bed on the sabbath day. But he had come here to set His people free from the shackles which religious zealots had forged. Never did He toady to the public opinion in His day; nor should we. There are thousands of His people who need to be reminded of Gal. 5:1: "Stand fast therefore in the liberty wherewith Christ hath made us free, and be not entangled again with the yoke of bondage". If the child of God is regulated by the Scriptures and knows that he is pleasing his Lord, it matters little or nothing what his fellow-men (or his fellow-Christians either) may think or say about him. Better far to displease them than to be brought into bondage to their rules. Sufficient for the Christian to heed the commandments of God.

"He answered them, He that made me whole, the same said unto me, Take up thy bed, and walk" (v. 11). This sets a fine example for us. How simply he met his critics. He did not enter into an argument about their perverted views of the sabbath: he did not charge them with want of sympathy for those who were sufferers, though he might have done both. Instead, he hid behind Christ. He fell back upon the Word of God. Well for us when we have a "Thus saith the Lord" with which to meet our critics.

"Then asked they him, What man is that which said unto thee, Take up thy bed and walk? And he that was healed wist not who it was" (vv. 12, 13). This illustrates the fact that there is much ignorance even in believers. We ought not to expect too much from babes in Christ. This man had been healed, and he had obeyed the command of his Benefactor; but not yet did he perceive His Divine glories. Intelligence concerning the person of Christ follows (and not precedes) an experimental acquaintance with the virtues of His work.

"For Jesus had conveyed Himself away, a multitude being in that place" (v. 13). This brings out the moral perfections of the Saviour. It evidences the meekness of the Divine Servant: He ministered without ostentation. He never sought to be the popular Idol of the hour, or the Center of an admiring crowd. Instead of courting popularity, He shunned it. Instead of advertising Himself, He "received not honor from men". This lovely excellency of Christ appears most conspicuously in Mark's Gospel: see 1:37, 38, 44; 7:17, 36; 8:26, etc.

"Afterward Jesus findeth him in the temple, and said unto him, Behold, thou art made whole: sin no more, lest a worse thing come upon thee" (v. 14). The Lord had withdrawn from the man. Christ had retired in order that he might be tested. New strength had been given him; opportunity was then afforded for him to use it. The restored sufferer did not falter. The One who had saved him was obeyed as Lord. The Jewish critics had not intimidated him. That a work of grace had been wrought in his soul as well as in his body is evidenced by the fact that he had gone to the House of Prayer and Praise. And there, we are told, the Lord Jesus found him. This is most blessed. Christ was not to be met with in the throng, but He was to be found in the temple!

Having dealt in "grace" with the poor helpless sufferer Christ now applied the "truth". "Sin no more" is a word for his conscience. Grace does not ignore the requirements of God's holiness: "awake to righteousness, and sin not" (1 Cor. 15:24) is still the standard set before us. "Lest a worse thing come unto thee" reminds us that the believer is still subject to the government of God. "Whatsoever a man soweth that shall he also reap" is addressed to believers, not unbelievers. If we sin we shall suffer chastisement. Bishop Ryle has pointed out that there is here an important message for those who have been raised from a bed of sickness. "Sin no more": renewed health ought to send us back into the world with a greater hatred of sin, a more thorough watchfulness over our ways, a greater determination to live for God's glory.

"The man departed, and told the Jews that it was Jesus, that had made him whole" (v. 15). This gives beautiful completeness to the whole incident. Here we see him who had been healed confessing with his lips the One who had saved him. It would seem that as soon as the Lord Jesus had revealed Himself to this newly-born soul, that he had sought out the very ones who had previously interrogated and criticized him, and told them it was Jesus who had made him whole.

In closing, we call attention to the striking typical picture found in our passage. Just as the one which engaged us last (John 4:43-54) was unmistakeably *Gentilish* in its character, the one before us here in John 5:1-15 is noticeably *Jewish*. The mention of "Jerusalem" in v. 1; the reference to the "Hebrew tongue" in v. 2; the "Jews" in v. 10; the "temple" in v. 14 all prove this. The time-mark in vv. 9, 10 and 16—"the sabbath"—show that it is another *millennial* foreshadowment which is here before us. Like the other prophetic pictures of John, this one also has seven lines in it:—First, the Lord Jesus was in Jerusalem "at the feast," cf. Zech. 14:16. Second, the fact that Bethesda was "by the sheep" (v. 2) tells of Mercy for the lost sheep of the house of Israel. Third, the great multitude of "impotent folk" (v. 3) shows Israel's *need* of Mercy, and depicts their condition at the time of Christ's return—in an attitude of "waiting". Fourth, in the words "I have no man to put me into the pool" (v. 7) we see the *friendlessness* of Israel: Israel always has been and will be still more so in the tribulation period, the friendless people among the nations. Fifth, Israel will be healed at the beginning of the great antitypical sabbath—the Millennium (v. 9). Sixth, Christ will then honor their temple worship (v. 14). Seventh, Israel will then confess Him as "**Jesus**", their Saviour (v. 15).

Study the following questions on the next lesson, 5:16-31:—

1. What is the force of Christ's answer in v. 17?
2. What is the meaning of Christ's words in v. 19?
3. How does v. 20 bring out the Deity of Christ?
4. What does v. 23 go to prove about Christ?
5. How does v. 24 establish the eternal security of the believer?
6. Why should the Son of Man be the Judge? v. 28
7. Does v. 30 speak of Christ's humanity or Deity?

—Arthur W. Pink.

11. ANTICHRIST IN THE APOCALYPSE

The scope of the Apocalypse is indicated by its place in the Sacred Canon. Coming as it does right at the close of the Scriptures, we should naturally expect to find it outlining the last chapters of the world's history. Such is indeed the case. The Revelation is mainly devoted to a description of the judgments which God will yet send upon the earth. It furnishes by far the most complete description of the conditions which are to obtain during the Tribulation period. It treats at greatest length with the character and career of the Antichrist, who will be the "Rod" in the hands of an angry God to chastise recreant Israel and apostate Christendom. All of this is, of course, preparatory to the establishment of Messiah's kingdom, which will exist during the last of earth's dispensations.

It is impossible to understand the Apocalypse without a thorough acquaintance with the books that precede it. The more familiar we are with the first sixty-five books of the Bible, the better prepared are we for the study of its sixty-sixth. There is little that is really new in the Revelation. Its varied contents are largely an amplification of what is to be found in the preceding scriptures. Each of its figures and symbols are explained if not on its own pages, then somewhere within the compass of the written Word. For Scripture is ever self-interpreting. Most of our difficulties with the Revelation grow out of our ignorance and lack of acquaintance with the earlier books. Daniel and Zechariah especially should be examined minutely, for they shed much light upon the visions and prophecies of the Patmos seer.

The Apocalypse not only reveals much concerning the person and work of the Man of Sin, but it describes his doom, as it also announces the complete overthrow of the Trinity of Evil. This, no doubt, accounts for much of the prejudice which obtains against the study and reading of this book. It is indeed remarkable that this is the only book in the Bible connected with which there is a distinct promise given to those who read and hear read its prophecy (1:3). And yet how very rarely *it is* read from the pulpits of those churches which are reputed as orthodox! Surely the great Enemy is responsible for this. It seems that Satan fears and hates above every book in the Bible this one which tells of his being ultimately cast into the Lake of Fire. But "we are not ignorant of his devices" (2 Cor. 2:11). Then let him not keep us from the prayerful and careful perusal of this prophecy which tells of those things "which must shortly come to pass".

1. We turn first to the sixth chapter of the Revelation, where a fourfold view is presented of the Son of Perdition. Just as at the beginning of the New Testament the Holy Spirit has given us a fourfold delineation of Christ in the Gospels, so at the commencement of His description of the judgments of God on the earth He has furnished us with a fourfold picture of Christ's great opponent. We believe that the contents of the first four of the "seals" describe four aspects of the Antichrist's character, and also outline four stages in his career. First, he is seen aping the Christ of God as the Righteous One. The *"white"* horse" on which he is seated, speaking of righteousness. Just as we are told in 2 Cor. 11:14 that "Satan himself is transformed into an angel of light", and "therefore it is no great thing if his ministers also be transformed as the ministers of *righteousness"*, so the Antichrist will pose as the friend of law and order. Second, he is seen mimicking the Christ of God as the mighty Warrior. Just as the Lord Jesus at His return will make a footstool of His enemies and trample in fury all

who defy Him (Isa. 63:3), so the Man of Sin shall slay all who dare to oppose him. Third, he is seen imitating Christ as the Bread of Life, for the third seal views him as the Food-controller. Fourth, he is seen with his mask off, depicted as one whose name is Death and Hades, that is, as the Destroyer of men's bodies and souls.

Let us see how the *identity* of this Rider of the various colored horses is established. In 6:2 we are told, "And I saw, and behold a white horse: and he that sat on him had a bow; and a crown was given unto him: and he went forth conquering, and to conquer". Notice first, that he is here viewed as seated upon a "white horse". This is in imitation of the Christ of God, who, at the time of His second advent to the earth, will also appear seated upon "a white horse" (Rev. 19:11). Second, it is said that "a crown was given unto him". This at once serves to connect him with the first Beast—the Anti-Christ—of Rev. 13, for of him it is written, "And they worshipped the Dragon which *gave power* unto the Beast" (v. 4). Again; in 6:4 we are told, "And there went out another horse that was red: and power was given to him that sat thereon to take peace from the earth, and that they should kill one another: and there was given unto him a great sword." Notice first, the last clause—"There was given unto him a great sword". This stamps him plainly as the pseudo christ, for of the true Christ it is written, "Out of His mouth goeth a sharp sword" (19:15). Second, it is said "power was given to him to take peace *from the earth*." So, too, of the first Beast of Rev. 13 we read, "And power was given him over *all* kindreds, and tongues, and *all* nations" (v. 7). In the third seal he is viewed as the Food-controller, weighing out the necessities of life at famine prices. This, no doubt, corresponds with what we read of in 13:17. Finally, in the fourth seal he is named "Death and Hell".

This double title removes all doubt as to who is in view. When God remonstrates with Israel for having made the seven-years' treaty, He does so in the following language: "And your covenant with Death shall be disannulled, and your agreement with Hell shall not stand" (Isa. 28:18). Thus the Riders of the four horses of Rev. 6 are not four different persons, but one person presented in a fourfold way, as the Lord Jesus is in the four Gospels.

Before we pass from Rev. 6 a few words should be added by way of amplification of our remarks above, namely, that in the first part of Rev. 6 we have outlined *four stages* in the Antichrist's career. The preparation of the Man Christ Jesus for His public ministry—the long years spent quietly at Nazareth—are passed over by the four Evangelists. So here in Rev. 6 the early days of the Man of Sin—in his "little horn" character—are not noticed. Under the first seal he is viewed as seated on a white horse, having a bow. The color of the horse and the fact that no arrow is seen attached to the bow, suggests bloodless victories, for he goes forth "conquering and to conquer". This first seal at once conducts us to the time when the Prince of Darkness poses as the Christ of God and presents himself to the Jews for their acceptance. He does not come out in his true satanic character, rather does he simulate the Prince of Peace. The first seal is parallel with Dan. 11:21, 23, where we learn that he will gain the kingdom by flatteries and political diplomacy. But not for long will he fill this pacific role. War is in his heart (Psa. 55:21), and nothing short of universal dominion will satisfy his proud ambitions. As God has plainly warned, at the very time when men shall be saying, **Peace and safety**, "then sudden destruction cometh upon them, as travail upon a woman with child; and they shall not escape" (1 Thess. 5:3).

It is to this the second seal brings us. Here the Antichrist is seen no longer upon a white horse, but upon a *red* horse. And in perfect accord with this, it is added, "And power was given to him that sat thereon to take peace from the earth. . . .and there was given to him a great sword" (v. 4). Little wonder that he is called "the Destroyer of the Gentiles" (Jer. 4:7). At the time of his overthrow it will be exclaimed, "Is this the man that made the earth to tremble, that did shake kingdoms; that made the world as a wilderness, and destroyed the cities thereof?" (Isa. 14: 17, 18). Jer. 25:29 throws light upon this "great sword" which is given to him—"For, lo, I begin to bring evil on the city which is called by my name, and should ye be utterly unpunished? Ye shall not be unpunished: for I will call for *a sword* upon *all* the inhabitants of the earth, saith the Lord of hosts" (read verses 15 to 33).

In the third seal he is portrayed as the Harbinger of famine conditions. This is intimated by the change of the color of the horse: for "black" in connection with famine see Jer. 14:1, 2 and Lam. 5:10. The symbolic significance of the "black" horse is intensified by the figure of the "pair of balances in his hand" (*compare* Hosea 12:7, Amos 8:4-6). What follows describes the wheat being doled out at famine prices. But it is added, "See thou hurt not the oil and the wine". This intimates that the famine is by no means universal: yea, it suggests that side by side with abject suffering there is abundance and luxury. We therefore regard this third seal as denoting the Antichrist's persecution of the godly Jews which, from other scriptures we learn, will be the fiercest during the last three and one half years of his career. Rev. 13:17 makes it known that they who will not be suffered to buy or sell are the ones who refuse to receive his mark. These, of course, are the faithful remnant of the Jews. But they who *do* render allegiance to the Beast will not want—"oil and wine" shall be their portion.

The fourth seal, plainly conducts us to the end of Antichrist's course. The fact that he is named Death and that we are told Hades (that which receives the soul) followed with him, makes known the awful doom which shall overtake this Son of Perdition and all his blinded followers—see Rev. 19: 20, 21.

2. The next allusion to the Antichrist is found in Rev. 9:11 where he is given a threefold appellation, namely, King over the locusts, The Angel of the Abyss, and the Destroyer. A few remarks upon the context are required if we are to expound, even briefly, the significance of these three titles. The majority of pre-millennial commentators are agreed upon the identity of the personage named in Rev. 9:11, though there is considerable difference of opinion among them concerning the meaning of the context. We can here only offer a few remarks on the preceding verses according to our present light and submit the reasons for our conclusions.

The immediate context takes us back to the opening verse of Rev. 9 where a "star" is seen falling from heaven unto the earth, unto whom is given the key of the Bottomless Pit. This we believe refers to Lucifer, or "Day-Star" (see Isa. 14:12 margin). The reference, we think, is not to his original fall, but to what is described in Rev. 12:9. The fact that the key of the Abyss is given to *him* is in keeping with the fact that during the Tribulation period God allows him free rein and suffers him to do his worst. The R. V. correctly renders verses one and two as follows—"And there was given to him the key of *the Pit of* the Abyss. And he opened *the Pit of* the Abyss", etc., or, as it may literally be rendered, *"the well of* the Bottomless Pit." This expression occurs nowhere else in Scripture. The "well of the Bottomless Pit" is to be distinguished from the

Bottomless Pit itself, mentioned in 9:11; 11:7; 17:8; 20:3. What the distinction is we shall presently suggest.

Out of *the well of* the Bottomless Pit issued a smoke, so great that the sun and the air were darkened (v. 2), and out of the smoke came "locusts upon the earth". We regard these "locusts" as identical with the creatures referred to in the prophecy of Joel (2:1-11). By noticing what is said of them in Joel 2 and Rev. 9 it is at once apparent that they are no ordinary locusts. Joel says of them, "A great people and a strong; there hath not been ever the like, neither shall be any more after it" (2:2). It is said, "When they fall upon the sword they shall not be wounded" (2:8). The fact that they issue from the Pit also denotes that they are supernatural beings. In the description furnished in Rev. 9 they seem to be a kind of *infernal cherubim*, for "the horse" (v. 7), the "man" (v. 7), the "lion" (v. 8), and "the scorpion" (v. 19) are combined in them. Their number is given as two hundred thousand thousand. Who, then, are these infernal beings? No commentator that we are acquainted with has attempted an answer. It is therefore with diffidence that we suggest, without being dogmatic, that they are, most likely, *fallen angels* now imprisoned in Tartarus. We give three reasons which, in our judgment, point to this conclusion.

First, we know from 2 Pet. 2:4 that the angels which sinned were "cast *down* to Tartarus", and in Rev. 9:2,3 we are told there *"arose* a smoke out of the Pit. . .and there came out of the smoke locusts upon the earth". Now, as pointed out, these infernal "locusts" issue from *"the well of* the Pit", an expression occurring nowhere else in Scripture, and only the "locusts" are said to come from *there*. So also the term "Tartarus" is found nowhere but in 2 Pet. 2:4. It seems likely, then, that *"the well of* the Pit" may be only another name for "Tartarus" (with which *only* fallen angels are connected), just as "the Lake of Fire" is only another name for "Gehenna". Who else could these locusts be *but* the fallen angels? To say we do not know may savor of humility, but shall the writer be deemed presumptuous because he has sought to furnish an answer by comparing scripture with scripture?

In the second place, it is surely significant that the "king"of these "locusts" is termed in Rev. 9:11 "the *angel* of the Bottomless Pit"! A title which is nowhere else given to him. Just as Christ, the "Angel of the Covenant" (Mal. 3:1—cf Isa. 63:3, etc.) is, again and again, termed an "angel" in the Apocalypse (see 8:3, 10:1, 20:1, etc.), so the Antichrist is here denominated "the Angel of the Bottomless Pit". And just as we learn from Matt. 25:31 that "the Son of Man shall come in His glory, and *all* the *holy angels* with Him" (cf Matt. 24:31), so when the Son of Perdition is manifested, *all* the unholy angels will be *with him!*

In the third place, let the language of 2 Pet. 2:4 be carefully examined: "For if God spared not the angels that sinned, but cast them down to Tartarus, and delivered them into chains of darkness, to be reserved unto judgment". It is to the last clause we wish to direct attention. Let it be compared with the 9th verse of the same chapter —"The Lord knoweth how to deliver the godly out of temptations, and to reserve the unjust unto the day of judgment *to be punished".* Wicked human beings are said to be reserved "unto *the Day of* Judgment to be *punished".* But this is not what is said of the angels that sinned, though, of course, eternal punishment awaits them as we learn from Matt. 25:41. 2 Pet. 2:4 simply says they are "reserved unto judgment", and we believe this means that God is holding them in Tartarus until His time comes for Him to use them as one of His instruments of *judgment* upon an ungodly world. The *time* when God will thus use them is stated in Jude 6—it will be in "the judgment of the great day" (compare Rev. 6:17 for "the great day"). Confirmatory of this, observe that in Joel 2:11 the Lord calls the supernatural locusts *"His* army", then employed to inflict sore punishments on apostate Israel.* If our interpretation of 2 Pet. 2:4 be correct, namely, that it makes no reference to the future punishment of the fallen angels, this explains why the Lord in Matt. 25:41 when referring to future punishment was careful to mention *them* specifically.

Returning now to Rev. 9:11 the Antichrist is here termed the "King over" the locusts. Let the reader pay careful attention to what is predicated of these infernal beings in Joel 2 and here in Rev. 9, and let him remember they number no less than two hundred millions, and then see if it does not throw new light on Rev. 13:4, where concerning the Antichrist the question is asked, "Who is able to make *war* with *him?*"!! How utterly futile to engage in conflict one who commands an "army" of two hundred millions, none of whom are subject to death! In the second place, he is here termed "the Angel of the Bottomless Pit", a title peculiarly appropriate as the leader of the fallen angels; and, as well, a title which denotes the superhuman nature of the Son of Perdition. In the third place, we are here told that his name "in the Hebrew tongue is Abaddon, but in the Greek tongue hath his name Apollyon". This title serves to establish beyond a shadow of doubt the identity of this "King" of the infernal "locusts", this "Angel of the Bottomless Pit". The Hebrew and the Greek names signify the same thing in English—the Destroyer. It is "the Destroyer of the Gentiles" of Jer. 4:7, translated "Spoiler" in Isa. 16:4 and Jer. 6:24. Suitable name is this for the one who is the great opponent of the *Saviour*. "Destroyer" is close akin to "Death" in Rev. 6:8. The reason why his name is given here in both Hebrew and Greek is because he will be connected with and be the destroyer of *both* Jews and Gentiles! But why give the Hebrew name first? Because the order in judgment, as in grace, is "the Jew first"—see Rom. 2:9 and 1:16 for each, respectively.

3. "And when they shall have finished their testimony, the Beast that ascendeth out of the Bottomless Pit shall make war against them, and shall overcome them, and kill them" (Rev. 11:7). This is the first time in the Revelation that the Antichrist is seen in his character of "the Beast". The last scripture which we have examined serves at once to identify him. He is termed "the Angel *of* the Bottomless Pit", because in a peculiar sense the Abyss is his home. There he has been during all the centuries of this Christian era. In Acts 1:23 (cf Article 3, Section 3) the Pit is called "his *own* place". Here the Beast is shown ascending out of the Bottomless Pit. What, then, is the Abyss? It appears to be the special abode of infernal creatures. As we have seen, out of its "well" issue the fallen angels. From it comes the Beast. And in it Satan himself is incarcerated for the thousand years (Rev. 20:3). The "Abyss" is quite distinct from "Hades" in which the souls of lost *human* beings are now being tormented; as it must also be distinguished from "Gehenna" or "the Lake of Fire" in which *all* the lost shall suffer for ever and ever.

4. We come now to Rev. 13. A lengthy paper might readily be devoted to its exposition, but as we have had occasion to refer to its contents so frequently in earlier articles, we shall here be as brief as possible. The contents of this chapter center around two "Beasts". As to which of them represent the Antichrist there is a dif-

---

* Psa. 78:49 speaks of God using "evil angels" (those mentioned in Rev. 12:7) in His judgments on Egypt.

ference of opinion. The majority of those who have written upon the subject regard the first Beast as the Man of Sin, and with them we are in hearty accord. We shall devote our next article to a setting forth of some of the many proofs that the first Beast *is* the Antichrist. Here we shall take the point for granted.

"And I stood upon the sand of the sea, and saw a beast rise up out of the sea, having seven heads and ten horns, and upon his horns ten crowns, and upon his heads the name of blasphemy" (v. 1). There is here, as frequently in Scripture, a *double* reference. Two objects quite distinct though intimately connected are in view. We believe that this "Beast" which arises from "the sea" points to the Roman Empire revived and in its final form, that is, resuscitated and confederated under the form of ten kingdoms. In Dan. 7:3 we read, "And four great beasts came up from the sea, diverse one from another". These "four great beasts" are interpreted in the verses which follow as four kingdoms. In v. 7 we are told this fourth Beast (the Roman Empire) "had ten horns". So the Beast of Rev. 13:1 also has "ten horns". Each of the successive Beasts or kingdoms of Dan. 7 retained the territory of the previous one, though enlarging on it. In the symbolic description there furnished the first Beast is likened unto "a lion" (v. 4); the second to "a bear" (v. 5); the third to "a leopard" (v. 6). So also in Rev. 13 the Beast there is "like unto a leopard", has feet like "a bear", and has the mouth of "a lion" (v. 2). Thus we learn that the Roman Empire in its final form will include within its borders the territory controlled by the earlier Empires and will also perpetuate the dominant characteristics of the ancient Babylonians, Medo-Persians, and Grecians.

But it is very clear from what follows in Rev. 13 that there is something more than the Empire here in view. In vv. 3-8 it is a *person* that is before us. We are satisfied that this same person is also described, symbolically, in the opening verses. As is frequently the case in the prophetic scriptures, the king and his kingdom are here inseparably united. Rev. 13:1, 2 portrays both the Empire and its last Emperor. One of the proofs for this is found in Dan. 9:26, 27, where (as we have shown in Article 9) the Antichrist is denominated "the prince" of that people who destroyed Jerusalem in A. D. 70. We shall therefore interpret here according to this principle.

"And I saw .... a Beast rise up out of the sea". In Scripture, the troubled "sea" is frequently a figure of restless humanity away from God. The Antichrist will come upon the scene at a time of unprecedented social disturbance and governmental upheaval. He will appear at a crisis in the history of the world. From other prophetic scriptures we gather that, following the removal of the Church from this earth and some time before Daniel's seventieth week begins, there will be a complete overthrow of law and order, both civil and political. All Divine restraint being removed, lawlessness will prevail. We have no doubt that Satan will designedly bring this about. It will create a situation beyond the diplomatic skill of earth's statesmen. This will provide the desired opportunity for the coming Superman, who will be a diplomatic genius. Just as many leaders today are satisfied that a League of Nations would be the best device for preserving peace, so in the day to come the Man of Sin will satisfy the world that this is the only solution to the baffling problems then confronting the Powers of earth. Thus will the Antichrist resurrect the old Roman Empire at a time of universal confusion and tumult. He will himself be the acknowledged head or Emperor, the last of the Cæsars. Hence the *double* significance of this figure—"a Beast rising out of *the sea*". Out of a state of anarchy will come forth this mighty Despot, who will speedily arrogate to himself *all* authority, both Divine and human; and in the end it will be seen that he embodies a lawlessness even worse and more fatal than that out of which he sprang. A *Beast* indeed will he soon appear to be. Pregnant with meaning is this title. Having rejected God's "Lamb"; a "Beast" shall be the world's ruler. *This* will be God's reply to the satanic teaching of "Evolution" now so popular almost everywhere. The leaders of modern thought insist on the *beastial* origin of man, and so a Beast shall yet lead the majority of his generation to Perdition!

"Having seven heads and ten horns". It is most significant that identically the same features are attributed to the Dragon in 12:3. He, too, is there said to have "seven heads and ten horns." This clearly implies his satanic origin: he will be a human replica of the Devil himself. As wrote the late G. H. Pember (from whom we have borrowed a number of valuable points), the Beast will be "the effulgence of the Antigod's glory, and the very image of his substance". We take it that the "seven heads" are symbolic of full intelligence, and the "ten horns" completeness of imperial dominion.

"And the Beast which I saw was like unto a leopard, and his feet were as the feet of a bear, and his mouth as the mouth of a lion" (v. 2). Like the "Beast rising up out of the sea" of the previous verse, we believe the terms of this second verse have a *double* significance. First, as intimated above, they denote that the Empire will include the territory and preserve the dominant features of the earlier Empires. Second, they supply a figurative description of the Emperor himself. The Antichrist will combine in his personality the characteristics of the leopard (beauty and subtlety), of the bear (strength and cruelty), and of the lion (boldness and ferocity).

"And the Dragon gave him his power, and his seat, and great authority" (v. 2). This is the Devil's travesty of what God the Father will yet do to His Son:—"I saw in the night visions, and, behold, one like the Son of Man came with the clouds of heaven, and came to the Ancient of Days, and they brought Him near before Him. And there was *given Him* dominion, and glory, and a kingdom, that all people, nations, and languages, should serve Him" (Dan. 7:13, 14).

"And I saw one of his heads as it were wounded to death; and his deadly wound was healed: and all the world wondered after the Beast" (v. 3). It is clear from a number of scriptures that during the early part of the second half of Daniel's seventieth "week" the Antichrist will be slain by the sword— cf Isa. 14:18, 19; 37:7; Ezek. 21:25 R. V.; Zech. 11:17: see our comments on these in the closing portion of Article 6. It is equally clear that this "wound of death" will be "healed" (Rev. 13:4) and that the Beast shall again "live" (Rev. 13:14). * Satan will be permitted to bring his son from the dead. This is no wild speculation of ours but a view which has been propounded by quite a number of devout students. In his "Coming Prince", Sir Robert Anderson said, "The language of Rev. 13:3, 12 suggests that there will be some impious travesty of the resurrection of our Lord". It is useless to reason about it: we simply believe the record of Scripture upon it. The raising of the Beast from the dead will remove whatever doubt men may have entertained concerning his supernatural character. "*All the world* wondered after him" is the statement which immediately follows the reference to the healing of his wound of death.

"And they worshipped the Dragon which gave power unto the Beast: and they worshipped the Beast, saying,

---

* "It is remarkable that just three times (the number of *resurrection)* the healing of the Antichrist's "wound of death" is referred to here in Rev. 13— see vv. 3, 12, 14!

Who is like unto the Beast? Who is able to make war with him?" (v. 4). This cry of the world, "Who is like unto the Beast?" is a travesty of the song of Moses. When celebrating Jehovah's overthrow of their enemies at the Red Sea, Israel sang, "Who is like unto Thee, O Lord, among the Gods! Who is like Thee, glorious in holiness, fearful in praises, doing wonders!" (Ex. 15:11). The additional exclamation, "Who is able to make war with him?" is evoked by the vast army of infernal creatures at his command, and by his own triumph over death in battle.

"And there was given unto him a mouth speaking great things and blasphemies" (v. 5). *This* is the one great distinguishing mark of the Antichrist—cf Psa. 52:1-4; Isa. 14:13, 14; Dan. 7:11, 20; 11:36; 2 Thess. 2:4, etc. But not for long will he be suffered to continue his God-defying course. Another "forty two months" and his career shall be ended. This number—here designedly used by the Holy Spirit, rather than three and one half years or twelve hundred and sixty days—is a very significant one. Its factors are 6 and 7, which stand for man and completeness. It is man in his fallen condition, here the Man of Sin, *fully* manifested. Forty-two stands for *intensified apostasy*. Thus Num. 33 gives the various stopping places of unbelieving Israel in the wilderness as forty-two in number. Judges 12:6 tells us that the number of the apostate Ephraimites which fell before the Gileadites were 42-thousand. See also 2 Kings 2:4 and 10:14. The official designation "the Christ" is found in Matthew (the theme of which is the rejection of their Messiah by apostate Israel) forty-two times.

"And it was given unto him to make war with the saints, and to overcome them: and there was given to him authority over every tribe and people and tongue and nation. And all they that dwell on the earth shall worship him, every one whose name hath not been written from the foundation of the world in the book of life of the Lamb that hath been slain" (vv. 7, 8, R. V.). The "saints" here mentioned are the godly Jewish remnant who will refuse to worship the Beast. Those "overcome" are they who disobeyed the command of Christ recorded in Matt. 24:16; those who obey will be preserved by God—see Rev. 12:6. Note how election is seen here: only they whose names were "written from the foundation of the world in the book of life" will be preserved from the unpardonable sin of worshipping the Antichrist—cf Matt. 24:22, 24.

"And I beheld another Beast coming up out of the earth; and he had two horns like a lamb, and he spake as a dragon" (v. 11). This brings before us the second Beast, called in 19:20 the False Prophet. He is the third person in the Trinity of Evil. As there is to be an Antichrist who will both counterfeit and oppose the Christ of God, so there will be an Anti-spirit who will simulate and oppose the Spirit of God. Just as the great work of the Holy Spirit is to glorify Christ, so the one aim of the Anti-spirit will be to magnify the false Christ (see 13:12). Just as the coming of the Holy Spirit at Pentecost was visibly attended by "cloven tongues like as of fire" (Acts 2:3), so we read of the Anti-spirit that "he doeth great wonders, so that he maketh *fire* come down from heaven on the earth in the sight of men" (v. 13). And just as it is the Holy Spirit who now *quickens* dead sinners into newness of life, so of the Antispirit we are told, "He had power to give *life* unto the image of the Beast" (v. 15).

5. "And the third angel followed them, saying with a loud voice, If any man worship the Beast and his image, and receive his mark in his forehead, or in his hand, the same shall drink of the wine of the wrath of God, which is poured out without mixture into

the cup of His indignation, and he shall be tormented with fire and brimstone in the presence of the holy angels, and in the presence of the Lamb" (Rev. 14:9, 10). This looks back to what we read of in the closing verses of the preceding chapter: "And he causeth all, both small and great, rich and poor, free and bond, to receive a mark in their right hand, or in their foreheads: and that no man might buy or sell, save he that had the mark, or the name of the Beast, or the number of his name" (13:16, 17). This "mark" will be the *official sign* of allegiance to the Emperor stamped either upon the hand or forehead of his loyal subjects. It will be the satanic travesty of the "seal" which the angel will stamp on "the foreheads of God's servants" (7:3). This "mark" on the persons of the subjects of the Beast will be, we believe, *the name of the Devil*, (cf Rev. 13:4), as the seal on the foreheads of God's servants is defined in 14:1 as "having their Father's name written on their foreheads". Here in Rev. 14:9-11 we have one of the most solemn warnings in all the Bible. An angel from heaven will announce the terrible punishment which shall be visited upon those who honor the Beast. It is set over against the threats of the Beast and the False Prophet, who will terrify men by the sentence of physical death for all who defy them. But here God, by His angel, declares that all who heed the Beast and his coadjutor will share their awful doom. This no doubt will strengthen the faith and patience of the saints, and enable them to "endure unto the end".

6. "And another angel came out from the altar, which had power over fire; and cried with a loud cry, to him that had the sharp sickle, saying, Thrust in thy sharp sickle, and gather the clusters of the Vine of the earth; for her grapes are fully ripe. And the angel thrust in his sickle into the earth, and gathered the Vine of the earth, and cast it into the great winepress of the wrath of God" (14:19, 20). The "Vine of the earth" refers, we believe, to the Man of Sin at the head of apostate Israel. This appellation points one more contrast. In John 15 we find the Lord Jesus saying, "I am the true Vine, ye are the branches". The true Vine, then, consists of the Christ of God and His people in fellowship with Him. Over against this is "the Vine of the earth", which is the Antichrist and those allied to him, particularly, renegade Israel. In Deut. 32 there is a reference to the "Vine of the earth"—"For their rock is not as our Rock, even our enemies themselves being judges. For their Vine is of the vine of Sodom, and of the fields of Gomorrah: their grapes are grapes of gall, their clusters are bitter" (vv. 31, 32). That this is speaking of apostate Israel is clear from v. 28—"For they are a nation void of counsel, neither is there any understanding in them". That the passage is speaking of apostate Israel in the days of the Antichrist appears from v. 35—"To me belongeth vengeance, and recompense; their foot shall slide in due time: for *the day of their calamity is at hand,* and the things which shall come upon them make haste" (v. 35).

7. In Rev. 15:2 there is a brief allusion to the Beast, in connection with the godly Remnant: "And I saw as it were a sea of glass mingled with fire: and them that had gotten the victory over the Beast, and over his image, and over his mark, and over the number of his name, stand on the sea of glass, having the harps of God", etc. The reference is to those who had been slain by the Antichrist because they had refused to render him any honor or worship. The same company is seen again in 20:4.

8. Rev. 16 describes the "vial" judgments which are executed just before the end of the Tribulation. The Beast is noticed several times in the chapter. In v. 2 we read, "And the first went, and poured out his vial upon the earth;

and there fell a noisome and grievous sore upon the men which had the mark of the Beast, and upon them which worshipped his image" (v. 2). This is a foretaste of the grievous torments awaiting the worshippers of the Beast. Again in v. 10 we read, "And the fifth angel poured out his vial upon the seat of the Beast; and his kingdom was full of darkness; and they gnawed their tongues for pain". Here the Beast himself receives intimation of the doom awaiting him. In vv. 13 and 14 we are told, "And I saw three unclean spirits like frogs come out of the mouth of the Dragon, and out of the mouth of the Beast, and out of the mouth of the False Prophet. For they are the spirits of demons, working miracles, which go forth unto the kings of the earth and of the whole world, to gather them to the battle of that great day of God Almighty". Here we behold, in symbolic guise, each of the persons in the Evil Trinity. The figure of the "frog" is very suggestive. Frogs are creatures which love the darkness rather than the light: they wallow in the mire and filth: their croaking is heard in the dusk of twilight and by night. Thus they are an apt symbol of the persons in the Trinity of Evil. Their very form suggests inflation by pride. The reference here in Rev. 16: 13, 14 indicates the superhuman character of the False Prophet as well as of the Beast and the Dragon.

9. Rev. 17 calls for a lengthy exposition, but our space is almost exhausted. The central figures in it are "the great whore" and the "Beast". While freely granting that, historically, the great whore has received its fulfilment in the Roman Catholic system, and while allowing that it will yet represent the whole of apostate Christendom, nevertheless, we believe that the ultimate reference is to apostate Israel. Here in Rev. 17 the "woman" is first seen sitting upon the scarlet colored Beast—the Antichrist in his imperial glory (v. 3); but later we see him suffering his ten kings to destroy her (v. 16). This accords perfectly with the dual relation of Antichrist to Israel: first posing as their Benefactor (here seen in v. 3 *supporting* her), later standing forth as her great Enemy. Upon this we shall have more to say in later articles, when we hope to consider at some length the future Babylon and its relation to Antichrist in the End-time. The eighth verse (see our comments on it in Article 3, Section III, 6) is one of the scriptures which show that Antichrist is a re-incarnation of Judas.

10. Rev. 19:19, 20 describes the end of Antichrist's career. We need not enlarge now upon these verses for we have already commented on them in Article 7. The final reference to the Antichrist is in Rev. 20:10 where we read of the Devil being cast into the Lake of Fire where the Beast and the False Prophet are, to be, with them, tormented for ever and ever.

—Arthur W. Pink.

THE LAW AND THE SAINT

1. Introduction.

It has been said that every unregenerate sinner has the heart of a Pharisee. This is true; and it is equally true that every unregenerate sinner has the heart of an Antinomian. That is the character which is expressly given to the carnal mind: it is "enmity against God"; and the proof of this is, that "it is *not subject to the law of God*, neither indeed can be" (Rom. 8:7). Should we be surprised, then, if we find the underlying principles of Phariseeism and Antinomianism *uniting* in the same mind? Surely not. There is no more real opposition between these apparently opposing principles, than there is between enmity and pride. Many a slothful servant has hated his master and his service, and yet had he pride and presumption enough to demand his wages. Phariseeism and Antinomianism unite, like Herod and Pilate did, against the Truth.

The term Antinomian signifies one who is against the Law, hence when we declare that ours is an age of lawlessness, it is only another way of saying that it is an age characterized by Antinomianism. There is little need for us to pause and offer proof that this *is* an age of lawlessness. In every sphere of life the sad fact confronts us. In the well-nigh total absence of any real discipline in the majority of the churches, we see the principle exemplified. Not more than two generations ago, thousands, tens of thousands, of the loose-living members whose names are now retained on the membership roles, would have been disfellowshipped. It is the same in the great majority of our homes. With comparatively rare exceptions, wives are no longer *in subjection* to their husbands (Eph. 5:22, 24); and as for *obeying* them (1 Pet. 3:1, 2, 5, 6), why, the majority of women demand that such a hateful word be stricken from the marriage ceremony. So it is with the children—how could it be otherwise? Obedience to parents is almost entirely a thing of the past. And what of conditions in the world? The abounding m a r i t a l unfaithfulness, Sunday trading, banditry, lynchings, strikes, and a dozen other things that might be mentioned, all bear witness to the frightful wave of lawlessness which is flowing over the country.

What, we may well inquire, is the *cause* of the lawlessness which now so widely obtains? For every effect there is a cause, and the character of the effect usually intimates the nature of the cause. We are assured that much of the present wide-spread contempt for human law is the inevitable outgrowth of disrespect for Divine Law. Where there is no fear of God, we must not expect there will be much fear of man. And why is it that there is so much disrespect for Divine Law? This, in turn, is but the effect of an antecedent cause. Nor is this hard to find. Do not the utterances of Christian teachers during the last twenty-five years go far to explain the situation which now confronts us?

History has repeated itself. Of old, God complained of Ephraim, "I have written to him the great things of My Law, but they were counted as a strange thing" (Hosea 8:12). Observe how God speaks of His Law: "The *great* things of My Law"! They are not precepts of little moment, to be lightly esteemed, and slighted; but are of great authority, importance, and value. But as then, so during the last few years—they have been "counted as a *strange* thing". Christian teachers have vied with each other in denouncing the Law as a "yoke of bondage", a "grievous burden", "a remorseless enemy". They have declared in trumpet tones that Christians *should* regard the Law as "a strange thing": that it was never designed *for them:* that it was given to Israel, and then made an end of at the Cross of Christ. They have warned God's people to have nothing to do with the Ten Commandments. They have denounced as "Legalists" Christians of the past, who, like Paul, *"served* the Law" (Rom. 7: 25). They have affirmed that Grace rules the Law out of the Christian's *life* as absolutely as it did out of his *salvation.* They have held up to ridicule those who contended for a Christian Sabbath, and have classed them with Seventh-Day Adventists. Having sown the wind, is it any wonder that we are now reaping the whirlwind?

The character of the cause determines the character of the effect. *Whatsoever* a man soweth *that* (the same in kind) shall he also reap. Unto them who of old regarded the great things of God's Law as a strange thing, God declared, "Because Ephraim hath made many *altars* to sin, *altars* shall be unto him to sin" (Hosea 8:11). And because many of our Christian leaders have publicly repudiated Divine Law, God has visited us with a wave of lawlessness in our churches, homes, and social life. "Be not deceived; God is not mocked"!! Nor have we any hope of stemming the onrushing tide, or of causing Christian leaders to change their position. Having committed themselves publicly, the examples of past history warn us that *pride* will keep them from making the humbling confession that they have erred. But we *have* a hope that some who have been under the influence of twentieth-century Antinomianism will have sufficient spiritual discernment to recognize the truth when it is presented to their notice; and it is for them we now write.

In the January 1923 issue of a contemporary, appeared the second article from the pen of Dr. McNicol, Principal of Toronto Bible School, under the caption of "Overdoing the Dispensations". The purpose of these articles is to warn God's children against the perils which lie "in the way of much of the positive pre-millennial teaching of the day". Quoting, Dr. McNicol says:

"1. *There is danger when the Law is set against Grace.* No scheme of prophetic interpretation can be safe which is obliged to represent the dispensations of Law and Grace as opposing systems, each excluding the other and contrary to it. If this were the case, it would mean that God had taken opposing and contradictory attitudes towards men in these two different ages. In the last analysis this representation of the relation of law and grace affects the character of God, as everything which perverts the Scriptures, disturbing thereby the mirror of His mind, ultimately does.

"So far from being opposing systems, law and grace as revealed in Scripture are parts of one harmonious and progressive plan. The present dispensation is spoken of as the age of grace, not because grace belongs to it exclusively, but because in it grace has been fully manifested. When John declared that 'the law was given by Moses, but grace and truth came by Jesus Christ', he was contrasting law and grace, not as two contrary and irreconcilable systems, but as two related parts of one system. The law was the shadow, Christ was the substance. The law was the pattern, Christ was the reality. The grace which had been behind the law came to light through Jesus Christ so that it could be realized. As a matter of fact grace had been in operation from the beginning. It began in Eden with the first promise of redemption immediately after the fall. All redemption is of grace; there can be no salvation without it, and even the law itself proceeds on the basis of grace.

"The law was given to Israel not that they might be redeemed, but because they had been redeemed. The nation had been brought out of Egypt by the power of God under the blood of the slain lamb, itself the symbol and token of His grace. The law was added at Sinai as the necessary standard of life for a ransomed people, a people who now belonged to the Lord. It began with a declaration of their redemption; 'I am the Lord thy God who brought thee out of the land of Egypt, out of the house of bondage' (Ex. 20:2). It rested on the basis of grace, and it embodied the principle that redemption implied a conformity to God's moral order. In other words, the very grace that redeemed Israel carried with it the necessity of revealing the law to Israel. The law was given that they might walk worthy of the relation in which they now stood to God, worthy of a salvation which was already theirs. The covenant of the law did not supersede the covenant of promise, but set forth the kind of life which those who were redeemed by the covenant of promise were expected to live.

"The law was not a covenant of works in the sense that Israel's salvation depended upon obedience to it. The devout Israelite was saved by faith in the promise of God, which was now embodied in the tabernacle services. He looked forward through the sacrifices to a salvation which they foreshadowed, and by faith accepted it, as we look back to the Cross and by faith accept the salvation which has been accomplished. The Old Testament saints and the New Testament saints are both saved in the same way, and that is, by the grace of God through Jesus Christ alone.

"Of course the people did not keep the law. It only brought sin to light and proved that righteousness could not come that way, as Paul points out in the Epistle to the Romans. It made all the more evident that there was a need for the work of Christ. But Christ came not to put the law aside and introduce another plan. 'I came not to destroy', He declared, 'but to fulfill'; not to dissolve the obligations of the law and release us from them, but to substantiate the law and make good all that it required. In the Sermon on the Mount He expounded and expanded the law, in all its depth and breadth, and in all its searching sweep. This sermon He spoke to His disciples; it was His law for them. It was not intended for another age and another people; it set forth the kind of life He expected His own people to live in the present age.

"Of course we cannot fulfill the law of the Sermon on the Mount as an outward standard of life. Our Lord did not leave it at that. He was Himself going to make it possible for His disciples to fulfill it, but He could not yet tell them how. When He died and rose again and ascended into heaven, and His Holy Spirit—the same Spirit which had fulfilled and exemplified that law completely in His own life—came flowing back into the lives of His disciples, then they had to keep it. The law was written on their hearts. Their lives were conformed to the law, not by slavish obedience to an outward standard, but by the free constraint of an inward spirit, The ordinance of the law was fulfilled in them when they walk not after the flesh but after the spirit.

"It is this very feature of grace which seems to make it an entirely different and separate system from the law, for it did not exist in the Old Testament dispensation. It could not be realized before the redemptive work of Christ was done and the Holy Spirit came. The Israelites occupied a different position towards the law from that occupied by the Christian now. The law demanded an obedience which the natural heart could not give. In its practical working, therefore, the law necessarily came to stand over man as a creditor, with claims of justice which had not been satisfied. These claims Christ met on the Cross and put out of the way. More than that, by virtue of our union with Him in His death and resurrection, He has brought us out of the sphere where the law as an outward authority demands obedience of the natural man, into the sphere where the law is written upon the heart by the power of the Holy Spirit. He has created for us 'a new man' whose nature it is to fulfill the law by an inward power and principle. This is what Paul meant when he said, 'I through the law died unto the law that I might live unto God' (Gal. 2:19), and when he wrote to the Romans, "Sin shall not have dominion over you, for ye are not under law but under grace' (6:14).

"This new relation to the law has been created by the grace of God through the work of Jesus Christ. *But the law still remains.* It is the reflex of His own character and the revelation of His moral order. He cannot set it aside, for then He would deny Himself.

The wonder and glory of grace consists in this, that it came in, not to oppose the law and substitute another plan, but to meet and satisfy all its claims and provide a way of fulfilling all its obligations. It has pleased the Lord by His grace to magnify the law and make it honorable".

With the above remarks we are in hearty accord*. It is a superficial and erroneous conclusion that supposes the Old and New Testaments are antagonistic. The Old Testament is full of grace: the New Testament is full of Law. The relation of the New Testament to the Old is like that of the oak tree to the acorn. It has been often said, and said truly, "The New is in the Old contained, the Old is by the New explained". And surely this *must be* so. The Bible as a whole, and in its parts, is not merely for Israel or the Church, but is a written revelation from God for *the whole human race*. It is indeed sad to see how little this elementary truth is grasped today, and what confusion prevails.

Even the late Mr. F. W. Grant in his notes on Exodus 19 and 20 was so inconsistent with himself as to say, First, "It is plain that redemption, as bringing the soul to God, sets up His throne within it, and obedience is the only liberty. It is plain too, that there is a 'righteousness of the law' which the law itself gives no power to fulfill, but which 'is fulfilled in us who walk not after the flesh but after the Spirit' (Rom. 8:4). What is merely dispensational passes, *but not that which is the expression of God's character and required by it. Nothing of that can pass.* . . .grace still must affirm this, therefore, not set it (obedience) aside; but it does what law does not—it provides for the accomplishment of the condition. First of all, the obedience of Another, who owed none, has glorified God infinitely with regard to those who owed but did not pay. Secondly,—for this even could not release (nor could there be blessing in release) *from the personal obligation*,—grace apprehended in the heart brings back the heart to God, and the heart brought back in love *serves* of necessity" (italics ours).

With the above quoted words from The Numerical Bible we are in entire accord, and only wish they might be echoed by Mr. Grant's followers. But second, and most inconsistently, and erroneously, Mr. Grant says: "In the wisdom of God, that same law, whose principle was 'do and live', could yet be the *type* of the obedience of faith in those who are the subjects of a *spiritual* redemption, the principle of which is 'live and do'. Let us remember, however, that law in itself retains none the less its character as opposed to grace, and that as a *type* it does not *represent* law any longer: we are not, as Christians, in any sense *under* the law, but under grace" (italics his). This is a mistake, the more serious because made by one whose writings now constitute in certain circles the *test* of orthodoxy in the interpreting of God's Word.

What has been said above reveals the need for a serious and careful examination of the teaching of Holy Scripture concerning the Law. But to what do we refer when we speak of "The Law"? This is a term which needs to be carefully defined. In the New Testament there are three expressions used, concerning which there has been not a little confusion. First, there is "the Law of God" (Rom. 7: 22, 25, etc.). Second, there is "the Law of Moses" (John 7:23; Acts 13: 39; 15:5, etc.). Third, there is "the Law of Christ" (Gal. 6:2). Now these three expressions are by no means synonymous, and it is not until we learn to distinguish between them, that we

---

* Except that in the closing paragraphs Dr. McNicol is somewhat confused about the present *relation* of the Law to the believer.

can hope to arrive at any clear understanding of our subject.

The "Law of God" expresses the mind of the *Creator*, and is binding upon all rational creatures. It is God's unchanging moral standard for regulating the conduct of all men. In some places "the Law of God" may refer to *the whole* revealed *will* of God, but in the majority it has reference to the Ten Commandments; and it is in this restricted sense we use the term. This Law was impressed on man's moral nature from the beginning, and though now fallen, he still shows the work of it written in his heart. This Law has never been repealed, and in the very nature of things, cannot be. For God to abrogate the moral Law would be to plunge the whole universe into anarchy. Obedience to the Law of God is man's *first* duty. That is why the *first* complaint that Jehovah made against Israel after they left Egypt was, "How long refuse ye to keep My *commandments* and My *laws*" (Ex. 16:27). That is why the *first* statutes God gave to Israel were the Ten Commandments, i. e. the moral Law. That is why in the *first* discourse of Christ recorded in the New Testament He declared, "Think not that I am come to destroy the Law, or the Prophets: I am not come to destroy, but to fulfill" (Matt. 5:17), and then proceeded to expound and enforce the moral Law. And that is why in the *first* of the Epistles, the Holy Spirit has taught us at length the relation of the Law to sinners and saints, in connection with salvation and the subsequent walk of the saved: the word "law" occurs in Romans no less than seventy-five times, though, of course, not every reference is to the Law of God. And that is why sinners (Rom. 3:19) and saints (Jas. 2:12) shall be *judged* by this Law.

The "Law of Moses" is the entire system of legislation, judicial and ceremonial, which Jehovah gave to Israel during the time they were in the wilderness. The Law of Moses, as such, is binding upon none but Israelites. This Law has not been repealed, and, in fact, will be enforced by Christ during the Millennium, when "out of Zion shall go forth the Law, and the word of the Lord *from Jerusalem*" (Isa. 2:3). That the Law of Moses *is not binding* on Gentiles is clear from Acts 15.

The "Law of Christ" is God's moral Law, but in the hands of the Mediator. It is the Law which Christ Himself was "made under" (Gal. 4:4). It is the Law which was "in His heart" (Psa. 40:8). It is the Law which He came to "fulfill" (Matt. 5:17). The "Law of God" is now termed "the Law of Christ" as it relates *to Christians*. As *creatures* we are under bonds to "serve the Law of God" (Rom. 7:25). As *redeemed sinners* we are "the bondslaves of Christ" (Eph. 6:6), and as such we are under bonds to "serve the Lord Christ" (Col. 3:24). The relation between these two appellations, "the Law of God" and "the Law of Christ", is clearly intimated in 1 Cor. 9:21, where the apostle states, that he *was not* "without Law to God", for *he was* "under the Law to Christ". The meaning of this is very simple. As a human creature, the apostle was still under obligations to obey the moral Law of God his Creator; but as a saved man he now belonged to Christ, the Mediator, by redemption. Christ had purchased him: he was His, therefore he was "under the Law of Christ". The "Law *of* Christ", then, is just the moral Law of God now in the hands of the Mediator and Redeemer—cf Ex. 34:1 and what follows!

Should any object against our definition of the distinction drawn between God's moral Law and "the Law of Moses" we request them to attend closely to what follows. God took special pains to show us the clear line of demarcation which He has Himself drawn between the two. The moral Law became incorporated in the

Mosaic Law,* yet was it sharply distinguished from it. The proof of this is as follows:—

In the first place, let the reader note carefully the words with which Ex. 20 opens: "And *God* spake all these words". Observe it is not "The *Lord* spake all these words", but "*God* spake". This is the more noticeable because in the very next verse He says, "I am the Lord thy God, which have brought thee out of the land of Egypt", etc. Now the Divine titles are not used loosely, nor are they employed alternately for the purpose of variation. Each one possesses a definite and distinct signification. "God" is the creatorial title (see Gen. 1:1). "Lord" is God in *covenant relationship,* that is why it is "Lord God" all through Gen. 2. In Gen. 1 it is God in connection with His creatures. In Gen. 2 it is the Lord God in connection with Adam, with whom He had entered into a covenant—see Hos. 6:7, margin. The fact, then, that Ex. 20 opens with "And *God* spake all *these* words", etc. proves conclusively that the Ten Commandments were not and are not designed solely for Israel (the covenant people), but *for* all mankind. The use of the title "God" in Ex. 20:1 is the more forceful because in vv. 2, 5, 7, 10, 11, 12 "the Lord" is named, and named there because *Israel is* being *addressed.*

In the second place, the Ten Commandments, *and they alone,* of all the laws Jehovah gave to Israel, were *promulgated* by the voice of God, amid the most solemn manifestations and tokens of the Divine presence and majesty.

In the third place, the Ten Commandments, *and they alone,* of all Jehovah's statutes to Israel, were *written directly* by the finger of God, written upon tables of stone; and written thus to denote their lasting and imperishable nature.

In the fourth place, the Ten Commandments were further distinguished from all those laws which had merely a local application to Israel, by the fact that *they alone* were *laid up in the ark.* A tabernacle was prepared by the special direction of God, and within it an ark was placed, in which the two tables of the Law were deposited. The ark, formed of the most durable wood, was overlaid with gold, within and without. Over it was placed the mercy-seat, which became *the throne* of Jehovah in the midst of His people. Not until the tabernacle had been erected, and the Law placed in the ark, did Jehovah take up His abode in Israel's midst. Thus did the Lord signify to Israel that the moral Law was *the basis* of all His governmental dealings with them.

Thus is it clear beyond any room for doubt that the Ten Commandments, the moral Law of God, were sharply distuingished from "the Law of Moses." The "Law of Moses," excepting the moral Law incorporated therein, was binding on none but Israelites, or Gentile proselytes. But the moral Law of God, unlike the Mosaic, is binding on *all men.* Once this distinction is perceived, many minor difficulties are cleared up. For example: someone says, If we are to keep the Sabbath day holy, as Israel did, why must we not observe the other Sabbaths—the Sabbatic *year,* for instance? The answer is, Because the moral Law *alone* is binding on Gentiles and Christians. Why, it may be asked, does not the death penalty attached to the desecration of the Sabbath day (Ex.

---

* And this of necessity. As already stated, the Ten Commandments reveal the will of the Creator for every human creature, and as Israelites were first God's creatures, before being brought into the relationship of His covenant people, the moral Law was given to them before the Mosaic Law. This explains why the Ten Commandments are *repeated* in Deut. 5. In Ex. 20 they are addressed to God's creatures; in Deut. 5, to Israel *as* Jehovah's covenant people. Mark the *absence* 'n Deut. 5 of *"God* spake all these words"!

31:14, etc.) still obtain? The answer is, Because though *that* was a part of the *Mosaic* Law, it *was not* a part of the *moral* Law of God, i. e. it was not inscribed on the tables of stone; therefore it concerned none but Israelites.

In the articles that will follow this, D. V., we propose to offer an exposition of the principal scriptures in the New Testament which refer to the Ten Commandments. First, we will take up the passages which are appealed to by those who deny that the Law is in any-wise binding on Christians. Second, we shall treat of some of the many passages which unmistakeably prove that all are under lasting obligations to obey the Law of God. Third, a separate article will be devoted to the Christian Sabbath. Fourth, we hope to discuss the nature of true Christian *liberty*. May Divine grace so illumine our understandings and rule our hearts that we shall run in the way of God's commandments.

—Arthur W. Pink.

EXPOSITION OF FIRST PETER

DISCOURSE III.

THE PRESENT AND FUTURE STATE OF THE CHRISTIAN CONTRASTED.

1 Pet. i. 6-9.—Wherein ye greatly rejoice, though now for a season (if need be) ye are in heaviness through manifold temptations; that the trial of your faith, being much more precious than of gold that perisheth, though it be tried with fire, might be found unto praise, and honor, and glory, at the appearing of Jesus Christ: Whom having not seen, ye love; in whom, though now ye see him not, yet believing, ye rejoice with joy unspeakable, and full of glory: Receiving the end of your faith, even the salvation of your souls.

The first step towards the satisfactory interpretation of a long, complicated parenthetical sentence like that just now read, is to analyze it. The sentence consists of a direct assertion, with a long parenthesis interposed. The direct assertion is, "In that time, the last time, ye greatly rejoice; ye rejoice with joy unspeakable and full of glory, receiving the end of your faith, even the salvation of your souls." The parenthetical statement is, "though *now* for a season, if need be" —or, "since there is need, ye are in heaviness through manifold temptations, that the trial of your faith, being more precious than that of gold which perisheth, though it be tried with fire, might be found unto praise, and honor, and glory, at the appearing of Jesus Christ, whom though you have not seen, ye love, not seeing him, but believing in him."

With respect to the direct assertion, a careful reader will easily perceive, that though expressed in the present time, it refers to the future.

The time of the Christian's joy unspeakable and full of glory, is the last time, contrasted with the time of his trial—"now;"[1] when he shall receive the end of his faith, even the salvation of his soul—the same period which is described as that of "the appearing" or manifestation "of Jesus Christ." Instances of an assertion made in the present tense, when it plainly refers to the future, are not unfrequent. "Yet a little while I am," that is, shall be, "with you, and then I go," that is, shall go, "unto him that sent me. Ye shall seek me, and shall not find me: and where I am," that is, shall be, "thither ye cannot," that is, shall not be able to, "come." "How are," that is, shall be, "the dead raised, and with what bodies do," that is, shall, "they come?" "And if any man will hurt them, fire proceedeth," that is, shall proceed, "out of their mouth, and devoureth," that is, shall devour, "their enemies."[2]

The phrases, "a joy unspeakable and full of glory," are too strong to describe the Christian's habitual feelings

---

[1] It is rendered by the future in the Latin Vulgate, and versions made from it.
[2] John vii. 33, 34. 1 Cor. xv. 35. Rev. xi. 5.

in the present state; and we find the very same words employed, in reference to the happiness of the final state, in an after part of the epistle. "But rejoice, inasmuch as ye are made partakers of Christ's sufferings; that when his glory shall be revealed, ye may be glad also with exceeding joy."

The meaning of the apostle would have been more evident to an English reader, had the assertion been rendered in the future time; "in which time," that is, in the last time, ye shall greatly rejoice—(though now for a season, since it is needful, ye are in heaviness through manifold temptations; that the trial of your faith, which is more precious than that of gold which perisheth, though it be tried with fire, might be found to praise, and honor, and glory, at the appearing of Jesus Christ: whom, not seeing him, but believing on him, ye love, though ye have not seen him)—"ye shall rejoice with joy unspeakable, and full of glory: receiving the end of your faith, the salvation of your soul."

The passage, thus interpreted, contains in it a beautiful and instructive comparison, or rather contrast, of the state of Christians in the present and in the last time, on earth and in heaven. The points of comparison or contrast are the following:—I. Now and here, Christ, the great object of their affection, is not bodily present with them, is but imperfectly known by them, and all their knowledge of him, and all their intercourse with him, are by means of faith—Then and there, he will be bodily present with them, intimately known by them, and their knowledge and intercourse will be direct and immediate. II. Now and here, they are exposed to manifold trials—Then and there, they will enjoy the glorious results of these trials. III. Now and here, complete salvation is a subject of faith and hope—Then and there, it shall be the subject of enjoyment. IV. Now and here, they are for a season in heaviness—Then and there, they shall "greatly rejoice;" they shall "rejoice with a joy unspeakable and full of glory." In the remaining part of the discourse I shall endeavor shortly to illustrate this contrasted view of the present and the future state of the true Christian.

I.—CHRIST ABSENT AND BELIEVED ON, CONTRASTED WITH CHRIST PRESENT AND SEEN.

The first point of contrast is, that now and here, Christ, the great object of their affection, is bodily absent from them—is but imperfectly known by them—and all their knowledge of him is by means of faith; then and there, Christ will be revealed—manifested: he will be bodily present with them; he will be intimately known by them, and their knowledge and intercourse will be direct and immediate.

Christ is the great object of his people's affection; he is, by way of eminence, HE whom they love. This is an essential element of the Christian character. When a person is brought under divine influence to understand and believe the Gospel, he perceives that in Christ Jesus centres every amiable excellence in absolute perfection; and that the benefits which he has obtained for us, are infinite in number, value, and duration. He appears at once infinitely lovely and infinitely kind. Contemplating his glory, "the glory as of the only begotten of the Father, full of grace and of truth," the believer says in his heart, "He is the chiefest among ten thousand, and altogether lovely." "This is my beloved, and this is my friend."[1] Reflecting on what he has done and what he has suffered; what he has given, and what he has promised—the believer says in his heart, "I love him, because he first loved me." I love him who "loved not his life to the death," for my salvation. I love him who hath "washed me from

[1] John i. 14. Cant. v. 10, 16.

my sins in his own blood, and made me a king and a priest to God, even his Father."[1] The Christian has other objects of affection besides his Saviour; but HE is the object of his supreme affection. In comparison of HIM, "he hates even his father and mother."[2]

It is of the essence of love to seek union with its object. We naturally wish to be present with, to become intimately acquainted with, to have frequent intimate intercourse with, the object of our affection. These wishes of the Christian, in reference to the great object of his affection, are—can be, but very imperfectly gratified in the present state. He whom we love was once a man among men. Yes, "the Word was made flesh, and dwelt among men." "Inasmuch as the children were partakers of flesh and blood, he also took part of the same."[3] There was a time when it was possible to have become, in the ordinary sense of the term, familiarly acquainted with Jesus Christ; and I believe very few Christians, not naturally deficient in the imaginative and affectionate parts of our nature, have ever read the history of his going out and in among his chosen followers, without in some measure envying their enjoyments. Who has not occasionally felt a wish rising in his heart that he had come into existence eighteen centuries sooner, and that he had had his lot cast in that land gladdened and dignified above all lands by the presence of the incarnate Divinity—that so he might have contemplated the humble shrine of the divine glory, and seen its radiance bursting through in miracles of power and mercy—that he might have gazed on that countenance which beamed with divine intelligence and benignity, and listened to that voice which poured forth a stream of divine wisdom, and truth, and kindness? Who has not sometimes said in his heart, O happy family of Bethany, all whose members were the objects of Jesus' peculiar love, and under whose hospitable roof he spent so many of his hours! O that, like the three favored disciples, we had been admitted to witness the glory on "the Holy Mount," and to watch and weep with him amid his agony in the garden of Gethsemane! O that we had seen him displaying at once the tokens of his unexampled love, and the proofs of the reality of his resurrection! O that we had been with the two disciples when he so opened the Scriptures about himself, as to make their hearts burn within them! O that we had heard the cheering salutation, "Peace be unto you," and felt his warm breath when he said, "Receive ye the Holy Ghost!" Such wishes are natural, I believe, to the renewed mind; and though they belong, it may be, to the weakness of regenerated humanity, I do not think they will be severely judged by Him "who knows our frame, and remembers we are dust."

In the present state, however, these longings cannot be gratified. On the day on which he "led out his disciples as far as to Bethany, and lifted up his hands, and blessed them," "the heavens received him," and they must "retain him till the times of the restitution of all things."[4] And with this arrangement we have good reason to be satisfied, both for his sake and our own. For his sake: for what has earth to offer in the shape of dignity and enjoyment, in comparison of that "name above every name," which he bears in the heaven of heavens, or of those "rivers of pleasures" that are at his Father's right hand? "If we loved him, we would rejoice that he has gone to the Father." For our own: for "it was expedient for us that he should go away; for if he had not gone away, the Comforter would not have come; but having gone, he has sent him to us." Yet still, though we know and

---

[1] Luke xiv. 26.
[2] John iv. 19. Rev. i. 5.
[3] John i. 14. Heb. ii. 14.

[4] Luke xxiv. 20, 21. Acts iii. 21.

believe all this, we feel that our happiness would be increased were we allowed to see his face, and to hear his voice; for we are sure "his voice is sweet, and his countenance is comely."[1]

But not merely is Jesus Christ, the great object of his people's love, bodily absent from them in the present state; while they are here, they can be but very imperfectly acquainted with him. They *are* acquainted with him, and they would not part with their knowledge of him for all the stores of human science. They feel that "it is life eternal to know him;" and they "count all things but loss for the excellency of the knowledge of Christ Jesus our Lord."[2] They know, and they are following on to know, him. They are studying his word, and they are studying his providence, which are both manifestations of him, and they are thus gradually becoming better acquainted with him. But there is much in his word that they but imperfectly comprehend. There is much in his providence which perplexes and confounds them. If it were not their own fault, they might know much more of him than they do; for he is not backward to manifest himself to his people in another way than he does to the world. A more careful study of the Bible, and a more careful study of providential dispensations in the light of the Bible, would be found exhaustless sources of satisfactory information about Him whom we love, affording most amazing displays of his wisdom and power, and faithfulness and kindness. Yet, however carefully these means might be improved, still would it be true that here "we see through a glass darkly; we know but in part,"[3] in reference to him whom we love.

While in the present state, our knowledge of him, and our intercourse with him, are through the medium of faith. "We do not see him—we believe in him." His mind and his heart are made known to us in his word. It is only so far as we understand this word that we know him; and it is only so far as we believe it that we have intercourse with him; his mind then becoming our mind, and his will our will. It is true that we have "the Spirit whom he hath given us;"[4] but that Holy Spirit does not directly give us information about Christ; he only, by his enlightening influence, enables us to understand and believe the information contained in the Scriptures; and while, if we are Christians, we are "joined to the Lord,"[5] and are "one Spirit" with him we love, the intercourse of holy desire and affection is carried on entirely by means of clear and impressive views of revealed truth. Such is the Christian's situation while here below, in reference to the object of his supreme love. He is not bodily present with us—he is but imperfectly known by us; and all our knowledge of him, and intercourse with him, are through the medium of faith.

It will be otherwise by-and-by. In "the last time" there will be "a revelation of Jesus Christ." At the appointed season he will bodily return to earth for the entire salvation of his chosen ones. He will then deliver them completely from "the last enemy" by raising them from the dead; and in his glorified body will forever dwell in the midst of his people, all of them possessed of bodies "fashioned like unto his glorious body." "Ye men of Galilee," said the angels to the disciples who stood gazing up to heaven, after the cloud had received the ascending Saviour out of their sight—"Ye men of Galilee, why stand ye here gazing up to heaven? this same Jesus, which is taken up from you into heaven, shall so come in like manner as ye have seen him go into heaven." "Behold,"

---

[1] Phil. ii. 9 Psal. xvi. 11. John xiv. 28; xvi. 7.
[2] John xvii. 3. Phil. iii. 8.
[3] 1 Cor. xiii. 12.
[4] 1 John iii. 24.
[5] 1 Cor. vi. 17.

says John the divine, hurried forward by the inspiring Spirit to "the last time," even "the time of the revelation of Jesus Christ,"—"Behold, he cometh with clouds, and every eye shall see him." The man Christ Jesus, ordained to be the judge of the world, shall descend from heaven, and having raised the dead, and pronounced and executed righteous judgment on all the living and the dead, shall return to heaven, and spend the endless years of eternity amid his reanimated and completely redeemed people, a glorified man amid glorified men, their Lord and yet their Brother, the visible Head of his visible body, the Church—"the fulness of him who filleth all in all."[1]

That the happiness of the saints will be greatly increased by the bodily presence of their Lord and Saviour, there can be no doubt. But "the Revelation of Jesus Christ" seems to me to import something more than this— something still more closely connected with the happiness of his people. He will not only be bodily present with them, but he will be much more extensively known by them. A much more complete manifestation will be made of his excellence and kindness, and they will be rendered much more capable of comprehending this manifestation. Every obscurity in his word will then be removed. Every dark dispensation will be explained. "In his light they shall see light clearly."[2] The excellencies of his personal character, the wisdom and benignity of his mediatorial administration, and the nature and transcendent dignity of his mediatorial honors, will all be apprehended to an extent, and with a clearness, of which at present we have no conception. The meaning of the scriptural descriptions of his excellencies will then be distinctly understood by his people; and they will find that he is excellent and amiable "above all that they have thought." The whole of his varied dispensations in the administration of universal government, shall appear a consistent display of infinite wisdom, righteousness, and benignity; and the glories of that higher order of administration which is to characterize the celestial state, shall be as fully displayed to them as the limited faculties of their glorified nature admit.

The only other idea which I wish to bring before your minds just now, in illustration of the point of contrast between the present and the future state of the Christian, is, that whereas now, all our knowledge of, and all our intercourse with Christ, is through the medium of faith, then it will be direct and immediate. How knowledge is then to be communicated to us by him, how our intercourse with him is to be carried on, we cannot distinctly say, we cannot clearly conceive. We know it will be as different from our present mode of obtaining knowledge and maintaining intercourse, as seeing a thing is from merely crediting a report about it. We shall live, not by faith, but by sight. We shall see no longer as "by means of a mirror,[1] but face to face; we shall know no longer in part; we shall know as we are known." Our knowledge will not be infinite, but it will be very extensive and perfectly clear, altogether unmixed with error or doubt. So much for the illustration of the first point of contrast.

---

[1] Acts i. 11.   Rev. i. 3.   1 Cor. xv. 26, 42-55.
1 Thess. iii. 15-17   Phil. iii. 20, 21.   Eph. i. 23.
[2] Psal. xxxvi. 9.

(Continued from page 129.)

to be delivered from it. It is not until the sunlight floods a room that the grime and dust are fully revealed. So, it is only as we really come into the presence of Him who is *light,* that we are made aware of the filth and wickedness which indwells us, and which defiles *every* part of our being. And such a discovery will *make us* cry "O wretched man that I am"!

"But", inquires some one, "Does not communion with Christ produce rejoicing rather than mourning?" We answer, that it produces *both.* It did with Paul. In v. 22 of our chapter he says, *"I delight* in the Law of God". Yet only two verses later he cries, "O wretched man that *I am!"* Nor does this passage stand alone. In 2 Cor. 6 the same apostle says, "As sorrowful, yet always rejoicing" (v. 10). *Sorrowful* because of his failures, because of his daily sins. *Rejoicing* because of the grace which still bore with him, and because of the blessed provision which God has made even for the sins of His saints. So again in Rom. 8: after declaring, "There is therefore now no condemnation to them which are in Christ Jesus" (v. 1); and after saying, "The Spirit Himself beareth witness with our spirit, that we are the children of God: And if children, then heirs; heirs of God, and joint-heirs with Christ" (vv. 16, 17); the apostle adds, "But ourselves also, which have the firstfruits of the Spirit, even we ourselves *groan* within ourselves, waiting for the adoption, the redemption of our body" (v. 23). Sorrow and groaning, then, are not absent from the highest spirituality.

In these days of Laodicean complacency and pride, there is considerable talk and much boasting about communion with Christ, but how little *manifestation* of it do we behold! Where there is no sense of our utter unworthiness, where there is no mourning over the total depravity of our nature, where there is no sorrowing over our *lack* of conformity to Christ, where there is no groaning over being brought into captivity to sin; in short, where there is no crying, "O wretched man that I am", it is greatly to be feared that there is *no fellowship with Christ* at all.

When Abraham walked with the Lord he exclaimed, "Behold now, I have taken upon me to speak unto the Lord, *which am but dust and ashes"* (Gen. 18:27). When Job came face to face with God, he said, "Behold *I am vile"* (40:4), and again, *"I abhor myself"* (42:6). When Isaiah entered the Divine presence he cried, *"Woe is me!* for I am undone; because I am *a man of unclean lips"* (Isa. 6:5). When Daniel had that wondrous vision of Christ (Dan. 10:5,6) he declared, "There remained no strength in me: for my comeliness was turned in me *into corruption"* (v. 8). And in one of the last epistles by the beloved apostle to the Gentiles, we read "This is a faithful saying, and worthy of all acceptation, that Christ Jesus came into the world to save *sinners;* of whom *I am chief"* (1 Tim. 1:15). These utterances proceed not from unregenerate men, but come from the lips of God's saints: nor were they the confessions of backslidden believers: rather were they voiced by the most eminent of the Lord's people. Where, today, shall we find any fit to be placed along side of Abraham, Job, Isaiah, Daniel and Paul? Where indeed! And yet *these* were the men who, as believers, were so conscious of their vileness and unworthiness.

May God in His mercy so deliver us from the spirit of pride which now defiles the air of modern Christendom, and grant us such an humbling view of our own uncleanness that we shall join the apostle in crying, with ever deepening fervor, "O wretched man that I am".

—Arthur W. Pink.

STUDIES in the SCRIPTURES

"Search the Scriptures" John 5:39.

A PERIODICAL (MONTHLY "IF THE LORD WILL") DEVOTED TO BIBLE STUDIES and EXPOSITIONS

Associate Editors and Publishers, I. C. HERENDEEN and ARTHUR W. PINK,
Swengel, Pa.

Price: 10 cents per copy; $1.00 per year. Foreign $1.00 per year.

TO OUR SCRIPTURE STUDY FAMILY

"O wretched man that I am! who shall deliver me from the body of this death" (Rom. 7:24).

In our last editorial we pointed out how that this is the language of a regenerate soul, and how that it is in harmony with the confessions of Abraham (Gen. 18:27); Job (40:4; 42:6); Isaiah (6:5); Daniel (10:8), and the apostle Paul (1 Tim. 1:15). We go further: this moan, "O wretched man that I am", expresses the *normal* experience of the Christian, and any Christian who does not so moan is in an *ab-*normal and *un-*healthy state spiritually. The man who does not utter this cry daily is either so out of communion with Christ, or so ignorant of the teaching of Scripture, or so deceived about his actual condition, that he knows not the corruptions of his own heart and the abject failure of his own life.

The one who bows to the solemn and searching teaching of God's Word, the one who *there* learns the awful wreckage which sin has wrought in the human constitution, the one who sees the exalted standard of holiness which God has presented before us, cannot fail to discover what a vile wretch he is. If he is given to behold how far short he falls of attaining to *God's* standard; if, in the light of the Divine sanctuary, he discovers how *little* he resembles the Christ of God, then will he find this language most suited to express his godly sorrow. If God reveals to him the coldness of His love, the pride of his heart, the wanderings of his mind, the evil that defiles his godliest acts, he will cry, 'O wretched man that I am". If he is conscious of his *ingratitude,* of how little he appreciates God's daily mercies; if he marks the *absence* of that deep and genuine fervor which ought ever to characterize his praise and worship of that One who is 'glorious in holiness"; if he recognizes that sinful spirit of *rebellion* which so often causes him to murmur or at least chafe against the dispensations of God in his daily life; if he attempts to tabulate not only the sins of commission but the sins of omission, of which he is daily guilty, he will indeed cry "O wretched man that I am".

It is remarkable that the only other time this word "wretched" (the only other time in the Greek too) is found in the New Testament occurs in Rev. 3:17, where to the Laodiceans Christ says, "And *knowest not that thou ART WRETCHED"!* Their boast was that *they* had "need of nothing". They were so puffed up with pride, so satisfied with their attainments, that they *knew not* their wretchedness. And is not this what we witness on every hand today? Is it not evident that we *are* now living in the Laodicean period of the history of Christendom? Many were conscious of a "need", but now they fancy they have received "the second blessing", or "the baptism of the Spirit", or that they have entered into "victory"; and, fancying this, they fondly imagine that *their* 'need" *has been* met. And the *proof* of this is, *they* are the very ones who 'know not" that *they* are *"wretched".* With an air of spiritual superiority they will tell you that *they* have "got out of Romans 7 into Romans 8". With pitiable complacency they will say that Romans 7 no longer depicts *their* experience. With smug satisfaction they will look down in pity upon the Christian who cries "O wretched man that I am", and like the Pharisee in the temple, they will *thank God* that it is otherwise with them. Poor blinded souls. It is to *just such* that the Son of God here says, "And knowest not that *thou* ART WRETCHED". We say 'blinded' souls, for mark it is to these very Laodiceans that Christ says, "Anoint thine eyes with eyesalve, *that thou mayest SEE"* (Rev. 3:18)!

How entirely different were the confessions and witnessings borne by eminent saints of the past from the ignorant and arrogant boastings of modern Laodiceans! How refreshing to turn from the present-day biographies to that written long ago. Ponder the following:

John Newton, writer of that blessed hymn, "Amazing grace, how sweet the sound, that saved a wretch like me; I once was lost, but now am found, was blind, but now I see"; when referring to the expectations he cherished at the outset of his Christian life wrote thus, "But alas! these my golden expectations have been like South Sea dreams. I have lived hitherto a poor sinner, and I believe I shall die one. Have I, then, gained nothing? Yes, I have gained that which I once would rather have been without—such accumulated proof of the deceitfulness and desperate wickedness of my heart, as I hope by the Lord's blessing has, in some measure, taught me to know what I mean when I say, Behold, I am vile . . . . I was ashamed of myself, when I began to seek Him, *I am more ashamed* now".

Mr. Bradford, of holy memory, who was martyred in the reign of bloody Queen Mary, in a letter to a fellow-prisoner in another penitentiary, subscribed himself thus: "The sinful John Bradford: a very painted hypocrite: the most miserable, hard-hearted, and unthankful sinner, John Bradford" (1555 A.D.).

Augustus Toplady, author of "Rock of Ages", wrote thus in his private diary under Dec. 31, 1767 —'Upon a review of the past year, I desire to confess that my unfruitfulness has been exceeding great; my sins still greater; God's mercies greater than both". And again, "My short-comings and my mis-doings, my unbelief and want of love, would sink me into the lowest hell, was not Jesus my righteousness and my Redeemer".

Listen to the words of that godly woman, the wife of that eminent missionary Adoniram Judson: 'Oh how I rejoice that I am out of the whirlpool! Too gay, too trifling for a missionary's wife! That may be, but after all, gaiety is my lightest sin. It is my coldness of heart, my listlessness, my want of faith, my spiritual inefficiency and inertness, my love of self, the inherent and every-day pampered *sinfulness of my nature,* that makes me such a mere infant in the cause of Christ—not the attractions of the world".

O that God in His sovereign mercy may grant to both writer and reader such a view of their own depravity and unworthiness that they may indeed grovel in the dust before Him, and there praise Him for such wondrous grace to such hell-deserving sinners.   —Arthur W. Pink.

IMPORTANT NOTICES

All new subscriptions will be dated back to January, 1923.

Set of twelve issues for 1922, unbound, $1.00. Bound, $1.50.

Note: We cannot break a set or now supply any **single** 1922 issues.

Subscription Price: $1.00 per year to any address in the world. Single copies 10 cents.

Change of Address: Please notify us promptly of any change of address, and be certain to give both old and new addresses.

Non-Subscribers receiving this Magazine regularly will understand their subscription has been entered by a friend.

Copies lost in the mail duplicated only if we are notified promptly.

Entered as second-class matter December 15th, 1921 at the post office at Swengel, Pa., under Act of March 3rd, 1879.

CONTENTS

John's Gospel (John 5:16-30) 162
Antichrist in Revelation 13 172
The Law and the Saint, #2 177
A Message of Cheer 186
Exposition of First Peter 189

JOHN'S GOSPEL

18. The Deity of Christ: Sevenfold Proof, John 5:16-30.

We present our customary Analysis of the passage which is to be before us. It sets forth the *absolute equality* of the Son with the Father:—

1. In Service, vv.16-18
2. In Will, v. 19
3. In Intelligence, v. 20
4. In Sovereign Rights, v. 21
5. In Divine Honors, vv. 22-23
6. In Imparting Life, vv. 24-26
7. In Judicial Power and Authority, vv. 27-30.

There is an intimate connection between the passage before us and the first fifteen verses of the chapter: the former provides the occasion for the discourse which follows. The chapter naturally divides itself into two parts: in the former we have recorded the sovereign grace and power of the Lord Jesus in healing the impotent man on the Sabbath day, and the criticism and opposition of the Jews; in the latter we have the Lord's vindication of Himself. The second half of John 5 is one of the profoundest passages in this fourth Gospel. It sets forth the Divine glories of the incarnate Son of God. It gives us the Lord's own teaching concerning His Divine Sonship. It, also, divides into two parts: in the former is contained the Lord's sevenfold declaration of His Deity; in the latter, beginning at v. 41, He cites the different witnesses to His Deity. We shall confine ourselves now to the former section. May the Spirit of Truth whose blessed work it is to "glorify" the One who is now absent from these scenes illumine our understandings and enable us to rightly divide this passage of God's inspired Word.

The miracle of the healing of the impotent man, which engaged our attention in the last article, has several outstanding and peculiar features in it. The abject misery and utter helplessness of the sufferer, the sovereign action of the Great Physician in singling him out from the multitude which lay around the Pool of Bethesda, the total absence of any indication of him making any appeal to Christ or exercising any faith in Him previous to his healing, the startling suddenness and spontaneity of the miracle, the Lord's command that he should "take up his bed" on the Sabbath day, are all so many items that at once arrest the attention. The turning of the healed man's steps toward the Temple, evidenced that a work of grace had been wrought in his soul as well as in his body. The grace of the Lord in seeking him out in the Temple and the faithful words there addressed to his conscience, give beautiful completeness to the whole scene. All of this but serves to emphasize the enormity of what follows:

As soon as the healed man had learned Who it was that had made him whole, he went and "told the Jews that it was Jesus" (v. 15). What, then, was their response? Did they immediately seek this Blessed One who must be none other than their long-promised Messiah? Did they, like the prophetess Anna, give thanks unto the Lord, and speak "of Him to all them that looked for redemption in Jerusalem" (Luke 2:38)? Alas, it was far otherwise. Instead of being filled with praise, they were full of hatred. Instead of worshipping the Sent One of God, they persecuted Him. Instead of coming to Him that they might have life, they sought to put Him to death. Terrible climax was this to all that had gone before. In chapter one we see "the Jews" ignorant as to the identity of the Lord's forerunner (1:19), and blind to the Divine Presence in their midst (1:26). In chapter two we see "the Jews" demanding sign from Him who had vindicated the honor of His Father's House (2:18). In chapter three we are shown "a ruler of the Jews" dead in trespasses and sins, needing to be born again (3:7). Next we see "the Jews" quibbling or quarreling with John's disciples about purifying (3:25). In chapter four we learn of their callous indifference toward their Gentile neighbors—"the Jews have no dealings with the Samaritans" (4:9). Then, in the beginning of chapter five, we read of "a feast of the Jews", but its hollow mockery is exposed in the scene described immediately afterwards—a "feast", and then "a great multitude of impotent folk, of blind, halt, withered"! Now the terrible climax is reached when we are told, "And therefore did the Jews persecute Jesus, and sought to slay Him, because He had done these things on the Sabbath day" (5:16). Beyond this they could not go, save, when God's time had come, for the carrying out of their diabolical desires.

"And therefore did the Jews persecute Jesus, and sought to slay Him, because He had done these things on the Sabbath day" (v. 16). Unspeakably solemn is this, for it makes manifest, in all its hideousness, that carnal mind which is enmity against God. Here was a man who had been afflicted for thirty and eight years. For a long time he had lain helplessly by the Pool of Bethesda, unable to step into it. Now, of a sudden, he had risen up in response to the quickening word of the Son of God. Not only so, he carried his bed, and walked. The cure was patent. That a wondrous miracle had been wrought could not be gainsaid. Unable to refute it, the Jews now vented their malice by persecuting the Divine Healer, and seeking to put Him to death. They sought to kill Him because He had healed on the Sabbath day. What a situation! They dared to pit themselves against the Lord of the Sabbath. The One who had performed the miracle of healing was none other than the Son of God. In criticising Him, they were murmuring against God Himself. Therefore, we say we have here an out and out exposure of that carnal mind which is enmity *against God:* that carnal mind which, my reader, is, by nature, in each of us. How this reveals the awful depravity of the fallen creature. How it demonstrates his deep need of a Saviour! How it makes manifest that wondrous grace of God which provided a Saviour for such incorrigible rebels.

"But Jesus answered them, My Father worketh hitherto, and I work" (v. 17). This was not the only occasion when the Lord Jesus was criticised for healing the sick on the Sabbath day, and it is most instructive to observe (as others before us have pointed out) the various replies He made to His opponents as these are recorded by the different Evangelists. Each of them narrates the particular incident (and the Lord's words, in connection with it) that most appropriately accorded with the distinctive design of His Gospel. In Matt. 12:2, 3 we find that Christ appealed to the example of David and the teaching of the Law, which was well suited for record in this pronouncedly Jewish Gospel. In Mark 2:24, 27 we read that He said, "The Sabbath was made for man", that is, it was designed to serve man's best interests—this in the Gospel which treats most fully of service. In Luke 13:15 we find the Lord Jesus asking, "Doth not each one of you on the Sabbath loose his ox or his ass from the stall, and lead him away to watering?": here, in the Gospel of Christ's humanity, we find Him appealing to human sympathies, but in John 5 Christ takes altogether higher ground and makes answer suited to His Divine glory.

"But Jesus answered them, My Father worketh hitherto, and I work". Here is the first of the seven proofs which Christ now gives for His absolute Deity. Instead of pointing to the example of David or appealing to human sympathies, Christ identifies Himself directly with "the Father". In saying *"My Father* worketh hitherto *and I* work" He affirms His absolute equality with the Father. It would be nothing short of blasphemy for a mere creature —no matter how exalted his rank or how great his antiquity—to couple himself with the Father thus. When He speaks of "My Father .... and I" there is no misunderstanding the claim that He made. But let us ponder first the *pertinency* of this affirmation.

"My Father worketh hitherto". It is true that on the seventh day God rested from all His creative works. As we read in Gen. 2:3, "And God blessed the seventh day, and sanctified it: because that in it He had rested from all His work which God created and made". That seventh day of rest was not needed by Him to recuperate from the toil of the six days' labor, for "the everlasting God, the Lord, the Creator of the ends of the earth, fainteth not, neither is weary" (Isa. 40:28). No; but it is otherwise with the creature. Work tires us, and rest is a physical and moral necessity, and woe be to the man or woman who ignores the merciful provision "made for man". If we refuse to rest throughout one day each week, God will compel us to spend at least the equivalent of it upon our backs on a bed of sickness—"Be not deceived; God is not mocked". God, at the beginning, set before His creatures a Divine example, and pronounced the Day of Rest a "blessed" one, and blessing has always attended those who have observed and preserved its rest. Contrawise, a curse has descended, and still descends, on those who rest not one day in seven. God not only blessed the seventh day, but He "hallowed" it, and the word "hallow" means to set apart for sacred use.

While it is true that God rested on that first seventh day from all His creative work, He has never since then rested from His governmental work, His providential work of supplying the needs of His creatures. The sun rises and sets, the tides ebb and flow, the rain falls, the wind blows, the grass grows on the weekly Rest Day as well as on any other. What we may term works of necessity and works of mercy —that is, upholding and sustaining the whole realm of creation and supplying the daily recurring needs of His creatures—God never rests from.

Now says Christ, "My Father worketh hitherto, and I work". All through the centuries has the Father been working. Nor had His working been restricted to the material realm. In illuminating the understandings of men, in convicting their conciences, in moving their wills, had He also "worked hitherto." If, then, it was meet that God the Father worked with unremitting patience and mercy, if the Father ministered to the wants of His needy creatures on the Sabbath day, then by parity of reason it must also be right for God the Son, the Lord of the Sabbath, to engage in works of necessity and mercy on the weekly Rest Day. Thus the Lord Jesus unequivocally claims absolute equality with the Father in service.

"Therefore the Jews sought the more to kill Him, because He not only had broken the Sabbath, but said also that God was His Father, making Himself equal with God" (v. 18). There was no mistaking the force of Christ's declaration. By saying "My Father ... and I" He had done what, without the greatest impropriety, was impossible to any mere creature. He had done what Abraham, Moses, David, Daniel, never dreamed of doing. He had placed Himself on the same level with the Father. His traducers were quick to recognize that He had "made Himself equal with God" and they were right. No other inference could fairly be drawn from His words. And mark it attentively, the Lord Jesus did not charge them with wresting His language and misrepresenting His meaning. He did not protest against their construction of His words. Instead of that He continued to press upon them His Divine claims, stating the truth with regard to His unique personality and presenting the evidence on which His claim rested. And thus did He vindicate Himself not only from the charge of Sabbath violation in having healed by His Divine word a poor helpless sufferer on that day, but also of blasphemy, in making an assertion in which by obvious implication, was a claim to equality with God.

Christ's claim to absolute equality with God only fanned the horrid flame of the enmity in those Jewish zealots— they "sought the more to kill Him". A similar scene is presented to us at the close of John 8. Immediately after being told that the Lord Jesus said "Before Abraham was I am" (another formal avowal of His absolute Deity) we read, "*Then* took they up stones to cast at Him" (vv. 58, 59). So again in the tenth chapter we find that as soon as He had declared "I and Father are one" "*Then* the Jews took up stones again to stone Him" (vv. 30, 31). Thus did the carnal mind of man continue to display its inveterate enmity against God.

"Then answered Jesus and said unto them, Verily, Verily, I say unto you, The Son can do nothing of Himself, but what He seeth the Father do: for what things soever He doeth, these also doeth the Son likewise" (v. 19). This is a verse which has been a sore puzzle to many of the commentators, and one used frequently by the enemies of Christ who deny His Deity. Even some of those who have been regarded as the champions of orthodoxy have faltered badly. To them the words "The Son can do nothing of Himself" seem to point to a blemish in His person. They affirm a limitation, and when misunderstood appear to call for a half apology. The only solution which seems to have occurred to these men who thus dishonor both the written and the incarnate Word, is that this statement must have reference to the humanity of Christ. But a moment's reflection should show that such a conclusion is wide of the mark. The second half of this 19th verse must be studied and interpreted in the light of the first half.

It is to be noted that the verse opens by saying "Then *answered* Jesus and said unto them, Verily, Verily, I say unto you, The Son can do nothing of Himself, but what He seeth the Father do". *What* was it that He was replying to? *Who* was it that He was here "answering"? The previous v e r s e quickly decides. He was replying to those who sought to kill Him; He was answering His enemies who were enraged because He had "made Himself equal with God". In what follows, then, we have the Lord's response to their implied charge of blasphemy. In v. 19 we have the second part of the vindication of His claim that He and the Father were one. Thus it will be seen that the words "The Son can do nothing of Himself" respect His Deity and not His humanity, separately considered. Or, more accurately speaking, they concern the Divine glory of the Son of God incarnate.

"The Son can do nothing of Himself but what He seeth the Father do". Does this mean that His ability was limited? or that His power was restricted? Do His words signify that when He "made Himself of no reputation (R. V. "emptied Himself") and took upon Him the form of a servant" (Phil. 2:7) that He was reduced to all the limitations of human nature? To all these questions we return an emphatic and dogmatic No. Instead of pointing to an imperfection, either in His person or power, they, rightly understood, only serve to bring out His peerless excellency. But here as everywhere else, Scripture must be interpreted by Scripture, and once we heed this rule, difficulties disappear like the mists before the sun.

It will be seen that in v. 30 we have a strictly parallel statement, and by noting what is added there the one in v. 19 is more easily understood. "The Son can do nothing of Himself" of v. 19 is repeated in the "I can do nothing of Myself" in v. 30, and then in the closing words of v. 30 we find that the Lord explains His meaning by giving us a reason—"Because I seek not mine own will, but the will of the Father which hath sent Me." The limitation is not because of any defect in His person (brought about by the incarnation) nor because of any limitation in His power (voluntary or imposed); it was solely a matter of *will*. "The Son can do *nothing of Himself*", literally, "nothing *out of* Himself", that is, "nothing" as proceeding from or originating with Himself. In other words, the force of what He said was this: 'I cannot act independently of the Father'. But was that a limitation which amounted to a defeat? Indeed no; the very reverse. Do the words *"God* that *cannot* lie" (Titus 1:2) and *"God cannot* be tempted with evil" (James 1:13) point to a blemish in the Divine nature or character? Nay, verily; they affirm Divine perfections. It was so here in the words of Christ.

But may it not be that Christ is here speaking in view of His mediatorial position, as the servant of the Father? We do not think so, and that for three reasons. In the first place, John's Gospel is not the one which emphasizes His servant-character; that is unfolded in Mark's. In this Gospel it is His Deity, His Divine glory, which is prominent throughout. Therefore, some explanation for this verse must be found consonant with that fact. In the second place, our Lord was not here defending His mediatorship. His Divinely-*appointed* works; instead, He was replying to those who deemed Him guilty of blasphemy, because He had made Himself equal with God. Our third reason will be developed below.

"The Son can do nothing of Himself". This we have attempted to show means, 'the Son cannot act independently of the Father'. And why could He not? Because *in will* He was absolutely *one* with the Father. If He were *God* the Son then His will must be in perfect unison with that of *God* the Father, otherwise, there would be two absolute but conflicting wills, which means that there would be two Gods, the one opposing the other; which, in plainer language still, would be affirming that there were two *Supreme* Beings which is, of course, a flat contradiction of terms. It was just because the Lord Jesus was the Son of *God*, that His will was in fullest harmony with the will of the Father. Man can will independently of God, alienated from Him as he is. Even the angels which kept not their first estate, yea, one above them in rank, the "anointed cherub" himself could, and did say, "I will" (see Isa. 14:13, and 14 five times repeated). But the Son of God could not, for He was not only very

Man of very man but also very God of very God.

It was this in the God-man which distinguished Him from all other men. *He* never acted independently of the Father. He was always in perfect subjection to the Father's will. There was no will in Him which had to be broken. From start to finish He was in most manifest agreement with the One who sent Him. His first recorded utterance struck the keynote to His earthly life —"Wist ye not that I must be about *My Father's* business?" In the temptation, when assailed by the Devil, He stedfastly refused to act independently of God. "My meat is to do the will of Him that sent Me" ever characterized His lovely service. And, as He nears the end, we have the same blessed excellency displayed, as we behold Him on His face in the Garden, covered with bloody sweat, as He faces the thrice awful Cup, yet does He say, "Not My will, but Thine be done".

"The Son can do nothing of Himself, but what He seeth the Father do". The word for "seeth" (blepo) signifies to contemplate, to perceive, to know. It is used in Rom. 7:23; 11:8; 1 Cor. 13:12; Heb. 10:25, etc. When, then, the Son exerts His Divine power, it is always in the conscious knowledge that it is the will of the Father it should be so exerted.

"The Son can do nothing of Himself, but what He seeth the Father doing: for what things soever He doeth, these also doeth the Son likewise." Here is an assertion which none but a Divine person (in the most absolute sense of the term) could truthfully make. Because the Son can do nothing but what the Father does, so, on the other hand, "What things soever the Father doeth, these also doeth the Son likewise". Note well this word "likewise". Not only does He do *what* the Father does, but He does it *as* He does it, that is, in a manner comporting with the absolute perfections of their common Divine nature. But what is even more striking is the all-inclusive "whatsoever". Not only does He perform His works with the same Divine power and excellency as the Father does His, but the Son also does *all* "whatsoever He (the Father) doeth". This is proof positive that He is speaking here not in His mediatorial capacity, as the servant, but in His essential character as one absolutely equal with God.

We cannot refrain from quoting here part of the most excellent comments of the late Dr. John Brown on this verse:—"All is *of* the Father—all is *by* the Son. Did the Father create the universe? So did the Son. Does the Father uphold the universe? So does the Son. Does the Father govern the universe? So does the Son. Is the Father the Saviour of the world? So is the Son. Surely the Jews did not err when they concluded that our Lord made Himself 'equal with God'. Surely He who is so intimately connected with God that He does what God does, does all God does, does all in the same manner in which God does it; surely such a person cannot but be equal with God". To this we would add but one word: Scripture also reveals that in the future, too, the will of the Father and of the Son will act in perfect unison, for, in the last chapter of the Bible we read that the throne of Deity on the new earth will be "the throne of God *and of the Lamb*" (Rev. 22:1). But before passing on to the next verse let us pause for a brief moment to make application to ourselves. "The Son can do nothing of Himself". How this rebukes the selfwill in all of us! Who is there among the saints who can truthfully say, I can do nothing at my own instance; my life is entirely at God's disposal?

"For the Father loveth the Son, and showeth Him all things that Himself doeth: and He will show Him greater works than these, that ye may marvel" (v. 20). Here again the carnal mind is puzzled. If Christ be the Son of God why does He need to be *"shown"*. When we "show" a child something it is because it is ignorant. When we "show" the traveller the right road, it is because he does not know it. Refuge is sought again in the mediatorship of Christ. But this destroys the beauty of the verse and mars the unity of the passage. What seems to point to an imperfection or limitation in Christ's knowledge only brings out once more His matchless excellency.

"For the Father loveth the Son and showeth Him all things that Himself doeth". The opening word "for" intimates there is a close connection between this and the verse immediately preceding, as well as with the whole context. It intimates that our Lord is still submitting the proof that He *was* "equal with God". The argument of this verse in a word is this: The Father has no secrets from the Son. Because He is the Son of God, the Father loveth Him that is to say, because they are in common possession of the same infinite perfections, there is an ineffable affection of the Father to the Son, and this love is *manifested* by the Father "showing the Son all things". There is no restraint and no constraint between them: there is the most perfect intimacy because of their co-equality. Let me try to reduce this profound truth to a simple level. If an entire stranger were to visit your home, there are many things you would not think of "showing" him—the family portrait-album for example. But with an intimate friend or a loved relative there would be no such reluctance. The illustration falls far short we know, but perhaps it may help some to grasp better the line of thought we are seeking to present.

But not only do the words "the Father showeth the Son" make manifest the perfect intimacy there is between them, but the additional words "showeth Him *all things* that Himself doeth" evidences another of the Divine glories of Christ, namely, the absolute *equality of intelligence* that there is between the Father and the Son. Let us again bring the thought down to a human level. What would be the use of discussing with an illiterate person the mathematics of the fourth dimension? What the value of taking a child in the first grade and "showing" *him* the solution of a problem in algebra? Who, then, is capable of understanding all the ways and workings of God? No mere creature. Fallen man is incapable of knowing God. The believer learns but gradually and slowly, and only then as he is taught by the Holy Spirit. Even the unfallen angels know God's mind but in part—there are things they desire "to look into" (1 Pet. 1:12). To whom then could God show the full counsel of His mind? And again we answer, To no mere creature, for the creature however high in rank has no capacity to grasp it. The finite cannot comprehend the infinite. Is it not self-evident, then, that if the Father showeth the Son *"all things* that Himself doeth" He *must be* of the *same* mind as the Father? that they are one, absolutely equal in intelligence! Christ *has* the capacity to apprehend and comprehend "all things that the Father doeth", therefore, He must be "equal with God", for none but God could measure the *Father's* mind perfectly.

"The idea seems to be this, that the love of the Father, and of the Son, their perfect complacency in each other, is manifest in the perfect knowledge which the Son has of the period *at* which, the purpose *for* which, and the manner *in* which, the Divine power equally possessed by them is to be put forth. It is in consequence of this knowledge, as if our Lord had said—'That in this case (the healing of the impotent man) I have exercised Divine power while My Father was exercising it!'

"And He adds, 'Still further—still more extraordinary manifestations of this community of knowledge, will, and operation of the Father, and of the Son, will be made'. 'He will show Him greater works than these, that ye may marvel', or, 'that ye shall marvel'; that is, we apprehend, 'the Son, in consequence of His perfect knowledge of the mind, and will, and operations of His Divine Father, will yet make still more remarkable displays of that Divine power which is equally His Father's and His *own*'—such displays as will fill with amazement all who witness them. What these displays were to be, appears from what follows: He had healed the impotent man, but He was soon to raise to life some who had been dead; nay, at a future period He was to raise to life all the dead and act as the Governor and Judge of all mankind" (Dr. John Brown).

"For as the Father raiseth up the dead, and quickeneth them; even so the Son quickeneth whom He will" (v. 21). This verse presents the fourth proof of Christ's Deity. Here He affirms His absolute equality with the Father *in sovereign rights*. This affords further evidence that the Lord Jesus was not here speaking as the dependent Servant, but as the Son of God. He lays claim to Divine sovereignty. The healing of the impotent man was an object lesson: it not only demonstrated His power, but it illustrated His absolute sovereignty. He had not healed the entire company of impotent folk who lay around the Pool; instead, He had singled out just one, and had made him whole. So He works and so He acts in the spiritual realm. He does not quicken (spiritually) all men, but those "whom He will". He does not quicken the worthy, for there are none. He does not quicken those who seek quickening, for being dead in sin, none begin to seek until they *are* quickened. The Son quickeneth whom He will: He says so, that ends the matter. It is not to be reasoned about, but believed. To quicken is to impart life, and to impart life is a Divine prerogative. How this confirms our intrepretation of the previous verses! It is the *Divine rights* of Christ which are here affirmed.

"For as the Father raiseth up the dead and quickeneth them; even so the Son quickeneth whom He will". The verse opens with the word "for", showing it is advancing a reason or furnishing a proof in connection with what had been said previously. In our judgment it looks back first to v. 19 and gives an illustration of "what things soever He (the Father) doeth, these also doeth the Son likewise"—the Father quickens, so does the Son. But there is also a direct connection with the verse immediately preceding. There He had referred to "greater works" than healing the impotent man. Here, then, is a specimen—quickening the dead: making alive spiritually those who are dead in sins. This is a further demonstration of His absolute equality with the Father.

"For the Father judgeth no man, but hath committed all judgment unto the Son: that all men should honor the Son, even as they honor the Father. He that honoreth not the Son honoreth not the Father which hath sent Him" (vv. 22, 23). This declaration that the Father judgeth no man—better "no one"—is especially noteworthy. The Father is the One whom we might most naturally expect to be the Judge. He is the first who was wronged. It is His rights (though not His exclusively) which have been denied. His governmental claims have been set at naught. He was the One who sent here the Lord Jesus, that has been despised and rejected. But instead of the Father being the Judge, He hath "committed all judgment unto the Son", and the reason for this is "that all should honor the Son, even as they honor the Father". There is then, or more correctly, there will be, absolute equality between the Father and the Son *in Divine honors*".

"Verily, verily I say unto you, He that heareth My word, and believeth on Him that sent Me, hath everlasting life, and shall not come into condemnation, **but is passed from death unto life**" (v. 24). Once more we find the Lord, as in v. 17, linking Himself in closest union with the Father: "Heareth *My* word, and believeth *Him that sent* Me". But as we have already dwelt at such length on the dominant thought running all through our passage, we turn now to consider other subordinate though most blessed truths. This verse has been a great favorite with the Lord's people. It has been used of God to bring peace and assurance to many a troubled soul. It speaks of eternal life as a present possession—"*Hath* everlasting life", not shall have when we die, or when the resurrection morning comes. Two things are here mentioned which are evidences and results of having everlasting life, though they are usually regarded as two conditions. The hearing ear and the believing heart are the consequences of having eternal life and not the qualifications for obtaining it. It is worse than folly to talk of meeting conditions when those without eternal life are *dead* in trespasses and sins. Then it is added, "And shall not come into condemnation": this guarantees the future—"There is therefore now no condemnation to them which are in Christ Jesus" (Rom. 8:1). No condemnation for the believer because it fell upon his Substitute. Another reason why the believer shall not come into condemnation is because he has "passed from death", which is the realm of condemnation, "into life".

"Verily, verily, I say unto you, The hour is coming, and now is, when the dead shall hear the voice of the Son of God: and they that hear shall live" (v. 25). This continues the same thought as in the previous verse, though adding further details. "The dead shall hear": what a paradox to the carnal mind! Yet all becomes luminous when we remember that it is the voice of the Son of God they hear. *His* voice alone can penetrate into the place of death, and because His voice is a life-giving voice, the dead hear it and live. Once again we press the point that "hearing" is not a *condition* which the sinner has to fulfill in order to be made alive; that would be to get things up-side-down. The capacity to hear accompanies the power of the Voice that speaks, and it is just because that Voice is a life-giving one that the *dead* hear it at all, and hearing, live. Here then is the sixth proof presented for the Deity of Christ: the Son claims absolute equality with the Father *in the power to give life.*

"For as the Father has life in Himself; so hath He given to the Son to have life in Himself" (v. 26). This confirms what we have just said above, while bringing in one further amplification. The Father hath "life in Himself". "It belongs to His nature; He has received it from no one; it is an essential attribute of His necessarily existing nature: He so has life that He can impart, withdraw, and restore it to whomsoever He pleases. He is the fountain of all life. All in heaven and in earth who have life, have received it from Him. They have not life in themselves" (Dr. Brown). Now in like manner the life of Christ is not a derived life. "In Him *was* life" (John 1:4). He is able to communicate life to others because the Father hath "given to the Son to have life in Himself". The word "given" must be understood figuratively and not literally, in the sense of appointed not imparted: see its usage in Isa. 42:6; 49:8; 55:4. So also the word "given Him to *have*", signifies to hold or administer. Thus, inasmuch as all creatures live and move and have their being in God, but in contrast from them Christ has "life *in Himself*", He cannot be a mere creature but must be "equal with God."

"And hath given Him authority to execute judgment also, because He is the Son of Man. Marvel not at this: for the hour is coming, in the which all that are in the grave shall hear His voice, and shall come forth; they that have done good, unto the resurrection of life; and they that have done evil, unto the resurrection of damnation" (vv. 27-29). This brings us to the seventh proof for the absolute Deity of Christ: He is co-equal with the Father *in judicial authority and power.*

"And hath given Him authority to execute judgment also, because He is the Son of Man". The "also" seems to point back to v. 22, where we are told, "The Father judgeth no man, but hath committed all judgment unto the Son". Judgment has been committed to the Son in order that all should honor Him even as they honor the Father. But here in v. 27 Christ gives an additional reason: the Father has also appointed the Lord Jesus to execute judgment "because He is the Son of Man". It was because the Son of God had become clothed with flesh and walked this earth as Man, that He was despised and rejected and His Divine glories disowned. This supplies a further reason why it is meet that the Son of man should be Judge in the last great day. The despised One shall be in the place of supreme honor and authority. All will be compelled to bow the knee before Him; and thus will He be glorified before them and His outraged rights vindicated.

Next follows a reference to the **resurrection of all that are in the graves.** These are divided into two classes. First, they that have done good unto the resurrection of life. This refers to the resurrection of the saints. They that have "done good" is a characteristic description of them. It has reference to their walk which manifests the new nature within them. In the previous verses (24, 25) we have had life, eternal life, imparted to the spiritually dead by the sovereign power of the Son of God. This is His own life which is communicated to them. The Christ-life within is seen by Christ-like acts without. This is forcibly and beautifully brought out in the language which the Lord Jesus uses when referring to His people. Just as in Acts 10:38 the apostle sums up the earthly life of Christ by saying He "went about *doing good*", so here the Lord Jesus speaks of His own as "they that have *done good*", that is, have manifested His own life. These will come forth at the time of His appearing (1 Cor. 15:23; 1 Thess. 4:16); come forth "unto a resurrection of life" for then they shall enter fully and perfectly into the unhindered activities and joys of that life which is life indeed.

"And they that have done evil", describes the great company of the unsaved. These, too, shall "come forth". All the ungodly dead will hear His voice, and obey it. They refused to hearken to Him while He spoke words of grace and truth, but then they shall be compelled to hear Him, as He utters the dread summons for them to appear before the great white throne. They would not believe on Him as *the Saviour of sinners,* but they will have to own Him as *Lord of the dead* (Rom. 14:9). They shall come forth a thousand years later than the redeemed (Rev. 20) unto "the resurrection of damnation". Unspeakably solemn is this. Not a vestage of hope is held out for them. It is not a resurrection of probation as some modern perverters of God's truth are now teaching, but it is the resurrection "unto damnation". Nothing awaits them but impartial judgment, the formal and public pronouncement of their sentence of doom, and after that nothing but an eternity of torment spent in the lake which burneth with fire and brimstone. As they had sinned in physical bodies so shall they suffer in physical bodies. Instead of having glorified bodies, they shall be raised in bodies marred by sin and made hideous by evil—"Shame and everlasting contempt" (Dan. 12:2) describes them. Though capable of enduring "tribulation and anguish" (Rom. 2:9) they shall not be annihilated by the flames (any more than were the physical bodies of the three Hebrews in Babylon's fiery furnace) but continue forever—"Salted with fire" (Mark 9:49): the "salt" speaks of a *preservative* element which prevents decay.

"I can of Mine own self do nothing: as I hear, I judge: and My judgment is just; because I seek not Mine own will, but the will of the Father which hath sent Me" (v. 30). The first part of the verse need not detain us, for it has already received consideration under our exposition of v. 19. The second half of the verse adds a further word concerning the Judgment. "My judgment is just": this is profoundly solemn. Christ will deal not in grace, but in inflexible righteousness. He will administer *justice*, not mercy. This, once more, excludes every ray of hope for all who are raised "unto damnation".

Two additional thoughts in connection with the Deity of Christ come out in these last verses. First, the fact that "all that are in the graves shall hear" the voice of Christ and shall "come forth", proves that He is far more than the most exalted creature. Who but *God* is able to regather all the scattered elements which have gone to corruption! Second, who but *God* is capable of acting as Judge in the Great Assize!

None but He can read the heart, and none but He possesses the necessary wisdom for such a stupendous task as determining the sentence due to each one of that vast assemblage which will stand before the great white throne. Thus we see that from start to finish this wonderful passage sets forth the Godhood of the Saviour. Let us then honor Him even as we honor the Father, and prostrate ourselves before Him in adoring worship.

Let the interested reader study carefully the following questions preparatory to our next lesson on John 5:31-47:—

1. How many witnesses are there here to the Deity of Christ?
2. What is the meaning of v. 31?
3. What is the significance of the first half of v. 34, after Christ had already referred to "John"?
4. What warning is there in the second half of v. 35?
5. What is the force of "Ye think" in v. 39?
6. Who is referred to in the second half of v. 43?
7. What is the moral connection between receiving honor of men and not believing in Christ? v. 44.

—Arthur. W. Pink

12. THE ANTICHRIST IN REVELATION 13.

In the thirteenth chapter of Revelation *two* "Beasts'" are there described. The first is the final Head of the last great Empire before the establishment of the millennial kingdom of our Lord. The second Beast is denominated, in other passages, "the False Prophet". There is a difference of opinion as to which of these "Beasts'" represent the Antichrist. In the Appendix to our book "The Redeemer's Return", where this subject is discussed and from which we shall here freely transcribe, we have stated that opinion is about equally divided. But during the last five years we have made a much wider investigation, and as the result we have found that the great majority of those who have written on the subject regard the *first* Beast as the Antichrist, and that only a comparative few—nearly all of whom belong to a particular school—favor the alternative view. However, the writings of the few have had a wide circulation and have exerted a considerable influence on students of prophecy, and therefore these papers on the

Antichrist would lack completeness, and probably some of our readers would be disappointed, if we said nothing on the subject. It is in no spirit of controversy that we now present our own reasons for believing it is the first Beast of Rev. 13 who is the Antichrist.

The book of Revelation makes known the fact that there is a Trinity of Evil. Each of these three evil persons comes into view in Rev. 13. First, there is "the Beast" (v. 2). Second, there is "the Dragon" (v. 2). Third, there is "another Beast" (v. 11). The fact that of this third Beast it is said "He spake as a dragon" (v. 11) at once intimates his satanic nature and character, for the speech corresponds to the heart. The demoniacal nature of each of these evil persons comes out clearly in Rev. 16:13, 14, where we read, "And I saw *three* unclean spirits like frogs come out of the mouth of the Dragon, and out of the mouth of the Beast, and out of the mouth of the False Prophet. For they are the spirits of demons, working miracles". Finally, in Rev. 19:19, 20 we are told, "And the Beast was taken, and with him the False Prophet. . . . these both were cast alive into a lake of fire burning with brimstone", and then in 20:10 we read, "And the Devil that deceived them was cast into the lake of fire and brimstone, where the Beast and the False Prophet are, and shall be tormented day and night for ever and ever."

The above scriptures clearly establish the fact that there is a Trinity of Evil. Now it surely needs no argument to prove that these three evil persons are opposed to and are the antithesis of the three Persons in the Godhead. The Devil stands opposed to God the Father—"Ye are of your *father*, the Devil", John 8:40, etc. The Antichrist stands opposed to God the Son—his very name shows this. The remaining evil person stands opposed to God the Spirit. If this be the case, then our present task is greatly simplified: it is merely a matter of noting what is separately predicated of the two Beasts in Rev. 13 so as to ascertain which of them stands opposed to Christ and which to the Holy Spirit.

Now there are only two arguments of any plausibility which have been advanced to support the view that it is the second Beast of Rev. 13 which is the Antichrist, but so far as we are aware *no one has endeavored to show that the first Beast represents the third Person in the Trinity of Evil!* Yet he *must* be so if the second is the Antichrist! This is unmistakeably clear from Rev. 16:13, 14 and 19:19, 20. The first argument used is drawn from the language of 13:11, where of the second Beast it is said, "He had two horns *like a lamb*, and he spake as a dragon". This, we are told, indicates that it is the Antichrist who is here in view, aping the Lamb of God. Personally, we are amazed that such an assertion should have been made in soberness. It is difficult to imagine anything more wide of the mark, seeing that not only is it not said this beast with the two horns was "like *the* lamb" but in this same book "the Lamb" is pictured with *"seven* horns" (see 5:6). But if this second Beast, the False Prophet, be the opponent of God the Spirit, then the *two* horns have a pertinent significance, for two is the number of *witness*, and just as Christ declared the Spirit of God should "testify (lit., bear witness) of Me" (John 15:26), so the third person in the Trinity of Evil bears witness to the first Beast—see 13:12, 14, 16. In the second place, it is said that the first Beast of Rev. 13 is presented as the *political* Head, while it is the second who is viewed as the *religious* Head. But if this is not a bad mistake, it certainly needs to be modified. It is the first Beast, not the second, who is *worshipped* (v. 12)! Having thus noticed briefly the two leading objections which have been brought against the position we are about to define and defend, we shall now present some of the many arguments on the other side.

In the first place, to regard the Antichrist as *limited* to the *religious* realm and *divorced* from the *political*, seems to us, to leave out entirely an essential and fundamental element of his character and career. The Antichrist will claim to be the true Christ, the Christ of God. Hence, it would seem that he will present himself to the Jews as their long-expected Messiah—the One foretold by the Old Testament prophets—and that before apostate Christendom, given over by God to believe the Lie, he will pose as the *returned* Christ. Therefore, must we not predicate, as an *inevitable corollary*, that the pseudo christ, will usher in a false millennium, and rule over a mock messianic kingdom? That this conclusion is fully borne out by Scripture we shall show in a moment.

Why was it (from the human side) t h a t, when our Lord tabernacled among men, the Jews rejected Him as their Messiah? Was it not because He failed to fulfill their expectations that He would take the government upon His shoulder and wield the royal sceptre as soon as He presented Himself to them? Was it not because they looked for Him to restore the Kingdom to Israel there and then? Is it not therefore reasonable to suppose that when the Antichrist presents *himself* to them, that *he will* wield great temporal power, and rule over a vast earthly empire? It would certainly seem so. Happily we are not left to logical deductions a n d conclusions. We have a "thus saith the Lord" to rest upon. In Dan. 11:36—a scripture upon which all are agreed concerning its application—the Antichrist is expressly termed *"The King* (which) shall do according to his will". Here then is unequivocal proof that Antichrist *will exercise* political or governmental power. He will be a king—"the king"—and if a king he must be at the head of a kingdom.

In the second place, if the Antichrist is to be *a perfect counterfeit* of the true Christ, if he is to ape the *millennial* Christ as set forth in Old Testament prophecy—for, of course, he will not mimick the "suffering" Christ of the first advent—then it necessarily follows that he will *fill the role of king*, yea, that he will reign as a King of kings, as Satan's parody of the Son of man seated upon "the throne of His glory". That the Antichrist will *also* be at the head of the religious world, that he will demand and receive Divine honors, is equally true. Just as in the Millennium the Lord Jesus will *"be a Priest upon His Throne"* (Zech. 6:13), so the Antichrist will *combine* in his person the headships of both the political and the religious realms—see our notes on Ezek. 21:25, 26 in Article 9. And just as the Son of Man will be the Head of the fifth world-empire (Dan. 2:44) so, the Man of Sin will be the Head of the revived fourth world-empire (Dan. 2:40).

In the third place, to make the Antichrist and "the False Prophet" one and the same person is to involve us in a difficulty for which there seems to be no solution. In Rev. 19:20 we read, "And the Beast was taken, and with him t h e False Prophet that wrought miracles before him. . . . These both were cast alive into a lake of fire burning with brimstone". Now, if the "False Prophet" is the Antichrist, then who is "the Beast" that is cast with him into the lake of fire? The Beast here cannot be the Roman Empire (the people in it), for no member of the human race (as such) is cast into the lake of fire until *after* the Millennium (see Rev. 20). That "the Beast" is a separate entity, another individual than "the False Prophet" is also clear from Rev. 20:10—"And the Devil that deceived them was cast into the lake of fire and brimstone, where the Beast and the False Prophet are". In this last quoted scripture, each of the three persons in the Trinity of Evil is specifically mentioned, and if "the Beast" is not the Antichrist, the Son of Perdition, the second person in the Trinity of Evil, who is he?

In the fourth place, what is predicated of the *first* "Beast" in Rev. 13 comports much better with what is elsewhere revealed concerning the Antichrist, than what is here said of the second "Beast". In proof of our assertion we submit the following:

Points of resemblance between the first Beast of Rev. 13 and the Man of Sin of 2 Thess 2:—

1. The first Beast receives his power, seat, and great authority from the Dragon, Rev. 13:2. Cf. 2 Thess. 2:9—"Him, whose coming is after the working *of Satan* with all power and signs and lying wonders".

2. "All the world" wonders after the first Beast, Rev. 13:2. Cf. 2 Thess. 2:11, 12—"And for this cause God shall send them strong delusion, that they should believe the Lie; that they *all* might be damned", etc.

3. The first Beast is *"worshipped"*, Rev. 13:4. Cf 2 Thess. 2:4—"He *as God* sitteth in the temple of God".

4. The first Beast has a mouth "speaking great things", Rev. 13:5. Cf 2 Thess. 2:4—"Who . . . *exalteth himself* above all that is called God". Note also that in Rev. 13:5 it is said of the *first* Beast, he "has a mouth speaking great things and *blasphemies*". Is not this one of the chief characteristic marks of the Antichrist?

5. The first Beast makes war on the saints, Rev. 13:7. Cf 2 Thess. 2:4—"Who *opposeth* . . . all that is called God", that is, he will seek to exterminate and obliterate everything on earth which bears God's name.

From these points of analogy it is evident that the first Beast of Rev. 13 and the Man of Sin of 2 Thess. 2 are one and the same person.

In the fifth place, that the *second* "Beast" is *not* "the Man of Sin" appears from the fact that the second Beast causeth the earth to worship the *first* Beast (Rev. 13:12), whereas the Man of Sin *"exalteth himself"* (2 Thess. 2:4), and compare Dan. 11:36: "And he *exalteth himself*". As already intimated, there are several things which show plainly that the second Beast is the *third* person in the Trinity of Evil, that is, the one who is the satanic parody of the Holy Spirit. The point now before us supplies further confirmation. There is nothing in Rev. 13, nor elsewhere, to show that this second Beast is worshipped, rather does he direct worship away from himself, to the first Beast. Therefore, he cannot be the pseudo christ, for the Lord Jesus *did*, again and again, receive worship (see particularly Matthew's Gospel), and will be worshipped on His return. But this second Beast, who directs worship *away from himself*, accurately imitates the Holy Spirit in this respect, for nowhere in the New Testament is the third Person of the Holy Trinity presented as a distinct Object of worship; instead, He is to "glorify" Christ (John 16:14) by drawing out our hearts unto that blessed One who loved us and gave Himself for us.

Again; it has been generally recognized by prophetic students that our Lord referred to the Antichrist when He said, "I am come in My Father's name, and ye receive Me not: if another shall come *in his own name,* him ye will receive" (John 5:43). If the one here mentioned as coming "in his own name" *is* the Antichrist, then it is certain that the *second* Beast of Rev. 13 cannot be the Antichrist, for he *does not* come "in his own name". On the contrary, the second Beast comes in the name of the first Beast as is clear from Rev. 13:12-15. Just as the Holy Spirit—the *third* Person in the Holy Trinity—speaks "not of H i m s e l f" (John 16:13), but is here to glorify

Christ, so the second Beast—the *third* person in the Evil Trinity—seeks to glorify the first Beast, the Antichrist.

If it should be objected that the second Beast is represented as *working miracles* (Rev. 13:13, 14) and, that as the Man of Sin is also said to come "after the working of Satan with all power and signs and lying wonders" (2 Thess 2:9), therefore, the second Beast must be the Antichrist, the answer is, This by no means follows. The power to work miracles *is common to each person* in the Trinity of Evil. Just as God the Father, God the Son, and God the Holy Spirit, each perform miracles, so does the Dragon, the Beast, and the False Prophet (see Rev. 16:13, 14 for proof). Three things are said in connection with the second Beast which correspond closely with the work of the Holy Spirit. First, "he maketh *fire* come down from heaven" (Rev. 13:13), cf Acts 2:1-4. Second, "he had power to *give life* unto the image of the Beast" (Rev. 13:15), cf John 3:6—"born of the Spirit". Third, "he causeth all, both small and great, rich and poor, free and bond, to *receive a mark* in their right hand, or in their foreheads" (Rev. 13:16), cf Eph. 4:30—"Grieve not the Holy Spirit of God, *whereby ye are sealed* unto the day of redemption".

Finally; the second Beast is clearly *subordinate* to the first Beast. But would the Jews receive as their Messiah and King one who was himself the vassal of a Roman? Was not this the very reason why the Jews of old *rejected* the Lord Jesus, i. e., because *He was* subject to Caesar, and because He refused to deliver the Jews *from* the Romans!

In the sixth place, as we have seen, in Dan. 11:36 the Antichrist is termed "the King", and if a king he must possess a kingdom, and can there be any doubt as to the identity of this kingdom? Will not Antichrist's kingdom be the very one which Satan offered in vain to Christ? namely, "all the kingdoms of the world, and the glory of them" (Matt. 4:8). That the kingdom of the Antichrist will be much wider than Palestine appears from Dan. 11:40-42—"And at the time of the end shall the king of the South push at him (the Antichrist): and the king of the North (the Antichrist, as King of Babylon) shall come against him (the King of the South) like a whirlwind, with chariots, and with horsemen, and with many ships; and he (the Antichrist) shall enter into the countries, and shall overflow and pass over. He (the Antichrist) shall enter also into the glorious land, and many countries shall be overthrown: but these shall escape out of his (the Antichrist's) hand, even Edom and Moab, and the chief of the children of Ammon. He (the Antichrist) shall stretch forth his hand upon the countries: and the land of Egypt shall not escape". From this scripture it is also clear that the Antichrist will be at the head of a great army and therefore be a *political* ruler as well as a religious chief.

In the seventh place, it is generally agreed among those students of prophecy who belong to the Futurist school, that the rider upon the four horses in Rev. 6 is the Antichrist. If this be the case, then we have further proof that the Antichrist and *the Head* of the revived Roman Empire are one and the same person. This may seem by comparing three scriptures. In Rev. 6:8, of the rider on "the pale horse", we read, "His name that sat on him was *Death* and *Hell* followed with him". In Isa. 28:18, those who will be in Jerusalem during the Tribulation period are addressed by Jehovah as follows: "And your covenant with *Death* shall be disannulled, and your agreement with *Hell* shall not stand". What "covenant" can this be, except the one mentioned in Dan. 9:27, where we read of the Roman Prince (the Head of the revived Roman Empire) confirming the covenant with the many for seven years? Now reverse the order of these three passages, and what do we learn? In Dan. 9:27 we learn that the Head of the Roman Empire makes a "covenant" with the Jews. In Isa. 28:18 this "covenant" is said to have been made with "Death and Hell". While in Rev. 6:8 the rider on the pale horse (whom it is generally admitted is the Antichrist) is named "Death and Hell". Hence, from whatever angle we approach the subject it is seen that the Antichrist is the Head of the fourth world-kingdom.

—Arthur W. Pink.

2. THE LAW AND THE SAINT.

What is the relation between the Law and the saint? By the Law we refer to the Ten Commandments engraven upon the tables of stone by the finger of God; by the saint we mean, the believer living in the present dispensation. What, then, is the relation between the Christian living today and the Ten Commandments formally proclaimed in the time of Moses? It is indeed sad that such a question needs to be raised, and that the Divine answer requires to be pressed upon the people of God. There was a time when it would not have been easy to find a Christian who was ignorant upon this subject; a time when the first thing committed to memory by the children of Christian parents was the Ten Commandments. But, alas, today it is far otherwise. Now, it is becoming increasingly difficult to find those who can give a clear and scriptural answer to our opening question. And as to finding children who can repeat the Ten Commandments, they are rare indeed.

The Law and the saint. Present-day teaching on this subject, as on almost every other scriptural theme, is conflicting and contradictory. There are indeed few Divine doctrines upon which even Christian teachers are uniform in their testimony. What differences of opinion exist concerning Church-truth and the ordinances! What a variety of interpretations of prophecy now confront us! What a lack of harmony concerning the doctrine of sanctification! The same confusion prevails concerning the relation of the Law to the saint. Just as the Confusion of Tongues (Gen. 11) immediately preceded God's call to Abraham (the father of us all) to leave his native home and go forth into that land which he was to receive for an inheritance (Gen. 12), so there is a *confusion of tongues* in the theological world just before the people of God are to be called away from this earth to their heavenly inheritance (1 Peter 1:4). That God has a good reason for permitting the present confusion of tongues, we doubt not—"For there *must be* factions among you; that they that are approved may be made manifest among you" (1 Cor. 11:19, R. V.).

What is the relation of the Law to the saint? Three answers have been given. First, that sinners *become saints* by obeying the Law. Second, that the Law is *a rule of life* for believers. Third, that the Law has *nothing whatever to do with* believers today. Those who give the first answer teach that, the Law defines what God requires from man, and therefore man must keep it in order to be accepted by God. Those who give the second answer teach that, the Law exhibits a standard of conduct, and that while this Old Testament standard receives amplification in the New, yet the latter does not set aside the former. Those who give the third answer teach that, the Law was a yoke of bondage, grievous to be borne, and that it has been made an end of so far as Christians are concerned. The first answer is

Legalism pure and simple: salvation by works; the second, relates to true Christian liberty; the third, is Antinomianism—lawlessness, a repudiation of God's governmental authority. The first view prevailed generally during the Medieval Ages, when Popery reigned almost supreme. The second view prevailed generally during the time of the Reformers and Puritans. The third view has come into prominence during the last century, and now is the popular belief of our day.

How thankful we should be that it is our happy privilege to retire from the theological bedlam that surrounds us, and enter the quiet sanctuary of God's truth; that we may turn away from the conflicting voices of men, to hear what God says on the subject. We trust that this is the hearty desire of our readers. We cherish the hope that few who have read the above paragraphs are so conceited as to suppose *they* have no *need* to examine or re-examine what *the Scriptures* teach about the relation of the Law to believers. We are persuaded, rather, that the reader shares the conviction of the writer, namely, that this is an imperative necessity. It is so easy to conclude that our views of certain Divine truths have been formed from our *own* study of God's Word, when, in reality, they are the products of what we have (correctly or incorrectly) imbibed from human teachers. Our need is that of the Bereans (Acts 17:11)—to "Search the Scriptures daily" to find out whether or not what we hear and read is in accord with the Word of Truth. Moreover, this is sure, "if *any man* think that he knoweth anything, he knoweth nothing yet as he ought to know" (1 Cor. 8:2). Therefore it behooves every one of us to definitely look to God for light and help, and then reverently turn to His Word for the needed instruction.

Before we present to the reader some of the leading scriptures which set forth the relation of the Law to believers of this dispensation, it will first be necessary to examine the passages which are appealed to by those who affirm that the Law has *no* relation to the people of God living today. Let us then turn to these passages, and without prejudice (as far as that is possible) seek to ascertain their true meaning.

1. "For as many as have sinned without Law shall also perish without Law . . . . for when the Gentiles, which have not the Law, do by nature the things contained in the Law, these, having not the Law, are a Law unto themselves" (Rom. 2:12-14). These verses really have no direct bearing on our present theme, inasmuch as they treat of other than saints. Yet, as this passage does relate to the wider subject of the Law in general, and as it is made use of by those who flatly and hotly deny that the Law has any relation to believers today, we give it a brief notice.

It is affirmed by some whom we respect, but from whom on this subject we are obliged to differ, that the Law was given to the nation of Israel and to none else, and therefore, that neither Gentiles nor Christians are under any obligation to keep it. That the Law was formally given to Israel at Sinai is freely granted. But does that prove it was meant for none other than the descendants of Jacob? Surely not. When writing to the saints at Rome (many of whom were Gentiles, see 1:13; 11:13; 15:15, 16, etc.). Paul said, "But now *we* are delivered from the Law" (7:6). Again; in 8:7 he declares, "The carnal mind is enmity against God: for it is not subject to the Law of God, neither indeed can be": mark, it is not "the Jewish mind", but the "carnal mind" in Jew and Gentile alike. Now, there would be no point to this statement if the mind of man, as man, is not obligated to be in subjection to the Law of God. Man's mind is not subject, and because of its innate depravity "cannot be"; nevertheless, it ought to be. Once more: note how in Eph. 2:2 the wicked are said to be "children of *disobedience*": this is meaningless if they are *not* under obligation *to obey* the commandments of God. These scriptures, then, are sufficient to establish the fact that Gentiles, as well as Jews, *are* "under the Law".

Returning now to Rom. 2:12, 13. The simple meaning of these verses is that, the Gentiles never had given to them the two tables of stone on which the Ten Commandments were inscribed, nor were they in possession of the Scriptures, wherein those Commandments were recorded. But it should be carefully noted that Rom. 2:15 goes on to state these very Gentiles "show the work of the Law written on their hearts". On these verses Prof. Stifler has well said, "The argument (of v. 14) lies in this, that Gentiles have what is tantamount to the moral Law". The fact that the Gentiles are "a law unto themselves" shows that God gave them the equivalent of what He gave the Jews, namely, *a standard* of right and wrong. In the case of the former, it was "written in their hearts", in the case of the latter, it was written on tables of stone, and afterwards in the Scriptures. "From this it is clear that the moral Law given to Israel by Moses was but a transcript, or compendium, of the Law which God, in the creation, had stamped upon the moral nature of man . . . . The moral Law, therefore, was not altogether new in the time of the exodus; nor was it something exclusively for Israel, but was a gift for the whole race, and therefore, must be of perpetual validity" (Mr. Wm. Mead).

2. "For ye are not under the Law, but under grace" (Rom. 6:14). This is the favorite verse with those who take the position that the Law has *no* relation to believers of this dispensation. "Not under the Law" is explicit, and seems final. What, then, have we to say concerning it? This: that like every other verse in the Bible, it must not be divorced from its setting, but is to be studied and faithfully interpreted *in the light of its context*. What, then, is the context about? First, what is the *remote* context concerned with? Second, what is the theme of the *immediate* context? By the remote context we mean, the Epistle as a whole. This is always the first thing to be weighed in connection with the exposition of any passage. Failure here is responsible for the great majority of misinterpretations and erroneous applications of Scripture. It should be carefully noted that the words "Ye are not under the Law" but "under grace" are found *not in Hebrews*, but in Romans. This, of itself, should warn us that "not under Law" needs to be understood in a modified sense. If it were true that the Law has been abrogated, then the Epistle to the Hebrews would be the one place of all others where we should expect to find this taught. The *theme* of Hebrews is, The superiority of Christianity over Judaism*. In the expansion of this theme the apostle, again and again, shows how the prominent things in Judaism are now obsolete—see chapter 7 for the changing of the priesthood, from the Aaronic to the Melchizedek order; chapters 8 and 9 for the substitution of the new covenant for the old, etc. And yet, not a word is said in it that the Law is now supplanted by grace.

"Not under the Law, but under grace" is found in Romans, the great theme of which is, The righteousness of God: man's need of God's righteousness, how it becomes the believer's, what are the legal consequences of this, and the effect it should have on our conduct. The prominent feature of the first eight chapters of Romans is that they treat of the *judicial*

---

*This theme is developed by showing the superiority of Christ—the Center and Life of Christianity—over angels, Adam, Moses, Joshua, Aaron, and the whole Levitical economy.

side of Gospel-truth, rather than with the experimental and practical. Romans 5 and 6, especially, treat of *justification* and its *consequences*. In the light of this fact it is not difficult to discover the meaning of 6:14. "Ye are not under Law, but under grace" signifies, Ye are under a system of *gratuitous justification*. "The whole previous argument explains this sentence. He refers to our *acceptance*. He goes back to *the justification of the guilty*, 'without the deeds of the Law', by the act of free grace; and briefly re-states it thus, that he may take up afresh the position that this glorious liberation means not license, but Divine order" (Bishop Moule—1893).

"Ye are not under the Law, but under grace". The contrast is not between the Law of Moses and the Gospel of Christ, as two economies or dispensations, rather is it a contrast between Law and grace as *the principles of two methods of justification*, the one false, the other true; the one of human devising, the other of Divine provision. "'Under Law' means, ruled by Law as a covenant of *works*" (Dr. Griffith-Thomas). "Law" and "grace" here are parallel with "the Law of *works*" and "the Law of *faith*" in 3:27! Rom. 6:14 was just as true of the Old Testament saints as of New Testament believers. Caleb, Joshua, David, Elijah, Daniel were no more "under Law" in the sense that these words bear in Rom. 6:14, than Christians are today. Instead, *they* were "under grace" in the matter of their justification, just as truly as we are.

. "'Not under the Law' does not mean, Not under obligation to obey the precepts of the moral Law; but signifies, Not keeping the Law in order to be saved. The apostle asserts in this verse that Christians are not under the Law, as an actual, effectual adequate means of justification or sanctification, and if they are so, their case is utterly hopeless; for ruin must inevitably ensue. That this is all that he means is apparent from the sequel of his remarks (6:15-8:39). What can be plainer, than that the moral Law as 'precept' is altogether approved and recognized by him. 'See chapter 7:12-14. Nay, so far is the apostle from pleading for oblivion or repeal of moral precepts, that he asserts directly (8:3, 4) that the Gospel is designed to secure obedience to these moral precepts; which the Law was unable to do. It is, then, from the Law viewed in this light, and this only, namely, as inadequate to effect the justification and secure the obedience of sinners that the apostle declares us to be free.

"Let no one, then, abuse this declaration by imagining that it in anywise affords ground to believe that Christians are freed from obligation to obey the precepts of the moral Law. What is the Divine Law but a transcript of the Divine will? And are not Christians to be conformed to this? Is not all the Law summed up in these two declarations: 'Thou shalt love the Lord with all thine heart; and thy neighbour as thyself'! And are Christians absolved from loving God and their neighbour? If not, then this part of the subject stands unembarassed by anything which the apostle has said in our text or context" (Prof. Moses Stuart).

The force of Rom. 6:14 becomes more apparent if we observe what follows it. In the very next verse we read, "What then? Shall we sin, because we are not under the Law, but under grace? God forbid". This anticipates an objection: If we are not under the Law as the ground of our justification, then are we to be *lawless?* The inspired answer is, God forbid. Nothing is more self-evidently certain, then, that if the moral Law is *not* a rule of life to believers, they *are* at liberty to disregard its precepts. But the apostle rejects this error with the utmost abhorrence. We quote here a part of Calvin's comments on Rom. 6:15: "But we are much deceived if we think, that the righteousness which God approves of in His Law is abolished, when the Law is abrogated; for the abrogation is by no means to be applied to the precepts which teach the right way of living, as Christ confirms and sanctions these, and does not abrogate them; but the right view is, that *nothing is taken away but the curse,* to which men without grace are subject".

In what follows, to the end of the chapter, the apostle shows that though the believer is *"not under Law"* as the ground of his justification, nevertheless, he *is* under the Law as a rule of his Christian life, that is, he is under obligations to obey its moral precepts. In v. 18 (which contains the positive answer to the question asked in v. 15) the apostle declares, "Being then made free from sin, ye became the *servants* (bond-slaves) of *righteousness*". Again, in v. 22 he says, "But now being made free from sin, and become *servants* to God, ye have your fruit unto holiness". Observe carefully, it is not here said "servants *of Christ*", nor "servants of *the Father*", which would bring in quite another thought, but "servants *of God*", which enforces the believer's responsibility to the Law-giver. That this is the meaning of Rom. 6:18 and 22 is clear from 7:25, where the apostle says, "So then with the mind I myself *serve* THE LAW OF GOD".

3. "Wherefore, my brethren, ye also are become dead to the Law . . . . Now we are delivered from the Law" (Rom. 7:4, 6). These statements really call for a full exposition of Rom. 7:1-6, but it would occupy too much space to give that here. Perhaps we can arrive at the meaning of these two verses by a shorter route. They occur in a section of the Epistle which treats of the *results* of Divine righteousness being imputed to the believer. Chapter 4 deals with the imputation of this righteousness; chapters 5 to 8 give the results. The results (summarized) are as follows:—5:1-11 Justification and Reconciliation; 5:12-6:23 Identification with Christ, the last Adam; 7:1-25 Emancipation from the Curse of the Law; 8:1-39 Preservation through time and eternity. Thus it will be seen that these chapters deal mainly with the *Divine* rather than the human side of things. "Dead to the Law" in 7:4 is parallel with "dead to sin" in 6:2: parallel in this sense, that it is objective "death" not subjective; the judicial and not the practical aspect of truth which is in view. Observe it is said, we "became dead to the Law *by the body of Christ*," not by a Divine repeal of the Law. In order words, we died to the Law *vicariously,* in the person of our blessed Substitute. So, too, we are "delivered from the Law", or as the R. V. more accurately puts it, "We have been discharged from the Law", because we have "died to that wherein we were held". In Christ *we* "died" to the judicial threatenings and ceremonial requirements of the Law.

"'Dead to the Law'. By the term the Law, in this place, is intended that Law which is obligatory both on Jews and Gentiles. It is the Law, the work of which is written in the hearts of all men; and that Law which was given to the Jews in which they rested, 2:17. It is the Law taken in the largest extent of the word, including the whole will of God in any way manifested to all mankind, whether Jew or Gentile. All those whom the apostle is addressing, had been under this Law in their unconverted state. . . . To the moral Law exclusively here and throughout the rest of the chapter, the apostle refers. . . . Dead to the Law means freedom from the power of the Law, as having endured its penalty, and satisfied its demands. It has ceased to have a claim on the obedience of believers in order to life (better, on believers it has ceased to pronounce its curse—A. W. P.), although *it still remains their rule of duty"* (Robert Haldane). On the words, "Now we are delivered from the Law", Mr. Haldane says: "Christ hath fulfilled the Law, and suffered its penalty for them, and they in consequence are free from its demands for the purpose of obtaining life, or that, on account of the breach of it, they should suffer death".

One further word needs to be said on Rom. 7:4-6. Some insist that the whole passage treats only of *Jewish* believers. But this is certainly a mistake. When Paul says in v. 1 "I speak to them that know Law"—there is no article in the Greek—he reasons on the basis that his readers were fully cognizant of the principle that "the Law hath dominion over a man so long as he liveth". If Paul was here *confining* his address to *Jewish* believers, he had said, "I speak to those *among you* who know the Law". When he says "Know ye not *brethren*" (v. 1) and "Wherefore, my *brethren*" (v. 4) he is addressing his brethren in Christ as is clear by a comparison of 1:13. When he is referring to the Jews, his brethren by nature, he is careful to so intimate, "My brethren, my kinsmen according to the flesh" (9:3)! Finally, it should be carefully noted how the apostle uses the pronouns "ye" and "we" *interchangeably* in vv. 4 and 5. The emphatic "ye also" in v. 4 seems specifically designed to show that his illustration in the previous verses, with its obvious suggestion of Israel's history, was strictly applicable to *all* Christians.

"The deliverance from Law in Galatians is that which leads to the sonship of all saints, while the deliverance in Romans leads to the union of all saints with Christ. But in both they are viewed as all alike having been in bondage under Law, and all alike delivered from it. For indeed it is the design of the Holy Spirit ever to lead the saints of all ages to regard themselves as delivered from a common guilt, redeemed from a common curse —'the curse of the Law'—rescued from a common doom; and all this as the result of the curse being fulfilled in the death of him in whom they all alike died" (Charles Campbell).

4. "For Christ is the end of the Law for righteousness to every one that believeth" (Rom. 10:4). Frequently, only the first half of this verse is quoted, "Christ is the end of the Law". But this is not all that is said here. Christ is the end of the Law *for righteousness*, that is, before God. The context unequivocally settles the scope and significance of this expression. Paul had just affirmed that Israel, who were ignorant of God's righteousness, had gone about "to establish *their own* righteousness". Once more it is *justification* which is in view, and not the walk of a believer. The meaning, then, of Rom. 10:4 is very simple. Says Dr. Thos. Chalmers: "There is one obvious sense in which Christ is the end of the Law, and that is, when the Law viewed as a schoolmaster brings us to the conclusion, as to its last lesson, that Christ is our only refuge, our only righteousness". So also Dr. G. Thomas: "With Christ before us *legal* righteousness is necessarily at an end, and in not submitting to Christ, the Jews were refusing to submit to the God who gave them the Law".

5. Another passage frequently appealed to by those who insist on the total abrogation of the Law is 2 Cor. 3. Such expressions as "That which is done away" (v. 11), and "that which is abolished" (v. 13) are regarded as alluding to the Ten Commandments "written and engraven in stones" (v. 7). That this is a mistake, is easily proven. For in Rom. 13:9 and Eph. 6:2 several of the Ten Commandments are quoted and enforced. This is quite sufficient to prove that the moral Law *is not* "done away". And such scriptures as Isa. 2:2, 3; Jer. 31:33, etc. make it plain that the Law *is not* "abolished", inasmuch as it will be in use during the Millennium.

In 2 Cor. 3 (and again and again throughout the Epistle) Paul is contending against false "apostles" (note

2:17 and see further 6:1; 11:3, 4, 13, 22) who, preaching the Law to the exclusion of Christ, were seducing the people of God from the blessings of the new covenant. Consequently, the apostle is not here treating of the Law as the moral standard of conduct for believers, but as that which condemns sinners. The inspired penman is pointing out the folly of turning back to the Law as the ground of acceptance before God—which was what the false apostles insisted on. The method he follows is to draw a series of contrasts between the old covenant and the new, showing the immeasurable superiority of the latter over the former. He shows that apart from Christ, the old covenant was but a ministration of condemnation and death; that just as the body without the spirit is dead, so the Law without Christ was but a lifeless "letter". 2 Cor. 3, then, contrasts Christianity from Judaism. That which has been "done away" is the old covenant; that which is "abolished" (for the Christian) is the ceremonial law.

6. In the Galatian Epistle there are quite a number of verses which are used by those who affirm the Law has no relation to believers today—e. g. 2:19; 3:13; 3:23-25; 4:5; 5:18. Now it is impossible to understand these verses unless we first see what is the theme and character of the Epistle in which they are found. The theme of Galatians is the Believer's Emancipation from the Law. The special character of the Epistle is that it was written to confirm the faith of Christians, who had been troubled and shaken by Judaisers. But a careful reading of the Epistle should show that the Emancipation here viewed is not from the Law as the standard of moral conduct, but from the *curse* or penalty of the Law; and the particular heresy of the Judaisers was not that they pressed the Ten Commandments upon the saints as a rule of life, but that they insisted the works of the Law must be fulfilled before a sinner could be saved.

(See Acts 15:1). "The trouble at Galatia was *legalism* and *ritualism*. Speaking strictly the two are one; for the attempt to secure Divine favor through law observance leads inevitably to ritualism in its worst form. That the Galatians were going over to the ground of law *for acceptance with God* is evident from the whole tenor of the Epistle" (Prof. W. G. Morehead on "Galatians"). "The object of the Epistle to the Galatians was to restore among them the pure Gospel which they had received, but which they had so mingled with human works and ceremonies and a notion of their own free will and merits, as to have wellnigh lost it" ("Grace in Galatians" by Dr. George S. Bishop).

The central issue raised in Galatians is not what is the standard of conduct for the believer's life, but what is the ground of a sinner's salvation. In proof of this assertion note carefully that in Gal. 1:7 Paul expressly says the Judaistic troublers were they who "would pervert the *Gospel* of Christ". Again, "That no man is *justified* by the Law in the sight of God is evident", etc. (3:11) shows the trend of the argument. Again; "For I testify again to every man *that is circumcised*, that he is a debtor to do the whole Law" (5:3 and cf 6:15) indicates wherein the Judaisers erred. So, "Christ is become of no effect unto you, whosoever of you are *justified* by the Law; ye are fallen from grace" (Gal. 5:4) evidences the subject of the Epistle. To "fall from grace" means not for a Christian to obey the Ten Commandments, but to do the works of the Law (moral and ceremonial) *in order to be* justified. The Law and the Gospel are irreconcilable. Every attempt to combine them strikes equally at the majesty of the Law and the grace of the Gospel.

On Gal. 3:25 Dr. George Bishop has this to say: "We are no longer 'under a schoolmaster' i. e., for discipline, for penalty. It does not mean for precept. It does not mean that the Ten

Commandments are abolished. It simply says, You are not saved by keeping the Commandments, nor are you lost if you fail. It is Christ who has saved you, and you cannot be lost. Now you will obey from the instinct of the new nature and from gratitude, for these are holiness". On 5:13, 14 he says, " 'By love serve one another'. Here the Law is brought in as a service. 'I am among you', said Jesus, 'as One that serveth'—'If ye love Me *keep My commandments*'. The New Testament repeats and enforces all the Ten Commandments. They were given to be kept, and kept they shall be. Matt. 5:19: 'For all the Law is fulfilled in one word, even in this, Thou shalt love thy neighbour as thyself'. 'The Law is fulfilled': the Law was given to be fulfilled, not only *for* us, but *in* us, who walk not after the flesh but after the Spirit. There is danger here of a mistake on either side—for if we do not preach faith alone for salvation, no one is saved; but if we preach a faith that does not *obey*, we preach that which nullifies the faith which saves us."

On Gal. 5:18 Dr. John Eadie has this to say: "The Galatians were putting themselves in subjection to Law, and ignoring the free government of the Spirit. To be led by the Spirit is incompatible with being under the Law. So the beginning of Gal. 3. To be under the Law is thus to acknowledge its claim and to seek to obey it *in hope of meriting eternal life*". To be led by the Spirit is incompatible with being under the Law because the Holy Spirit leads a sinner to trust in Christ alone for salvation.

7. "Blotting out the handwriting of ordinances that was against us, which was contrary to us, and took it out of the way, nailing it to His cross" (Col. 2:14). Here it is assumed that the "handwriting of ordinances" refers to the Ten Commandments, and, that "which was contrary *to us*", refers to Christians. Such a distortion is quickly discovered once this interpretation is exposed to the light. Observe, in the first place, that at the beginning of the previous verse the apostle refers to *Gentile* believers—"And *you*, being dead in your sins and the uncircumcision of your flesh", etc. The "us" of v. 14 refers, then, to *Jewish* believers. But *between* the "you" and the "us" is a word which supplies the key to what follows, namely, the word "together", which here, as in Eph. 2:5, 6, points to the spiritual union of believing Gentiles with believing Jews. Believing Jews and Gentiles were "quickened together". And how could that be? Because they were "quickened together *with Him*". Christ acted vicariously, as the Representative of all His people, so that when He died they all died (judicially); when He was quickened they all were; when He rose again they all rose: not merely one part of them did, but all *together*. But in order for Jew and Gentile to enjoy fellowship, in order for them to be brought "together", that which had hitherto *separated* them must be made an end of. And it is *this* which is in view in Col. 2:14. The "handwriting of ordinances" was *"against us"*, i. e. against the Jews, for their Divinely-given Law prohibited them from all religious intercourse with the Gentiles. But that which *had* been against the Jews, was *taken out of the way*, being nailed to the Cross. Nor does this interpretation stand unsupported: it is indubitably confirmed by a parallel passage.

It is well-known among students of the Word that the Epistles of Ephesians and Colossians are largely complementary and supplementary; and it will frequently be found that the one is absolutely indispensable to the interpretation of the other. Now in Eph. 2 there is a passage which is strictly parallel with this portion of Col. 2. In v. 11 the apostle addresses the Gentile saints, who were of the Uncircumcision—note the reference to "uncircumcision" in Col. 2:13. Then in v. 12 he reminds them of how in their unconverted state they had been "aliens from the commonwealth of Israel", etc. But in v. 13 he tells them that they had been "made nigh" by the blood of Christ. The result of this is stated in v. 14: "For He is our peace who hath made *both* one" (i. e. both believing Jews and believing Gentiles): the "made both *one*" being parallel with the "quickened *together*" of Col. 2:13. Next the apostle tells how this had been made possible: "And hath broken down the middle wall of partition" (that had separated Jew from Gentile); which is parallel with "and took it out of the way", etc. Then the apostle declares, "having *abolished* in His flesh the enmity, the Law of commandments contained in *ordinances*", which is parallel with *"blotting out* the handwriting of *ordinances"!* Thus has God most graciously made us entirely independent of all human interpretations of Col. 2:13, 14, by interpreting it for us in Eph. 2:11-15. How much we lose by failing to compare scripture with scripture.

8. One other verse we must consider, and that is 1 Tim. 1:9: "Knowing this, that the Law is not made for a righteous man, but for the lawless and disobedient, for the ungodly and for sinners", etc. The key to this is supplied in the immediate context. In vv. 3 and 4 the apostle bids Timothy to "charge some that they preach no other doctrine, neither give heed to fables and endless genealogies", etc. It is clear that he has in mind those who had been infected by Judaisers. In v. 5 the apostle tells his son in the faith what was *the "end"*, of "the commandments"—i. e. the moral Law, as is clear from what precedes and what follows. The design or aim of that Law which is "holy and just and good" (Rom. 7: 12) was to direct and advance love to God and men; but this love ("charity") can spring only "out of a pure heart and a good conscience, and faith unfeigned".

Next, in vv. 6 and 7 the apostle taxes the Judaisers and those affected by them, as having "swerved" from love and faith, turning aside to "vain jangling", and setting themselves up as teachers of the Law, understanding neither what they said nor affirmed. Then, in v. 8, the apostle guards against his readers drawing a false inference from what he had just said in v. 7, and so he declares "But we know that the Law is good, if a man use it lawfully"; thus amplifying what he had affirmed in v. 5. Lest they should think that because he had reflected upon the Judaisers, he had also disparaged the Law itself, he added this safeguard in v. 8. To "use" the Law "lawfully", is to use it as God intended it to be used: not as a means of salvation, but as a standard of conduct; not as the ground of our justification, but as the director of our obedience to God. The Law is used *unlawfully*, not when presented as the rule of the believer's life, but when it is opposed to Christ!

Finally, in vv. 9 and 10 the apostle contrasts the design of the Law as it respected believers and unbelievers: "The Law is not made for a righteous man, but for the lawless and disobedient", etc. That is to say, the Law as an instrument of terror and condemnation, was not made for the righteous but for the wicked. "The Law, threatening, compelling, condemning, is not made for a righteous man, because he is pushed forward to duty of his own accord, and is no more led by the spirit of bondage and fear of punishment" (Turretin). "By the Law is to be understood, the moral Law, as it is armed with stings and terrors, to restrain rebellious sinners. By the righteous man, is meant, one in whom a principle of Divine grace is planted, and who, for the knowledge and love of God, chooses the things that are pleasing to Him. As the Law has annexed so many severe threatenings to the transgression of it, it is evidently directed to the wicked, who will only be compelled by fear from the outrageous breaking of it" (Poole's Annotations).

We have now examined every passage of any importance in the New Testament which is used by modern Antinomians. And not one of them has a word to say against believers in this dispensation *using the Law* as the standard of their moral conduct. In our next article, we shall treat of the positive side of the subject, and show that the children of God *are* obligated to obey the Ten Commandments, not as a condition of salvation, but as the director of their obedience to God.

In this article we have departed from our usual custom, in that we have quoted from quite a number of the commentators of the past. This has been done, not because we desired to buttress our expositions by an appeal to human authorities—though the interpretations of godly men of the past are not to be scorned and regarded as obsolete, rather should they receive the careful examination which they merit, for it was under such teaching was produced Christian conduct that puts to unutterable shame the laxity of the present-day Christian walk. No, we have appealed to the writings of Christian exegetes of the past that it might be seen we have not given a forced and novel interpretation of those passages which stood in the way of what we deem to be the truth on the subject of the relation of the Law to Christians; but instead, an interpretation which, though the result of personal study, is in full accord with that given by many, who for piety, scholarship, spiritual discernment, and knowledge of the Scriptures, few living today are worthy to be compared.

A MESSAGE OF CHEER

"And we know that all things work together for good to them that love God, to them who are the called according to His purpose" (Rom. 8:28).

How many of God's children have, through the centuries, drawn strength and comfort from this blessed verse. In the midst of trials, perplexities, and persecutions, this has been a rock beneath their feet. Though to outward sight things *seemed* to work *against* their good, though to carnal reason things *appeared* to be working for their *ill*, nevertheless, faith knew it was far otherwise. And how great the loss to those who *failed* to rest upon this inspired declaration: what unnecessary fears and doubtings were the consequence.

"*All things* work together". The first thought occurring to us is this: What a glorious Being must our God be, who is able to make all things so work!

What a frightful amount of evil there is in constant activity. What an almost infinite number of creatures there are in the world. What an incalculable quantity of opposing self-interests at work. What a vast army of rebels fighting against God. What hosts of super-human creatures ever opposing the Lord. And yet, high above all, is GOD, in undisturbed calm, complete master of the situation. There, from the throne of His exalted majesty, He worketh all things after the counsel of His own will (Eph. 1:11). Stand in awe, then, before this One in whose sight "all nations are as nothing; and they are counted as less than nothing, and vanity" (Isa. 40:17). Bow in adoration before this "High and Lofty One that inhabiteth eternity" (Isa. 57:15). Lift high your praise unto Him who from the direst evil can educe the greatest good.

"All things *work*". In nature there is no such thing as a vacuum, neither is there a creature of God that fails to serve its designed purpose. Nothing is idle. Everything is energized by God so as to fulfill its intended mission. All things are laboring toward the grand end of their Creator's pleasure: all are *moved* at His imperative bidding.

"All things *work together*". They not only operate, they co-operate; they all act in perfect concert, though none but the anointed ear can catch the strains of their harmony. All things work together, not singly but conjointly, as adjunct causes and mutual helps. That is why afflictions seldom come solitary and alone. Cloud rises upon cloud: storm upon storm. As with Job, one messenger of woe quickly succeeded by another, burdened with tidings of yet heavier sorrow. Nevertheless, even here *faith* may trace both the wisdom and love of God. It is the compounding of the ingredients in the recipe that constitutes its beneficent value. So with God: His dispensations not only "work", but they work together." So recognized the sweet singer of Israel—"He drew me out of *many* waters" (Psa. 18:16).

"All things work together *for good* to", etc. These words teach believers that no matter what may be the number nor how overwhelming the character of adverse circumstances, they are all contributing to conduct them into the possession of the inheritance provided for them in heaven. How wonderful is the providence of God in over-ruling things most disorderly, and in turning to our good things which in themselves are most pernicious! We marvel at His mighty power which holds the heavenly bodies in their orbits; we wonder at the continually recurring seasons and the renewal of the earth; but this is not nearly so marvellous as His bringing good out of evil in all the complicated occurrences of human life, and making even the power and malice of Satan, with the naturally destructive tendency of his works, to minister good for His children.

"All things work together *for good*". This *must be so* for three reasons. First, because *all things* are under the absolute control of the Governor of the universe. Second, because *God desires* our good, and nothing but our good. Third, because even Satan himself cannot touch a hair of our heads without God's permission, and then only for our further good. Not all things are good in themselves, nor in their tendencies; but God makes all things *work* for our good. Nothing enters our life by blind chance: nor are there any accidents. Everything is being *moved* by God, with this end in view, our *good*. Everything being subservient to God's eternal purpose, works blessing to those marked out for conformity to the image of the Firstborn. All suffering, sorrow, loss, are used by our Father to minister to the benefit of His elect.

"To them that *love God*". This is the grand distinguishing feature of every true Christian. The reverse marks all the unregenerate. But the saints are those who *love God*. Their creeds may differ in minor details; their ecclesiastical relations may vary in outward form; their gifts and graces may be very unequal; yet, in *this* particular there is an essential unity. They all believe in Christ, they all love God. They love Him for the gift of the Saviour: they love Him as a Father in whom they may confide: they love Him for His personal excellencies—His holiness, wisdom, faithfulness. They love Him for His conduct: for what He withholds and for what He grants; for what He rebukes and for what He approves. They love Him even for the rod that disciplines, knowing that He doeth all things well. There is nothing in God, and there is nothing from God, for which the *saints* do not love Him. And of this they are all assured, "We love Him *because* He first loved us".

"To them that *love* God". But, alas, how little I love God! I so frequently mourn my lack of love, and chide myself for the coldness of my heart. Yes, there is so much love of self and love of the world, sometimes I seriously question if I have any real *love* for God at all. But is not my very desire to love God a good symptom? Is not my very grief that I love Him so little a sure evidence that I do not hate Him? The presence of a hard and ungrateful heart has been mourned over by the saints of all ages. "Love to God is a heavenly aspiration, that is ever kept in check by the drag and restraint of an earthly nature; and from which we shall not be unbound till the soul has made its escape from the vile body, and cleared its unfettered way to the realm of light and liberty" (Dr. Chalmers).

"Who are *called*". The word "called" is never, in the New Testament Epistles, applied to those who are the recipients of a mere external invitation of the Gospel. The term always signifies an inward and *effectual* call. It was a call over which we had no control, either in originating or frustrating it. So, in Rom. 1:6, 7 and many other passages: "Among whom are ye also the called of Jesus Christ: to all that be in Rome, beloved of God, called saints". Has this call reached you, my reader? Ministers have called you; the Gospel has called you; conscience has called you; but has the Holy Spirit called you with an inward and irresistible call? Have you been spiritually called from darkness to light, from death to life, from the world to Christ, from self to God? It is a matter of the greatest moment that you should know whether you have been *truly* called of God. Has, then, the thrilling, life-giving music of that call sounded and reverberated through all the chambers of your soul? But *how* may I be sure that I *have* received such a call? There is one thing right here in our text which should enable you to ascertain. They who have been efficaciously called, *love God*. Instead of hating Him, they now esteem Him; instead of fleeing from Him in terror, they now seek Him; instead of caring not whether their conduct honored or dishonored Him, their deepest desire now is to please and glorify Him.

"According to *His purpose*". The call is not according to the merits of men, but according to the Divine purpose: "Who hath saved us, and called us with an holy calling, not according to our works, but according to His own purpose and grace, which was given us in Christ Jesus before the world began" (2 Tim. 1:9). The design of the Holy Spirit in bringing in this last clause, is to show that the reason some men love God and others do not, is to be attributed solely to the mere sovereignty of God: it is not for anything in themselves, but due alone to His distinguishing grace.

There is also a *practical* value in this last clause. The doctrines of grace are intended for a further purpose than that of making up a creed. One main design of them is to move the affections; and more especially to reawaken that affection to which the heart oppressed with fears, or weighed down with cares, is wholly insufficient —even the love of God. That this love may flow perennially from our hearts, there must be a constant recurring to that which inspired it and which is calculated to increase it; just as to re-kindle your admiration of a beautiful scene or picture, you would return again to gaze upon it. It is on this principle that so much stress is laid in Scripture on keeping the truths which we believe in memory: "By which also ye are saved, if ye *keep in memory* which I preached unto you" (1 Cor. 15:2). "I stir up your pure minds *by way of remembrance*", said the apostle (2 Pet. 3:1). "Do this in *remembrance* of Me" said the Saviour. It is, then, by going back in memory to that hour when, despite our wretchedness and utter unworthiness, God *called* us, that our affection will be kept fresh. It is by recalling the wondrous *grace* that then reached out to a hell-deserving sinner and snatched you as a brand from the burning, that your heart will be drawn out in adoring gratitude. And it is by discovering this was due alone to the sovereign and eternal *"purpose"* of God that you were called when so many others are passed by, that your love for Him will be deepened.

Returning to the opening words of our text, we find the apostle (as voicing the normal experience of the saints) declares, *"We know"* that all things work together for good". It is something more than a speculative belief. That all things work together for good is even more than a fervent desire. It is not that we merely *hope* that all things *will* so work, but that we are fully assured all things *do* so work. The knowledge here spoken of is spiritual, not intellectual. It is a knowledge rooted in our hearts, which produces confidence in the truth of it. It is the knowledge of faith, which receives everything from the benevolent hand of Infinite Wisdom. It is true that we do not derive much comfort from this knowledge when out of fellowship with God. Nor will it sustain us when faith is not in operation. But when we are in communion with the Lord, when in our weakness we do lean hard upon Him, then is this blessed assurance ours: "Thou wilt keep him in perfect peace, whose mind is stayed on Thee: because he trusteth in Thee" (Isa. 26:3).

A striking exemplification of our text is supplied by the history of Jacob—one whom in several respects each of us closely resembles. Heavy and dark was the cloud which settled upon him. Severe was the test, and fearful the trembling of his faith. His feet were almost gone. Hear his mournful plaint: "And Jacob their father said unto them, Me have ye bereaved of my children: Joseph is not, and Simeon is not, and ye will take Benjamin away: all these things are *against* me" (Gen. 42:36). And yet those circumstances, which to the dim eye of his faith wore a hue so sombre, were at that very moment developing and perfecting the events which were to shed around the evening of his life the halo of a glorious and cloudless sunset. All things *were* working together for his *good!* And so, troubled soul, the *"much tribulation"* will soon be over, and as you enter the "kingdom of God" you shall then see, no longer "through a glass darkly" but in the unshadowed sunlight of the Divine presence, that *"all things" did* "work together" for your personal and eternal good.

—Arthur W. Pink.

EXPOSITION OF FIRST PETER
II.—THE TRIALS OF CHRISTIANS IN THE PRESENT STATE CONTRASTED WITH THEIR RESULTS IN THE FUTURE STATE.
(1 Peter 1:6-9).

The second point of contrast between the present and future state of Christians is, that now and here, Christians are exposed to numerous and varied trials; then and there, they shall enjoy the glorious results of these trials. Christians in the present state are exposed to "temptations," to "manifold"—that is, numerous and varied, "temptations." Temptation is ordinarily used to signify enticement to sin; but in the New Testament it frequently signifies afflictions generally, viewed as trials, and this is obviously its meaning in the passage before us. The apostolical assertion then is, Christians are exposed in the present state to numerous and varied afflictions, and these numerous and varied afflictions are trials of the reality and strength of their faith, and hope, and love, and patience, and other graces.

An abstract consideration of the divine character, and of the relation in which true Christians stand to God, would lead us to expect that they should be completely exempted from affliction. He is infinitely powerful, and wise, and good. They are the objects of his peculiar love. Is it not natural, then, to conclude, that from the moment they are brought into the relation of children to him by faith in Christ Jesus, they should be freed from evil in all its forms and degrees, and made happy up to their largest capacity of happiness? But "his ways are not our ways; nor are his thoughts our thoughts. As the heavens are high above the earth; so are his thoughts above our thoughts, and his ways above our ways." [1]

Christians are not exempted from the ordinary evils of life. It is true of them, as of mankind generally, that they are "born to trouble as the sparks fly upward." They are "of few days and full of trouble." Poverty, reproach, sickness, disappointment, sorrow, pain, and death, are the lot of the saint as well as the sinner. Many who are "rich in faith," are "poor in this world," strangers to the comforts and conveniences, and but scantily furnished with even the necessaries of life. They may be, they often are, the subjects of the most painful and loathsome diseases, and the general law of mortality holds in their case equally as in that of their irreligious neighbors,—"Dust thou art, and unto dust shalt thou return." Indeed, in very many cases a larger proportion of suffering than ordinary seems to fall to the lot of the children of God. "Whom the Lord loveth he chasteneth, and he scourgeth every son whom he receiveth." [2]

Besides the afflictions which are common to the saint as a man, there are others which are peculiar to him as a Christian. He is exposed to suffering from the world "lying under the wicked one," and he is exposed to suffering from the wicked one himself. "In the world," said our Lord to his followers, "ye shall have tribulation;" and the faithful witness did not lie. All who have lived godly in this world have suffered, "all who will live godly must suffer, persecution." Some of them have "had trial of cruel mockings and scourgings; yea, moreover, of bonds and imprisonments. They were stoned, they were sawn asunder, they were tempted, they were slain by the sword, they wandered about in sheep's skins and goat's skins—destitute, afflicted, tormented, they wandered in deserts and in mountains, in dens and caves of the earth." [3] And even where they are not exposed to open violence, they find that "this world is not their friend, nor this world's law;" that the world which hated their Lord and Master does not love them; and that a malignant influence in reference to their best interests is constantly proceeding forth from "the present evil world."

In addition to trials from the world, the Christian is exposed to affliction from the assaults of his unseen enemies. He has to strive, not only "with flesh and blood, but with principalities and powers, with the rulers of the darkness of this world, with spiritual wickedness in high places." "His enemy, the devil, goeth about like a roaring lion, seeking whom he may devour." [4] His fiery darts, when not warded off by the shield of faith, sink deep into the heart, and inflict, though not a deadly, yet a most painful wound; and the buffetings of some of his messengers are all but intolerable

All these afflictions, from whatever quarter they come, are "trials." They are intended to prove and to improve the Christian, to try at once the reality and the vigor of his gracious prin-

---

[1] Isa. lv. 8, 9.
[2] Job v. 7; xiv. 1. James ii. 5. Gen. iii. 19. Heb. xii. 6.
[3] John xvi. 33. 2 Tim. iii. 12. Heb. xi. 36-38.
[4] Eph. vi. 12. 1 Pet. v. 8.

ciples; and not only to try them, but to strengthen them. This, then, is the state of the Christian; while here, he is exposed to numerous and varied afflictions, by means of which he is tried and improved.

But in the state of final happiness there will be no affliction. The trial, having served its purpose, shall cease, and nothing but the glorious result of the trial will remain. "The trial of the Christian's faith" by means of these manifold afflictions, "is more precious than the trial of gold." The apostle does not here directly contrast faith and gold, but the trial of faith and the trial of gold. Trial by fire improves gold; it frees it from all debasing alloy, but it does not render it indestructible. Refine gold as you will, it is, after all, a perishing thing. But the trial of the faith of the Christian has a nobler result. Purified and strengthened by the trials it is exposed to under the influence of the Holy Spirit, faith, with all the graces which grow out of it, survives the wreck of all material things, and, "at the revelation of Jesus Christ, is found to praise, and honor, and glory." The results of all the trials to which they have been exposed in the present state, will be found in that character of perfect conformity to the image of God, in which consist at once their perfect holiness and their perfect happiness.

"Praise, honor, and glory," are synonymous expressions, and are equivalent to a very strong superlative. The praise, glory, and honor, may be referred either to the saints themselves or to their Lord and Saviour; to the saints themselves, for we know that "praise, and honor, and glory," shall be to every saint "in the day when Jesus Christ shall judge the secrets of all hearts;" to their Lord and Saviour, for we know that "he shall be glorified in his saints, and admired in all them that believe."[1] It has been beautifully remarked, "These two will well agree together; that it be both to their praise and to the praise of Christ; for certainly all their praise and glory will end in the praise and glory of their head, Christ who is God over all, blessed forever. They have each their crown, but their honor is to cast them all down before HIS throne."

III.—THE CHRISTIAN'S PRESENT STATE A STATE OF EXPECTATION—HIS FUTURE STATE, A STATE OF ENJOYMENT.

The third point of comparison or contrast between the present and future state of Christians is, that now and here complete salvation is the object of faith and hope; then and there it will be the object of enjoyment.

Saints in the present state are made partakers of many of the blessings of the Christian salvation. So far as the purchase of salvation is concerned, immediately on believing the truth they are interested indefeasibly in that all-perfect work of Christ which secures their everlasting happiness. They obtain the forgiveness of all their sins. "In him they have redemption through his blood—the forgiveness of sins." They obtain deliverance from the prevailing power of sin. "Sin shall not have dominion over them."[2] They obtain a joy, and peace, and satisfaction, to which, till they believed, they were strangers. But still they are but very imperfectly possessed of the Christian salvation—complete deliverance from evil in all its forms and all its degrees.

We have seen, that they are still exposed to the ordinary calamities of life, to the persecution of the world, and to the temptations of Satan. They are still but imperfectly delivered from their innate depravity. Sin, though it no longer reigns, yet dwells in them. There is still much darkness in the

---

[1] Rom. ii. 10. 2 Thess. i. 10.   [2] Eph. i. 7. Rom. vi. 14.

understanding, much disorder in the affections, much perversity in the will. They are far, very far, from being "holy as God is holy, perfect as he is perfect." This mortal has not yet put on immortality. This corruptible has not yet put on incorruption. In one word, perfect holy happiness—complete salvation, is, in the present state, the object, not of enjoyment, but of faith and hope. "We ourselves," says the apostle, "who have the first fruits of the Spirit, even we ourselves groan within ourselves, waiting for the adoption, to wit, the redemption of our body"—the final deliverance on the day of the resurrection; "for we are saved by hope"—that is, our salvation at present is not in possession, but in expectation: we are not so much saved as we hope to be saved: "For hope that is seen is not hope; for what a man seeth, why doth he yet hope for?"[1]

In the future state, however, Christians shall obtain, in all its extent and perfection, "the salvation that is in Christ with eternal glory." They shall receive "the end of their faith, even the salvation of their soul."

The final salvation is termed the salvation of "the soul," not to exclude the salvation of the body; "for we look for the Saviour from heaven, the Lord Jesus Christ, who shall change these vile bodies, and fashion them like unto his own glorious body;" but because the soul in itself, immaterial and immortal, is both the nobler part of human nature, and the immediate seat of that holy happiness in which the Christian salvation essentially consists.[2]

This salvation is said to be "the end of their faith"—that is, I apprehend, the termination of their faith. The attainment of complete salvation shall no more be a matter of faith; it shall be a matter of experience. They will no more believe that they shall be saved; they will know that they are saved. We are persuaded that faith will continue forever in heaven; but the object of faith will then be, not the attainment of a complete salvation, but the eternal continuance of the enjoyment of a complete salvation already attained. In one word—here Christians believe they shall be saved, here they hope to be saved; there they are saved.   Dr. John Brown.

Unless we take absolute election into the account, we must either suppose that God saves no man whatever, or that those He saves, are saved at random and without design. But His goodness forbids the first; and His wisdom excludes the latter. Absolute election, therefore, must be taken into account; or you at once, *ipso facto*, strike off either goodness or wisdom from the list of Divine perfections. That scheme of doctrine must necessarily be untrue which represents the Deity as observing no regular order, no determinate plan, in an affair of such consequence as the everlasting salvation of His people. I cannot acquit of blasphemy that system which likened the Deity to a careless ostrich which, having deposited her eggs, leaves them in the sand, to be hatched, or crushed, just as chance happened. Surely He, who numbers the very hairs of His people's heads, does not consign their souls and their eternal interests to precarious hazard! the blessings of grace and glory are too valuable and important to be shuffled and dealt out by the hand of chance. Besides, if one thing come to pass, either without, or contrary to, the will of God, another thing, nay, all things, may come to pass in the same manner: and then good bye to Providence.

—Augustus Toplady, 1768. Author of "Rock of Ages".

---

[1] Rom. viii. 23-25.
[2] Phil. iii. 20, 21.

Vol. II   JULY, 1923   No. 7

STUDIES in the SCRIPTURES

"Search the Scriptures" John 5:39.

A PERIODICAL (MONTHLY "IF THE LORD WILL")
DEVOTED TO BIBLE STUDIES and EXPOSITIONS

Associate Editors and Publishers, I. C. HERENDEEN and ARTHUR W. PINK, Swengel, Pa.

Price: 10 cents per copy; $1.00 per year. Foreign $1.00 per year.

TO OUR SCRIPTURE STUDY FAMILY

"O wretched man that I am! Who shall deliver me from the body of this death?" (Rom. 7:24).

As pointed out in our last editorials, this is the language of a regenerate soul. The substance of it may be found in the recorded utterances of Old and New Testament saints, as well as in the writings of the most eminent Christians who have lived during the last five hundred years. Dr. Jonathan Edwards, in whose home died that remarkable man Mr. David Brainerd—the first missionary to the Indians, and whose devotion to Christ was witnessed to by all who knew him —and with whom he was intimately acquainted, says in his "Memoirs of Mr. Brainerd", "His religious illuminations, affections, and comfort, seemed to a great degree to be attended with evangelical humiliation; consisting in a sense of his own utter insufficiency, despicableness, and odiousness; with an answering disposition and frame of heart. *How deeply affected was he* almost continually with *his great defects* in religion; with his *vast distance from* that spirituality and holy frame of mind that become a child of God; with his ignorance, pride, deadness, barrenness! He was not only affected with the remembrance of his former sinfulness, before his conversion, but with the sense of his *present* vileness and pollution. He was not only disposed to think other saints better than he; yea to look on himself as the worst and least of saints; but, very often, as the vilest and worst of mankind".

Jonathan Edwards himself, than whom few men have been more honored of God, either in their spiritual attainments or in the extent to which God has used them in blessing to others, near the end of his life, wrote thus: "When I look into my heart and take a view of its wickedness it looks like an abyss infinitely deeper than hell. And it appears to me, that, were it not for free grace, exalted and raised up to the infinite height of all the fulness and glory of the great Jehovah, I should appear sunk down in my sins below hell itself; far below the sight of everything, but the eye of sovereign grace, that alone can pierce down to such a depth. And it is affecting to think how ignorant I was, when a young Christian, (alas, that so many older Christians are still ignorant of it—A.W.P.) of the bottomless depths of wickedness, pride, hypocrisy and deceit *left* in my heart" (1743).

Godly Rutherford wrote, "This body of sin and corruption embitters and poisons our enjoyment. O that I were where I shall sin no more." (1650).

James Ingliss (Editor of "Waymarks in the Wilderness") at the close of his life, wrote to Dr. Brookes, "As I am brought to take a new view of the end, my life seems so made up of squandered oppor-

(Continued on page 224.)

IMPORTANT NOTICES

All new subscriptions will be dated back to January, 1923.

Set of twelve issues for 1922, unbound, $1.90. Bound, $1.50.

Note: We cannot break a set or now supply any single 1922 issues.

Subscription Price: $1.00 per year to any address in the world. Single copies 10 cents.

Change of Address: Please notify us promptly of any change of address, and be certain to give both old and new addresses.

Non-Subscribers receiving this Magazine regularly will understand their subscription has been entered by a friend.

Copies lost in the mail duplicated only if we are notified promptly.

Entered as second-class matter December 15th, 1921 at the post office at Swengel, Pa., under Act of March 3rd, 1879.

CONTENTS

John's Gospel (John 5:31-47) 194
Types of the Antichrist 202
Assurance 210
The Law and the Saint, #3 212
Exposition of First Peter 221

JOHN'S GOSPEL

19. The Deity of Christ: Threefold Witness to it: John 5:31-47.

We begin with our usual Analysis of the passage which is to be before us:—

1. Christ's Witness not independent of the Father: vv. 31, 32.
2. The Witness of John: vv. 33, 34.
3. Christ's Witness to John: v. 35.
4. The Witness of Christ's Works: v. 36.
5. The Witness of the Father: vv. 37, 38.
6. The Witness of the Scriptures: v. 39.
7. Christ's Witness against the Jews: vv. 40-47.

As we pass from chapter to chapter it is ever needful to keep in mind the character and scope of this fourth Gospel. Its chief design is to present the Divine glories of Christ. It was written, no doubt, in its first and local application to refute the heresies concerning the person of the Lord Jesus which flourished toward the end of the first century. Less than fifty years after the Lord departed from these scenes and returned to His Father in heaven, the horrible system of Gnosticism, which denied the essential Deity of the Saviour, spread widely throughout those lands where the Gospel had been preached. Whilst it was generally allowed that Christ was a unique personage, yet, that He was "equal with God" was denied by many. Nor is that very surprising when we stop to think how much there was which would prove a stumbling block to the natural man.

Outwardly, to human eyes, Christ appeared to be an ordinary man. Born into a peasant family; cradled amid the most humble surroundings; carried away into Egypt to escape the cruel edict of Herod, and returning later, only to grow to manhood's estate in obscurity; working for years, most probably, at the carpenter's bench— what was there to denote that He was the Lord of Glory? Then, as He began His public ministry, appearing not as the great of this world are accustomed to appear, with much pomp and ostentation; but, instead, as the meek and lowly One. Attended not by an imposing retinue of angels, but by a few poor and unlettered fisherman. His claims rejected by the religious leaders of that day; the tide of popular opinion turning against Him; the very ones who first hailed Him with their glad Hosannas, ending by crying, "Away with Him: crucify Him". Finally, nailed in shame to the cruel tree; silent to the challenge to descend from it; and there breathing out His spirit —that, *that* was the last the world saw of Him.

And now by the year A. D. 90 almost all of His original disciples would be dead. Of the twelve apostles who had accompanied Him during His public ministry, only John remained. On every side were teachers denying the Deity of Christ. There was thus a real need for an inspired, authoritative, systematic presentation of the manifold glories of His Divine person. The Holy Spirit therefore moved John—the one who of all the early disciples knew Christ best, the one whose spiritual discernment was the keenest, the one who had enjoyed the inestimable privilege of leaning on the Master's bosom —to write this fourth Gospel. In it abundant evidence is furnished to satisfy the most credulous of the Deity of the Lord Jesus. It is to the written Word God now refers all who desire to know the truth concerning His beloved Son, and in it are presented the "many infallible proofs" for the Godhood of our blessed Redeemer. Chiefest of these are to be found in John's Gospel.

In the chapter we are now studying we find record of a remarkable miracle performed by the Lord Jesus which signally displayed His Divine power. He had singled out a most hopeless case and by a word had made whole, instantly, one that had suffered with an infirmity for thirty and eight years. Because this miracle had been performed on the Sabbath day, the Jews persecuted the Lord Jesus. In gracious condescension the Lord replied to their criticism by giving them a sevenfold declaration of His equality with the Father. This we examined at some length in our last article; now, in the passage before us, we find that He closed by bringing in the evidence of various unimpeachable witnesses who testified to the veracity of His claims. In view, then, of what is to be found here, there can be no excuse whatever for ignorance, still less for unbelief, upon this all-important subject. So bright was Christ's glory, so concerned was the Father in maintaining it, so immeasurable is the blessing when received, so tremendous is the stake involved in its loss, God has vouchsafed us the amplest, clearest, fullest evidence.

"If I bear witness of Myself, My witness is not true" (v. 31). Every commentator we have consulted expounds this verse as follows: The witness which I have just borne to Myself would not be valid, unless it is supported by that of others. The law of God requires two or three witnesses for the truth to be established. Therefore if I bear witness of Myself, says Christ, and there is none to confirm it, it is "not true", i. e. it is not convincing to others. But we must humbly dissent from any such interpretation. The word of a mere man *does* need confirmation: but not so that of God the Son. To affirm or suggest that *His* witness must be ratified by the testimony of others so as to establish its validity, is deeply dishonoring to Him. And we are both amazed and saddened that such a view should be put forth by many excellent men.

"If I bear witness of Myself, My witness is not true". The key to this verse lies in what has gone before. Divorce it from its context, and we must expect to find it difficult; but examine it in the light of its setting, and all becomes clear. This verse simply reiterates in another form what we find the Saviour saying at the beginning of the previous verse. "I can of Mine own self do nothing" which means, I cannot act independently of the Father: I am so absolutely one with Him that His will is My will; Mine, His. So, now, He declares, "If I bear witness of Myself, My witness is not true". He speaks hypothetically—"if". "If I bear witness of Myself" means, If I bear witness *independently* of the Father. In such a case, "My witness is not true". And why? Because such would be insubordination. The Son can no more bear *witness* of Himself independently of the Father, than He can of Himself *work* independently of the Father.

"There is another that beareth witness of Me; and I know that the witness which He witnesseth of Me is true" (v. 32). This explains the previous verse and confirms our interpretation of it. The "other" who is here referred to as "bearing witness" of Him, is not John the Baptist, as some have strangely supposed, but the Father Himself. Reference, *not appeal*, is made to John in vv. 33,34. Observe now that our Lord did not here say, "There is *One* that beareth witness of Me" and *His* witness is true, but "there is *Another* that beareth witness of Me". He would no more dissever the Father's witness to Himself, than He would bear witness to Himself independently of the Father. This is strikingly confirmed by what we read in John 8: "The Pharisees therefore said unto Him, Thou bearest record of Thyself; Thy record is not true. Jesus answered and said unto them, Though I bear record of Myself, yet My record is true . . . . Ye judge after the flesh; I judge no man. And yet if I judge, My judgment is true: *for I am not alone*, but *I and the Father* which sent Me" (vv. 13-16).

"Ye sent unto John, and he bare witness unto the truth" (v. 33). Here our Lord reminds "the Jews" (v. 16) how, when they had sent an embassy unto His forerunner (see 1:19), that he bare witness unto the truth". Notice the abstract form in which this is put. Christ did not say, "He bore witness unto *Me*", but "unto the truth". This witness is recorded in John 1:20-27. First, John confessed that he was not the Christ, but simply "the voice of one crying in the wilderness, Make straight the way of the Lord". Then, he testified to the presence of One in their midst whom they knew not, One of whom he said, "He it is, who coming after me, is preferred before me, whose shoe's latchet I am not worthy to unloose". Such was the Baptist's witness to the delegates of these same Jews.

"But I receive not testimony from man: but these things I say, that ye might be saved" (v. 34). The Son of God continues to occupy the same high ground from which He had spoken throughout this interview. "I receive not testimony from man" shows that He had *not appealed* to the witness of John in confirmation of His own declarations. His purpose was quite otherwise: "These things I say, that ye might be saved." The witness which John had borne to "the truth" was fitted to have a salutary effect on those who heard him. John's testimony was a merciful concession which God had made to the need of Israel. Christ Himself did not stand in need of it; but *they* did. God sent His messenger before His Son to prepare the way for Him. His ministry was designed to arouse men's attention and to produce in them a sense of their deep need of the One who was about to be manifested.

"But I receive not testimony from man". This word "receive" is explained to us in v. 44 where it is interchanged with "seek". It means to lay hold of, or grasp at. Christ would not bemean Himself by subpoening human witnesses. His claim to be equal with God rested on surer ground that the testiony of a man. But He had *reminded* these Jews of what John had said to their representatives on an earlier occasion, and this that they "might be saved", for salvation comes by believing God's "witness unto the truth".

"He was a burning and a shining light: and ye were willing for a season to rejoice in his light" (v. 35). This was most gracious of Christ. John had given faithful witness to the One who was to come after him; and now the Son of God bears witness to *him*. A beautiful illustration is this of the promise that if we confess Christ before men, so He will yet confess us before God. "A burning and shining light"—more correctly, "lamp", see R. V.—the Lord calls him. Burning inwardly, s h i n i n g outwardly. John's light had not been hid under a bushel, but it had shone "before men". Ah, dear reader, will the Saviour be able to say of *you*, in a coming day, "He was a burning and shining lamp"? Is the light that is within thee "burning" or is it just *flickering?* Is your lamp "trimmed", and so "shining", or is it shedding but a *feeble* and *sickly* glow? Great is the need for burning and shining "lamps" in the world today. The shadows are fast lengthening, the darkness increases, and the "midnight" hour draws on apace. "And that, knowing the time, that now it is high time to awake out of sleep: for now is our salvation nearer than when we believed. The night is far spent, the day is at hand: let us therefore cast off the works of darkness, and let us put on the armour of light" (Rom. 13:11,12).

"And ye were willing for a season to rejoice in his light" (v. 35). This provides us with an illustration of the stony-ground hearers of the parable of the Sower. Concerning t h i s class Christ says, "But he that received the seed into stony places, the same is he that heareth the Word, and anon *with joy receiveth it;* yet hath he not root in himself, but dureth for a while" (Matt. 13:20, 21). Such were these Jews: "for a season" they rejoiced in John's light. But the difference between real believers and mere professors is not in how they begin but how they end. "He that endureth to the end shall be saved": enduring to the end is not a condition of salvation, but an evidence of it. So, again, when Christ says, "If ye continue in My word, then are ye My disciples indeed" (8:31): continuing in Christ's word is a proof that we are His disciples. We take it that that which caused these Jews to "rejoice" for a season in John's light was the testimony which he bore to the Messiah, then about to appear. This was good news indeed, for they thought this meant deliverance from the Roman yoke and the destruction of all their enemies. But when the Messiah was actually manifested and instead of setting up His kingdom at once, He announced that He had come to save the lost, and when He demanded repentance and faith, their joy soon faded away.

"But I have greater witness than that of John: for the works which the Father hath given Me to finish, the same works that I do, bear witness of Me, that the Father hath sent Me" (v. 36). Here is the first witness to which Christ appeals in proof of His Deity. His "works" bore unmistakeable witness to Him. He gave hearing to the deaf, speech to the dumb, sight to the blind, cleansing to the leper, deliverance to the captives of the Devil, life to the dead. He walked the waves, stilled the wind, calmed the sea. He turned water into wine, cleansed the Temple single-handed, and fed a great multitude with a few loaves and fishes. And these miracles were performed by His own inherent power. To these works He now directs attention as furnishing proof of His Deity. Quite frequently did He a p p e a l t o His "works" as affording Divine testimony, see John 10:25, 38; 14:11; 15:24.

The late Bishop Ryle called attention to five things in connection with our Lord's miracles. "First, their *number:* they were not a few only, but very many. Second, their *greatness:* they were not little, but mighty interferences with the ordinary course of nature. Third, their *publicity:* they were not done in a corner, but generally in open day, and before many witnesses, and often before e n e m i e s. Fourth, their *character:* they were almost always works of love, mercy and compassion, helpful and beneficent to man, and not merely barren exhibitions of power. Fifth, their *direct appeal to man's senses:* they were visible, and would bear any examination. The difference between them and the boasted miracles of Rome, on all these points, is striking and conclusive". To these we might add two other features: Sixth, their *artlessness.* They were not staged mechanically: they happened in the natural course of our Lord's ministry. There was nothing pre-arranged about them. Seventh, their *efficacy*. There was as much difference between the miracles of healing performed by Christ and those of His miserable imitators which are being so widely heralded in our day, as there is between *His teaching* and that given out by these pretenders who claim to heal in His name. Christ's cures were instantaneous, not gradual; complete and perfect, not faulty and disappointing.

"The same works that I do, bear witness of Me". Ere passing on to the next verse, we pause to apply these words to ourselves. *Our* works, too, bear witness of us. If ours are "dead works", wood, hay, and stubble, which shall be burned up in the coming Day, that proves we are carnal, walking after the flesh; and such a witness will dishonor and grieve Him whose name we bear. But if we abound in "good works" this will show that we are walking after the spirit, and men (our fellow-believers) s e e i n g o u r good works will glorify our Father which is in heaven. What, then, my reader, is the "witness" which *your* "works" are bearing? What the writer's? Let us "be careful to *maintain* good works" (Titus 3:18).

"And the Father Himself, which hath sent Me, hath borne witness of Me. Ye have neither heard His voice at any time, nor seen His shape" (v. 37). The miracles performed by our Lord were not the only nor the most direct evidence which proved His Deity. The Father Himself had borne witness. The majority of the commentators refer this to the baptism of Christ, when the Father's voice declared, This is My beloved Son, in whom I am well pleased. But we scarcely think this is correct. Immediately following, our Lord went on to say, "Ye have neither heard His voice at any time, nor seen His shape". What, then, would be the force of Christ here appealing to the Father's witness at the Jordan if these detractors of His had not heard that Voice? Personally, we think that Christ refers, rather, to the witness which the Father had borne to His Son through the prophets during Old Testament times. This seems to give more meaning to what follows—the Old Testament economy was characterized by an *invisible* God, neither His voice being heard, nor His shape seen.

"And ye have not His word abiding in you: for whom He hath sent, Him ye believe not" (v. 38). Here our Lord begins to make solemn application of what He had said to the consciences and hearts of these Jews. Note the awful charges which He brings against them: "Ye *have not* His word abiding in you" (v. 38); "Ye *will not* come to Me" (v. 40); "Ye *have not* the love of God in you" (v. 42); "Ye *receive Me not*" (v. 43); ye "*seek not* the honor that cometh from God only (v. 44); "Ye *believe not*" (v. 47). But notice carefully the basic charge: "Ye have not His word abiding in you". *This* explained all the others. This was the cause, of which the others were but the inevitable effects. If God's Word has no place in men's hearts they will not come to Christ, they will not receive Him, they will not love God, and they will not seek the honor that cometh from God only. It is only as the Word is hidden in our hearts that we are preserved from sinning against God.

"Search the Scriptures; for in them ye think ye have eternal life: and they are they which testify of Me" (v. 39). This is the last witness which our Lord cites, and, for us, it is the most important. John has long since passed away; the "works" of Christ are no longer before men's eyes; the voice of the Father is no more heard; but the testimony of the Scriptures abides. The Scriptures testified of Christ, and affirmed His Deity. Their witness was the climax. The Holy Writings, given by inspiration of God, were the Final

Court of appeal. What dignity does the Lord of Glory here give to them! What importance and authority does He attach to them? Beyond them there was no appeal: above them no higher authority: after them no further witness. It is blessed to note the *order* in which Christ placed the three witnesses to which He appealed in proof of His equality with God. First, there was the witness of His own Divine works. Second, there was the witness which the Father had borne to Him through the prophets. Third, there was the testimony of the Holy Scriptures, written by men moved by the Holy Spirit. Thus in these three witnesses there is a remarkable reference made to each of the three persons in the Holy Trinity.

"Search the Scriptures" was both an appeal and a command. It is to be read, as in our A. V., in the imperative mood. The proof for this is as follows: First, the *usage* of the word. The Bible is its own interpreter. If scripture be compared with scripture its meaning will be plain. In John 7:52 we find the only other occurrence of the Greek word (ereunao) in John's Gospel, here translated "search": "They answered and said unto him, Art Thou also of Galilee? *search*, and look: for out of Galilee ariseth no prophet". When the Pharisees said to Nicodemus "search and look", they were *bidding* him search the Scriptures. Thus, in both instances, the word has the imperative and not the indicative force. Again; to give the verb here the indicative force in John 5:39 is to make the first half of the verse pointless; but to render it in the imperative gives it a meaning in full accord with what precedes and what follows. "For in them ye think ye have eternal life". The pronoun "ye" is emphatic. The word "think" does not imply it was a doubtful point, or merely a matter of human opinion. It is rather as though Christ said unto them, 'This is one of the articles of *your* faith: ye think (are persuaded), and rightly so; then act on it. Search the Scriptures (in which you are assured there is eternal life) and you will find that they, too, testify of Me'. The word "think" does not imply a doubt, but affirms an assurance.

"Search the Scriptures". Here is a command from the Lord. The authority of His Godhood is behind it. "Search", He says; not merely "read". The Greek word is one that was used in connection with hunting. It referred to the hunter stalking game. When he discovered the tracks of an animal, he concentrated all his attention on the ground before him, diligently searching for other marks which would lead him to his quarry. In a similar way, *we* are to study God's Word, minutely examining each expression, tracing every occurrence of it, and ascertaining its meaning from its usage. The grand motive for such earnest study is, that the Scriptures "testify" *of Christ*. May writer and reader give daily heed to this Divine admonition, to *"search"* the Scriptures.

"And ye will not come to Me, that ye might have life" (v. 40). It was not lack of evidence but perversity of will which kept these Jews from coming to Christ. And it is so still. The Lord Jesus stands ready to receive all who come to Him; but by nature men are unwilling, unwilling to come to Him that they "might have life". But why is this? It is because they fail to realize their awful peril: did they but know that they are standing on the brink of the Pit, they would flee from the wrath to come. Why is it? It is because they have no sense of their deep and desperate need: did they but apprehend their awful condition—their wickedness, their blindness, their hardheartedness, their depravity—they would hasten to the Great Physician to be healed by Him. Why is it? It is because the carnal mind is enmity *against God,* and Christ is God.

"I receive not honor from men" (v. 41). Here again the Lord maintains

His dignity and insists upon His Divine self-sufficiency. I "receive not" signifies, as in vv. 34 and 44, "I seek not" honor from men. "When I state My claims, and complain that you disregard them, it is not because I wish to ingratiate Myself with you; not because I covet your approbation, or that of any man, or set of men. He did not need their sanction: He could receive no honor from their applause. His object was to secure the approbation of His Divine Father, by faithfully executing the commission with which He was entrusted; and so far as they were concerned, His desire was not that He should be applauded by them, but that they should be saved by Him. If He regretted, and He did most deeply regret their obstinate unbelief and impenitence, it was for their own sakes, and not for His own. Such was the unearthly, unambitious spirit of our Lord, and such should be the spirit of all His ministers" (Dr. John Brown).

"But I know you, that ye have not the love of God in you" (v. 42). How this makes manifest the *omniscience* of Christ! He who searcheth the heart knew the state of these Jews. They posed as worshippers of the true and living God. They appeared to be very jealous of His honor. They claimed to be most punctilious in the observance of His Sabbath. But Christ was not deceived. He knew they had not the love of God in them, and this was why they refused to come to Him for life. It is so now. The reason why men despise the claims of Christ is not because of any want of evidence on the side of those claims, but because of a sinful indisposition on their part to attend to those claims. They have not the love of God in them; if they had, they would receive and worship His Son.

"I am come in My Father's name, and ye receive Me not: if another shall come in his own name, him ye will receive" (v. 43). Unspeakably solemn is this. Israel's rejection of Christ has only prepared the way for them to accept the Antichrist, for it is to him our Lord referred in the second part of this verse. Just as Eve's rejection of the truth of God laid her open to accept the Devil's lie, so Israel's rejection of the true Messiah has thoroughly prepared them, morally, to receive the false Messiah; who will come in his own name, doing his own pleasure, and seeking glory from men. Thus will he thoroughly expose the corrupt heart of the natural man. How this exhibits what is in the fallen creature and demonstrates his depravity!

"How can ye believe, which receive honor one of another, and seek not the honor that cometh from God only" (v. 44). "Honor" signifies approbation or praise. While these Jews were making it their chief aim to win the good opinion of each other, and remained more or less indifferent to the approval and approbation of God, they would not come to Christ for life. To come to Christ they must humble themselves in the dust, by taking the place of lost sinners before Him. And to receive Him as their Saviour and Lord, to live henceforth for the glory of that One who was despised and rejected of men, would at once separate them from the world, and would bring down upon them contempt and persecution. But there is no middle ground: "the friendship of the world is enmity with God". If we are determined to be honored and smiled upon by our fellowmen, we shall remain alienated from God.

"Men are deceived today by the thought of building up man, the improvement of the race, the forming of character, holding on to themselves as though all that man needed was change of direction. Man is himself evil, a sinner in nature, utterly alienated from the life of God. He needs life, a new one. For what else did Christ come but that He might give it? He is not to be received with honors such as men pay to high officals. for they are like the men who pay the honor, but He is from above and above all, and has eternal life to give. He needs emptiness for His fulness, sinfulness for His holiness, sinners for His salvation, death for His life; and he who can make out his case of being lost and helpless gets all. It is not that men should do their best by leaving off vices and reforming, and pay devout respect to the name of Jesus and to religious rites, adding this to their goodness for God's acceptance. It is that they should be as the poor man in the beginning of this chapter, indebted to Christ for everything: they must be receivers instead of givers. Receiving honor from one another vitiates the whole idea in regard to God and His Christ. We honor Him only when we are saved by Him; then, as saved, worshipping and rejoicing in Christ Jesus the Lord" (M. Taylor).

"Do not think that I will accuse you to the Father: there is one that accuseth you, even Moses, in whom ye trust. For had ye believed Moses, ye would have believed Me: for he wrote of Me" (vv. 45, 46). Our Lord concludes by intimating to these Jews that they would yet have to give an account of their rejection of Him before the tribunal of God, and there they would meet as their accuser the great legislator of whom they boasted, but whose testimony they rejected. Here, then, was the final reason why they would not come to Him for life—they believed not the written Word of God.

"There is one that accuseth you, even Moses, in whom ye trust. For had ye believed Moses, ye would have believed Me: for he wrote of Me". How solemn and searching is this! If there is one thing those Jews *thought* they believed, it was Moses and his writings. They contended earnestly for the law: they venerated the name of Moses above almost all of their national heroes. They would have been ready to die for what Moses taught. And yet here is the Son of God solemnly declaring that these Jews *did not* believe Moses, and furnishing proof by showing that if they had really believed Moses' writings they had believed in Christ, of whom Moses wrote. How terribly deceptive is the human heart! "There is a way *that seemeth right unto a man,* but the end thereof are the ways of death" (Prov. 14:12). O, dear reader, make certain that *you* believe, *really* believe, on the Son of God.

"But if ye believe not his writings, how shall ye believe My words?" (v. 47). How this exposes the "Higher Critics"! If they believe not the writings of Moses, no matter what their ecclesiastical connections or religious professions, it is sure proof that they are unsaved men—men who have not believed in Christ. The Old Testament Scriptures are of equal authority with the teaching of Christ: they are equally the Word of God.

Let the following questions be studied for the next article (John 6:1-13):—

1. What do the opening words of v. 1 denote?

2. In what respects is v. 2 repeated today?

3. What is the significance of v. 4 coming just before the feeding of the multitude?

4. How may we apply to ourselves Christ's question in v. 5?

5. Wherein do Philip and Andrew represent us? Vv. 7-9.

6. What are the spiritual lessons suggested by v. 11?

7. What dispensational picture can you discern in John 6:1-13?

—Arthur W. Pink.

This completes Vol. I of our exposition of John's Gospel. These 19 articles are attractively bound in book form (380 pages), and can now be obtained for $1.50. Order a copy and thus preserve them in permanent form for *future* reference.

13. TYPES OF THE ANTICHRIST.

"In the volume of the book it is written of Me" (Heb. 10:7), said the Lord Jesus. Christ is the key to the Scriptures—"Search the Scriptures .... they are they which testify of Me", are His words; and the "Scriptures" to which He had reference were not the four Gospels, for they were not then written, but the writings of Moses and the prophets. The Old Testament Scriptures, then, are something more than a compilation of historical narratives, something more than the record of a system of social and religious legislation, or a code of ethics. The Old Testament Scriptures are, fundamentally, a stage on which is shown forth, in vivid symbolry, stupendous events then future. The events recorded in the Old Testament were actual occurrences, yet were they also typical prefigurations. Throughout the Old Testament dispensations God caused to be shadowed forth things which must yet come to pass. This is in full accord with a basic law in the economy of God. Nothing is brought to maturity at once. As it is in the natural world, so it is in the spiritual: there is first the blade, then the ear, and then the full corn in the ear. So there is first the shadow, and then the substance; the type, and then the antitype.

"Whatsoever things were written aforetime were written for our learning" (Rom. 15:4). Israel's tabernacle was *"a figure* for the time then present" (Heb. 9:8, 9), as well as the example and *"shadow of heavenly things"* (Heb. 8:5). Concerning the history of Abraham, his wives and his children, the apostle was inspired to write "which things are *an allegory*" (Gal. 4:24). These and other passages which might be quoted witness plainly to the typical meaning of portions of the Old Testament. But there are some brethren who will own the typical significance of *these* things, who refuse to acknowledge that anything else in the Old Testament has a typical meaning save those which are expressly interpreted or mentioned in the New. But surely this is a mistake. Ought we not to regard those Old Testament types which *are* expounded in the New Testament as *samples* of others which are not explained? Are there no more prophecies in the Old Testament than those which in the New Testament are expressly said to be "fulfilled"? Assuredly there are. Then why not admit the same in connection with the types? Nothing is said in the New Testament that the history of Joseph has a profound and wonderful typical significance, yet who with anointed eyes can fail to see in the experiences of Jacob's favorite son a remarkable foreshadowing of the person and work of Christ!

There will probably be few who read this article that will dispute what we have said above. No doubt the majority of our readers have already been instructed in much of the typology of the Old Testament. Many of God's servants have written at length upon the Passover, the brazen serpent, the Tabernacle, etc., as well as upon the many ways in which such men as Abel, Noah, Isaac, Moses, David, etc. prefigured the Saviour. But strange to say, very little seems to have been written upon those who adumbrated the Antichrist. So far as we are aware practically nothing has been given out concerning the many Bible characters of ill fame, who foreshadowed that coming one, that occupies such a prominent place in the prophetic scriptures. A wide field is here opened for study, and we take pleasure in now submitting to the careful perusal of the reader the results of our own imperfect researches, hoping that it may lead others to make a more complete examination of the subject for themselves.

It was well said by one of the Continental Puritans that "When we read the Scriptures, we are to judge beforehand, that then only do we understand them, when we discover in them a wisdom unsearchable and worthy of God" (Witsius). Such is the inexhaustible fulness of the written Word of God that not only are its words significant of things, but even the things, which are first signified by the words, also represent other things, which they were appointed to prefigure long before they happened. Besides the plain and literal sense of Scripture, there is also a mystical sense, hidden beneath the surface and which can only be discovered as we, in dependance on the Holy Spirit, diligently compare scripture with scripture. In pursuing the latter we need not only to proceed with due caution, but with "fear and trembling", lest we devise mysteries out of our own imagination, and thus pervert to one use what belongs to another. The principle which will safeguard us is to thoroughly acquaint ourselves with the antitypes. Let nothing be regarded as a type unless we are sure there is an exact correspondence with the antitype. This will preserve us from erroneously supposing that any person who is clearly a type of either Christ or the Antichrist is so in *every* detail of his life. Thus Moses was plainly a type of Christ as our Mediator, and in many other respects too, but in his failures and in other details of his personal history he was not a type of Christ. So, too, with those who foreshadowed the Antichrist: not everything recorded of them prefigured the character or deeds of the Man of Sin. Should it still be inquired, How are we to ascertain *in which* respects the actions of Old Testament characters were, and were not, typical? the answer, as given above, is, By comparing the antitype. This will save us from the wild allegorizing of Origen and others of the "Fathers". We shall now look at ten Bible characters, each of whom strikingly typified the Antichrist.

1. *Cain*. It is indeed solemn to discover that the very first man born into this world prefigured the Man of Sin. He did so in at least seven respects. First, we may observe that in 1 John 3:12 we are told "Cain was of that Wicked one", i. e. the Devil. Of none other is this particular expression used. The Antichrist will also, in a special sense, be "of that Wicked one", for the Devil is said to be his "father" (John 8:44). Second, Cain was a religious hypocrite. This is seen in the fact that at first he posed as a worshipper of God, but the emptiness of his pretensions were quickly evidenced; for, when the Lord refused his offering, Cain was "very wroth" (Gen. 4:5). As such he clearly prefigured that one who will first claim to be the Christ, only to stand forth later as His denier (1 John 2:22). Third, by his primogeniture Cain occupied the position of *ruler*. Said the Lord to him, "Unto thee shall be his desire, and thou shalt *rule over* him", that is, over Abel (Gen. 4:7). Such, too, will be the position filled by the Antichrist—he shall be a Ruler over men. Fourth, in murdering his brother Abel, Cain foreshadowed the wicked martyrdom of the Tribulation saints by the Son of Perdition. Fifth, Cain was a *liar*. After the murder of Abel, when the Lord asked Cain, "Where is Abel thy brother?", he answered, "I know not" (Gen. 4:9). In like manner deceit and falsehood will characterize him who is appropriately named "the Lie" (2 Thess. 2:11). Sixth, God's judgment descended upon Cain. So far as we know from the Scripture record, no human eye witnessed the dastardly murder of Abel, and doubtless Cain deemed himself secure from any penal consequences. But if so, he reckoned without God. The Lord announced to him, "Thy brother's blood crieth unto Me from the ground", and then He declared, "And now art thou cursed from the earth" (Gen. 4:10). So, too, in his reckless conceit, the Antichrist will

imagine that he can defy God and slay His people with impugnity. But his blasphemous delusions will be quickly dispelled. Seventh, Cain was made to exclaim, "My punishment is greater than I can bear" (Gen. 4:13). Such indeed will be the awful portion meted out to the Antichrist—he shall be "cast alive into the lake of fire burning with brimstone" (Rev. 19:20).

2. *Lamech.* And Lamech said unto his wives: Adah and Zillah, hear my voice; Ye wives of Lamech, hearken unto my speech: For I have slain a man for wounding me, and a young man for bruising me. If Cain shall be avenged sevenfold, Truly Lamech seventy and seven fold" (Gen. 4:23, 24, R. V.). The record of this man's life is exceedingly brief, but from the little that is recorded about him we may discover at least seven parallelisms between him and the Antichrist. First, the meaning of his name. Lamech signifies "powerful". This was an appropriate name for one who foreshadowed the Man of Sin who, as the Head of the United States of the World, will be powerful governmentally. He will also be mighty in his person, for we are told that the Dragon shall give power unto him (Rev. 13:4). Second, in the fact that Lamech was a descendant of Cain (Gen. 4:17-19), not Seth, we see that he sprang from the *evil* line. Third, he was the *seventh* from fallen Adam, as though to intimate that the cycle of depravity was *completed in him*. So the Antichrist will be not only the culmination of satanic craft and power, but as well, the climax of human wickedness—the Man of Sin. Fourth, the first thing predicted of Lamech is his "lawlessness". "Lamech took unto him *two wives*" (Gen. 4:19). As such he violated the marriage-law and disobeyed the command of God (Gen. 2:24). Clearly, then, he foreshadowed the "Lawless One" (2 Thess. 2:8, R. V.). Fifth, like Cain before him, Lamech was a murderer. His confession is, "I have *slain* a man for wounding me, and a young man for bruising me" (Gen. 4:23). In this, too, he foreshadowed the Man of blood and of violence. Sixth, he was *filled with pride*. This comes out in two details. First, he says to his wives, "Hear *my* voice; Ye wives of Lamech, hearken unto *my* speech" (Gen. 4:23). Second, in his arrogant self-importance—"If Cain shall be avenged sevenfold, *truly* LAMECH seventy and seven fold" (Gen. 4:24). This appears to mean that Lamech had slain a man for wounding him, and mad with passion, he jeered ironically at God's dealings with Cain. Seventh, in the fact that the very next thing recorded after the brief notice of Lamech is the *birth of Seth* (the one from whom, according to the flesh, Christ descended) who *set aside* the line of Cain—for on his birth Eve exclaimed, "God hath appointed me another seed instead of Abel whom Cain slew" (Gen. 4:25)—thus we have a beautiful foreshadowing of the millennial reign of the Lord Jesus following the *overthrow* of the Antichrist.

3. *Nimrod.* This personal type of the Antichrist is deeply interesting and remarkably full in its details. His exploits are recorded in Gen. 10 and 11, and it is most significant that his person and history are there introduced at the point immediately preceding God's call of Abraham from among the Gentiles and His bringing him into the promised land. Thus will history repeat itself. Just before God again gathers Abraham's descendants from out of the lands of the Gentiles (many, perhaps the majority of whom, will be found dwelling in Chaldea, in Assyria, the "north country"—see Isa. 11:11; Jer. 3:18, etc.) there will arise one who will fill out the picture here typically outlined by Nimrod.

Let us examine the details of this type. First, the meaning of his name is most suggestive. Nimrod signifies "The Rebel". A fit designation was this for a man that foreshadowed the

Lawless One, who shall *oppose* and exalt himself above all that is called God (2 Thess. 2:4), and who shall "stand up against the Prince of princes" (Dan. 8:25). Second, we are told that he was a son of Cush—"And Cush begat Nimrod" (Gen. 10:8), and Cush was a son of Ham, who was cursed by Noah. Nimrod, then, was not a descendant of Shem, from whom Christ sprang, nor of Japheth; but he came from Ham. It is remarkable that these men who typified the Antichrist came from the *evil* line. Third, we are told that Nimrod "began to be a mighty one in the earth" (Gen. 10:8). Four times over is this term "mighty" connected with this one who prefigured him "whose coming is after the working of Satan, *with all power* and signs and lying wonders" (2 Thess. 2:9). But observe that it is first said, "He *began* to be mighty", which seems to suggest the idea that he *struggled for the pre-eminence* and obtained it by mere force of will. How this corresponds with the fact that the Man of Sin first appears as "the *little* horn" and by force of conquest attains to the position of King of kings needs only to be pointed out. It is also significant that the Hebrew word for "mighty" in Gen. 10:9 is "gibbor" which is translated several times "Chief" and "Chieftain". Fourth, it is also added, "Nimrod the mighty hunter *before the Lord"*, which means that he pushed his designs in brazen defiance of his Maker. The words "mighty hunter before the Lord" are found twice in Gen. 10:9. This repetition in so short a narrative is highly significant. If we compare the expression with a similar one in Gen. 6:11,—"The earth also (in the days of Noah) was corrupt *before God"*—the impression conveyed is, that this "Rebel" pursued his impious designs in open defiance of the Almighty. The contents of Gen. 11 abundantly confirm this interpretation. In like manner, of the Antichrist it is written, "And the King shall do according to *his* will, and he shall exalt himself and magnify himself above every god (ruler), and shall speak marvelous things against the God of gods" (Dan. 11:36). Fifth, Nimrod was a "Man of Blood". In 1 Chron. 1:10—"And Cush begat Nimrod; he began to be *mighty* upon the earth". The Chaldea paraphrase of this verse says, "Cush begat Nimrod who began to prevail in wickedness for he slew innocent blood and rebelled against Jehovah". This, coupled with the expression "a mighty Hunter before the Lord", suggests that he relentlessly sought out and slew God's people. As such, he accurately portrayed the *bloody* and *deceitful* Man (Psa. 5:6), the *violent* Man (Psa. 140:1). Sixth, Nimrod was a King—"the beginning of his *kingdom* was Babel" (Gen. 10:10). Thus he was King of Babylon, which is also one of the many titles of the Antichrist (Isa. 14:4). In the verses which follow in Gen. 10 we read, "He went out into Assyria and builded Ninevah, and the city Rehoboth, and Calah", etc. (Gen. 10:11). From these statements it is evident that Nimrod's ambition was to establish a *world-empire*. Seventh, mark his inordinate desire for *fame*. His consuming desire was to make for himself *a name*. Here again the antitype marvellously corresponds with type, for the Man of Sin is expressly denominated "King over all the children of pride" (Job 41:34).

What is recorded in Gen. 10 about Nimrod supplies the key to the first half of Gen. 11 which tells of the building of the Tower of Babel. Gen. 10:10 informs us that the beginning of Nimrod's kingdom was *Babel*. In the language of that day Babel meant "the gate of God", but afterwards, because of the judgment which the Lord there inflicted, it came to mean "Confusion". That at the time Nimrod founded Babel this word signified "the gate (the figure of official position) *of God"* intimates that he not only organized an imperial government over which he presided as king, but that he also instituted a new and idolatrous system of worship. If the type is perfect, and we are fully assured it is so, then, as the Lawless One will yet do, Nimrod demanded and received *Divine honors*. In all probability, it was at this point that idolatry was introduced.

Nimrod is not directly mentioned in Gen. 11, but from the statements made about him in chap. 10 there cannot be any doubt that *he* was the "Chief" and "King" who organized and headed the movement and rebellion there described: "And they said, Go to, let us build us a city and a tower, whose top may reach unto heaven; and let us make us a name, lest we be scattered abroad upon the face of the whole earth" (11:4). Here we behold a most blatant defiance of God, a deliberate refusal to obey His commands given through Noah—"Be fruitful, and multiply, and replenish *the earth*" (9:1). But they said, "Let us make us a name *lest we be* scattered upon the face of the whole earth". As we have seen, Nimrod's ambition was to establish a *world-empire*. To accomplish this two things, at least, were necessary. First, a *center*, a great headquarters; and second, a *motive* for the inspiration and encouragement of his followers. The former was furnished in the city of Babylon: the latter was to be supplied in the "let us make us a name". It was inordinate desire for fame. The idea of the "Tower" (considered in the light of its setting) seems that of *strength*, a stronghold, rather than eminence.

To sum up. In Nimrod and his schemes we behold Satan's initial attempt to raise up an universal ruler of men. In his inordinate desire for fame, in the mighty power that he wielded, in his ruthless and brutal methods, in his blatant defiance of the Creator, in his founding of the kingdom of Babel, in his assuming to himself Divine honors, in the fact that the Holy Spirit has placed the record of these things *just before* the inspired account of God's bringing Abraham into Canaan —pointing forward to the re-gathering of Israel in Palestine, immediately after the overthrow of the Lawless One —and finally, in the Divine destruction of his kingdom—described in the words, "Let Us *go down* and there confound their language" (Gen. 11:7) which so marvellously pictures the *descent* of Christ from heaven to vanquish His impious rival—we cannot fail to see that we have a wonderfully complete typical picture of the person, the work, and the destruction of the Antichrist.

4. *Chedorlaomer*. The history of this man is recorded in Gen. 14 which is a chapter of deep interest to the student of typology. The chapter opens with the words "And it came to pass in the days" of. "This is an expression which occurs six times (in the Hebrew) and always marks a time of trouble ending in blessing—cf Ruth 1:11; Isa. 7:1; Jer. 1:3; Esther 1:1; 2 Sam. 21:1" (Companion Bible). Such is plainly the case here. The first half of Gen. 14 depicts Tribulation conditions, and this is followed by a scene foreshadowing millennial glory. The *time* when Chedorlaomer lived is the first point in the type. His history is recorded just before the first mention of Melchizedek, the priest-king, who came forth and blessed Abraham—an unmistakeable foreshadowment of Christ in millennial glory, blessing Israel. Second, the name of this man is highly significant. Gesenius, in his lexicon, says of the meaning of his name, "If it be a Phoenicio—Shemetic word 'a handful of sheaves' . . . . perhaps its true etymology should be sought in the *ancient* Persian". The latter is doubtless correct, for "Elam", of which Chedorlaomer was king (Gen. 14:1), is the ancient name for Persia. Col. Rawlinson searched for his name on the tablets of ancient Assyria, and there he found that his official title was, "Ravager of the west"! Thus

was he a true type of the coming one who shall wade through a sea of blood to his coveted position as Emperor of the world. Third, it is indeed remarkable to find that just as Rev. 13:1 shows us that the empire of which the Antichrist will be the Head (see our notes on this verse in Article 11) includes within it the territory and perpetuates the characteristics of the earlier empires (Babylon, Persia, Greece and Rome), so in Gen. 14 Chedorlaomer is seen connected with *the same dominions:* "And it came to pass in the days of Amraphel king of Shinar, Arioch king of Ellasar, Chedorlaomer king of Elam, and Tidal king of nations". Now "Shinar" is one of the names of *Babylon* (see Dan. 1:2); "Elam" is the ancient name of *Persia;* "Ellasar" is translated "Hellas" in the Sept., which is the ancient name of *Greece;* while "Tidal king of the nations" evidently stands for *Rome,* the last of the world empires. Fourth, but what is even more striking, is the fact that in Gen. 14:5 Chedorlaomer is seen *at the head of* the kings mentioned in v. 1. They act as his vassals, and thus bow to the superiority of this one who was evidently a King of kings. Fifth, Chedorlaomer was a Warrior of renown. He was the Attila, the Napoleon of his day. He defeated in battle the kings of Sodom and Gomorrah and brought them into subjection and servitude (see 14:2-4). Later, they rebelled, and gathering his forces together he went forth, vanquished, and slew them (14:9, 10). Thus did he foreshadow the "Destroyer of the Gentiles" (Jer. 4:7). Sixth, in Gen. 14:12 we read, "And they took Lot, Abraham's brother's son, who dwelt in Sodom, and his goods, and departed". This prefigured the persecution of Israel by Antichrist and his subordinates in a coming day. Finally, we learn how that Abraham and his servants pursued Chedorlaomer and his forces, and that "Chedorlaomer and the kings that were with him" were slain "in the kings dale" (14:17), which strikingly adumbrated the future overthrow of Antichrist and the kings who shall be with him, in the dale of Megiddo (see Rev. 19:19).

5. *Pharaoh.* We have in mind the Pharaoh of the book of Exodus. His history and character are described at much greater length than the other personal types of the Antichrist which have been before us, and therefore more parallelisms are to be found here. We shall aim to be suggestive rather than exhaustive. First, Pharaoh was king of Egypt which, in Scripture, is the lasting symbol of the world. In like manner, the one whom he so strikingly prefigured will be Head of the world-kingdom. Second, the Pharaoh of Exodus came from Assyria (Isa. 52:4); so also will the Antichrist first rise in that land. Third, Ex. 1 presents him to our view as the merciless persecutor of the Hebrews, embittering their lives by hard bondage. Fourth, he is next seen as the one who sought to cut off Israel from being a nation, giving orders that all the male children should be slain in infancy. Fifth, he was the blatant defier of God. When Moses and Aaron appeared before him and said, "Thus saith the Lord God of Israel, Let My people go, that they may hold a feast unto Me in the wilderness", his arrogant reply was, "Who is the Lord, that I should obey His voice to let Israel go?" (Ex. 5:1, 2). Sixth, God's *two witnesses* performed miracles before Pharaoh (Ex. 7:10); so, too, will God's two witnesses in the Tribulation period work miracles before the Beast (Rev. 11:6, 7). Seventh, Pharaoh had magical resources at his disposal (Ex. 7:11), as the Antichrist will have at his (2 Thess. 2:9). Eighth, Pharaoh made fair promises to the Hebrews, only to break them (Ex. 8:8, 15). In this, too, he foreshadowed the Antichrist in his perfidy and treachery toward Israel. Ninth, he met with a drastic end at the hands of God (Psa. 136:15). Tenth,

he was overthrown at the time that Israel started out for the promised land: so Antichrist will be cast into the Lake of Fire just before Israel enters into everlasting possession of their promised inheritance. In all of these ten respects (and in others which the student may search out for himself) Pharaoh was a striking and accurate type of the Antichrist.

6. *Abimelech.* First, Abimelech signifies "father of the king". Gideon, deliverer of Israel, was his father. But his mother was a concubine, and this name was given to him, no doubt, for the purpose of hiding the shame of his birth. Looking from the type to the antitype—"*Father* of the King"—calls attention to the satanic origin of the Antichrist. Second, Abimelech slew seventy of his own brethren (Judges 9:5), and was therefore a bloody persecutor of Israel. Third, Judges 9:6, 22 tell us that he was "king over Israel". Fourth, it is significant to note that he occupied the throne at the time of Israel's apostasy (see Judges 8:33, 34). Fifth, it is also most suggestive that we are told he commenced his career at the stone (Judges 9:6), or pillar, which Joshua erected in Ebal (facing Gerizim), the mount where all the *curses* of a broken law were announced—Deut. 11:29; 27:4, 12, 13; Josh. 8:30. Sixth, he was a mighty warrior, a violent man (see Judges 9: 40-50, and cf Psa. 140, v. 1 for the Antichrist as such). Seventh, he was slain by the *sword* (Judges 9:54 and see Zech. 11:7; Rev. 13:3 for the antitype).

7. *Saul.* In at least ten respects Saul foreshadowed the Antichrist. Almost the first thing told us about Saul is that he was "from his shoulders and upward higher than any of the people" (1 Sam. 9:2, which is repeated in 10: 23). As such he fitly prefigured the coming Super-man, who in intelligence, governmental power, and satanic might, will so tower above all his contemporaries that men shall exclaim, "Who is like unto the Beast?" (Rev. 13:4). Second, Saul was king of Israel (1 Sam. 10:24), so also will the Antichrist be. Third, Saul was a priest-king, blatantly performing the office of the Levite (see 1 Sam. 13:9, and cf Ezek. 21:25, 26 R.V.). Fourth, the *time* of his reign was immediately before that of David, as that of the Antichrist will immediately precede that of David's Son and Lord. Fifth, he was a mighty Warrior (see 1 Sam. 11:11, 13:1-4, 15:4, 7;8). Sixth, he was a rebel against God (1 Sam. 15:11). Seventh, he hated David (1 Sam. 18:7, 8, 11; 26:2, etc.). Eighth, he slew the servants of God (1 Sam. 22:17, 18). Ninth, he had intercourse with the powers of evil (1 Sam. 29). Tenth, he died by the *sword* (1 Sam. 31:4).

8. *Goliath.* First, his name means "Soothsayer" which at once connects him with the powers of evil. Second, he was a giant, and thus, like Saul, prefigured the Super-man. Third, he was the enemy of Israel. Fourth, his consuming egotism was displayed in his blatant challenge, "I defy the armies of Israel" (1 Sam. 17:10). Fifth, the mysterious number 666 (the number of the Antichrist) is connected with Goliath. Note the three sixes. (a) He was "*six* cubits high" (1 Sam. 17:4). (b) *Six* pieces of armor are enumerated—helmet, coat of mail, greaves, target, staff, and shield (1 Sam. 17:5-7). (c) His spear's head weighed "*six* hundred shekels of iron (1 Sam. 17:7). Sixth, he was slain by the *sword* (see 1 Sam. 17:51). Seventh, he was slain by David—type of Christ. In each of these respects he foreshadowed the Antichrist.

9. *Absalom.* First, the meaning of his name is very significant. "Absalom" means "father of peace". A careful reading of his history reveals the fact that, again and again, he posed as a man of peace, while war was in his heart. So the Antichrist will pose as the promised Prince of peace, and for a time it will appear that he has ac-

tually ushered in the Millennium. But ere long his violent and bloody character will be revealed. Second, Absalom was the son of David, and therefore a Jew. Third, but Absalom was a son of David by Maacah, the daughter of the Gentile king of Jeshur (2 Sam. 3:3). So, too, will the Antichrist also be connected with the Gentiles. Fourth, Absalom was a man of imposing personality (2 Sam. 14:25). So the Antichrist will be a veritable king among men. Fifth, Absalom was a man of blood (2 Sam. 13, etc.). Sixth, Absalom sought to obtain the kingdom by flatteries (2 Sam. 15:2-6); cf Dan. 11:21, 23. Seventh, he cloaked his rebellion by a pretense of religion (read 2 Sam. 15:7, 8). Eighth, he was the immediate cause of the faithful followers of David being driven from Jerusalem into the wilderness (2 Sam. 15:14-16). Ninth, he reared up a "pillar" unto himself (2 Sam. 18:18), which clearly foreshadowed the "image" which the Antichrist will cause to be set up unto himself. Tenth, he met with a violent end (2 Sam. 18:14).

There are quite a number of others who foreshadowed the Antichrist in one or more of the outstanding features of his character and career. For instance, there is Balak who, accompanied by Baalam the prophet sought to curse and destroy Israel—a striking foreshadowing of the Beast with his ally the False Prophet. There is Adoni-zedek, mentioned in Joshua 10, and who headed a federation of ten kings; it is remarkable that his name signifies "lord of righteousness" which is what the Antichrist will claim to be as he comes forth on "the *white* horse" (Rev. 6). Then there is Adoni-kam, with whom is associated the mystical number 666—see Ezra 2:13; and how profoundly significant that his name signifies "the Lord hath risen". We believe that this mystic number in connection with the Antichrist will apply to him only after his resurrection —666 is *three* sixes, and three is the number of *resurrection*, and six the number of man! Sennacherib (2 Kings 18) prefigured the Antichrist in a number of ways: as the king of Assyria, the blatant defier of God, smitten by the sword, etc. Haman, four times denominated "the Jews' enemy" (Esther 3:10 etc.), and termed "the adversary" (Esther 7:6), was another typical character. Nebuchadnezzar, king of kings, who demanded universal worship, who set up an image to himself, and decreed that all should worship it under pain of death, etc., manifestly pointed forward to the Man of Sin, and so we might continue. Almost every prominent feature of the Antichrist's person and career was foreshadowed by some Old Testament character. The subject is intensely interesting, and we trust that many of our readers will be encouraged to pursue it further for themselves. In closing this paper we shall look at one New Testament type of the Antichrist.

10. *Herod.* At the beginning of the New Testament there meets us a typical foreshadowing of the Antichrist. We refer to what is recorded in Matt. 2. The description there furnished of Herod obviously contains a prophetic adumbration of his great prototype. Notice, first, that three times over he is denominated *"the king"* (vv. 1, 3, 9), as such he prefigured the last great king, before the appearing of the King of kings. Second, observe his *hypocrisy*. When the "wise men", who had followed the star which heralded the Saviour's birth, were summoned into Herod's presence, we are told that he said unto them, "Go and search diligently for the young child; and when ye have found Him, bring me word again, *that I may come and worship Him also*" (v. 8). That nothing could have been further from his mind is plain from his subsequent acts. But, nevertheless, he first posed as a devout worshipper. Such is the role that the Antichrist will first fill in Palestine. Third, next he *threw off* his religious

mask and displayed his wicked heart: "Then Herod, when he saw that he was mocked of the wise men, was exceeding wroth, and sent forth, and slew all the children that were in Bethlehem", etc. (v. 16). Similarly will the Antichrist act in Jerusalem. Three and one half years before his end comes he will discard his religious pretensions and stand forth in his true character. Fourth, in this edict of slaying the young children in Bethlehem and the coasts thereof, he was aiming, of course, at Christ Himself. Thus did he accurately foreshadow that one who will yet fulfill the terms of Gen. 3:15, where we read of a *double* "enmity"—between Satan and the woman (Israel), and between her Seed (Christ) and the Serpent's "seed" (the Antichrist). In the fifth place, we may also discover in Herod's destruction of the children, a forecast of the fiendish assaults which the Antichrist will make upon *the Jews,* when he seeks to cut them off from being a nation. In the sixth place, we may note how *the consequence* of Herod's cruelty will reappear in the future—"In Ramah was there a voice heard, lamentation, and weeping, and great mourning, Rachel weeping for her children, and would not be comforted, because they are not" (Matt. 2:18). This is a quotation from Jer. 31:15. But like most, if not all, prophecies, this will receive another and final fulfillment at the close of the Tribulation period. Our authority for this is found in the words which immediately follow in Jer. 31: "Thus saith the Lord, Refrain thy voice from weeping, and thine eyes from tears: for thy work shall be rewarded, saith the Lord; and they shall come again from the land of The Enemy. And there is hope in *thine end,* saith the Lord, that thy children shall come again to their own border". Thus it is clear that "bitter weeping and lamentation" will again be heard in Ramah just before Christ returns and restores Israel. Seventh, the accuracy of the typical picture supplied by Matt. 2 may be discovered in *the failure* of Herod to destroy the Christ-child. Just as God foiled Herod, so will He yet bring to nought the wicked designs of the Antichrist; and just as we read of Christ coming and dwelling at Nazareth after the *death* of Herod, so Christ shall again dwell in that land after the death of the false King. Surely, this remarkable typical picture of the Antichrist should cause us to search more diligently for other esoteric allusions to him in the New Testament. —Arthur W. Pink.

3. THE LAW AND THE SAINT.

What is the relation of the Law (the Ten Commandments) to Christians? In our previous article we pointed out how that three radically different answers have been returned to this question. The first, that sinners *become saints* by obeying the Law. This is Legalism pure and simple. It is heresy of the most dangerous kind. All who really believe and act on it as the ground of their acceptance by God, will perish eternally. Second, others say that the Law *is not binding* on Christians because it has been abolished. This is, we are fully assured, a serious error. It arises from a mistaken interpretation of certain passages in the Epistles. The inevitable tendency of such an error is toward Antinomianism, the "turning of the grace of God into lasciviousness" (Jude 4). Third, others affirm, and the writer is among the number, that the Ten Commandments are an expression of the unchanging character and will of God: that they are a moral standard of conduct which we disregard at our peril: that they are, and will ever be, *binding* upon every Christian.

In our last article we sought to prepare the way for the present one. There, we dealt with the negative side; here, we shall treat of the positive. In the former, we sought to give the true meaning of the principal passages in the New Testament appealed to by those who *deny* that the Ten Commandments are now binding on Christians. In the present article, we shall endeavor to expound some of the many passages in the New Testament which *affirm* that the Ten Commandments are now binding on Christians. We, therefore, invite the reader's most diligent and prayerful attention to the scriptures cited and our comments upon them.

1. "Think not that I am come to destroy the Law, or the Prophets: I am not come to destroy, but to fulfill. For verily I say unto you, Till heaven and earth pass, one jot or one tittle shall in nowise pass from the Law, till all be fulfilled. Whosoever therefore shall break one of these least commandments, and shall teach men so, he shall be called the least in the kingdom of heaven: but whosoever shall do and teach them, the same shall be called great in the kingdom of heaven" (Matt. 5:17-19). It might appear to the disciples of Christ that their Master intended to set aside Moses and the Prophets, and introduce an entirely new standard of morality. It was true indeed that He would expose the error of depending on the works of the Law for acceptance with God (as Moses and the prophets had done before Him); but it was no part of His design to set aside the Law itself. He was about to correct various corruptions, which obtained among the Jews, hence He is careful to preface what He has to say by cautioning them not to misconstrue His designs. So far from having any intention of repudiating Moses, He most emphatically asserts: first, that He had not come to destroy the Law; second, that He had come to "fulfill" it; third, that the Law is of perpetual obligation; fourth, that whoso breaks one of the least of the Law's commandments and teaches others so to do, shall suffer loss; fifth, that he who kept the Law and taught men to respect and obey it should be rewarded.

"I am not come to destroy the Law"—the Prophets simply expounded the Law, and rebuked Israel for their failure to keep it, and forewarned them of the consequences of continued disobedience. "I am *not come* to destroy the Law". Nothing could be more explicit. The word "destroy" here means "to dissolve or overthrow". When, then, our Lord said that He had not come to destroy the Law He gave us to understand that it was not the purpose of His mission to repeal or annul the Ten Commandments: that He had not come to free men from their obligations to them. And if *He* did not "destroy" the Law, then no one has destroyed it; and if no one has destroyed it, then the Law still stands with all its Divine authority; and if the Law still abides as the unchanging expression of God's character and will, then every human creature is under lasting obligations to obey it; and if every human creature, then the Christian!

Second, the Son of God went on to say "I am not come to destroy, but to fulfill". The word "fulfill" here means "to fill up, to complete". Christ "fulfilled" the Law in three ways: first, by rendering personal obedience to its precepts. God's Law was within His heart (Psa. 40:8), and in thought, word, and deed, He perfectly met its requirements; and thus by *His* obedience He magnified the Law and made it honorable (Isa. 42:21). Second, by suffering (at the Cross) it's death-penalty on behalf of His people who had transgressed it. Third, by exhibiting its fulness and spirituality and by amplifying its contents. Thus did Christ, our Exemplar, "fulfill the Law".

So far from Christ having repealed

the Law, He expressly affirmed, "Till heaven and earth pass, one jot or one tittle shall in nowise pass from the Law, till all be fulfilled". In these words He announces the *perpetuity* of the Law. So long as *heaven* and earth shall last, the Law will endure, and by necessary implication, the lasting obligations of all men to fulfill it.

But this is not all that our Lord here said. With omniscient foresight He anticipated what Mr. Mead has aptly termed "The Modern Outcry against the Law", and proceeds to solemnly warn against it. He said, "Whosoever therefore shall break one of these least commandments, and *shall teach men so*, he shall be called *the least* in the kingdom of heaven". The "kingdom of heaven" (in its ultimate form) refers, we believe, to Christ's millennial kingdom. In that kingdom, whosoever has slighted the Law—broken even one of its least commandments and taught men to do the same—shall be called least; that is, shall occupy a position of least honor (cf Matt. 11:11). But on the other hand, whoso honors the Law—by obeying and teaching others to—shall be called great; that is, shall have a position of honor in the kingdom (cf Matt. 18:4).

2. "Do we then make void the Law through faith? God forbid: yea, we establish the Law" (Rom. 3:31). In the previous part of the chapter the apostle had proven that "there is none righteous, no not one" (v. 10); second, he had declared "By the deeds of the Law there shall no flesh be justified" (v. 2); then in vv. 21-26 he had set forth the Divine way of salvation —"through faith in Christ's blood". In v. 28, he sums up his argument by affirming "a man is justified by faith without the deeds of the Law". In vv. 29, 30 he proves that this is true for Jew and Gentile alike. Then, in v. 31, he anticipates an objection: What about the Law, then? This was a very pertinent question. Twice had he said that justification was apart from the deeds of the Law. If, then, the Law served no purpose in effecting the salvation of sinners, has it no office at all? If we are saved "through *faith*" is the Law useless? Are we to understand you to mean (Paul) that the Law has been annulled? Not at all, is the apostle's answer: "We *establish* the Law".

What did the apostle mean when he said "We establish the Law"? He meant that, as saved men, Christians are under *additional* obligations to obey the Law, for they are now furnished with new and more powerful motives to serve God. Righteousness imputed to the believer produces in the justified one a kind and an extent of obedience which could not otherwise have been obtained. So far from rendering void or nullifying the authority and use of the Law, it *sustains* and *confirms* them. *Our* moral obligation to God and our neighbour have not been weakened, but strengthened. Below we offer one or two brief exerpts from other expositors:

"Does not the doctrine of faith evacuate the Old Testament of its meaning, and does it not make law void, and lead to disregard of it? Does it not open the door to license of living? To this the apostle replies, that it certainly does not; but that, on the contrary, the Gospel puts law on a proper basis and esfablishes it on its foundation as a revelation of God's will" (Dr. Griffith-Thomas).

"We cancel law, then, by this faith of ours? We open the door, then, to moral license? We abolish code and precept, then, when we ask not for conduct, but for faith? Away with the thought; nay, we establish law; we go the very way to give a new sacredness to its every command, and to disclose a new power for the fulfillment of them all. But *how* this is, and is to be, the later argument is to show" (Dr. Handley Moule).

"Objection. If man is justified by

faith without works, does not that do away with law entirely, i. e. teach lawlessness? *Answer:* By no means. It establishes the law. When a man is saved by grace, that does not make him lawless. There is a power within him which does not destroy, but it strengthens the law, and causes him to *keep* it, not through fear, but through love to God" (H. S. Miller, M.A.).

3. "For I delight in the Law of God after the inward man . . . . with the mind I myself serve the Law of God" (Rom. 7:22-25). In this chapter the apostle does two things: first, he shows what is not and what is the Law's relation to the believer—judicially, the believer is emancipated from the curse or penalty of the Law (7:1-6); morally, the believer is under bonds to obey the Law (vv. 22, 25). Secondly, he guards against a false inference being drawn from what he had taught in chapter 6. In 6:1-11 he sets forth the believer's *identification with Christ* as "dead to sin" (vv. 2, 7, etc.). Then, from v. 11 onwards, he shows the effect this truth should have upon the believer's walk. In chapter 7 he follows the same order of thought. In 7:1-6 he treats of the believer's *identification with Christ* as "dead to the law" (see vv. 4 and 6). Then, from v. 7 onwards he describes the experiences of the Christian. Thus the first half of Rom. 6 and the first half of Rom. 7 deal with the believer's *standing*, whereas the second half of each chapter treats of the believer's *state;* but with this difference: the second half of Rom. 6 reveals what our state *ought* to be, whereas the second half of Rom. 7 (vv. 13-25) shows what our state *actually is**.

The controversy which has raged over Rom. 7 is largely the fruitage of the Perfectionism of Wesley and his followers. That brethren, whom we have cause to respect, should have adopted this error in a modified form, only shows how widespread today is the spirit of Laodiceanism. To talk of "getting out of Rom. 7 into Rom. 8" is excuseless folly. Rom. 7 and 8 *both* apply with undiminished force and pertinency to every believer on earth today. The second half of Rom. 7 describes the *conflict* of the two natures in the child of God: it simply sets forth in detail what is summarised in Gal. 5:17. Rom. 7:14, 15, 18, 19, 21 are now true of *every* believer on earth. *Every* Christian falls far, far short of the standard set before him—we mean *God's* standard, not that of the so-called "victorious life" teachers. If any Christian reader is ready to say that Rom. 7:19 does not describe *his* life, we say in all kindness, that he is sadly deceived. We do not mean by this that every Christian breaks the laws of men, or that he is an overt transgressor of the laws of God. But we do mean that his life is far, far below the level of the life our Saviour lived here on earth. We do mean that there is much of "the flesh" still evident in every Christian—not the least in those who make such loud boastings of their spiritual attainments. We do mean that *every* Christian has urgent need to daily pray for the forgiveness of his daily sins (Luke 11:4), for "in many things we all stumble" (James 3:2, R. V.).

The second half of Rom. 7, then, is describing the *state* of the Christian, i. e. the conflict between the two natures within him. In v. 14 the apostle declares, "We know that the Law is spiritual". How different is this language from the disparaging way that many now refer to God's Law! In v. 22 he exclaims, "I *delight* in the Law of God after the inward man". How far removed is this from the delusion that the Law has been abolished, and that it no longer serves any purpose for the Christian! The apostle Paul did not ignore the Law, still less did he regard it as an enemy. The new

---
* Vv. 8-12 are more or less in the nature of a parenthesis.

nature within him delighted in it: so, too, did the Psalmist, see Psa. 119:72, 97, 140. But the old nature was still within him too, warring against the new, and bringing him into captivity to the law of sin, so that he cried, "O wretched man that I am! Who shall deliver me from the body of this death?" (v. 24)—and we sincerely pity every professing Christian who does not echo this cry. Next, the apostle thanks God that he *shall be* delivered yet "through Jesus Christ our Lord" (v. 25), not "by the power of the Holy Spirit" note! The deliverance is future, at the return of Christ, see Phil. 3:20, etc. Finally, and mark that this comes *after* he had spoken of the promised "deliverance", he sums up his *dual* experience by saying, "So then with the mind I myself serve the Law of God; but with the flesh the law of sin". Could anything be plainer? Instead of affirming that the Law had nothing to do with him as a Christian, nor he with it, he expressly declared that he *served* "the Law of God". This is sufficient for us. Let others refuse to "serve" the *Law of God* at their peril.

4. "For what the Law could not do, in that it was weak through the flesh, God sending His own Son in the likeness of sinful flesh, and for sin, condemned sin in the flesh: That the *righteousness of the Law* might be *fulfilled in us,* who walk not after the flesh but after the spirit" (Rom. 8:3, 4). This throws light on Rom. 3:31, showing us, in part, *how* the Law is "established". The reference here is to the new nature. The believer now has a heart that loves God, and therefore does it "*delight*" in the Law of God". And it is ever at *the heart* that God looks, though, of course, He takes note of our actions too. But in heart the believer "fulfills" the holy requirements of God's Law, inasmuch as his innermost desire is to serve, please, and glorify the Law-giver. The righteous requirements of the Law are "fulfilled" *in* us because we now "obey from the heart" (Rom. 6:17).

5. "He that loveth another hath fulfilled the Law. For this, Thou shalt not commit adultery, Thou shalt not kill, Thou shalt not steal, Thou shalt not bear false witness, Thou shalt not covet; and if there be any other commandment, it is briefly comprehended in this saying, namely, Thou shalt love thy neighbour as thyself. Love worketh no ill to his neighbour: therefore love is the fulfilling of the Law" (Rom. 13:8-10). Here again, the apostle, so far from lending the slightest encouragement to the strange delusion that the Ten Commandments have become obsolete to Christians, actually *quotes* five of them, and then declares, "Love is the fulfilling of the Law". Love is not a substitution for Law-obedience, but *it is that which prompts the believer to render obedience to it.* Note carefully, it is not "love is the *abrogating* of the Law", but "love is the *fulfilling* of the Law". "The whole Law is grounded on love to God and love to man. This cannot be violated without the breach of Law; and if there is love, it will influence us to the observance of all God's commandments" (Haldane). Love is the fulfilling of the Law because love is what the Law demands. The prohibitions of the Law are not unreasonable restraints on Christian liberty, but the just and wise requirements *of love.* We may add that the above is another passage which serves to explain Rom. 3:31, for it supplies a practical exemplification of the way in which the Gospel establishes the Law as the expression of the Divine will, which love alone can fulfill.

6. "For though I be free from all men, yet have I made myself servant unto all, that I might gain the more. And unto the Jews I became as a Jew, that I might gain the Jews; to them that are under the Law, as under the Law, that I might gain them that are under the Law; to them that are

without Law, as without Law, (being not without Law to God, but under the Law to Christ,) that I might gain them that are without Law" (1 Cor. 9:19-22). The central thought of this passage is how the apostle forewent his Christian liberty for the sake of the Gospel. Though "free" from all, he nevertheless, made himself "the servant" of all. To the unconverted Jews he "became a Jew"; Acts 16:3 supplies an illustration. To those who deemed themselves to be yet under the ceremonial law, he acted accordingly: Acts 21:26 supplies an example of this. To them without Law: that is, Gentiles without the ceremonial law, he abstained from the use of all ceremonies as they did: cf Gal. 2:3. Yet, he did not act as "without Law *to God*," but instead, as *"under Law* to Christ"; that is, as still under the moral Law of God. He never counted himself free from *that*, nor would he do anything contrary to the eternal Law of righteousness. To be "under Law to God", is, without question, to be under the Law of God. Therefore, to be under the Law to Christ, is to be under the Law of God, for the Law was not abrogated but re-inforced by Christ. This text, then, gives a plain and decisive answer to the question, *How* the believer is under the Law of God, namely, as he is "under the Law to Christ", belonging to Christ, as he does, by redemption.

7. "For, brethren, ye have been called unto liberty; only use not liberty for an occasion to the flesh, but by love serve one another. For all the Law is fulfilled in one word, even in this; Thou shalt love thy neighbour as thyself" (Gal. 5:13, 14). Here the apostle first reminds the Galatian saints (and us) that they had been called unto "liberty", i. e., from the *curse* of the moral Law (3:13). Second, he defines the bounds of that liberty, and shows that it must not deteriorate to fleshly license, but that it is bounded by the requirements of the unchanging moral Law of God, which requires that we love our neighbours as ourselves. Third, he repeats here, what he had said in Rom. 13:8-10, namely, that love is the fulfilling of the Law. The new commandment of love to our brethren is comprehended in the old commandment of love to our neighbour, hence the former is *enforced* by an appeal to the latter.

"For, brethren, ye have been called unto liberty; only use not liberty for an occasion to the flesh, but by love serve one another" (Gal. 5:13). We quote here part of the late Dr. George Bishop's comments on this verse: "The apostle here emphasizes a danger. The believer before believing, relied upon his works to save him. After believing, seeing he is in no way saved by his works, he is in danger of despising good works and minifying their value. At first he was an Arminian living by law; now he is in danger of becoming an Antinomian and flinging away the law altogether.

"But the law is holy and the commandment holy, and just, and good. It is God's standard—the eternal Norm. Fulfilled by Christ for us, it still remains the swerveless and unerring rule of righteousness. We are without the law for salvation, but not without the law for obedience. Angels are under the law 'doing God's commandments, hearkening to the voice of His word' (Psa. 103:20). The law then is immutable—its reign universal and without exception. The law! It is the transcript of the Divine perfections: the standard of eternal justice: the joy and rapture of all holy beings. The law! We are above it for salvation, but under it, or rather in it and it in us, as a principle of holiness" (Grace in Galatians).

8. "Children obey your parents in the Lord: for this is right. Honour thy father and mother; which is the first commandment with promise; That it may be well with thee, and thou mayest live long on the earth" (Eph. 6:1-

3). Once more we have a direct quotation from the tables of stone as the regulator of the *Christian* conscience. First, the apostle bids children obey their parents in the Lord. Second, he *enforces* this by an appeal to the fifth commandment in the Decalogue. What a proof this is that the Christian *is* under the Law (for the apostle is writing *to* Christians), under it "to Christ". Third, not only does the apostle here quote the fifth commandment, but he reminds us that there is *a promise* annexed to it, a promise concerning the prolongation of *earthly* life. How this refutes those who declare that *our* blessings are *all* spiritual and heavenly (Eph. 1:3). Let the ones who are constantly criticising those who press on the children of God the scriptures which have to do with our *earthly walk,* and who term this a "coming down from our position in the heavenlies" weigh carefully Eph. 6:2, 3 and also 1 Tim. 4:8—"For bodily exercise profiteth little: but godliness is profitable unto all things, having promise of *the life that now is,* and of that which is to come"; and let them also study 1 Pet. 3:10. In the administration of His government, God acts upon *immutable* principles*.

9. "But we know that the Law is good, if a man use it lawfully" (1 Tim. 1:8). The Law is used *unlawfully,* when sinners rest on their imperfect obedience to it as the ground of their acceptance by God. So, too, believers use it *unlawfully,* when they obey its precepts out of servile fear. But used lawfully, the Law is *good.* This could never have been said if the Law is an enemy to be shunned. Nor could it have been said if it has been repealed for the Christian. In that case, the apostle would have said, "The Law is not binding upon us". But he did not so say. Instead, he declared "The Law *is* good". He said more than that, he affirmed, "We *know* that the Law is good". It is not a debateable point, rather is it one that has been Divinely settled for us. But the Law is only "good" if a man (Greek, any one) use it lawfully. To use the Law lawfully is to regard it as the unchanging expression of the will of God, and therefore to "delight" in it, To use the Law lawfully is to receive it as the corrector of our conduct. To use the Law lawfully is to "fulfill" it in love.

10. "Behold, the days come, saith the Lord, when I will make a new covenant with the house of Israel and with the house of Judah .... this is the covenant that I will make with the house of Israel after those days, saith the Lord; I will put My laws into their mind, and write them in their hearts: and I will be to them a God, and they shall be to Me a people" (Heb. 8:8, 10). Ah, says the carping objector, This concerns Israel in a coming day, not Christians in this dispensation. True, it has reference to millennial Israel, but is it to be *limited to them?* Before we answer this question, let it be carefully noted that this passage unmistakeably demonstrates two things: first, it proves conclusively that the Law *has not been* "abolished"! Second, it proves that the Law *does have* a use and value for those that are *saved,* for it is saved Israel that is here in view! Nor is there any possible room for doubt as to whether or not this applies to Gentile Christians now.

The passage just quoted refers to "the *new covenant*". Is the new covenant *restricted to Israel?* Emphatically no. Did not our Saviour say at the Holy Supper, "This is My blood of the new covenant, which is poured out for many for the remission of sins?" (Matt. 26:28, R. V.). Was Christ's

---

* That some obedient children are shortlived no more belies the Word of God than that some *diligent* men are poor, yet Prov. 10:4 says, "The hand of the diligent maketh rich". The truth is, that these promises reveal the *general purpose* of God, but He always reserves to Himself the sovereign right to make whom He pleases *exceptions* to the general rule.

blood of the new covenant limited to Israel? Certainly not. Note how the apostle quotes our Lord's words when writing to the *Corinthians*, see 1 Cor. 11:25. So, too, in 2 Cor. 3:6 the apostle Paul declares that God has made us (not is going to make us) "ministers of the *new* covenant". This is proof positive that *Christians* are under the new covenant. The new covenant is made with all that Christ died for, and therefore Heb. 8:8-10 assures us that God puts His laws into the minds and writes them upon the hearts of every one of His redeemed. That the passage here in Heb. 8 uses the future tense is because Israel is in view, and Israel is not yet saved. But Gentile believers, even now, have God's *laws* in their minds and hearts. Proof of this is found in Rom. 8:4—"That the righteousness of the Law might be fulfilled *in* us".

But so anxious are some to grasp at everything which they imagine favors their contention that in no sense are believers under the Law, this passage is sometimes appealed to in support. It is argued that since God has now (by regeneration) written the Law on the believer's heart, He no longer needs any *outward* commandments to rule and direct him. Inward principle, it is said, will now move him spontaneously, so that all need for *external* law is removed. This error was so ably exposed fifty years ago by Dr. Martin, we transcribe a part of his refutation:

"How was it with our first parents? If ever outward law, categorical and imperative, might have been dispensed with, it might in Adam's case. In all the compass of his nature, there was *nothing* adverse to the law of God. He was a law unto himself. He was the moral law unto himself; loving God with all his heart, and his neighbour as himself, in all things content, in nothing coveting. Was imperative, authoritative, sovereign commandment therefore utterly unnecessary? Did God see it to be needless to say to him, Thou shalt, or, Thou shalt not? It was the very thing that infinite wisdom saw he needed. And therefore did He give commandment—'Thou shalt not eat of it'.

"How was it with the last Adam? All God's law was in His heart operating there, an inward principle of grace; He surely, if any, might have dispensed with strict, imperative, authoritative law and commandment. 'I delight to do Thy will, O God; Thy law also is within My heart'. Was no commandment, therefore, laid upon —no obedience-statute ordained—unto Him? Or did He complain if there was? Nay; I hear Him specially rejoicing in it. Every word He uttered, every work He did, was by commandment: 'My Father which sent me, He gave Me *commandment* what I should say and what I should do; as He gave Me *commandment* therefore, so I speak'.

"And shall His members, though the regenerating Spirit dwells in them, claim an exemption from what the Son was not exempt? Shall believers, because the Spirit puts the law into their hearts, claim a right to act merely at the dictate of inward gracious principle, untrammelled, uncontrolled by outward peremptory statute. I appeal to Paul in the seventh chapter of the Romans, where he says, 'The law is holy', and adds, as if to show that it was no inward actuating law of the heart, but God's outward commanding law to the will: 'the law is holy, and the *commandment* is holy, and just, and good'. And I appeal to the sweet singer of Israel, as I find him in the 119th Psalm, which is throughout the breathing of a heart in which the law of God is written, owning himself with joy as under peremptory external law: 'Thou hast *commanded* us to keep Thy precepts diligently'".

11. "If ye fulfill the royal Law according to the scripture, Thou shalt love thy neighbour as thyself, ye do well" (James 2:8). The immediate

purpose of the apostle was to correct an evil—common in all climes and ages—of which his brethren were guilty. They had paid deference to the wealthy, and shown them greater respect than the poor who attended their assembly (see preceding verses). They had, in fact, "despised the poor" (v. 6). The result was that the worthy name of Christ had been "blasphemed" (v. 7). Now it is striking to observe the *method* followed and the *ground* of appeal made by the apostle James in correcting this evil.

First, he says, "If ye fulfill the royal law according to the scripture, Thou shalt love thy neighbour as thyself, ye do well: but if ye have respect of persons, ye commit sin, and are convinced of the Law as transgressors" (vv. 8, 9). He shows that in despising the poor they had transgressed the Law, for the Law says, "Thou shalt *love* thy neighbour as thyself". Here, then, is proof positive that the Law was binding upon those to whom James wrote, for it is impossible for one who is in *every* sense "dead to the Law" to be a transgressor" of it. And here, it is probable that some will raise the quibble that the Epistle of James is *Jewish*. True, the Epistle is addressed to the twelve tribes scattered abroad. Yet it cannot be gainsaid that the apostle was writing to men of faith (1:3); men who had been regenerated—"begotten" (1:18); men who were called by the worthy name of Christ (2:7), and therefore *Christians*. And it is *to them* the apostle here appeals to the Law!—another conclusive proof that the Law *has not been* "abolished".

The apostle here terms the Law, "the royal Law". This was to emphasize its *authority*, and to remind his regenerated brethren that the slightest deflection from it was rebellion. The "royal Law" also calls attention to the supreme *dignity* of its Author. This royal Law, we learn, is transcribed "in the Scriptures"—the reference here was, of course, to the Old Testament Scriptures.

Next, the apostle says, "For whosoever shall keep the whole Law, and yet offend in one point, he is guilty of all. For He that said, Do not commit adultery, said *also*, Do not kill. Now if thou commit *no* adultery, yet if thou *kill*, thou art become a transgressor of the Law" (vv. 10, 11). His purpose is evident. He presses on those to whom he writes that, he who fails to love his neighbor is just as much and just as truly a *transgressor* of "the Law" as the man who is guilty of adultery or murder, for he has *rebelled* against *the authority* of the One who gave the whole Law. In this quotation of the 6th and 7th commandments all doubt is removed as to *what* "Law" is in view in this passage.

Finally, the apostle says, "So speak ye, and so do, as they that shall be judged by the Law of liberty. For he shall have judgment without mercy, that hath showed no mercy; and mercy rejoiceth against judgment" (vv. 12, 13). This is solemn and urgently needs pressing upon the Lord's people today: *Christians* are going to be "judged by the Law"! The Law is God's unchanging standard of conduct for all, and all alike, saints and sinners, are going to be weighed in *its* balances; not, of course, in order to determine their eternal destiny, but to settle the apportionment of reward and punishment. It should be obvious to all that the very word "reward" implies *obedience* to the Law! Let it be repeated, though, that this judgment for Christians has nothing whatever to do with their salvation. Instead, it is to determine the measure of reward which they shall enjoy in the kingdom. Should any object against the idea of any future judgment (*not* "punishment" but "judgment") for Christians, we would ask them to carefully ponder 1 Cor. 11:31, 32; 2 Tim. 4:1; Heb. 10:30—in each case the Greek word is the same as here in James 2:12.

It should be noted that the apostle here terms the Law by which we shall be judged "the Law of liberty". It is, of course, the *same* as "the royal Law" in v. 8. But why term it the Law *of liberty?* Because such it is to the Christian. He obeys it (or should do) not from fear, but out of love. The only *true* "liberty" lies in complete subjection to God. There was, too, a peculiar propriety in the apostle James here styling the Law of God "the Law of liberty". His brethren had been guilty of "respecting persons", showing undue deference to the rich; and this was indeed *servility* of the worst kind. But to "love our neighbor" will *free* us from this.

12. Other passages in the New Testament which show more directly the bearing of the Law on believers might be quoted, but we close, by calling attention to 1 John 2:6: "He that saith he abideth in Him *ought* himself also *so* to walk, *even as* He walked" (1 John 2:6). This is very simple, and yet deeply important. The believer is here exhorted to regulate his "walk" by that of the walk of *Christ*. *How* did He "walk"? We answer, in perfect obedience to the Law of God. Gal. 4:4 tells us, "God sent forth His Son, made of a woman, *made under the Law*". Psa. 40:8 declares that God's *Law* was in His heart. Everything recorded about the Saviour in the four Gospels evidences His complete subjection to the Law. If, then, the Christian desires to honor and please God, if he would walk as Christ walked, then must he regulate his conduct by and render obedience to *the Ten Commandments*. Not that we would for a moment insist that the Christian has *nothing more* than the Ten Commandments by which to regulate his conduct. No; Christ came to "fulfill" the Law, and as we have intimated, one thing this means is that, He has brought out the fulness of its contents, He has brought to light its exceeding spirituality, He has shown us (both directly and through His apostles) its manifold application. But whatever amplification the Law has received in the New Testament, nothing has been given by God which in any wise conflicts with what He first imprinted on man's moral nature and afterwards wrote with His own finger at Sinai, nothing that in the slightest modifies its authority or our obligation to render obedience to it.

May the Holy Spirit so enlighten our sin-darkened understanding and so draw out our hearts unto God, that we shall truthfully say, "The law of Thy mouth is better unto me than thousands of gold and silver .... O how I love Thy Law! It is my meditation all the day" (Psa. 119:72-97).
—Arthur W. Pink.

EXPOSITION OF FIRST PETER
IV.—THE SORROWS OF THE CHRISTIAN'S PRESENT STATE CONTRASTED WITH THE JOYS OF HIS FUTURE STATE.
(1 Pet. 1:6-9)

The fourth point of contrast is, Now, and Here, Christians are "for a season in heaviness" on all these accounts; Then, and There, they will "rejoice, greatly rejoice, rejoice with a joy that is unspeakable and full of glory." The bodily absence of Jesus Christ, their imperfect knowledge of him, their indirect and interrupted intercourse with him, their manifold trials, their imperfect enjoyment of the blessings of the Christian salvation—all these naturally produce, to a certain degree, a depression of spirit. The Christian is "in heaviness." He mourns the absence of his Lord, and says in his heart, "Oh! that I knew where I could find him, that I might come even to his seat." Under the pressure of bodily affliction or mental distress, he is constrained to cry out, "I am oppressed—undertake for me." Harassed with the movements of remaining corruption, he groans out, "Wretched man that I am; who will deliver me?" And feeling that he is saved but in hope, he sighs out, "How long, O Lord, how long?" "When shall I come and appear before God?"[1]

This heaviness of heart is but for a season—it is, at least in an oppressive degree, not constant, but only occasional, and at any rate it is only for the season, the short season, of mortal life. And what should still further prevent Christians from murmuring, is the thought that, if they are in heaviness even for a season for these causes, it is "since there is need for it." All is ordered, and all is well ordered. HE does not "afflict willingly, nor grieve without a cause."[2] Everything in the saint's lot is arranged in the way best suited to promote his true, his everlasting welfare.

But in the future state there will be no heaviness, no, not even "for a season." It will no more be needful. Affliction will have served its purpose, and will forever cease. There, then, will be nothing but unmingled happiness and unending rejoicing. "They shall rejoice; they shall rejoice with a joy which is unspeakable," which cannot be adequately expressed, "and full of glory"—that is, either in the highest degree glorious and excellent, or full of gloriation or triumph. It is needless for us to attempt to illustrate this subject; we can do nothing but quote a few passages of Scripture, which, in all their extent of meaning, seem applicable only to this final state of happiness. "The ransomed of the Lord shall return and come to Zion, with songs, and with everlasting joy on their head; they shall obtain joy and gladness, and sorrow and sighing shall flee away." "Thy sun shall no more go down, neither shall thy moon withdraw her shining; for the Lord God shall be thy everlasting light, and the days of thy mourning shall be ended." "God himself shall be with them, and be their God; and there shall be no more death, neither sorrow, nor crying; neither shall there be any more pain, for the former things are passed away. The Lamb who is in the midst of the throne shall feed them, and lead them to fountains of living waters; and God shall wipe away all tears from their eyes."[3]

Thus have I shortly considered the beautiful and instructive contrast contained in the text between the saint's condition on earth and in heaven. And now, in conclusion, ought not all Christians, with the apostle, to "reckon," judge, conclude, on the most satisfactory premises, "that the sufferings of the present time are not worthy to be compared with the glory that shall be revealed in them"—and that, however heavy and long continued, that "affliction" is but "light," and "for a moment," which "worketh out for them such a far more exceeding and eternal weight of glory."[4]

Who would not be a Christian? For ah! how different are the prospects of the unbeliever? He, too, must see Christ Jesus, whom he does not love, but it will be as a righteous judge, coming "in flaming fire to take vengeance" on him as an adversary of God. His afflictions here will prove to have been but "the beginning of sorrows;" what he now fears he will then feel, and feel to be far worse than he feared; and, instead of joy unspeakable and full of glory, there will be woe, unutterable but in "weeping, and gnashing of teeth."[5]

Let Christians live like those who

---

[1] Job xxiii. 3. Isa. xxxviii. 14. Rom. vii. 24. Rev. vi. 10. Psal. xlii. 2.
[2] Lam. ii. 33.
[3] Isa. xxxv. 10. Ibid. lx. 19, 20. Rev. xxi. 3, 4.
[4] Rom. viii. 18. 2 Cor. iv. 17.
[5] 2 Thess. i. 8. Matt. viii. 12.

have such prospects. Let them "be steadfast, immovable, always abounding in the work of the Lord, forasmuch as they know their labor is not in vain in the Lord;" and, "having such promises," let "them cleanse themselves from all filthiness of the flesh and spirit, and perfect holiness in the fear of God."

DISCOURSE IV.

THE FINAL HAPPINESS OF CHRISTIANS THE SUBJECT OF OLD TESTAMENT PREDICTION, NEW TESTAMENT REVELATION, AND ANGELIC STUDY.

1 PET. i. 10-12.—Of which salvation the prophets have inquired and searched diligently, who prophesied of the grace that should come unto you: searching what, or what manner of time, the Spirit of Christ which was in them did signify, when it testified beforehand the sufferings of Christ, and the glory that should follow. Unto whom it was revealed, that not unto themselves, but unto us, they did minister the things, which are now reported unto you by them that have preached the gospel unto you with the Holy Ghost sent down from heaven; which things the angels desire to look into.

If we would satisfactorily understand any book, or any passage in a book, there are two points which we must distinctly apprehend and never lose sight of. These are, what is the subject of which the author treats, and what is the object which he has in view in treating it. Let us endeavor to ascertain those two points with regard to that paragraph which I have just read, and which I intend to make the subject of the following discourse.

The subject of the apostle is, plainly, the final deliverance and complete happiness which Christians are to obtain at the second coming of Jesus Christ. This is spoken of as "the inheritance incorruptible, undefiled, and that fadeth not away, reserved in heaven;" as "the salvation prepared to be revealed in the last times;" as "the grace which is to be brought to Christians at the revelation of Jesus Christ." This is plainly the subject of the paragraph.

With regard to the object of the apostle in treating this subject, it is obviously to sustain the minds of the Christians to whom he wrote, amid the manifold trials to which they were exposed—to enable them to remain "steadfast and immovable" in the profession of the faith, and in the practice of the duties of their high and holy calling. He states the truth with regard to the immeasurable grandeur, and absolute certainty, of this final salvation, that they might be induced to "gird up the loins of their mind, be sober, and hope to the end," that they might "fashion themselves as obedient children," and "be holy in all manner of conversation, as he who had called them is holy."

No means could be better fitted to gain the end proposed, than that adopted by the apostle; for if they firmly believed that such a salvation certainly awaited every one who "held fast the beginning of his confidence steadfast to the end,"[1] it is obvious that the smiles and the frowns, the allurements and the terrors of the world, would be equally powerless to shake their attachment to that Lord who will in due time so munificently reward all his faithful followers.

The manner in which the apostle brings the magnitude and certainty of this salvation before their minds, shows that he, as well as his "beloved brother Paul," speaks "according to the wisdom given to him."[2] He first describes it generally, as "an inheritance incorruptible, undefiled, and that fadeth not away, reserved in heaven for them, while they are kept to it by the power of God through faith." Then he brings out more prominently its characteristic excellencies, by describing it in contrast with the present state of the people of God. In opposition to a state in which Jesus Christ,

[1] Heb. iii. 14.
[2] 2 Pet. iii. 15.

the object of the Christian's supreme affection, is bodily absent from him, in which his knowledge of him is limited and obscure, and his intercourse with him carried on entirely through the medium of believing—it is exhibited as a state in which Christ is bodily present with his people, in which their knowledge of him is extensive and distinct, and their communion with him direct and immediate; in opposition to a state in which they are exposed to numerous and varied trials—it is exhibited as a state in which, freed from all trials, they shall enjoy the glorious results of those trials to which in a previous state they had been subjected; in opposition to a state in which complete deliverance and happiness are objects merely of faith and hope—it is exhibited as a state in which they are the objects of enjoyment; and, in fine, in opposition to a state in which they are "for a season, since it is needful, in heaviness"—it is exhibited as a state in which they shall forever "greatly rejoice; rejoice with a joy which is unspeakable, and full of glory."

In the paragraph which forms our text, the apostle takes another and an equally efficient method of bringing before the minds of his readers, the greatness and the certainty of this final salvation, by representing it as one great or leading subject of Old Testament prophecy, apostolic preaching, and angelic study. "Of this salvation the prophets prophesied"—of this salvation "they who preached the Gospel with the Holy Ghost sent down from heaven made a report"—and "into this salvation the angels desire to look." In the remaining part of this discourse, then, I shall turn your attention to the view which the apostle gives us of the final salvation of Christians, first, as the subject of Old Testament prophecy; secondly, as the subject of apostolical preaching; and, thirdly, as the subject of angelic study.

1.—THE FINAL HAPPINESS OF CHRISTIANS THE SUBJECT OF OLD TESTAMENT PROPHECY.

Let us first, then, attend to the statement which the apostle makes as to this final salvation being the subject of Old Testament prophecy.

"Of," or concerning, "this salvation the prophets inquired and searched diligently, who prophesied of the grace that should come unto you; searching what, or what manner of time, the Spirit of Christ which was in them did signify, when it testified beforehand the sufferings of Christ, and the glory that should follow. Unto whom it was revealed, that not to themselves, but to us, they did minister."

The truths taught us in these words are the following:—The ancient prophets, inspired by the Spirit of Christ, predicted that final salvation which remains for the people of God; they diligently inquired into the meaning of their own predictions; and they obtained information that these predictions referred to blessings not to be conferred during the economy under which they were placed, but during that higher one which was to supersede it. The first of these truths is taught us in these words, "The prophets prophesied of the grace which should come to you"—"The Spirit of Christ which was in them did testify beforehand of the sufferings of Christ, and the glory that should follow." The second of these truths is taught us in these words—"Concerning this salvation the prophets inquired and searched diligently, searching what, or what manner of time, the Spirit of Christ which was in them did signify." And the third truth is taught in these words—"To them it was revealed, that not to themselves, but to us, they did minister."[1]

The ancient prophets predicted that final salvation which will be bestowed

---
[1] John i. 17.

on the people of God at the coming of Jesus Christ. "They prophesied of the grace which should come to us." "The grace which should come to us" has often been considered as a general expression for the blessings of the New Testament economy, on earth as well as in heaven—"the grace which came by Jesus Christ;" but if we look closely at the passage, we shall find the sole subject to be the final and complete salvation awaiting Christians, or, as it is expressed more fully, "the grace that is to be brought to Christians at the revelation of Jesus Christ." The words, "they prophesied of the grace which should come to us," are then just equivalent to, 'they predicted the final salvation which awaits the people of God.'

The same sentiment is, I apprehend, repeated in another form of words, when it is said, "the Spirit of Christ which was in them did testify beforehand of the sufferings of Christ, and the glory that should follow."

"All Scripture is given by divine inspiration." "Prophecy came not in old time by the will of man, but holy men of God spake as they were moved by the Holy Ghost."[1] The Holy Ghost is termed "the Spirit of Christ," inasmuch as he is essentially related to the second person of the Trinity, who is Christ, as well as to the Father; and inasmuch as previously, no less than subsequently to his incarnation, all communications of the divine will were made by the Son through the Spirit. Never was there a time when the Father immediately revealed himself. "The only begotten Son, who is in his bosom, he declared him"—declared him by the Spirit. This divine person, inspiring the prophets, taught them what things to reveal, and in what words to reveal them. To use the language of one of themselves, "He spake by them, and his word was on their tongue."[2]

The Spirit of Christ, then, "testified of the sufferings of Christ, and the glory that should follow them." These words naturally suggest, and have been ordinarily understood of, the personal sufferings and glories of Jesus Christ, the degradation and sorrows to which the incarnate Son was exposed, when, "being found in fashion as a man, he humbled himself, and became obedient unto death, even the death of the cross;" and the high dignity and inconceivable happiness to which he was raised when "God highly exalted him, and gave him a name which is above every name," "angels, and authorities, and powers, being made subject to him."[3] I am persuaded, however, that if we attend to the connection of the words, and to the words themselves, we will find they do not refer to the personal sufferings and glories of Christ, but to the sufferings of his people during the present state, and the glories which are to follow "in the last time," "at the revelation of Jesus Christ." It is not the sufferings of Christ personally, and the subsequent glories, which are the subject of the apostle's discussion, but the manifold trials to which Christians are exposed for a season, and the glory which is to be theirs in the last time. Looking at the construction of the passage, we naturally conclude that the clauses, "the prophets prophesied of the grace which is to be brought to us," and, "the Spirit of Christ testified beforehand of the sufferings of Christ, and the glory which should follow," are parallel—that the prophecy of the prophets, and the testimony of the Spirit of Christ, refer to the same thing.

[1] 2 Tim. iii. 16. 2 Pet. i. 21.
[2] 2 Sam. xxiii. 2.
[3] Phil. ii. 8, 9. 1 Pet. iii. 22.

(Continued from page 193.)

tunities, and so barren of results, that it is sometimes very painful; but grace comes in to meet it all, and He will be glorified in my humiliation also" (1872). On which Dr. Brookes remarked, "How like him, and how unlike the boastings of those who are glorying in their fancied attainments!"

Other testimonies from the lips and pens of men equally pious and eminent might be given, but sufficient has been quoted to show what cause the saints of all ages have had to make their own these words, "O wretched man that I am". But it is on the closing words of Rom. 7 we would now offer a few comments in conclusion.

"Who shall deliver me from the body of this death?" "Who shall deliver me?": this is not the language of despair, but of earnest desire for help from without and above himself. That from which the apostle desired to be delivered, is termed "the body of this death". This is a figurative expression for the carnal nature. Note how in Rom. 6:6 the carnal nature is termed "the *body* of sin", and as having "members" (Rom. 7:23). We, therefore, take the apostle's meaning to be, Who shall deliver me from this deadly and noxious burden—my sinful self!

In the next verse the apostle answers his question, "I thank God through Jesus Christ our Lord". It should be obvious to any impartial mind that this looks forward to *the future*. His question was, "Who *shall* deliver me?" His answer is, Jesus Christ *will*. How this exposes the error of those who teach a *present* "deliverance" by the power of the Holy Spirit. In his answer, the apostle says *nothing* about the Holy Spirit; instead, he mentions only "Jesus Christ our Lord". It is not by the *present* work of the Spirit *in* us that Christians will be delivered "from this body of death", but by the yet *future* coming of the Lord Jesus Christ *for* us. It is *then* that this mortal shall put on immortality, and this corruptible shall put on incorruption.

But, as though to remove all doubt that this "deliverance" *is* future, the apostle concludes by saying, "So *then* with the mind I myself serve the Law of God; but with the flesh the law of sin". Let every reader note carefully that this comes *after* he had thanked God that he *would be* "delivered". The last half of Rom. 7:25 sums up what he had said in this second part of Rom. 7. It describes the Christian's *dual* life. The new nature serves the Law of God; the old nature, to the end of its history, will *serve* "the law of sin". That it was so with Paul himself is clear from what he wrote at the close of his life, when he termed himself the *"chief"* of sinners (I Tim. 1:15). That was not the exaggeration of evangelical fervor, still less was it the mock modesty of hypocrisy. It was the assured conviction, the felt experience, the settled consciousness of one who saw deeply into the depths of corruption within himself, and who knew how far, far short he attained to the standard of holiness which God set before him. Such, too, will be the consciousness and confession of every other Christian who is not blinded by conceit. And the *outcome* of such a consciousness will be to make him long more ardently and thank God more fervently for the promised deliverance at the return of our Saviour and Lord, when He shall "change our vile body, that it may be fashioned like unto His glorious body, according to the working whereby He is able even to subdue all things unto Himself" (Phil. 3:20); and having done so, He will "present us *faultless* before the presence of His glory with exceeding joy" (Jude 24). Hallelujah, what a Saviour!—Arthur W. Pink.

STUDIES in the SCRIPTURES

"Search the Scriptures" John 5:39.

A PERIODICAL (MONTHLY "IF THE LORD WILL") DEVOTED TO BIBLE STUDIES and EXPOSITIONS

Associate Editors and Publishers, I. C. HERENDEEN and ARTHUR W. PINK,
Swengel, Pa.

Price: 10 cents per copy: $1.00 per year. Foreign $1.00 per year.

TO OUR SCRIPTURE STUDY FAMILY

The subject on which we write this time is a rather delicate one, inasmuch as our motive and object are likely to be misconstrued. For some time past the matter of benevolences has become more and more of a problem to the writer. It is his desire to have fellowship with others engaged in the Lord's work, but invidious as it must sound, he has to confess that it is becoming increasingly difficult to locate those he can give to with a clear conscience.

It is greatly to be feared that few of us are sufficiently careful in our inquiries. To have financial fellowship with those who profess to be engaged in the Lord's work is to incur a grave responsibility (see 2 John 11). A man may be a Christian, and stand for the fundamentals of the faith, yet on some important points he may be giving out error. Or, an institution may be sound in the faith, but employing methods (both in raising money and in conducting its work) which are condemned by the Word and dishonoring to God.

As the end of this dispensation draws rapidly nearer and the great apostasy swiftly approaches—already casting its dark and dreadful shadows across Christendom—it is to be expected that false teachers will abound more and more. Nor will they be easily recognized: Satan is seeing to it that the wolves are well disguised in sheep's clothing. Scripture plainly warns us that the days in which we are living are "perilous times" (2 Tim. 3:1), and not the least of the perils now confronting the Lord's people is the very real danger all of us face lest we be found contributing to the support of that which is *dishonoring to Christ*.

The path which the believer treads is a "narrow" one, and the more he is brought into subjection to the mind of God, the narrower will he find it to be. The more familiar he becomes with Scripture, and the more he is truly taught of the Spirit, the less will he find of that which will really stand the test of those Scriptures. Many a book that he once thought was sound and helpful he will see to contain much that is erroneous. Preaching, institutions, societies that he formerly regarded as being conducted in a spiritual manner, he will now discover are far from being in accord with God's Word.

What, then, is such an one to do? Must he satisfy himself with the plea that nothing is perfect down here, and therefore he must support that which has the least error in it? Surely not. The Word of God is plain: "Believe not every spirit, but *try* the spirits wherever they are of God: *because* many false prophets have gone out into the world" (1 John 4:1). And not only so,

(Continued on page 256.)

IMPORTANT NOTICES

All new subscriptions will be dated back to January, 1923.

Set of twelve issues for 1922, unbound, $1.00. Bound, $1.50.

Note: We cannot break a set or now supply any **single** 1922 issues.

Subscription Price: $1.00 per year to any address in the world. Single copies 10 cents.

Change of Address: Please notify us promptly of any change of address, and be certain to give both old and new addresses.

Non-Subscribers receiving this Magazine regularly will understand their subscription has been entered by a friend.

Copies lost in the mail duplicated only if we are notified promptly.

Entered as second-class matter December 15th, 1921 at the post office at Swengel, Pa., under Act of March 3rd, 1879.

CONTENTS

John's Gospel (John 6:1-13) 226
Babylon and the Antichrist 237
The Christian Sabbath 246

JOHN'S GOSPEL

20. CHRIST FEEDING THE MULTITUDE.

John 6:1-13.

Of all the miracles performed by the Lord Jesus the feeding of the five thousand is the only one recorded by each of the four Evangelists. This at once intimates that there must be something about it of unusual importance, and therefore it calls for our most diligent study. The Holy Spirit has—if we may reverently employ such language—described this miracle in the most matter-of-fact terms. No effort is made to emphasize the marvel of it. There is an entire absence of such language as an uninspired pen would naturally have employed to heighten the effect on the reader. And yet, notwithstanding the simplicity and exceeding brevity of the narrative, it is at once evident that this incident of the feeding of the hungry multitude was a signal example of Christ's almighty power. As Bishop Ryle has noted, of all the wonderful works which our Saviour did none was quite so public as this, and none other was performed before so many witnesses. Our Lord is here seen supplying the bodily needs of a great crowd, by means of five loaves and two small fishes. Food was called into existence which did not exist before. To borrow another thought from Bishop Ryle: In healing the sick and in raising the dead, something was amended or restored which *already* existed; but here was an absolute creation. Only one other miracle in any wise resembles it—His first, when He made wine out of the water. These two miracles belong to a class by themselves, and it is surely significant, yea most suggestive, that the one reminds us of His precious blood, while the other points to His holy body, broken for us. And here is, we believe, the chief reason why this miracle is mentioned by all of the four Evangelists: it shadowed forth *the gift of Christ Himself*. His other miracles exhibited His power and illustrated His work, but this one in a peculiar way sets forth the *person* of Christ, the Bread of Life.

Why, then, was this particular miracle singled out for special prominence? Above, three answers have been suggested, which may be summarized thus: First, because there was an *evidential value* to this miracle which excelled that of all others. Some of our Lord's miracles were wrought in private, or in the presence of only a small company; others were of a nature that made it difficult, in some cases impossible, for sceptics to examine them. But here was a miracle, performed in the open, before a crowd of witnesses which were to be numbered by the thousand. Second, because of the *intrinsic nature* of the miracle. It was a creation of food: the calling into existence of what before had no existence. Third, because of *the typical import* of the miracle. It spoke directly of the *person* of Christ. To these may be added a fourth answer: The fact that this miracle of the feeding of the hungry multitude is recorded by all the Evangelists intimates that it has a *universal application*. Matthew's mention of it suggests to us that it foreshadows Christ, in a coming day, feeding Israel's poor—cf Psa. 132:15. Mark's mention of it teaches us what is the chief duty of God's servants—to break the Bread of Life to the starving. Luke's mention of it announces the sufficiency of Christ to meet the needs of all men. John's mention of it tells us that Christ is the Food of God's people.

Before we consider the miracle itself we must note its setting—the manner in which it is here introduced to us. And ere doing this we will follow our usual custom and present an Analysis of the passage which is to be before us:—

1. Christ followed into Galilee by a great multitude, vv. 1, 2.
2. Christ retires to a mountain with His disciples, v. 3.
3. Time: just before the Passover, v. 4.
4. The testing of Philip. vv. 5-7.
5. The unbelief of Andrew, vv. 8, 9.
6. The feeding of the multitude, vv. 10, 11.
7. The gathering up of the fragments, vv. 12, 13.

"After these things Jesus went over the sea of Galilee, which is the sea of Tiberias" (v. 1). "After these things": the reference is to what is recorded in the previous chapter—the healing of the impotent man, the persecution by the Jews because this had been done on the Sabbath day, their determination to kill Him because He had made Himself equal with God, the lengthy reply made by our Lord. After these things the Lord left Jerusalem and Judea, and "went over the sea of Galilee". It is similar to what was before us in John 4:1-3. The Son of God would not remain and cast precious pearls before swine. He departed from those who despised and rejected Him. Very solemn is this, and a warning to every unbeliever who may read these lines.

"And a great multitude followed Him, because they saw His miracles which He did on them that were diseased" (v. 2). How completely these people failed in their discernment and appreciation of the person of Christ! They saw in Him only a wonderful Magician who could work miracles, a clever Physician that could heal the sick. They failed to perceive that He was the Saviour of sinners and the Messiah of Israel. They were blind to His Divine glory. And is it any otherwise with the great multitude today? Alas, few of them see in Christ anything more than a wonderful Teacher and a beautiful Example.

"And a great multitude followed Him, because they saw His miracles which He did on them that were diseased" (v. 2). How sadly true to life. It is still idle curiosity and the love of excitement which commonly gathers crowds together. And how what we read of here is being repeated before our eyes in many quarters today. When some professional evangelist is advertised as a 'Faith-healer' what crowds of sick folk will flock to the meetings! How anxious they are for physical relief, and yet, what little real concern they seem to have for their *soul's* healing!

"And Jesus went up into a mountain, and there He sat with His disciples" (v. 3). This may be regarded as the sequel to what we read of in v. 2, or it may be connected with v. 1, and then v. 2 would be considered as a parenthesis. Probably both are equally permissible. If we take v. 2 as giving the cause *why* our Lord retired to the mountain with His disciples, the thought would be that of Christ withdrawing from the unbelieving world. The miracles drew many *after* Him, but only a few *to* Him. He knew why this great multitude "followed Him", and it is solemn to see Him withdrawing to the mountain with His disciples. He will not company with the unbelieving world: His place is among His own. If v. 3 be read right on after v. 1, then we view the Saviour departing from Judea, weary (cf Mark 6:31) with the unbelief and self-sufficiency of those in Jerusalem. "He went up into a mountain into another atmosphere, setting forth the elevation with the Father to which He retired for refreshment of spirit" (Malachi Taylor). Compare John 6:15 and 7:53 to 8:2 for other examples in John's Gospel.

"And the Passover, a feast of the Jews, was nigh" (v. 4). This seems introduced here in order to point again to the empty condition of Judaism at this time. The Passover was nigh, but the Lamb of God who was in their midst was not wanted by the formal religionists. Yea, it was because they were determined to "kill Him" (5:18), that He had withdrawn into Galilee. Well, then, may the Holy Spirit remind us once more that the Passover had degenerated into "a feast *of the Jews*". How significant is this as an introductory word to what follows! The Passover looks back to the night when the children of Israel feasted on the lamb; but here we see their descendants hungering! Their physical state was the outward sign of their emptiness of soul. Later, we shall see how this verse supplies us with one of the keys to the dispensational significance of our passage.

"When Jesus then lifted up His eyes, and saw a great company come unto Him, He saith unto Philip, Whence shall we buy bread, that these may eat?" (v. 5). While the multitude did not know Christ, His heart went out in tender pity to them. Even though an unworthy motive had drawn this crowd after Christ, He was not indifferent to their need. Matthew, in his account, tells us "And Jesus went forth, and saw a great multitude, and was *moved with compassion* toward them"(14:14). So also Mark (6:34). The absence of this sentence here in John is one of the innumerable evidences of the Divine authorship of Scripture. Not only is every word inspired, but every word is in its suited place. The "compassion" of Christ, though noted frequently by the other Evangelists, is *never* referred to by John, who dwells upon the dignity and glory of His Divine person. Compassion is more than pity. Com-passion signifies to suffer with, along side of, another. Thus the mention of Christ's compassion by Matthew tells us how near the Messiah had come to His people; while the reference to it in Mark shows how intimately the Servant of Jehovah entered into the sufferings of those to whom He ministered. The absence of this word in John, indicates His elevation above men. Thus we see how everything is most suitably and beautifully placed. And how much we lose by our ungodly haste and carelessness as we fail to mark and appreciate these lovely little touches of the Divine Artist! May Divine grace constrain both writer and reader to handle the Holy Book more reverently, and take more pains to acquaint ourselves with its exhaustless riches. It would be a delight to tarry here, and notice other little details mentioned by the different evangelists which are omitted from John's account—such as the fact that Matthew tells us (*before* the miracle was performed) that "it was evening", and that the disciples bade their Master "send the multitude away"—but perhaps more will be accomplished if we leave the reader to search them out for himself.

"When Jesus then lifted up His eyes, and saw a great multitude come unto Him, He saith unto Philip, Whence shall we buy bread, that these may eat? And this He said to prove him: for He Himself knew what He would do" (vv. 5, 6). In reading the Scriptures we fail to derive from them the blessings most needed unless we apply them to our own hearts and lives. Unlike all others, the Bible is a *living* book. It is far more than a history of the past. Stript of their local and incidental details, the sacred narratives depict characters living and incidents transpiring *today*. God changes not, nor do the motives and principles of His actions. Human nature also is the same in this twentieth century as it was in the first. The world is the same, the Devil is the same, the trials of faith are the same. Let, then, each Christian reader view Philip here as representing himself. Philip was confronted with a trying situation. It was *the Lord* who caused him to be so circumstanced. The Lord's design in this was to "prove" or test him. Let us now apply this to ourselves.

What happened to Philip is, in principle and essence, happening daily in *our* lives. A trying, if not a difficult, situation confronts us; and we meet with them constantly. They come not by accident or by chance; instead, they are each arranged by the hand of the Lord. They are God's testings of our faith. They are sent to "prove" *us*. Let us be very simple and practical. A bill comes unexpectedly; how are we to meet it? The morning's mail brings us tidings which plunge us into an unlooked-for perplexity; how are we to get out of it? A cog slips in the household's machinery, which threatens to wreck the daily routine; what shall we do? An unanticipated demand is suddenly made upon us; how shall we meet it? Now, dear friends, *how* do such experiences find us? Do we, like Philip and Andrew did, look at our resources? Do we rack our minds to find some solution? or do our first thoughts turn to the Lord Jesus, who has so often helped us in the past? *Here,* right here, is the test of our faith.

O, dear reader, have we learned to spread each difficulty, as it comes along, before God? Have we formed the habit of instinctively turning to Him? What is your feebleness in comparison with His power! What is your emptiness in comparison with His ocean fulness? Nothing! Then look daily to Him in simple faith, resting on His sure promise, "My God *shall* supply *all* your *need*" (Phil. 4:19). Ah, you may answer, It is easy to offer such advice, but it is far from easy to *act* on it. True. Yea, of yourself, it is impossible. Your need, and my need, is to *ask* for faith, to *plead* for grace, to *cry* unto God for such a sense of helplessness that you will lean on Christ, and on Him alone. Thus, ask and *wait*, and you shall find Him as good as His word. "Why art thou cast down, O my soul? And why art thou disquieted within me? Hope thou in God: for I shall yet praise Him, who is the health of my countenance, and my God".

"The birds without barn,
Or storehouse are fed;
From them let us learn
To trust for our bread.
His saints what is fitting
Shall ne'er be denied,
So long as, 'tis written
'The Lord will provide'.

When Satan appears,
To stop up our path,
And fills us with fears,
We triumph by faith:
He cannot take from us,
Though oft he has tried,
The heart-cheering promise,
'The Lord will provide' ".

"Philip answered him, Two hundred pennyworth of bread is not sufficient for them, that every one of them may take a little" (v. 7). Let us see in Philip, once more, a portrait of ourselves. First, what does this answer of Philip reveal? It shows he was occupied with circumstances. He was looking on the things which are seen—the size of the multitude—and such a look is always a barrier in the way of faith. He made a rapid calculation of how much money it would require to provide even a frugal meal for such a crowd; but he calculated without Christ! His answer was the language of unbelief—"Two hundred pennyworth of bread is not sufficient for them, that every one of them may *take a little*". Fancy talking of "a little" in the presence of Infinite Power and Infinite Grace! His unbelief was also betrayed by the very amount he specified—two hundred pennyworth.

Nowhere in Scripture are numbers used haphazardly. Two hundred is a multiple of twenty, and in Scripture twenty signifies *a vain expectancy*, a coming short of God's appointed time or deliverance. For example, in Gen. 31:41 we learn how that Jacob waited *twenty* years to gain possession of his wives and property; but it was not until the twenty-first that God's appointed deliverance came. From Judges 4:3 we learn how that Israel waited *twenty* years for emancipation from Jabin's oppression; but it was not until the twenty-first that God's appointed deliverance came. So in I Sam. 7:2 we learn how that the ark abode in Kirjath-Jearim for *twenty* years, but it was in the twenty-first that God delivered it. As, then, twenty speaks of *insufficiency*, a coming short of God's appointed deliverance, so two hundred conveys the same idea in an *intensified* form. Two hundred is always found in Scripture in an *evil* connection. Let the reader consult (be sure to look them up) Josh. 7:21; Jud. 17:4; 1 Sam. 30:10; 2 Sam. 14:26; Rev. 9:16. So the number here in John 6:7 suitably expressed Philip's *unbelief*.

How surprising was this failure in the faith of Philip. One would have supposed that after all the disciples had witnessed of the Lord's wonder-working power they had learned by this time that all fulness dwelt in Him. We should have supposed their faith was strong and their hearts calm and confident. Ah—*should* we? Would not our own God-dishonoring unbelief check such expectations? Have we not discovered how weak *our* faith is! How obtuse our understandings! How earthly our minds and hearts! In vain does the Lord look within us sometimes for even a ray of that faith which glorifies Him. Instead of counting on the Lord, we, like Philip, are occupied with nature's resources. Beware, then, of condemning the unbelief of Philip, lest you be found condemning yourself too.

How often has the writer thought, after some gracious manifestation of the Lord's hand on his behalf, that he *could* trust Him for the future; that the remembrance of His past goodness and mercy would keep him calm and confident when the next cloud should drapen his landscape. Alas! When it came how sadly he failed. Little did we know our treacherous heart. And little do we *know* it even now. O dear reader, each of us need the upholding hand of the Lord *every* step of our journey through this world that lieth in the Wicked one; and, should that hand be for a single moment withdrawn, we should sink like lead in the mighty waters. Ah, nothing but *grace* rescued us; nothing but *grace* can sustain us; nothing but *grace* can carry us safely through. Nothing, *nothing* but the distinguishing and almighty grace of a sovereign God!

"One of His disciples, Andrew, Simon's Peter's brother, saith unto Him, There is a lad here, which hath five barley loaves, and two small fishes: but what are they among so many?" (vv. 8, 9). Unbelief is *infectious*. Like

Philip before him, Andrew, too, seemed blind to the glory of Christ. "What are they among so many?" was the utterance of the same old evil heart of unbelief which long ago had asked, "Can God furnish a table in the wilderness?" (Psa. 78:10). And how the *helplessness* of unbelief comes out here! "That every one may take *a little*", said Philip; *"What are these among so many?"*, asked Andrew. What mattered the "many" when the Son of God was there! Like Philip, Andrew calculated without Christ, and, therefore he saw only a hopeless situation. How often we look at God through our difficulties; or, rather, we *try* to, for the difficulties *hide* Him. Keep the eye on Him, and the difficulties will not be seen. But alas! What self-centered, skeptical, sinful creatures we are at best! God may lavish upon us the riches of His grace —He may have opened for us many a dry path through the waters of difficult circumstances—He may have delivered us with His outstretched arm in six troubles, yet, when the *seventh* comes along, instead of resting on Job 5:19, we are distrustful, full of doubts and fears, just as if we had never known Him. Such frail and depraved creatures are we, that the faith we have this hour may yield to the most dishonoring distrust in the next. This instance of the disciples' unbelief is recorded for our "learning"—for our humbling and watchfulness. The same unbelief was evidenced by Israel in the wilderness, for the human heart is the same in all ages. All of God's wonders in Egypt and at the Red Sea were as nothing, when the trials of the wilderness came upon them. Their testings in "the wilderness *of Sin*" (Ex. 16:1) only brought out of their hearts just what this testing brought out of Philip's and Andrew's, and just what similar testing brings out of ours —blindness and unbelief. The human heart, when proved, can yield nothing else, for nothing else is there. O with what fervency should we daily pray to our Father, "Lead us not into temptation" (trial)!

"And Jesus said, Make the men sit down" (v. 10). How thankful we should be that God's blessings are dispensed according to the riches of His grace, and not according to the poverty of our faith. What would have happened to that multitude if Christ had acted according to the faith of His disciples? Why, the multitude would have gone away unfed! Ah, dear reader, God's blessings *do* come, despite all our undeserving. Christ never fails, though there is nothing but failure in us. His arm is never withdrawn for a moment, nor is His love chilled by our skepticism and ingratitude. To hear or read of this may encourage one who is merely a professing Christian to *continue* in his careless and God-dishonoring course; but far otherwise will it be with a *real* child of God. The realization of the Lord's unchanging goodness, His unfailing mercies—despite our backslidings—will melt him to tears with godly sorrow.

"And Jesus said, Make the men sit down" (v. 10). How patient was the Lord with His disciples. There was no harsh rebuke for either Philip or Andrew. Ah, the Lord knoweth our frame and remembers that we are dust. "Make the men sit down", was a further test; this time of their *obedience*. And a searching test it was. What was the use of making a hungry multitude sit down when there was nothing to feed them with? Ah, but *God* had spoken; *Christ* had given the command, and that was enough. When He commands it is for us to obey, not to reason and argue. Why must not Adam and Eve eat of the tree of knowledge? Simply because God had forbidden them to. Why should Noah, in the absence of any sign of an approaching flood, go to all the trouble of building the ark? Simply because God had commanded him to. So, today. Why should the Christian be baptized? Why should the women keep silence in the churches? Simply because God has *commanded* these things—Acts 10:48; 1 Cor. 14:34.

It is indeed blessed to note the response of the disciples to this command of their Master. Their faith had failed, but their obedience did not. Where both fail, there is grave reason to doubt if there is spiritual life dwelling in such a soul. Their obedience evidenced the genuineness of their Christianity. "If faith is weak, obedience is the best way in which it may be strengthened. 'Then shall *ye know*', says the prophet, 'If ye *follow on* to know the Lord'. If you have not much light, walk up to the standard of what you have, and you are sure to have more. This will prove that you are a genuine servant of God. Well, this is what the disciples seemed to do here. The light of their faith was low, but they heard the word of Jesus, 'Make the men sit down'. They can act, if they cannot see. They can obey His word, if they cannot see that all fulness dwells in Him to meet every difficulty. So they obey His command. The men sit down, and Jesus begins to dispense His blessings. And thus by their act of obedience, their faith becomes enlightened, and every want is supplied. This is always the result of walking up to the light we have got. 'To him that hath shall more be given'. That light may be feeble, it may be only a single ray irradiating the darkness of the mind; nevertheless, it is what God has given you. Despise it not. Hide it not. Walk up to it, and more shall be added.

"And we may notice here how all blessings come down to us through the channel of obedience. The supply for every want had been determined beforehand in the Saviour's mind, for 'He Himself knew what He would do' (v. 6). Yet though this were so, it was to flow through this medium—so intimately and inseparably is the carrying out of all God's purposes of grace toward us connected with obedience to His commands. This is the prominent feature in all God's people. '*Obedient children*' is the term by which they are distinguished from those who are of the world. 'He became obedient' was the distinguishing feature in the character of the divine Master, and it is the mark that the Holy Spirit sets upon all His servants. Obedience and blessing are inseparably connected in God's Word. 'If any man will *do* His will, he shall know of the doctrine whether it be of God'. 'He that hath My commandments and *keepeth* them, he it is that loveth Me; and he that loveth Me shall be loved by My Father, and *I will love him and will manifest Myself to him*'" (Dr. F. Whitfield).

"And Jesus said, Make the men sit down" (v. 10). But why "sit down"? Two answers may be returned. First, because God is a God of order. Any one who has studied the works of God knows that. So, too, with His Word. When His people left Egypt, they did not come forth like a disorderly mob; but in ranks of fives—see Ex. 13:18 margin. It was the same when they crossed the Jordan and entered Canaan—see Josh. 1:14 margin. It was so here. Mark says, "They sat down in ranks, by hundreds, and by fifties" (6:40). It is so still: "Let all things be done decently and in order" (1 Cor. 14:40). Whenever there is confusion in a religious meeting—two or more praying at the same time, etc.—it is a sure sign that the Holy Spirit is not in control of it. "God *is not* the Author of confusion" (1 Cor. 14:33).

"Make the men sit down". Why? Secondly, may we not also see in this word the illustration of an important principle pertaining to the spiritual life, namely, that we must sit down if we would be fed—true alike for sinner and saint. The activities of the flesh must come to an end, if the Bread of life is to be received by us. How much all of us need to ask God to teach us to be quiet and sit still. Turn to and ponder Psa. 107:30; Isa. 30:15; 1 Thess. 4:11; 1 Pet. 3:4. In this crazy age, when almost everybody is rushing hither and thither, when the standard of excellency is not how well a thing is done, but how quickly, when the Lord's people are thoroughly infected by the same spirit of haste, this is indeed a timely word. And let not the reader imagine that he has power of himself to comply. We have to be *"made"* to "sit down"—frequently by sickness. Note the same word in Psa. 23—"He *maketh me* to lie down in green pastures".

"Now there was much grass in the place" (v. 10). How gracious of the Holy Spirit to record this. Nothing, however trifling or insignificant, is unknown to God or beneath His notice. The "much cattle" in Ninevah (Jonah 4:11) had not been forgotten by Him. And how minutely has the Word of God recorded the house, the situation of it, and the name and occupation of one of the Lord's disciples (Acts 10:5, 6)! Everything is before Him in the registry of heaven. God's eye is upon every circumstance connected with our life. There is nothing too little for Him if it concerns His beloved child. God ordered nature to provide cushions for this hungry multitude to sit upon! Mark adds that the grass was "green" (6:39), which reminds us that we must rest in the "green pastures" of His Word if our souls are to be fed.

"So the men sat down, in number about five thousand" (v. 10). This is another beautiful line in the picture (cf the *five* loaves in v. 9), for five is ever the number which speaks of *grace,* that is why it was the dominant numeral in the Tabernacle where God manifested His grace in the midst of Israel. Five is four (the number of the creature) plus one—God. It is God adding His blessing and grace to the works of His hand.

"And Jesus took the loaves" (v. 11). He did not scorn the loaves because they were few in number, nor the fish either because they were "small". How this tells us that God is pleased to use small and weak things! He used the tear of a babe to move the heart of Pharaoh's daughter. He used the shepherd-rod of Moses to work mighty miracles in Egypt. He used David's sling and stone to overthrow the Philistine giant. He used a "little maid" to bring the "mighty" Naaman to Elisha. He used a widow with a handful of meal to sustain His prophet. He used a "little child" to teach His disciples a much needed lesson in humility. So here, He used the five loaves and two small fishes to feed this great multitude. And, dear reader, He is ready to use you—weak, insignificant, and ignorant though you be—and make you "mighty through God, to the pulling down of strongholds" (2 Cor. 10:4). But mark it carefully, it was only as these loaves and fishes were placed in the *hands of Christ* that they were made efficient and sufficient!

"And Jesus took the loaves". He did not despise them and work independently of them. He did not rain manna from heaven, but used the means which were to hand. And surely this is another lesson that many of His people need to take to heart today. It is true that God is not limited to means, but frequently He employs them. When healing the bitter waters of Marah, God used a tree (Ex. 15:23-25). In healing Hezekiah of his boil, He employed a lump of figs (2 Kings 20:4-7). Timothy was exhorted to use a "little wine for his stomach's sake and his often infirmities" (1 Tim. 5:23). In view of such scriptures let us, then, beware of going to the fanatical lengths of some who scorn the use of drugs and herbs when sick.

"And when He had given thanks" (v. 11). In all things Christ has left us a perfect example. He here teaches us to acknowledge God as the Giver of every good gift, and to own Him as the One who provides for the wants of all His creatures. This is the least that we can do. To fail at this point is the basest ingratitude.

"He distributed to the disciples, and the disciples to them that were set down" (v. 11). Here we are taught, again, the same lesson as the first miracle supplied, namely, that God is pleased to use human instruments in accomplishing the counsels of His grace, and thus give us the inestimable honor and privilege of being "laborers together with God" (1 Cor. 3:9). Christ fed the hungry multitude *through His disciples*. It was their work as truly as it was His. His was the increase, but theirs was the distribution. God acts according to the same principle today. Between the unsearchable riches of Christ and the hungry multitudes there is need of consecrated service and ministry. Nor should this be regarded as exclusively the work of pastors and evangelists. It is the happy duty of every child of God to pass on to others that which the Lord in His grace has first given to him. Yea, this is one of the *conditions* of receiving more for ourselves. This is one of the things that Paul reminded the Hebrews of. He declared he had many things to say unto them, and they were hard to be interpreted because they had become dull (*slothful* is the meaning of the word) of hearing, and unskilled in using the Word. Consequently, instead of teaching others—as they ought—they needed to be taught again themselves (Heb. 5:11-13). The same truth comes out in that enigmatical utterance of our Lord recorded in Luke 8:18: "For whosoever hath, to him shall be given; and whosoever hath not, from him shall be taken even that which he seemeth to have".

The one who "hath" is the believer who makes *good use* of what he has received, and in consequence more is given him; the one who "seemeth to have" is the man who hides his light under a bushel, who makes not good use of what he received, and from him this is "taken away". Be warned then, dear reader. If we do not use to God's glory what He has given us, He may withhold further blessings from us, and take away that which we fail to make good use of.

"He distributed to the disciples, and the disciples to them that were set down" (v. 11). One can well imagine the mingled feelings of doubt and skepticism as the twelve left the Saviour's side for the hungry multitude, with the little store in their baskets. How doubt must have given place to amazement, and awe to adoration, as they distributed, returned to their Master for a fresh supply, and continued distributing, giving a portion of bread and fish to each till all were satisfied, and more remaining at the close than at the beginning! Let us remember that Jesus Christ is "the same yesterday and today and forever", and that all fulness dwells in Him. By comparing Mark 6:41 it will be found that there the Holy Spirit has described the *modus operandi* of the miracle: "He looked up to heaven, and blessed, and *brake* the loaves, and *gave* to His disciples". The word "brake" is in the aorist tense, intimating an instantaneous act; whereas "gave" is in the imperfect tense, denoting the continuous action of giving. "This shows that the miraculous power was in the hands of Christ, between the breaking and the giving" (Companion Bible).

"He distributed to the disciples, and the disciples to them that were set down". What a lesson is there here for the Christian servant. The apostles first received the bread from the hands of their Master, and then "distributed" to the multitude. It was not *their* hands which made the loaves increase, but *His!* He provided the abundant supply, and their business was to humbly receive and faithfully distribute. In like manner, it is not the business of the preacher to make men value or receive the Bread of life. *He* can not make it soul-saving to any one. This is not his work; for this he is not responsible. It is *God* who giveth the "increase"! Nor is it the work of the preacher to *create* something new and novel. His duty is to *seek* "bread" at the hands of his Lord, and then *set it* before the people. What *they* do with the Bread is *their* responsibility! But, remember, that we cannot give out to others, except we have first received ourselves. It is only the full vessel that overflows!

"And likewise of the fishes as much as they would" (v. 11). "Precious, precious words! The supply stopped only with the demand. So, when Abraham went up to intercede with God on behalf of the righteous in Sodom, the Lord never ceased granting till Abraham had ceased asking. Thus also in the case of Elisha's oil; so long as there were empty vessels to be found in the land, it ceased not its abundant supply (2 Kings 4:6). Likewise also here: so long as there was a single one to supply, that supply came forth from the treasuries of the Lord Jesus. The stream flowed on in rich abundance till all were filled. This is grace. This is what Jesus does to all His people. He comes to the poor bankrupt believer, and, placing in His hand a draft on the resources of heaven, says to him, 'Write on it what thou wilt'. Such is our precious Lord still. If we are straitened, it is not in Him, but in ourselves. If we are poor and weak, or tried and tempted, it is not that we cannot help ourselves—it is because we do not ("All things *are* yours", in Christ, 1 Cor. 3:22 A.W.P.). We have so little faith in things unseen and eternal. We draw so little on the resources of Christ. We come not to Him with our spiritual wants—our empty vessels—and draw from the ocean fulness of His grace.

"As much as they would'. Precious, precious words. Remember them, doubting, hesitating one, in all thy petitions for faith at the throne of grace. 'As much as they would'. Remember them, tried and tempted one, in all thy pleadings for strength to support thee on thy wilderness way. 'As much as they would'. Remember them, bereaved and desolate one, whose eyes are red with weeping, bending over the green sod, beneath which all thy earthly hopes are lying, and with a rent in thine heart that shall never be healed till the morning of resurrection—remember these words as thy wounded and desolate spirit breaks forth in mournful accents on a Saviour's ear for help and strength. And, guilty one, bowed down with a lifetime's load of sin, traversing the crooked by-paths of the broad road to ruin; a wilful wanderer from thy God; as the arrow of conviction penetrates thy soul, and as thine agonizing voice is heard crying for mercy—remember these precious, precious words, 'as much as they would'. 'Him that cometh unto Me I will in no wise cast out'" (Dr. F. Whitfield).

"When they were filled" (v. 12). God gives with no niggardly hand. "When they were *filled*", what a contrast is this from the words of Philip, "That every one of them may take *a little*"! The one was the outpouring of Divine grace, the other the limitation of unbelief. Christ had fed them from His own inexhaustible resources, and when *He* feeds His people He leaves no want behind. Christ, and He alone, *satisfies*. His promise is, "He that cometh to Me shall never hunger, and he that believeth on Me shall never thirst" (John 6:35). Do you know, dear reader, what it is to be "filled" from His blessed hand—

filled with peace, filled with joy, filled with the Holy Spirit!

"Gather up the fragments that remain, that nothing be lost" (v. 12). All were filled and yet abundance remained! How wonderful and how blessed this is. All fulness dwells in Christ, and that fulness is exhaustless. Countless sinners have been saved and their souls satisfied, and yet the riches of grace are as undiminished as ever. Then, too, this verse may be considered from another angle. "Gather up the fragments". There was abundance for all, but the Lord would have no waste. How this rebukes the wicked extravagance that we now behold on every hand! Here, too, the Holy One has left us a perfect example. "Gather up the fragments" is a word that comes to us all. The "fragments" we need to watch most are the fragments of our time. How often these are wasted! "Let nothing be lost"! "Gather them up" —your mis-spent moments, your tardy services, your sluggish energies, your cold affections, your neglected duties. Gather them up and use them for His glory.

"Therefore they gathered them together, and filled twelve baskets with the fragments of the five barley loaves, which remained over and above unto them that had eaten" (v. 13). How this confirms what we have said above about giving out to others. The loaves were augmented by division and multiplied by substraction! We are never impoverished, but always enriched by giving to others. It is the *liberal* soul that is made fat (Prov. 11:25). We need never be anxious that there will not be enough left for our own needs. God never allows a generous giver to be the loser. It is miserliness which impoverishes. The disciples had more left at the finish than they had at the beginning! They "filled twelve baskets", thus the twelve apostles were also provided with an ample supply for their own use too! *They* were the ones who were enriched by ministering to the hungry multitude! What a blessed encouragement to God's servants today!

In closing, let us call attention to another of the wonderful typical and dispensational pictures which abound in this Gospel. The passage which has been before us supplies a lovely view of the activities of God during this dispensation. It should be carefully noted that John 6 opens with the words, "After these things". This expression always points to the beginning of a *new* series—cf 5:1; 7:1; 21:1; Rev. 4:1, etc. In John 4 we have two typical pictures which respect *the Gentiles*—see the closing portions of articles 15 and 16. Hence John 5 *begins* with "After this". John 5 supplies us with a typical picture of *Israel*—see article 17. Now as John 6 opens with "After these things", we are led to expect that the dispensational view it first supplies will respect *the Gentiles* again and not the Jews. This is confirmed by the fact that the remainder of the verse intimates that Christ had now left Judea and had once more entered Galilee of the Gentiles. Further corrobation is found in that Philip and Andrew figure so prominently in the incident which follows—cf John 12:20-22 which specially links *them* with the *Gentiles*. In the remainder of the passage we have a beautiful view of Christ and His people during the present dispensation. Note the following lines in the picture:—

First, we behold the Lord *on high* and His people "seated" *with Him* (v. 3). This, of course, typifies our *standing;* what follows contemplates our *state*. Second, we are shown the *basis* of our blessings: "And the Passover, a feast of the Jews, was nigh" (v. 4). The Passover speaks of "Christ our Passover sacrificed for us" (1 Cor. 5: 7). But note, it is not only "the Passover" which is mentioned here, but also "the Passover, a *feast*" (note the absence of this in John 2:13!), which beautifully accords with what follows—typically, believers *feeding* on Christ! But we are also told here that this "Passover" was "a feast of *the Jews*". This is parallel with John 4:22—"Salvation is *of* the Jews". It is a word to humble us, showing our indebtedness to Israel, cf Rom. 11:18: "Thou bearest not the root, but the root thee". Third, the people of God, those who in this dispensation are fed, are they who "come unto Him" (v. 5)—Christ. Fourth, Christ's desire (v. 5) and purpose (v. 6) to feed His own. Fifth, His saints are a people of little faith (cf Matt. 8:26), who fail in the hour of testing (vv. 5-9). Sixth, His people must "sit down" in order to be "fed". Seventh, Christ ministers to His people in sovereign *grace* ("Five loaves" and "five" thousand men, vv. 10, 11) and gives them a satisfying portion—"They were *filled*" (v. 12).

It is beautiful to observe that *after* the great multitude had been fed, there "remained" *twelve* full baskets, which tells of the abundance of grace reserved for *Israel*, after this dispensation is over. This also gives meaning to, "A feast of the Jews *was nigh*" (v. 4), for only a comparatively brief interval intervenes between the ending of this dispensation and the happy time of the Millennium!

Let the following questions be studied with a view to the next article:—

1. *Why* did Christ "depart"? v. 15.
2. Why were the disciples "afraid"? v. 15.
3. What dispensational picture can you discover in vv. 15 to 21?
4. What spiritual lessons may be drawn from vv. 17 to 21?
5. What dispensational picture can you find in vv. 22 to 27?
6. How harmonize the first half of v. 27 with Eph. 2:8, 9?
7. What is meant by Christ being "sealed"? v. 27.

—Arthur W. Pink.

14. BABYLON AND THE ANTICHRIST.

We arrive now at a branch of our subject upon which the Lord's people are in evident need of instruction: they have less light here than on most prophetic themes. And perhaps we should not be surprised at this. The very name Babylon means *confusion*, and widely prevails the confusion concerning it. Yet here and there God has raised up individuals who have borne faithful testimony to the teaching of His Word concerning the past and future of Babylon, and to their witness the writer acknowledges his indebtedness. In view of the ignorance which generally obtains we shall proceed the more cautiously. We here propose to examine carefully the principal scriptures in the Old Testament bearing upon our present theme.

"Babylon was a mighty city of old; its beginnings were in Shinar in the days shortly after the flood; it played an important part in the history of Israel and of Judea; it was the head of the kingdoms of the earth in the days of Nebuchadnezzar; after its capture by the Medes and Persians it fell from its high estate, but for some centuries after Christ it was still a city of importance, and the head of a district. In the New Testament it is first mentioned by Peter (1 Pet. 5:13), and here in the book that tells of the events that occur in the *Day of the Lord* we read of it as a city again dominating the world, and that at a time when Israelites are again prominent in the story of the earth. Here, too, Babylon reappears in its ancient dual aspect, political and social, the first city of earth and also the leader of the worship and religion of the world powers. The site of old Babylon is known at the present day; it covers a wide extent of ground, and parts of it are inhabited, as for instance Hillah, where there are some five or six thousand people. When the long-talked-of Euphrates Valley Railway becomes a reality, Babylon will be one of the most important places on the line" (Col. VanSomeron —"The Great Unfolding"). This quotation supplies a brief but fairly comprehensive outline of our subject.

The earliest mention of Babel in Scripture is in connection with the name of him who first after the deluge attained to greatness in the earth—greatness apart from God. Nimrod was the grandson of Ham, who called down upon him the curse of his father, Noah. "The sons of Ham were Cush . . . . and Cush begat Nimrod: he began to be a mighty one in the earth. He was a mighty hunter before the Lord, and the beginning of his kingdom was *Babel, in the land of Shinar*" (Gen. 10:7-10). Let the reader turn back to the previous article for our comments on Nimrod as a type of the Antichrist. "Thus mightiness in the earth and commencement of kingly rule are first mentioned in connection with one, the seat of whose power was Babylon and the land of Shinar. Nimrod—Nebuchadnezzar—Antichrist, are, as we shall see, the three great names connected with that region and with that city" (B. W. Newton: "Babylon; Its Revival and Final Destruction"—1859).

The first mention of anything in Scripture always calls for the most particular attention, inasmuch as the initial occurrence of any term or expression in the Word of God invariably defines its meaning and forecasts its subsequent significance and scope. The passage just quoted from Gen. 10 is inseparably connected with and is in fact the key to what is found in Gen. 11. There we learn that the land of Shinar is mentioned as the place where men first united in confederate action against God. God had commanded that men should spread abroad—Gen. 9:1. But they, in blatant defiance, preferred to centralize. They determined to make for themselves a name, saying, "Go to, Let us build us *a city* and a tower, whose top may reach unto heaven; and let us make us a name, lest we be scattered abroad upon the face of the whole earth" (Gen. 11:4). And this, we are told, was "In the *land of Shinar*" (11:2). But the Lord interfered, came down, confounded their speech, and scattered them—"And they left off to build the city. Therefore is the name of it called *Babel;* because the Lord did there confound the language of all the earth", etc. (Gen. 11:8,9). Thus we see that at the beginning, the land of Shinar and the city of Babylon were the scene of confederate evil, and of judgment from the hand of God.

Shinar, then, was the land around Babel. Now, though the building of the city of Babylon was checked during the days of Nimrod, yet his kingdom was not overthrown. In Gen. 14:1 we read of "Amraphal king of Shinar". It would appear from several scriptures that "the land of Chaldea"—the capital of which was the city of Babylon—is but another name for "the land of Shinar". In Dan. 5:30 Belshazzar is termed "the king of the Chaldeans", while in 7:1 he is called "the king of Babylon"—cf Isa. 47:1; Jer. 50:8; 51:54; Ezek. 12:13. In addition to these passages, Dan. 1:2, 3 seems to positively establish this conclusion, for there we are expressly told that the Babylon of Nebuchadnezzar's day was situated in "the land of *Shinar*"! This serves to confirm the fact that Chaldea or Babylonia was the most ancient of the early empires. It was from "Ur" *of Chaldea*

(Gen. 11:28) that Abram was called; and it was "the *Chaldeans*" who plundered Job (Job 1:17); and in Josh. 7:21 we read of the "goodly *Babylonish* garment" which tempted A c h a n, among the spoils of Jericho. In striking accord with this is the statement found in Jer. 5:15, where the Holy Spirit terms the Babylonians an *"ancient"* as well as a "mighty" nation. After the days of Joshua, Babylon was not directly referred to again till the days of Esar-Haddan, of whom it is said, "And the king of Assyria brought men from Babylon, and from Cuthah, and from Ava, and from Hamath, and from Sepharvaim, and placed them in the cities of Samaria instead of the children of Israel: and they possessed Samaria, and dwelt in the cities thereof" (2 Kings 17:24), and cf Ezra 4:2. Closely connected with the land of Shinar is *Assyria*. For a time the supremacy alternated between Assyria and Babylonia, until in the days of Nabapolasser, the father of Nebuchadnezzar, Ninevah was conquered and Assyria became subject to Babylon.

But though Shinar and its capital are referred to in Gen. 10 and 11, and though there are occasional allusions to them in the centuries that followed, it was not until Israel's apostasy had been fully manifested that we find Babylon coming into the place of prominence and dominion. "Until Jerusalem had been sufficiently tried, to see whether she would prove herself worthy of being God's city, Babylon was kept in abeyance. The founder of Babylon's greatness was that great king who was raised up to scourge Jerusalem, and who commenced the 'Times of the Gentiles', by receiving from God that endowment of power which was taken from Israel, and remains vested in the Gentiles, till Jerusalem shall be forgiven and cease to be trodden down. It was Nebuchadnezzar who 'walked in the palace of the kingdom of Babylon. The king spoke and said, Is not this great Babylon which I have built for the house of the kingdom by the might of my power and for the honor of my majesty?' (Dan. 4). The *greatness* of Babylon dates only from Nebuchadnezzar" (B.W.N.).

The fifth chapter of Daniel tells how Belshazzar, the successor of Nebuchadnezzar, was slain by Darius, who took over the kingdom. Neither the city nor the kingdom was then destroyed, and so far from it being made desolate and without inhabitant, it remained for long centuries a city of note. Two hundred years after its capture by Darius, Alexander the Great, after his conquest over the Persians, selected Babylon as the intended capital of his vast dominion, and, in fact, died there. In the first century of the Christian era Babylon still stood, for Peter refers to a church there! (See 1 Pet. 5:13). Several of the church "Fathers" refer to Babylon, and at the beginning of the sixth century A.D. the famous Babylonian Talmud was issued by the Academies of Babylonia. Mr. Newton tells us that "Ibn Hankel in A. D. 917 speaks of Babylon as a small village. Even in the tenth century, therefore, it had not wholly disappeared". Slow and almost undiscernible was its decline and decay. Even in this day there is still a small town, Hillah, standing on the original site of ancient Babylon. What, then, of the future?

That there will yet be another Babylon, a Babylon eclipsing the power and glory of that of Nebuchadnezzar's day, has long been the firm conviction of the writer. Nor are we by any means alone in this conviction. A long list of honored names might be given of those who have arrived, independently, at the conclusion that the Scriptures plainly teach that Babylon is going to be re-built. But there is no need to buttress our conviction by an appeal to human authority. Better that the faith of the reader rest on the Word of God, than in the wisdom of the best of men. Before we set forth some of the many scripture *proofs* on which our conviction rests, let us ask, Would it not be passing strange if Babylon had no place in the Endtime? Scripture tells us that Jerusalem, which has been so long trodden down by the Gentiles, is to be restored by human agency, and have a re-built temple (Matt. 24:15). Egypt and Assyria have yet an honored future before them, as is clear from Isa. 19: 23, 24. Moab, Edom, and Seir are to figure in the coming day, as is intimated in Num. 24:17, 18. Greece awaits her final judgment from God (Zech. 9:13). And so we might go on. Why, then, should *Babylon* be exempted from the general renovation of the East?

But we are not left to logical deductions, the Word of God expressly affirms that Babylon *will* play a prominent part at the time of the End. The empire over which the Antichrist will reign is described in the identical symbols which were applied to the four world-kingdoms of Dan. 7. In Dan. 7:3 Daniel beheld "four great beasts" come up from *the sea*, and in Dan. 7:17 we are told "these great beasts, which are four, are four kings (or kingdoms) which shall arise out of the earth". These four beasts or kingdoms were the Babylonian, the Medo-Persian, the Grecian, and the Roman. Dan. 7:4 says "The first was like a *lion*". 7:5 says "The second was like a *bear*". 7:6 says the third was "like a *leopard*". 7:7 says the fourth was "dreadful and terrible". Now, in Rev. 13:1,2, where we have a symbolical description of the empire which the Antichrist shall head, we are told that John saw "a Beast rise up out of *the sea*", and then it is added, "the Beast . . . was like unto a *leopard*, and his feet were as the feet of a *bear*, and his mouth as the mouth of a *lion*". Of the fourth beast of Dan. 7 we read, "It had *ten horns*" (7: 7); so in Rev. 13:1 the Beast there has *"ten horns"*. Who, then, can doubt that Rev. 13:1, 2 is given for the express purpose of teaching us that the four great world-kingdoms of the past —not merely the fourth but *all* of the four—are to be revived and restored at the time of the End? But as this point is disputed by some, we tarry to advance further proof.

It is to be noted that the Beast (kingdom) of Rev. 13:1 is said to have "seven heads". This has puzzled many of the commentators, but once it is seen that the Beast of Rev. 13:1, 2 is a symbolic description, first of a *composite* kingdom, made up of and perpetuating the features of the four world-empires of old; and second, a symbolic description of the one who shall head it, all difficulty disappears. That we have here in Rev. 13: 1, 2 a *composite* kingdom is clear from the "seven heads". Now note that in Dan. 7 the first, second and fourth kingdoms are not said to have more than one head, but the third has *"four heads"* (Dan. 7:6). Thus the beasts of Dan. 7 have, three of them one head each, and the third four heads, or *seven* in all; which tallies perfectly with Rev. 13:1. But even this does not exhaust the proofs that the *four kingdoms* of Dan. 7 are to be restored, and play their final parts immediately before the Millennium.

If the reader will turn to Dan. 2, which is parallel with Dan. 7—the "image" in its *four parts* (the head, the breast and arms, the belly and thighs, the legs and feet) corresponding with the *four beasts*—it will be found that when we come to v. 45, which speaks of Christ (under the figure of "the Stone cut out of the mount without hands") returning to earth to destroy the forces of evil, and then set up His kingdom, we discover that the Stone "brake in pieces the iron (Rome), the brass (Greece), the clay (apostate Israel), the silver (Medo-

Persia), and the gold (Babylon). What we desire the reader to note particularly is that the Stone strikes not only the iron, but the brass, clay, silver, and gold; in fact, v. 35 tells us, expressly, they shall be "broken to pieces *together*"! If, then, they are destroyed "together", they *must* all be on the scene at the time of Christ's return to earth to inaugurate His millennial reign, and if so, each of them must have been *revived* and *restored!!* As our present inquiry concerns not the renovation of Persia, Greece and Rome, but only that of Babylon, we shall confine ourselves to the scriptures which speak of the last mentioned.

1. Isa. 13 and 14 contain a remarkable prophecy bearing directly on the theme before us. It is termed in the opening verse, "The burden of Babylon". It tells of the terrible judgment which God shall send on this city. It speaks of the total and final destruction of it. It declares that "Babylon, the glory of kingdoms, the beauty of the Chaldees' excellency, shall be as when God overthrew Sodom and Gomorrah". It shall never be inhabited, neither shall it be dwelt in from generation to generation (vv. 19, 20). Now the one point pertinent to our present inquiry is, Whether Isa. 13 describes the doom which befell the Babylon of Belshazzar's day, or the judgment which shall overtake the Babylon of the coming day. Upon this point there is, for those who desire to be subject to God's Word, no room for uncertainty. The sixth verse expressly declares that this "burden of Babylon" is to receive its fulfillment in "the Day of the Lord". This, we need hardly add, is the name for that Day which follows the present Day of Salvation (2 Cor. 6:2). If the reader will consult a concordance he will find that "the Day of the Lord" never refers to a period now past, but always has reference to one which is yet future! If any doubt remains as to whether or not Isa. 13 is speaking of a *future* Day, the contents of v. 10 should forever remove it. There we are told that "the stars of heaven and the constellation thereof shall not give their light: the sun shall be darkened in his going forth, and the moon shall not cause her light to shine". All students of prophecy will see at a glance that these cosmic phenomena are what are to be witnessed during the Tribulation period—cf Matt. 24: 29. There is not a hint anywhere either in Scripture or (so far as we are aware) in secular history, that such disturbances among the heavenly bodies occurred at the captivity of Babylon by Darius. And it is at *that* time, in "the Day of the Lord" when the sun is darkened and the moon shines not, that Babylon is overthrown (v. 19). This one scripture is quite sufficient to establish the futurity of Babylon and its coming overthrow*.

2. The 14th of Isaiah reads right on from 13, completing the "burden of Babylon" there begun. It supplies further proof that there is to be another Babylon. The chapter opens with a declaration of Israel's coming restoration. It declares "the Lord will have mercy on Jacob, and will yet choose Israel, and set them in their own land" (v. 1). It goes on to say, "It shall come to pass *in the day that* the Lord shall give thee rest from thy sorrow, and from thy fear, and from the hard bondage wherein thou wast made to serve, That thou shalt take up this taunting speech against the king of *Babylon*, and say, How hath the oppressor ceased! the golden city ceased!" (vv. 3, 4). Should the quibble be raised that these verses are speaking of the restoration of Israel to Palestine following the captivity of Nebuchadnezzar's time, it is easily silenced. The verses that follow those

---
* There is no room for a quibble about the meaning of "Babylon", for v. 19 expressly terms it "The beauty of the *Chaldees'* excellency".

just quoted make it unmistakeably clear that this prophecy *yet awaits* its fulfillment. Thus we read in vv. 7, 8, "The whole earth is at rest, and is quiet: they break forth into singing. Yea, the fir trees rejoice at thee, and the cedars of Lebanon, saying, Since thou art laid down, no feller is come up against us". The whole earth never has been "at rest" since the days of Cain (except it were during the brief period when the Word tabernacled among men). But it will be during the Millennium! Notice, too, that following the overthrow of "the golden city", Israel exclaims, "Since thou art laid down, (laid low) *no* feller (no *cutter off*) is come up against us"! This establishes, unequivocally, the time of which this prophecy treats. Long after the days of Belshazzar, the Romans came up against Israel and cut them off. But none shall do this again when the *last* king of Babylon is destroyed!

Above, we have quoted to the end of the 8th verse of Isa. 14. In the 9th verse the prophet suddenly turns from Babylon to its last king. Verses 9 to 20 contain a striking portrait of the lofty arrogance and fearful doom of the Man of Sin. Then, in verse 21, the "burden" returns again to the *subjects* of the Antichrist: "Prepare slaughter for his children for the iniquity of their fathers; that they do not rise, nor possess the land, nor fill the face of the world with cities. For I will rise up against them, saith the Lord of hosts, and cut off from Babylon the name, and remnant, and son, and nephew, saith the Lord. I will also make it a possession for the bittern, and pools of water: and I will sweep it with the besom of destruction, saith the Lord of hosts" (vv. 21-23). Finally, the prophet concludes with a parting word concerning the Antichrist: "The Lord of hosts hath sworn, saying, Surely as I have thought, so shall it come to pass; and as I have purposed, so shall it stand:

That I will break the Assyrian in my land, and upon my mountains tread him under foot: then shall his yoke depart from off them, and his burden depart from off their shoulders. This is the purpose that is purposed upon the whole earth: and this is the hand that is stretched upon all the nations. For the Lord of hosts hath purposed, and who shall disannul it? And His hand is stretched out, and who shall turn it back?" (vv. 24-27). Well has it been said, "These are remarkable and significant words, and certainly we cannot say they have been fulfilled. Will any one affirm that God's purpose which He hath purposed upon the whole earth was accomplished when Babylon was overthrown by the Medes and Persians? Did the hand that was stretched out over all the nations, *then* fulfill its ultimate designs? Was the Assyrian then trodden under foot in THE LAND, AND ON THE MOUNTAINS OF ISRAEL, and, that at a time when the yoke of bondage is finally broken from off the neck of Israel? If this were so we should no longer see Jerusalem trodden down now. 'The times of the Gentiles' would have ended. Israel would be gathered, and Jerusalem be 'a praise in the earth'. The concluding words of this prophecy, therefore, might alone convince us that it yet remains to be fulfilled" (B. W. N.).

3. We appeal next to the 50th chapter of Jeremiah. The opening verses contain a prophecy which certainly has not received its complete fulfillment in the past. It declares, "The words that the Lord spake against Babylon and against the land of the Chaldeans by Jeremiah the prophet. Declare ye among the nations, and publish, and set up a standard; publish, and conceal not: say, Babylon is taken, Bel is confounded, Merodach is broken in pieces; her idols are confounded, her images are broken in pieces. For out of the north there

cometh up a nation against her, which shall make her land desolate, and none shall dwell therein: they shall remove, they shall depart, both man and beast. In those days, *and in that time*, saith the Lord, the children of Israel shall come, they and the children of Judah *together*, going and weeping: they shall go, and seek the Lord their God. They shall ask the way to Zion with their faces thitherward, saying, Come, and let us join ourselves to the Lord in a perpetual covenant which shall not be forgotten" (vv. 1-5). Mark carefully three things in these verses. First, it is announced that the *land* of Babylon shall be made so desolate that neither man nor beast shall dwell therein. Second, the time for this is defined as being when Israel and Judah *together* (and since the days of Rehoboam they have never been united) shall "seek the Lord". Third, it is when Israel and Judah shall join themselves to the Lord in "a perpetual covenant"! Still more explicit is the time-mark in v. 20: "*In those days, and in that time,* saith the Lord, the iniquity of Israel shall be sought for, and there shall be *none;* and the sins of Judah, and they shall not be found".

4. The whole of Jer. 51 should be carefully studied in this connection. Much in it we reserve for consideration in the two papers which will follow this. Here we simply call attention to vv. 47-49: "Therefore, behold, the days come, that I will do judgment upon the graven images of Babylon: and her whole land shall be confounded, and all her slain shall fall in the midst of her. Then the heaven and the earth, and all that is therein, shall sing for Babylon: for the spoiler shall come upon her from the north, saith the Lord. As Babylon hath caused the slain of Israel to fall, so at Babylon shall fall the slain of all the earth". Surely little comment is needed here. When did the slain "of all the earth" (i. e. of all nations) fall in the midst of Babylon? And when did heaven and earth and all that is therein rejoice at her overthrow? "When Babylon passed into the hands of the Medes there was little occasion for such joy. It made little difference to the earth whether Babylon was reigned over by Chaldeans, or by Persians, or Greeks, or Romans. There was little cause for thanksgiving in *such* transfer of authority from one proud hand to another. But if there be a fall of Babylon that is to be immediately succeeded by the kingdom of Him, of whom it is said, 'All nations shall call Him blessed' .... then there is indeed sufficient reason why heaven and earth, and all that is therein should sing" (B. W. N.).

5. "Be in pain, and labour to bring forth, O daughter of Zion, like a woman in travail: for now shalt thou go forth out of the city, and thou shalt dwell in the field, and thou shalt go even to *Babylon;* there shalt thou be delivered; *there* the Lord shall redeem thee from the hand of thine enemies" (Micah 4:10). In the light of such scriptures as Micah 5:3, Matt. 24:8 ("sorrows" literally means "birthpangs"), etc., there can be no room for doubt as to the time to which this prophecy refers. It is at the close of the Great Tribulation. And at that time a remnant of Israel will be found in *Babylon* and they shall be delivered by the Lord.

6. Both the prophecies of Isaiah and Jeremiah as well as the Apocalypse speak of the *immediateness* of the blow which is to destroy Babylon. "Come down, and sit in the dust, O virgin daughter of Babylon, sit on the ground: there is no throne, O daughter of the Chaldeans: for thou shalt no more be called tender and delicate .... therefore hear now this, thou that art given to pleasures, that dwellest carelessly, that sayest in thine heart I am, and none else besides me; I shall not sit as a widow, neither shall I know the loss of children: But

these two things shall come to thee *in a moment, in one day*, the loss of children, and widowhood: they shall come upon thee in thy perfection for the multitude of thy sorceries, and for the great abundance of thine enchantments" (Isa. 47:1, 8, 9). "Babylon is *suddenly* fallen and destroyed: howl for her" (Jer. 51:8). "Alas, alas, that great city Babylon, that mighty city! for *in one hour* is thy judgment come" (Rev. 18:10). There has been nothing in the past history of Babylon which in any-wise corresponds with these prophecies.

7. Isaiah, Jeremiah, and the Revelation each declare that Babylon shall be *burned* with fire. "And Babylon, the glory of kingdoms, the beauty of the Chaldees' excellency shall be *as* when God overthrew *Sodom and Gomorrah*" (Isa. 13:19). "The mighty men of Babylon have forborne to fight, they have remained in their holes: their might hath failed; they became as women: they have *burned* her dwelling places; her bars are broken.... Thus saith the Lord of hosts; the broad walls of Babylon shall be utterly broken, and her high gates shall be *burned with fire*" (Jer. 51:30, 58). "And cried when they saw the smoke of her *burning*, saying, What city is like unto this great city!" (Rev. 18:18). We know of nothing in either Scripture or secular history which shows that Babylon was "burned" *in the past.*

"But it will be said, perhaps, How can this be? Has not Babylon already been smitten? Has it not already been swept with the besom of destruction? Our answer is—Not at the time and with the concomitant circumstances specified in the passages just quoted. It is true indeed that the Euphratean countries have been smitten—sorely smitten under the hand of God. God is wont in His goodness to give premonitory blows—He is accustomed to warn before He finally destroys. Egypt, Jerusalem, and many other places, have all experienced premonitory desolations, and so has Babylon. Its present ruin (which came on it slowly, and if I may so speak, gently), is a memorial of what God's righteous vengeance can do, and a warning of what it will more terribly do, if human pride in contempt of all His admonitions, shall again attempt to rear its goodly palaces when He has written desolation. But if it be the habit of God thus graciously to warn, it is equally the habit of man to say, 'The bricks are fallen down, but we will build with hewn stone; the sycamores are cut down, but we will change them into cedars'. Unbidden, the hand of man revived what God had smitten (that is what happened in Chicago and San Francisco! A.W.P.). Without therefore undervaluing the lesson given by past visitations of God's judgments—without hiding, but rather seeking to proclaim the reality and extent of the ruin, His holy hand has wrought, we have also to testify, that the hand of man uncommissioned from above will, sooner or later, reconstruct the fabric of its greatness—its last evil greatness, on the very plains which teem with the memorials of a ruin entailed by former and yet unrepented of transgressions. Egypt, Damascus, Palestine, and in a measure, Jerusalem, are already being revived. And if these and neighboring countries which have been visited by inflictions similar to those which have fallen on Babylon, are yet to revive and flourish with an evil prosperity at the time of the end, why should *Babylon* be made an exception?" (B.W.N.).

That the Antichrist will be intimately connected with the land of Chaldea is clear from a number of scriptures, notably, those which speak of him as "the Assyrian" and "the king of Babylon". But as this is a disputed point we are obliged to pause and make proof of it. Let us turn, then, first to Isa. 10 and 11 which form one continuous prophecy. We can not now attempt even an outline of this long and interesting prediction, but must merely single out one or two statements from it which bear on the point now before us.

In the fifth verse of Isa. 10, the Lord addresses the Antichrist as follows: "O Assyrian, the rod of mine anger, and the staff in their hand is mine indignation". This intimates, as pointed out in a previous article, that the Son of Perdition is but a tool in the hands of the Almighty, His instrument for threshing Israel. His consuming egotism and haughtiness come out plainly in the verses that follow (7-11). But when God has accomplished His purpose by him, He "will punish the fruit of the stout heart of the king of Assyria, and the glory of his high looks" (v. 12). How this serves to identify him with the "little horn" of Dan. 7:20, the Man of Sin of 2 Thess. 2:4!—cf further his proud boastings recorded in Isa. 10: 13, 14. In v. 23 is another statement which helps us to fix with certainty the period of which the prophet is speaking, and the central actors there in view: "For a consummation, and that determined, shall the Lord, the Lord of hosts, make in the midst of all the earth" (R. V.). The words "consummation" and "that determined" occur again in Dan. 9:27—"He (Antichrist) shall make it (the temple) desolate, even until *the consummation*, and *that determined* shall be poured upon the Desolator". The "King of Assyria" and "the Desolator" are thus shown to be the same. In Isa. 10, vv. 24 and 25 we read, "Therefore thus saith the Lord God of hosts, O My people that dwellest in Zion, be not afraid of the Assyrian: he shall smite thee with a rod, and shall lift up his staff against thee, after the manner of Egypt. For yet a very little while, and *the indignation shall cease*, and Mine anger in their destruction." Clearly this is parallel with Dan. 11:36: "And the King shall do according to his will; and he shall exalt himself, and magnify himself above every god, and shall speak marvellous things against the God of gods, and shall prosper till *the indignation be accomplished*." In the 11th chapter of Isaiah there is a statement even clearer, a proof conclusive and decisive: "And He shall smite the earth with the rod of His mouth and with the breath of His lips shall He slay the wicked" (11:4). These very words are applied to the Man of Sin in 2 Thess. 2:8.

In Isa. 14 we have a scripture which very clearly connects the Antichrist with Babylon. The opening verses (which really form a parenthesis) tell of the coming restoration of Israel to Jehovah's favor, and then in v. 4 they are bidden to take up "a taunting speech (marginal rendering) against the King of Babylon". The taunting speech begins thus: "How hath the Oppressor ceased! the golden city ceased! the Lord hath broken the staff of the Wicked" (vv. 4, 5). As to *who* is in view here there is surely no room for doubt. He is Israel's Oppressor in the End-time; he is the Wicked One. In the verses which follow there are many marks by which he may be positively identified. In v. 6 this "King of Babylon" is said to be "He who smote the people (i. e. Israel) in wrath with a continual stroke". In v. 12 he is called "Lucifer (Daystar), Son of the morning", a title which marks him out as none other than the Son of Perdition. Whatever backward reference to the fall of Satan there may be in this verse and the ones that follow, it is clear that they describe the blasphemous arrogance of the Antichrist. In v. 13 we read, "For thou hast said in thine heart, I will ascend into heaven, I will exalt my throne above the stars of God: I will sit also upon the mount of the congregation, in the sides of the north". Then, in vv. 15 and 16 we are told, "Yet thou shalt be brought down to hell, to the sides of the Pit. They that see thee shall narrowly look upon thee, and consider thee, saying, Is this the *man* that made the earth to tremble, that did shake kingdoms?" Clearly it is the Man of Sin that is here in view.

In Isa. 30 we have another scripture which links Antichrist with Babylonia. Beginning at v. 27 we read: "Behold, the name of the Lord cometh from far, burning with His anger, and the burning thereof is heavy: his lips are full of indignation, and his tongue as a devouring fire: And his breath, as an over-flowing stream, shall reach to the midst of the neck, to sift the nations with the sieve of vanity: and there shall be a bridle in the jaws of the people, causing them to err. Ye shall have a song, as in the night when a holy solemnity is kept; and gladness of heart, as when one goeth with a pipe to come into the mountain of the Lord, to the mighty One of Israel". Clearly it is the very end of the Tribulation period which is here in view. The reference is to the return of the Lord to earth in great power and glory, when He shall overthrow those who are gathered together against Him, and put an end to the awful career of the Antichrist. Continuing, we find this passage in Isa. 30 closes as follows: "For through the voice of the Lord shall *the Assyrian* be beaten down, which smote with a rod. And in every place where the grounded staff shall pass, which the Lord shall lay upon him, it shall be with tabrets and harps: and in battles of shaking will he fight with it. For Tophet is ordained of old; yea, for the King it is prepared; He hath made it deep and large: the pile thereof is fire and much wood; the breath of the Lord, like a stream of brimstone, doth kindle it"—cf "the breath of the Lord" here with Isa. 11:4. For further references to Antichrist and Assyria see Isa. 7:17-20; 8:7, etc.

The next two articles will be devoted to a consideration of Babylon in the New Testament, when Rev. 17 and 18 will come before us. May the Lord in His grace give us the wisdom we so sorely need, and preserve the writer and reader from all error.—Arthur W. Pink.

THE CHRISTIAN SABBATH.

What does God's Word teach about the Sabbath? When was the Sabbath instituted: at Sinai, or before? Was it appointed for Israel, or does it impose a binding obligation upon all men? Has the fourth commandment in the Decalogue been repealed, or is it still in force? What did Christ teach concerning the Sabbath? What have the Epistles to say upon the Sabbath? If the Sabbath-law has not been revoked, *which day* ought we to keep holy? If the Sabbath observance is a duty binding upon Christians, *how* does God require us to spend that day? These are questions which ought to arouse God's people, who should desire, above all things, a knowledge of His will and grace to conform thereto. But before we seek to furnish answers to these questions, we must prepare the way by first asking, *Is there* a "Christian Sabbath"?

Is there such a thing as *a Christian "Sabbath"?* Some of the leading Bible teachers of the day answer, emphatically, There is not. They say that such an expression is a contradiction in terms. They challenge us to find the words anywhere in the Bible. And because this cannot be done, many people rashly conclude that there is no such thing as a Christian Sabbath. And yet, these same people speak frequently of "Christian baptism". What will happen when we declare that nowhere in the Bible is *that* expression to be found! Will *that* prove there is no such thing *as* Christian baptism? In like manner, we read nowhere in the New Testament of the Christian dispensation, of the Christian life, or of the Christian anything. The fact is that the word "Christian" as an adjective is never used once in God's Word. Therefore, *the absence* of such an expression as "the Christian Sabbath" *proves nothing,* one way or the other.

But if "the Christian Sabbath" is a non-scriptural expression are we justified in *using* it? Does not the fact that *man* has coined the term prove, or at least go far to show, that that for which it stands is also *a human invention?* Not necessarily. "Christian baptism" is a non-scriptural term, but does this *forbid* our use of it? Certainly not. How, then, are we to decide on such matters? Is each man to be a law unto himself? Is it to be left to an arbitrary decision? Surely not. What, then, is the principle which is to determine the *legitimacy* of such non-scriptural expressions? Plainly it is this: Does the thing which we designate "Christian" have an objective existence in the New Testament? We speak of "the Holy Trinity", of "the Divine Incarnation", of "the substitutionary work of Christ", yet none of these *expressions* are found in Scripture. Nevertheless, the realities are; and it is *this* which justifies our use of them. To speak of Christian baptism is perfectly in order, because the New Testament describes baptisms, under Divine authority, after the Christian dispensation had commenced.

Our inquiry, then, narrows itself down to this: Does God require His people to keep a "Sabbath" *during this Christian dispensation?* If He does, then such a Sabbath is, necessarily, a *Christian* Sabbath. If He does not, then that is the end of the matter. The issue is very simple. It is not an academical one, where a knowledge of Hebrew and Greek are essential to the settlement of it. It is not a matter of terms at all, and those who seek to make it such are simply *evading* the real issue. Nor does our *fundamental* inquiry concern *which* particular day of the week is to be set apart for rest and worship, though that phase of our subject will be carefully examined in its proper place. No, we repeat, it is simply a question as to whether or not *God requires* those living today to keep the Sabbath holy. And those who have read carefully our previous papers on the Law, ought to have no difficulty in anticipating the scriptural answer.

The question as to whether or not God requires those living today to keep the Sabbath day holy is only a part of a larger question, namely, Has the moral Law of God been abolished, or is it still in force? Are the Ten Commandments now binding on all who live during this Christian dispensation? In our previous articles we have shown that God still imposes the obligation of conformity to the demands of His moral Law on all rational creatures, inasmuch as that Law has never been revoked. Hence, it follows that the keeping of the Sabbath is still a moral obligation resting on all alive on earth today, for the fourth of those commandments expressly says, "Remember the Sabbath day to keep it holy". There is only one possible way by which our previous arguments on the perpetuity of the Law, now applied to the Christian Sabbath, could be overthrown; and that is by pointing to some verse in the New Testament in which we read that the fourth commandment of the Decalogue has been *repealed.* And this we confidently affirm *cannot be done.* The New Testament may be read diligently from cover to cover, but it will be searched in vain to find one single categorical declaration that the Sabbath-law has been abrogated. As, then, the fourth commandment *has not been repealed,* and as the New Testament teaches explicitly, again and again, that the moral Law *is binding* on Christians, then it follows of invincible necessity that *there is* a "Christian Sabbath", and that Christians are under bonds to keep it holy.

And right here we might rest our case, fully assured that none can successfully assail it from Scripture. But as the New Testament does not leave the matter at the point we have now reached, neither shall we. We propose, therefore, to show that not only does the New Testament contain no word which declares the Sabbath has been abolished, but that it *does* teach that the Sabbath *remains* for this dispensation, yea, and in that which follows it. But before examining the New Testament scriptures, we shall go first to the Old Testament, principally for the purpose of showing how entirely erroneous are the oft-made assertions that the Sabbath was never designed for any but Israelites and that the Sabbath-law was first promulgated at Sinai.

1. THE INSTITUTION OF THE SABBATH.

"And on the seventh day God ended His work which He had made; and He rested on the seventh day from all His work which He had made. And God blessed the seventh day, and sanctified it: because that in it He had rested from all His work which God created and made" (Gen. 2:2, 3). This passage records the *institution* of the Sabbath. Lest any should wish to cavil because the word "Sabbath" is not found in Gen. 2:2, 3, we call attention to the fact that in Ex. 20:11 Jehovah Himself expressly terms that *first* "seventh day" the "Sabbath day": "For in six days the Lord made heaven and earth, the sea, and all that in them is, and rested *the seventh day:* wherefore the Lord blessed *the Sabbath day* and hallowed it".

The second chapter of Genesis opens with the words, "Thus the heavens and the earth were finished, and all the host of them". And then, the very next thing we read of is the institution of the Sabbath rest. Thus, to institute the Sabbath was God's *first* act after the earth had been made fit for human habitation! Let us now point out four things in connection with this first scripture in which the Sabbath is referred to.

1. The primal Sabbath was a *rest day*. Emphasis is laid upon this feature by the repetition in thought which is found in the two parts of Gen. 2:2. First, on the seventh day "God *ended His work*" which He had made"; second, "And He *rested* on the seventh day *from all His work* which He had made". Therefore the prime element and basic truth connected with the Sabbath is *rest*. Before raising the question as to *why* God "rested", let us offer a few words upon the *nature* of His rest.

It has been said repeatedly by a certain class of expositors, that this rest of God consisted of His *satisfaction* in the work of His hands; that it was God looking out in *complacency* over His fair creation. But, we are told, that this "rest" of God did not last for long: it was rudely broken by the entrance of sin, and ever since man fell God has been "working": John 5:17 being appealed to in proof. That such a definition of the "rest" of God in Gen. 2:2 should have been received by a large number of the Lord's people, only goes to show how few of them ever do much thinking or studying for themselves. It also proves how the most purile interpretations of Scripture are likely to be accepted, providing they are made by reputable teachers, who on other matters are worthy of respect. Finally, it demonstrates what a real need there is for every one of us to humbly, prayerfully, and diligently bring *everything* we read and hear to a rigid examination in the light of Holy Scripture.

That God's "rest" in Gen. 2:2 *was not* the complacence of the Creator prior to the entrance of sin, is unequivocally evidenced by the fact that Satan had fallen before the time contemplated in that verse. How could God look abroad upon creation with Divine contentment when the highest creature of all had become the basest and blackest of sinners? How could God find satisfaction in all the works of His hands when the anointed cherub had apostatized, and in his rebellion had dragged down with him "the third part" of the angels (Rev. 12:4)? No; this is manifestly untenable. Some other definition of God's "rest" must therefore be sought.

Now we need to pay very close attention to the exact wording here (as everywhere). Gen. 2:2 *does not* say (nor does Ex. 20:10) that God rested from *all* work, for that was not true. Gen. 2:2 is careful to say, "On the seventh day God ended His work *which He had made*", and "He rested on the seventh day from all His work which He *had made*". And *this* brings out and calls attention to the basic feature and primal element in the Sabbath: *it is a resting from the activities commonly pursued during the six working days*. But the Sabbath day is not appointed as a day for the cessation of *all* activities—to remain in bed and sleep through that day would not be spending the Sabbath as God requires it to be spent. What particular works *are* required and are permissible, we shall show later; but what we now press upon the reader is the fact that, according to Gen. 2:2, the Sabbath rest consists of resting from the labors of the working week.

Gen. 2:2 does not state that on the seventh day God did no work, for, as we have said, that would not have been true. God *did* work on the seventh day, though His activities on the seventh day were of a different nature from the ones in which He had been engaged during the preceding days. And herein we see not only the marvellous accuracy of Scripture, but the perfect example God here set before His creatures, for as we shall yet see *there are* works suited to the Sabbath. For God to have ceased *all* work on that first seventh day in human history, would have meant total destruction of all creation. God's *providential* working could not cease, or no provision would be made for the supply of His creatures' wants. "All things" needed to be "upheld" or they would have passed back into nonentity.

Let us fix it firmly in our minds that *rest is not inertia*. The Lord Jesus has entered into "rest" (Heb. 4:10), yet is He not inactive, for He ever liveth "to make intercession". And when the saints shall enter their eternal rest, *they* shall not be inactive, for it is written, "And His servants shall *serve* Him" (Rev. 22:3). So here with God. His rest on that first day was not a rest of total inactivity. He rested from the work of creation and restoration, but He then began (and has never ceased) the work of Providence—the providing of supplies for His myriad creatures.

But now the question arises, *Why* did God rest on the seventh day? Why did He so order it that all the works recorded in Gen. 1 were completed in six days, and that then He *rested?* Certainly it was not because the Creator *needed* rest, for "the Creator of the ends of the earth *fainteth not*, neither is weary" (Isa. 40:28). Why, then, *did* He "rest", and why is it so recorded on the top of the second page of Holy Writ? Surely there can be only one answer: As an *example* for man! Nor is this answer merely a logical or plausible inference of ours. It rests on Divine authority. It is based directly upon the words of none other than the Son of God, for He expressly declared, "The Sabbath was made for man" (Mark 2:27): made not for God, but *for man*. Nothing could be plainer, nothing simpler, nothing more unequivocal.

2. The next thing that we would carefully note in this initial reference to the Sabbath is, that Gen. 2:3 tells us this day was *blessed* by God: "And God blessed the seventh day". The reason why God *blessed* the seventh day was not because it *was* the *seventh,* but because "in it He had *rested*". Hence, when the Sabbath law was written upon the tables of stone, God did not say, "Remember the *seventh* day to keep it holy", but, "Remember the *Sabbath* day to keep it holy". And again, He did not say, "He blessed the *seventh* day and hallowed it" but "He blessed the *Sabbath* day and hallowed it".

But why should He? Why single out the seventh day thus? Young's Concordance defines the Hebrew word for "blessed" here as "to *declare* blessed". But why should God have "declared" the *seventh* day 'blessed'? for there is no hint that He pronounced any of the other days blessed. Surely it was not for the mere *day's* sake. Only one other alternative remains: God declared the seventh day blessed because it was *the Sabbath* day, and because He would have every reader of His Word know, right at the beginning, that special Divine *blessing* marks its observance. This at once refutes a modern heresy and removes an aspersion which many cast upon God. The Sabbath was not appointed to bring man into bondage. It was not designed to be a burden, but a blessing! And if history demonstrates anything, it demonstrates beyond a peradventure that the family or nation which has kept the Sabbath day holy, has been markedly *blest* of God; and contrariwise, that the family or nation which has desecrated the Sabbath, has been *curst* of God. Explain it as we may, the fact remains.

3. Gen. 2:3 teaches us that the Sabbath was a day *set apart for sacred use*. This comes out plainly in the words, "And God blessed the seventh day and *sanctified* it"—"And God blessed the seventh day and *hallowed* it" (R. V.). The prime meaning (according to its scriptural usage) of the Heb. word rendered "sanctified" and "hallowed", is *"to set apart for a sacred use"*. This shows that here in Gen. 2:3 we have something more than a historical reference to the resting of God on the seventh day, and something more, even, than God setting an *example* before His creatures. The fact that we are told God "sanctified" it, proves conclusively that here we have the original *institution* of the Sabbath, the Divine appointment of it for man's use and observance. As exemplified by the Creator Himself, the Sabbath day is *separated* from the six preceding days of manual labor.

4. Let us call attention to a notable *omission* in Gen. 2:3. If the reader will turn to Gen. 1 he will find that at the close of each of the six working days the Holy Spirit says "And the evening and the morning were", etc.—see Gen. 1:5, 8, 13, 19, 23, 31. But here in Gen. 2:2, 3 we do not read, "And the evening and the morning were the seventh day"; nor are we told what took place in the eighth day. In other words, the Holy Spirit has not *mentioned* the *ending* of the "seventh day". Why is this? There is a reason for every omission in Scripture, a Divine reason: and there is a reason why the Holy Spirit omitted the usual formula at the close of the seventh day. We suggest that this omission is a silent but most significant intimation that the *observance* of the Sabbath never would end—it was to be perpetuated as long as time should last*.

Before we proceed further, let it be said that Gen. 2 contains nothing

---

* No doubt there is a *dispensational* reason too for the omission of "the evening and the morning were the seventh day".

whatever which enables us to determine *which* day of our week this primal "seventh day" was. We have absolutely no means of knowing whether that original seventh day fell on a Saturday, a Sunday, or any other day of the week; for the simple reason that we are quite unable to ascertain on which day that first week began. All we do know, and it is all which is *necessary* for us to know, is, that the seventh day was the day which followed six days of manual work. As to *which* day of the week is the Christian Sabbath will be considered later.

Ere passing from Gen. 2 let us duly weigh the fact that this notice of the Divine institution of the Sabbath *is placed almost at the very beginning of Holy Writ*. Nothing takes precedence save the brief announcement in the first two verses of Gen. 1 and the description of the six days' work of creation and restoration. This at once impresses us with the great importance which God Himself places upon the Sabbath and its observance. *Before* a single page of human history is chronicled, before a single act of Adam is described, the Holy Spirit places before us the institution of the Sabbath! Does not this signify, plainly, that the observance of the Sabbath —the sanctifying of a seventh day—is a *primary* duty! Moreover, are we not thereby plainly warned that failure to keep the Sabbath day holy is a sin of the first magnitude! Let us consider next,

II. THE PRIMITIVE OBSERVANCE OF THE SABBATH.

By the primitive observance of the Sabbath we refer to the recognition and keeping of a Sabbath *before* the formal proclamation of the Decalogue at Sinai. It is frequently asserted that the Sabbath Law originated at the time when Jehovah wrote the Ten Commandments on the two tables of stone. But as we have already shown, this is an error. The Sabbath was instituted before the fall. It is one of the two things (the marriage tie and the Sabbath) which come to us out of Eden. But in this second section we are to discuss the primitive observance of the Sabbath.

Is there any inspired record of men keeping the Sabbath before Israel reached Sinai? In seeking an answer to this, we have to turn to the book of Genesis and the first eighteen chapters of Exodus, and ere we consult them, it is well to remember their general character. No less than twenty-five hundred years of human history are covered by those first sixty-eight chapters of the Bible. Thus it is evident at once that the Holy Spirit has seen fit to give us little more than a fragmentary account of what transpired during the infancy of our race. Therefore, we must not expect to find here anything more than a *few* references to the Sabbath, and these of the *briefest* nature. The same will apply to almost any other theme. If we confined ourself to the first sixty-eight chapters of the Bible, and took up the study of the person of the Holy Spirit, the light possessed by believers on what lies beyond death, the subject of prayer, angels, temperance, or any other moral virtue, while we should find *something* said about each of these subjects, we should not find *very much*, in fact, little more than hints and fragmentary notices. So it is in connection with the Sabbath. There *are* unmistakeable references to the Sabbath, but they are few in number and incidental in character.

1. We ask the reader to turn to Gen. 4:3 and note thoughtfully the marginal reading—which, as usual, is to be preferred to the reading in the text. "And *at the end of days* it came to pass, that Cain brought of the fruit of the ground an offering unto the Lord". Here the Holy Spirit has seen well to call our attention to the *time* when Cain (and Abel likewise: see Gen. 4:4, "And Abel he *also*", etc.)

brought his offering to the Lord. The bringing of offerings by Cain and Abel was the formal recognition of God. It was an act of worship. Now, why has the Holy Spirit told us that the sons of Adam and Eve worshipped God at "the end of days", if it is not to intimate that they worshipped at the *Divinely appointed* season? And when was that? What is signified by "the end of days"? Surely the unprejudiced reader who comes to the Scriptures in childlike simplicity, desiring to learn the mind of God, will form only one conception here. Surely he will naturally say, Why, the end of days must be *the end of the week*, and that, of course, is *the Sabbath*. Very ingenious, says the objector; but altogether lacking in proof. Not so, is our reply; for in this article we shall not base our appeal upon anything that is not backed up by clear Scripture proof.

What is meant by "the *end* of days"? We have suggested above, that it signifies the end of the week, that is, the end of the work-days. How can this be proven? In a very simple way: by an appeal to the context. If the first three chapters of Genesis be read through, it will be found they mention one "end" and *one only*, and that is in Gen. 2:2. There we read, "And on the seventh day God *ended* His work which He had made". Thus the only "ending" referred to in the context is the ending of *the six days' work*. Now, as Scripture ever interprets Scripture, as it defines its terms by the way they are used in other passages, and as the law of the context is what ever fixes the meaning of any given clause, so here in Gen. 4:3; the *"end* of days" means, *and can only mean*, the end of the working week; therefore, it was on the Sabbath day, that Cain and Abel, according to Divine appointment, brought their offerings to the Lord as an expression of their worship. We say *by Divine appointment*, and we appeal to Heb. 11:4 in proof. It was *"by faith"* that Abel offered unto God, and as faith "cometh by *hearing"* (Rom. 10:17), Abel must have heard *what* God required and *when* He required this formal recognition and worship of Himself.

Here, then, in Gen. 4:3 we have a scripture which proves four things: first, that previously to the days of Cain and Abel a Sabbath had been instituted. Second, that this Sabbath came at the end of a week of work. Third, that it was recognized by the sons of Adam and Eve. Fourth, that it was set apart for sacred use, namely, the worship of God.

2. We turn next to Gen. 5:29: "And he called his son Noah (rest), saying, This same shall comfort us concerning *our work* and *toil of our hands*, because of the ground which the Lord hath cursed". Let it be said that, we do not *base* any argument on this verse, nor do we adduce it as one of our proof texts for the primitive observance of the Sabbath. We simply call attention to it as a scripture of interest in this connection; though personally, the writer regards it as one of significance and as one that contains more than a hint that there *was* a Sabbath instituted and recognized long before the time of Moses.

The verse just quoted above gives us the reason *why* Lamech named his son "Noah". The fact that the Holy Spirit has recorded this at all at once shows there must be some good reason for it. Names were not given in those early days at the idle caprice of the parents. They were pregnant with meaning; they were frequently given under Divine guidance, and they often memorialized some event of importance. Plainly this was so in our present instance. Lamech belonged to the godly line. He was the son of Methuselah (whose name was certainly given under Divine impulse*);

---

* See the author's article in "Gleanings in Genesis".

the grandson of Enoch. Now Lamech called his son Noah, which means *rest*, and his avowed reason for thus naming him was, "This same shall comfort us concerning *our work* and *toil* of our hands". In the light of Gen. 2:2, 3 is not this profoundly suggestive? Was there not here a reference to the weekly Sabbath? Did not Lamech, in the name given his son, express his gratitude to the great Creator for having provided a weekly Sabbath, as a rest *from* "work" and "toil"?! It was a pious heart looking forward to the *Rest* of which the weekly Sabbath was both the type and pledge.

3. "And it came to pass *on the seventh day*, that the waters of the flood were upon the earth" (Gen. 7:10, margin). This verse records the beginning of the great deluge. It is all the more noteworthy because in the next verse we read, "In the six hundredth year of Noah's life, in the second month, in the seventeenth day of the month, the same day were all the fountains of the great deep broken up and the windows of heaven were opened". Now surely the Holy Spirit has some good reason for giving us *both* of these time-marks. He tells us that the flood commenced in the six hundredth year of Noah's life, which was on the seventeenth day of the second month. This is clearly an *historic* reference. Nothing could be more definite. Why, then, has He *also* told us, *first*, that the waters of the flood were on the earth "on the *seventh* day"? Clearly, because the reference here is a *moral* one. It is an explanatory word. It gives us to see one of the reasons, perhaps one of the chief ones, *why* God visited the earth in such sore judgment. And it conveys a solemn message to us. *The flood began on the Sabbath day!* Is not the inference inescapeable? Is there not only one conclusion we can possibly draw from this? Was it not an act of, what men term, poetic justice? Or, to use a figure of Scripture, were not the antediluvians now commencing to reap *what* they had sown? Without a doubt, they had flouted the Sabbath institution, as they had every other law of God. They had desecrated the holy day. Therefore, when God visited them in judgment, it was on *the Sabbath day* that the flood commenced!!

4. "And he stayed yet other *seven days* .... and he stayed yet other *seven days*" (Gen. 8:10, 12). These references (and to them may be added Gen. 29:27) afford further proof that back in Noah's days the division of time into *weeks* was a recognized custom. This fact has not received the attention it deserves. How was it, why was it, and when originated *this* division of time? We quote here from the late Dr. B. H. Carroll, President of the S. W. Baptist Seminary:—

"I ask you to notice this strange historical fact, that for all other divisions of time we have a reason in the motions of the heavenly bodies. The revolution of the earth around the sun marks the division of time into years. The moon's revolution around the earth gives us the month. The day comes from the revolution of the earth upon its axis. But from what suggestion of nature do you get the division of time into weeks? It is a positive and arbitrary division. It is based on authority. The chronicles of the ages record its recognition. But how did it originate?

"Here in the oldest book, in the first account of man, you will find its origin and purpose. Noah twice recognized it in the ark, when he waited *seven days* each time to send out his dove. Jacob in the days of his courtship, found it prevalent when he looked for satisfaction in the laughing eyes of Rachel, and the stern father said, 'Fulfill her week'. Why *a week?* How did he get it? It was *God's* division of time."

Yes, it *was* God's division of time;

and there is only one way of accounting for it, and that is, the Maker of man set apart one seventh of his days for the worship of the Lord Almighty. And while time shall last—and it shall never end—this will not be changed. Even when this earth has passed away, and there has been created the new earth, wherein righteousness shall dwell, and in which no trace of sin shall be found, the same division of time into weeks will obtain, and (as we shall yet *prove)* the Sabbath will still be observed.

5. We ask the reader to turn now to Ex. 16, from which we may learn several things of importance concerning the Sabbath. This chapter records the sending of the manna, as Israel's daily food while they were in the wilderness. Ex. 16 treats of a point in Israel's history *prior* to their arrival at Sinai. This cannot be gainsaid. And yet, in this very chapter, the *Sabbath* is expressly mentioned!

Look first at vv. 4 and 5: "Then said the Lord unto Moses, Behold, I will rain bread from heaven for you; and the people shall go out and gather a certain rate every day, that I may prove them, whether they will walk in My law or no. And it shall come to pass, that on the sixth day they shall prepare that which they bring in; and it shall be twice as much as they gather daily". These verses plainly anticipate what is said later in vv. 22 and 23. God was about to give Israel a daily supply of manna. But on the sixth day the supply would be a *double* one—"twice as much"—because on the seventh day none would be sent. In this respect Ex. 16 is parallel with Gen. 2:2, 3, inasmuch as once more God condescends to be the Examplar of His people. Jehovah evidenced *His* respect for the Sabbath, by withholding the manna on that day. "We may here observe that three miracles in honor of the Sabbath, and to secure it against desecration, were wrought every week before the promulgation of the Law at Sinai. Double the quantity of manna fell on the sixth day. None fell on the Sabbath. The manna preserved for that day did not corrupt" (Robert Haldane).

In the second place, observe carefully God's avowed purpose in thus withholding manna from Israel on the seventh day. His express design was, "to *prove* them, whether they will walk in My law, or no". And mark it, this was said to Moses *before* they had reached Sinai! There *was*, then, a *"Law"* of God in existence *before* the Ten Commandments were inscribed on the tables of stone! And, unequivocally, the observance of the Sabbath was part of that Law! In no other way can these words of God to Moses be explained. How this exposes the widely received error of our day, that the Ten Commandments were given at Sinai for the *first* time, is evident.

In the third place, let us ponder v. 23: "And he said unto them, This is that which the Lord hath said, Tomorrow is the rest of the holy Sabbath unto the Lord: bake that which ye shall bake today, and seethe that which ye will seethe; and that which remaineth over lay up for you to be kept until the morning". Note, Moses did not say, "This is that which the Lord *will say*", but "This is that which the Lord *hath said*". What was it, then, that the Lord *had* said? This: "Tomorrow is the rest of the holy Sabbath unto the Lord". These words *repeat* the three primal features of the Sabbath: first, it is designed for "rest"; second, it is "holy"—set apart from the six working days; third, it is to be kept "unto the Lord"; that is, it is a day for Divine worship.

In the fourth place, note carefully vv. 27 and 28: "And it came to pass, that there went out some of the people on the seventh day for to gather, and they found none. And the Lord said unto Moses, How long refuse ye to keep My commandments and My laws?" Here we have illustrated the universal rebellion of the human heart. Here we have exemplified the common tendency to desecrate God's holy day. Even after the most explicit instructions to *rest* on the seventh day (v. 23), some of the people went out "*for* to gather". And mark God's response—"*How long* refuse ye *to keep* My commandments and My laws?" This was not the first time Israel had profaned the Sabbath. The words "How long" prove this! They also confirm what we said above on v. 4: "*long*" *before Sinai* was reached, Israel *had* God's "commandments" and "laws"! Jehovah Himself says so, and the man who denies, no matter what his standing or reputation, is guilty of the awful sin of making God a liar. "How long refuse ye" look back to the wicked conduct of Israel while in Egypt*.

Finally, observe how v. 29 supplies one more proof that Sabbath-observance was no new thing at this time: "See, for that the Lord hath given you the Sabbath, therefore He giveth you on the sixth day the bread of two days; abide ye every man in his place, let no man go out of his place on the seventh day". Mark the careful distinction observed in the verbs here: "The Lord *hath given* you the Sabbath, therefore He *giveth* you on the sixth day the bread of two days". What excuseless ignorance, then, is betrayed by those who affirm that the Sabbath was first instituted at Sinai. It is either ignorance or wilful perversion of the Scriptures, and charity requires us to conclude that it must surely be the former.

(To be continued, D. V.)
—Arthur W. Pink.

O Lord Jehovah, how little is it that we poor mortals know of Thy supreme Deity, and Thy incomprehensible perfections! How little do

* Let the reader consult Lev. 17:7; Josh. 24:14; Ezek. 20:8.

our thoughts of Thee correspond to the immensity of Thy essence, of Thy perfections, and of Thy sovereignty over the creatures! What mortal can take upon him to circumscribe within his own limits where Thou dost not lead the way! This we know, Lord, that Thou art indebted to none, and that there is none who can say to Thee, What doest Thou, and why Doest Thou so? that Thou art also holy, and infinitely good, and therefore a lover and rewarder of holiness. May the consciousness of our ignorance in other things kindle in our hearts an ineffable desire of that beautific vision, by which, knowing as we are known, we may, in the abyss of Thy infinity, behold those things, which we cannot now reach by force of thought.

—Herman Witsius, 1693.

Our Lord affirmed that such or such an event *should* come to pass. Its accomplishment, therefore, was unavoidable. The antecedent is infallible: by parity of argument, the consequent is so too. For the consequent is not in the power of a created being, forasmuch as Christ affirmed these things. Neither did Christ affirm anything accidentally. Seeing, then, that His affirmation was not accidental, but necessary; it follows, that the event affirmed by Him must be necessary likewise. This argument receives additional strength, by observing, that, in what way soever God may declare His will by His after-discoveries of it in time; still, His determination, concerning the event, took place before the world was made: *ergo*, the event will surely follow. The necessity, therefore, of the antecedent, holds no less irrefragably for the necessity of the consequent. And who can either promote or hinder the inference, namely, that this was decreed of God before the foundation of the world?

—John Wickliff, 1360.

(Continued from page 225.)

"have no fellowship with the unfruitful works of darkness" (Eph. 5:11). Better not give at all, than give to any one or any thing which is displeasing to the Lord. Our line of duty then is clear; first, to make most *careful investigation;* second, to have *no fellowship* with any thing we are not certain is thoroughly in accord with God's Word.

The writer is having less and less *direct* financial fellowship with men or with institutions. Numbers of the Lord's servants, both in the home land and abroad, are known to him personally, and while in many respects they are preaching the truth, in a number of important particulars they are teaching contrary to the truth, and to have fellowship with these brethren would also be to have fellowship with their erroneous teaching, and this he is sure is displeasing to God. What alternative, then, offers itself? This: if he knows of a really helpful book, in which after a careful reading (i. e. testing it by the Word of God) he fails to find any false teaching, he makes careful inquiries in the endeavor to locate young preachers (the great majority of the older preachers seem too self-sufficient to be helped) who are in need of such a work, and make them a gift of it.

It is this side of the work which we are particularly desirous of developing in connection with the magazine. Studies in the Scriptures is now being sent out free to about one hundred missionaries, and fifty more have been approached to see if they desire to be placed on our free list. Pages might be filled with the letters we have already received from almost every part of the earth, telling what a blessing this little publication has proved, under God, to their souls. Several of our readers have had fellowship with us in this sending forth of the magazine to the Lord's servants in distant lands, and we feel sure that others would do so if they would definitely look to the Lord about it. Let not this be construed as an indirect appeal for ourselves. It is not. If our friends sent in gifts to enable us to send out the magazine to another hundred missionaries, we should not make a single cent of profit. It is for the sake of those who are now cut off from all oral ministry, and who are hungering for soul food, that this suggestion is submitted to our readers.

Here, then, is a way by which Christians may contribute to the Lord's work, and yet have *no fellowship* with any errors the Lord's servants may be propagating. Locate a magazine or a book that is thoroughly sound, and then send *it* to those who need it. And we do not ask you to make an exception of us. *Test* our writings rigidly by God's Word, and if you find they do not measure up to that Word, then do not have any fellowship with us. But if, according to the light you have, you find our writings scriptural and profitable to the soul, weigh this suggestion *before the Lord.*

One friend recently received such a blessing from our book on "The Sovereignty of God", they ordered seventy copies to be sent to as many foreign countries. Another friend ordered one hundred and twenty-five copies of our book on "The Divine Inspiration of the Scriptures" to be sent to as many students and preachers. The Bible Truth Depot of Swengel, Pa. (which is conducted *solely* for God's glory, the edification of the saints, and the salvation of sinners) is willing to make special prices on any of its own publications which are to be used in *free* distribution—this must be definitely specified. May the Lord be pleased to prompt some who read this article to emulate the example set by those named above. If this is a message from God pray over it, and then act as *He* guides.—Arthur W. Pink.

STUDIES in the SCRIPTURES

"Search the Scriptures" John 5:39.

A PERIODICAL (MONTHLY "IF THE LORD WILL")
DEVOTED TO BIBLE STUDIES and EXPOSITIONS

Associate Editors and Publishers, I. C. HERENDEEN and ARTHUR W. PINK,

Swengel, Pa.

Price: **10** cents per copy: **$1.00** per year. Foreign **$1.00** per year.

TO OUR SCRIPTURE STUDY FAMILY—

"It is not meet to take the children's bread and cast it to dogs" (Matt. 15:26).
In these words our Lord uttered a warning which many of our present-day preachers and teachers need to take to heart. The conditions under which this statement was made by Christ were exceptional, but its principle is of general application. A Gentile woman approached Him, crying, "Have mercy on me, O Lord, *Thou Son of David*". In thus addressing Him she was excluding herself from the desired blessing. As "Son of David" (King of the Jews) He is related to none but Israelites. It was not until she dropt "the Son of David", and owned Him simply as "Lord", that her request was granted. In answering her "It is not meet to take the children's bread and to cast it to dogs", she was reminded that a Gentile had no right to what was the exclusive property of the Jews.

"It is not meet to take the children's bread and cast it to dogs". Reducing these words to a simple principle we may paraphrase them thus: It is unlawful to take that which belongs alone to the people of God and give it to the unregenerate. There are many truths which God has graciously made known for the comfort of His saints that are not for the unsaved at all. Many of these truths are found in the Epistles—which are addressed exclusively to the children of God—and it is a most serious perversion of God's Word to take and apply them to God's enemies. To take the promises and many of the doctrinal declarations found in the Church Epistles, and expound them as though they belonged to saint and sinner alike, is not only to take the *children's* "bread" and cast it to *dogs*, but it is also to be guilty of casting pearls before swine!

"Work out your own salvation with fear and trembling" (Phil. 2:12), is addressed not to the human race at large, but exclusively to those who have already passed from death unto life. This is evidenced by the fact (to mention no other proofs) that the text says, "Work out *your own* salvation". They are to "work out" a salvation *already theirs*. But this passage has not been so flagrantly mis-applied as many others. For example: the wellknown text, "God is love". This occurs in an epistle addressed to the family of God, but from the modern use made of it one would suppose it was to be found in the book of Acts, in the sermons of Peter and Paul to unsaved people. Apart from John 3:16 (which we have expounded at length elsewhere) God's love is *never mentioned* in the New Testament outside of the Epistles. To preach God's love to the unsaved is to take the children's bread and cast it to dogs. What sinners need to hear about is the holy wrath of a sin-hating God: they need arousing and alarming, not soothing.

(Continued on page 288.)

IMPORTANT NOTICES

All new subscriptions will be dated back to January, 1923.

Set of twelve issues for 1922, unbound, $1.00. Bound, $1.50.

Note: We cannot break a set or now supply any single 1922 issues.

Subscription Price: $1.00 per year to any address in the world. Single copies 10 cents.

Change of Address: Please notify us promptly of any change of address, and be certain to give both old and new addresses.

Non-Subscribers receiving this Magazine regularly will understand their subscription has been entered by a friend.

Copies lost in the mail duplicated only if we are notified promptly.

Entered as second-class matter December 15th, 1921 at the post office at Swengel, Pa., under Act of March 3rd, 1879.

CONTENTS

John's Gospel (John 6:14-27) ... 258
Antichrist and Babylon 268
The Sabbath (Continued) 279
Exposition of First Peter 284

JOHN'S GOSPEL

21. CHRIST WALKING ON THE SEA: John 6:14-27.

We begin with our customary Analysis of the passage which is to be before us:

1. The Response of the people to the miracle of the loaves: vv. 14, 15.

2. The Retirement of Christ to the mount: v. 15.

3. The Disciples in the Storm: vv. 16-19.

4. The Coming of Christ to them: vv. 20, 21.

5. The people follow Christ to Capernaum: vv. 22-25.

6. Christ exposes their motive: v. 26.

7. Christ presses their spiritual need upon them: v. 27.

The opening verses of the passage before us contain the sequel to what is described in the first thirteen verses of John 6. There we read of the Lord ministering, in wondrous grace, to a great multitude of hungry people. They had no real appreciation of His blessed person, but had been attracted by idle curiosity and the love of the sensational—"Because they saw His miracles which He did on them that were diseased" (v. 2). Nevertheless, the Son of God, in tenderest pity, had supplied their need by means of the loaves and the fishes. What effect, then, did this have upon them?

Christ had manifested His Divine power. There was no gainsaying that. The crowd were impressed, for we are told, "Then those men, when they had seen the miracle which Jesus did, said, This is of a truth that prophet which should come into the world" (v. 14). The title "that prophet" has already been before us in 1:21. The reference is to Deut. 18:15, where we read that, through Moses God declared, "The Lord thy God will raise up unto thee a prophet from the midst of thee, of thy brethren, like unto Me; unto Him ye shall hearken". These men, then, seemed ready to receive the Lord as their Messiah. And yet how little they realized and recognized what was due Him as "that prophet"—the Son of God incarnate. Instead of falling down before Him as undone sinners, crying for mercy; instead of prostrating themselves at His feet, in reverent worship; instead of owning Him as the Blessed One, worthy of their hearts' adoration, they would "take Him by force and make Him a king" (v. 15); and this, no doubt, for *their own ends*, thinking that He would lead them in a successful revolt against the hated Romans. How empty, then, were their words! How little were their consciences searched or their hearts exercised! How blind they still were to the Light! Had their hearts been opened, the light had shone in, revealing their wretchedness; and then, they would have taken their place as lost and needy sinners. It is the same today.

Many there are who regard our Lord as a Prophet (a wonderful Teacher), who have never seen their need of Him as a Refuge from the wrath to come—a doom they so thoroughly deserve. Let us not be misled, then, by this seeming honoring of Christ by those who eulogize His precepts, but who despise His Cross. It is no more a proof that they are saved who, today, own Christ as a greater than Buddha or Mohammed, than this declaration by these men of old—"This is of a truth that prophet which should come into the world," evidenced that they had "passed from death unto life".

"When Jesus therefore perceived that they would come and take Him by force" (v. 15). This is very solemn. Christ was not deceived by their fair speech. Their words sounded very commendable and laudatory, no doubt, but the Christ of God was, and is, the Reader of hearts. He knew what lay behind their words. He discerned the spirit that prompted them. "Jesus therefore *perceived*", is parallel with John 2:24, 25: "But Jesus did not commit Himself unto them, *because He knew* all, and needed not that any should testify of man: for He *knew* what was in man". "Jesus therefore perceived" is a word that brings before us His Deity. The remainder of v. 15 is profoundly significant and suggestive.

"When Jesus therefore perceived that they would come and take Him by force, to make Him a king, He departed again into a mountain Himself alone" (v. 15). These Jews had owned Him (with their lips) as *Prophet,* and they were ready to crown Him as their *King,* but there is another office that comes in between these. Christ could not be their King until He had first officiated as *Priest,* offering Himself as a Sacrifice for sin! Hence the doctrinal significance of "He departed again into a mountain Himself *alone*", for in His priestly work He is unattended—cf Lev. 16:17!

But there was also a moral and dispensational reason why Christ "departed" when these Jews would use force to make Him a King. He needed not to be *made* "a King", for He was *born* such (Matt. 2:2); nor would He receive the kingdom at *their* hand. This has been brought out beautifully by Mr. J. B. Bellet in his notes on John's Gospel:—"The Lord would not take the kingdom from zeal like this. This could not be the source of the kingdom of the Son of Man. The 'beasts' may take their kingdoms from the winds striving upon the great sea, but Jesus cannot (Dan. 7:2 and 25). This was not, in His ear, the shouting of the people bringing in the headstone of the corner (Zech. 4:7); nor the symbol of His people made willing in the day of His power (Psa. 110:3). This would have been an appointment to the throne of Israel on scarcely better principles than those on which Saul had been appointed of old. His kingdom would have been the fruit of their revolted heart. But that could not be. And besides this, ere the Lord could take His seat on Mount Zion, He must ascend the solitary mount; and ere the people could enter the kingdom, they must go down to the stormy sea. And these things we see reflected here as in a glass".

The time for the reign of Christ had not arrived. First, because the way to the Throne was via the Cross. Moreover, the present parenthetical dispensation must first run its course, during which time Israel are set aside for their unbelief, and God is now visiting the Gentiles, to take out of them a people for His name (Acts 15:14); during which time Christ is on high as our great High Priest making intercession for His people below. Second, because Israel are not yet ready for their King. As a nation they continue in unbelief till this present dispensation is ended: hence, we see Christ "retiring", ascending the mount *alone*, which intimates that the Lord would be on high during the postponement of the kingdom. And before He comes back to the earth, before the kingdom is established in Zion, Israel must "repent"—"I will go and return to My place, till they acknowledge their offence, and seek My face: in their affliction they will seek Me early" (Hosea 5:15, and cf Matt. 3:2). Then, when the Father's time has come (Acts 1:6, 7), and Israel has said "Blessed is He that cometh in the name of the Lord" (Matt. 23:39), Christ shall return, receiving the kingdom not at the hands of man, but from the Father—see Psa. 2:6; Dan. 7:13, 14; Luke 19:12.

It should be noted that Matthew tells us how Christ "went up into a mountain apart *to pray*" (14:23); so, too, Mark (6:46). The absence of this word in John is in beautiful accord with the character and theme of this fourth Gospel, and supplies us with another of those countless proofs for the Divine and verbal inspiration of the Scriptures. In this Gospel we never see Christ *praying* (John 17 is *intercession*, giving us a sample of His priestly ministry on our behalf in heaven: note particularly vv. 4 and 5, which indicate that the intercession recorded in the verses that follow was *anticipatory* of Christ's return to the Father!), for John's special design is to exhibit the *Divine* glories of the Saviour.

"And when even was now come, His disciples went down unto the sea, and entered into a ship" (vv. 16 and 17). Matthew explains the reason for this: "And straightway Jesus constrained His disciples to get into a ship, and to go before Him unto the other side, while He sent the multitudes away" (14:22). The Lord desired to be alone, so He caused the disciples to go on ahead of Him. It would seem, too, that He purposed to teach them another lesson on faith. This will appear in the sequel.

"And entered into a ship, and went over the sea toward Capernaum, and it was now dark, and Jesus was not come to them" (v. 17). Here, as constantly in the Gospels, we need to distinguish carefully between the spiritual application and the dispensational typification. We shall treat first of the former. What we have here, and in the verses that follow, speaks unmistakeably *to us*. It describes the conditions through which we must pass as we journey to our Home above. Though not of the world, we are necessarily in it: *that* world made up of the wicked, who are like "the troubled sea". The world in which we live, dear reader, is the world that rejected and still rejects the Christ of God. It is the world which "lieth in the Wicked One" (1 John 5:19), the friendship of which is enmity with God (James 4:4). It is a world devoid of spiritual light: a world over which hangs the shadow of death. Peter declares the world is "a dark place" (2 Pet. 1:19). It is dark because "the Light of the world" is absent.

"It was now dark, and Jesus was not come to them" (v. 17). Sometimes Christ withholds the light of His countenance even from His own. Job cried, "When I waited for light, there came darkness" (30:26). But, thank God, it is recorded, "Unto the upright there ariseth light *in* the darkness" (Psa. 112:4). Let us remember that the darkness is not created by Satan, but by God (Isa. 45:7). And He has a wise and good reason for it. Sometimes He withholds the light from His people that they may discover "the *treasures* of darkness" (Isa. 45:3).

"Jesus was not come to them, and the sea arose by reason of the great wind that blew" (v. 18). This tested the faith and patience of the disciples.

The longer they waited the worse things became. It *looked* as though Christ was neglectful of them. It *seemed* as though He had forgotten to be gracious. Perhaps they were saying, If the Master had been here, this storm would not have come up. Had He been with them, even though asleep on a pillow, His presence would have cheered them. But He was not there; and the darkness was about them, and the angry waves all around them—fit emblems of the opposition of the world against the believer's course. It was a real test of their faith and patience.

And similarly does God often test us today. Frequently our circumstances are dark, and conditions are all against us. We cry to the Lord, but He "does not come". But let us remind ourselves, that God is never in a hurry. However much the petulance of unbelief may seek to hasten His hand, He waits His own good time. *Omnipotence* can afford to wait, for it is always sure of success. And because omnipotence is combined with infinite wisdom and love, we may be certain that God not only does everything in the right way, but also at the best time: "And therefore will the Lord *wait*, that He may be gracious unto you, and therefore will He be exalted, that He may have mercy upon you: for the Lord is a God of judgment: blessed are all they that *wait* for Him" (Isa. 30:18).

Sometimes the Lord "waits" until it is eventide before He appears in His delivering grace and power. The darkness becomes more gloomy, and still He *waits*. Yes, but He *waits* "to be gracious". But why? Could He not be gracious without this waiting, and the painful suspense such waiting usually brings to us? Surely; but one reason for the delay is, that *His* hand may be the more evident; and another reason is, that *His* hand may be the more appreciated, when He does intervene. Sometimes the darkness becomes even more gloomy, well-nigh unbearable; and still He *waits*. And again, we wonder, Why? Ah, is it not that all *our* hopes may be disappointed; that *our* plans may be frustrated, till we reach our wit's *end* (Psa. 107:27)! And, then, just as we had given up hope, He breaks forth unexpectedly, and we are startled, as were these disciples on the storm-lashed sea.

"So when they had rowed about twenty-five or thirty furlongs, they see Jesus walking on the sea" (v. 19). These lines will, doubtless, be read by more than one saint who is in a tight place. For you, too, the night is fearfully dark, and the breakers of adverse circumstances look as though they would completely swamp you. O tried and troubled one, read the blessed sequel of John 6:17, 18. It contains a word of cheer for *you*, if your faith lays hold of it. Notice that the disciples did not give up in despair—they continued "rowing" (v. 19)! And ultimately the Lord came to their side and delivered them from the angry tempest. So, dear saint, whatever may be the path appointed by the Lord, however difficult and distasteful, *continue therein*, and in His own good time the Lord *will* deliver you. Again we say, Notice that the disciples continued their "rowing". It was all they could do, and it was all that was required of them. In a little while the Lord appeared, and they were at the land. Oh may God grant both writer and reader, perseverance in the path of duty. Tempted and discouraged one, remember Isa. 30:18 (look it up and memorize it) and *continue rowing!*

There is another thing, a blessed truth, which is well calculated to sustain us in the interval *before* the deliverance comes; and it *will* if the heart appropriates its blessedness. While the storm-tossed disciples were pulling at the oars and making little or no progress, the Lord was on high —not below, but above them—master of the situation. And, as Matthew tells us, He was "praying". And on high He is now *thus* engaged on *our* behalf. Remember this, O troubled one, your great High Priest who is "touched with the feeling of your infirmities" is above, ever living to intercede. *His* prayers undergird you, so that you cannot sink. Mark adds a word that is even more precious— "And *He saw* them toiling in rowing" (6:48). Christ was not indifferent to their peril. His eye was upon them. And even though it was "dark" (John 6:17) He *saw them*. No darkness could hide those disciples from Him. And this, too, speaks to *us*. We may be *"toiling* in rowing" (the Greek word means "fatigued"), weary of the buffeting from the unfriendly winds and waves, but there is One above who is not unconcerned, who sees and knows our painful lot, and who, even now, is preparing to come to our side. Turn your eyes away from your frail barque, away from the surrounding tempest, and "look off unto Jesus, the Author and Finisher of faith" (Heb. 12:1).

"So when they had rowed about five and twenty or thirty furlongs, they see Jesus walking on the sea, and drawing nigh unto the ship: and they were afraid" (v. 19). This shows how little faith was in exercise. Matthew tells us, "And when the disciples saw Him walking on the sea, they were *troubled*" (14:26). Think of it, "troubled" and "afraid" of Jesus! Does some one say, That was because the night was dark and the waves boisterous, consequently it was easy to mistake the Saviour for an apparition? Moreover, the sight they beheld was altogether unprecedented: never before had they seen one walking on the water! But if we turn to Mark's record we shall find that it was not dimness of physical sight which caused the disciples to mistake their Master for a spectre, but dulness of spiritual vision: "They considered not the miracle of the loaves: for *their heart was hardened*". Their fears had mastered them. They were not expecting deliverance. They had already forgotten that exercise of Divine grace and power which they had witnessed only a few short hours before. And how accurately (and tragically) do they portray us—so quickly do we forget the Lord's mercies and deliverances in the past, so little do we really expect Him to answer our prayers of the present.

"But He saith unto them, It is I; be not afraid" (v. 20). This is parallel in thought with what we had before us in v. 10. The scepticism of Philip and the unbelief of Andrew did not prevent the outflow of Divine mercy. So here, even the hardness of heart of these disciples did not quench their Lord's love for them. O how deeply thankful we ought to be that "He hath not dealt with us after our sins; nor rewarded us according to our iniquities" (Psa. 103:10). From beginning to end He deals with us in wondrous, fathomless, sovereign grace. "It is I", He says. He first directs their gaze to Himself. "Be not afraid", was a word to calm their hearts. And this is His unchanging order. Our fears can only be dispelled by looking in faith to and having our hearts occupied with Him. Look around, and we shall be disheartened. Look within, and we shall be discouraged. But look unto Him, and our fears will vanish.

"Then they willingly received Him into the ship: and immediately the ship was at the land whither they went" (v. 21). Now that He had revealed Himself to them; now that He had graciously uttered the heart-calming "Be not afraid"; now that He had (as Matthew and Mark tell us) spoken that wellknown word "Be of good cheer": they "willingly received Him into the ship". Christ does not force Himself upon us: He waits to be "received". It is the welcome of our hearts that He desires. And is it not just because this is so often withheld, that He is so slow in coming to our relief—i. e. "manifesting Himself" to us (John 14:21)! How blessed to note that as soon as *He* entered the ship, the end of the voyage was reached for them. In applying to ourselves the second half of this twenty-first verse, we must not understand it to signify that when Christ has "manifested" Himself unto us that the winds will cease to blow or that the adverse "sea" will now befriend us; far from it. But it means that the *heart* will now have found a Haven of rest: our fears will be quieted; we shall be occupied not with the tempest, but with the Master of it. Such are some of the precious spiritual lessons which we may take to ourselves from this passage. But this is not by any means all that is to be found in it. This portion of God's Word contains a striking dispensational picture, which gives a perfect portrayal of the experiences of the godly Jewish Remnant in the Great Tribulation. Let us now re-examine our passage from this angle.

The first line of the picture is found in v. 15. Here we see the King "departing" from Israel, which suggests, of course, the postponement of the kingdom. Second, the King retires to a "mountain", which was a figure of Him taking His place on high. Third, we are told that "even was now come". It was the end of the day. So, too, the Tribulation period will be "the end of the Age" (Matt. 24:3, etc.). Fourth, the disciples, representing the godly Jewish Remnant, "went down unto the sea" (v. 16), which is ever a figure of the Gentiles. It tells of the Jews, *outside* of their land, scattered among the Nations. Fifth, they "entered into a ship". Thus they were in the sea, but not of it. Among the waves and yet separated by the ship from them. So, too, God has placed a wall around Israel, and prevented them from being assimilated by the Gentiles.

Sixth, they went over the sea "toward Capernaum" (v. 17). Capernaum means, place of consolation, and it is toward the true Place of Consolation that the godly Remnant will have their faces turned at the End-time. Seventh, it was "dark" (v. 17). Since the Light of life departed, it has been particularly dark for Israel; but in the coming Night, to which this dispensational panorama points, it will be doubly so. As Isa. 60:2 tells us, "Behold, the darkness shall cover the earth, and gross darkness *the* people". Eighth, "Jesus was not come *to them*" (v. 17). Intensely pathetic is this. During the present dispensation God is visiting the Gentiles, to take out of them a people for His name (Acts 15:14). Afterwards, as Acts 15 assures us, He will return and build again the tabernacle of David, which is now in ruins. But this will not be until the commencement of the Millennium. During the Tribulation period, which our picture views, Jesus (the Saviour) will not yet have "come" to Israel.

Ninth, "The sea arose by reason of a great wind that blew" (v. 18). Compare Dan. 7:2, and note how that the remainder of the chapter carries us to the end of the Tribulation period. The raging of the sea, symbolizes the final turning of the Gentiles against the Jews, when they will seek to "cut them off from being a nation" (Psa. 83:4). Tenth, those in the ship rowed "about twenty-five or thirty furlongs" (v. 19). This, in which no writer that we have consulted sees any particular significance, is very striking. "Twenty-five *or* thirty furlongs" suggests that we take the midway figure—twenty-seven and one half furlongs, and that gives us *three and one half* miles; and who can fail to see in this a veiled but perfect prefigurement of the Tribulation period, which will last for precisely *three and one half* years!! But why should not the Holy Spirit have *said* "three and one half miles", rather than twenty-five or thirty furlongs? For precisely the same reason that He speaks of the 1260 *days* (Rev. 12:6) when referring to the trials of Israel in the coming Night; rather than the forty-two "months" which He uses when defining the final stage in the career of the Antichrist (Rev. 13:5). The forty-two *months* will seem of brief duration to the Wicked One; but the 1260 *days* will be a well-nigh interminable length of time to the poor persecuted Jews. So, three and one half miles seems a short trip across the waters on a smooth day; but twenty-five or thirty furlongs (twenty-seven and one half to be precise) would be wearisome to those rowing against the tide, with an angry sea battling against them.

Eleventh, the next thing we read is that "they see Jesus walking on the sea, and drawing nigh unto the ship" (v. 19). Here again the picture is Divinely perfect. Note this was *after* they had rowed the twenty-five or thirty furlongs, which, being interpreted, means, that this next line in the picture introduces us to an event *following* the Tribulation period. And what will that be? "Jesus *walking on the sea*", drawing nigh *to the ship* makes answer. The sea, which in its angry rage had been attacking the ship, is here seen *beneath* the feet of Christ. As we have said, the "sea" is a figure of the Gentiles. The Tribulation will terminate with the return of Christ to Israel, when His enemies shall be made *His footstool!!* Twelfth, but as Jesus drew nigh to the ship, those in it were "afraid": they were discomforted. How evidently this foreshadows what we read of in Zech. 12:10: when Israel shall "look upon" Christ, they shall "mourn" and "be in bitterness" as godly sorrow will work repentance in them.

Thirteenth, then Christ addressed His disciples, and said, "It is I". It is passing strange, and greatly to be deplored, that the meaning of the original has been hidden from the English reader by this clumsy translation. To us, this word of Christ here is the most striking line in this wonderful typical and dispensational picture. In John 8:58 we read that our Lord said, "Before Abraham was, *I am*". Here, when speaking to those in the ship, He uses *identical language!* And it is this which gives the real significance to this incident and "sign". The only One who can deliver Israel is the great I AM! It is the striving of the four winds of heaven which will bring about for Israel the "Time of Jacob's Trouble"; yet, as the prophet declared, "he shall be saved out of it" (Jer. 30:7); saved, as signified here, by the personal coming into the midst of their danger of the Lord Jesus Christ, the "I am" of the Old Testament. Then shall Israel exclaim, "Lo, this is *our God*, we have waited for Him" (Isa. 25:9). Fourteenth, next we read, "Then they willingly received Him into the ship" (v. 21). "*Then*", observe, when He stood revealed before them as the great "I am". Then will John 1:11 be reversed. There we read, that "the Word" who "was God", "came unto His own, and His own *received Him not*". But when He presents Himself to them the second time, they will "willingly receive Him". Fifteenth, "And immediately the ship was at the land whither they went" (v. 21). How beautiful is this closing touch to the picture! The danger is now passed. The rough voyage of Israel, through the long dark night, is now over. "*The* Land" is now theirs! The coming to them of the now absent but exalted Messiah, will both hush the storm that threatens Israel's complete destruction, and bring them to the desired Haven of rest!!

It is surely significant that we have in the above typical view not seven, but *fifteen* lines to the picture—not one of which can be left out, and we do not think an additional one can be discovered in John 6:15-21—for fifteen is 3 multiplied by 5. 3 is the number of full manifestation, and 5 of grace: and it is not until Christ comes back and saves Israel that *grace* will be *fully manifested*. Then shall it *be seen*, as never before, that where sin abounded, *grace* has "much more abounded".

"The day following, when the people which stood on the other side of the sea saw that there was none other boat there, save that one whereinto His disciples were entered, and that Jesus went not with His disciples into the boat, but that His disciples were gone away alone; (Howbeit there came other boats from Tiberias nigh unto the place where they did eat bread, after that the Lord had given thanks:) When the people therefore saw that Jesus was not there, neither His disciples, they also took shipping, and came to Capernaum, seeking for Jesus" (vv. 22-24). The multitude, whose hearts were set on making the Miracle-worker their "king", apparently collected early in the morning to carry their purpose into effect. But on seeking for Jesus, He was nowhere to be found. This must have perplexed them. They knew that on the previous evening there was only one boat on their side of the sea, and they had seen the disciples depart in this, alone. Where, then, was the Master? Evidently, He who had miraculously multiplied five loaves and two fishes so as to constitute an abundant meal for more than five thousand people, must also in some miraculous manner have transported Himself across the sea. So, availing themselves of the boats which had just arrived from Tiberias, they crossed over to Capernaum, in the hope of finding the Lord Jesus there; for they knew that this city had, for some time, been His chief place of residence. Nor was their expectation disappointed.

"And when they had found Him on the other side of the sea, they said unto Him, Rabbi, when camest Thou hither? Jesus answered them and said, Verily, verily, I say unto you, Ye seek Me, not because ye saw the miracle, but because ye did eat of the loaves, and were filled" (vv. 25, 26). There was, perhaps, nothing wrong in their question, "Rabbi, when camest Thou hither?" But to have answered it would not have profited them, and that was what the Lord sought. He, therefore, at once showed them that He was acquainted with their motives, and knew full well what had brought them thither. Outwardly at least, these people appeared ready to honor Him. They had followed Him across the sea of Galilee, and sought Him out again. But He read their hearts. He knew the inward springs of their conduct, and was not to be deceived. It was the Son of God evidencing His Deity again. He knew it was temporal, not spiritual blessing, that they sought. When He tells them, "Ye seek Me, not because ye *saw* the miracles (or "signs") but because ye did eat of the loaves", His evident meaning is that they realized not the spiritual significance of those "signs". Had they done so, they would have prostrated themselves before Him in worship. And let us remember that "Jesus Christ is the same yesterday, and today, and forever". Christ still reads the human heart. No secrets can be withheld from Him. He knows why different ones put on religious garments when it suits their purpose—why, at times, some are so loud in their religious pretensions—why they profess to be Christians. Hypocrisy is very sinful, but its folly and uselessness are equally great.

"Labor not for the meat which perisheth, but for that meat which endureth unto everlasting life, which the Son of Man shall give unto you" (v. 27). The expression used here by Christ is a relative and comparative one: His meaning is, Labour for the latter rather than for the former. The word "labour" is very expressive. It signifies that men should be in deadly earnest over spiritual things; that they should spare no pains to obtain that which their souls so imperatively need. It is used *figuratively*, and signifies making salvation the object of intense desire. O that men would give the same diligence to secure that which is imperative, as they put forth to gain the things of time and sense. That to which Christ bids men direct their thoughts and energies is "meat which endureth"—*abideth* would be better: it is one of the characteristic words of this Gospel.

When our Lord says, *"labour . . . . for that meat (satisfying portion) which endureth unto everlasting life"*, He was not inculcating salvation by works. This is very clear from His next words—"which the Son of Man shall *give* unto you". But He was affirming that which needs to be pressed on the half-hearted and those who are occupied with material things. It is difficult to preserve the balance of truth. On the one hand, we are so anxious to insist that salvation is by grace alone, that we are in danger of failing to uphold the sinner's responsibility to *seek* the Lord with all his heart. Again; in pressing the total depravity of the natural man, his *deadness* in tresspasses and sins, we are apt to neglect our duty of calling on him to repent and believe the Gospel. This word of Christ's, "labour .... for the meat which endureth" is parallel (in substance) with *"strive* to enter in at the strait gate" (Luke 13:24), and "every one *presseth into* the kingdom of God (Luke 16:16).

"For Him hath God the Father sealed" (v. 27). What is meant by Christ being "sealed" by God the Father? First, notice it is as "Son *of man"* that He is here said to be "sealed". That is, it was as the Son of God, but *incarnate.* There are two prime thoughts connected with "sealing": identification, and attestation or ratification. In Rev. 7 we read of God's angel "sealing" twelve thousand from each of the tribes of Israel. The sealing there consists of placing a mark on their foreheads, and it is for the purpose of identification: to distinguish and separate them from the mass of apostate Israel. Again; in Esther 8:8 we read, "Write ye also for the Jews, as it liketh you, in the king's name, and seal it with the king's ring: for the writing which is written in the king's name, and *sealed* with the king's ring, *may no man reverse".* Here the thought is entirely different. The *king's* "seal" there speaks of authority. His seal was added for the purpose of confirmation and ratification. These, we doubt not, are the principal thoughts we are to associate with the "sealing" of Christ.

The historical reference is to the time when Christ was baptized—Acts 10:38. When the Lord Jesus, in marvellous condescension, had identified Himself with the believing Remnant in Israel, taking His place in that which spoke of death, the Father there singled Him out by "anointing" or "sealing" Him with the Holy Spirit. This was accomplished by His audible voice, saying, "This is My beloved Son, in whom I am well pleased". Thus was the Christ, now about to enter upon His mediatorial work, publicly *identified* and *accredited* by God. The Father *testified* to the perfections of His incarnate Son, and communicated official authority, by "sealing" Him with the Holy Spirit. This declaration of Christ here in v. 27 anticipated the question or challenge which we find in v. 52, "How can *this man* give us His flesh to eat?" The sufficient answer, already given, was *"for* Him hath God the Father sealed". So, too, it anticipated and answered the question of v. 30: "What sign showest *Thou* then, that we may see, and believe Thee?" Just as princes of the realm are often authorized by the king to act in governmental and diplomatic affairs on his behalf, and carry credentials that bear the king's seal to confirm their authority before those to whom they are sent, so Christ gave proof of His heavenly authority by His miracles: "God anointed Jesus of Nazareth with the Holy Ghost *and with power*" (Acts 10:38).

It is blessed to know that we, too, have been "sealed": Eph. 1:13. Believers are "sealed" as those who are *approved* of God. But observe, carefully, that it is *in Christ* we are thus distinguished: "*In whom* also after that ye believed, ye were *sealed* with that Holy Spirit of promise". Christ was "sealed" because of His own intrinsic perfections; we, because of our identification and union with Him! "Accepted *in the Beloved*" (Eph. 1:6) gives us the same thought. Mark, though, it is not said (as commonly misunderstood) that the Holy Spirit *seals us*, but that the Holy Spirit Himself *is* God's "Seal" upon us—the distinguishing sign of identification, for sinners do not have the Holy Spirit (Jude 19).

In conclusion, it should be pointed out that in this second half of our passage (vv. 22-27) we have another dispensational picture. Its position in our chapter at once indicates its scope. Vv. 15-21 present us with a view of Israel in the Tribulation period: the verses that follow contain a striking, if veiled, portrayal of Israel *in the Millennium*. There are seven details which we point out below:—

1. In v. 22: "The day following". Let the reader turn back and compare our notes on the various "days" in John 1 and in 2:1. Here, as in the previous instances, it is a *dispensational* "day" that is in view. The preceding foreshadowment treats of the "even" (6:16), or end of the present Age. This Age closes with the Tribulation period. "The day *following*", then, brings us to the Millennium.

2. In the passage now being considered, Christ is owned as "the Lord" (v. 23). This is the more noticeable and striking if we observe the contrast in v. 11. There we read, "And *Jesus* took the loaves, and when He had given thanks", etc. But here we are told, "After that *the Lord* had given thanks". As we showed in our last article, v. 11 forms part of a dispensational portrayal of this *present* dispensation, and during it Israel do not own Jesus as "the Lord". But in the Millennium—the "Day following" —they will!

3. Here we read that "the people ....*came to* Capernaum", or "place of consolation." In v. 17, where the godly Remnant in the Tribulation are in view, they are going "toward Capernaum"; but here, "the day following" "the people .... came to Capernaum". In the Millennium "Consolation" will be Israel's indeed.

4. The people "came to Capernaum, *seeking for Jesus*" (v. 24). Thus will it be in that blessed Day. God will have removed from Israel "the heart of stone", and in its stead, given them "a heart of flesh". Then shall the One they so long "despised and rejected", be the Object of their hearts' desire.

5. Next we see Christ *teaching* Israel (v. 27). This is precisely what the prophets declare Christ shall do in the Millennium. We quote now but a single passage in proof: "O thou afflicted, *tossed with tempest*, and not comforted, behold, I will lay thy stones with fair colors, and lay thy foundations with sapphires .... and all thy children shall be *taught* of the Lord". It is indeed striking to observe the order of the two things which we have placed in italics. The order is the same here in John 6. In v. 18 we have a vivid picture of tempest-tossed Israel; in v. 27 Christ teaching them!

6. We now find Christ presenting Himself as the Satisfier of the soul (v. 27). And this accurately accords with the passage last quoted from Isaiah. After assuring tempest-tossed Israel, at the close of chapter 54, that the Lord will be merciful unto them and will teach them, the very next thing we read of, in the opening verses of chapter 55 is, "Ho, every one that thirsteth, come ye to the waters .... wherefore do ye spend money for that which is not *bread?* and your *labour* for that which *satisfieth* not? Hearken diligently unto Me, and eat ye that which is good, and let your soul delight itself in fatness". How marvellously this corresponds with John 6:27!

7. Christ is presented to the people as the One "sealed"—attested by—God the Father (v. 27). So will it be in the Millennium. Psa. 2:6-8 shows us how Christ will be publicly accredited by His Father. Thus do we have here in John 6:22-27 a rehearsal of the coming Day of Christ's glory.

Let the student ponder the following questions, preparatory to our next lesson:—

1. What does the question in v. 28 intimate?

2. What is the meaning of v. 29?

3. What do verses 30 and 31 demonstrate in connection with those people?

4. In how many different respects is "bread" a suited emblem of Christ?

5. What is the meaning of v. 35— Does a believer ever "hunger" or "thirst"?

6. *Who* have been given to Christ by the Father? V. 37.

7. What comforting truth is found in v. 39?

—Arthur W. Pink.

15. ANTICHRIST AND BABYLON

Continued.

In the last article we confined ourself to the Old Testament, in this and the one that follows we shall treat mainly of Babylon in Rev. 17 and 18, though, of necessity, we shall examine these in the light of Old Testament passages. In the previous article, we briefly reviewed the Old Testament evidence which proves there is to be a re-built Babylon, over which the Antichrist shall reign during the Time of the end. Now as both the Old and New Testaments have one and the same Divine Author, it cannot be that the latter should conflict with the former. "If the Old and New Testaments treat of the circumstances which are immediately to precede the Advent of the Lord in glory, the substantive facts of that period must be alike referred to in both. If the Old Testament declares that Babylon and 'the Land of Shinar' is to be the focus of influential wickedness at the time of the end, it is impossible that the Revelation, when professedly treating of the same period, should be silent respecting such wickedness, or respecting the place of its concentration. If the Old Testament speaks of an individual of surpassing power who will connect himself with this wickedness, and be the king of Babylon, and glorify himself as God, it is not to be supposed that the Revelation should treat of the same period and be silent respecting such an event. If, therefore, in the Old Testament, the sphere be fixed—the locality named—the individual defined —it is impossible that the Revelation, when *detailing the events of the same period,* should alter the localities, or change the individuals. There cannot be two sovereign individuals, nor two sovereign cities in the same sphere at the same time. If the mention of the 'Land of Shinar', and of

'Assyria', and of 'the king of Babylon', be intended in the Old Testament to render our thoughts fixed and definite, why should similar terms, applied in the Revelation to a period avowedly the same, be less definite?" (B.W.Newton).

Of Rev. 17 and 18 it has been well said, "There is, perhaps, no section of the Apocalypse more fraught with difficulty than the predictions concerning Babylon. Enigmatical and inconsistent with each other as, at first sight, they seem to be, we need to give careful attention to every particular, and much patient investigation of other scriptures, if we would penetrate their meaning and possess ourselves of their secret" (Mr. G. H. Pember, M.A.). In prosecuting our present study we cannot do better than borrow again from the language of Mr. Pember, "Nor is the present necessarily brief and imperfect essay written in any spirit of dogmatic certainty that it solves the mystery; but only as the conclusion, so far as light has been already vouchsafed, to one who, having received mercy of the Lord, has been led to much consideration of this and kindred subjects".

An exposition of the Revelation or any part thereof should be the last place for dogmatism. Both at the beginning and close of the book the Holy Spirit expressly states that the Apocalypse is a "prophecy" (1:3; 22:19), and prophecy is, admittedly, the most difficult branch of Scripture study. It is true that during the last century God has been pleased to give His people not a little light upon the predictive portions of His Word, nor is the Apocalypse to be excepted. Yet, the more any one reads the literature on the subject, the more should he become convinced that dogmatism here is altogether unseemly. During the last fifteen years the writer has made it a point to read the Revelation through carefully at least three times a year, and during this period he has also gone through over thirty commentaries on the last book of the Bible. A perusal of the varied and conflicting interpretations advanced have taught him two things: First, the wisdom of being cautious in adopting any of the prevailing views; second, the need of patient and direct waiting on God for further light. To these may be added a third, namely, the possibility, yea, the probability, that many of the prophecies of the Revelation are to receive a double, and in some cases, a treble, fulfillment.

"*All* Scripture is given by inspiration of God. and is *profitable*". This applies equally to the Prophets as to the Epistles, and it was just as true five hundred years ago as it is today. That being so, the right understanding of the *final* fulfillment of the prophecies in the Revelation cannot be the only value that book possesses. There must also be that in it which had a pertinent and timely message for the people of God of this dispensation in *each* generation. There must be that in it which strengthened the faith of those saints who read it during the "Dark Ages", and that which enabled them to detect and keep clear from that which was opposed to God and His Christ. In other words, its prophecies must have received a gradual and partial fulfillment all through the centuries of the Christian era, though their final fulfillment be yet future. Such is the case with Rev. 17 and 18. Ever since John received the Revelation there has always existed a system which, in its *moral features,* has corresponded to the Babylon of the 17th chapter. There exists such a system today; there will exist such a system after the Church is raptured to heaven. And there will also come into existence another and final system which will exhaust the scope of this prophecy.

The position which the Apocalypse occupies in the Sacred Canon is surely indicative of the character of its contents. The fact that it is placed at the close, at once suggests that it treats of that which concerns the *end* of things. Moreover, it is taken for granted that the student of this sixty-sixth book of the Bible is already acquainted with the previous sixty-five books. Scripture is self-interpreting, and we may rest assured that whatever appears vague or difficult in the last book of Scripture is due to our ignorance of the meaning of the books preceding, and particularly of the Prophets. In the Apocalypse the various streams of prediction, which may be traced through the Old Testament Scriptures, are seen emptying themselves in the sea of historical accomplishment. Or, to change the figure, here we are given to behold the last act of the great Dispensational Drama, the earlier acts of which were depicted in the writings of the seers of Israel. And yet, as previously intimated, these final scenes have already had a preliminary rehearsal during the course of the Christian centuries.

It will thus be seen that we are far from sharing the views of those who *limit* the prophecies of the Revelation to a *single* fulfillment. We believe there is much of truth in both the Historical and Futurist interpretations. We are in entire accord with the following words from the pen of our esteemed brother, Mr. F. C. Jennings: "How many of the controversies that have ruled, alas, amongst the Lord's people, have been due to a narrow way of limiting the thoughts of God, and seeking to confine or bend them by our own apprehension of them. How often two, or more, apparently opposing systems of interpretation may really both be correct; the breadth, the length, and height, and depth, of the mind of God, including and going beyond both of them". Let us now come more directly to our present theme.

The first time that Babylon is mentioned in the Apocalypse is in 14:8: "And there followed another angel, saying, Babylon is fallen, is fallen, that great city, because she made all nations drink of the wine of the wrath of her fornication". Now what is there here to discountenance the natural conclusion that "Babylon" means *Babylon?* Two or three generations ago, students of prophecy received incalculable help from the simple discovery that when the Holy Spirit spoke of Judea and Jerusalem in the Old Testament Scriptures He meant Judea and Jerusalem, and not England and London; and that when He mentioned Zion He did not refer to the Church. But strange to say, few, if any of these brethren, have applied the same rule to the Apocalypse. Here they are guilty of doing the very thing for which they condemned their forebears in connection with the Old Testament—they have "spiritualised". They have concluded, or rather, they have accepted the conclusions of the Reformers, that Babylon meant Papal Rome, ultimately being refined to signify apostate Christendom. But what is there in Rev. 14:8 which gives any hint that "Babylon" there refers to the Papal system? No; we believe that this scripture means what it says, and that we need not the annals of secular history to help us to understand it. What then? If to regard "Jerusalem" as meaning *Jerusalem* be a test of intelligence in Old Testament prophecy, shall we be counted a heretic if we understand "Babylon" to mean *Babylon,* and not Rome or apostate Christendom?

The next reference to Babylon is in Rev. 16:18, 19: "And there were voices, and thunders, and lightenings; and there was a great earthquake, such as was not since men were upon the earth, so mighty an earthquake, and so great. And the great city was divided into three parts, and the cities of the nations fell: and great Babylon came in remembrance before God, to give unto her the cup of the wine of the fierceness of His wrath". The remarks just made above apply with equal force to this passage too. Surely it is a literal city which is in view, and which is divided into three parts by a literal earthquake. If it does not mean this then the simple reader might as well turn from the Apocalypse in dismay. More than a hint of the literalness of this great city Babylon is found in the context, where we read of the river *Euphrates* (v. 12). This is sufficient for the writer: whether or not it is for the reader, we must leave with him.

We come now to Rev. 17, and as soon as we read its contents we are at once struck with the noticeable difference there is between it and the other passages which have just been before us. Here the language is no longer to be understood literally, but symbolically; here the terms are not plain and simple, but occult and mysterious. But God, in His grace, has provided help right to hand. He *tells us* that here is "mystery" (v. 5). And what is more, He *explains* most (if not all) of the symbols for us—see vv. 9, 12, 15, 18. With these helps furnished it ought not to be difficult to grasp the general outline.

The central figures in Rev. 17 are "the great whore", the "scarlet-colored Beast", and the "ten horns". The Beast is evidently the first Beast of Rev. 13. The "ten horns" are stated to be "ten kings" (v. 12). Who, then, is figured by "the great Whore"? There are a number of statements made concerning "the great Whore" —"the woman"—"the Mother of harlots"—which are of great help toward supplying an answer to this question. First, it is said that she "sitteth upon many waters" (v. 1), and in v. 15 these are said to signify "peoples, and multitudes, and nations, and tongues". Second, it is said, "The kings of the earth have committed fornication" with her (v. 2). Third, she is supported by "a scarlet-colored Beast" (v. 3), and from what is said of this Beast in v. 8 it is clear that he is the Antichrist, here viewed at the head of the last world-empire. Fourth, the woman "was arrayed in purple and scarlet color and decked with gold and precious stones" (v. 4). Fifth, "Upon her forehead was a name written—Mystery: Babylon the great", etc. (v. 5). Sixth, the woman was "drunken with the blood of the saints and with the blood of the martyrs" (v. 6). Seventh, in the last verse it is said, "And the woman which thou sawest is that great city, which reigneth over the kings of the earth". These seven points give an analysed summary of what is here told us about this "woman".

Now the interpretation which has been most widely accepted is, that the "Whore" of Rev. 17 pictures the Roman Catholic system. Appeal is made to the fact that though she poses as a virgin, yet has she been guilty of the most awful spiritual fornication. Unlike the blessed One, who, in His condescension and humiliation, had "not where to lay His head", Romanism has coveted silver and gold, and has displayed herself in meretricious luxury. She has had illicit intercourse with the kings of the earth, and she has made herself drunken with the blood of saints. Other parallelisms between the woman of Rev. 17 and the Roman Catholic system may be pointed out. What, then, shall we say to these things?

The points of correspondence between Rev. 17 and the history of Romanism are too many and too marked to be set down as mere co-incidences. Undoubtedly the Papacy has supplied *a* fulfillment of the symbolic prophecy found in Rev. 17. And therein has lain its practical value for God's people all through the dark ages. It presented to them a warning too plain to be disregarded. It was the means of keeping the garments of the Waldenses (and many others) unspotted by her filth. It confirmed the faith of Luther and his contemporaries, that they were acting according to the revealed will of God, when they separated themselves from that which was so manifestly opposed to His truth. But, nevertheless, there are other features in this prophecy which *do not* apply to Romanism, and which compel us to look elsewhere for the *complete* and *final* fulfillment. We single out but two of these.

In Rev. 17:5 Babylon is termed *"the Mother* of harlots and abominations of the earth". Is this an accurate description of Romanism? Were there no "harlot" systems before her? Is the Papacy the *mother* of the "abominations of the earth"? Let scripture be allowed to interpret scripture. In 1 Kings 11:5-7 we read of "Ashtoreth the goddess of the Zidonians, and after Milcom the *abomination* of the Ammonites . . . . then did Solomon build an high place for Chemosh, the *abomination* of Moab, in the hill that was before Jerusalem, and for Molech, the *abomination* of the children of Ammon"! The Papacy had not come into existence when John wrote the Revelation, so that *she* cannot be held responsible for all the "abominations" which preceded her. Again; in Rev. 17:2 we read of "the great Whore" that "the kings *of the earth* have committed fornication" with her. Is that applicable in its fulness to Rome? Have the kings of Asia and the kings of Africa committed fornication with the Papacy? It is true that the Italian pontiffs have ruled over a wide territory, yet it is also true that there are many lands which have remained untouched by their religious influence.

It is evident from these two points alone that we have to go back to something which long antedates the rise of the Papacy, and to something which has exerted a far wider influence than has any of the popes. What, then, is this something? and where shall we look for it? The answer is not hard to find: the word "Babylon" supplies us with the needed key. Babylon takes us back not merely to the days of Nebuchadnezzar, but to the time of *Nimrod*. It was in the days of the son of Cush that "Babylon" began. And from the Plain of Shinar has flown that dark stream whose tributaries have reached to *every* part of the earth. It was then, and there, that idolatry began. In his work on "The Two Babylons"* Dr. Hislop has proven conclusively that all the idolatrous systems of the nations had their origin in what was founded by that mighty Rebel, the beginning of whose kingdom was Babel (Gen. 10:10). But into this we cannot now enter at length. We refer the reader back to our comments on Nimrod in article 13. Babylon was founded in rebellion against God. The very name Nimrod gave to his city, proves him to have been a idolator —the *first* mentioned in Scripture— for Bab-El signified "the gate of God"; thus he, like his anti-type, determined to exalt himself above all that is called God (2 Thess. 2:4). This, then, was the source and origin of all idolatry. Pagan Rome, afterwards Papal Rome, was only one of the polluted streams from this corrupt source—one of the filthy "daughters" of this unclean Mother of Harlots. But to return to Rev. 17.

In v. 5 we read, "And upon her forehead was a name written—mystery: Babylon the great, the Mother of harlots and abominations of the earth". We believe that the English translators have misled many by printing (on their own authority) the word "mystery" in large capital letters, thus making it appear that this was a part of "the woman's" name.

* A book of intense interest for the antiquarian, but dull and wearisome for the average reader.

This we are assured is a mistake. That the "mystery" is connected with the "Woman" herself and not with her "name" is clear from v. 7, where the angel says unto John, "I will tell thee *the mystery of the Woman*, and of the Beast which carrieth her".

The word "mystery" is used in the New Testament in two ways. First, as a *secret*, unfathomable by man but explained by God: see Matt. 13:11; Rom. 16:25, 26; Eph. 3:3, 6, etc. Second, the word "mystery" signifies a *sign* or *symbol*. Such is its meaning in Eph. 5:32, where we are told that a man who is joined to his wife so that the two become "one flesh" is a "great mystery, (that is, a "great sign" or "symbol") of Christ and the Church". So, again, in Rev. 1:20 we read of "the mystery (sign or symbol) of the seven stars", etc.

As we have seen, the term "mystery" has *two* significations in its New Testament usage, and we believe it has a *double* meaning in Rev. 17:5, where it is connected with the "Woman". It signifies both a *symbol* and a *secret*, that is, something not previously revealed. It should also be noted that, in keeping with this, the name given to the Woman is a *dual* one— "Babylon the great", *and* "the Mother of harlots and abominations of the earth". Who, then, is symbolized by the Woman with this dual name? V. 18 tells us, "And the Woman which thou sawest is that great city, which reigneth over the kings of the earth". Now to get the force of this it is essential that we should bear in mind that, in the Apocalypse, the words "is" and "are" almost always (in the symbolical sections) signify *"represent"* Thus, in 1:20 "the seven stars *are* the seven churches" means "the seven stars *represent* the seven churches;" and "the seven candlesticks *are* the seven churches", signifies, "the seven candlesticks *represent* the seven churches". So in 17:9 "the seven heads *are* (represent) seven mountains"; 17:12 "the ten horns *are* (represent, ten kings"; 17:15 "the waters .... *are* (represent) peoples", etc. So in 17: 18 "the woman which thou sawest *is* that great city" must mean "the woman *represents* that great city". What, then, is signified by the "great city"?

In keeping with what we have just said above, namely, that the term "mystery" in Rev. 17:5 has a two-fold significance, and that the woman has a dual name, so we believe "that Great City" has a *double* force and application. First, it signifies a *literal* city, which shall yet be built in "the Land of Shinar", on the banks of the "Euphrates". Proof of this was furnished in our last article so that we need not pause here to submit the evidence. *Six* times (significant number!) is "Babylon" referred to in the Apocalypse, and nowhere is there a hint that the name is not to be understood literally. In the second place, the "great city" (unnamed) signifies an *idolatrous system*—"mother of harlots" a system of idolatry which originated in the Babylon of Nimrod's day, and a system which is to culminate and terminate in another Babylon in a day soon to come. This we think is clear and on the surface. What, then, is the *secret* here disclosed, which had hitherto been so closely guarded?

In seeking the answer to our last question it is important to note that there is another "Woman" in the Revelation, between whom and this one in chapter 17 there are some striking comparisons and some vivid contrasts. Let us note a few of them. First, in Rev. 12:1 we read of "a Woman clothed with the sun, and the moon under her feet, and upon her head a crown of twelve stars", which symbolically signifies that she occupies a position of *authority* and *rule* (cf Gen. 37:9); so also the Woman of chapter 17 is pictured as "ruling over the kings of the earth" (v. 18). Second, this Woman of Rev. 12 is a mother, for she gives birth to the

Man-child who shall rule all nations (v. 5); so the Woman of chapter 17 is "the *Mother* of harlots". Third, in 12:3 we read of a great red Dragon "having seven heads and ten horns", and he *persecutes* the Woman (v. 14); but in striking contrast, the Woman of chapter 17 is seen *supported by* a scarlot-colored Beast "having seven heads and ten horns" (v. 3). Fourth, in Rev. 19:7 the Woman of chapter 12 is termed the Lamb's Wife (v. 7); whereas the Woman of chapter 17 is the Devil's Whore. Fifth, the Wife of Rev. 19 is "arrayed in fine linen, clean and white" (v. 8); but the Whore of chapter 19 is arrayed in purple and scarlet, and has in her hand a golden cup "full of abominations and filthiness of her fornication" (v. 4). Sixth, the Lamb's Wife is also inseparably connected with a great city, even the holy Jerusalem (21:10); so the Whore of Rev. 17 is connected with a great city, even Babylon. Seventh, the chaste Woman shall dwell with the Lamb forever; the Whore shall suffer endless torment in the Lake of Fire.

Once we learn who is symbolized by the chaste Woman, we are in the position to identify the corrupt Woman, who is compared and contrasted with her. As to whom is signified by the former, there is surely little room for doubt—it is the faithful portion of Israel. *She* is the one who gave birth to the Man-child—i. e. Judah, in contrast from the unfaithful ten tribes, who because of idolatry were, at the time of the Incarnation, in captivity. So in Rev. 19 and 21 there are a number of things which show clearly (to any unprejudiced mind) that the Bride, the Lamb's Wife, is redeemed Israel, and not the Church. For example, in Rev. 19:6, 7, when praise bursts forth because the marriage of the Lamb is come, a great multitude cry, *"Alleluia:* for the Lord God omnipotent reigneth. Let us be glad and rejoice, and give honor to Him: *for* the marriage of the Lamb is come". "Alleluia (which occurs nowhere in the New Testament but in this chapter) is a peculiarly *Hebrew* expression, meaning "Praise the Lord". In the second place, the word for "marriage" (gamos) or "wedding-feast" is the same as is used in Matt. 22:2, 3, 8, 11, 12, where, surely, it is *Israel* that is in view. In the third place, note that we are told "His wife hath *made herself ready"* (v. 7). Contrast this with Eph. 5:26, where we learn that *Christ* will make the Church ready—see Matt. 23:39 for *Israel* making herself "ready". In the fourth place, in 19:8 we read, "And to her was granted that *she should be* arrayed in fine linen, clean and white, for the fine linen is the righteousness of saints". The Church will have been arrayed years before the time contemplated here. In the fifth place, note it is said that "the marriage of the Lamb is come" (v. 7), just as He is on the point of leaving heaven for earth (v. 11); but the Church will have been with Him in the Father's House for at least seven years (probably forty years or more) when that hour strikes. In the sixth place, in Rev. 21:9, 10 the Lamb's Wife is inseparably connected with that great city, the holy *Jerusalem,* and in the description which follows we are told that on the twelve gates of the city were written "the names of the twelve tribes of the children *of Israel"* (v. 12)! Surely that is conclusive evidence that it is not the Church which is in view. In the seventh place, in Rev. 21:14 we are told that in the twelve foundations of the City's wall were "the names of the twelve apostles of the Lamb" (cf Matt. 19:28!). Is it thinkable that the name of the apostle *Paul* would have been omitted if the Church was there symbolically portrayed?*

---

* "He that *hath* the Bride" (John 3:29), spoken by John the Baptist—the "friend of the Bridegroom"—demonstrates that "the Bride" was in view during our Lord's ministry unto the lost sheep of the house of Israel. The be-

If, then, the Chaste Woman of Rev. 12, 19, 21, symbolizes *faithful* Israel, must not the Corrupt Woman (who is compared and contrasted with the former) represent *faithless* Israel? But if so, *why* connect her so intimately with Babylon, the "great city"? It will help us here to remember that the Chaste Woman of the Apocalypse is also indissoluably united to a city. In Rev. 21: 9 we read that one of the seven angels said to John, "Come hither, *I will show thee the Bride*, the Lamb's Wife". And immediately following we read, "And he carried me away in the spirit to a great and high mountain, *and showed me that great city*, the holy Jerusalem, descending out of heaven from God". Thus, though separate, the two are intimately connected. The Bride *will dwell* in the holy Jerusalem. So here in Rev. 17, though distinct, the Whore is intimately related to the City, Babylon. One of the many proofs that the Harlot of Rev. 17 is apostate Israel is found in Isa. 1, where we read, "How is the faithful city become an *harlot*!" (v. 21). In the verses which follow it will be seen that the Lord of hosts is addressing Israel, and describing conditions which will prevail in the End-time. After indicting Israel for her sins, the Lord declares, "I will ease Me of Mine adversaries, and avenge Me of Mine enemies". Clearly, this has reference to the Tribulation period. Then the Lord continues, "And I will turn Mine hand upon thee, and purely purge away thy dross", etc., and then He adds, "Afterwards thou shalt be called, The city of righteousness, the *faithful* city". How clear it is then that God calls Israel "an *Harlot*" for her unfaithfulness. For further proofs see Jer. 2:20; 3:6,8; Ezek. 16:15; 20:30; 43:8,9; Hosea 2:5, etc.

We would next call attention to some of the scriptures which prove that there will be Israelites dwelling in Babylon and the land of Assyria at the End-time. In Jer. 50:4-7 we read, "In those days, and in that time, saith the Lord, the children of Israel shall come, they and the children of Judah together, going and weeping: they shall go, and seek the Lord their God. They shall ask the way to Zion with their faces thitherward, saying, Come, and let us join ourselves to the Lord in a perpetual covenant that shall not be forgotten", etc. Clearly these verses treat of the closing days of the time of "Jacob's trouble". Immediately following we read, "Remove out of the midst of *Babylon*, and go forth out of the land of the *Chaldeans*" (v. 8). Then, in the next verse, a reason is given, showing the urgency of this call for the faithful Jews in Babylon to come out: "For lo, I will raise and cause to come up against Babylon an assembly of great nations from the north country: and they shall set themselves in array against her; from thence she shall be taken" (v. 9). Again, in Jer. 51:44, the Lord says, "And I will punish Bel in *Babylon*, and I will bring forth out of his mouth that which he hath swallowed up: and the nations shall not flow together any more unto him: yea, the wall of Babylon shall fall". And then follows the Call for the faithful Jews to separate themselves from the mass of their apostate brethren in Babylon—"My people, go ye out of the midst of her, and deliver ye every man his soul from the fierce anger of the Lord". Isa. 11:11; 27:13; Micah 4:10, all show that Israel will be intimately connected with Babylon in the End-time.

It was of incalculable help to students of the past when they discovered that *Israel* is the key which unlocks prophecy, and that the Nations are referred to only as they affect the fortunes of Jacob's descendants. There were other mighty peoples of old besides the Egyptians and the Chal-

lieving Remnant who "received" Him, form the nucleus and were representative of redeemed Israel, millennial Israel, the Bride of the Lamb.

deans, but the Holy Spirit has passed them by, because their history had no bearing on that of the chosen Nation. The same reason explains why the empires of Babylon, Medo-Persia, Greece, and Rome, *do* occupy such a prominent notice in the book of Daniel—they were the enemies into whose hands God delivered His wayward people. These principles have received wide recognition by prophetic students, and therefore it is the more strange that so few have applied them in their study of the final prophetic book. *Israel* is the key to the Revelation, and the Nations are only mentioned therein as they immediately affect *Israel's* fortunes. The **ultimate** design of the Apocalypse is not to take notice of such men as Nero and Charlemagne and Napoleon, nor such systems as Mohammedanism and the Papacy. Nor would so much be said about Babylon unless this "great city" was yet to be the home of apostate Israel. After these preliminary considerations, which though lengthy were necessary, we are now prepared to examine a few of the details supplied by Rev. 17 and 18. Nor can we now do more than offer a bare outline, and even that will require a further article on Rev. 18.

"And there came one of the seven angels which had the seven vials, and talked with me, saying unto me, Come hither; I will show unto thee the judgment of the great whore that sitteth upon many waters: with whom the kings of the earth have committed fornication, and the inhabitants of the earth have been made drunk with the wine of her fornication" (Rev. 17:1, 2). The "great whore", in the final accomplishment of this prophecy, describes apostate Israel in the Endtime—i. e. Daniel's seventieth week. The figure of an unfaithful woman to represent apostate Israel is a common one in the Scriptures: see Jer. 2:20; 3:6,8; Ezek. 16:15; 20:30; 43:8,9; Hosea 2:5, etc. She is here termed "the *great* whore" for two reasons: first, because (as we shall show later) she will, at the end, worship Mammon as she never has in the past; second, because of her idolatrous alliance with the Beast. The apostle is here shown her "judgment". This is in contrast from what we have in Rev. 12, where we learn that the chaste "Woman" will be preserved. That apostate Israel will yet sit "upon many waters" ("peoples", etc., v. 15), and that the kings of the earth will commit fornication with her, we reserve for consideration in our next article.

"So he carried me away in the spirit into the wilderness: and I saw a woman sit upon a scarlet colored Beast, full of names of blasphemy, having seven heads and ten horns. And the woman was arrayed in purple and scarlet color, and decked with gold and precious stones, and pearls, having a golden cup in her hand full of abominations and filthiness of her fornication" (vv. 3 and 4). The Woman seated on the Beast does not signify that she will rule over him, but intimates that he will support her. The ultimate reference here is to the Devil's imitation of the Millennium, when the Jews (even now rapidly coming into prominence) shall no longer be the tail of the Nations, but the head. How the Devil will bring this about will appear when we examine Rev. 18. As the result of the Beast's *support* (v. 3), apostate Israel will be lifted to heights of worldly power and glory (v. 4).

"And upon her forehead was a name written, mystery: BABYLON THE GREAT, THE MOTHER OF HARLOTS AND ABOMINATIONS OF THE EARTH" (v. 5). In a re-built Babylon will culminate the various systems of idolatry which had their source in the first Babylon of Nimrod's day. It is in this city that the most influential Jews will congregate at the Time of the End. From there, Jewish financiers will control the governments of earth. That apostate Israel, in Babylon, should be clothed in "purple and scarlet" (emblems of royalty and earthly glory) *before* the Kingdom of Messiah is set up, was indeed a "mystery" (secret) disclosed by none of the Prophets, but now made known in *the Revelation*.

"And I saw the woman drunken with the blood of the saints, and with the blood of the martyrs of Jesus: and when I saw her, I wondered with a great wonder" (v. 6, R.V.). The final reference is, again, to apostate Israel in the End-time. The most relentless enemies of the godly Jews will be their own apostate brethren—cf our notes on Luke 18 in article 9. The second half of v. 6, correctly rendered in the R. V., "And when I saw her I wondered with a great wonder", ought to show us that it is not Romanism which is here in view. Why should John, who was himself then suffering from the hatred of Rome (Pagan) wonder at Rome (Papal) being clothed with govermental power and glory, and drunken with the blood of saints? But that the kings of the earth (her worst enemies for three thousand years) should commit fornication with Israel, and that the apostate portion of the Nation should be drunken with the blood of their own brethren according to the flesh, was well calculated to fill him with amazement.

"And the angel said unto me, Wherefore didst thou marvel? I will tell thee the mystery of the woman, and of the Beast that carrieth her, which hath the seven heads and ten horns" (v. 7). It should be noted that in the interpretation which follows, far more is said about "the Beast" than about "the Woman". We believe the chief reason for this is because the 18th verse tells us the Woman represents "that great city, which reigneth over the kings of the earth", and the City receives fuller notice in the chapter that follows—Rev. 18.

"And here is the mind which hath wisdom. The seven heads are seven mountains, on which the woman sitteth. And there are seven kings: five are fallen, and one is, and the other is not yet come; and when he cometh, he must continue a short space. And the Beast that was, and is not, even he is the eighth, and is of the seven, and goeth into perdition" (vv. 9-11). Here is the mind which hath wisdom (v. 9): "This repetition of 13:18 identifies and connects these two chapters. The word rendered 'mind' in 17:9 and 'understanding' in 13:18 is the same. This 'wisdom' is, to understand that, though a 'Beast' is seen in the vision, it is not a wild beast that is meant, but one great final superhuman personality; namely, a man energized by satanic power" (Dr. E. W. Bullinger).

The 9th verse should end with the word "wisdom": what follows belongs to v. 10. The R. V., which in this verse follows a number of reliable translations, renders thus: "The seven heads are seven mountains, on which the woman sitteth, *and they are* seven kings". This at once disposes of the popular interpretation which regards these "seven *mountains*" as referring to the seven *hills* on which the city of Rome is built. The Holy Spirit expressly tells us that the seven mountains are (*represent*) seven kings. Of these seven kings it is said, "five are fallen, and one is (i. e. the sixth existed when John wrote the Apocalypse), and the other (the seventh) is yet to come; he must continue a short space". And then in v. 11 we read, "And the Beast that was, and is not, is himself also an eighth, and is of the seven, and he goeth into perdition". Upon these verses we cannot do better than give extracts from Mr. Newton's "Thoughts on the Apocalypse":

"This passage is evidently intended to direct our thoughts to the various forms of executive government or kingship which have existed, or shall exist in the prophetic earth, **until the hour when the sovereignty of the world shall become the sovereignty of the Lord and of His Christ.** We might expect to find such a reference in a chapter which professedly treats of him who is to close the history of human government by the introduction of a new and marvellous form of power—a form new as to its mode of administration and development, yet not unconnected with the past, for it will be constructed upon principles drawn from the experience of preceding ages, and will have the foundations of its greatness laid by the primeval efforts of mankind. He will be the eighth; but he is *of* (ek) the seven.

"The native energy and intrepidity of him who is said to have been a mighty hunter before the Lord—an energy essential to men who were settling in a forlorn and unsubdued earth, surrounded by beasts of the forest and countless other difficulties and dangers, very naturally gave the first form to *kingship*, and hence its parentage may be said to spring. 'The beginning of his kingdom was Babel'. The supremacy of Nimrod was not derived from any previously existing system. He neither inherited his power from others, nor did he, like Nebuchadnezzar afterwards, receive it as a gift from God. He earned it for himself, by the force of his own individual character—but it was without God. Great progress was made in the kingdom which he founded in the land of Shinar, in civilization and refinement; for we early read of the goodly Babylonish garment, and of the skill and learning of the Chaldees; but their dominion was repressed and kept, as it were, in abeyance by the hand of God, until the trial of Israel, His people, had been fully made, that it might be seen whether they would prove themselves worthy of *supremacy* in the earth.

"The form of government in Israel was a theocracy; as was seen in the reigns of David and Solomon, who were types *(imperfect* types indeed) of Him that is to come. The monarch was independent of and uncontrolled by those whom he governed, but he was dependent upon God, who dwelt in the temple, ever near to be consulted, and whose law was given as the final standard of appeal. He stood between God and the people, not to be their functionary and slave—not to be the expression of *their* judgments, and the reflection of *their* will; but as set *over* them by God, his office was to mould *them* and to fashion *them* by principles which he himself had received from above. But the possession of power like this, held in companionship with God, required a holiness that was not found in man in the flesh, and therefore it was soon forfeited. Divine sanction, however, has many times since been coveted, and the name of 'the Lord's annointed' assumed. The last great king of the Gentiles, indeed, will do more than this, for he will take the place of Divinity itself, and sit upon the mount of the congregation on the sides of the north, saying he is like the Most High. But all this is unauthorized assumption.

"The third form is developed when the Gentile dynasty was formally constituted by God in the person of Nebuchadnezzar. He, like the monarchs of Israel, had absolute sovereignty granted to him—but God was not with him in it. He and his successors received it as delegated power, to be exercised according to their own pleasure, though in final responsibility to God. It is not necessary here to pursue the painful history of the Gentiles. It is sufficient to say, as regards the history of power, that the Gentile monarchs from the beginning, not knowing God so as to lean upon Him, and too weak to stand alone; exposed to the jealousy and hatred of those whom they governed—a jealousy not unfrequently earned by their own evil, found it necessary to lean upon something inferior to themselves: and thus the character of power has been deteriorated from age to age, until at last the monarchy of these latter days has consented not only to own the people as the basis and source of its power, but has also submitted to be directed in the exercise of that power by given rules prescribed by its subjects.

"The native monarchy of Nimrod, the theocracy of Israel, the despotic authority of Nebuchadnezzar, the aristocratic monarchy of Persia, and the military monarchy of Alexander and his successors, had all passed away when John beheld this vision. All these methods had been tried—none had been found to answer even the purposes of man; and now another had arisen, the half military, half popular monarchy of the Caesars,—the iron empire of Rome. 'Five have fallen, and one is, and the other is not yet come; and when he cometh he must continue a little space'.

"That other (though it cannot yet be said to have *come* so as to fulfill this verse)* has nevertheless appeared and is found in the constitutional monarchy of this present hour. This is the seventh, (we are rather inclined to believe that the "seventh" is *commercialism*, that is, the moneyed-interests in control—A.W.P.) and, with one brief exception, the last form that is to be exhibited before the end shall come, and it is under this form that the system of Babylon is matured. It is obvious that a monarchy, guided not by the people numerically, but by certain classes of the people, and those classes determined by the possession of property, must be the form adapted for the accumulation of wealth, and the growth of commercial power; for it gives (which pure democracy has ever failed to do), the best security for property without unduly fettering the liberty of individual enterprise".

For lack of space we are obliged to pass over the intervening verses now, and in closing this paper we offer a brief word on v. 18. "And the woman which thou sawest is that great city, which reigneth over the kings of the earth". This verse tells us that the Whore represents a City. This city is named in 14:8; 16:19; 17:5; 18:2; 10, 21; and it is surely significant that it is thus named in the Apocalypse *six* times—the number of *man;* whereas the new Jerusalem is referred to *three* times (3:12; 21:2, 10) the *Divine* number. Babylon, must therefore be understood *literally*, otherwise we should have the anomaly of a figure representing a figure. But from the very fact that we are here told the Woman represents the City, we learn that she is not literal, but *figurative*. In our next, we shall further review Rev. 17 and offer some comments on Rev. 18.
—Arthur W. Pink

THE SABBATH (Continued).

III. The Sabbath During the Mosaic Economy.

1. "Remember the Sabbath day, to keep it holy. Six days shalt thou labor, and do all thy work: But the seventh day is the Sabbath of the Lord thy God: in it thou shalt not do any work, thou, nor thy son, nor thy daughter, thy manservant, nor thy maidservant, nor thy cattle, nor thy stranger that is within thy gates: For in six days the Lord made heaven and earth, the sea, and all that in them is, and rested the seventh day: wherefore the Lord blessed the Sabbath day, and hallowed it" (Ex. 20:8-11). These words form part of the Decalogue, and, as shown in our previous article, that Decalogue is last-

---

* It will not have come in the sense of this verse, until it pervades the Roman world. When *all* the ten kingdoms have been constitutionalized, it may be said to have come.

ingly binding on every member of the human race. Before commenting upon the fourth commandment let us first offer a few brief remarks upon the Decalogue as a whole.

In the first place, let the reader note carefully the words with which Exodus 20 opens: "And God spake all these words". Observe it is not *"The Lord* spake all these words", but *"God* spake". This is the more noticeable because in the very next verse He says, "I am the Lord thy God, which have brought thee out of the land of Egypt", etc. Now the Divine titles are not used loosely, nor are they employed alternately for the purpose of variation. Each one possesses a definite and distinct signification. "God" is the creatorial title (see Gen. 1:1). "Lord" is God *in covenant relationship,* that is why it is "Lord God" all through Gen. 2. In Gen. 1 it is God in connection with His creatures. In Gen. 2 it is the Lord God in connection with Adam, with whom He had entered into a covenant—see Hosea 6:7, margin. The fact, then, that Ex. 20 opens with "And *God* spake all these words", etc. proves conclusively that the Ten Commandments were not and are not designed solely for Israel (the covenant people), but for all mankind. The use of the title "God" in Ex. 20:1 is the more forceful because in vv. 2, 5, 7, 10, 11, 12 "the Lord" is named, and named there because Jehovah was Israel's *covenant* God.

In the second place, the Ten Commandments, and they alone, of all the laws Jehovah gave to Israel, were promulgated by the voice of God, amid the most solemn manifestations and tokens of the Divine presence and majesty.

In the third place, the Ten Commandments, and they alone, of all Jehovah's statutes to Israel, were *written* directly by the finger of God, written upon tables of stone; and written thus to denote their lasting and imperishable nature.

In the fourth place, the Ten Commandments were further distinguished from all those laws which had merely a local application to Israel, by the fact that they alone were laid up in the ark. A tabernacle was prepared by the special direction of God, and within it an ark was placed, in which the two tables of the Law were deposited. The ark, formed of the most durable wood, was overlaid with gold, within and without. Over it was placed the mercy-seat, which became the throne of Jehovah in the midst of His people. Not until the tabernacle had been erected, and the Law placed in the ark, did Jehovah take up His abode in Israel's midst. Thus did the Lord signify to Israel that the moral Law was the basis of all His governmental dealings with them.

"The fourth commandment is closely connected with the other commandments. But so far from having any Jewish origin, it is the first and only commandment announced in the opening of the sacred record, and was imposed on our first parents in their state of uprightness and innocence. It thus stands in a peculiar manner at the head of all the commandments, and involves in its breach the abandonment equally of the first and second tables of the decalogue. It is placed at the end of the first table, as the tenth is at the end of the second, as the safeguard of all the rest. It stands between the two tables of our duty to God and our duty to man, as the great foundation and corner stone binding both together—its observance supporting and conducing to our obedience to the whole" (Robert Haldane).

A few words now concerning the fourth commandment itself. The commandment opens with the word "Remember". This intimates two things: first, this commandment was not here given for the first time—the word "remember" looks back to Gen. 2:2, 3; second, there is more danger of forgetting *this* commandment than any of the ten. Then follows a description of how the Sabbath is to be kept: in it no work is to be done. This is not to be taken absolutely, but is modified by other scriptures. What works *are* permissible we shall see later. In v. 11 a reason is given *why* the Sabbath must be kept holy: it memorializes God's work of creation. It recognizes Him as earth's Proprietor and owns Him as man's Sovereign.

2. The next time the Sabbath is mentioned is in Ex. 31:13, 14. "Speak thou also unto the children of Israel, saying, Verily My sabbaths ye shall keep: for it is a sign between Me and you throughout your generations; that ye may know that I am the Lord that doth sanctify you. Ye shall keep the Sabbath therefore; for it is holy unto you: every one that defileth it shall surely be put to death: for whosoever doeth any work therein, that soul shall be cut off from among his people". Two things are to be noted here. First, the Sabbath was God's appointed "sign" between Himself and Israel throughout their generations. The meaning of this is very simple. At the time when God entered into covenant relations with Israel, all other nations had been given up by God (Rom. 1). Not liking to retain Him in their knowledge, they had abandoned themselves to idolatry. For this cause, God had given them up to a reprobate mind. The heathen nations, therefore, kept no Sabbath, and, by this time, in all probability knew not that their Creator required them to. But to Israel, God had made known His laws. He had favored them with a written revelation of His will. He had blessed them in many other ways. And now He tells them the "sign" or "token" (as the Hebrew word is frequently rendered) that they were His people—a people separated from all others (note "sanctify *you*"

in v. 13)—would be their observance of His Sabbath. Thus, by singling out from all of the Ten Commandments *the fourth*, and making obedience *to it* the "sign" of Israel's privileged relation to Jehovah, God once more signified (as in Gen. 2, and Ex. 16) the supreme importance *He* attaches to the keeping holy of the seventh day!

The second point we would note in this passage from Ex. 31 is, that God here attached the death penalty to the desecration of the Sabbath. Now in connection with this there are several things which need to be carefully borne in mind. First, this *was not* a part of the Decalogue, which, as we have seen, is binding on all men. Second, this death penalty was attached to the Sabbath *only* as that Sabbath was a "sign" between Jehovah and Israel! Third, this death penalty, therefore, is not a part of the moral Law proper, and consequently, does not apply to Gentiles or Christians who are guilty of disobedience to the fourth commandment. To show that this is no *invention* of ours to dispose of a difficulty, we ask the reader to note carefully the contents of Lev. 20:10: "And the man that committeth adultery with another man's wife, even he that committeth adultery with his neighbour's wife, the adulterer and the adulteress shall *surely be put to death*". Now, "Thou shalt not commit adultery" was one of the Ten Commandments engraven upon the tables of stone, but *no* death penalty was attached to it *there*. That it was so *here* shows, again, that this was peculiar to Israel. "Marriage was an ordinance of God from the beginning, coeval with that of the sanctification of the seventh day; but marriage had some peculiarities among the Jews, such as the marrying the brother's wife, which is done away. Shall we say, because these peculiarities are done away, that the ordinance of marriage which was established in the garden of Eden, is also done away?" (Robert Haldane). Once it is clearly perceived that it is not the Mosaic Law which is binding on men today, but the *moral* Law, inscribed on the tables of stone, many (if not all) difficulties will vanish like mists before the sun.

There is no need for us to examine now every scripture in the Old Testament where the Sabbath is mentioned, for most of the references pertain to that which was peculiar to Israel. What we are here concerned with is the Sabbath as an intrinsic part of God's moral Law, which is of perpetual force and binding upon all. We shall, therefore, confine ourselves to passages bearing more or less directly on our present inquiry.

3. "Thou camest down also upon Mount Sinai, and spakest with them from heaven, and gavest them right judgments, and true laws, good statutes and commandments: And madest known unto them Thy holy Sabbath" (Neh. 9:13, 14). These words formed part of Nehemiah's address to the remnant of the Jews who had returned to Jerusalem after their captivity in Babylon. Here Nehemiah reviews Jehovah's past dealings with their fathers. Observe closely a distinction with he drew between the Sabbatic Law and the other laws. He says, "Thou . . . . *gavest* them right judgments, and true laws", etc.; and then declares, "And *madest known* unto them Thy holy Sabbath". This supplies us with another proof that the Sabbath *was not newly appointed* when promulgated at Sinai. It proves that the Sabbath had been previously instituted, or why distinguish it thus from the commandments "God gave" at Sinai? It shows there was a need for God to say, "*Remember* the Sabbath day". It evidences the fact that the Sabbath had been forgotten, yea, *lost* to Israel, during their four hundred year sojourn in Egypt. It reveals the fact that God now *restored* to Israel their full knowledge of it.

It is indeed a sad commentary on human nature to read in this same book of Nehemiah the lack of respect some of those Israelites paid to the fourth commandment, "In those days, saw I in Judah some treading winepresses *on the Sabbath,* and bringing in sheaves, and lading asses; as also wine, grapes, and figs, and all manner of burdens, which they brought into Jerusalem on *the Sabbath day:* and I testified against them in the day wherein they sold victuals. There dwelt men of Tyre there also therein, which brought fish, and all manner of ware, and sold on *the Sabbath* unto the children of Judah, and in Jerusalem. Then I contended with the nobles of Judah, and said unto them, What evil thing is this that you do, and *profane the Sabbath day?* Did not your fathers thus, and did not our God bring all this evil upon us, and upon this city? yet ye bring more wrath upon Israel by profaning the Sabbath" (13:15-18).

As we pass along, it is interesting to note that the inscription to Psa. 92 is, "A Song for the Sabbath Day". It contains instruction upon the way in which we should occupy ourselves on the holy Sabbath.

4. "Blessed is the man that doeth this, and the son of man that layeth hold on it; that keepeth the Sabbath from polluting it, and keepeth his hand from doing any evil" (Isa. 56:2). Here the Lord pronounces the man *"blessed"* that polluteth not His holy day. Therefore, by necessary implication, the one who defiles it is *cursed.*

5. "If thou turn away thy foot from the Sabbath, from doing thy pleasure on My holy day,—and call the Sabbath a delight, the holy of the Lord, honorable; and shalt honor Him, not doing thine own ways, nor finding thine own pleasure, nor speaking thine own words; Then shalt thou delight thyself in the Lord; and I will

cause thee to ride upon the high places of the earth, and feed thee with the heritage of Jacob thy father: for the mouth of the Lord hath spoken it" (Isa. 58:13, 14). Notice carefully the words, "Call the Sabbath *a delight*". How this rebukes the blasphemies of men, who, today, speak of the Sabbath as a yoke of bondage, a burden grievous to be borne!

IV. Christ and the Sabbath.

What attitude did the incarnate Son of God take to the Sabbath? How did He act in regard to it, and what was His teaching concerning it? We answer, unhesitatingly, He honored it; He kept it; He upheld its claims upon men. First, He was Himself "made under the Law" (Gal. 4:4); therefore, did He keep it perfectly, in thought and word and deed. Second, nowhere did Christ so much as hint at the repeal of the Sabbath, instead, He expressly declared, "Think not that I am come to destroy the Law, or the prophets; I am not come to destroy, but to fulfill" (Matt. 5:17). Thus, did He "magnify the Law and make it honorable" (Isa. 42:21). But to consider His attitude to the Sabbath in detail:

"And He came to Nazareth, where He had been brought up: and, as His custom was, He went into the synagogue on the Sabbath day" (Luke 4: 16). This is the first passage, chronologically. It casts light on the pre-ministerial life of Christ. It shows that before He entered upon His great mission, that it had been His *custom* to attend the synagogue on the Sabbath day. Therefore, it informs us *how* Christ had been wont to spend the Sabbath during those quiet years in Nazareth, before His public work commenced. It proves that He *honored* the Sabbath. And mark it carefully, this is recorded not in Matthew, the distinctively Jewish Gospel; but in Luke, the distinctively *Gentile* Gospel. Not simply as "Son of David" did He honor the Sabbath, but as "Son of *man*". Nor was it only during His *official* ministry as the Minister of the Circumcision, that He thus observed the Sabbath; but *before* He presented Himself to Israel as their Messiah. Another clear intimation is this that the Sabbath is binding not only upon Jews, but upon *all men!*

2. "At that time Jesus went on the Sabbath day through the corn; and His disciples were an hungered, and began to pluck the ears of corn, and to eat. But when the Pharisees saw it, they said unto Him, Behold, Thy disciples do that which is not lawful to do upon the Sabbath day" (Matt. 12:1, 2). This is one of several passages which record the criticism which the Saviour encountered from His enemies. And it is instructive and important to note the different answers He gave in self-vindication. Here, He reminded His detractors that the Scriptures furnished examples—in the case of David and of the priests in the Temple—that *works of necessity* were permissible. Those works which are required in order to supply *real* human wants *are not* a violation of the Sabbath law. Similarly, in Matt. 12: 11, 12 we read, "And He said unto them, What man shall there be among you, that shall have one sheep, and if it fall into a pit on the Sabbath day, will he not lay hold on it, and lift it out? How much then is a man better than a sheep? Wherefore it is lawful to do well on the Sabbath days". These words of the Son of God affirm that *works of mercy* performed on the Sabbath day are "lawful".

Thus, we have scriptural authority for saying that, the words "In it thou shalt not do any work" in Ex. 20:10, are not to be taken absolutely, but are to be understood in the light of these qualifications of Christ. All works which are not works of mercy and works of absolute necessity for man's wellbeing are Divinely forbidden. But those acts which are essential for the good of ourselves and others, are sanctioned by the example and teaching of the Law-giver Himself. In the *application* of these two qualifications to our lives, each one must seek Divine guidance for himself. "If any of you lack wisdom, let Him ask of God" (James 1:5). Works done in the seeking of pleasure are plainly sinful. Cooking food on Sunday is unnecessary, and is, therefore, a breach of the Sabbatic law. Travelling in trains or on street cars is not an absolute necessity, and hence, when used on the Sabbath, is wrong. Writing business letters on Sunday—no matter how important—is a desecration of the Lord's day. The reading of Sunday newspapers is a "polluting" of the Sabbath. But there is no need to enter further into details.

3. "He said unto them, The Sabbath was made for man, and not man for the Sabbath: Therefore the Son of man is Lord also of the Sabbath" (Mark 2:27, 28). There are three points in this passage we desire to emphasize. First, our Lord declares, "The Sabbath was made for *man*". This at once refutes those who say that the Sabbath was designed for none but Israel. The Sabbath was made for man's blessing. The Sabbath was made for man, that he might be a *man* in the highest sense of the word—something nobler than a beast of burden; something more than a cash register. The Sabbath was made for man because he *needed* it: his body needs it, his soul needs it. "His mind is finite; his body mortal. His powers of endurance and of persistent application are limited. He cannot work unceasingly. He needs regular periods of rest for his body and his mind. He must also have stated periods for enjoying and worshipping God, that his soul may be fed and nourished" (Dr. Carroll).

In the second place, note well the force of the "therefore"—"*Therefore* the Son of man is Lord also of the Sabbath". It signifies that since the Sabbath is made not merely for Israel, but for *man,* that consequently "the Son of man", not "the Son of David", is it's *Lord.* Because Jesus was more than a Jew, because in becoming incarnate He touched all humanity, then, as "Son of *man*" He is "Lord *also*" of the Sabbath.

In the third place, mark how Christ here speaks of Himself in relation to the Sabbath. He says that He is "Lord", *not* the "Destroyer" of the Sabbath, but *"Lord* of the Sabbath". He is not the Repealer or the Abolisher of the Sabbath, but its Sovereign. He is its "Lord" because *He* instituted it—John 1:1-3 proves this: *He* was the Creator. As the Creator, then, He instituted the Sabbath "for man", that is, for his *benefit,* to be a blessing to him. And this supplies another unanswerable a r g u m e n t which proves that the Sabbath originated not at Sinai, but in Eden. We may state it thus: The Sabbath was made for man: it was made for man because he needed it: therefore, it would have been *unmerciful* if the Maker of man had withheld it for twenty-five hundred years! This argument may be avoided, but it cannot be answered.

(To be concluded).
—Arthur W. Pink.

EXPOSITION OF FIRST PETER

Besides, the original expression is quite peculiar, and is altogether different from that ordinarily rendered "the sufferings of Christ." It is literally—"the sufferings in reference to Christ," that is, on Christ's account, in Christ's cause—or the sufferings till Christ, that is, the sufferings to be undergone by his body the Church, and by every member in particular, till he come "the second time, not as a sin-offering, but for their salvation." The sufferings till Christ, and the subsequent glories, are then just "the afflictions of the present time, and the glory which shall be revealed in us,"[1] and the apostle's statement is, the 'prophets, under the influence of the Spirit of Christ, predicted the sufferings to which Christians are to be exposed in the present state, and the glories which are to be bestowed on them at the second coming of their Lord.'

Let us then show, by the quotation of particular passages from the Jewish Scriptures, that the final salvation of the people of God was indeed the subject of Old Testament prediction. Before commencing these quotations, however, let us recollect that we are not in the Old Testament declarations to expect what, for perspicuity and distinctness, can compare with the declarations "which they who have preached the gospel with the Holy Ghost sent down from heaven," have made to us. It is enough that we meet with declarations of a completeness of deliverance and a perfection of happiness, far surpassing anything ever yet enjoyed by the Church on earth—far surpassing anything the New Testament warrants her to expect till her Lord return. I think it right also to add, that I am not prepared to assert that all the passages which I quote have a *direct* reference to the *heavenly* state, though it is only in that state that the blessings predicted will be enjoyed in that perfection which will completely exhaust the meaning of the prophetic oracles.

The first prediction I quote, of the final and complete salvation of the people of God, is the prophecy of Enoch, "Behold the Lord cometh with ten thousand of his saints."[2] This may seem a prophecy rather of the destruction of God's enemies than of the salvation of his people; but the two events are closely connected, and it seems to me probable that the apostle refers to this prophecy when he says, "Them who sleep in Jesus, God will bring with him."[3]

The next prediction that I shall refer to, is that wonderful passage in the 19th chapter of Job, "Oh that my words were now written—Oh that they were printed in a book—that they were graven with an iron pen, and with lead in the rock forever: For I know that my Redeemer liveth, and that he shall stand at the latter day upon the earth; and though, after my skin, worms destroy this body, yet in my flesh shall I see God, whom I shall see for myself, and mine eyes shall behold, and not another, though my reins be consumed within me."[4]

I now turn your attention to a passage in the 8th Psalm, "What is man, that thou art mindful of him? and the son of man, that thou visitest him? for thou hast" (after he had been in a state equal to the angels as to immortality) "made him a little" (rather for a short season) "lower than the angels; and" (then, afterwards) "hast crowned him with glory and honor; thou hast made him to have dominion over the works of thy hand—thou hast put all things under his feet"[5] That this refers to the final salvation of the redeemed from among men, is obvious from the apostle's commentary on it in the Epistle to the Hebrews. He plainly applies it to redeemed man, "For unto the angels hath he not put in subjection the world to come, whereof we speak? But one in a certain place testified, saying, What is man, that thou art mindful of him? or the son of man, that thou visitest him? Thou madest him a little lower than the angels; thou crownedst him with glory and honor, and didst set him over the works of thy hands: thou hast put all things in subjection under his feet.

---

[1] Rom. viii. 18.
[2] Jude 14.
[3] 1 Thess. iv. 14.
[4] Job xix. 23-27.
[5] Psal. viii. 4-6.

For in that he put all things in subjection under him, he left nothing that is not put under him. But we see not yet all things put under him" (redeemed man): "But we see Jesus" (who was a man—the head of the ransomed race), "who was made a little" (for a season) "lower than the angels, for the suffering of death, crowned with glory and honor; that he by the grace of God might taste death for every man." He suffered, and then was glorified, and thus shall it be with all his people.[1]

There are other quotations from the Psalms that deserve notice: "As for me, I shall behold thy face in righteousness: I shall be satisfied, when I awake in thy likeness." "Surely goodness and mercy shall follow me all the days of my life, and I shall dwell in the house of the Lord forever." "How excellent is thy lovingkindness, O God! therefore the children of men put their trust under the shadow of thy wings. They shall be abundantly satisfied with the fulness of thy house; and thou shalt make them drink of the river of thy pleasures. For with thee is the fountain of life; in thy light shall we see light."[2]

The following quotations from the prophets Isaiah, Daniel, Hosea, and Malachi, will serve as further specimens of the manner in which the prophets prophesied of the grace which is to be brought to us, and in which the Spirit of Christ, which was in them, testified beforehand of the glories which were to follow the sufferings till Christ: "Then the moon shall be confounded and the sun ashamed, when the Lord of hosts shall reign in Mount Sion, and before his ancients gloriously." "He shall swallow up death in victory, and the Lord God shall wipe away tears from off all faces, and the rebuke of his people shall he take away from off all the earth, for the Lord hath spoken it." "Thy dead men shall live; together with my dead body shall they arise: Awake and sing, ye that dwell in dust; for thy dew is as the dew of herbs, and the earth shall cast out the dead." "The sun shall be no more thy light by day, neither for brightness shall the moon give light unto thee: but the Lord shall be thy everlasting light, and the days of thy mourning shall be ended." "And many of them who sleep in the dust of the earth shall awake, some to everlasting life, and some to shame and everlasting contempt." "I will ransom them from the power of the grave: I will redeem them from death: O death! I will be thy plague: O grave! I will be thy destruction; repentance shall be hid from mine eyes." "They shall be mine, saith the Lord of hosts, in that day when I make up my jewels; and I will spare them as a man spareth his own son that serveth him. Then shall ye return and discern between the righteous and the wicked, between him that serveth God and him that serveth him not."[3] All these oracles speak of "suffering" as the lot of a peculiar people down to a particular period, and of "glory that is to follow" that period.

These prophetic oracles were but imperfectly understood by those who uttered them. We are not to suppose, however, that in uttering them, their minds were entirely passive, and that the Holy Spirit employed only their organs of speech to express words to which they attached no idea. They understood the meaning of the words; they were the expression of thoughts communicated to their minds. They knew that they referred to great blessings to be bestowed on the Church; but as to the precise nature and extent of these blessings, and as to the period when, and the manner in which, they were to be bestowed, they

---

[1] Heb. ii. 5-9.
[2] Psal. xvii. 15; xxiii. 6; xxxvi. 7-9.
[3] Isa. xxiv. 23; xxv. 8; xxvi. 19; lx. 19, 20. Daniel xii. 2. Hosea xiii. 14. Mal. iii. 18, 19.

were much in the dark. "The prophecy came not by their own will." "It was not of *self-interpretation.*" Either the event referred to, or another explicatory revelation, was necessary to unfold fully its meaning.

These holy men were desirous of knowing all that could be known on the subject. They "inquired and searched diligently" concerning the salvation—the grace which was to come to us; "they searched what, or what manner of time, the Spirit of Christ did signify, when he testified beforehand the glory which was to follow the sufferings until Christ." They wished to know when, and in what circumstances, these glorious predictions were to be fulfilled; and the means they employed for that purpose were the study of the Scriptures—comparing one passage with another, and fervent supplication to God. We have an example of this in the case of Daniel, in reference to another class of prophecies: "I, Daniel, understood by books the number of the years; and I set my face unto the Lord God, to seek" (further insight as to what and what manner of time) "by prayer and supplications, with fasting, and sackcloth, and ashes."[1]

The prophets did not obtain all the information they desired; but it was revealed to them, that "not to themselves, but to us, they did minister those things which have been reported to us by those who preached the gospel with the Holy Ghost sent down from heaven." "Those things which have been reported," &c.—are, I apprehend, the statements made by the apostles with regard to the final salvation of the people of God. It was revealed to the ancient prophets, that this glorious salvation was not to be enjoyed under the Jewish economy—that it was to take place "in the latter days"—"in the last times"—in the days of the Messiah. They were made to perceive that their predictions would be better understood, and therefore would be more useful to those who lived under the Messiah, than they were to themselves. "They ministered not to themselves, but to us;" that is, these predictions, uttered by them, though not useless to them (for they, like Abraham, wished to see the day of Christ, and "saw it afar off, and were glad,") are still more useful to us who have had them explained by a further revelation. The apostle's idea has been very finely illustrated by the following beautiful figure—"The sweet stream of their doctrine made its own banks fertile and pleasant, as it ran by and flowed still forwards to after ages, and, by the confluence of more such prophecies, grew larger as it proceeded, till it fell in with the main current of the gospel revelation; and thus united into one river clear as crystal, this doctrine of salvation hath still refreshed the city of God, and shall continue to do so till it empty itself into the ocean of eternity."[2]

How strikingly does the fact, that the *final* salvation was the subject of prophetic testimony from the beginning, illustrate at once the grandeur of this salvation, and the certainty that it shall in the appointed season be conferred on the people of God! That must be a glorious object to which God, by his Spirit, directed the admiring eyes of inspired prophets, while at the distance of so many thousand years. The highest conceptions we can form of it must come inconceivably short of the truth, when we think of it as the glorious termination of the whole wondrous systems of nature, and providence, and grace, which have been in operation for nearly six thousand years.

And the fact that it is the subject of Old Testament prophecies, proves not only its grandeur, but its security. We have "the word of prophecy more

---

[1] Dan. ix. 2, 3.
[2] Leighton.

confirmed" than the Old Testament believers. They had enough to make it most reasonable in them to believe, that whatever was predicted in the Scriptures should be fulfilled; but we have far more evidence than they had for the second coming of the Lord, and the complete salvation that is to accompany it. We have the fulfilment of the predictions as to the first coming, and many succeeding events, to confirm our faith. The final salvation of believers, at the second coming of the Lord, is one of those things which ought to be "most surely believed among us." If we do not believe it, it is not for want of evidence. "He will come the second time; and to all who look for him, he will come unto salvation."

If it was the duty of the ancient prophets to inquire into the meaning of the oracles revealed by them, respecting the great salvation of the people of God at the coming of the Lord, it certainly must be our duty to do so. Every part of divine revelation deserves and requires study; and, surely, those portions of it which have a reference to the coming of Christ, and the complete salvation of his people, have a peculiar claim on our attention. The extravagances into which some students of prophecy have run, ought not to prevent us from imitating the ancient prophets in "inquiring and searching diligently concerning this salvation," knowing that a blessing is pronounced on him "that readeth, and on them that hear the words of that prophetic book which is the revelation of Jesus Christ."[1] "Were the prophets not exempted from the pains of search and inquiry, that had the Spirit of God not only in a high degree, but after a singular manner—how unbecoming, then, is slothfulness and idleness in us! Whether is it, that we judge ourselves advantaged with more of the Spirit than those holy men, or that we esteem the doctrines and mysteries of salvation, on which they bestowed so much of their labor, unworthy of ours? We do ourselves much injury, if we bar ourselves from sharing in our measure of the search of those same things that were the study of the prophets, and which, by their studying and publishing them, are made more accessible and easy to us. These are the golden mines in which the abiding treasures of eternity are to be found, and therefore worthy of all the digging and pains we can bestow upon them."[2]

(Continued from page 257.)

Take again the oft-quoted language of 1 Pet. 2:24: "Who His own self bare *our* sins in His own body on the tree". When the apostle, under Divine inspiration, penned that sentence, he was not writing to a miscellaneous company, but to those who had been "born again" (see 1 Pet. 1:23). Therefore, common honesty, to say nothing of exegetical accuracy, requires us to limit this statement to the people of God. To stand before a mixed audience and announce that the Son of God "bore" *their* sins, is to take the children's bread and cast it to dogs.

What we have written above is designed to expose one of the favorite devices of the Enemy. More error is fostered, and more souls are injured and destroyed by a *distortion* of Scripture, than by the open denial of it. A *false application* is more dangerous (because less liable to be detected) than an erroneous interpretation. Therefore, let each of us seek daily wisdom and grace from God that we may be preserved from taking the *children's* bread and casting it to *dogs*. May we "tremble at the Word" (Isa. 66:2) lest we be found using a single sentence of it in any other way than as *He* has designed.

—Arthur W. Pink.

---

[1] Rev. i. 3.
[2] Leighton.

STUDIES in the SCRIPTURES

"Search the Scriptures" John 5:39.

A PERIODICAL (MONTHLY "IF THE LORD WILL") DEVOTED TO BIBLE STUDIES and EXPOSITIONS

ssociate Editors and Publishers, I. C. HERENDEEN and ARTHUR W. PINK,
Swengel, Pa.

Price: **10** cents per copy; **$1.00** per year. Foreign **$1.00** per year.

TO OUR SCRIPTURE STUDY FAMILY—

The first three issues of this magazine contained 20 pages each, and then the Lord made it plain He would have us increase it to 24. At this size it remained to the end of last year. We were so encouraged by the response we received that we believed it would be pleasing to God and also to our subscribers if we made further enlargement to 32 pages. We announced in the December 1922 issue that this would entail additional expense, calling for another 300 subscriptions to take care of it. But by now it seems plain that we have run before the Lord. Instead of an increased circulation we are slightly below what we had this time last year, and therefore it is wisest to cut down the cost of production and go back to 24 pages again. We have no sympathy with those who incur debts in the Lord's work and then call on God's people to pay the deficit. Consequently this October number contains only 24 pages, as will the remaining issues of this year. By thus reducing expenses we hope to "come out even" by the end of the year.

Perhaps some of our readers will be glad that the size of Studies in the Scriptures is being reduced. The contents are much heavier than what are found in many other religious periodicals; and in this busy age, when most people have so many calls on their time, it is better to furnish **24 pages** monthly to be read prayerfully than 32 to be skimmed carelessly.

Having explained the reason for cutting down our magazine to 24 pages, there is one other matter we would speak of at this time. It would be *a great help* to us if our subscribers would send in their renewals for 1924 during the *present* month. Our orders to the printers have to be sent in weeks ahead, and unless we receive renewals not later than Nov. 15, we are quite in the dark as to how many of the January 1924 copies to have printed. It will therefore simplify matters very much if our subscribers will remit AT ONCE. Please do not put this off, but send in your subscription (and if possible that of a friend with it) during *October*.

We believe that next year (D. V.) our magazine will be of more general interest. The Antichrist series will have been completed. In their place will be a series of shorter articles on the book of *Exodus*—similar in style to our "Gleanings in Genesis". The expositions of John's Gospel will be continued, but those by John Brown on First Peter will be discontinued through lack of space. The balance of each number will then be made up of *short* articles of a helpful nature to the spiritual life. Definite efforts will be made to provide *comfort* for those in distress and *stimulus* to those whose faith is weak and wavering. In short, we shall aim at greater *simplicity, brevity,* and *variety.* Thanking our friends for their past support, and hoping for their future co-operation and fellowship, we remain, Yours in His service,

Arthur W. Pink
I. C. Herendeen

IMPORTANT NOTICES

All new subscriptions will be dated back to January, 1923.

Set of twelve issues for 1922, unbound, $1.00. Bound, $1.50.

Note: We cannot break a set or now supply any **single** 1922 issues.

Subscription Price: $1.00 per year to any address in the world. Single copies 10 cents.

Change of Address: Please notify us promptly of any change of address, and be certain to give both old and new addresses.

Non-Subscribers receiving this Magazine regularly will understand their subscription has been entered by a friend.

Copies lost in the mail duplicated only if we are notified promptly.

Entered as second-class matter December 15th, 1921 at the post office at Swengel, Pa., under Act of March 3rd, 1879.

CONTENTS

John's Gospel (John 6:28-40)	290
Antichrist and Babylon	298
The Sabbath (Concluded)	303
Exposition of First Peter	308

JOHN'S GOSPEL

22. CHRIST, THE BREAD OF LIFE: John 6:28-40.

Below we give an Analysis of the passage which is to be before us:—

1. The Inquiry of the legalistic heart: v. 28.
2. The Divine answer thereto: v. 29.
3. The Scepticism of the natural heart: vv. 30, 31.
4. Christ the true Bread: vv. 32-34.
5. Christ the Satisfier of man's heart: v. 35.
6. The Unbelief of those who had seen: v. 36.
7. Christ's Submission to the Father's will: vv. 37-40.

It is both important and instructive to observe the connection between John 5 and John 6: the latter is, doctrinally, the sequel to the former. There is both a comparison and a contrast in the way Christ is presented to us in these two chapters. In both we see Him as the Source of life, Divine life, spiritual life, eternal life. But, speaking of what is characteristic in John 5, we have life *communicated* by Christ, whereas in John 6 we have salvation *received* by us. Let us amplify this a little.

John 5 opens with a typical illustration of Christ imparting life to an impotent soul: a man, helpless through an infirmity which he had had for thirty-eight years, is made whole. This miracle Christ makes the basis of a discourse in which He presented His Divine glories. In v. 21 we read, "As the Father raiseth up the dead, and quickeneth them: even so the Son *quickeneth whom He will*". The same line of thought continues through to the end of v. 26. Thus, Christ there presents Himself in full Godhead title, as the Source and Dispenser of life, sovereignly imparted to whom He pleases. The one upon whom this Divine life is bestowed, as illustrated by the case of the impotent man, is regarded as entirely *passive;* he is called into life by the Almighty, creating voice of the Son of God (v. 25). There is nothing in the sinner's case but the powerlessness of death, until the deep silence is broken by the word of the Divine Quickener. *His* voice makes itself heard in the soul, hitherto dead, but no longer dead as it hears His voice. But nothing is said of any searchings of heart, any exercises of conscience, any sense of need, any felt desire after Christ. It is simply Christ, in Divine sufficiency, speaking to spiritually dead souls, empowering them (by sovereign "quickening") to hear.

In John 6 Christ is presented in quite another character, and in keeping with this, so is the sinner too. Here our Lord is viewed not in His essential glories, but as the Son incarnate. Here He is contemplated as "the Son of Man" (vv. 27, 53), and therefore, as in the place of humiliation, "come down from heaven" (vv. 33, 38, 51, etc.). As such, Christ is made known as the Object of desire, and as the One who can meet the sinner's need. In John 5 it was Christ who *sought out* the "great multitude" of impotent folk (vv. 3, 6), and when Christ presented Himself to the man who had an infirmity thirty and eight years, *he* evidenced no desire for the Saviour. He acted as one who had no heart whatever for the Son of God. As such he accurately portrayed the dead soul when it is first quickened by Christ. But in John 6 the contrast is very noticeable. Here the "great multitude" *followed Him* (vv. 2, 24, 25), with an evident desire for Him—we speak not now of the unworthy motive that prompted that desire, but the desire itself as *illustrative* of a truth. It is this contrast which indicates the importance of noting the relation of John 5 and 6. As said in our opening sentences, the latter is the sequel to the former. We mean that *the order* in the contents of the two chapters, so far as their contents are typical and illustrative, set forth the *doctrinal order* of truth. They give us the *two* sides: the Divine and the human; and here, as ever, the Divine comes first. In John 5 we have the *quickening* power of Christ, as exercised according to His sovereign prerogative; in John 6 we have illustrated the *effects* of this in a soul already quickened. In the one, Christ approaches the dead soul; in the other, the dead soul, now quickened, *seeks* Christ!

In developing this illustration of the truth in John 6, the Holy Spirit has followed the same order as in John 5. Here, too, Christ works a miracle, on those who typically portray the doctrinal characters which are in view. These are sinners already "quickened," but not yet saved; for, unlike quickening, there is a *human* side to salvation, as well as a Divine. The prominent thing brought before us in the first section of John 6 is *a hungry multitude*. And how forcibly and how accurately they illustrate the condition of a soul just quickened, is obvious. As soon as the Divine life has been imparted, there is a stirring within; there is a sense of need awakened. It is the life turning toward its Source, just as water ever seeks its own level. The illustration is Divinely apt, for there are few things of which we are more *conscious* than when we are assailed by the pangs of hunger. But not so with a *dead* man, for he is unconscious; or with a *paralyzed* man, for he is incapable of feeling. So it is spiritually. The one who is dead in trespasses and sins, and paralyzed by depravity, has no hunger for God. But how different with one who has been Divinely "quickened"! The first effects of quickening is that the one quickened awakes to consciousness. The Divine life within gives capacity to discern his sinfulness and his need of Christ.

Mark, too, what follows in the second section of John 6. The same line of truth is followed further. Here we see the disciples in darkness, in the midst of a storm, rowing towards the Place of Consolation. What a vivid illustration does this supply of the experiences of the newly quickened and so *awakened* soul! It tells of the painful experiences through which he passes ere the Haven of Rest is reached. Not yet is he really saved; not yet does he understand the workings of Divine grace within him. All he is conscious of is his deep sense of need. And it is then that Satan's fiendish onslaughts are usually the fiercest. Into what a storm is he now plunged! But the Devil is not permitted to completely overwhelm the soul, any more than he was the disciples in the illustration. When God's appointed time arrives, Christ draws nigh and says, "I am: be not afraid". *He* stands revealed before the one who was seeking Him, and *then* is He *"willingly* received into the ship"—He is gladly embraced by faith, and received into the heart! *Then* the storm is over, the desired haven is reached, for the next thing we see is Christ and the disciples *at* "Capernaum" (place of consolation). Thus, in the feeding of the *hungry* multitude, and in the delivering of the disciples from *the storm-tossed sea*, we have a most blessed and wonderful illustration of Christ meeting and satisfying the conscious need of the soul previously quickened.

It will thus be seen that all of this is but introductory to the great theme unfolded in the middle section of John 6. Just as the healing of the impotent man at the beginning of John 5 introduced and prepared the way for the discourse that followed, so it is in John 6. Here the prominent truth is Christ in the place of humiliation, which He had voluntarily entered as man, "come down from heaven"; and thus as "the Bread of life" presenting Himself as the Object who alone can supply the need of which the quickened and awakened soul is so conscious*.

"Then said they unto Him, What shall we do, that we might work the works of God? (v. 28). This question appears to be the language of men temporarily impressed and aroused, but still in the dark concerning the way to Heaven. They felt, perhaps, that they were on the wrong road, that something was required of them, but what that something was they knew not. They supposed they had to *do* some work;

* We do not think the time would be wasted if the above paragraphs were *re-read* before proceeding farther.

but *what* works they were ignorant. It was the old self-righteousness of the natural man, who is ever occupied with his own doings. The carnal mind is flattered when it is consciously *doing* something for God. For his doings man deems himself entitled to reward. He imagines that salvation is due him, because he has *earned* it. Thus does he reckon the reward "not of grace, but of debt". Man seeks to bring God into the humbling position of debtor *to him*. How unbelief and pride degrade the Almighty! How they rob Him of His glory!

"What shall we do, that we might work the works of God" (v. 28). It seems almost incredible that these men should have asked such a question. Only a moment before, Christ had said to them "Labour not for the meat which perisheth, but for that meat which endureth unto everlasting life, which the Son of Man shall *give* unto you" (v. 27). But the carnal mind, which is enmity against God, is unable to rise to the thought of a gift. Or, rather, the carnal heart is unwilling to *come down* to the place of a beggar and a pauper, and receive everything for nothing. The sinner wants to do something to earn it. It was thus with the woman at the well: until Divine grace completed its work within her, she knew not the "gift of God" (John 4:10). It was the same with the rich young ruler: "Good Master, what shall I *do* to inherit eternal life?" (Luke 18:8). It was the same with the stricken Jews on the day of Pentecost: "Men and brethren, what shall we *do?*" (Acts 2:37). It was the same with the Philippian jailer: "Sirs, what must I *do* to be saved?" (Acts 16:30). So it was with the prodigal son—"Make me as one of thy *hired servants*" (one who *works* for what he receives) was his thought (Luke 19:15). Ah, dear friends, God and man are ever the same wherever you find them!

"Jesus answered and said unto them, This is the work of God, that ye believe on Him whom He hath sent" (v. 29). In what lovely patient grace did the Lord make reply! In blessed simplicity of language, He stated that the one thing that God requires of sinners is that they *believe* on the One whom He has sent into the world to meet their deepest need. "This is the work of God" means, this is what God requires. It is not the works of the Law, nor the bringing of an offering to His temple altar; but faith in Christ. Christ is the Saviour appointed by God, and *faith in Him* is that which God approves, and without which nothing else can be acceptable in His sight. Paul answered the question of the Philippian jailor as the Lord before him had done—"What must I *do* to be saved?": "*Believe* on the Lord Jesus Christ and thou shalt be saved", was the reply (Acts 16:31). But again we say, Man had rather *do* than "believe". And why is this? Because it panders to his pride: because it repudiates his utter ruin, inasmuch as it is a denial that he is "without strength" (Rom. 5:6): because it provides for him a platform on which he can boast and glory. Nevertheless, the one and only "work" which God will accept is faith in His Son.

But, perhaps some one will raise the question, Is it possible that I can ever enter heaven without good works? Answer: No; you cannot enter heaven without a good character. But those good works and that character of yours must be *without a flaw*. They must be as holy as God, or you can never enter *His* presence. But how may I secure such a character as that? Surely that is utterly impossible! No, it is not. But how then? By a series of *strivings* after holiness? No; that is *doing* again. Do nothing. Only believe. Accept the Work already done—the finished work of the Lord Jesus on our behalf. This is what God asks of you—give up your own doings and receive that of My beloved Son. But are you ready to do this? Are you willing to abandon your own doings, your own righteousness, and to accept His? You will not till you are thoroughly convinced that *all* your doings are faulty, that all your efforts fall far short of God's demands, that all your own righteousness is tarnished with sin, yea, is as filthy rags. What man will renounce his own work in order to trust to that of another, unless he be first convinced that his own is worthless? What man will repose for safety in another till he be convinced that there is no safety in trusting to himself? It is impossible. Man cannot do this of himself: it takes "the work of God". It is the convicting power of the Holy Spirit, and that alone, which brings the sinner to *renounce* his own works and *lay hold* on the Lord Jesus for salvation.

O dear reader, we would solemnly press this upon you. Is the finished work of

Christ the *only* rock on which your soul is resting for eternal life, or are you still secretly trusting to your own doings for salvation? If so, you will be eternally lost, for the mouth of the Lord hath spoken it —"He that believeth not shall be damned". Your own doings, even if they were such as you wish them to be, could never save you. Your prayers, your tears, your sorrowings for sin, your alms-givings, your church-goings, your efforts at holiness of life—what are they all but *doings* of your own, and if they were all perfect they could not save you. Why? Because it is written, "By the deeds of the law there shall no flesh be justified in His sight". Salvation is not a thing to be *earned* by a religious life, but is a free gift received by faith—Rom. 6:23.

"They said therefore unto Him, What sign showest Thou then, that we may see, and believe Thee? What dost Thou work?" (v. 30). How this exhibits the workings of unbelief! How difficult it is yea impossible, for the natural man, of himself, to accept Christ and His finished work by simple faith! Truly, nothing but the Spirit of God can enable a man to do it. The Lord had said, "believe". They replied, "Show us *a sign*". Give us something we can *see* along with it. Man must either see or feel *before* he will believe. "We do not mean to say that salvation is not by believing on Christ, but we want some *evidence* first. We will believe if we can have some evidence on which to believe. Oh, perfect picture of the natural heart! I come to a man—one who has probably for years been making a profession of religion—and I say to him, 'Have you got eternal life dwelling in you? Do you know that you are a saved man, that you have passed from death unto life?' The reply is, 'No, I am not sure of it.' Then you do not believe on the Lord Jesus. You have not accepted the finished work of Christ as yours. He replies, 'Yes, I do believe on Christ'. Then remember what He has said, 'He that believeth *hath* everlasting life'. He does not *hope* to have it. He is not *uncertain* about it. 'He *hath* it,' says the Son of God. The man answers, 'Well, I would believe this if I could only feel better. If I could only see in myself some *evidences* of a change, then I could believe it, and be as certain of it as you are'. So said these people to the Lord—give us some evidence that we may see and believe.

Do you not see that you are thus making salvation depend on the evidences of the Spirit's work *within* you, instead of the finished work of the Lord Jesus *for* you? You say, I would believe if I could only *feel* better—if I could only *see* a change. God says, Believe *first*, then you shall feel —then you shall see. God reverses your order, and you must reverse it too, if you would ever have peace with God. Believe, and you will then have in your heart a *motive* for a holy life, and not only so, you will walk in liberty, and peace, and joy" (Dr. F. Whitfield).

"They said therefore unto Him, What sign showest Thou then, that we may see, and believe Thee? What dost Thou work?" (v. 30). The force of that is this: You have asked us to receive you as the One sent of God. What sign, then do you show; where are your credentials to authorize your mission? And this was asked, be it remembered, on the morning following the feeding of the five thousand! It seems unthinkable. Only a few hours before, they had witnessed a miracle, which in some respects, was the most remarkable our Lord had performed, and from which they had themselves benefitted. And yet, does not our own sad history testify that this is true to life? Men are surrounded by innumerable evidences for the existence of God: they carry a hundred demonstrations of it in their own persons, and yet how often do they ask, What *proof* have we that there *is* a God? So, too, with believers. We enjoy countless tokens of His love and faithfulness; we have witnessed His delivering hand again and again, and yet when some fresh trial comes upon us—something which completely upsets *our* plans, the removal, perchance, of some earthly object around which we had entwined our heart's affections—we ask, Does God really care? And, maybe, we are sufficiently callous to ask for another "sign" in proof that He does!

"Our fathers did eat manna in the desert; as it is written, He gave them bread from heaven to eat" (v. 31). Here they drew a disparaging contrast between Christ and Moses. It was the further workings of their unbelief. The force of their objection was this: What proof have we that Thou art greater than Moses? They sought to deprecate the miracle they had witnessed on the previous day by comparing Moses and the manna. It was as though they had said, 'If you would have us believe on you as the sent One of God, you must show us greater works. You have fed five thousand *but once,* whereas in Moses' day, our fathers ate bread for forty years! It is striking to note how they harped back to their "fathers". The woman at the well did the same thing (see 4:12). And is it not so now? The experiences of "the fathers", what *they* believed and taught, is still with many the final court of appeal.

"Our fathers did eat manna in the desert; as it is written, He gave them bread from heaven to eat" (v. 31). Their speech betrayed them, as is evident from their use of the word "manna." The late Malachi Taylor pointed out how this was "a name always used by their fathers, of wilfulness, persistently ignoring Jehovah's word 'bread', and now uttered by them, because it was so written. It is notable that they of old never called it anything at all but 'manna' (meaning 'What is this?'), except when they despised it (Num. 21:5); and then they called it 'light bread'. And Jehovah named it 'manna' in Num. 11:7 when the mixed multitude fell a lusting for the flesh pots of Egypt. What lessons for us as to our thoughts of Christ, the Bread of God! In Psa. 78:24, where God is recounting the *evil ways* of Israel through the wilderness, He calls it 'manna'; but in Psa. 105:40, where all *His mercies* pass in review, calling for praise, it is called 'bread'. Again we say, What lessons for us!"

"Then Jesus said unto them, Verily verily, I say unto you, Moses gave you not that bread from heaven; but My Father giveth you the true bread from heaven" (v. 32). With good reason might our blessed Lord have turned away from His insulting challengers. Well might He have left them to themselves. But as another has said, "Grace in Him was active. Their souls' interests He had at heart" (C. E. S.). And so, in wondrous condescension, He speaks to them of the Father's "Gift", who alone could meet their deep need, and satisfy their souls. And has He not often dealt thus with thee, dear reader? Cannot you say with the Psalmist, "He hath not dealt with us after our sins; nor rewarded us according to our iniquities" (Psa. 103:10)? Instead of turning away in disgust at our ingratitude and unbelief, He has continued to care for us and minister to us. O how thankful ought we to be for that precious promise, and the daily fulfillment of it in our lives, "I will *never* leave thee, nor forsake thee".

"Then Jesus said unto them, Verily, verily, I say unto you, Moses gave you not that bread from heaven; but My Father giveth you the true bread from heaven" (v. 32). The error of the Jews here should be a warning to us. They thought Moses gave them the manna. But it was God and not Moses. He was only the humble instrument. They ought to have looked through the instrument to God. But the eye rested, where it is ever so prone to rest —on the human medium. The Lord here leads them to look beyond the human instrument to God—"Moses gave you not that bread but My Father", etc. O what creatures of sense we are. We live so much in the outward and visible, as almost to forget there is anything beyond. All that we gaze upon here is but the avenue to what eye hath not seen, nor ear heard. All the temporal gifts and blessings we receive are but the finger of the Father beckoning us in within the inner shrine. He is saying to us, 'If My works be so beautiful, if My gifts be so precious, if My footprints be so glorious, what must *I* be?' Thus should we ever look through nature, to nature's God. Thus shall we enjoy God's gifts, when they lead us up to Him; and then shall we not make idols of them, and so run the risk of their removal. Everything in nature and in providence is but the "Moses" between us and God. Let us not be like the Jews of old, so taken up with Moses as to forget the "greater than Moses", whence they all proceed.

"For the bread of God is He which cometh down from heaven, and giveth life unto the world" (v. 33). The Father's provision for a dying world was to send from heaven His only begotten Son. There is another suggestive contrast here, yea, a double one. The manna had no power to ward off death—the generation of Israel that ate it in the wilderness died! How, then, could *it* be the "true bread"? No; Christ is the "true bread", for He bestows "life". But again: the manna was only for Israel. No other people in the desert (the Amorites, for instance) partook of the manna; for it fell only in Israel's camp. But the true Bread "giveth life unto the world". The "world" here does not include the whole human race, for Christ does not *bestow* "life" on every descendant of Adam. It is not here said that the true

Bread *offereth* "life unto the world", but He *"giveth* life". It is the world of believers who are here in view. The Lord, then, designedly employs a word that reached beyond the limits of Israel, and took in elect Gentiles, too!

"For the bread of God is He which cometh down from heaven, and giveth life unto the world" (v. 33). Three different expressions are used by our Lord in this passage, each having a slightly varied meaning; the three together, serving to bring out the fulness and blessedness of this title. In v. 32 He speaks of Himself as the "true bread from heaven": "true" speaks of that which is real, genuine, satisfying; "from heaven" tells of its celestial and spiritual character. In v. 33 He speaks of Himself as "the bread of God", which denotes that He is Divine, eternal. Then, in v. 35 He says, "I am the bread of life": the One who imparts, nourishes and sustains life.

"Then said they unto Him, Lord, evermore give us this bread" (v. 34). This was but the outcome of a fleeting impression which had been made by His words. It reminds us very much of the language of the woman at the well, "Sir, give me this water, that I thirst not, neither come hither to draw" (4:15), and those who recall our comments on that verse will remember the motive that prompted her. The words of these men but served to make their rejection of Him more manifest and decisive when they fully grasped His meaning: v. 36 proves this conclusively—"But I said unto you, that ye also have seen Me, and believed not".

"And Jesus said unto them, I am the bread of life" (v. 35). The Lord places Himself before us under the figure of bread. The emblem is beautifully significant, and like all others used in Scripture calls for prolonged and careful meditation. First, bread is a *necessary* food. Unlike many other articles of diet which are more or less luxuries, this is essential to our very existence. Bread is the food we cannot dispense with. There are other things placed upon our tables that we can do without, but not so with bread. Let us learn the lesson well. Without Christ we shall perish. There is no spiritual life or health apart from the Bread of God.

Again, bread is a food that is *suited to all.* There are some people who cannot eat sweets; others are unable to digest meats. But *all* eat bread. The physical body may retain its life for a time without bread, but it will be sickly, and soon sink into the grave. Bread, then is adapted to all. It is the food of both king and artisan. So it is with Christ. He meets the need of all alike; He is able to satisfy every class of sinners—rich or poor, cultured or illiterate.

Again; bread is a *daily* food. There are some articles of food which we eat but occasionally; others only when they are in season. But bread is something we need every day of our lives. It is so spiritually. If the Christian fails to feed on Christ daily, if he substitutes the husks of religious forms and ceremonies, religious books, religious excitement, the glare and glitter of modern Christianity, he will be weak and sickly. It is failure at this very point which is mainly responsible for the feebleness of so many of the Lord's people.

Again; bread is a *satisfying* food. We quickly tire of other articles of diet, but not so with this. Bread is a staple and standard article, which we must use all our lives. And does not the analogy hold good again spiritually? How often have we turned aside to other things, only to find them but husks! None but the Bread of life can satisfy.

Finally, let us note *the process* through which bread passes before it becomes food. It springs up—the blade, the ear, the full corn in the ear. Then it is *cut down,* winnowed, and *ground* into flour, and finally subjected to the *fiery* process of the oven. Thus, and only thus, did it become fit to sustain life. Believer in Christ, such was the experiences of the Bread of God. He was *"bruised* for our iniquities". He was subjected to the fierce fires of God's holy wrath, as He took our place in judgment. O how wonderful—God forbid that we should ever lose our sense of wonderment over it. The Holy One of God, was "made a curse for us". "It pleased the Lord to bruise Him". And this in order that He might be the *Bread* of life to us! Let us then feed upon Him. Let us draw from His infinite fullness. Let us ever press forward unto a more intimate fellowship with Him.

"And Jesus said unto them, I am the bread of life: he that cometh to Me shall never hunger; and he that believeth on Me shall never thirst" (v. 35). In v. 33 Christ had spoken of giving life to "the world"— the world of believers, the sum total of the saved. Now He speaks of the individual

—"*He* that cometh to Me . . . . *He* that believeth". A similar order is to be observed in v. 37—note the "all" is followed by "him". There is, no doubt, a shade of difference between "believing on" Christ, and "coming to" Him. To "believe on" Christ is to receive God's testimony concerning His Son, and to rest on Him alone for salvation. To "come to" Him—which is really the effect of the former—is for the heart to go out to Him in loving confidence. The two acts are carefully distinguished in Heb. 11:6: "without faith it is impossible to please Him: for he that cometh to God must believe that He is: and that He is the rewarder of them that diligently seek Him". I must know who the physician is, and believe in his ability, before I shall go to him to be cured.

But what are we to understand by "shall never hunger" and "shall never thirst"? Does the Christian *never* "hunger" or "thirst"? Surely; then, how are we to harmonize his experience with this positive declaration of the Saviour? Ah, He speaks here according to the fulness and satisfaction there is *in Himself*, and not according to our imperfect apprehension and appreciation of Him. If we are straitened it is in ourselves, not in Him. If we *do* "hunger" and "thirst", it is not because He is unable, and not because He is unwilling, to satisfy our hunger and quench our thirst, but because we are of "little faith", and fail to draw daily from His fulness.

"But I said unto you, that ye also have seen Me, and believe not" (v. 36). Even the sight of Christ in the flesh, and the beholding of His wondrous miracles, did not bring men to believe on Him. O the depravity of the human heart! "Ye also have seen Me, and believe not". This shows how valueless was their request: "Lord, evermore give us this bread" (v. 34). It is unspeakably solemn. They trusted in Moses (9:28), they had rejoiced for a season in John the Baptist's light (5:35); they could quote the Scriptures (6:31), and yet they believed not on Christ! It is difficult to say how far a man may go, and yet come short of the one thing needful. These men were not worse than many others, but their unbelief was manifested and declared; consequently, Christ addresses them accordingly. This, indeed, would be the result in every case, were we left to our own thoughts of Christ. Be warned then, dear reader, and make sure that *yours* is a *saving* faith.

"But I said unto you, that ye also have seen Me, and believe not" (v. 36). Was, then, the incarnation a failure? Was His mission fruitless? That could not be. There can be no failure with God, though there is much failure in all of us to understand His purpose. Christ was not in anywise discouraged or disheartened at the apparent failure of His mission. His next word shows that very conclusively, and to it we turn.

"All that the Father giveth to Me shall come to Me" (v. 37). Here the Lord speaks of a definite company which have been given to Him by the Father. Nor is this the only place where He makes mention of this people. In John 17 He refers to them seven times over. In v. 2 He says, "As Thou hast given Him power over all flesh, that He should give eternal life to *as many as Thou hast given Him*". So again in v. 6 He says, "I have manifested Thy name unto the men *which Thou gavest Me* out of the world: Thine they were, and Thou gavest them Me". And again in v. 9 He declares, "I pray not for the world, but *for them which Thou hast given Me*; for they are Thine". See also verses 11, 12, 24. Who those are that the Father gave to Christ we are told in Eph. 1:4—"According as He hath *chosen* us in Him before the foundation of the world". Those given to Christ were God's *elect*, singled out for this marvellous honor before the foundation of the world: "God hath from the beginning chosen you to salvation" (2 Thess. 2:13). But let us notice the exact connection in our passage wherein Christ refers to the elect.

In v. 36 we find our Lord saying to those who had no heart for Him, "Ye also have seen Me, and believe not." Was He, then, disheartened? Far from it. And why not? Ah, mark how the Son of God, here the lowly Servant of Jehovah, *encourages* Himself. He immediately adds, "All that the Father giveth Me *shall* come to Me". What a lesson is this for every under shepherd. Here is the true haven of rest for the heart of every Christian worker. Your message may be slighted by the crowd, and as you see how many there are who "believe not" it may appear that your labor is in vain. Nevertheless **"the foundation of God** *standeth sure,* having this seal, the Lord knoweth *them that are*

His" (2 Tim. 2:19). The eternal purpose of the Almighty cannot fail; the sovereign will of the Lord most high cannot be frustrated. *All*, every one, that the Father gave to the Son before the foundation of the world "*shall* come to Him". The Devil himself cannot keep one *of them* away. So take heart fellow-worker. You may seem to be sowing the Seed at random, but God will see to it that part of it falls onto ground which He has prepared. The realization of the invincibility of the eternal counsels of God will give you a calmness, a poise, a courage, a perseverance which nothing else can. "Therefore, my beloved brethren, be ye steadfast, unmoveable, always abounding in the work of the Lord, forasmuch as *ye know* that your labor is *not in vain* in the Lord" (1 Cor. 15:58).

"All that the Father giveth Me shall come to Me" (v. 37). But while this is very blessed, it is solemnly tragic and deeply humbling. How humiliating for us, that in the presence of incarnate life and love in the person of the Lord of glory, no one would have come to Him, *none* would have benefitted by His mission, had there not been those who were given to Him by the Father, and on whose coming He could, therefore, reckon. Man's depravity is so entire, his enmity so great, that in *every* instance, his will would have resisted and rejected Christ, had not the Father determined that His Son *should have* some as the trophies of His victory and the reward of His coming down from heaven. Alas that our deadness to such love should have called forth such sighs as seem to breathe in these very words of Christ!

"And him that cometh to Me I will in no wise cast out" (v. 37). Let us not miss (as is so commonly done) the connection between this clause and the one which precedes it. "Him that cometh to Me" is explained by "all that the Father giveth Me". *None* would come to Him unless the Father had first predestinated that they should, for it is only "*as many as* were ordained to eternal life" that believe (Acts 13:48). Each one that the Father has given to Christ in eternity past, "cometh" to Him in time—comes as a lost sinner to be saved; comes having nothing, that he may receive everything.

The last clause "I will in no wise cast out", assures the eternal preservation of every one that truly cometh to Christ. These words of the Saviour do not signify (as generally supposed) that He promises to *reject none* who really come to Him, *though that is true;* but they declare that under no imaginable circumstances will He ever expel any one that *has* come. Peter came to Him and was saved. Later, he *denied* his Master with an oath. But did Christ "cast him out"? Nay, verily. And can we find a more extreme case? If Peter *was not* "cast out", *no* Christian ever was, or ever will be. Praise the Lord!

"For I came down from heaven, not to do Mine own will, but the will of Him that sent Me" (v. 38). This is most instructive. The force of it is this: Those whom the Father had given the Son—*all* of them—*would* come to Him. It was no longer the Son in His essential glory, quickening whom *He* would, as in 5:21, but the Son incarnate, the "Son of man" (6:27), *receiving* those the Father "drew" to Him (6:44)! "Therefore be it who it might, He would in no wise cast him out: enemy, scoffer, Jew or Gentile, they would not come if the Father had not sent them" (J. N. D.). Christ was here to do *the Father's* will. Thus does Christ assure His own that He will save to the end *all* whom the Father had given Him.

"For I came down from heaven, not to do Mine own will, but the will of Him that sent Me" (v. 38). How greatly does this enhance the value of the precious words at the close of the preceding verse, when we see that our *coming to Christ* is not attributed to man's fickle will, but as the effect of the Father's drawing to the Saviour each one given to Him in the counsels of that Father's love before the foundation of the world! So, too, the *reception* of them is not merely because of Christ's compassion for the lost, but as the obedient Servant of the Father's will, He welcomes each one brought to Him— brought by the unseen drawings of the Father's love. Thus our security rests *not upon anything in us or from us,* but upon the Father's choice and the Son's obedient love!

"And this is the Father's will which hath sent Me, that of all which He hath given Me I should lose nothing, but should raise it up again at the last day" (v. 39). How blessedly this, too, explains the closing words of v. 37! *Eternal predestination guarantees eternal preservation.* The "last day" is, of course, the last day of the Christian dispensation. *Then* it shall *appear* that

He *hath not* lost a single one whom the Father gave to Him. Then shall He say, "Behold I and the children which God hath given Me" (Heb. 2:13).

"And this is the will of Him that sent Me, that every one which seeth the Son, and believeth on Him, may have everlasting life: and I will raise Him up at the last day" (v. 40). Christ had just spoken of the Father's counsels. He had disclosed the fact that the success of His ministry depended not on man's will—for that was known to be, in every case, so perverse as to *reject* the Saviour—but on the drawing power of the Father. But here He leaves, as it were, the door wide open to any one any where who is disposed to enter: "That *every one* which seeth the Son, and believeth on Him, may have everlasting life". Yet it is instructive to note the order of the two verbs here: "believing" on Christ is the result of "seeing" Him. He must first be *revealed* by the Spirit, *before* He will be received by the sinner. Thus did our Lord disclose to these men that a far deeper and infinitely more important work had been entrusted to Him than that of satisfying Israel's poor with material bread—no less a charge than that of raising up at the last day all that had been given to Him by the Father, without losing so much as one.

The following questions are submitted to help the student for the next lesson on John 6:31-59:—

1. Wherein does v. 44 rebuke their "murmuring"?
2. What ought to have been their response to v. 44?
3. Who are the "all" that are "taught of God" (v. 45)?
4. What is meant by "not die" (v. 50)?
5. What are the various thoughts suggested by "eat" (v. 51)?
6. What is the difference in thought between vv. 53 and 56?
7. What is meant by "I live by the Father" (v. 57)?

—Arthur W. Pink.

16. ANTICHRIST AND BABYLON
(Rev. 18)

In our last article we sought to show that in Rev. 17 "the great Whore", and "Babylon the great", though intimately connected, are yet distinct; the former being the representative of the latter. While allowing, yea insisting upon it, that many features of the symbolic prophecy contained in Rev. 17 have had a striking fulfillment already, still *that* in which *all* its varied terms are to find their complete realization is yet future. We also reminded our readers that *Israel* supplies the solution to most of the problems of prophecy, and this is becoming more and more evident as the last prophetic book in the Bible is receiving wider and closer study. Fifty years ago the majority of the commentators "spiritualised" the first half of Rev. 7 and made the "twelve tribes of Israel", there mentioned, to refer to the Church. But this has long since been discredited. So, the popular interpretation of Rev. 12 which made the "woman" there a figure of the Church has also been abandoned by many. An increasing number of Bible students are recognizing the fact that "the Lamb's Wife," "the Bride" of Rev. 19 and 21 also contemplates Israel rather than the Church. That the Church is the Bride (a statement nowhere affirmed in Scripture) has been sedulously proclaimed by the Papacy for over a thousand years, and the tradition has been echoed throughout Protestantism. But, as we have said, there is a steadily increasing number who seriously question this, yea, who are bold to repudiate it, and declare in its stead that the new Israel, saved Israel, will be "the Bride". As this truth becomes more clearly discerned, we believe it will also be apparent that the great Whore is not the apostate church but *apostate Israel*.

The future of Israel is a wide subject, for numerous are the scriptures which treat of it. It is, moreover, a subject of profound interest, the more so because what is now prophetic is so soon to become historic. The Zionist movement of the last twenty-five years is something more than the impracticable ideal of a few visionaries; it is steadily preparing the way for the reestablishment of the Jews in Palestine. It is true that the Zionists have been frowned upon by many in Jewry, and that, for a very good reason. God's time is not yet fully ripe, and He has permitted the mercenary spirit of many of Jacob's descendants to hold it, temporarily, in check. The millions of Jews now comfortably settled and prospering in this land, and in the capitals of the leading European countries, are satisfied with their present lot. The love of money outweighs sentimental considerations. Zionism has made no appeal to their avarice. To leave the markets and marts of New York, London, Paris, and Berlin in order to become *farmers* in Palestine is not sufficiently alluring. Mammon is now the god of the vast majority of the descendants of those who, of old, worshipped the golden calf.

At present, it is (with few exceptions) only those who are oppressed in greater Russia, Hungary, etc. who are really anxious to be settled in Palestine. But soon there will be a change of attitude. Even now there are faint indications of it. As Palestine becomes more thickly populated, as the prospects of security from Turkish and Arabian depredations grow brighter, as the country is developed and the possibilities of commercial aggrandizement loom on the horizon, the better class of Jews will be quick to see and seize the *golden* opportunity. Few American Jews are anxious to emigrate to Palestine when there is nothing more than a spade and a hoe at the end of the journey. But as hospitals, colleges, universities, banking-houses are opened, and all the commercial adjuncts of civilization find a place in the land of David, then rapidly increasing numbers of David's descendants will turn their faces thitherward. High finance is the magnet which will draw the covetous Hebrews.

Once Palestine becomes a thorough Jewish State it is not difficult to forecast the logical corollary. We quote from the excellent exposition on Zechariah by Mr. David Baron—his comments on the fifth chapter*. "Without any spirit of dogmatism, and without entering at this place into the question of the identity and significance of the Babylon in the Revelation—whether mystical or actual—we would express our conviction that there are scriptures which cannot, according to our judgment, be satisfactorily explained except on the supposition of a revival and yet future judgment of literal Babylon, which for a time will be the center and embodiment of all the elements of our godless 'civilization', and which especially will become the chief *entrepot* of commerce in the world.

"To this conviction we are led chiefly by the fact that there are prophecies in the Old Testament concerning the literal Babylon which have never in the past been exhaustively fulfilled, and that Scripture usually connects the final overthrow of Babylon with the yet future restoration and blessing of Israel.

"And it is very striking to the close observer of the signs of the times how things at the present day are rapidly developing on the very lines which are forecast in the prophetic scriptures. 'The fears and hopes of the world—political, commercial, and religious,' writes one in a monthly journal which lies before me, 'are at the present day being increasingly centered upon the home of the human race—Mesopotamia .... As the country from which the father of the Jewish nation emigrated to the land of promise, it is also occupying the thoughts and aspirations of the Jews'.

"Whatever may be the outcome of the negotiations which have been carried on recently with the Turkish Government by the Jewish Territorialists 'for the establishment of a Jewish autonomous State' in this very region, in which many Zionists and other Jews were ready to join, there is so much truth in the words of another writer that when once a considerable number of such a commercial people as the Jews are re-established in Palestine, '*the Euphrates would be to them as necessary as the Thames to London or the Rhine to Germany. It would be Israel's great channel of communication with the Indian seas, not to speak of the commerce which would flow towards the Tigris and Euphrates from the central and northern disticts of Asia! It would be strange, therefore, if no city should arise on its banks of which it might be said that her merchants were the great men of the earth'*".

Zech. 5 is most intimately connected with Rev. 18, and a grasp of the former i of such importance in studying the latter that we must here give it a brief consideration. But first let us outline in the fewest possible words the contents of the first four chapters of Zechariah. After a brief introduction we learn, first, that God's eye is ever upon Israel (1:7-17). Second, that His eye is also upon her enemies and

---
* Mr. Baron is probably the ablest and most widely known and esteemed Hebrew Christian alive today.

desolators (1:18-21). Third, assurance is given of her future blessing (2) and of her cleansing (3). Fourth, we learn of the blessings which shall follow her restoration (4). Fifth, we are taken back to behold the punishment of apostate Israel: the "flying roll" symbolizes the destruction of wicked Jews (5:1-4). Then follows the vision of "the Ephah" in 5:5-11—let the reader please turn to it.

We cannot do more than now call attention to the prominent features in this vision. First, the prophet sees an "ephah" (or "bath") which was the largest measure for dry goods among the Jews. It would, therefore, be the natural symbol for *Commerce*. Next, we note that twice over it is said that the ephah "goeth forth" (vv. 5,6). As the whole of the preceding visions concern *Jerusalem and her people*, this can only mean that the center of *Jewish* commerce is to be transferred from Palestine elsewhere. Next, we are told that there was a "woman" concealed in the midst of the ephah (v. 7). We say "concealed", for in vv. 5 and 6 the "woman" is not seen— the leaden cover (cf v. 8) had to be "lifted" before she could be beholden. The writer is satisfied that this hidden "woman in the ephah" is "the Woman" which is fully *revealed* in *Revelation* 17 and 18. Next, we are told that "wickedness" (lawlessness) was cast into the ephah, before its cover was closed again. Then, in what follows, we are shown this ephah, with the "woman" and "wickedness" shut up therein, being rapidly conveyed from Palestine to *"the land of Shinar"* (v. 11). The purpose for this is stated to be, "to build it a house", i.e. a settled habitation. Finally, we are assured, "it shall be established, and set *there* (in the land of Shinar) upon her own base". This vision or prophecy contains the germ which is afterwards expanded and developed in such detail in Rev. 17 and 18, where it is shown that "the house" which is established for this system of commerce is "Babylon the great". Let it be remembered, that this vision is found in the midst of a series of prophecies which have to do with, first the faithful, and then the faithless in Israel, and we have another clear and independent proof that the Corrupt Woman of the Apocalypse is none other than apostate Israel!

In his helpful and illuminative work on the Babylon of the future, the late Mr. Newton devoted a separate chapter to Zech. 5. His remarks are so excellent that we cannot forbear from making an extract: "If human energy is to be permitted again to make the Euphratean regions the scene of its operation—if prosperity is to be allowed for a brief moment to re-visit the Land of Babylon, it might be expected that the Scriptures would somewhere allude, and that definitely, to such an event. And we find it to be so. The Scripture does speak of an event yet unaccomplished, of which the scene is to be the Land of Babylon. The passage to which I refer is at the close of the fifth chapter of Zechariah.

"That the event predicted in this remarkable passage remains still unaccomplished, is sufficiently evident from the fact of Zechariah's having prophesied *after* Babylon had received that blow under which it has gradually waned. Zechariah lived after Babylon had passed into the hands of the Persians, and since that time, it is admitted by all, that declension—not 'establishment'—has marked its history. From that hour to the present moment there has been no 'preparation of an house', no establishment of anything—much less of an Ephah in the Land of Shinar. But an Ephah is to be established *there*, and a house to be built for it *there*, and *there* it is to be set firmly upon its base.

"An Ephah is the emblem of commerce. It is the symbol of the merchants. In the passage before us the Ephah is described as 'going forth'; that is, its sovereign influence is to pervade the nations, and to imprint on them a character derived from itself, as the formative power of their institutions. In other words, *commerce is for a season to reign.* It will determine the arrangements, and fix the manners of Israel, and of the prophetic earth. The appearance of every nation that falls under its control is to be mercantile. 'He said, moreover, this is their appearance (or aspect) throughout all the earth' ".

The theme is of deep interest, and we are tempted to enter at length into details. But that is scarcely necessary. Every one who has a general knowledge of the past, and who is at all in touch with political conditions in the world today, knows full well the radical change which the last two or three centuries have witnessed. For a thousand years the Church (the professing church) controlled the governments of Europe. Following the Reformation, the aristocracy (the nobility) held the reins.

During the first half of last century democratic principles obtained more widely. But in the last two or three generations the governmental machines of this country and of the leading European lands have been run by the Capitalists. Of late, Labor has sought to check this, but thus far with little success. In the light of Zech. 5 and Rev. 18 present-day conditions are profoundly significant. It is *commerce* which is more and more dominating the policies and destinies of what is known as the civilized world. "If we turn our eyes abroad upon the world, we shall find that the one great object before the nations of the earth today is this image of commerce, drawing them with all the seductive influence a siren woman might exercise upon the heart of men. The one great aim on the part of each is to win the favor of this mighty mistress. The world powers are engaged in a Titanic struggle for commercial supremacy. To this end mills are built, factories founded, forests felled, lands sown, harvests reaped, and ships launched. Because of this struggle for mastery of the world's market the nations reach out and extend their borders" (Dr. Haldeman). The recent war was caused by commercial jealousies. The root trouble behind the "reparation" question, the "Strait's" problem, the cancellation or demanding repayment of United States loans to Europe, each go back to commercial considerations.

Sixty years ago it was asked, "Is not commerce the sovereign influence of the day? If we were asked to inscribe on the banners of the leading nations of the earth, an emblem characteristically expressive of their condition, could we fix on any device more appropriate than an ephah?" With how much greater pertinency may this be said today! And how this is preparing the way for and will shortly head up in what is portrayed in Rev. 18, it is not difficult to see. There we read, "Thy *merchants* were the *great* men of the earth" (v. 23). This was not true four hundred years ago: for then the ecclesiastics were "the great men of the earth". Nor was it true one hundred years ago, for then the nobility were "the great men of the earth". But today. Ah! Ask the man on the street to name half a dozen of the "great men" now alive, and whom would he select? And who are behind and yet one with the "merchants"? Is it not the financiers? And who are the leading ones among them? Who are the one that are more and more controlling the great banking-systems of the world? And, as every well-informed person knows, the answer is, *Jews.* How profoundly significant, then, that the head on the image in Nebuchadnezzar's dream (which symbolized the *Babylonian* Empire) should be of *gold,* and that the final Babylon should be denominated "the *golden* city" (Isa. 14:4). And how all of this serves, again, to confirm our interpretation of Rev. 17, namely, that "the great Whore" with "the *golden* cup in her hand" (17:4) is apostate Israel, whose final home shall be that "great city", soon to be built on the banks of the Euphrates. Not yet is it fully evident that the wealth of the world is rapidly filling Hebrew coffers—only a glimpse of the "woman" in *"the midst of the Ephah"* was obtained before it became established in the Land of Shinar. But it cannot be long before this will become apparent. At the End-time it will fully appear that *"the woman* .... is (represents) that great city" (17:18). This explains the words of Rev. 17:5, where we learn that the words "Babylon the great" are written upon "her *forehead"*—it will be obvious then to all! Apostate Israel, then controlling the wealth of the world, will personify Babylon.

And what part will the Antichrist play in connection with this? What will be his relation to Babylon and apostate Israel? The Word of God is not silent on these questions, and to it we now turn for the Divine answer. As to Antichrist's relation to Babylon, Scripture is very explicit. He will be "the King of Babylon" (Isa. 14:4); the "King of Assyria" (Isa. 10:12). As to his relation to apostate Israel, that is a more intricate matter and will require more detailed consideration. We shall therefore devote a separate article (the next one) to this interesting branch of our subject. Here we shall deal briefly with what Rev. 17 and 18 say thereon.

Rev. 17 presents the relation of apostate Israel to the Antichrist in three aspects. First, she is *supported by* him. This is brought before us in 17:3, where we are shown the corrupt Woman seated upon the scarlet-colored Beast. This, we believe, is parallel with Dan. 9:27, which tells us that "the Prince that shall come" will make a Covenant with Israel. This covenant, league, or treaty, will insure her protection. It is significant that Dan. 9:27 tells us the "covenant" is made by the one who is then at the head of the revived Roman Empire, which corresponds with the fact that Rev. 17:3 depicts him as a "scarlet colored Beast .... having seven heads and *ten horns*". It is the Antichrist no longer in his "little horn" character, but as one that has now attained earthly glory and dominion. As such, he will, for a time, uphold the Jews and protect their interests.

Second, Rev. 17 depicts apostate Israel as *intriguing with* "the kings of the earth". In v. 2 we read that the kings of the earth shall commit fornication with her. Note how this, as an item of importance, is *repeated* in 18:3. This, we believe, is what serves to explain 17:16 which, in the corrected rendering of the R. V. reads, "And the ten horns which thou sawest *and the Beast,* these shall *hate* the Harlot, and shall make her desolate and naked, and shall eat her flesh, and shall burn her utterly with fire". What it is which causes the Beast to turn against the Harlot and hate and destroy her is her *unfaithfulness* to him. Not content with enjoying the protection the Beast gives her, apostate Israel will aspire to a position of rivalry with the one over the ten horns. That she succeeds in this we learn from the last verse of the chapter—"And the woman which thou sawest is (represents) that great city, which *reigneth over* the kings of the earth". As to how apostate Israel will yet "reign over" the kings of the earth we hope to show in our next article.

Third, Rev. 17 makes it known that apostate Israel will ultimately be *hated by* the Beast and his "ten horns" (v. 16). The 12th verse tells us that the ten horns are "ten kings". This has presented a real difficulty to many. In 17:16 it says that the ten horns (kings) and the Beast *hate* the Whore, and make her desolate and naked, and shall eat her flesh (that is, appropriate to themselves her substance, her riches), and burn her with fire; whereas in 18:9 we read, "The kings of the earth who have committed fornication and lived deliciously with her, shall *bewail* her, and lament for her, when they shall see the smoke of her burning". Yet the solution of this difficulty is very simple. The difficulty is created by confusing "the kings of the earth" with the "ten horns", whose kingdoms are within the limits of the old Roman Empire (see Dan. 7:7). The "kings of the earth" is a much wider expression, and includes such kingdoms as North and South America, China and Japan, Germany and Russia, etc., all in fact, outside the bounds of the old Roman Empire. It is the intriguing of apostate Israel with "the kings of the earth" which brings down upon her the hatred of the Beast and *his* "ten kings".

In closing this article we wish to call attention to some of the many and striking verbal correspondencies between Rev. 17 and 18 and the Old Testament Prophets:—

1. In Rev. 17:1 we are told the great Whore "sitteth upon many waters".

In Jer. 51:13 Babylon (see previous verse) is addressed as follows: "O thou that dwellest upon many waters".

2. In Rev. 17:2 it is said that, "The inhabitants of the earth have been made drunk with the wine of her fornication".

In Jer. 51:7 we read, "Babylon hath been a golden cup in the Lord's hand, that made all the earth drunken: the nations have drunk of her wine".

3. In Rev. 17:4 the great Whore has "a golden cup in her hand".

In Jer. 51:7 Babylon is termed "a golden cup in the Lord's hand".

4. In Rev. 17:15 we are told, "The waters which thou sawest, where the Whore sitteth, are peoples, and multitudes, and nations, and tongues".

In Jer. 51:13 we read, "O thou that dwellest upon many waters, abundant in treasures".

5. Rev. 17:16 tells us that Babylon shall be burned with fire—cf 18:8.

So in Jer. 51:58 we read, "The broad walls of Babylon shall be utterly broken, and her high gates shall be burned with fire".

6. In Rev. 17:18 we are told that the woman who represents the great city "reigneth over the kings of the earth".

In Isa. 47:5 Babylon is denominated "the lady of kingdoms".

7. Rev. 18:2 tells us that after her fall, Babylon becomes "the habitation of demons, and the hold of every foul spirit, and a cage of every unclean and hateful bird".

Isa. 13:21 says, "But wild beasts of the desert shall lie there; and their houses shall be full of doleful creatures; and owls shall dwell there, and satyrs shall dance there".

8. Rev. 18:4 records God's call to the

faithful Jews—"Come out of her My people".

In Jer. 51:45 God also says, "My people, go ye out of the midst of her".

9. In Rev. 18:5 it is said, "Her sins have reached unto heaven".

In Jer. 51:9 it reads, "For her judgment reacheth unto heaven".

10. In Rev. 18:6 we read, "Reward her as she rewarded you".

In Jer. 50:15 it says, "Take vengeance upon her; as she hath done, do unto her".

11. In Rev. 18:7 we find Babylon saying in her heart, "I sit a queen, and am no widow, and shall see no sorrow".

In Isa. 47:8 we also read that Babylon says in her heart, "I am, and none else beside me; I shall not sit as a widow, neither shall I know the loss of children".

12. In Rev. 18:8 we read, "Therefore shall her plagues come in one day".

Isa. 47:9 declares, "But these two things shall come to thee in a moment, in one day".

13. In Rev. 18:21 we read, "And a mighty angel took up a stone like a great millstone, and cast it into the sea, saying, Thus with violence shall that great city Babylon be thrown down, and be found no more at all".

So in Jer. 51:63, 64 we are told, "And it shall be, when thou hast made an end of reading this book, that thou shalt bind a stone to it, and cast it into the midst of the Euphrates: And thou shalt say, Thus shall Babylon sink, and shall not rise from the evil that I will bring upon her".

14. In Rev. 18:23 we read, "And the light of the candle shall shine no more at all in thee, and the voice of the bridegroom and of the bride shall be heard no more at all in thee".

In Isa. 24:8, 10 it is said of Babylon, "The mirth of tabrets ceaseth, the noise of them that rejoice endeth, the joy of the heart ceaseth . . . . the City of Confusion is broken down: every house is shut up, that no man may come in . . . . all joy is darkened, the mirth of the land is gone".

15. In Rev. 18:24 we read, "And in her was found the blood of prophets, and of saints, and of all that were slain upon the earth".

In Jer. 51:49 we read, "As Babylon hath caused the slain of Israel to fall, so at Babylon shall fall the slain of all the earth".

These parallelisms are so plain they need no comments from us. If the reader still insists that the Babylon of Rev. 17 and 18 is the ultimate development of the Papacy as it envelopes apostate Christendom, it is useless to discuss the subject any farther. But we believe that the great majority of our readers—who have no traditions to uphold—will be satisfied that the Babylon of the Apocalypse is the Babylon of Old Testament prophecy, namely, a literal, rebuilt city in "the land of Nimrod" (Micah 5:6), a city which shall be the production of covetousness ("which is *idolatry*"—Col. 3:5), and a city which shall yet be the home of apostate Israel.

—Arthur W. Pink.

THE SABBATH (Concluded)

V. THE SABBATH IN THE EPISTLES.

1. "Let no man therefore judge you in meat, or in drink, or in respect of an holy day, or of the new moon, or of the Sabbath days" (Col. 2:16). This is the favorite verse with those who insist that the Sabbath is not binding on Christians. That they appeal to such a scripture shows how untenable is their position. In the first place, the Greek word here for "Sabbath" is in the plural number, not in the singular as in Mark 2:27, 28. This at once intimates that it is not the weekly Sabbath of the moral Law which is in view. In the second place, "Sabbath*s*" here has no article before it, which is proof positive that the *weekly* Sabbath is not under discussion. To what, then, is the apostle referring? A glance at the context will show us.

That Col. 2:16 looks back to what has been said in the previous verses and contains a conclusion drawn from their contents is manifest from the word "therefore": "Let no man *therefore* judge you", etc. On what, then, does the "therefore" rest? If we go back to v. 13 we read, "And you, being dead in your sins and the *uncircumcision* of your flesh, hath He quickened together with Him, having forgiven you all trespasses". Then in v. 14 he says, "Blotting out the handwriting of *ordinances* that was against us, which was contrary to us, and took it out of the way, nailing it to His Cross". The words we have placed in italics show plainly the trend of the apostle's line of thought. He was referring to the *ceremonial* law, which had walled off the Jews from the Gentiles. But for believers in Christ this has been "taken out of the way", see Eph. 2:14. *Therefore,* says the apostle, let no man *judge* you in connection with meat, and drink, nor with "respect of an holy day, or of the new moon, or of the Sabbaths", for these all pertain to the ceremonial law. If further proof of the correctness of this interpretation be required, it is supplied in the very next verse: "Which are a shadow of things to come; but the body is of Christ". It was not the moral law, but the ceremonial, which contained the shadows of which the "body", or reality, is now found in Christ!

2. "There remaineth therefore a Sabbath-keeping to the people of God" (Heb. 4:9, see margin). The Greek word here rendered "Sabbath-keeping" is "sabbatismos". It speaks for itself.* As Dr. Carroll affirmed, "No *scholar* will deny the legitimacy of this translation, however he may interpret its import". The Revised Version gives, "There remaineth therefore a Sabbath rest for the people of God". Other important translations might be quoted, but that is not necessary.

"There remaineth therefore a Sabbath-keeping to the people of God". The first thing to which we would here direct attention is the word "remaineth". Note it does not say, "There awaiteth", or "There is yet to be a Sabbath-keeping"; but "There *remaineth*". The reference is not to something future, but to what is present. The Greek verb (in its passive form) is never rendered by any other English equivalent than "remaineth". It occurs again in Heb. 10:26. The word 'remain' signifies "to be left after others have withdrawn, to continue unchanged". Here then is a plain, positive, unequivocal declaration by the Spirit of God: "There *remaineth* therefore a Sabbath-keeping". Nothing could be simpler; nothing less ambiguous. The striking thing is that this statement occurs in the very epistle whose theme is the superiority of *Christianity* over Judaism—a theme developed by showing the superiority of Christ (the Center and Life of Chris-

* The Greek word for "rest" in vv. 1, 3, 5, etc. is an entirely different one.

tianity) over angels, Adam, Moses, Joshua, Aaron, and the whole Levitical economy. It is an epistle addressed to "Holy brethren partakers of the *heavenly* calling" (3:1). Therefore, it cannot be gainsaid that Heb. 4:9 is referring directly to *the Christian Sabbath.* Hence, we solemnly and emphatically declare that the man who says there is *no* Christian Sabbath takes direct issue with the *New Testament* Scriptures.

The second point of importance for our consideration in connection with Heb. 4:9 is to ascertain the force of the "therefore". It would consume too much space for us now to give even a brief exposition of the whole passage of which this verse forms a part, though such an exposition is greatly needed by God's people today. A glance at the context will show that the first eleven verses of Heb. 4 are treating of "Rest", see vv. 1, 3, 4, 5, 6, etc. The purpose of the whole passage is to contrast the rest of Christianity with the rest of Judaism, and the argument centers in an antithesis between Christ and Joshua. The point of the contrast is, that Joshua did not conduct Israel into rest, but Christ does His people. Vv. 1 and 3 show that Israel had the *promise* of rest, but the thing promised they never entered into. The *proof* and the *pledge* that there *is* a rest for "the people of God" is found in the recorded facts that *"God* did *rest* the seventh day from all His works" (v. 4). The "therefore" of v. 9, then, looks back to what we read of in v. 4, which is a quotation from Gen. 2. Believers are "the people of God", *therefore* as *"God"* rests, they must too. But the rest of God referred to in v. 4 was a *Sabbath* rest, hence the Holy Spirit says, "There remaineth therefore a *Sabbath-keeping* to the people of God."

In the third place, notice the *proof for this* furnished in the verse which immediately follows: *"For* He that is entered into His rest, He also hath ceased from His own works, as God did from His" (v. 10). Here the reference is to Christ Himself. The evidence for this is right to hand. The Holy Spirit does not say, "For *they* that have entered into His rest", but *"He* that is entered". Moreover the "also" is still more conclusive: "He that is entered into His rest, He *also* hath ceased from His own works *as God* did from His". Surely none but the Lord Jesus could be thus compared with "God"! Thus the Holy Spirit here teaches us to look upon Christ's rest from His Work of Redemption as *parallel* with God's Work in Creation. They are spoken of as parallel in *this* particular respect: the relation which each Work has *to the keeping of a Sabbath!*

The connection between vv. 9 and 10 is obvious. Christ's finished work and the resting from His labors is expressly and directly assigned as *the reason why* His people must keep a Sabbath. This invests the Christian Sabbath with a fuller meaning than the Sabbath had in Old Testament times. It is now not only a memorial of God's work of creation, and a recognition of the Creator as our Proprietor, but it is also an emblem of the rest which Christ entered as a memorial of His finished work. And inasmuch as Christ ended *His* work and entered upon His "rest" by rising again on the *first* day of the week, we are thereby notified that the Christian's six work days must run from Monday to Saturday and that his Sabbath must be observed on Sunday. This is confirmed by the additional fact that the New Testament shows that after the crucifixion of Christ the first day of the week was the one set apart for Divine worship.

"Then the same day at evening, being the first day of the week, when the doors were shut where the disciples were assembled for fear of the Jews, came Jesus and stood in the midst, and saith unto Him, Peace be unto you" (John 20:19). This was the first assembling together of the disciples on a Christian Sabbath, and it was occasioned by the glorious testimony to the *resurrection* of their Saviour, and there is no record of the disciples again assembling together until the following Sunday! "And after eight days again His disciples were within, and Thomas with them: then came Jesus, the doors being shut, and stood in the midst, and said, Peace be unto you" (John 20: 26). But why wait until then? Why assemble again on the Sunday? It is also most significant that there is no hint of any of the eleven having seen the risen Saviour during the intervening days! But as the apostles assembled on the second Christian Sabbath He appeared in their midst!!

In the fourth place, it is most significant and solemn to note the closing words of this passage in Heb. 4: "Let us labor therefore to enter into that rest, lest any man fall after the same example of unbelief" (v. 11). Here the Holy Spirit sums up with a searching application. The reference is twofold. First and generally, to the central thought of the whole passage, which treats of the *spiritual* rest which remains (v. 6), for those who believe, but which is not entered into by unbelievers; second and more particularly, to the *Sabbath-keeping* of v. 9. To enter into either the rest of Christianity, or the rest of the Sabbath which is now the emblem of it, the Holy Spirit bids us "labor". The Revised Version more accurately renders it, "Let us therefore *give diligence* to enter into that rest". Plainly the Holy Spirit is here anticipating the modern deflection from the truth. He hereby warns us not to follow the false teaching of those who *deny* that "there *remaineth* a *Sabbath-keeping* to the people of God". He bids us "give diligence" that we may not be robbed of our rightful heritage. He tells us not to allow Satan to filch from us the Sabbath rest, but to labor to *enter* it.

Ere passing from this section perhaps a few words should be said to show that in observing the *first* day of the week we in no wise fail to keep the very letter of the fourth commandment of the Decalogue, which declares that "the *seventh* day is the Sabbath of the Lord thy God". As already stated in an earlier section, there is nothing whatever to show on *which* day of our present week God "rested" at the beginning. All that the fourth commandment enjoins is that the seventh day *following six working days* must be kept holy unto the Creator. In addition to this, it remains to be pointed out that the Holy Spirit uses *two distinct words:* "hebdomas" the seventh day; "sabbaton" the Sabbath. They are *not* synonymous terms; that is to say, a Gentile could have kept the fourth commandment by working from Saturday till Thursday and then resting on the Friday just as strictly as if he had started working on Sunday and rested on Saturday. The first day of the week, Sunday, is a "Sabbath", a scriptural Sabbath, if it be observed as a day of rest following six days of work.

VI. THE SABBATH IN THE MILLENNIUM.

That there *will be* a Sabbath observed weekly in Millennial times is proof positive that our moderns err greatly in their interpretation of 2 Cor. 3, when they take such expressions as "the letter that killeth" (v. 6), "that which is done away" (v. 11), and "that which is abolished" (v. 13), as referring to the Ten Commandments. If the Ten Commandments *have been* "abolished", then has "the Sabbath" been abolished, and if the Sabbath has been abolished the Lord Jesus would never permit saved Israel, under "the new covenant", to observe it. So, too, it proves how untenable and erroneous are their strictures on Rom. 6:14 and similar passages, for if it is now incongruous and impossible for those saved by grace to be in any sense under the Law, then, since the Sabbath forms an intrinsic part of the Law, it would be equally incongruous and impossible for Israel in the Millennium, who will have been *saved by grace,* to keep any Sabbath! That the Sabbath *will be* observed during the Millennium, supplies one more proof of the perpetuity of God's moral Law and the lasting obligations on man to obey it.

We offer two proof texts to show there will be a Sabbath kept during Millennial times. The first is in Isa. 56:4-8, "For thus saith the Lord unto the eunuchs that keep My Sabbaths, and choose the things that please Me, and take hold of My covenant; Even unto them will I give in Mine house and within My walls a place and a name better than of sons and of daughters: I will give them an everlasting name, that shall not be cut off. Also the sons of the stranger, that joined themselves to the Lord, to serve Him, and to love the name of the Lord, to be His servants, every one that keepeth the Sabbath from polluting it, and taketh hold of My covenant; Even them will I bring to My holy mountain, and make them joyful in My house of prayer: their burnt offerings and their sacrifices shall be accepted upon Mine altar; for Mine house shall be called an house of prayer for all people. The Lord God which gathereth the outcasts of Israel saith, Yet will I gather others to Him, beside those that are gathered unto Him". The closing verses in this quotation make it clear that it is a passage describing conditions which will obtain during the Millennium, for not till then will God's House, the re-built Temple in Jerusalem (cf Isa. 2:2, etc.), be called "An House of prayer for *all* people".

It will be noted that in the above passage the Lord makes a special promise to the eunuchs, namely, that He will give them "a place and a name better than of sons and daughters". In the preceding verse He states the conditions on which the fulfillment of this promise rests, namely, "the eunuchs that (1) keep My Sabbaths, and (2) choose the things which please Me, and (3) take hold of My covenant". The *order* of these three conditions shows us, once more, the importance which *God* attaches to the keeping of His Sabbaths: Sabbath observance is placed *first!*' The force of this will be appreciated still more if we observe that in v. 7 the Lord makes a promise to "the stranger", that is, to the Gentiles: "He shall be made joyful in My house of prayer". But to this promise also conditions are attached, namely, (1) "That every one that keepeth the Sabbath from polluting it (2) and taketh hold of My covenant" (v. 6). Thus are we shown that not only will the Sabbath be observed during the Millennium but that the faithful keeping of it is made a fundamental condition of blessing, and that, to Jew *and Gentile* alike!

The second scripture to which we would refer the reader is in Ezek. 46. There we read, "Thus saith the Lord God; The gate of the inner court that looketh toward the east shall be shut the six working days; but on the Sabbath it shall be opened" (v. 1). The reference is to the re-built Temple: see the previous chapters of Ezekiel. This scripture intimates that, as from the beginning, the Sabbath is appointed especially for *Divine worship.* It also provides positive proof that the *day* for the Sabbath is the one that follows "the six working days". Let the reader ponder the verses that follow in Ezek. 46.

VII. THE SABBATH ON THE NEW EARTH.

It will no doubt come as a surprise to many when they hear that there will be a Sabbath observed on the *new* earth. Yet so the Scriptures plainly teach. In Isa. 66: 22-24 we read, "For as the new heavens and the new earth, which I will make, shall remain before Me, saith the Lord, so shall your seed and your name remain. And it shall come to pass, that from one new moon to another, and from one *Sabbath* to another, shall all flesh come to *worship* before Me, saith the Lord. And they shall go forth, and look upon the carcases of the men that have transgressed against Me: for their worm shall not die, neither shall their fire be quenched; and they shall be an abhorring unto all flesh".

The above scripture refers to the new heavens and the new earth which shall be *"created"* (see Isa. 65:17) *after* "the first heavens and the first earth were passed away" (Rev. 21:1). On the new earth, God declares, Israel's "seed" and "name" shall *"remain".* And on that new earth, we are told, it shall come to pass, "that from one new moon to another (i. e. from one month to another—cf "every *month"* in Rev. 22:2), and from one Sabbath to another, shall all flesh come to worship before Me, saith the Lord". This passage shows: first, that on the new earth time will be divided into months and weeks, as now; second, that there will be a "Sabbath" observed; third, that this Sabbath will be not only for redeemed Israel, but for *"all flesh"*—thus does the Holy Spirit refute, once more, the modern heretics who say that the Sabbath is only for Israel; fourth, that the Sabbath is appointed, then as now, for the formal recognition and public worship of the Lord. Whatever objections men may bring against this, it stands written in the infallible Word of truth, "It *shall* come to pass".

CONCLUSION.

Let us now sum up the different reasons why men in general and Christians in particular are under solemn obligations to keep the Sabbath day holy. First, because the Creator Himself condescended to set us an example so to keep it (Gen. 2). Second, because the Creator has expressly commanded us to (Ex. 20:8-11). Third, because He has shown us the supreme importance He attaches to it, by making it the "sign" between Himself and Israel, and by recording in His Word that the pollution of His Sabbaths was the chief reason why He visited Israel with such sore judgments in the past. Fourth, because the Lord Jesus Himself kept the Sabbath (Luke 4:16). Fifth, because we need it (Mark 2:27). Sixth, because the Epistle to the Hebrews—addressed to "Holy brethren, partakers of the heavenly calling" (3:1)—expressly declares, "There *remaineth* therefore a Sabbath keeping to the people of God". Seventh, because all history witnesses to the fact that those who keep the Sabbath are signally blest of God, and that those who break it are manifestly curst of God.

It is true that though death was the Divinely-ordained penalty for the Israelite who polluted the Sabbath, it is not threatened against us today; nevertheless, let not any proud rebel suppose he shall escape the anger of his offended Creator. Gal. 6:7 applies here with its full solemn force: "Be not deceived; God is not mocked: for whatsoever a man soweth, that shall he also reap." No, God is not mocked. He has *commanded* man to spend one day out of each seven in rest from all unnecessary work, and if he disobeys. God will *make him rest,* rest on a bed of sickness, and if that does not suffice, rest in death!

"A Sabbath well spent,
Brings a week of content,
And strength for the toils of the morrow;
But a Sabbath profaned,
Whate'er may be gained,
Is a certain forerunner of sorrow".

"The three articles on "The Saint and the Law" have been neatly bound in booklet form and can be supplied at 15¢ per copy, $1.50 per dozen, postpaid. The three articles on "The Sabbath" also in booklet form at the same price.

—Arthur W. Pink.

God is with us in our sorrows. There is no pang that rends the heart, I might almost say not one which disturbs the body, but what Jesus Christ has been with us in it all. Feel you the sorrows of poverty? He "had not where to lay His head." Do you endure the griefs of bereavement? Jesus "wept" at the tomb of Lazarus. Have you been slandered for righteousness' sake, and has it vexed your spirit? He said "Reproach hath broken Mine heart." Have you been betrayed? Do not forget that He, too, had His familiar friend, who sold Him for the price of a slave. On what stormy seas have you been tossed which have not also roared around His boat? Never glen of adversity so dark, so deep, apparently so pathless, but what in stooping down you may discover the foot-prints of the Crucified One. In the fires and in the rivers, in the cold night and under the burning sun, He cries, "I am with thee: be not dismayed; for I am both thy Companion and thy God."—*C. H. Spurgeon.*

EXPOSITION OF FIRST PETER

II.—THE FINAL HAPPINESS OF CHRISTIANS THE SUBJECT OF APOSTOLICAL PREACHING.

The final salvation of the people of God, at the second coming of Jesus Christ, is the subject of apostolical preaching. Things in reference to that salvation, concerning which the prophets prophesied and made inquiry, "have been reported to us by those who preached the gospel with the Holy Ghost sent down from heaven."

"Those who preached the gospel with the Holy Ghost sent down from heaven," are, we apprehend, the apostles and other miraculously gifted teachers of the primitive age. They "preached the gospel;" that is, they published the glad tidings of a full, free, and everlasting deliverance from sin and all its dreadful consequences, through the mediation of the incarnate Son of God, who having expiated sin by the shedding of his own precious blood, which cleanses from all sin, has been raised from the dust of death, and invested with all power in heaven and earth, that he may be able to save to the uttermost all coming to God by him.

They preached this gospel "with the Holy Ghost sent down from heaven." These words intimate, either that their preaching the gospel was accompanied with miraculous works, proving the truth and the divinity of what they taught,—works which they were enabled to perform by the Holy Ghost, whose miraculous influence was "sent down from heaven," —that is, communicated to them by God: —or that their preaching was accompanied by the influence of the divine Spirit on the minds and hearts of those to whom it was addressed, leading them to attend to, to understand, and to believe it; "opening their understandings" to understand the truth, and "their hearts to receive the love of the truth, so as to be saved by it." Both these statements are true, and I think it not improbable that the words of the apostle were meant to include both. "The Lord the Spirit" "bore testimony to the word of grace" in both ways. "The great salvation was begun to be spoken by the Lord, and was confirmed unto us by them who heard him; and God bore witness by signs and wonders, and divers miracles, and gifts of the Holy Ghost, according to his will."[1] When Peter was preaching the gospel to Cornelius and his friends, "the Holy Ghost fell on all them which heard the word." When Paul preached to the Thessalonians, "Our gospel," says he, that is, the gospel as preached by us, "came not to you in word only, but in power, and with the Holy Ghost, and with much assurance:"[2] with abundant evidence given by him, and apprehended by them.

These holy apostles of our Lord Jesus, who, in words taught not by men but by the Holy Ghost, preached the gospel with evidence and efficacy both derived from the divine Spirit, "made a report" concerning the things of which the prophets had prophesied, and into which they had inquired; that is, they made a report concerning the final salvation which is to be bestowed on believers at the second coming of their Lord. Much of their preaching was occupied in telling us what is the nature of that salvation; what Jesus Christ had done and suffered in order to procure that salvation; how the individual sinner is to become a partaker of its blessings; and in showing that there is a present salvation from guilt and the dominion of sin, and the tormenting fear of divine displeasure and everlasting misery. But it also included in it a plain statement of the fact, that the full salvation of the Christian is not to be bestowed on him till the second coming of his Lord, and a description more or less particular of the varied and complete blessedness which was then to become his portion.

They "reported" these things. In making these declarations, they did not utter the dreams of their own imagination, or the deductions of their own reason. They merely "spoke the things which they had heard." They made known to others what had been made known to themselves. This was true of all they said; and, in particular, in reference to things which they reported concerning the final salvation of the people of God. "They did not follow cunningly devised fables when they made known the power and coming of our Lord Jesus." "The things which God had laid up for them who love him, were things which eye had not seen, which ear had not heard, and which it never could have

---
[1] Heb. ii. 3, 4.
[2] Acts x. 44. 1 Thess. i. 5.

entered into the mind of man to conceive; but God revealed them to them by his Spirit;"[1] and of this revelation they made a faithful report.

Let us attend, then, to the report which those men who preached the gospel with the Holy Ghost sent down from heaven have made respecting this salvation, which is to be brought to Christians at the revelation of Jesus Christ. Their report refers both to what their Lord and Master revealed on this subject when he was on earth, and to what was revealed to them by that Holy Spirit whom he promised to send to them, to "lead them into all the truth."

Let us attend first, then, to the report they have given us of what our Lord, when on earth, revealed respecting this salvation. The following passages of Scripture contain that report:—"Verily I say unto you, that ye which have followed me in the regeneration, when the Son of man shall sit on the throne of his glory, ye also shall sit upon twelve thrones, judging the twelve tribes of Israel. And every one that hath forsaken houses, or brethren, or sisters, or father, or mother, or wife, or children, or lands, for my name's sake, shall receive an hundred-fold, and shall inherit everlasting life." "When the Son of man shall come in his glory, and all the holy angels with him, then shall he sit upon the throne of his glory; and before him shall be gathered all nations; and he shall separate them one from another, as a shepherd divideth his sheep from the goats: And he shall set the sheep on his right hand, but the goats on the left. Then shall the King say unto them on his right hand, Come, ye blessed of my Father, inherit the kingdom prepared for you from the foundation of the world: For I was an hungered, and ye gave me meat: I was thirsty, and ye gave me drink: I was a stranger, and ye took me in: Naked, and ye clothed me: I was sick, and ye visited me: I was in prison, and ye came unto me. Then shall the righteous answer him, saying, Lord, when saw we thee an hungered, and fed thee? or thirsty, and gave thee drink? When saw we thee a stranger, and took thee in? or naked, and clothed thee? Or when saw we thee sick, or in prison, and came unto thee? And the King shall answer and say unto them, Verily I say unto you, Inasmuch as ye have done it unto one of the least of these my brethren, ye have done it unto me; and the righteous shall go away into life eternal." "In the end of the world the Son of man shall send forth his angels, and they shall gather out of his kingdom all things that offend, and them who do iniquity, and cast them into a furnace of fire; there shall be weeping and gnashing of teeth. Then shall the righteous shine forth as the sun in the kingdom of their Father." "God so loved the world, that he gave his only begotten Son, that whosoever believeth on him might not perish, but have everlasting life." "He that believeth my word, and believeth on him who sent me, hath everlasting life, and shall not come into condemnation; but is passed from death to life. The hour is coming when all that are in their graves shall hear the voice of the Son of God, and come forth; they who have done good to the resurrection of life." "This is the will of him that sent me, that every one which seeth the Son, and believeth on him, may have everlasting life; and I will raise him up at the last day." "In my Father's house are many mansions: if it were not so, I would have told you. I go to prepare a place for you. And if I go and prepare a place for you, I will come again, and receive you unto myself; that where I am there ye may be also. And whither I go ye know, and the way ye know."[2]

The following passages embody revelations made directly to the apostles by the Holy Ghost sent down from Heaven:— "God will render to every man according to his deeds—to them who, by patient continuance in well-doing, seek for glory, and honor, and immortality, eternal life. Glory, honor, and peace shall be to every man that worketh good, in the day when God shall judge the secrets of men by Jesus Christ." "The sufferings of this present time are not worthy to be compared with the glory which shall be revealed in us. For the earnest expectation of the creature waiteth for the manifestation of the sons of God. For the creature was made subject to vanity, not willingly, but by reason of him who hath subjected the same, in hope that the creature itself also shall be delivered from the bondage of corruption into the glorious liberty of the children of God. For we know that the whole creation groaneth and travaileth in pain together

[1] 2 Pet. i. 16. 1 Cor. ii. 7–10.

[2] Matt. xix. 27–29; xxv. 31–40, 46; xiii. 41, 43. John iii. 16; v. 24, 26, 29; vi. 38, 40; xiv. 2–4.

until now: And not only they, but ourselves also, which have the first-fruits of the Spirit, even we ourselves groan within ourselves, waiting for the adoption, the redemption of our body." "Christ is risen from the dead, and become the first-fruits of them that slept. For since by man came death, by man came also the resurrection of the dead; for as in Adam all die, so in Christ shall all be made alive. The last enemy, death, shall be destroyed. It is sown in corruption, it is raised in incorruption: it is sown in dishonor, it is raised in glory: it is sown in weakness, it is raised in power: it is sown a natural body, it is raised a spiritual body. This corruptible must put on incorruption, and this mortal must put on immortality. The saying that is written shall be brought to pass, Death is swallowed up in victory." "We know that if our earthly house of this tabernacle were dissolved, we have a building of God, a house not made with hands, eternal in the heavens." "Your life is hid with Christ in God. When Christ, who is our life, shall appear, we also shall appear with him in glory." "The Lord shall descend with a shout, with the voice of the archangel, and with the trump of God; and the dead in Christ shall first arise. Then we which are alive, and remain, shall be caught up together with them in the clouds to meet the Lord in the air, and so shall we be forever with the Lord." "It is a righteous thing with God to recompense to you who are troubled rest with us, when the Lord Jesus shall be revealed from heaven." "An entrance shall be ministered unto us abundantly into the everlasting kingdom of our Lord and Saviour Jesus Christ." "We, according to his promise, look for a new heaven and a new earth, wherein dwelleth righteousness." "To him that overcometh will I give to eat of the tree of life in the midst of the paradise of God. I will give him a crown of life. He shall not be hurt with the second death. I will give him to eat of the hidden manna, and will give him a white stone, and in the stone a new name, which no man knoweth save he who receiveth it; and I will give him the morning star. He shall be clothed in white raiment, and I will not blot his name out of the book of life; but will confess his name before my Father, and before his angels. I will make him a pillar in the temple of my God, and he shall no more go out. I will grant him to sit with me on my throne, even as I also overcame, and am set down with my Father on his throne." "And God shall wipe away all tears from their eyes; and there shall be no more death, neither sorrow nor crying, neither shall there be any more pain; for the former things are passed away." "And there shall be no more curse; and there shall be no night there; and they shall reign forever and ever."[1]

These are "the things which have been reported to us by them who have preached the Gospel with the Holy Ghost sent down from heaven." There is a good deal in those descriptions which is dark through excessive brightness,—imperfectly intelligible by us, because descriptive of a state more pure, and felicitous, and glorious, than our limited, obtuse, sensualized faculties can distinctly apprehend; but what is clear, and what is dark, equally prove that this happiness, with the love in which it originates, has a height, and a depth, a length and a breadth, that pass knowledge. And O, delightful, solemnizing thought! this is no airy dream. "These are the true and faithful sayings of God." The period referred to is hastening on apace; and all this happiness must either be gained or lost by every one of us—gained or lost forever.

III.—THE FINAL HAPPINESS OF CHRISTIANS THE SUBJECT OF ANGELIC STUDY.

It only remains that I turn your attention to the last view which the apostle gives us of the final salvation of Christians,—as the subject of angelic study: "Into these things the angels desire to look."

Into what things? Obviously into the things "of which the prophets prophesied, and into which they inquired"—into the things "reported to us by them who preached the Gospel with the Holy Ghost sent down from heaven," that is, into the things respecting "the salvation prepared to be revealed in the last time"—into the things respecting "the grace to be brought to Christians at the revelation of Jesus Christ"—into those things the angels desire to look. The meaning of these words is obviously, the angels have an intense desire to understand the whole truth in reference to the final salvation of the people of God.

The angels here spoken of are, without

---

[1] Rom. ii. 6, &c.; Rom. viii. 18–25. 1 Cor. xv. 20, &c. 2 Cor. v. 2, 3. Col. iii. 3, 4. 1 Thess. iv. 13. 2 Thess. i. 6, &c. 2 Pet. i. 11. Rev. ii. passim; Rev. iii. passim; xxi. 4; xxii. 1–5.

doubt, "the elect angels,"—those holy, happy, unembodied spirits who retain their original integrity, who, infinitely beneath God, are yet far superior to men in the scale of being, who excel in wisdom and strength, and who find their happiness in contemplating the divine excellencies, and in doing the divine will.

These exalted spiritual beings are represented as "desirous to look" into the things which respect the final salvation of the redeemed from among men. The original expression is very beautiful. They are with earnest desire bending down, fixing their intensest gaze on these things. The peculiar mode of expression probably alludes to the figures of the cherubim above the mercy-seat, who with downcast eyes were represented as looking on the mercy-seat, as if seeking to penetrate the mystery of wisdom and kindness which the fiery law, covered by the blood-sprinkled golden propitiatory, embodied.

We have no reason to think that the angels directly know anything more about the final salvation of the redeemed among men than we do. It is "by the Church," that is, by the dispensations of God to the Church, that "the principalities and powers in the heavenly places" become acquainted with that revelation of "the manifold wisdom of God"[1] contained in the plan of human redemption. We have no doubt that they know all that is revealed in the Bible on this subject; and that, from their higher faculties, and their more diligent study, and their juster and more extended views of the divine perfections, and of what constitutes the happiness of intelligent creatures, they understand what is revealed there much better than we do.

But still they are not satisfied—they are desirous to understand these wondrous divine declarations more completely, and they are looking forward with intense desire to the period when fulfilment shall develop the full extent of their meaning. Nor is it at all difficult to divine what are the principles in the minds of angels which make them thus desire to look into these things. Enlightened curiosity, piety, and benevolence, all combine in turning their attention with unwearied interest towards this subject.

Enlightened curiosity, or the desire of useful knowledge, is one of the characteristic features, we have reason to believe, of angelic as well as human minds. They know far more than we do, but there is much they do not know; and it is probable their thirst for knowledge exceeds ours just in a similar proportion to their possession of knowledge. It is easy to conceive how desirous they must be of knowing what it is for "corruption to put on incorruption," what it is for "mortality to be swallowed up of life." Enlightened philosophers have great pleasure in witnessing, and in expecting to witness, experiments tending to throw light on the processes of nature. A world in flames, the elements melting with fervent heat, and the heavens flying away like a scroll, and a new heaven and a new earth rising out of the fiery chaos, are spectacles which it is not wonderful the angels should look forward to, with eager desire and almost holy impatience.

Their piety interests them still more deeply in the subject. This salvation is to be the full manifestation of the divine excellencies, as displayed in the whole of that wonderful economy which shall then be completed. Angels will then see more of the power, and wisdom, and holiness, and benignity of God, than they had ever seen, than they had ever conjectured; and then, in the final pulling down of everything which opposes his will or obscures his glory, they will obtain the fullest gratification of the strongest wish of a loyal creature's heart—"that God may be all in all."

Their benevolence, too, keeps their minds fixed on the subject. "They are all ministering spirits, sent forth to minister to those who shall be heirs of salvation." They "encamp round about them that fear God, and deliver them."[2] They have a kind interest in, a tender affection for, those committed to their care. They regard their manifold trials with a benignant pity, though themselves strangers to pain; and they take a generous interest in those events which are to consummate their blessedness. They wonder at the height of glory reserved for the redeemed among men; and, completely free from envy, they desire to understand what is meant by "all things being put under their feet," and by men who have overcome through the blood of the Lamb, sitting down with him on his throne, as he, when he overcame, sat down on his Father's throne.

[1] Eph. iii. 10.
[2] Heb. i. 14. Psal. xxxiv. 7.

Vol. II   NOVEMBER, 1923   No. 11

STUDIES in the SCRIPTURES

"Search the Scriptures" John 5:39.

A PERIODICAL (MONTHLY "IF THE LORD WILL")
DEVOTED TO BIBLE STUDIES and EXPOSITIONS

Associate Editors and Publishers, I. C. HERENDEEN and ARTHUR W. PINK,
Swengel, Pa.

Price: 10 cents per copy; $1.00 per year. Foreign $1.00 per year.

NO CONDEMNATION.

"There is therefore now no condemnation to them which are in Christ Jesus" (Rom. 8:1).

"(There is) *therefore* now no condemnation". The eighth chapter of the epistle to the Romans concludes the first section of that wonderful epistle. Its opening word "Therefore" ("There is" is in italics, because supplied by the translators) may be viewed in a twofold way. First, it connects with *all* that has been said from 3:21. An inference is now deduced from the whole of the preceding discussion, an inference which was, in fact, the grand conclusion toward which the apostle had been aiming throughout the entire argument. Because Christ has been set forth "a propitiation through faith in His blood" (3:25); because He was "delivered for our offences and raised again for our justification" (4:25); because by the obedience of the One the many (believers of all ages) are "made righteous", constituted so, legally, (5:19); because believers have "died (judicially) to sin" (6:2); because they have "died" to the condemning power of the law (7:4), there is, "*therefore*, NO CONDEMNATION".

But not only is the "therefore" to be viewed as a conclusion drawn from the whole of the previous discussion, it is also to be considered as having a close relation to what immediately precedes. In the second half of Rom. 7 the apostle had described the painful and ceaseless conflict which is waged between the antagonistic natures in the one who has been born again, illustrating this by a reference to his own personal experiences as a Christian. Having portrayed with a master pen—himself sitting for the picture—the spiritual struggles of the child of God, the apostle now proceeds to direct attention to *the Divine consolation* for a condition so distressing and humiliating. The transition from the despondent tone of the seventh chapter to the triumphant language of the eighth, appears startling and abrupt, yet is it quite logical and natural. If it is true that to the saints of God belongs the *conflict* of sin and death, under whose effects they mourn, equally true is it that their *deliverance* from the curse and the corresponding condemnation is a victory in which they rejoice. A very striking contrast is thus pointed. In the second half of Rom. 7 the apostle treats of the *power* of sin, which operates in believers as long as they are in the world; in the opening verses of chapter eight, he speaks of the *guilt* of sin from which they are completely delivered the moment they are united to the Saviour by faith. Hence in 7:24 the apostle asks "Who *shall* deliver me" from the power of sin; but in 8:2 he says, "*hath* made me free*", i. e. hath delivered me, from the guilt of sin.

"(There is) therefore *now* no condemnation". It is not here a question of *our* heart condemning us (as in 1 John 3:21), nor of *us* finding nothing within which is worthy of condemnation; instead, it is the far more blessed fact that *God* condemns not the one who has trusted in Christ to the saving of his soul. We need to distinguish sharply between subjective and objective truth; between that which is judicial and that which is experimental; otherwise, we shall fail to draw from such scriptures as the one now before us the comfort and peace they are designed to convey. There is no condemnation to them who are *in Christ Jesus*. "In Christ" is the believer's *position before God*, not his condition in the flesh. "In Adam" I was condemned (Rom. 5:12); but "in Christ" is to be forever freed from all condemnation.

(Continued on page 336.)

IMPORTANT NOTICES

All new subscriptions will be dated back to January, 1923.
Set of twelve issues for 1922, unbound, $1.00. Bound, $1.50.
Set of twelve items for 1923, unbound, $1.00 Bound (ready December 1st) $1.50.
Note: We cannot break a set or now supply any **single** 1923 issues.
Subscription Price: $1.00 per year to any address in the world. Single copies 10 cents.
Change of Address: Please notify us promptly of any change of address, and be certain to give both old and new addresses.
Non-Subscribers receiving this Magazine regularly will understand their subscription has been entered by a friend.
Copies lost in the mail duplicated only if we are notified promptly.

Entered as second-class matter December 15th, 1921 at the post office at Swengel, Pa., under Act of March 3rd, 1879.

CONTENTS

John's Gospel (John 6:41-59) 314
Israel and the Antichrist 323
Exposition of First Peter 328

JOHN'S GOSPEL

23. CHRIST IN THE CAPERNAUM SYNAGOGUE. John 6:41-59.

The following is submitted as an Analysis of the passage which is to be before us:

1. The murmuring of the Jews: vv. 41, 42.
2. Christ's rebuke: vv. 43-45.
3. The glory of Christ: v. 46.
4. Christ, the Life-giver: vv. 47-51.
5. The criticism of the Jews: v. 52.
6. Christ's solemn reply: v. 53.
7. The results of feeding on Christ: vv. 54-59.

The first thirteen verses of John 6 describe the feeding of the multitude, and in vv. 14 and 15 we are shown what effect that miracle had upon the crowd. From v. 16 to the end of v. 21 we have the well-known incident of the disciples in the storm, and the Lord walking on the sea and coming to their deliverance. In vv. 22 to 25 we see the people following Christ to Capernaum, and in vv. 26 to 40 we learn of the conversation which took place between them and our Lord—most probably in the open air. At v. 41 there is a break in the chapter, and a new company is introduced, namely, "the Jews"; and from v. 59 it is clear that *they* were in the synagogue. In this Gospel "the Jews" are ever viewed as antagonistic to the Saviour—see our notes on 5:15. Here they are represented as "murmuring" because the Lord had said, "I am the bread which came down from heaven". This does not prove that *they* had heard His words which are recorded in v. 33. Note it does not say in v. 41 that the Lord had said *this* "unto them": contrast vv. 29, 32, 35! Most probably, the words He had spoken to "the people" of v. 24—words which are recorded in the verses which follow, to the end of v. 40—had been *reported* to "the Jews". Hence, vv. 41 to 59 describe the conversation between Christ and the Jews in the Capernaum synagogue, as the preceding verses narrate what passed between the Saviour and the Galileans. The Holy Spirit has placed the two conversations side by side, because of the similarity of their themes.

"The Jews then murmured at Him, because He said, I am the bread which came down from heaven" (v. 41). "In John 'the Jews' are always distinguished from the multitude. They are the inhabitants of Jerusalem and Judea. It would, perhaps, be easier to understand this Gospel, if the words were rendered 'those of Judea', which is the true sense" (J. N. D.). These Jews were "murmuring", and it is a significant thing that the same word is used here as in the Septuagint (the first Gentile translation of the Hebrew Old Testament) of Israel murmuring in the wilderness. In few things does the depravity of the human heart reveal itself so plainly and so frequently as in *murmuring* against God. It is a sin which few, if any, are preserved from.

The Jews were murmuring against Christ. They were murmuring against Him because He had said, "I am the bread which came down from heaven". This was a saying that offended them. And why should *that* cause them to murmur? They were, of course, completely blind to Christ's Divine glory, and so were ignorant that this very One whom some of them had seen grow up before their eyes in the humble home of Joseph and Mary in Nazareth, and the One that some of them, perhaps, had seen working at the carpenter's bench, should make a claim which they quickly perceived avowed His Deity. It was the pride of the human heart disdaining to be indebted to One who had lain aside His glory, and had taken upon Him the form of a servant. They refused to be beholden to One so lowly. Moreover, they were far too self-satisfied and self-righteous to see any need for One to come down from heaven *to them*, much less for that One to die upon the Cross to meet their need and thus become their Saviour. *Their* case, as they thought, was by no means so desperate as that. The truth is, they had *no hunger* for "the bread which came down from heaven". What light this casts on the state of the world today! How it serves to explain the common treatment which the Lord of glory still receives at the hands of men! Pride, the wicked pride of the self-righteous heart, is responsible for unbelief. Men despise and reject the Saviour because they feel not their deep need of Him. Feeding upon the husks which are fit food for swine, they have no appetite for the true bread. And when the claims of Christ are really pressed upon them they still "murmur"!

"And they said, Is not this Jesus, the son of Joseph, whose father and mother we know? How is it then that He saith, I came down from heaven?" (v. 42). This shows that these Jews understood Christ's words "I am the bread which came down from heaven" as signifying that He was of Divine origin; and in this they were quite right. None but He could truthfully make the claim. This declaration of Christ meant that He had personally existed in heaven before He appeared among men, and, as His forerunner testified, "He that cometh from above is above all" (John 3:31): above all, because the first man and all his family are of the earth, earthy; but "the second Man is the Lord from heaven" (1 Cor. 15:47). And for the Lord to become Man required the miracle of the virgin birth: a supernatural Being could only enter this world in a supernatural manner. But these Jews were in total ignorance of Christ's superhuman origin. They supposed Him to be the natural son of Joseph and Mary. His "father and mother", said they, "we *know*". But they did not. His Father, they knew not of, nor could they, unless the Father revealed Himself unto them. And it is so still. It is one thing to receive, intellectually, as a religious dogma, that Jesus Christ is the Son of God; it is altogether another to *know* Him as such for myself. Flesh and blood cannot reveal this to me (Matt. 16:17).

"Jesus therefore answered and said unto them, Murmur not among yourselves. No man can come to Me, except the Father which hath sent Me draw him: and I will raise him up at the last day" (vv. 43, 44). This word is very solemn coming just at this point, and it is necessary to note carefully its exact connection. It was a word which at once exposed the moral condition and explained the cause of the "murmuring" of these Jews. Great care must be taken to observe what Christ did not say, and precisely what He did say. He did not say, "No man can come to Me, except the Father hath given him to Me", true as that certainly is. But He spoke here so as to address their human responsibility. It was not designed as a word to repel, but to humble. It was not closing the door in their face, but showed how alone that door could be entered. It was not intended as an intimation that there was no possible hope for them, rather was it a pointing out the direction in which hope lay. Had Saul of Tarsus then been among the number who heard these searching words of Christ, they would have applied in full force to his own case and condition; and yet it became manifest, subsequently, that *he* was a vessel of mercy, given by the Father before the foundation of the world to the Son. And it is quite possible that some of these very Jews, then murmuring, were among the number who, at Pentecost, were drawn by the Father to believe on the Son. The Lord's language was carefully chosen, and left room for that. John 7:5 tells us that the Lord's own brethren (according to the flesh) did not believe on Him at first, and yet, later, they ranked among His disciples, as is clear from Acts 1:14. Let us be careful, then, not to read *into* this 44th verse what is not there.

"No man can come to Me, except the Father which hath sent Me draw him" (v. 44). These words of Christ make manifest the depths of human depravity. They expose the inveterate stubbornness of the human will. They explain the "murmuring" of these Jews. In answering them thus, the obvious meaning of the Saviour's words was this: By your murmuring you make it evident that *you* have not come to Me, that you are not disposed to come to Me; and with your present self-righteousness, you never will come to Me. Before you come to Me you must be converted and become as little children. And before that can take place, you must be the subjects of Divine operation. One has only to reflect on the condition of the natural man in order to see the indubitable truth of this. Salvation is most exactly suited to the sinner's needs, but it is not at all suited to his natural inclinations. The Gospel is too spiritual for his carnal mind: too humbling for his pride: too exacting for his rebellious will: too lofty for his darkened understanding: too holy for his earthbound desires.

"No man can come to Me, except the Father which hath sent Me draw him" (v. 44). How can one who has a high conceit of himself and his religious performances admit that all his righteousnesses are as filthy rags? How can one who prides himself on his morality and his religiousness, own himself as lost, undone, and justly condemned? How can one who sees so little amiss in himself, who is *blind* to the fact that from the crown of his head to the soul of his foot there is no soundness in him (Isa. 1:6), earnestly seek the great Physician? No man with an *unchanged* heart and mind will ever embrace God's salvation. The inability here, then, is a moral one. Just as when Christ also said, "*How can ye,* being evil, speak good things?" (Matt. 12:34). And again, "*How can ye believe,* which receive honor one of another?" (John 5:44). And again, "Even the Spirit of truth; whom the world *cannot* receive" (John 14:17). Water will not flow uphill, nor will the natural man act contrary to his corrupt nature. An evil tree cannot bring forth good fruit, and equally impossible is it for a heart that loves the darkness to also love the light.

The depravity of man is, from the human side, the only thing which will explain the general rejection of the Gospel. The only satisfactory answer to the questions, Why is not Christ cordially received by all to whom He is presented? Why do the majority of men despise and reject Him? is—Man is a fallen creature, a depraved being who loves sin and hates holiness. So, too, the only satisfactory answer which can be given to the questions, Why is the Gospel cordially received by any man? Why is it not obstinately rejected by all? is, In the case of those who believe, God has, by His supernatural influence, counteracted against the human depravity; in other words, the Father has "drawn" to the Son.

The condition of the natural man is altogether beyond human repair. To talk about exerting the will is to ignore the state of the man behind the will. Man's will has not escaped the general wreckage of his nature. When man fell, *every* part of his being was affected. Just as truly as the sinner's heart is estranged from God and his understanding darkened, so is his will enslaved by sin. To predicate the freedom of the will is to *deny* that man is totally depraved. To say that man *has* the power within himself to either reject or accept Christ, is to *repudiate* the fact that he is the captive of the Devil. It is to say *there is* at least one good thing in the flesh. It is to flatly contradict this word of the Son of God—"No man *can* come to Me, except the Father which hath sent Me draw him."

Man's only hope lies *outside* of himself, in Divine help. And this is what we meant above when we said that this word of Christ was not intended to close the door of hope, but pointed out the direction in which hope lay. If it be true that I cannot get away from myself; if it be true that my whole being is depraved, and therefore at enmity with God; if it be true that I am powerless to reverse the tendency of my nature, what then can I do? Why, *acknowledge* my helplessness, and *cry* for help. What should a man do who falls down and breaks his hip? He cannot rise: shall he, then, lie there in his misery and perish? Not if he has *any desire* for relief. He will lift up his voice and summon assistance. And if these murmuring Jews had *believed* what Christ told them about their helplessness, this is what *they* had done. And if the unsaved today would only believe God when He says that the sinner is *lost,* he, too, will call for a Deliverer. If I cannot come to Christ without the Father "draws" me, then, my responsibility is to *beg* the Father *to* "draw" me.

In what, we may inquire, does this "drawing" consist? It certainly has reference to something more than the invitation of the Gospel. The word used is a strong one, signifying, the putting forth of power and *obliging* the object seized to respond. The same word is found in John 18:10; 21:6, 11. If the reader consults these passages he will find that it means far more than "to attract". *Impel* would give the true force of it here in John 6:44.

As said above, the unregenerate sinner is so depraved that with an unchanged heart and mind he will never come to Christ. And the change which is absolutely essential is one which God alone can produce. It is, therefore, by Divine "drawing" that any one comes to Christ. *What* is this "drawing"? We answer, It is the power of the Holy Spirit overcoming the self-righteousness of the sinner, and convicting him of his lost condition. It is the Holy Spirit awakening within him a sense of need. It is the power of the Holy Spirit overcoming the pride of the natural man, so that he is ready to come to Christ as an empty-handed beggar. It is the Holy Spirit creating within him an *hunger* for the bread of life.

"It is written in the prophets, And they shall be all taught of God" (v. 45). Our Lord confirms what He had just said by an appeal to the Scriptures. The reference is to Isa. 54:13: "And all thy children shall be taught of the Lord". This serves to explain, in part at least, the meaning of "draw". Those drawn are they who are "taught of God". And who are these, so highly favored? The quotation from Isa. 54 tells us: they are God's "children"; His own, His elect. Notice carefully *how* our Lord quoted Isa. 54:13. He simply said, "And they shall be *all* taught of God". This helps us to define the "all" in other passages, like John 12:32: "I, if I be lifted up from the earth, will draw *all* unto Me". The "all" *does not mean* all of humanity, but all of God's children, all His elect.

"Every man therefore that hath heard, and hath learned of the Father cometh unto Me" (v. 45). This also throws light on the "drawing" of the previous verse. Those drawn are they who have "heard" and "learned of the Father". That is to say, God has given them an ear to hear and a heart to perceive. It is parallel with what we get in 1 Cor. 1:23, 24: "But we preach Christ crucified, but unto the Jews a stumblingblock, and unto the Greeks foolishness: But unto them which are *called*, both Jews and Greeks, Christ the power of God, and the wisdom of God". "Called" here refers to the effectual and irresistible call of God. It is a call which is heard with the inward ear. It is a call which is instinct with Divine power, drawing its object to Christ Himself.

"Not that any man hath seen the Father, save He which is of God, He hath seen the Father" (v. 46). This is very important. It guards against a false inference. It was spoken to prevent His hearers (and us today) from supposing that some *direct* communication from the Father is necessary before a sinner can be saved. Christ had just affirmed that only those come to Him who had heard and learned of the Father. But this does not mean that such characters hear His *audible* voice or are *directly* spoken to by Him. Only the Saviour was and is in *immediate* communication with the Father. We hear and learn from the Father *only* through His written Word! So much then for the primary significance of this verse according to its local application. But there is far more in it than what we have just sought to bring out.

"'Not that any man hath seen the Father, save He which is of God, He hath seen the Father" (v. 46). How this displays the *glory* of Christ, bringing out, as it does, the infinite distance there is between the incarnate Son and all men on earth. No man had seen the Father; but the One speaking *had,* and *He* had because He is "of (not "the Father" but) God". *He* is a member of the Godhead, Himself very God of very God. And because He had "seen the Father", He was fully qualified to speak of Him, to reveal Him—see John 1:18. And who else *could* "declare" the Father? How else could the light of the Father's love and grace have shined into our hearts, but through and by Christ, His Son?

"Verily, verily, I say unto you, He that believeth on Me hath everlasting life" (v. 47). Christ still pursues the line of truth begun in v. 44. This forty-seventh verse is not an invitation to sinners, but a doctrinal declaration concerning saints. In v. 44 He had stated what was essential from the Divine side if a sinner come to Christ: he must be "drawn" by the Father. In v. 45 He defined, in part, what this "drawing" consists of: it is hearing and learning of the Father. Then, having guarded against a false inference from His words in v. 45, the Saviour now says, "He that believeth on Me hath everlasting life". Believing *is not* the cause of a sinner obtaining Divine life, rather is it the *effect* of it. The fact that a man believes, is the evidence that he *already* has Divine life within him. True, the sinner *ought* to believe. Such is his bounden duty. And in addressing sinners from the standpoint of human responsibility, it is perfectly proper to say 'Whosoever believeth in Christ shall not perish *but have* eternal life'. Nevertheless, the fact remains that *no* unregenerate sinner ever did or ever will believe. The unregenerate sinner ought to *love* God, and love Him with all his heart. He is commanded to. But he *does not*, and *will not*, until Divine grace gives him a new heart. So he ought to believe, but he will not till he has been quickened into newness of life. Therefore, we say that when any man *does* believe, is found believing, it is proof positive that he is *already* in possession of eternal life. "He that believeth on Me *hath* (already has) eternal life": cf John 3:36; 5:24; 1 John 5:1, etc.

"I am that bread of life" (v. 48). This is the first of the seven "I am" titles of Christ found in this Gospel, and found nowhere else. The others are, "I am the Light of the world" (8:12); "I am the Door" (10:9); "I am the Good Shepherd" (10:11); "I am the Resurrection and the Life" (11:35); "I am the Way, the Truth, and the Life" (14:6); "I am the True Vine" (15:1). They all look back to that memorable occasion when God appeared to Moses at the burning bush, and bade him go down into Egypt, communicate with his people, interview Pharaoh, and command him to let the children of God go forth into the wilderness to worship Jehovah. And when Moses asked, Who shall I say hath sent me?, the answer was, "Then shalt thou say unto the children of Israel I AM hath sent me unto you" (Ex. 3:14). Here in John, we have a *sevenfold* filling out of the "I am"—I am the Bread of life, etc. Christ's employment of these titles at once identifies Him with the Jehovah of the Old Testament, and unequivocally demonstrates His absolute Deity.

"I am that bread of life" (v. 48). Blessed, precious words are these. 'I am that which every sinner needs, and without which he will surely perish. I am that which alone can satisfy the soul and fill the aching void in the unregenerate heart. I am that because, just as wheat is ground into flour and then subjected to the action of fire to fit it for human use, so I, too, have come down all the way from heaven to earth, have passed through the sufferings of death, and am now presented in the Gospel to all that hunger for life.'

"Your fathers did eat manna in the wilderness, and are dead. This is the bread which cometh down from heaven, that a man may eat thereof, and not die" (vv. 49, 50). This is an amplification of v. 48. There He had said, "I am that bread of life"; here He describes one of the characteristic qualities of this "life". The Lord draws a contrast between Himself as the Bread of life and the manna which Israel ate in the wilderness; and also between *the effects* on those who ate the one and those who should eat the other. The fathers did eat manna in the wilderness, but they died. The manna simply ministered to a temporal need. It fed their bodies, but was not able to immortalize them. But those who eat the true bread, shall not die. Those who appropriate Christ to themselves, those who satisfy their hearts by feeding on Him, shall live forever. Not, of course, on earth, but with Him in heaven.

"This is the bread which cometh down from heaven, that a man may eat thereof, and not die" (v. 50). It is obvious that Christ gives the word "die" a different meaning here from what it bears in the previous verse. There He had said that they, who of old ate manna in the wilderness, "are dead": natural death, physical dissolution being in view. But here He says that a man may eat of the bread which cometh down from heaven, and "not die": that is, not die spiritually and eternally, not suffer the "second death". Should any object to this interpretation which gives a different meaning to the word "death" as it occurs in two consecutive verses, we would remind him that in a single verse the word is found twice, but with a different meaning: "Let the dead bury their dead" (Luke 9:60).

This is one of the many, many verses of Scripture which affirms the eternal security of the believer. The life which God imparts in sovereign grace to the poor sinner, is not a life that may be forfeited; for, "the gifts and calling of God are without repentance" (Rom. 11:29). It is not a life which is perishable, for it is "hid with Christ in God" (Col. 3:3). It is not a life which ends when our earthly pilgrimage is over, for it is "eternal life". Ah, what has the world to offer in comparison with this?

Do the worldling's fondest dreams of happiness embrace the element of unending continuity? No, indeed; *that* is the one thing lacking, the want of which spoils all the rest!

"I am the living bread which came down from heaven" (v. 51). How evident it is then that Christ is here addressing these Jews on the ground, not of God's secret counsels, but, of their human responsibility. It is true that none will come to Him save as they are "drawn" by the Father; but this does not mean that the Father refuses to "draw" any poor sinner that really *desires* Christ. Yea, that very desire *for* Christ is the proof the Father has commenced to "draw". And how Divinely simple is the way in which Christ is received—"If any man (no matter who he be) *eat* of this bread he shall live forever". The figure of "eating" is very suggestive, and one deserving of careful meditation.

In the first place, eating is *a necessary act* if I am to derive that advantage from bread which it is intended to convey, namely, bodily nourishment. I may look at bread and admire it; I may philosophize about bread and analyze it; I may talk about bread and eulogize its quality; I may handle bread and be assured of its excellency—but unless I *eat* it, I shall not be nourished by it. All of this is equally true with spiritual bread, Christ. Knowing the truth, speculating about it, talking about it, contending for it, will do me no good. I must *receive* it into my heart.

In the second place, eating is *responding to a felt need.* That need is hunger, unmistakeably evident, acutely felt. And when one is *really* hungry he asks no questions, he makes no demurs, he raises no quibbles, but gladly and promptly partakes of that which is set before him. So it is, again, spiritually. Once a sinner is awakened to his lost condition; once he is truly conscious of his deep, deep need, once he becomes aware of the fact that without Christ he will perish eternally; then, whatever intellectual difficulties may have previously troubled him, however much he may have procrastinated in the past, *now* he will need no urging, but promptly and gladly will he receive Christ as his own.

In the third place, eating implies *an act of appropriation.* The table may be spread, and loaded down with delicacies, and a liberal portion may be placed on my plate, but not until I commence to *eat* do I make that food my own. Then, that food which previously was without me, is taken inside, assimilated, and becomes a part of me, supplying health and strength. So it is spiritually. Christ may be presented to me in all His attractiveness, I may respect His wonderful personality, I may admire His perfect life, I may be touched by His unselfishness and tenderness, I may be moved to tears at the sight of Him dying on the cruel Tree; but, not until I *appropriate* Him, not until I *receive* Him as mine, shall I be saved. Then, He who before was outside, will indwell me. Now, in very truth, shall I know Him as the bread of life, ministering daily to my spiritual health and strength.

In the fourth place, eating is an intensely *personal act:* it is something which no one else can do for me. There is no such thing as eating by proxy. If I am to be nourished, I must, myself, eat. Standing by and watching others eat will not supply *my* needs. So, dear reader, no one can believe in Christ for you. The preacher cannot; your loved ones cannot. And you may have witnessed others receiving Christ as theirs; you may later hear their ringing testimonies; you may be struck by the unmistakeable change wrought in their lives; but, unless *you* have "eaten" the bread of life, unless you have personally received Christ as yours, it has all availed you nothing. "If any man eat of this bread, he shall live forever". Divinely simple and yet wonderfully full is this figure of eating.

"And the bread which I will give is My flesh" (v. 51). Exceedingly solemn and exceedingly precious is this. To "give" His "flesh" was to offer Himself as a sacrifice, it was to voluntarily lay down His life. Here, then, Christ presents Himself, not only as One who came down from heaven, but as One who had come here to die. And not until we reach this point do we come to the heart of the Gospel. As an awakened sinner beholds the person of Christ, as he reads the record of His perfect life down here, he will exclaim, "Woe is me; I am undone". Every line in the lovely picture which the Holy Spirit has given us in the four Gospels only condemns me, for it shows me how *unlike* I am to the Holy One of God. I admire His ways: I marvel at His perfections. I wish that I could be like Him. But, alas, I am altogether *unlike* Him. If Christ be the One that the Father delights in, then verily, He can never delight in me; for His ways and mine are as far apart as the east is from the west. O what is to become of me, wretched man that I am! Ah, dear reader, what had become of every one of us if Christ had *only* glorified the Father by a brief sojourn here as the perfect Son of man? What hope had there been if, with garments white and glistering, and face radiant with a glory surpassing that of the midday sun, He had ascended from the Mount of Transfiguration, leaving this earth forever? There is only one answer: the door of hope had been fast closed against every member of Adam's fallen and guilty race. But blessed be His name, wonderful as was His descent from heaven, wonderful as was that humble birth in Bethlehem's lowly manger, wonderful as was the flawless life that He lived here for thirty-three years as He tabernacled among men; yet, that was not all, that was not the most wonderful. Read this fifty-first verse of John 6 again: "I am the living bread which came down from heaven: if any man eat of this bread, he shall live forever: and the bread that I will give is My flesh, which I will give for the life of the world". Ah, it is only in a *slain* Christ that poor sinners can find that which meets their dire and solemn need. And His "flesh" He gave in voluntary and vicarious sacrifice "for the life of the world": not merely for the Jews, but for elect sinners of the Gentiles too. His meritorious life was substituted for our forfeited life. Surely this will move our hearts to fervent praise. Surely this will cause us to bow before Him in adoring worship.

"The Jews therefore strove among themselves, saying, How can this man give us His flesh to eat?" (v. 52). "It is difficult, or rather impossible, to say what was the precise state of mind which this question indicated on the part of those who proposed it. It is not unlikely that it expressed different sentiments in different individuals. With some it probably was a contemptuous expression of utter incredulity, grounded on the alleged obvious absurdity of the statement made: *q. d.*, 'The man is mad; can any absurdity exceed this? We are to live for ever by eating the flesh of a living man!' With others, who thought that neither our Lord's words nor works were like those of a madman, the question probably was equivalent to a statement—'These words must have a meaning different from their literal signification, but what can that meaning be?'

"These 'strivings' of the Jews about the meaning of our Lord's words, were 'among themselves'. None of them seemed to have stated their sentiments to our Lord, but He was perfectly aware of what was going on among them. He does not, however, proceed to explain His former statements. They were not ready for such an explication. It would have been worse than lost on them. Instead of illustrating His statement, He reiterated it. He in no degree explains away what had seemed strange, absurd, incredible, or unintelligible. On the contrary, He becomes, if possible, more paradoxical and enigmatical than ever, in order that His statement might be more firmly rooted in their memory, and that they might the more earnestly inquire, 'What can these mysterious words mean?' He tells them that, strange and unintelligible, and incredible, and absurd, as His statements might appear, He had said nothing but what was indubitably true, and incalculably important" (Dr. John Brown).

"Then Jesus said unto them, Verily, verily, I say unto you, Except ye eat the flesh of the Son of man, and drink His blood, ye have no life in you" (v. 53). This verse and the two that follow contain an amplification of what He had said in v. 51. He was shortly to offer Himself as a substitutionary victim, an expiatory sacrifice, in the room of and in order to secure the salvation, of both Jews and Gentiles. And this sacrificial death must be appropriated, received into the heart by faith, if men are to be saved thereby. Except men "eat the flesh" and "drink" the blood of Christ, they have "no life" in them. For a man to have "no life" in him means that he continues in spiritual death: in that state of condemnation, moral pollution, and hopeless wretchedness into which sin has brought him.

Observe that it is as Son of man He here speaks of Himself. How could He have suffered death if He had not become incarnate? And the incarnation was in order to His death. How this links together the mysteries of Bethlehem and Calvary; the incarnation and the Cross! And, as we have said, the one was in order to the other. He came from heaven to earth in order to die: "but now once in the end of the age hath He appeared to put away sin by the sacrifice of Himself" (Heb. 9:26). "But we see Jesus, who was made a little lower than the angels *for* the suffering of death" (Heb. 2:9).

"Except ye eat the flesh of the Son of man, and drink His blood, ye have no life in you" (v. 53). Difficult as this language first appears, it is really blessedly simple. It is not a dead Christ which the sinner is to feed upon, but on the *death of* One who is now alive forever more. His *death* is mine, when appropriated by faith; and thus appropriated, it becomes *life* in me. The figure of "eating" looks back, perhaps, to Gen. 3. Man *died* (spiritually) by "eating"—of the forbidden fruit; and he is *made alive* (spiritually) by an act of eating!

"Whoso eateth My flesh, and drinketh My blood, hath eternal life; and I will raise him up at the last day" (v. 54). Notice the change in the tense of the verb. In the previous verse it is, "Except ye *eat*"; here it is "whoso *eateth*". In the former, the verb is in the aorist tense, implying a single act, an act done once for all. In the latter, the verb is in the perfect tense, denoting that which is continuous and characteristic. V. 53 defines the difference between one who is lost and one who is saved. In order to be saved, I must "eat" the flesh and "drink" the blood of the Son of man; that is, I must appropriate Him, make Him mine by an act of faith. This act of receiving Christ is done once for all. I cannot *receive* Him a second time, for He never leaves me! But, having received Him to the saving of my soul, I now feed on Him constantly, daily, as the Food of my soul. Ex. 12 supplies us with an illustration. First, the Israelite was to *apply* the shed blood of the slain lamb. Then, as protected by that blood, he was to *feed* on the lamb itself.

"Whoso eateth My flesh, and drinketh My blood, hath eternal life; and I will raise him up at the last day" (v. 54). This confirms our interpretation of the previous verse. If we compare it with v. 47 it will be seen at once the "eating" is equivalent to "believing". Note, too, that the tense of the verbs is the same: v. 47 "believeth", v. 54 "eateth". And observe how each of these are *evidences* of eternal life, already in possession of the one thus engaged: "He that believeth on Me *hath* eternal life"; "Whoso eateth My flesh, and drinketh My blood, *hath* eternal life".

This passage in John 6 is a favorite one with Ritualists, who understand it to refer to the Lord's Supper. But this is certainly a mistake, and that for the following reasons. First, the Lord's Supper had not been instituted when Christ delivered this discourse. Second, Christ was here addressing Himself to unbelievers, and the Lord's Supper is for saints, not unregenerate sinners. Third, the eating and drinking here spoken of are in order to salvation; but eating and drinking at the Lord's table is for those who have been saved.

"For My flesh is meat indeed, and My blood is drink indeed" (v. 55). The connection between this and the previous verse is obvious. It is brought in, no doubt, to prevent a false inference being drawn from the preceding words. Christ had thrown the emphasis on the "eating". Except a man ate His flesh, he had no life in him. But now our Lord brings out the truth that there is nothing *meritorious* in the act of eating; that is to say, there is no mystical power in faith itself. The nourishing power is in the *food* eaten; and the potency of faith lies in its *Object*.

"For My flesh is meat indeed, and My blood is drink indeed" (v. 55). Here Christ throws the emphasis on *what it is* which must be "eaten". It is true in the natural realm. It is not the mere eating of anything which will nourish us. If a man eat a poisonous substance he will be killed; if he eat that which is innutritious he will starve. Equally so is it spiritually. "There are many strong believers in hell, and on the road to hell; but they are those who believed a lie, and not the truth as it is in Christ Jesus" (Dr. J. Brown). It is Christ who alone can save: Christ as crucified, but now alive for evermore.

"He that eateth My flesh, and drinketh My blood, dwelleth in Me, and I in him" (v. 56). In this, and the following verse, Christ proceeds to state some of the blessed *effects* of eating. The first effect is that, the saved sinner is brought into vital union with Christ, and enjoys the most intimate *fellowship* with Him. The word "dwelleth" is commonly translated "abideth". It always has reference to *communion*. But mark the tense of the verb: it is only the one who "eateth" and "drinketh", constantly, that abides in unbroken fellowship with Christ.

"He that eateth My flesh, and drinketh My blood, dwelleth in Me, and I in Him" (v. 56). This language clearly implies, though it does not specifically mention the fact, that Christ would *rise* from the dead, for only as risen could He dwell in the believer, and he believer in Him. It is, then, with Christ risen, that they who feed on Him as slain, are identified: so marvellously identified that Scripture here, for the first time, speaks of *union* with our blessed Lord.

"As the living Father hath sent Me, and I live by the Father: so he that eateth Me, even he shall live by Me" (v. 57). How evident it is, again, that Christ is here speaking of Himself as the Mediator, and not according to His essential Being: it is Christ not in Godhead glory, but as the Son incarnate, come down from heaven. "I live by the Father" means He lived His life in *dependence* upon the Father. This is what He stressed in replying to Satan's first assault in the temptation. When the Devil said, "If Thou be the Son of God, command", etc. He was not (as commonly supposed) casting doubt on the Deity of Christ, but asking Him to make a wrong use of it. "If" must be understood as "since", same as in John 14:2; Col. 3:1, etc., etc. The force of what the Tempter said is this: Since you *are* the Son of God, *exercise* your Divine prerogatives, *use* your Divine power and supply your bodily need. But this ignored the fact that the Son had taken upon Him the "form of a servant" and had entered (voluntarily) the place of subjection. Therefore, it is of *this* the Saviour reminds him in His reply—"*Man* shall not *live* by bread alone, but by every word that proceedeth out of the mouth of *God*". How beautifully this illustrates what Christ says here, "I live by the Father"! Let us then seek grace to heed its closing sentence: "So he that eateth Me, even he shall live by Me". Just as the incarnate Son, when on earth, lived in humble dependence on the Father, so now the believer is to live his daily life in humble *dependence* on Christ.

"This is that bread which came down from heaven: not as your fathers did eat manna, and are dead: he that eateth of this bread shall live forever" (v. 58). There is an important point in this verse which is lost to the English reader. Two different words for eating are here employed by Christ. "Your fathers did *eat* (ephazon) manna"; "he that *eateth* (trogon) of this bread shall live forever". The verb "phago" means "to eat, consume, eat up". "Trogo" signifies "to feed upon", rather than the mere act of eating. The first, Christ used when referring to Israel eating the manna in the wilderness: the second, was employed when referring to believers feeding on Himself. The one is a carnal eating, the other a spiritual; the one ends in death, the other ministers life. The Israelites in the wilderness saw nothing more than an objective article of food. And they were like many today, who see nothing more in Christianity than the objective side, and know nothing of the spiritual and experimental! How many there be who are occupied with the externals of religion—outward performances, etc. How few really *feed* upon Christ. They admire Him objectively, but receive Him not into their hearts.

"These things said He in the synagogue, as He taught in Capernaum" (v. 59). What effect this discourse of Christ had on those who heard Him will be considered in our next article. Meanwhile, let the interested reader meditate upon the following questions:—

1. At what, in particular, were the disciples "offended": vv. 60, 61?
2. What is the meaning of v. 63?
3. What is the force of the "therefore" in v. 65?
4. What does the "going back" of those disciples prove: v. 66?
5. Why did Christ challenge the twelve: v. 67?
6. What was the assurance of Peter based on: v. 68?
7. Why was there a Judas in the apostolate: v. 71? How many reasons can you give?

—Arthur W. Pink.

HAVE You Renewed Your Subscription?

natural to men while they are unrenewed, are the principles which regulate their conduct and form their character. One man loves pleasure, another loves money, another loves power, another loves fame. The ruling desire, or lust, is the principle which forms the character and guides the conduct.

Now the Christian, being no longer in ignorance, but knowing and believing the revelation God has made of his will, must no longer permit his character to be fashioned by those desires, to the guidance of which, when in a state of ignorance, he delivered himself up. All these desires, so far as they are sinful, must be mortified, and, even so far as they are innocent, they must cease to be governing principles, and must be subordinated to a higher principle —the principle of submission of mind and heart to the will of God.

The objects of these desires are sensible and present things—things which are "in the world;" so that the not fashioning ourselves according to our former lusts in our ignorance, and our not being "conformed to this world," are but two different modes of expressing the same thing. An unregenerated man's character is entirely formed by the desires of his fallen nature, excited by their appropriate objects in the present world. It was once so with the Christian, but it must be so with him no longer. On the contrary, "as he who has called him is holy, so must he be holy in all manner of conversation."

(2.) This is the apostle's positive statement with respect to Christian duty. There is no word, I apprehend, to which more indistinct ideas are generally attached, than holiness; yet, surely, there is no word of the meaning of which it is of more importance we should have a clear and accurate conception; for "without holiness no man shall see the Lord."[1] The clearest and the justest idea we can form of holiness, as a quality of an intelligent creature, is conformity of mind and will with the Supreme Being, who alone is, in all the extent of meaning belonging to the word, holy. Holiness does not consist in mystic speculations, enthusiastic fervors, or uncommanded austerities; it consists in thinking as God thinks, and willing as God wills. God's mind and will are to be known from his word; and, so far as I really understand and believe God's word, God's mind becomes my mind, God's will becomes my will, and, according to the measure of my faith, I become holy.

And this conformity of mind and will to God—this holiness—is to be manifested "in all manner of conversation." "Conversation," here, as usually in the New Testament, signifies not colloquial intercourse, but general conduct. In every part of your character and conduct, let it appear that the ruling principles of your conduct, the forming principles of your character, are no longer what they once were—your lusts, your natural desires, but the mind and the will of him who has called you, even God, who is holy; his mind and will having become your mind and will, through the knowledge and belief of the truth, make it evident, that these are now the principles by which your character is formed and your life governed. In everything show that you think as God thinks, that you will as God wills, that you love what God loves, that you hate what he hates, that you choose what he chooses, that wherein he finds enjoyment, you seek enjoyment. Such is a short account of the Christian's duty.

There are two conclusions to which these observations necessarily conduct us, highly worthy of considerate reflection. First, that there are many who call themselves Christians, who have no title to that name, habitual violators of God's law, strangers to the very principle of obedience, still "walking according to the course of this world, serving divers lusts and pleasures."[2] How vain—how much worse than vain, is their profession—how dangerous their circumstances—how awful, if they continue in their present state, their final doom! The second conclusion is, that those who are really Christians are still very far, indeed, from being what they ought to be— from being what they might be. The best Christians, then, need to have such exhortations addressed to them as these: "Follow holiness," seek growing conformity of mind and heart to God, and recollect this can be obtained only by growing knowledge and faith of the truth. Though already not of the world, even as their Lord is not of the world, they need the great Intercessor continually to pray for them, "Sanctify them through thy truth, thy word is truth."[3]

[1] Heb. xii. 14.
[2] Eph. ii. 2, 3. Tit. iii. 3.
[3] John xvii. 7.

will soon be over, and it shall be followed by "the great Day of His Wrath" (Rev. 6:17; Joel 2:11). Then will God visit the earth with His sore judgments, and though the Nations shall by no means escape the righteous retribution due them for their part in the crucifixion of Christ, yet, the ones who will be punished the most severely will be they who took the lead in that crime of crimes.

The form which God's judgment will take upon the Jews is to be in full accord with the unchanging law of recompense—what they have sown, *that* shall they also reap. This was expressly affirmed by our Lord Jesus: "I am come in My Father's name, and ye receive Me not: if another shall come in his own name, him ye will receive" (John 5:43). Because they rejected God's Christ, Israel shall receive the Antichrist. The same thing is stated in 2 Thess. 2:7—"For this cause (i. e. "because they received not the love of the Truth, that they might be saved") *God shall send them strong delusion that they should believe the Lie*". The immediate reference here, we believe, is to the Jews, though the principle enumerated will also have its wider application to apostate Christendom. The chief reason why God suffers the Man of Sin to come on the scene and run his awful course, is in order to *inflict punishment upon guilty Israel*. This is clearly taught in Isa. 10:5, where of the Antichrist God says, "O Assyrian, the rod (the instrument of chastisement) of Mine anger, and the staff in their hand is Mine indignation. *I will send him* against an hypocritical nation, against *the people of My wrath* will I give him a charge, to take the spoil, and to take the prey, and to tread them down like the mire of the street", and cf our brief comments on Jer. 6:26, 27 and 15:8 in article nine.

It must be borne in mind that the Jews are to return to Palestine and there re-assume a national standing whilst yet unconverted. There are a number of passages which establish this beyond question. For example, in Ezek. 22:19-22 we are told, "Therefore thus saith the Lord God; because ye are all become dross, behold, therefore I will gather you into the midst of Jerusalem, as they gather silver, and brass, and iron, and lead, and tin, into the midst of the furnace, to blow the fire upon it, to melt it; so will I gather you in Mine anger and in My fury, and I will leave you there, and melt you. Yea, *I will gather you*, and blow upon you in the fire of My wrath, and ye shall be melted in the midst thereof". The first six verses of Isa. 18 describe how the Lord will gather the Jews to Jerusalem, there to be the prey of "fowls and beasts". The closing chapters of Zechariah lead to the inevitable conclusion that the Jews return to their land in unbelief, for if their national conversion takes place in Jerusalem (Zech. 12:10), they must have returned to it unconverted.

When the Antichrist is manifested, great companies of the Jews will already be in Palestine, and in a flourishing condition. What, then, will be his relations with them? It is by no means easy to furnish a detailed answer to this question, and at best we can reply but tentatively. Doubtless, there are many particulars respecting this and all other related subjects, which will not be cleared up until the prophecies concerning them have been fulfilled. We, today, occupy much the same position with regard to the predictions concerning the Antichrist, as the Old Testament saints did to the many passages which foretold the coming of the Christ. Their difficulty was to arrange those passages in the order they were to be fulfilled, and to distinguish between those which spoke of Him in humiliation and those which foretold His coming glory. A similar perplexity confronts us. To ascertain the *sequence* of the prophecies relating to the Antichrist is a real problem. Even when we confine ourselves to those passages which speak of him in his connections with Israel, we have to distinguish between those which concern only the godly remnant, and those which relate to the great apostate mass of the Nation; and, too, we have to separate between those prophecies which concern the time when Antichrist is posing as the true Christ, and those which portray him in the final stage of his career, after he has thrown off his mask of religious pretension.

It would appear that the first thing revealed in prophecy concerning the Antichrist's dealings with Israel is the entering into a "covenant" with them. This is mentioned in Dan. 9:27: "And he shall confirm the covenant ("make a firm covenant", R. V.) with many for one week" i. e. seven years. The "many" here can be none other than the mass of the Jewish people, for they are the principal subjects of the prophecy. The one who makes this covenant is the "Prince that shall come" of the previous verse, the Head of the restored Roman Empire. Thus the relations between this Prince, the Antichrist, and the mass of the Jews shall, at the first, be relations of apparent friendship and public alliance. That this covenant is not forced upon Israel, but rather is entered into voluntarily by them, as *seeking Antichrist's patronage,* is clear from Isa. 28:18, where we find God, in indignation, addressing them as follows—"And *your* covenant with Death shall be disannulled, and *your* agreement with Hell shall not stand; when the overflowing scourge shall pass through, then ye shall be trodden down by it". And this, we believe, supplies the key to Dan. 2:43.

Nebuchadnezzar's vision of the great image and the interpretation given to Daniel, outlines the governmental history of the earth *as it relates to Palestine,* further details being supplied in the other visions found in the book of Daniel. "The earthly dispensations of God revolve around Jerusalem as their center. The method which it hath pleased God to adopt in giving the prophetic history of these nations, is in strict accord with this principle. As soon as they arose into supremacy and supplanted Jerusalem, prophets were commissioned, especially Daniel; to delineate their course. We might perhaps, have expected that their history would have been given minutely and consecutively from its beginning to its close. But instead of this, it is only given in its connection with Jerusalem; and as soon as Jerusalem was finally crushed by the Romans and ceased to retain a national position, all detailed history of the Gentile Empires is suspended. Many a personage most important in the world's history has since arisen. Charlemagne has lived, and Napoleon—many a monarch, and many a conqueror—battles have been fought, kingdoms raised and kingdoms subverted—yet Scripture passes silently over these things, however great in the annals of the Gentiles. Because Jerusalem has nationally ceased to be, 1800 years ago, the *detail* of Gentile history was suspended—it is suspended still, nor will it be resumed until Jerusalem reassumes a national position. Then the history of the Gentiles is again minutely given, and the glory and dominion of their last great King described. He is found to be especially connected with *Jerusalem and the Land* . . . . The subject of the book of Daniel as a whole, is the indignation of God directed through the instrumentality of the Gentile Empires upon Jerusalem" (B. W. Newton "Aids to Prophetic Enquiry", first Series).

The method which the Holy Spirit has followed in the book of Daniel is to give us, first, a general outline of Gentile dominion over Jerusalem, and this is found in the vision of the Image in chapter 2; and second, to fill in this outline, which is given in the last six chapters of that book. It is with the former we are now more particularly concerned. Much of the prophetic vision of Dan. 2 has already become history. The golden head (Babylon), the silver breast and arms (Medo-Persia), the brazen belly and thighs (Greece), the iron legs (Rome), have already appeared before men. But the *feet* of the Image, "part of iron and part of clay", have to do with a time yet future. The break between the legs and feet corresponds with the break between the sixty-ninth and seventieth "weeks" of Dan. 9:24-27. The present dispensation comes in as a parenthesis during the time that Israel is outside the Land, dispersed among the Gentiles.

What, then, is represented by the "iron and the clay" toes of the feet of the Image? If we bear in mind that this portion of the Image exactly corresponds to the seventieth week, we have an important key to the interpretation. Dan. 9:26,27 treats of the seventieth week—the "one week" yet remaining. These verses speak of the Prince (of the restored Roman Empire) making a seven years' Covenant with the Jews. Thus, the prophecy concerning the seventieth week presents to us two prominent subjects—the Romans, at whose head is the Antichrist, and apostate Israel, with whom the Covenant is made. Returning now to Dan. 2 we find that when interpreting the king's dream about the Image, the prophet declares that the "iron" is the symbol for the "fourth kingdom" (v. 40), which was Rome, that succeeded Babylon, Persia, and Greece; the "feet" with their ten toes forecasting this Empire in its final form. Thus, we have Divine authority for saying that the "iron" in the feet of the Image represents the peoples who shall yet occupy the territory controlled by the old Roman Empire. In a word, the "iron" symbolizes *the Gentiles*—specifically those found in the lands which shall be ruled over by the "ten kings."

Who, then, is symbolized by "the clay"?

Here we are obliged to part company with the commentators, who unanimously take the clay to be the figure of democracy. So far as we are aware none of them has offered a single proof text in support of their interpretation, and as the Word is the only authority, to it we must look. Assured that Scripture is its own interpreter, we turn to the concordance to find out what the "clay" signifies elsewhere, when used symbolically. In Isa. 64, which records the Cry of the Remnant at the End-time, we find them saying, "But now, O Lord, Thou art our Father; *we are the clay*, and Thou our Potter; and we all are the work of Thy hand". Again, in Jer. 18 the same figure is employed. There, the prophet is commanded to go down to the potter's house, where he beheld him manufacturing a vessel. The vessel was marred in the hands of the potter, so he "made it again another vessel". Clearly, this is a picture of Israel in the past and in the future. The interpretation is expressly fixed in v. 6: "O house of Israel, cannot I do with you as this potter? saith the Lord. Behold, *as the clay* is in the potter's hand, *so are ye* in Mine hand, *O house of Israel*". How clear it is then that "clay" is God's symbol for *Israel**.

In its final form, then, the revived Roman Empire—the kingdom of Antichrist—will be partly Gentilish and partly Jewish. And is not this what we must expect? Will not that be the character of the kingdom of that One which the Antichrist will counterfeit? Such scriptures as Psa. 2: 6-8; Isa. 11:10; 42:6; Rev. 11:15, etc., make plain the *dual* character of the kingdom over which our Lord will reign during the Millennium. That the Antichrist *will be* intimately related to both the Jews and the Gentiles we have proven again and again in the previous articles—Rev. 9:11 is quite sufficient to establish the point. Therefore, we should not be surprised to find that that part of the Image which specifically depicts the kingdom over which the Man of Sin shall reign, should be composed of both "iron" *and* "clay". It would be passing strange were it otherwise. It is indeed striking to note that the "clay" is mentioned in Dan. 2 just *nine* times—the number of judgment!

In Dan. 2:43 we read, "And whereas thou sawest iron mixed with miry clay, they shall mingle themselves with the seed of men: but they shall not cleave one to another, even as iron is not mixed with clay"—a verse that has sorely puzzled the expositors. We believe that the reference is to the coming intimacy between Jews and Gentiles. The apostate Jews (members of the Corrupt *Woman*) shall "mingle themselves with the seed of men"—the Gentiles. This is amplified in Rev. 17, where we read of the great Whore "with whom the kings of the earth have committed fornication, and the inhabitants of the earth have been made drunk with the wine of her fornication". "But they shall not cleave one to another" (Dan. 2:43) is explained in Rev. 17:16—"And the ten horns which thou sawest upon the Beast, these shall *hate* the Whore, and shall make her desolate and naked," etc.! There is a remarkable verse in Hab. 2 which confirms our remarks above, and connects the Antichrist himself with the "clay". The passage begins with the third verse, which, from its quotation in Heb. 10:37,38 we know, treats of the period immediately preceding our Lord's return. In vv. 4 and 5 we have a description of the Antichrist, and then in v. 6 we read, "Shall not all these take up a parable against him, and a taunting proverb against him, and say, Woe to him that increaseth that which is not his! how long? and to him that ladeth himself with *thick clay*". The reference is clearly to this "proud Man's" fellowship with apostate Israel. We are satisfied that Hab. 2:6-8 is parallel with Isa. 14:9-12. Isa. 14 gives us a glimpse of the Antichrist being scoffed at in Hell, by the "chief ones of the earth" because he, too, was unable to escape *their* awful fate. So in Hab. 2, after stating that he "gathereth unto him all nations" (v. 5) the prophet goes on to say; "Shall not all *these* take up a taunting proverb against him". The taunt is, that though he had leagued himself with the mass of Israel (*laden himself* "with thick clay"), yet it will be "the remnant" of this *same people* that shall "spoil" him (v. 8).

---

* That the Hebrew word for "clay" in these passages is a different one from that employed in Dan. 2 is exactly what a reflecting mind would naturally expect. Isa. 64 and Jer. 18 treat of the Israel that shall be restored, whereas Dan. 2 speaks of the *apostate* portion of Israel, irrevocably given up to judgment. In striking accord with this, we may add, that the word used in Isa. 64 and Jer. 18 refers to clay in its native and mouldable stage; but the word in Dan. 2 signifies "*burnt* clay", which denotes its *final* condition—here, as always, "burning" tells of Divine *judgment?*

Another scripture which shows that in the End-time apostate Israel will no longer be divided from and hated by the Gentiles is found in Isa. 2, where we are told, "They strike hands with the children *of strangers*" (v. 6 R. V.). As the context here is of such deep interest, and as the whole chapter supplies us with a most vivid picture of the Jews in Palestine just before the Millennium, we shall stop to give it a brief consideration. The first five verses present to us a millennial scene, and then, as is so frequently the case in the prophecies of Isaiah, we are taken back to be shown something of the conditions which shall precede the establishing of the Lord's house in the top of the mountains. This is clear from the twelfth verse, which defines this period, preceding the Millennium, as "the Day of the Lord". The section, then, which describes the conditions which are to obtain in Palestine *immediately before* the Day of the Lord dawns, begins with v. 6. We therefore quote from v. 5 to the end of v. 10:—

"For thou hast forsaken thy people the house of Jacob, because they be filled with customs from the east, and are soothsayers like the Philistines, and they strike hands with the children of strangers. Their land also is full of silver and gold, neither is there any end of their treasures; their land also is full of horses, neither is there any end of their chariots. Their land also is full of idols; they worship the work of their own hands, that which their own fingers have made. And the mean man is bowed down, and the great man is brought low; therefore forgive them not. Enter into the rock, and hide thee in the dust, from before the terror of the Lord, and from the glory of His majesty". This most interesting passage shows us that apostate Israel will be on terms of intimacy with the Gentiles; that she will be the mistress of vast wealth; that she will be given up to idolatry. Their moral condition is described in vv. 11 to 17—note the repeated references to "lofty looks", "haughtiness of men", "high and lifted up", etc.

If Zech. 5 be read right after Isa. 2:6-9 we have the connecting link between it and Rev. 17. Isa. 2 shows us the Jews as the owners of fabulous wealth, as being in guilty fellowship with "strangers", and as universally given to idolatry. Zech. 5 reveals the emigration of apostate Israel (the "woman" in the midst of the Ephah) and the transference of her wealth to the land of Shinar. Rev. 17 and 18 give the ultimate outcome of this. Here we see apostate Israel in all her corrupt glory. She is pictured, first, as sitting upon many waters (v. 1), which signifies "peoples, and multitudes, and nations and tongues" (v. 15). These will support her by contributing to her revenues. The huge bond issues made by the nations to obtain loans, are rapidly finding their way into Jewish hands; and doubtless, it is the steadily accumulating interest from these which will soon make them the wealthiest nation of the world. That which has half-bankrupted Europe will soon be used to array the Woman in purple and scarlet color and gold and precious stones and pearls (v. 4).

Second, the Woman is seen supported by the Beast (v. 3), which means that the Antichrist will use his great governmental power to insure her protection. How this harmonizes with Dan. 9:27, where we read of him making a seven-year *Covenant* with them, needs not to be pointed out. Then will poor blinded Israel believe that the Millennium has come. No longer the people of the weary foot, and homeless stranger, but mistress of the greatest city in the world. No longer poor and needy, but possessor of the wealth of the earth. No longer the "tail" of the nations, but reigning over them as their financial Creditor and Dictator. No longer despised by the great and mighty, but sought after by the kings of the earth. Nothing withheld that the flesh can desire. The false Prince of Peace their benefactor. Yes, blinded Israel will verily conclude that at long last the millennial era has arrived, and such will be the Devil's imitation of that blessed time which shall be ushered in by the return of God's Son to this earth.

But not for long shall this satanic spell be enjoyed. Rudely shall it be broken. For, third, Rev. 17 shows us the ten horns and the Beast turning against the Whore, stripping her of her wealth, and despoiling her of her glory (v. 16). This, too, corresponds with Old Testament prophecy, for there we read of the Antichrist *breaking* his Covenant with Israel! As we are told in Psa. 55:20, "He hath put forth his hands *against* such as be at peace with him: he has broken his covenant", cf Isa. 33:8. And this very breaking of the Covenant is but the fulfillment of the Divine counsels. Thousands of years ago, Jehovah addressed Himself through Isaiah to apostate Israel, saying, "And your Covenant with Death shall be disannulled, and your agreement with Hell shall not stand; when the overflowing scourge shall pass through, then *ye shall be trodden down by it*".

Concerning Antichrist's relations with the godly Jewish Remnant, that has already been discussed in previous papers, as also his final attack upon Jerusalem and his defeat and overthrow in the Valley of Armageddon. Apostate Israel, the Beast, and all his Gentile followers shall be destroyed. The faithful remnant of Israel, and those Gentiles who befriend them in the hour of their need, shall have their part in the millennial kingdom of David's Son and Lord (Matt. 25). Thus has God been pleased to unveil the future and make known to us the things which "must shortly come to pass". May it be ours to reverently search the more sure Word of Prophecy with increasing interest, and may an ever-deepening gratitude fill our hearts and be expressed by our lips, because all who are now saved by grace through faith shall be with our blessed Lord in the Father's House, when the Great Tribulation with all its attendant horrors shall come upon the world. —Arthur W. Pink.

This unique series of seventeen papers on "The Antichrist" have been neatly bound, making a book of approximately 300 pages. It would make an excellent gift to any one interested in the study of prophecy. Price only $1.25 per copy, postpaid.

EXPOSITION OF FIRST PETER

The practical use to be made of these truths it is not difficult to discover. If these things have been reported to us by men who preached the gospel with the Holy Ghost sent down from heaven, surely we should believe them. And if we believed them—if we really believed them—O what an influence would they have on our temper and conduct! A faith of this truth would induce the man, who is yet uninterested in the christian salvation, immediately to seek a share in its heavenly and spiritual blessings, and would make those who are interested in it very holy, very happy, very active, and perfectly contented amid all the calamities and trials of life.

What is the subject of the constant, intense contemplation of angels, surely deserves our most careful study. We are far more closely connected with, far more deeply interested in, the subject of study, than they. The salvation they desire to look into will promote, but it will but indirectly promote their happiness. Their happiness may be secure without reference to it. But as to us, this salvation must be ours, or we are undone forever and ever. It is *now* that an interest is to be obtained in it, if obtained at all. It is only by knowing and believing the truth about this salvation, that an interest in it can be obtained. Oh, then, let us, with intensest ardor, seek the knowledge of this salvation! If we die unacquainted with it, we die uninterested in it; and if we die uninterested in it, it never, never can become ours. "Now is the accepted time, now is the day of salvation."

DISCOURSE V.
CHRISTIAN DUTY—MEANS OF, AND MOTIVES TO, ITS PERFORMANCE.

1 PET. i. 13-21.—Wherefore gird up the loins of your mind, be sober, and hope to the end, for the grace that is to be brought unto you at the revelation of Jesus Christ: as obedient children, not fashioning yourselves according to the former lusts in your ignorance: but as he which hath called you is holy, so be ye holy in all manner of conversation; because it is written, Be ye holy; for I am holy. And if ye call on the Father, who without respect of persons judgeth according to every man's work, pass the time of your sojourning here in fear: forasmuch as ye know that ye were not redeemed with corruptible things, as silver and gold, from your vain conversation received by tradition from your fathers; but with the precious blood of Christ, as of a lamb without blemish and without spot: who verily was fore-ordained before the foundation of the world, but was manifest in these last times for you, who by him do believe in God, that raised him up from the dead, and gave him glory; that your faith and hope might be in God.

Among the numerous mistaken notions of Christianity which prevail among its professors, few are more common, and none more fatal, than that in which it is viewed merely as a theory—a system of abstract principles, which, however true, are but remotely connected with human interests; and which, therefore, can but feebly influence human character and conduct. It is but too evident that the grand characteristic doctrines of Christianity, such as the trinity, the incarnation, the atonement, justification by faith, sanctification by divine influence, are, with many who readily admit their truth, and who would indeed be shocked at having their orthodoxy called in question, mere inoperative opinions, which exercise no more practical influence over their temper and conduct than the philosophical doctrines respecting the nature of space and time, or the size and distance of the celestial bodies, or the historical facts respecting the victories of Alexander or the discoveries of Columbus.

It is painful to think that it is no uncommon thing for a person to be able to talk plausibly about these principles of Christianity, to reason conclusively in their support, and to be zealous even to rancor against those who deny, or even doubt, their truth; while he yet continues a total stranger to their transforming efficacy, the slave of selfishness, malignity and worldliness. And what is the most lamentable part of this sad history, the infatuated man seems in a great measure unaware of the shocking inconsistency he is exhibiting, in displaying the most unchristian tempers in defence of christian truth. He mistakes his knowledge and zeal about certain propositions—which, it may be, embody christian truth—for Christianity itself; and looking, it would seem, on orthodoxy of opinion as the sum and substance of religious duty, wraps himself up in an overweening conception of his own attainments, and resigns himself to the pleasing dreams of a fancied security, from which but too frequently he is first and forever awakened by hearing the awful mandate, "Depart from me, I never knew you;" and by finding his place assigned him with the hypocrites, in the regions of hopeless misery.

It is an interesting inquiry, and, if properly conducted, would certainly elicit some important results—How comes it that men, with the Bible in their hands, can practise such fatal impositions on themselves? How comes it that the mere speculator should so readily conclude himself a sound believer? How comes it that the truth of doctrines should not only be readily admitted, but zealously maintained, while their appropriate influence is altogether unfelt, and indeed, steadily resisted? It would lead us too far out of our way just now to engage in such an inquiry; but I must be permitted to observe, that whatever influence deficient human representations of divine truth may have had in producing so mischievous and lamentable a result (and I believe that influence has been extensive and powerful), the truths of the Gospel themselves, and the scriptural representation of them, cannot be justly charged as in any degree the cause of this evil. The doctrines of the Gospel are of such a nature, that, if apprehended in their meaning and evidence, —if understood and believed,—they must, from the constitution of the mind of man, have a commanding influence over its principles of action; and these doctrines, as taught in the Bible, are not exhibited as mere abstract propositions, but are stated in such a manner as distinctly to show, how closely the belief of them is connected with everything that is good in disposition, and right in conduct. The speculatist in religion must not seek, for he will not find, in the Bible, an apology for his infatuation and inconsistency. On the contrary, he will meet with much to prove him altogether inexcusable.

The principles of Christianity are never in the New Testament exhibited in an abstract systematic form. They are interwoven with the injunctions to the cultivation of right dispositions, and to the practice of commanded duties, to which in truth they form the most powerful motives. The Author of Revelation, who is also the Author of our nature, and who is intimately acquainted with all its intellectual and moral obliquities in its present fallen state, has mercifully and wisely led those "holy men who spoke as they were moved by his Spirit," to guard their readers against that tendency to consider the doctrines of Christianity as mere matters of speculation, to which we have been adverting, by almost invariably following a statement of doctrine, with a statement of the practical consequences which that doctrine, understood and believed, is at once calculated and intended to produce.

Of this we have a very striking and instructive exemplification in the passage which we have here chosen as the subject of this discourse. In the preceding paragraph we have a statement of some of the most sublime and delightful peculiarities of Christian doctrine. We are instructed respecting that state of ineffable purity, dignity, and happiness, to which it is the purpose of God ultimately to raise men, through the mediation of his incarnate only begotten. This state is described as "salvation"—deliverance from evil, in all its forms and degrees, forever—a holy happiness, filling to an overflow all the capacities of enjoyment during the entire eternity of man's being—as "an *inheritance*," intimating at once the gratuitousness of the nature, and the security of the tenure, of this happiness—"an inheritance incorruptible," having nothing in its own nature which can lead to decay or termination—"undefiled," its pure elements unmingled with any inferior or heterogeneous ingredients—"unfading," retaining unimpaired its power to communicate happiness—"laid up in heaven," pure and ethereal in its nature, and secured beyond the reach of fraud or of violence; while those for whom it is destined, those who, according to the divine fore-knowledge, have been selected by a spiritual separation from the world lying under the wicked one, that they may obey the truth, and be sprinkled by the blood of Jesus—that is, possess the blessings secured by his atoning sacrifice—are preserved for its enjoyment amid all the dangers they are exposed to, by the power of God and through the instrumentality of believing.

Still further to illustrate the glories of this salvation, this final state of blessedness, we are told, that unlike the present state, in which Jesus Christ is bodily absent from his chosen ones, and in which the imperfect knowledge they have of him is obtained entirely through the medium of believing, in which they are exposed to numerous and severe trials, in which complete deliverance from evil is the object of faith and hope, and in which, owing to these causes, they are often in heaviness—the future state of Christians is a state in which Christ Jesus is bodily present with them, and maintains intimate and uninterrupted intercourse with them—a state in which nothing of their trials but their blissful and glorious results remain—a state in which complete deliverance is the object of enjoyment—a state in which, in consequence of all these things, they "rejoice with a joy which is unspeakable and full of glory;" and, as if even all this were not enough to give us just ideas of the glories and felicities "which God has laid up for those who love him," we are told, that this state of final happiness is a leading subject of Old Testament prophecy, apostolical preaching, and angelical study.

These delightful and wonderful announcements are not brought forward as abstract principles—things to speculate and to talk about. They are no sooner stated than the apostle proceeds to urge them on Christians as most powerful motives to the duties of their high and holy calling, and equally powerful supports and consolations under the afflictions to which the discharge of those duties might expose them. "Wherefore," for those reasons, since these things are so—"Wherefore gird up the loins of your mind, be sober, and hope to the end, for the grace that is to be brought unto you at the revelation of Jesus Christ: As obedient children, not fashioning yourselves according to the former lusts in your ignorance: But as he which hath called you is holy, so be ye holy in all manner of conversation; because it is written, Be ye holy; for I am holy. And if ye call on the Father, who without respect of persons judgeth according to every man's work, pass the time of your sojourning here in fear. Forasmuch as ye know that ye were not redeemed with corruptible things, as silver and gold, from your vain conversation received by tradition from your fathers; but with the precious blood of Christ, as of a lamb without blemish and without spot: Who verily was fore-ordained before the foundation of the world, but was manifest in these last times for you, who by him do believe in God, that raised him from the dead, and gave him glory; that your faith and hope might be in God."

In this admirable paragraph we have a most instructive view—I. Of Christian duty; II. Of the means of performing it; and III. Of the motives to its performance. Of CHRISTIAN DUTY—described, first, generally, as obedience, Christians being exhorted to act "as obedient children," rather, children of obedience; and then described more particularly—first negatively, "Not fashioning yourselves according to your former lusts in your ignorance;" and then positively—"Be holy in all manner of conversation." Of the MEANS OF PERFORMING CHRISTIAN DUTY; first, determined resolution—"Gird up the loins of your mind;" secondly, moderation in all our estimates, and desires, and pursuit of worldly objects —"Be sober;" thirdly, hope—"Hope to the end," hope perfectly; fourthly, fear—"Pass the time of your sojourning here in fear." OF THE MOTIVES TO THE PERFORMANCE OF CHRISTIAN DUTY; first, the grandeur and excellence and security of the Christian inheritance, the full possession of which we can attain only by Christian obedience—"Wherefore," referring to the whole of the preceding description of the final state of happiness which awaits the saints; secondly, the holiness of God—"Be ye holy, for I am holy;" thirdly, the equity of God—"The Father on whom we call, without respect of persons, judgeth every man according to his works;" and fourthly, the wonderful provision which had been made for securing this holiness, in their having been redeemed, or bought back to God, by the blood of his own Son—"Forasmuch as ye know that ye were not redeemed with corruptible things, as silver and gold, from your vain conversation received by tradition from your fathers; but with the precious blood of Christ, as of a lamb without blemish and without spot: Who verily was fore-ordained before the foundation of the world, but was manifest in these last times for you, who by him do believe in God, that raised him up from the dead, and gave him glory; that your faith and hope might be in God."

Such is the outline which I shall attempt to fill up in the subsequent illustrations.

I.—CHRISTIAN DUTY.

§ 1.—*General view—obedience.*

According to the plan which has just been sketched, our attention must be first directed to the view of Christian duty with which we are presented in the passage before us.

Christian duty is in this paragraph represented generally as obedience. The apostle calls on Christians to conduct themselves "as obedient children," or rather children of obedience, which is the literal rendering of the original terms. The apostle's meaning does not seem to be "Behave yourselves towards God as obedient children do towards their father," but act the part not of children of disobedience—a strong idiomatic phrase for disobedient persons; but of children of obedience—a strong idiomatic phrase for obedient persons. Obedience, then, is the great duty of the Christian.

Obedience has always a reference to a law to be obeyed. Christians are often, in the epistolary part of the New Testament, represented as not only completely delivered from subjection to the law of Moses; but the state into which they are brought by the faith of the gospel is described as a being "not under law, but under grace."[1] Their pardon and salvation are not to be procured by their own obedience to any law, but to be received as the "gift of God, through Jesus Christ our Lord." But though delivered from the Mosaic law, and though "not under law," in the sense of their final salvation being the stipulated reward of stipulated labor, they are "not without law to God; they are under the law to Christ."[2]

The law to which the Christian owes obedience is the revelation of the divine will contained in the Holy Scriptures. This law is, like its Author, "spiritual" and "holy," both "just and good."[3] It reaches not merely to action, but to the principles of action, and requires obedience of *mind*, obedience of *heart*, and obedience of *life*.

Obedience of mind consists in the implicit belief of whatever is revealed in the Holy Scriptures. It is counting true whatever God has said, just because God has said it. A Christian is not left to think as he pleases. The command of God is, "Let the mind be in you which was also in Christ Jesus."[4] We must think in conformity to the mind of God, as made known in his word. We must receive what is written there, "not as the word of man, but as it is in truth the word of the living God."[5]

This submission of mind to the authority of God is the fundamental part of christian obedience, and naturally leads to that obedience of heart which is equally required by that law, which is exceeding broad. By obedience of heart, I understand a state of the affections corresponding to the character of God as revealed in the manifestation he has made of his will. He appears in that manifestation infinitely venerable and estimable, and amiable and trustworthy; and reverence and esteem, and love and confidence, are the dispositions which these excellencies ought to excite in our minds. To "sanctify the Lord God in our hearts," to "make him our fear and dread," to "love him with our heart, and our soul, and our strength, and our mind," and "to trust in him at all times,"[6]—this is the obedience of the heart.

As the obedience of the mind naturally

---
[1] Rom. vi. 14.
[2] 1 Cor. ix. 21.
[3] Rom. vii. 12, 14.
[4] Phil. ii. 5.
[5] 1 Thess. ii. 13.
[6] 1 Pet. iii. 15. Isa. viii. 13. Matt. xxii. 37. Psal. lxii. 8.

leads to the obedience of the heart, as it is impossible to venerate and esteem, and love and trust God, without knowing and believing that he is venerable and excellent, and amiable and trustworthy, and impossible to believe him possessed of those excellencies without exercising those dispositions, so the obedience of the mind and of the heart naturally express themselves in the obedience of the life.

The obedience of the life is twofold—active and passive: the one consisting in conscientiously doing whatever God commands; and the other consisting in cheerfully submitting to whatever God appoints. It is the duty of the Christian to "walk in all God's commandments and ordinances blameless," to be "patient in tribulation," and even to "count it all joy when brought into manifold trials."[1] Such is the general idea of obedience as the duty of the Christian: a conformity of mind and heart and conduct to the revealed will of God.

There are certain general characters which belong to this obedience when it is genuine, and which distinguish it from all counterfeits. It is *implicit* obedience. The Christian not only believes what God reveals, but he believes it because God has revealed it; he not only does what God commands, but he does it because God has commanded it; he not only submits to what God appoints, but he submits to it because God has appointed it. It is obviously just so far as the faith and conduct of a Christian have this character, that they deserve the name of obedience at all.

The obedience which forms the sum and substance of Christian duty, is *impartial* and *universal* obedience. If it be implicit, it will be impartial and universal. If I really regard the will of God at all, I will regard it whenever I see it clearly manifested. I will not, among duties commanded with equal clearness, choose which I will perform, and which I will neglect. I will "esteem all his precepts concerning all things to be right, and I will hate every false way."[2]

Cheerfulness is another essential character of Christian obedience. External obedience may often be constrained and mercenary; but the obedience of the life, which proceeds from, and is the expression of, the obedience of the mind and heart, cannot be either. In obeying, the Christian is doing what he knows to be right; and what he feels to be good. He "consents to the law that it is good." He "delights in the law after the inward man." When his heart is enlarged by just and impressive views of the reasonableness and excellence of the divine law, he runs in the ways of God's commandments, and finds that "in keeping them there is great reward."[3]

The obedience which is the sum of the Christian's duty, in fine, is not an occasional and temporary, but a *habitual* and a *persevering* obedience. It is the business of his life: "Whatsoever he does, whether in word or in deed," ought to be done "in the name of the Lord Jesus, giving thanks to God the Father by him." "Whether he eats or drinks, or whatsoever he does," he ought to do "all, to the glory of God." His obedience ought to be "a patient continuance in well-doing," "a steadfast, immovable, constant abounding in the work of the Lord," "a forgetting the things which are behind, a reaching forth to those which are before, a pressing to the mark for the prize of the high calling of God in Christ Jesus."[4]

§ 2.—*Particular view of Christian Duty.*
(1.) *Negative.* (2.) *Positive.*

The duty of Christians is not only described generally as obedience, but more particularly, first, negatively, as a "not fashioning themselves according to the former lusts in their ignorance," and then, positively, as a "being holy in all manner of conversation." Let us shortly attend to these very instructive descriptions of Christian duty.

(1.) The apostle's negative statement is, that Christians ought not to fashion themselves "according to the former lusts in their ignorance." While a man continues unacquainted with the meaning and evidence of the revelation which God has made of himself in his word—and this is the case with every unbeliever,—he is in a state of ignorance respecting the most important of all subjects, the character and will of God—the duty and happiness of man. While in that state, he does not "fashion himself," that is, regulate his conduct—form his character, "according to the will of God," but according to his "lusts,"—his desires. The desires which are

---
[1] Luke i. 6. Rom. xii. 12. James i. 2.
[2] Psal. cxix. 128.
[3] Rom. vii. 16, 22. Psal. cxix. 32; xix. 11.
[4] Col. iii. 17. 1 Cor. x. 31. Rom. ii. 7. 1 Cor. xv. 58. Phil. iii. 13, 14.

natural to men while they are unrenewed, are the principles which regulate their conduct and form their character. One man loves pleasure, another loves money, another loves power, another loves fame. The ruling desire, or lust, is the principle which forms the character and guides the conduct.

Now the Christian, being no longer in ignorance, but knowing and believing the revelation God has made of his will, must no longer permit his character to be fashioned by those desires, to the guidance of which, when in a state of ignorance, he delivered himself up. All these desires, so far as they are sinful, must be mortified, and, even so far as they are innocent, they must cease to be governing principles, and must be subordinated to a higher principle—the principle of submission of mind and heart to the will of God.

The objects of these desires are sensible and present things—things which are "in the world;" so that the not fashioning ourselves according to our former lusts in our ignorance, and our not being "conformed to this world," are but two different modes of expressing the same thing. An unregenerated man's character is entirely formed by the desires of his fallen nature, excited by their appropriate objects in the present world. It was once so with the Christian, but it must be so with him no longer. On the contrary, "as he who has called him is holy, so must he be holy in all manner of conversation."

(2.) This is the apostle's positive statement with respect to Christian duty. There is no word, I apprehend, to which more indistinct ideas are generally attached, than holiness; yet, surely, there is no word of the meaning of which it is of more importance we should have a clear and accurate conception; for "without holiness no man shall see the Lord."[1] The clearest and the justest idea we can form of holiness, as a quality of an intelligent creature, is conformity of mind and will with the Supreme Being, who alone is, in all the extent of meaning belonging to the word, holy. Holiness does not consist in mystic speculations, enthusiastic fervors, or uncommanded austerities; it consists in thinking as God thinks, and willing as God wills. God's mind and will are to be known from his word; and, so far as I really understand and believe God's word, God's mind becomes my mind, God's will becomes my will, and, according to the measure of my faith, I become holy.

And this conformity of mind and will to God—this holiness—is to be manifested "in all manner of conversation." "Conversation," here, as usually in the New Testament, signifies not colloquial intercourse, but general conduct. In every part of your character and conduct, let it appear that the ruling principles of your conduct, the forming principles of your character, are no longer what they once were—your lusts, your natural desires, but the mind and the will of him who has called you, even God, who is holy; his mind and will having become your mind and will, through the knowledge and belief of the truth, make it evident, that these are now the principles by which your character is formed and your life governed. In everything show that you think as God thinks, that you will as God wills, that you love what God loves, that you hate what he hates, that you choose what he chooses, that wherein he finds enjoyment, you seek enjoyment. Such is a short account of the Christian's duty.

There are two conclusions to which these observations necessarily conduct us, highly worthy of considerate reflection. First, that there are many who call themselves Christians, who have no title to that name, habitual violators of God's law, strangers to the very principle of obedience, still "walking according to the course of this world, serving divers lusts and pleasures."[2] How vain—how much worse than vain, is their profession—how dangerous their circumstances—how awful, if they continue in their present state, their final doom! The second conclusion is, that those who are really Christians are still very far, indeed, from being what they ought to be—from being what they might be. The best Christians, then, need to have such exhortations addressed to them as these: "Follow holiness," seek growing conformity of mind and heart to God, and recollect this can be obtained only by growing knowledge and faith of the truth. Though already not of the world, even as their Lord is not of the world, they need the great Intercessor continually to pray for them, "Sanctify them through thy truth, thy word is truth."[3]

[2] Eph. ii. 2, 3. Tit. iii. 3.
[3] John xvii. 7.

[1] Heb. xii. 14.

II.—MEANS FOR THE PERFORMANCE OF CHRISTIAN DUTY.

We now proceed to direct your minds to the view here given us of the means of performing this duty. If we would be "children of obedience, not fashioning ourselves after our former lusts in our ignorance"—if we would be "holy in all manner of conversation," it is necessary that we should "gird up the loins of our mind"—that we should be "sober"—that we should "hope to the end"—and that we should "pass the time of our sojourning here in fear." Determined resolution, moderation, hope, and fear, are the means here prescribed for our realizing, in our own character and conduct, those views of Christian duty presented to us by the apostle. Let us shortly attend to them in their order.

§ I.—*Determined Resolution a means of Christian Obedience.*

Determined resolution is one of the instrumental means which we ought to employ, in order to our complying with the apostle's exhortation. "Gird up," says he, "the loins of your mind." The ancients were accustomed to wear loose, flowing garments, which, though graceful and agreeable on ordinary occasions, were found inconvenient when strenuous and long-continued exertion became necessary. In such cases it was usual to gather together the folds of the flowing drapery, and, having wrapped them round the waist, to confine them by a belt or girdle. This was termed girding up the loins.

The phrase is here used figuratively. To inquire, as some have done, what are meant by the loins of the mind, and to reply—the sensual affections and appetites, the lower propensities of human nature; and to inquire what is meant by girding up the loins of the mind, and to reply—the restraint and mortification of these debasing propensities, is rather ingeniously to play with, than satisfactorily to explain, the phraseology of the sacred writer. "To gird up the loins of the mind," is to gird up the loins mentally; that is, to cultivate that state of mind of which the girding up of the loins is the natural emblem. When a man has nothing to do, or nothing which requires any thing like exertion, he permits his robes to flow in graceful negligence around him; or, even if called on to a sudden, transient, though vigorous effort, he may not think it worth his while to make any change in his dress; but if he has a work to perform, which requires at once strenuous and continued exertion,—if he is about, not to take a walk for pleasure, but to undertake a journey on business, then he girds up his loins. The action is naturally emblematical of that state of mind in which a person contemplates a course of conduct, which, while he considers it as highly eligible and indispensably obligatory, he plainly perceives to involve in it serious difficulty, and to demand the persevering putting forth of all his active energies.

The apostolical command, "Gird up the loins of your mind," is equivalent to 'Set yourselves with resolute determination to the performance of these duties. Impress on your minds a sense of their importance, obligation, advantages, and necessity. Let there be no "halting between two opinions." Considering Christian obedience as the business of life; a business, the right discharge of which will require all the care you can devote to it; a business, in the prosecution of which no exertion must be spared, no sacrifice grudged; enter on it with a determination, that whatever may be neglected this shall be attended to; and with a distinct understanding, that this is not to be an occasional employment for your by-hours, but the habitual occupation to which all your time and all your faculties are to be devoted.[1]

Such a spirit of determined resolution is absolutely necessary to the proper performance of the duties involved in a life of Christian obedience. These duties are numerous, varied, and laborious. They are all in the highest degree reasonable, and to a being whose moral constitution is in a completely sound state, none of them would be in the slightest degree grievous. The yoke of Christian duty should be very easy —the burden of Christian duty should be very light. But who that believes the declarations of Scripture—who that is in any degree conversant with the realities of Christian experience, needs to be told that the remains of native depravity, acted on by the temptations of Satan, and by the influence of a world lying under his power, often make irksome what ought to be delightful, difficult what should be easy, la-

---

[1] Exod. xii. 11. 1 Kings xviii. 46. Job xxxviii. 3; xl. 7. Luke xii. 35.

borious what should be spontaneous? How endless, varied, and diversified are the circumstances which have a tendency to induce spiritual sloth, and make us become "weary in well-doing!" How apt are we to turn out of the way, instead of proceeding right onwards; to loiter, when we should quicken our pace; to think we have "attained, and are already perfect," when we have little more than entered on our Christian course! How often, when the spirit is willing, is the flesh weak! Oh, how does "the flesh war against the spirit, so that we cannot do the things that we would!"[1]

To meet this state of things, nothing is more necessary than that resolute determination here recommended by the apostle. Without it we shall make but little progress in our Christian course, and the little progress we make, will be productive of but little comfort to ourselves—little glory to our Lord; everything will be a difficulty; we shall be constantly stumbling, and but too often falling. But with it, our progress will be steady and rapid, delightful to ourselves, comfortable to our brethren, honorable to our Lord; we shall "forget the things which are behind, reach forward to those which are before, and press toward the mark for the prize of the high calling of God in Christ Jesus."[2]

This resolute determination must not rest on the mistaken opinion of our possessing in ourselves all the energies, which are necessary for the successful performance of all the duties implied in Christian obedience, but on an humble yet confident reliance on the promises of God, securing for us all those supplies of divine influence which are requisite for this purpose. It is the faith of the truth, and that alone, that can brace the mind for spiritual work and warfare. It is this which makes us "strong in the Lord, and in the power of his might."[3]

Let us, then, like the Israelites when leaving Egypt, "gird up our loins," resolved to prosecute our journey, undeterred by the fury of our spiritual enemies endeavoring to bring us again into bondage, by the billows of the Red Sea of persecution, or by the endless toils and troubles of the wilderness of this world, till, having passed the Jordan of death, we shall lay by the staff and the sword for the palm and the harp, and exchange the humble garb of the pilgrim for the flowing robes of the victor. Meanwhile, to use the language of the heavenly Leighton, "Let us remember our way, and where we are, and keep our robes girt up, for we walk among briers and thorns, which, if we let them down, will entangle and stop us, and possibly tear our garments; we walk through a world where there is a great mire of sinful pollutions, and which therefore cannot but defile them: and the crowd we are among will be ready to tread on them; yea, our own feet may be entangled in them, and so make us stumble and possibly fall." Our only safety is in girding up the loins of our mind.

[1] Gal. v. 17.
[2] Phil. iii. 13.
[3] Eph. vi. 10.

Have you renewed your subscription? Remember that "Gleanings in Exodus" and a series of articles on "How to Study the Bible" by Arthur W. Pink will commence with the January 1924 issue, D. V. Don't miss these.

(Continued from page 313.)

"(There is) therefore *now* no condemnation". The qualifying "now" implies there was a time when Christians, before they believed, *were* under condemnation. This was before they died *with* Christ, died judicially (Gal. 2:20) to the penalty of God's righteous law. This "now", then, distinguishes between two states or conditions. By nature we were "under the (sentence of) law", but *now* believers are "under grace" (Rom. 6:14). By nature we were "children of wrath" (Eph. 2:2), but *now* we are "accepted in the Beloved" (Eph. 1:6). Under the first covenant we were "in Adam" (1 Cor. 15:22), but *now* we are "in Christ" (Rom. 8:1). As believers in Christ we have everlasting life, and because of this we "shall not come into condemnation".

Condemnation is a word of tremendous import, and the better we understand it the more shall we appreciate the wondrous grace that has delivered us from its power. In the halls of a human court this is a term which falls with fearful knell upon the ear of the convicted criminal and fills the spectators with sadness and horror. But in the court of Divine Justice it is vested with a meaning and content infinitely more solemn and awe-inspiring. To that Court every member of Adam's fallen race is cited. "Conceived in sin, and shapen in iniquity" each one enters this world under arrest—an indicted criminal, a rebel manacled. How, then, is it possible for such an one to escape the *execution* of the dread sentence? There was only one way, and that was by the *removal* from us of that which called forth the sentence, namely, *sin*. Let *guilt* be *removed* and there can be "no condemnation".

Has guilt been removed, removed, we mean, from the sinner who believes? Let the following scriptures answer: "As far as the east is from the west so far hath He removed our transgressions from us" (Psa. 103:12). "I, even I, am He that blotteth out thy transgressions" (Isa. 43:25). "Thou hast cast *all* my sins behind Thy back" (Isa. 38:17). "Their sins and iniquities will I remember no more" (Heb. 10:17).

But *how* could guilt be *removed?* Only by it being *transferred*. Divine holiness could not ignore it; but Divine grace could and did transfer it. The sins of believers were transferred *to Christ:* "The Lord hath laid on Him the iniquity of us all" (Isa. 53:6). "For He hath made Him to be sin for us" (2 Cor. 5:21).

"(There is) therefore now no condemnation". The "no" is emphatic. It signifies there is no condemnation whatsoever. No condemnation from the law, or on account of inward corruption, or because Satan can substantiate a charge against me; there is none from any source or for any cause at all. *"No* condemnation" means that none at all is possible; that none ever will be. There is no condemnation because there is *no accusation* (see 8:33), and there can be no accusation because there is *no imputation* of sin (see 4:8).

"(There is) therefore now no condemnation *to them* which are in Christ Jesus". When treating of the conflict between the two natures in the believer the apostle had, in the previous chapter, spoken of himself in his own person, in order to show that the highest attainments in grace do not exempt from the internal warfare which he there describes. But here in 8:1 the apostle changes the number. He does not say, There is no condemnation to *me*, but "to *them* which are in Christ Jesus". This was most gracious of the Holy Spirit. Had the apostle spoken here in the singular number, we should have reasoned that such a blessed exemption was well suited to this honored servant of God who enjoyed such wondrous privileges; but could not apply to us. The Spirit of God, therefore, moved the apostle to employ the plural number here, to show that "no condemnation" is true of *all* in Christ Jesus.

"(There is) therefore now no condemnation to them which are *in Christ Jesus"*. To be in Christ Jesus is to be perfectly identified with Him in the judicial reckoning and dealings of God; and it is also to be one with Him as vitally united by faith. Immunity from condemnation does not depend in any-wise upon our "walk", but solely on our being "in Christ". "The believer is in Christ as Noah was enclosed within the ark, with the heavens darkening above him, and the waters heaving beneath him, yet not a drop of the flood penetrating his vessel, not a blast of the storm disturbing the serenity of his spirit. The believer is in Christ as Jacob was in the garment of the elder brother when Isaac kissed and blessed him. He is in Christ as the poor homicide was within the city of refuge when pursued by the avenger of blood, but who could not overtake and slay him" (Dr. Winslow, 1857). And *because* he *is* "in Christ" there is, therefore, *no condemnation* for him. Hallelujah!

—Arthur W. Pink.

Vol. II   DECEMBER, 1923   No. 12

STUDIES in the SCRIPTURES

"Search the Scriptures" John 5:39.

A PERIODICAL (MONTHLY "IF THE LORD WILL")
DEVOTED TO BIBLE STUDIES and EXPOSITIONS

Associate Editors and Publishers, I. C. HERENDEEN and ARTHUR W. PINK,
Swengel, Pa.

Price: 10 cents per copy; $1.00 per year. Foreign $1.00 per year.

CHRIST IN THE MANGER.

"And she brought forth her firstborn son and wrapped him in swaddling clothes, and laid him in a manger; because there was no room for them in the inn" (Luke 2:7). Luke is the only one of the four Evangelists who tells us of this—a point of touching interest concerning His humanity, and one that is worthy of our reverent contemplation. *Why* was it the Father suffered His blessed Son, now incarnate, to be born in a stable? *Why* were the cattle of the field His first companions? What spiritual lessons are we intended to learn from His being placed in a manger? Weighty questions are these, admitting, perhaps, of at least a sevenfold answer:—

1. He was laid in a manger because there was *no room in the inn.* How solemnly this brings out *the world's estimate* of the Christ of God. There was no appreciation of His amazing condescension. He was not wanted. It is so still. There is no room for Him in the schools, in society, in the business world, among the great throngs of pleasure-seekers, in the political realm, in the newspapers, nor in many of the churches. It is only history repeating itself. All that the world gave the Saviour was a stable for His cradle, a cross on which to die, and a borrowed grave to receive His murdered body.

2. He was laid in a manger to demonstrate *the extent of His Poverty.* "For ye know the grace of our Lord Jesus Christ, that, though He was rich, yet for your sakes He became poor, that ye through His poverty might be rich" (2 Cor. 8:9). *How* "poor" He became, was thus manifested at the beginning. The One who, afterwards, had not where to lay His head, who had to *ask for* a penny when He would reply to His critics about the question of tribute, and who had to use another man's house when instituting the Holy Supper, was, from the first, a homeless Stranger here. And the "manger" was the earliest evidence of this.

3. He was laid in a manger in order to be *Accessible to all.* Had He been born in a palace, or in some room in the temple, few could have reached Him without the formality of first gaining permission from those who would have been in attendance at such places. But none would have any difficulty

(Continued on page 360.)

IMPORTANT NOTICES

All new subscriptions will be dated from January, 1924.
Set of twelve issues for 1922, unbound, $1.00. Bound, $1.50.
Set of twelve issues for 1923, unbound, $1.00 Bound $1.50.
Note: We cannot break a set or now supply any single 1923 issues.
Subscription Price: $1.00 per year to any address in the world. Single copies 10 cents.
Change of Address: Please notify us promptly of any change of address, and be certain to give both old and new addresses.
Non-Subscribers receiving this Magazine regularly will understand their subscription has been entered by a friend.
Copies lost in the mail duplicated only if we are notified promptly.
Entered as second-class matter December 15th, 1921, at the post office at Swengel, Pa., under Act of March 3rd, 1879.

CONTENTS

John's Gospel (John 6:60-71). 338
The Antichrist (Concluded) 345
Christian Liberty 347
Exposition of First Peter 353

JOHN'S GOSPEL

24. CHRIST AND HIS DISCIPLES: John 6:60-71.

The following is submitted as an Analysis of the passage which is to be before us:

1. Many disciples offended at Christ's discourse: v. 60.
2. Christ's admonition: vv. 61-65.
3. Many disciples leave Christ: v. 66.
4. Christ's challenge to the Twelve: v. 67.
5. Simon Peter's confession: vv. 68, 69.
6. Christ corrects Peter: v. 70.
7. The betrayer: v. 71.

The passage before us is one that is full of pathos. It brings us to the conclusion of our Lord's ministry in Galilee. It shows us the outcome of His ministry there. Here, He had performed some wonderful miracles, and had given out some gracious teachings. It was here, that He had turned the water into wine; here, He had healed the nobleman's son, without so much as seeing him; here, He had fed the hungry multitude. Each of these miracles plainly accredited His Divine mission, and evidenced His deity. None other ever performed such works as these. Before such evidence unbelief was excuseless. Moreover, He had presented Himself, both to the crowd outside and to the Jews inside the synagogue, as the Bread of life. He had freely offered eternal life to them, and had solemnly warned that, "except ye eat the flesh of the Son of man, and drink His blood, ye have no life in you" (v. 53). What, then, was their response to all of this?

It is indeed pathetic to find that here in Galilee Christ met with no better reception than had been His in Judea, and it is striking to see how closely the one resembled that of the other. He had begun His ministry in Judea, and, for a season, His success there, judged by human standards, seemed all that could be desired. Crowds followed Him, and many seemed anxious to be His disciples. But all is not gold that glitters. It soon became evident that the crowds were actuated by motives of an earthly and carnal character. Few gave evidence of any sense of *spiritual* need. Few, if any, seemed to discern the real purpose of His mission. A spirit of partizanship was rife, so we read, "When therefore the Lord knew how the Pharisees had heard that Jesus made and baptized more disciples than John, He left Judea, and departed again into Galilee" (John 4:1, 3).

How was it, then, in Galilee? It was simply a repetition of what had happened in Judea. Human nature is the same wherever it is found: that is why history so constantly repeats itself. Here in Galilee, the crowds had followed Him. For a brief season, He was their popular idol. And yet, few of them manifested any signs that their consciences were stirred or their hearts exercised. Fewer still understood the real purport of His mission. And now that He had declared it, now that He had pressed upon them their spiritual need, they were offended: many who had posed as His disciples, turned back, and walked no more with Him.

How many of the Lord's servants have had a similar experience. They entered some field of service, and for a time the crowd thronged their ministry. For a season they were popular with those among whom they labored. But, then, if the servant was faithful to his Master, if he pressed the claims of Christ, if he shunned not to declare *all* the counsel of God,—then, how noticeable the change! Then, arose a "murmuring" (6:41); there was a "striving" among those who heard him (6:52); there was a querulous "This is a *hard* saying" (v. 61); there was a "many" of "the disciples" going back, and walking "no more with him" (v. 66). But sufficient for the servant to be as his Master. Let him thank God that there *is* a little company left who recognize and appreciate "the words of eternal life" (v. 64), for *they* are of far greater price in the sight of God than "the many" who "went back". Ah, dear reader, this is indeed a *living* Word, mirroring the fickle and wicked heart as faithfully today as it did two thousand years ago!

"Many therefore of His disciples, when they heard this, said, This is an hard saying; who can hear it?" (v. 60). The wonderful discourse in the synagogue, following the one given to the people on the outside, was now over. We are here shown the effect of it on the disciples. A "disciple" means one who is a learner. These "disciples" are carefully distinguished from "the twelve". They were made up of a class of people who were, in measure, attracted by the person of Christ and who were, more especially, imprest by His miracles. But how *real* this attraction was, and how *deep* the impression made, we are now given to see. When Christ had presented Himself not as the Wonder-worker, but as the Bread of God; when He had spoken of giving His flesh for the life of the world, and of men drinking His blood, which signified that He would die, and die a death of violence; when He insisted that except they ate His flesh and drank His blood "they had no life" in them; and, above all, when He announced that man is so depraved and so alienated from God, that except the Father draw him, he would never come to Christ for salvation: they were all offended. It will be seen, then, that we take the words, "This is an hard saying; who can hear it?" as referring to the whole of the discourse which Christ had just delivered in the Capernaum synagogue.

"Many therefore of His disciples, when they had heard this, said, This is an hard saying; who can hear it?" (v. 60). The simple meaning of this is, that these disciples were offended. It was not that they found the language of Christ so obscure as to be unintelligible, but what they had heard was so irreconcilable with *their own* views, they would not receive it. What their own views were, comes out plainly in John 12. When Christ signified what death He should die, "The people answered Him, We have heard out of the Law that Christ *abideth for ever:* and how sayest Thou, The Son of man must be lifted up?" (v. 34).

In applying the above verse to ourselves, two things should be noted. First, that when today professing Christians criticize a servant of God who is really giving out Divine truth, and complain that his teaching is "An hard saying", it is always to be traced back to the same cause as operated here. Many disciples will still reject the Word of God when it is ministered in the power of the Spirit, and they will do so because it *conflicts* with their own views and contravenes the traditions of their fathers! In the second place, note that these men complained among themselves. This is evident from the next verse: "When Jesus *knew in Himself* that His disciples murmured at it". They did not come directly to Christ and openly state their difficulties. They did not ask Him to explain His meaning. And why? Because they were not really anxious *for* light. Had they been so, they would have sought it from Him. Again we say, How like human nature today! When the Lord's messenger delivers a word that is distasteful to his hearers, they are not manly enough to come *to him* and tell him their grievance, far less will they approach him seeking help. No, like the miserable cowards they are, they will skulk in the background, seeking to sow the seeds of dissension by criticizing what they have heard. And such people the servant of God will have no difficulty in placing: they may wear the badge of disciples, but he will know from their actions and speech that they are not believers!

"When Jesus knew in Himself that His disciples murmured at it, He said unto them, Doth this offend you?" (v. 61). How solemn this is! These men could not deceive Christ. They might have walked with Him for a time (v. 66); they might have posed as His disciples (v. 60); they might have taken their place in the synagogue (v. 59), and listened with seeming attention and reverence while He taught them; but He knew their hearts: those they could not hide from Him. Nor can men do so today. *He* is not misled by all the religiousity of the day. His eyes of fire pierce through every mask of hypocrisy. Learn, then, the consummate folly and utter worthlessness of "a form of godliness" without its power (2 Tim. 3:5).

"When Jesus *knew in Himself* that His disciples murmured at it, He said unto them, Doth this offend you?" (v. 61). How this evidenced, once more, His deity! At the beginning of our chapter, He had been regarded as a "Prophet"; but a greater than a prophet was here. Later, an insulting contrast had been drawn between Moses and Christ; but a greater than Moses was before them. Neither Moses nor any of the prophets had been able to read the hearts of men. But here was One who knew *in Himself* when these disciples murmured. He knew, too, *why* they murmured. He knew they were *offended*. Plainly, then, this must be God Incarnate, for none but the Lord Himself can read the heart.

"What and if ye shall see the Son of man ascend up where He was before?" (v. 62). Here we have the third great fact which this chapter brings out concerning Christ. First, He referred to the Divine incarnation: He was the Bread which had "come down from heaven" (v. 41). Second, He was going to die, and die a death of violence: the repeated mention of His "blood" showed that (vv. 52, 55, etc.). Third, He would ascend to heaven, thus returning to that place from whence He had come. His ascension involved, of necessity, His resurrection. Thus does our chapter make clear reference to each of the vital crises in the history of Christ.

"What and if ye shall see the Son of man ascend up where He was before?" (v. 62). Soon would the Son of God return to that sphere of unmingled blessedness and highest glory, from whence He came to Bethlehem's manger; and that, in order to go to Calvary's Cross. But He would return there as "the Son of Man". This is indeed a marvel. A *man* is now seated upon the throne of the Father—the Godman. And because of His descent and ascent, heaven is the home of every one who, by eating His flesh and drinking His blood, becomes a partaker of His life. And because of this, earth becomes a wilderness, a place of exile, through which we pass, the children of faith, as strangers and pilgrims. Soon, thank God, shall His prayer be answered: "Father, I will that they also, whom Thou hast given Me, be *with Me* where I am" (John 17:24).

"What and if ye shall see the Son of man ascend up where He was before?" (v. 62). This is one of several intimations that during the days of His earthly ministry the Lord Jesus looked beyond the Cross, with all its dread horror, to the joy and rest and glory beyond. As the apostle tells us in Heb. 12:2, "Looking unto Jesus the Author and Finisher of our faith; who for *the joy that was set before Him* endured the Cross, despising the shame". It is striking to note how the *ascension* is made typically prominent at the beginning of John 6: see vv. 3 and 15—"Jesus went up into *a mount*".

It is to be observed that Christ did not positively declare that these murmurers *should* "see" Him as He ascended, but He merely asked them if they would be offended at such a sight. It seems to us He designedly left the door open. There is no room for doubt but that many became real believers for the first time *after* He had risen from the dead. The fact that 1 Cor. 15:6 tells us He was seen of "above five hundred *brethren*" proves this. It is quite likely that some of these very men who had listened to His blessed teaching in the Capernaum synagogue were among that number. But at the time of which our lesson treats they were unbelievers, so He continued to address them accordingly.

"It is the Spirit that quickeneth" (v. 63). The Lord here presses upon His critics what He had first said in v. 44. To believe on Him, to appropriate the saving value of His death, was not an act of the flesh: to do this, they must first be "drawn by the Father", that is, be "quickened by the Spirit". There *must* be life before there can be the activities of life. Believing on Christ is a manifestation of the Divine life already in the one that believes. The writer has no doubt at all that the words, "It is the Spirit that quickeneth", refer to the regenerating power of the Holy Spirit. John 6:63 is complementary to 5:21. In the former, "quickening" is referred to both God the Father, and God the Son; here, to God the Holy Spirit. Thus by linking the two passages together we learn that regeneration is the joint work of the three Persons in the Holy Trinity. So, in like manner, by linking together Eph. 1:20, John 10:18 and Rom. 8:11, we learn that each Person of the Trinity was active in the resurrection of the Lord Jesus.

"It is the Spirit that quickeneth: the flesh profiteth nothing" (v. 63). This is indeed a searching word and one that greatly needs emphasizing today. The flesh "profiteth *nothing*". The flesh has *no part* in the works of God. All fleshly activities amount to nothing where the regeneration of dead sinners is concerned. Neither the logical arguments advanced by the mind, hypnotic powers brought to bear upon the will, touching appeals made to the emotions, beautiful music and hearty singing to catch the ear, nor sensuous trappings to draw the eye—none of these are of the slightest avail in stirring *dead* sinners. It is not the choir, nor the preacher, but "the Spirit that quickeneth". This is very distasteful to the natural man, because so humbling; that is why it is completely ignored in the great majority of our modern evangelistic campaigns. What is urgently needed today is not mesmeric experts who have made a study of how to produce a religious "atmosphere", nor religious showmen to make people laugh one minute and weep the next, but faithful preaching of God's Word, with the saints on their faces before God, humbly praying that He may be pleased to send His quickening Spirit into their midst.

"The words that I speak unto you, they are spirit, and they are life" (v. 63). This confirms our interpretation of the first part of the verse. Christ is speaking of regeneration, which was the one great need of those who were offended at His teaching. They could not discern spiritual things till they had spiritual life, and for *that* they must be "quickened" by the Spirit of God. First, He told them *who* did the quickening—"the Spirit"; now He states *what* the Spirit uses to bring about that quickening—the "words" of God. The Spirit is the Divine Agent; the Word is the Divine instrument. God begets "with the Word of truth" (James 1:18). We are born again of incorruptible seed, "by the Word of God" (1 Pet. 1:23). We are made partakers of the Divine nature by God's "exceeding great and precious promises" (2 Pet. 1:4). And here in John 6:63 Christ explains how this is: the words of God are "spirit, and they are life". That is, they are spiritual, and employed by the Holy Spirit to impart life. Thus, we say again, The great need of today, as of every age, is the faithful preaching of *God's* Word; "not with enticing words of man's wisdom, but in demonstration of the Spirit and of power" (1 Cor. 2:4). What is needed is less anecdotal preaching, less rhetorical embellishment, less reliance upon logic, and more direct, plain, pointed, *simple* declaration and exposition of the Word itself. Sinners will never be saved without this—"the flesh profiteth *nothing*"!

"The words that I speak unto you, they are spirit, and they are life" (v. 63). How Christ here maintained the *balance* of truth! "It is the Spirit that quickeneth" speaks of the *Divine* side. In connection with *it* man has no part. There, the "flesh" is ruled out entirely. Are we, then, to fold our arms and act as though we had no obligations at all? Far from it. Christ guards against this by saying, "The words that I speak *unto you*, they are spirit, and they are life." This was addressed to *human responsibility*. These "words" are given to be *believed;* and we are under direct obligation to set to our seal that God is true. Let then the sinner read God's Word; let him see himself mirrored in it. Let him take its searching message to himself; let him follow the light whithersoever it leads him; and if he be sincere, if he is truly seeking God, if he longs to be saved, the Holy Spirit shall quicken *him* by that same Word of life.

"But there are some of you that believe not" (v. 64). This affords further confirmation of what we have said above. Christ was addressing human responsibility. He was pressing upon His hearers their need of *believing* on Him. He was not deceived by outward appearances. They might pose as His disciples, they might seem to be very devoted to Him, but He knew that they *had not* "believed". The remainder of the verse is a parenthetical statement made by John (under the inspiration of God) at the time he wrote the Gospel. "For Jesus knew from the beginning who they were that believed not, and who should betray Him". Very striking is this. It is one more of the many evidences furnished by this fourth Gospel, that Christ is none other than the Son of God.

"And He said, Therefore said I unto you, that no man can come unto Me, except it were given unto him of My Father"

(v. 65). Here He repeats what He had said in v. 44. He is still addressing their responsibility. He presses upon them their moral inability. He affirms their need of Divine power working within them. It was very humbling, no doubt. It furnished *proof* that "the flesh profiteth nothing". It shut them up to God. To the Father they must turn; from Him they must seek that drawing power, without which they would never come to Christ and be saved. Not only "would not" but *could not*. The language of Christ is unequivocal. It is not "no man will", but "no man *can* come unto Me, except it were given him of My Father". The will of the natural man has nothing to do with it. John 1:13 expressly declares that the new birth is "*not* of the will of the flesh". Contrary this may be to *our* ideas; distasteful to *our* minds and hearts; but it is *God's* truth, nevertheless, and all the denials of men will never alter it one whit.

"'From that time many of His disciples went back, and walked no more with Him" (v. 66). While the preceding verses contain words of Christ which were addressed to human responsibility, we must not overlook the fact that they also expressed the Divine side of things. The "drawing" of the Father is exercised according to His *sovereign* will. He denies it to none who sincerely seek; but the truth is, that the seeking itself, the desire *for* Christ, is the initial *effect* of this "drawing". That all men do not seek Christ may be explained from two viewpoints. From the human side the reason is that, men are so depraved they love the darkness and hate the light. From the Divine side, that any *do* seek Christ, is because God in His sovereign grace has put forth a power in them which overcomes the resistence of depravity. But God does not work thus in all. He is under no moral obligation so to do. Why *should* He make an enemy love Him? Why should He "draw" to Christ, one who wants to remain away? That He *does* so with particular individuals is according to His own eternal counsels and sovereign pleasure. And once this is pressed upon the natural man he is offended. It was so here: "From that time many of His disciples went back, and walked no more with Him". What a contrast was this from what occurred at the beginning of that day! Then, the many had crossed the Sea and sought Him out; now, the many turned their backs upon Him: so unreliable and so fickle is human nature.

"From that time many of His disciples went back, and walked no more with Him" (v. 66). This verse is parallel with what we read of in Luke 4: "But I tell you of a truth, many widows were in Israel in the days of Elias, when the heaven was shut up three years and six months, when great famine was throughout all the land; but unto *none of them* was Elias sent, *save* unto Sarepta, a city of Sidon, unto a woman which was a widow. And many lepers were in Israel in the time of Eliseus the prophet; and *none of them* was cleansed *saving Naaman* the Syrian" (vv. 25-27). Here Christ, in the synagogue of Nazareth, pressed upon His hearers how in the past God had most evidently acted according to His mere sovereign pleasure. And what was the effect of this on those who heard? The very next verse tells us: "And all they in the synagogue, when they heard *these things*, were filled with *wrath*". And human nature has not changed. Let the sovereign rights of God be emphasized today, and people will be "filled with wrath"; not only the men of the world will be, but the respectable attenders of the modern synagogue. So it was here in our lesson: *"From that time* many of His disciples went back". From what time? From the time that Christ had declared, "No man can come unto Me, except it were given unto him of My Father" (v. 65). *This* was too much for them. They would not remain to hear any more. And mark it carefully, that those who left were "many of *His disciples*". Then let not the one who faithfully preaches the sovereignty of God today be surprised if he meets with a similar experience.

"Then said Jesus unto the twelve, Will ye also go away?" (v. 67). Christ desires no unwilling followers; so, on the departure of the "many disciples", He turns to the twelve and inquires if they also desire to leave Him. His question was a test, a challenge. Did they prefer to be found with the popular crowd, or would they remain with what was, outwardly, a failing cause? Their answer would evidence whether or not a Divine work of grace had been wrought *in them*.

"Will *ye also* go away?". The same testing question is still being put to those who profess to be the followers of Christ. As He sees some being carried along by the different winds of erroneous doctrines, now blowing in every direction; as He beholds others going back into the world, loving pleasure more than they love God; as He marks others offended by the faithful and searching ministry of His servants, He says to you and to me, "Will ye also go away?" O that Divine grace may enable us to stand and to withstand. O that we may be so attracted by the loveliness of His person that we shall gladly go forth "unto Him, without the camp (the camp of Christianized Judaism) bearing His reproach" (Heb. 13:13).

"Then Simon Peter answered Him, Lord, to whom shall we go? Thou hast the words of eternal life" (v. 68). A blessed reply was this. The wondrous miracles had attracted the others, but the *teaching* of Christ had repelled them. It was the very opposite with the apostles, for whom, as usual, Peter acted as spokesman. It was not the supernatural works, but the Divine *words* of the Lord Jesus which held them. Peter had, what the "many disciples who went back" had not—the hearing ear. Christ had said, "The *words* that I speak unto you, they are spirit, and they are life" (v. 63), and Peter believed and was assured of this: "Thou *hast* the *words* of eternal life" he confessed. "The words of Christ had sunk deep into his soul. He had felt their power. He was conscious of the blessing they had imparted to him" (C.E.S.). It is ever this which distinguishes a true Christian from the formal professor.

"And we believe and are sure that Thou art that Christ, the Son of the living God" (v. 69). Notice carefully the *order* here: "We believe and are sure". It is the Divinely appointed and unchanging order in connection with spiritual things. It supplies one out of a thousand illustrations that God's thoughts and ways are *different*, radically different, always different, from ours. Whoever heard of believing in order to be sure? Man wants to make sure first, before he is ready to believe. But God always reverses man's order of things. It is impossible, utterly impossible, to be *sure* of Divine truth, or of any part thereof, until we have *believed* it. Other illustrations of this same principle may be adduced from Scripture. For example, the Psalmist said, "I had fainted, unless I had *believed to see* the goodness of the Lord in the land of the living" (27:13). This also is the very opposite of human philosophy. The natural man says, 'Seeing is believing'; but the spiritual man believes in order to see. So, again, in Heb. 11:3 we read, "Through faith we understand". How many desire to *understand* the mystery of the Trinity or the doctrine of election, *before* they will believe it. They might live to be as old as Methuselah, and they would "understand" neither the one nor the other until they had *faith* in what God had revealed thereon. It is *through* faith that we do understand any part of Divine truth. "We believe *and* are sure". To sum up: assurance, vision, knowledge, are the *fruits* of "believing". God rewards our faith by giving us assurance, discernment and understanding; but the unbelieving are left in the darkness of ignorance so far as spiritual things are concerned.

"And we believe and are sure that Thou art that Christ, the Son of the Living God" (v. 69). Certainty that Christ is "the Son of the living God" comes not by listening to the labored arguments of seminary professors, nor by studying books on Christian Evidences, but by *believing* what God has *said* about His Son in the Holy Scriptures. Peter was *sure* that Christ was the Son of God, because he had believed "the *words* of eternal life" which he had heard from His lips. It is indeed striking to note that in Matthew's Gospel this confession is placed right after the apostles had *seen* Christ walking on the waters and after they had received Him into the ship (14:33); for it is thus that Israel, in a coming day, will be brought to believe on Him (cf Zech. 12:10). But here in John's Gospel, which treats of the *family* of God, this confession is evoked by the assurance which comes from believing His *words*. How beautifully this illustrates the opening verse of John's Gospel, and how evident it is that God Himself has *placed* everything in these Gospels!

"Jesus answered them, Have not I chosen you twelve, and one of you is a devil? He spake of Judas Iscariot, the son of Simon: for he it was that should betray Him, being one of the twelve" (vv. 70, 71). "Jesus *answered* them". This was in reply to Peter's avowal, *"We believe and are sure"*. Christ showed that *He* knew better than His disciple. It was the omniscience of the Lord Jesus displayed once more. He was not deceived by Judas, though it is evident that all the apostles were. Proof of this is found in the fact that when He said, "One of you shall betray Me," instead of them answering, Surely you refer to Judas, they asked, "Lord, is it I?". But from the beginning Christ *knew* the character of the one who should sell Him to His enemies. Yet not now will Christ openly identify him. What we read of in v. 71 is the apostle's inspired comment, written years afterwards.

That Judas was *never* saved is clear from many considerations. Here in our text Christ is careful to *except* him from Peter's confession—"*We* believe". So, too, in John 13. After washing the feet of His disciples, which symbolized the removal of every defilement which hindered communion with Him, He said, "Ye are clean", but then He was careful to add, "But *not all*" (13:10), and then John supplies another explanatory comment—"For He knew who should betray Him; therefore said He, Ye are not all clean" (v. 11). Again; the fact that Christ here calls him a "devil"—and this was six months before he betrayed Him—proves positively that he *was not* a child of God. Acts 1:25—"Judas by transgression fell"—is sometimes appealed to in proof that he fell from grace. But the first part of the verse makes quite clear *what* it was from which Judas fell: it was "ministry and apostleship". This raises the question, Why was there a Judas in the apostolate?

The Divine answer to our question is furnished in John 17:12, where Christ tells us plainly that "the son of perdition" was lost in order that "the Scriptures might be fulfilled". The reference was to Psa. 41:9 and similar passages. When that prophecy was uttered it seemed well-nigh incredible that the Friend of sinners should be betrayed by one intimate with Him. But no word of God can fall to the ground. It had been written that, "Mine own familiar friend, in whom I trusted, which did eat of My bread, hath lifted up his heel against Me", and the son of perdition was lost in order that this scripture might be accomplished. But why did God ordain this? Why should there be a Judas in the apostolate? Mysterious as this subject is, yet, a number of things seem clear. The following ends, at least, were accomplished:—

1. *It furnished an opportunity for Christ to display His perfections.* When the Son became incarnate, He declared, "Lo I come to do *Thy will*, O God" (Heb. 10:7), and this will of God for Him was written "in the volume of the book". Now in that book it was recorded that a familiar friend should lift up his heel against Him. This was indeed a sore trial, yet was it part of the Divine will for God's Servant. How, then, does He act? John 6:70 answers: He deliberately "chose" one to be His apostle, whom He knew at the time was a "devil"! How this displays the perfections of Christ! It was in *full subjection* to the Divine will, "written in the book", that He thus acted. Even though it meant having Judas in closest association with Him for three years (and what must *that* have meant to the Holy One of God!), though it meant that even when He retired from His carping critics to get alone with the twelve, there would then be *a devil* next to Him, He hesitated not. He bowed to God's will and "chose" him!

2. *It provided an impartial witness to the moral excellency of Christ.* His Father, His forerunner, His saved apostles, bore testimony to His perfections; but lest it should be thought that these were *ex parte* witnesses, God saw to it that an *enemy* should also bear testimony. Here was a man that was "a devil"; a man who was in the closest possible touch with the life of Christ, both in public and in private; a man who would have seized eagerly on the slightest flaw, if it had been possible to find one; but it was not: "I have betrayed the *innocent* blood" (Matt. 27:4), was the unsought testimony of an impartial witness!

3. *It gave occasion to uncover the awfulness of sin.* The fulness of Redemption must bring to light the fulness of the wickedness of that for which atonement is to be made: only thus could we thoroughly see what is that terrible thing from which we are saved. And how could the heinousness of sin be more fittingly exposed at that time than by allowing a man to company with the Saviour, to be inside the circle of greatest earthly privilege, and to be himself convinced of the innocency of that One who was to be the sacrificial victim; and yet, notwithstanding, for *him* to basely betray that One and sell Him into the hands of His enemies! Never was the vileness of sin more thoroughly uncovered.

4. *It supplies sinners with a solemn warning.* The example of Judas shows us how near a man may come to Christ and

yet be lost. It shows us that outward nearness to Christ, external contact with the things of God, is not sufficient. It reveals the fact that a man may witness the most stupendous marvels, may hear the most spiritual teaching, may company with the most godly characters, and yet himself never be born again.

5. *It tells us we may expect to find hypocrites among the followers of Christ.* A hypocrite Judas certainly was. He was not a deceived soul, but an out and out imposter. He posed as a believer. He forsook the world and followed Christ. He went out as a preacher and heralded the Gospel (Matt. 10:4). He did not manifest any offence at the teaching of Christ, and did not follow those who turned back and walked no more with Him. Instead, he remained by the Saviour's side right up to the last night of all. He even partook of the passover supper, and yet all the time, he was an hypocrite; and his hypocrisy was undetected by the eleven. And history repeats itself. There are still wolves in sheep's clothing.

6. *It shows us that a devil is to be expected among the servants of God.* It was thus when Christ was here on earth; it is so still. Scripture warns us plainly against "false prophets", and "false apostles" who are "the ministers of Satan". And the case of Judas gives point to these warnings. Whoever would have expected to find a "devil" among the twelve! Whoever would have dreamed of finding a Judas among the apostles chosen by Christ Himself! But there was. And this is a solemn warning to us to place confidence in *no man.*

7. *It affords one more illustration of how radically different are God's thoughts and ways from ours.* That God should appoint a "devil" to be one of the closest companions of the Saviour; that He should have selected "the son of perdition" to be one of the favored twelve, seemed incredible. Yet so it was. And as we have sought to show above, God had *good* reasons for this selection; He had *wise* reasons for this appointment. Let this, then, serve to show us that, however mysterious may be God's ways, they are ever dictated by omniscience!

The following questions are to help the student prepare for the next lesson on John 7:1-13:—

1. What relation does v. 1 have to the rest of the lesson?
2. What do you know about the feast of tabernacles (v. 2)? Look up Old Testament references.
3. Who are "His brethren" (v. 3)?
4. Why did His brethren make the request of v. 4?
5. To what was Christ referring in vv. 6 and 8?
6. In view of vv. 1 and 8, why did Christ go to the feast at all (v. 10)?
7. What is the meaning of the last clause of v. 10?

—Arthur W. Pink.

THE ANTICHRIST.

Conclusion

In bringing to a close our series of articles on the Antichrist we are conscious that "there remaineth yet very much land to be possessed" (Josh. 13:1). We have sought to present as comprehensive an outline of the subject as our present light and somewhat limited space would permit. But little more than an outline has been given. Abundant scope is still left for the interested reader and student to work out and fill in the details for himself. This, we trust, is what many will do. The subject, though solemn, is one full of interest.

No doubt the subject is new, and hence, mysterious, to some of our readers. These we would ask to turn back to the first article, and re-read to the end of the series. That God will yet permit the Devil to bring forth his satanic Masterpiece, who shall defy God and persecute His people, should scarcely be surprising. In each succeeding age there has been a Cain for every Abel; a Jannes and Jambres for every Moses and Aaron; a Babylon for every Jerusalem; an Herod for every John the Baptist. It has been so during this dispensation: the sowing of the Wheat, was followed by the sowing of the Tares. It will be so in the Tribulation period: not only will there be a faithful remnant of Israel, but there shall be an unfaithful company of that people, too. And just before the Christ of God returns to this earth to set up His kingdom, God will suffer His arch-enemy to bring forth the false christ, who will establish his kingdom.

And God's hour for this is not far distant. It was when "the iniquity of the Amorites" was come to the "full" (Gen. 15:16) that God gave orders for their extermination (Deut. 7:1, 2). And Israel's transgressions (Dan. 8:23) and the transgressions of Christendom (2 Thess. 2: 11, 12), will only have come to "the full" when those who rejected the Christ of God, shall have received the christ of Satan. Then, shall God say to His avenging angel, "Thrust in thy sickle, and reap: for the time has come for thee to reap; for *the harvest of the earth is ripe*" (Rev. 14:15). It is this which makes the subject so solemn.

What God has been pleased to make known concerning the Antichrist is not revealed in order to gratify carnal curiosity, but is of great moment for our daily lives. In the first place, a proper apprehension of these things should cause us to seriously search our hearts, and to examine carefully the foundation upon which our hopes are built, to discover whether or not they rest on the solid Rock Christ Jesus, or whether they stand upon nothing more stable than the shifting sands of human feelings, human resolutions, human efforts after self-improvement. Incalculably serious is the issue at stake, and we cannot afford to be uncertain about it. A mere *"hope I am saved"* is not sufficient. Nothing short of the full assurance of faith ought to suffice.

Unspeakably solemn is what we read of in 2 Thess. 2:8-12: "And then shall that Wicked be revealed, whom the Lord shall consume with the spirit of His mouth, and shall destroy with the brightness of His coming: Even him, whose coming is after the working of Satan, with all power and signs and lying wonders, and with all deceivableness of unrighteousness in them that perish; because they *received not the love of the truth,* that they might be saved. And for this cause God shall send them strong delusion, that they should believe the Lie: That they all might be damned who *believed not the truth,* but had *pleasure in unrighteousness*".

There are three points in the above verses by which the writer and the reader may *test* himself. First, have I *"believed the Truth"*? *"Thy Word* is Truth". Have I set to my seal that God is true? Have I applied the Word of God *to myself,* and taken it to *my own* heart? Have I *personally* received the Saviour that it reveals?

Second, do I have *"pleasure* in unrighteousness"? There is a vast difference between *doing* an act of unrighteousness, and having "pleasure" therein. Scripture speaks of Moses "choosing rather to suffer affliction with the people of God, than to enjoy *the pleasures of sin* for a season" (Heb. 11:25). And again, it speaks of some who "knowing the judgment of God that they who commit such things are worthy of death, not only *do* the same, but *have pleasure* in them that do them" (Rom. 1:32). So it is here in the passage before us. They who "believe not the Truth", have *"pleasure* in unrighteousness". And here is one of the vital differences between an unbeliever and a genuine believer. The latter may be overtaken by a fault, his communion with Christ may be broken, he may sin grievously, but if he does, *he* will have no "pleasure" therein! Instead, he will *hate* the very unrighteousness into which he has fallen, and mourn bitterly for having done that which was so dishonoring to his Saviour.

Third, have I "received *the love* of the Truth"? Do I read God's Word daily, not simply as a duty, but as a delight; not merely to satisfy conscience, but because it rejoices my heart; not simply to gratify an idle curiosity, that I may acquire some knowledge of its contents, but because I desire above everything else to become better acquainted with its Author. Can I say with the Psalmist, "I will *delight myself* in Thy statutes . . . . Thy commandments are *my delights"* (Psa. 119:16, 143). The wicked *love* the "darkness"; but God's people *love* "the light"!

Here, then, are three tests by which we earnestly entreat every reader to honestly examine himself, and see whether he be in the faith. Awful beyond words is the only alternative, for Scripture declares of those who have "believed not the Truth", who have "pleasure in unrighteousness", and who have "received not the love of the Truth", that "for this cause God shall send them strong delusion, that they should believe the Lie: *that they all might be damned".*

Again; if we diligently search the Scriptures to discover what they teach concerning the Antichrist—his personality, his career, his ways, etc.—the more we are informed about him the better shall we be prepared to detect the many antichrists who are in the world today, now preparing the way for the appearing and career of the Man of Sin. There is no reason why we should be *ignorant* of Satan's "devices". There is no valid excuse if we are deceived by his "false apostles", who transform themselves into the apostles of Christ (2 Cor. 11:13). Christians ought not to be misled by the many false prophets who are gone out into the world (1 John 4:1). Nor will they be, if they study diligently those things which God has recorded for our enlightenment and to safeguard us against the subtle deceptions of the great Enemy.

Again; as we give diligent heed to the prophetic Word, as we take its solemn warnings *to heart*, the effect must be that we shall *separate ourselves* from everything which is anti-Christian. "Be not unequally yoked together with unbelievers: for what fellowship hath righteousness with unrighteousness? and what communion hath light with darkness? And what concord hath Christ with Belial? or what part hath he that believeth with an infidel? And what agreement hath the temple of God with idols? for ye are the temple of the living God; as God hath said, I will dwell in them, and walk in them; and I will be their God, and they shall be My people. Wherefore come out from among them, and be ye separate, saith the Lord, and touch not the unclean thing; and I will receive you" (2 Cor. 6:14-17).

This Call is not directed toward Christians separating themselves from their fellow-Christians. How could it be? Scripture does not contradict itself. God's Word explicitly says, "Not forsaking the assembling *of ourselves together,* as the manner of some is; but exhorting one another: and so much the more, as ye see the day approaching" (Heb. 10:25). But the same Word which tells us not to forsake the assembling of ourselves together, commands us to have *"no fellowship* with the unfruitful works of darkness" (Eph. 5:11). God forbid that His people should be found helping forward the plans of the Prince of Darkness.

Finally; as we read prayerfully the teaching of Scripture concerning this Coming One, who shall embark upon the most awful course that has ever been run on this earth; as we learn of how he will ascend the Throne of the World, and be the director and dictator of human affairs; as we discover how he will employ the mighty power with which Satan invests him, to openly defy God and everything which bears His name; and, as we are made aware of the unspeakably dreadful judgments which God will pour upon the world at that time, and the fearful doom which shall overtake the Antichrist and all his followers; our hearts will be stirred within us, and we shall not hesitate to lift up our voices in warning. The world is in complete ignorance of what awaits it. The nations know not what is in store for them. Even Israel discern not the dark night which lies before them. But as God instructs us concerning what He is about to do, it is positively criminal to remain silent. The voices of all whom God has been pleased to enlighten ought to be raised in solemn and united testimony to the things which He has declared *"must* shortly come to pass".

—Arthur W. Pink.

CHRISTIAN LIBERTY

In the opening article of this series* we affirmed that the unregenerate sinner is, in heart and practise, an Antinomian; that is, one who is *opposed to* the Law of God. Proof of this is furnished by Rom. 8:7, which tells us, "The carnal mind is enmity against God: for it is not subject to the Law of God, neither indeed can be." It

* See "The Law" and "The Sabbath".

needs to be remembered that the "carnal mind" still remains in the believer. It is true that the Christian has a new mind (2 Tim. 1:7), which is part of the new nature—a mind which *"serves* the Law of God" (Rom. 7:25); and it is this, alone, that explains the *conflict* waged daily within every saint. But the presence of the carnal mind within, reveals the urgent need there is for the "casting down imaginations, and every high thing that exalteth itself against the knowledge of God, and bringing into captivity every thought *to the obedience of Christ*" (2 Cor. 10:5). This can be accomplished *only* as the believer yields his members (not only the members of his body, but *every* "member" of his complex personality) "*servants* to righteousness unto holiness" (Rom. 6:19).

But does not this expression "yielding our members as *servants* to righteousness" savor of *legality*, and is not that entirely at variance with Christian *liberty?* And here we reach, perhaps, what has seemed a real difficulty to many who have read the previous articles. Probably our readers have felt the force of what has been set before them. The various scriptures cited are so plain that their meaning is not open to question. The binding obligations of the Law of God upon every Christian has, we trust, been unequivocally established. But now the question naturally arises, What, then, of Christian liberty? Did not the Lord Himself promise, "If the Son therefore shall make you free, ye shall be *free indeed*" (John 8:36)? Did not the apostle Paul, under the Holy Spirit, write, "Stand fast therefore in *the liberty wherewith Christ hath made us free,* and be not entangled again with the yoke of bondage" (Gal. 5:1)? How are we to understand these statements? Are they to be evacuated of all meaning? If not, how is it possible to fairly and satisfactorily harmonize them with the affirmation that Christians *are* under bonds to obey the Ten Commandments?

In seeking an answer to the above questions several things need to be borne in mind. First, we may be fully assured that the Holy Scriptures contain no contradictions. Second, we need to be very careful in defining our terms: and to define them correctly, we must make a patient and thorough search of the Word. In the third place, whatever true Christian liberty is, certainly, *obedience to God* does not conflict with it. It was to men whom He had *already* "made free" that the Son said, "If ye love Me, *keep My commandments*" (John 14:15). And it was to those who *were* in the enjoyment of Christian liberty that one of His apostles was moved to write, "And whatsoever we ask, we receive of Him, because we *keep His commandments*" (1 John 3:22). Thus, it is evident that we must distinguish sharply between Christian liberty and lawlessness.

The term "Christian liberty", like many another, is used very loosely by our moderns. We greatly fear that to many, who though bearing the name of Christians have never been born again, Christian liberty means *license to do as one pleases.* We are far from affirming, or even insinuating, that this is true of *all* those who deny that believers are under obligations to "serve the Law of God". With many their hearts are better than their heads: their lives superior to their creeds. But, nevertheless, it cannot be gainsaid, that to the popular mind Law and Liberty are opposing terms. Many of the Lord's own people are being taught that legal restrictions are incompatible with true Christian liberty, and this in the face of the words of the Saviour—"teaching them to observe all things whatsoever I have *commanded you*" (Matt. 28:20)!

It is now being proclaimed on almost every side that grace rules out all Law. Nor is this to be wondered at, for Christ plainly foretold that lawlessness *should* abound (Matt. 24:12). But though it is not to be wondered at, it is to be deeply deplored that some, whom we have good reasons to look upon as the Lord's servants, should be found lending themselves to forwarding this incoming tide of spiritual anarchy. The Word of truth declares that "grace reigns *through righteousness*" (Rom. 5:21), not at the expense of it; and there can be no righteousness apart from law. Righteousness is right doing; and right doing is conformity to law. The only other alternative is what the writer of the book of Judges speaks of, namely, "Every man doing that which was right in *his own eyes*" (21:25), which is a state of anarchy.

Liberty and license are as far apart as the poles. True liberty is *subjection to Law,* paradoxical as that may sound. To the unregenerate mind the terms of Christian life must appear to abound in paradoxes. "When I am *weak,* then am I *strong*" (2 Cor. 12:10), will seem a contradiction in terms to one who is devoid of spiritual intelligence. But is it meaningless to the real Christian? We trow not. Whether he understands it or not, he knows full well that it is the inspired declaration of God's Word. Equally foolish must it appear to the unbeliever to read, that, When a man becomes the *slave* of Christ, then is he *free!* Nevertheless, that is what God's Word affirms, and it is what Christian experience confirms. Little as the mind of the flesh may be able to grasp it, is it not nevertheless a fact that, when we are the *most elevated* spiritually, we take the *lowest* place before God? that when we are the holiest, we are most conscious of our sinful defilements? Equally so is it true that we enjoy the greatest spiritual freedom when we are most in subjection to God's Law. What saith the Scriptures? This: "I will walk at liberty, *for* I seek Thy *precepts*" (Psa. 119:45). The natural man imagines that to be subject to God's "precepts" is to be confined to a narrow place; but the mind illumined by the Holy Spirit will acknowledge, "Thy commandment is *exceeding broad*" (Psa. 119:96).

After these preliminary considerations we shall now attempt to define the scriptural import of *Christian liberty*. Not that we profess to give here a complete or exhaustive definition, nevertheless, we believe it will include the primary elements and aspects of it.

1. Christian liberty is *deliverance from the Wrath of God*. The relation which the Christian, before conversion, stood to God (because of sin) was that of a condemned criminal. By nature he was a child "of wrath, even as others" (Eph. 2:3). By birth he belonged to a race which is under the curse of God. In Adam he sinned, and upon him rested the righteous condemnation of a sin-hating God (Psa. 58:3). Because of this, he was, together with all others of Adam's race, looked at as a criminal in prison, awaiting execution. But, all praise to His peerless name, it was to deliver just such that the Son of God became incarnate. He was sent "to proclaim liberty *to the captives*, and *the opening of the prison* to them that are bound" (Isa. 60:1). This was His *first* ministerial utterance (see Luke 4:16-18). Nor was this to be confined to Jewish sinners. Of old the Lord declared, I will "give thee for a covenant of the people, for a light of *the Gentiles*. To open the blind eyes, *to bring out the prisoners from the prison,* and them that sit in darkness out of the prison house" (Isa. 42:7).

The Gospel, then, proclaims "*liberty* to the captives" (Isa. 61:2), and the one who believes its joyous message is immediately and forever freed from that awful prison in which he lay as a culprit condemned. The Gospel tells him *how* this could be righteously accomplished. Another took his place; a Substitute suffered in his stead. And of Him it is written, *"He* was taken *from prison* and *from judgment"* (Isa. 53: 8). He entered, for His people, the place of condemnation, and from it He was taken to judgment—that is one reason why He was crucified between two "malefactors", to show us the more plainly, *the place* He took! Only thus could we be liberated. When the Judge delivers the culprit to the officer and he is "cast into prison", the Divine sentence is, "Thou shalt by no means come out thence, till thou hast paid the uttermost farthing" (Matt. 5:25,26). And because *we* had "nothing (with which) to pay" (Luke 7:42), the Lord Jesus paid the full redemption-price for us, by suffering in our stead 'the whole of wrath Divine'. In consequence of this, we are delivered. No longer prisoners, but free men are we. No longer under God's righteous wrath, but delivered from all condemnation (Rom. 8:1). Here, then, is the first aspect of Christian liberty: deliverance from the wrath of God. The disobedient are "spirits *in prison*" (1 Pet. 3:19); but those who have obeyed God's command to believe on His Son have been "made free" (John 8:36), free from the sentence of condemnation.

2. Christian liberty is *deliverance from the Power of the Devil*. Christians, in their unregenerate state, "walked according to the course of this world, according to the Prince of the power of the air, the spirit that now worketh in the children of disobedience" (Eph. 2:2). The ungodly are the slaves of Satan. Said our Lord to the Pharisees, "Ye are of your father the Devil, and the lusts of your father ye will do" (John 8:44). Men are "taken *captive* by him (the Devil) at his will" (2 Tim. 2:26).

Now the Gospel is God's appointed agency for delivering men from their awful bondage to the Devil. When the Lord commissioned the apostle Paul to go unto the Gentiles, He sent him "to open their eyes, and to turn them from darkness to light, and *from the power of Satan* unto God" (Acts 26:18). Christians are a people who have been delivered from "the Power of darkness (Satan) and translated into the kingdom of God's dear Son" (Col. 1:13). Heb. 2:14,15 tells how this was made possible for us: "Forasmuch then as the children are partakers of flesh and blood, He also Himself likewise took part of the same; that He might destroy him that had the power of death, that is, the Devil; and deliver them who through fear of death were all their lifetime subject to bondage." Here, then, is the second aspect of Christian liberty: believers in Christ have been *delivered* from that *bondage* to which they had been, all their lifetime, subject. Consequently, to them the promise now is "Resist the Devil, and he will *flee* from you" (Jam. 4:7).

3. Christian liberty is *deliverance from the Bondage of Sin*. The unregenerate are the *slaves* of sin: "Whosoever committeth sin is the bond-slave of sin" (John 8:34). So completely are the wicked under the dominion of sin they *cannot* of themselves think a godly thought, beget a godly aspiration, or perform a godly deed. They *cannot* come to Christ (John 6:44). They *cannot* hear His word (John 8:43). They *cannot* believe (John 12:39). They *cannot* receive the Holy Spirit (John 14:17). They *cannot* please God (Rom. 8:8). And in each case the reason why they cannot is because they are the bond-slaves of sin. And in that condition they will remain unless the Son shall "make them free".

That the natural man is ignorant of this bondage only evidences how completely he is under the dominion of sin. His understanding is darkened. That he boasts of being a free-agent only demonstrates the derangement of his mind. The same men who call darkness light, and light darkness; who term wisdom, folly, and deem folly to be wisdom; also regard true freedom as bondage, and consider their own bondage, freedom. Ever since man drank in that deadly poison, "Ye shall be *as God*" (Gen. 3:5), his descendants have affected a dominion over themselves, and have disregarded the Lordship of their Maker. Their boast is, "With our tongue will we prevail; our lips are our own: *who* is lord over us?" (Psa. 12:4). They suppose that the only true liberty is to be at the command and under the control of none above themselves. They think that to live according to their own heart's desire is to assert their free-agency. But *that* is bondage and thraldom of the worst kind.

The natural man may cherish the delusion that *he* is not hampered by the bonds which restrict the liberty of the saints. He may think himself free to go where he wills, and free to do as he pleases, untrammeled by Divine restraints. But this only proves that the god of this world (Satan) *has* "blinded his mind" (2 Cor. 4:4). Instead of being free he *"serves* divers lusts" (Titus 3:3). Instead of carving his own career, he is simply walking "according to the Prince of the power of the air, the spirit that now worketh in the children of disobedience" (Eph. 2:2). Instead of being master of himself, he is doing the desires of his father, the Devil (John 8:44). And little as he knows it, *God Himself* "restrains" him (Psa. 76:10). The truth is, that the most awful punishment which God ever inflicts upon men in this world is to abandon them to themselves: "So I *gave them up* unto their own hearts' lust: and they walked in their own counsels" (Psa. 81:12).

But believers have been *delivered* from the dominion of sin: "Being then made free from sin" (Rom. 6:18). Christians have been emancipated from their former bondage: "Sin shall not have *dominion over* you" (Rom. 6:14) is now the Divine promise to them. It is not that the sinful nature has been removed from them, but that its sovereign power has been broken. Sin may harass them, but they are no more its slaves. Believers may fall, but they shall not be utterly cast down (Psa. 37:24). Here, then, is the third aspect of Christian liberty: believers have been delivered from the bondage of sin, and if they will but avail themselves of God's all-sufficient grace, they will find that full provision has been made for them to enjoy *complete* deliverance from the servitude of sin. That we do not enjoy this, is entirely our own fault.

4. Christian liberty is *deliverance from the Authority of man*. The Christian belongs to Christ. He has been bought with a price. He is "the Lord's freeman" (1 Cor. 7:22). Consequently no man and no set of men, have any right to impose any restraints on his conscience. No man and no set of men have any right to tell the Christian what he must believe or what he must do (his civic life excepted). For the State to interfere in connection with spiritual things is iniquitous tyranny. If the State were to demand my subscription to a man-made creed, that would be an attack upon my Christian freedom. If the State were to demand that my children should be baptized and join some church, that would be an unlawful infringement of my Christian liberty. The Lord's people in the United States cannot be sufficiently

thankful to God for the religious liberty which is granted them in this favored land. And the least they can do in return is to earnestly pray the Lord for His blessing to rest on the President and the members of his Senate, that such privileges may be continued.

It is this particular aspect of Christian freedom which the apostle pressed upon the Galatian saints. They had been harassed by certain Judaizers who demanded that they be circumcised; and it was in view of *this* (and of this alone) that the apostle said to them, "Stand fast therefore in the liberty wherewith Christ hath made us free, and be not entangled again with the yoke of bondage" (5:1). He hereby reminds them that to submit to the demand of the Judaizers would be to repudiate the liberty wherewith Christ had made them free. Mark that Paul is not here addressing Jewish believers, but Gentile believers. Proof of this is found in the very next verse: *"If ye be circumcised"*.

From *what*, then, had the Galatian believers been "made free" by Christ? The answer is, from the requirements and commandments, from the rites and ceremonies of man-made religions. "When ye knew not God", said the apostle, "ye did service ("ye were *in bondage*", Bagster's Interlinear) unto them which by nature are no gods" (4:8). They had been slaves to human traditions and authority. In principle, then, these Judaizers, *un*-authorized by God, were seeking to drag them back again into that from which they had been delivered. Hence, continues the apostle, "after that ye have known God, or rather are known of God, how turn ye *again* to the weak and beggarly elements, whereunto ye desire *again* to be in bondage?" (Gal. 4:9). To submit to circumcision at the hands of men, was no better than a return to their heathen rites. Therefore said the apostle, "Stand fast in the liberty wherewith Christ hath made you free, and *be not* entangled again with the yoke of bondage". Disdain these Judaizers. Refuse to heed them. Do not allow them to rob you of your Christian liberty. *They* have no right to issue commandments nor impose ordinances. You belong to Christ: heed *His* commandments and submit to *His* ordinances.

Our comments above on Gal. 5:1 are confirmed by what we read of in 5:11-13: "And I, brethren, if I yet preach *circumcision*, why do I yet suffer persecution? Then is the offence of the Cross ceased. I would *they* were even cut off *which trouble you*. For, brethren, ye have been called unto liberty". Thus it is clear that the "liberty" of which the apostle treats in this epistle is emancipation from all human authority in religious matters, for it was not the moral Law but *circumcision* that these Judaistic "troublers" were pressing upon these Galatian saints.

It is this particular aspect of Christian freedom which the apostle also pressed on the Colossian saints. The Colossian church had been troubled by Gnostics, who sought to impose their system of asceticism upon the Lord's people. They had drawn up a series of prohibitions which the apostle summarizes in the words, "Touch not; taste not; handle not, which are all to perish with the using" (Col. 2:21, 22). With these saints the apostle expostulates, "Wherefore if ye be dead with Christ from the rudiments of the world, why, as though living in the world, are ye subject to ordinances, after the commandments and doctrines *of men?*" (vv. 20, 22). His argument here is parallel with the one he used with the Galatians. You belong to Christ, he reminds them ("dead with Him"), why then descend from this privileged place and heed the rules of *men*. Such rules, admits the apostle, "have indeed a *show* of wisdom in will worship, and humility, and neglecting of the body", etc. But a "show" is *all* they have, for they are *"to perish* with the using." Well would it be if many of our moderns would study these verses, for there are not a few today who are seeking to impose *their own* "commandments and doctrines" of "touch not, taste not, handle not". Insofar as Christians heed them they are robbed of their liberty. When a man believes the Gospel, with enlightened faith, he accepts Christ as the alone Lord of his conscience, faith and conduct. "One is your Master, even Christ" (Matt. 23:8), therefore, should he refuse to allow any man (or any woman) to dictate to him what he should touch or taste or handle. Let him give himself, unreservedly, to learning the mind of *Christ* and responding to it, and leave others to be brought into bondage to "the commandments and doctrines *of men*" if they are so determined. Let others "neglect" their "bodies" if they wish to; for our part, we believe that "Every creature of God is good, and nothing to be refused, if it be received with thanksgiving" (1 Tim. 4:4); and we desire grace to use them all to God's glory.

5. Christian liberty is *deliverance unto the service of God*. Thus far we have considered only the negative side—what Christians have been delivered from. Now we take up the positive—what Christians are delivered unto. True liberty is not the right to live as we please, but the power to live as we ought. It is being delivered from the bondage of condemnation, Satan, sin, and men, so that the Christian is now free to serve *God*. Regeneration effects *a change of masters*. The one who before was the captive of Satan and the slave of sin is now free to serve God. The lawless rebel has become a loyal subject. This is the central truth in the second half of Rom. 6. We confine ourself now to vv. 16-18 and 22, and as these are so pertinent we give a brief, but clause by clause, exposition:

Verse 16. "Know ye not?": I appeal to a common fact of observation. "That to whom ye yield yourselves servants to obey, his servants ye are to whom ye obey". If I see a number of laborers working in a field, I at once conclude they are the servants of the proprietor of that field. This illustrates the principle which the apostle here develops and applies. If men are doing the work of Satan, they must be his servants; if they are engaged in the work of God, they must be *His* servants. Sin is here personified, and sinners are termed its "slaves". "Whether of sin unto death, or of obedience unto righteousness". Death is the wages which sin pays its servants. "Obedience" is also personified here.

V. 17. "But God be thanked, that ye were the servants of sin, but ye have obeyed from the heart that form of doctrine whereto ye were delivered". Those who had formerly been the slaves of sin were now the servants of righteousness, and for this the apostle returns thanks to God. They had obeyed "from the heart", for Christian obedience is spontaneous and cordial, not constrained by fear or produced by force. "That form of doctrine whereto ye were delivered". The Greek words here refer to the moulding of metal. When the melted metal is transferred to a mould, it obeys or conforms to its shape. So believers respond to and take their form of character from the mould of Divine doctrine.

V. 18. "Being then made free from sin". In their unregenerate state, God's saints were the slaves of sin; but the Gospel has emancipated them. This emancipation is an intrinsic part of their freedom, though it is far from signifying a state of sinless perfection, or even entire deliverance from the influence of sin. "Ye became the servants of righteousness". Servants of righteousness are men obedient to righteousness.

V. 22. "But now being made free from sin, and become servants to God, ye have your fruit unto holiness, and the end everlasting life". Believers have been emancipated from the state of sin's slavery, and have become the bond-slaves of God. There has been a complete change of masters. The subjection of a slave is absolute and continuous. The slave does not obey his own will, but that of his master. He is under an influence which secures obedience. This is as true in spiritual as in natural and external relations. But there is this vital difference: the slaves of sin are in the most direful bondage; whereas the bondslaves of God enjoy true liberty. The slave of sin is the helpless victim of his depraved nature; but the bond-slave of God serves freely—his obedience is from *the heart!**

"Christians are free in reference to God. They are 'the Lord's freeman' (1 Cor. 7:22). By this we do not mean that they are not under the strongest obligations to conform their minds and wills to the mind and will of God, and to regulate the whole of their temper and conduct according to the revelation of that mind and will revealed in His Word. They are not free in the sense of being without law to God; to be so, would be the reverse of a privilege; they are 'under the law to Christ' (1 Cor. 9:21)" (Dr. John Brown).

In a word, then, Christian liberty is the freedom of *children* in contrast from the bondage of *prisoners,* and just as children are (normally) subject to the government of their parents, so are God's children subject to His government; and the Law is for the regulation of their conduct.

But one more question needs to be faced ere we conclude, namely, If we *are* under the Law as a rule of life, are we not then subject to its *curse?* If we break it, must

---
* In this brief exposition we have given a digest of Mr. R. Haldane's.

not its curse, necessarily, come upon us? Decidedly not, is our answer. And why? Because Christ suffered its "curse" in the stead of His people (Gal. 3:13). David, Elijah, Daniel were "under the Law" (not for salvation, but governmentally), and they broke it. Were *they*, then, under its curse? Surely not. On what principle, then, (governmental principle) does God act toward His *children* who break the Law? A pertinent question, and one to which a clear scriptural answer may be returned. Let the reader turn to Psalm 89 and there he will read, "If His children forsake My Law, and walk not in My judgments; if they break My statutes, and keep not My commandments; Then will I visit their transgression with the rod, and their iniquity with stripes, Nevertheless My lovingkindness will I not utterly take from him, nor suffer My faithfulness to fail" (vv. 30-33)!

In closing, let us repeat, that Christian liberty is not only emancipation from sin and Satan, but it is deliverance unto the service of God: "Circumcision is nothing, and uncircumcision is nothing, but *the keeping of the commandments of God* * * he that is called, being free, is Christ's *servant*", that is, "bondslave" (1 Cor. 7:19-22). Freedom that does not issue in "keeping the commandments of God" is a delusion. "As free, and not using your liberty for a cloke of maliciousness, but as *the bond-slaves of God*" (1 Pet. 2:16). The greatest freedom is enjoyed by him who is most subject to the Law of God, which is "holy, and just, and good". That is why God's Law is termed "the Law *of liberty*" (James 2:12), an expression which must be utterly unintelligible to the carnal mind, but one that is perfectly simple to the man who is controlled by the Holy Spirit. Anything short of this complete subjection to the Law is bondage. Let us not be deceived, then, by those who promise a *spurious* liberty, for "they themselves are the slaves of corruption" (2 Pet. 2:19). Let us not be found "turning the grace of our God into lasciviousness" (Jude 4). Rather let us heed that word of the apostle Paul, "For, brethren, ye have been called unto liberty; only use not liberty for an occasion to the flesh, but by love serve one another" (Gal. 5:13). Be these the breathings of our soul: Lord, my sweetest liberty is obedience to Thee; my highest freedom wearing Thy yoke; my greatest rest bearing Thy burden. O, how love I Thy Law after the inward man! I delight to do Thy will, O my God! The Lord grant unto us that we "being *delivered* out of the hand of our enemies might *serve Him* without fear, in holiness and righteousness before Him, all the days of our life" (Luke 1:74, 75).

EXPOSITION OF FIRST PETER

§ 2.—*Moderation a means of Christian Obedience.*

Moderation is another of the instrumental means which the apostle recommends for the performance of the duty of Christian obedience. "Be sober." To be sober, in ordinary language, is descriptive of that particular variety of the duty of temperance which is opposed to the undue use of intoxicating liquors. But the word used by the apostle has a much more extensive meaning. The sobriety or temperance of the apostle is another word for *moderation,* and is descriptive of that state of the mind, and affections, and behavior, in reference to "things seen and temporal," "the present world," by which a Christian should be distinguished.

The foundation of true christian sobriety or moderation lies in a just estimate of the intrinsic and comparative value of "all that is in the world, the lust of the flesh, the lust of the eye, and the pride of life,"[1] —all that the eye or the flesh desires—all of which living men are apt to be proud. The Christian does not consider the wealth, and the honor, and the pleasures of this world, as destitute of value; but he sees that that value is by no means what the deluded worshippers of Mammon suppose it to be. He sees that the possession of them cannot make him happy, nor the want of them make him miserable. They cannot obtain for him the pardon of his sin, they cannot pacify his conscience, they cannot transform his character, they cannot give him life in death, they cannot secure him of happiness forever. They appear to him polluted with sin, replete with temptation, pregnant of danger.

With these views, he is moderate in his

---
[1] 1 John ii. 6.

desires for them, moderate in his pursuit of them, moderate in his attachment to them while he enjoys them; moderate in his regrets for them; when he is deprived of them. This is christian sobriety. It is for those who have earthly relatives to be as if they had them not; for "those who weep to be as though they wept not; for those who rejoice to be as though they rejoiced not; for those who use this world to use it as not abusing it, knowing that the fashion of this world passeth away."[1]

The cultivation of this sobriety is of the utmost importance to the proper performance of the duties of christian obedience. The supreme love of the world is inconsistent with christian obedience altogether. "No man can serve two masters: for either he will hate the one, and love the other; or else he will hold to the one, and despise the other; ye cannot serve God and Mammon."[2] And, as the supreme love of the world necessarily makes and keeps men "children of disobedience," so the undue love of the world prevents even those who are "the children of God, through faith in Christ Jesus," from being, in so high a degree as they ought to be, "the children of obedience." What is it that makes obedience so often to be felt a tiresome task, but the undue love of the world: and how do the commandments of our Lord become to us not grievous, but by our victorious faith overcoming the world?[3] It has been finely said, that "the same eye cannot both look up to heaven and down to earth at the same time." And the heart must be emptied of the love of the world, that it may be filled with that love of God, which is at once the seminal principle and the concentrated essence of all christian obedience. Those who are quite engrossed with earth's business and pleasures cannot be "seeking a country—a better country, that is, an heavenly." They who, by their immoderate attachment to earth, show they are at home, cannot be "strangers and sojourners." The Captain of the Lord's host, our New Testament Gideon, will not own as his soldiers those who lie down to drink of the streams of earth's delight, but only those who, in passing, drink of them with their hand, as of the brook in the way.[4]

It is much to be desired that professors of Christianity were more deeply impressed with this truth,—that the supreme love of the world is utterly inconsistent with the very existence of Christianity; and that real Christians were more deeply impressed with the kindred truth, of the utter inconsistency of an undue love of the world with a healthy, thriving Christianity, a Christianity bringing forth the fruits of true holiness and true peace, fruits which are to the glory of God, and to the happiness of the believer. It is, my brethren, this worldliness, this want of christian sobriety, which spreads such a withering blight over the blossoms of fair profession, and prevents their ever ripening into fruit. To quote again the spiritual commentator already referred to: "All immoderate use of the world and its delights injures the soul in its spiritual condition, makes it sickly and feeble, full of spiritual distempers and inactivity, benumbs the graces of the Spirit, and fills the soul with sleepy vapors, makes it grow secure and heavy in spiritual exercises, and obstructs the way and motion of the Spirit of God in the soul."[5] If we would, then, be children of obedience, if we would not fashion ourselves according to the former lusts, if we would be holy in all manner of conversation, let us "be sober."

Let each of us, ere we proceed further, examine himself. Am I girding up the loins of my mind? Am I, in a dependence on the promised aids of divine influence, honestly, heartily, determined to make the service of God, through Christ Jesus, my great business, and to make the life I live in the flesh a life of subjection to his will, and obedience to his law, by making it a life of faith in his Son? Am I sober, temperate, moderate, in all things, in my estimates, my desires, my pursuits, my enjoyments, my sorrows? If we are not girding up the loins of our minds, if we are not sober, we are not Christians. We may be calling Christ Lord, Lord; but we are not doing the things which he says to us; and unless a thorough change take place, to us, at last, must be addressed these heart-withering words—"Depart from me, I never knew you, ye workers of iniquity."

§ 3.—*Hope a means of Christian Obedience.*

We proceed now to observe, that Hope is the third means recommended by the apostle for securing the proper per-

---
[1] 2 Cor. vii. 29-31.
[2] Matt. vi. 24.
[3] 1 John v. 4.
[4] Leighton. Heb. xi. 13, 14. Judges vii. 4-7.
[5] Leighton.

formance of the duty of christian obedience. If you would be "children of obedience," if you would "not fashion yourselves according to your former lusts in your ignorance," if you would "be holy in all manner of conversation," you must "hope to the end; for the grace which is to be brought to you at the revelation of our Lord Jesus Christ."

"The grace," or favor, "which is to be brought to Christians at the revelation of Christ Jesus," that is, when Christ Jesus is revealed, is that perfection of holy happiness to which they are to be raised at the close of the present state of things —"the salvation that is ready," prepared, "to be revealed in the last time"—"the inheritance incorruptible, undefiled, and that fadeth not away, reserved in heaven for them"—"the glory that is to follow" the second coming of the Lord.

For this "grace," this manifestation of his sovereign favor,—for the salvation of Christ from the beginning to the end is of grace—the apostle exhorts Christians to "hope," and to "hope to the end."

He exhorts them to hope for it, to expect it, to consider it as something that is absolutely secure, something that in due season they shall certainly enjoy; and he exhorts them to "hope to the end," that is, either to hope perfectly, to cherish an undoubting confidence, or to persevere in hoping to the very close of life, "not casting away their confidence," but "holding it fast to the end," knowing that "they have need of patience," that is, "the patience of hope;" in other words, knowing that they must persevere in hoping, in order that they may do the will of God, and that "they may obtain the promise," that is, the promised blessing. [1]

The practical truths here taught by the apostle are these—that it is the duty of Christians to cultivate a persevering, confident hope of final salvation; and that the cultivation of this persevering, confident hope of final salvation, is a necessary and important means of enabling them to perform the duties of christian obedience.

(1.) That it is the duty of Christians, believers of the truth as it is in Jesus, to cherish the hope of eternal happiness, is exceedingly plain. God has distinctly stated, that "whosoever believeth on Christ Jesus shall not perish, but shall have everlasting life;" and surely it must be the duty of the Christian to believe what God says, and to expect what God has promised. [2] For an unbelieving and impenitent person, continuing in unbelief and impenitence, to hope for eternal life is the extreme of presumption. That were to believe something which God has never said—that were to expect something which God has never promised. Nay, that were to believe the reverse of what God says—to expect the reverse of what God has declared. His declarations are, "Except ye repent, ye shall perish." "He that believeth not, shall be damned." [3] The unbeliever who is cherishing the hope of "*grace* to be brought" to him, continuing an unbeliever "at the revelation of Jesus Christ," is trusting to a hope which will make him "ashamed and confounded world without end." For he will be "revealed then in flaming fire, to take vengeance on such as know not God, and obey not the gospel of his Son." [4]

But let this impenitent man change his mind; let this unbeliever but credit the testimony of God, counting it a faithful saying, that "God is in Christ, reconciling the world to himself, not imputing to men their trespasses; seeing he hath made him who knew no sin to be sin in our room, that we may be made the righteousness of God in him," [5]—and immediately that hope which, in his previous state, it would have been absurdity and error, folly and presumption, in him to cherish, naturally grows up in his mind; its enjoyment is one of his highest privileges, and its cultivation one of his most important duties.

When we call on Christians to cultivate hope, we would press upon their attention the importance of three things. First, let them endeavor to obtain clear and ever-extending views of that holy happiness which is the object of their hope, of that "grace which is to be brought to them at the coming of our Lord Jesus." Let them not rest satisfied with some indistinct general notion of it as a state of deliverance from all suffering, and of the enjoyment of every species of blessedness; but let its character as a state of holy happiness be familiar to their minds; a state of endearing and transforming communion with the Holy, Holy, Holy One, a seeing Him as he is, a being like him, a beholding his face in righteousness, a being satisfied with his

---
[1] Heb. x. 35, 36.
[2] John iii. 16.
[3] Luke xiii. 3, 5. Mark xvi. 16.
[4] 2 Thess. i. 7, 8.
[5] 2 Cor. v. 19-21.

likeness, a being holy as he is holy, perfect as he is perfect.

Secondly, let them never forget that the holy ground on which their hope of obtaining this blessedness rests, is the sovereign mercy of Him whose nature as well as name is love, exercised in perfect consistency with, in glorious illustration of, his righteousness, through the obedience to death of his only begotten Son, made known to them in the word of the truth of the gospel. That appeared to them the only ground of hope, when, in the hour of conviction, every refuge of lies was swept away, and they were made to see that, so far as depended on themselves, so far as depended on the universe of creatures, there was no hope for them. They were then absolutely "without hope" till "the hope set before them in the gospel" was disclosed to their mind. There is no other ground of hope. Never, Christians, shift from this foundation—never attempt to add to this foundation. "Hold fast the beginning of your confidence, steadfast to the end." Let your hope of eternal life be that of a sinner who knows that eternal death is his merited portion, but who, believing, because God has said it, that "eternal life is the gift of God through Jesus Christ our Lord," gladly and gratefully receives what is freely given him of God, and setting to his seal that God is true, confidently trusts, humbly expects, that God will do as he has said.

Thirdly, in hoping for this holy happiness entirely on the ground of sovereign mercy, let Christians expect to obtain it only in the way in which God has promised to bestow it on them. To expect eternal life in a course of thoughtlessness and sin, is to expect what God has never promised. It is "through faith and patience" that the promised blessing is to be inherited. It is "in a patient continuance in well-doing," that "glory, honor, and immortality" are to be expected. It is "after doing the will of God that we are to receive the promise."[1] Let Christians, keeping these three things in view, expect only what God has promised—expect this only on the ground that He who is infinite in kindness, and wisdom, and power, and faithfulness, has promised it—and expect it only in the way and by the means which he has appointed for obtaining it; and it is impossible for them to be too confident in that

[1] Rom. ii. 7. Heb. vi. 12; x. 36.

"hope for the grace which is to be brought to them at the revelation of our Lord Jesus Christ."

(2.) This confident, persevering hope of final salvation, is one of the most necessary and important means for enabling a Christian to perform the duties of christian obedience. There are some theologians who would represent the performance of the duties of christian obedience as the ground of the hope of eternal life. These are not wise builders. They turn things upside down, and place the superstructure in the room of the foundation. Till a man has, through the faith of the gospel, obtained the hope of eternal life, he will never take a step in that path of filial obedience which is the only road to heaven, and the more he has of a well-grounded hope of eternal life, the more rapidly will he run along that road, the more easily will he master the difficulties, and surmount the obstacles which threaten to prevent his progress. When by a lively hope the Christian is enabled to feast on the clusters of the grapes of the promised land, which faith has furnished him with in the wilderness, he is disposed to say with Caleb, 'It must be a good land; and, seeing it is a good land, let us go up and possess it. What though hosts of spiritual enemies oppose our progress; what though the Jordan of death, that river over which there is no bridge, roll his waters deep and dark between us and the Canaan above, He who is infinite in power and in faithfulness, hath promised to make us "more than conquerors," and to bring us to, and make us reside forever in, that good land.'

"It is," to borrow the well-considered language of Leighton, "a foolish misgrounded fear, and such as argues inexperience of the nature and workings of divine grace, to imagine that the assured hope of salvation will beget unholiness and presumptuous boldness in sin. Our apostle is not so sharp-sighted as these men think themselves: he apprehends no such matter: he, indeed, supposes the contrary as unquestionable: he takes not assured hope and holiness as enemies, but joins them as near friends. Hope perfectly, in order to your being holy in all manner of conversation. The more assurance of salvation, the more holiness—the more delight in it, the more study of it, as the only way to that end; and as labor is then most pleasant when we are made surest that it shall not be lost, nothing doth make the soul so nimble and active in obedience as this oil of gladness, this assured hope of glory." Accordingly, the apostle John says, "It doth not yet appear what we shall be; but when he shall appear we shall be like him, for we shall see him as he is. Every man that hath this hope in him purifieth himself, even as he is pure." In perfect accordance with these two apostles, their beloved brother Paul, in his Epistle to the Hebrews, declares his desire "that every one of them would give all diligence to the full assurance of hope to the end;" would sedulously cultivate an unshaken, confident, persevering hope of eternal life, in order that they might not be "slothful, but followers of them who, through faith, and patience, are now inheriting the promises."[1]

This is, I am persuaded, the only way of securing habitual christian obedience. Let Christians, then, learn to say with the Psalmist, "But I will hope continually; and I will go in the strength of the Lord, making mention of his righteousness, even of his only."[2]

It may be proper, before leaving this part of the subject, to remark, that as the hope of eternal life has a powerful influence on Christian obedience, so christian obedience has a powerful influence on the hope of eternal life. We have seen that christian obedience is not the ground of the hope of eternal life, but it is its evidence. It is in the nature of things impossible that a Christian, while negligent about the duty of obedience, should enjoy in any high degree the privilege of hope. It is the same truth which inspires hope and stimulates to obedience; and if it is not present to the mind doing the latter, it cannot be present doing the former. It has been finely said, "The greatest affliction does not damp the hope of eternal life, so much as the smallest sin; affliction often renders hope more vigorous, sin uniformly weakens it."[3] If Christians would be "obedient children," they must "hope to the end;" and if they would "hope to the end," they must be "obedient children." These two things are linked together by divine appointment; and "what God has thus joined, let no man attempt to put asunder."

[1] 1 John iii. 2, 3. Heb. vi. 11, 12.
[2] Psal. lxxi. 14-16.
[3] Leighton.

§ 4.—*Fear a means of Christian Obedience.*

Fear is the fourth and last instrumental means which the apostle prescribes for securing the performance of the duties of christian obedience. If we would be "children of obedience," if we would not "fashion ourselves according to the former lusts in our ignorance, if we would "be holy in all manner of conversation," then must we "pass the time of our sojourning here in fear."

This injunction may not at first view appear to harmonize well with that which we have just been illustrating. It may be said, "does not perfect love cast out fear?"[4] and must not "the full assurance of hope," which the apostle has been recommending, cast it out also? The discrepancy is apparent only, not real. The fear which the apostle recommends, so far from being inconsistent with love and hope, and destructive of that comfort and happiness to which they give origin, naturally grows out of those views of the divine character which excite love and hope, and acts the part of guardian to the comfort and happiness which they produce in the mind.

The fear recommended by the apostle is beyond doubt the fear of offending God, and of the consequences of offending God. Such a fear is not only consistent with love and hope, but is their inseparable companion. The more highly I value the favor of God, the more must I fear that which, in the degree in which it prevails, deprives me of the sense of this favor. The more I delight in the anticipation of the holy happiness of heaven, the more must I be afraid of that, the direct and certain effect of which is to deprive me of this delight. The happiness of Christians is in the love of God, and the light of his countenance is the life of their life. It matters little to them that the world frowns on them, if he smiles; and it matters little to them that the world smiles, if he frowns. Nothing in the world can deprive them of the tokens of their Father's love but sin; and, therefore, they consider it as of all things the most terrible. "By this fear of the Lord they are made to depart from evil." It is implanted in their hearts by God for this express purpose, "I will put my fear in their hearts, and they shall not depart from me."[5] It naturally leads them to keep at a distance from sin; to guard against temptation, to beware

[4] 1 John iv. 18.
[5] Prov. xvi. 6. Jer. xxxii. 40.

of what may lead to the interruption of their delightful communion with their reconciled Father; and involve in clouds of perplexity and doubt the prospect of future blessedness. "Happy is the man who *thus* feareth always."[1] When a Christian believer thinks of the remains of corrupt principle within, and the number and force of temptation without; when he sees how many fall before these temptations, and make shipwreck of faith and a good conscience, surely it must be good for him to "be not high-minded, but fear."[2]

There is a system which passes with many for a peculiarly pure Christianity, the object of which seems to be to set believers free from every species of fear as inconsistent with faith, which, according to them, consists in believing that, at all events, the individual shall be saved. Every species of fear is run down under the name of unbelief. Now, it is quite plain the apostles had a very different view of the subject, since Paul exhorts the Hebrew Christians to "fear, lest, a promise of entering into God's rest being left to them, any of them should seem to come short of it,"[3] and since Peter, in the words of our text, exhorts Christians to "pass the time of their sojourning here in fear." They inculcate fear as a means of preventing unbelief and its consequences.

It is justly remarked by a judicious divine,[4] that both "believers and unbelievers have their fears, but they arise from very different sources, and have quite opposite effects. The fears of unbelievers arise from unworthy thoughts of God; a distrust of his power, faithfulness, and goodness; and, also, from a prevailing love of the present world and its enjoyments, which makes them more afraid of worldly losses and sufferings for righteousness' sake, than of forfeiting the divine favor," or incurring the divine displeasure. "Such fears not only indispose the mind to obedience, but lead directly to sin. But that godly fear which is proper to believers, arises from a just view, reverence, and esteem of the character of God, and a supreme desire of his favor, as their chief happiness; and is a fear lest they offend him and incur his just displeasure. Such a fear outweighs all the allurements of sin on the one hand, and all the terrors of the present sufferings on the other."

Such is the fear inculcated by the prophet when he says, "Sanctify the Lord God in your heart, and let him be your fear and your dread, and he shall be for a sanctuary." Such is the fear enjoined by our Lord on his disciples: "Fear not him who, after he has killed the body, hath no more that he can do; but fear him who, after he hath killed the body, can cast both soul and body into hell fire; yea, I say unto you, fear him." Such is the fear prescribed by the apostle in the passage before us, as an instrumental means for securing christian obedience: "Pass the time of your sojouring here in fear."[5]

This fear must be habitually exercised during the whole continuance of our mortal life. None are so highly advanced in grace here below, as to be out of the need of this principle; but when their pilgrimage is finished, and they are come home to their Father's house above, there shall be no more fearing. There are no dangers there, and therefore no fear. They shall indeed have, in a higher degree than ever, a holy reverence of the Divine Majesty, but the fear of offending God will pass away with the possibility of offending him. In that blessed world there is neither sin, nor temptation to sin; no more conflict, no more danger; the victory is complete, the peace secure, the triumph eternal.[6]

These observations have been addressed exclusively to Christians. But I am afraid there are persons now hearing me who are not Christians. I call on them to fear: they have good reason; I dare not call on them to hope, while they continue in unbelief and impenitence. "There is no peace to the wicked, saith my God,"[7]—no hope for the unbelieving. But I present to them "the hope set before us" in the gospel. I tell them, Christ Jesus died for sinners; for the chief of sinners. I assure them that "eternal life is the gift of God, through Jesus Christ our Lord." I put them in mind of the solemn oath of God, that he has no pleasure in their death; I put them

---

[1] Prov. xxviii. 14.
[2] Rom. xi. 20.
[3] Heb. iv. 1.
[4] The late Archibald M'Lean from whose writings I have derived much advantage. It may be worth stating, that when introduced to the late Robert Hall, one of the first things he said to me was, "Sir, you have found me reading your countryman, Archibald M'Lean. He was a man mighty in the Scriptures, sir: mighty in the Scriptures."
[5] Isa. viii. 13. Matt. x. 28.
[6] Leighton.
[7] Isa. lvii. 21.

in mind of the most condescending expostulation, "Why, why, will ye die?" I beseech them to despair of salvation in themselves; I assure them that Jesus is "able to save them to the uttermost," and as willing as able.[1] Oh, if they would but believe "these true and faithful sayings of God," a hope that will never make them ashamed would spring up in their hearts; and, along with that fear of the Lord by which men depart from evil, a fear in which there is sweet awful pleasure, not torment, in delightful harmonious operation, would induce them, from "children of disobedience," to become children of obedience; and, instead of continuing to "fashion themselves according to their lusts in their ignorance," would lead them to "be holy in all manner of conversation."

III.—MOTIVES TO THE PERFORMANCE OF CHRISTIAN DUTY.

Let us now illustrate the motives to Christian duty, which are unfolded in the paragraph under consideration. These are four in number. (1.) The grandeur, excellence, and security of that inheritance, the full possession of which can be attained only in a course of christian duty: "Wherefore," says the apostle, referring to the whole of the preceding description of the final happiness which awaits Christians at the second coming of their Lord. (2.) The holiness of God: "Be ye holy, for I am holy." (3.) The equity of God: "The Father on whom ye call, or he whom ye call Father, judgeth every man according to his works." And, (4.) The provision made for sanctification, by the sacrifice of the Son of God: "Ye are redeemed, not with such corruptible things as silver and gold, from your vain conversation received by tradition from your fathers; but with the precious blood of Christ, as of a lamb without blemish and without spot; who verily, was fore-ordained before the foundation of the world, but was manifest in these last times for you, who by him do believe in God, that raised him from the dead, and gave him glory; that your faith and hope might be in God."

[1] Rom. vi. 23. Ezek. xxxiii. 11.

Let me turn your attention to these powerful motives in their order.

§ 1.—*The grandeur, excellence, and security of the Christian salvation, a motive to Christian duty.*

The grandeur, excellence, and security of the inheritance, the full posession of which can be attained only in a course of christian duty, is a most powerful motive to obedience, and to the employment of all the means which are fitted to secure it. When the apostle says, "Wherefore," for these reasons, we naturally ask, for what reasons? and we readily find an answer. The preceding context is principally occupied with a description of the final happiness, the eternity of holy blessedness, which awaits the genuine followers of Jesus Christ in the last time, at the revelation of the Saviour.

Now, is not the attainment of this eternity of holy happiness well worthy of every exertion that man is capable of?—will it not infinitely more than compensate for privations however great, sacrifices however costly, sufferings however severe, that may be required in pursuing it? When we look around us, and see "all things so full of labor, that man cannot utter it;" when we see men, in order to obtain some worldly advantage, the value of which is in a great measure imaginary, and the possession of which must be insecure and shortlived, rising early, sitting late, eating the bread of carefulness, compassing sea and land, straining to the utmost every faculty of exertion, and tasking to the utmost every power of endurance, we cannot help being painfully struck at the disproportion between the worthlessness of the object, and the multitude and mightiness of the means. It "resembles ocean into tempest tost, to waft a feather or to drown a fly." We feel disposed to ask the infatuated laborer, "Wilt thou set thine heart on things which are not?" "Why do you spend your money for that which is not bread, and your labor for that which satisfieth not?"[2]

[2] Prov. xxiii. 5. Isa. lv. 2.

Have you renewed your subscription? Remember that "Gleanings in Exodus" and a series of articles on "How to Study the Bible" by Arthur W. Pink will commence with the January 1924 issue. D. V. Don't miss these.

(Continued from page 337.)

in obtaining access to a *stable;* there He would be within easy reach of poor and rich alike. Thus, from the beginning, He was easy of approach. No intermediaries had first to be passed in order to reach Him. No priest had to be interviewed before *entre* could be obtained to His presence. Thus it was then; and so it is now, thank God.

4. He was laid in a manger so as to foreshadow *the Character of those among whom He had come.* The stable was the place for beasts of the field, and it was into *their* midst the newly-born Saviour came. And how well did they symbolize the moral character of men! The beasts of the field are devoid of any spiritual life, and so have no knowledge of God. Such, too, was the condition of both Jews and Gentiles. And how *beast-like* in character were those into whose midst the Saviour came: stupid and stubborn as the ass or mule, cunning and cruel as the fox, groveling and filthy as the swine, and ever thirsting for His blood as the more savage of the animals. Fittingly, then, was He placed amid the beasts of the field at His birth.

5. He was laid in a manger to show *His contempt for Worldly riches and pomp.* We had thought it more fitting for the Christ of God to be born in a palace, and laid in a cradle of gold, lined with costly silks. Ah, but as He Himself reminds us in this same Gospel, "That which is highly esteemed among men, is abomination in the sight of God" (Luke 16:15). And what an exemplification of this truth was given when the infant Saviour was placed, not in a cradle of gold, but, in a humble manger!

6. He was laid in a manger to mark *His identification with human suffering and wretchedness.* The One born was "the Son *of Man*". He had left the height of heaven's glory and had descended to our level, and here we behold Him entering the human lot at its lowest point. Adam was first placed in a garden, surrounded by the exquisite beauties of Nature as it left the hands of the Creator. But sin had come in, and with sin all its sad consequences of suffering and wretchedness. Therefore, does the One who had come here to recover and restore what the first man lost, appear first, in surroundings which spoke of abject need and wretchedness; just as a little later we find Him taken down into Egypt, in order that God might call His Son from the same place as where His people Israel commenced their national history in misery and wretchedness. Thus did the Man of Sorrows identify Himself with human suffering.

7. He was laid in a manger because such speaks of *the place of sacrifice.* The manger was the place where vegetable life was sacrificed to sustain animal life. Fitting place was this, then, for Him who had come to be the great Sacrifice, laying down His life for His people, that we might through His death be made alive. Remarkably suggestive, therefore, and full of emblematic design, was the place appointed by God to receive the infant body of the incarnate Saviour.

—Arthur W. Pink.

Vol. I. Studies in the Scriptures	$1.50
Vol. II. Studies in the Scriptures:	$1.50
Vol. I. Exposition of John's Gospel:	$1.50
The Antichrist	$1.50

Printed in the United States of America

www.ingramcontent.com/pod-product-compliance
Lightning Source LLC
Chambersburg PA
CBHW071154230426
43668CB00009B/952